ADVANCED PHYSICS

Keith Gibbs

Head of Science, Queen's College, Taunton

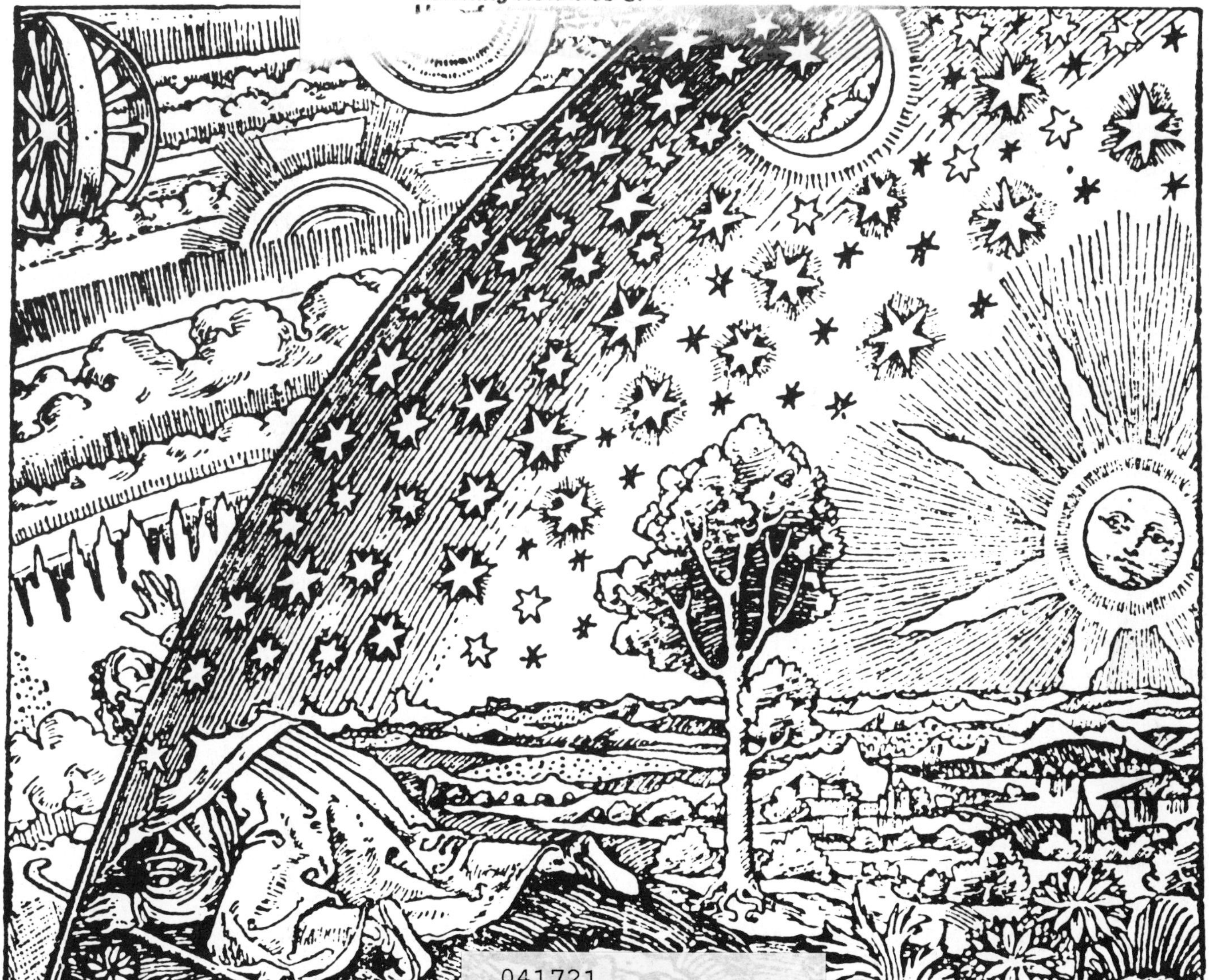

A medieval conception of the universe

CAMBRIDGE
UNIVERSITY PRESS

Preface

This is the morning I would not forget
For then we stood in awe
And saw the world created in a day *F.S.Bourne*

This book is a full A level text covering the A level syllabi of all the major examining boards. The double page layout has been followed wherever possible and the language has been kept straightforward within the restrictions of an A level course.

Particular attention has been paid to the common core A level Physics material published by the examinations boards in 1983, all of which will be found in the text. Many examples are given throughout and these have been boxed with important facts highlighted. The examples show the use of formulae and also give ideas of the values of quantities to be expected in real life situations. Practical applications of the subject are referred to throughout the text since this is thought to be a vital part of the study of the subject at this level. I would like to thank all those who have provided information here.

There is also a large number of Student investigations within the text. These are both theoretical and practical tasks, many of the practical tasks being of an open-ended nature. There is a full section that deals with experimental technique and data handling for both traditional and open-ended experiments.

Full exam-style questions have been placed at appropriate points within the text. They immediately follow the relevant work and are not isolated at the end of a chapter. They have been carefully selected and edited to remove the purely recall type of formula quotation and experiment description. Since this would simply mean copying out the text teachers have been left to devise these for themselves. There is also a section on the comprehension of Physics texts. I must thank all the examining boards who have given me permission to reproduce these questions.

Particular care has been paid to the layout of the book so that it is easy to follow and attractive to look at. Many diagrams have been included as an aid to understanding and also to make the book more attractive. Tables of useful values appear at relevant places in the text to give the student an idea of the properties of real materials. The section on particle Physics goes rather beyond A level but I felt that it should be there as it represents the frontiers of the subject, as does the work on micro-processors and computing. There is a section on formulae as a useful aid to revision although pupils should be sure that they understand the meaning of a formula rather than simply learning it.

The book has not been written to suggest a teaching sequence and can be used in any order although some sections naturally follow others. Some topics of a GCSE standard are included as either a basis or an introduction to further work.

My thanks must go to all those who have helped in the preparation of this book in a great many ways. Particular mention must be made of Dr Jean Macqueen for the arduous task of editing my initial manuscript, to all those at Cambridge University Press for their encouragement throughout, to Dr. John Sanders of Oriel College, Oxford for his many helpful comments and suggestions in preparing the second edition and last but not least to my family for their interest, patience and understanding.

Keith Gibbs
Queen's College
Taunton
1990

Published by the Press Syndicate of the University of Cambridge
The Pitt Building, Trumpington Street, Cambridge CB2 1RP
40 West 20th Street, New York, NY 10011-4211, USA
10 Stamford Road, Oakleigh, Melbourne 3166, Australia

First published 1988
Second edition 1990
Reprinted 1994

Printed in Great Britain by Ebenezer Baylis, Worcester

British Library cataloguing in publication data

Gibbs, Keith, 1944–
Advanced Physics. – 2nd ed.
1. Physics
I. Title
530 20

ISBN 0 521 39985 8
0 521 39652 2 (CAMBISE)

MU

[First edition ISBNS: 0 521 33583 3; 0 521 34763 7 (CAMBISE)]

Contents

Introduction

A view of the earth from a weather satellite showing cyclones in the North Pacific (By courtesy of the Japan Meteorological Agency)

1 · Physics and physicists

Physics has an impact on our lives in a great number of ways and I will start this book by looking at some of these applications. I do not think that a study of Physics should ever be separated from a study of the real world around us.

If you become a physicist you must be prepared to investigate, to observe, to carry out experiments and then record your results. You must then be able to explain these results to others and discuss your ideas and their opinions. You must be prepared to be adaptable in the rapidly changing world of technology and you must have sufficient mathematical ability to express your results and ideas in precise terms rather than broad generalisations.

Physicists may work in many fields and the list below shows some of these. (I am most grateful to the Institute of Physics for permission to print these.)

None of these careers may be undertaken without knowledge and it is the study of this knowledge and its application that will concern us in the rest of the book. When you are trying to grasp a formula or solve a problem, try not to forget the wider applications of the subject.

Knowledge of Physics is needed:

to set up satellite communications
to investigate 'black holes'
to take scans of the human body
to construct a computer
to detect flaws in structures
to make new materials
to study pollution of air, land and water
to reduce the noise in vehicles
to harness energy of all kinds
to solve crimes

Physics provides answers to questions such as:

why is the sky blue but sunsets red?
how can we save premature babies from dying?
what makes glass transparent?
what holds parts of the atom together?
how can we predict earthquakes?

and many more – this list can only give you just a small insight into the possibilities when working as a physicist.

Careers in Physics

Medical Physics

Health Service
Instrumentation
Health physics
Physics for the handicapped

Education

Schools
Colleges
Universities
Polytechnics

Geophysics

Mineralogy
Petrology
Prospecting
Mineral processing

Environmental Physics

Radiation protection
Conservation
Noise control
Pollution control

Computing

Computer design
System design
Computer aided design
Robotics
Microprocessor control

Meteorology

Oceanography
Weather forecasts
Radio
Travel

Alternative energy

Geothermal
Solar
Wave
Wind

Engineering

Chemical
Civil
Control
Electrical
Mechanical

Scientific Civil Service

Defence
Energy and resources
Patents
Research labs.
Science policy
Standards

Materials science

Metallurgy
New materials
Thin films

Communications

Fibre optics
Satellites
Telecommunications

Industry

Aerospace
Chemical
Electronics
Food
Petroleum
Semiconductor

2 · Basic measurements in Physics

Physics is a science of observation of the world around us. It aims to give an understanding of this world both by observation and by prediction of the way in which objects will behave. It is a science of measurement, but before any measurements can be made we must define the units on which our measurements are made.

The units used in this book are the **International System of Units** (SI) based on the seven base units defined below.

Base units

The **metre** is the distance travelled by electromagnetic waves in free space in 1/299 792 458 second.

The **kilogram** is the mass equal to that of the international prototype kilogram kept at the Bureau International des Poids et Mesures at Sèvres, France.

The **second** is the duration of 9 192 631 770 periods of the radiation corresponding to the transition between two hyperfine levels of the ground state of the caesium-137 atom.

The **ampere** is that constant current which, if maintained in two parallel straight conductors of infinite length and of negligible circular cross-section placed 1 metre apart in a vacuum, would produce a force between them of 2×10^{-7} N per metre of length.

The **kelvin** is 1/273.16 of the thermodynamic temperature of the triple point of water.

The **candela** is the luminous intensity in a given direction of a source that emits monochromatic radiation of frequency 540×10^{12} Hz that has a radiant intensity of 1/683 watt per steradian.

The **mole** is the amount of substance of a system that contains as many elementary particles as there are in 0.012 kg of carbon-12.

The accurate measurement of length

We shall consider two instruments here, the micrometer and the vernier scale; it is likely, however, that digital and interference methods will become more popular in the years to come.

The micrometer (Figure 2.2)

This is a device for the measurement of distances up to a few millimetres with an accuracy of about 0.01 mm. It has an accurately threaded screw fixed to a drum so that when the drum rotates once the screw advances a known distance, usually 0.5 mm, and the jaws close by this amount. The body of the drum is graduated from 0 to 50 so that measurements

Student investigation

Measure the following quantities using what you consider to be the most appropriate measuring device that you have available, and record your results:

(*a*) the volume of the laboratory,
(*b*) the diameter of a marble,
(*c*) the length of the line *l* (Figure 2.1),
(*d*) the separation of the dots A and B,
(*e*) the thickness of one page of this book,
(*f*) the radius of 28 gauge wire,
(*g*) the area of the rectangle PQRS,
(*h*) the mass of one rice grain,
(*i*) the radius of the circle D.

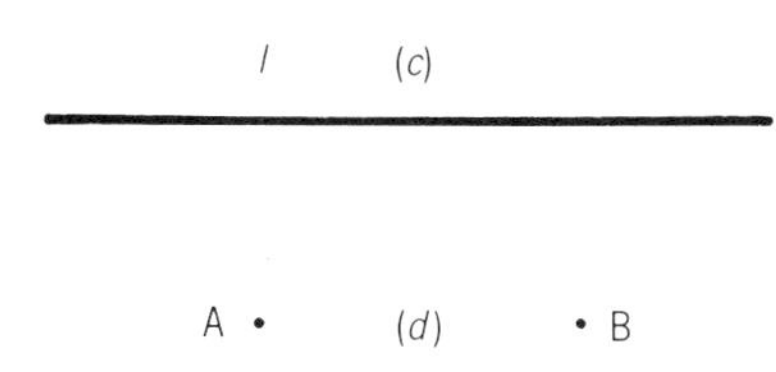

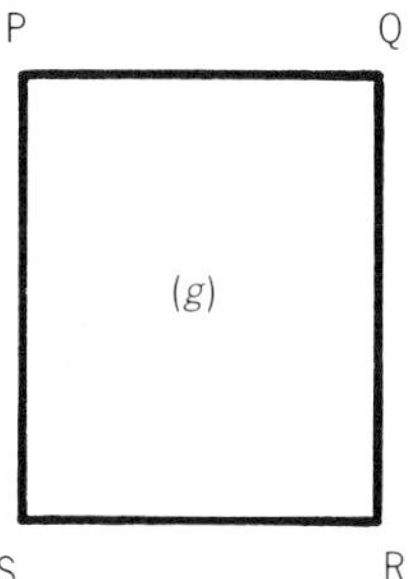

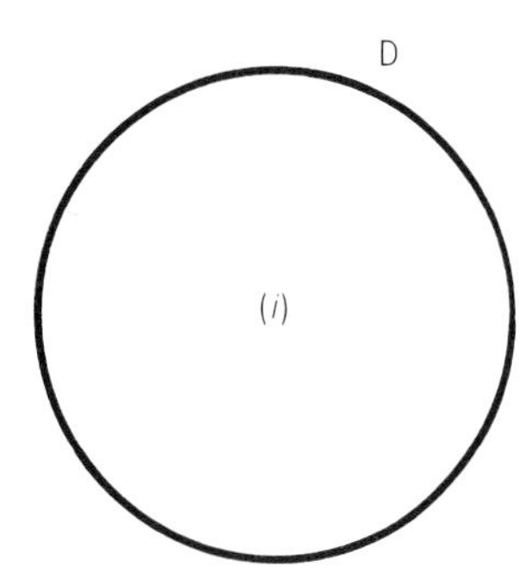

Figure 2.1

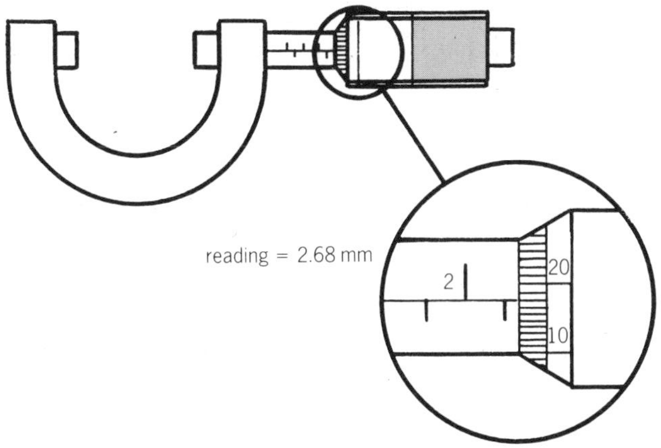

Figure 2.2

of 1/50 of a rotation or 0.01 mm may be made. A ratchet screw is provided so that the object being measured is not squashed and the jaws are not strained.

Before making any measurement it is important to check that the micrometer reads zero when the jaws are closed. If it does not then this **zero error** must be allowed for when the reading is taken.

The vernier scale (Figure 2.3)

A vernier scale is a useful extension of the main scale and is usually used for lengths of a few centimetres. It is accurate to about 0.1 mm.

The vernier scale is divided into ten parts and is the same length as nine parts on the main scale. This means that if the main scale is graduated in millimetres, each vernier division is 0.9 mm long. The reading on the vernier scale that exactly matches a scale division gives the next decimal place in the measurement.

In Figure 2.3 the reading is 12.7 mm. Vernier scales are frequently found on travelling microscopes and Fortin barometers. An angular vernier scale is used on the table of accurate spectrometers.

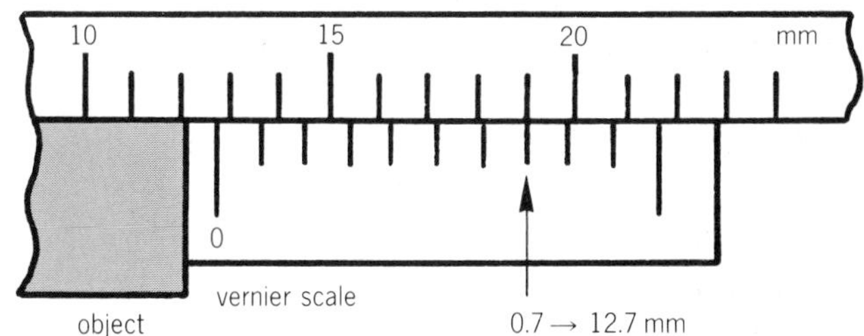

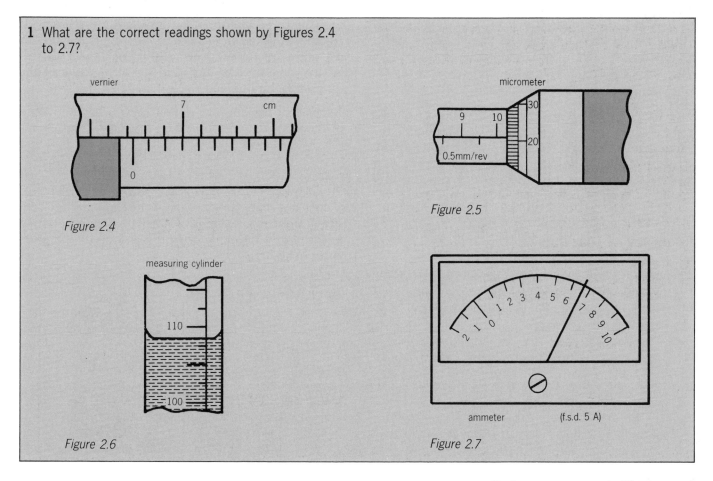

Figure 2.3

1 What are the correct readings shown by Figures 2.4 to 2.7?

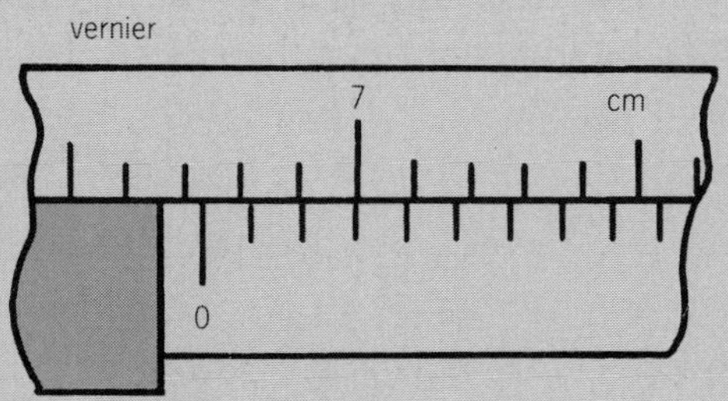

vernier

Figure 2.4

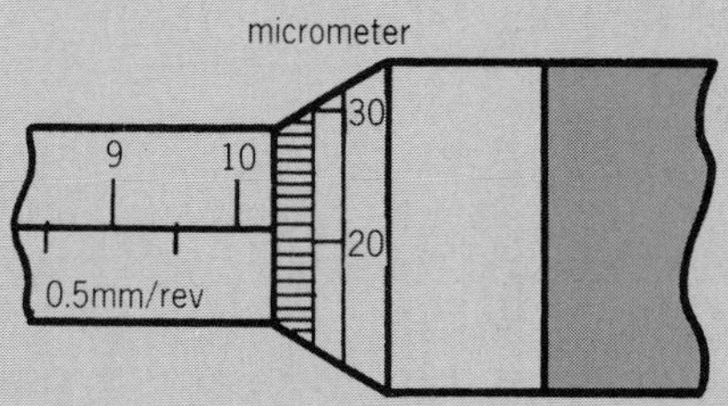

micrometer

Figure 2.5

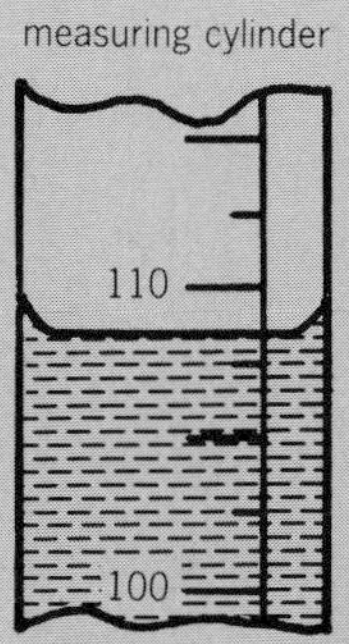

measuring cylinder

Figure 2.6

ammeter (f.s.d. 5 A)

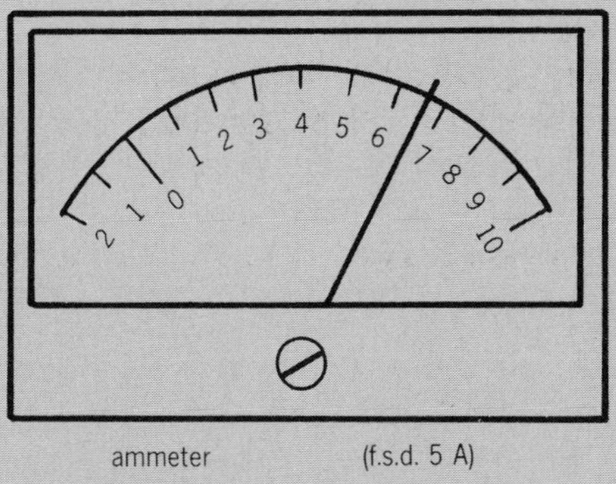

Figure 2.7

3 · Dimensions and errors

Any experiment will involve a series of measurements, and each of these measurements will be made to a certain degree of accuracy. For example, the calculation of a velocity requires the measurement of a time and a distance.

Using a stopwatch you may measure the time to the nearest tenth of a second, and using a metre rule you may find the distance to the nearest millimetre (if it is a fairly small distance measured in the laboratory).

It is very useful to have a rough idea of the kind of result that you might expect before starting an experiment, although of course in research this is not always possible.

There are two basic types of error that may appear in the result.

Systematic errors

These occur due to faulty apparatus such as an incorrectly labelled scale, an incorrect zero mark on a meter or a stopwatch running slowly. Repeating the measurement a number of times will have no effect on this type of error and it may not even be suspected until the final result is calculated. The only way to eliminate this type of error is to change or recalibrate the measuring instrument.

Random errors

The size of these errors depends on how well the experimenter can *use* the apparatus. The better the experimenter you are, the smaller will be the random error that you will introduce into an experiment. Making a number of readings of a given quantity and taking an average will reduce the overall error.

Accuracy of readings

The accuracy with which you can quote any reading will depend upon the smallest scale division on your measuring instrument and it is quite wrong to give results to much greater accuracies than this, especially when the final answer may contain a number of different measurements.

Let us start with a very simple example. If you measure a length with a ruler and get an answer of 6.8 cm, then we assume that you have been able to measure to ±1 mm since that is the last figure in your answer. This means that that reading is accurate to 1 part in 68, i.e., 1.5 %. Now if that reading forms part of an experiment in which there are other measurements then it is useful if the other quantities can be found to the same degree of accuracy. Taking one reading to a very high degree of accuracy is little help if others will be much more inaccurate. In any experiment you should be aware of which readings are the inaccurate ones.

Quoting an answer

When you have made your set of readings, you must be careful when you quote the result. You will probably use a calculator to work out a formula containing perhaps three or four different quantities; your calculator will give an answer to nine digits but do *not* use this as an answer. The accuracy of the answer will always be less than the accuracy of any one of the quantities used to find it.

A word of warning here: small quantities may only be ignored *in comparison with large ones*. For example, in an answer such as 6.700 002 the 0.000 002 may be ignored but this is *not* the case in an answer such as 0.000 012 where the 0.000 002 is 17 % of the answer! Think: if you are sat on by an elephant it does not matter very much if the elephant has a fly sitting on its back (Figure 3.1) – but if an isolated fly is sat on by another fly, then this second fly is important to the first one!

Figure 3.1

Calculating the error

In this section we will imagine that we wish to find the value of a quantity Q that involves the measurement of two other quantities a and b.

(i) A **sum** or **difference** of two quantities, i.e. $Q = a + b$ or $Q = a - b$

Let Q be the length of an object found by taking two readings (a and b) from a ruler (see Figure 3.2).

Therefore $Q = b - a$

Let $a = 16.5$ cm $\pm$ 0.1 cm and $b = 25.4$ cm $\pm$ 0.1 cm.

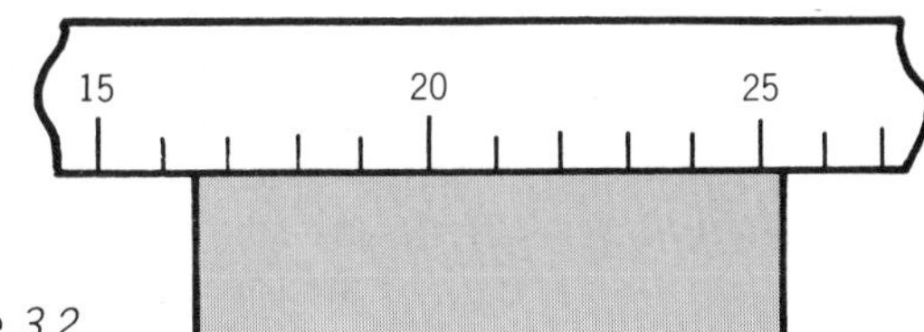

Figure 3.2

Q has its *average* value when both a and b have their average values:

i.e. $Q = 25.4 - 16.5 = 8.9$ cm

Q has its *maximum* value when a has its smallest value and b its largest:

i.e. $Q = 25.5 - 16.4 = 9.1$ cm

Q has its *minimum* value when a has its largest value and b its smallest:

i.e. $Q = 25.3 - 16.6 = 8.7$ cm

The error in Q is therefore simply the *sum* of the errors in a and b.

We write this as: $\Delta Q = \Delta a + \Delta b$

This formula applies for a sum or difference.

In this example the answer should be written as:

$$Q = 8.9 \pm 0.2 \text{ cm}$$

The percentage error in Q would be $(0.2/8.9) \times 100 = 2.2$ %.

(ii) The **product** or **quotient** of two quantities: $Q = ab$ or $Q = a/b$

An example is shown in Figure 3.3.

Let the error in Q be ΔQ
the error in a be Δa
the error in b be Δb

Therefore if $Q = ab$, the maximum value for Q is:

$$Q + \Delta Q = (a + \Delta a)(b + \Delta b)$$
$$= a\Delta b + b\Delta a + \Delta a\, \Delta b + ab$$

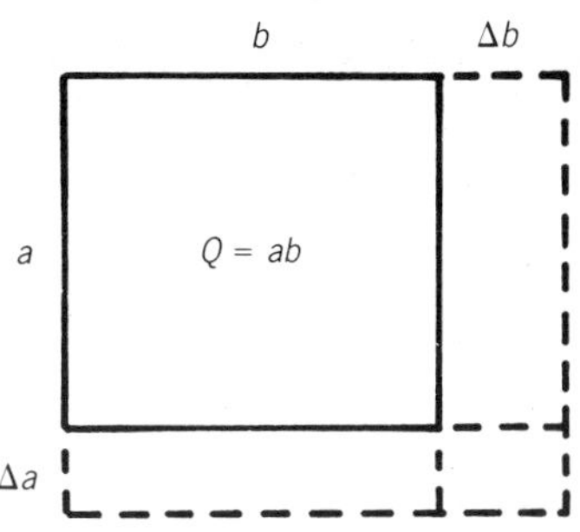

Figure 3.3

Now we can ignore the term $\Delta a \Delta b$, since it is the product of two small quantities and is therefore small *in comparison* with the other terms. Then

$$\Delta Q = a\Delta b + b\Delta a$$

or, expressed as a fractional error:

$$\frac{\Delta Q}{Q} = \frac{\Delta a}{a} + \frac{\Delta b}{b}$$

This will apply to both a product and a quotient. You can also show that if one or more of the quantities (a,b) is raised to a power, say n (i.e., $Q = ab^n$) then:

$$\frac{\Delta Q}{Q} = \frac{\Delta a}{a} + \frac{n\Delta b}{b}$$

Notice that pure numbers have no errors; this can also be assumed for quantities such as π and e.

Example

Find the maximum possible error in the measurement of the force on an object (mass m) travelling at velocity v in a circle of radius r if $m = 3.5$ kg $\pm$ 0.1 kg, $v = 20$ m s^{-1} $\pm$ 1 m s^{-1} and $r = 12.5$ m $\pm$ 0.5 m.

$$\text{Force } (F) = \frac{mv^2}{r}$$

Therefore
$$\frac{\Delta F}{F} = \frac{\Delta m}{m} + \frac{2\Delta v}{v} + \frac{\Delta r}{r}$$
$$\frac{\Delta F}{F} = \frac{0.1}{3.5} + \frac{2 \times 1}{20} + \frac{0.5}{12.5}$$
$$= 0.03 + 0.1 + 0.04$$
$$= 0.17$$

Therefore $F = 112 \pm 19$ N

The percentage error can be expressed as the sum of the percentage errors in the quantities. In the above example the percentage error in F is 3 % + 10 % + 4 % = 17 %. So the error F is 17 % of 112 = 19 N.

Taking a number of readings

In an experiment taking a number of readings will reduce the error in the final answer. Consider the measurement of the thickness of a hacksaw blade made at a number of places with a micrometer, such that each reading is accurate to ± 0.01 mm.

Suppose that the six readings taken are: 0.65, 0.66, 0.63, 0.66, 0.64 and 0.65 mm. The mean of these will be their sum divided by 6, which is 0.65 mm.

To calculate the final error we need to find the differences between each reading and the mean value, square these differences, add them, divide by the number of readings and take the square root of the result. This quantity is called the **standard deviation** of the readings.

The likely error in the mean of these readings is the standard deviation divided by $(n-1)^{½}$, where n is the number of readings.

In the above example, the standard deviation is 0.011 mm and the likely error in the mean is $0.011/(6-1)^{½} = 0.005$.
The thickness should be quoted as 0.65 ± 0.005 mm.

Errors in graphs

If a graph is plotted then the error in the result is found as follows. Consider the graph shown in Figure 3.4. The best fit line to the points is drawn and its slope found (m). The average value of all the x- and y-coordinates is found; this will give the **centroid** of the line. The lines of greatest and least slope through the centroid are then drawn and their respective slopes found (m_1 and m_2).

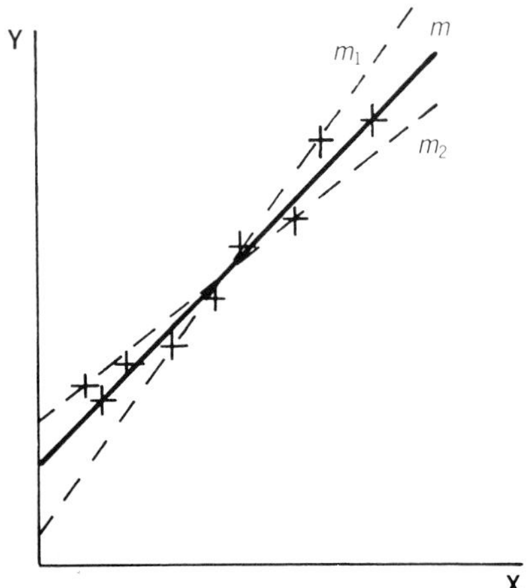

Figure 3.4

The final error in the slope is then given by $\frac{\Delta m}{m}$

where Δm is the difference between either m_1 or m_2 (whichever is the greater) and m.

1 Explain what is meant by
(*a*) a *random* error,
(*b*) a *systematic* error.
Give a practical example of each and discuss how they may be reduced or eliminated.

2 A ticker timer giving 50 dots per second is used to measure the velocity of a trolley running down a friction-compensated runway 2 m long.
If the velocity of the trolley is found to be 1.5 m s^{-1}, give an estimate of the accuracy that might be achieved in this result. Show in detail how you arrived at such a figure.

3 The density of a rectangular solid block is found by measuring three of the sides with a ruler which can be read to ± 0.5 mm and then finding its mass from a balance accurate to ± 1 g.
The readings obtained were
Length: 4.56 cm and 2.35 cm Width: 3.52 cm and 1.26 cm
Height: 3.04 cm and 2.61 cm Mass: 32 g
(*a*) Find
(i) the average volume of the block in mm^3, cm^3 and m^3,
(ii) the maximum and minimum values possible for the volume,
(iii) the average value for the density of the block,
(iv) the maximum fractional error in the volume,
(v) the maximum fractional error in the density,
(vi) the maximum error in the volume in mm^3,
(vii) the maximum error in the density in kg m^{-3}.
(*b*) Express the volume of the block correctly, showing the error.
(*c*) Express the density of the block correctly, showing the error
(*d*) Repeat the calculations for the volume but assume that a pair of vernier calipers reading to ± 0.1 mm had been used instead.

Student investigation

Repeat the experiments on page 4 giving an estimate of the accuracy of your results.

Dimensions

The basic quantities in Physics are those of mass, length, time, electric current, temperature, luminous intensity and amount of a substance (see page 4). Other related quantities such as energy, acceleration and so on can be derived from combinations of these basic quantities and are therefore known as **derived** quantities.

The way in which the derived quantity is related to the basic quantity can be shown by the **dimensions** of the quantity. In considering dimensions we will restrict ourselves to those used in mechanics and properties of matter only.

The dimensions of mass are written as [M]
The dimensions of length are written as [L]
The dimensions of time are written as [T]

Note the square brackets round the letter to show that we are dealing with the dimensions of a quantity.

The dimensions of any other quantity will involve one or more of these basic dimensions. For instance, a measurement of volume will involve the product of three lengths and the dimensions of volume are therefore $[L]^3$.

In the same way a measurement of velocity requires a length divided by a time, and so the dimensions of velocity are $[L][T]^{-1}$.

The table below shows the dimensions of various common quantities in mechanics.

Quantity	Dimension
area	$[L]^2$
velocity	$[L][T]^{-1}$
force	$[M][L][T]^{-2}$
energy	$[M][L]^2[T]^{-2}$
power	$[M][L]^2[T]^{-3}$
volume	$[L]^3$
acceleration	$[L][T]^{-2}$
pressure	$[M][L]^{-1}[T]^{-2}$
momentum	$[M][L][T]^{-1}$

Dimensions have two important uses in Physics:

to check equations,
to derive equations.

Use of dimensions to check equations

The dimensions of the quantities of each side of an equation must match: those on the left-hand side must equal those on the right (remember the classic problem of not being able to give the total when five apples are added to three oranges – see Figure 3.5).

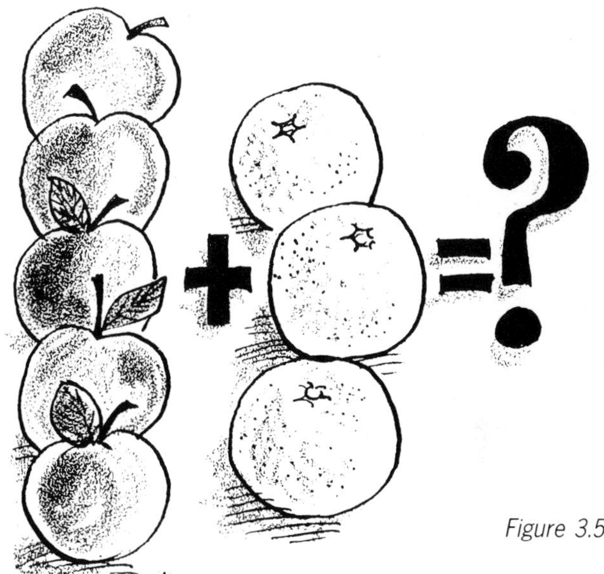

Figure 3.5

For example, consider the equation:

$$s = ut + \tfrac{1}{2}at^2$$

Writing this in dimensional form we have:

$$[L] = [L][T]^{-1}[T] + [L][T]^{-2}[T]^2$$

therefore $[L] = [L] + [L]$

This proves the equation, since the length on the left-hand side of the equation is obtained by adding together the two lengths on the right-hand side.

Notice that $\frac{1}{2}$ is a pure number having no dimensions and is therefore omitted in the dimensional equation.

A further example is shown below.

> **Example**
>
> Show that the equation for impulse $Ft = mv - mu$ is dimensionally correct.
>
> Writing this in dimensional form we have:
>
> $$[M][L][T]^{-2}[T] = [M][L][T]^{-1} + [M][L][T]^{-1}$$
>
> Therefore $[M][L][T]^{-1} = [M][L][T]^{-1}$ and the equation is correct, both sides having the dimensions of momentum.

Use of dimensions to derive equations

If we have some idea upon which quantities a further quantity might depend, then we can use the method of dimensional analysis to obtain an equation relating the relevant variables. You should appreciate that since numbers are dimensionless we cannot use this method to find these in equations, however.

Consider the oscillation of a simple pendulum. We will assume that the period of the pendulum (t) depends in some way on the following quantities:
(i) the mass of the pendulum bob (m)
(ii) the length of the string of the pendulum (l), and
(iii) the gravitational intensity (g).

We therefore write the equation as:

$$t = km^x l^y g^z$$

where x, y and z are unknown powers and k is a dimensionless constant.

Writing this in dimensional form gives:

$$[\mathrm{T}] = [\mathrm{M}]^x[\mathrm{L}]^y[\mathrm{L}]^z[\mathrm{T}]^{-2z}$$

Equating the indices for M, L and T on both sides of the equation we have:

M: $0 = x$
L: $0 = y + z$
T: $1 = -2z$

Therefore:

$x = 0$, $y = \frac{1}{2}$ and $z = -\frac{1}{2}$.

The original equation therefore becomes:

$$t = k\left(\frac{l}{g}\right)^{\frac{1}{2}}$$

which is what we would expect for a simple pendulum. Dimensional analysis does not give us the value of the dimensionless constant k which can be shown by other methods to be 2π in this case (see page 78).

Further examples of the use of dimensional analysis to derive equations are found in the discussions later in this book of
(i) viscosity – Stokes's and Poiseuille's laws (pages 124 and 122),
(ii) wave velocity on a stretched string (page 176).

4 Use the method of dimensional analysis to deduce equations for the following:
(*a*) the period of oscillation of a mass suspended on a vertical spiral spring,
(*b*) the velocity of waves on a stretched string,
(*c*) the frictional drag on a sphere falling through a liquid,
(*d*) the rate at which liquid flows through a pipe.

5 Use the method of dimensional analysis to check the validity of the following equations:
(*a*) $E = mc^2$, where E is the energy obtainable from a mass m, and c is the velocity of light.
(*b*) Energy stored in a wire $= -\frac{1}{2}\frac{EAe^3}{l}$ where E is the Young modulus, A the cross-sectional area, e the extension and l the original length.
(*c*) Escape velocity from a planet = $2Rg_0$, where R is the radius of the planet and g_0 is the gravitational intensity at its surface.
(*d*) Period of oscillation of a floating cylinder with its axis vertical and length h immersed in a liquid of density d:

$$T = 2\pi\sqrt{\frac{hd}{g}}$$

6 What are the dimensions of the following quantities?
(*a*) work
(*b*) energy
(*c*) power
(*d*) momentum
(*e*) impulse
(*f*) force
(*g*) coefficient of viscosity
(*h*) modulus of elasticity
(*i*) density
(*j*) coefficient of restitution

7 What are the maximum percentage errors in the following:
(*a*) the area of a rectangle whose sides are measured to ± 8% and ± 5%,
(*b*) the resistance of a piece of wire when the voltage across it is measured to ± 6% and the current through it to ± 3.2%.

8 What are the maximum possible errors in the following:
(Give your answers both in percentages and actual values.)
(*a*) the velocity of an object that travels 25 m ± 0.5 m in a time of 8.0 ± 0.1 s.
(*b*) the density of a block of sides 2.5 ± 0.1 cm, 4.8 ± 0.1 cm and 10.2 ± 0.1 cm and of mass 245 g ± 2 g.

4 · Experimental work in Physics

Since much of Physics is experimental it is important to know how to perform experiments properly and how to present observations and work out conclusions. How much faith can be put in a theory if it can never be backed up by an experiment? In this chapter we will look at these techniques.

The appendix includes a list of experiments that might form part of a sixth form Physics course although the exact content will depend on the interests and facilities in any particular school (see page 480). Most of the experiments are of a standard nature but the value of open-ended investigations should not be overlooked. After all, the whole purpose of experimental research is that experiments are performed that nobody has done before, and although some are designed to confirm a theoretical prediction many unexpected results are found. For this reason some investigations of this type should form part of the course.

Suggested procedure for practical work

Practical work is of great importance in Physics, and you should treat all experiments carefully no matter how simple they appear to be. A good experimental technique can often be gained from such work.

Read all instructions carefully and plan your work before doing anything. Ask for help if you are in any doubt – this is better than damaging expensive apparatus!

Plan the number and spread of readings that you are going to take. If you have to draw a graph as part of the experiment then be sure to take at least eight readings, and make sure that these cover the full range. Do not attempt to set your readings to particular numbers (e.g. every 10 cm); adjust the variable and then read its value.

Always take more than one measurement if there is time and record the accuracy of each. Results should normally be recorded in table form, the units and accuracy being recorded at the top of each column.

A full and correct conclusion should be written at the end of each experiment, together with a comment on the errors and difficulties and how you would overcome them.

A calculation of the experimental error may be required in some experiments.

Remember that experiments without a mathematical answer are just as important as those that do have a numerical result, and a clearly written conclusion is still required.

Practical investigations

Some experiments are designed to verify a principle and others to measure a numerical quantity. There is, however, a third type: those that serve to examine a property or a situation, and seek to explain it or investigate how things will behave under different sets of circumstances. They are experiments which you would design yourselves, ones where the results are not known to you and which you have not looked up in books. Such experiments are known as **open-ended** – we cannot be sure what we will find! Many such investigations are described elsewhere in the book, but we will mention here some suggestions about how to tackle such investigations.

Before starting an experiment of this type you should be sure of the following:

What am I going to measure or investigate?
Do I need a control experiment?
What is my plan of action?
What apparatus will I need, and is it available?
Are my aims realistic?
Will the readings be taken manually or automatically?
How much time will I be able to allow for the investigation?
How will I present my results?

Having decided on these points you will have a better chance of success. Remember that a null result is not necessarily a wrong result; if you are seeing if something will happen and it doesn't then that is itself a valid experimental result. Don't let yourself be put off if things do not happen in quite the way that you expected.

Graphical methods in Physics

The presentation of experimental results or theories in the form of a graph has two main advantages:

(i) the variation of one quantity with another may be seen easily, and
(ii) the average value of a constant may be determined from the graph.

Before looking at graphs in detail you should realise that certain guidelines should be followed when plotting graphs:

1 The axes should be labelled with both the quantity and units.
2 The graph should be given a title.
3 It should fill the space available on the graph paper or page as far as possible.
4 Suitable scales should be chosen – something like 5 squares to 10 units, *not* 7 to 3!
5 The points should be plotted accurately and clearly.
6 The best fit line to the points should be drawn clearly but finely.

Probably the most useful form of graph is one in the form of a straight line and so we will begin by considering this type.

$y = mx + c$

This is the general equation for a straight line, where y and x are variables and m and c are constants. A general example of the graph produced by such an equation is shown in Figure 4.1. You should notice the following points:

(*a*) When $x = 0$ the intercept on the y-axis is c.
(*b*) When $y = 0$ the intercept on the x-axis is $-c/m$.
(*c*) The slope of the line (the change in y with x (dy/dx) is m.

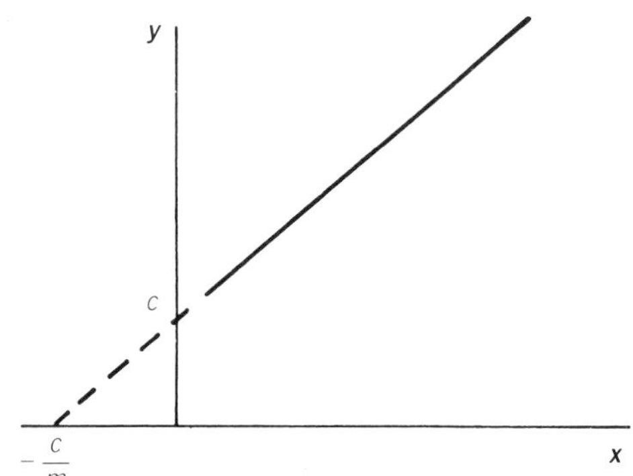

Figure 4.1

There are of course a large number of graphs but we will consider just a few other basic types. The equations and the relevant graphs are shown below.

$y = mx^2 + c$ (Figure 4.2)

This is a basic quadratic; if $c = 0$ the graph passes through the origin. An example of this would be the variation of the kinetic energy of a body with its velocity.

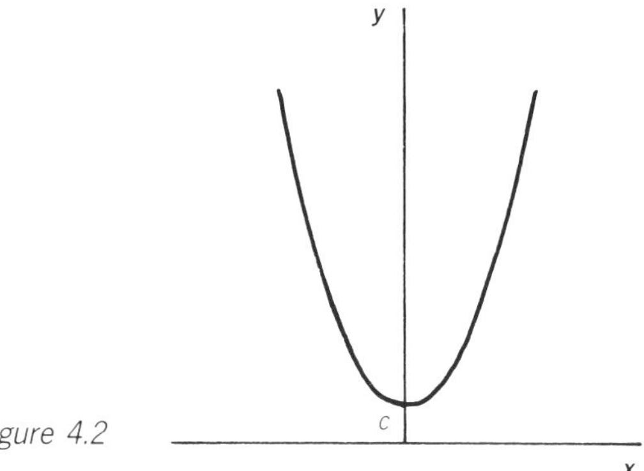

Figure 4.2

$y = ke^x$ (Figure 4.3)

This shows an exponential increase in y with respect to x; k is a constant. An example of this would be the increase in the pressure of air with depth.

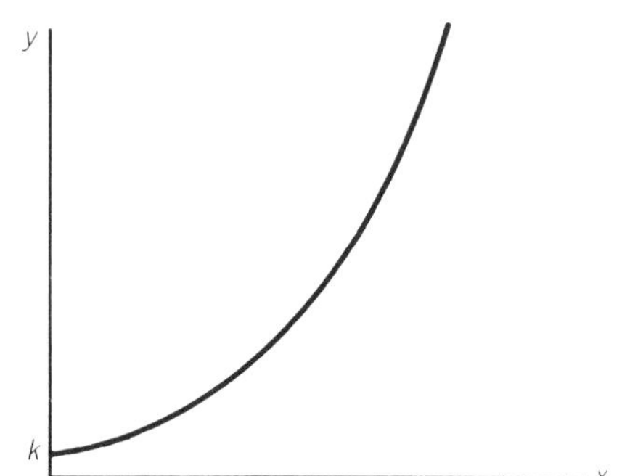

Figure 4.3

$y = ke^{-x}$ (Figure 4.4)

A rather more common form is the exponential decrease of y with respect to x. Once again k is a constant. This equation applies to radioactive decay, the discharge of a capacitor and many other physical phenomena.

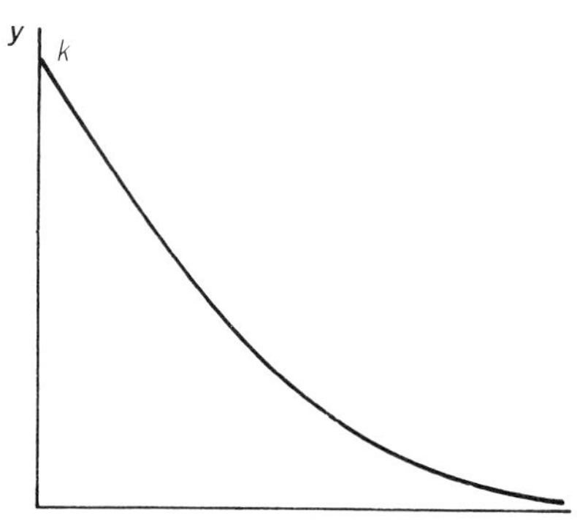

Figure 4.4

It is much more useful to plot the results of an experiment in the form of a straight line and so a means has to be found by which the equations above can be altered to give a linear relation between a function of y and a function of x. This is quite simply done:

For $y = mx^2 + c$: plot y against x^2 (Figure 4.5).

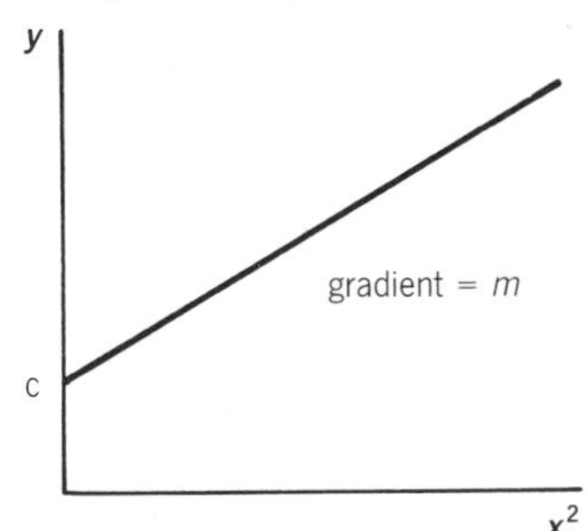

Figure 4.5

For $y = ke^x$: plot y against e^x (Figure 4.6).

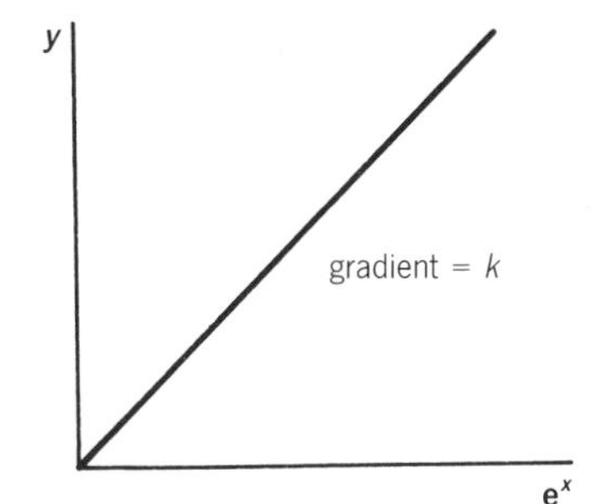

Figure 4.6

For $y = ke^{-x}$: plot y against e^{-x} (Figure 4.7).

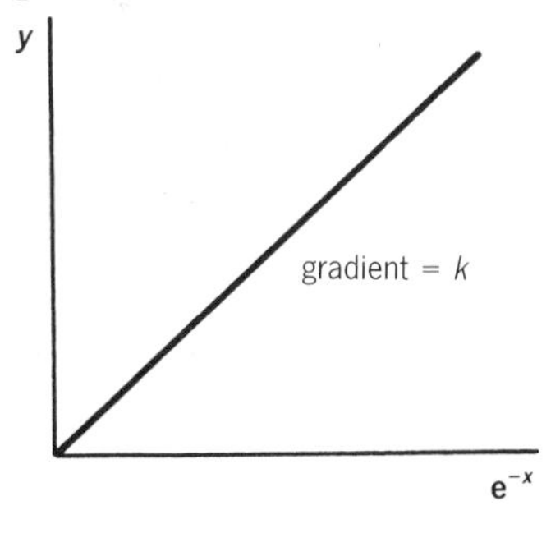

Figure 4.7

$y = ke^{cx}$

Here c is another constant. Taking natural logs gives:

$$\ln y = \ln k + cx$$

Plotting $\ln y$ against x gives a straight line with slope c and intercept on the $\ln y$ axis of $\ln k$ (Figure 4.8).

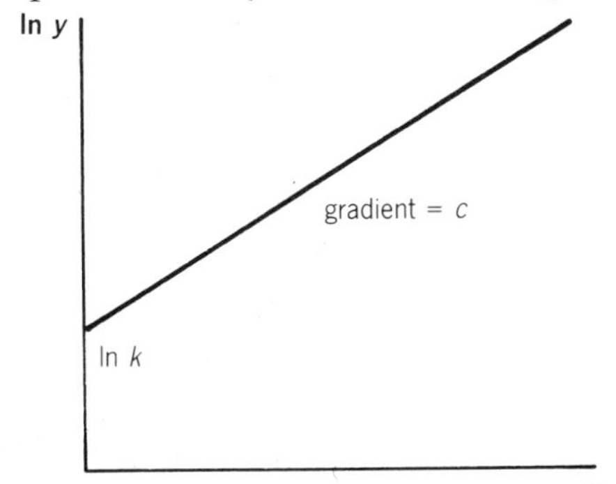

Figure 4.8

Notice that if we have an exponential *decrease*, c is negative.

An alternative method is to take logs of both sides of the equation; this is also useful when one is attempting to derive an unknown equation from a set of experimental results. We will consider first two versions where the equation is known and then one where it is not.

$y = kx^2$

Taking logs gives:

$$\log y = \log k + 2 \log x$$

Plotting $\log y$ against $\log x$ (Figure 4.9) will give a straight line of slope 2, with intercept on the $\log y$ axis of $\log k$.

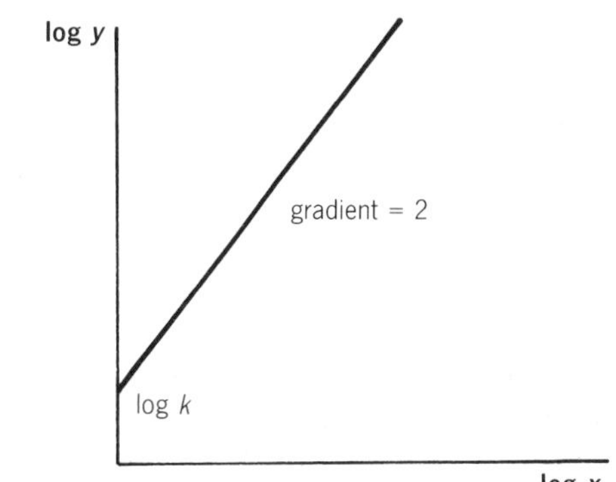

Figure 4.9

$y = ax^b$

Here a and b are constants but both are unknowns. Once again take logs of both sides:

$$\log y = \log a + b \log x$$

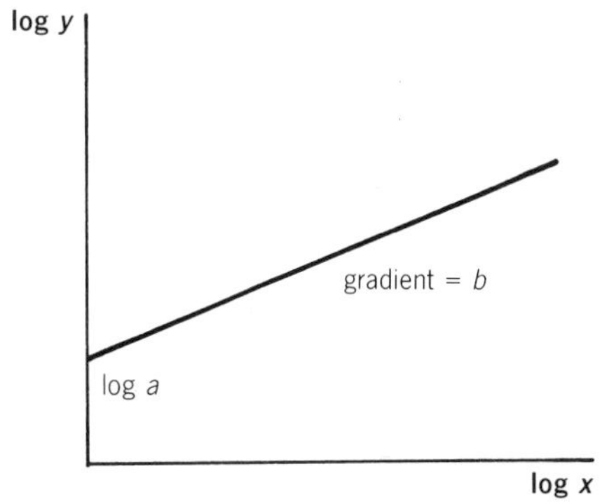

Figure 4.10

Plotting $\log y$ against $\log x$ will give a straight line of slope b and intercept on the $\log y$ axis of $\log a$ (Figure 4.10). Hence both a and b may be found and the form of the equation determined.

An example of the use of these methods may be found on page 76.

1 The following set of results were obtained from an experiment to determine the acceleration due to gravity (g) using a simple pendulum.

Plot a graph of the length of the pendulum (l) against the square of the period of oscillation (T) and thence calculate a mean value for g.

Length l/m	0.1	0.25	0.37	0.45	0.67	0.75	0.82
Time for 10 swings/s	6.3	10.4	12.2	13.8	16.7	17.6	18.4

2 Sketch the graphs that would be obtained by plotting y against x for each of the following equations (k, c and m are constants):

(*a*) $y = kx + m$ (*b*) $mx = k - y$
(*c*) $ky = c - mx$ (*d*) $xy = c$
(*e*) $y = x^2 - k$ (*f*) $y = me^x$
(*g*) $y = ke^{-mx}$ (*h*) $yx^2 = k$

For all linear graphs state the gradient (y/x).

If the graph is not linear state which two variables must be plotted on the two axes to obtain a straight line graph.

3 The following equation is suggested for the variation of two quantities x and t:

$$x = at^b$$

where a and b are constants. Use the data below to plot a suitable linear graph and thence determine the values of a and b.

x	1.86	2.45	3.16	4.07	5.37	6.61	8.71
t	1.60	2.50	4.00	6.40	10.0	15.9	25.1

4 The following set of data was obtained from a radioactive decay experiment:

N	6630	3650	2000	1000	600	330	165	90	50	30	15
T	0	5	10	15	20	25	30	35	40	45	50

N is the number of counts per second and t is the time in seconds. The equation for such a decay is:

$$N = N_0e^{-kt}$$

where N_0 and N represent the initial activity and the activity after a time t, and k is a constant.

Plot a graph of ln N against t and thence determine the time taken for the activity of the source to fall to half its original value (the half-life of the source).

Also determine the value of the constant k, and comment on this value.

5 A 100 μF capacitor is charged and then allowed to discharge through a large resistor (R) and the voltage (V) across it is recorded every five seconds. The following set of results were obtained:

Time/s	0	5	10	15	20	25	30	35	40
Voltage/V	9.0	6.9	5.0	3.7	2.6	2.0	1.4	1.05	0.8

The voltage across a capacitor during discharge is given by the equation:

$$V = V_0e^{-(t/RC)}$$

where V_0 is the initial voltage at a time $t = 0$ and C is the capacitance of the capacitor.

Plot a graph of the voltage against time and use it to find the time for the voltage to decrease to $0.368V_0$ (the time constant (T) for the circuit).

Since $T = RC$, determine the resistance of the resistor (R).

Also plot a graph of ln V against t and determine the value of R from this graph.

Compare your two values of R.

6 Using the data given in question 1, determine the maximum possible error in the value for the acceleration due to gravity obtained.

7 The following readings are taken for the thickness of a single sheet of paper, using a micrometer accurate to 0.01 mm. Calculate the mean value and the likely error in your answer.

Reading	1	2	3	4	5	6	7	8
Thickness/mm	0.11	0.13	0.12	0.11	0.10	0.11	0.09	0.11

8 The following set of results were obtained by a student in an experiment to determine g using a pendulum bob swinging from a non-rigid support.
They have not been well presented. Make your own results table based on these results and comment on any aspects in the original presentation which you consider to be poor.

Length of pendulum (l) (±0.001 m)

l/m	(±0.01 s)	Time for 10 swings T/S	T^2
0.1	8.85	0.89	0.792
0.2	10.81	1.08	
0.3	12.5	1.25	1.563
0.4	14.06	1.406	1.988
0.5	15.31	1.531	
0.25	11.79	1.18	
0.35	13.15	1.315	1.729

Use your results to plot a graph of T^2 against l and find the intercept on the T^2 axis.

The practical examination

In a practical examination, all the preceding points concerning practical work in general should be kept in mind, but there are some additional points that may apply to examination conditions only.

All results should be recorded *as they are made*; no time will be available to make a fair copy afterwards. For this reason it is important that you *plan* the readings that you wish to take and therefore the results table.

All results should be quoted to a sensible degree of accuracy and this accuracy recorded.

At least six different values should be taken for a variable, over the full range asked for in the question, if the graph is thought to be a straight line. Eight different values should be taken if it is thought to be a curve.

If the slope of line is asked for it is likely that the line will be straight, but if the slope *at a specified point* is requested then it is likely that the line will be a curve.

Any 'odd' points that fall well off the line should be checked for their accuracy.

You should not attempt to 'set' measurements to exact values but record the values as they are.

The presentation of the results table is of great importance and therefore an example of how the columns should be headed is shown.

9 The graph shown in Fig.4.11 was obtained by a student in an experiment to measure how the current (I) through a silicon diode varies with the applied voltage (V).
The variation of current with voltge is given by the equation:

$$I = I_0 e^{(eV/kT)}$$

where T is the absolute temperature (372 K in this experiment), k is Boltzmann's constant (1.38×10^{-23} J K^{-1}) and e is the charge on the electron.
Use the graph and the data given above to determine the charge on the electron.

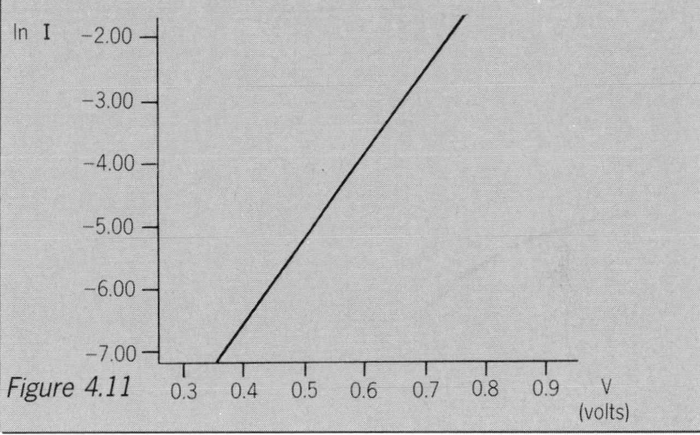

Figure 4.11

name —— (unless defined elsewhere)	Period of oscillation	
symbol ——	T	
unit ——	(s)	
accuracy ——	±0.05	
reading ——	16.10	

It is vital that you read the complete question paper, since if you omit something it may not always be possible to go back and repeat that section – even if you have time to do so.

If the experiment requires the measurement of a property of a substance then do check that your answer is reasonable. For example, refractive indices are never less than 1, the viscosity of water is about 10^{-3} kg s^{-1} m^{-1} and the resistance of a metre length of resistance wire will be a few ohms. For this reason do browse through the section in the book relating to data before such an exam.

Be careful not to claim an unreasonably high degree of accuracy. One of the commonest examples of this is the use of a digital clock to measure the period of an oscillation. Although the clock may be accurate to within 0.01 s, you may not be able to judge to better than 0.5 s when to press it!

Work carefully and methodically, and don't panic! If you do, the only person to suffer will be you.

A level Physics practical: Example one

This experiment is concerned with the oscillations of a loaded ruler in two perpendicular directions.

Figure 4.12 shows a metre rule AB of length $2l$ from which a pendulum bob P is hung by two equal length threads AP and BP, so that the centre of the bob is at a distance h below the centre O of the rod. The whole system is suspended by a short thread from O.

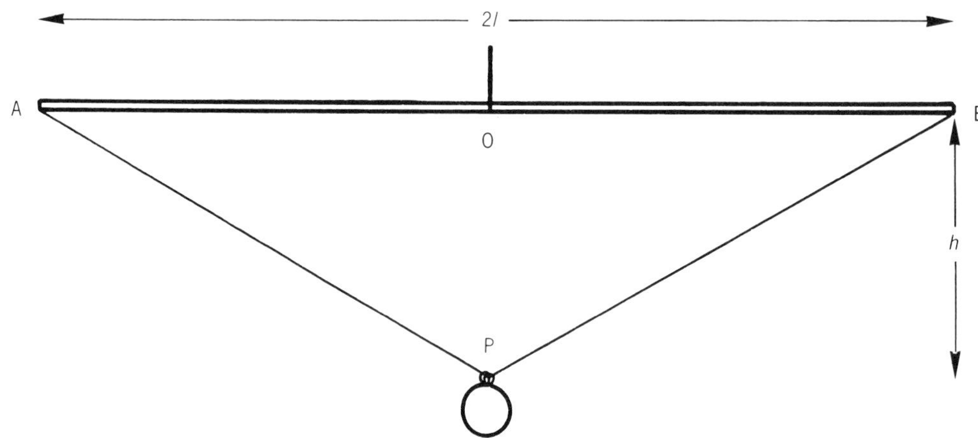

Figure 4.12

In this arrangement a small displacement of the bob followed by its release gives two main modes of oscillation for the system:

(*a*) in the plane APB (so that the rod AB performs a see-saw motion), with period T_1,

(*b*) perpendicular to the plane of APB (so that the rod AB is stationary), with period T_2.

The relationship between the periods T_1 and T_2 and the physical parameters of the system is:

$$T_1^2 - T_2^2 = \frac{4\pi^2}{g}\frac{I}{mh}$$

where g is the acceleration due to gravity, m the mass of the bob, and I is the moment of inertia of the rod (of mass M) about an axis through its centre and perpendicular to its length.

(*a*) (i) Set up the apparatus as described, and measure the periods T_1 and T_2 for various values of h between $h = 0.10$ m and $h = 0.60$ m.

(ii) Plot a graph of $(T_1^2 – T_2^2)$ against $(1/h)$.

(iii) Determine the slope of the graph and from it a value for I/m. How accurate is your value of I/m?

(iv) Given that $I = \frac{1}{3}Ml^2$ and assuming that l is exactly 0.50 m calculate a value of the ratio M/m of the masses of the rod and bob.

(*b*) Describe briefly any difficulties encountered in carrying out the experiment and list any precautions taken. [o]

Sample results

The table of results shows the quantity, units and accuracy of each reading.

h/m ±0.01	$1/h$/m^{-1}	$10T_1$/s ±0.1	T_1/s	$10T_2$/s ±0.1	T_2/s	T_1^2/s^2	T_2^2/s^2	$T_1^2 - T_2^2$
0.67	1.49	18.8	1.88	17.0	1.70	3.55	2.89	0.66
0.59	1.69	18.0	1.80	16.0	1.60	3.25	2.56	0.69
0.51	1.96	17.5	1.75	14.7	1.47	3.08	2.16	0.92
0.47	2.13	17.6	1.76	14.4	1.44	3.11	2.08	1.03
0.43	2.35	17.0	1.70	13.5	1.35	2.89	1.83	1.06
0.39	2.56	16.4	1.64	13.0	1.30	2.72	1.69	1.03
0.34	2.99	17.0	1.70	12.0	1.20	2.89	1.45	1.44
0.28	3.57	17.0	1.70	11.1	1.11	2.89	1.24	1.65
0.21	4.76	17.8	1.78	9.90	0.99	3.17	0.99	2.18
0.18	5.71	18.7	1.87	9.20	0.92	3.50	0.84	2.66
0.13	8.00	20.0	2.00	7.90	0.79	4.04	0.63	3.41

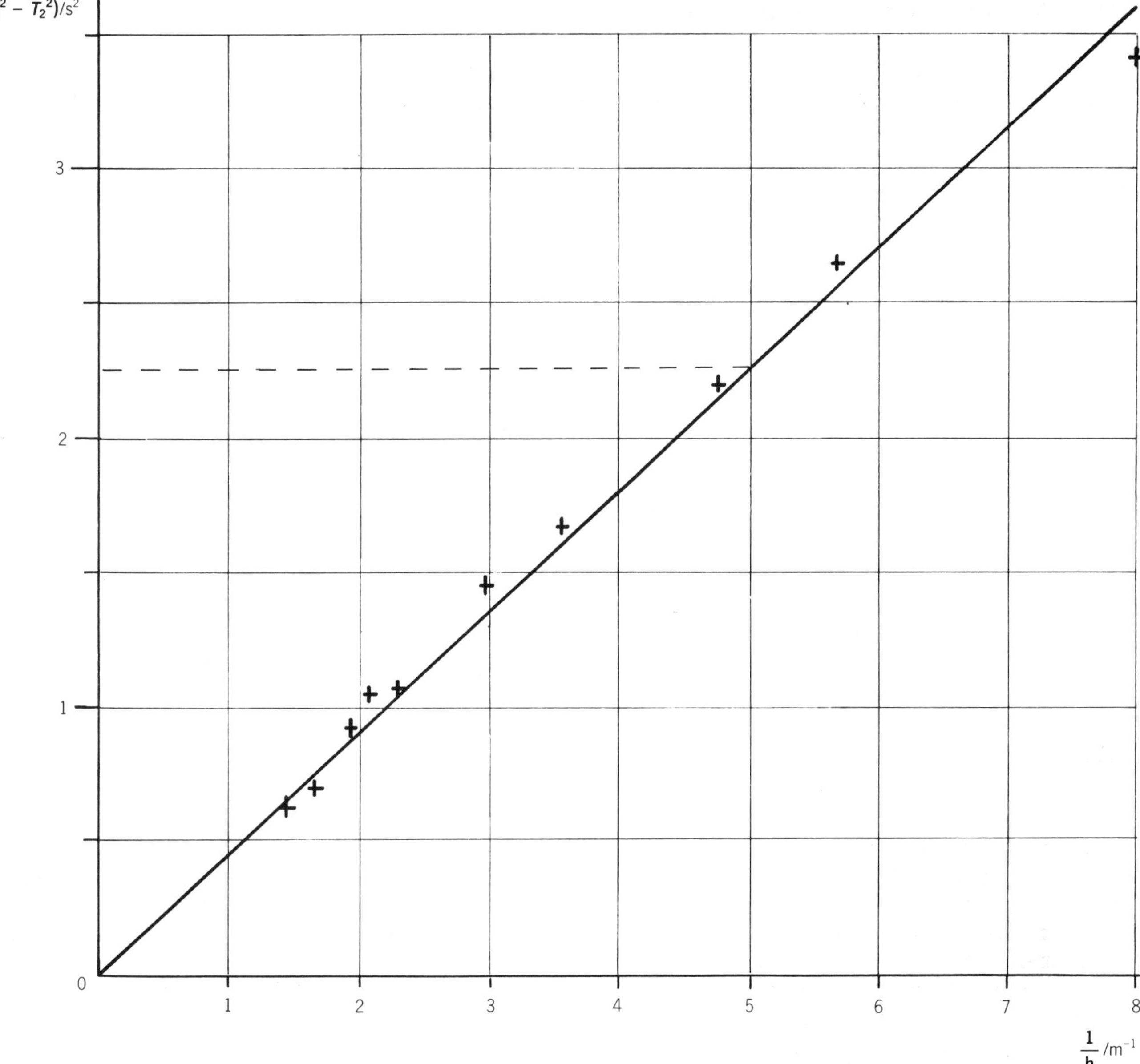

Figure 4.13

From the graph (Figure 4.13) we can determine the slope of the line:

$$\text{Slope} = (T_1^2 - T_2^2)/(1/h) = 2.25/5 = 0.45$$

$$= \frac{4\pi^2 I}{g\,m}$$

Therefore $\frac{I}{m} = 0.11$. But we are given that $I = \frac{1}{3}Ml^2$

Therefore $\frac{M}{m} = \frac{13.24}{9.87} = 1.34$

Comments on the experiment

(*a*) The ruler oscillated in two planes at once and also turned about the cotton suspension. Both these problems were reduced by having a short suspension cotton and timing for a maximum of 10 oscillations, those oscillations being of small amplitude.

(*b*) It was found difficult to change the value of h, and so the cotton was fixed at one end and looped through the bob eye so that only one end had to be adjusted.

A level Physics practical: Example two

For a silicon diode, the relationship between the forward current I passing through it and the potential difference V applied across it is, for low values of forward current,

$$I = I_0 \exp(eV/2kT)$$

where I_0 is a constant, e the electronic charge, k the Boltzmann constant and T the absolute temperature.

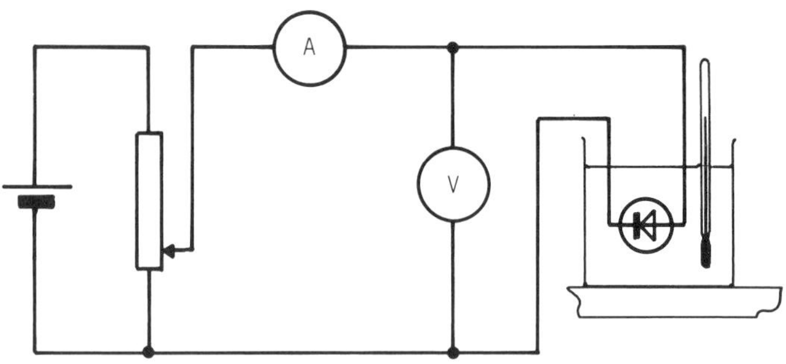

Figure 4.14

(*a*) Set up the apparatus, as shown in Figure 4.14, with the silicon diode immersed in the water bath at room temperature θ. (Take care to ensure that the positive terminal of the power supply is connected to the positive end of the silicon diode, both of which are clearly marked.) Measure the temperature θ_1 and calculate the absolute temperature T_1, of the water bath.

Measure the potential difference V across the diode as the current I is varied in the range 0 to 50 mA.

(*b*) Heat the water bath to boiling point, measure its temperature θ_2 and calculate the absolute temperature T_2 of the water bath. Repeat the measurements of V and I for currents in the range 0 to 50 mA, maintaining the water bath at boiling point.

(*c*) On the same sheet of squared paper, plot graphs of ln I (on the y-axis) against V for the sets of results at T_1 and T_2.

(*d*) Determine the slopes of the two graphs (which are equal to $e/2kT$), and hence calculate the values of the electronic charge e in each case. What is the accuracy of each value?

[Take the value of the Boltzmann constant k to be 1.38×10^{-23} J K $^{-1}$.]

(*e*) List the experimental precautions taken in your measurements. Describe any difficulties encountered and how you overcame them.

The following results were obtained:
(*a*) at AH° C T = 291 K

$I(A) \times 10^{-3}$ $\pm 0.2 \times 10^{-3}$	V (volts) ± 0.005	ln I
3	0.6	−5.81
25.5	0.7	−3.67
50	0.73	−3.00
47	0.725	−3.06
40	0.72	−3.22
33.5	0.71	−3.40
28.5	0.705	−3.56
10	0.66	−4.61
13.4	0.67	−4.31
6.5	0.64	−5.04

(*b*) at 99° C T = 372 K

$I(A) \times 10^{-3}$ $\pm 0.2 \times 10^{-3}$	V (volts) ± 0.005	ln I
18	0.54	−4.02
10.5	0.51	−4.56
28.5	0.56	−3.56
35	0.58	−3.35
48.5	0.60	−3.03
41.5	0.59	−3.18
3.5	0.45	−5.66
8.0	0.49	−4.83
30.5	0.57	−3.49
1	0.33	−6.91

The experiment was simple to perform and no difficulties were experienced. The water was stirred and care was taken not to allow the leads of the diode to get near the flame.

The student should use the results and the graphs to find the following:

(*a*) the slopes of the two graphs

(*b*) the value of the electronic charge for each experiment

(*c*) the accuracy of each measurement

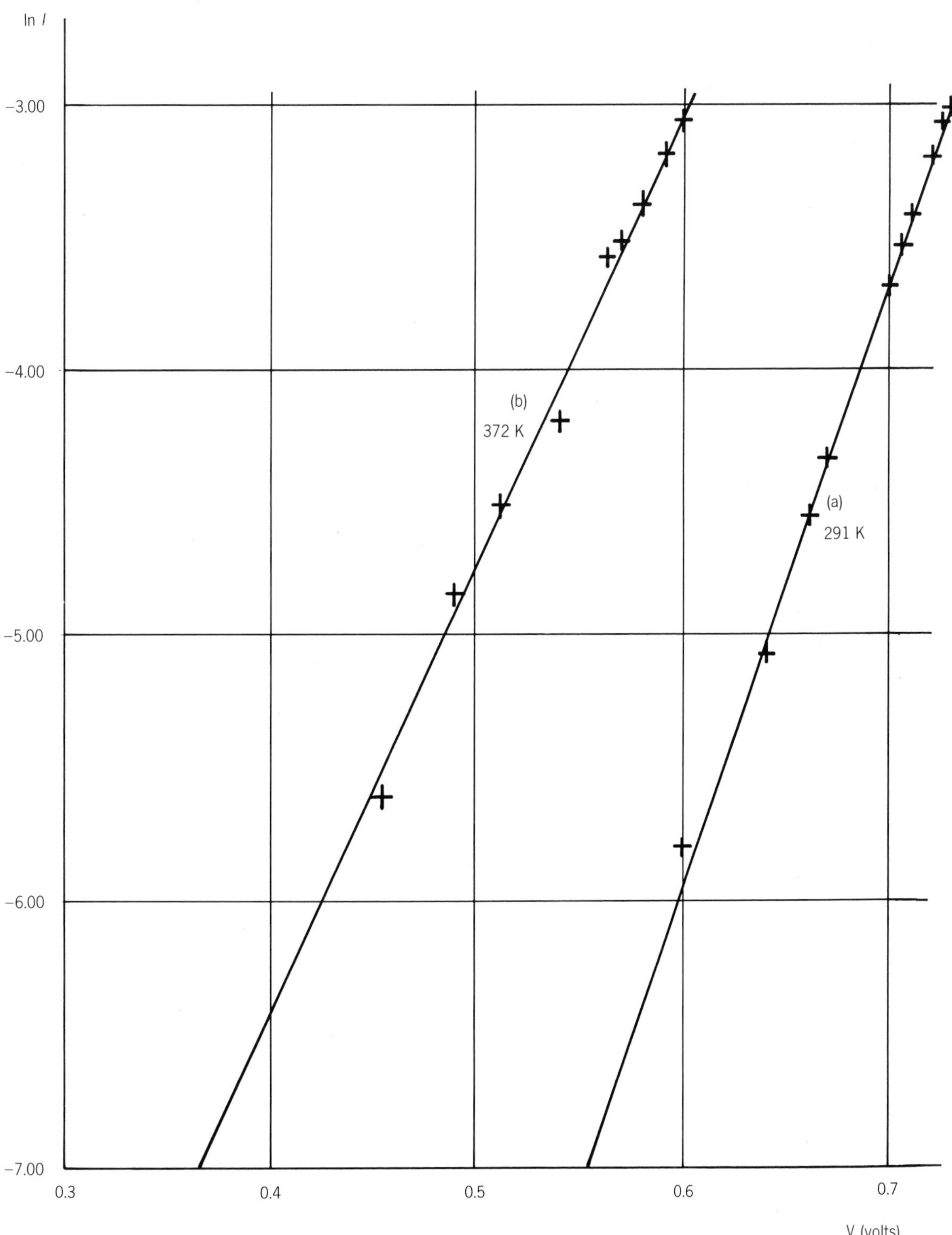

Figure 4.15

5 · Reading Physics

The following passage is based on an article entitled 'Clear paths in Geneva: the vacuum requirements for proton accelerators and storage rings at CERN'.

The equipment discussed is used to produce beams of very high energy protons using electric fields to accelerate them. Initially they are accelerated while travelling in a straight line but at higher energies the magnetic field from very large electromagnets is used to cause them to travel in circles while their speed is being increased. The high-energy protons are then 'stored' by allowing them to circulate in rings so that very high particle concentrations gradually build up in the beams.

In the article proton energies are given in electronvolt (eV) and pressures in torr.

$1 \text{ eV} \approx 1.6 \times 10^{-19} \text{ J}$
$1 \text{ GeV} = 10^{9} \text{ eV}$
$1 \text{ torr} \approx 130 \text{ Pa}$

Read the passage carefully and then answer the questions at the end.

Accelerators and storage rings obviously need some sort of clear path for the beams which they create and maintain. A certain degree of vacuum is therefore necessary which will depend on the type of particle, its energy and the time spent or path length to be covered in the machine. In this article I shall concentrate on proton beams and, in particular, discuss the vacuum requirements of the large proton accelerator and storage ring complex at CERN, Geneva.

In all cases a vacuum is needed to reduce the number of collisions between the charged particles of the beam and the atoms of the residual gas. Such collisions may cause direct loss of particles from the beam or, more usually, some broadening of the beam. The total degradation of the beam will depend on the total number of collisions or, other things being constant, on the product of the residual gas density and the total distance travelled in the machine. This is basic – small machines involving short total path lengths will usually have modest vacuum requirements. Thus the residual gas density must be chosen accordingly for each machine along the accelerator–storage ring complex to maintain the necessary beam quality.

Accelerator vacuum system

Let us now consider the problem in practice as illustrated by the CERN accelerator complex, shown schematically in Figure 5.1. The protons are produced by an arc discharge in hydrogen inside a duoplasmatron operating at the relatively high pressure of about 1 torr.

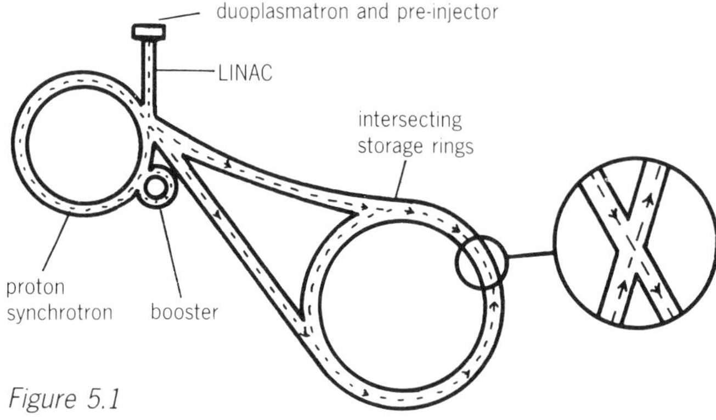

Figure 5.1

The protons are extracted by an electrode system from the duoplasmatron before being accelerated to 0.5 MeV by the electrostatic 'pre-injector'. From the pre-injector the beam enters the LINAC, a linear accelerator about 30 m long, which accelerates the protons to 50 MeV. The path length of 30 m at 10^{-6} torr, even at these low energies, produces negligible broadening of the beam.

The 'booster' is a proton synchroton which accepts the 50 MeV beam from the LINAC and accelerates the protons up to 800 MeV before injection into the main proton synchroton (PS) accelerator. The necessary vacuum in the booster is obtained in a stainless steel system with all-metal joints. The system reaches the design pressure of 10^{-7} torr in eight hours and finally settles at about 2×10^{-8} torr; hydrogen accounts for 90 per cent of the residual gas.

The final and major stage of acceleration from 800 MeV up to a maximum of 31 GeV is achieved in the main PS accelerator. The acceleration period from injection to ejection into a storage ring is, as in the booster, about 1 s. As the protons gain energy the beam becomes 'stiffer', i.e. less affected by collisions, and the vacuum requirement can be relaxed to 10^{-6} torr.

There are, however, other disturbing effects from electrons which are produced in ionising collisions and the performance of the PS has been greatly improved by reducing the average pressure around its 650 m circumference to approximately 2×10^{-7} torr.

Vacuum for storage rings

Storage rings are devices in which beams of high energy particles are accepted from an accelerator and kept circulating in orbits, often for many hours. The much longer time spent and the greater distance travelled by a particle in a storage ring compared to that in an accelerator require a much lower residual gas density in this part of the vacuum chamber.

The CERN intersecting storage rings (ISR) consist of two quasi-circular tubes in the same horizontal plane, each about 1 km in circumference, which intersect at eight symmetrical points (see Figure 5.1 inset; the individual tubes are not shown in the main part of the diagram). At these intersections the two counter-circulating beams of up to 31 GeV collide almost 'head-on'. A vacuum improvement factor of some 10^4 over that in the PS accelerator, i.e. pressures of the order of 10^{-11} torr, is necessary for good operation of proton storage rings.

In general, colliding beam devices suffer, in comparison with accelerators using conventional solid targets, from a relatively low beam–beam interaction rate (or 'luminosity') at the intersection. The luminosity clearly varies as the product of the two beam currents (I_1, I_2) and, for beams crossing in the horizontal plane, it varies inversely as the beam height, h. The flatter a given beam current the denser it appears as a target to the other beam. Thus, for the simple case of equal beams, the luminosity is proportional to I^2/h. (The horizontal beam dimension is only relevant insofar as it enlarges the volume of the collision region.)

1 Sketch the paths of the proton beam shown in Figure 5.1. (The vacuum chambers are not required.) Mark on your diagram
(*a*) the particle energies, where known,
(*b*) the pressure, where known, in the vacuum chamber round each part of the beam under steady conditions,
(*c*) the approximate value of the diameter of the PS and of the ISR.

2 If the mean cross-section of the vacuum system of the ISR is about 1.0×10^{-2} m^2, estimate the volume of this system and the number of molecules of gas in this system during use.
(There are approximately 2.0×10^{25} molecules in 1.0 m^3 of any gas at standard atmospheric pressure [approximately 1.0×10^5 Pa] at the temperature of the vacuum chamber.)

3 The protons in the ISR have a speed of nearly 3.0×10^8 m s^{-1} and a typical beam current is 20 μA. How many protons are circulating in each ring? (Each proton has a charge 1.6×10^{-19}C.)

4 Explain why the luminosity for equal beams 'is proportional to I^2/h'.
(You should assume that the horizontal width of the beam remains unchanged as I and h vary.)

5 Give a general indication of the maximum pressure which you think would be acceptable in the approximately straight links between the PS and the ISR, giving reasons for your value.
(Institute of Physics) [L]

6 · Vectors and scalars

The quantities measured in Physics may be divided into two groups:

(*a*) **scalars** – these are quantities that have magnitude (size) only. Examples are mass, length, energy, temperature and speed.

(*b*) **vectors** – these are quantities with both magnitude and direction. Examples are force, velocity, acceleration and momentum.

Scalars may be added together by simple arithmetic but when vectors are added the *direction* of the vector must also be considered.

A vector may be represented by a line, the length of the line being the magnitude of the vector and the direction of the line the direction of the vector.

The addition of vectors

If we wish to know the sum of two vectors such as the resultant of two forces acting on a body we must use vector addition. We show here how two vectors may be added together.

(i) Vectors acting in the same line
In Figure 6.1, the sum or **resultant** of the two vectors is 50 N, acting from left to right.

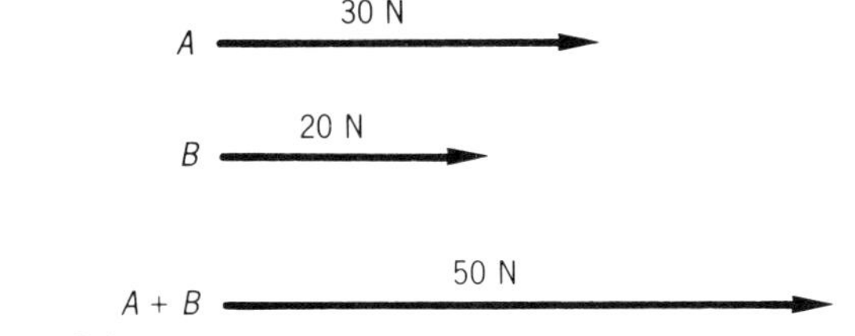

Figure 6.1

(ii) Vectors acting in different directions
The **triangle of vectors** is used in Figure 6.2 to find the resultant. It is given by the line that completes the triangle, in this case 30 N acting along a bearing of 140°.

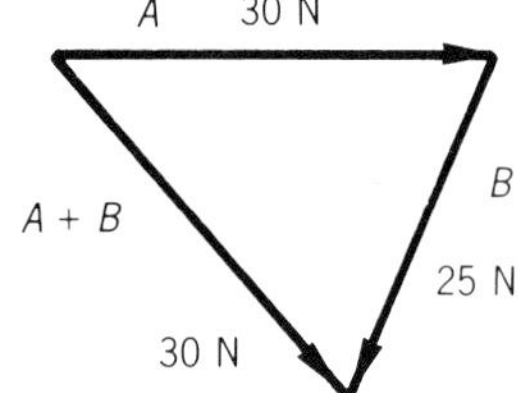

Figure 6.2

Components of vectors

It is often necessary to find the **components** of a vector, usually in two perpendicular directions. This process is known as **resolution** of a vector, usually along two directions at right angles to each other.

The component of the vector along any direction is the magnitude of the vector multiplied by the cosine of the angle between its direction and the direction of the component (Figure 6.3).

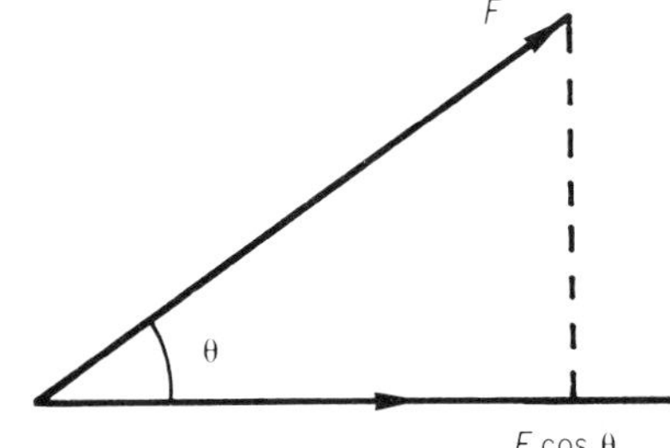

Figure 6.3

A component is the effective value of a vector along a particular direction. Imagine pulling a truck along a railway track by a rope inclined at an angle to the track (Figure 6.4). The force that you apply to the rope has a component along the direction of the track which is less than the force in the rope.

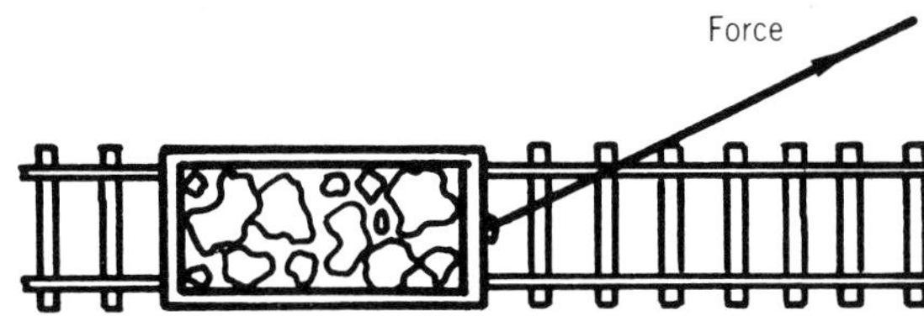

Figure 6.4

Figure 6.5 shows the magnitudes of the components of a vector in two directions at right angles to each other:

Component $F_x = F \cos \theta$
Component $F_y = F \cos(90 - \theta) = F \sin \theta$

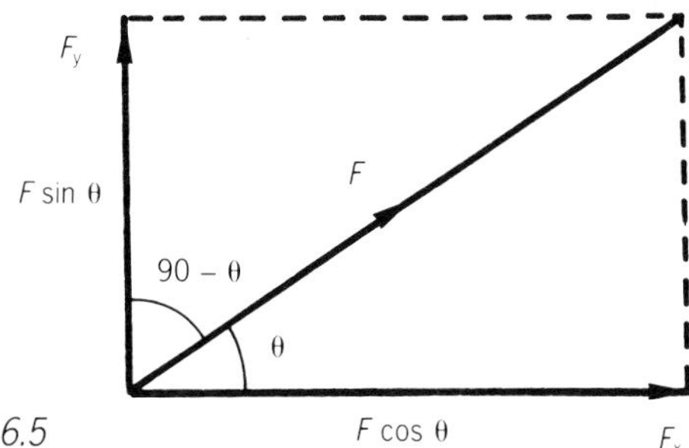

Figure 6.5

1 Discuss and explain the following:
(*a*) Can two vectors be added to give a zero resultant? What about three vectors?
(*b*) Can the direction of motion of a body change while its acceleration is constant?

Mechanics

Testing a Rolls-Royce Pegasus engine at a Ministry of Defence establishment in England (Rolls-Royce)

7 · Kinematics

The motion of any object such as a person, a car, a raindrop or a planet is likely to be very complex. This is because each is made up of a large number of particles of different mass linked together and all subject to a number of forces.

It is for this reason that we begin our study of motion by considering the motion of individual massless particles. This branch of Physics is known as **kinematics** (as distinct from dynamics, where the masses of the moving particles are also considered).

Motion with uniform velocity

Velocity is defined as the rate of change of distance with time or:

$$v = \frac{ds}{dt}$$

and if this is constant the body is said to move with uniform velocity.

Strictly speaking we should write **displacement** instead of distance, since displacement is the distance measured in a particular direction.

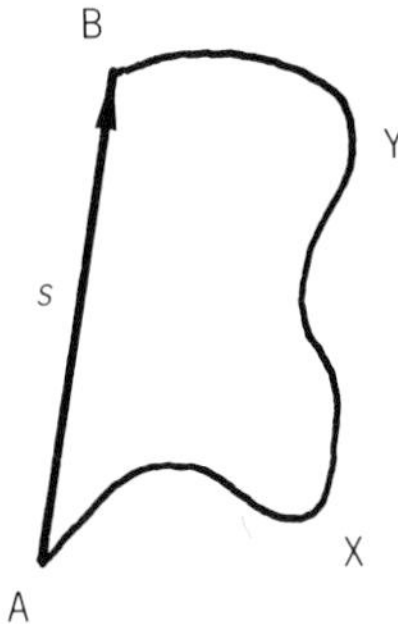

Figure 7.1

The difference between displacement and distance is shown by Figure 7.1. An object moves from A to B along the line AXYB. The *distance* travelled from A to B is shown by the line AXYB while the *displacement* is shown by the vector AB.

Notice that since velocity is a vector, uniform velocity requires there to be no change in either the *magnitude* or *direction* of the velocity.

This type of motion is virtually impossible to achieve in practice. Theoretically, however, the velocity of a body (v) is related to the distance (s) that it travels in a time (t) by the equation:

$$s = vt$$

and a graph of velocity against time will look like Figure 7.2. It should be clear that the distance travelled is equal to the area under the line on the velocity–time graph.

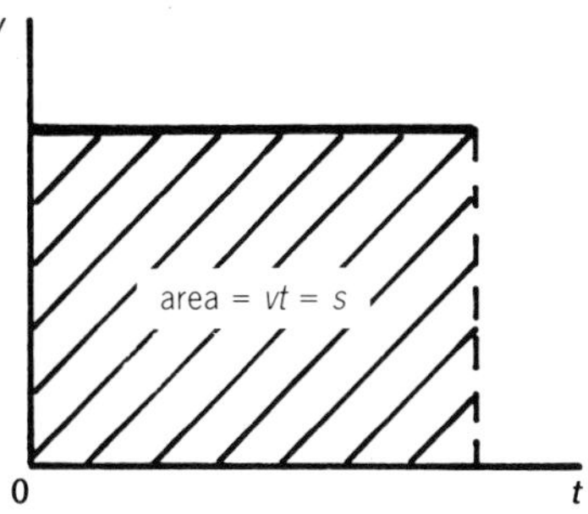

Figure 7.2

Student investigation

The major difficulty when measuring high velocities is the determination of short time intervals.

(*a*) Devise and carry out experiments to measure the time of contact that a ball makes with the ground when dropped on to it from a height of 1 m.
You should carry out *two* separate methods of measuring this time.

(*b*) Measure the rate of rotation of an electric vacuum cleaner motor.

Velocity measurement

The measurement of velocity normally requires the measurement of two quantities (displacement and time) but it can be found directly as the following investigation shows.

Student investigation

The police radar speed trap measures the velocity of a car by the doppler effect using the beats between the transmitted and reflected signals (see page 173). Using the apparatus shown in Figure 7.3, measure the velocity of a trolley.

The frequency (f) that you hear is related to the velocity (v) of the trolley by the formula:

$$f = \frac{2vF}{c}$$

where F is the frequency emitted by the transmitter and c is the velocity of electromagnetic radiation (3×10^8 m s^{-1}).

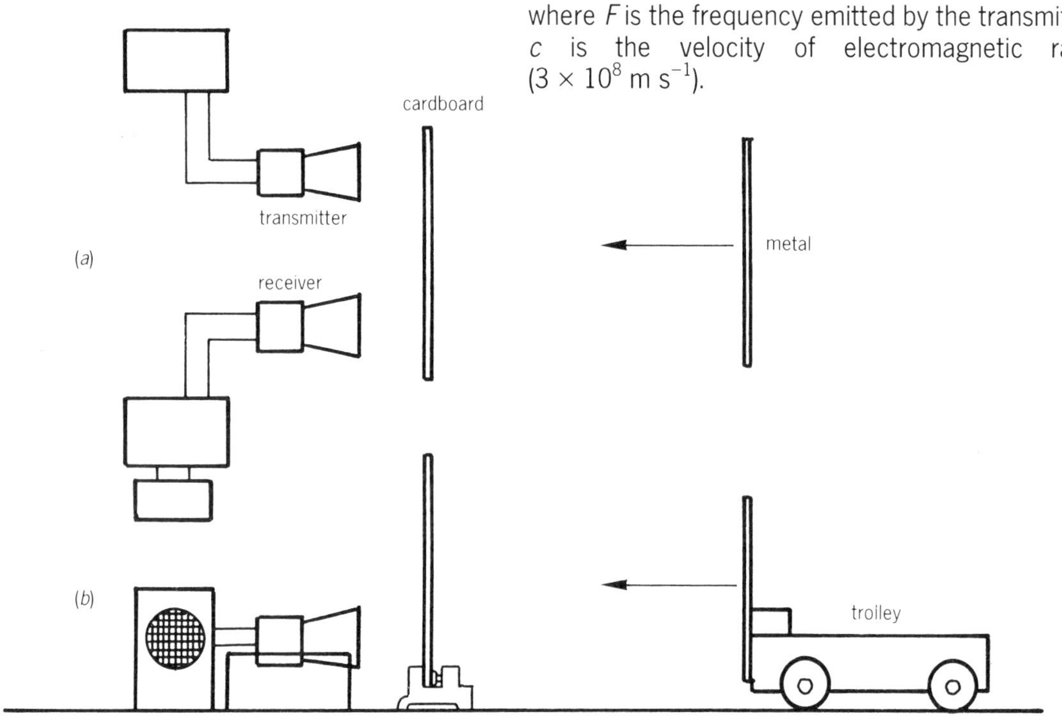

Figure 7.3

Motion with non-uniform velocity

This type of motion is **accelerated motion**, and our definition of instantaneous velocity still holds here. The **acceleration** of an object is defined as:

$$\text{acceleration} = \text{rate of change of velocity} = \frac{dv}{dt}$$

The acceleration at a given time is therefore the gradient of the velocity–time curve at that time (see Figure 7.4).

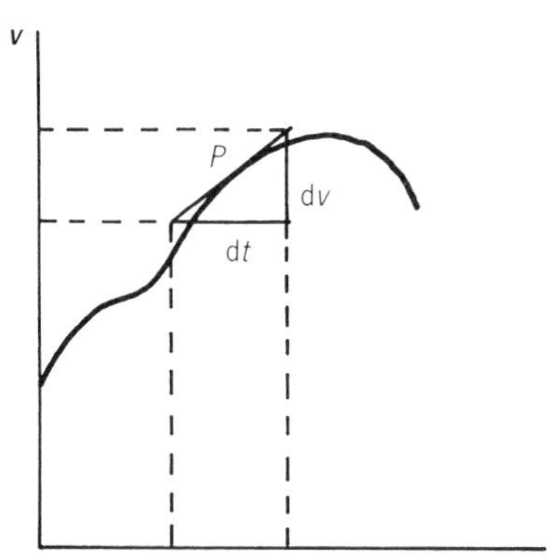

Figure 7.4

By referring to the section concerning Newton's laws of motion (page 34) you might realise that the human body is not sensitive to velocity (if you shut your eyes!) but it can feel acceleration: the rate of acceleration is therefore of some importance in all transport systems.

Some animals experience large accelerations, a perch may reach 33 m s^{-2}, a bush baby 180 m s^{-2}, a woodpecker 1000 m $^{-2}$ when pecking and when a flea jumps it may achieve 1400 m s^{-2}!

The ticker timer

A simple method of calculating the velocity of an object is to use a ticker timer. This makes a series of dots on a length of tape, usually 50 per second. This means that there is 1/50 s between one dot and the next. A section of tape with 5 spaces on it has therefore passed through the timer in 5/50 or 0.1 s and if its length is measured the average velocity of the tape may be found.

Velocity–time graphs

The set of graphs in Figure 7.5 show how the velocity varies with time for several different situations.

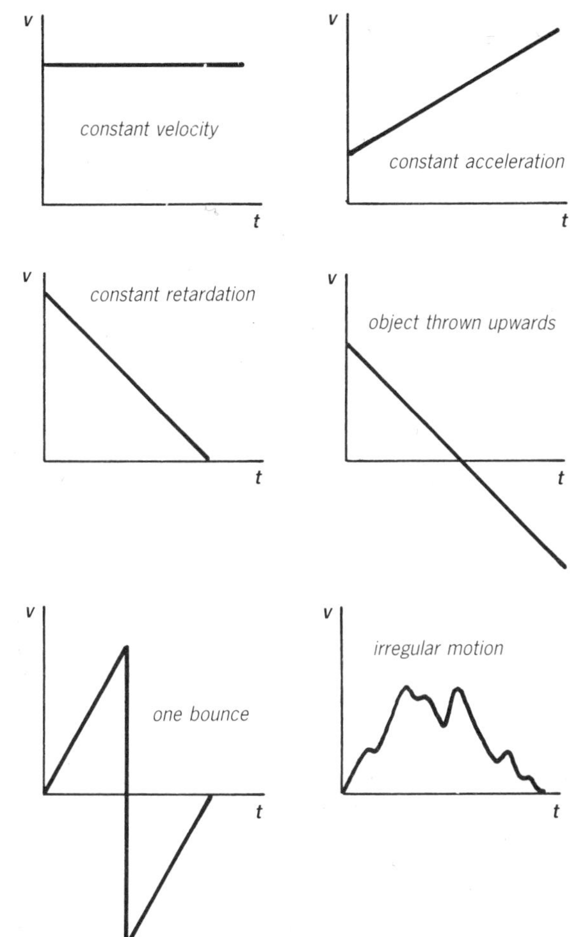

Figure 7.5

The area below the line still represents the distance travelled in a certain time, whether the acceleration is uniform or not. As stated before, the slope of the line at any point (dv/dt) gives the instantaneous acceleration. The average acceleration is found by dividing the velocity change by the time taken.

We consider two types of accelerated motion:

(*a*) uniform acceleration where the velocity changes steadily with time, and

(*b*) non-uniform acceleration where the rate of change of velocity is changing with time.

Student investigation

Pilots and astronauts have to withstand large accelerations and decelerations. Find out the biological affects of such accelerations.

Equations of motion for uniform acceleration

If the acceleration of a particle is uniform the following equations apply to its motion:

$$\text{average velocity} = \frac{v+u}{2}$$

$$a = \frac{v-u}{t}$$

$$s = ut + \tfrac{1}{2}at^2$$

$$v^2 = u^2 + 2as$$

where u is the initial velocity, v the final velocity, a the acceleration and s the displacement.

Example

A balloon is going up at a steady velocity of 12 m s^{-1} at a height of 32 m above the ground when an object is dropped from it. How long does it take for the object to reach the ground?

Consider first the time taken to return to the 32 m level. $v = 12$ m s^{-1}, $u = -12$ m s^{-1}; therefore from $v = u + at$ we have:

$$12 = -12 + 10t$$

Therefore $t = 2.4$ s.

Now it falls to the ground:

$$32 = 12t + 5t^2$$

This is solved to give $t = 1.6$ s or -4.00 s. The negative value indicates a time before it passed the 32 m level, which is clearly of no physical significance here.

Therefore the total time = 1.6 s + 2.4 s = 4 s.

Student investigation

It is often stated in physics questions that the acceleration due to gravity is about 10 m s^{-2}, but is it?

Devise and carry out two experiments based on different principles to measure the acceleration due to gravity.

Suggest where improvements may be made to improve the accuracy if you are not able to carry out the most accurate versions of your investigations.

1 A tortoise travels half the distance from its nose to a lettuce leaf every second. Will the tortoise ever reach the leaf? Explain.

Acceleration due to gravity = 10 m s^{-2}.

2 Discuss the theoretical ways in which the distance travelled by a body can be found for
(*a*) uniform accelerated motion, and
(*b*) non-uniform accelerated motion.

3 Starting from rest, a car travels for 2 minutes with a uniform acceleration of 0.3 m s^{-2}, after which the speed is kept constant until the car is brought to rest with a uniform retardation of 0.6 m s^{-2}. If the total distance covered is 4500 m, what is the time taken for the journey?

4 A sandbag is released from a balloon which is ascending with a steady vertical velocity of 8 m s^{-1}. If the sandbag hits the ground 15 s later, what was the height of the balloon above the ground when it was released?

5 A ball is thrown vertically upwards from the ground with a velocity of 30 m s^{-1}. Exactly 0.5 s later another ball is dropped from rest from a cliff 40 m above the point from which the first stone was projected. Find
(*a*) the time after the first stone was thrown when the two stones meet, and
(*b*) how far above the ground they are at this time.

6 What is meant by the statement that space is three-dimensional? [A–W]

7 Light takes 4.5 years to reach us from the nearest star. If the velocity of light is $3 \times 10^8 \text{ m s}^{-1}$, how far away is the star? A rocket just outside the Earth's atmosphere in space accelerates at 30 m s^{-2} for a week (7 days). How long will it take for the rocket to reach the star? (Ignore any gravitational attraction.)

8 A body dropped from rest falls half its total path in the last second before it strikes the ground. From what height was it dropped?

9 The data below was taken for part of a car's journey. Plot a graph of the velocity of the car against time, drawing the best fit line through the points, and from the graph determine the following:
(*a*) the total distance travelled,
(*b*) the average velocity over the whole journey,
(*c*) the velocity at $t = 10$ s,
(*d*) the average acceleration between $t = 10$ s and $t = 20$ s,
(*e*) the instantaneous acceleration at $t = 14$ s, and
(*f*) the instantaneous acceleration at $t = 25$ s.

Time/s	0	4	6	8	12	15	18	20	22	23	26	30
Velocity/m s^{-1}	0	2.5	4.0	6.5	8.0	8.0	8.5	9.0	7.5	5.2	4.0	2.5

10 An electron in a TV tube reaches a velocity in the region of 10^7 m s^{-1}. If the distance between the filament and the accelerating anode is 5 cm, what is the acceleration of the electron? (Assume that this is uniform.)

Example

A light rubber ball of mass 0.08 kg is thrown vertically upwards at 14 m s^{-1}, and Figure 7.6 represents the velocity–time graph for part of the resulting motion.

(*a*) Describe the motion briefly.

(*b*) Estimate the acceleration at A, and the accelerations at B and C. How do you account for the differences between them?

(*c*) Estimate the height to which the ball rises above the point of projection and hence the gain in potential energy at this stage of the motion. Write down the loss of kinetic energy and account for the difference between these values.

(*d*) Find the loss of potential energy and the gain in kinetic energy of the ball during its downward motion.

(*e*) Find the momentum change, and the average force acting on the ball between A and B. Find also the momentum change and the average force acting on the ball between B and C. Comment on these two sets of results. [O]

(*a*) The ball is thrown upwards and decelerates with a decreasing acceleration until it reaches the top at B. It then descends to the bottom at C when it bounces.

(*b*) The accelerations at A, B and C are found by taking the gradient of the curve at those points.

Acceleration at A = -17.5 m s^{-2}
Acceleration at B = -10.0 m s^{-2}
Acceleration at C = -3.3 m s^{-2}

(*c*) Since the acceleration is not uniform we cannot use the simple equations of motion to calculate the distance travelled; the area under the curve must be used instead.
This gives height to which the ball rises = 6.3 m (area AOB)

Gain in potential energy = $0.08 \times 10 \times 6.3 = 5.04$ J
Loss in kinetic energy = $\frac{1}{2} \times 0.08 \times 196 = 7.84$ J

The difference is due to the energy lost due to air friction.
(*d*) Loss in potential energy = $0.08 \times 10 \times 6.3$
= 5.04 J (area BCD)
Gain in kinetic energy = $\frac{1}{2} \times 0.08 \times 64 = 2.56$ J
(*e*) Momentum change (A – B) = 0.08×14
= 1.12 N s
Average force = 1.12/1.0 = 1.12 N
Momentum change (B – C) = $0.08 \times 8 = 0.64$ N s
Average force = 0.64/1.4 = 0.457 N

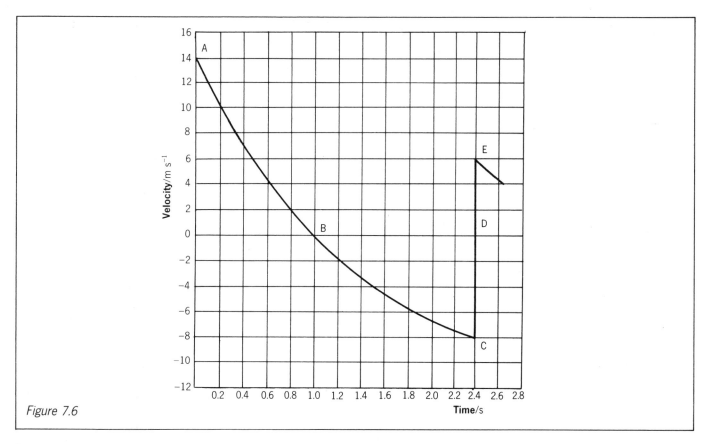

Figure 7.6

Relative velocity

The velocity of an object only really has meaning when it is expressed relative to a set of axes or 'frame of reference'.

We usually consider the motion of objects moving relative to the Earth, but since the Earth is orbiting the Sun and the Sun is moving through the Galaxy this is a purely arbitrary concept. When dealing with more than one body in motion the problem is complex – consider the difficulties in sending the space probe Giotto to rendezvous with Halley's comet many millions of miles away!

We should always specify the frame of reference relative to which an object is moving.

The velocity of one body relative to another is called its **relative velocity**.

Think about the case where *both* bodies are moving relative to a third. A simple example would be where the motions of both bodies are in the same straight line – for instance, two cars travelling along a motorway. If both cars are travelling in the same direction, one at 25 m s^{-1} and the other at 35 m s^{-1}, then their relative velocity is 10 m s^{-1} (by vector addition). If they are moving in opposite directions, however, the relative velocity of one car with respect to the other is 60 m s^{-1}.

What we are effectively doing is considering one car to be at rest and finding the velocity of the other car in that frame of reference. To do this we must add the negative of the velocity of one car to both cars' velocities. This effectively brings one to rest and we then consider the velocity of the other car relative to it.

The situation is a little more complex when the motion of the two objects is not in the same straight line. Consider the case shown in Figure 7.7(*a*).

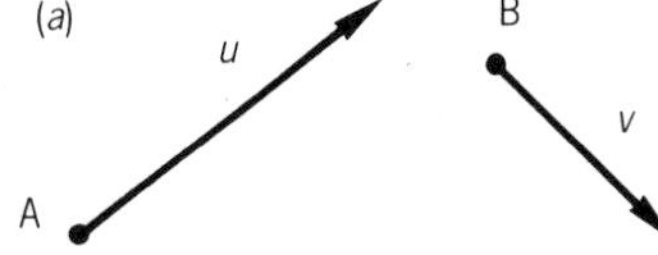

Let object A be moving with velocity u and object B be moving with velocity v. (Note that both these velocities are relative to an external frame of reference.)

If we add the negative of the velocity of A ($-u$) to A and B, we can imagine A to be at rest and then find the velocity of B relative to it. (See Figure 7.7(*b*)). This is most easily done by drawing the vector diagram and finding the resultant shown by the vector R.

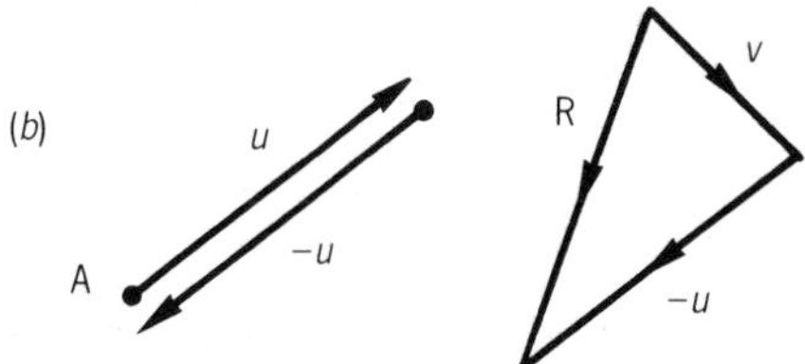

Figure 7.7

Example

Two cars are moving along a road at right angles to each other as shown in Figure 7.8(*a*). Car A is moving due west at 20 m s^{-1} and car B is moving due north at 30 m s^{-1}. At a given moment B is exactly 1.5 km due south of A.

Find the relative velocity of car B to car A, and the distance of closest approach (*d*) of the two cars.

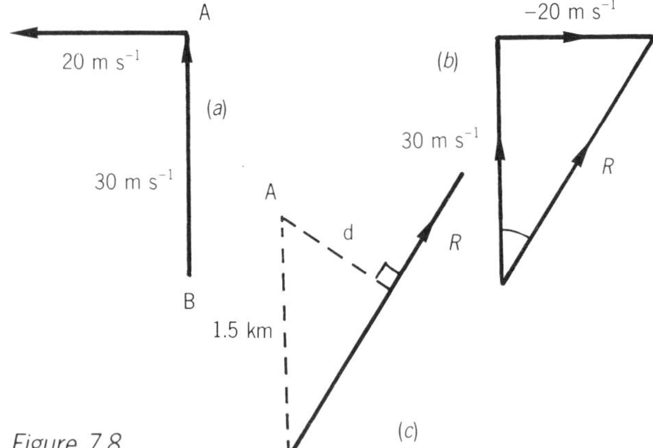

Figure 7.8

From Figure 7.8(*b*), the relative velocity is found to be 36.1 m s^{-1} in a direction N 33.7° E.

Using Figure 7.8(*c*) we can find the distance of closest approach, using the relative velocity just calculated. Remember that this velocity assumes A to be at rest; Figure 7.8(*c*) is not a vector diagram but simply a *map* showing the positions of the two cars.

Distance of closest approach $= 1.5 \sin(33.7)$
$= 0.83$ km

The time to the point of closest approach is given by $\frac{1250}{36.1} = 34.5$ s.

11 A rower whose speed of rowing is *u* crosses a river of width *s* to a point exactly opposite. Find the time of the journey if the speed of the stream is *V* (less than *u*).

12 A submarine moving due north at a speed of 5 m s^{-1} is sighted at 10.00 a.m. from a ship steaming due east at 10 m s^{-1}. The submarine is then 6 km north-east of the ship. Find, by calculation or scale diagrams,

(*a*) the relative velocity of the submarine to the ship,

(*b*) the relative velocity of the ship to the submarine,

(*c*) the distance of closest approach.

13 A car is travelling due north. Is it possible for it to have a velocity to the north and at the same time an acceleration due south? Explain your answer.

Projectiles

A body that is projected through a gravitational field is known as a **projectile**. We will look for the present at the case of an unpowered projectile such as a stone, and ignore the effects of air resistance.

Consider first the case of an object that is projected vertically upwards or dropped vertically downwards.

The vertical acceleration is due to the gravitational attraction of the Earth and is called the **acceleration due to gravity** (*g*). The value of *g* decreases as the distance from the centre of the Earth increases, but if we restrict our considerations to points close to the Earth's surface its value is sensibly constant and has a value of about 9.81 m s^{-2} (often simplified to 10 m s^{-2}).

Since this acceleration is produced by the gravitational field of the Earth it may also be called the **gravitational intensity** (units N kg^{-1}) (see page 35 on Newton's laws). The value of *g* can vary due to the following factors (see also Chapter 16 on Gravitation):

(*a*) distance above sea level – *g* is less up a mountain or in a satellite or plane;

(*b*) on the equator – the distance from the centre of the Earth is greater here, because of the non-spherical shape of the Earth, and *g* is smaller;

(*c*) above mineral deposits – there is a greater attraction and so *g* is larger;

(*d*) the centripetal force of the rotating Earth causes a variation in *g* from Equator to pole.

Example

A ball is thrown vertically upwards with a velocity of 30 m s^{-1}. Calculate:

(*a*) the maximum height reached,

(*b*) the time taken for it to return to the ground.

(*a*) Using $v^2 = u^2 + 2as$,

$$0 = 900 - 2 \times 10 \times s$$

$$20s = 900$$

$$s = 45 \text{ m}$$

Notice that at the maximum height the vertical velocity is zero and that the acceleration due to gravity is negative since it acts to retard the ball.

(*b*) Using $v = u + at$,

$$30 = -30 + 10t$$

$$t = 6 \text{ s}$$

Notice that the ball must return to the ground with the same speed with which it left it.

Object projected at an angle

Consider now the case of an object that is projected at an angle to the horizontal other than 90°.

It is helpful to treat the horizontal and vertical components of velocity separately. A diagram of the motion is shown in Figure 7.9.

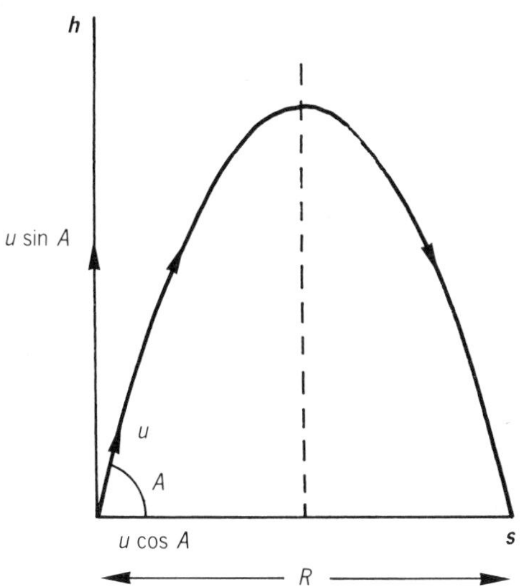

Figure 7.9

Consider an object projected with velocity u at an angle A to the horizontal.

Vertical component of velocity = u sin A
Horizontal component of velocity = u cos A

If we ignore the effects of air resistance, the horizontal velocity is constant and the vertical velocity changes with a uniform acceleration. The path that the body follows is a **parabola** as can be seen from the proof below.
Vertical motion: $h = ut \sin A - \frac{1}{2}gt^2$
Horizontal motion: $s = ut \cos A$

(*a*) Range

The object will hit the ground again when $h = 0$, i.e. when $ut \sin A = \frac{1}{2}gt^2$.

Therefore it will hit the ground after a time t, where $t = 2u \sin A/g$.

Therefore the range R is given by:

$$\begin{aligned} R &= \text{horizontal velocity} \times \text{time} \\ &= (u \cos A \times 2u \sin A)/g \\ &= (u^2\, 2 \sin A \cos A)/g \\ &= \frac{u^2}{g} \sin 2A \end{aligned}$$

We can therefore see that the maximum range for a given velocity of projection is when $\sin 2A = 1$, that is, when $2A = 90°$ or when $A = 45°$.

(*b*) Height

The projectile will reach its maximum height when the vertical component of its velocity is zero, that is, when $u \sin A - gt = 0$, or $t = u \sin A/g$

This gives the maximum height reached as:

$$h = \frac{u^2 \sin^2 A}{2g}$$

Figure 7.10 shows the parabolic path of an object projected horizontally. The time taken for the object to reach the ground along the parabolic path is the same as if it were dropped vertically.

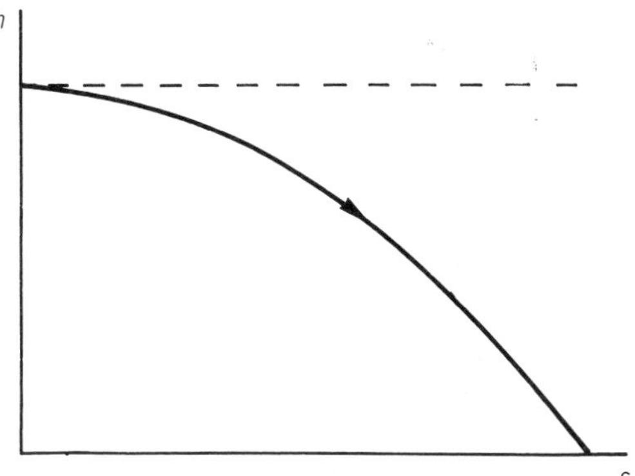

Figure 7.10

14 A man stands on the edge of a cliff and throws a stone vertically upwards with an initial speed *u*. He then throws another stone vertically downwards with the same vertical velocity. Which stone, if either, has the greater velocity when it hits the ground?

15 A tennis ball is returned from a point close to the ground on the base line and just clears the net, hitting the ground on the base line at the other side of the net. If the net is 1.0 m high and the distance from the net to either base line is 12 m, find the velocity with which the ball left the racquet.

Student investigation

Make three model car tracks, one straight and two in the shape of a catenary. Try allowing model cars to run down each track and explain what you observe.

Start two cars at different points on the two catenary tracks. Which one gets to the bottom first? Try to explain the results.

Example

A stone is projected at an angle of 60° to the horizontal with a velocity of 30 m s^{-1}. Calculate (*a*) the highest point reached, (*b*) the range, (*c*) the time taken for the flight, (*d*) the height of the stone at the instant that the path makes an angle of 30° with the horizontal.

(*a*) Highest point $= \dfrac{30^2 \sin^2 60°}{2g} = \dfrac{900 \times 0.75}{20} = 33.75$ m.

(*b*) Range $= \dfrac{30^2 \sin 120°}{10} = \dfrac{900 \times 0.866}{10} = 78$ m.

(*c*) Time of flight $= \dfrac{2 \times 30 \sin 60°}{10} = 5.2$ s.

(*d*) At the point when the path makes an angle of 30° to the horizontal we have:

$$\tan 30° = \frac{\text{vertical component of velocity}}{\text{horizontal component of velocity}} = \frac{\text{vertical component}}{30 \cos 60°}$$

The vertical component (v) is given by the formula: $v^2 = 30^2 \sin^2 60° - (2 \times 10 \times h) = (900 \times 0.75) - 20h$ where h is the height reached at that point.

$$\text{Therefore } \tan 30° = \frac{675 - 20h}{15}$$

$$15 \times 0.58 = 675 - 20h$$
$$8.66 = 675 - 20h$$
$$20h = 666$$
$$h = 33.3 \text{ m}$$

Trajectory – parabolic path

The shape of the trajectory can be found by combining the equations for vertical and horizontal velocity.

Taking the vertical displacement as y and the horizontal displacement as x, we have:

$$x = ut \cos A$$
$$y = ut \sin A - \tfrac{1}{2}gt^2$$

This gives:

$$y = x \tan A - \frac{gx^2}{2u^2 \cos^2 A}$$

For a given angle of projection and projection velocity, this becomes:

$$y = Bx - Cx^2$$

where B and C are constants; this is the equation of a parabola.

Example

An aeroplane flies at a height h at a constant speed u in a straight horizontal line, so as to pass vertically over a certain gun. At the instant when the aeroplane is directly over it the gun fires a shell which hits the plane (Figure 7.11). Find the minimum muzzle velocity (v) of the shell and the correct angle of elevation (A) of the gun at this velocity (neglecting air resistance).

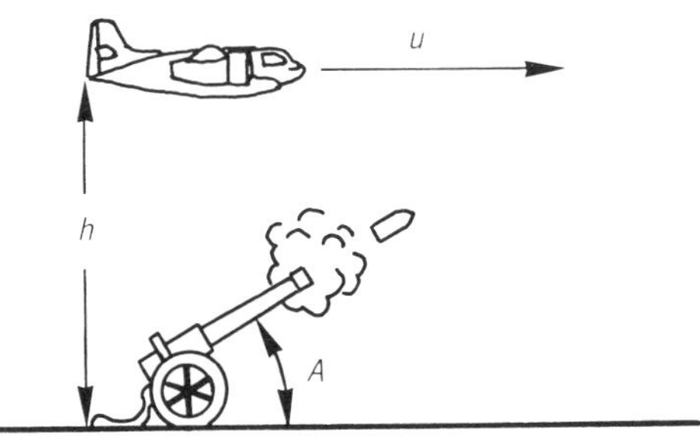

Figure 7.11

If we require the minimum muzzle velocity, then the height of the plane when it is hit must be the maximum height reached by the shell, in other words the vertical component of its velocity must be zero when it hits the plane.

Therefore $0 = v^2 \sin^2 A - 2gh$

But $u = v \cos A$.

Therefore

$$0 = v^2(1 - \cos^2 A) - 2gh$$
$$v^2 = u^2 + 2gh$$
$$v = \sqrt{(u^2 + 2gh)}$$

and this gives

$$\tan (A) = \frac{2gh}{u^2}$$

The above equations only refer to projectiles where the effects of air resistance have been ignored. Quite different paths may be found in practice for such objects as golf balls, javelins and disci.

16 A shot is projected at an angle of 55° to the horizontal with a velocity of 8 m s^{-1}. Calculate
(*a*) the highest point reached,
(*b*) the range,
(*c*) the time taken to return to the ground,
(*d*) the height of the shot when its path makes an angle of 30° with the horizontal, and
(*e*) the velocity of the shot when it hits the ground.
(Neglect the effects of air resistance.)

8 · Mass in motion

Up to this point we have considered the motion of massless particles; we now move on to think about how the mass of the body affects its state of motion.

It was Galileo who first realised that the motion of a body is independent of its mass. It is the *change* of this state of motion that is affected by the mass of the body.

We all know that if we are in a car that brakes suddenly we seem to be flung forwards, and that if the car corners we seem to move to the outer edge of the curve. There is also the beautiful party trick where a magician removes a cloth from under a tea set and the tea set remains where it was. Both these results are due to the lack of any large force acting on the body.

A body is said to possess a property called inertia. This can be simply defined as follows:

The inertia of a body is measured by its reluctance to change its state of motion.

The more massive the body, the more inertia it has.

The period of vibration of an object is also affected by its inertia. The simple inertia balance that you may have used in your GCSE courses has a period that depends solely on the inertia of the masses in the end.

Galileo was the first to appreciate the effect of a force on the motion of a massive body. For example, the force acting on a shell due to the gun stops the instant it leaves the barrel – longer gun barrels therefore allow the force to act for longer.

The object shown in Figure 8.1 is resting on a frictionless slope.

When the object is released it will slide down the slope and go up the opposite side to the same height from which it was released. If we decrease the angle of the slope on the right-hand side, then the object will move further before it reaches the original height.

If we were to reduce the slope to zero the object would theoretically go on moving for ever. The resultant forces on the object in this case are zero, however. This therefore shows that a force is needed to change the motion of the object.

Experiments where there is no resultant force are difficult to achieve, since frictional forces always affect the result. The best that can be done in school would be with a linear air track.

Student investigation

The Victorians were fond of a parlour demonstration using inertia. A needle was fixed in the two ends of a broom handle and then balanced with the two needles resting on two wine glasses (see Figure 8.2). The trick was to break the broom handle by hitting it sharply in the centre with another broom handle.

Suggest why this might be possible and devise your own version of the experiment, without using wine glasses. Can you measure the forces on the two supports at the moment of impact?

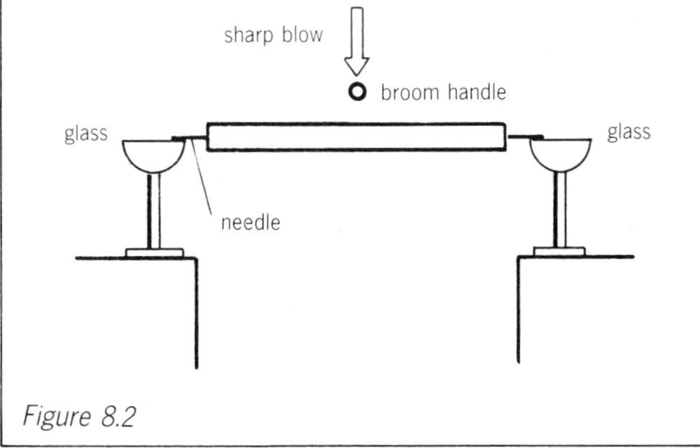

Figure 8.2

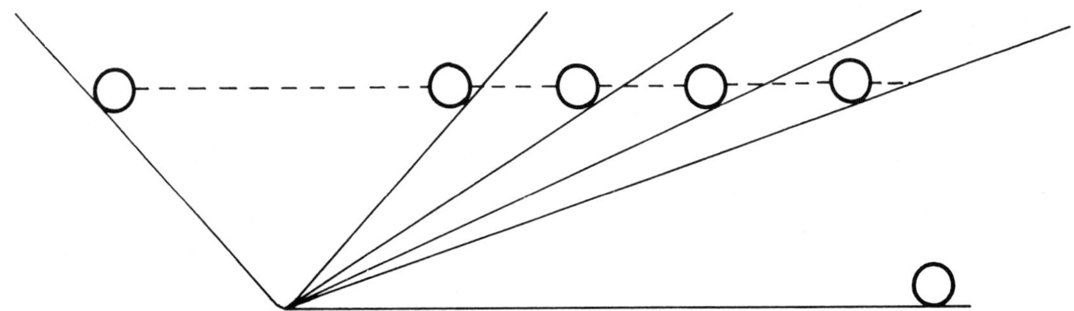

Figure 8.1

Newton's laws of motion

For many centuries the problem of motion and its causes had puzzled scientists – it was not until the time of Galileo and Newton that real progress in its explanation was made.

It was thought that a 'force' was needed to keep a body moving, and that if this force was removed the body would naturally come to rest. However, Galileo (1564–1642) (see page 33) proposed that a force was only needed to *change* the state of motion of a body, thus laying the foundation for Newton's work.

In 1687 Newton published his famous treatise on mechanics, *Principia Mathematica*. In it he proposed his three laws of motion, adopting many of the ideas already suggested by Galileo.

Experimental investigation of Newton's laws

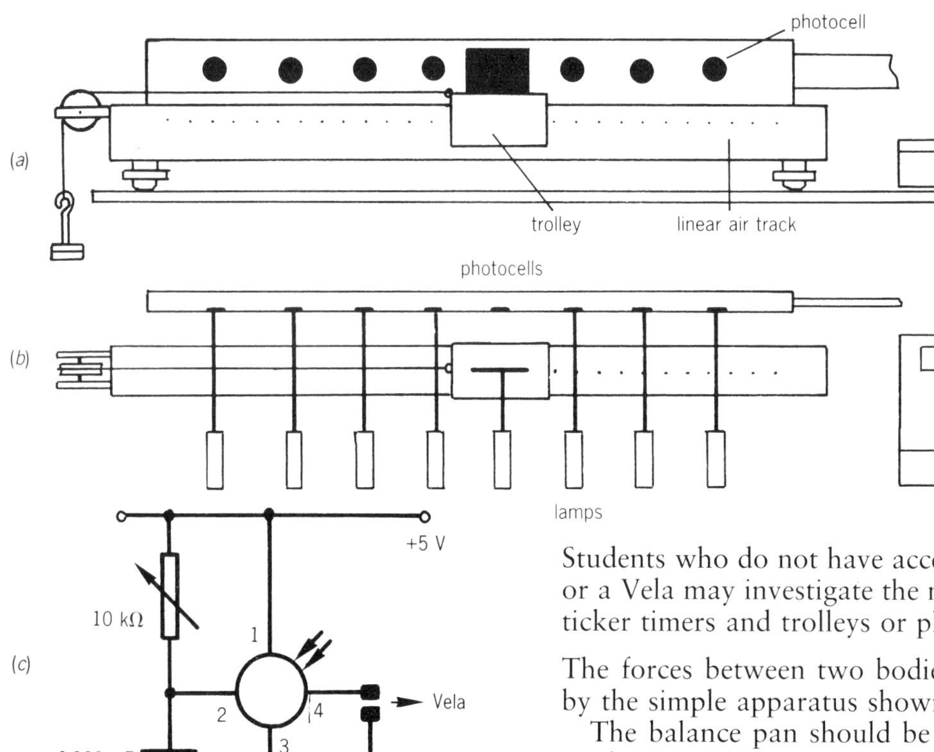

Figure 8.3

The laws of motion may best be investigated using a linear air track.

If the track is carefully levelled it may be shown that the trolley will remain at rest or move with a constant velocity since no resultant force acts on it. (The constant velocity may be checked using either two photodiode assemblies or a modification of the experiment using a Vela, below.)

The effect of a resultant force on the acceleration of a body may be investigated using the apparatus in Figure 8.3.

The outputs from the light-sensitive gates are connected to the digital inputs of the Vela. The time for the card to pass in front of each gate is recorded and hence the change in velocity and therefore the acceleration may be found.

Students who do not have access to a linear air track or a Vela may investigate the motion of masses using ticker timers and trolleys or photodiode assemblies.

The forces between two bodies may be investigated by the simple apparatus shown in Figure 8.4.

The balance pan should be pushed down and the readings on the compression balance and the spring balance recorded.

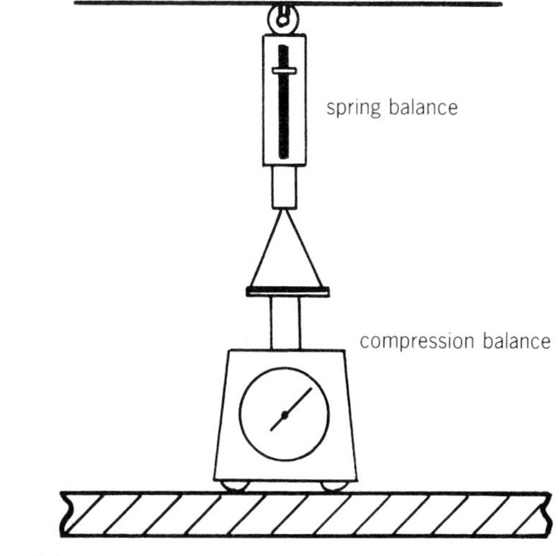

Figure 8.4

Student investigations

The preceding experiment is subject to several errors which limit its accuracy. What are they, how will they affect the result, and how would you try and reduce them?

Use a linear air track with magnets fixed to the trolleys to investigate the effects of the force between two bodies.

Newton's laws now form the basis of what is known as Newtonian mechanics. Newton realised that the effect of a force on a body changed the **momentum** of a body. Momentum is defined as *mass* × *velocity*, and a full treatment of this is given on page 42.

1. A body remains in a state of rest or uniform motion unless acted on by a resultant force.
2. The rate of change of momentum is directly proportional to the applied force and in the direction of that force.
3. When a force acts on a body an equal and opposite force acts on another body.

In the statement of the third law it is important to realise that the forces act on *different* bodies. If they were to act on the *same* body we could never have accelerated motion because the resultant force on any body would always be zero.

Mathematical consideration of the second law

The second law can be written as:

$$F = \frac{d(mv)}{dt} = \frac{m\,dv}{dt}, \quad \text{or } F = ma$$

$$F = \frac{mv - mu}{t}$$

where u and v are the initial and final velocities, or

Force = mass × acceleration

This follows only if the mass of the object remains constant. This is true for normal velocities but is invalid at very high velocities where relativistic effects must be considered.

The unit of force is the newton (N), such that a force of 1 newton will give a mass of 1 kg an acceleration of 1 m s^{-2}.

The interaction between one body and another is due to the forces between them.

Student investigations

(*a*) Design an accelerometer that will indicate the acceleration of a dynamics trolley.

(*b*) Consider the different forms of tracked transport systems from the following standpoints: economics, propulsion systems, environmental considerations, magnetic levitation.

(*c*) What would be the maximum comfortable acceleration in a transport system? How would you investigate this, and what are the limitations?

Example

A man of mass 85 kg stands on a lift of mass 30 kg, as shown in Figure 8.5. When he pulls on the rope he exerts a force of 400 N on the floor of the lift. Calculate the acceleration of the lift.

Force on the man : $T - 850 + 400 = 85a$
Force on the lift : $T - 300 - 400 = 30a$

where T is the tension in the rope and a is the acceleration.
Therefore:

$$-700 + 450 = -55a$$
$$a = +4.55 \text{ m s}^{-2}$$

Figure 8.5

Student investigation

A woman stands in a lift. Predict how her weight and the reaction at the floor of the lift will vary when the lift is:

(*a*) at rest,
(*b*) moving upwards with a constant velocity,
(*c*) accelerating upwards, and
(*d*) freely falling.

How would you test this *in a laboratory simulation*?

9 · The forces of nature

There are at present only four certainly known types of force, and these are listed below. The relative importance of each force in an interaction depends on the type of interaction being considered.

(*a*) The **gravitational force** acts between all particles, and is responsible for holding planets in orbit around the Sun.
(*b*) The **electromagnetic force** acts between charged particles, and is the binding force of atoms and molecules.
(*c*) The **weak force** is responsible for radioactive decay.
(*d*) The **strong force** holds neutrons and protons together in a nucleus.

There may be another stronger force called the **colour force** that holds quarks together in a proton.

In this section of the book on mechanics we will be considering only the first two of these, since it is the electromagnetic force that is responsible for collisions between objects from the atomic to the cosmic scale.

The electromagnetic force in action – a simulated lightning strike on the tip of an aircraft propeller blade (AEA Technology, Culham Laboratory)

1 A 20 kg monkey hangs from a rope that passes over a frictionless pulley. The other end of the rope is tied to a 20 kg bunch of bananas. The monkey sees the bananas and begins to climb up the rope (Figure 9.1).
(*a*) As the monkey climbs do the bananas move up, move down or remain at rest?
(*b*) As the monkey climbs, does the distance between the monkey and the bananas get bigger, get smaller or remain the same?
(*c*) The monkey lets go of the rope. What happens to the distance between the monkey and the bananas while the monkey is falling?
(*d*) Before the monkey reaches the ground the monkey grabs the rope to stop the fall. What happens to the bananas? [A–W]

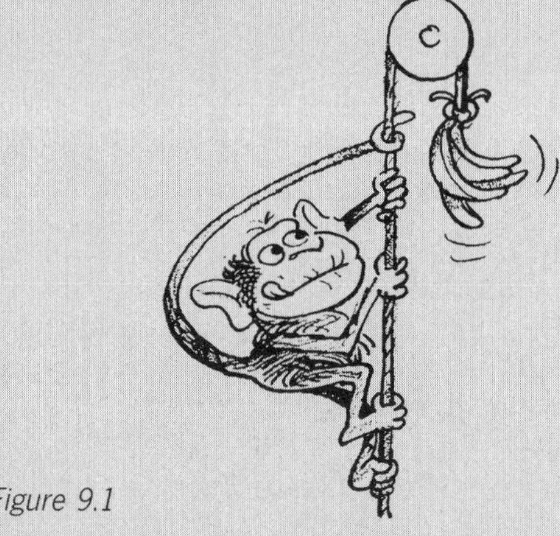

Figure 9.1

2 A stone of mass 500 g is thrown with a velocity of 15 m s^{-1} across the frozen surface of a lake and comes to rest in 40 m. What is the average force of friction between the stone and the ice?

3 A 5000 kg engine pulls a train of 5 trucks, each of 2000 kg along a horizontal track. If the engine exerts a force of 50 000 N and the frictional resistance is 5000 N calculate:
(*a*) the net accelerating force
(*b*) the acceleration of the train
(*c*) the force of truck 1 on truck 2

4 A man of mass 70 kg and a bucket of bricks of mass 100 kg are tied to the opposite ends of a rope which passes over a frictionless pulley so that they hang vertically downwards.
(*a*) what is the tension in the section of rope supporting the man
(*b*) what is the acceleration of the bucket

10 · Energy and power

There are about 20 million households in Britain alone and on average each one of these uses some 21 000 kW h of energy annually! The study of energy is therefore of vital importance in our lives.

When a body on which a force is acting moves in the direction of the force *work* is done and *energy* is transformed. Work is defined as the product of force and distance, and although force is a vector work itself is a scalar quantity.

A more general case is shown by Figure 10.1, giving:

work done = $Fs \cos \theta$

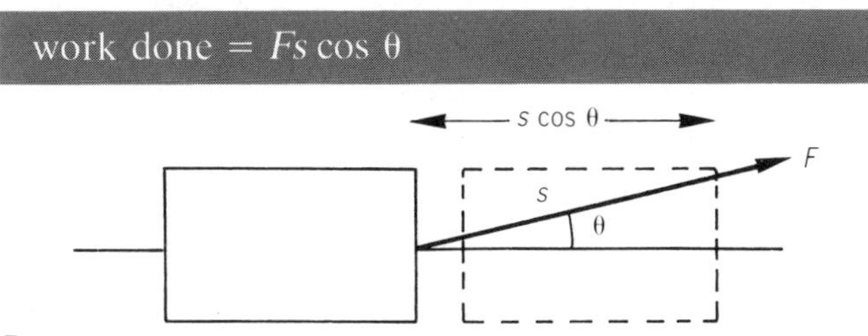

Figure 10.1

where θ is the angle between the line of action of the force and the direction of motion.

The unit of work and energy is the **joule**, which is defined as follows:

One joule of work is done, and one joule of energy transformed from one form to another, if the point of action of a force of one newton is moved a distance of one metre along the line of action of the force.

Conservation of energy

You should notice that we talk about the *conversion* of energy from one form to another and not its *use*. This is because although we may use up energy in one form it always reappears as another. This is a most important principle of Physics: that of the **conservation of energy**. The principle states that:

Energy is never created or destroyed but only changed from one form to another.

The enormous increase in demand for energy this century makes the production and conversion of energy a most important topic. But you may ask: why worry, if energy is always conserved? The trouble is that it is changed from useful or high-grade forms such as chemical or electrical energy to relatively useless forms such as low-grade heat.

World energy use

An account of the growth in world energy consumption makes sobering reading. If we define a quantity of energy (Q) as 10^{21} J then in the 2000 years up to 1850 the world is thought to have used between 6 and 9 Q. In the following hundred years up to 1950 it had burned a further 6 Q and from then on we have been using at least 1Q every ten years. Fortunately in recent years this rate of increase has slowed down considerably, partly because of the high cost of energy.

Energy conservation is also important. Some 5 per cent of the total energy bill of the western world could be saved by conservation measures such as the proper use of insulation!

To give you some idea of the value of energy, the table below shows the energy used in a number of situations.

Typical energy values (J)

moonlight on face for 1 s	10^{-3}
pressing down a typewriter key	1
house brick raised to shoulder height	30
burning a match	1000
potential energy of a person at the top of the stairs	1500
kinetic energy of a car travelling at 70 mph	500 000
electrical energy in a fully charged car battery	2 000 000
chemical energy in a day's food intake	11 000 000
chemical energy in one litre of petrol	35 000 000
first atomic bomb	10^{13}
very severe earthquake	10^{20}
world energy consumption (1964)	1.4×10^{21}
Earth's annual share of the Sun's heat	10^{25}
rotational kinetic energy of the Earth	10^{29}

Student investigation

The conversion of energy from one form to another is of considerable importance and in this conversion energy is often wasted, the process being less than 100% efficient. Investigate, either theoretically or practically, the efficiency of the following energy conversion processes.

(*a*) the internal combustion engine
(*b*) the steam engine
(*c*) the bicycle
(*d*) an electric kettle
(*e*) a meths or paraffin stove
(*f*) a solar cell

Energy sources

Energy is available from a number of sources:

Fossil fuels:
Coal
Oil
Gas

Other forms:

Wind	Solar energy
Waves	Biochemical energy
Hydroelectricity	Tides
Peat	Nuclear fission and nuclear fusion
Geothermal	Wood

Since there is a limit to the reserves of fossil fuels considerable work is being done to develop other alternative sources of energy.

The major need of the western world is to use one of the primary sources of energy to generate electricity. Some of the various primary sources are considered below.

Wood

Gasification of wood produces a gas that can be used for combustion.

Biochemical energy

Alcohol can be produced from cane sugar, maize, cassava, sago palms, yams and other root crops and then used to generate heat and finally electricity. The growth of some bacteria may also be a way of producing flammable gases.

Geothermal energy

This results from the flow of heat up through the rocks from hotter rocks beneath the surface. In Iceland 50 per cent of domestic hot water is produced using geothermal energy. In Britain the average thermal gradient appears to be about 40 °C km^{-1} and the average potential for heat extraction is some 6×10^{-2} W m^{-2}. The maximum value found globally is some 10 W m^{-2}.

Wind

Offshore 'wind farms' are now a source of renewable energy being favourably considered by the CEGB. Windmills with vanes of diameter 130 m can give up to 7.2 MW.

Hydroelectricity

Hydroelectricity now generates some 20–25 per cent of the world's electricity and there are about 100 schemes of 100 MW capacity throughout the world. The pumped storage system as used in Snowdonia is a useful variation of the normal hydroelectric power system: the water flows down through the turbines during the day and is then pumped back uphill overnight during periods of low electricity demand.

Waves

Wave energy is thought to be able to generate about 5 kW m^{-1} in accessible positions from the shore. On this basis about 8 GW may be achieved from the shores of the United Kingdom.

Tides

The tidal barrage across the river Severn is still being considered as a potential large energy source. This scheme, which would be the biggest of its kind in the world would use 192 turbines with an installed capacity of over 7000 MW. A smaller scheme for the River Mersey would have a capacity of some 500 MW.

Solar energy

The heat from the Sun may be used to produce steam, and this steam used to drive turbines. One array of mirrors in Southern California has an area of 7.3×10^4 m^2 and the steam produced by it gives an electrical output of 10 MW. This facility assumes 300 cloudless days a year! An alternative form of solar power is to convert the sunlight to electricity directly using photovoltaic cells. Cost is a problem here (at the time of writing it is some $0.7 per watt) but this method may still be attractive in very sunny positions.

Nuclear energy

The use of nuclear fission for the generation of electricity has become very important in this century. Many countries in the world such as the USA, Great Britain, France, Canada and the Soviet Union have a well developed nuclear fission reactor programme although the reactors are of different types. The nuclear fusion reaction may be a source of energy in the future although this may not be until after the year 2000. A fuller description of both types of nuclear energy is given on pages 456 and 458.

The large requirement of energy means that these alternative energy facilities have to be large if they are to replace conventional plant to any substantial extent. For example, to generate the 1000 MW produced by many large power stations would need one of the following:

300 windmills each with a 100 m diameter rotor
a large tidal barrage
a very large dam in a hydroelectric scheme
a 400 km^2 solar collector
a 100 km ocean wave-powered generator

The B.P. photo-voltaic array at Marchwood, Southampton, England, at peak times this array produces 30 kW of electricity (Reproduced with the kind permission of Powergen.)

Student investigation

Following the very brief survey of energy sources given here, write an essay about the most useful forms of alternative energy. Tidal and combined heat and power systems were not mentioned in detail; how effective do you consider these to be?

Do you consider that our actual way of life will have to alter in the next 200 years to take into account this shift in energy use?

In what ways can energy be saved? How much could the average household in Britain save in the course of an average year?

Ultimate recoverable energy deposits (thousands of millions of tonnes or equivalent)

	Cumulative production to 1975	*Proven or probable reserves*	*Possible additional reserves*
Petroleum	48.4	114.8	142.7
Tar sands	0.025	300	–
Shale oils	–	460.3	1415.6
Natural gas	21	54	185
Hard coal	n/a	339.9	4904
Lignite	n/a	99.3	1656
Total	n/a	1368.3	8303.3

(*Interdisciplinary Science Reviews* 1983)

Energy types

Energy exists in the following forms:

mechanical { potential, kinetic

chemical
heat
light
nuclear
magnetic
electrical

Almost everything that happens in the world is a result of a change of energy from one form to another, although the conversion is never 100 per cent efficient. The following table shows the amounts of power used by an adult male of mass 76 kg when doing various activities.

Activity	*Power used/W*	*Activity*	*Power used/W*
Sleeping	83	Swimming (breaststroke, 1.6 km h^{-1})	475
Sitting	120	Skating	535
Riding in a car	140	Stairs (116 steps min^{-1})	685
Walking (4.8 km h^{-1})	265	Cycling (21.3 km h^{-1})	700
Cycling (15 km h^{-1})	410	Basketball	800
Tennis	440		

Efficiency

The efficiency of a machine in its conversion of energy from one form to another is defined as:

$$\text{Efficiency} = \frac{\text{useful energy output}}{\text{energy input}}$$

The conversion may never be 100 per cent, and in fact for many machines it falls well short of this. For the human body the efficiency varies depending on the job; you can see some examples in the table below, which also includes some other machines for comparison.

Activity	*Efficiency/%*
Cycling	20
Swimming	2
(underwater)	4
Shovelling	3
Steam engine	17
Petrol engine	38

Kinetic and potential energy

Potential energy

The energy associated with the position of a body in a gravitational field is the **gravitational potential energy** of the body

$$\text{potential energy} = mgh$$

compared with some reference point where $h = 0$, usually the surface of the Earth. This may also represent the *change* in potential energy, where m is the mass of the body, g the intensity of the gravitational field (assumed uniform here) and h is the vertical distance moved in the field.

Kinetic energy

The energy possessed by a body by virtue of its motion is called the **kinetic energy** of the body.

Suppose that a body of mass m moving with velocity u is brought to rest in a distance s by a constant retarding force F (Figure 10.2).

The original kinetic energy of the body is equal to Fs, and this must therefore be the work done in bringing it to rest.

Since $F = ma$ however, we have (from $v^2 = u^2 + 2as$)

$$\text{kinetic energy} = Fs = mas = \frac{mu^2}{2}$$

$$\text{kinetic energy} = \tfrac{1}{2}mu^2$$

1 A lift has a mass of 400 kg. A man of mass 70 kg stands on a weighing machine fixed to the floor of the lift. Four seconds after starting from rest the lift has reached its maximum speed and has risen 5 m.
(*a*) What will be the reading on the weighing machine during the period of acceleration?
(*b*) How may it be decided whether the acceleration was uniform?
(*c*) How much energy will be used by the lift motor in (i) the first four seconds, (ii) the next four seconds? [O]

2 A dummy is used in a test crash to test the suitability of a selt belt. If the dummy had a mass of 65 kg and it was brought to rest in a distance of 65 cm from a velocity of 12 m s^{-1}, calculate
(*a*) the mean deceleration during the crash, and
(*b*) the average force exerted on the dummy during the crash.

3 In a colliding beams accelerator, two beams of protons travelling in opposite directions are made to collide head on. If the mass of a proton is 1.6×10^{-27} kg and the protons have been accelerated to an energy of 10 GeV, calculate the kinetic energy in joules lost in the collision.
Compare this with the energy available when a single proton of energy 10 GeV strikes a stationary target.

4 Two scale pans each of mass 12.0 g are connected together by a light string which passes over a frictionless pulley. A mass of 20 g is placed in one of the pans which then starts to move downwards. Calculate
(*a*) the tension in the string,
(*b*) the acceleration of the pans and
(*c*) the force exerted by the 20 g mass on the scale pan.

Figure 10.2

Student investigation

The following data refers to some production model cars. Use it to calculate:

(a) the mean acceleration from 0–60 mph
(b) the maximum kinetic energy
(c) the force produced by the engine at top speed

	0–60 mph	*Max. Power*	*Mass*
CAR 1	11.8 s	51 kW	1300 kg
CAR 2	7.2 s	110 kW	1700 kg
CAR 3	13.5 s	77 kW	1750 kg

Power

The rate at which work is done, or the rate at which energy is converted from one form to another is the **power**, simply defined as:

$$\text{power} = \frac{\text{work done}}{\text{time taken}}$$

The units of power are watts (W) where one watt is one joule per second.

Since work done = energy converted = force × distance, we may express power as:

$$\text{power} = \frac{\text{force} \times \text{distance}}{\text{time}}$$

and you should see that this is equal to force × velocity. So power may be expressed as:

$$\text{power} = \frac{\text{work done}}{\text{time taken}} = \text{force} \times \text{velocity}$$

Example

A lorry of mass 2000 kg moving at 10 m s^{-1} on a horizontal surface is brought to rest in a distance of 12.5 m by the brakes being applied. Calculate the average retarding force (F).

What power must the engine produce if the lorry is to travel up a hill of 1 in 10 at a constant speed of 10 m s^{-1}, the frictional resistance being 200 N?

Kinetic energy of lorry $= \frac{1}{2} \times 2000 \times 100 = 10^5$ J
$= F \times 12.5$

Therefore: $F = 8000$ N

On the hill, height risen per second = 1 m and distance travelled along the slope = 10 m.

Potential energy gained by lorry per second
= 2000 × 10 × 1 = 20 000 J.

Work done against friction per second
= 200 × 10 = 2000 J.

Total energy required per second
= 22 000 W = 22 kW.

5 A car travelling at 30 m s^{-1} along a level road is brought to rest in a distance of 35 m by its brakes. If the car has a mass of 900 kg calculate the average force exerted by the brakes.

If the same car travels up a slope of 1 in 15 at a constant speed of 25 m s^{-1} what power does the engine develop if the total frictional resistance is 120 N?

6 What is the maximum speed at which an earth-mover of mass 250 000 kg can descend a slope of 1 in 10, if the brakes can dissipate energy at a maximum rate of 2000 kW? [O]

7 A rope tied to a trolley is pulled so that the trolley accelerates. However, according to Newton's third law, the trolley pulls back on the rope with an equal and opposite force.

(*a*) Is the total work done zero?

(*b*) If so how can the trolley's kinetic energy change?

8 The total annual energy consumption of the United States is of the order of 10^{19} J.

(*a*) What area of solar collector would be needed to produce this energy, given that the power falling on the Earth's surface due to solar radiation is 1400 W m^{-2}? (Assume 100 per cent efficiency.)

(*b*) What mass of deuterium would be required to supply that need?
(Mass defect when two deuterium nuclei fuse to give one nucleus of helium = 0.0255 u)

9 A lift is raised at a constant speed. Is the total work done on the lift positive, negative or zero?

10 A girl bounces on a trampoline getting higher and higher each time she bounces. How is she able to increase her total mechanical energy?

11 A gun is powered by a spring that requires a force of 500 N to compress it by 1 m. It is compressed by 0.05 m and a ball of mass 0.01 kg is put in the barrel against the compressed spring. Calculate:

(*a*) the maximum velocity with which the ball leaves the barrel when the gun is fired

(*b*) the initial acceleration of the ball

11 · Momentum and impulse

When a force is applied to a body it can change the body's velocity, the size of this change depending on the magnitude of the force and the time for which it acts. For example, a javelin-thrower will apply a force to the javelin for the longest possible time, and the longer the barrel of a gun the greater the muzzle velocity of the bullet since the explosive forces will be acting on it for a longer time.

We therefore define a quantity called the **impulse** of a force where:

impulse = force × time for which it acts

The velocity change due to a given impulse depends on the mass of the body, a small mass clearly experiencing a larger change in velocity.

The quantity mass × velocity is called the **momentum** of the body.

We can therefore see that an impulse will produce a change in the momentum of a body.

impulse = momentum change

If a body of mass m has its velocity changed from u to v by the application of a force F for a time t, then:

$$Ft = mv - mu$$

The units for both impulse and momentum are newton seconds (N s) or kilogram metre per second (kg m s^{-1}).

An impulse can either accelerate a body or slow it down, and therefore momentum is a vector quantity. You can see from the following example that a given change of momentum (a given impulse) can be due to a small force acting for a long time or a large force acting for a short time.

Because the sand is soft the time taken to come to rest is increased and therefore the force on the long jumper is reduced (ZEFA)

Student investigation

When a ball is dropped on to the ground it experiences an impulse during the time for which it is in contact with the ground and deformation of the ball takes place. This is shown in Figure 11.1.

Devise and carry out an experiment to measure the time of contact; hence calculate the change of momentum of the ball and hence the impulse.

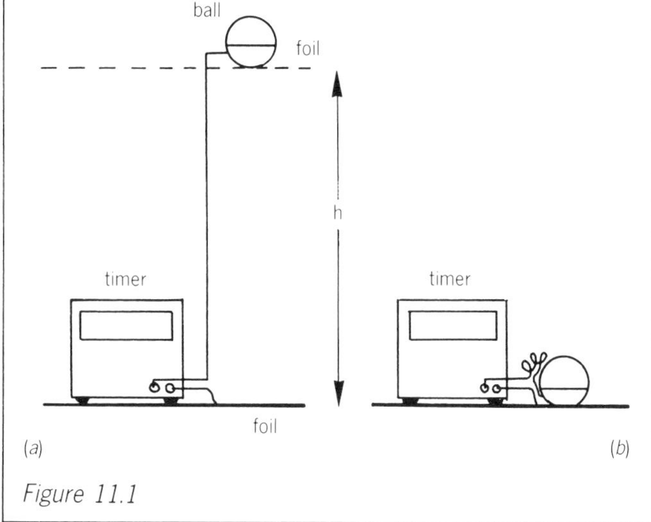

Figure 11.1

Example

A girl of mass 50 kg jumps on to the ground from a 2 m high wall. Calculate the force on her when she lands (*a*) if she bends her knees and stops in 0.2 s, and (*b*) if she keeps her legs straight and stops in 0.05 s.

(*a*) Velocity on impact $= (2 \times 10 \times 2)^{\frac{1}{2}} = 6.3$ m s^{-1}.
Momentum change $= 50 \times 6.3 = 315$ N s.
Therefore force $= \dfrac{315}{0.2} = 1575$ N.

(*b*) Force $= \dfrac{315}{0.05} = 6300$ N.

1 Why is it much more painful to be hit by a hailstone of mass 5×10^{-3} kg falling at 5 m s^{-1} which bounces off your head than by a raindrop of the same mass and falling at the same velocity but which breaks up on hitting you and does not bounce? (A numerical answer is required.)

Conservation of momentum

When two bodies collide the momentum is conserved, as long as no external forces act on the system during collision. This is expressed in the **law of conservation of momentum** for bodies moving in the same straight line as:

> The algebraic sum of the momenta before collision is equal to the algebraic sum of the momenta after the collision.

You will notice from the way that the law is stated that momentum is a vector quantity.

Consider a collision as shown in Figure 11.2.

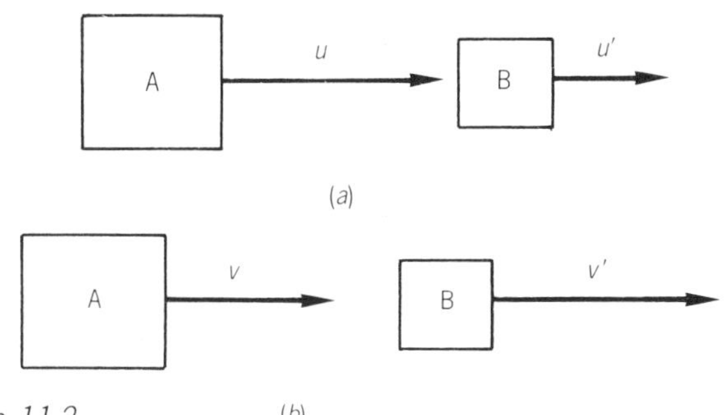

Figure 11.2

Let the body A have a mass m, and let u and v be the velocities of A before and after the collision respectively.

Let the mass of B be m', and let the velocities of B before and after the collision be u' and v' respectively.

By the law of conservation of momentum we can write:

$$mu + m'u' = mv + m'v'$$

Proof of the law of conservation of momentum from Newton's laws

Let two bodies A and B with masses m and m' moving with velocities u and u' collide and let their velocities after collision be v and v', as shown by Figure 11.3.

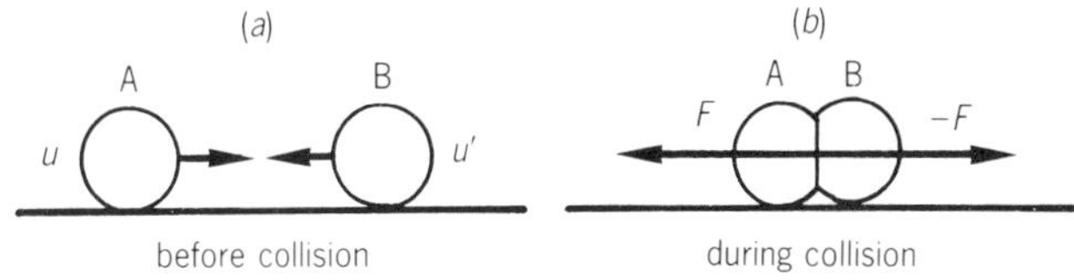

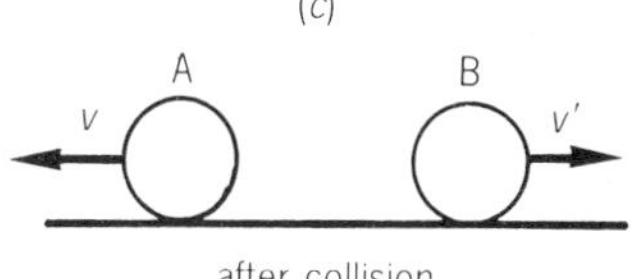

Figure 11.3

During the collision:

Force on A is given by

$$F = \frac{m(v - u)}{t}$$

Force on B is given by

$$F' = \frac{m'(v' - u')}{t}$$

But by Newton's third law: $F = -F'$, and therefore we have:

$$m(v - u) = -m'(v' - u')$$

giving $mu + m'u' = mv + m'v'$

and this is the law of conservation of momentum.

2 A bullet of mass 50 g is fired horizontally into a block of wood of mass 8 kg which is suspended by strings 2.5 m long. After the impact the block swings upwards through an angle of 30°. Calculate the velocity of the bullet.

3 When a person fires a rifle it is advisable to hold the butt firmly against the shoulder rather than a little way from it, to minimise the impact on the shoulder. Explain why. [A–W]

4 Use your knowledge of impulse and momentum change to explain the working of the Newton's cradle shown in Figure 11.4.

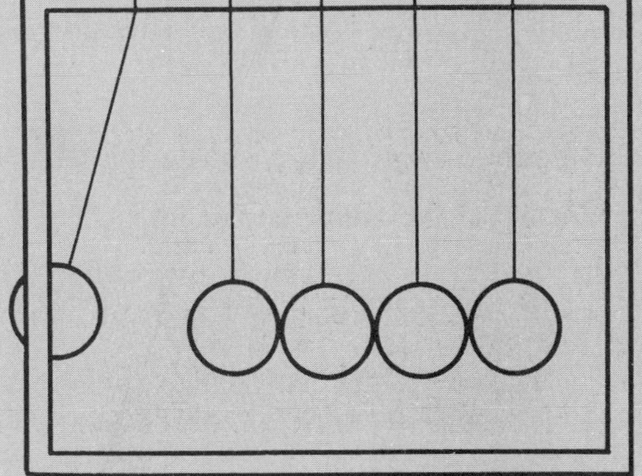

Figure 11.4

Collisions

Although the momentum is always conserved in isolated collisions, this is not always true of the kinetic energies of the colliding bodies. In many collisions some of the kinetic energy is converted into other forms such as sound and heat.

A collision where *some* or *all* of the kinetic energy is lost is called an **inelastic** collision: an example in which all the kinetic energy is lost is a lump of putty falling on to the floor. One where *none* of the kinetic energy is lost is called an **elastic** collision and this can be demonstrated fairly closely by dropping a steel ball-bearing on to a steel plate.

The amount of kinetic energy lost depends on *both* surfaces and can be considered as follows.

Suppose a mass A moving at velocity u collides with a mass B moving with velocity u' such that after the collision they have velocities v and v' respectively (see Figure 11.5).

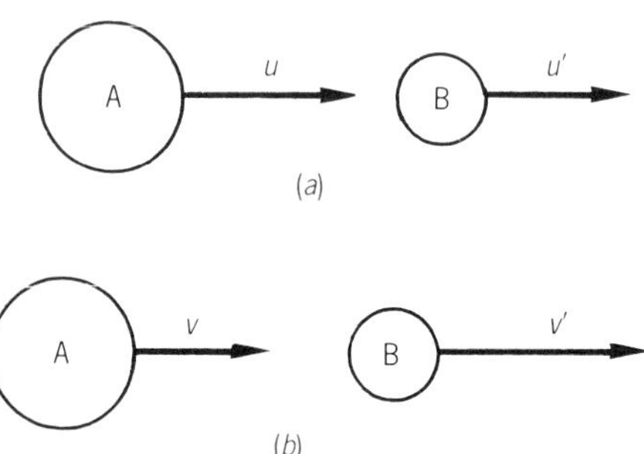

Figure 11.5

Newton described the elasticity of the collision by considering the velocities of approach and separation.

Velocity of approach $= u - u'$
Velocity of separation $= v - v'$

He defined a quantity known as the **coefficient of restitution** (e) as:

$$e = \frac{\text{velocity of separation}}{\text{velocity of approach}} = \frac{v - v'}{u - u'}$$

This is known as **Newton's law of impact.**

The ratio $(v - v')/(u - u')$ must always be ≤ 1; for a perfectly elastic collision $e = 1$ and for a perfectly inelastic collision $e = 0$.

The coefficient of restitution between a ball and the ground can be found as follows. Suppose that a ball falls from rest on to the ground from a height h and bounces to a height h'. By considering the loss of potential energy and the gain of kinetic energy we have:

Velocity of approach $= \sqrt{2gh}$
Velocity of separation $= \sqrt{2gh'}$

Therefore

$$\text{coefficient of restitution} = \sqrt{\frac{2gh'}{2gh}} = \sqrt{\frac{h'}{h}}$$

Example

A 4 kg ball moving at 8 m s^{-1} collides with a stationary ball of mass 12 kg, and they stick together. Calculate the final velocity and the kinetic energy lost in the impact.

By the conservation of momentum,

$$\text{final velocity} = \frac{(8 \times 4) + (12 \times 0)}{16} = 2 \text{ m s}^{-1}$$

Therefore

kinetic energy lost in the impact
$= \frac{1}{2} \times 4 \times 64 - \frac{1}{2} \times 16 \times 4$
$= 128 - 32$
$= 96$ J

Student investigation

From measurements of the time of contact of a person's foot with the road, make an estimate of the force in the hip joint in the following activities: (*a*) walking, (*b*) running, (*c*) high jumping, (*d*) long jumping.

How would these values be altered if the surface had been a yielding one such as sand? (Actual measurements are required.)

5 A body of mass 50 g falls from a height of 30 cm on to a horizontal surface and rebounds to a height of 20 cm. If the time of collision was 0.05 s, calculate
(*a*) the average force experienced by the body during the impact,
(*b*) the kinetic energy lost by the body on impact, and
(*c*) the coefficient of restitution between the two surfaces.

Elastic collisions between equal masses

1 Collisions in a straight line
Let a mass A moving with velocity u collide with a stationary mass B as shown in Figure 11.6. Let the velocities of A and B after collision be v and w respectively.

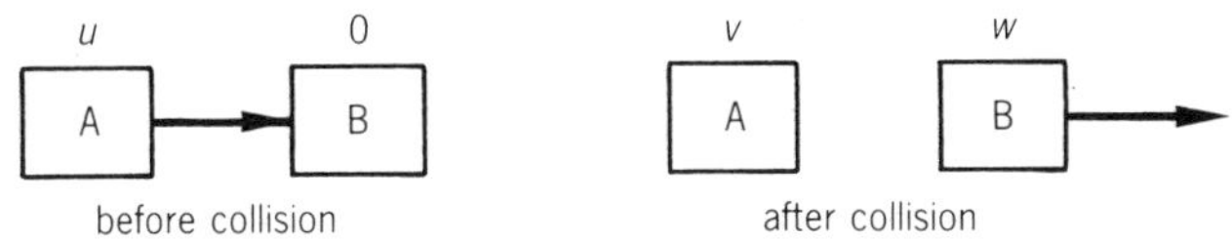

Figure 11.6

By the law of conservation of momentum:

$$mu = mv + mw$$

By the law of conservation of energy:

$$\tfrac{1}{2}mu^2 = \tfrac{1}{2}mv^2 + \tfrac{1}{2}mw^2$$

Therefore

$$v = u - w \text{ and } u^2 = v^2 + w^2$$

Substituting for v gives

$$u = w$$

and therefore $v = 0$.

Therefore A comes to rest and B moves off with the original velocity of A. A beautiful example of this is shown in Newton's cradle (see Figure 11.4) where a series of suspended ball-bearings can be made to collide with each other.

2 Oblique collisions
In any collision between a moving mass A and a stationary mass B, the mass B always moves off along the line joining the centres of mass at the moment of collision (Figure 11.7(a)). This can be of real importance in a game like snooker!

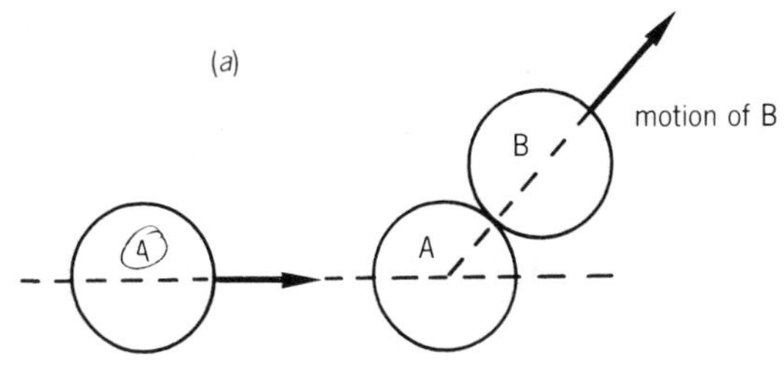

Figure 11.7(a)

Let the velocities be as shown in Figure 11.7(b).

By the law of conservation of energy:

$$\tfrac{1}{2}mu^2 = \tfrac{1}{2}mv^2 + \tfrac{1}{2}mw^2$$

Therefore

$$u^2 = v^2 + w^2$$

Thus (by Pythagoras' theorem) the velocities v and w are at right angles to each other.

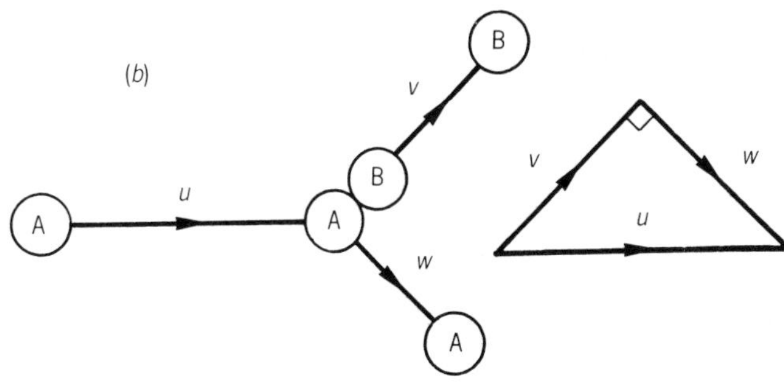

Figure 11.7(b)

Collisions between two unequal masses

1 Collisions in a straight line
Let mass A of mass m and moving with a velocity u collide with a stationary mass B of mass M. Let the velocity of A after collision be v and that of B be w.

It is left for the reader to show that for an elastic collision the kinetic energy lost by A is:

(a) maximum when $m = M$,
(b) zero when M = infinity or zero.

This is important in nuclear physics where two sub-atomic particles collide with each other (see page 441).

2 Oblique collisions
If a mass m collides obliquely with a stationary mass M then the two masses will move off at an angle to the original path.

It is left as an exercise for the reader to show that if θ is the angle between the paths of the two masses after collision then

(a) if $m < M$ then $\theta > 90°$
(b) if $m = M$ then $\theta = 90°$
(c) if $m > M$ then $\theta < 90°$

Collisions of this type can often be seen in cloud chambers and bubble chambers, and enable the masses of unknown nuclear particles to be found.

Examples

1 A mass A of 6 kg moving with a velocity of 5 m s^{-1} collides with a mass B of 8 kg moving in the opposite direction at 3 m s^{-1}. Calculate the final velocity if the masses stick together on impact.

Momentum before collision $= (6 \times 5) + (8 \times (-3))$
$= 6$ N s.

Therefore momentum after collision = 6 N s.

Therefore velocity $= \frac{6}{14} = 0.43$ m s^{-1}

2 Now assume that the masses above do not stick together but that mass A moves on with a velocity of 0.5 m s^{-1}. Calculate the velocity of B.

Momentum after collision $= 6 = (6 \times 0.5) + 8v$ where v is the velocity of B after the collision.

Velocity of B $= \frac{6-3}{8} = 0.38$ m s^{-1}

You may think that the example of the girl jumping on to the ground (see page 42) violates the law of conservation of momentum, but this is not the case. Although there appears to be a loss of momentum we have neglected the recoil of the Earth as she lands on it!

Motion of the centre of mass

Some quite complex problems can be solved by considering the motion of the centre of mass of a body or system of bodies.

If an irregular object such as a hammer is thrown, then – although the motion of some parts of the hammer will be complex – its centre of mass (see page 53) will move in a straight line in the absence of any external forces (Figure 11.8(*a*)). In an explosion if the centre of mass was at rest before the explosion the centre of mass of the fragments must also be at rest after the explosion (Figure 11.8(*b*)).

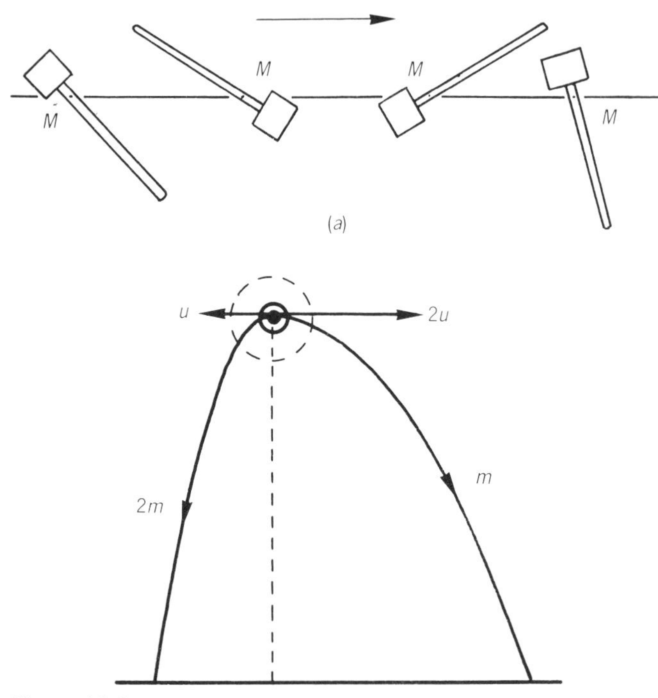

Figure 11.8

6 Two trolleys are involved in a collision. Trolley A (mass 2 kg), initially travelling at 10 m s^{-1} collides with trolley B which was initially at rest. Trolley B eventually reaches a velocity of 6 m s^{-1} in the same direction in which trolley A was travelling, while trolley A eventually rebounds at 2 m s^{-1}. If the time spent in collision is 1 ms and trolley A travels 0.02 m in the collision while trolley B travels 0.015 m, calculate:

(*a*) the mass of trolley B,

(*b*) the average force exerted on both trolleys during the collision, and

(*c*) the kinetic energy change of both trolleys.

Comment on the fact that the two trolleys travel through different distances during the collision. What quantities are the same for both trolleys during the collision?

7 A proton travelling at 3×10^7 m s^{-1} collides with the nucleus of a stationary oxygen atom and rebounds in a direction at 90° to its original path. Calculate the velocity and direction of the oxygen nucleus, assuming that the collision is perfectly elastic and ignoring relativistic effects. (Mass of proton = 1.6×10^{-27} kg; mass of oxygen atom = 2.56×10^{-26} kg.)

8 A body of mass m makes a head-on, perfectly elastic collision with a body of mass M initially at rest.

(*a*) What quantities are conserved in the collision?

(*b*) Show that:

$$\frac{\Delta E}{E_0} = \frac{4(M/m)}{(1 + M/m)^2}$$

where E_0 is the original kinetic energy of the mass m and ΔE the energy it loses in the collision.

(*c*) Plot a graph of $\Delta E/E_0$ against M/m for values of M/m from 0 to 20. Hence, or otherwise, find the value of M/m for which $\Delta E/E_0$ is a maximum.

(*d*) On the basis of your answer to (*c*), which of the elements of mass number 0 to 16 appears to be the best as a moderator in a nuclear reactor? What other factors must be considered? [c]

Kinetic energy in explosions

Consider an explosion that produces two fragments of masses m and M with velocities u and v respectively (as in Figure 11.9). By the law of conservation of momentum these must move off in opposite directions.

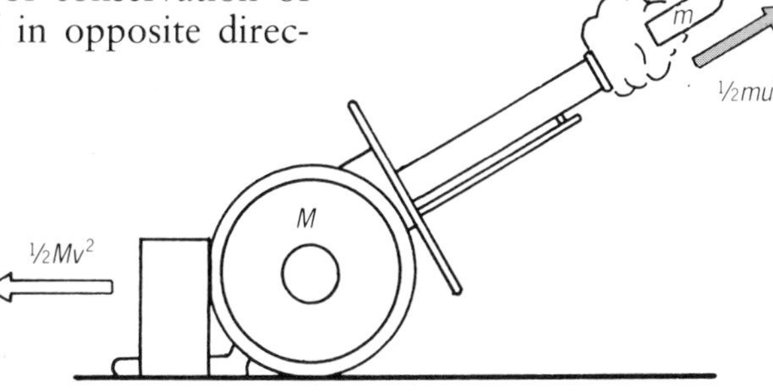

Figure 11.9

Let the kinetic energy of m be E and that of M, E'.

Now

$$E = \tfrac{1}{2}mu^2 \text{ and } E' = \tfrac{1}{2}Mv^2$$

By the conservation of momentum $mu = -Mv$ and therefore:

$$E = \tfrac{1}{2}mu^2 \text{ and } E' = \tfrac{1}{2}\frac{m^2u^2}{M}$$

This gives

$$\frac{E}{E'} = \frac{M}{m}$$

and so the fragment with the smaller mass has the larger kinetic energy.

> **Example**
>
> A rifle of mass 3 kg fires a bullet of mass 0.025 kg at 100 m s^{-1}. Calculate the kinetic energies of the rifle and bullet.
>
> Kinetic energy of bullet
> $= 0.5 \times 0.025 \times 100 \times 100 = 125$ J.
>
> Kinetic energy of rifle $= \dfrac{125 \times 0.025}{3} = 1.04$ J.

> **9** Uranium-235 is an alpha-emitter, the resulting nucleus having a mass of 231. If a stationary uranium-235 nucleus emits an alpha-particle, what is the ratio of the kinetic energy of the alpha-particle to that of the residual nucleus?

It is often very useful to use the idea of relative velocity in a collision problem. One of the objects involved is considered to be at rest, the relative velocity of the other is found and then the final velocities of the objects relative to the frame of reference can be calculated.

The following example demonstrates the use of relative velocity in a collision problem.

> **Example**
>
> A mass m moving to the right with velocity v collides elastically with a mass M moving in the opposite direction also at velocity v (see Figure 11.10). If M is very much greater than m, calculate:
>
> (*a*) the velocity of m immediately after the collision,
> (*b*) the change in the momentum of m, and
> (*c*) the change in the kinetic energy of m.
>
> 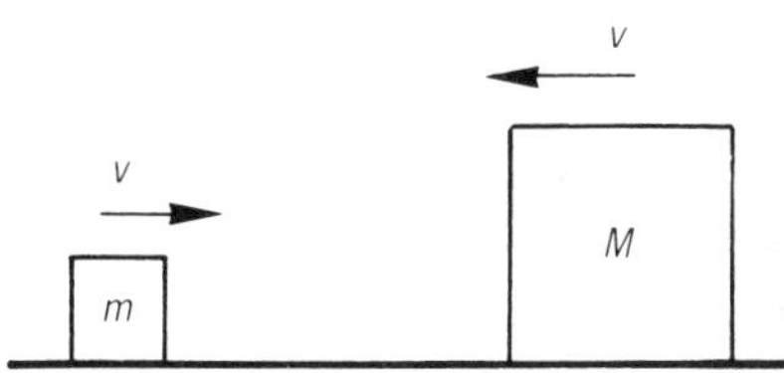
>
>
> *Figure 11.10*
>
> (*a*) Consider M to be at rest; then the velocity of m relative to M is $2v$. After collision the velocity of m relative to M must be $-2v$, since the collision is perfectly elastic.
>
> Therefore (since $M >> m$) the velocity of M will be virtually unchanged by the collision, and hence the velocity of m relative to the external observer will be $(-2v) + (-v) = -3v$.
>
> (*b*) The momentum change is then $mv - m(-3v) = -4mv$.
>
> (*c*) The kinetic energy change is $4mv^2$.

Rockets

The propulsion systems of rockets depend on the laws of momentum conservation. For a solid or liquid fuel rocket, the greater the velocity of the exhaust gases the greater is their momentum and hence the greater the momentum of the rocket.

The table below gives the exhaust gas velocity for a variety of different fuels.

Fuel	Exhaust gas velocity/m s^{-1}
hydrogen and oxygen	5800
acetylene and oxygen	5500
petrol and oxygen	5000
kerosene and oxygen	5000
alcohol and oxygen	4850
smokeless gunpowder	3500
black gunpowder	2600

Alternative propulsion systems have been proposed and they include nuclear engines, ion drives and even explosive drives!

Student investigation

Astronauts and fighter-pilots have been trained on rocket-powered trolleys to test their ability to withstand high accelerations. In your GCSE courses you may well have seen a carbon dioxide powered version of the rocket trolley, such as the one shown in Figure 11.11. It consists of a small carbon dioxide cylinder such as those used in a soda syphon, mounted on a small trolley. The trolley is propelled by releasing the gas from the cylinder by piercing the end with a needle.

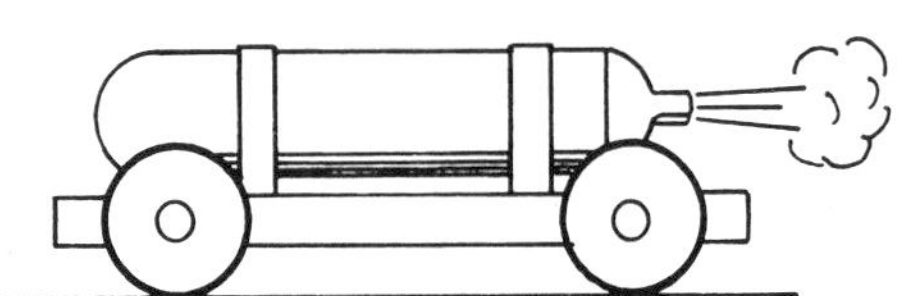

Figure 11.11

Using such a trolley, devise and carry out experiments to measure the following:

(*a*) the average velocity of the trolley,
(*b*) the maximum velocity of the trolley,
(*c*) the average force exerted by the gas, and
(*d*) the average exhaust gas velocity.

The calculation of the velocity of a rocket some time after its launch is a difficult problem, since the mass of the rocket is constantly changing and therefore even with a constant thrust the acceleration will not be constant. The velocity of the rocket when its mass is M can be shown to be:

$$v = u - \omega \ln (M/M_0)$$

where u and M_0 are the initial velocity and mass of the rocket and ω is the velocity of the exhaust gases relative to the rocket.

10 A space rocket with fuel of total mass 1.9×10^3 kg stands on a launch pad (Figure 11.12). On ignition gas is ejected from the rocket at a speed of 2.5×10^3 m s^{-1} and fuel is consumed at a constant rate of 7.4 kg s^{-1}. Find the thrust of the rocket and explain why there is a delay between ignition and lift-off.

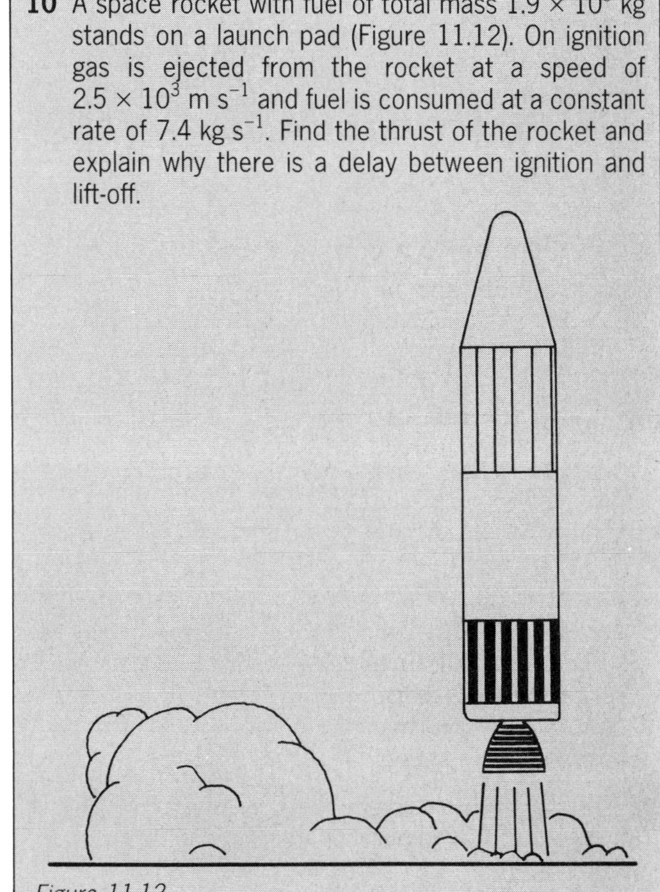

Figure 11.12

Further applications of the law of conservation of momentum

Hose pipe

Consider a hose pipe of cross-sectional area A giving a water jet of velocity v (see Figure 11.13). If the water hits a wall and comes to rest then:

mass of water striking the wall per second $= \rho v A$

where ρ is the density (see page 54) of water.

momentum change per second $= \rho v^2 A$
force on wall = momentum change per second
$= \rho v^2 A$

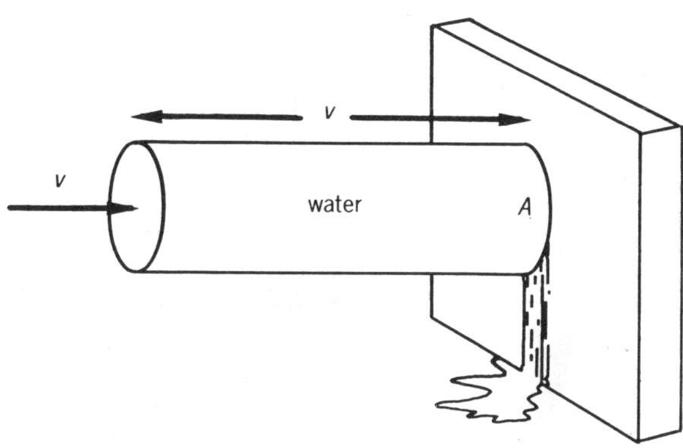

Figure 11.13

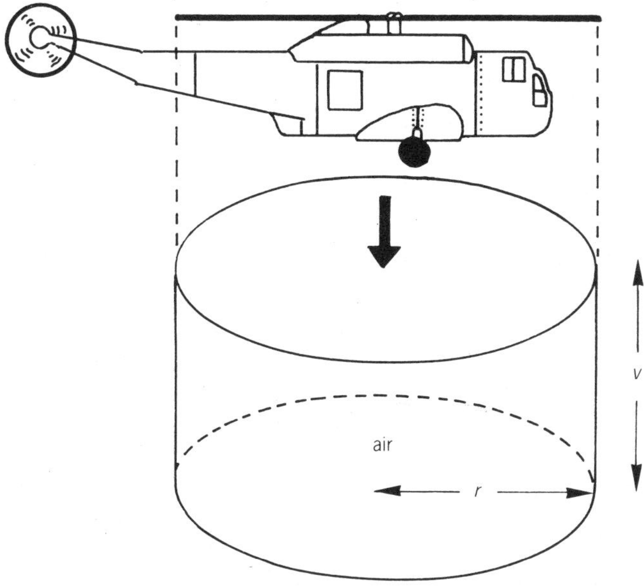

Figure 11.14

Sand falling on to a conveyor belt

Let a mass of sand m fall on to the conveyor belt every second. If the velocity of the belt is v then:

gain in momentum per second = mv

But this is the rate of change of momentum of the sand, that is, the force on the belt. Therefore:

force = mv

Helicopter

Consider a helicopter of mass m with rotor blades of radius r, hovering above the ground. The rotor produces a column of air moving vertically with velocity v. If the helicopter is stationary the weight of the aircraft is balanced by the rate of change of momentum of the air (see Figure 11.14). Then:

volume of air moved per second = $\pi r^2 v$
mass of air moved per second = $\pi r^2 v\rho$

where ρ is the density of the air.
Therefore:

momentum change per second = $\pi r^2 v^2 \rho$

Therefore:

weight of helicopter = $mg = \pi r^2 v^2 \rho$

Example

A horizontal jet of water leaves the end of a hose pipe and strikes a wall horizontally with a velocity of 20 m s^{-1}. If the end of the pipe has a diameter of 2 cm, calculate the force that will be exerted on the wall (assuming that the water loses all its kinetic energy on impact).

Force = density × velocity^2 × area
= 1000 × 400 × 0.00031 = 125.7 N

11 Water flows at 3 m s^{-1} from a pipe 0.1 m in diameter and then strikes a vertical plate near the outlet of the pipe. If the stream of water strikes the plate normally, calculate the force exerted on the plate. (Density of water = 1000 kg m^{-3})

12 During a storm, rain falls steadily at an angle of 45° on to a flat roof. If 5 cm of rain fell in an hour and the mean terminal velocity of the raindrops was 6 m s^{-1}, what was the additional pressure on the roof assuming that no rain collects on it?

13 Coal is deposited at a uniform rate of 25 kg s^{-1} and with negligible kinetic energy on to a conveyor belt moving horizontally at 1.5 m s^{-1}. Calculate

(*a*) the force required to maintain the belt's constant velocity,

(*b*) the power required to maintain constant velocity, and

(*c*) the rate of change of kinetic energy of the moving coal.

Why are these last two quantities not equal?

14 Show that when a collision takes place between a neutron and a stationary nucleus the energy lost by the neutron is

(*a*) maximum when the nucleus has the same mass as the neutron,

(*b*) very small when the nucleus has a much larger mass than the neutron.

Why are these results important in the effects of neutron radiation on the human body and the choice of materials used to protect us from this radiation?

12 · Statics

A body is at rest or in a state of uniform motion if no resultant force acts on it (see Newton's first law, page 35).

We will deal here with the case of bodies at rest, that is, those not in linear motion – there may be some rotation, however, as we will see.

Forces acting through the centre of mass

It should be clear that if only one force acts on a body then it cannot be in equilibrium (see page 51). Figure 12.1(*a*) shows one force acting through the centre of mass of the object (see below) and the body will therefore accelerate in the direction of action of the force.

If two or more forces act, however, then equilibrium is possible as Figure 12.1(*b*) shows. The two forces F_1 and F_2 are equal and opposite and act in the same line and so the resultant force is zero; the body is at rest.

Figure 12.1

The moment of a force, or torque

If the line of action of a force does *not* pass through the centre of mass then it will exert a turning effect on the body (see Figure 12.2).

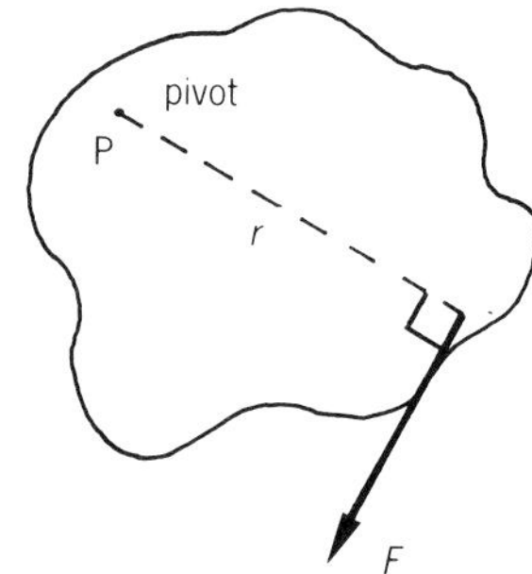

Figure 12.2

The measure of this turning effect is known as the **moment** of the force or the **torque**. The true effects of torque on a body can be seen in the space stations, where gravitational forces do not mask the effect.

The torque is defined as follows:

$$\text{torque} = Fr$$

where r is the perpendicular distance from the point of rotation to the line of action of the force F.

Torque is measured in newton metres (N m).

Couples

A **couple** is said to exist when two antiparallel forces whose lines of action do not coincide act on a body (Figure 12.3(*a*)). A true couple will produce rotation only and no translation.

Examples of couples are the forces in the driver's hands applied to a steering wheel, and the forces experienced by two sides of a suspended rectangular coil carrying a current in a magnetic field.

The moment of a couple or torque of a couple

The **torque of a couple** is defined as the product of one of the forces and the perpendicular distance between the lines of action of the forces. Therefore from Figure 12.3(*b*):

$$\text{moment of couple or torque of couple} = Fd$$

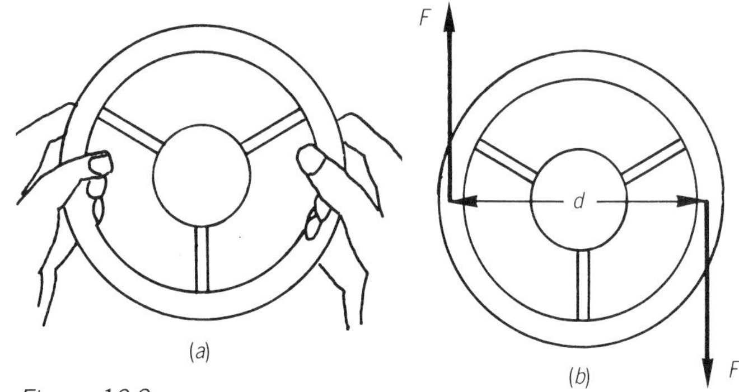

Figure 12.3

Figure 12.4 shows that a force on a body may be replaced by a force through the centre of mass and a couple.

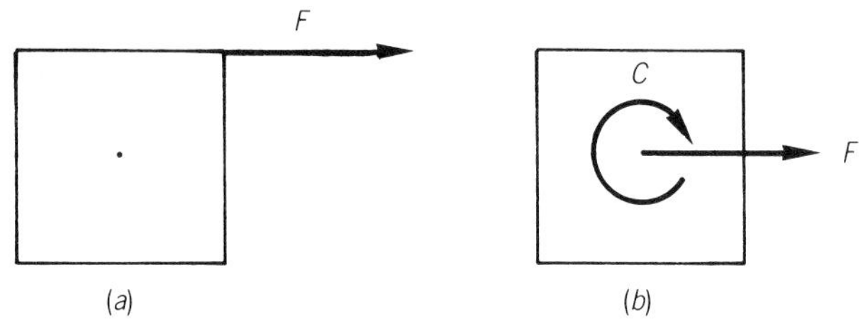

Figure 12.4

Equilibrium

A particle will be **in equilibrium** if there is no resultant force or couple acting on it. The equilibrium is **static** if the particle's velocity is also zero and **dynamic** if it isn't.

In Figure 12.5(*a*) the two forces acting on the body cancel out, but since their lines of action are different there will be a resultant couple.

In Figure 12.5(*b*) the reverse is true and a resultant force will act.

In Figure 12.5(*c*), however, both conditions are satisfied and the body is truly in equilibrium.

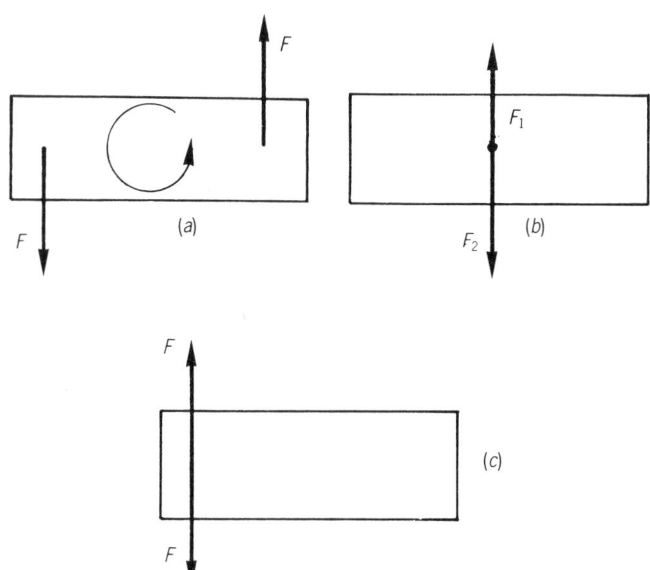

Figure 12.5

Two conditions are therefore required for a body to be in equilibrium:

1 The vector sum of the forces acting on the body must be zero.
2 The vector sum of the moments taken about any point must be zero (this point need not actually be on the body in question).

Example

Consider a simple example such as the rod AB shown in Figure 12.6. Let the rod be rigid and of negligible mass and let a force of 20 N ($=W_1$) act on end A. The rod is pivoted about O such that AO = 1.2 m and OB = 1.6 m.

Find the value of the force at B (W_2) such that the rod is in equilibrium.

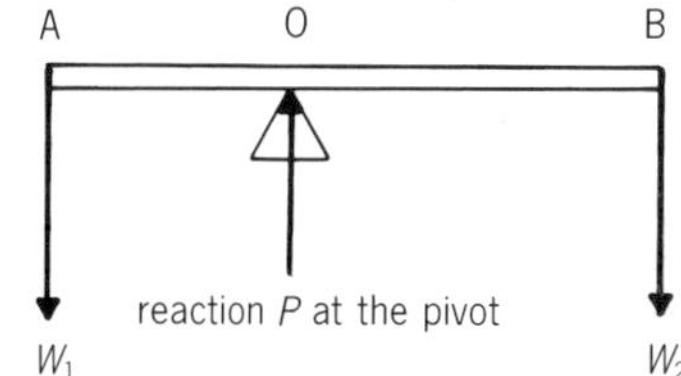

Figure 12.6

If the rod is in equilibrium then:
Summing the force vectors:

$$P - W_1 - W_2 = 0 = P - 20 - W_2$$

Taking moments about O:

$$(20 \times 1.2) - (W_2 \times 1.6) = 0$$

This gives: $P = 35$ N and $W_2 = 15$ N

If any other point is chosen about which to take moments it will be found that the resultant moment is zero, even if the point does not lie on the rod itself.

1 A man of mass 70 kg walks at a uniform speed of 2 m s^{-1} across a rigid bridge which is 40 m long and has a mass of 1000 kg. Draw graphs to show the following:
(*a*) the variation of the reaction at both ends of the bridge with the man's distance from one end, and
(*b*) the variation of the torques at both ends of the bridge with the man's distance from one end.

2 A horse is required to pull a cart, but being an intelligent horse, it quotes Newton's third law: 'The pull of the horse on the cart is equal and opposite to the pull of the cart on the horse'. 'If I can never exert a bigger force on the cart than it exerts on me, how can I ever move it?' asks the horse. What would you reply? Explain your answer.

3 Some bricks are used to make part of an overhang as shown in Figure 12.7. Each brick is of length *l*.

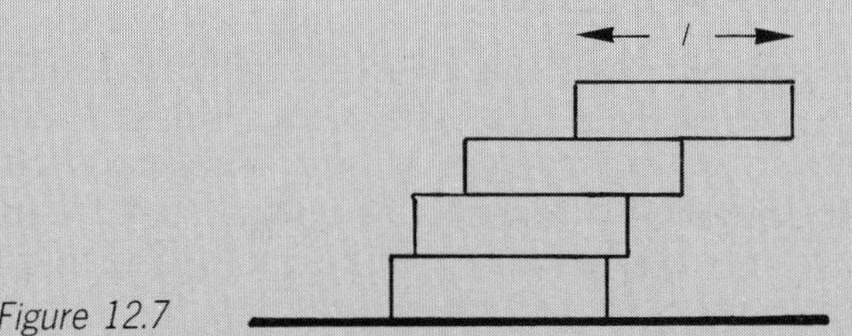

Figure 12.7

Show that for equilibrium the largest overhang distances are:
(*a*) the top brick overhanging the one below it by $l/2$,
(*b*) that one overhanging the next by $l/4$, and
(*c*) that one overhanging the next by $l/6$.

4 (*a*) Why is it much easier to balance a metre rod on your finger tip than to balance a matchstick?
(*b*) Why is the *torque* specified in car repair manuals for tightening nuts and not the *force*?

Forces applied at an angle to each other

If the forces are applied at an angle to each other then clearly it is the components of these forces in two perpendicular directions that must balance to give equilibrium, as shown in Figure 12.8. Using the notation shown, for equilibrium:

$$F_1 \cos \theta_1 + F_2 \cos \theta_2 = 0$$
$$F_1 \sin \theta_1 + F_2 \sin \theta_2 = F_3$$

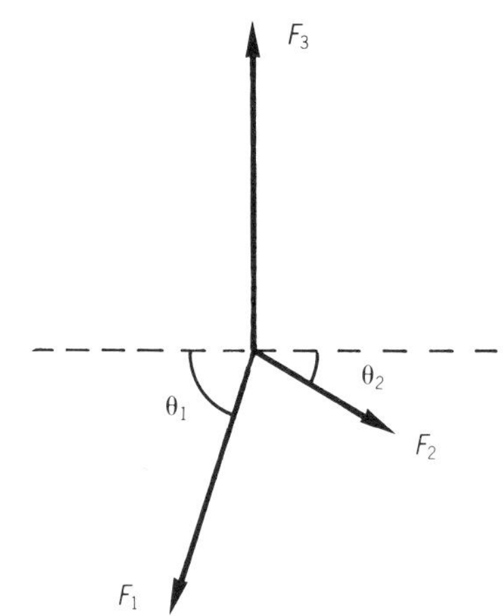

Figure 12.8

Example

A uniform ladder 10 m long and with a mass of 40 kg (weight 400 N) rests in equilibrium against a frictionless vertical wall at an angle of 60° to the horizontal (Figure 12.9).

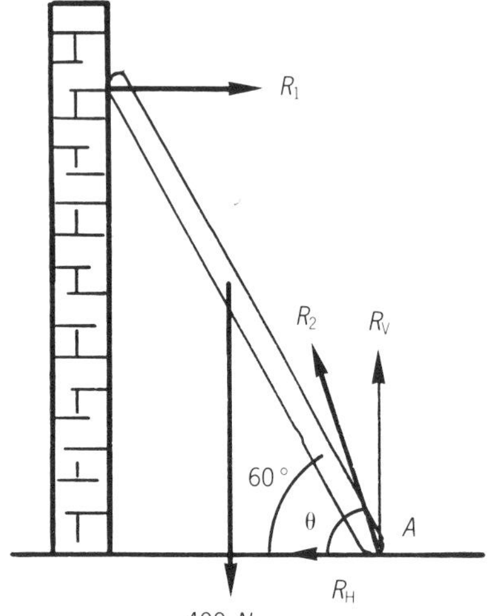

Figure 12.9

Calculate the magnitude and direction of the reactions R_1 and R_2 at the two ends of the ladder.

Since the wall is frictionless R_1 is at 90° to it, but the direction of R_2 is unknown. We will therefore treat R_2 in two components: R_H horizontally and R_V vertically.

Resolving vertically: $R_V = 400$ N
Resolving horizontally: $R_H = R_1$

Taking moments about A:

$$R_1 \times 10 \sin 60 = 400 \times 5 \cos 60$$

Therefore:

$$R_1 = \frac{1000}{8.66} = 115.4 \text{ N, giving } R_H = 115.4 \text{ N}$$

Therefore $R_2 = \sqrt{(400^2 + 115.4^2)} = 416.3$ N at an angle θ to the vertical, where

$$\tan \theta = \frac{400}{115.4} \text{ giving } \theta = 74°.$$

Student investigation

The equilibrium conditions for a set of forces acting on a body may easily be investigated using a set of masses hung on a system of pulleys, as shown in Figure 12.10. The equilibrium is found and the vertical components of each force are then calculated; the sum of the vertical components should be zero.

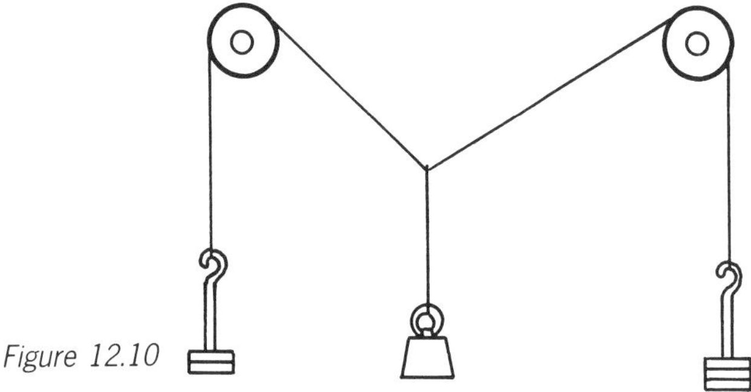

Figure 12.10

A more interesting investigation, however, is to consider a normal bicycle.

Mount the bicycle upside down as shown in Figure 12.11. Suspend a 1 kg mass from the pedal and measure the force which needs to be applied tangentially to the rim of the wheel to just make the wheel turn. Investigate this with various gearings.

Calculate the efficiency of the bicycle for various gearings.

Figure 12.11

5 A ladder is at rest with its upper end resting against a vertical wall such that the ladder is inclined at an angle θ to the vertical. Is the ladder more likely to slip when a person stands on the top or the bottom of the ladder? Explain your answer.

6 A light uniform metre stick 1 m long is suspended horizontally by two vertical strings A and B which are tied to it at the zero and 80 cm marks respectively. The string A will break when the tension in it exceeds 0.5 N and B when the tension in it exceeds 1 N. Find the range of positions on the stick where a load of 110 g may be placed without either string breaking.

Centre of mass and centre of gravity

The **centre of mass** M of a body is that point where the mass of the body can be thought to be concentrated.

The **centre of gravity** G is the point through which the total gravitational attraction can be considered to act on the body.

The centre of gravity coincides with the centre of mass in uniform gravitational fields such as those found close to the surface of the Earth (Figure 12.12(*a*)). This is not the case in non-uniform fields, however, such as those near a black hole where the gravitational intensity changes markedly with distance (Figure 12.12(*b*)).

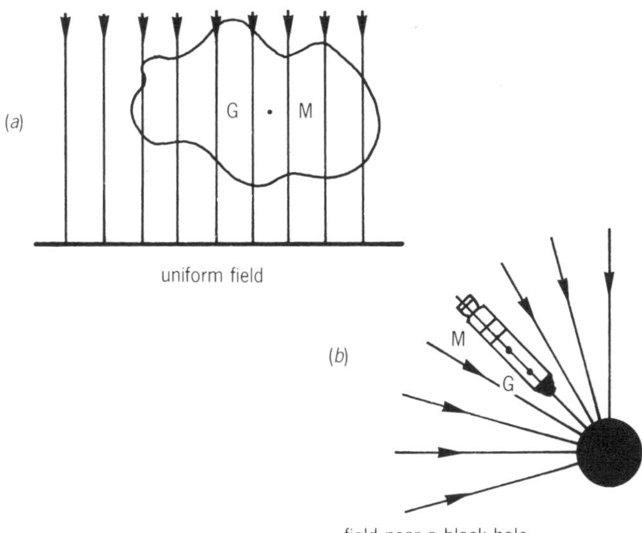

Figure 12.12

The sum of the moments about the centre of mass of a body is zero, and it therefore follows that if a body is suspended from any point and is in equilibrium the centre of mass must lie on a vertical line through the point of suspension.

Student investigation

Construct a bar such as that shown in Figure 12.13. It has a nut on a screw thread mounted below the pivot. Investigate how the stability of the bar depends on the position of the nut and hence the position of the centre of mass.

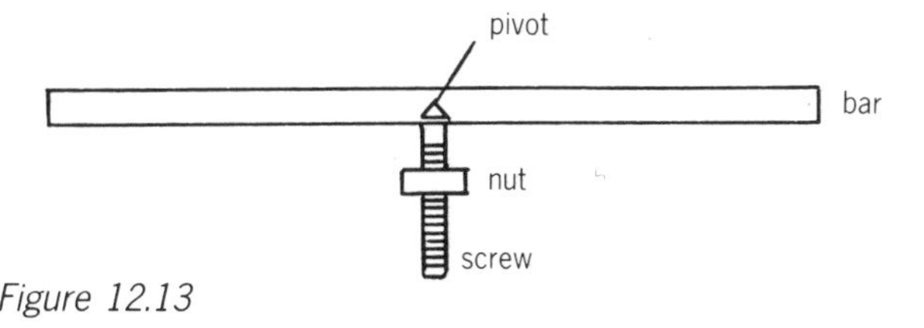

Figure 12.13

7 A forearm is held horizontally with the upper part of the arm vertical, and a load of 2 kg is placed in the hand so that its centre of gravity is 30 cm from the elbow joint. Assuming that the upper and lower ends of the biceps muscle are attached at points 12 cm and 5 cm respectively from the elbow joint, find

(*a*) the tension in the muscle, and

(*b*) the horizontal and vertical components of the reaction at the joint.

Neglect the weight of the forearm itself.

8 It is found that during a gale the mooring cable of a captive balloon is at an angle of 20° to the vertical and the tension in the cable is 1000 N. Calculate

(*a*) the horizontal force exerted by the wind, and

(*b*) the net vertical upthrust experienced by the balloon.

9 A uniform ladder 8 m long and of mass 75 kg stands on the pavement resting at an angle of 30° against a smooth vertical wall. A boy of mass 50 kg climbs the ladder to a point 3 m above the ground. Calculate the magnitudes and directions of the forces exerted by the ladder

(*a*) on the wall,

(*b*) on the ground.

10 A large uniform cylindrical drum stands on its flat base and is filled with water. The height of its centre of gravity above the ground is unchanged. Explain carefully with the help of diagrams and equations whether the drum is more stable when it is empty or full of water.

11 A mass of 60 kg hangs by two strings AC and BC inclined at 60° to the horizontal. A horizontal pull of 200 N is applied to the mass in the plane ABC. Calculate

(*a*) the tension in the strings, and

(*b*) the value of the horizontal pull when the string BC just becomes slack.

Density and pressure

The density (units kg m^{-3}) of a substance is defined as

$$\text{density} = \frac{\text{mass}}{\text{volume}}$$

The pressure (units N m^{-2} or Pascal (Pa)) on a surface is given by

$$\text{Pressure} = \frac{\text{force at right angles to surface}}{\text{area of contact}}$$

Pressure in fluids

We will deal here with the pressure in fluids at rest, considering both compressible and incompressible fluids. An incompressible fluid may be defined as one in which the density of the fluid does not change with depth – water being a good example of such a fluid. Air is an example of a compressible fluid where the density changes markedly with depth.

Incompressible fluids

The fluid pressure below the surface of the fluid is given by the equation:

$$\text{pressure } (p) = \text{depth } (d) \times \text{density } (\rho) \times g$$

Therefore the pressure 10 m below the surface of water is approximately $10 \times 1000 \times 10 = 10^5$ Pa, which is roughly equal to that due to the Earth's atmosphere.

Compressible fluids

If the fluid is compressible there will be a change of density with height. Consider the case of air.
Let the change in pressure due to a small change in height δh be δp. Consider the density at this point to be ρ (Figure 12.14).

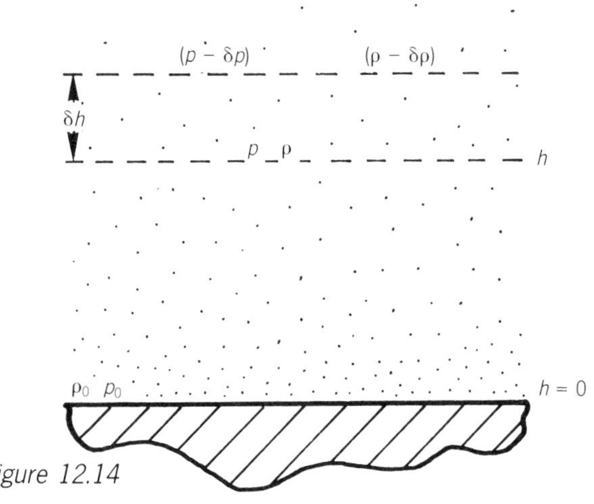

Figure 12.14

Let g be constant near the surface of the Earth. Since, if T is constant, ρ is proportional to p we have

$$p/p_o = \rho/\rho_o$$

where p_o and ρ_o are the pressures and densities of the air at sea level.

Therefore $\dfrac{\delta p}{\delta h} = -\rho g$, giving $\dfrac{\delta p}{\delta h} = -g\rho_o \dfrac{p}{p_0}$

so that $\dfrac{\delta p}{p} = \dfrac{-g\rho_0 \delta h}{p_0}$

In the limit this becomes $\dfrac{dp}{p} = -\dfrac{g\rho_0}{p_0}\, dh$

Integrating gives

$$p = p_0 e^{-g(\rho_0/p_0)h} \quad \text{or} \quad \rho = \rho_0 e^{-g(\rho_0/p_0)h}$$

Substituting the accepted values for p_0 and ρ_0 we have

$$p = p_0 e^{-0.116h}$$

with h in kilometres.

> **Example**
>
> Calculate the distance below the surface of the Earth at which a piece of iron (density 7870 kg m^{-3}) will float in air if the density of air at sea level is 1.3 kg m^{-3}.
>
> $7870 = 1.3e^{-0.116h}$
>
> Therefore $6053 = e^{-0.116h}$, giving $h = 75$ km!

Flotation and Archimedes' principle

When an object is in a fluid it will displace a certain amount of the fluid. The effect of this is to produce an upward force on the body and the apparent weight of the body is therefore less in the fluid than it would be in a vacuum (Figure 12.15). The magnitude of this upward force, or upthrust, depends on

(*a*) the volume of the body – the more fluid that is displaced the greater the upthrust;

(*b*) the density of the fluid – the greater the density the greater the upthrust.

Archimedes, a Greek physicist of the third century B.C., is said to have been pondering the problems of flotation when he suddenly realised *why* objects appear to weigh less when immersed in a denser fluid.

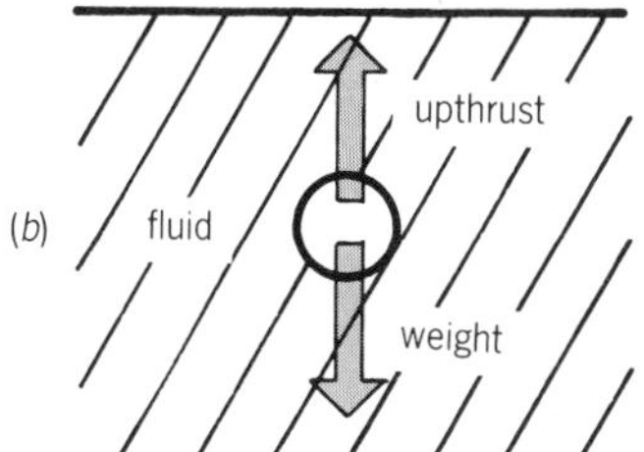

Figure 12.15

Leaping from the bath, he cried, 'Eureka!' (meaning, 'I have it!'), and rushed off naked down the street.

More formally, he stated **Archimedes' principle** as:

> When a body is wholly or partially immersed in a fluid there is an upthrust which is equal to the weight of fluid displaced.

It should be clear from the above that a floating body will displace its own weight of fluid such that there is no vertical resultant force on the body.

Therefore if a sphere of radius r made of material of density ρ is fully immersed in a liquid of density σ the apparent weight of the sphere is given by:

$$\begin{aligned}\text{apparent weight} &= \text{actual weight} - \text{upthrust}\\ &= \tfrac{4}{3}\pi r^3 g(\rho - \sigma)\end{aligned}$$

The fluid may be a liquid, such as water, or a gas, such as air, although due to the low density of air (about 1 kg m^{-3}) the upthrust in air in usually small, but sufficient to support a helium-filled balloon.

12 A boat is lowered by a crane on to a river and then slowly filled with concrete until it sinks. Sketch a graph of the variation of the tension in the cable supporting the boat.

13 A hollow steel buoy in the form of a sphere of radius 0.5 m is fixed by a wire to the base of a river. If the mass of the buoy is 20 kg, calculate the tension in the cable. (Density of water = 1000 kg m^{-3})

14 A certain hot air balloon has a volume of 600 m^3 and hovers just clear of the ground when the air in it is heated so that its density is 0.80 kg m^{-3}. If the density of the air outside the balloon is 1.25 kg m^{-3}, calculate

(*a*) the total mass of the balloon including the air inside it,

(*b*) the mass of the envelope of the balloon and its load.

Take g = 10 m s^{-2}.

15 A small boat floats in a swimming pool. In the boat there is a swimmer, a length of cord and two blocks of equal volume, one of wood (which will float) and one of concrete (which won't).

Describe and explain what happens to the water level in the swimming pool when each of the following things happens on its own:

(*a*) the swimmer throws out the wood;

(*b*) the swimmer throws out the concrete;

(*c*) the swimmer throws out the concrete but holds on to the cord which is tied to the concrete;

(*d*) the swimmer throws out both the concrete and the wood.

16 The volume of a deep sea diver enclosed in a diving suit is 0.15 m^3 and the total mass is 95 kg. Find the mass of lead that must be attached to the feet so that the diver will just sink in sea water of density 1030 kg m^{-3}. (Density of lead = 11 400 kg m^{-3}).

Example

A 20 kg spherical hollow steel buoy of volume 0.06 m^3 is tethered to the bottom of a fast flowing river by a cable so that the cable makes an angle of 40° with the base of the river. Calculate the tension in this cable.

Resolving vertically

Forces on the buoy:

	Upthrust	=	$mg + T\cos 40$
But	Upthrust	=	$0.06 \times 1000 \times 10 = 600$ N
Therefore	$T\cos 40$	=	$600 - 200 = 400$
	T	=	522 N

13 · Circular motion

This is the special case of the generalised motion in a curve which may be elliptical, parabolic, hyperbolic and so forth, as well as circular.

To move an object from a straight line path a force must be applied to it, since velocity is a vector: a change of direction means a change of velocity, and thus a force is required.

Examples of circular motion are given below, together with the force that makes them move in a path other than a straight line:

centrifuge – reaction at the walls
gramophone needle – friction with grooves
aircraft banking – lift on the wings
planetary orbit – gravitation
electron orbits – electrostatic force
car cornering – friction at wheels
car cornering on banked track – component of gravity
object on string – tension in string (Figure 13.1)
rotating liquid surface – gravity
governor – tension in bars
variation of *g* with latitude – gravity

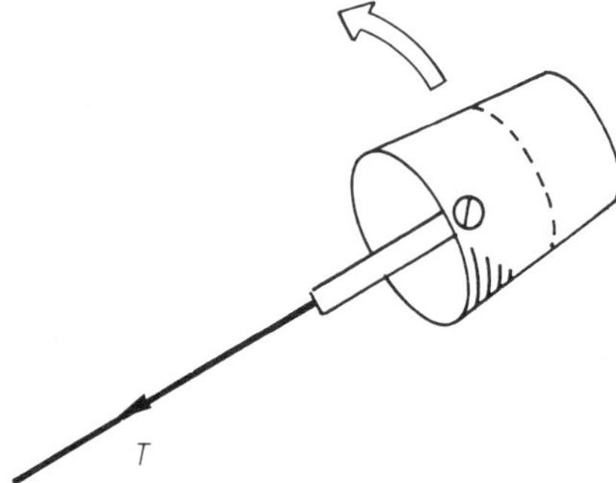

Figure 13.1

When a body is travelling in a circle it has an instantaneous linear velocity but also an **angular velocity**.

The angular velocity (ω) is defined as the rate of change of angle with time, and is expressed in radians per second. For a rotating rigid body such as a wheel the angular velocity is the same at all points on the body, but the linear velocity at a point depends on its distance from the axis of rotation.

If we take T to be the time for one complete rotation – called the **period** of the motion – then:

$$T = \frac{2\pi r}{v} = \frac{2\pi}{\omega}$$

where v is the linear velocity at a distance r from the axis of rotation.

Since T is the period then the number of revolutions per second (n) is $1/T$.

When an object moves with constant angular velocity in a circle its linear velocity is continually changing; there must therefore be an acceleration and thus a force must be acting. This force is called the **centripetal force**.

This is the force that makes the body move out of its straight line path into a curve. In the case of circular motion this force is directed towards the centre of the circle.

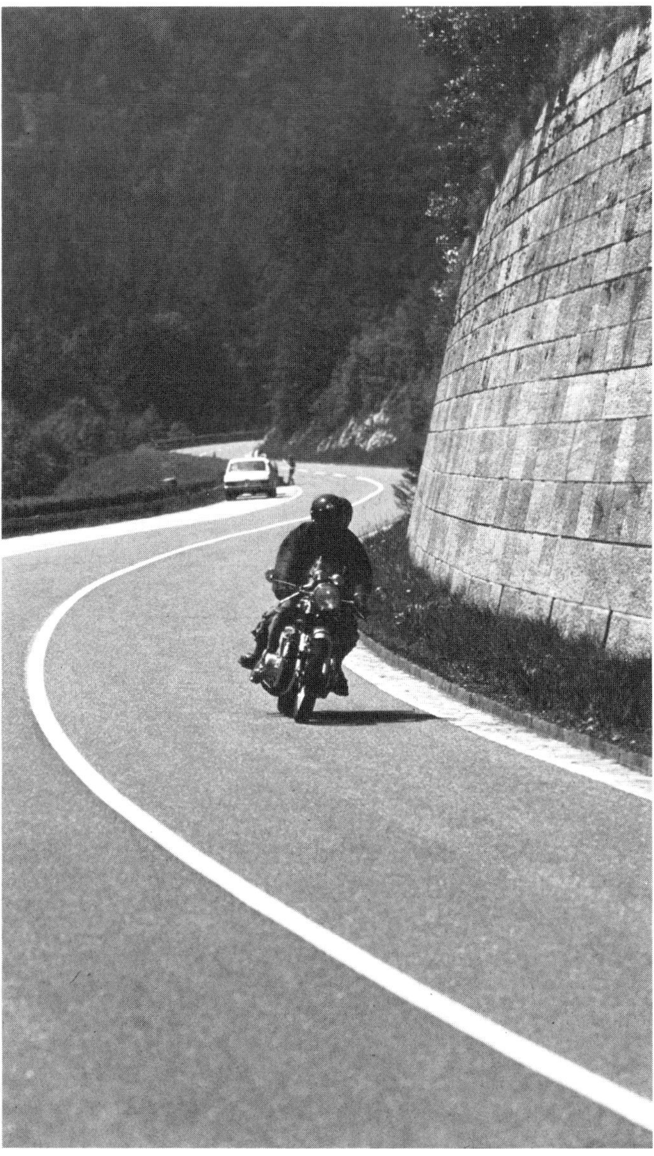

Describe the forces acting as the cyclist turns the bend (ZEFA)

Proof of the formula for centripetal acceleration and force

Consider an object of mass m moving at constant speed v and constant angular velocity ω round a circle of radius r with centre O as shown in Figure 13.2. We consider that it moves from P to Q in a time t.

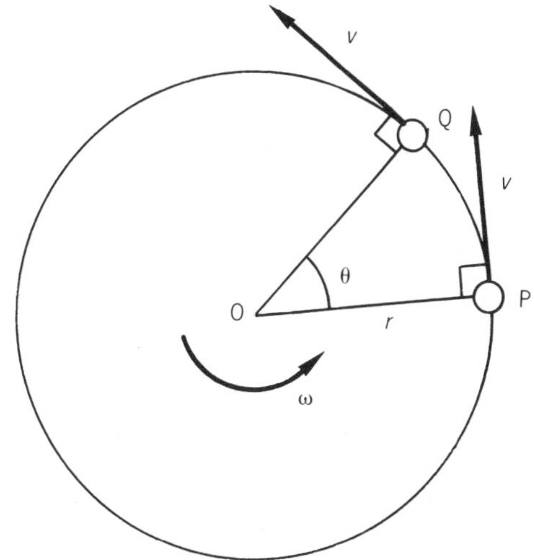

Figure 13.2

Change in velocity parallel to PO = $v \sin\theta - 0$

Change in velocity perpendicular to PO = $v \cos\theta - v$

When θ becomes small (that is, when Q is very close to P) $\sin\theta$ tends to θ in radians and $\cos\theta$ tends to 1. The equations become:

Change in velocity along PO = $v\theta - 0 = v\theta$

Change in velocity perpendicular to PO = $v - v = 0$

Therefore acceleration along PO = $v\theta/t = v\omega = v^2/r$

$$\text{centripetal acceleration} = \frac{v^2}{r} = \omega^2 r$$

But since $F = ma$, the centripetal force is given by:

$$\text{centripetal force} = \frac{mv^2}{r} = m\omega^2 r$$

Note that the force is directed towards the centre of the circle; if the force is removed the object will continue to move in a straight line along the tangent to the circle at that point.

In fact, since the force is always at right angles to the motion the object will move in a circle, since the radius of a circle is always at right angles to the tangent.

If we think of an object being swung round in a circle on a piece of string then the action of the centripetal force on the object causes a reaction on the hand – this is known as the **centrifugal force.**

The centrifugal force is equal and opposite to the centripetal force.

Example 1

Find the maximum speed with which an unpowered car of mass 1000 kg can take a corner of radius 20 m if the coefficient of friction between the tyres and the road is 0.5.

$$v = \sqrt{\frac{Fr}{m}} = \sqrt{\frac{5000 \times 20}{1000}} = 10 \text{ m s}^{-1}$$

This is a reasonable result for a car going round a motorway island.

Example 2

Calculate the tension in the wire of a hammer thrower's hammer of mass 7 kg, if it is being swung round at 1 rev per second in a circle of radius 1.5 m.

$$F = \frac{mv^2}{r} = \frac{7 \times 88.8}{1.5} = 414 \text{ N}$$

1 An astronaut is trained in a centrifuge that has an arm of length 6 m. If the astronaut can stand an acceleration of 9 *g*, what is the maximum number of revolutions per second that the centrifuge may make?

2 A helicopter's rotor blades rotate such that the speed at the tip is 200 m s^{-1}. This is roughly the same for all helicopters regardless of the length of the blades. Calculate the frequency of rotation for the following:
(*a*) Boeing Chinook – rotor blade length 9.14 m;
(*b*) Sikorsky Black Hawk – rotor blade length 8.45 m;
(*c*) Westland Lynx – rotor blade length 6.40 m.
Calculate also the maximum tension in (c) if the mass of the blade is 46 kg.

Student investigation

The groove in a long-playing record is a spiral. The record rotates at a constant rate of 33.33 r.p.m. Consider how the force on the needle varies as it crosses the record and how the velocity of the record relative to the pickup alters during the playing of the record.

Motion in a vertical circle

It is interesting to consider the motion of an object in a vertical circle (see Figure 13.3). It should be clear that for a given velocity of rotation the centripetal force must be constant; however, since the contribution due to gravitational attraction varies as the object makes one revolution so does the tension in the string. At the top of the circle the centripetal force is provided by both the tension in the string (T_1) and the gravitational attraction (mg)

$$\frac{mv^2}{r} = T_1 + mg \qquad \text{and so } T_1 = \frac{mv^2}{r} - mg$$

However, at the bottom of the circle the tension (T_2) and the gravitational attraction act in opposite directions and therefore:

$$\frac{mv^2}{r} = T_2 - mg \qquad \text{and so } T_2 = \frac{mv^2}{r} + mg$$

Clearly the value of T must be greatest at the bottom of the circle and it is therefore here that the string is most likely to break. A pilot in a plane that is looping the loop, someone riding a big wheel at a fairground and a person at the top of the big dipper are all undergoing circular motion in a vertical circle.

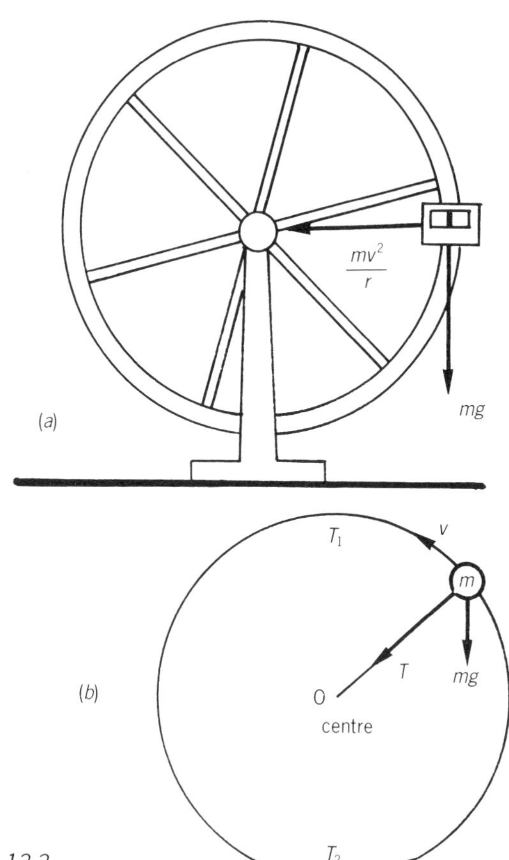

Figure 13.3

3 A roundabout accelerates from rest with a steady acceleration of 0.03 rad s^{-2}. After 0.75 minutes it reaches its maximum speed and continues to rotate steadily for a further 5 minutes, after which time it slows down steadily to a stop in a further 1.5 minutes.
(*a*) What is the maximum angular velocity?
(*b*) What was the acceleration during the last 1.5 minutes?
(*c*) How many revolutions did the roundabout make?

4 A stone of mass 0.5 kg is whirled round on the end of a 0.8 m long string in a vertical circle. If the speed of the stone is 4 m s^{-1}:
(*a*) at which point in the circle is the tension in the string a minimum and what is its value?
(*b*) at which point in the circle is the tension in the string a maximum and what is its value?

5 A motorway interchange includes a bend with a radius of 200 m. At what angle must the road be banked so that a car will take the curve automatically in an unpowered state at 25 m s^{-1}?

6 Explain why a centrifuge may be used to separate particles of different densities in a liquid.

7 A pilot in a plane loops the loop in a vertical circle of diameter 0.6 km at a constant speed of 250 km hr^{-1}. The pilot has a mass of 70 kg. Draw an accurate graph showing the magnitude of the force exerted on him during one complete loop.

8 A stunt pilot who has been diving vertically at 150 m s^{-1} pulls out of the dive into a circle in the vertical plane.
(*a*) What is the minimum radius of this circle, if the force on the pilot is not to exceed 6*g*?
(*b*) If the pilot has a mass of 80 kg, what is the apparent weight of the pilot at the lowest point of the circle?

9 A singly charged ion in a cyclotron moves in a circle of radius 0.3 m. If the mass of the ion is 10^{-27} kg and the flux density of the magnetic field is 0.1 T, calculate the velocity of the electron. ($e = 1.6 \times 10^{-19}$ C)

10 Calculate the angular velocity with which a space station of radius 50 m must be rotated to produce the effect of artificial Earth's gravity at its rim. Find the velocity of the rim.

11 A conical pendulum consists of a bob of mass 2.5 kg tied to a cord of length 1.5 m. The bob describes a horizontal circle of radius 0.2 m.
Draw a diagram to show the forces acting on the bob. Calculate the tension in the string and the number of revolutions per minute made by the bob.

Strength of rotating objects

If the tension in a material becomes too great it may not be able to hold itself together. This applies to things like car tyres and helicopter blades, although since the masses of these objects are not concentrated at a point complete analysis of the problem is difficult.

Example

A wire of mass 0.4 kg and length 2.0 m (Figure 13.4) is spun in a horizontal circle. If the breaking stress of the wire is 8×10^9 Pa and the cross-sectional area is 8×10^{-6} m, calculate the maximum frequency of rotation before the wire breaks and find at which point it will break.

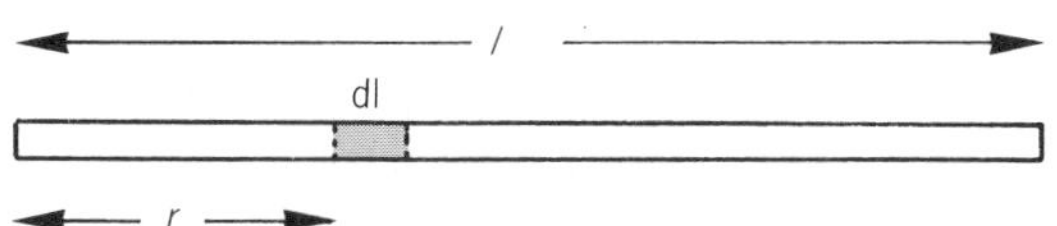

Figure 13.4

Let the mass per unit length be ρ. Then $m = \rho l$, where l is the length of the wire.

Considering the forces acting on a short length of the wire:

$$(T + \mathrm{d}T) - T = -\mathrm{d}m\, r\,\omega^2 \qquad \text{giving } \mathrm{d}T = -\rho\omega^2 r\,\mathrm{d}r$$

Integration gives:

$$T = -\tfrac{1}{2}\rho\omega^2 r^2 + c$$

Therefore:

$$T = \tfrac{1}{2}m\omega^2(l - r^2/l)$$

giving the maximum tension of $\frac{1}{2}m\omega^2 l$ when $r = 0$, that is, the wire will break at the point of attachment.

Substitution of the above figures gives a frequency of rotation of

$f = 63.6$ revs per second

Student investigation

Set up a candle inside a vertical glass tube with a diameter of about 5 cm mounted on a circular horizontal table. Using a variable-speed electric motor, rotate the table. Record the effect on the candle flame. (A table of 30 cm radius and rotating at 1 Hz will show the effects well.)

12 Discuss the forces that may be set up in a car tyre rotating at high speed. What might happen if cars had wheels double the normal diameter which rotated at the same angular velocity as before?

13 A wall of death motorcyclist at a fair rides round in a horizontal circle of diameter 10 m.
(*a*) Draw a diagram to show the forces acting on the rider.
(*b*) If the rider and the motorbike have a total mass of 140 kg, calculate the speed at which the rider must ride to avoid slipping down the wall. (Assume that the coefficient of friction between the tyres and the wall is 0.35.)

Motion in a circle – particular cases

The following examples of objects moving in circles will now be considered.

(i)	conical pendulum	(iv)	wall of death
(ii)	car on flat track	(vi)	aircraft banking
(iii)	car on banked track	(vii)	cyclist cornering
(iv)	variation of g	(viii)	rotating liquid surface

(i) Conical pendulum

Consider a mass m fixed to a string of length l rotating in a horizontal circle of radius r at a constant speed v, the string being at an angle θ to the vertical (Figure 13.5).

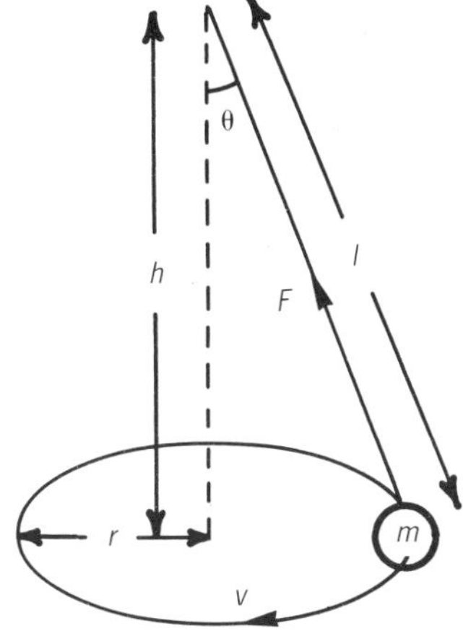

Figure 13.5

Resolving horizontally and vertically,

$$F \sin\theta = \frac{mv^2}{r} \qquad \text{and} \qquad F\cos\theta = mg$$

where F is the tension in the string. Therefore

$$\tan\theta = \frac{v^2}{rg} \qquad \text{and so } v = \sqrt{(rg\tan\theta)}$$

If the period of the motion is T, then

$$T = \frac{2\pi r}{v} = \frac{2\pi r}{\sqrt{(rg\tan\theta)}} = 2\pi\sqrt{\frac{(l\cos\theta)}{g}} = 2\pi\sqrt{\frac{h}{g}}$$

(ii) Car on a flat track

Consider a car of mass m travelling round a circle of radius r with a velocity v. The height of the car's centre of gravity is h and the distance between the wheels is $2b$ (Figure 13.6).

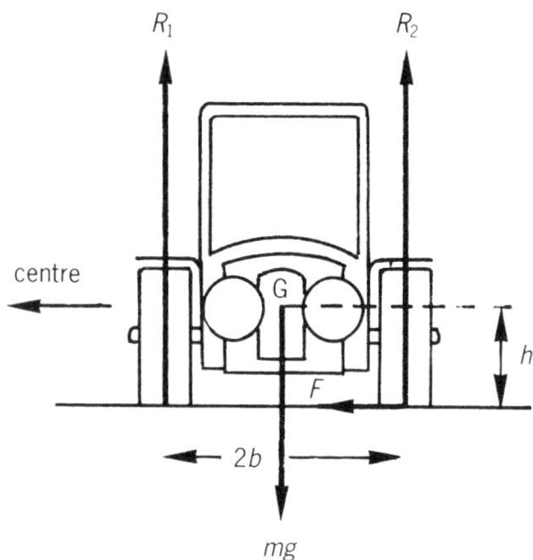

Figure 13.6

The frictional force between the road and the tyres is F and the reactions at the inner and outer pairs of wheels are R_1 and R_2 respectively.

When the car is just about to fail to take the curve R_1 will become zero as the inner wheels lift off the road. Resolving vertically:

$$R_2 = mg$$

Taking moments about the centre of gravity G:

$$R_2 b = Fh$$

Therefore, since $F = mv^2/r$,

$$mgb = \frac{hmv^2}{r}$$

and so the maximum possible velocity (v) is given by:

$$v^2 = \frac{brg}{h}$$

(iii) Car on a banked track

Consider the same car as in (ii), travelling on a track banked at an angle θ (Figure 13.7). If we assume that the track is frictionless, then the car is held in a circular path by the component of the reaction at the wheels (R).

Resolving vertically and horizontally gives:

$$R \cos\theta = mg \qquad \text{and} \qquad R \sin\theta = \frac{mv^2}{r}$$

where v is the maximum speed that the car can have so that it may just take the corner of radius r. Therefore

$$\tan\theta = \frac{v^2}{rg}$$

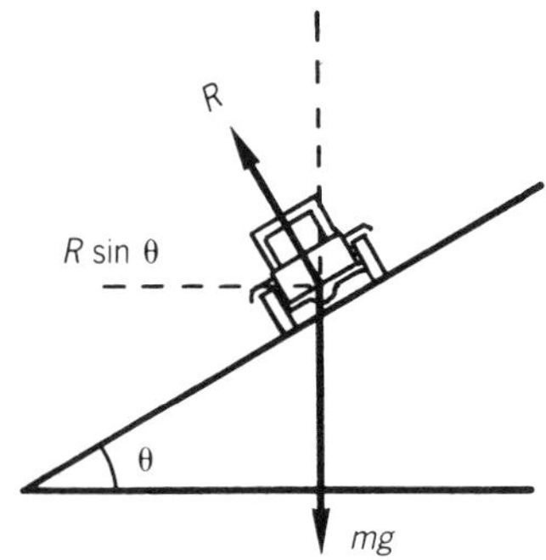

Figure 13.7

If friction is taken into account as well then the car will be able to corner at a greater speed, since the frictional force will also have a component towards the centre of the circle and the centripetal force will be greater.

(iv) Variation of g

The circular motion of any point on the Earth's surface will tend to reduce the actual effect of the gravitational acceleration of gravity at that point.

The resultant acceleration g is given by the following equations for a latitude θ.

$$mg' \cos\theta = mg - m\omega^2 r \cos\theta$$

$$mg \sin\theta = m\omega^2 r \sin\theta$$

$$g' = g - r\omega^2 \cos^2\theta$$

The value of g is 9.78 m s^{-2} at the equator, 9.81 m s^{-2} at latitude 45° and 9.83 m s^{-2} at the poles.

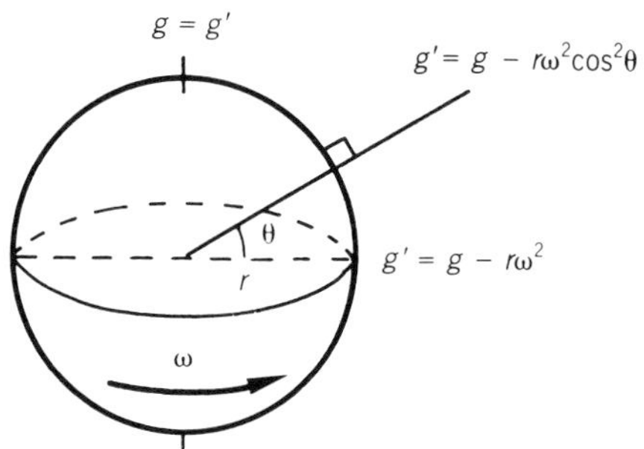

Figure 13.8

(v) Wall of death
Consider a rider of mass m going round a circle of radius r (Figure 13.9). There must be a frictional force between the rider and the wall, otherwise the rider could not stay up (as you can see from the equations). The slower the rider goes the more upright the rider will have to ride.

$$mg = \mu R$$

$$R = \frac{mv^2}{r} \qquad \text{and so} \qquad \frac{rg}{\mu} = v^2$$

For a person on a wall of death μ is about 0.5.

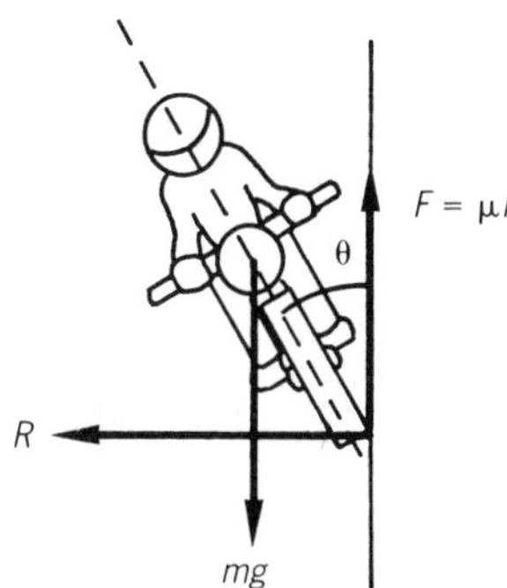

Figure 13.9

(vi) Aircraft banking
Consider an aircraft of mass m with a lifting force on the wings L (this is provided by the Bernouilli effect – see page 127) as shown in Figure 13.10.

Resolving vertically and horizontally we have

$$L \cos \theta = mg \qquad \text{and} \qquad L \sin \theta = \frac{mv^2}{r}$$

Therefore

$$\tan \theta = \frac{v^2}{rg}$$

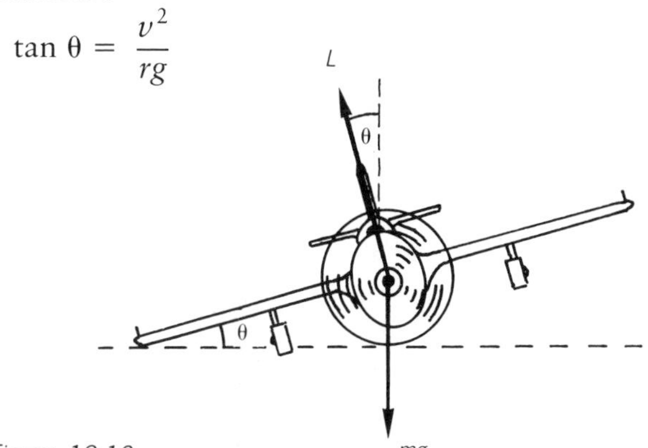

Figure 13.10

(vii) Cyclist cornering
The cyclist leans over at an angle so that there is a couple opposing the turning effect of the frictional couple and the bike experiences a reaction at the wheels (Figure 13.11).

Resolving vertically and horizontally:

$$R = mg \qquad \text{and} \qquad F = \frac{mv^2}{r}$$

Taking moments about the centre of gravity:

$$Rh \sin \theta = Fh \cos \theta$$

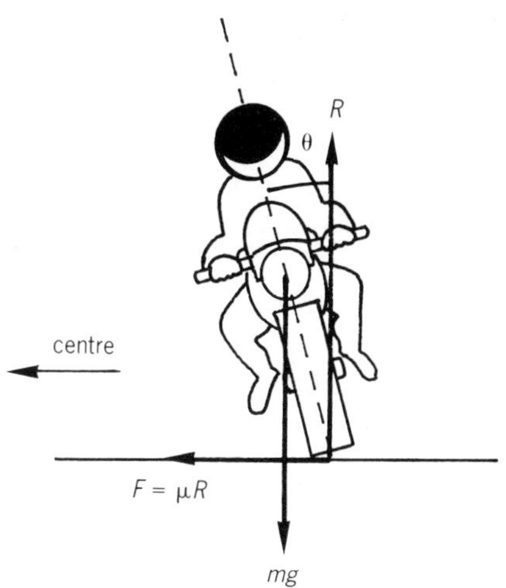

Figure 13.11

(viii) Rotating liquid surface
Consider a point on the liquid surface a distance x from the centre of rotation. At this point the surface makes an angle θ with the horizontal (Figure 13.12).

Consider the effect of the centripetal force and the weight.

$$\tan \theta = \frac{m\omega^2 x}{mg} = \frac{\omega^2 x}{g}$$

But $\tan \theta = dy/dx$, and so $dy/dx = \omega^2 x$.

Therefore

$$y = \frac{\omega^2 x^2}{2g} + C$$

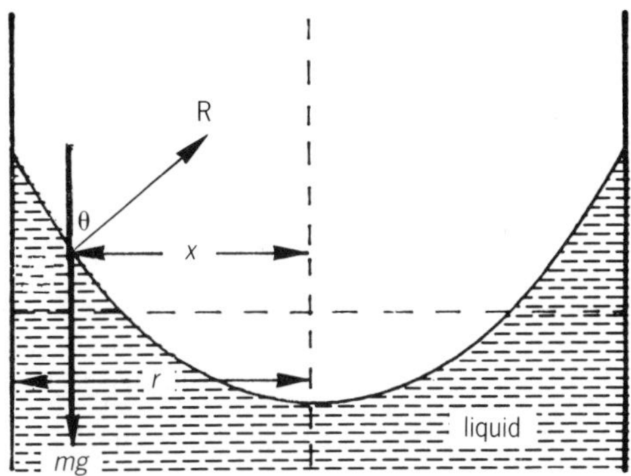

Figure 13.12

But $y = 0$ when $x = 0$. Therefore $C = 0$.

This is the equation of a parabola and so the liquid surface is parabolic.

It is left as an exercise for the reader to consider the production of artificial gravity in a rotating space station.

14 · Rotation of rigid bodies

We have so far considered the motion of point masses in a circle and we must now look at the case of rigid bodies whose mass is spread over a definite area. The behaviour of rotating objects is of considerable importance in our lives: the results of our considerations can be applied to rotating car wheels, flywheels, the rotation of high divers and many other things.

A rotating object has kinetic energy associated with it. Flywheels can be used to store rotational kinetic energy; for example, current to energise the electromagnets of the proton accelerator at the Rutherford laboratory in Oxfordshire is provided by a generator that is driven by a 5 m diameter flywheel; this allows large pulses of electricity to be obtained without putting a sudden large drain on the mains supply.

Rotational energy is also important in stability, which is due to the angular momentum of the body (discussed below); many washing machines have a disc of concrete fixed to the base of the drum to prevent vibrations due to uneven loading with clothes.

If we think of a mass m on a string being swung round in a circle of radius r (Figure 14.1) then its kinetic energy at any instant is given by:

$$\tfrac{1}{2}mv^2 = \tfrac{1}{2}m\omega^2r^2$$

where ω is the angular velocity of the mass. (Think of the action of a hammer thrower: he may spin a 7.5 kg hammer round his head once a second and use the kinetic energy so gained to project it some 80 m when released.)

Moment of inertia

We can think of a solid rigid body as made up of many particles of masses m_1, m_2, m_3... at distances r_1, r_2, r_3... from the centre of rotation (Figure 14.2): the total rotational kinetic energy of the body will be the sum of the energies of all the particles. Then

total kinetic energy =

$$\tfrac{1}{2}m_1\,\omega^2r_1^2 + \tfrac{1}{2}m_2\,\omega^2r_2^2 + \tfrac{1}{2}m_3\omega^2r_3^2 + ...$$

Notice that since the body is rigid the *angular* velocity (ω) is the same for all particles although the *linear* velocity will be greater for particles further from the axis of rotation. We can write this as:

$$\text{kinetic energy} = \tfrac{1}{2}\omega^2\Sigma mr^2$$

where Σmr^2 represents the sum of all terms like $m_1r_1^2$.

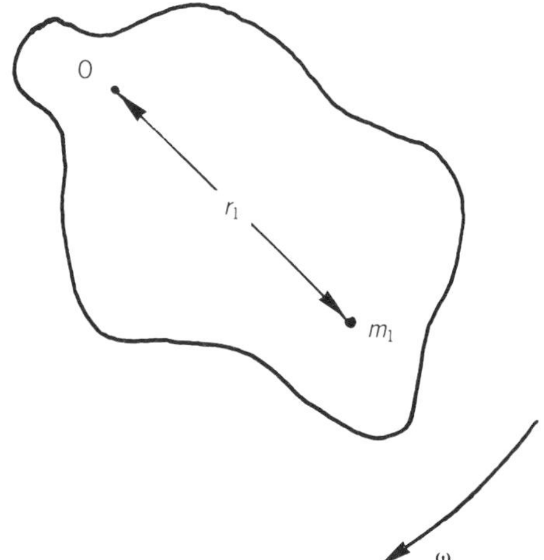

Figure 14.2

If we now compare the expression with that for linear kinetic energy we see that they are very similar. The term Σmr^2 takes the place of mass in the linear equation and it is known as the **moment of inertia** of the body (I). The units for moment of inertia are kg m^2.

$$\text{rotational kinetic energy} = \tfrac{1}{2}I\omega^2$$

Since power is the rate at which work is done, or at which energy is transformed from one type to another, we can write:

$$\text{energy} = \text{power} \times \text{time} = \tfrac{1}{2}I\omega^2$$

Unlike mass, the moment of inertia of a body may be variable; it depends on how the mass is distributed about the axis of rotation. A wheel with a heavy rim will have a bigger moment of inertia than a uniform disc of the same mass and radius.

Example

Consider two wheels, both of mass 4 kg and both of radius 0.3 m. One wheel has all its mass concentrated in a heavy rim and the other is a uniform thin flat disc (Figure 14.3). Calculate the rotational kinetic energy of both if they are rotated at 10 rev s^{-1}.

(a) *Disc with heavy rim:*
Kinetic energy $= \frac{1}{2} mr^2\omega^2$

Since all the mass is concentrated in the rim

k.e. = 710.6 J

(b) *Uniform disc:*
Kinetic energy $= \frac{1}{2} I\omega^2 = 355.3$ J.

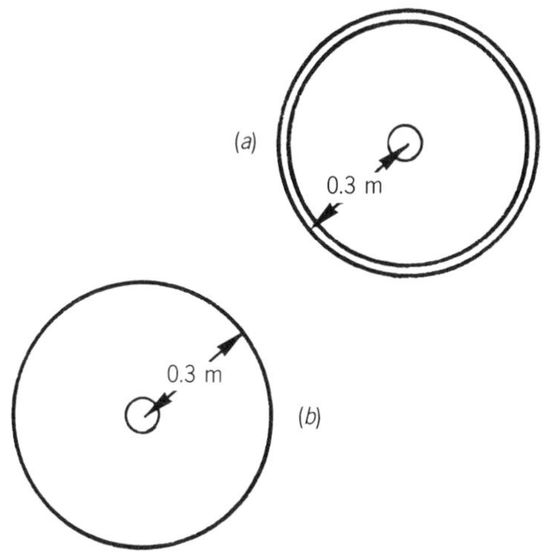

Figure 14.3

(The formula for the moment of inertia of a flat disc is given on page 64.)

Student investigation

The effect of moment of inertia may be studied using the apparatus shown in Figure 14.4. It consists of a bar, pivoted at the centre, along which two masses may be moved and fixed at varying distances.

The bar is fixed to an axle and may be set in rotation by wrapping a string round the axle and fixing a weight to the free end of the string and allowing the weight to fall to the ground. Investigate the following:

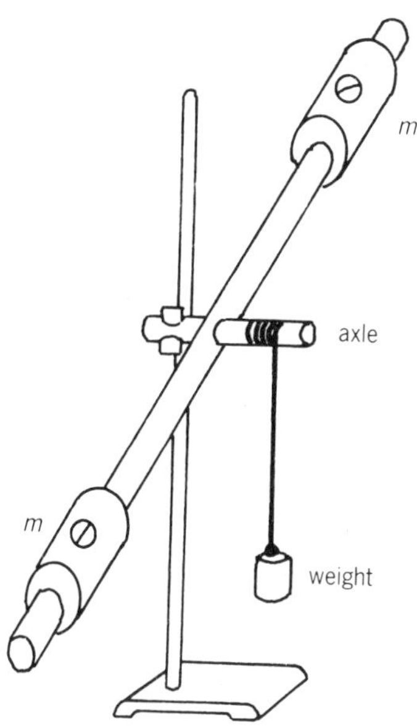

Figure 14.4

(*a*) the angular velocity of the system after varying times with the masses in a fixed position, and

(*b*) the angular velocity after the string has left the axle for different positions of the masses.

1 A uniform disc of mass 100 g has a diameter of 10 cm. Calculate the total energy of the disc when rolling along a horizontal table with a velocity of 20 cm s^{-1}.

2 A hammer of mass 6 kg is swung round an athlete's head in a horizontal circle of radius 1.5 m with a velocity of 8 m s^{-1}. Calculate
(*a*) the moment of inertia of the hammer,
(*b*) its kinetic energy, and
(*c*) the tension in the wire.

3 Calculate the kinetic energy stored in a helicopter rotor consisting of four blades each 8 m long and with a mass of 50 kg if the tips of the blades are moving at 200 m s^{-1}.

Student investigation

Make a detailed study of the effects of moment of inertia in athletics. If possible, obtain numerical values of the angular velocity in events such as the hammer, the discus and the long jump.

What rotational problems might there be in the different methods of high jumping, that is, the flop technique and the straddle?

Formulae for moments of inertia

The list that follows gives the more important moments of inertia for some common simply shaped objects (see Figure 14.5).

(*a*) Uniform thin rod about one end $\frac{ml^2}{3}$

(*b*) Uniform thin rod about the middle $\frac{ml^2}{12}$

(*c*) Circular disc about the centre $\frac{mr^2}{2}$

(*d*) Cylinder about the axis of symmetry:
 (i) solid cylinder $\frac{mr^2}{2}$
 (ii) hollow cylinder mr^2

(*e*) Sphere about a diameter $\frac{2mr^2}{5}$

Figure 14.5

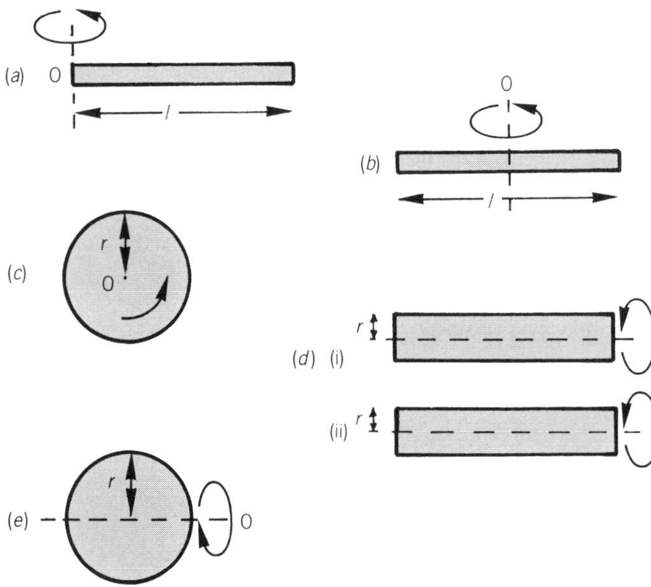

Figure 14.5

Calculation of the moment of inertia of a body

We give here a method for finding the moment of inertia of a uniform thin rod about the centre by calculation.

Consider a rod of mass m and cross-sectional area A, and let ρ be the mass of the rod per unit volume. Let the rod be divided into slices perpendicular to XY.

For one elementary slice the moment of inertia about O is $A\rho\, dx.x^2$

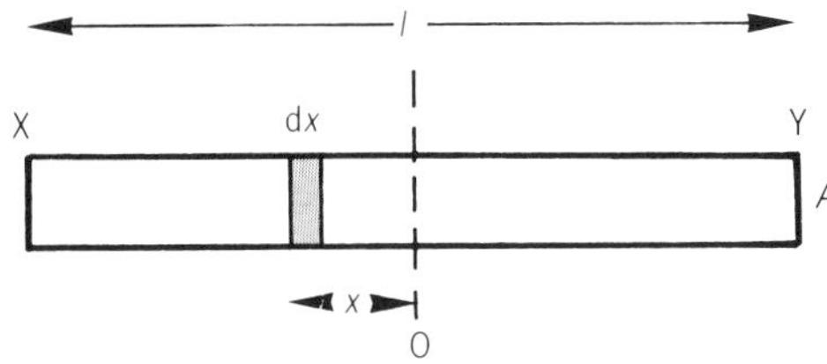

Figure 14.6

For the whole rod:

$$I = A\rho \int_{-l/2}^{+l/2} x^2\, dx$$

$$= A\rho l \frac{l^2}{12} = \frac{ml^2}{12}$$

Similar proofs may be carried out for other simply shaped bodies.

4 A cricket ball of mass 0.15 kg and diameter 8 cm is bowled at 12 m s^{-1}, spinning about an axis through its centre with angular velocity 80 rad s^{-1}. Calculate
 (*a*) its rotational energy,
 (*b*) its total kinetic energy.

5 A uniform rod is pivoted with a movable pivot so that the time of oscillation of the rod may be taken at different positions along the rod. The minimum time period of oscillation is found to be 1.85 s. What is the length of the rod?

6 Make sensible estimates of the rotational kinetic energy of the following:
 (*a*) a record single rotated at its normal speed,
 (*b*) the second hand of a laboratory wall clock.
In each case explain any assumptions made in your calculation.

Student investigation

A braking system on a wheel destroys the rotational kinetic energy of the wheel, converting it into heat.

Make an estimate of the forces in a bicycle braking system by finding the angle through which the wheels of a bike rotate after the brakes are applied. (It is suggested that the bike is mounted upside down or clear of the ground for this investigation.)

Couples and angular acceleration

In just the same way that a body's linear velocity can be changed by the application of a force, its angular velocity can be changed by a couple acting on it for a time t.

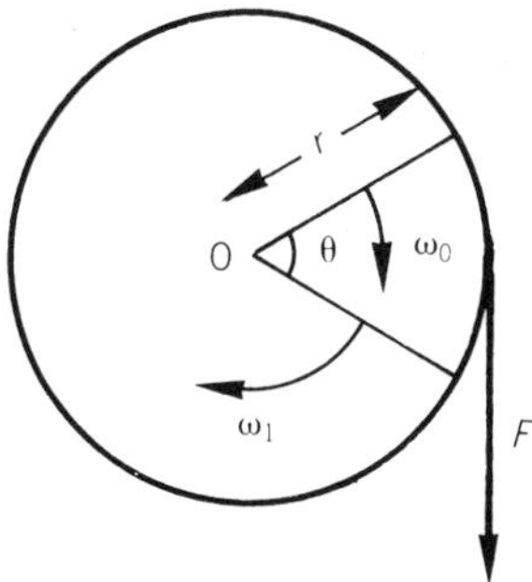

Figure 14.7

If a couple is applied for a time t as shown in Figure 14.7, the angular velocity of the body will be changed from ω_0 to ω_1; this means the body experiences an angular acceleration of α.

Suppose that the body rotates through an angle θ during the acceleration, then

$$\theta = \omega_0 t + \tfrac{1}{2}\alpha t^2$$
$$\omega_1^2 = \omega_0^2 + 2\alpha\theta$$
$$\alpha = \frac{\omega_1 - \omega_0}{t}$$

The work done by the couple is given by the equation:

$$\text{work done} = T\theta = F \times 2\pi r n$$

where r is the distance of the force from the axis of rotation and n is the number of rotations.

If a continuous input of energy is required to maintain a constant angular velocity ω against a frictional couple T then:

$$\text{energy used per second} = \text{power} = \frac{T\theta}{t} = T\omega$$

The torque T, the moment of inertia I and the angular acceleration α are related by the equation:

$$T = I\alpha$$

These equations can be compared with the similar ones for linear motion.

Linear motion	*Angular equivalent*
Displacement, s	Angular displacement, θ
Velocity, v	Angular velocity, $\omega = v/r$
Acceleration, a	Angular acceleration, α
Momentum $= mv$	Angular momentum $= I\omega$
Kinetic energy $= \frac{1}{2}mv^2$	Rotational k.e. $= \frac{1}{2}I\omega^2$
Force $= ma$	Torque $= I\alpha$
$s = vt$	$\theta = \omega t$
$s = ut + \frac{1}{2}at^2$	$\theta = \omega_0 t + \frac{1}{2}\alpha t^2$
$v^2 = u^2 + 2as$	$\omega_1^2 = \omega_0^2 + 2\alpha\theta$

Example

A force of 5 N is applied for 3 s to the rim of a uniform stationary wheel of mass 4 kg and radius 0.5 m (Figure 14.8). Calculate:

(*a*) the angular acceleration,
(*b*) the final angular velocity,
(*c*) the number of revolutions in that time,
(*d*) the energy gained by the wheel, and
(*e*) the work done by the couple.

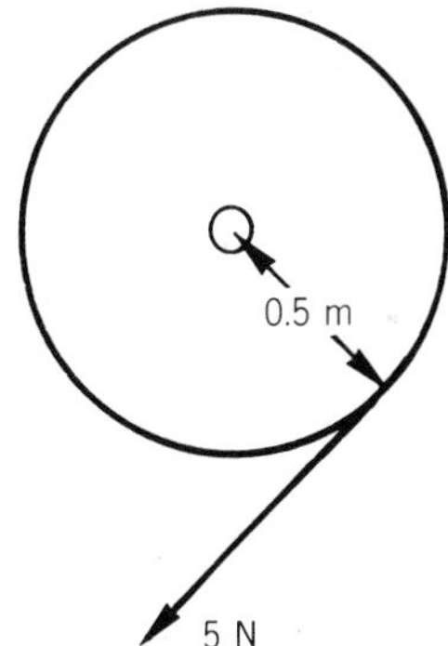

Figure 14.8

(*a*) $C = I\alpha \quad 5 \times 0.5 = (4 \times 0.5^2)\,\alpha/2$
$\alpha = 5$ rad s^{-2}.
(*b*) $\omega_1 = \omega_0 + \alpha t = 5 \times 3 = 15$ rad s^{-1}.
(*c*) Average velocity = 7.5 rad s^{-1}.
Therefore wheel turns through = 3 × 7.5
= 22.5 rads.
Therefore number of revs = 22.5/2π = 3.58.
(*d*) Energy gained $= \frac{1}{2}I\omega^2 = 0.5 \times 0.5 \times 15 \times 15$
= 56.25 J.
(*e*) Work done = 5 × 2π × 0.5 × 3.58 = 56.25 J.

Angular momentum

Rotating bodies show the same reluctance to a change in their angular velocity as bodies moving in a straight line do to a change in their linear velocity. This is due to the **angular momentum** of the object.

A body can possess angular momentum as you can see from Figure 14.9.

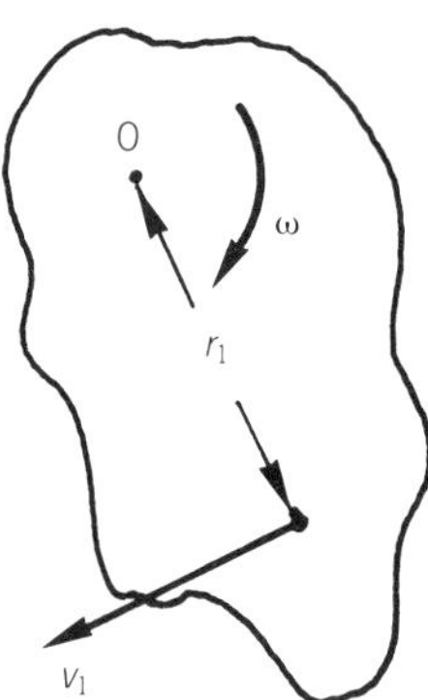

Figure 14.9

Consider a mass m_1 rotating at a distance r_1 from the centre of rotation; its linear momentum at that instant is $m_1v_1 = m_1r_1\omega$.

The angular momentum of the mass is defined as the **moment of the momentum about the centre of rotation.** Therefore the angular momentum of m_1 is:
$= r_1\ (m_1r_1\ \omega)$.

If we sum this for all the particles of the body then:

$$\text{angular momentum of the body} = \omega\Sigma mr^2 = I\omega$$

The units for angular momentum are kg m^2 radian s^{-1}.

You should have expected this result as it is similar to that for linear momentum (mv).

The application of a couple C for a certain time t will produce a change of angular momentum such that

$$Ct = I\omega_1 - I\omega_0$$

7 It has been suggested that it might be possible to design a bus that is powered from the energy stored in a flywheel. This flywheel would be accelerated to 3000 r.p.m. by electric motors placed at stopping points along its route.

If the flywheel has a mass of 1000 kg and a diameter of 1.8 m, calculate the following:

(*a*) the maximum kinetic energy that may be stored in the flywheel,

(*b*) the maximum time of one journey if the power needed to run the bus is 19 kW,

(*c*) the maximum distance between any stopping points at an average speed of 40 km per hour.

(The flywheel may be taken as a uniform disc.)

8 A flywheel of moment of inertia 0.32 kg m^2 is rotated steadily at 120 rad s^{-1} by a 50 W electric motor. Find

(*a*) the kinetic energy of the flywheel,

(*b*) the angular momentum of the flywheel,

(*c*) the value of the frictional couple opposing rotation, and

(*d*) the time taken for the wheel to come to rest after the motor has been switched off. [0]

Radius of gyration

We can write the moment of inertia I of a body as Mk^2, where M is the mass of the body and k is a distance called the **radius of gyration** of the body. For example, for a disc the moment of inertia is $Mr^2/2$, and so $k = (r^2/2)^{\frac{1}{2}} = r/\sqrt{2}$ (Figure 14.10).

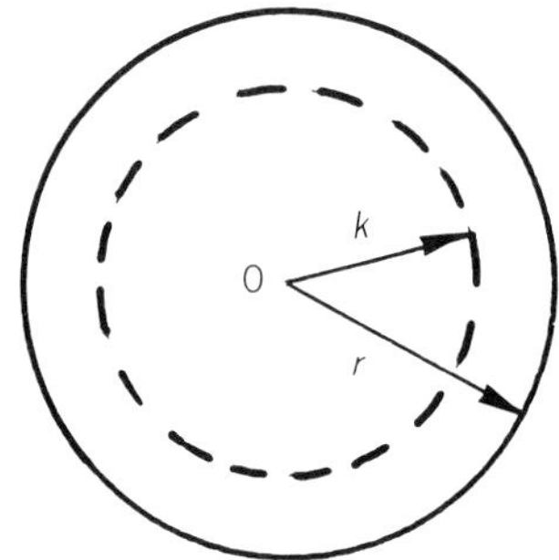

Figure 14.10

The radius of gyration can be defined as the distance from the centre of rotation of a rotating body to the point where the mass can be considered to be concentrated (not to be confused with the centre of mass).

Conservation of angular momentum

As with linear momentum angular momentum is conserved in an isolated system where no external couples act.

The angular momentum of an isolated system is constant.

This may be expressed in a formula as:

$$I_0\omega_0 = I_1\omega_1$$

where $I_0\omega_0$ and $I_1\omega_1$ are the initial and final angular momenta of the system.

A very simple demonstration of this law can be shown by a person standing on a rotating platform (Figure 14.11). If they first rotate with their arms outstretched and then bring their arms in, their angular velocity will increase. This happens because their angular momentum must remain constant; the decrease in their moment of inertia as they drop their arms results in an increase in their angular velocity.

Figure 14.11

Many of you will have experienced the effects of the conservation of angular momentum when riding a bike. It is very hard to keep the bike upright when it is stationary, but as soon as the bike is moving and its wheels are rotating it becomes much easier. The rotation of the wheels produces angular momentum and prevents the bike from falling sideways, because this would give a change in the angular momentum (since this is a vector quantity).

A helicopter is prevented from rotating about a vertical axis either by the small tail rotor or by a sideways jet of air ducted through the tail boom.

Stability of rotating objects

Since angular momentum is a vector quantity a couple is needed to change the angular momentum of a body. It therefore follows that spinning objects are more stable than ones that do not spin, and keep pointing in a fixed direction. A rugby ball does not tumble in flight if it is spinning, and a spinning bullet from a rifle keeps pointing in the forward direction. For this reason, satellites are given a spin when they are launched from the space shuttle.

9 In a playground there is a small stationary roundabout with a radius of 1.5 m and a mass of 120 kg. The radius of gyration is 1 m. A child of mass 30 kg runs at a speed of 3 m s^{-1} along a tangent to the roundabout and then jumps on. Neglecting friction, find the resulting angular velocity of the child and roundabout.

10 An electric sanding wheel and a large circular saw will coast for a minute or more when either is switched off, but an electric drill will only coast for a few seconds. Explain why this is so.

11 Two hollow tin cans of identical dimensions are allowed to roll down a slope. One is empty and the other is filled with water. Which reaches the bottom first? Explain your answer.

12 A flywheel in the form of a uniform solid disc is mounted on a light axle of radius 2 cm round which is wound a cord to which is attached a mass of 0.5 kg. If the thickness of the flywheel is 4 cm, its radius 10 cm and its density 7800 kg m^{-3}, find the tension in the cord and the kinetic energy of the flywheel when the attached mass has descended a distance of 20 cm from rest. (T)

13 A hub cap with a mass of 1.2 kg comes off the wheel of a car that is travelling at 30 m s^{-1}. The wheel has a diameter of 60 cm and the frictional force between the hub cap and the road is 10 N.

(*a*) How far will the hub cap go before it comes to rest?

(*b*) Is the estimate of the frictional force reasonable?

Measurement of the moment of inertia of a flywheel

A flywheel of radius R is set up on a horizontal axle of radius r. A string of length h is wrapped round the axle with a mass m tied to the end (Figures 14.12 and 14.13). The moment of inertia of the flywheel and axle is I. The flywheel is accelerated by the couple applied by the mass m. The mass is allowed to fall through a height h, at which point the string leaves the axle. The velocity of the falling mass at this instant is v and the angular velocity of the flywheel ω.

The potential energy lost by the weight is converted into kinetic energy of the weight, kinetic energy of the flywheel and heat due to friction in the bearings.

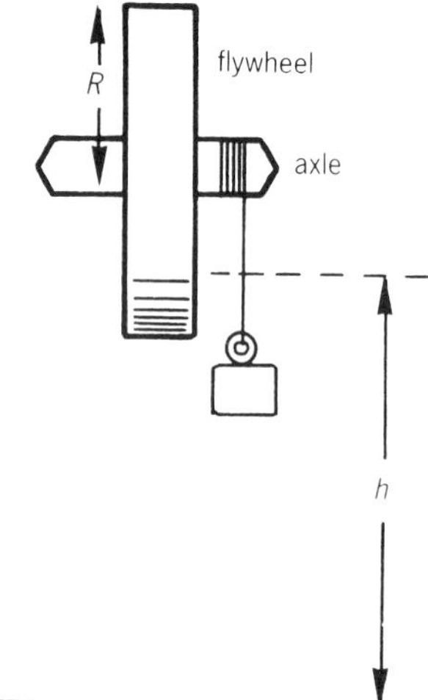

Figure 14.12

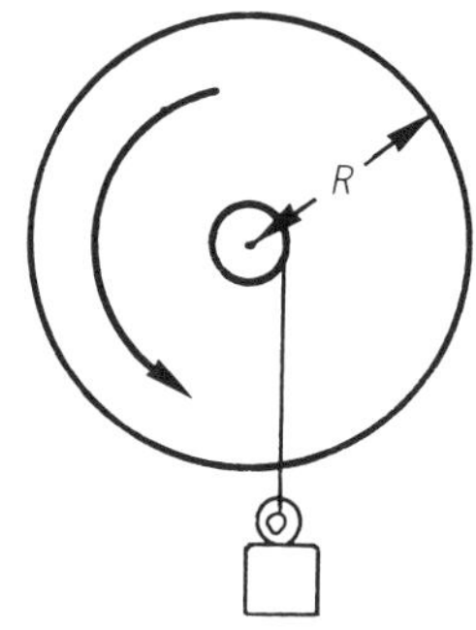

Figure 14.13

If the energy lost per revolution due to friction is E and the flywheel makes n_1 revolutions during acceleration, then

$$mgh = \tfrac{1}{2}mv^2 + \tfrac{1}{2}I\omega^2 + n_1E$$

The flywheel is then allowed to come to rest due to the frictional couple. If it stops after a further n_2 revolutions, then

$$\tfrac{1}{2}I\omega^2 = n_2E$$

Therefore:

$$\begin{aligned} mgh &= \tfrac{1}{2}mv^2 + \tfrac{1}{2}I\omega^2 + (n_1/n_2)\,\tfrac{1}{2}I\omega^2 \\ &= \tfrac{1}{2}mv^2 + \tfrac{1}{2}I\omega^2\,(1 + n_1/n_2) \end{aligned}$$

We could convert v into ω if we wished.

Now the angular velocity ω at the end of the period of the acceleration is given by:

$$\frac{\omega}{2} = \frac{2\pi n_1}{t}$$

Since $\omega/2$ is the average angular velocity and $2\pi n_1$ is the angular distance covered in a time t.

Parallel and perpendicular axes theorems

These two theorems may be useful in considering problems on moments of inertia.

(*a*) Parallel axes theorem

The moment of inertia I of a body about any axis is equal to the moment of inertia I_G about a parallel axis through the centre of gravity of the body plus Mh^2, where M is the mass of the body and h is the distance between the two axes.

(*b*) Perpendicular axes theorem

For any plane body (e.g. a rectangular sheet of metal) the moment of inertia about any axis perpendicular to the plane is equal to the sum of the moments of inertia about any two perpendicular axes in the plane of the body which intersect the first axis.

This theorem is most useful when considering a body which is of regular form (symmetrical) about two out of the three axes. If the moment of inertia about these axes is known then that about the third axis may be calculated.

14 Meteoric material amounting to about 1×10^7 kg falls on the Earth's surface every day equally from all directions. The Earth is approximately a sphere of radius 6×10^6 m and moment of inertia 8×10^{37} kg m^2.

(*a*) Explain why this arrival of material causes the Earth's rate of rotation to decrease.

(*b*) By what fraction would the Earth's angular speed have changed in the last 10^6 years? The moment of inertia of a thin spherical shell about a diameter is $\frac{2}{3}mr^2$.

Angular momentum and athletics

Long jumpers make use of the conservation of angular momentum when they jump. As jumpers leave the board they keep their bodies long in the hang style of long jump in order to slow down forward rotation (Figure 14.14). If they use the hitch kick techniques and rotate their legs in the opposite direction this will have the same effect.

The reverse is true of a diver or a trampolinist; they go into the tuck position to speed up their rotation. In the same way spinning skaters will speed up their rate of rotation if they bring their arms into a vertical position.

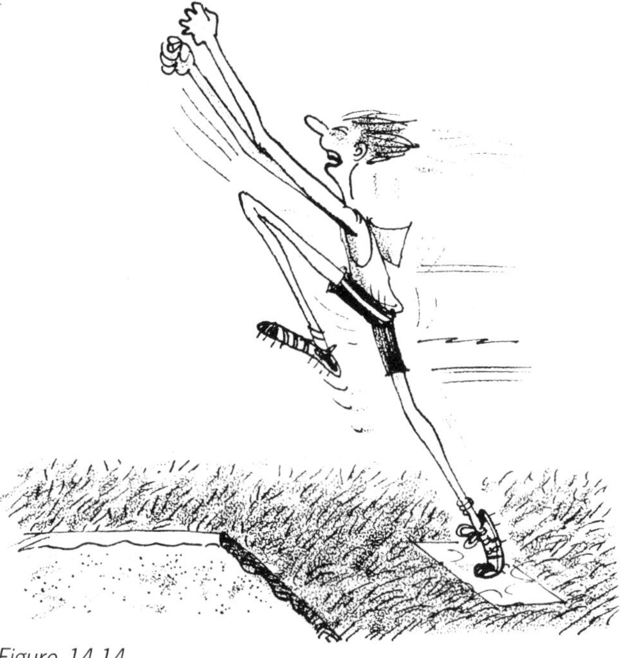

Figure 14.14

Measurement of the moment of inertia of a disc

The conservation of angular momentum may be used to measure the moment of inertia of a disc.

If a disc of moment of inertia I_1 is dropped coaxially on to a freely rotating table of known moment of inertia I_0 and angular velocity ω_0 (Figure 14.15) then

momentum before = momentum after

$$I_0\omega_0 = (I_0 + I_1)\omega_1$$

where ω_1 is the angular velocity after the disc has been dropped on to the rotating table.

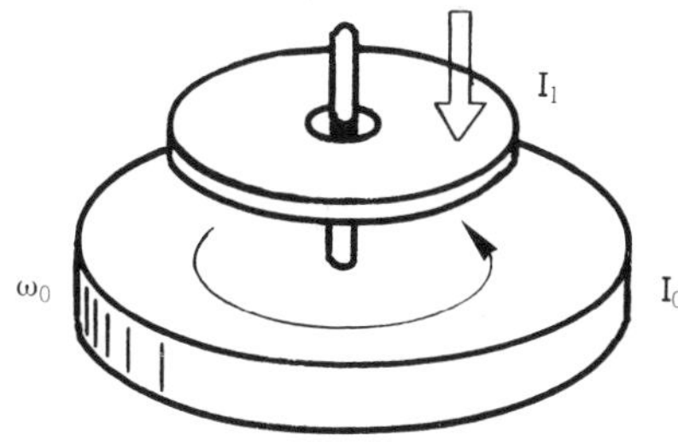

Figure 14.15

This is thus a very simple method of determining I_1, the moment of inertia of the disc.

If a disc is dropped on to a table that is maintained at a constant angular velocity (such as a record deck) then a frictional couple must act to accelerate the disc. The energy while the disc is accelerating goes both to accelerate the disc and to maintain the constant velocity of the table.

15 The turntable of a record player rotates at a steady angular speed of 3.5 rad s^{-1}. A record is dropped from rest on to the turntable. Initially the record slips but eventually it moves with the same angular speed as the turntable.

(*a*) The angle through which the table turns while the record is slipping is 0.25 rad. Find the average angular acceleration of the record while it is attaining the steady speed of the turntable.

(*b*) The moment of inertia of the record about its axis of rotation is 1.1×10^{-3} kg m^2. What additional torque must be applied by the turntable motor to maintain the constant angular speed of the turntable while the record is accelerating?

16 The wheel of a car may be represented by a uniform disc of mass 2 kg and radius 0.16 m to the rim of which the tyre is fitted. Assuming for the purpose of the calculation that the tyre can be treated as a thin uniform ring of mass 8 kg and radius 0.22 m which is concentric with the disc, find the combined moment of inertia of the wheel and tyre about the axle.

When the wheel with its tyre is mounted on its axle for 'balancing' it always comes to rest with one point P in the lowest position. When displaced slightly it oscillates with a period of 7 s.

Find the mass which should be attached at 0.16 m from the axis in order that the wheel may come to rest in any position. The period of oscillation T of a solid object of mass m and moment of inertia I is given by

$$T = 2\pi\sqrt{\frac{I}{mgh}}$$

where h is the distance from the centre of gravity of the object to the axis of rotation. [O]

Example

Figure 14.16 shows an object rolling down a hill. Such an object will gain rotational as well as translational kinetic energy as it loses potential energy.

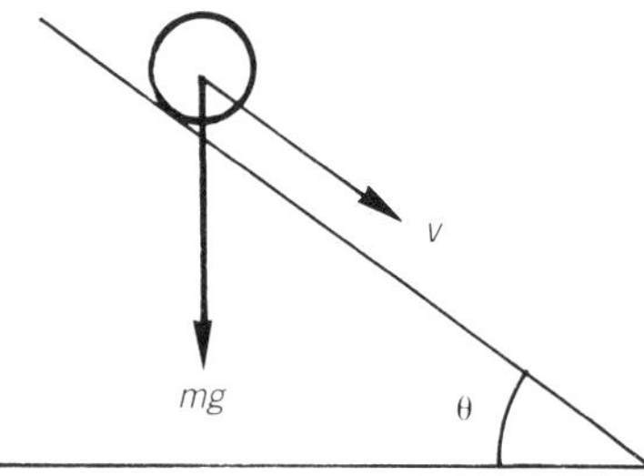

Figure 14.16

Loss of potential energy = mgh = gain in kinetic energy $= \frac{1}{2}mv^2 + \frac{1}{2}I\omega^2 = \frac{1}{2}mv^2 + \frac{1}{2}I(v^2/r^2)$

Show that the acceleration of a rolling cylinder is less than that of one that slides down a slope without rolling providing there is no friction.

For a cylinder of mass m rolling down a slope of angle θ the kinetic energy is

k.e. $= \frac{3}{4}mv^2$

The loss of potential energy is $mgs \sin\theta$ where s is the distance travelled down the slope. Therefore $mgs \sin\theta = \frac{3}{4}mv^2$ and this gives the acceleration as $\frac{2}{3}g \sin\theta$.

Now for a body that does not roll the acceleration is $g \sin\theta$, which is more than that of the rolling body.

Application to Kepler's laws

Kepler's second law (see page 84) states that a line drawn from the Sun to a planet sweeps out equal areas in equal times. This is illustrated in Figure 14.17. The angular momentum of the planet is also conserved since it moves fastest when closest to the Sun and slowest when at its greatest distance.

It can easily be shown that the ratio of the maximum and minimum velocities of a planet in orbit are in the inverse ratio to the maximum and minimum distance of the planet from the Sun.

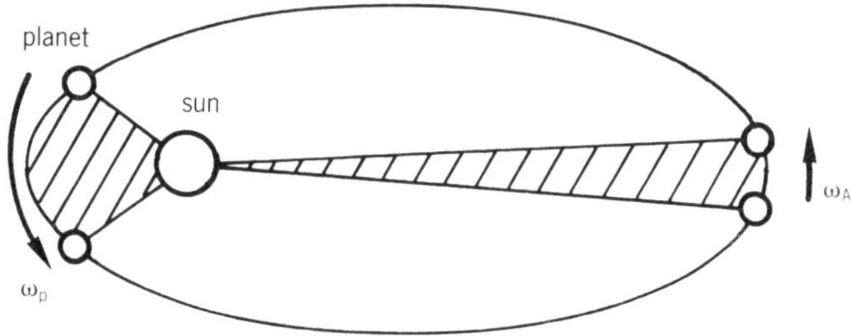

Figure 14.17

17 A flywheel rotates about a horizontal axle fitted into friction-free bearings. A light string, one end of which is looped over a pin on the axle, is wrapped ten times round the axle and has a mass of 1.5 kg attached to its free end. Discuss the energy changes as the mass falls. If the moment of inertia of the wheel and axle is 0.10 kg m^2 and the diameter of the axle 5.0 cm, calculate the angular velocity of the flywheel at the instant when the string detaches itself from the axle after ten revolutions. [AEB 1984]

15 · Simple harmonic motion

Any motion that repeats itself after a certain period is known as a **periodic** motion, and since such a motion can be represented in terms of sines and cosines it is called a **harmonic** motion.

Simple harmonic motion (s.h.m.) is the name given to a particular type of harmonic vibration. The following are examples of simple harmonic motion:

- a test-tube bobbing up and down in water (Figure 15.1)
- a simple pendulum
- a compound pendulum
- a vibrating spring
- atoms vibrating in a crystal lattice
- a vibrating cantilever
- a trolley fixed to two springs
- a marble on a concave surface
- a torsional pendulum
- liquid oscillating in a U-tube
- a small magnet suspended over a horseshoe magnet
- an inertia balance

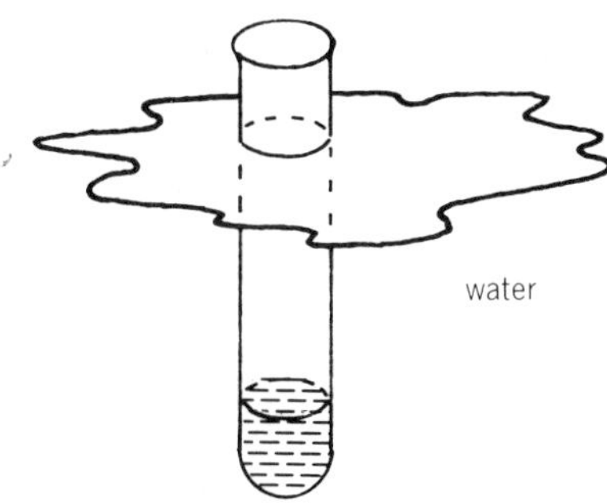

Figure 15.1

Simple harmonic motion is defined as follows:

> A body is undergoing simple harmonic motion if it has an acceleration which is
> (*a*) directed towards a fixed point, and
> (*b*) proportional to the displacement of the body from that point.

The equations for simple harmonic motion can be written as follows:

acceleration $a = -kx$

or $\dfrac{d^2x}{dt^2} = -kx$

or $\ddot{x} = -kx$

where k is a constant and x is the displacement of the body from the fixed point at any time t (Figure 15.2).

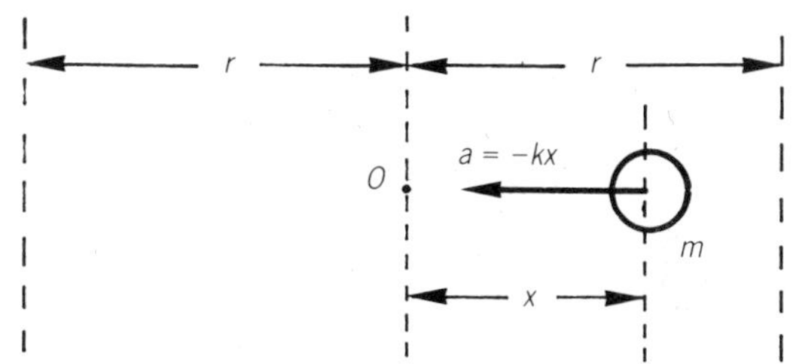

Figure 15.2

The maximum displacement of the body on either side of its central position is called the **amplitude** (r).

The **period** of the motion (T) is the time it takes for the body to make one *complete* oscillation.

The equation for s.h.m. is usually written as

$$\text{acceleration } (a) = -\omega^2 x$$

where ω is a constant (not to be confused with angular velocity). The value of ω depends on the particular system of oscillation.

The solution to this equation can be shown to be of the form

$$x = r \sin \omega t$$

since the equation for acceleration can be obtained by twice differentiating the equation for displacement against time.

We will prove later that the period of the motion is given by the equation

$$T = \frac{2\pi}{\omega}$$

Student investigation

The oscillation of a trolley fixed to rigid supports by two springs is s.h.m. Using the apparatus shown in Figure 15.3, find out whether this is true. Using an instrument such as a Vela, the variation of displacement and velocity with time may be found. Plot graphs of the values that you obtain. Do they agree with the results that you would expect?

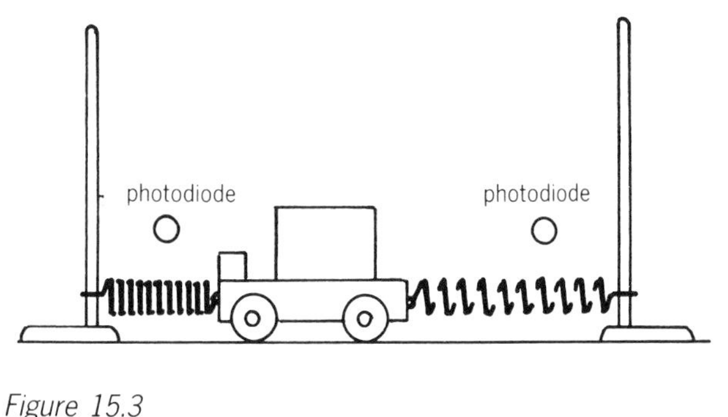

Figure 15.3

Proof of the formulae for s.h.m. (1)

There are two alternative proofs. We will give the mathematical one first because it is the more satisfactory of the two.

S.h.m. is defined by the equation:

$$a = -\omega^2 x \qquad \text{or} \qquad \frac{dv}{dt} = -\omega^2 x$$

Therefore

$$v\frac{dv}{dx} = -\omega^2 x$$

which when integrated becomes

$$v^2/2 = -\omega^2 x^2/2 + C$$

Using the limits $v = 0$ when $x = r$, and $v = r\omega$ when $x = 0$, we have $C = \omega^2 r^2/2$.

Therefore

$$v = \pm\, \omega \sqrt{(r^2 - x^2)}$$

Note the $\pm$ sign, showing that the velocity can be in either direction about the midpoint. Therefore

$$\frac{dx}{dt} = \pm\, \omega \sqrt{(r^2 - x^2)} \qquad \omega dt = \frac{dx}{(r^2 - x^2)^{\frac{1}{2}}}$$

which when integrated becomes

$$x = r \sin \omega t$$

with the limits $x = \pm\, r$ when $t = \pi/2\omega$ or $3\pi/2\omega$, and $x = 0$ when $t = 0$, π/ω or $2\pi/\omega$.

If we differentiate this equation we have alternative equations for both v and a:

$$v = r\omega \cos \omega t \qquad \text{and} \qquad a = -\, r\omega^2 \sin \omega t$$

Example

An object performs s.h.m. of amplitude 5 cm and period 4 s. If timing is started when the object is at the centre of an oscillation (i.e. $x = 0$) calculate

(*a*) the frequency of the oscillation,
(*b*) the displacement 0.5 s after the start,
(*c*) the maximum acceleration of the system and
(*d*) the velocity at a displacement of 3 cm.

(*a*) Since $T = 1/f$, $f = 0.25$ Hz.

(*b*) Since $\omega = 2\pi f$, $\omega = 1.6$ and therefore $\omega t = 1.6 \times 0.5 = 0.8$ radians $= 45°$.

Therefore, from $x = r \sin \omega t$,

$$x = 5 \times \sin 45° = 3.54 \text{ cm}$$

(*c*) The maximum acceleration occurs when $x = r$. Therefore maximum acceleration $= -\omega^2 r = -1.6 \times 1.6 \times 5 = -12.8$ cm s^{-2}.

(*d*) Velocity v is given by the formula

$$v = \pm\omega\sqrt{(r^2 - x^2)}$$
$$v = \pm 1.6\sqrt{(5^2 - 3^2)}$$
$$= \pm 1.6 \times 4$$
$$= \pm 6.4 \text{ cm s}^{-1}$$

Note the conversion of radians to degrees in part (*b*), and the + and − signs in part (*d*).

1 The balance wheel of a watch vibrates with angular amplitude of π radians and a period of 0.5 s. Calculate

(*a*) the maximum angular speed,

(*b*) the angular speed when the displacement is $\pi/2$, and

(*c*) the angular acceleration when the displacement is $\pi/4$.

2 The displacement x of a body moving with simple harmonic motion is given by the equation:

$x = 3.5 \sin (4t + 0.2)$

(*a*) What is the amplitude of the motion?

(*b*) What is the value of the constant ω?

(*c*) What is the frequency of the motion?

(*d*) What is the period of the motion?

(*e*) What will be the displacement 0.2 s after measurements are begun?

(*f*) What will be the velocity at time $t = 1.5$ s?

Period and amplitude

The period of a body undergoing simple harmonic motion can be shown to be independent of the amplitude of the motion.

We will start by assuming an equation for T that depends on the force on the body F, its displacement x and its mass m. This can be written as:

$$T = KF^p x^q m^r$$

where K is a constant. Using the method of dimensions (see page 10) this gives

$$T = K(mx/F)$$

and therefore if the period is to be independent of amplitude then x/F must be a constant.

Therefore x is proportional to F, and since m is constant x is proportional to the acceleration. This is the definition of simple harmonic motion.

Therefore for s.h.m. the period is independent of the amplitude, providing that the motion is not damped (see below). This motion is also known as **isochronous** motion.

If the displacement at a time t is x_1, then x_1 is given by the formula

$$x_1 = r \sin \omega t$$

and the displacement at a time $(t + 2\pi/\omega)$ is x_2, where

$$\begin{aligned} x_2 &= r \sin \omega(t + 2\pi/\omega) = r \sin (\omega t + 2\pi) \\ &= r \sin \omega t \cos 2\pi + r \cos \omega t \sin 2\pi \\ &= r \sin \omega t = x_1 \end{aligned}$$

That is, the motion repeats itself after a time T where $T = 2\pi/\omega$, and T is therefore the period of the motion:

period of s.h.m. = $2\pi/\omega$

Proof of the formulae for s.h.m. (2)

The next proof is slightly less mathematical, and uses the projection on a diameter of a circle of the motion of a point P round the circle. Let the velocity of the particle round that circle be u and the velocity of the projection on AB be v (Figure 15.4). We wish to show that the motion of the projection of P on AB is s.h.m.

The displacement x of the projection of P from O along AB is given by

$$\begin{aligned} x &= r \sin \theta \\ &= r \sin \omega t \end{aligned}$$

Consider the component of velocity of P parallel to AB: this will be the velocity of the projection of P on AB.

$$\begin{aligned} \text{Component parallel to AB} &= u \cos \omega t \\ &= r\omega \cos \omega t \\ &= r\omega\, (1 - \sin^2 \omega t) \\ &= r\omega\, (1 - x^2/r^2) \end{aligned}$$

Therefore

$$v = \pm\omega\sqrt{(r^2 - x^2)}$$

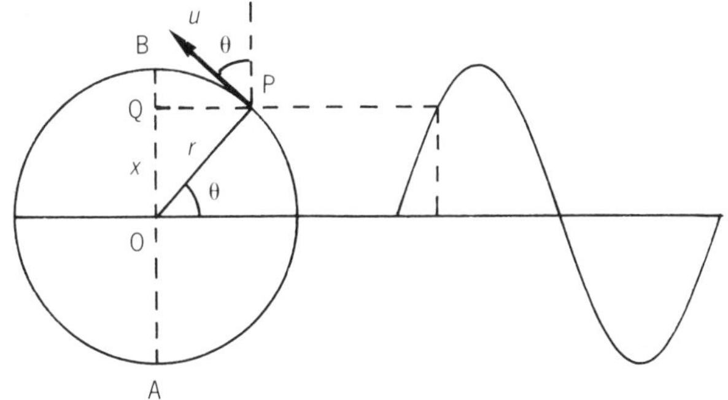

Figure 15.4

Now the acceleration of P will be towards the centre of the circle and therefore its component parallel to AB will be:

$$\begin{aligned} \text{acceleration} &= -\omega^2 r \sin \omega t \\ &= -\omega^2 x \end{aligned}$$

This is s.h.m., since we have shown that the acceleration of Q is directed towards θ and proportional to OQ.

Phase shift

In both these proofs we have assumed that timing was started when the displacement of the body was zero, that is, that $t = 0$ when $x = 0$. If this is not the case then we have to introduce a **phase shift** (ϵ) into the equations giving:

$$x = r \sin (\omega t + \epsilon)$$

This means that $t = 0$ when $x = r \sin \epsilon$. The phase shift can clearly be seen from Figure 15.5.

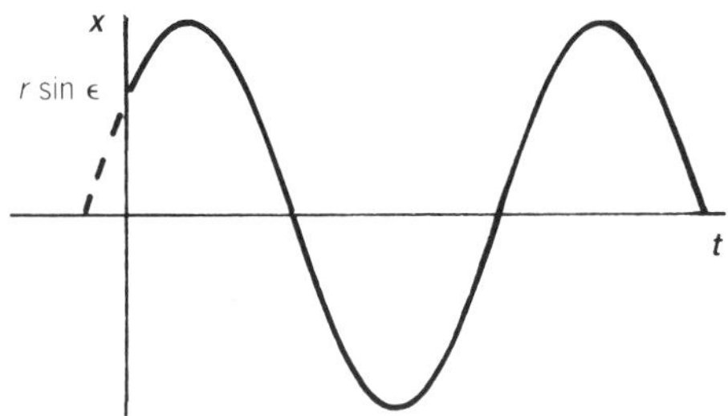

Figure 15.5

> **3** A dock has a tidal entrance at which the water is 10.0 m deep at 12.00 noon when the tide is at its lowest. The water is 30.0 m deep when the tide is at its highest which follows next at 6.15 p.m. A tanker needing a depth of water of 15.0 m requires to enter the dock as soon as possible that afternoon.
>
> (*a*) Calculate the earliest time that it could just clear the dock entrance.
>
> (*b*) State what you have assumed about the tidal motion, and discuss critically what other factors might affect the earliest possible entry time in practice. [c]
>
> **4** A small coin rests on a horizontal table which performs oscillations in the vertical plane. If the amplitude of these oscillations is 10 cm calculate the maximum frequency of oscillation such that the coin remains in contact with the table surface.

Graphical representation of s.h.m.

Figure 15.6 shows the variation of a, v and x with t, and of a and v with x. The exact shape of the curves depends upon the value of ω.

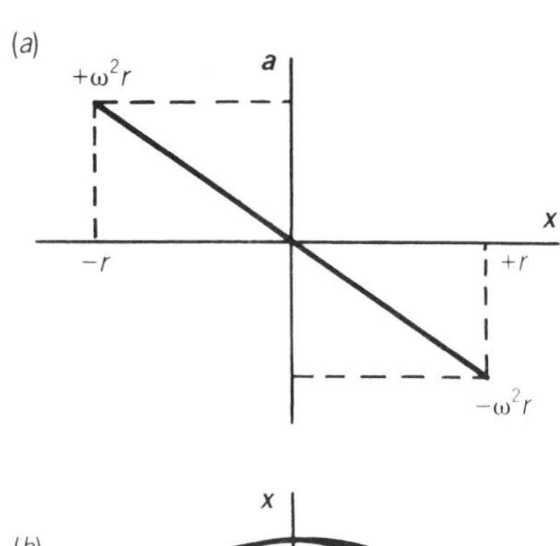

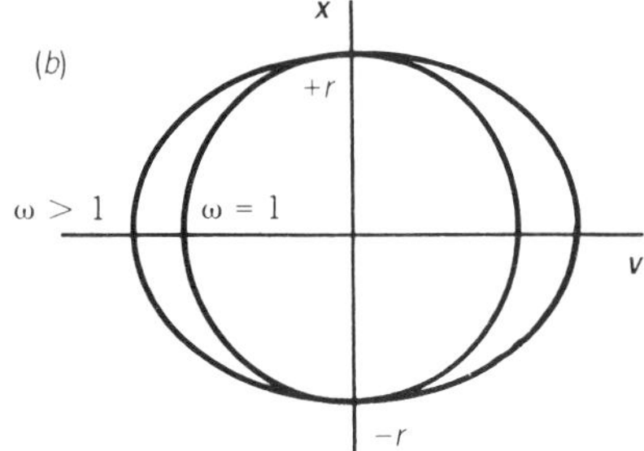

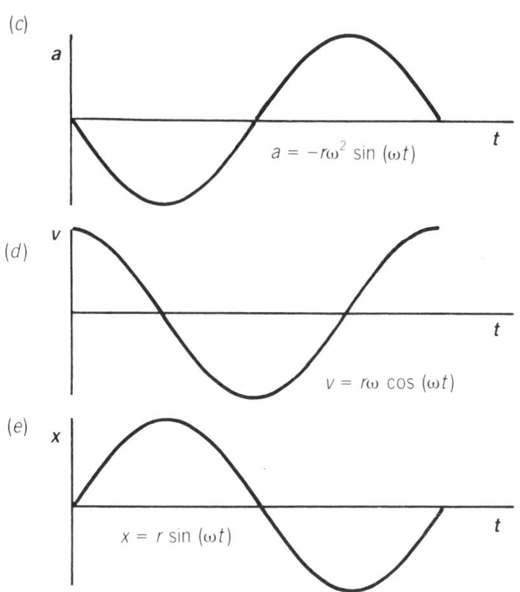

Figure 15.6

Student investigation

Some vibrating mechanical systems can be thought of as a bar fixed at one end and with the other end free to oscillate (Figure 15.7). This is known as a **vibrating cantilever**. Set up such an arrangement and determine the period of oscillation for

(*a*) a number of different lengths with a fixed load,

(*b*) a variety of different loads with a fixed length.

Plot suitable linear graphs that enable you to suggest an equation for the oscillation.

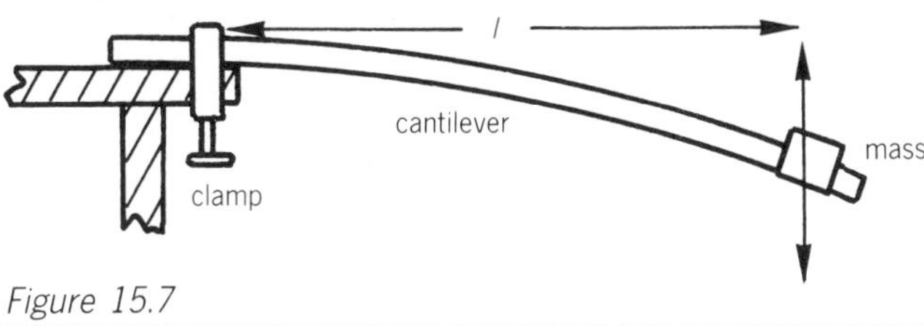

Figure 15.7

Energy in s.h.m.

The kinetic energy of any body is given by

$$\text{k.e.} = \tfrac{1}{2}mv^2$$

So, in s.h.m.,

$$\text{k.e.} = \tfrac{1}{2}m\omega^2(r^2 - x^2)$$

Now the maximum value of the kinetic energy will occur when $x = 0$, and this will be equal to the total energy of the body. Therefore:

$$\text{total energy} = \tfrac{1}{2}m\omega^2r^2$$

Therefore, since p.e. = total energy − k.e., the p.e. at any point will be given by

$$\text{p.e.} = \tfrac{1}{2}m\omega^2x^2$$

Graphs of the variation of p.e., k.e. and total energy are shown in Figure 15.8.

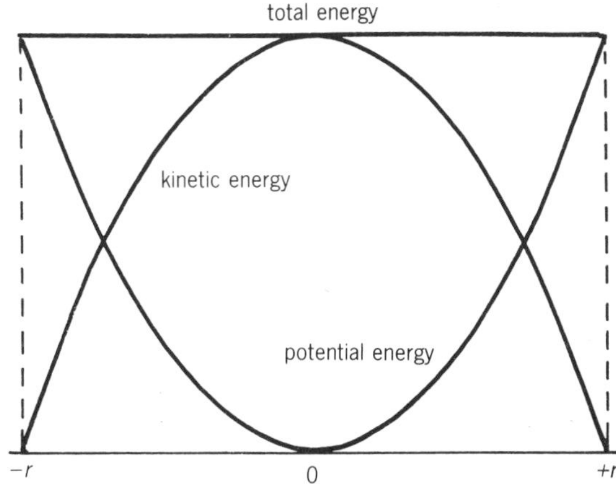

Figure 15.8

Example

A 2 kg body panel of a car oscillates with a frequency of 2 Hz and amplitude 2.5 cm. If the oscillations are assumed to be s.h.m. and undamped, calculate

(*a*) the maximum velocity of the panel,

(*b*) the total energy of the panel,

(*c*) the maximum p.e. of the panel, and

(*d*) the kinetic energy of the panel 1.0 cm from its equilibrium position.

(*a*) From $v = +\omega\sqrt{(r^2 - x^2)}$ the maximum velocity occurs when $x = 0$, at the centre of the oscillation. Therefore

maximum velocity
$= +12.6 \times 2.5 = 31.5 \text{ cm s}^{-1} = 0.315 \text{ m s}^{-1}$

(*b*) Total energy =
$\tfrac{1}{2}m\omega^2r^2 = \tfrac{1}{2} \times 2 \times 12.6 \times 12.6 \times 0.025 \times 0.025$
$= 0.1 \text{ J}$

(*c*) Maximum p.e = total energy = 0.1 J

(*d*) Kinetic energy $= \tfrac{1}{2}m\omega^2(r - x^2)$
$= \tfrac{1}{2} \times 2 \times 12.6 \times 12.6\ (0.025^2 - 0.01^2)$
$= 0.0833 \text{ J}$

Note the conversion of centimetres to metres for the energy calculations.

5 A ship's siren vibrates with a displacement x where $x = r \sin 200\pi t$. This sound causes vibrations in the diaphragm of an eardrum of an observer 500 m away. If the speed of sound is 335 m s^{-1}, calculate

(*a*) the frequency of the sound,

(*b*) the number of wavelengths of sound between the siren and the ear,

(*c*) the phase difference between the motion of the siren and that of the eardrum, and

(*d*) the maximum kinetic energy of the eardrum due to the sound if its mass is 1.00×10^{-5} kg and the amplitude of its motion is 1.00×10^{-8} m. [C]

Proof that objects are undergoing s.h.m.

For all the following proofs we have to show that the acceleration of the object is directed towards a fixed point and is proportional to the displacement of the body from that point. The following cases will be considered:

(*a*) helical spring
(*b*) cylinder floating in liquid
(*c*) liquid in a U-tube
(*d*) simple pendulum
(*e*) piston in gas-filled cylinder
(*f*) compound pendulum
(*g*) torsional oscillations
(*h*) bifilar suspension

The first three are examples of exact s.h.m., while the rest are approximate s.h.m. only, with certain limitations on their amplitude. The examples (*a*), (*b*), (*d*) and (*f*) are dealt with in full; the remainder are left as an exercise for the student to prove the equations given.

We will assume zero damping for all cases (damped s.h.m. is dealt with later in this chapter).

(*a*) The helical spring

Consider a mass m suspended at rest from a spiral spring and let the extension produced be e. If the spring constant is k we have:

$mg = ke$ (see page 112)

The mass is then pulled down a small distance x and released. The mass will oscillate due to both the effect of the gravitational attraction (mg) and the varying force in the spring ($k(e + x)$) (Figure 15.9).

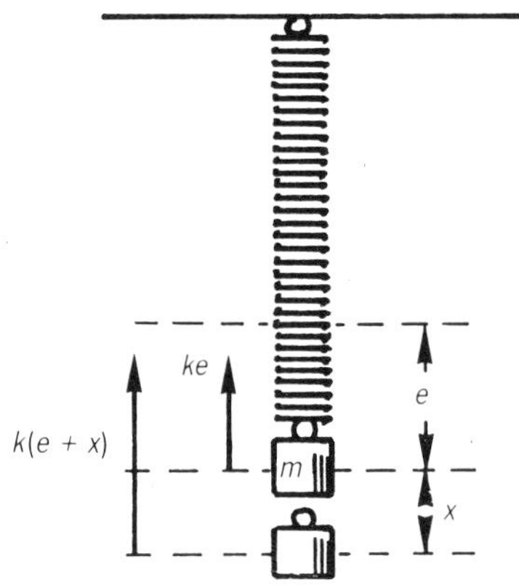

Figure 15.9

At any point distance x from the midpoint:

restoring force $= k(e + x) - mg$

But $F = ma$, so

$$ma = -kx$$

the equation for s.h.m.

The negative sign shows that the acceleration acts in the opposite direction to increasing x.

From the defining equation for s.h.m. we have

$$\omega^2 = k/m = g/e$$

and therefore the period of the motion T is given by:

$$T = 2\pi/\omega = 2\pi\sqrt{\frac{m}{k}} = 2\pi\sqrt{\frac{e}{g}}$$

A graph of e against T^2 can be used to determine g (Figure 15.10).

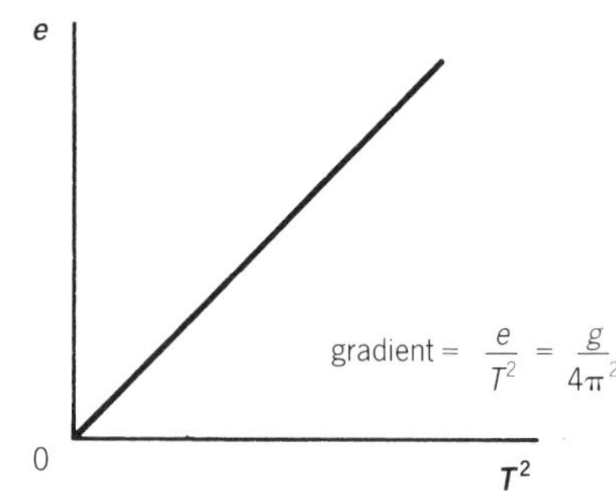

Figure 15.10

If the mass of the spring is significant we can allow for it and in fact the corrected equation becomes:

$$T = 2\pi\sqrt{\frac{m + M}{k}}$$

where M is one-third of the mass of the spring.

The mass must be sufficiently large to keep the coils open.

6 A light helical spring with spring constant (k) of 30 N m^{-1} is suspended vertically with a mass of 0.30 kg fixed to its lower end. If the mass is now pulled down a distance of 0.015 m and then released calculate

(*a*) the maximum kinetic energy of the mass,

(*b*) the maximum and minimum values of the tension in the spring during the motion.

If the same spring with the same mass attached were taken to the Moon what would be the effect, if any, on the period of the oscillation? Explain your answer.

What would be observed if the period of a simple pendulum were measured first on the Earth and then on the Moon?

7 An elastic string extends by 1 cm when a small mass is attached at the lower end. If the weight is pulled down by 0.25 cm, calculate the period of the resulting simple harmonic motion.

Student investigation

The true equation for an oscillating spring that cannot be considered massless is best investigated using a Slinky spring.

Suspend the Slinky so that it has an extended length of about 1 m when hanging freely. Measure the extension (*e*) (Figure 15.11).

Pull the lower end downwards a little and allow the spring to perform small oscillations in the vertical plane. Record the period of oscillation (*T*). Repeat the procedure with the spring loaded with a series of small masses.

Plot a graph of *T* against e^2 and use it to determine the value of *g* and the true equation for the spring.

Also plot a graph of the spacing between the spring coils against distance from the top of the spring.

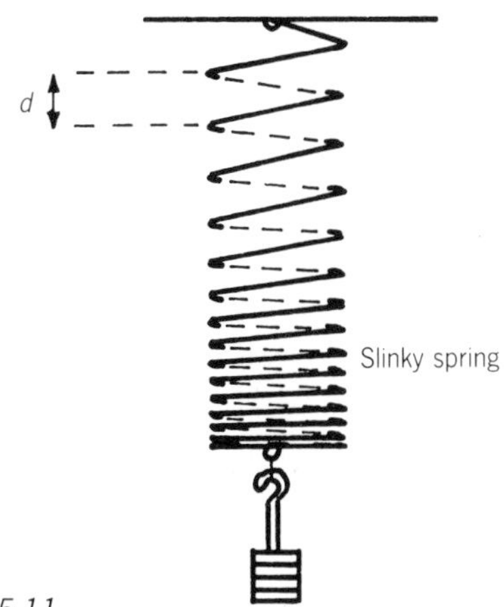

Figure 15.11

8 A stunt man of mass 70 kg jumps off a high bridge, tied to the bridge by a 10 m elastic rope. If a static load of 20 kg extends the elastic rope by 0.8 m, calculate

(*a*) the maximum extension that the falling man produces in the elastic rope,

(*b*) the maximum force in the elastic rope, and

(*c*) the potential energy stored in the elastic rope at maximum extension.

9 Discuss the following:

(*a*) Does a tuning fork vibrate with s.h.m.? Why is this important for musicians?

(*b*) Is the bouncing of an elastic superball s.h.m.? Explain your answer.

(*c*) If a large rectangular box resting on the floor is slightly tilted and then released, is the resulting motion s.h.m.? Explain your answer.

(*d*) Why is the springiness of a diving board adjusted for different dives and different divers? How is this adjustment made?

(*e*) If a pendulum clock is taken to the top of the mountain does it gain or lose? Explain.

(*b*) The floating cylinder

Consider a cylinder of length *l* and density *r* floating in a liquid of density *s*. Let the cylinder have a cross-sectional area *A*, and let a length *h* be below the surface when the cylinder is at rest (Figure 15.12).

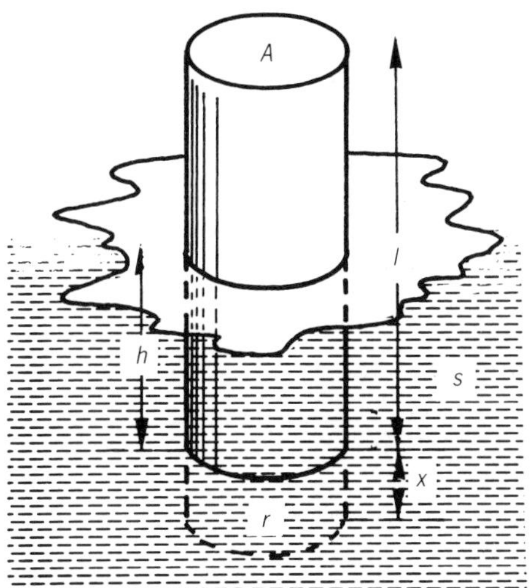

Figure 15.12

The cylinder is now pushed downwards a little (x) and allowed to bob up and down, the forces causing the oscillation being gravity and the varying upthrust on the cylinder.

$$\text{extra upthrust} = \text{extra weight of liquid displaced} = Asgx$$

$$\text{force} = Asgx$$

$$\text{acceleration} = -\frac{Asgx}{Arl} = -\frac{sgx}{rl}$$

and the cylinder therefore moves with s.h.m.

The value of ω^2 is $\frac{sg}{rl}$, so the period T is:

$$T = 2\pi/\omega = 2\pi\sqrt{\frac{h}{g}}$$

since for a floating body the upthrust = the weight of the body, that is, $Alr = Ahs$.

(*c*) Liquid in a U-tube

If the liquid in a U-tube is displaced slightly and then released it will oscillate with simple harmonic motion. The period of the motion $T = 2\pi\sqrt{h/g}$, where h is half the length of the liquid in the U-tube.

(*d*) The simple pendulum

Consider a pendulum of length l with a mass m at the end displaced through an angle θ from the vertical (Figure 15.13). The restoring force F is the component of the weight of the bob. Therefore

$$F = -mg \sin \theta = ma$$

giving $a = -g \sin \theta$

But for small angles $\sin \theta$ tends to θ, and therefore

$$a = -g\theta$$
$$= -\frac{gx}{l}$$

where x is the distance of the bob from the midpoint of the oscillation. The pendulum therefore moves with s.h.m.

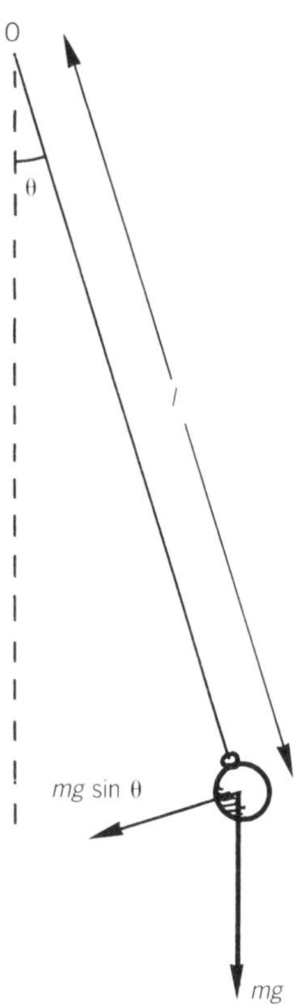

Figure 15.13

The value of ω^2 is g/l, and so the period of a simple pendulum is

$$T = 2\pi\sqrt{\frac{l}{g}}$$

(this formula is only accurate for small angles of swing, however).

An alternative treatment uses the idea of the moment of inertia of the bob (ml^2) and the restoring couple ($C = -mg \sin \theta\, l$). Since $C = I\alpha$ (see page 64) we have

$$-mg \sin \theta l = I\alpha = ml^2\alpha$$

Therefore,

$$\text{angular acceleration } (\alpha) = \frac{-g\theta}{l} \text{ for small } \theta,$$

giving the same result as the first proof.

Example

Calculate the length of a simple pendulum that will have a period of exactly one second, taking $g = 9.81 \text{ m s}^{-2}$.

$$l = \frac{T^2g}{4\pi^2} = \frac{1 \times 9.81}{39.47} = 0.25 \text{ m}$$

The measurement of the acceleration due to gravity
A simple pendulum may be used to measure the acceleration due to gravity (g). The period is measured for a series of different values of l and a graph plotted of T^2 against l (Figure 15.14). From this the value of g can be found. Very accurate determinations by this method have been used in geophysical prospecting.

For large angles of swing (θ) the period of the simple pendulum is:

$$T = 2\pi\sqrt{\frac{l}{g}\left(1 + \frac{1}{2^2}\sin^2\theta + \frac{1.3^2}{2^2.4^2}\sin^4\theta + \ldots\right)}$$

although the simple formula is accurate to ± 0.5 per cent for $\theta \leqslant 15°$.

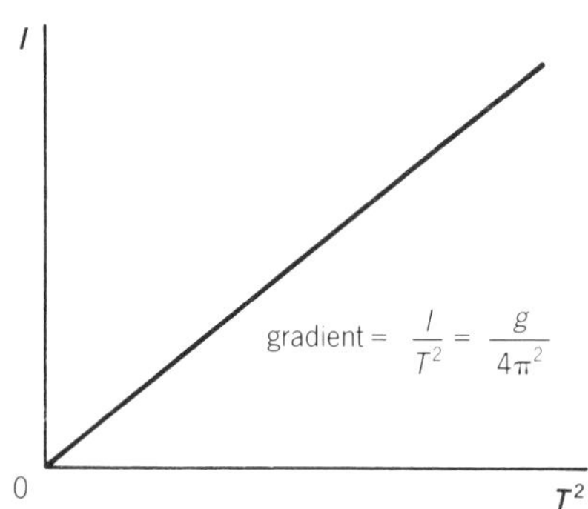

Figure 15.14

10 A simple pendulum has a period of 4.2 s. When the pendulum is shortened by 1 m the period is 3.7 s. From these measurements calculate
(*a*) the acceleration due to gravity, and
(*b*) the original length of the pendulum.

Student investigation

Use a pendulum at least 2 m long with a small but heavy bob to make a determination of the acceleration due to gravity. Include in your results an estimate of the accuracy, taking into account the angle of swing if you consider it to be an important factor.

11 The total energy of an atom oscillating in a crystal lattice at a temperature T is, on average, $3kT$ where k is the Boltzmann constant (1.38×10^{-23} J K^{-1}). Assuming that copper atoms, each of mass 1.06×10^{-25} kg, execute simple harmonic motion of amplitude 8×10^{-11} m at 300 K, calculate the corresponding frequency of the motion. [o]

12 The period of a certain simple pendulum is 2.0 s and the mass of the pendulum bob is 50 g. The bob is pulled aside through a horizontal distance of 8 cm and then released. Find the displacement and kinetic energy of the bob 0.7 s after its release.

13 A spiral spring extends 0.2 m when a load is placed on it. The mass is then pulled down a short distance and released. Calculate

(*a*) the period of the motion, and

(*b*) the period of the motion if the same mass was used but the spring was cut in half and only half of it used.

14 A pendulum and a spiral spring are both suspended from the ceiling of a lift. If the lift now accelerates upwards, what happens to the period of oscillation of both systems?

15 The following question concerns the trolley shown in Figure 15.15.

Figure 15.15

A trolley of mass 3.0 kg oscillates with simple harmonic motion on a frictionless horizontal surface due to the forces in the two springs. The displacement after a time t is given by the equation:

$$x = 0.6 \cos 0.5\pi t$$

Calculate:

(*a*) the amplitude of the motion,

(*b*) the period of oscillation of the trolley,

(*c*) the displacement after 4 s,

(*d*) the velocity when $t = 0$ and 1 s, and

(*e*) the maximum kinetic energy of the trolley.

The trolley's motion is described by the equation given only if the trolley had a maximum displacement to the right when $t = 0$. If this condition is not true then the motion may be represented by the equation:

$$x = 0.6 \cos (0.5\pi t + \epsilon)$$

where ϵ is the initial phase angle. Calculate the value of ϵ if

(*f*) $t = 0$ when the trolley is at the left-hand end of its motion,

(*g*) $t = 0$ when $x = 0$ and the trolley is moving to the right,

(*h*) $t = 0.5$ s and the trolley has a displacement of -0.1 m moving to the left. [H]

16 Why do you think that the 'springiness' of diving boards is adjusted for divers of different weights? How would this adjustment be made?

(*e*) Heavy piston in a gas-filled cylinder

The period of the motion $T = 2\pi\sqrt{h/g}$, where h is the height of gas in the cylinder with the piston in its equilibrium position.

(*f*) The compound pendulum

A simple pendulum theoretically has the mass of the bob concentrated at one point, but this is impossible to achieve exactly in practice. Most pendulums are **compound**, with an oscillating mass spread out over a definite volume of space.

Let G be the centre of gravity of a compound pendulum of mass m that oscillates about a point O with OG = h. If the pendulum is moved so that the line OG is displaced through an angle θ (Figure 15.16), the restoring couple is $-mgh \sin\theta = -mgh\theta$ if θ is small. Therefore

$$I\alpha = -mgh\theta \qquad \text{and so} \qquad \alpha = -\frac{mgh}{I}\theta$$

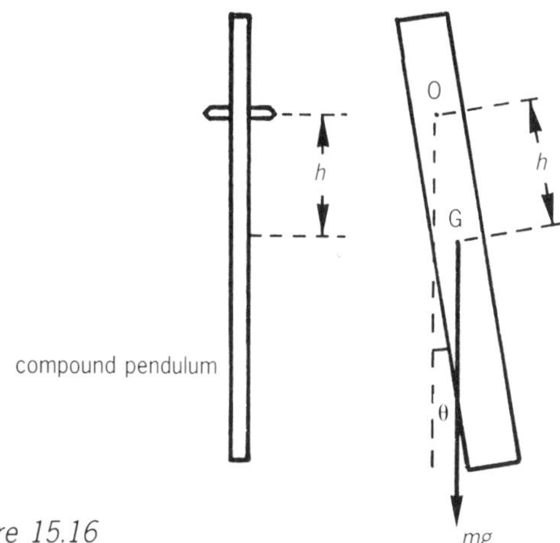

Figure 15.16

This is therefore s.h.m. of period T where

$$T = 2\pi\sqrt{\frac{I}{mgh}}$$

But I is the moment of inertia about an axis through O, and therefore

$$I = I_G + mh^2 = mk^2 + mh^2$$

where k is the radius of gyration about a parallel axis through G. The period can therefore be written as:

$$T = 2\pi\sqrt{\frac{k^2 + h^2}{hg}}$$

If a uniform rod is used as a compound pendulum and the period of oscillation T measured for different values of h on either side of the centre of gravity then a graph may be obtained like the one in Figure 15.17.

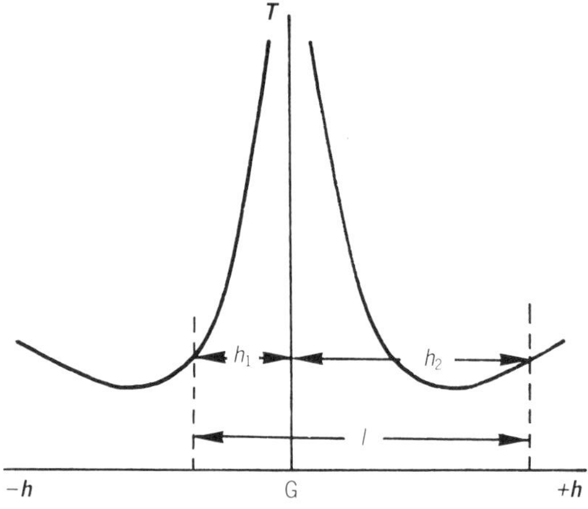

Figure 15.17

Since the formula for a simple pendulum is $T = 2\pi\sqrt{l/g}$, we can define a quantity l called the length of the **simple equivalent pendulum**. This is given by

$$l = \frac{k^2 + h^2}{h}$$

For two distances h_1 and h_2 on either side of the centre, $l = h_1 + h_2$ (as can be seen from the graph) and $h_1h_2 = k^2$. At the minimum $h_1 = h_2$ and $h = k$.

A value of g can be determined by measuring l from the graph.

(*g*) Torsional oscillations

If an object of moment of inertia I is hung from the lower end of a torsion wire of length l, radius r and modulus of rigidity (shear modulus) G (Figure 15.18); then the period is given by:

$$T = 2\pi\sqrt{\frac{2Il}{Gr}}$$

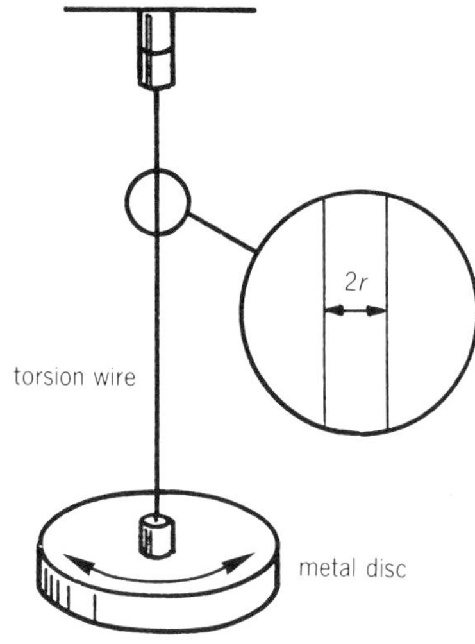

Figure 15.18

(*h*) Bifilar suspension

If a rod of moment of inertia I and mass m is hung from two threads separated by a distance d (Figure 15.19) is oscillated in a horizontal plane about a vertical axis through its centre, then the period is given by:

$$T = 2\pi\sqrt{\frac{2I}{mgd}}$$

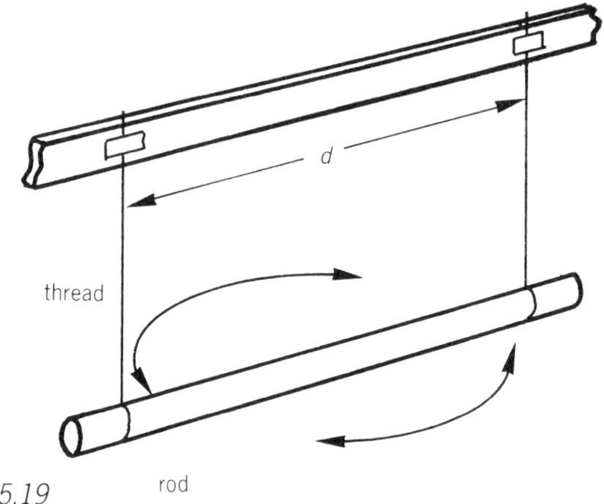

Figure 15.19

Student investigation

This investigation is based on the centre of percussion of an object.

Suspend a metre rule by hanging it on a matchstick passed through a hole at the 5 cm mark. Now strike the ruler a sharp blow with a hammer two-thirds of the way down. What happens to the matchstick?

Now try hitting it at other points.

Find out why this experiment gives the results that it does. How do the results apply to ball games such as rounders, baseball and cricket?

Free, damped and forced oscillations

There are three main types of oscillation:

(*a*) free oscillations – s.h.m. with a constant amplitude and period and no external influences

(*b*) damped oscillations – s.h.m. but with a decreasing amplitude and varying period due to external or internal damping forces

(*c*) forced oscillations – s.h.m. but driven externally

(*a*) Free oscillations

These oscillations only occur in theory since in practice there will always be some damping. The displacement will follow the formula $x = r \sin \omega t$ where r is the amplitude.

It is interesting to look at the superposition of two s.h.m.s and this is best done on the oscilloscope or using a computer.

(i) If two s.h.m.s act along the same direction with the same frequency, then their resultant is a s.h.m. with the same frequency along that line. The amplitude will be constant but will depend on the phase difference between the two s.h.m.s.

(ii) If their frequencies are different but they still act along the same line then **beats** will be produced, the variation in amplitude depending on the difference in frequency (for a full treatment see page 170).

(iii) If they act in perpendicular directions then there are two sets of possibilities:

(1) The frequencies are the same and of equal amplitude:
phase difference 0 gives a straight line,
phase difference $\pi/2$ gives a circle,
phase difference π gives a straight line.

(2) The frequencies are different but of equal amplitude:
this gives **Lissajous figures**, three examples of which are shown in Figure 15.20 for a phase difference of $\pi/2$. The numbers of loops in the x- and y-directions can be counted, and this will give the frequency ratio of the two s.h.m.s:

$$\text{frequency ratio } (f_y/f_x) = \frac{\text{number of loops in } x\text{-direction}}{\text{number of loops in } y\text{-direction}}$$

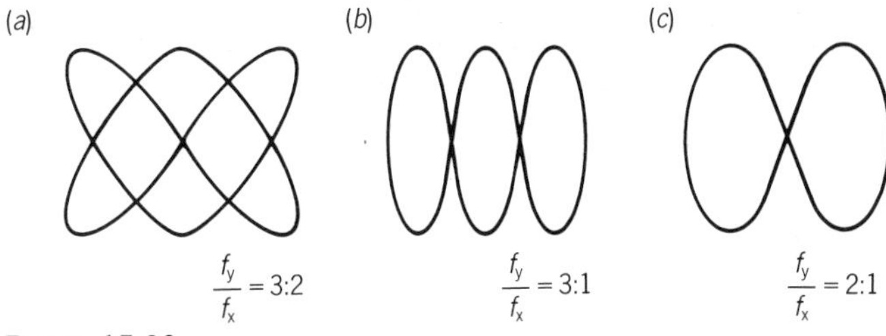

Figure 15.20

(*b*) Damped oscillations

These are oscillations where energy is taken from the system and so the amplitude decays. They may be of two types:

(i) Natural damping, examples of which are:
internal forces in a spring,
fluids exerting a viscous drag.

(ii) Artificial damping, examples of which are:
electromagnetic damping in galvanometers,
the coating of panels in cars to reduce vibrations,
shock absorbers in cars,
interference damping – gun mountings on ships.

Artificial damping can be *light*, in which case the system oscillates about the midpoint (Figure 15.21(*a*)), *heavy*, in which the system takes a long time to reach equilibrium (Figure 15.21(*b*)) or *critical*, where the system reaches equilibrium in about $T/4$ where T is the natural period of vibration of the system (Figure 15.21(*c*)).

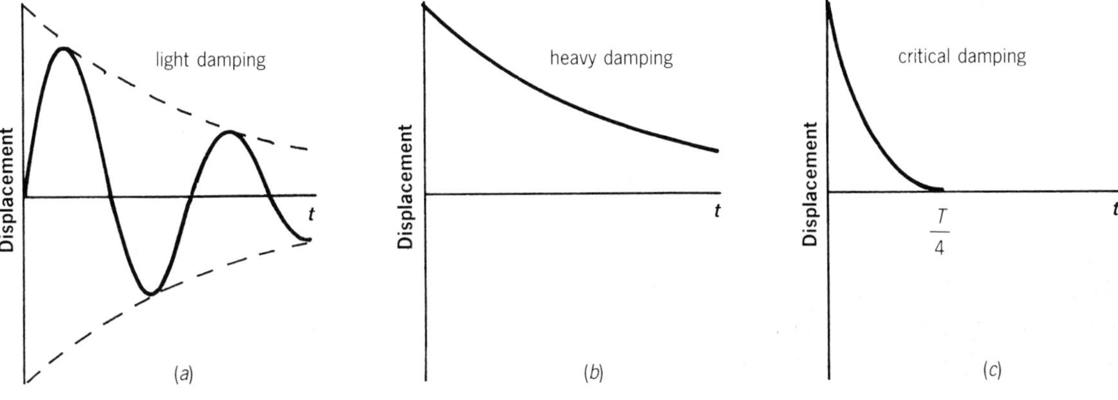

Figure 15.21

Student investigation

The damping of the oscillations of a system can be very important. Investigate the damping in the two following examples.

(*a*) Air damping

The effect of air damping on the oscillations of a helical spring may be carried out using a large disc of light but rigid cardboard fixed to the spring as shown in Figure 15.22. You should displace the spring by a given amount and then record the amplitude of the subsequent oscillations. It may be possible to investigate the dependence of the damping on the size of the cardboard. Plot suitable linear graphs to present your results. Would a card with turned-up or turned-down edges be as good or better than the flat card?

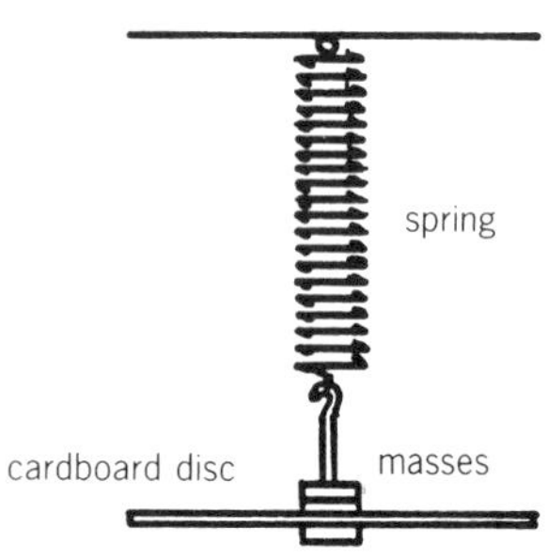

Figure 15.22

(*b*) Liquid damping

Once again a spring may be used, but this time a metal cylinder should be fixed to the end. This cylinder should be allowed to oscillate in a cylindrical container of liquid (Figure 15.23). As before, attempt to record the variation of amplitude of the oscillations.

Investigate the dependence of the damping on (i) the liquid in the cylindrical container, (ii) the diameter of the cylindrical container.

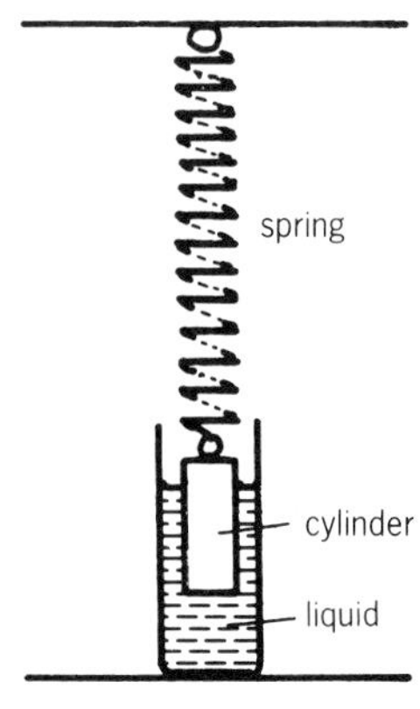

Figure 15.23

A good example of damping can be seen in the **moving coil galvanometer.** Electromagnetic damping is used here: the coil moves in a magnetic field and the current flowing in it can be shorted with a resistor, thus varying the damping. The system is either

(i) *dead beat* – that is, critically damped, or

(ii) *ballistic* – the damping is as small as possible.

As the damping is increased the time period is increased and the oscillations die away more rapidly.

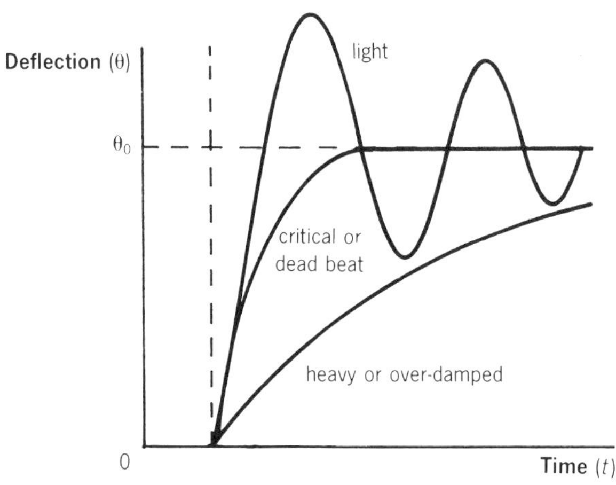

Figure 15.24

(*c*) Forced oscillations

These are vibrations that are driven by an external force. A simple example of forced vibrations is a child's swing: as you push it the amplitude increases and you will find that if you push in time with the natural frequency of the swing then the oscillations build up rapidly. This last fact is an example of **resonance.** All systems have their own natural frequency, and if you apply a driving force of the same frequency and in phase with the initial oscillations then resonance results. If you walk across a small suspension bridge timing your footsteps at a particular rate you can make the bridge swing! The most alarming example of the effect of resonance on a suspension bridge was when the Tacoma Narrows suspension bridge collapsed in a gale, due to resonance. The rebuilt bridge was redesigned to limit the amplitude of horizontal oscillation and is now safe!

Barton's pendulums (Figure 15.25) are a very good demonstration of forced vibrations and resonance.

A heavy driving pendulum X is hung from a thread fixed to a cord between two retort stands. Hanging from the cord are five other pendulums, each with a light paper cone as the bob.

As X is swung all the other pendulums begin to vibrate, but pendulum C has the greatest amplitude

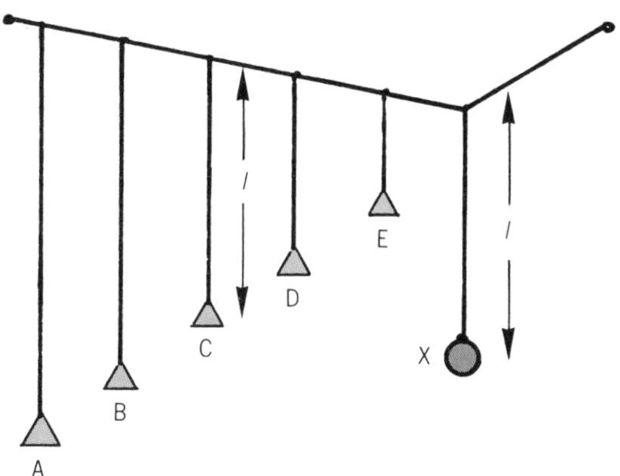

Figure 15.25

as it has the same natural frequency as X. It is found that:

A and B are about half a period behind X,
C is about a quarter of a period behind X,
D and E are nearly in phase with X.

The effects of resonance can be demonstrated in several areas of Physics. You may find that the internal mirror in a car vibrates strongly when travelling at one particular speed over a rough road. If a cello is played near a piano, the sounding of the cello note may make a string of the same frequency on the piano resonate. The breaking of a wine glass by a loud note of a particular frequency is also due to this effect. The absorption of light by a gas depends on a resonance effect within the atom (see page 418) and the tuned LCR circuit (see page 355) resonates at one particular frequency. The variation of amplitude of the system with input frequency is shown in Figure 15.26.

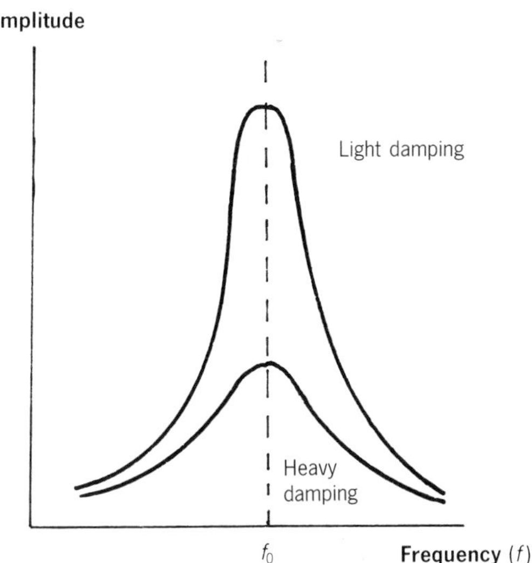

Figure 15.26

Student investigation

This investigation enables you to study the effect of resonance in a simple mechanical system.

Set up the apparatus as shown in Figure 15.27, and connect the vibrator to a signal generator set at a frequency of about 10 Hz. Observe the maximum amplitude of the top of the hacksaw blade. Slowly increase the frequency and record the amplitude at intervals of 5 Hz. Plot a graph of double the amplitude against frequency. It should show resonant peaks and harmonics.

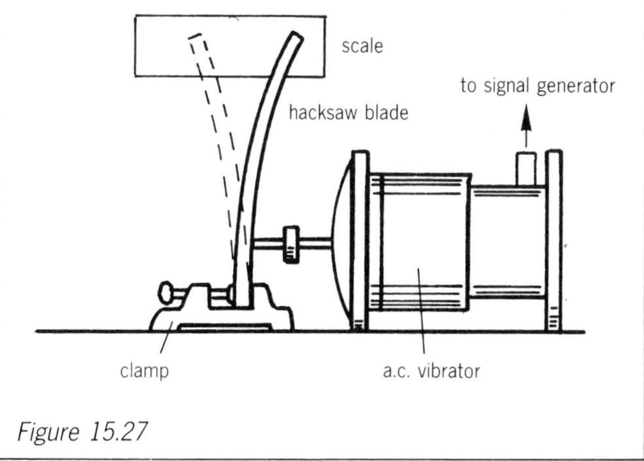

Figure 15.27

Student investigation

Study the effects of the transfer of energy between two coupled pendulums when one is displaced. Explain why there is a difference if both are displaced on opposite sides of the centre of oscillation.

16 · Gravitation

An accurate knowledge of gravitation is of vital importance in these days of space flight. It governed the flight of the space probe *Giotto* to its rendezvous with Halley's comet in 1986 and helped to explain the wobble in the orbits of spacecraft round the Moon due to high mass concentrations (mascons) in the lunar surface.

Gravitation was investigated initially to explain the motion of the planets around the Sun. The first true 'laws' of planetary motion were those due to Johannes Kepler. These laws were proposed between 1609 and 1619 as a result of his work on the observations of the Dutch astronomer Tycho Brahe. Brahe had worked for the King of Denmark, and when he died he left Kepler his records of twenty years of planetary observation. This work is all the more remarkable if you remember that the telescope was not invented until after Brahe's death! Kepler knew nothing of the nature of the forces that held the planets in their orbits but he deduced the following laws to describe their motion:

1 The planets orbit the Sun in ellipses, with the Sun at one focus of the ellipse.

2 A line joining the planet to the Sun (the radius vector) sweeps out equal areas in equal times.

3 The square of the time of revolution about the Sun is directly proportional to the cube of the mean radius of the planet's orbit.

These laws can be checked as follows:

Law 1 – either observe the change in the diameter of the Sun as the Earth makes one orbit round it, or plot the orbit of one component of a double star.

Law 2 – observe the orbit of one component of a double star.

Law 3 – record the data for any planet travelling around the Sun.

1 Explain the following:

(*a*) an astronaut may feel weightless in orbit round the Earth although the gravitational attraction of the Earth still acts on the astronaut;

(*b*) a comet spends a large part of the time for one orbit a large distance from the Sun;

(*c*) geostationary satellites must be placed above the equator;

(*d*) why objects at the equator do not get flung off into space. Calculate the speed at which the Earth would have to rotate in order that this does begin to happen.

2 Given that the period of the Earth about the Sun is one year and that the mean distance between the Earth and the Sun is 1.5×10^{11} km, calculate the periods of revolution of the following planets:

Planet	Orbit radius/km
Mercury	5.8×10^{10}
Venus	1.1×10^{11}
Mars	2.3×10^{11}
Jupiter	7.8×10^{11}
Saturn	1.4×10^{12}
Uranus	2.9×10^{12}
Neptune	4.5×10^{12}
Pluto	5.9×10^{12}

Gravitation and the orbit of the Moon

Kepler's laws stated *how* the planets orbited the Sun, but they gave no indication as to *why* they moved in this way. It was Newton's analysis of these laws that was to lead to an explanation of the orbits and also formed part of the basis for his law of universal gravitation.

Newton considered the orbit of the Moon round the Earth and assumed it to be approximately circular. He reasoned that the Moon was held in orbit by some kind of attraction between the Moon and the Earth and set about finding a relation between the magnitude of this force and the separation of the bodies.

Now for a body of in an orbit of radius r and moving with a velocity v there must be a centripetal acceleration a towards the centre of the circle, given by the equation:

$$a = \frac{v^2}{r}$$

Now Newton knew that the acceleration at the Earth's surface (g) was approximately 9.81 m s^{-2} and using the above equation he calculated that the centripetal acceleration of the Moon in its orbit is 0.0027 m s^{-2}.

Clearly the acceleration decreases with separation. In fact the radius of the Moon's orbit is roughly one-sixtieth of the radius of the Earth and at the distance of the Moon's orbit from the centre of the Earth the acceleration, and therefore the force, has reduced by a factor of 3600 (60×60) times. This suggested to Newton that the force reduces as the inverse square of the separation of the two bodies.

Newton's law of gravitation and Kepler's laws

In about 1666 (when he was still only twenty-four years old) Isaac Newton, attempting to find a law of force that would be consistent with Kepler's third law, proposed his **law of universal gravitation**.

Consider a planet moving round the Sun in a circular orbit of radius r. Let the mass of the planet be m, that of the Sun M and let the angular velocity of the planet be ω (Figure 16.1).

$$\text{Force on the planet } F = m\omega^2 r = mr(2\pi/T)^2 = \frac{4\pi^2 mr}{T^2}$$

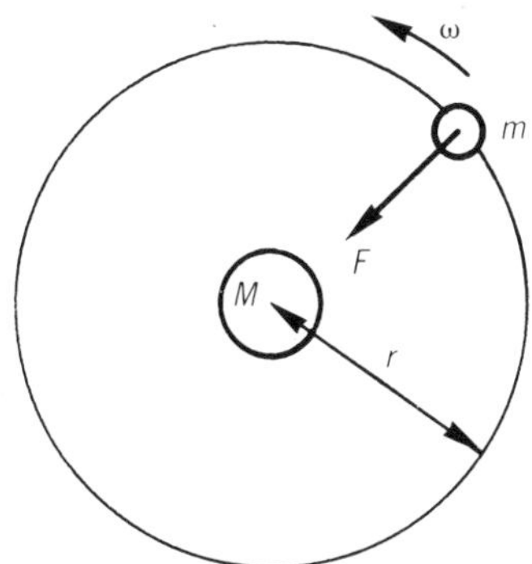

Figure 16.1

Newton then took a crucial step and *assumed* an inverse square law of force between the bodies, that is,

$$F = \frac{km}{r^2}$$

where k is a constant. This assumption formed the basis of his law of universal gravitation.

$$\frac{km}{r^2} = \frac{4\pi^2 mr}{T^2} \quad \text{and so} \quad T^2 = \frac{4\pi^2 r^3}{k}$$

and therefore $T^2 \propto r^3$. This shows that the inverse square law of force is consistent with Kepler's third law and it appears to be a sound assumption.

For the Moon, with an orbit around the Earth of radius r, we have:

$$F = \frac{4\pi^2 mr}{T^2}$$

but the force on a mass m at the Earth's surface $= mg_0$; therefore

$$\frac{4\pi^2 mr}{T^2} : mg_0 = \frac{1}{r^2} : \frac{1}{R^2}$$

where R is the radius of the Earth, and

$$g_0 = \frac{4\pi^2 r^3}{R^2 T^2}$$

and this gave a good result for g_0 as soon as Newton had obtained a satisfactory value for r.

Weightlessness

We often speak of astronauts being weightless and it is important to understand exactly what we mean by this.

Since weight is a force, 'weightlessness' implies the absence of this force. But this will only be true for a point out in space infinitely distant from a star or planet. The condition could also apply at a point where two or more gravitational fields cancel each other, however. If we ignore the attraction of the Sun then there will be a point between the Earth and the Moon where true weightlessness would occur.

We usually describe a feeling of weightlessness when there is no reaction on a body from the floor. If we stand in a lift that is falling freely we still have weight but we *feel* weightless because the reaction has been removed. The same feeling is experienced in orbit, since both the spacecraft and the astronaut have the same centripetal acceleration. During training astronauts fly in a plane that describes a parabolic trajectory, and they therefore experience free fall and feel weightless.

Consider a person of weight W standing in a stationary lift, and let the reaction of the lift floor on the person's body be R. Then in the following five cases R and W are related thus:

(*a*) lift stationary: $W = W, R = W$;
(*b*) lift moving up or down with uniform velocity: $W = W, R = W$;
(*c*) lift accelerating upwards: $W = W, R > W$;
(*d*) lift accelerating downwards: $W = W, R < W$;
(*e*) lift falling freely: $W = W, R = 0$.

> **3** As you know, the gravitational attraction of the Earth on an object is proportional to the mass of the object. Why don't heavy objects fall faster than light ones do?

The universal law of gravitation

Newton extended his ideas to relate to any two bodies and not just those in orbit about each other. He proposed that the force between two point masses was:

(*a*) proportional to the product of their masses, and

(*b*) inversely proportional to the square of the distance between their centres.

Therefore for two point masses of mass m and M separated by a distance d (Figure 16.2), the force of attraction may be written as:

$$F \propto mM \quad \text{and} \quad F \propto \frac{1}{d^2}$$

Therefore:

$$F = \frac{GmM}{d^2}$$

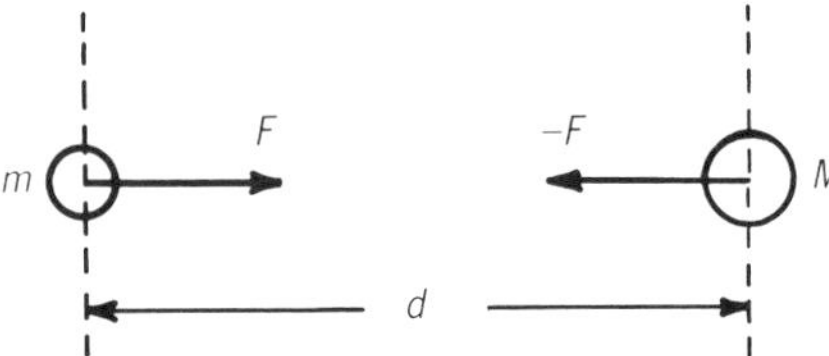

Figure 16.2

where G is the universal constant of gravitation, its value being:

$$G = 6.67 \times 10^{-11}\ \text{N m}^2\ \text{kg}^{-2}.$$

(A dimensional analysis of the equation gives alternative units for G of $\text{m}^3\ \text{kg}^{-1}\ \text{s}^{-2}$.)

You can see that G is a very small number, and therefore gravitational forces are small unless the masses of the two attracting bodies are large.

Example 1

Calculate the gravitational attraction of two cars 5 m apart if the masses of the cars are 1000 kg and 1200 kg. (A very approximate treatment.)

$$F = \frac{6.67 \times 10^{-11} \times 1000 \times 1200}{25}$$

$$= 3.2 \times 10^{-6}\ \text{N}$$

Example 2

Calculate the force between the Sun and Jupiter. Assume that the mass of the Sun = 2×10^{30} kg, the mass of Jupiter = 1.89×10^{27} kg, and the radius of Jupiter's orbit = 7.73×10^{11} m.

$$F = \frac{6.67 \times 10^{-11} \times 2 \times 10^{30} \times 1.89 \times 10^{27}}{5.98 \times 10^{23}}$$

$$= 4.22 \times 10^{23}\ \text{N}$$

This enormous force is sufficient to hold Jupiter in its orbit round the Sun.

Example 3

A mass of 5 kg is first weighed on a balance at the top of a tower 20 m high. The mass is then suspended from a fine wire 20 m long and reweighed. Find the difference in weight. Assume that the radius of the Earth is 6400 km, the mass of the Earth 6×10^{24} kg and G 6.67 $\times 10^{-11}\ \text{N m}^2\ \text{kg}^{-2}$.

$$\text{Original force} = \frac{6.67 \times 10^{-11} \times 6 \times 10^{24} \times 5}{(6400.02 \times 10^3)^2}$$

$$= 48.8522\ \text{N}$$

$$\text{Force at surface} = \frac{6.67 \times 10^{-11} \times 6 \times 10^{24} \times 5}{(6400 \times 10^3)^2}$$

$$= 48.8525\ \text{N}$$

Therefore change in weight = 0.0003 N.
Calling $g = 10\ \text{N kg}^{-1}$, this is equivalent to the weight of a 0.03 g mass at the Earth's surface.

4 Calculate the force of attraction between two masses, one of 5 kg and one of 8 kg, whose centres are 10 cm apart.

5 A binary star consists of two dense spherical masses of 10^{30} kg and 2×10^{30} kg whose centres are 10^7 km apart and which rotate together with angular velocity ω about an axis which intersects a line joining their centres.

Assuming that the only forces acting on the stars arise from their mutual gravitational attraction and that each mass may be taken to act at its centre, show that the axis of rotation passes through the centre of mass of the system, and find the value of ω.

[O and C]

The measurement of the universal constant of gravitation

During the eighteenth century many ingenious methods were devised to measure G. Accurate results were extremely difficult to obtain, however, because of its very small value.

The first experiment was performed in 1740 by Bouguer, who measured the deflection of a plumb line from the vertical due to the attraction between the plumb bob and a mountain (Chimborazo in the Andes) and from this calculated the mass of the Earth and hence G.

Other experimenters were Airy (1854), who measured the change in the acceleration of gravity down a mine, and von Jolly (1878) and Poynting (1891) who used the deflection of a large balance. All these experiments led to values of G but they are now really only of historical interest.

The basis of the modern method for G was an experiment carried out in 1789 on Clapham Common by Henry Cavendish. He used a large torsion balance and measured the twist in the torsion wire due to the attraction between two large fixed lead spheres 30 cm in diameter and two small lead spheres 5 cm in diameter attached to a beam at the base of the torsion wire. This experiment was greatly improved in 1895 by Boys, and it is this method that will be described fully.

Boys' method for the determination of G

The apparatus is shown diagrammatically in Figure 16.3(*a*). Two gold spheres (a and b) 5 mm in diameter and with a mass of 3 g were suspended at different heights from either end of a 2.3 cm bar. This bar was hung from a quartz fibre torsion wire, 0.43 m long and with a diameter of 0.000 5 cm! This arrangement was placed in a draughtproof box, and outside this were hung two large lead spheres (A and B), 115 mm in diameter and each with a mass of 7 kg. These were then enclosed in an outer box. The spheres were mounted at different levels to minimise cross-attractive forces between a and B and between b and A. The whole apparatus had to be mounted on a stable base to prevent vibrations.

The plan view (Figure 16.3(*b*)) shows the forces acting on the spheres. The forces between the small masses and the large masses cause the beam to twist through an angle θ as shown in the diagram.

Let the separation of the centres of A and a and B and b be d, and let the beam have a length l. Then

$$\text{torque on the beam} = \frac{GmMl}{d^2} = c\theta$$

where c is the torque in the torsion wire per radian twist. Therefore:

$$G = \frac{c\theta d^2}{mMl}$$

The torsional constant was determined by allowing the beam to oscillate and measuring the period of oscillation (T). Using the equation

$$T = 2\pi\sqrt{\frac{I}{c}}$$

c can be found if the moment of inertia of the beam and the small spheres is known.

The period was found to be about 2 minutes compared with the 7 to 8 minutes that Cavendish had found with his apparatus, which had a 1.8 m beam!

Heyl repeated the experiment in 1942 using a lamp and scale 7 m away as a pointer and claimed an accuracy of 0.75 minutes of arc, giving G to better than one part in 10 000. Heyl and Brown also devised a method where a large mass was brought up briefly to a small mass suspended on a beam and the period of the resulting oscillations measured.

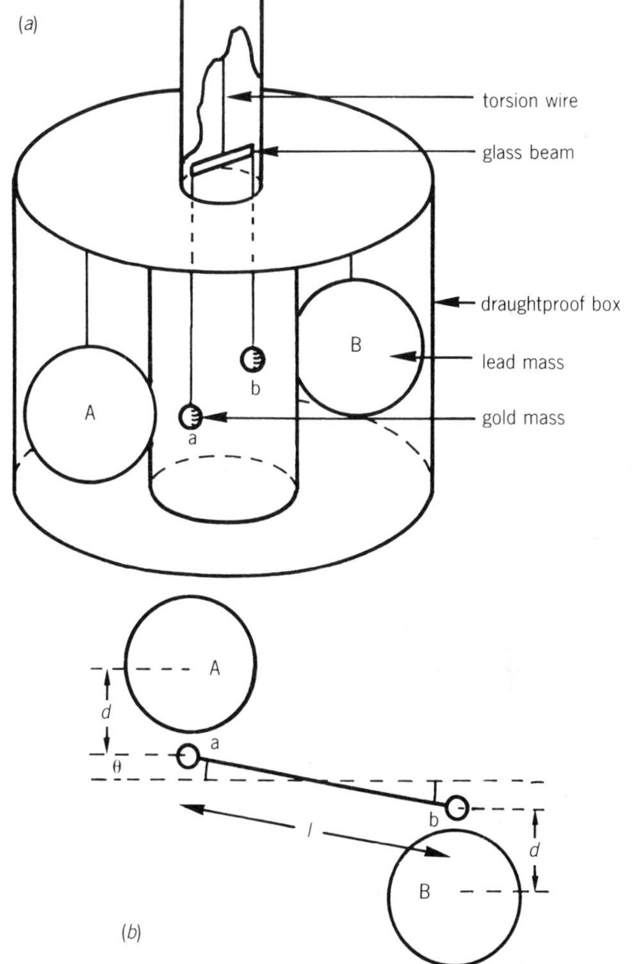

Figure 16.3

Up to the time of writing no substance has been discovered that shows a screening effect for the gravitational force and it is assumed that this force travels with the speed of light. Efforts to detect gravity waves (see page 95) or quanta of gravitational force (gravitons) have also been unsuccessful.

Explanation of symbols used

For all the subsequent work on gravitation we will use the following notation:

Acceleration due to gravity at the Earth's surface	g_0
Acceleration due to gravity at any other point	g
Radius of the Earth	R
Distance of any other mass from the centre of the Earth	r
Mass of the Earth	M
Mass of any other mass	m

Relation between g_0 and G

Consider a mass m on the surface of the Earth. It will experience a gravitational force:

$$F = \frac{GmM}{R^2}$$

but this force is also its weight (mg_0). Therefore (Figure 16.4):

$$\frac{GmM}{R^2} = mg_0$$

and so

$$g_0 = \frac{GM}{R^2}$$

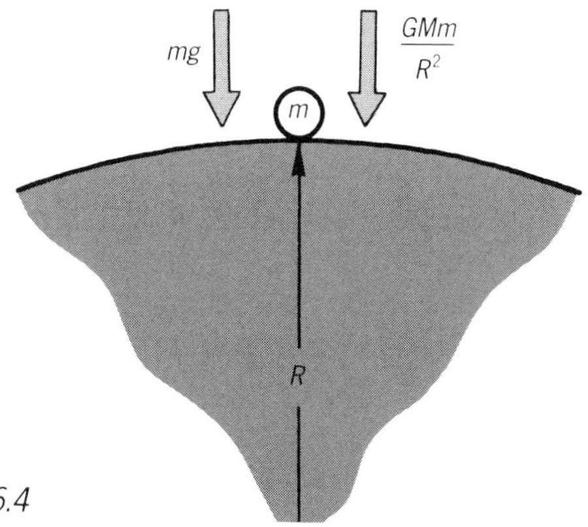

Figure 16.4

6 If the acceleration due to gravity at the Earth's surface is 10 m s^{-2} and the radius of the Earth is 6400 km, calculate a value for the mass of the Earth.

7 The length of a certain 1 m simple pendulum can be measured to ± 0.1 cm and its period to ± 0.01 s. Calculate the height above the Earth's surface where a change in period could be measured with certainty. Take g_0 = 10 m s^{-2}

8 The planet Neptune makes one complete orbit of the Sun in 165 years. Calculate the mean radius of its orbit.

Gravitational and inertial mass

So far we have thought of the mass of an object in two different ways, and it is important to see how they are connected. We have considered

(*a*) the mass that governs how fast an object will accelerate when a given force acts on it, known as the **inertial mass** (m_i);

(*b*) the mass that governs the gravitational attractive force between two bodies, known as the **gravitational mass** (m).

The two equations giving these quantities are:

$$F = m_i a \quad \text{and} \quad F = \frac{GmM}{R^2}$$

but $\frac{GM}{R^2} = g_0$

Therefore $F = mg_0 = W$ (the weight of the mass).

We can derive the simple pendulum equation using $W = mg_0$:

$$-mg_0xl = m_i a$$

So the period (T) is given by

$$T = 2\pi\sqrt{\frac{m_i l}{mg_0}}$$

Experiments show that $m_i/m = 1$ to a high degree of accuracy and so $m_i = m$. Thus inertial mass and gravitational mass are equivalent.

Gravitational field

The gravitational field strength (g) at a point at a distance r from a mass M is defined as the force on unit mass placed at that point, that is:

$$g = \frac{GM}{r^2}$$

Therefore for an object placed on the surface of the Earth:

$$\text{gravitational field strength} = \frac{GM}{R^2} = g_0$$

The units are N kg^{-1}.

We will now consider two special cases of the gravitational field strength, one above and one below the surface of the Earth.

9 Calculate the approximate ratio of the mass of the Sun to that of the Earth, stating clearly any data that you assume.

(a) Field inside the Earth

Consider a point inside the Earth at distance r from the centre ($r < R$). Let the field strength at that point be g (Figure 16.5). Therefore

$$g = \frac{GM'}{r^2}$$

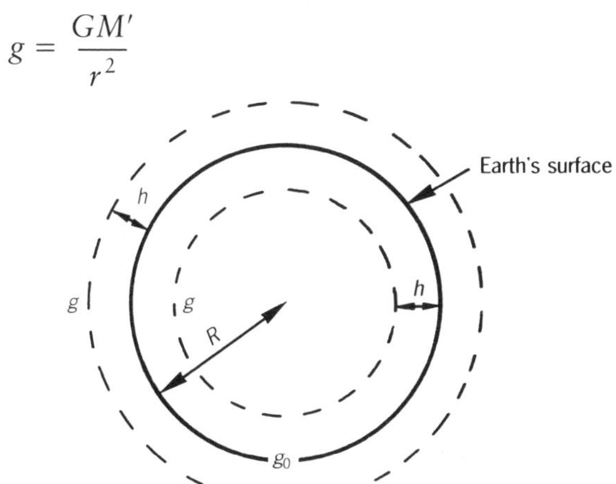

Figure 16.5

where M' is the mass of the Earth within radius r. But $M' = r^3M/R^3$. Therefore $mg = GmMr/R$; hence

$$g = g_0 \frac{r}{R}$$

This means that – theoretically – the gravitational field intensity decreases linearly inside the Earth; however, this is only true if we assume that the Earth has a uniform density.

In fact the density increases with depth, the density of the Earth's crust being about 2.8×10^3 kg m^{-3} while that of the surface of the core is 9.7×10^3 kg m^{-3}.

This actually results in an increase in g for a short distance below the surface. The theoretical and actual variations are shown in Figure 16.6. If $R - r = h$, then the theoretical reduction in gravitational intensity at a depth h *below* the surface is given by:

$$g_0 - g = \frac{hg_0}{R}$$

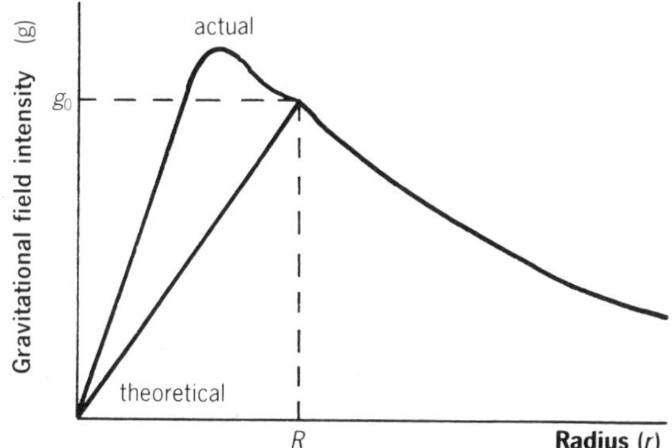

Figure 16.6

10 The variation of g in the Earth's interior is given by the following table:

Depth/km	g/m s^{-2}	Depth/km	g/m s^{-2}
0	9.82	1400	9.88
33	9.85	1600	9.86
100	9.89	1800	9.85
200	9.92	2000	9.86
300	9.95	2200	9.90
413	9.98	2400	9.98
600	10.01	2600	10.09
800	9.99	2800	10.26
1000	9.95	2900	10.37
1200	9.91	4000	8.00

Plot a graph of the variation of g with depth and suggest how the density of the Earth might vary to give such a variation in g.

(b) Field above the Earth's surface

Consider a point a distance r from the centre of the Earth where $r > R$.

$$g = \frac{GM}{r^2} \quad \text{but} \quad g_0 = \frac{GM}{R^2}$$

Therefore

$$g = g_0 \frac{R^2}{r^2}$$

For a height h *above* the Earth's surface, $r = R + h$. Using the result above, and assuming that h is small compared with the radius of the Earth R, we can show that:

$$g_0 - g = \frac{2h}{R} g_0$$

Thus the value of g at a depth h below the Earth's surface is greater than that at the same distance above the surface.

Example

Find the gravitational intensity at a point 1000 m above mean sea level. Take R = 6400 km and g_0 = 9.81 m s^{-2}.

$$g_0 - g = \frac{2 \times 10^3 g_0}{6.4 \times 10^6} = 0.31 \times 10^{-3} g_0 = 0.003 \text{ m s}^{-2}$$

$$\therefore g = 9.807 \text{ m s}^{-2}$$

The synchronous satellite

We have already shown for Kepler's laws that

$$\frac{4\pi^2 r^3}{T^2} = g_0 R^2 \quad \text{Therefore} \quad T^2 = \frac{4\pi^2 r^3}{g_0 R^2}$$

Since $g_0 = GM/R^2$ the period T of a satellite in an orbit of radius r above the Earth (radius R) is therefore

$$T = 2\pi\sqrt{\frac{r^3}{g_0 R^2}} = 2\pi\sqrt{\frac{r^3}{GM}}$$

A **synchronous satellite** is one that always remains above the same point on the equator, that is, it has a period of exactly one day (86 400 s).

Therefore this gives for the orbit radius (r):

$r = 42\ 400$ km

which is very nearly equal to the circumference of the Earth. Remember that this distance, as with all satellite orbits used in these problems, must be measured from the centre of the Earth.

11 A preliminary stage of the spacecraft Apollo 11's journey to the Moon was to place it in a parking orbit 189 km above the Earth's surface. Calculate
(*a*) the gravitational intensity at this height,
(*b*) the speed of the spacecraft, and
(*c*) the time to complete one orbit. [L]

12 Calculate the height of the orbit for a geostationary satellite above the Earth, given that the period of revolution of the Moon is 27.3 days and that its mean distance from the Earth is 3.8×10^8 m.

13 Calculate the value of the gravitational intensity at a point
(*a*) 8000 m above sea level,
(*b*) 8000 m below sea level.
What difference would it make to the period of a simple pendulum of length 1 m if it were taken from one point to the other? (Assume that the gravitational intensity at the surface of the Earth is 10 N kg^{-1}.)

14 It has been calculated that the 'diameter' of a black hole with the same mass as the Earth is about 1.0 cm. Calculate
(*a*) the distance from the surface of the black hole where the gravitational intensity would be the same as that at the Earth's surface,
(*b*) the gravitational intensity 1 m from the centre of the black hole.
(Assume that our laws of Physics are still obeyed near black holes!)

Student investigation

The following extract is adapted from the NASA booklet *Gravitational Field* describing the Apollo–Soyuz series of spaceflights in the 1970s.

Gravitational field

After four years of preparation by the US National Aeronautics and Space Administration (NASA) and the USSR Academy of Sciences the Apollo and Soyuz spacecraft were launched on 15 July 1975. Two days later, after Apollo manoeuvred into the same orbit as Soyuz, the two spacecraft were docked.

Thirty-four experiments were performed while the Apollo and Soyuz were in orbit. These experiments were selected from 161 proposals from scientists in nine countries. The orbit of a spacecraft is controlled by the Earth's gravitational field. If the Earth's gravity is 'smooth' the spacecraft moves in an elliptical orbit at a predictable velocity. However, if there are irregularities in the Earth's gravity a spacecraft in low orbit will speed up and slow down as it passes over them. Such irregular motion has been observed for spacecraft in orbit around the Moon and has been looked for on NASA missions passing other planets.

For many years the acceleration of gravity g was thought to be the same on all parts of the Earth's surface. Then it was discovered that g is higher than normal in some regions and lower than normal in others. These regions are called 'gravity anomalies' and they are caused by high or low density in the Earth's crust. Detecting them is useful in locating ore deposits, coal, oil and gas. Two of the Apollo–Soyuz experiments were designed to detect gravity anomalies from the motions of spacecraft. One of these used the doppler effect (see page 172). The effect uses the change of frequency produced by a moving source or observer of waves to determine the velocity of the source or observer.

A satellite at very high altitude is almost unaffected by gravity anomalies because of the inverse square nature of Newton's law of gravitation. Therefore doppler tracking of a low satellite (accelerated by gravity anomalies) from a high satellite should make measurements of these accelerations possible. The situation is complicated because the low satellite (Apollo) moves at changing angles to the high–low line (see Figure 16.7). When Apollo was directly under the high satellite there was no doppler shift because there was no component of orbital velocity along the high–low line.

The ATS-6 communications satellite was used as the high satellite. It was in a 24 hr geosynchronous orbit 35 900 km above Lake Victoria in East Africa. At a height of 42 280 km from the Earth's centre it circles the Earth once every 24 hours and therefore remains over the same point on the equator.

The Apollo spacecraft in low orbit, the ATS-6 satellite in high orbit (actually more than 160 times higher than Apollo) are shown in Figure 16.7. The 2.25 GHz radio signals from Apollo to ATS-6 have a doppler shift of $f = 2.25 \times 10^9 v/c$ where v is the component of orbital velocity along the Apollo–ATS-6 line. The doppler shift was zero when Apollo passed directly under ATS-6. The doppler shift was at maximum when Apollo was near the horizon as seen from the ATS-6. These doppler-shifted signals were then radioed to the ATS receiver in Madrid on a 3.8 GHz circuit with almost no doppler shift, because the position of the ATS-6 is nearly fixed in the sky.

The object of one experiment was to measure gravity anomalies as small as 0.05 mm s^{-1} over features as small as 300 km. Two areas were selected: the centre of Africa which has positive gravity anomalies and the Indian Ocean trough which has a negative gravity anomaly.

The radiofrequency crystal oscillators were stable enough that velocity changes as small as 1 mm s^{-1} were detected. Errors in measurement were about 0.5 mm s^{-1}.

Changes in v (the component of Apollo's velocity towards the ATS-6 during three orbits over the Indian Ocean and the Himalayan Mountains) are shown in Figure 16.8. If changes in v are converted to the strength of the anomalies, the two largest anomalies correspond to changes in g of about 0.6 and 1.0 mm s^{-2}.

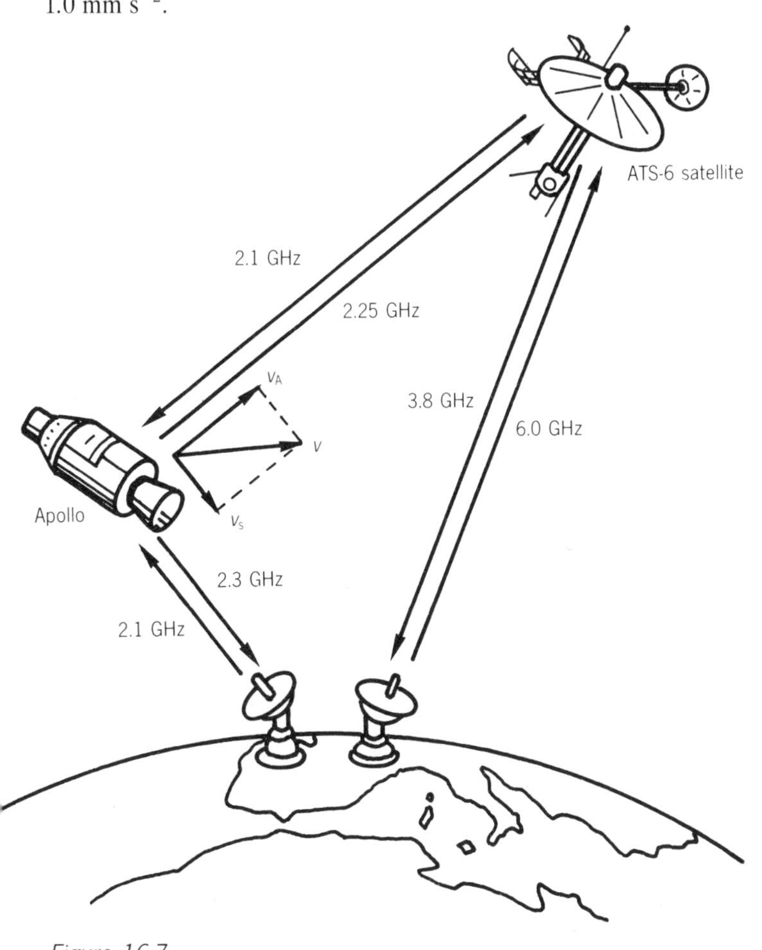

Figure 16.7

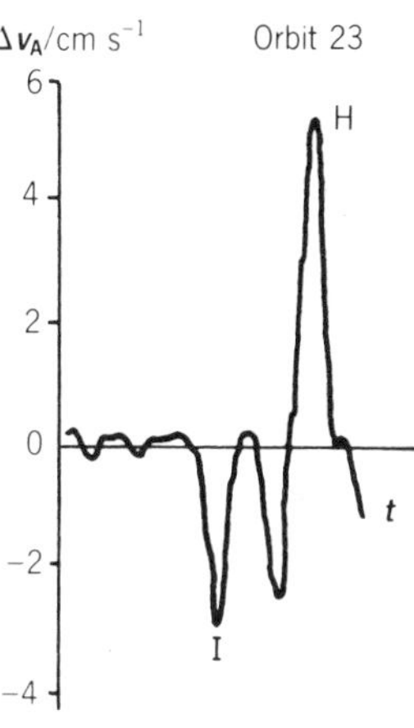

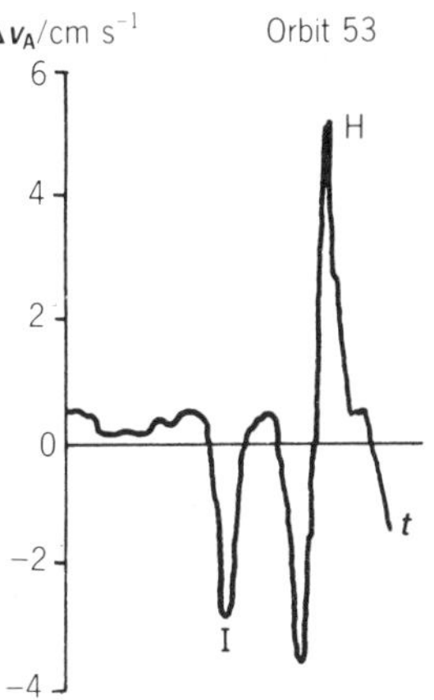

I = Indian Ocean

H = Himalayas

Figure 16.8

Answer the following questions.

1 With crystal oscillators controlling radiofrequency to 1 mHz in 334 Hz, what is the smallest velocity along the line of sight that can be detected?

2 At which positions relative to the ATS-6 would the doppler shift be (*a*) a maximum, (*b*) a minimum?

3 Would you consider this to be a good method for the detection of gravitational anomalies?

4 How would the roll of the Apollo spacecraft affect the doppler-shifted readings?

Gravitational potential

The gravitational potential at a point in a field is defined as the work done (W) in bringing unit mass from infinity to that point. Since the gravitational force is attractive this work will be negative.

Note that the zero for potential is at infinity. All other points have a negative potential and work must be done on a body to remove it *to* infinity.

The potential at a point is defined as W/m. Therefore if the work done in moving mass m from P + dx to P is dW (Figure 16.9),

$$\mathrm{d}W = F\mathrm{d}x = \frac{GmM\mathrm{d}x}{x^2}$$

Therefore the potential V at P is given by:

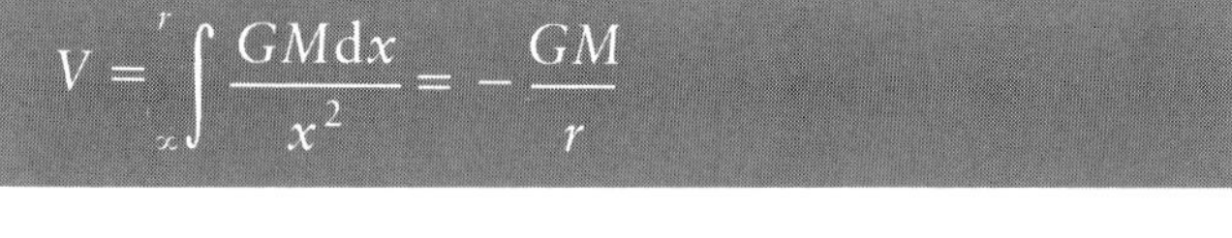

$$V = \int_{\infty}^{r} \frac{GM\mathrm{d}x}{x^2} = -\frac{GM}{r}$$

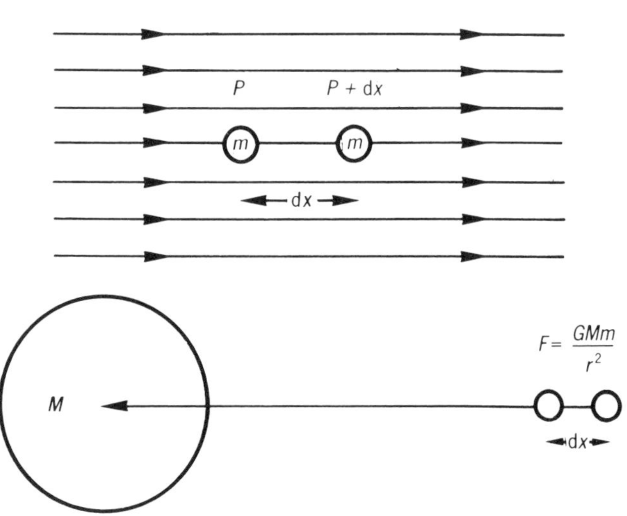

Figure 16.9

This is the work done in moving unit mass from infinity *to* that point. Notice that it is negative.

To move the mass *away* from a planet will require a positive amount of work. At the surface of the Earth the potential is:

$$\text{gravitational potential} = -\frac{GM}{R}$$

If we consider a mass m then the work done in bringing it to a point in the field is equal to the potential energy gained (Figure 16.10):

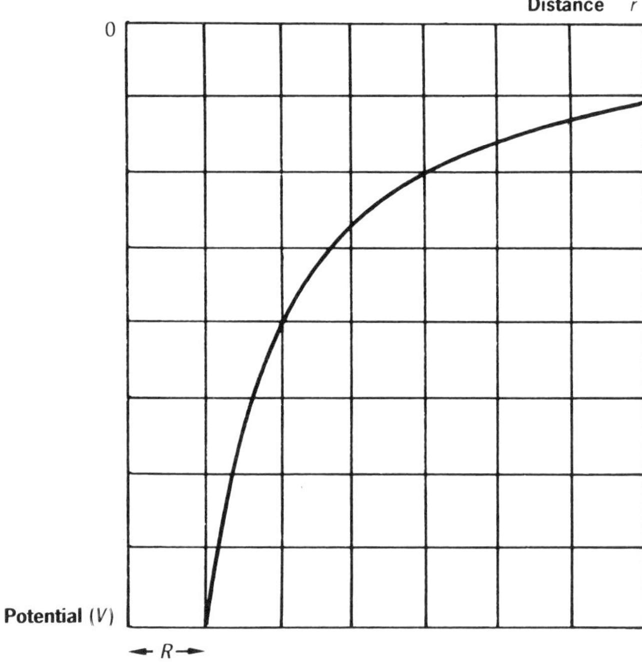

Figure 16.10

$$\text{gravitational potential energy} = -\frac{GmM}{r}$$

The minus sign in this expression may seem strange if we think of the former way of expressing potential energy (mgh), since mgh is taken as positive. We can show that there is no dilemma, however, since mgh represents a *change* of potential energy compared with the Earth's surface.

Consider a mass m being raised to a height h above the Earth's surface:

$$\text{potential energy at surface} = -\frac{GmM}{R}$$

$$\text{potential energy at height } h = -\frac{GmM}{(R+h)}$$

Therefore the difference in potential energy

$$= -\frac{GmM}{(R+h)} - \left\{-\frac{GmM}{R}\right\}$$

$$= GmM\left\{\frac{1}{R} - \frac{1}{(R+h)}\right\}$$

and this result is positive.

Energy in satellite orbits

When a satellite is placed in orbit above the Earth two factors must be taken into account in an energy consideration.

(*a*) the potential energy required to raise the satellite to that height, and

(*b*) the kinetic energy required for the orbit at that height.

At the required height an orbit injection manoeuvre is performed to put the satellite into the desired orbit.

In calculating the total energy required to place a satellite in orbit, the kinetic energy needed to give it the correct tangential velocity for the orbit at that height must also be found.

Example

When a body is moved from the Earth's surface to a height *h* we can write the change in gravitational potential energy as

$$\Delta\,(\text{p.e.}) = +\frac{GmM\,h}{R(R+h)}$$

So for a mass of 2 kg moved through 100 m we have

$$\Delta\,(\text{p.e.}) = \frac{6.3 \times 10^7 \times 2 \times 100}{6400 \times 10^3}$$

$$= 1969 \text{ J}$$

which is very close to the value obtained using *mgh*.

15 The USA space shuttle orbiter has a mass of 68 000 kg. Calculate

(*a*) the energy required to place the orbiter in an orbit 1000 km above the Earth's surface, and

(*b*) the volume of fuel needed if 1 gallon of fuel produces 200 MJ. (Density of fuel = 800 kg m^{-3}).

Comment on your answers and suggest why the volume required would be very much greater in practice.

16 If a signal rocket rose to a height of 200 m on the Earth, to what height would it rise on the Moon?

Variation in potential between two objects

We can use these ideas to sketch the variation in potential between the Earth and the Moon (Figure 16.11).

You can work out the values of potential at the surfaces of the Earth and the Moon:

potential at Earth $= 6.3 \times 10^7$ J kg^{-1}
potential at Moon $= 2.8 \times 10^6$ J kg^{-1}

Notice that to escape from either body a satellite must go over the potential hill. The diagram shows that more energy is needed to escape from the gravitational attraction of the Earth than from the Moon.

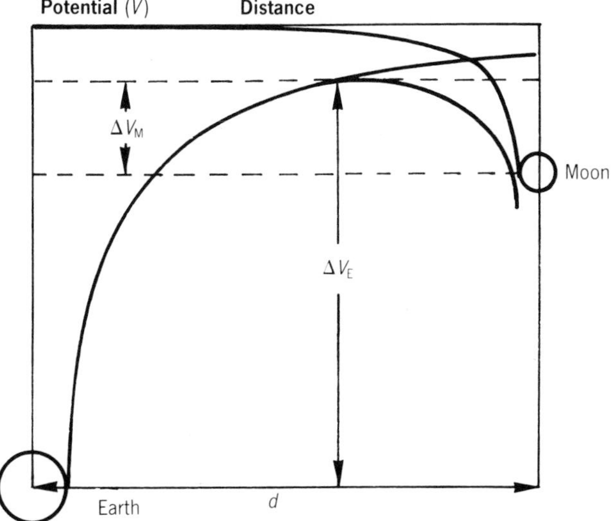

Figure 16.11

Student investigation

You wish to launch a spacecraft of mass 1000 kg to a moon from a planet.

Using the graph of the gravitational potential plotted against distance (Figure 16.12), find the following:

(*a*) the energy needed to reach the moon,

(*b*) the energy needed to reach the moon starting at an orbital height of 1000 km, and

(*c*) the energy needed to return to the planet from the lunar surface.

Comment on your results in the light of the Apollo Moon flights, giving reasons for the vehicles used in various parts of the flight.

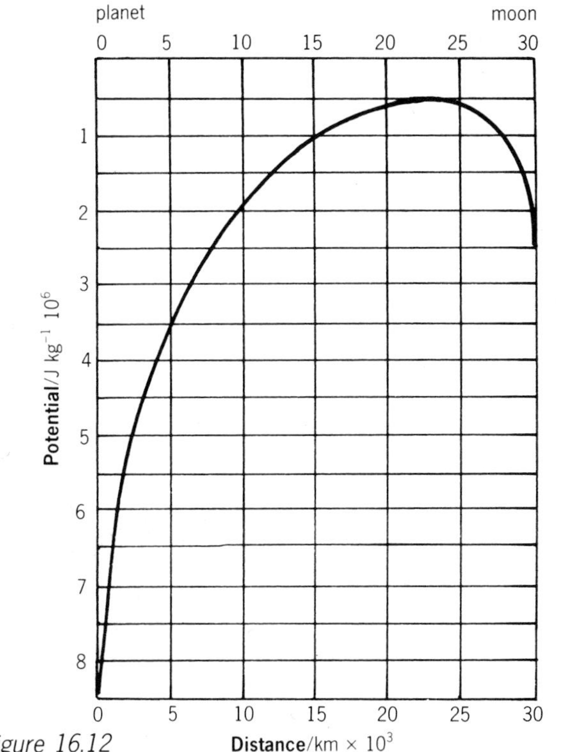

Figure 16.12

Energy and satellite orbits

We must consider the p.e., k.e. and total energy of a satellite in orbit of radius r about the Earth:

$$\text{p.e.} = -\frac{GmM}{r}$$

But since $\dfrac{GmM}{r^2} = \dfrac{mv^2}{r}$

$$\text{k.e.} = \tfrac{1}{2}mv^2 = \frac{GmM}{2r}$$

Therefore the total gravitational potential energy of a satellite E is

$$E = -\frac{GmM}{2r}$$

This is negative (because of the convention about zero p.e. at infinity).

Figure 16.13 shows how the k.e., p.e. and total energy change with distance.

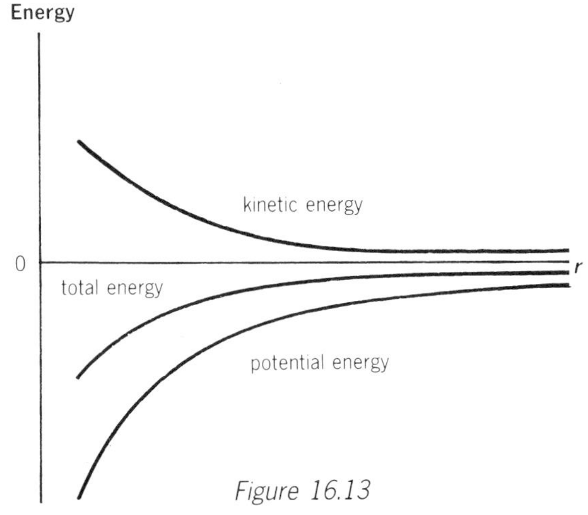

Figure 16.13

Example

Calculate the change in the energy of a 500 kg satellite when it falls from an altitude of 200 km to 199 km. If this change takes place during one orbit, calculate the retarding force on the satellite.

Change in energy

$$= \Delta\left\{\frac{GMm}{r}\right\} = 6.67 \times 10^{-11} \times 6 \times 10^{24}$$

$$\times 500\left\{\frac{1}{6.6 \times 10^6} - \frac{1}{6.599 \times 10^6}\right\}$$

$$= 2 \times 10^{17}(1.5152 \times 10^{-7} - 1.5154 \times 10^{7})$$

$$= -4 \times 10^6\ \text{J}$$

If this occurs during one orbit then the energy lost = force × distance. If we take the distance as being the circumference of one orbit, then:

$$\text{retarding force} = \frac{4 \times 10^6}{2\pi 6.6 \times 10^6} = 0.1\ \text{N}$$

Escape velocity

Since we have talked about escaping from the Earth, it is interesting to work out the **escape velocity**. The escape velocity is the vertical velocity that a body must be given at the surface of a planet so that it will just escape from the gravitational attraction of that planet. We must assume that after reaching that velocity its engines are switched off.

If we consider a rocket of mass m, then it must be given enough energy to escape from the potential well produced by the planet. Therefore

$$\text{work done} = \text{energy gained} = \frac{GmM}{R}$$

Therefore

$$\text{k.e. required} = \tfrac{1}{2}mv^2 = \frac{GmM}{R}$$

This gives the escape velocity (v_e):

$$v_e = \sqrt{\frac{2GM}{R}} = \sqrt{2Rg_0}$$

(see Figure 16.14). For the Earth we can show that this is 1.13×10^4 m s^{-1} or 11.3 km s^{-1}.

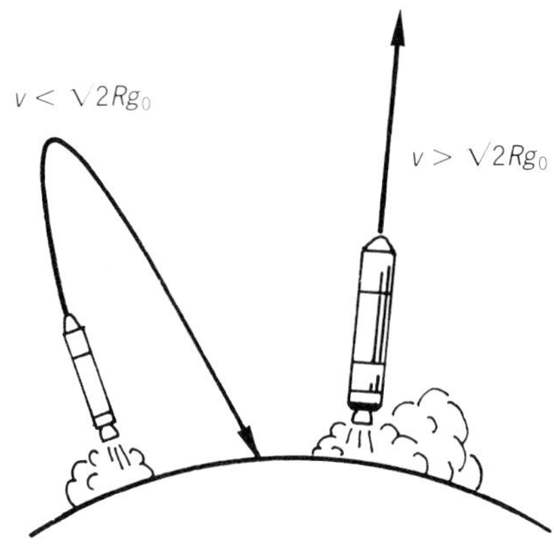

Figure 16.14

Example

Consider the possibility of the loss of atmosphere from the Earth. For this to happen the velocity of the molecules (v) must be greater than v_e.

For air at 273 K the root mean square velocity of the oxygen molecules is 0.48 km s^{-1}. Read the section on page 255 and decide whether any oxygen molecules would be lost from the upper atmosphere. Would any hydrogen molecules be lost?

Orbit injection

Figure 16.15 shows the orbit shapes for various launching velocities.

(*a*) If $v = v_e$ then the orbit will be parabolic.
(*b*) If $v < v_e$ then the orbit will be elliptical.
(*c*) If $v = \sqrt{Rg_0}$ the orbit will be circular (since $mv^2/R = GmM/R^2$).
(*d*) If $v > v_e$ the orbit will be hyperbolic.

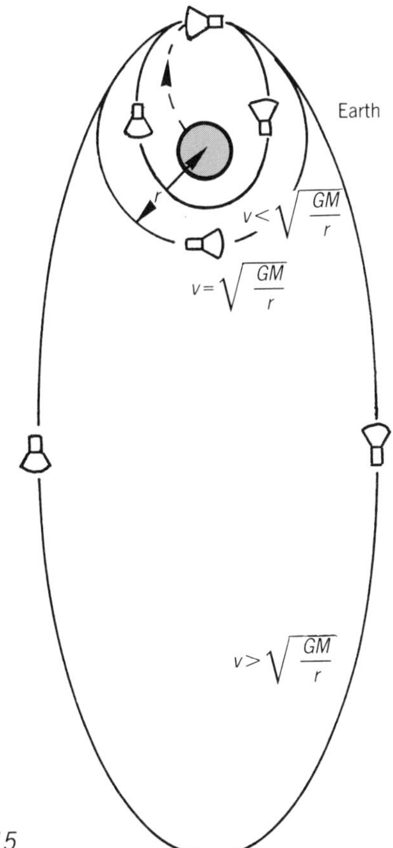

Figure 16.15

The velocity with which a satellite is launched into an orbit which is initially parallel to the surface of the Earth at that point will determine the subsequent shape of the orbit.

17 The period of the Martian satellite Phobos is 7.65 hours and the mean height of its orbit about the planet is 5920 km. If Mars has a diameter of 6720 km, calculate the density of Mars.

18 Calculate (*a*) the gravitational intensity at the surface of (i) the Sun, (ii) Jupiter, (iii) Deimos; (*b*) the escape velocities of the bodies in (*a*)
Mass of the Sun = 1.99×10^{30} kg; radius = 6.96×10^8 m
Mass of Jupiter = 1.90×10^{27} kg; radius = 7.14×10^7 m
Mass of Deimos $\approx 1.72 \times 10^{16}$ kg; radius $\approx 1.27 \times 10^4$ m

19 Using only the values quoted for the universal constant of gravitation and the radius and mean density of the Earth, calculate the escape velocity of the Earth.

20 What is the minimum radius of a planet of the same density as the Earth that could just retain an atmosphere of air at a temperature of 300 K, if the root mean square velocity of air molecules at this temperature is 450 m s^{-1}?

21 Calculate the minimum distance from the Earth where a satellite will fall towards the Moon with no further input of energy.

22 A stone is dropped down a hole that goes through the centre of the Earth. Neglecting air resistance, how long will it take for the stone to fall to the other side?

Gravity waves

One conclusion that can be drawn from Einstein's general theory of relativity is that space is curved in regions where a gravitational field exists (see page 469). As a result of this packets of curved space – tidal ripples of gravity – should flow through empty space far from the bodies that created them. This has given rise to the search for 'gravity waves' which would pass through space in much the same way as shock waves pass through the Earth after an earthquake.

The most intense sources of gravity waves would be star-swallowing black holes, or even a collision between two large black holes.

The first builder of gravity wave detectors was Joseph Weber at the University of Maryland in the mid-1960s. He used a massive cylinder of aluminium with a mass of some 1500 kg. This cylinder should vibrate slightly as a gravity wave passes through it.

Although gravity waves were detected in Maryland, however, nobody else has been able to reproduce these results, and so at present their existence is the subject of some doubt.

Molecular properties

Intermolecular forces in practice – the construction of the Sydney Opera House. Client: Government of New South Wales; Architect: Stages 1 and 2 – Jorn Utzon; Stage 3 – Hall, Todd and Littlemore; Consulting Engineers: Ove Arup and Partners.

17 · Intermolecular forces

In a solid all the molecules exert a force on each other and these forces can give an explanation of some of the elastic and thermal properties of a material.

Figure 17.1 shows how the potential energy of two molecules and the force between them changes with their separation. The force at any point is found from $F = -\mathrm{d}V/\mathrm{d}r$, where V is the potential energy. Two forces act between the molecules:

(*a*) the repulsive force which predominates at short distances

(*b*) the attractive force which predominates at long distances

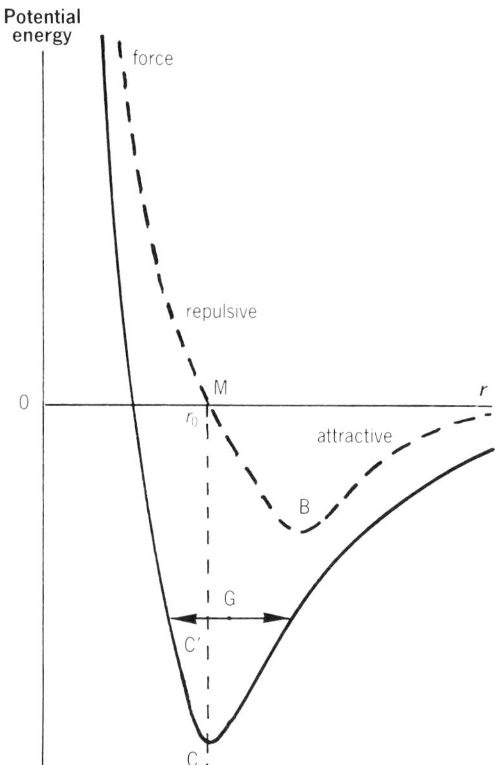

Figure 17.1

You can see from the graph that when the molecules are close to each other the repulsive force predominates, while at greater distances the attractive force is larger. The resultant force is:

(*a*) *repulsive* from O to M,

(*b*) *attractive* from M to B but increasing with distance, and

(*c*) *attractive* from B to infinity but decreasing with distance.

There is a position where the two forces balance, shown by M on the graph. This is the equilibrium position for molecules in the solid.

The potential energy is a minimum at this point (as would be expected). Any disturbance from this position would produce a force tending to return the molecules to M. The force of attraction between the molecules increases as the molecules are separated from M to B. The breaking point is at B, since beyond this point the force of attraction decreases with increasing separation.

For a molecule to be completely separated from its neighbour it must gain an amount of energy E, represented by CM on the diagram. The latent heat of vaporisation for the two molecules is CM when there is no residual attractive force. This length also represents the latent heat of vaporisation for the whole material.

In a solid the distance OM is some $2\text{–}3 \times 10^{-10}$ m and you can see that around this point the force between the molecules varies approximately linearly with distance.

The curves also explain the expansion of a solid with increasing temperature. If an amount of energy E is added to a molecule at C its p.e. will rise to the level C′, the energy appears as kinetic and potential energy and the molecule oscillates about G. However, since the p.e.–distance curve is not symmetrical this centre of oscillation is further from O than from M. This results in a mean separation of the molecules – that is, an expansion.

The oil drop experiment

We have considered the forces that exist in a solid between adjacent molecules and have therefore assumed the existence of these molecules. The following simple experiment can be used to give a rough idea of the *size* of a molecule.

The radius r of a small drop of oil is found and the volume of the drop calculated. The drop is now placed on the surface of some dust-covered water and the drop spreads out into a roughly circular patch, the diameter of which is measured, and hence the radius R is found. This patch must be at least one molecule thick, but clearly cannot be less. Now the volume of the original drop is the same as that of the film; therefore, if h is the thickness of the film,

$$\tfrac{4}{3}\pi r^3 = \pi R^2 h$$

and from this the thickness of the film can be found. Therefore the size of a molecule of oil must be equal to or less than the thickness of the film.

Results from this experiment suggest the diameter of a molecule of oil to be about 10^{-9} m, and this has been confirmed by X-ray diffraction (see page 436).

18 · Solids, liquids and gases

The evidence for molecular structure is based on such observations as Brownian motion, diffusion of gases and X-ray diffraction. These are considered separately and in detail on pages 250, 252 and 436.

We will consider here the size of molecules and the forces that hold them together in different materials.

The mole and the Avogadro constant

The unit for the amount of a substance is the **mole**. It is defined as the amount of a substance that contains the same number of particles (atoms or molecules) as the number of atoms in 12 g of the isotope carbon-12. This number is known as the **Avogadro constant** (L) and is 6.02×10^{23} particles per mole.

The ratio of the mass of one mole of the substance to one-twelfth of the mass of one mole of carbon-12 is called the **relative molecular mass** of the substance – it is 32 for oxygen, 2 for hydrogen and so on.

A knowledge of the Avogadro constant enables us to calculate the number of molecules in any mass of a substance and therefore to get an idea of the size of one molecule. For example, a drop of water of volume $1.0\ \text{cm}^3$ has a mass of 1 g. The relative molecular mass of water is 18, and therefore this drop of water must contain $\frac{6.02 \times 10^{23}}{18} = 3.34 \times 10^{22}$ molecules.

The average volume of a water molecule must therefore be $2.99 \times 10^{-23}\ \text{cm}^3$, and if we assume the molecules to be spherical the diameter of a water molecule is about 2×10^{-8} cm or 2×10^{-10} m, a result confirmed by X-ray diffraction.

The value of the Avogadro constant can be deduced from the following example.

Forces between solids

Having looked at the sizes of atoms and molecules, we must now consider the forces that hold them together into a solid. (If you refer to page 36 you should realise that all are types of the basic electromagnetic force.) The forces in solids are of four types:

(*a*) **ionic** – this is the electrostatic attraction of two oppositely charged ions and occurs in crystals such as sodium chloride.

(*b*) **covalent** – this force results from electrons being shared between the shells of adjacent atoms as in diamond, silicon and methane.

(*c*) **metallic** – this force is due to the free electron cloud that exists in metals such as copper. The electrons move freely between the atoms and are not fixed to any pair of atoms as they are in the covalent bond.

(*d*) **van der Waals** – these are electric dipole forces formed by the electron cloud and the nucleus; they operate in all matter and are responsible for the attractive force between molecules in a gas. They can be observed in solid neon, simply because none of the others operate there.

1 Using graphs of force against distance, and of potential energy against distance, explain:
(*a*) Hooke's law,
(*b*) the breaking point,
(*c*) disassociation energy,
(*d*) why solids expand when they are heated, and
(*e*) why energy can be stored in a solid both when the solid is extended and when it is compressed.

2 (*a*) How many moles are there in a glass of water (0.2 kg)?
(*b*) How many molecules are there in the same glass of water?
(The Avogadro constant is $6.0 \times 10^{23}\ \text{mol}^{-1}$.)

Example

A sample of 2 mg of polonium is found to emit 2.90×10^{18} alpha-particles during one half-life. If the relative atomic mass of polonium is 210, calculate a value for the Avogadro constant.

During a half-life one half of the polonium atoms will have decayed. Therefore 2 mg of polonium would emit 5.80×10^{18} alpha-particles before it decayed completely.

Therefore

$$\text{number of moles in 2 mg} = \frac{2 \times 10^{-3}}{210} = 9.52 \times 10^{-6}$$

Therefore one mole contains

$$\frac{5.80 \times 10^{18}}{9.52 \times 10^{-6}} = 6.09 \times 10^{23}\ \text{particles}$$

a good approximation to the Avogadro constant.

The structure of solids

In a liquid or a gas the atoms and/or molecules are relatively free and can move round at will. In solids, however, they are almost completely lacking mobility; all they can do is to vibrate about a mean position when energy is added to the solid. This lack of mobility gives a solid its most characteristic property – that of retaining whatever shape it is given.

The way in which a solid behaves depends on its internal structure and there are three main types of solid:

(*a*) crystalline solids such as sugar,
(*b*) amorphous solids such as glass,
(*c*) polymeric solids such as rubber.

We will consider some of the properties of these types of solid in more detail.

(*a*) Crystalline solids

A **crystalline** solid is one where the internal structure is regular in nature, the atoms within it being set in well-defined patterns. Some crystals are **isotropic** – that is, their physical properties are the same in whichever direction they are measured, while others are **anisotropic** – their properties are different in different directions.

Metals are generally **polycrystalline** materials, being composed of a large number of small crystals or grains aligned in a variety of different directions.

Figure 18.1 shows the structures of the four most common types of crystal (for the moment we will assume that they are perfect and contain no impurities or dislocations). The four types are listed below together with one example of each:

(i) face-centred cube – sodium chloride,
(ii) hexagonal close-packed – zinc,
(iii) body-centred cube – potassium,
(iv) tetrahedral – silicon.

The characteristics of each structure can be investigated using the techniques of X-ray diffraction mentioned on page 436. In general, if the solid exhibits a regular structure as shown by the first three crystalline states mentioned the X-ray diffraction pattern will show a series of dots. If it is irregular, however, as in graphite in which the layers are free to slide one over the other, a series of rings will result. (This can also be seen by the electron diffraction through graphite – see page 462).

The face-centred cube and the hexagonal close-packed crystals are the most closely packed structures, and 60 per cent of all metals exist in one or other of these forms.

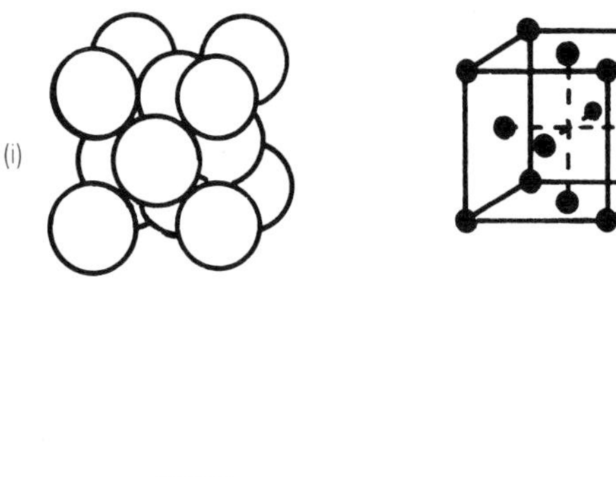

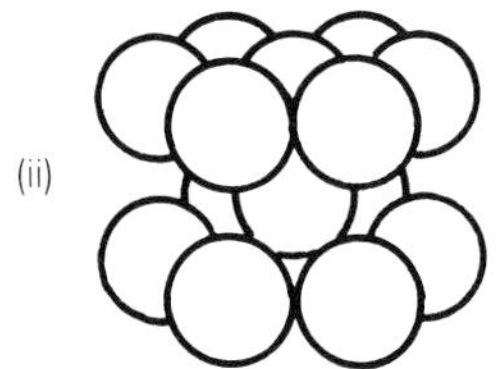

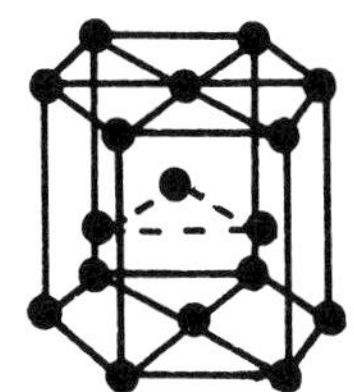

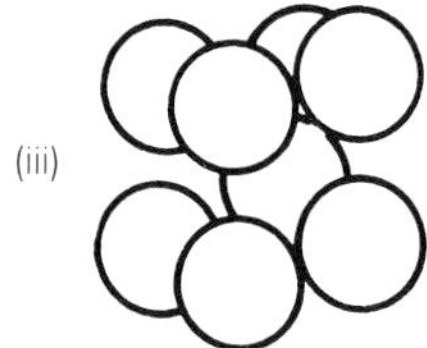

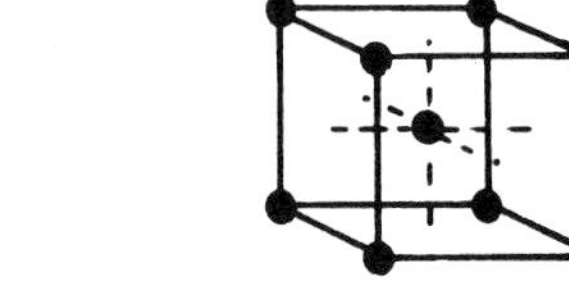

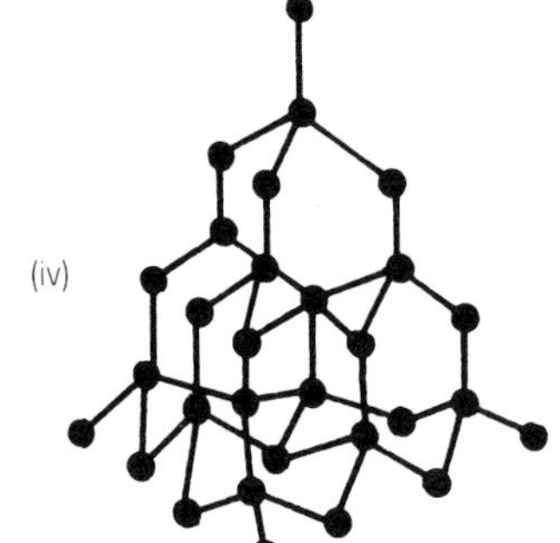

Figure 18.1

Bubble rafts

A very useful two-dimensional model of the three-dimensional crystal can be made with a bubble raft. The basic apparatus is shown in Figure 18.2(*a*).

A Petri dish is partly filled with a bubble solution of 1 part 'Teepol', 8 parts glycerol and 32 parts water by volume. Using the 25-gauge hypodermic syringe connected to the gas tap a raft of bubbles may be blown. The appearance will be similar to that shown in Figure 18.2(*b*). You will notice how all the bubbles pack together just like atoms in a crystal. The surface tension (see page 102) between the bubbles pulls them together, and the pressure inside them prevents them from getting too close.

These bubble rafts behave like real solids: if they are compressed slightly they will return to their original state but if too great a force is applied they will rupture, or one plane of bubbles will slide past another.

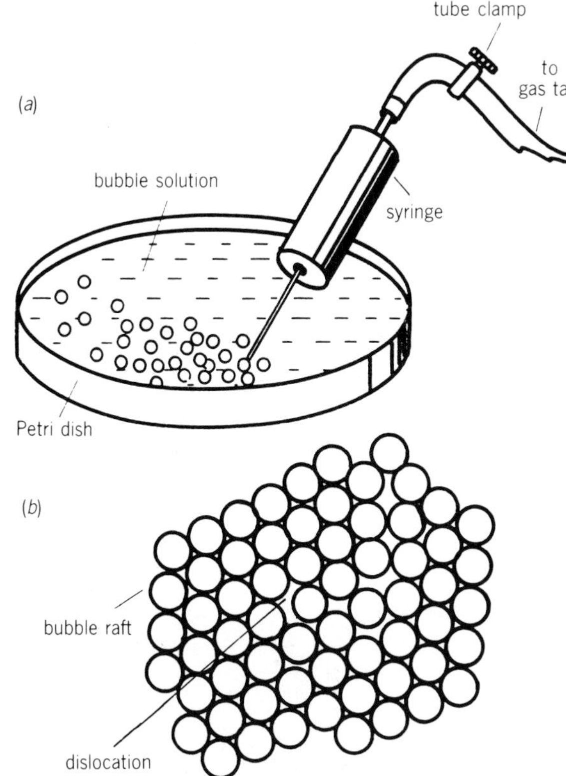

Figure 18.2

Very rarely will a perfect raft of bubbles be formed; more usually, large bubbles or missing bubbles will show as discontinuities – a model of **dislocations** in a three-dimensional crystal. Figure 18.3(*a*) to (*c*) illustrate the formation of a dislocation in a crystal. They also illustrate how the dislocation may move through the solid as one crystal plane slides over the other.

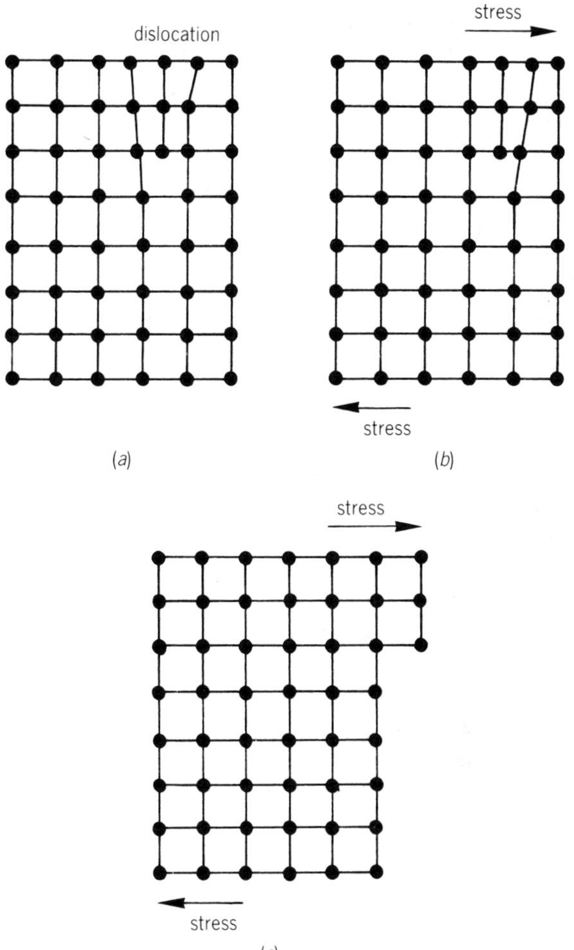

Figure 18.3

(*b*) Amorphous solids

An amorphous solid exhibits no regular internal structure; glass and soot are examples. In a way such a solid is like an instantaneous snapshot of a liquid, although one with an enormously great viscosity.

(*c*) Polymeric solids

In these solids the molecules form long chains which may contain anything between 1000 and 10 000 molecules. Many are natural organic materials such as plant constituents but there are many synthetic polymers, one example being polythene. The precise properties of the polymer depend on just how tightly these chains of molecules are bound together. They may be tangled together in a haphazard way or lie side by side; any cross-chainlinking will enormously increase the strength of the material – the vulcanising of rubber, for example, eventually produces the hard material ebonite: this is the result of cross-chainlinking by sulphur atoms. Below a critical temperature polymers behave much like glass (but with a greater degree of ductility) but above it they are more rubber-like. Cooling rubber in liquid nitrogen strikingly illustrates this change of properties (see page 112).

19 · Surface tension

The properties of a liquid surface give very good evidence for the existence of molecules and tell us quite a lot about the behaviour of these molecules.

The free surface of a liquid can show many interesting properties due to a phenomenon known as **surface tension.** Surface tension explains why liquid drops are spherical (in the absence of a gravitational field), why water rises up a capillary tube, why the insects called pond-skaters can walk on water, why your waterproof tent will not let in rain, why small pieces of camphor behave erratically when dropped on water and why the bristles of a paint brush cling together when it is lifted out of water. The motion of ripples on a water surface is also governed by surface tension.

Surface tension is known to be due to intermolecular attractions in the liquid surface and these forces produce a skin effect on the surface. The forces between individual pairs of molecules are very small, and so in a definition of the surface tension we consider the effect of a large number of molecules in a line in the surface.

Consider a line of unit length drawn in the surface of the liquid and think of the forces acting on the molecules in that line. Clearly the forces will act in all directions in the surface but we will consider only those components of force acting at right angles to the line. The force on the whole line is the sum of all the forces on the individual molecules (see Figure 19.1). Notice that any given molecule is in equilibrium due to equal and opposite forces acting on it.

We define the **coefficient of surface tension** of the liquid as follows:

> The coefficient of surface tension of a liquid is the force acting in the surface of the liquid and at right angles to a line of unit length drawn in the surface of the liquid.

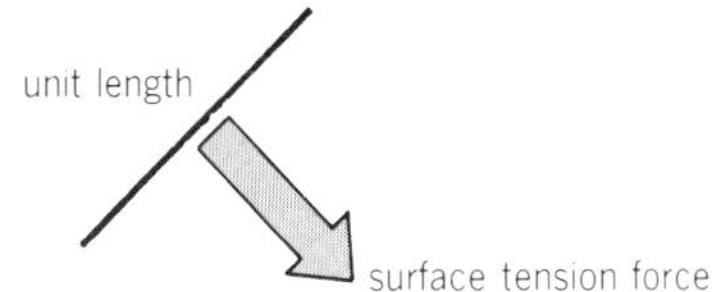

Figure 19.1

The units for surface tension are therefore newtons per metre ($N\ m^{-1}$) and the dimensions are ML^0T^{-2}. The following table gives the surface tensions of some common liquids.

Liquid	*Surface tension* $/N\ m^{-1} \times 10^{-3}$	*Liquid*	*Surface tension* $/N\ m^{-1} \times 10^{-3}$
Methylated spirits	22.6	Mercury	472
Glycerol	63.4	Olive oil	32
Water	72.7	Ether	17
Benzene	28.9	Gold	1102

The surface tension of a liquid decreases with increase in temperature and vanishes at the critical temperature. All values given in the table are for temperatures of 20 °C, except that for gold which is for 1130 °C.

1 Explain the following observations in terms of surface tension:

(*a*) A pond-skater can walk on water but a person cannot.

(*b*) A wet tent will let in water if the inside is touched.

(*c*) Water will rise up the capillaries inside a plant stem (surface tension only partly explains this effect, however).

(*d*) A needle may be made to float on water.

(*e*) A small piece of soap fixed to the back of a piece of cardboard that is floating on water will cause the cardboard to move over the water surface.

(*f*) Lead shot is made by pouring a molten stream of lead from a tall tower.

An application of surface tension (ZEFA)

Surface energy

The molecules exert an attraction on each other, and therefore when a liquid surface such as a soap film is stretched the surface gains potential energy since the molecules are being separated from each other. All free liquid surfaces are said to possess energy.

Consider a soap film (Figure 19.2). If the film is bounded by a movable wire at the right-hand edge, then the molecules along that edge will experience a surface tension force acting only towards the left. To prevent the film from contracting an equal and opposite force must be applied.

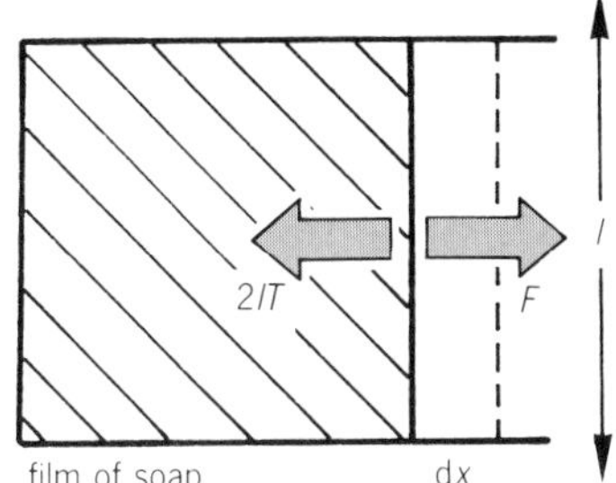

Figure 19.2

If the wire has a length l, then this force is $2lT$ where T is the surface tension of the liquid. Notice the 2 in this formula. This must be included because the film has *two sides*, and therefore the surface tension acts on both sides of it and we have to maintain equilibrium on both these two sides.

If the wire is moved a distance dx to the right then the work done is $2lTdx$, and this is equal to the energy gained by the surface. However, $2ldx$ is the increase in the surface area of the film and therefore the energy gained is equal to the surface tension multiplied by the increase in surface area. This provides an alternative definition for the surface tension, namely:

Surface tension is the energy per unit area of a free liquid surface.

One important difference between the behaviour of a liquid surface or soap film and that of an elastic sheet is that the tension of the film is constant while that of the elastic sheet increases with increasing area.

Any liquid surface will try to exist in the lowest state of potential energy that it can; this explains the spherical shape of liquid drops, the sphere having the minimum surface area for a given volume. It also explains the way in which soap films can be used to solve such mathematical problems as finding the shortest series of roads that could connect a number of towns.

The energy of a liquid surface can be explained in terms of the forces of attraction between the molecules. The molecules in the liquid surface are attracted only to molecules at their sides and below, while molecules within the body of the liquid are attracted to liquid molecules all around. To bring a molecule from the body of the liquid to the surface these forces have to be opposed and therefore net work must be done on the molecule. Consequently the molecules at the surface have a greater potential energy than those beneath it. A molecule in the surface would need further energy to remove it to infinity against the attraction of the liquid – this is provided in evaporation.

2 A circular ring of thin wire of mean radius 2 cm is suspended horizontally by a thread passing through the 5 cm mark on a metre ruler pivoted at its centre, and the ring is balanced by a 5 g mass suspended from the 70 cm mark. A beaker of liquid is then placed so that the ring just touches the liquid surface when the ring is horizontal. If the 5 g mass is moved to the 80 cm mark the ring just parts from the surface.

Find the surface tension of the liquid.

The theoretical spherical shape of droplets is often distorted by gravitational effects; in practice, droplets show a flattened shape. Drops of oil in an alcohol–water mixture of the same density show true spherical shapes, however.

Student investigation

Take a kitchen sieve and immerse it in molten candle wax. Remove it quickly, shaking off excess wax, so that the wires of the sieve get a thin coating of wax.

Now pour some water into it. Explain what happens.

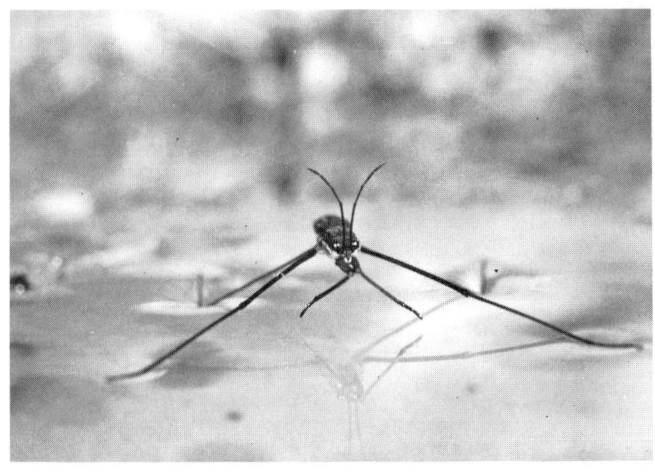

Pond skaters rely on surface tension to enable them to move across the surface of the water and catch their prey (Science Photo Library)

The angle of contact

When a liquid surface meets a solid surface the angle (ϕ) between the two surfaces is important.

This angle is known as the **angle of contact**, and its size determines whether the liquid will spread over the surface or whether it will form droplets on it. If ϕ is less than 90° the liquid will spread, while if it is greater than 90° it will form droplets (Figure 19.3). This effect can be seen clearly with water on glass. For a clean glass–water boundary the angle of contact is nearly zero but this increases to well over 90° if the surface is waxed.

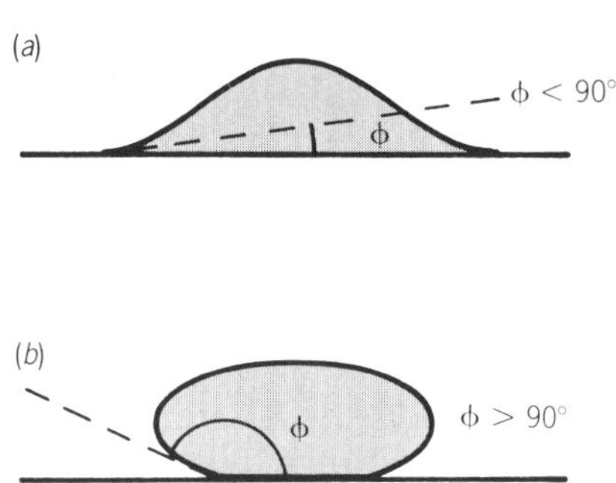

Figure 19.3

In fact a surface will be wetted by water if the angle of contact is less than 90°, and so waterproofing is designed to produce this. Addition of soap to water will reduce the angle of contact and is therefore useful in washing!

Student investigation

Using the apparatus shown in Figure 19.4, investigate the effect on the angle of contact between water and glass when measured amounts of concentrated soap solution are added to it. The microscope slide should be rotated until the liquid meets the glass at a zero angle.

If possible the angle of contact for different surfaces should be studied, by replacing the microscope slide with other materials.

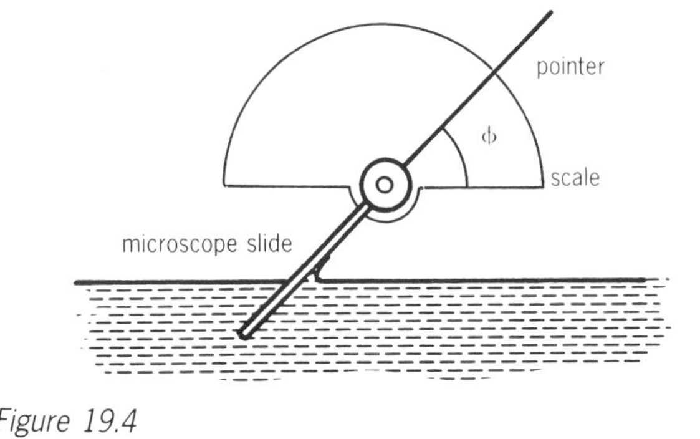

Figure 19.4

Molecular consideration of surface tension

You can easily understand why the surface of a liquid behaves like a skin by considering Figure 19.5. A molecule such as A within the body of the liquid will experience a force of attraction due to all other molecules within a small distance of A: this is called the **sphere of molecular activity**. The resultant force on A is therefore zero. However, a molecule such as B very close to the surface will experience a net inward force; so too will a molecule such as C that is actually *in* the surface.

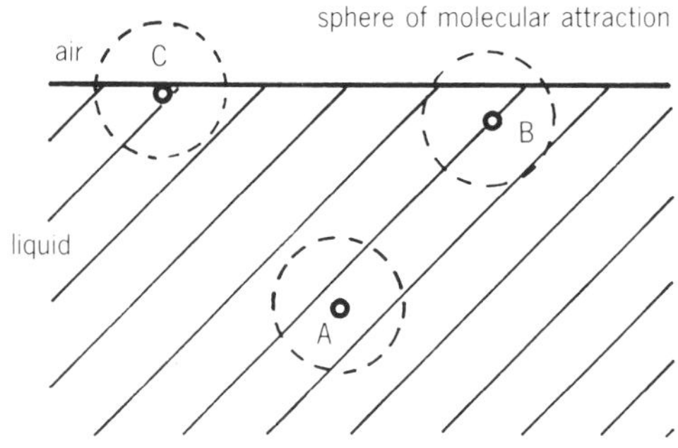

Figure 19.5

The molecules cannot move downwards because there are molecules below them but they do resist being separated from each other, thus giving the skin effect. To call it an elastic skin is misleading, since the surface tension does not vary with the size of the surface as it would in the case of an elastic sheet.

Molecular explanation of the shape of liquid surfaces

Figure 19.6 shows a section of a liquid surface close to the walls of a container. A liquid molecule at P will experience a force downwards due to gravitational

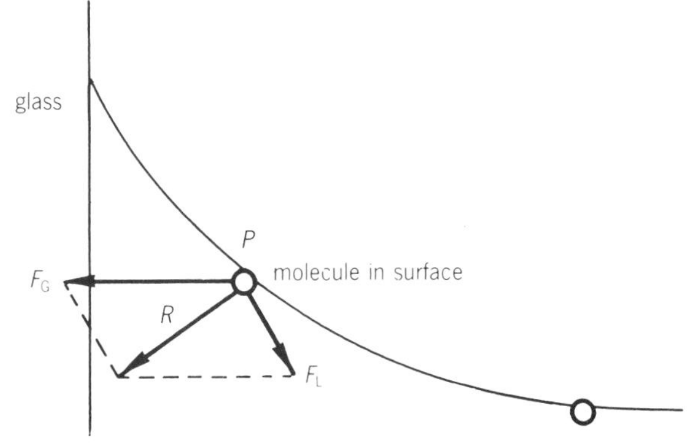

Figure 19.6

attraction, a force F_L towards the centre of the liquid due to the attractive force of the other liquid molecules and a horizontal force F_G due to the attraction of the molecules of the material of the walls.

The resultant force R shows that in this case the molecules will be drawn towards the walls, 'piling up' there to give a concave liquid surface. In the case of mercury the intermolecular attraction between liquid molecules is greater, and a convex surface results.

The excess pressure within a bubble

The fact that air has to be blown into a drop of soap solution to make a bubble should suggest that the pressure within the bubble is greater than that outside. This is in fact the case: this excess pressure creates a force that is just balanced by the inward pull of the soap film of the bubble.

Consider a soap bubble of radius r as shown in Figure 19.7. Let the external pressure be P_0 and the internal pressure P_1.

The excess pressure P within the bubble is therefore $P_1 - P_0$.

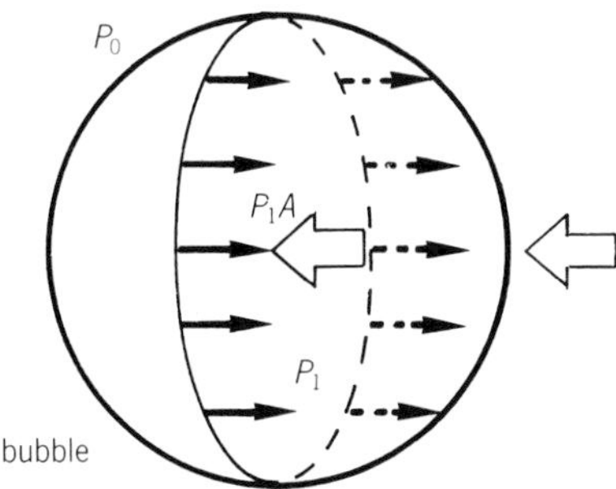

Figure 19.7

Consider the left-hand half of the bubble. The force acting from right to left due to the internal excess pressure can be shown to be PA, where A is the area of a section through the centre of the bubble. If the bubble is in equilibrium this force is balanced by a force due to surface tension acting from left to right. This force is $2 \times 2\pi rT$ (the factor of 2 is necessary because the soap film has two sides) where T is the coefficient of surface tension of the soap film. Therefore

$$2 \times 2\pi rT = PA = P\pi r^2$$

giving

$$P = \frac{4T}{r}$$

A bubble of air within a liquid has only one liquid–air surface and the excess pressure within such a bubble is simply

$$P = \frac{2T}{r}$$

Both these formulae show that the excess pressure within a small bubble is greater than that within a larger bubble.

Example

Calculate the excess pressure within a bubble of air of radius 0.1 mm in water.

$$\text{Excess pressure} = \frac{2T}{r} = \frac{2 \times 72.7 \times 10^{-3}}{10^{-4}} = 1454 \text{ Pa.}$$

If this bubble had been formed 10 cm below the water surface on a day when the atmospheric pressure was 1.013×10^5 Pa the total pressure within the bubble would have been $(1.013 \times 10^5) + (0.1 \times 1000 \times 10) + 1454 = 1.039 \times 10^5$ Pa.

3 A soap bubble of radius 8 cm is blown on the end of a tube which is connected to a U-tube containing water.

(*a*) What difference in water levels would be produced?

(*b*) If another soap bubble is now allowed to make contact with the first so that the radius of curvature of the common surface is 2 cm, calculate the radius of the second bubble.

(Surface tension of soap solution = 3.5×10^{-2} N m^{-1}; density of water = 1000 kg m^{-3}.)

4 (*a*) What is the excess pressure inside a spherical soap bubble of radius 5 cm if the surface tension of the soap film is 3.5×10^{-2} N m^{-1}?

(*b*) What is the work done in blowing the bubble?

5 A tube has a soap bubble blown on each end as shown in Figure 19.8. Describe and explain what happens when the tap is opened.

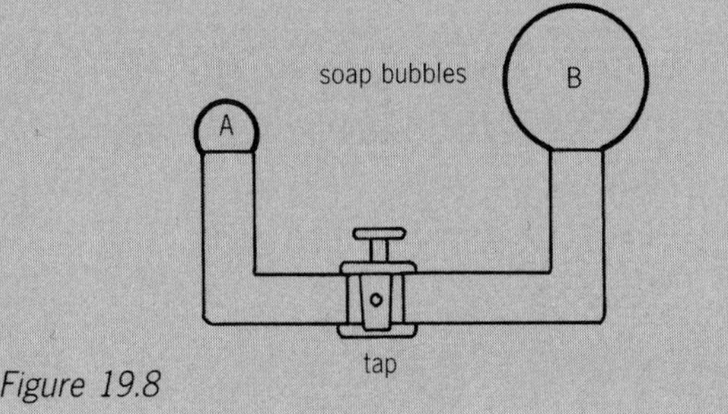

Figure 19.8

Capillary action

The rise of a column of liquid within a fine capillary tube is also due to surface tension. Capillary action causes liquid to soak upwards through a piece of blotting paper and it also partly explains the rise of water through the capillaries in the stems of plants. (In this last case osmotic pressure accounts for a large part of the rise.)

There are two alternative proofs for the formula for capillary rise and we will consider Figure 19.9(*a*) first.

Let the radius of the glass capillary tube be r, the coefficient of surface tension of the liquid be T, the density of the liquid be ρ, the angle of contact between the liquid and the walls of the tube be θ and the height to which the liquid rises in the tube be h. Consider the circumference of the liquid surface where it meets the glass.

Along this line the vertical component of the surface tension force will be $2\pi r \cos\theta\, T$.

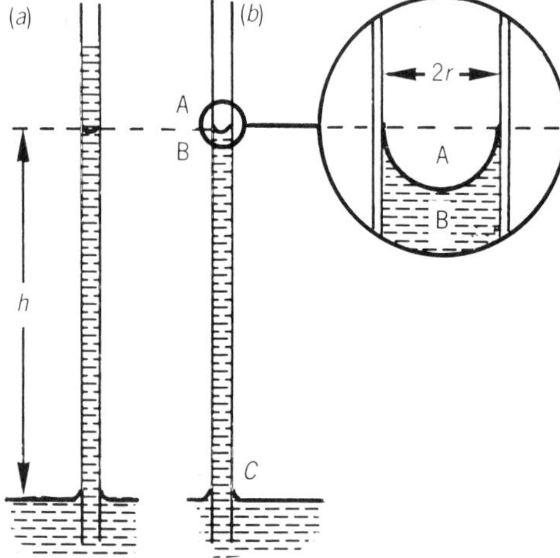

Figure 19.9

This will draw the liquid up the tube until this force is just balanced by the downward force due to the column of liquid of height h, that is, $\pi r^2 \rho g h$. Therefore at equilibrium:

$$2\pi r \cos\theta\, T = \pi r^2 \rho g h$$

which gives

$$h = \frac{2T\cos\theta}{r\rho g}$$

For a clean water–glass surface $\theta = 0$ and therefore $h = 2T/r\rho g$.

For the alternative proof consider Figure 19.9(*b*). We will assume that if the radius of the tube is small the shape of the liquid surface is very nearly hemispherical.

The pressure at A must be atmospheric, but since A is within a hemispherical surface the pressure at B must be less than A by an amount $2T/r$. The pressure at C is also atmospheric but it is greater than the pressure at B by the hydrostatic pressure $h\rho g$. Therefore at equilibrium we have $h = 2T/r\rho g$, as above.

Both these methods show that the rise is greater in small tubes and for zero angles of contact. In fact when the coefficient of surface tension is measured by capillary rise in the laboratory the values obtained are nearly always too small because of the difficulty of getting perfectly clean apparatus. The angle of contact can rarely be made zero.

With a mercury–glass surface the angle of contact is $>90°$ and therefore $\cos\theta$ is negative. This means that the mercury level is not raised but *depressed* below the level of the surrounding liquid.

Example

Calculate the radius of a capillary tube if water rises to a height of 12.5 cm within it, assuming the angle of contact between the water and glass to be 0°.

$$\text{Radius of tube} = \frac{2 \times 72.7 \times 10^{-3}}{0.125 \times 1000 \times 10} = 0.11 \text{ mm.}$$

6 A glass capillary tube with a uniform internal diameter is placed vertically with one end dipping into paraffin, for which the surface tension is 2.7×10^{-2} N m^{-1}, the angle of contact 26° and the density 865 kg m^{-3}.

If the paraffin rises 4.5 cm up the tube, what is the diameter of the tube?

7 A U-tube which has its ends open and its limbs vertical contains a liquid of surface tension 2.4×10^{-2} N m^{-1} and density 800 kg m^{-3}, the angle of contact between the tube and the liquid being 20°. The internal diameter of one limb is 0.4 mm and the other 0.2 mm.

Calculate the difference in the liquid levels in the two limbs.

Forces between two plates

If two flat plates are placed in contact with a thin film of water between them it is found difficult to pull the two apart. This is due to the reduced pressure within the water film, since the edges will be hemispherical (Figure 19.10).

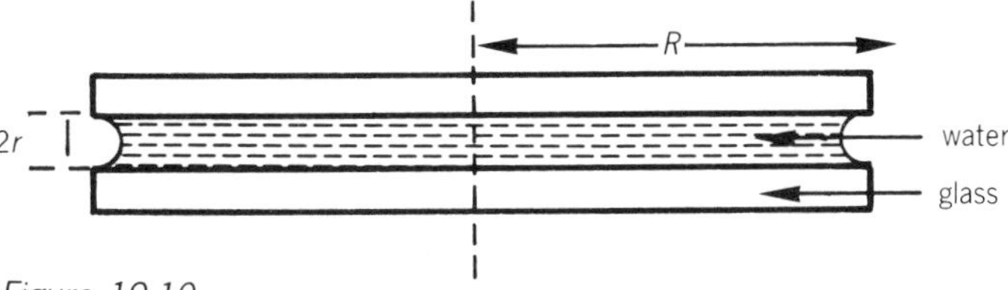

Figure 19.10

Since the film is convex in one direction and concave in the other the pressure difference (ΔP) is given by:

$$\Delta P = T(1/r - 1/R)$$

and the force (F) required to separate two plates of area A is given by

$$F = AT(1/r - 1/R)$$

For example, for two circular plates of radius 5 cm with a 0.01 mm thick film of water between them we have:

$$F = \pi(5 \times 10^{-2})^2 \times 72.7 \times 10^{-3} \times 199\,980$$
$$= 110\ \text{N}$$

Variation of surface tension with temperature

As might be expected, the coefficient of surface tension decreases with increasing temperature. It becomes zero at the critical temperature (see page 256).
The variation of surface tension with temperature can be studied by Jaeger's method using the apparatus shown in Figure 19.11.

Water is allowed to drip slowly into the large flask, so forcing bubbles of air out of the capillary tube which dips into a beaker of water. The lower end of the capillary tube is a depth h below the water surface. It can be shown that the bubble will break free from the end of the tube when its radius is equal to the internal radius of the tube.

Using a manometer the total pressure within the apparatus may be found; this is equal to the hydrostatic pressure ($h_1\rho_1 g$) plus the excess pressure within the air bubble due to the surface tension of the water. The total pressure is given by the equation:

$$h_2\rho_2 g = h_1\rho_1 g + \frac{2T}{r}$$

where ρ_1 is the density of water, ρ_2 the density of the liquid in the manometer, r the radius of the capillary tube and h_2 the difference in levels within the manometer. The surface tension T can therefore be found.

Heating the water enables the value of T to be determined at a range of temperatures.

Student investigation

Using the above apparatus, investigate the effect on the surface tension of the liquid of adding known amounts of methylated spirits to the water. Plot a graph of surface tension against the concentration of the water–meths mixture.

8 A small drop of water is placed between two glass plates and the plates are then squeezed together until the drop forms a thin circular film. If the radius of the film is 0.03 m and its thickness 0.10 mm, calculate the force required at right angles to the glass plates to pull them apart. (Surface tension of water = 7.2×10^{-2} N m^{-1})

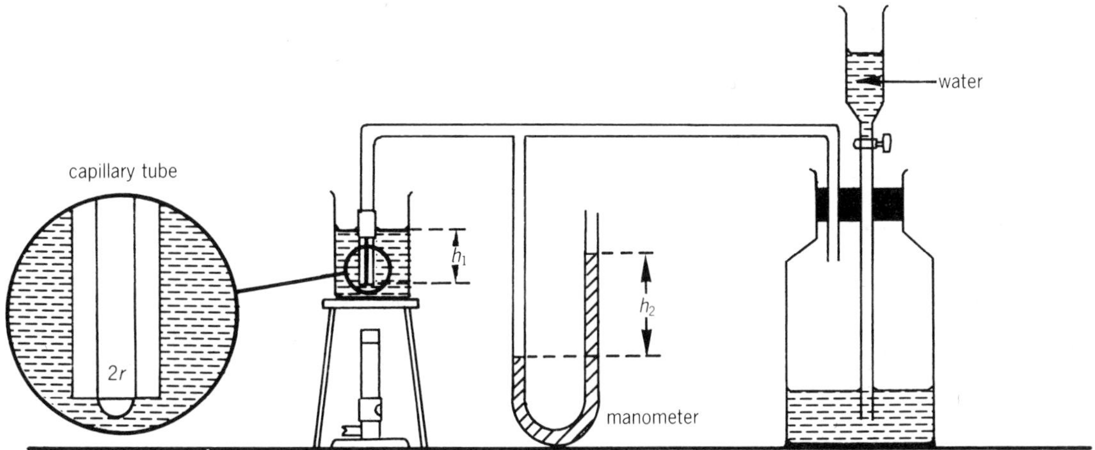

Figure 19.11

20 · Elasticity

When a force acts on a body one of the things it can do is to change the shape or size of the body. This will change the relative positions of the molecules within the body and the property of the material that governs such changes is called the **elasticity** of the body.

Clearly elasticity is of vital importance in our lives, from the elastic in our clothes to the strength of the cables in a suspension bridge!

Many materials behave quite normally when subjected to forces – a copper wire will stretch, a steel hacksaw blade will bend and so on. But there are some oddities. A squash ball has different elastic properties when it is hot, and although glass will shatter if it is given a sudden blow a glass fibre can be made to bend and stretch by the gentle application of a force. Rubber stretches at room temperature but shatters when cooled to the temperature of liquid nitrogen and hit with a hammer. You can buy a substance in shops called 'Silly putty' which will creep (stretch under its own weight) if hung up, will bounce like a rubber ball if dropped on the ground, behave like Plasticine under medium stress but shatter like glass if given a sharp blow with a hammer. A plastic straw will bend if pressed on to a potato but can be driven right through it if hit sharply.

Student investigation

Knowledge of the elastic properties of materials is of vital importance in bridge design. Practical bridges are difficult to analyse but the following investigations will give you some idea of the factors involved.

For both arrangements of the beam illustrated in Figure 20.1, record the depression y for *either* constant length and varying load *or* constant load and varying length.

Plot suitable graphs to enable you to suggest a formula for the depression of each arrangement.

A further investigation might be to use the arrangement in Figure 20.1(*a*) but to measure the depression for the load at different points along the beam.

Design and build a bridge from balsa wood to span a 2 m gap.

The carriageway must be 150 mm wide, no thicker than 1.5 mm and with a minimum headroom of 90 mm. It may be reinforced by wires and must be capable of supporting a load of 150 N m^{-1}. The centre 500 mm of the bridge must be capable of being raised. The ground pressure at the supports must not be greater than 7×10^3 N m^{-2}, and no member must have a cross-sectional area greater than 50 mm^2.

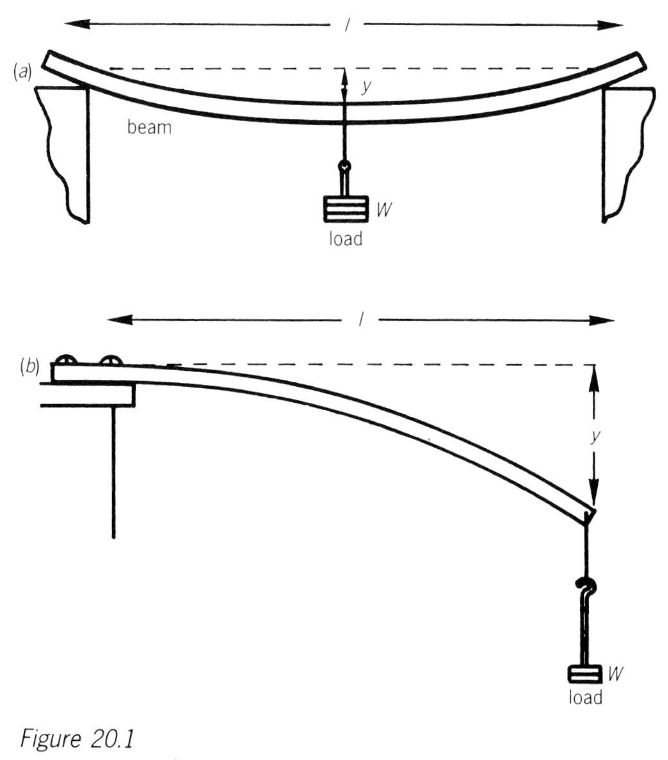

Figure 20.1

Student investigation

How elastic are stretchy socks or tights?

As was stated on page 98 the elastic properties of a solid, in particular a metallic one, depend on the variation in the forces between the molecules in that solid. The following two theoretical investigations are concerned with this property.

Student investigation

Figures 20.2 and 20.3 represent the forces between a pair of molecules and their potential energy.

Use Figure 20.2 to plot a second graph that shows the variation of the *resultant* force between these molecules. Use this graph to determine

(*a*) the equilibrium separation of these two molecules, and

(*b*) the separation when the intermolecular force is a maximum.

(*c*) What do these two results mean?

Use Figure 20.3 to find

(*d*) the energy required to squeeze the molecules together from a separation of 1.0 molecular diameter to a separation of 0.9 molecular diameter, and

(*e*) the energy required to separate the molecules from each other.

(*f*) If the pair of molecules is initially at their equilibrium separation and is given 3.0 eV of energy, calculate their new separation. [L]

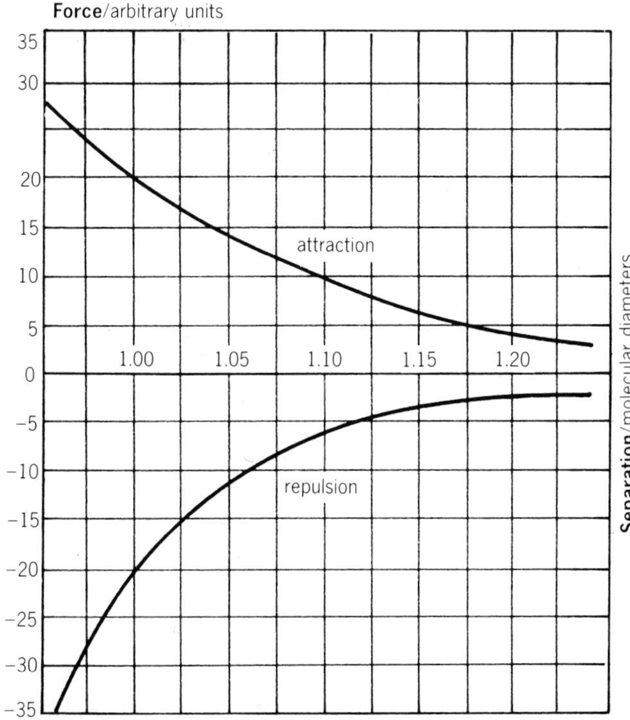

Figure 20.2

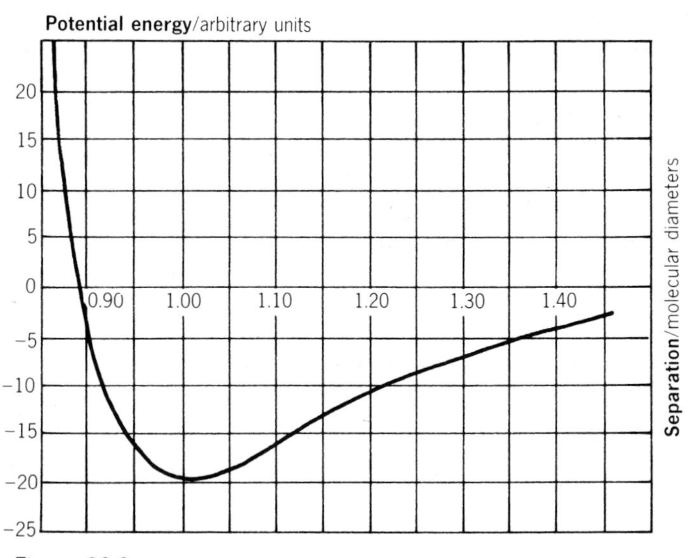

Figure 20.3

Student investigation

Figure 20.4 shows how the binding energy E of an ion pair depends upon the separation r of the ions. Make a copy of the graph.

(*a*) Write down the value of r when E is a minimum

(*b*) Draw tangents to the curve at points where $r = 28$, 35, 40, 50 and 70 nm. Measure the slope F of the curve at each of these points and present your results in a table.

(*c*) Plot a graph of F (y-axis) against r (x-axis). This shows how the force between the ions depends on their separation.

(*d*) For values of r greater than 40 nm, E and r are related by the equation

$$-E = ar^n$$

where a and n are constants.

The value of n can be found by plotting an appropriate graph. State the quantities that you would plot, draw up a table of values, plot the graph and determine the value of n. [AEB 1983]

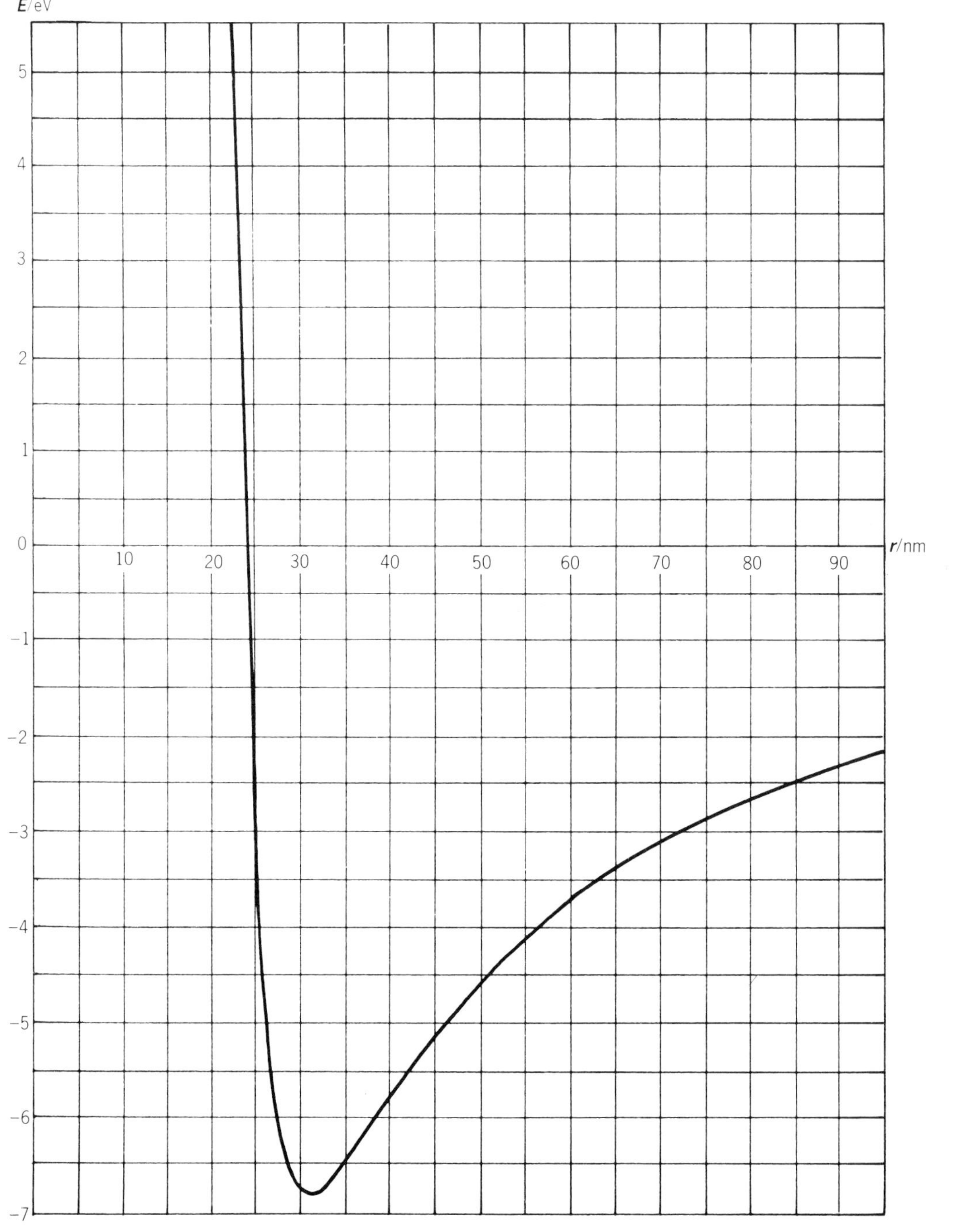

Figure 20.4

Stress and strain

We define the **stress** on a body as a measure of the cause of the deformation caused by a force:

$$\text{stress} = \frac{\text{force}}{\text{area}}$$

so stress has units N m^{-2} or Pa.

The maximum stress that a material can stand without fracture is called the **breaking stress** of the material. We will consider two types of breaking stress:

(*a*) compressive breaking stress – the maximum squashing stress before fracture, and

(*b*) tensile breaking stress – the maximum stretching stress before fracture.

An example of some compressive and tensile breaking stresses are given in the following table.

	Compressive breaking stress /N m^{-2}	*Tensile breaking stress /N m^{-2}*
Steel	552×10^6	$400–800 \times 10^6$
Rubber		2.1×10^6
Granite	145×10^6	4.8×10^6
Concrete	21×10^6	2.1×10^6
Oak	59×10^6	117×10^6
Porcelain	552×10^6	55×10^6
Bone (compact)	170×10^6	120×10^6
Nylon		70×10^6
Glass		$3.5–150 \times 10^6$
Carbon fibre		1000×10^6
Cast iron		$30–140 \times 10^6$

Strain is a measure of the extent of the deformation:

$$\text{strain} = \frac{\text{change in size}}{\text{original size}}$$

so strain is a pure number with no units.

The variation of stress and strain

If a ductile material such as copper is stretched until it breaks and its stress and strain measured and plotted, a graph like that in Figure 20.5 may be obtained.

There are a number of important points about such a graph:

(*a*) OP is a straight line – in this region Hooke's law (discussed below) is obeyed.

(*b*) P is the **limit of proportionality** – up to P strain ∝ stress.

(*c*) E is the **elastic limit** – up to E, if the load is removed the material will return to its original length (although the stress may not be proportional to the strain up to this point).

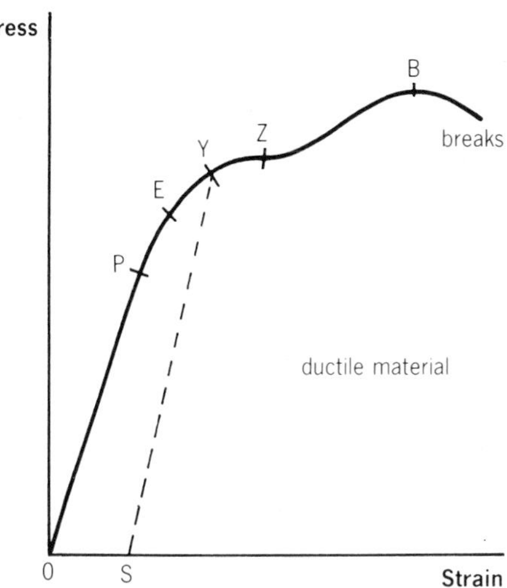

Figure 20.5

(*d*) Y is the **yield point** – between E and Y the material becomes **plastic**, that is, if the load is removed the material will contract but all the extension is not recoverable. The material follows the dotted line YS on the graph during contraction and the remaining extension is known as a **permanent set.**

(*e*) Z – after this point none of the extension is recoverable.

(*f*) B – this is the breaking stress beyond which the material will break.

A material like copper is known as **ductile** – that is, it will flow, and can be drawn out into a wire without fracture. Materials such as glass that can be extended but do not show plastic deformation and will easily fracture are known as **brittle** materials. A stress–strain curve for such a material is shown in Figure 20.6.

The stress–strain relationship for some common materials should now be investigated.

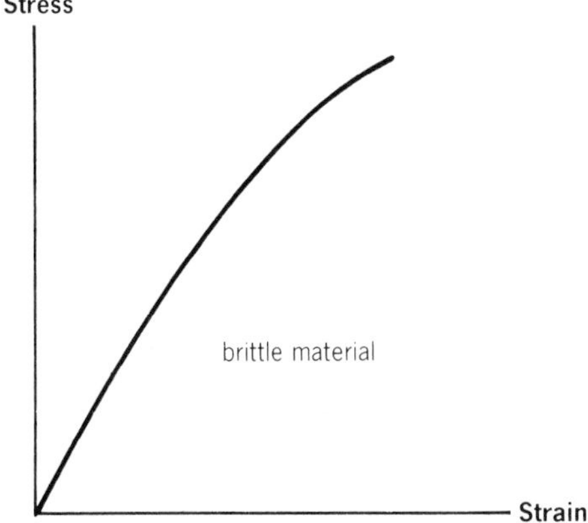

Figure 20.6

Elastic moduli

We need to define a property that will indicate how a specimen will behave when subjected to a given stress. We will call this property the **elastic modulus** of the material, and define it as:

$$\text{elastic modulus} = \frac{\text{stress}}{\text{strain}}$$

You can see that it must have the same dimensions as stress, that is, N m^{-2} or Pa.

There are three kinds of elastic modulus, each one corresponding to a different type of stress:

Modulus	*Nature of stress*	*Nature of strain*
Bulk modulus (K)	change of pressure	change of size but not shape
Shear modulus (G) (or rigidity modulus)	$\frac{\text{tangential force}}{\text{area}}$	change of shape but not size
Young modulus (E)	$\frac{\text{longitudinal force}}{\text{area}}$	change of shape and size

The bulk modulus refers to a change of volume with pressure, the shear modulus to a twisting and the Young modulus to a stretching or compression.

Some examples of the value of the different moduli are given below, in Pa.

	K	G	E
Typical metal	1×10^{11}	4×10^{10}	1×10^{11}
Water	2×10^{9}		
Gas at 10^5 Pa	1×10^{5}		

If you think about the values of the bulk modulus for water and a metal you should see why it is so painful to do a 'belly flop' in diving. The bulk modulus of water is only some 100 times less than that of a metal – and you wouldn't consider diving on to a sheet of steel!

Student investigation

Devise and carry out experiments to test the elastic properties of:

(*a*) a squash ball
(*b*) a cricket ball
(*c*) a table tennis ball
(*d*) a tennis ball
(*e*) a power ball
(*f*) a golf ball

The experiments should attempt to measure the strain produced for a given stress: this might be done statically by loading with weights or dynamically by dropping them. In the case of the squash ball, study how the temperature of the ball affects its elastic properties.

Student investigation

In the previous investigation the effects of temperature on a squash ball were considered. If your school has access to liquid nitrogen you should see how a rubber ball behaves after being immersed in this liquid at −192°C (81 K). If liquid nitrogen is unavailable carry out the following experiment as an alternative.

Take a thick elastic band and cool a section about 1 cm long with an aerosol freezer spray. Now stretch the band sharply and observe the widths of the warm and cold sections.

It has been stated that when an object is stretched it cools – can you verify this?

One exception is apparently our lips – kissing somebody will stretch your lips and therefore warm them up – do you think this is true?

Hooke's law

This law was proposed by Robert Hooke, the founder of the Royal Society, in 1676. He showed that **the extension of an elastic body is directly proportional to the force that produces it**, providing that the extension is small.

We can see that this is true by referring to the force–distance curve; since the line is nearly straight near the equilibrium position the force at this point is directly proportional to the extension.

In the region where Hooke's law is obeyed $F = -ke$ where e is the extension, and therefore if a molecule is displaced from its equilibrium position it will oscillate with s.h.m.

Student investigation

Draw out a piece of glass rod so that you have a piece as shown in Figure 20.7 – some 20 cm long, with a central section about 10 cm long and a diameter a little less than 1 mm. Carefully suspend weights from the centre and record the resulting depression.

Protect your eyes from flying glass.

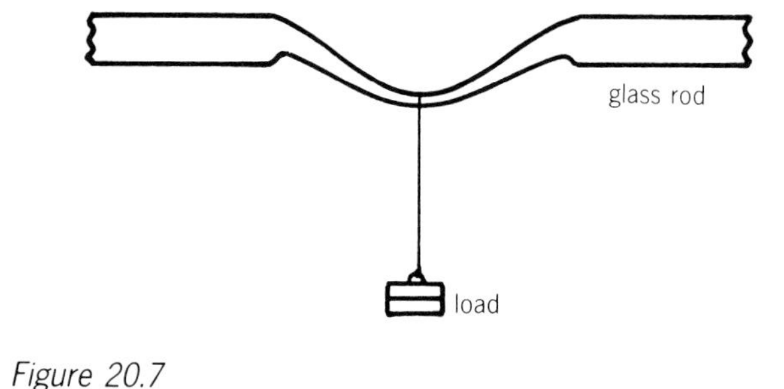

Figure 20.7

The Young modulus

We define the Young modulus (E) as:

$$E = \frac{\text{longitudinal stress}}{\text{longitudinal strain}}$$

Consider a wire as shown in Figure 20.8.

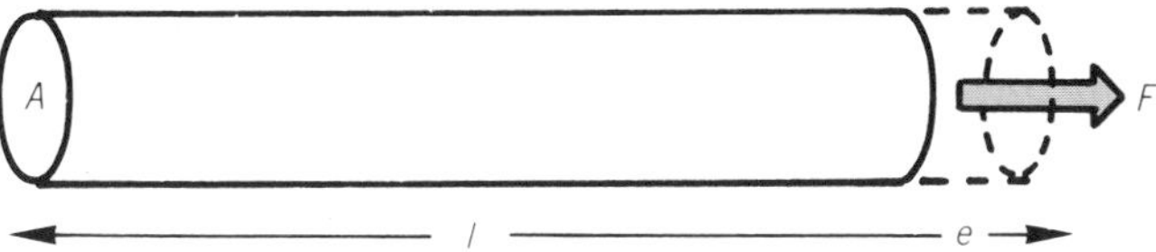

Figure 20.8

Let the original length be l and the cross-sectional area be A, and let a force F produce an extension e. Then

longitudinal (or tensile) stress = F/A
longitudinal (or tensile) strain = e/l

Therefore the Young modulus is given by the equation:

$$E = \frac{F/A}{e/l} = \frac{Fl}{eA}$$

The values of the Young modulus for some common materials are given in the table below.

Material	*Young modulus /GPa*	*Material*	*Young modulus /GPa*
Diamond	1200	Bone	18
Mild steel	210	Concrete	16.5
Copper	120	Beech wood	15
Cast iron	110	Oak	11
Aluminium	70	Plastic	2.0
Granite	50	Nylon	2.0
Lead	18	Rubber	0.02
Sandstone	6.3	Slate	110

(1 GPa = 10^9 Pa.)

Example

A steel wire 10 m long and with a cross-sectional area of 0.01 cm^2 is hung from a support and a mass of 5 kg is hung from its end. Calculate the new length of the wire. The Young modulus for steel = 210 GPa.

$$\text{Extension } (e) = \frac{Fl}{EA} = \frac{50 \times 10}{2.1 \times 10^{11} \times 1 \times 10^{-6}} = 2.38 \text{ mm}$$

$\therefore$ new length = 10.0024 m

Student investigation

Investigate the stretching of a length of fishing line (Figure 20.9), first when loads are applied gently and then when there is a sudden jerk (obtained by dropping the load) as you would have when a fish pulls sharply on the line. Compare the breaking stress in the two cases with the manufacturer's specifications. How does the fishing line compare with copper wire of the same original dimensions?

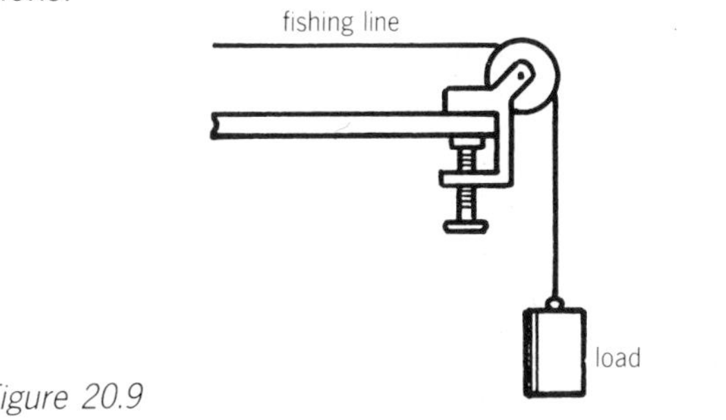

Figure 20.9

1 If the Young modulus for steel is 2.00×10^{11} N m^{-2}, calculate the work done in stretching a steel wire 100 cm in length and of cross-sectional area 0.030 cm^2 when a load of 100 N is slowly applied, the elastic limit not being exceeded.

2 A gymnast of mass 70 kg hangs by one arm from a high bar. If the gymnast's whole weight is assumed to be taken by the humerus bone (in the upper arm), calculate the stress in the humerus if it has a radius of 1.5 cm.

3 Find the maximum load that can be supported by a steel cable 1.5 cm in diameter without its elastic limit being exceeded when the load is:
(*a*) in air,
(*b*) immersed in water.

4 A hammer thrower swings a 7.25 kg hammer in a horizontal circle at one revolution per second. If the hammer wire is 1.20 m long, 1.5 mm in diameter and made of steel, calculate the extension produced in it. (The mass of the wire itself may be neglected.)

5 A copper wire 200 cm long and 1.22 mm in diameter is fixed horizontally between two supports 200 cm apart. Find the mass in grams of the load which, when suspended at the midpoint of the wire, produces a sag of 2 cm at that point. (The Young modulus for copper = 1.2×10^{11} N m^{-2}.)

6 The gravitational field strength at the surface of a certain neutron star is 1.34×10^{12} N kg^{-1}.
What would be the theoretical maximum height of a cylindrical granite column which could support its own weight without crushing when exposed to a field of this magnitude? (Density of granite = 2700 kg m^{-3}; crushing strength = 3.6×10^6 Pa.) [o]

Measurement of the Young modulus

The Young modulus may be measured for a material in the form of a wire using the apparatus shown in Figure 20.10.

Two identical wires are hung from a beam; a scale is fixed to one wire and a mass hung on the end to remove kinks in it. This wire is used as a reference standard.

The other wire has a small load placed on it to straighten it and a vernier scale which links with the scale on the reference wire.

The original length l of the test wire is measured and its diameter is found for various points along its length and an average diameter calculated. Hence its mean radius r can be found.

Loads are then placed gently on the wire and the extension of the wire found for each one. They should *not* be dropped as this would subject the wire to a sudden shock. After each reading the load should be removed to check that the wire returns to its original length, showing that its elastic limit has not been exceeded.

A graph is plotted of stress against strain and from this the value of the Young modulus may be found. The wires should be long and thin to give as large an extension as possible for a given load while retaining its elastic properties.

Two wires are used to eliminate errors due to changes of temperature and sagging of the beam.

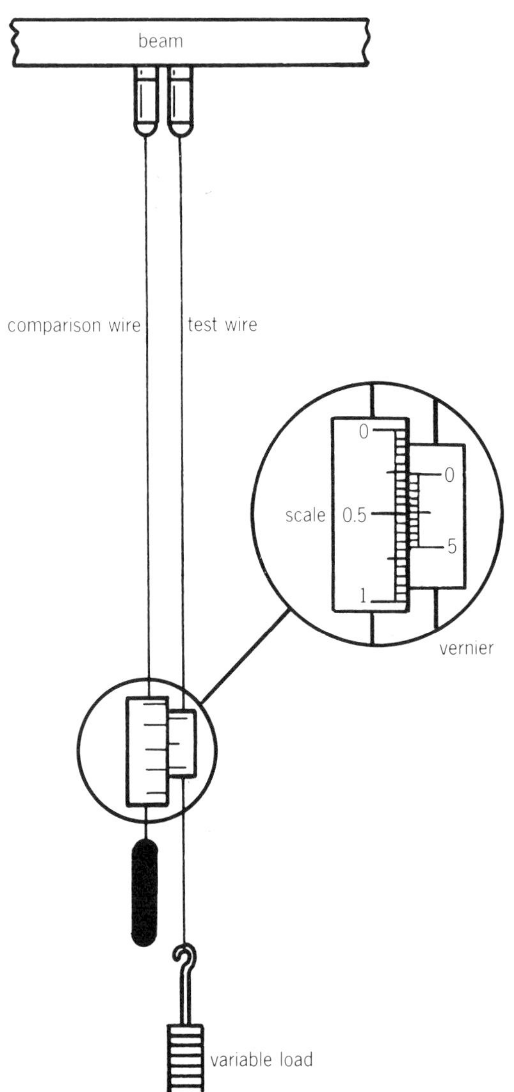

Figure 20.10

Student investigation

Much delicate equipment is transported around the country every day. Investigate the strength and protective capacity of (*a*) foam rubber, (*b*) polystyrene, (*c*) air bubbles in polythene.

Consider the connection between thickness and effectiveness and also the cost and waste of the packaging and how easily it is disposed of after use.

7 It has been calculated that during running the force on the hip joint is about five times the body weight. Estimate the compression of the femur during each running stride for a sprinter of mass 70 kg.

You may assume that the femur is 0.40 m long and has a mean diameter of 2.0 cm.

Student investigation

You will probably remember the classic experiment where a cast iron peg is broken by the large forces set up in a steel bar due to thermal expansion or compression (Figure 20.11).

Look up the breaking stress for an iron peg such as one used in the experiment (diameter 4 mm) and use it to estimate the mean temperature of the steel bar.

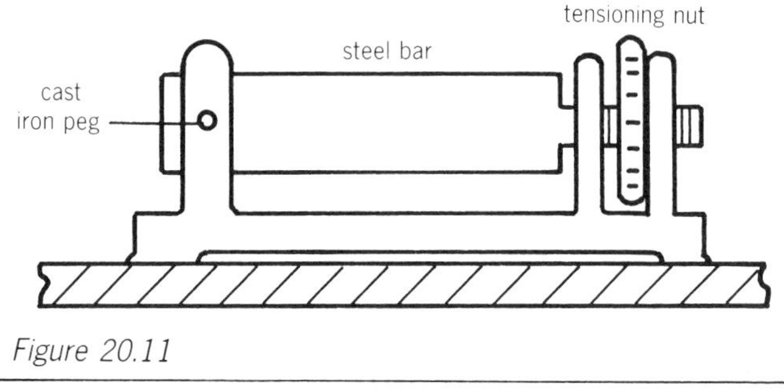

Figure 20.11

Force in a bar due to thermal expansion or compression

If a metal bar is heated it will expand, but if we prevent it from expanding then large forces will be set up within the bar. The force will be that which would be needed to compress the bar to its original length from the expanded position.

Consider the bar shown in Figure 20.12.

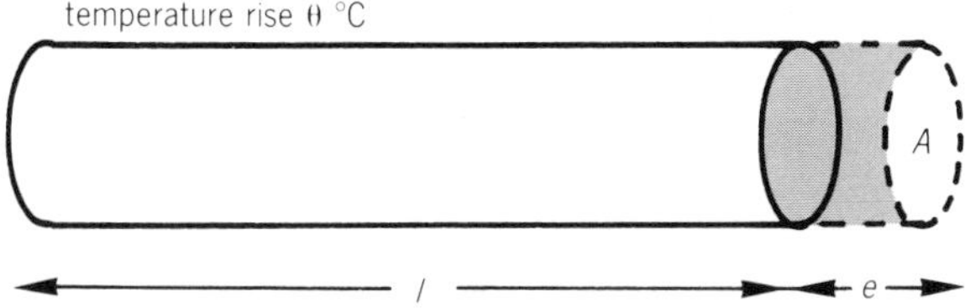

Figure 20.12

Let the linear expansivity of the material be α and the Young modulus be E. For a rise in temperature θ the bar will expand by an amount e, given by

$e = l\alpha\theta$ (see page 229)

but the extension produces a force in the wire given by

$$F = \frac{EeA}{l}$$

Therefore

$$l\alpha\theta = \frac{Fl}{EA} \quad \text{and so} \quad F = EA\alpha\theta$$

These forces can be very large, as is shown by the following example.

Example

A steel bar with a cross-sectional area of 2 cm^2 is heated, raising its temperature by 120 °C and prevented from expanding. Calculate the resulting force in the bar.

$$\text{Force } (F) = EA\alpha\theta = 2.1 \times 10^{11} \times 2 \times 10^{-4} \times 0.000\,012 \times 120 = 6.05 \times 10^4 \text{ N}$$

8 A steel tyre is heated and slipped on to a wheel of radius 40 cm, which it fits exactly at a temperature θ °C.

(*a*) What is the maximum value of θ if the tyre is not to be stretched beyond its elastic limit when it has cooled to air temperature (17 °C)?

(*b*) What will then be the tension in the tyre, assuming it to be 4 cm wide and 3 mm thick?

The elastic limit for steel occurs at a tension of 2.75×10^8 Pa. The wheel may be assumed to be at air temperature throughout and to be incompressible.

Elastic energy stored in a stretched wire

When a person jumps up and down on a trampoline it is clear that the bed of the trampoline stores energy when it is in a state of tension. This energy is converted to kinetic and potential energy of the jumper when the tension is removed.

Similarly, when a piece of elastic in a catapult is stretched energy is stored in it, and when the catapult is fired this energy is converted into the kinetic energy of the projectile.

These examples may be complex, but we can calculate the energy stored in a stretched wire as follows.

Let the wire be of unstretched length l and let a force F produce an extension e. (Assume that the elastic limit of the wire has not been exceeded and that no energy is lost as heat.)

The work done by F is equal to the energy gained by the wire. Therefore

$$\text{work done} = \text{average force} \times \text{extension} = \tfrac{1}{2}Fe$$

Substituting from the Young modulus formula gives

$$\text{work done} = \text{energy stored} = \tfrac{1}{2}Fe = \tfrac{1}{2}\frac{EAe^2}{l}$$

If the extension is increased from e_1 to e_2 then the extra energy stored is given by

$$\text{energy stored} = \tfrac{1}{2}\frac{EA}{l}(e_2^2 - e_1^2)$$

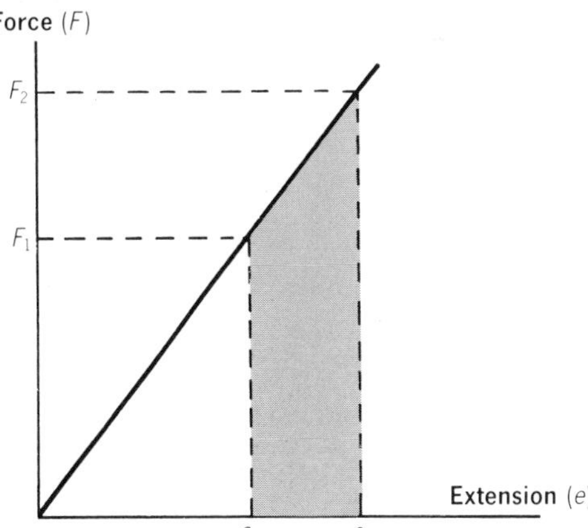

Figure 20.13

This is the shaded area on the graph in Figure 20.13, and in general the energy stored in an extension is the area below the line in the force–extension graph.

A striking example of the amount of energy that can be absorbed by a stretched material is seen in the action of the arrester wire that halts a plane when it lands on the deck of an aircraft carrier. As the plane lands its kinetic energy is converted to stored potential energy in the arrester wire.

> **Student investigation**
>
> 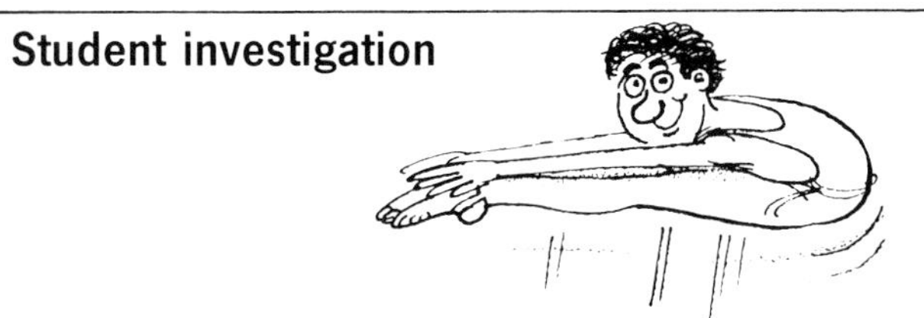
>
> What are the elastic properties necessary for a good trampoline? Investigate the relation between the height to which the trampolinist rises and the resulting depression of the trampoline bed (Figure 20.14).
>
> 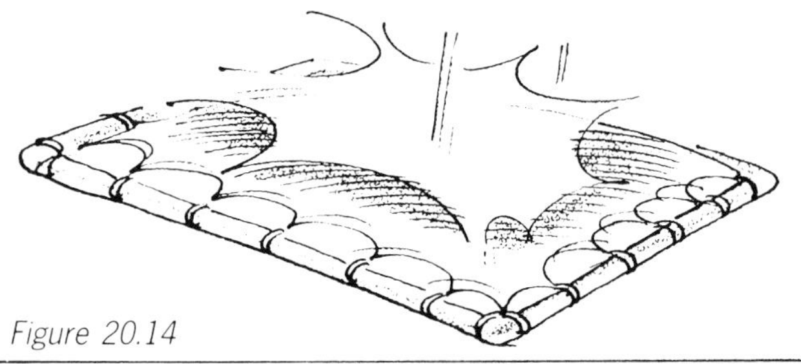
>
> *Figure 20.14*

If the wire has been extended beyond the elastic limit then if the force is removed the extension is only partially recoverable. Energy is therefore lost due to heat and this phenomenon is known as **hysteresis**. The force–extension curve for the wire will follow the line AN on the graph in Figure 20.15, where area OAX is the energy input, AXN the recoverable energy and the shaded area OAN represents the energy lost. The larger this area the bigger the energy loss due to hysteresis.

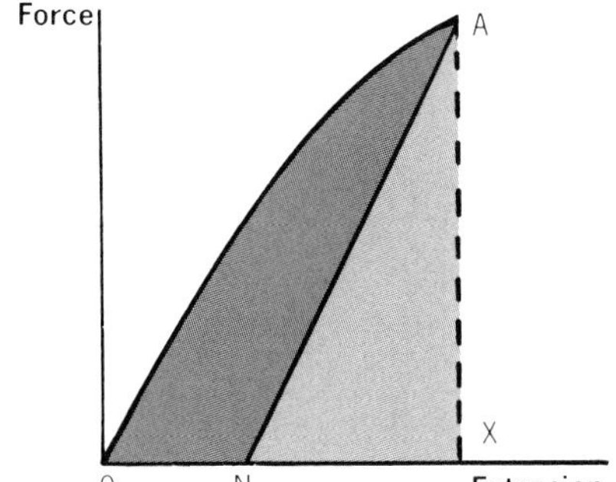

Figure 20.15

The effect of hysteresis is usually very small for metals, but is noticeable for polythene and glass.

> **Example**
>
> Calculate the energy stored in a 2 m long copper wire of cross-sectional area 0.5 mm^2 if a force of 50 N is applied to it.
>
> Energy stored $= \frac{1}{2}Fe$
>
> $$\text{Extension} = \frac{Fl}{EA} = \frac{50 \times 2}{1.2 \times 10^{11} \times 0.5 \times 10^{-6}} = 1.67 \text{ mm}$$
>
> $$\text{Therefore energy stored} = \tfrac{1}{2} \times 50 \times 1.67 \times 10^{-3} = 0.04 \text{ J}$$

> **Student investigation**
>
> Investigate the energy storage properties of a catapult by measuring the distance that a given mass may be projected. (Air resistance may be ignored.)

9 A steel rod of mass 97.5 g and of length 50 cm is heated to 200 °C and its ends securely clamped. Calculate the tension in the rod when its temperature is reduced to 0 °C, explaining how the calculation was made.

10 The rubber cord of a catapult has a cross-sectional area of 1.0 mm^2 and a total unstretched length of 10.0 cm. It is stretched to 15 cm and then released to project a missile of mass 5.0 g. Calculate
(*a*) the energy stored in the rubber,
(*b*) the velocity of projection, and
(*c*) the maximum height that the missile could reach.
Take the Young modulus for rubber to be 5.0×10^8 Pa, and state any assumptions made in your calculation.

11 A solid copper wire of cross-sectional area 8 mm^2 and original length 110 m is set up as a telephone line with a uniform tension of 3.6×10^3 N. Assuming that the wire stretches elastically calculate
(*a*) the extension of the wire, and
(*b*) the elastic energy stored in the wire.
During cold weather the temperature falls by 15 K. Calculate
(*c*) the heat lost by the wire in this cooling, and
(*d*) the change in elastic energy, assuming that the elastic properties of copper are unaffected by the temperature change. [o]

12 A steel arrester wire mounted on the deck of an aircraft carrier is designed to stop a 20 000 kg plane in a distance of 10 m. If the landing speed of the plane is 50 m s^{-1} and the distance between the points of suspension of the wire is 20 m, calculate the minimum diameter of wire needed.

13 A metal spring is compressed, clamped in a compressed position and then dissolved in acid. What has happened to the potential energy stored in the coils of the spring? [z]

14 A fishing line will support a given load but will break when the same load is applied to it sharply. Why is this?

Other elastic moduli

These will only be considered briefly here.

The bulk modulus (K)

Figure 20.16

$$\text{The stress} = \frac{\text{change in normal force}}{\text{area}} = \Delta p.$$

$$\text{The strain} = \frac{\text{change in volume}}{\text{original volume}} = \frac{\Delta V}{V_0}.$$

$$\text{Bulk modulus} = \frac{-\Delta p}{\Delta V/V_0}$$

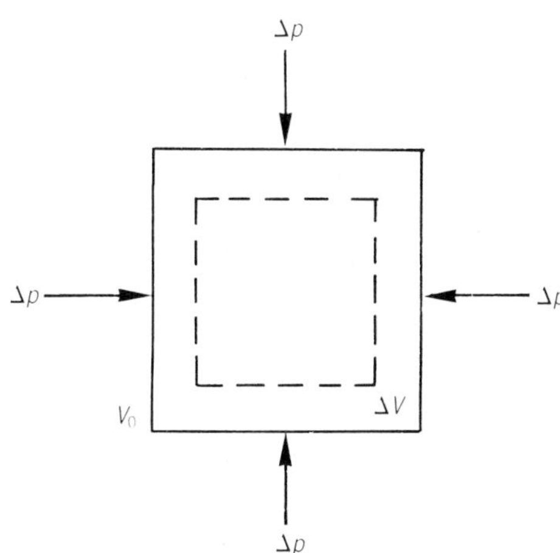

Figure 20.16

A material is therefore easily compressed if it has a small bulk modulus. Gases obviously have a much smaller bulk modulus than solids.

The table below shows the bulk moduli for a number of materials.

Material	*Bulk modulus /GPa*	*Material*	*Bulk modulus /GPa*
Tungsten	200	Steel	166
Iron (wrought)	143	Copper	125
Brass	63	Iron (cast)	100
Aluminium	67	Polystyrene	5
Rubber	2.5	Water	2
Benzene	1		

Student investigation

If you have ever watched a tree bending in a gale you will appreciate that plants of all types are subject to many and varied forces.

Investigate the bending of specimens such as grass and plant stems. How do their elastic properties compare with similarly sized specimens of nylon or copper?

The rigidity or shear modulus (G)

Figure 20.17

$$\text{The stress} = \frac{\text{tangential force}}{\text{area over which applied}} = \frac{F}{A}$$

$$\text{The strain} = \text{angle of shear} = \frac{x}{y} \quad \text{for small angles.}$$

Therefore

$$G = \frac{F/A}{\theta}$$

For a wire the restoring torque when twisted through an angle θ is

$$T = c\theta$$

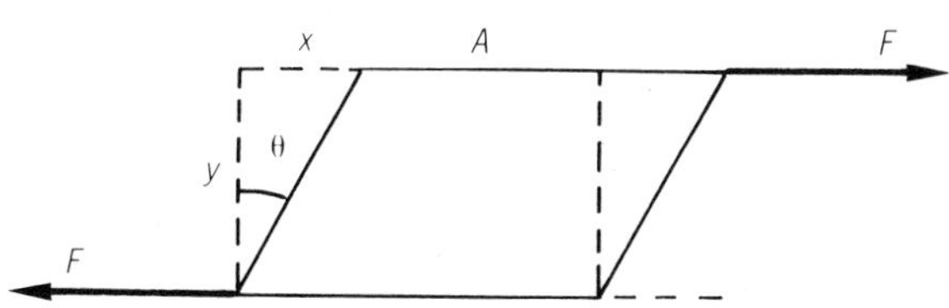

Figure 20.17

This means that a wire will twist by a large amount for a given torque if its modulus of rigidity is small. The ability to resist or allow twisting is of vital importance in the design of buildings and in the materials used for drive shafts in engines and suspensions in meters. Clearly a drive shaft with low rigidity would be useless, as would a meter suspension with a very high rigidity.

If a spiral spring is stretched all parts of the spring will become twisted. The extension of the spring therefore depends on both its modulus of rigidity and its size.

15 A cello C string has a length of 0.82 m, a diameter of 1.5 mm and a mass of 10 g.
(*a*) Calculate the tension in the string.
(*b*) If the string is basically nylon, find the change in tension when the string becomes one semitone flat.

16 A ship's propellor shaft 10 m in length and 15 cm radius twists through an angle of 1° when the shaft is rotating at 60 revolutions per minute. If the modulus of rigidity of the material of the shaft is 9×10^{11} Pa, calculate the power transmitted by the shaft.

21 · Friction and viscosity

Solid friction

Life as we know it would be very strange without friction. Friction is useful in brakes – indeed, without the frictional force between our feet and the ground we could not walk! Frictional forces play a large part in the losses of energy from machinery and in this area great efforts have been made to reduce them.

To move one body over another which is at rest requires a force. This is needed both to change the momentum of the first body and also to overcome the frictional force between the two surfaces. The force needed to overcome the frictional force when the bodies are at rest is called the **limiting friction**.

By experiment it has been found that the limiting frictional force between two surfaces depends on

(*a*) the nature of the two surfaces, and

(*b*) the normal reaction between them.

This can be expressed as an equation as

> frictional force (F) =
> coefficient of friction (μ) × normal reaction (R)
> (Figure 21.1)

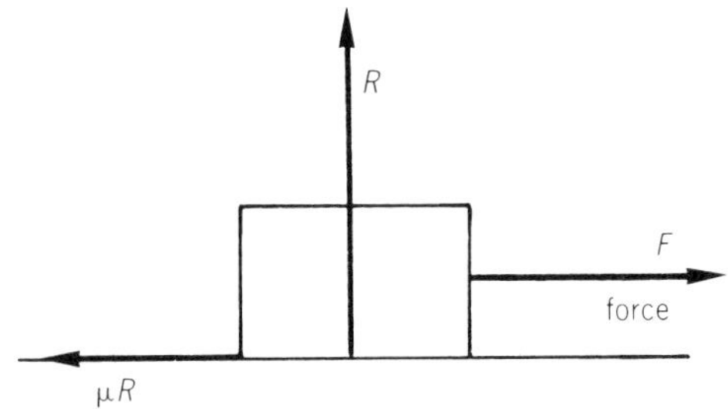

Figure 21.1

Since the coefficient of friction depends on *both* surfaces we will simply quote two values here:

coefficient of friction between wood and wood = 0.3
coefficient of friction between steel and steel = 0.74

When the object is moving the friction between the two surfaces is usually less than the limiting friction. It is known as the coefficient of kinetic friction. Further values are shown in the table below.

Coefficients of friction

Materials	*Static*	*Kinetic*
Steel on steel	0.74	0.57
Aluminium on steel	0.61	0.47
Copper on steel	0.53	0.36
Brass on steel	0.51	0.44
Zinc on cast iron	0.85	0.21
Copper on cast iron	1.05	0.29
Glass on glass	0.94	0.4
Copper on glass	0.68	0.53
Teflon on Teflon	0.04	0.04
Teflon on steel	0.04	0.04
Steel on air	0.001	0.001
Heel on road	0.15	
Steel on ice	0.03	
Tendon and sheath	0.013	
Lubricated bone joint	0.003	

You will see later that it is very simple to calculate the coefficient of friction from the slope down which an object will slide. Remember that a frictional force always acts to oppose the motion.

The frictional forces between glass fibres and the resins in which they are embedded are vital factors in the strength of these materials.

Careful study of friction has shown that the frictional force between two surfaces is independent of the area of contact. This can be explained as follows.

Think of two surfaces of steel which have been polished. When they are placed together we think that they are in contact over their whole surface area but this is not the case. In fact, they only touch at something like one-tenthousandth of their actual area as shown in Figure 21.2.

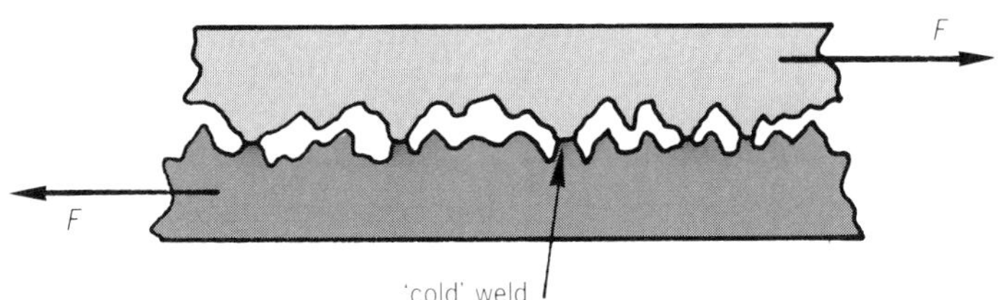

Figure 21.2

At the points of contact the surfaces are actually 'cold-welded' together and it requires energy to break the welds.

The motion of the top surface over the other is a 'stick–slip' movement: the small projections have to be broken as the object moves.

Measurement of the coefficient of friction between two solid surfaces

(i) Direct method
A mass A is pulled across a horizontal surface by a newtonmeter and the force required is recorded. If the weight of the object is known, the coefficient of friction may be determined.

(ii) Using a slope
The object is placed on a slope as shown in Figure 21.3 and the tilt of the slope (θ) is slowly increased

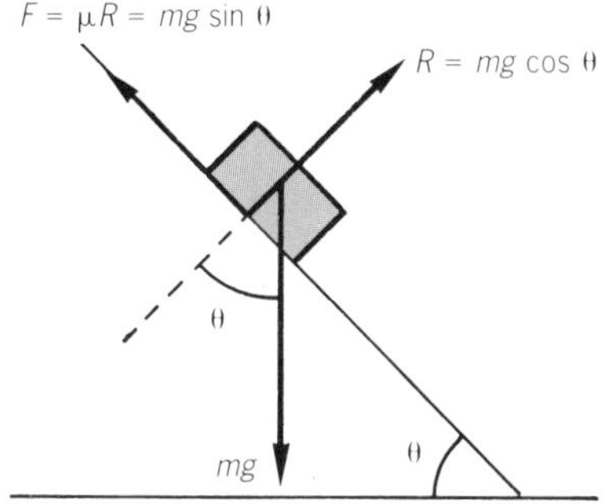

Figure 21.3

until the object begins to slide down. At the moment of slip the forces on the object are given by:

along the plane: $F = mg \sin\theta$
perpendicular to the plane: $R = mg \cos\theta$

Therefore:

$$\text{coefficient of friction} = \frac{F}{R} = \tan\theta$$

Student investigation

The friction between a rubber tyre and the surface of a road is of considerable importance in safety. In normal use the tyres have a tread to allow the passage of water but in dry racing-car tyres, the so-called 'slicks', the tyre is perfectly smooth and relies on the heat generated due to friction to melt a little of the tyre and so increase the road-holding ability.

Devise and carry out an experiment to test the frictional forces between a tyre and a road surface. The effect of a thin layer of water should also be studied.

1 Estimate the coefficients of friction between the following surfaces:

(a) a wood block and a slope that has to be tilted to 60° before the block will slide down it;

(b) a person's body and a 'wall of death' in a fairground of radius 5 m rotating at 0.4 revolutions per second.

When the smooth tyres spin round friction causes heat to build up which partially melts the tyres, the soft rubber then sticks and increases the grip on the road (ZEFA)

Liquid friction

As we have seen, solids surfaces in contact exert a frictional force on each other when they are moved. In a similar way, the relative motion of layers of liquid is restricted by friction.

The frictional forces within a liquid is known as the **viscosity** of the liquid. The greater the viscosity the less easy it is for the fluid to flow and the more sticky it feels. The viscosity of a liquid also affects how easily solids can move through it – try and imagine the difference between swimming in water and in treacle!

Consider the flow of liquid down a pipe (Figure 21.4). The liquid will be moving from left to right due to the pressure difference between the ends of the tube. The liquid in the centre of the pipe will be travelling faster than that at the edges.

Imagine that the liquid is moving in layers, rather like the cards in a pack, and assume that no one layer crosses another layer. The frictional forces within the liquid act between one layer and another. Such motion is called **laminar flow**. The velocity of particles at a given distance from the centre of motion is constant. If the layers do intermix we get **turbulent flow**.

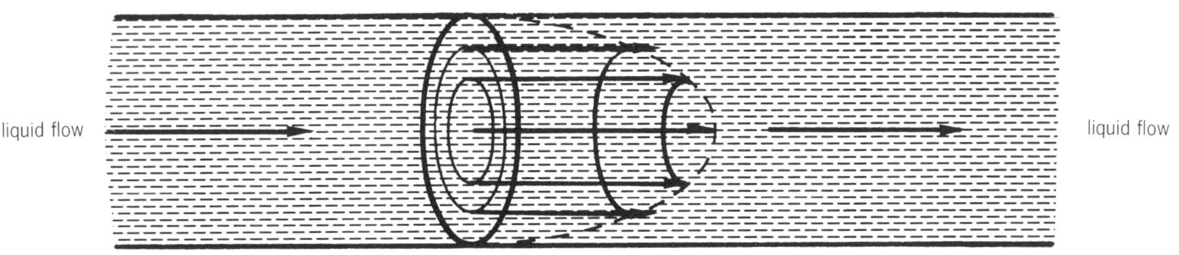

Figure 21.4

Streamlines

A **streamline** is a curve whose tangent always lies along the direction of motion of the fluid at that point. The streamlines never cross and in laminar flow they do not alter with time. (Figure 21.5(*a*)) but this is not the case with turbulent flow (Figure 21.5(*b*)). Clearly it is important for a vehicle moving through a fluid that the flow of the fluid around it is laminar so that the drag on it may be reduced to a minimum.

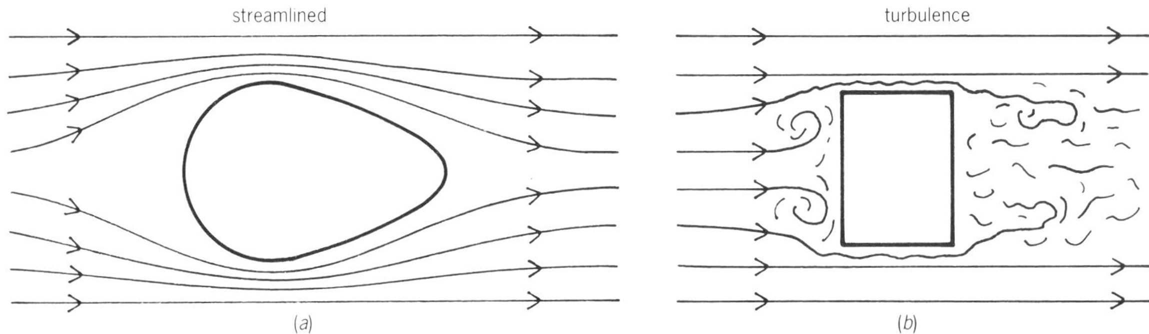

Figure 21.5

Student investigation

Construct a series of solid shapes with cross-sections as shown in Figure 21.6. Place them one at a time into a tank and allow water to flow round them. A few crystals of potassium manganate(VII) (potassium permanganate) should be introduced into the stream to show the direction of flow. Investigate the nature of the flow of water round these obstacles noting the streamlines. The effect of the speed of water flow should be studied by varying the pressure head of the water flowing into the tank.

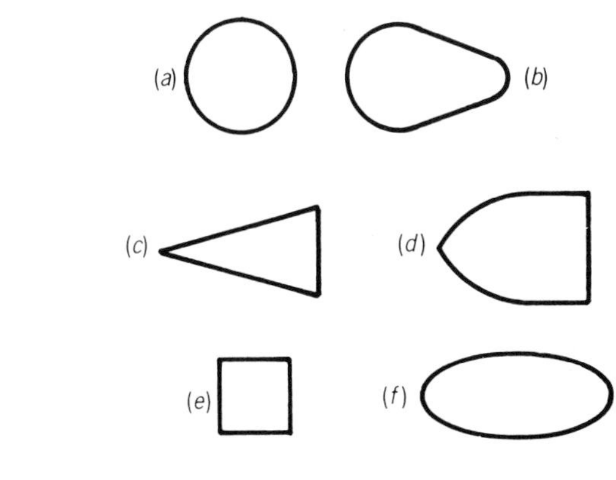

Figure 21.6

We could consider a stationary fluid and a moving tube. It is then clear that the tube will drag some fluid along with it while the fluid at the centre of the tube will lag behind. There is therefore a larger relative velocity between the tube and the central fluid than there is between the tube and the fluid in contact with it. It has been found that for laminar flow:

The frictional force is directly proportional to the product of velocity gradient and the cross-sectional area of the tube.

The **velocity gradient** is defined as the change in velocity across the tube (Figure 21.7).

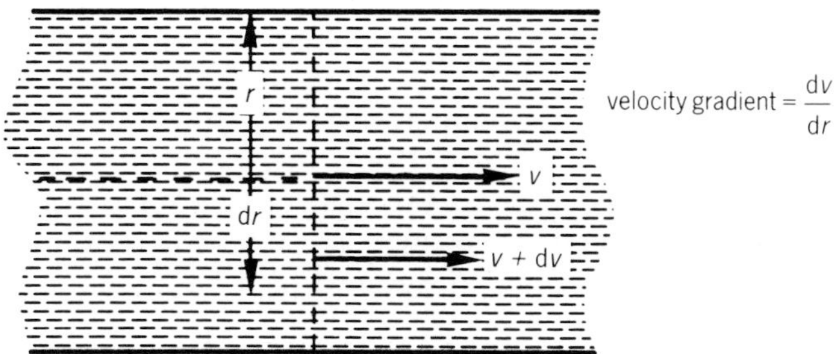

Figure 21.7

You can write the formula:

$$F = \eta A \times \text{velocity gradient}$$

where η is the **coefficient of viscosity** for the fluid. Fluids that behave in this way are known as **Newtonian fluids.**

η is defined as

$$\eta = \frac{\text{tangential stress}}{\text{velocity gradient}}$$

and is therefore very similar to the shear modulus for a solid. The units of the coefficient of viscosity are $N\,s\,m^{-2}$, $kg\,m^{-1}s^{-1}$ or Pa s, and it has dimensions $[M][L]^{-1}[T]^{-1}$.

The values of some coefficients of viscosity are given in the table below. Since viscosity varies with temperature they are all given for 20 °C.

Fluid	*Viscosity/Pa s*	*Fluid*	*Viscosity/Pa s*
Air	1.8×10^{-5}	Water	1.0×10^{-3}
Glycerol	8.3×10^{-1}	Golden syrup	100
Castor oil	2.42	Mercury	1.5×10^{-3}
Blood	$3\text{–}4 \times 10^{-3}$		

(The viscosity of blood depends on the concentration of the red blood corpuscles and therefore can be used to detect red blood corpuscle deficiency.)

Some illustrations of the variation of viscosity with temperature are shown below:

Pitch	5×10^{10}	Pa s at 273 K
	1×10^{1}	Pa s at 373 K
An oil	5.3	Pa s at 273 K
	0.99	Pa s at 293 K
	0.23	Pa s at 313 K
Water	0.0018	Pa s at 273 K
	0.0010	Pa s at 293 K
	0.0007	Pa s at 310 K

Oil used as a lubricant in engines must have a standard viscosity to comply with government regulations. An interesting allowance for the variation of the viscosity of water with temperature was made in the 1984 Olympic Games in Los Angeles. The swimming events were held in an outdoor pool and the water had to be cooled with blocks of ice to prevent the temperature from rising too much. This would have lowered the viscosity of the water, thus giving the swimmers an unfair advantage compared with times set in a cooler pool!

The flow of liquid through a tube

The rate at which fluid flows through a tube is likely to depend on

(*a*) the viscosity of the fluid,
(*b*) the dimensions of the tube, and
(*c*) the pressure difference between its ends.

This flow rate is of great importance in our lives since it governs things like the flow of blood round our bodies and the transmission of gas, water or oil through long distances in pipelines.

The proof of the relationship was first produced by Poiseuille in 1844 using dimensional analysis (a different proof based on the mechanics of fluids is available, but is outside the scope of this book). Consider a fluid of viscosity η flowing through a tube of length l and radius r due to a pressure difference Δp between its ends (Figure 21.8).

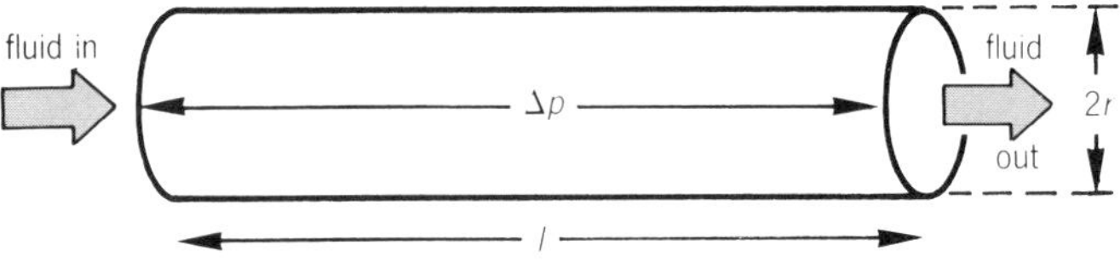

Figure 21.8

Assume that the volume v passing through the tube per second is given by the equation

$$v = k\eta^x r^y \frac{\Delta p^z}{l}$$

where the quantity $\frac{\Delta p}{l}$ is called the **pressure gradient** down the tube. Using dimensional analysis:

$$[L]^3[T]^{-1} = ([M][L]^{-1}[T]^{-1})^x[L]^y([M][L]^{-1}[T]^{-2})^z$$

and this gives $x = -1$, $y = 4$ and $z = 1$. Therefore the volume per second is

$$v = \frac{kr^4\Delta p}{\eta l}$$

The value of k can be shown to be $\pi/8$ and therefore:

$$v = \frac{\pi\Delta p r^4}{8\eta l}$$

This formula only applies to laminar flow, not to turbulent motion. It is interesting that warm-blooded animals regulate the heat loss from their bodies by changing the diameter of their blood vessels (varying r) and hence controlling the rate of blood flow.

Example

Calculate the pressure difference between the two ends of a hosepipe 20 m long and of radius 0.5 cm if the rate of flow of water through it is 0.8 litres per second. (Viscosity of water = 1×10^{-3} Pa s.)

$$\text{Pressure difference} = \frac{0.8 \times 10^{-3} \times 8 \times 10^{-3} \times 20}{\pi(0.5 \times 10^{-2})^4}$$

$$= 6.5 \times 10^4 \text{ Pa}$$

2 Oil having a viscosity of 0.3 Pa s and a density of 900 kg m^{-3} is pumped from one large open tank into another through a smooth steel pipe 1 km long and 15 cm in internal diameter. The outlet point is 30 cm above the inlet point. Calculate the pump pressure needed to maintain a flow rate of 0.05 m^3 s^{-1}.

3 Two capillary tubes AB and BC are joined end to end at B. AB is 16 cm long with a bore 0.4 cm in diameter and BC is 4 cm long with a bore 0.2 cm in diameter. The composite tube is held horizontally with the end A connected to a reservoir giving a constant pressure head of 3 cm of water above the open end (C). Calculate the pressure differences between A and B and between B and C.

Measurement of the viscosity of a liquid

The apparatus shown in Figure 21.9 may be used to determine the viscosity of a liquid such as water. The water flows from a constant head apparatus through a horizontal capillary tube and is then collected by a beaker, the time for a given volume to be collected is measured. The pressure difference between the two ends of the capillary tube is $h\rho g$ where ρ is the density of the liquid. The internal diameter of the capillary tube is measured with a travelling microscope. It is important that the temperature of the water is measured and that the water only drips from the free end of the tube, since in the rigorous proof of the formula the water is assumed to have no residual kinetic energy. Laminar flow must also be assumed.

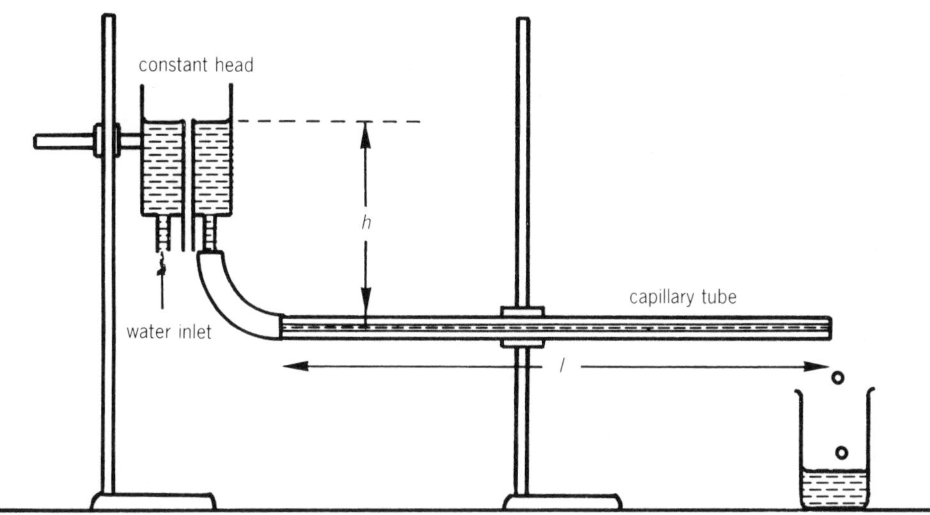

Figure 21.9

Student investigation

The variation of viscosity with temperature may be studied by the following experiment. The ease with which a liquid may be stirred at a given rate depends on the viscosity of the liquid and therefore the difficulty of stirring treacle will vary with temperature.

Set up the apparatus as shown in Figure 21.10, and record the power that must be applied to the motor to maintain a steady stirring rate as the treacle is slowly heated.

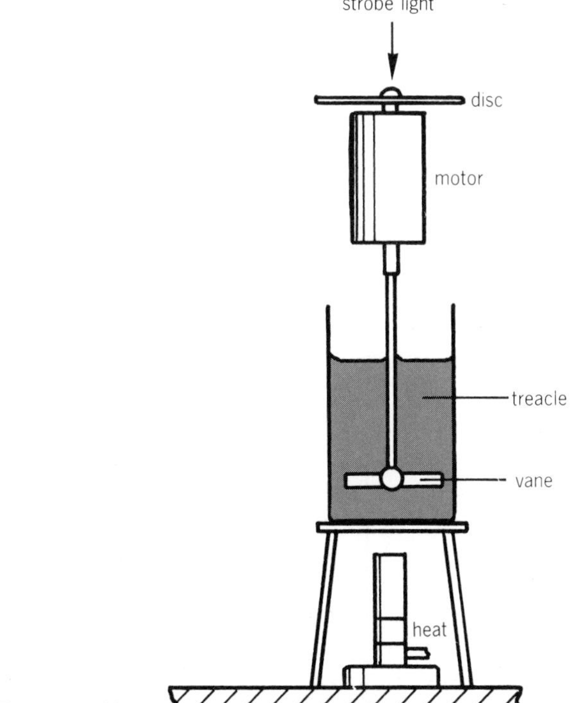

Figure 21.10

Plot a graph of power against temperature. If possible suggest a form for the equation of the variation of power with temperature.

4 A reservoir containing water is attached to a vertical capillary tube 50 cm long with a bore 0.8 mm diameter. The water level in the reservoir is maintained at a height of 20 cm above the top end of the tube and it is found that water flows out at 8 ml per minute.
Calculate the viscosity of water from this data.

The flow of mass, heat energy and charge

Comparison of the equations for the transfer of mass, heat energy (page 262) and charge (page 281) show that they are all of basically the same form, that is:

$$\text{flow rate} \propto \frac{\text{pressure causing flow}}{\text{resistance to flow}}$$

The three specific equations are:

$$(a)\ \text{Mass flow rate} = \frac{p\pi r^4}{8\eta l} = \frac{p}{R_M}$$

where R_M is a constant containing the viscosity, which is the resistance to the flow of the fluid.

$$(b)\ \text{Heat flow rate} = \frac{kA(\theta_1-\theta_2)}{x} = \frac{\Delta\theta}{R_H}$$

where R_H is a constant containing the inverse of thermal conductivity, which is the resistance to the flow of heat energy.

$$(c)\ \text{Charge flow rate} = \frac{V_2-V_1}{R_E}$$

where R_E is the electrical resistance of the conductor.

Stokes' law and terminal velocity

When any object rises or falls through a fluid it will experience a viscous drag, whether it is a parachutist or spacecraft falling through air, a stone falling through water or a bubble rising through fizzy lemonade. The mathematics of the viscous drag on irregular shapes is difficult; we will consider here only the case of a falling sphere. The formula was first suggested by Stokes and is therefore known as Stokes' law.

Consider a sphere falling through a viscous fluid. As the sphere falls so its velocity increases until it reaches a velocity known as the **terminal velocity**. At this velocity the frictional drag due to viscous forces is just balanced by the gravitational force and the velocity is constant (Figure 21.11).

Suppose that the sphere has radius r and falls through a fluid of viscosity η. Let the terminal velocity be v (Figure 21.12). We can calculate the viscous drag F on the sphere by dimensional analysis. If

$$F = kr^x\eta^y v^z$$

We have

$$MLT^{-2} = L^x(ML^{-1}T^{-1})^y(LT^{-1})^z$$

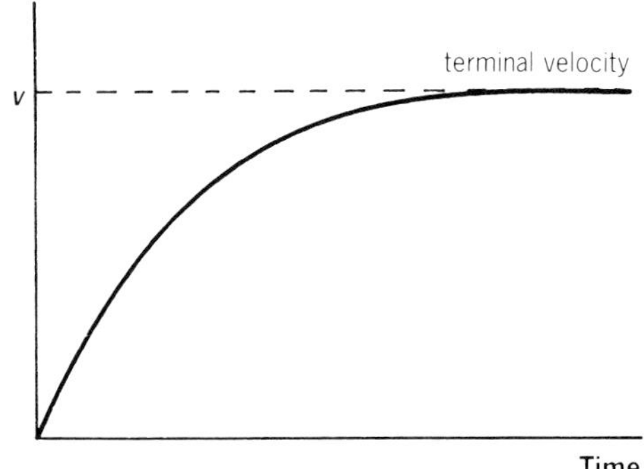

Figure 21.11

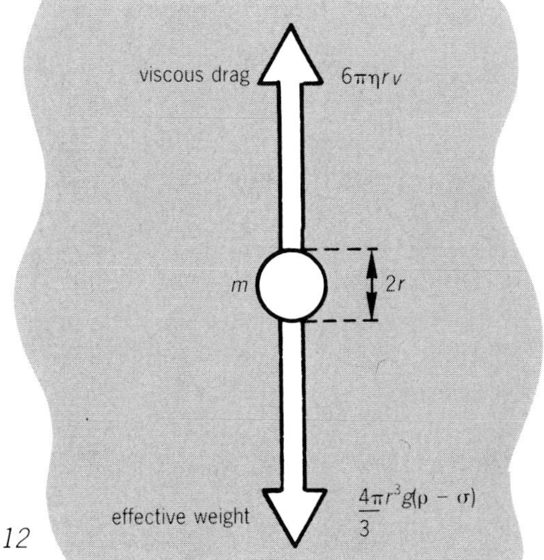

Figure 21.12

Solving this gives $x = 1$, $y = 1$ and $z = 1$. By other methods k can be shown to be 6π, and this gives for the frictional force:

$$F = 6\pi r\eta v \qquad \text{(Stokes' law)}$$

If the density of the material of the sphere is ρ and that of the liquid σ, then

effective gravitational force = weight − upthrust

$$= \frac{4\pi r^3}{3}(\rho-\sigma)g$$

Therefore we have for the viscosity η:

$$\eta = \frac{2gr^2(\rho-\sigma)}{9v}$$

where v is the terminal velocity of the sphere.

From the formula it can be seen that the frictional drag is smaller for large spheres than for small ones, and therefore the terminal velocity of a large sphere is greater than that for a small sphere of the same material.

Stokes' law is important in Millikan's experiment for the measurement of the charge on an electron (see page 410), and it also explains why large raindrops hurt much more than small ones when they fall on you – it's not just that they are heavier, they are actually falling faster.

Measurement of the viscosity of glycerol

A one-litre measuring cylinder is filled with glycerol and two rubber bands are placed around it a known distance apart (say 20 cm) as shown in Figure 21.13. The diameter of a small steel ball-bearing is measured with a micrometer and it is then released from just above the glycerol surface and allowed to fall through the fluid, the time for it to pass from the level of one band to that of the other being taken. The velocity of

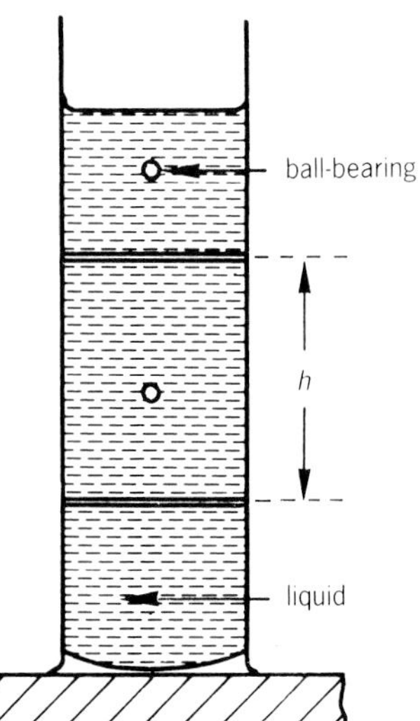

Figure 21.13

the ball-bearing between the bands can then be found, and it is assumed that this is its terminal velocity. From the equation above the viscosity of the fluid may be found. The temperature of the glycerol should be recorded and the experiment should be repeated with ball-bearings of different radii.

For accurate work allowance should be made for the effects of the walls of the container and for this reason the experiment should always be carried out with cylinders of large radii compared with the ball-bearings.

5 Calculate the terminal velocities of the following raindrops falling through air:
(*a*) one with a diameter of 0.3 cm,
(*b*) one with a diameter of 0.01 mm.
(Take the density of water to be 1000 kg m^{-3} and the viscosity of air to be 1×10^{-3} Pa s. The buoyancy effect of the air may be ignored.)

Example

Calculate the terminal velocity of a raindrop of radius 0.2 cm (raindrops with radii much greater than this will become unstable and break up). (Density of water = 1000 kg m^{-3} and that of air about 1 kg m^{-3})

$$\text{Terminal velocity } v = \frac{2gr^2(\rho - \sigma)}{9\eta}$$

$$= \frac{2 \times 9.81 \times (0.2 \times 10^{-2})^2 \times 999}{9 \times 10^{-3}}$$

$$= \frac{7.04 \times 10^{-2}}{9 \times 10^{-3}}$$

$$= 8.7 \text{ m s}^{-1}$$

We can use this law to calculate either the size of small particles or the time it will take a particle to fall through a given fluid if the radius of the particle is known.

Example

Find the time taken for a particle of carbon (density 2300 kg m^{-3}) with a radius of 0.0001 m to fall 2 m through air (viscosity 0.001 Pa s).

$$\text{Terminal velocity} = \frac{2 \times 10 \times 10^{-10} \times 2300}{10^{-2}}$$

$$= 4.6 \times 10^{-4} \text{ m s}^{-1}$$

$$\text{Time to fall 2 m} = \frac{2}{4.6 \times 10^{-4}} = 4348 \text{ s} = 72 \text{ min}$$

$$= 1.2 \text{ h}$$

6 An explosion occurs at an altitude of 1000 m where there is a constant horizontal wind speed of 10 m s^{-1}. It is estimated that the smallest particles produced by the explosion have a diameter of 0.01 mm and a density of 2000 kg m^{-3}. Calculate
(*a*) the time taken for the smallest particles to fall to the ground,
(*b*) the horizontal distance travelled from the point of the explosion.
Assume the viscosity and density of the air to be uniform over the distances considered. (Viscosity of air 1.8×10^{-5} Pa s; density of air 1.2 kg m^{-3})

7 Calculate the viscous drag on a drop of oil of 0.1 mm radius falling through air at its terminal velocity. (Viscosity of air = 1.8×10^{-5} Pa s; density of oil = 850 kg m^{-3})

8 Discuss the following statements:
(*a*) Large ball-bearings fall through glycerol faster than do smaller ones of the same material.
(*b*) The acceleration of a sphere falling through a fluid varies with the distance that it has fallen in the fluid.
(*c*) The size of the vessel through which an object falls also affects its motion.
(*d*) The viscosity of a liquid could be used to measure temperature.

9 Powdered chalk (density 2800 kg m^{-3}) is vigorously shaken up in a bottle containing 15 cm depth of water. It is found that it is half an hour before all the chalk has finally settled to the bottom of the bottle. If the coefficient of viscosity of water is 1.1×10^{-3} Pa s, find the diameter of the smallest particles (assumed spherical) of the chalk.
How would your answer differ if the suspension had been placed in a centrifuge to give an acceleration ten times that of gravity?

10 Compare the speed at which a steel ball (density 7800 kg m^{-3}) of radius 2 mm will fall through treacle, with that at which an air bubble (density 1.3 kg m^{-3}) of radius 1 mm will rise through the same liquid. (Take the density of treacle to be 1600 kg m^{3}.)

11 Two spherical raindrops of equal size are falling through air at a velocity of 0.08 m s^{-1}. If the drops join together forming a large spherical drop, what will be the new terminal velocity?

Laminar and turbulent flow

In the nineteenth century Reynolds investigated the conditions that would give turbulence in the flow of a fluid. He showed that the velocity for liquid flow in a tube is given by:

$$v_c = \frac{R_e\eta}{2\rho r}$$

where η is the viscosity of the liquid and ρ its density, and r the radius of the tube. The constant R_e is the **Reynolds number.**

It can be found from experiment that if $R_e < 2000$ the flow is streamlined (laminar), if $R_e > 3000$ the flow is turbulent and if it lies between these two the flow is unstable. The flow of liquid can easily be demonstrated with the apparatus shown in Figure 21.14. A dye flows from the tube into the tank and by altering the pressure head the flow can be made either turbulent or laminar. As you can see from the graph in Figure 21.15, the flow becomes turbulent when the line ceases to be straight.

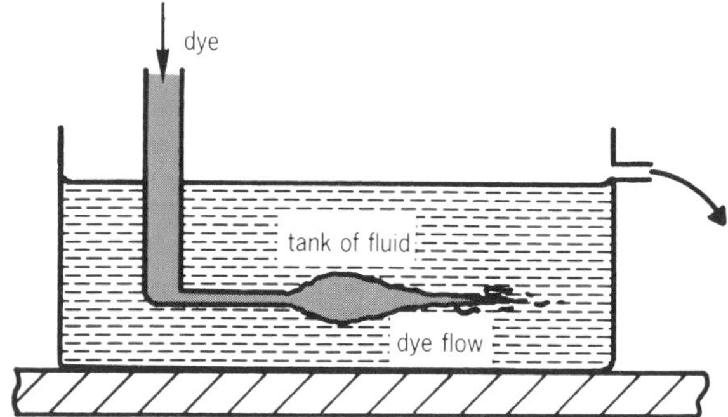

Figure 21.14

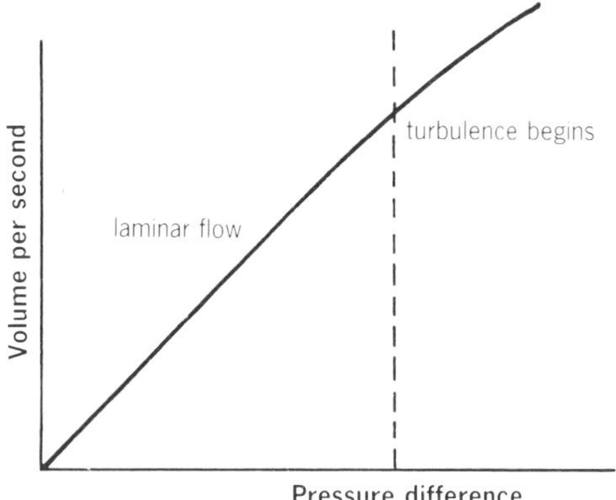

Figure 21.15

The streamlining of bodies is most important in the design of cars, submarines and the nose cones of aircraft and rockets, since a reduction in drag can reduce vibration and also save large amounts of fuel. Figure 21.16 shows the best shapes for rocket cones for subsonic, supersonic and hypersonic flight.

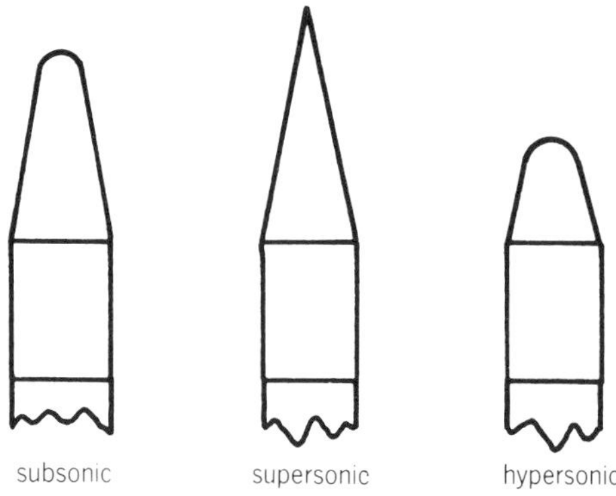

Figure 21.16

Molecular theory of viscosity

Viscosity in gases is due to the transfer of momentum between neighbouring layers of gas. The viscosity of a gas is given by

$$\eta = \frac{nm\lambda v}{3}$$

where n is the number of molecules per unit volume, v is the average velocity of the gas molecules, and λ is the mean free path of the molecules, given by

$$\lambda = \frac{1}{\sqrt{2}\pi\sigma^2 n}$$

where σ is the effective diameter of a molecule.

It can be seen that the viscosity of a gas is directly proportional to the average velocity of the gas molecules. Since the average velocity of the molecules is related to the temperature of the gas, the viscosity of a gas *increases* with increasing temperature. This is explained by the greater rate of transfer of momentum between layers in the gas at higher temperatures. The viscosity of a gas is independent of pressure, except at very low pressure.

Streamlined flow over a test car in a wind tunnel (Ford Motor Co. Ltd)

22 · Fluids in motion

When a fluid is in motion the pressure within the fluid varies with the velocity of the fluid if the flow is streamlined. This pressure variation is a consequence of **Bernouilli's theorem** proposed in 1740. This states that

> The pressure within a fast-moving fluid is lower than that in a similar fluid moving slowly.

A proof of this theorem is shown on page 128.

The forces generated by this pressure difference were first explained in 1852 by the German physicist Gustav Magnus, who solved the problem of why projectiles spinning about an axis other than their direction of motion will veer off course.

Applications and effects of the Bernouilli effect

One of the simplest demonstrations of the Bernouilli effect can be seen by blowing down between two sheets of paper. The air stream between the paper creates an area of low pressure here and so the sheets are drawn together. This effect can be observed when two tall heavy lorries travel along rapidly side by side and are drawn together. The same effect has also been experienced at sea between two ships.

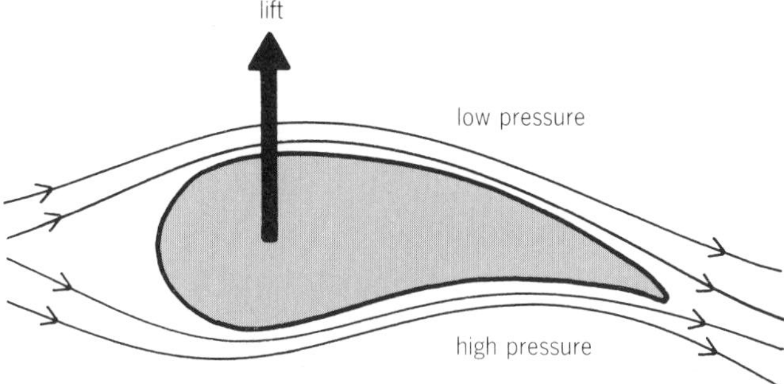

Figure 22.1

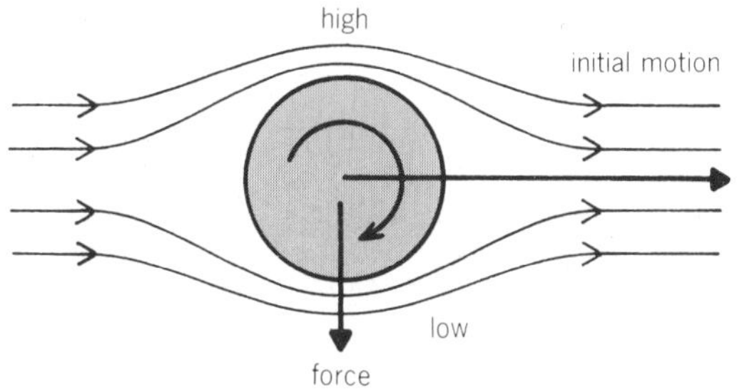

Figure 22.2

The shape of the cross-section of an aircraft wing is designed so that the velocity of the air above the wing is greater than that below it. A region of low pressure is therefore created above the wing and so the aircraft experiences an upward force known as **lift** (Figure 22.1).

Racing cars have inverted aerofoils so that the force is downwards, thus increasing the force between the car and the road.

A striking example is the movement in the air of a smooth, spinning ball such as a table tennis ball (see Figure 22.2).

As the ball moves through the air it will drag some of the air round with its spin. This will increase the velocity of the air on one side of the ball and decrease it on the other, creating areas of low and high pressure. The ball therefore moves into the region of low pressure.

(This explanation does not apply to a spinning cricket ball, however, where the smoothness of different faces and the seam will all affect its motion.)

The scent spray, the carburettor and the bunsen burner work because of the Bernouilli effect. For example, in the bunsen burner the high velocity of a jet of gas draws air into the burner (Figure 22.3).

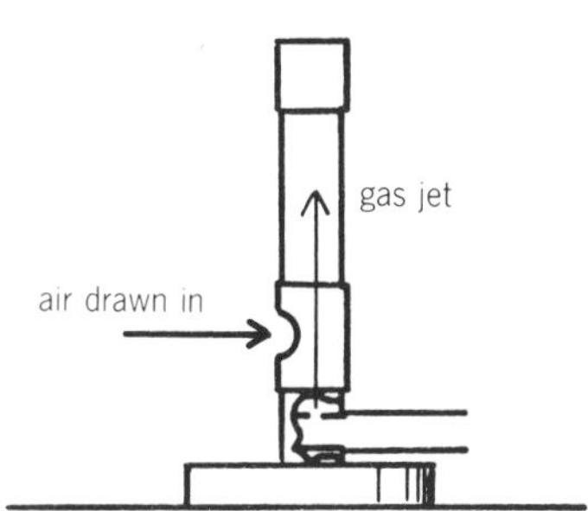

Figure 22.3

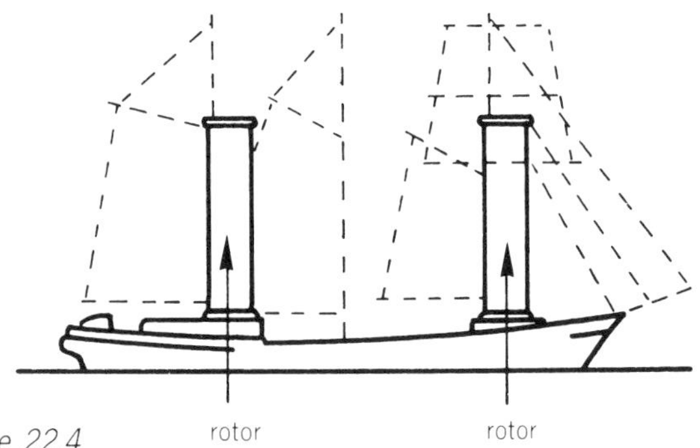

Figure 22.4

One final fascinating application of the principle is the rotor-driven ship designed by the German naval engineer Anton Flettner and built in 1925. The ship, the *Buckau*, had its masts and sails replaced by two vertical cylindrical rotors 12 m tall and with a diameter of 2.7 m. They were rotated about a vertical axis by two 11 kW electric motors below decks to a maximum speed of 125 r.p.m. (Figure 22.4). Just like the spinning ball, the combination of wind speed and rotor speed produced a force that propelled the ship through the water.

It was found that the *Buckau* could sail a full 20° closer to the wind than a traditional sailing ship, and that she could reach a speed of 14.3 km hr^{-1} when driven by rotors alone compared with 14.5 km hr^{-1} when using a traditional propellor.

Proof of Bernouilli's theorem

Consider a fluid of negligible viscosity moving with laminar flow, as shown in Figure 22.5.

Let the velocity, pressure and area of the fluid column be v_1, P_1, and A_1 at Q and v_2, P_2 and A_2 at R. Let the volume bounded by Q and R move to S and T where QS = l_1 and RT = l_2. If the fluid is incompressible:

$$A_1 l_1 = A_2 l_2$$

The work done by the pressure difference per unit volume = gain in k.e. per unit volume + gain in p.e. per unit volume. Now

work done = force × distance = p × volume

net work done per unit volume = $P_1 - P_2$

k.e. per unit volume = $\frac{1}{2}\rho v^2$

Therefore:

k.e. gained per unit volume = $\frac{1}{2}\rho(v_2^2 - v_1^2)$

p.e. gained per unit volume = $\rho g(h_2 - h_1)$

where h_1 and h_2 are the heights of Q and R above some reference level. Therefore:

$$P_1 - P_2 = \frac{1}{2}\rho(v_2^2 - v_1^2) + \rho g(h_2 - h_1)$$

$$P_1 + \frac{1}{2}\rho v_1^2 + \rho g h_1 = P_2 + \frac{1}{2}\rho v_2^2 + \rho g h_2$$

Therefore:

$P + \frac{1}{2}\rho v^2 + \rho g h$ is a constant

For a horizontal tube $h_1 = h_2$ and so we have

$P + \frac{1}{2}\rho v^2$ = constant

This is Bernouilli's theorem. You can see that if there is a increase in velocity there must be a decrease of pressure and vice versa.

No fluid is totally incompressible in practice, but the general qualitative assumptions still hold for real fluids.

Example

Water leaves the jet of a horizontal hose at 10 m s^{-1}. If the velocity of water within the hose is 0.4 m s^{-1}, calculate the pressure P within the hose. (Density of water = 1000 kg m^{-3} and atmospheric pressure = 100 000 Pa)

Using Bernouilli's theorem we have:

$$10^5 + \frac{1}{2} \times 1000 \times 100 = P + \frac{1}{2} \times 1000 \times 0.16$$

Therefore P = 1 49 920 Pa $\approx 1.5 \times 10^5$ Pa

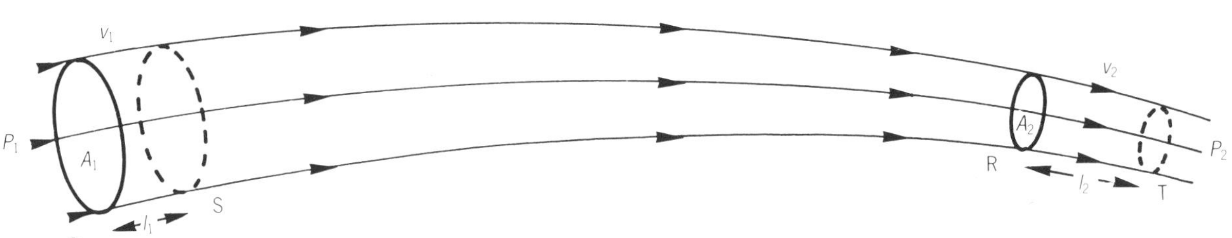

Figure 22.5

The Pitot static tube

This is a device for measuring the velocity of a moving fluid – Figure 22.6 is a simplified diagram.

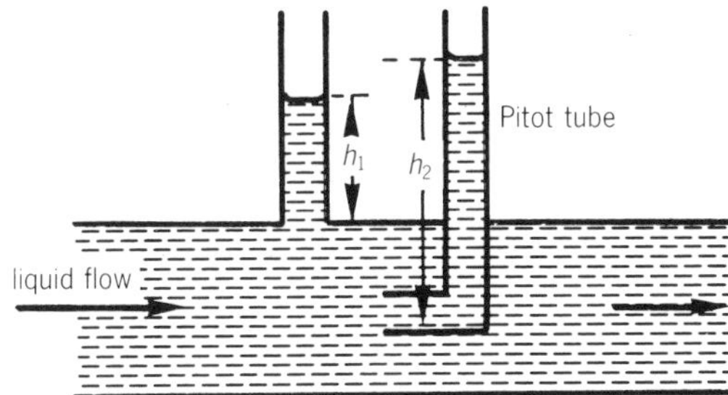

Figure 22.6

The total pressure within the moving fluid can be considered to have two components:

(*a*) the static pressure which it would have if the fluid was at rest, and

(*b*) the dynamic pressure which is the pressure equivalent of its velocity.

The dynamic pressure is therefore the total pressure – the static pressure. Now from Bernouilli's equation:

$$\text{total pressure} = p + \tfrac{1}{2}\rho v^2$$

Therefore

$$\text{dynamic pressure} = \tfrac{1}{2}\rho v^2$$

and the velocity v may be found from the equation:

$$v = \sqrt{\frac{2}{\rho}(\text{total pressure} - \text{static pressure})}$$

The total pressure is measured by the pressure head h_2 and the static pressure by pressure head h_1. Therefore the formula may be written:

$$v = \sqrt{2g(h_2 - h_1)}$$

Torricelli's theorem

This applies to a fluid flowing from a drum with a horizontal opening near the base (Figure 22.7). It states that, if the difference in levels between the hole and the upper liquid surface is h, then

$$v_2 = \sqrt{2gh}$$

taking $v_1 = 0$ in the Bernouilli equation and equal pressures at the top and the hole.

This theorem applies to the flow of fluid from a drum with a horizontal opening near the base. The relation may be deduced from Bernouilli's equation by taking the velocity v_1 to be zero and assuming equal static pressures at the top of the fluid and outside the hole.

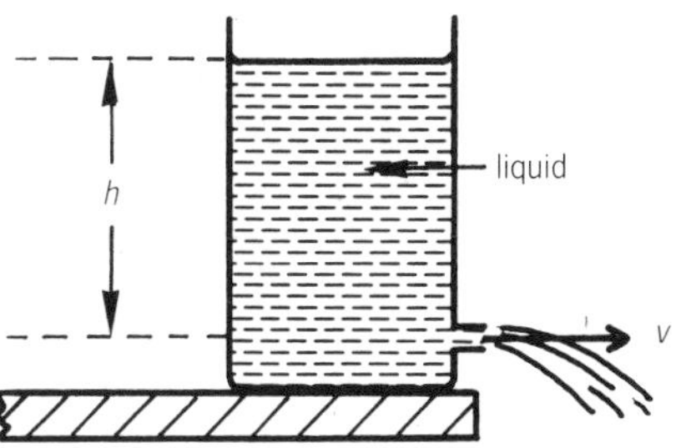

Figure 22.7

If the difference in levels between the hole and the upper liquid surface is h, then the velocity with which fluid emerges from the hole is given by:

$$v_2 = \sqrt{2gh}$$

1 A large tank containing water has a small hole near the bottom of the tank 1.5 m below the surface of the water.

(*a*) What is the velocity of the water flowing from the hole?

(*b*) Where must a second hole be drilled so that the velocity of water leaving this hole is half that of water flowing through the first hole?

2 Water flows along a horizontal pipe of cross-sectional area 30 cm^2. The speed of the water is 4 m s^{-1}, but this rises to 7.5 m s^{-1} in a constriction in the pipe. What is the area of this narrow part of the tube?

3 What is the maximum weight of an aircraft with a wing area of 50 m^2 flying horizontally, if the velocity of the air over the upper surface of the wings is 150 m s^{-1} and that over the lower surface 140 m s^{-1}? (Take the density of air to be 1.29 kg m^{-3}.)

4 Water flows steadily along a horizontal tube of cross-sectional area 25 cm^2. The static pressure within the pipe is 1.3×10^5 Pa and the total pressure 1.4×10^5 Pa.

Calculate the velocity of the water flow and the mass of water flowing past a point in the tube per second.

Optical properties

The 2.5 m Isaac Newton Telescope sited at the Roque de los Muchachos Observatory in the Canary Islands by the Royal Greenwich Observatory (Royal Greenwich Observatory)

23 · Reflection

Much of the work in this section will have been covered in a GCSE course and it is therefore intended to give only a summary here.

Plane mirrors

The reflection of light from a plane surface can be summarised by the following laws of reflection (Figure 23.1):

(*i*) The angle of incidence i equals the angle of reflection r.

(*ii*) The incident ray, the reflected ray and the normal all lie in the same plane.

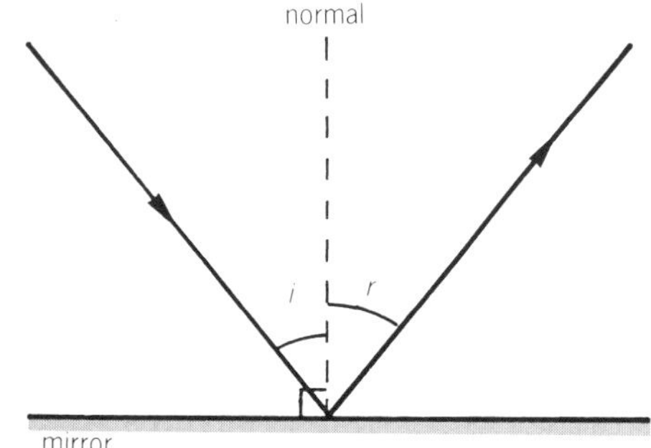

Figure 23.1

Images

A **real** image is one through which the rays of light actually pass and which can be formed on a screen, while a **virtual** image is one through which the rays do not actually pass, although they appear to come from it.

A consequence of the laws of reflection is that, for a real object, the image produced by a plane mirror is virtual and its distance behind the mirror is the same as the object's distance in front of it (Figure 23.2).

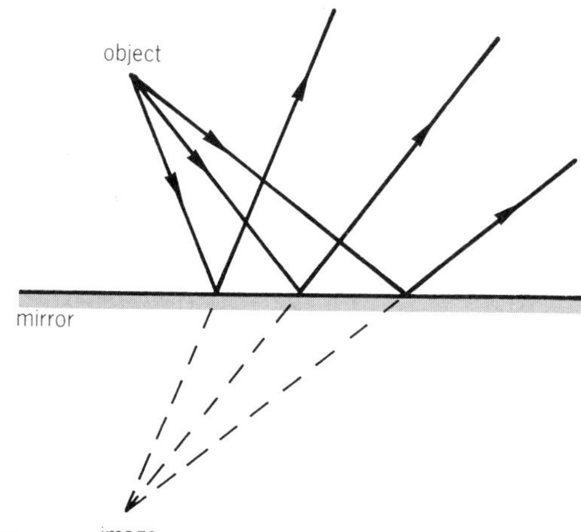

Figure 23.2

Inclined mirrors

The number of images formed in two plane mirrors inclined at an angle θ to each other is given by:

$$\text{number of images} = \frac{360}{\theta} - 1$$

Rotating mirror

When a mirror rotates through an angle θ the reflected light from it will turn through an angle 2θ (Figure 23.3).

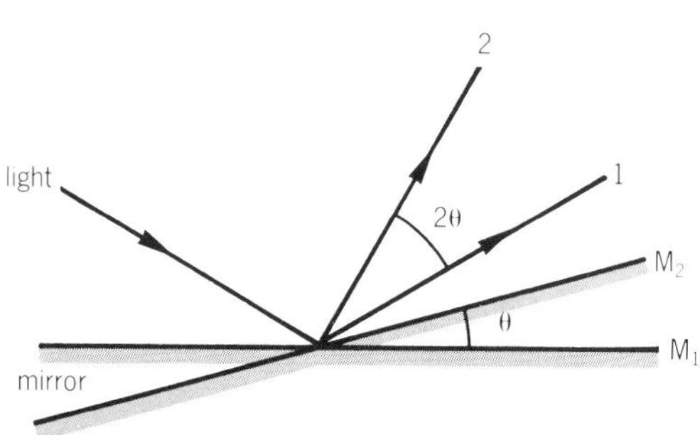

Figure 23.3

Lateral inversion

The image produced by a plane mirror is laterally inverted, that is, it is reversed left to right.

Uses of plane mirrors

Optical lever	Sextant
Kaleidoscope	Periscope (Figure 23.4)
Telescope flat	Dental mirror
Seeing round corners	

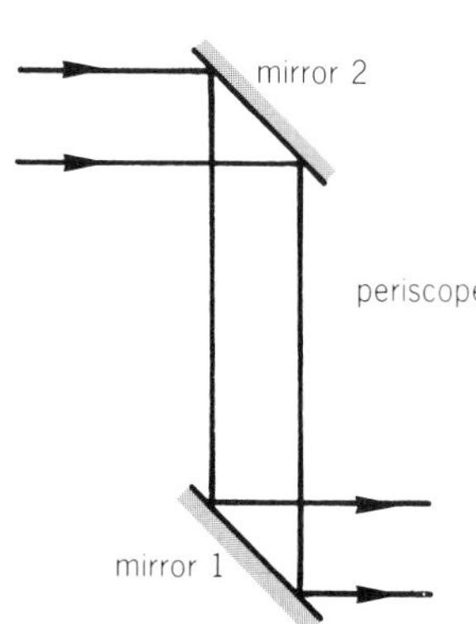

Figure 23.4

Student investigation

Use the principle of the optical lever to measure the bending of the following objects:

(*a*) a laboratory bench when a person sits on one end,

(*b*) a metre rule when it is fixed as a cantilever and loaded with its thin edge uppermost, and

(*c*) a glass window when it is pressed in the centre with one finger.

Reflection properties

When light falls on a surface three things may happen (Figure 23.5):

(*a*) a fraction r will be reflected

(*b*) a fraction a will be absorbed

(*c*) a fraction t will be transmitted

Therefore:

$$r + a + t = 1$$

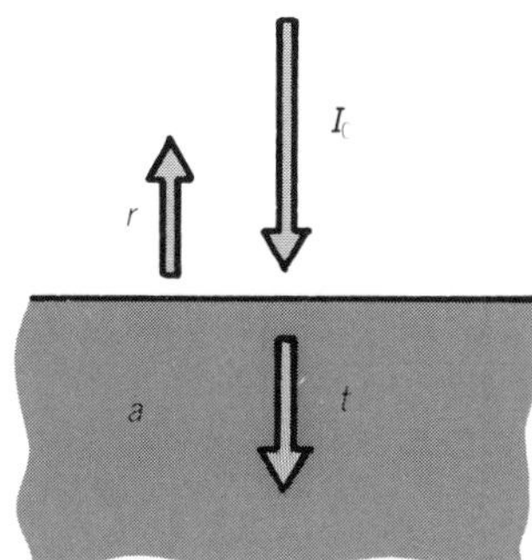

Figure 23.5

Magnesium oxide will reflect some 98 per cent of the incident light, silver is also very good over a fairly limited range of wavelengths while aluminium, although not quite so effective, gives a better reflection over a wide range of wavelengths.

The intensity of light (I) transmitted through a material of thickness x is given by the equation:

$$I = I_0 e^{-\mu x}$$

where μ is a constant for the material. For a specimen of glass μ could be $4\ m^{-1}$ at 600 nm wavelength (yellow light) rising to $1000\ m^{-1}$ at a wavelength of 250 nm (ultra-violet). The larger the value for μ, the more the light is absorbed.

Mirrors used for reflecting telescopes are made with front-silvered surfaces to prevent unwanted multiple reflections from within the glass.

One-way mirrors are an interesting application of reflection. A thin metal film is deposited on a glass sheet so that only part of the incident light is transmitted. Standing on the poorly lit side of such a mirror enables you to see through to the bright side but when viewed from the other side it looks like a perfect mirror.

Student investigation

The intensity of two light sources may be compared using the following simple experiment. Make a drop of grease about 1 cm in diameter on a piece of white paper. Place a standard source, say a candle, a measured distance from one side of the paper and move the source whose brightness is to be compared on the other side of the paper until the grease spot seems to disappear. At this point the intensities of illumination due to the two sources are equal. Measure the distance of the second light source from the paper.

Repeat with a series of different sources.

Student investigation

It is possible to buy pieces of plastic that have been coated on one side with a very thin layer of aluminium. They behave as one-way mirrors: objects can be seen clearly through the sheet only if they are on the more highly illuminated side.

Investigate the optical properties of such a sheet for various light levels. Use a phototransistor to measure the intensity of the incident, transmitted and reflected light from both sides of the film. How does the ratio of these three quantities depend on the initial light level?

1 A plane mirror is fixed to the suspension of a moving coil galvanometer with a sensitivity of 5° per microamp. A beam of light incident on the mirror is reflected on to a scale 3 m away.

Calculate the movement of the spot of light on the scale if a current of 0.8 μA passes through the meter.

2 Find the deviation D of a ray of light reflected from two plane mirrors inclined at an angle θ to each other and show that it is the same for all rays.

Calculate this deviation when θ is (*a*) 45° and (*b*) 90°.

3 What is the minimum length of plane mirror in which a man 1.8 m high can see his full length?

4 Discuss the problems of using a back-silvered mirror in place of a front-silvered mirror in a reflecting astronomical telescope.

Why don't back-silvered mirrors present any problem in everyday life?

The study of geometrical optics such as the reflection of light is of crucial importance in laser physics. Knowledge of this work may be applied to fibre optic communications, laser energy transfer, and so on.

Curved mirrors

There are very many types of mirror but initially we will consider only spherical and parabolic reflectors.

The effects of a narrow parallel beam of light on a concave and a convex surface are shown in Figure 23.6.

Some important definitions

The **principal axis** is a line through the centre of the mirror which passes through the centre of curvature.

The **pole** of the mirror P is where the principal axis meets the mirror.

The **principal focus** F is the point where parallel light close to the axis converges to a focus.

The **focal length** (f) is the distance from the principal focus to the pole of the mirror.

The **centre of curvature** C is the centre of curvature of the mirror surface.

The **radius of curvature** is the distance of the centre of curvature from the pole of the mirror.

The **paraxial ray** is one that lies close to the principal axis and may make a small angle with it.

Sign convention

Adopting a sign convention means that we decide to assign either a positive or a negative sign to all measurements of length.

In this book we will take all **real** distances as **positive** and all **virtual** distances as **negative**. Notice the following:

(*a*) for a concave mirror the principal focus and the focal length are real;

(*b*) for a convex mirror the principal focus and focal length are virtual.

Uses of curved mirrors

Concave mirrors	**Convex mirrors**
Reflecting telescope	Safety viewers at dangerous corners and on upper deck of buses
Dental mirror	Anti-shoplifting devices
Headlamp reflectors	Car wing mirrors
Shaving and make-up mirrors	

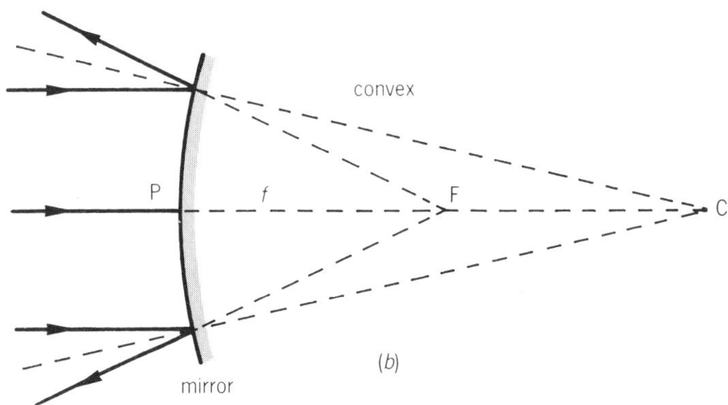

Figure 23.6

Graphical method for finding the position of an image

Using Figure 23.7, consider an object placed on the principal axis in front of a concave mirror of focal length f. (Mirror diagrams – see p.138.)

To locate the image we must draw three rays from the object:

1 the principal axis,

2 a ray from the top of the object parallel to the principal axis which when it strikes the mirror will be reflected through the principal focus,

3 a ray from the axis through the principal focus which after reflection will emerge parallel to the principal axis.

The image of the top of the object will be at the point where rays 2 and 3 cross. The image of the bottom of the object will lie on the principal axis such that the final image is perpendicular to that axis if the object is also perpendicular to the principal axis.

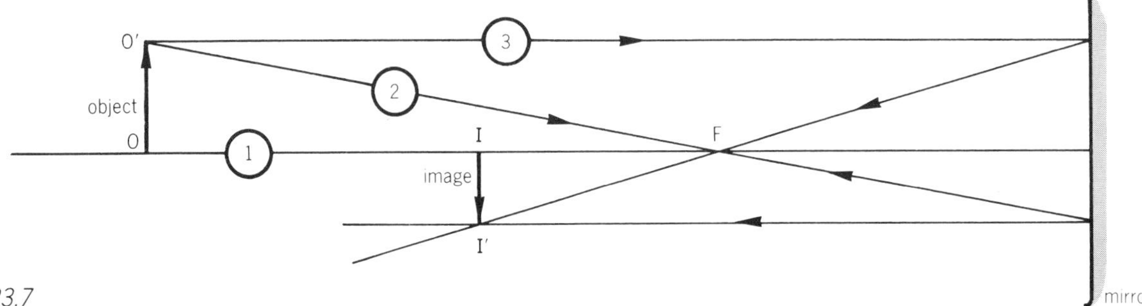

Figure 23.7

Let the object distance be u and the image distance be v. A summary of the results for a range of *real* objects is given in the table below.

	Concave	*Convex*
$\infty > u > 2f$	real/inverted $f < v < 2f$	virtual/erect $f > v > 2f/3$
$u = 2f$	real/inverted $v = 2f$	virtual/erect $v = 2f/3$
$2f > u > f$	real/inverted $\infty > v > 2f$	virtual/erect $2f/3 > v > f/2$
$u = f$	real/inverted $v = \infty$	virtual/erect $v = f/2$
$f > u > 0$	virtual/erect $\infty > v > 0$	virtual/erect $f/2 > v > 0$
$u = \infty$	real/inverted $v = f$	virtual/erect $v = f$

Formulae for curved mirrors

For an object distance u, an image distance v and focal length f we have:

$$\frac{1}{u} + \frac{1}{v} = \frac{1}{f}$$

This formula applies to both convex and concave mirrors, but of course the distances must be entered with their correct sign.

Transverse magnification

Consider an object and image as shown in Figure 23.8.

Light from the top of the object strikes the mirror at an angle θ and therefore must be reflected at an angle θ.

The transverse or linear magnification m is defined as:

$$m = \frac{\text{image height}}{\text{object height}}$$

From Figure 23.8 this is a/b but (by similar triangles) $a/b = v/u$ and so the linear magnification can be written as:

$$m = \frac{\text{image distance } (v)}{\text{object distance } (u)}$$

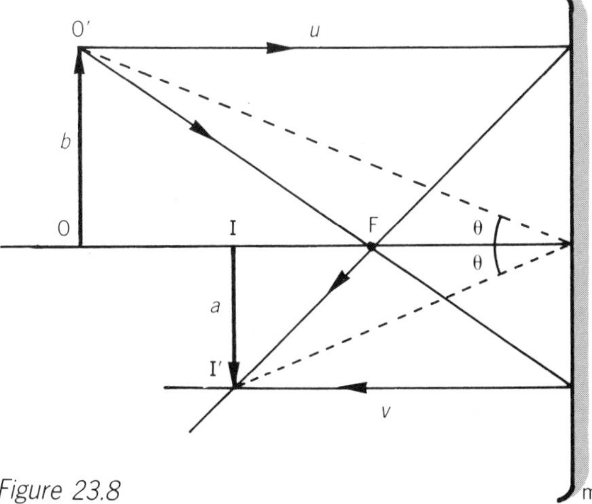

Figure 23.8

The superficial or area magnification is written as:

$$m = \frac{v^2}{u^2}$$

Newton's formula

Another useful formula is known as Newton's formula.

Let the distance of the object and image from the principal focus be x and y respectively (Figure 23.9). Then

$$u = f + x \quad \text{and} \quad v = f + y$$

Using the mirror formula:

$$\frac{1}{u} + \frac{1}{v} = \frac{1}{f} \quad \text{gives} \quad \frac{1}{f + x} + \frac{1}{f + y} = \frac{1}{f}$$

Therefore

$$f^2 = xy$$

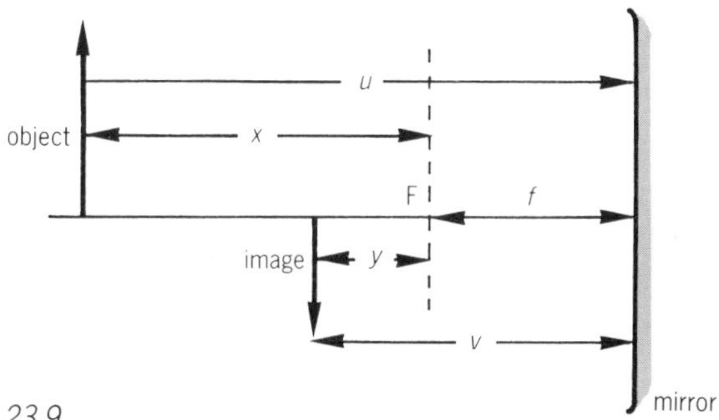

Figure 23.9

Magnification – demonstrated here by the refraction of light through the side of a water-filled beaker

Spherical and parabolic mirrors

You can consider a spherical mirror as being made up of an infinite number of plane mirrors, each one obeying the laws of plane reflection.

If a wide beam of light is incident on a spherical mirror, then the light does not return to one focus, as Figure 23.10(*a*) shows. The reflected lines form a pattern, and this has an envelope known as the **caustic curve**. You will see this effect in the reflection from the inside of a teacup (Figure 23.10(*b*)).

Because of this distortion large astronomical telescope mirrors are made parabolic, so that they give one clearly defined focus whatever width of beam of parallel light is incident upon them (Figure 23.10(*c*)). The largest optical reflectors have diameters of over five metres!

From now on we will confine ourselves to the study of spherical surfaces and rays close to the axis.

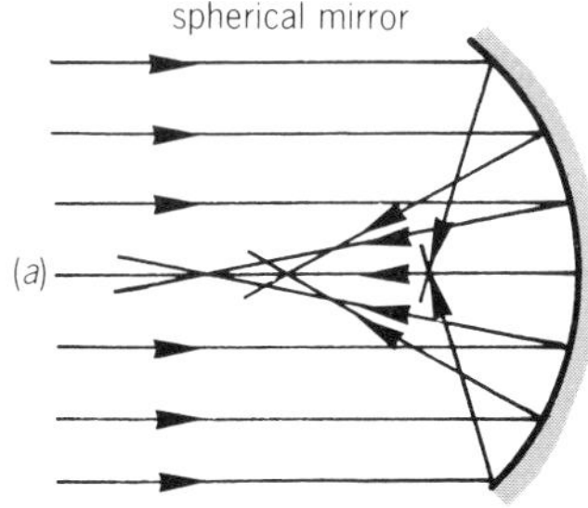

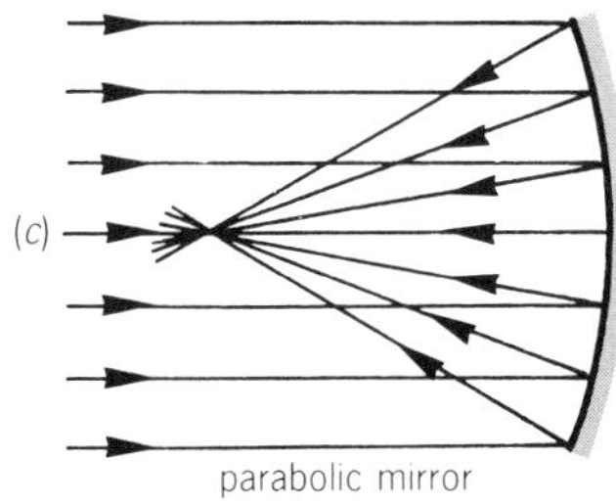

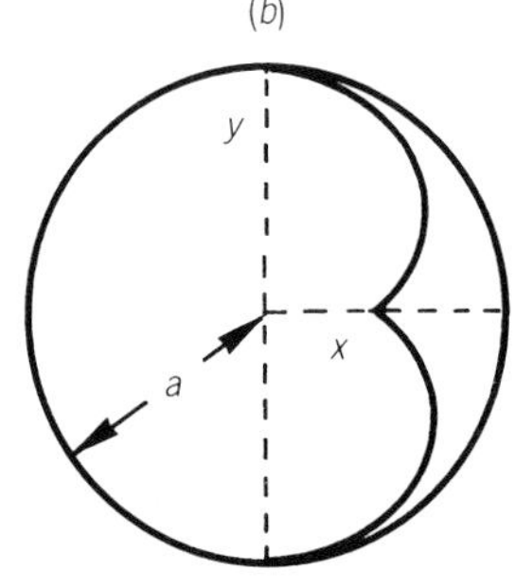

caustic curve: $\{4(x^2 + y^2) - a^2\}^3 = 27a^4y^2$

Figure 23.10

Relation between the radius of curvature (R) and the focal length (f)

If a parallel beam of light hits a mirror, then at the point of incidence of one ray it will make an angle of incidence i with the surface at that point. The angle of reflection will also therefore be i (by the laws of plane reflection). This reflected light will pass through the principal focus and therefore make an angle $2i$ with the axis (Figure 23.11).

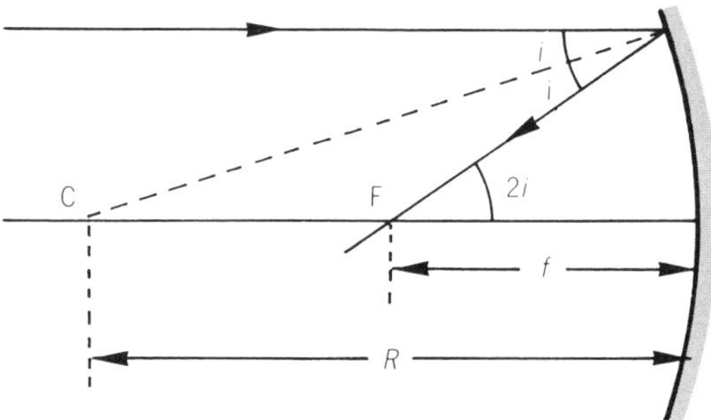

Figure 23.11

For small angles – that is, for a beam close to the principal axis – we can show that

$$R = 2f$$

Longitudinal magnification

It is left for the student to show that the longitudinal magnification (the magnification along the axis) is given by

$$m = \frac{v^2}{u^2}$$

5 A small object placed in front of a concave spherical mirror gives an image that is real and four times the size of the object. When the object is moved 10 cm towards the mirror a similarly magnified virtual image is formed.
Find the focal length of the mirror.

6 A large concave mirror has a radius of curvature of 1.5 m. A person stands 10 m in front of the mirror.
(*a*) Where is the person's image?
The person walks towards the mirror at a constant velocity of 2 m s^{-1}.
(*b*) What is the velocity of the person's image? [o]

Examples

1 A mirror forms an erect image 40 cm from the object and one-third its height. Where must the mirror be situated? What is its radius of curvature? If the object is real, is the mirror concave or convex?

Using the mirror formula and that for transverse magnification we have

$$\frac{1}{u} + \frac{1}{v} = \frac{1}{f} \quad \text{and} \quad v = -\frac{u}{3}$$

but since the image is erect it is virtual and so

$$v + u = 40$$

Therefore $-3v - v = 40$, giving $u = 30$ cm and $v = -10$ cm.
Therefore

$$\frac{1}{30} - \frac{1}{10} = \frac{1}{f}$$

Then

$f = -15$ cm, $R = -30$ cm.

Since then the focal length is negative and therefore real, the mirror is convex.

2 A concave mirror forms a sharply focused image of the Sun 1 cm diameter on a screen. If the Sun subtends an angle of 30′ of arc at the Earth, calculate the radius of curvature of the mirror.

This type of problem can be easily solved by considering Figure 23.12. In the triangle PFS:

$$\tan(30') = \frac{1}{f}$$

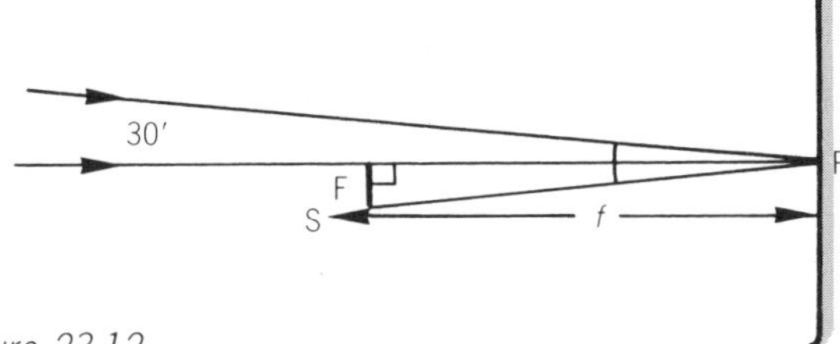

Figure 23.12

since the image of the Sun will be formed at the principal focus of the mirror.

Therefore $f = 114.6$ cm, giving $R = 229$ cm.

Mirror graphs

Figures 23.13 and 23.14 show how the object and image distances change for convex and concave mirrors respectively.

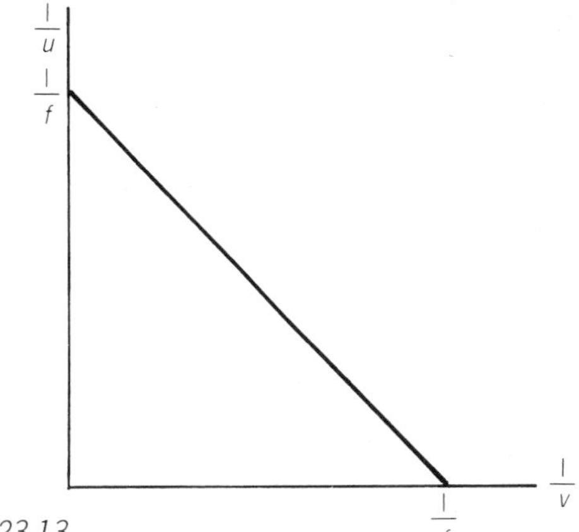

Figure 23.13

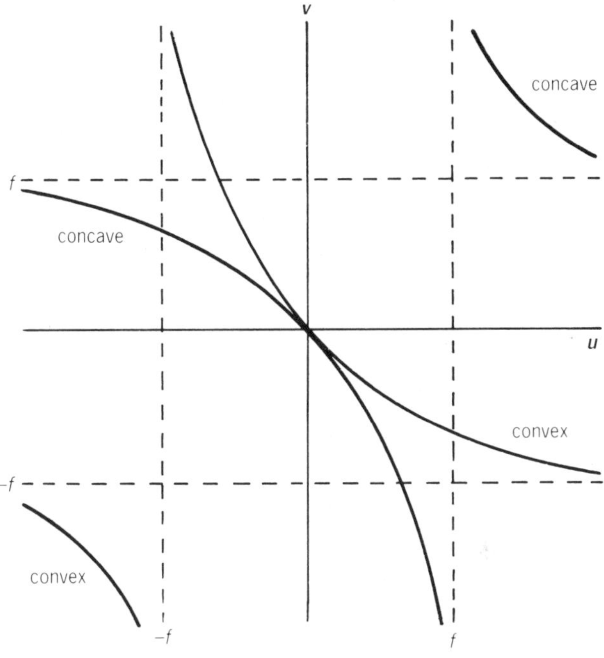

Figure 23.14

7 A Cassegrain reflecting telescope has a small convex mirror with its reflecting surface facing towards a large concave mirror mounted coaxially with the convex mirror. The focal length of each mirror is 1.20 m.

Calculate the distance by which these two mirrors must be separated if a real image is to be formed at the surface of the concave mirror when light from a distant object is incident upon it.

8 A solar telescope with a mirror focal length 8 m is used to project a real image of the Sun on to a screen. If the angular diameter of the Sun when seen from the Earth is 0.5°, calculate the diameter of the solar image formed by the telescope.

Measurement of the focal length of a mirror

The radius of curvature R of a spherical mirror can be measured directly with a sphereometer and the focal length f found from $R = 2f$. The following methods are alternatives to this and measure the focal length directly.

(i) Concave mirror

1 A simple method is to focus the image of a distant object such as the Sun on to a screen. The distance of the mirror from the screen is the focal length of the mirror.

2 A rather more accurate method is to adjust the position of an illuminated object until it coincides with its image (no parallax). The object is then at the centre of curvature of the mirror and hence R and then f may be found.

3 A series of values of u and v can be found and the focal length found either graphically or from the mirror formula.

(ii) Convex mirror

Clearly the methods described above for the concave mirror will be of no use for a convex mirror since it does not give a real image for a real object. An alternative method is described below.

Using a convex lens of greater power than the mirror an image I of the object O is produced.

The convex mirror is then placed between the lens and the screen and moved until the object coincides with its image I_1 (Figure 23.15). To do this the light must hit the mirror at right angles, and so I must be at the centre of curvature of the mirror. The distance between the mirror and I is therefore the radius of curvature of the mirror.

9 A dentist's mirror has a radius of curvature of 3 cm. How far must it be placed from a small dental cavity to give a virtual image of the cavity that is magnified five times?

10 A mirror forms an erect image which is 30 cm from a real object and twice its height.
(*a*) Where must the mirror be situated?
(*b*) What is its radius of curvature?
(*c*) Is the mirror convex or concave? [L]

11 (*a*) If a piece of photographic film is placed at the position of a real image it will record that image. Explain why this can't be done with a virtual image. How would you record a virtual image?
(*b*) Why does a plane mirror reverse left to right but not top to bottom?
(*c*) If a concave mirror is immersed in water, does its focal length change?
(*d*) If two opposite walls of a room are covered with plane mirrors a series of images can be seen. Explain how this occurs and why the more distant images are dimmer than the closer ones.

12 An object is 20 cm from the centre of a spherical silvered Christmas tree ornament which is 8 cm in diameter. Where is the image of this object?

Mirror diagrams

Since we are dealing with rays close to the axis we have adopted a simple representation for both concave and convex mirrors in most of the preceding diagrams.

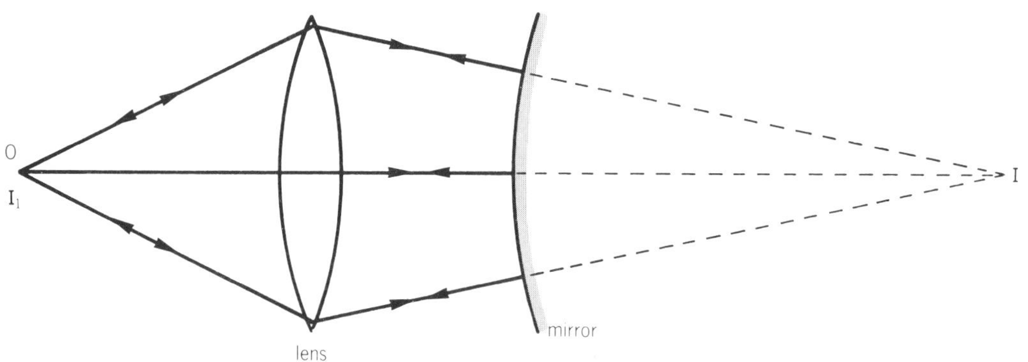

Figure 23.15

24 · Refraction

When light passes from one material to another its velocity is altered, and if it meets the boundary with an angle of incidence other than 0° the direction of travel of the light is also changed as shown in Figure 24.1. A consideration of this in terms of the wave theory is given on page 189.

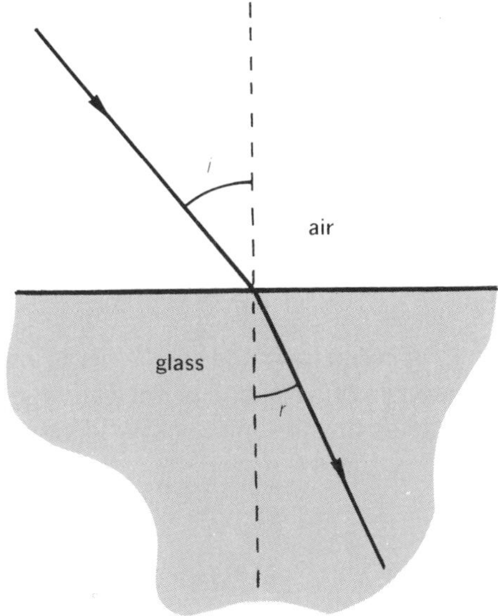

Figure 24.1

This phenomenon is known as **refraction** and the two angles *i* and *r* are known as the angle of incidence and the angle of refraction. The relation between these angles was discovered by Snell in 1621 and is known as **Snell's law**. It states that

the ratio $\frac{\sin i}{\sin r}$ is a constant for light passing from one medium to the other and is known as the **refractive index** (n) for the material into which the light passes.

The value of the refractive index is usually taken as being for light travelling from a vacuum into the material and is properly written as the **absolute refractive index,** a vacuum being defined to have a refractive index of 1. Some values for the absolute refractive index for different substances are quoted in the table.

Material	*Refractive index*
Diamond	2.42
Ruby	1.76
Glass (flint)	1.53–1.96
Glass (crown)	1.48–1.61
Glycerol	1.47
Water	1.33
Ice	1.31
Air at STP	1.000 298
Carbon disulphide	1.63
Diiodomethane	1.74

The refractive index for air is so close to 1.00 that we will assume it to be 1.00 for calculations in which light passes from air into a solid or liquid. Note that when light passes from air into a solid or liquid the refractive index is *always* > 1.

For light travelling from a medium of absolute refractive index n_1 to another of absolute refractive index n_2 the refractive index of the interface is given as ${}_1n_2$.

The refractive index of a material depends on the wavelength of radiation being considered. The relation is given by **Cauchy's formula:**

$$n = 1 + \frac{A}{\lambda^2}$$

where λ is the wavelength of the light and A a constant for the material.

1 The following set of results are the oldest recorded physical measurements. They were made by Ptolemy at Alexandria towards the end of the first century A.D. and show the angles of incidence (θ_1) and refraction (θ_2) for a ray of light passing from air into water.

Are they consistent with Snell's law? If so what value for the refractive index of water do they give?

θ_1	θ_2	θ_1	θ_2
10° 0′	7° 45′	50° 0′	35° 0′
20° 0′	15° 30′	60° 0′	40° 30′
30° 0′	22° 30′	70° 0′	45° 30′
40° 0′	29° 00′	80° 0′	50° 0′

Light passing from one transparent material to another

Consider a beam of light passing from material 1 to material 2 (Figure 24.2). Let the absolute refractive indices of the materials be n_1 and n_2 respectively. We have

$$ {}_1n_2 = \frac{\sin\theta_1}{\sin\theta_2} $$

and also, if the direction of the light is reversed,

$$ {}_2n_1 = \frac{\sin\theta_2}{\sin\theta_1} $$

Therefore

$$ {}_1n_2 = \frac{1}{{}_2n_1} $$

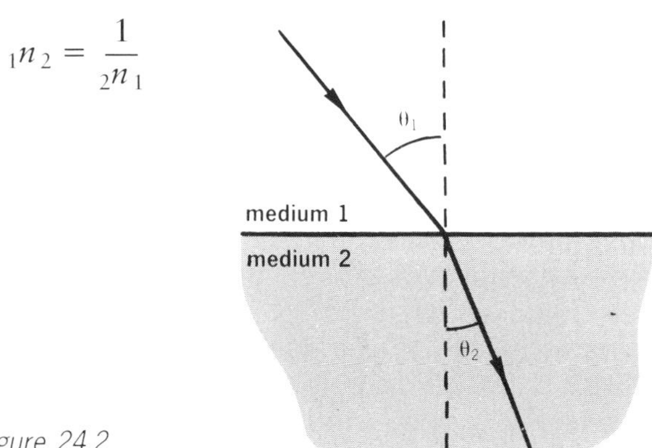

Figure 24.2

Notice that we have made an important assumption here, namely that the light will follow the same path whether it is travelling in one direction or the other. This is known as the **principle of reversibility of light.**

Light passing through a composite block

Consider light passing through the composite block shown in Figure 24.3. Considering the refractions at the three boundaries, we have

$$ {}_vn_1 = \frac{\sin i}{\sin i_1} \qquad {}_1n_2 = \frac{\sin i_1}{\sin i_2} \qquad {}_2n_v = \frac{\sin i_2}{\sin i} $$

and this gives us the important relationship that

$$ n_1 \sin i_1 = n_2 \sin i_2 $$

This can be extended to cover the passage of light through a multiple block. Notice also that if the block is parallel-sided (as shown in the diagram) then the light emerges travelling in the same direction as its original path but displaced sideways (see diagram). You should expect this result from the principle of reversibility of light.

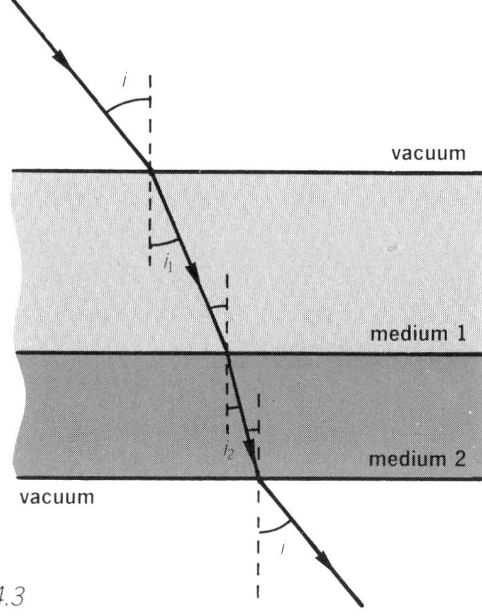

Figure 24.3

Example

A film of oil of refractive index 1.40 floats on water. Calculate the angle of refraction in the water for a beam of light that strikes the oil surface at 35°. (The refractive index of water is 1.33.)

We have

$$ n_a \sin i_1 = n_o \sin\theta = n_w \sin i_2 $$

$$ \sin 35 = 1.4 \sin\theta = 1.33 \sin i_2 $$

and so

$$ \sin i_2 = \frac{\sin 35}{1.33} = 0.43 $$

Therefore

$$ i_2 = 25.5° $$

Notice that the oil layer has no effect on the direction of the light in the water.

2 A beam of light is incident on the plane boundary between two materials of refractive indices 1.60 and 1.40. If the angle of incidence is 30° and the light originates in the medium of higher refractive index, what is the angle of refraction?

3 A dolphin is viewed through the 10 cm thick plate glass of the underwater viewing window in an oceanarium. If the eye of the dolphin is 1 m behind the glass, where does it appear to be to a person standing the other side of the glass? (Refractive index of glass = 1.50; refractive index of water = 1.33)

Lateral displacement

Although the direction of the light is not altered when it passes through a parallel-sided block, it is displaced sideways. This displacement is known as **lateral displacement** (AB = d in Figure 24.4). From the diagram:

$$BC = \frac{t}{\cos r}$$

Therefore

$$AB = \sin(i - r) \times BC$$

$$= \frac{t \sin(i - r)}{\cos r}$$

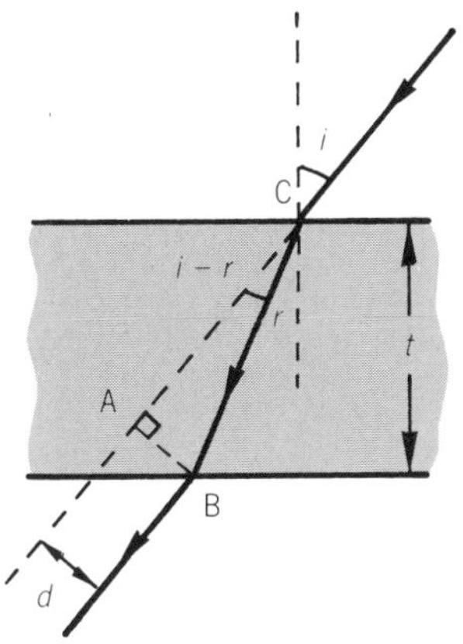

Figure 24.4

Real and apparent depth

When you look into a pool of water or a block of glass the material does not appear to be as deep or as thick as it really is, and this is due to the refraction of the light passing through it. It can be shown that

$$\text{refractive index of the material} = \frac{\text{real depth}}{\text{apparent depth}}$$

This formula is only strictly true when the eye is placed vertically over the object. At other positions the pool will appear even shallower since the angle of incidence with the water–air surface is larger. If the vertical displacement is d (Figure 24.5),

$$d = t - h$$

But $h = t/n$. Therefore

$$d = t(1 - 1/n)$$

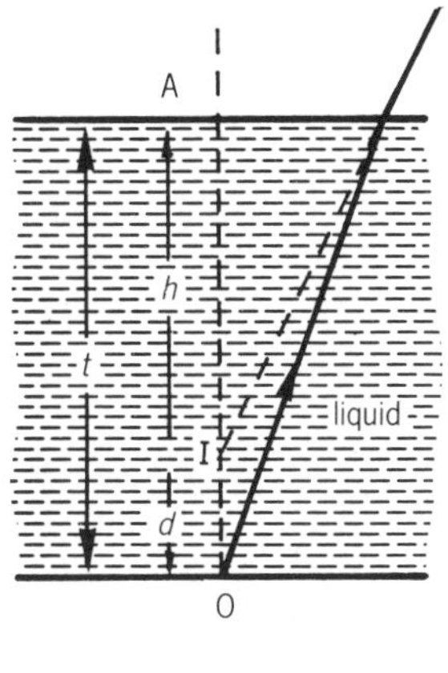

Figure 24.5

Example

Calculate the real depth of a swimming pool if the apparent depth is 1.2 m. (Refractive index of water = 1.33)

Real depth = 1.33 × apparent depth
∴ apparent depth = 1.6 m.

Student investigation

The author was once asked the following question by a science advisor in an interview for one of his teaching posts: 'How would you explain to an average fifteen year old why a rainbow is curved?'

Well, and how would you do it? A mathematical proof of the shape of the rainbow follows: can you re-write it in simple language to explain to the student in question – no difficult mathematics, please!

Figure 24.6 shows a ray of light from the Sun being *partially* internally reflected by a spherical raindrop. The amount of light reflected will vary with the deviation but will be maximum at, or near minimum deviation (see page 143).

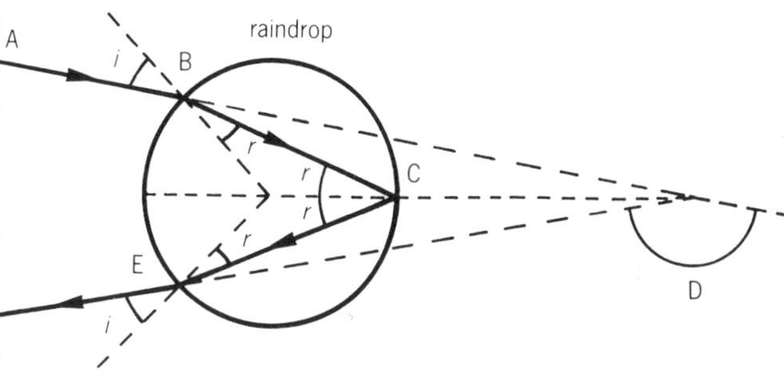

Figure 24.6

For one internal reflection (the primary rainbow) we have

$$D = 180 + 2i - 4r$$

Also for minimum deviation ($dD/di = 0$) we can show that

$$\cos i = \sqrt{\frac{n-1}{3}}$$

where n is the refractive index of the water of the raindrop.

The deviation for yellow light ($n = 1.34$) is about 138° and so the observer will see a rainbow in a direction that makes 180° – 138° = 42° with the Sun's altitude (Figure 24.7).

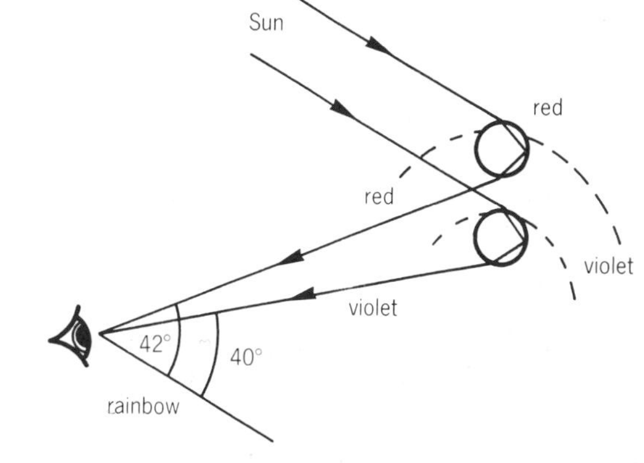

Figure 24.7

Total internal reflection and critical angle

When light passes from a material such as water into one of lower refractive index such as air it is found that there is a maximum angle of incidence in the water that will give a refracted beam in the air, that is, the angle of refraction is 90°. The angle of incidence in the denser medium corresponding to an angle of refraction of 90° is known as the **critical angle** (c) (Figure 24.8). The reason for this is clear if we consider the formulae. For an angle of refraction of 90° we have

$$_2n_1 = \frac{\sin i}{\sin r} = \frac{\sin c}{\sin 90^\circ} = \frac{1}{_1n_2}$$

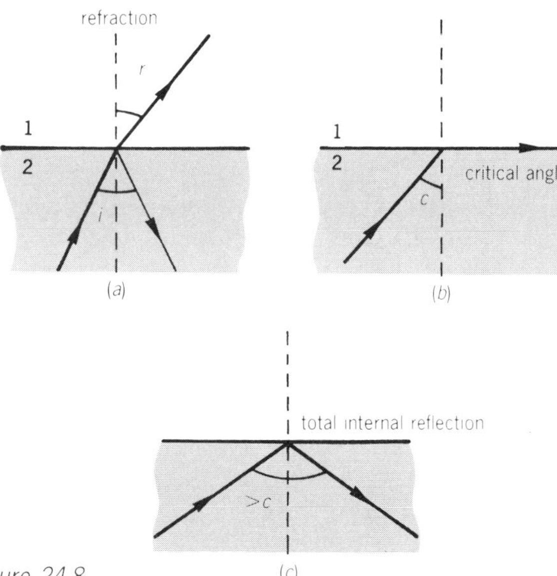

Figure 24.8

For an air–glass boundary, with $n = 1.5$, $c = 42°$ and for an air–water boundary $c = 48.5°$.

For angles of incidence greater than the critical angle *all* the light is reflected back into the optically more dense material, that is, the one with the greater refractive index. This is known as **total internal reflection** and the normal laws of reflection are obeyed.

Total internal reflection explains the shiny appearance of the water surface of a swimming pool when viewed at an angle from below. The phenomenon is used in prismatic binoculars (see page 159).

(Mirages are caused by continuous internal reflection.)

4 A man stands at the edge of the deep end of a swimming pool, the base of which is covered with square tiles. Describe and explain how the tiles will appear to him. [O and C]

Example

If the refractive indices from air to glass and from air to water are 1.50 and 1.33 respectively, calculate the critical angle for a water–glass surface.

The refractive index for light passing from water to glass $_wn_g$ is given by

$$_wn_g = \frac{n_g}{n_w} = \frac{1.5}{1.33} = 1.13 = {_wn_g}$$

Therefore the critical angle (c) can be found from

$$_wn_g = \frac{1}{\sin c}$$

$$\sin c = \frac{1}{_wn_g} = 0.89 \qquad \text{and so} \qquad c = 62.5^\circ$$

It is left as an exercise for the reader to prove that light cannot pass across the corner of a right-angled glass block if the refractive index of the glass is 1.5.

5 Explain or comment on the following:

(*a*) An empty test-tube placed in water may show a silvery appearance.

(*b*) The stars twinkle.

(*c*) Mirages occur in the Arctic.

(*d*) A diamond will sparkle more than an identically shaped piece of glass.

6 A student claims that because of atmospheric refraction the Sun can be seen after it has set, and that the day is therefore longer than if the Earth had no atmosphere.

(*a*) What does the student mean by saying that the Sun can be seen after it has set?

(*b*) Comment on whether you think the student's conclusions are valid. [Z]

Fibre optics

The transmission of light through glass fibres is one of the most important uses of total internal reflection. This use of glass fibres is known as **fibre optics**.

A beam of light travels through a bundle of fibres and as long as the angle of incidence with the walls of a fibre is great enough it will be reflected along the fibre as shown in Figure 24.9 (the bundles are often called **light pipes**). The fibres may be between 0.01 mm and 0.002 mm in diameter and may be arranged at the same relative positions at both ends of the light pipe so that a clear image may be seen through it.

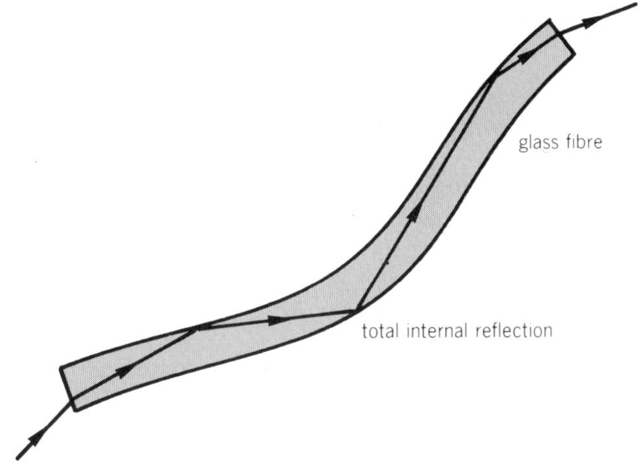

Figure 24.9

Such fibres can be made to carry information such as TV channels or telephone conversations. Other applications of fibre optics include its use in medicine to see inside the human body and in road signs where one light bulb and a set of fibres is used to illuminate different parts of the sign thus saving electrical energy. A further recent application is in security fences. The metal strands of the fence contain a piece of fibre optic material down which a beam of light passes. If the strand is cut the light beam is interrupted and an alarm sounds. It is thought that this type of system is impossible to bypass.

Refraction through prisms

We will consider the refraction of monochromatic light through prisms. The effect of different wavelengths is considered on page 154.

When light passes through a prism it is deviated, and the angle of deviation d depends upon the angle of incidence i of the light on the first face of the prism. If d is plotted against i then a graph like that in Figure 24.10 will be obtained. You will notice that there is a minimum deviation D for a certain value of incidence.

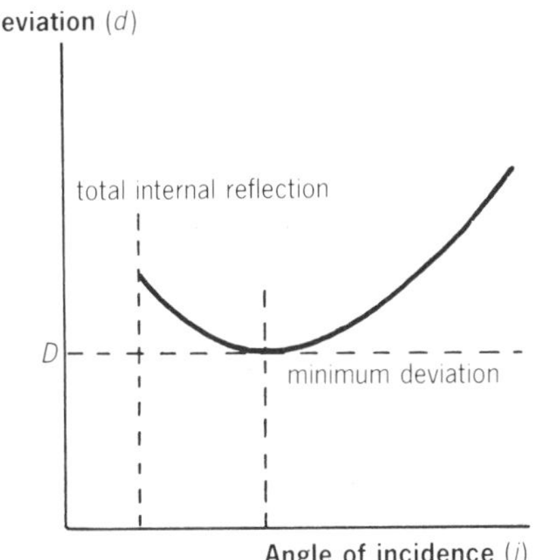

Figure 24.10

By the principle of reversibility it should be clear that this point of minimum deviation occurs when the light passes symmetrically through the prism.

This minimum deviation can be used to find the refractive index of the material of the prism. If a hollow glass prism filled with liquid is used, the refractive index of the liquid can be measured. The theory is shown below.

Let the angle of minimum deviation be D and the refracting angle of the prism be A. Therefore, from Figure 24.11,

$$A = 2r \quad \text{and} \quad n = \frac{\sin i}{\sin r}$$

and so
$$D = (i - r) + (i - r) = 2i - 2r$$

Therefore
$$i = \frac{D + A}{2}$$

and
$$n = \frac{\sin((D + A)/2)}{\sin (A/2)}$$

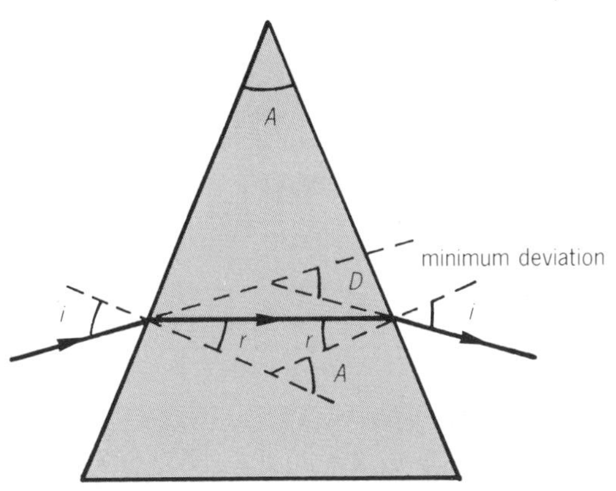

Figure 24.11

Example

A glass prism of refracting angle 60° gives a minimum deviation of 47°. What is the refractive index of the glass?

$n = \sin 53.5/\sin 30 = 1.61$.

7 A glass prism with angles 45°, 45° and 90° is immersed in water (refractive index 1.33). What is the minimum refractive index of the glass such that a ray of light may be totally internally reflected at one of its shorter sides?

8 A light pipe has a plane end as shown in Figure 24.12.

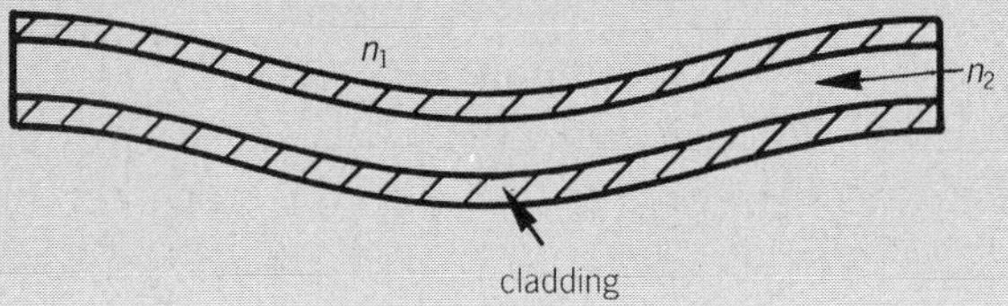

Figure 24.12

The refractive index of the cladding of the pipe is n_1 and that of the core of the pipe n_2. The pipe is in air which has a refractive index that can be considered to be 1. Find an expression for the maximum angle of incidence at the end of the pipe so that light will be transmitted down it.

9 A glass prism has a refracting angle of 60° and is made of material of refractive index 1.45. Calculate the angle of incidence at the first face that will just give total internal reflection at the second face.

10 A layer of turpentine floats on some water. The refractive indices of water and turpentine are 1.33 and 1.47 respectively. From which direction must a ray of light come so that it will be totally internally reflected at the boundary?

11 A glass prism with a refracting angle of 60° has a refractive index of 1.50. Calculate the minimum deviation produced.

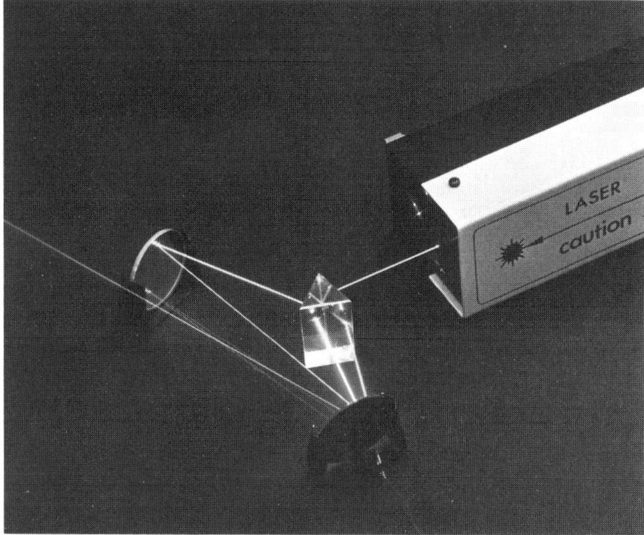

Refraction of laser light through a prism and total internal reflection at its faces (UNILAB Ltd.)

Prisms of small angle

Consider now a small-angled prism as shown in Figure 24.13. The deviation $d = (i - r) + (i' - r')$ and $A = r + r'$.

If the refracting angle of the prism (A) is small then i, i', r and r' are also small, and so

$$i = nr \qquad \text{and} \qquad i' = nr'$$

Therefore
$$\begin{aligned} d &= nr + nr' - A \\ &= n(r + r') - A \\ &= nA - A \\ &= (n - 1)A \end{aligned}$$

The deviation is therefore independent of the angle of incidence and depends only on the refracting angle of the prism and the refractive index for monochromatic light.

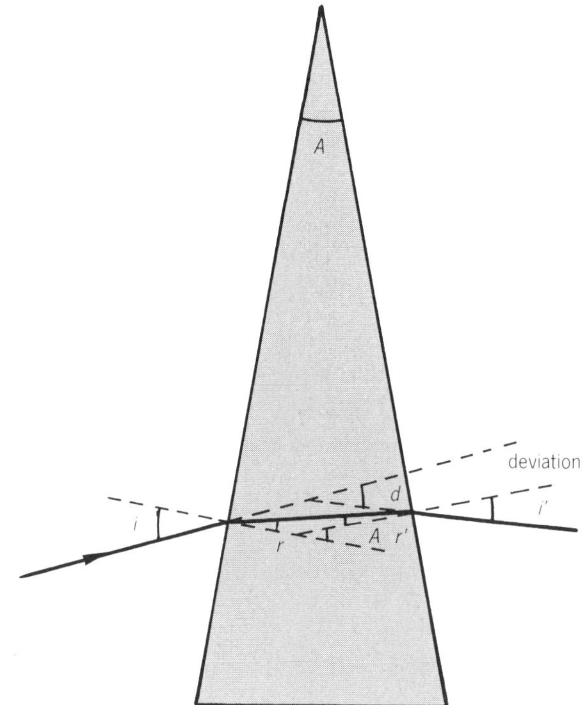

Figure 24.13

Measurement of refractive index

The refractive index of a solid may be found by direct measurement of the angles of incidence and refraction or by real depth/apparent depth measurements.

Several methods are available for finding the refractive indices of liquids. They include real/apparent depth measurements, the air cell method and the concave mirror method. The refractive index of a gas is usually found by an interference method.

The refractive index of a liquid may also be found by a modification of a Newton's rings experiment (see page 207). Only a small amount of liquid is needed for this method.

The air cell method

The air cell consists of two glass plates with a narrow air gap between them (Figure 24.14(*a*)). This cell is placed in a plane-sided container containing the liquid whose refractive index is to be measured.

A monochromatic light source is viewed through two slits placed either side of the container, and the air cell rotated until no light passes through the apparatus. A reading is taken of the orientation of the air cell at this position. The air cell is now rotated past the straight-through position until the light is cut out again. The angle of rotation from one position to the other is found (Figure 24.14(*b*)).

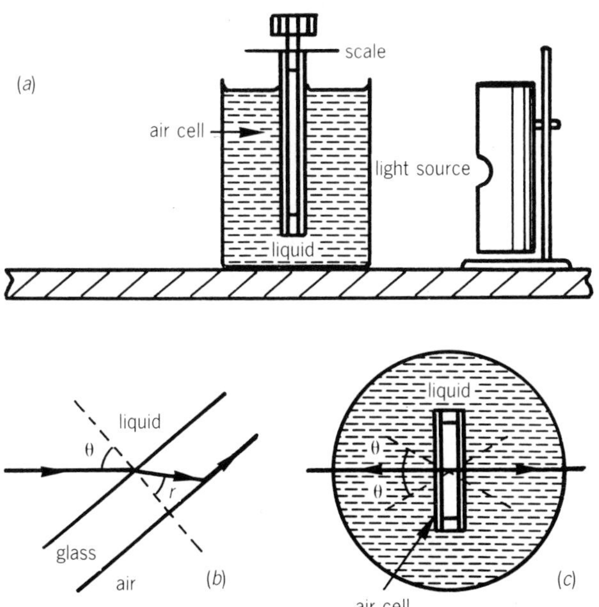

Figure 24.14 .

The light does not pass through the air cell because it is totally internally reflected when it travels from the first glass plate towards the air gap. Figure 24.14(*c*) shows the conditions that apply when the light is just cut off. At this point

$$n_L \sin \theta = n_g \sin r = n_a \sin 90 = n_a$$

$$n_L = \frac{n_a}{\sin \theta} = \frac{1}{\sin \theta}$$

where θ is half the angle through which the air cell is turned between cut-off positions.

Notice that the refractive index of the glass is not required.

The concave mirror method

A pin is held vertically above a concave mirror and its position adjusted until there is no parallax between the object and image. The distance from the mirror to the pin is then measured (h_1). A small quantity of liquid is placed on the mirror and the procedure repeated giving a new, smaller distance h_2 (Figure 24.15).

It can be shown that the refractive index n of the liquid is given by

$$n = \frac{h_1}{h_2}$$

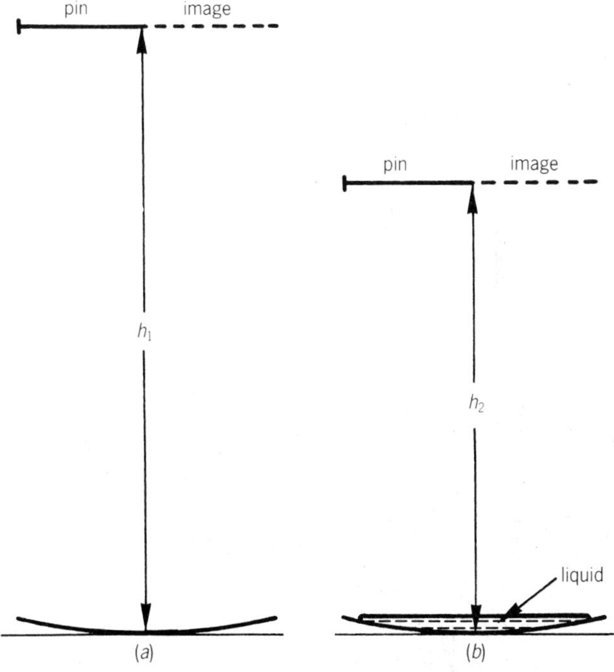

Figure 24.15

25 · Lenses

The action of a lens has been known for thousands of years – Aristophanes in 424 B.C. used a lens as a burning glass – but it has only been in the last 300 years that they have been put to much practical use (the refracting telescope, for example, was not invented until 1609). They are the basis of all optical instruments, including the eye (see page 157)!

A lens is simply a piece of transparent material such as glass, plastic or liquid with one or more curved faces, and the effect that it has on a beam of light depends on the extent and nature of this curvature. The five important types of lens are shown in Figure 25.1.

The curvatures of the surfaces are measured from within the solid so:

convex lens surfaces have a *real* and therefore *positive* radius of curvature;
concave lens surfaces have a *virtual* and therefore *negative* radius of curvature;
a convex lens has a real and therefore positive focal length;
a concave lens has a virtual and therefore negative focal length.

All distances are measured from the pole of the lens and for a thin lens (defined on page 147) this is almost coincident with the centre of the lens.

The strength of a lens is described in terms of either its focal length or its **power**. The power of a lens is defined as:

$$\text{power} = \frac{1}{\text{focal length in metres}}$$

Convex lenses have positive powers while concave lenses have negative powers. The power of a meniscus lens depends on which face of the lens is the more sharply curved.

For example, a convex lens with a focal length of 10 cm will have a power of +10, while a concave lens with a focal length of −5 cm will have a power of −20.

Uses of lenses

The uses of lenses are covered in most GCSE books. A brief survey is given here as a practical guide.

Convex lenses:
Eye (variable focal length)
Glasses to correct for long sight
Microscope
Telescope objective
Camera (single lens system)
Projector

Concave lenses:
Wide-angle spyhole in doors
Glasses to correct for short sight
Wide-angle lens in coach rear windows
Eye lens in Galilean telescope

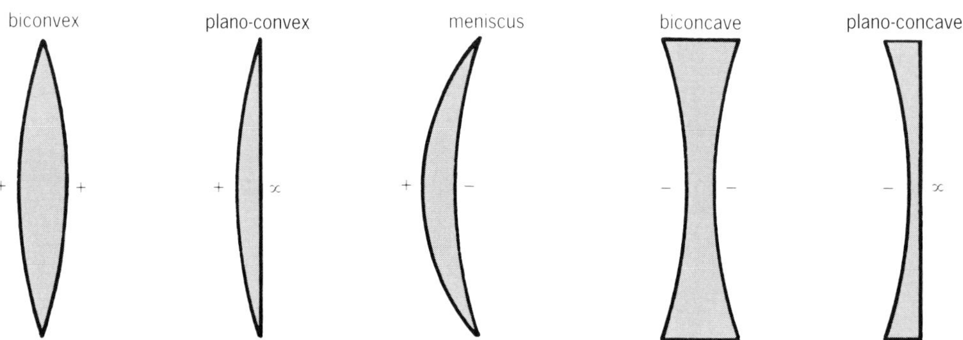

Figure 25.1

The thin lens

We can consider a lens to be made up of a number of prisms, each of small angle (Figure 25.2). If we restrict ourselves to a region near the principal axis of the lens then the refracting angle of these prisms and hence the angle of the face of the lens to a beam of parallel light is very small. From the formula for the deviation of light by a thin prism you can appreciate that as long as we consider only rays close to the axis and travelling at a small angle to it, then the deviation produced by the lens is constant and independent of the direction of the ray.

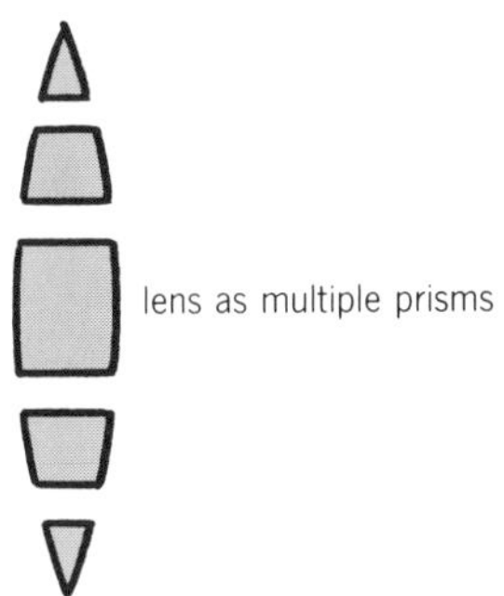

Figure 25.2

The effect on a beam of light of the two basic types of lens is shown in Figure 25.3. The principal focus, focal length, centre of curvature and radius of curvature are also shown.

The position of an image can be found graphically for a lens in a similar manner to that for a mirror. Four lines have to be drawn to represent respectively

(*a*) the principal axis,

(*b*) a ray from the top of the object that passes undeviated through the centre of the lens (notice that at this point the lens behaves like a parallel-sided block of glass),

(*c*) a ray from the top of the object, parallel to the axis that goes through the principal focus after passing through the lens, and

(*d*) a ray from the top of the object through the principal focus that emerges parallel to the axis.

The image of the top of the object is at the point where rays *b*, *c* and *d* cross.

The convex lens will give inverted real images for real objects if $u > f$ and erect virtual images if $u < f$. The virtual images are always magnified while the real images are magnified if $f < u < 2f$.

The concave lens will always give real, erect and diminished images for real objects.

Some examples are shown in Figure 25.4.

1 Use the method of graphical construction to solve the following problems:

(*a*) An object 1 cm high is placed on the axis 10 cm from a thin lens of focal length 25 cm. Find the position and size of the image.

(*b*) A lens forms a real image 3 cm high of an object 1 cm high. If the separation of object and image is 15 cm, find the focal length of the lens.

(*c*) A convex lens of focal length 5 cm forms a virtual image 5 cm high and 10 cm from the lens. Find the position and size of the object.

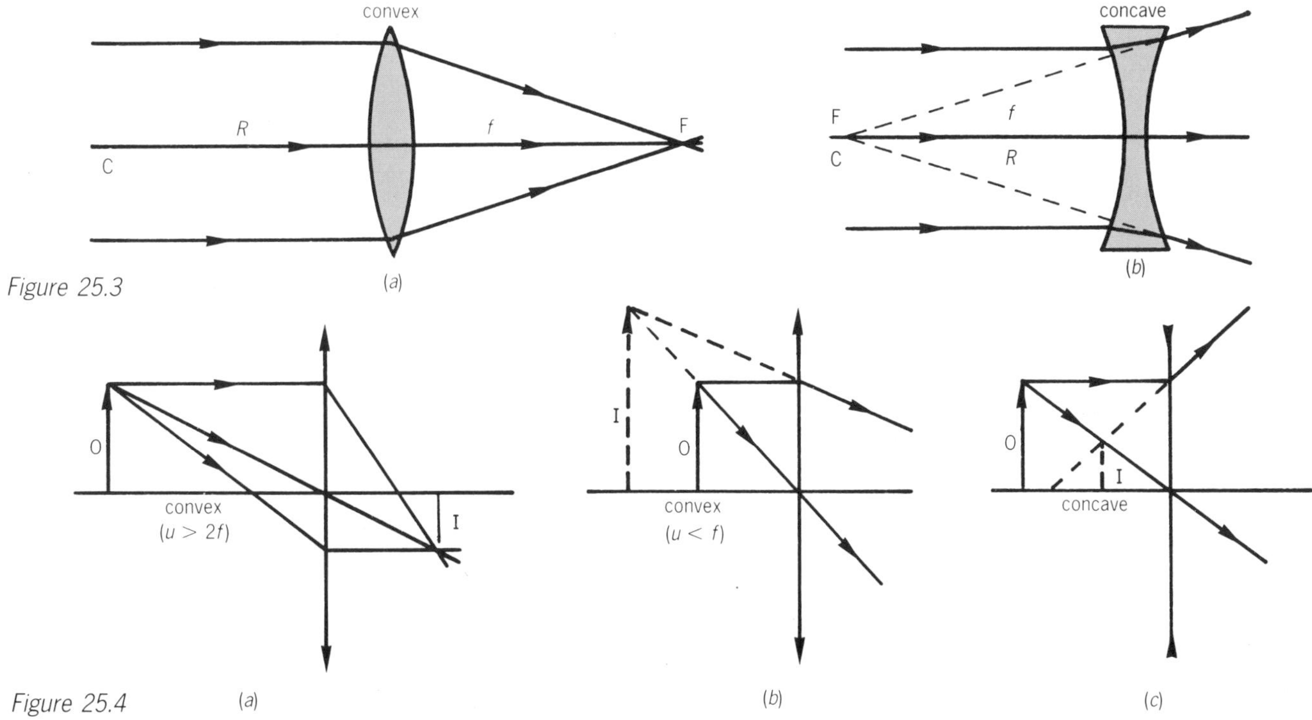

Figure 25.3

Figure 25.4

Magnification

The magnification of a lens, like that of a curved mirror, is given by

$$\text{magnification} = \frac{\text{image distance } (v)}{\text{object distance } (u)}$$

Formula for a thin lens

The formula for a thin lens can be shown to be:

$$\frac{1}{f} = \frac{1}{u} + \frac{1}{v}$$

This applies to all types of lens as long as the correct sign convention is used when substituting values for the distances.

(*Reminder:* we use the 'real is positive, virtual is negative' sign convention in this book.)

Two proofs of the formula will be given here, one a geometrical proof and the other an optical version.

(*a*) Geometrical proof of the lens formula

Consider a plano-convex lens, as shown in Figure 25.5.

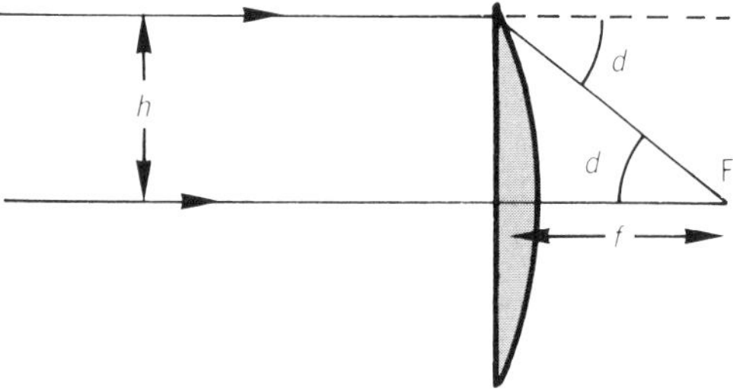

Figure 25.5

If we consider the action of the lens to be like that of a small-angle prism, then all rays have the same deviation. Therefore, in Figure 25.6,

$$d = \alpha + \beta$$

and so, for small angles,

$$\frac{h}{f} = \frac{h}{u} + \frac{h}{v}$$

We therefore have $\dfrac{1}{f} = \dfrac{1}{u} + \dfrac{1}{v}$

and the formula is proved.

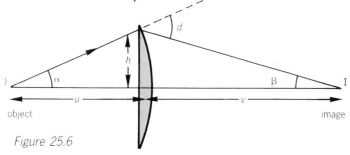

Figure 25.6

Example

An object is placed in front of a converging lens and gives a real image with magnification 5; when the object is moved 6 cm along the axis of the lens a real image of magnification 2 is obtained. What is the focal length of the lens?

Let the initial object and image distances be u and v respectively. Therefore $v/u = 5$, $v = 5u$, and $v'/u + 6 = 2$ where v' is the new image distance. Also

$$\frac{1}{u} + \frac{1}{5u} = \frac{1}{f} \quad \text{and} \quad \frac{1}{u+6} + \frac{1}{2u+12} = \frac{1}{f}$$

These equations give:
$6f = 5u$ and $3f = 2u + 12$, and so $f = 20$ cm.

The lens-maker's formula

The refractive index of the material of the lens n can be introduced into the formula. Consider Figure 25.7:

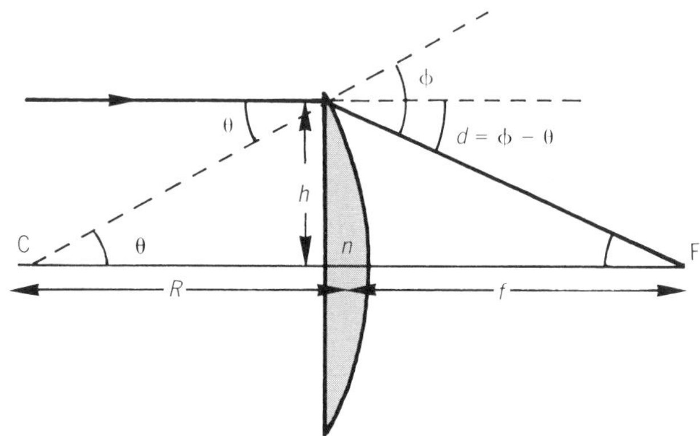

Figure 25.7

The radius of curvature $R = h/\theta$, but $n = \sin\phi/\sin\theta$ and therefore $n = \phi/\theta$, so $\phi = n\theta$ for small θ

But $d = \phi - \theta$. Therefore

$$(n-1)\theta = \frac{h}{f} \quad \text{and} \quad \theta = \frac{h}{R}$$

and $$\frac{n-1}{R} = \frac{1}{f} = \frac{1}{u} + \frac{1}{v}$$

For a lens we have

$$\frac{1}{f} = (n-1)\left(\frac{1}{R} + \frac{1}{S}\right)$$

where R and S are the radii of curvature of the two faces of the lens. This formula is known as the **lens-maker's formula.**

Example

A lens made of glass of refractive index 1.52 has a focal length of 10 cm in air and 50 cm when completely immersed in a liquid. Calculate the refractive index of the liquid (*n*).

Using the formula above we have

$$\frac{2(1.52-1)}{R} = \frac{1}{10} \quad \text{and} \quad \frac{2(1.52-1)}{Rn} = \frac{1}{50}$$

since R = S.

Therefore $R = 10.4$, and so $1.104 = 1.52/n$ giving $n = 1.38$.

Power of a lens

We can now obtain a simple expression for the power of a lens, which we previously defined as $1/f$. Since

$$\frac{1}{f} = (n-1)\left(\frac{1}{R}+\frac{1}{S}\right)$$

we can now define the power as

$$(n-1)\left(\frac{1}{R}+\frac{1}{S}\right)$$

(*b*) Optical proof of the lens formula

The case for a biconvex lens only will be considered (see Figure 25.8).

Consider the two spherical surfaces of the lens. For the first surface we have

$$\frac{n_2}{v'} + \frac{n_1}{u} = \frac{n_2 - n_1}{R_1}$$

For the second surface we have

$$\frac{n_2}{-v'} + \frac{n_1}{v} = \frac{n_2 - n_1}{R_2}$$

(note the negative sign denoting a virtual object for the second surface). Combining these two equations gives

$$\frac{n_1}{u} + \frac{n_1}{v} = (n_2 - n_1)\left(\frac{1}{R_1}+\frac{1}{R_2}\right) = \frac{n_1}{f}$$

This formula could be used to calculate the refractive index of the glass of the lens.

Example

Calculate the focal length of a glass lens of refractive index 1.5 placed in water of refractive index 1.33, the radii of both surfaces of the lens being 0.10 m.

We have $\frac{1.33}{f} = (1.5 - 1.33)(1/0.1 + 1/0.1)$

$1.33 = 3.4f$

Therefore $f = 0.39$ m

Compare this with the result for the lens in air, which would be 0.1 m!

2 A lens fixed somewhere inside a tube gives a clear image of a distant object on a screen when one end of the tube is 20 cm from the screen. When the tube is turned round an image is obtained with the other end of the tube 12 cm from the screen. If the tube is 10 cm long, where is the lens and what is its focal length?

3 A screen is placed 1.2 m from an illuminated object and an image is formed on the screen using a convex lens placed between the object and screen. When the lens is moved 20 cm another image is formed. Calculate

(*a*) the focal length of the lens,
(*b*) the magnification of the two images, and
(*c*) the two positions of the lens.

4 A lens is held 50 cm in front of the eye and a movement of 1.0 cm of the lens moves the image of a star through an angle of 1′ in the same direction.
Calculate the sign and power of the lens. [O]

5 The radii of curvature of a certain lens are +10 cm and −30 cm and it is made of glass of refractive index 1.5.

(*a*) Is the lens converging or diverging? Explain.
(*b*) What is the focal length of the lens (i) in air, (ii) in water (refractive index 1.33)?
(*c*) An object 1 cm high is placed on the axis of the lens and 25 cm from it. What are the position, size and nature of the image formed?
(*d*) The object is now moved 4 cm nearer the lens. How far does its image move, and in which direction?

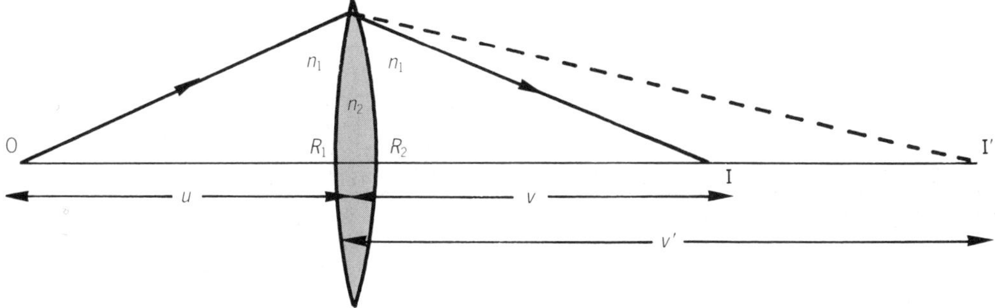

Figure 25.8

Two thin lenses in contact

In many optical instruments there may be compound lenses, that is, two or more lenses in contact. We will deal here with the case of two thin lenses in contact.

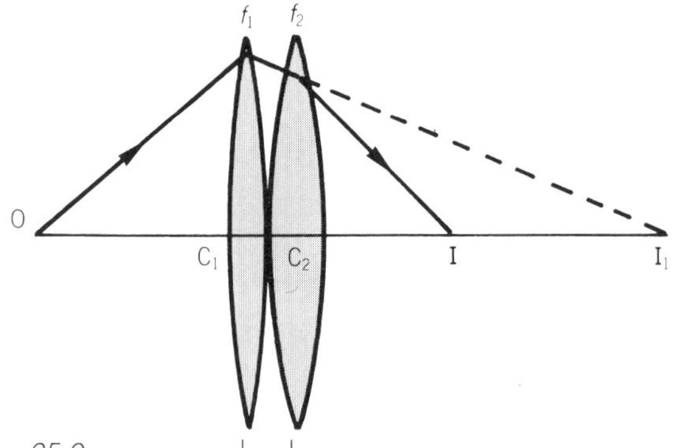

Figure 25.9

In Figure 25.9, let the focal lengths of the two lenses be f_1 and f_2.
$u_1 = OC_1$ and $v_1 = I_1C_1$
$u_2 = -C_1I_1 \approx -C_2I_1$ and $v_2 = C_2I \approx C_1I$

Therefore

$$\frac{1}{u_1} + \frac{1}{v_1} = \frac{1}{f_1} \quad \text{and} \quad \frac{1}{u_2} + \frac{1}{v_2} = \frac{1}{f_2}$$

$$\frac{1}{OC_1} + \frac{1}{I_1C_1} = \frac{1}{f_1} \quad \text{and} \quad \frac{1}{-I_1C_1} + \frac{1}{C_1I} = \frac{1}{f_2}$$

Therefore

$$\frac{1}{OC_1} + \frac{1}{IC_1} = \frac{1}{f_1} + \frac{1}{f_2} = \frac{1}{F}$$

where F is the focal length of the combination.

The focal length for two thin lenses separated by a distance a (Figure 25.10) is given by

$$\frac{1}{F} = \frac{1}{f_1} + \frac{1}{f_2} - \frac{a}{f_1f_2}$$

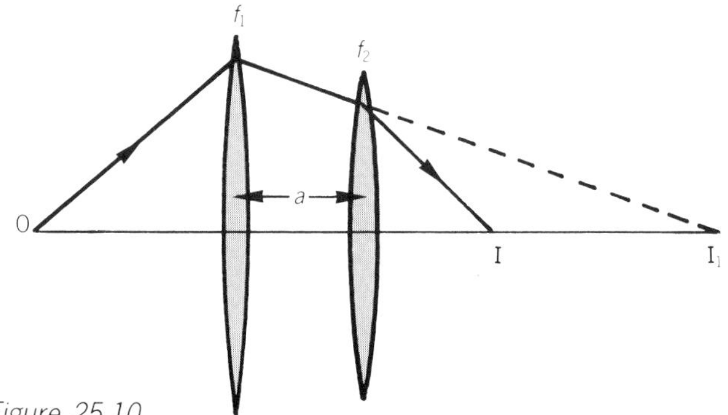

Figure 25.10

6 Calculate the following:

(*a*) the minimum separation of object and image for a convex lens of power +5 D,

(*b*) the refractive index of the material of a lens of focal length −25 cm and with sides of an equal radius of curvature of −24 cm, and

(*c*) the focal length of a lens where the object lies 5 cm from one principal focus and the image 10 cm from the other.

7 It is proposed to use a plastic bag full of air immersed in water as an underwater lens. Is this possible? If the lens is to be a converging lens explain what shape the air pocket should have. [z]

8 Two thin lenses are placed in contact so that their axes coincide. The focal lengths of the two lenses are 15 cm and 25 cm respectively. An object is viewed through the combination and the final image produced is 2 cm high, erect and 20 cm behind the lenses.

What is the position, size and nature of the object?

9 An eye positioned 15 cm from a convex lens sees an image of itself by parallel rays when looking through the lens towards a plane mirror placed 20 cm behind the lens. Calculate possible focal lengths for the lens and give the corresponding ray diagrams.

10 Two convex lenses A and B, of focal lengths 10 cm and 15 cm respectively, are arranged coaxially a distance of 20 cm apart. An object placed in front of lens A is viewed through the lens system. Find the nature and position of the image when the object is

(*a*) at an infinite distance,
(*b*) 20 cm in front of A,
(*c*) 10 cm in front of A, and
(*d*) 5 cm in front of A.

The measurement of the focal length of a lens

Knowledge of the focal length of a lens is vital in the construction of all optical instruments, from spectacles to large astronomical telescopes. The range of possible focal lengths is very large, from a few millimetres for the objective lens of a microscope to 20 m in a large telescope. Several simple methods are described because they all illustrate different aspects of the lens formula.

Convex lenses

(i) The focusing method
A rough guide to the focal length of a lens can be obtained by focusing light from a distant object, such as the Sun, on to a screen.

(ii) The graphical method
A graph of $1/u$ against $1/v$ can be plotted and the focal length f found from this.

(iii) The plane mirror method
The lens is placed on the mirror as shown in Figure 25.11, and the object is moved until object and image coincide. This point is the principal focus, since light from it will emerge parallel from the lens and so be reflected back along its original path when it strikes the mirror. The object can be either a pin or a point source.

Since $R = 2f$, the value of f can be found.

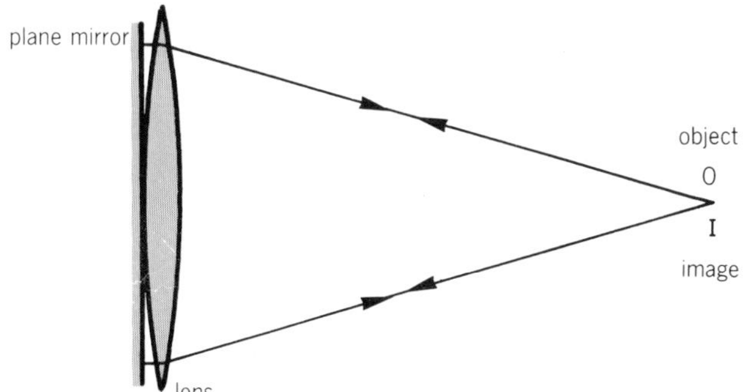

Figure 25.11

(iv) The two-position or displacement method
An illuminated object is set up in front of a lens and a focused image is formed on a screen.

For a given separation of the object and screen it will be found that there are two positions where a clearly focused image can be formed (Figure 25.12). By the principle or reversibility these must be symmetrical between O and I. Using the notation shown:

$$d = u + v \qquad \text{and} \qquad a = v - u$$

Therefore

$$u = \frac{d-a}{2} \qquad \text{and} \qquad v = \frac{d+a}{2}$$

Substituting in the lens equation gives:

$$\frac{2}{d-a} + \frac{2}{d+a} = \frac{1}{f} \qquad \text{and hence} \qquad f = \frac{d^2 - a^2}{4d}$$

(v) The minimum distance method
This more mathematical method derives from the fact that there is a minimum separation for object and image for a given lens. This can be shown if $u + v$ is plotted against either u or v. As in Figure 25.13, a minimum is formed and this can be shown to occur at the point where $u = v = 2f$ and $u + v = 4f$, that is, the minimum separation for object and image is $4f$.

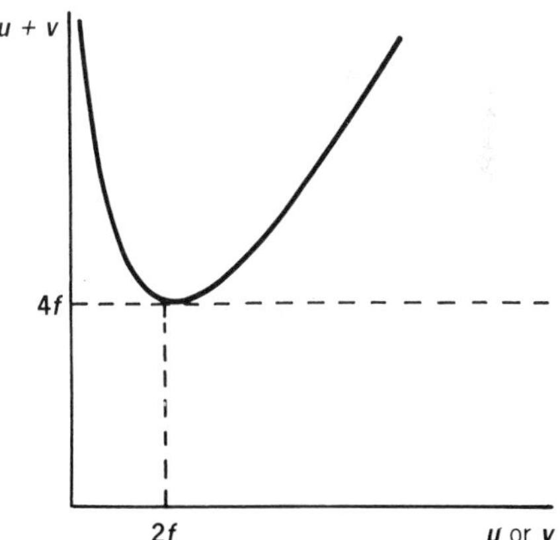

Figure 25.13

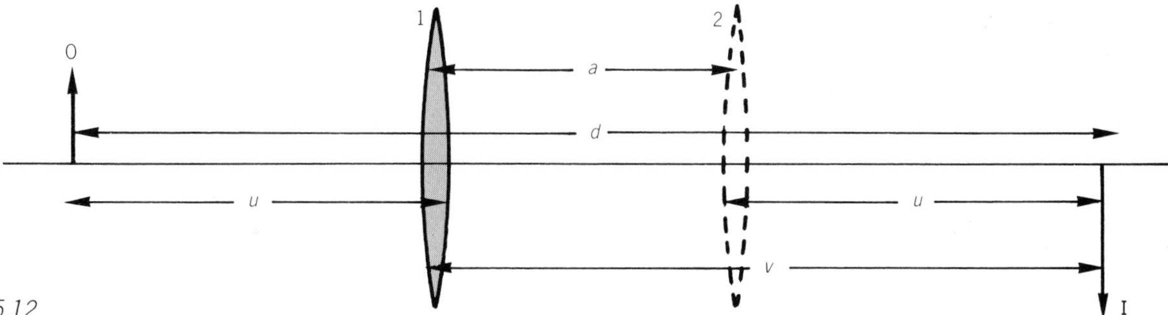

Figure 25.12

$$\frac{1}{u} + \frac{1}{v} = \frac{1}{f}$$

Therefore:

$$u + v = \frac{uv}{f} \text{ and } v = \frac{fu}{u - f} \text{ so } u + v = \frac{u}{u - f}$$

Therefore differentiating with respect to u gives

$$\frac{\mathrm{d}(u + v)}{\mathrm{d}u} = \frac{u^2 - 2uf}{(u - f)^2}$$

For a minimum, $\frac{\mathrm{d}(u + v)}{\mathrm{d}u} = 0$, or $u^2 - 2uf = 0$.

Therefore $u^2 = 2uf$, or $u = 2f$, and $u + v = 4f$.

Concave lenses

So far all the methods have been for convex lenses where a real image can be produced. We will now consider some methods for concave lenses.

(i) An auxiliary convex lens is used, in contact with the concave lens. It must be of greater power than the concave lens with one of its faces having the same radius of curvature as one of the faces of the concave lens. The focal length of the combination is then given by

$$\frac{1}{F} = \frac{1}{f} + \frac{1}{f'}$$

where the focal length of the convex lens f' can be found by the methods described above.

(ii) A convex lens of greater power is used to give a virtual object for the concave lens (Figure 25.14).

The position of this initial image (I′) is found and then the concave lens placed in position and the final image position (I) is located. The focal fore $v = R$he concave lens is then found using the lens equation.

(iii) A similar method to the above can be used, replacing the convex lens with a concave mirror.

Radius of curvature

The radius of curvature of a lens surface may be found either directly, using a sphereometer, or by **Boys' method**. In this method the lens of known focal length f is floated on mercury so that the lower surface acts as a mirror. An object is placed above the lens and moved until the image and object coincide. There is then a virtual image of the object at the centre of curvature of the lower surface (Figure 25.15).

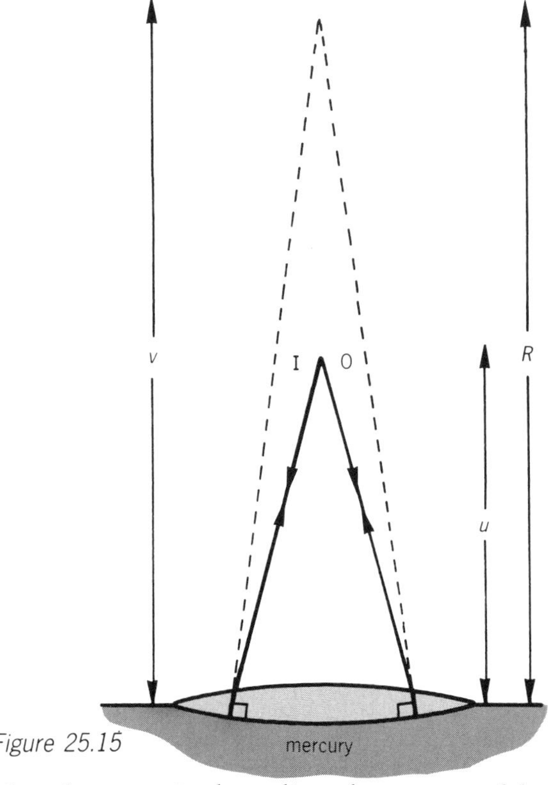

Figure 25.15

Therefore $v = R$, the radius of curvature of the lower surface, and so

$$\frac{1}{f} = \frac{1}{u} + \frac{1}{R}$$

Thus the radii of curvature of both faces of the lens may be found.

Mercury vapour is dangerously toxic and this experiment is unsafe to perform without the most rigorous precautions.

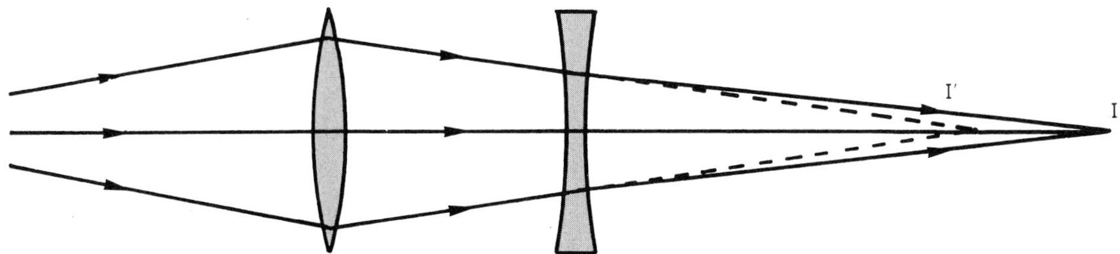

Figure 25.14

Focal length and magnification of a spherical surface

Figures 25.16 and 25.17 show how light is affected by a single spherical surface of radius R separating two media of refractive indices n_1 and n_2 with $n_2 > n_1$.

Consider Figure 25.17:

$$\frac{n_1}{u} + \frac{n_2}{v} = \frac{n_2 - n_1}{R} \qquad \text{but if } u = f_1, v = \infty$$

Therefore:

$$\frac{n_1}{f_1} = \frac{n_2 - n_1}{R} \quad \text{and so } f_1 = \frac{n_1 R}{n_2 - n_1}$$

for Figure 25.16, $u = \infty$ and $v = f_2$, giving

$$f_2 = \frac{n_2 R}{n_2 - n_1}$$

Therefore:

$$\frac{f_1}{f_2} = \frac{n_1}{n_2}$$

The magnification of the surface can be found using Figure 25.18.

Consider an object OO′ in a medium of refractive index n_1 giving an image II′ in medium of refractive index n_2.

$$\frac{\text{II}'}{v} = \tan r \approx r \text{ for small } r \text{ and } \frac{\text{OO}'}{u}$$

$= \tan i \approx i$ for small i

But also $n_1 i = n_2 r$ and therefore:

$$\text{magnification } (m) = \frac{\text{II}'}{\text{OO}'} = \frac{vr}{ui} = \frac{vn_1}{un_2}$$

11 A piece of capillary tubing has an external diameter of 0.5 cm and is made of glass of refractive index 1.48. What is the apparent diameter of the bore of the capillary tube if its actual diameter is 0.05 mm?

12 The refractive index of a certain type of glass is 1.523 for blue light and 1.510 for red light. Find the dispersion given by a 60° prism made of this glass when the angle of incidence is 70°.

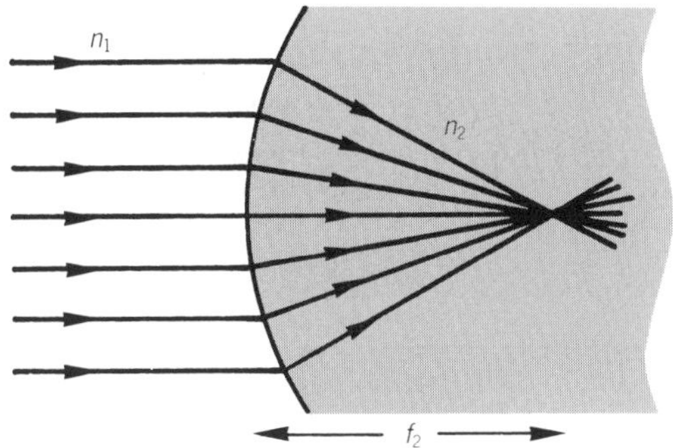

Figure 25.16

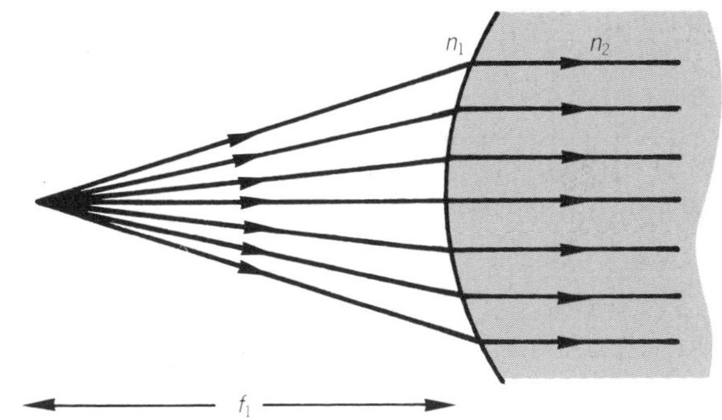

Figure 25.17

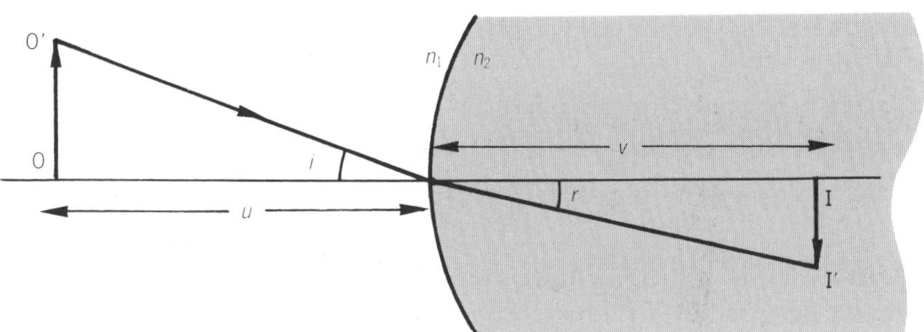

Figure 25.18

Dispersion

When light passes through a prism the amount of deviation depends on the refractive index, and since the refractive index is different for different wavelengths the deviation differs for different colours of light.

If a beam of white light is shone on a prism as shown in Figure 25.19 the refracted beam is separated into a spectrum (for the present we will restrict ourselves to a consideration of the visible spectrum).

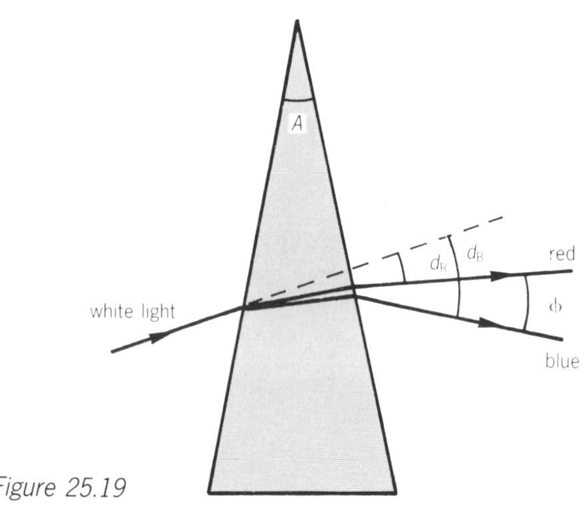

Figure 25.19

This spreading of the beam is called **dispersion** and can be shown to depend both on the refracting angle of the prism and on the refractive index of the material of which it is made.

If n_R and n_B are the refractive indices for red and blue light at the extreme ends of the visible spectrum, then the deviations for red and blue light are:

$$d_R = (n_R - 1)A \qquad \text{and} \qquad d_B = (n_B - 1)A$$

respectively.

Therefore for a prism of small angle the angular dispersion ϕ is given by the formula:

$$\phi = (n_B - n_R)A$$

The **mean deviation** for a prism is taken as being that produced with yellow light and is given by:

$$d_Y = (n_Y - 1)A$$

where n_Y is the refractive index of the glass of the prism for yellow light.

'Blue', 'red' and 'yellow' are rather vague terms, however, since each colour represents a range of wavelengths and so for accurate work we choose one particular wavelength within each area of the spectrum:

for red, the C line of hydrogen with a wavelength of 656 nm
for yellow, the D line of sodium with a wavelength of 589 nm
for blue, the F line of hydrogen with a wavelength of 486 nm

The refractive indices of two types of glass for these three standard wavelengths are given in the table below:

	n_C	n_D	n_F
Crown glass	1.5150	1.5175	1.5233
Flint glass	1.6434	1.6550	1.6648

Example

Calculate the angular dispersion produced by a flint glass prism of refracting angle 20°. (Take the refractive indices for red and blue light to be as shown in the table above.)

Angular dispersion $= (1.6648 - 1.6434) \times 20$
$= 0.428°$

A useful property to consider when calculating the dispersion is the **dispersive power** of a material. This depends only on the type of material of which a prism or lens is made and not on its shape. Dispersive power is defined as:

$$\text{dispersive power } (\omega) = \frac{\text{angular dispersion}}{\text{mean deviation}}$$

$$\omega = \frac{(n_F - n_C)}{(n_D - 1)}$$

Dispersion of white light through a prism (Science Photo Library)

Achromatic prisms and lenses

It is often necessary to deviate light without dispersing it, and prisms and lenses that do this are called **achromatic** (Greek, 'without colour').

(*a*) The achromatic prism

Such a prism is a compound prism made of two prisms of materials with different refractive indices, say n and n'.

The dispersion for prism 1 will be $(n_B - n_R)A$ and that for prism 2 $(n'_B - n'_R)A'$.

For there to be zero dispersion the algebraic sum of these must be zero, and therefore

$$(n_B - n_R)A + (n'_B - n'_R)A' = 0$$

Therefore

$$\frac{A}{A'} = -\frac{(n'_B - n'_R)}{(n_B - n_R)}$$

The negative sign indicates that the prisms must be placed as shown in Figure 25.20.

A single ray of white light passing through an achromatic prism will give rise to a parallel beam of light which when brought to a focus will appear white again. If we take more than one incident ray then the colours will overlap, giving a white centre with coloured edges.

> **Example**
>
> A crown glass prism of refracting angle 6° is combined with a flint glass prism to give an achromatic combination. Calculate the refracting angle of the flint glass prism. What deviation will the compound prism produce? (Take the refractive indices to be those in the table above.)
>
> Let θ be the angle of the flint glass prism. Then
>
> $$\frac{\theta}{6} = -\frac{1.523 - 1.515}{1.665 - 1.643} \text{ giving } \theta = -2.2°$$
>
> Deviation of red light =
> $(1.515 - 1) \times 6 - (1.643 - 1) \times 2.2 = 1.68°$.

(*b*) The achromatic lens

The dispersion of lenses can be a serious problem in large astronomical instuments – for example, the difference in focal length for red and blue light for a telescope with a mean focal length of around 15 m can be as much as 45 cm. Such a difference is obviously quite unacceptable when a clearly focused image is required.

This defect of lenses is known as **chromatic aberration.**

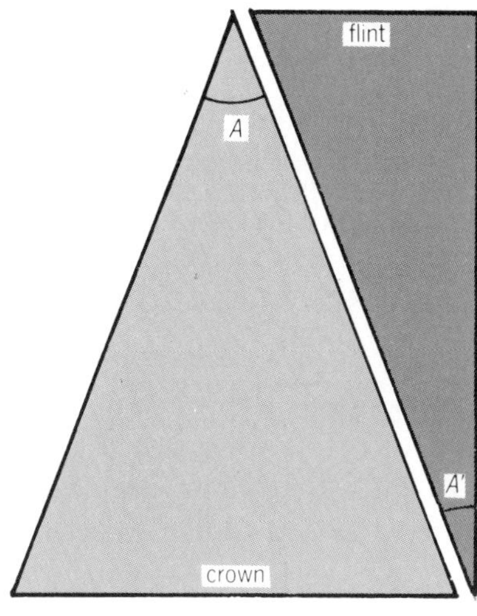

Figure 25.20

For a lens to be achromatic the focal length for red light (F_R) must be the same as that for blue light (F_B).

As with the achromatic prism this can be produced by using a 'doublet' made of two thin lenses of different refractive indices (Figure 25.21).

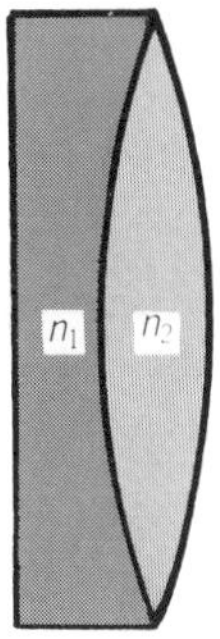

n_1 n_2

Figure 25.21

For blue light:

$$\frac{1}{F_B} = \frac{1}{f_B} + \frac{1}{f'_B}$$

For red light:

$$\frac{1}{F_R} = \frac{1}{f_R} + \frac{1}{f'_R}$$

and also we have for each lens:

$$\frac{1}{f_B} - \frac{1}{f_R} = (n_B - n_R)(1/R_1 + 1/R_2) \quad \text{and}$$

$$\frac{1}{f_Y} = (n_Y - 1)(1/R_1 + 1/R_2)$$

Therefore:

$$\frac{1}{f_B} - \frac{1}{f_R} = \frac{\omega}{f_Y} \quad \text{and} \quad \frac{1}{f_B'} - \frac{1}{f_R'} = \frac{\omega'}{f_Y'}$$

This gives:

$$\frac{\omega}{f_Y} + \frac{\omega'}{f_Y'} = 0$$

Therefore:

$$\frac{\omega}{f_Y} = -\frac{\omega'}{f_Y'}$$

In this formula the negative sign means that one of the lenses is convex and the other concave.

Notice that we have only made the lens truly achromatic for two colours, red and blue. There will still be a spread of colour due to the other wavelengths.

It is possible to make an achromatic lens using two thin lenses of the same material if they are separated by a distance equal to the mean of their focal lengths.

Defects of lenses

In addition to chromatic aberration described above, lenses suffer from several other defects.

(*a*) Spherical aberration

This is a result of the inner and outer portions of a lens having different focal lengths, that of the outside being shorter than that of the centre.

One way of reducing this is to make the deviation at the two surfaces as nearly equal as possible. Spherical aberration is therefore particularly marked when using a plano-convex lens with parallel light hitting the plane face.

Spherical aberration is also reduced by decreasing the aperture of a lens and by increasing its focal length.

(*b*) Coma

This defect produces a comet-like tail added to all images. It results from off-axis objects coupled with the different magnifications of different zones of the lens.

(*c*) Astigmatism

If the object point lies off the axis of the lens then the rays from the horizontal and vertical planes come to a focus at different distances from the lens as shown in Figure 25.22.

The rays from the vertical plane intersect in a horizontal line while those from a horizontal plane intersect in a vertical line.

(*d*) Distortion

The magnification of the lens varies from its centre to its edge and so the magnification of the image will vary as well. This gives rise to distortion.

Student investigation

Some of the effects of the defects of lenses may be studied using the following experiments.

(*a*) **Chromatic aberration**
Use a convex lens with a focal length of 20 cm, a white light source such as a filament lamp and a set of colour filters, the transmission wavelengths of which are known. With the object distance of 30 cm record the image distances for each colour of light. Plot a graph of wavelength against image distance.

(*b*) **Spherical aberration**
Record the image distance for a fixed object distance when first the centre and then the outside of the lens is covered.

(*c*) **Astigmatism**
For a fixed object distance record the image distances for the horizontal and vertical lines for different angles of rotation of the lens.

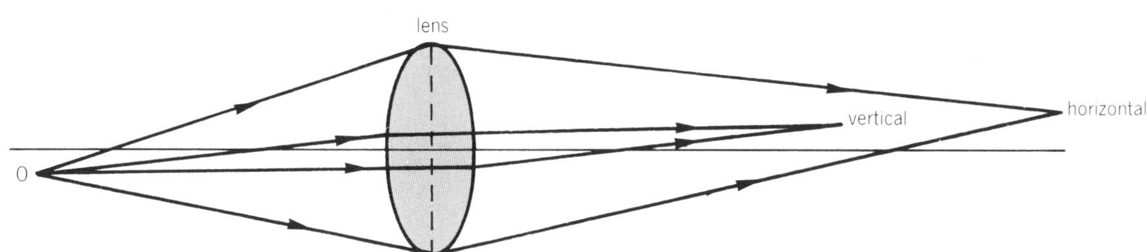

Figure 25.22

26 · Optical instruments

The following instruments will be considered:

the eye
the camera
the spectrometer
prismatic binoculars
the telescope – terrestial and astronomical
the microscope

The eye

The eye is for us probably the most important of optical instruments. Figure 26.1 is a simplified diagram of the human eye.

The human eye is about 2.5 cm in diameter and its near-spherical shape is maintained by the pressure of the fluid within it. The eye as a whole behaves like a thick lens. We will consider here only the Physics of various parts of the eye. For a more detailed account of the biology you should consult a biology textbook.

Parts of the eye:

cornea – a curved transparent membrane at the front of the eye; most of the refraction takes place here
iris – the coloured part of the eye
pupil – this is simply a hole through which light passes; it acts like a diaphragm and its diameter can be changed from about 3 mm to about 8 mm depending on the light intensity
lens – this is flexible and it focuses the image on the retina; the ciliary muscles around it contract to view near objects so squashing it and thus shortening its focal length
retina – the light-sensitive surface on which the image is formed; it is composed of many millions of light-sensitive nerve endings, rods that are sensitive to detail and cones that detect colour

The refractive indices of the aqueous humour and the vitreous humour are equal (1.337), and that of the lens is 1.437.

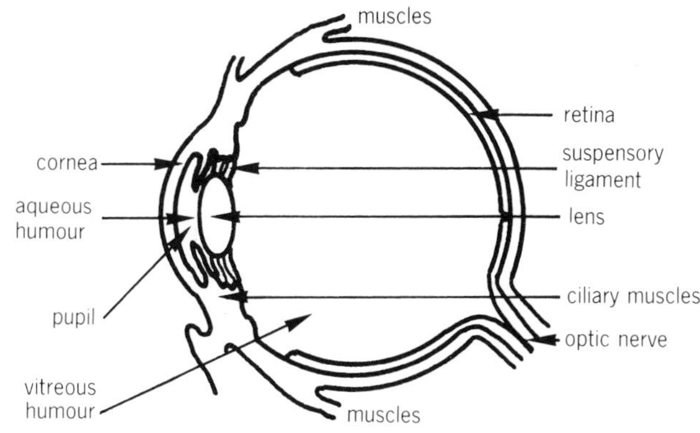

Figure 26.1

Defects of vision

(i) Short sight or myopia
The eye can see *near* objects clearly but not *distant* ones. This is due to the eyeball being too long (even a very small elongation is enough to produce myopia) and/or the eye lens being too strong (Figure 26.2(*a*)).

In a myopic eye the image of a distant object is formed in front of the retina and this can be corrected by using a concave lens (Figure 26.2(*b*)).

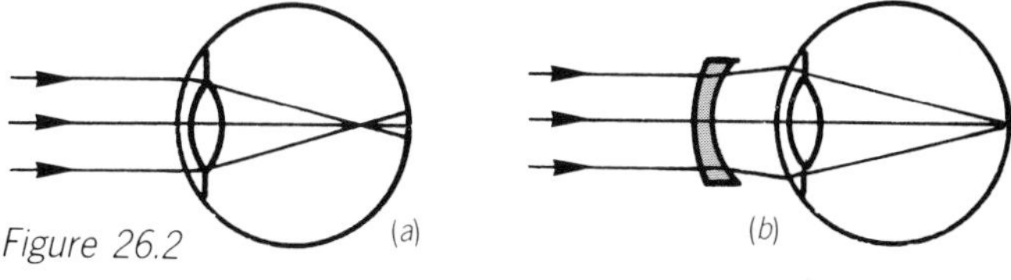

Figure 26.2

(ii) Long sight or hypermetropia
The eye can see *distant* objects clearly but not *close* ones. The eyeball is too short or the lens is too weak. The image of a near object is formed behind the retina (Figure 26.3(*a*)) and this defect can be corrected by using a convex lens (Figure 26.3(*b*)).

The **far point** of the eye is the most distant point that the eye can see clearly and this should ideally be at infinity.

The **near point** is the closest point that the eye can see clearly without strain and usually this is 25 cm from the eye (sometimes this is called the **least distance of distinct vision**).

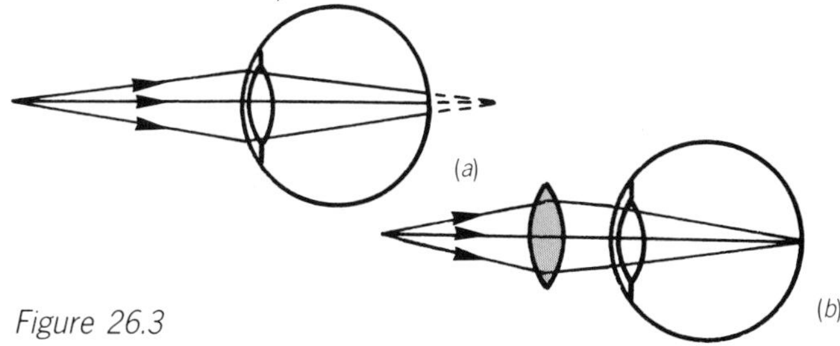

Figure 26.3

The camera

The camera in its simplest forms uses a single convex lens to form a real inverted image on a film. The film is coated with a light-sensitive material such as an emulsion of silver bromide on a transparent or paper base. Figure 26.4 is a diagram of a simple camera.

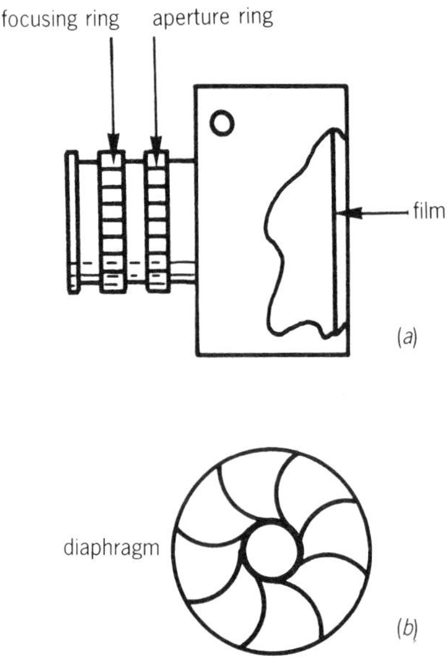

Figure 26.4

The important parts of the camera are:

(*a*) the lens that produces the image,

(*b*) the shutter that controls the time for which light is incident on the film (this time may vary from a thousandth of a second to a few seconds), and

(*c*) the diaphragm which controls the amount of light falling on to the film per second by using more or less of the aperture of the lens. The aperture of the camera lens is usually described by the **f-number** or **relative aperture** which is defined as follows:

$$\text{relative aperture (f-number)} = \frac{\text{focal length of lens}}{\text{diameter of aperture}}$$

that is, a camera with an f/8 lens is one with a focal length 8 × the diameter of the lens. You will find that the aperture control on a camera has the following f-numbers on it:

f-number	2	2.8	4	5.6	8	11	16	22	32
square	4	7.8	16	31.4	64	121	256	484	1024

The reason for this rather curious series of f-numbers is that the square of each is approximately double that of the previous one. Therefore changing from one to the next will double the aperture of the camera (since the area of the lens is proportional to the square of its diameter).

(*d*) The film that 'collects' the image.

An important property of a camera is its **depth of focus**, this is the distance that the film can be moved without spoiling the image. This will correspond to a **depth of field**, which is the range of object distance that will still give a satisfactory image. This is greater for a lens with a short focal length and for larger f-numbers.

Example

Calculate the diameter of an image of the Sun formed by a camera with a lens of focal length 50 mm, if the angular diameter of the Sun when seen from the Earth is 0.5°.

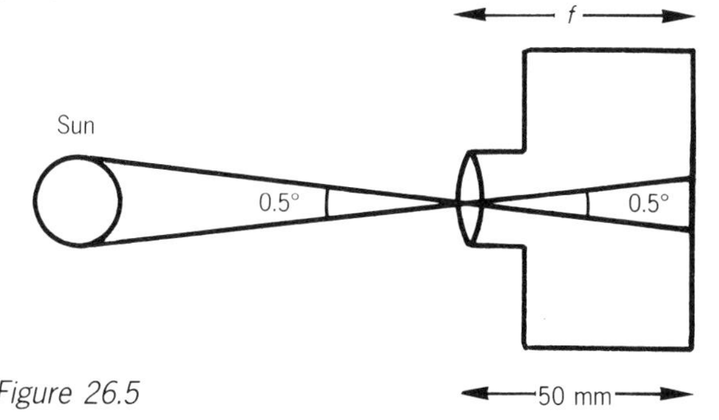

Figure 26.5

The image of the Sun must therefore also subtend an angle of 0.5° with the axis of the lens of the camera (as you can see from Figure 26.5) and therefore:

diameter of image = 50 × tan 0.5 = 0.44 mm

1 A camera with a shutter speed of 0.01 s and a lens of focal length 50 mm is used to photograph a car 100 m away and moving at 50 m s^{-1} perpendicular to the line of sight. By how much will the image on the film be blurred?

2 The telephoto lens system of a camera consists of two lenses: a convex lens of focal length 12 cm mounted 4 cm in front of a concave lens of focal length 10 cm. How much larger will the image of a distant object be if the telephoto lens system is used compared with the image produced by the convex lens alone?

The spectrometer

As its name suggests, the spectrometer is basically an instrument for observing spectra but it can also be used to view other optical effects such as the Fraunhofer diffraction at a single slit to measure the deviation of light by a prism, and so on.

Figure 26.6 shows the essential parts of a spectrometer of the type used in most schools. The main component parts are as follows.

(*a*) The **collimator**, which is a tube with an adjustable slit at one end and convex lens at the other. The distance between the slit and the lens can be varied. The slit is usually placed at the principal focus of the lens so that when it is illuminated a beam of parallel light emerges from the lens.

(*b*) The **spectrometer table**, which is a circular metal plate that may be rotated about a vertical axis and levelled by means of three adjusting screws. It is on this table that the prism, diffraction grating or single slit is placed.

(*c*) The **vernier scale**, on which the base of the table is fixed, and which moves over a circular scale that is mounted on the rest of the spectrometer. It enables angular movements of the table to be read to 0.1°. Ideally there should be two verniers, one at either side of the spectrometer table.

(*d*) The **telescope**, which is mounted horizontally and is free to rotate about the same vertical axis as the spectrometer table. It may be focused to receive parallel light from the collimator. The telescope eyepiece contains a set of cross-wires. Both the telescope and collimator usually have slow-motion movements to enable their position to be altered by small amounts.

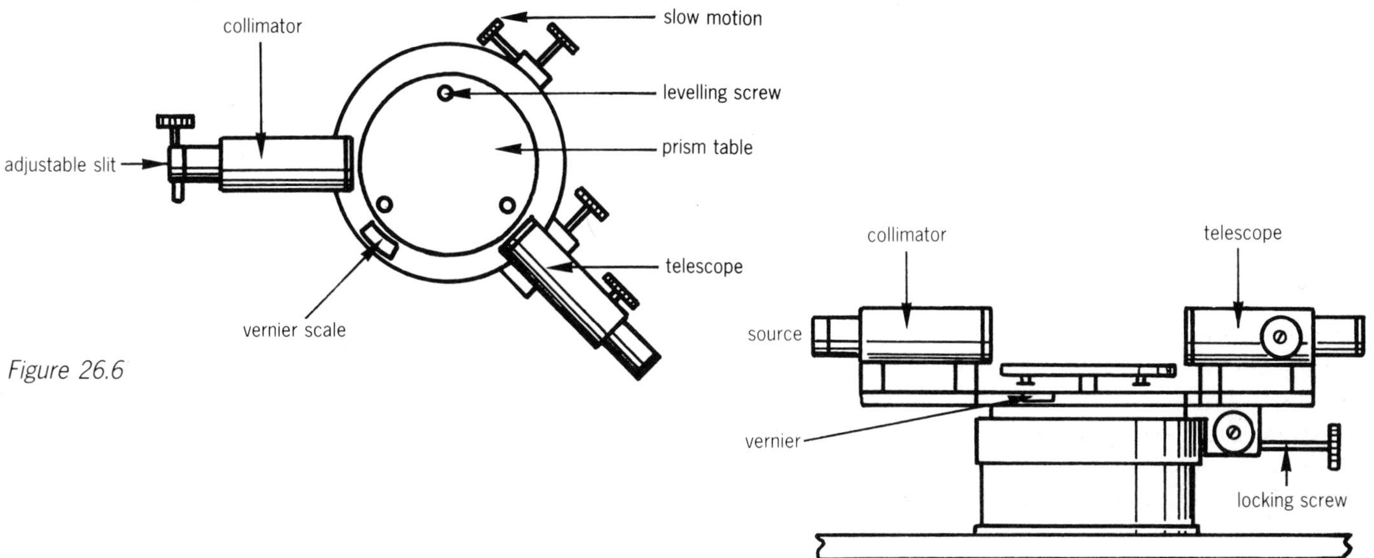

Figure 26.6

Figure 26.7

Prismatic binoculars

These instruments are worth mentioning here since the property of total internal reflection is used to reduce the length. They are really just two terrestrial telescopes (see below) mounted side by side with a totally internally reflecting prism in each tube (Figure 26.8). It is easy to see how this reflection reduces the overall length for a given set of focal lengths of the lenses.

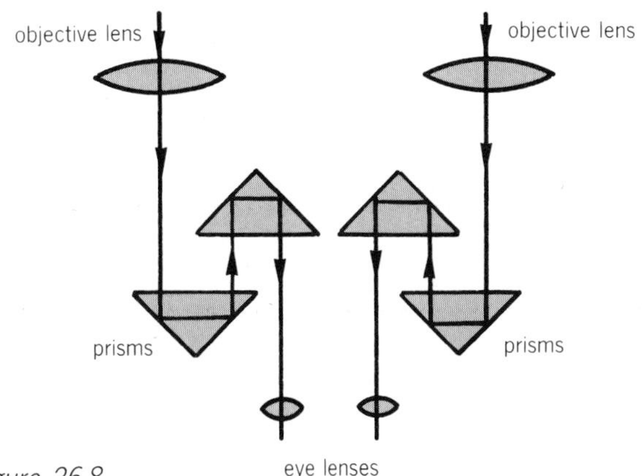

Figure 26.8

The astronomical telescope

The purpose of a telescope is to make distant objects appear closer and therefore larger. What they do is to increase the angle that the final image subtends at our eye. They do *not* make the image bigger than the object. You can appreciate this if you think of a telescope being used to look at a distant planet such as Jupiter. The image of Jupiter appears to be much bigger when viewed through a telescope simply because the angle it subtends with our eyes is larger. The telescope does not produce a real image of Jupiter which is bigger than the planet itself – if it did the image would not fit on the Earth!

Figure 26.9 is a diagram of a simple astronomical telescope

The telescope consists of two biconvex lenses, the **objective lens** and the **eye lens**. (Do not confuse the latter with the lens of the eye!) In many telescopes a compound eyepiece takes the place of the eye lens. The purpose of the objective lens is to gather as much light as possible from the object and to produce a real, inverted image of the object. The eye lens is then used to magnify this image, producing a final image.

The telescope is usually adjusted so that this final image is formed at infinity so that the eye may be completely relaxed when viewing it. Such adjustment is called **normal adjustment**.

The **angular magnification** (or **magnifying power**) of the telescope is defined as:

$$\text{angular magnification} = \frac{\text{angle subtended by image at eye}}{\text{angle subtended by object at unaided eye}} = \frac{\beta}{\alpha}$$

With the telescope in normal adjustment the final image is at infinity and since the object is effectively at infinity the lenses are separated by the sum of their focal lengths.

Therefore if f_o is the focal length of the objective and f_e the focal length of the eye lens then the angular magnification is:

$$\text{angular magnification} = \frac{\beta}{\alpha} = \frac{f_o}{f_e}$$

This can be very large with a telescope with an objective of focal length up to 20 m but because of diffraction effects, the difficulty of building a perfectly stable mounting and warm air currents round the telescope it is usually limited to 50 × the aperture in centimetres.

It is clear that only those rays of light that pass through the objective will go towards forming the image and the eye should be placed where it will receive as much as possible of the light coming from the eye lens. This position is called the **eye ring** or **exit pupil** of the telescope. The **exit pupil** is the image of the objective formed by the eye lens (Figure 26.10). The eye ring provides a very simple means of finding the magnifying power of a telescope. The telescope is used to view a ground glass screen or clear window and a piece of paper moved behind the eye lens until a clear eye ring is seen. Then

$$\text{angular magnification} = \frac{f_o}{f_e} = \frac{\text{diameter of objective}}{\text{diameter of eye ring}}$$

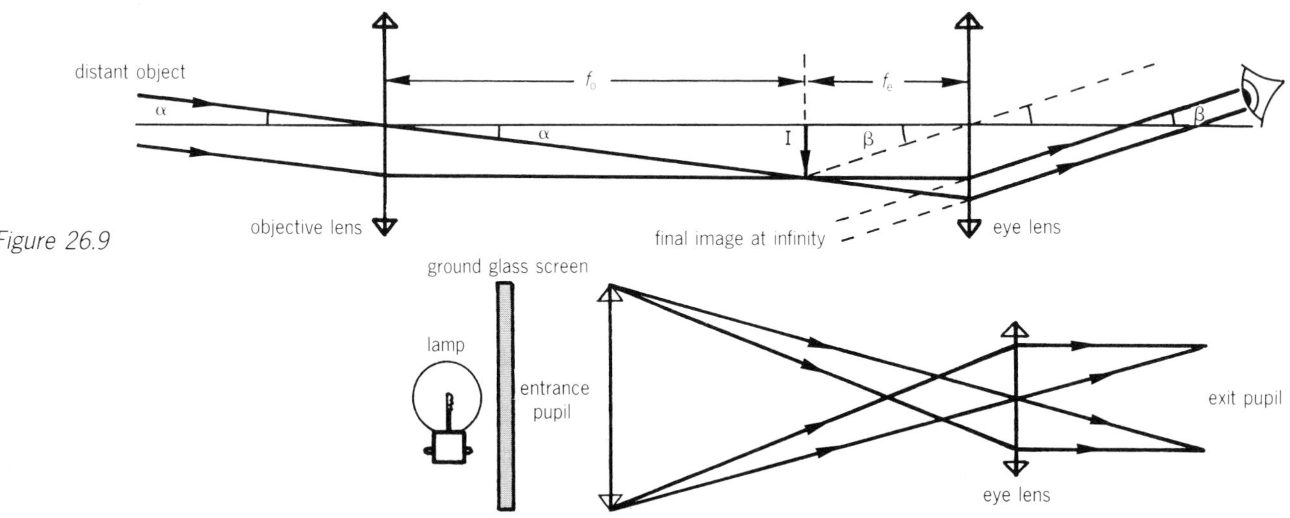

Figure 26.9

Figure 26.10

Example

An astronomical telescope with an objective lens of focal length 1.00 m and an eye lens of focal length 3 cm is used to project an image of the Sun on to a screen 20 cm from the eye lens.

If the diameter of this image is 4.9 cm, calculate the angle subtended by the Sun at the centre of the objective of the telescope.

Using the lens equation for the eye lens:

$$\frac{1}{u} + \frac{1}{20} = \frac{1}{3}$$

Therefore $u = 3.52$ cm. The size of the object for the eye lens is $\dfrac{4.9 \times 3.52}{20} = 0.86$ cm.

But this object is the initial image produced by the objective, and the angle that it subtends at the objective is equal to the angle that the Sun subtends at the objective.

$$\text{Angle subtended by the Sun} = \frac{0.86}{100} = 0.0086^c = 0.49^\circ.$$

3 When an astronomical telescope is used to view a star the distance between the objective and the eyepiece is 75 cm. When used to view a flagpole the eyepiece has to be pulled out 2 cm to give a clearly focused image. If the focal length of the eyepiece is 5 cm, what is the distance of the pole from the objective?

If the image subtends an angle of 10° at the eyepiece, find the height of the pole. (Assume that the final image is at infinity in each case.)

The Galilean telescope

In about 1610 Galileo designed a telescope that gave an erect image by using a concave lens as shown in Figure 26.11.

The objective lens forms a real image (I′) which acts as a virtual object for the eye lens. This is then adjusted to give the final image at infinity.

The length of such a telescope is then $f_o - f_e$ and it is therefore shorter than an astronomical telescope of similar magnification of the type described above. One disadvantage of the Galilean telescope is that the field of view is small, however.

The terrestrial telescope

Another method of giving a final erect image is to use a third convex lens (Figure 26.12).

The objective lens gives an image I_1 which becomes a real object for the lens L. This lens is often called the **erecting lens** because it simply produces an inverted image of I_1. The eye lens is then used to magnify this image and so the final image at infinity is erect.

Such a telescope is longer than the Galilean type, because of the additional lens.

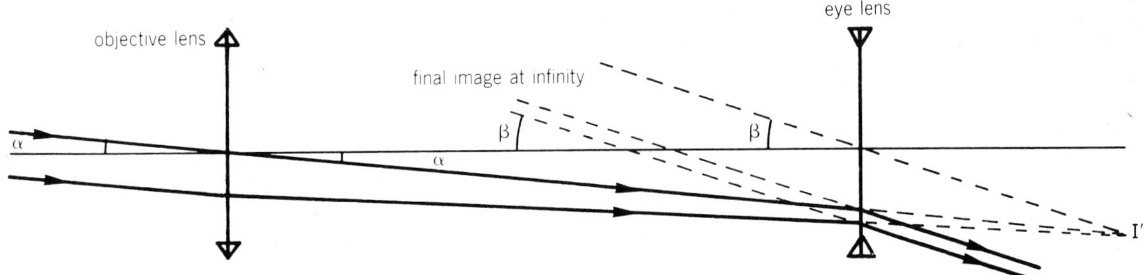

Figure 26.11

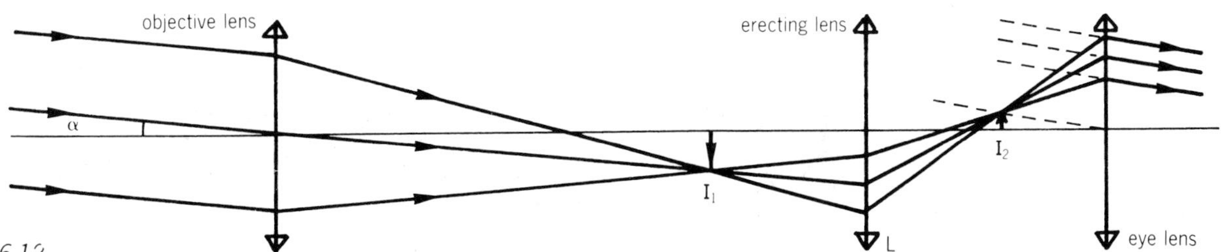

Figure 26.12

The reflecting telescope

The first reflecting telescope was made by Sir Isaac Newton in 1668. This used a spherical concave mirror as the objective instead of a convex lens. The modern reflecting telescopes use parabolic mirrors: mirrors with diameters greater than 5 metres have been constructed like those for the telescopes on Mount Palomar in the USA and at Mount Semirodriki in the Caucasus mountains. This telescope, with a mirror 5.99 m in diameter, has a light-gathering power over 300 000 times that of the human eye, and could detect the light from a candle 15 000 miles away. Even larger telescopes with mirror diameters of up to 10 m are now being planned.

There are three main types of reflecting telescope, differing from each other mainly in the position of their prime focus. Figure 26.13(*a*) shows the Newtonian arrangement, and Figure 26.13(*b*) and (*c*) show versions due to Cassegrain and Coudé.

(*b*) Since light does not have to pass through the glass of the mirror it can be made slightly less perfect than would be needed for a lens and it is therefore cheaper.

(*c*) No refraction occurs at the mirror surface and therefore a reflector does not suffer from chromatic aberration.

Today all large astronomical telescopes are reflectors, the largest having an aperture of almost 6 m compared with the largest refractor, that at Yerkes Observatory, which has an objective lens a mere 91 cm in diameter – a very large lens but small in comparison with the mirrors!

These telescopes are located at the top of mountains (as is the Sir Isaac Newton telescope in the Canary Islands) since the viewing conditions are better there. One telescope has even been placed in orbit so that there is no atmospheric absorption.

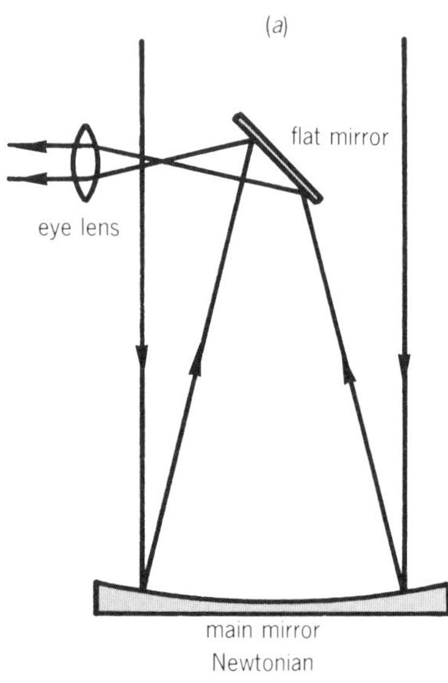

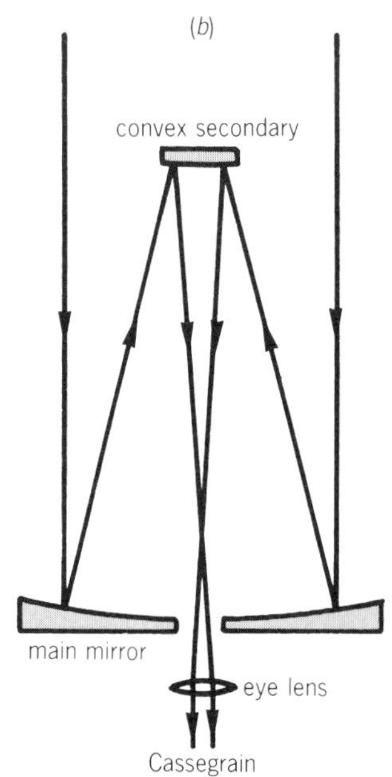

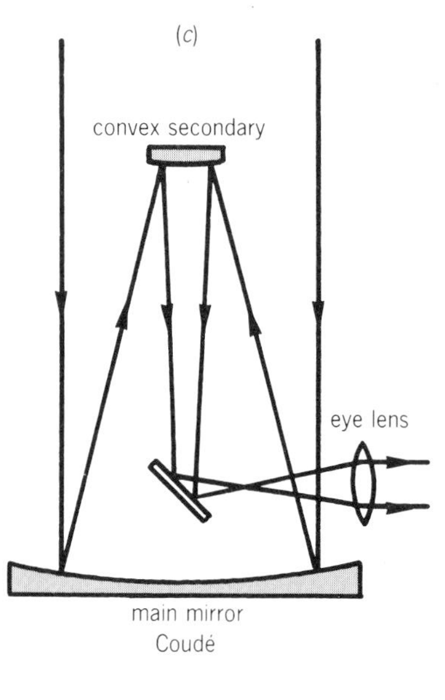

Figure 26.13

Mirror diameters:

Mount Semirodriki	5.99 m
Mount Palomar	5.08 m
William Herschel	4.20 m
Mount Wilson	2.54 m
Isaac Newton	2.49 m

The different types have their primary foci at different points for different positions of observation.

Reflectors have several advantages over refractors.

(*a*) The mirrors can be supported from behind as well as at the edge and therefore can be made much larger, thus improving the resolving power and light-gathering power.

Under ideal conditions the Mount Palomar telescope can resolve a double star with an angular separation of only 0.0297″ of arc while a 15 cm reflector will give a resolution of 0.99″ of arc.

The most recent large telescope to be opened is the William Herschel telescope which began observations in May 1987 at the observatory in the Canary Islands. Its modern 4.2 m diameter mirror makes it one of the most powerful telescopes in the world at the present time (1987).

The space telescope

The Hubble space telescope, launched by NASA in 1990, will be of great importance to the development of optical astronomy. Although it has a main mirror of only 2.4 m in diameter it will orbit at a height of about 500 km and this will put it well above the Earth's atmosphere. This will mean that it will not suffer from atmospheric distortion and at that altitude it will be able to receive the ultraviolet radiation that is absorbed before it reaches the Earth's surface. It is hoped that it will be able to detect objects some fifty times fainter than those visible at present with the largest Earth-based telescopes.

4 An astronomical telescope has an objective with a focal length of 100 cm and a diameter of 5 cm. If the eyepiece has a focal length of 20 cm and the telescope is used in normal adjustment, calculate
(*a*) the magnifying power,
(*b*) the diameter of the eye ring, and
(*c*) the separation of the lenses.

5 The Moon subtends an angle of 0.5° at the Earth's surface. What is the diameter of the image of the Moon produced by the 102 cm Lick Observatory refractor, which has a focal length of 18 m?
Calculate the resolving power of this instrument when light of wavelength 600 nm is used. [z]

6 A certain Cassegrain reflector with a main mirror of focal length 6 m is used to view a planet such that the final image formed by the mirrors is at the pole of the concave mirror. It is viewed there by means of an eyepiece lens of focal length 7.5 cm. The distance between the poles of the mirrors is 5.5 m and the angular diameter of the planet when viewed without a telescope is 10^{-4} radian. Calculate
(*a*) the diameter of the real image formed by the mirrors,
(*b*) the magnifying power of the telescope when in normal adjustment, and
(*c*) the magnifying power when the final virtual image is formed 25 cm from the eyepiece. [o and c]

7 (*a*) An astronomer has two telescopes of the same magnifying power but of different apertures. Discuss the advantages and disadvantages of each.
(*b*) What would be the result of using a back-silvered mirror as the flat in a Newtonian reflecting telescope?
(*c*) Describe with the aid of a labelled diagram the structure and purpose of a Schmidt telescope.

The microscope

The simple magnifying glass was in use in the thirteenth century but it was another three hundred years before it was used extensively and two or more lenses were used together to give a compound microscope.

A magnifying glass or microscope is an instrument used for looking at objects close to the eye and the image is usually formed at the least distance of distinct vision (D) from the eye.

You can see from Figure 26.14 that at this distance the image will subtend the largest possible angle at the eye and yet still remain clearly visible without strain.

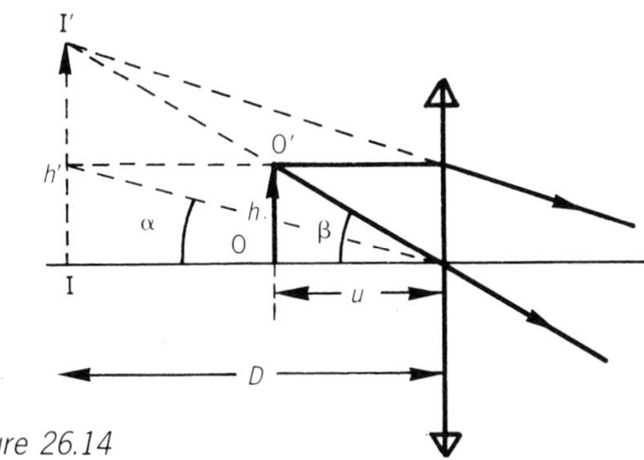

Figure 26.14

The object will also be seen most clearly when it is placed at the near point, and therefore the angular magnification of a microscope is defined as follows:

$$\text{angular magnification } (M) = \beta/\alpha$$

where β is the angle subtended at the eye by the image at the near point and α is the angle subtended at the unaided eye by the object at the near point.

The simple microscope or magnifying glass

A diagram of this is shown in Figure 26.14.

A convex lens of focal length f produces a magnified, erect and virtual image (II') of the object (OO').

The lens is adjusted so that the image is at the near point and so the image distance is the least distance of distinct vision D, about 25 cm. From the diagram:

$$\text{angular magnification } (M) = \frac{\beta}{\alpha} = \frac{h'}{h}$$

as long as the angles β and α are small.

However, the linear magnification of the lens is $h'/h = v/u$, and since $\frac{1}{u} + \frac{1}{v} = \frac{1}{f}$ and $v = D$ we have that.

$$\frac{v}{u} = \frac{v}{f} - 1 \qquad \text{Therefore:} \qquad M = \frac{D}{f} - 1$$

The compound microscope

The compound microscope (Figure 26.15) uses several lenses to produce a highly magnified image of an object.

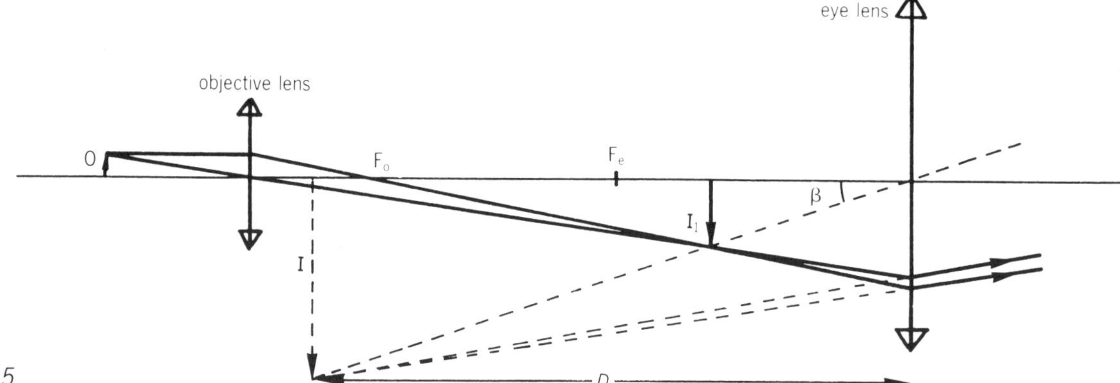

Figure 26.15

The diagram shows the microscope in **normal adjustment**, that is, with the final image at the near point (25 cm from the eye). This setting gives the maximum angular size of image without eye strain.

The objective lens produces a real, inverted image of the object O at I_1. This is then viewed by the eye lens and this gives a final virtual image at I. The magnifying power M of the instrument is given by the formula:

$$M = \left(\frac{D}{f_e} - 1\right)\left(\frac{v}{f_0} - 1\right)$$

and therefore you can see that the smaller the focal lengths of the objective and eye lens, the greater is the magnifying power. If the focal length of the objective is too small, however, the object will subtend too great an angle with it and the image will be distorted due to off-axis rays. This is the reason for using the oil immersion objective to reduce the amount of refraction at the first lens surface.

The resolving power of a microscope can be shown to depend on both the wavelength of light used (λ), the refractive index of the medium above the slide (n) and the angle subtended at the objective (α) (Figure 26.16):

$$\text{resolving power of microscope} = \frac{\lambda}{2n \sin \alpha}$$

This is the minimum separation of two points which can be seen as separate.

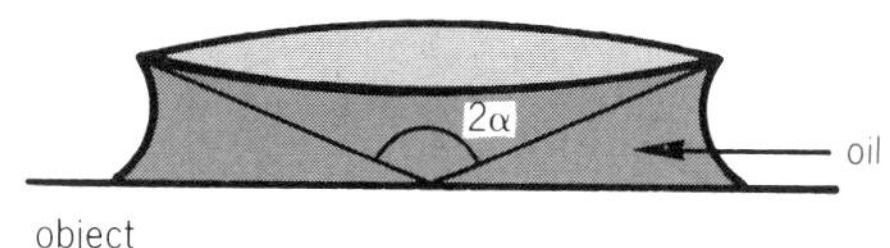

Figure 26.16

> **8** Two thin convex lenses are used to form a compound microscope. An object 3 cm in front of the objective lens gives a final image at the same position as the object and 25 cm from the eye lens, the magnification being 15.
>
> Calculate the focal lengths of both the objective lens and the eye lens.

An alternative and very useful formula for the magnifying power M of a compound microscope is:

$$M = m_o \times m_e$$

where m_o and m_e are the magnifications of the objective lens and eyepiece lens respectively.

> **9** A compound microscope is formed from two convex lenses, an eyepiece of focal length 5.0 cm and an objective of focal length 1.0 cm. If an object is placed 1.1 cm from the objective, the final image is formed 32.0 cm from the eye lens.
>
> Calculate the magnifying power of the instrument if the near point is 25 cm from the observer's eye.

Wave motion and sound

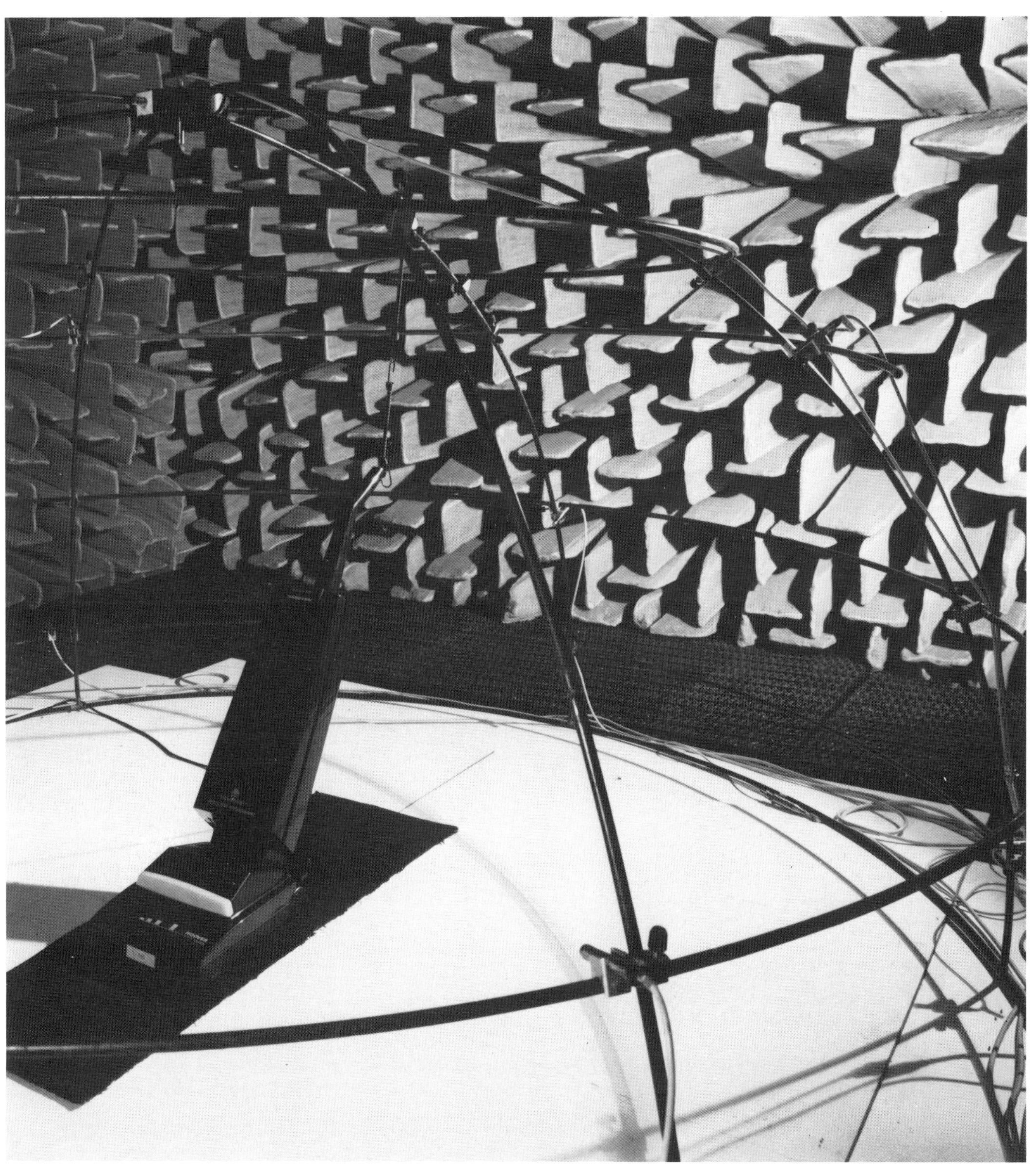

Testing a Hoover vacuum cleaner in an anechoic chamber at the National Engineering Laboratory, Scotland.

27 · Wave motion

A wave motion is the transmission of energy from one place to another through a material or a vacuum. Wave motion may occur in many forms such as water waves, sound waves, radio waves and light waves, but waves are basically of only two types:

(*a*) **transverse** waves – the oscillation is at right angles to the direction of propagation of the wave (Figure 27.1(*a*)). Examples of this type are water waves and most electromagnetic waves.

(*b*) **longitudinal** waves – the oscillation is along the direction of propagation of the wave (Figure 27.1(*b*)). An example of this type is sound waves.

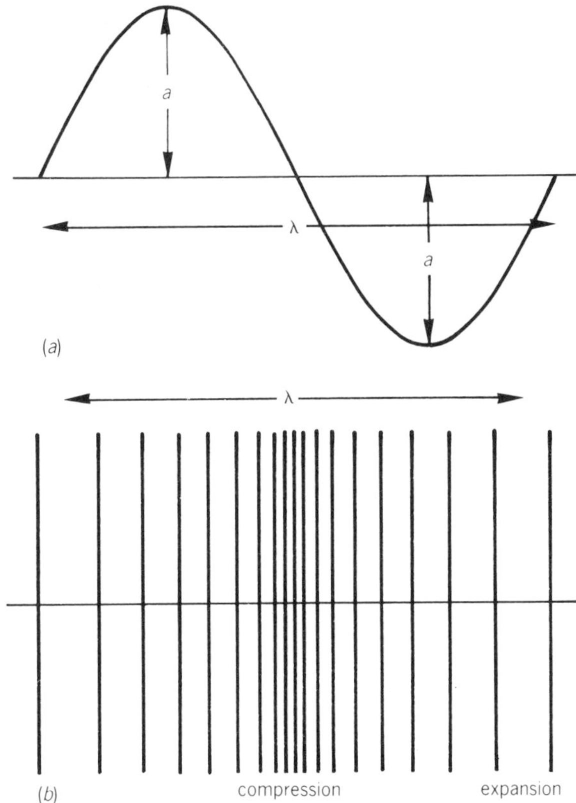

Figure 27.1

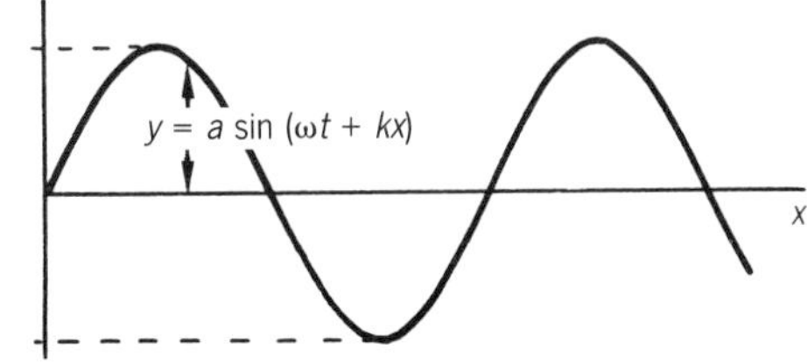

Figure 27.2

Basic definitions:

Wavelength:	the distance between any two successive corresponding points on the wave, that is, between two maxima or two minima (λ)
Displacement:	the distance from the mean, central, undisturbed position at any point on the wave (y)
Amplitude:	the maximum displacement (a)
Frequency:	the number of vibrations per second made by the wave (f)
Period:	the time taken for one complete oscillation ($T = 1/f$)
Phase:	a term related to the displacement at zero time (ϵ) (see below)

We will consider here the motion of a sine wave (Figure 27.2), since this type is the most fundamental. It can be shown that any other wave may be built up from a series of sine waves of differing frequency.

We can express a wave travelling in the positive x-direction by the equation:

$$y = a \sin (\omega t - kx)$$

and for one travelling in the opposite direction:

$$y = a \sin (\omega t + kx)$$

where k is a constant and $\omega = 2\pi f$.

The sign gives the direction of the motion. We can separate each equation into two terms:

(*a*) a term showing the variation of displacement with time at a particular place – for example, when $x = 0$ $\;y = a \sin (\omega t)$, that is, the variation of displacement with time at the particular place $x = 0$;

(*b*) a term showing the variation of displacement with distance at a particular time – for example, when $t = 0$ $\;y = a \sin (kx)$, that is, the variation of displacement with distance at a particular time $t = 0$.

An alternative form of the equation can be proved as follows.

Since the period $T = 1/f$ where f is the frequency and $\omega = 2\pi f$, we have $T = 2\pi/\omega$. Also when $t = 0$ $y = 0$ at $x = 0, \lambda/2, \lambda \ldots$ and so on, and so $k = 2\pi/\lambda$. The equation may therefore be written:

$$y = a \sin 2\pi(t/T + x/\lambda)$$

Phase shift

This is denoted by ϵ. A phase shift arises if we start timing the wave motion at an instant when the amplitude is not zero (see Figure 27.3), and when $t = 0$ $y = a \sin \epsilon$.

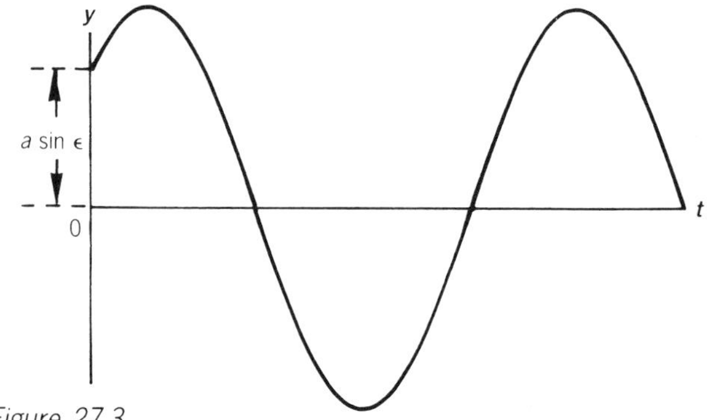

Figure 27.3

For the present we will take ϵ to be 0.

The reflection and refraction of waves

The reflection and refraction of waves at a series of different boundaries are shown in Figure 27.4. (For the present diffraction effects have been ignored.)

One of the most important diagrams is Figure 27.4(*g*). This shows that when waves pass from deep to shallow water, or when light passes from an optically less dense to an optically more dense material, there is refraction and also a change of wavelength. This is due to a change of wave velocity – the velocity in the more dense medium being less than that in the less dense medium. A full proof is given in the discussion of Huygens' wave theory on page 188, but the results will be summarised here as follows:

When a light wave passes from a less dense to a more dense material:

(*a*) there is a decrease in wave velocity,
(*b*) there is a decrease in wavelength,
(*c*) the frequency of the wave remains constant, and
(*d*) the ratio of the velocities in the two media is equal to that of the two wavelengths.

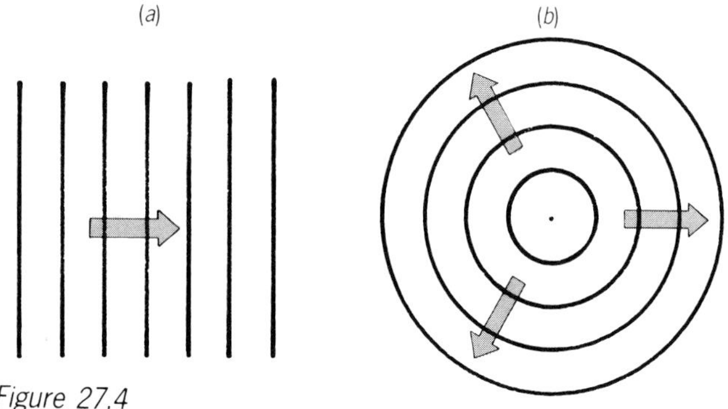

Figure 27.4

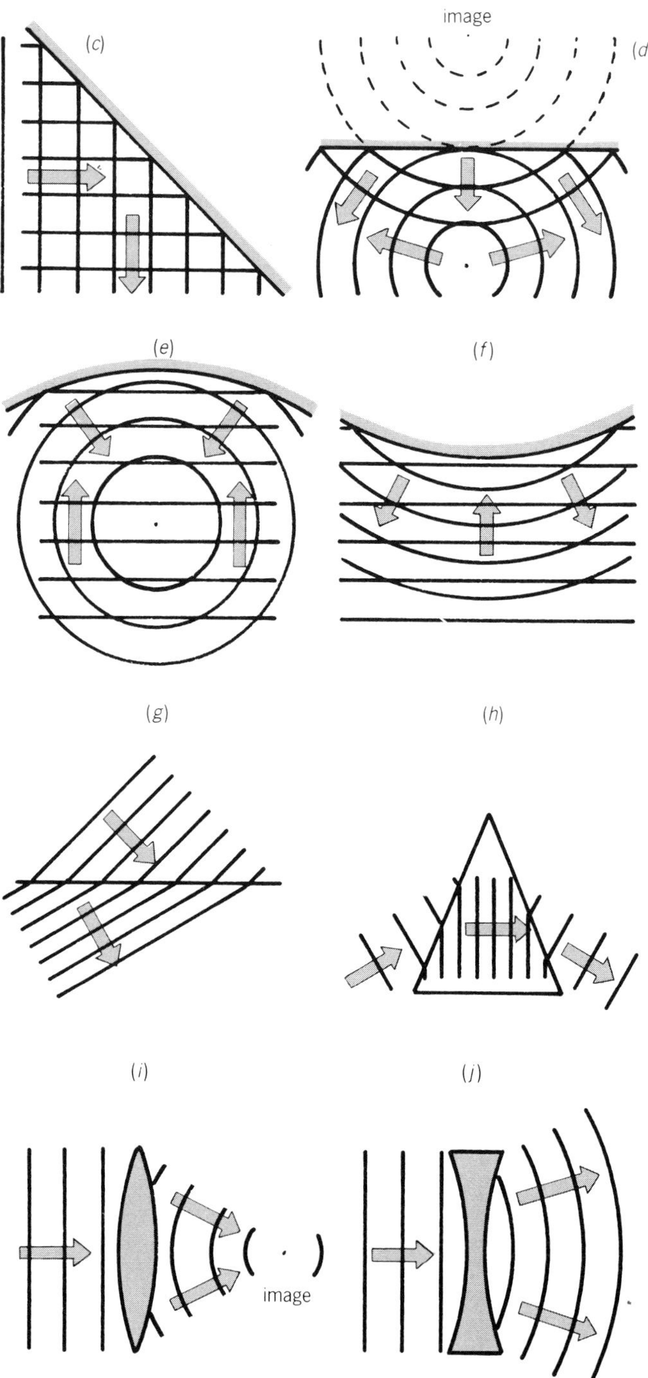

Phase change on reflection

It is important to realise the difference between longitudinal (or compression) waves and transverse waves when they are reflected at a boundary.

With the longitudinal wave there is no phase change on reflection if the reflection takes place at a fixed boundary. The particles carrying the vibration rebound elastically from a solid barrier and a compression is reflected as a compression. A phase change of π occurs at a free boundary, such as the open end of a tube, however.

With a transverse wave the phase change also depends on the nature of the boundary. If the boundary is fixed there is a phase change of π but if it is flexible the phase change is less than π; it is zero at a free boundary.

1 The equation $y = r \sin(\omega t - kx)$ represents a wave travelling in a medium along the x-direction, r being the amplitude and y the displacement at a time t.

(*a*) Is the wave travelling in the positive or negative x-direction?

(*b*) If $r = 1.0 \times 10^{-7}$ m, $\omega = 6.6 \times 10^2$ s^{-1} and $k = 20$ m^{-1}, calculate (i) the velocity of the wave, (ii) the maximum speed of a particle of the medium due to the wave.

(*c*) What is the displacement when $x = 0$ at a time t = 10 s,

(*d*) What is the displacement when $t = 0$ at a position $x = 8$ m.

Standing waves

A **stationary** or **standing** wave is one in which the amplitude varies from place to place along the wave. Figure 27.5 is a diagram of a stationary wave. Note that there are places where the amplitude is zero and, halfway between, places where the amplitude is a maximum; these are known as nodes and antinodes respectively.

A **node** is a place of zero amplitude.
An **antinode** is a place of maximum amplitude.

Any stationary wave can be formed by the addition of two travelling waves moving in opposite directions. A wave moving in one direction reflects at a barrier and interferes with the incoming wave:

$y_1 = a \sin(\omega t - kx)$ (say right–left)
$y_2 = a \sin(\omega t + kx)$ (say left–right)

Therefore:

$$y_1 + y_2 = a \sin(\omega t - kx) + a \sin(\omega t + kx) = 2a \sin(\omega t).\cos(kx) = A \sin(\omega t)$$

where $A = 2a \cos(kx)$.

Note that this expression is composed of two terms:

(*a*) $\sin(\omega t)$ – this shows a varying amplitude with *time* at a particular *place*.

(*b*) $\cos(kx)$ – this shows a varying amplitude with *position* at a particular *time*.

When $x = 0, \lambda/2 \ldots A$ is a maximum and we have an antinode;
When $x = \lambda/4, 3\lambda/4, 5\lambda/4 \ldots A$ is a minimum and we have a node.

Notice that the maximum value of A is $2a$.

Student investigation

The standing waves on a string may be studied using an experiment due to Melde and shown in Figure 27.6(*a*). A 0.5 m long rubber cord of 3 mm^2 cross-section is clamped at one end, stretched to twice its length and fixed to a vibrator. The vibrator is connected to a signal generator which can give a range of frequencies between 10 Hz and 100 Hz.

Observe the effects of slowly increasing the vibrator frequency from 10 Hz to 100 Hz and explain what you see. The experiment is best done in a darkened laboratory with the cord illuminated with a stroboscope.

Standing waves may also be investigated using the 2.8 cm wavelength microwave equipment used by most schools (Figure 27.6(*b*)).

The transmitter is set up facing a vertical metal plate about 50 cm away. If a probe detector connected to a meter is moved along the line between transmitter and plate a series of nodes and antinodes can be found. The distance between successive nodes or antinodes is half the wavelength of the microwaves.

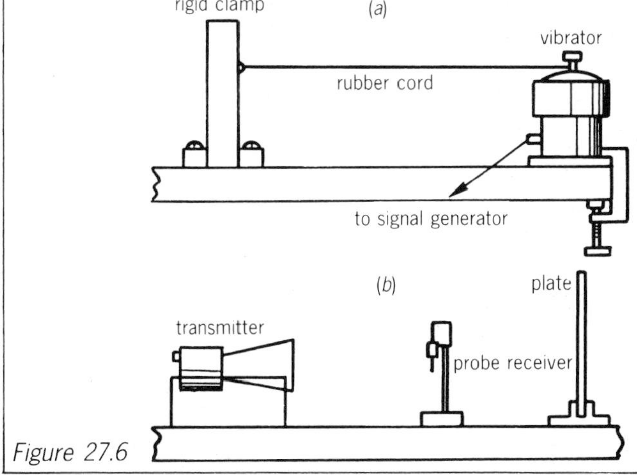

Figure 27.6

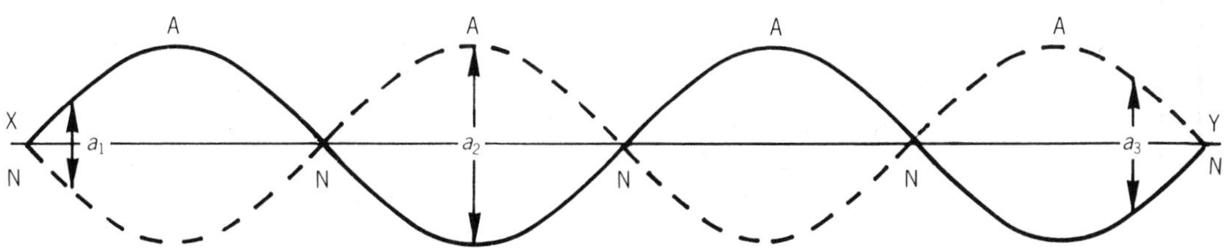

Figure 27.5

Beats

When two waves of slightly different frequency overlap a phenomenon known as **beats** results. The effect is a kind of throbbing sensation, which can sometimes be heard when two musicians such as oboeists are playing together.

If they are attempting to play the same note but are fractionally out of tune with each other beats will be heard: the frequency will vary about a mean value. The closer the two frequencies the lower will be the **beat frequency**, and this will become zero when they are perfectly in tune. The human ear is normally very sensitive to pitch and the two notes have to be well within one semitone for true beats to be heard.

Even if we take C and B on the musicians' scale, one semitone apart, the beat frequency would be 261.6 − 247 = 14.6 Hz, that is, nearly fifteen beats per second! This would not give audible beats, only an unpleasant discord.

Consider two waves of slightly different frequencies f_1 and f_2 ($f_1 > f_2$) but of the same amplitude. Figure 27.7 is a diagram of the two waves and their resultant for a frequency ratio of 1.25. (A computer program to generate such a pattern is given at the end of this section.)

Proof of the formula for beat frequency

Let the two displacements at a point be y_1 and y_2.

$$y_1 = a \sin 2\pi f_1 t$$
$$y_2 = a \sin 2\pi f_2 t$$

The final displacement (y) is given by:

$$y = a(\sin 2\pi f_1 t + \sin 2\pi f_2 t)$$
$$= 2a \cos 2\pi \frac{(f_1 - f_2)}{2} t . \sin 2\pi \frac{(f_1 + f_2)}{2} t$$

The first term shows a slow amplitude variation and the second a rapid displacement variation.

> **2** Two tuning forks A and B are sounded together, producing beats with a frequency of 10 Hz. If a small piece of Plasticine is fixed to fork B the beat frequency decreases. If A has a frequency of 300 Hz, what is the original frequency of B?

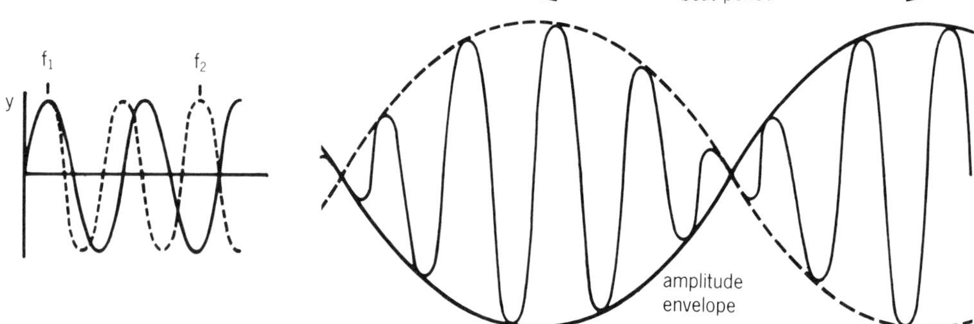

Figure 27.7

(*a*) The *amplitude* varies with time with a frequency $(f_1 - f_2)/2$.

(*b*) Since the ear is sensitive to the *intensity* and not the amplitude of a vibration, the beat frequency f is the number of times that the magnitude of the amplitude reaches a maximum each second (positive or negative):

> beat frequency (f) = 2 × amplitude frequency
> $= f_1 - f_2$

The effect can easily be observed in the laboratory with two signal generators and loudspeakers.

Beats are used in police radar speed traps. The outgoing and reflected signals are fed to the detector and the speed of the car is determined from the beat frequency using the doppler shift (see page 173).

Principle of superposition

The addition of two or more waves at a point to give a resultant disturbance uses the **principle of superposition**. This states that the final disturbance is simply the vector sum of each disturbance at that point. The principle is used in the equations for standing waves, beats, diffraction and interference.

Beats program

This simple computer program for the BBC microcomputer will generate the beat waveforms between two waves of differing frequency and amplitude.

```
 10 CLS
 20 MODE7
 30 PRINT TAB(13,10)CHR$145;"BEATS"
 40 PRINT TAB(3,11)CHR$141;CHR$145;
    "BEATS"
 50 PRINT TAB(3,23)CHR$132"PRESS THE
    SPACE BAR TO CONTINUE"
 60 REPEAT UNTIL GET = 32:CLS
 70 PRINT:PRINT"BEATS"
 80 PRINT "Beats are formed between two waves of
    differing frequency. You can hear beats between
    musical notes of similar pitch, the closer they are
    in pitch the slower the beats. When the beat
    frequency is zero they are exactly in tune."
 90 PRINT "This phenomenon is used by musicians
    to tune their instruments"
100 PRINT "The program shows the addition of two
    waves. Each wave is plotted and then the resultant
    wave is shown, the variation in amplitude
    showing the beats."
110 PRINT TAB(3,23)"PRESS THE SPACE BAR TO
    CONTINUE"
120 REPEAT UNTIL GET = 32:CLS
130 PRINT TAB(0,59);"Please type in the frequency
    ratio"
140 INPUT A
150 PRINT "Please type in the amplitude ratio (<1)"
160 INPUT B
170 PRINT TAB(0,20)"The space bar should be
    pressed to move to the graph and pressed again
    to move to the rest of the program"
180 REPEAT UNTIL GET = 32
190 CLS
200 MODE1
210 MOVE0,800:FORX% = 1 TO 2400 STEP 8:
    DRAW X%/2,800+160*SIN(X%/50):
    NEXT X%
220 GCOL0,2
230 MOVE0,800:FORX% = 1 TO 2400 STEP 8:
    DRAW X%/2,800+160*B*SIN((A*X%)/50):
    NEXT X%
240 GCOL0,3
250 MOVE0,320
260 FORX% = 1 TO 2400 STEP 8
270 DRAW X%/2,320+160*SIN(X%/50)
    +160*B*SIN((A*X%)/50)
280 NEXT X%
290 REPEAT UNTIL GET = 32
300 MODE7
310 PRINT:PRINTCHR$157CHR$135"RESULTS
    OF THE GRAPH" CHR$156
320 TAB(0,4);"FREQUENCY RATIO";A
330 PRINT TAB(0,6);"AMPLITUDE RATIO";B
340 PRINT TAB(5,20);"DO YOU WANT
    ANOTHER GO?"
350 INPUT P$
370 IF P$=Y CLS:GOTO130
380 END
```

Student investigation

A striking example of standing waves and resonance may be observed using a Slinky spring hanging vertically with its lower end fixed to a vibrator. Set up the apparatus as shown in Figure 27.8 and investigate the relation between frequency and wavelength for the standing waves on the spring.

What happens if the tension is altered, either by raising or lowering the support or by using a shorter length of spring?

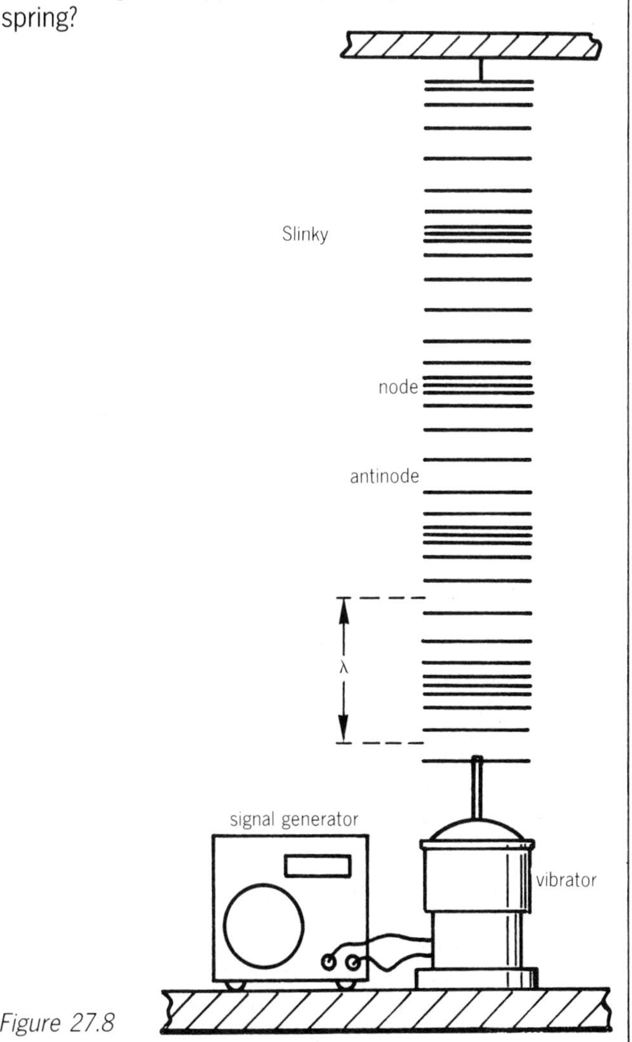

Figure 27.8

The doppler effect

The doppler effect is the apparent change of frequency and wavelength of a wave when a source or observer move relative to each other. These effects were explained by Doppler in 1842 as a bunching-up or a spreading-out of waves. To demonstrate his theory he persuaded some trumpeters to stand in an open railway carriage and play while the carriage travelled across the Dutch countryside, and the observers heard a change of pitch of the trumpet note as the truck passed them!

The effect can be observed in the following cases:

by whirling a whistle round your head on a string
in the change of pitch of a train siren as it passes through a station
in the shift of frequency in the light from the two sides of the Sun due to rotation
in spectroscopic binaries
in the red shift of the galaxies
in the use of radar by aircraft
in police speed traps
doppler broadening in plasmas

We can think of a simple analogy to explain this effect. Imagine that you are working in a chocolate factory packing chocolates that come to you down a steadily moving conveyor belt. At the other end of the belt another person puts the chocolates on the belt at a steady rate. The chocolates therefore reach you at the same steady rate that they were put on.

Now the other person starts to walk slowly towards you alongside the conveyor belt, still putting chocolates on at the original steady rate. You can see that you will receive the chocolates at a faster rate because after putting one chocolate on your partner walks after it and when the next chocolate is put on the belt it will be closer to the first chocolate than if he or she had not moved.

You will also receive the chocolates faster if you walk towards the other end of the conveyor belt collecting chocolates as you go.

Now the rate at which chocolates are put on the belt corresponds to the original frequency of the source of waves, the velocity of the belt corresponds to the wave velocity (which is constant and is unaffected by the motion of either the source or the observer) and the rate at which you receive them corresponds to the observed frequency.

We will now consider the doppler effect in wave motion. Consider a source S moving from left to right as shown in Figure 27.9.

Initially it is at position 1 and some time later it will be at positions 2 and 3. If it is emitting a wave then the three circles represent the positions of the

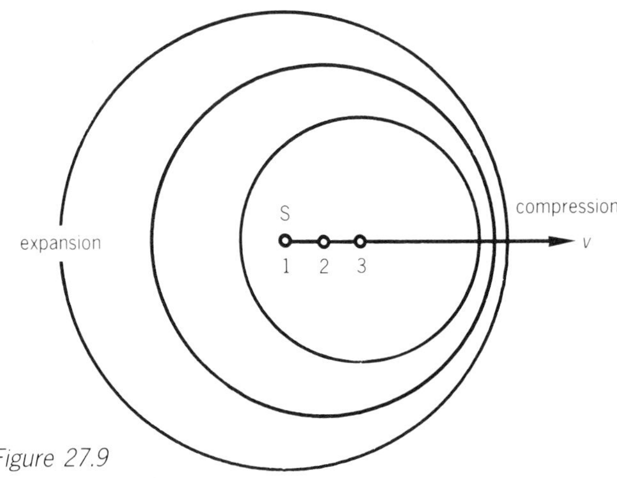

Figure 27.9

waves emitted at points 1, 2 and 3 some time after the source was at position 3. You will see that the waves on the right are closer together than those on the left; if the source is approaching an observer the wavelength will therefore be decreased and the frequency increased, while if it is moving away the reverse will be true.

Proof of the formulae for the doppler effect

(i) Moving source
Consider a source S moving at velocity v towards an observer O exactly one wavelength away. Let the source emit a continuous series of waves of wavelength λ, frequency f and velocity c.

In the time t that the wave travels from S to O the source travels from S to S′, a distance vt (Figure 27.10).

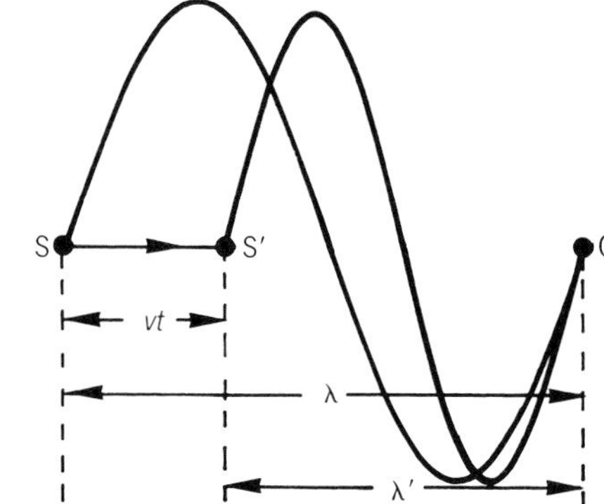

Figure 27.10

Therefore the observed wavelength λ' is

$$\lambda' = \lambda - vt$$

But $t = \lambda/c$, therefore

$$\lambda' = \lambda(1 - v/c)$$

If the source is receding we have

$$\lambda' = \lambda(1 + v/c)$$

A useful result here is that the wavelength change $\Delta\lambda$ is given by

$$\Delta\lambda = \lambda v/c$$

Alternatively, we can consider a source emitting f waves per second. In one second the waves will move forward a distance c and the source will move forward a distance v. Therefore f waves are now contained in a distance $(c - v)$. Therefore the new wavelength $\lambda' = (c - v)/f$.

Both these approaches show an apparent reduction in frequency and an increase in wavelength for the receding source.

(ii) Moving observer

In one second f waves will pass a stationary observer, but an observer who is moving forwards will pass through more waves per second and thus the observed frequency will increase. Let the observer move from O to O′ in one second (Figure 27.11).

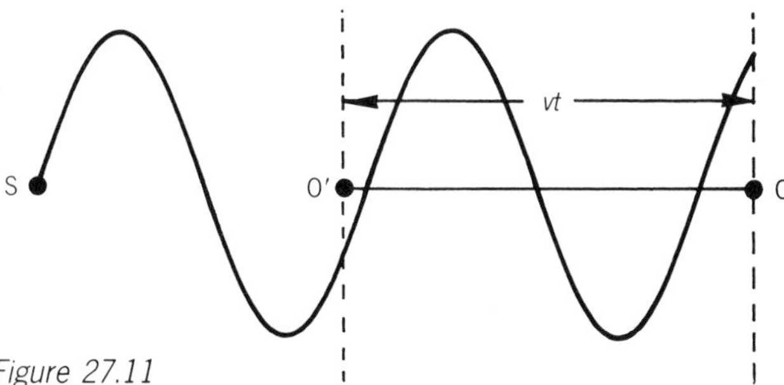

Figure 27.11

Now OO′ = v with $t = 1$, and so the extra number of waves received per second is v/λ. Therefore the new frequency f' is given by

$$f' = f(1 + v/c)$$

For a receding observer we have:

$$f' = f(1 - v/c)$$

If we compare the results for moving source and moving observer we see that there is a slight difference between them.

Example

Find the apparent wavelength change for light from a star moving away from the Earth at 20 km s^{-1}. Take the original wavelength as 600 nm. Then

$$\begin{aligned}\Delta\lambda &= \lambda v/c \\ &= (600 \times 10^{-9} \times 20 \times 10^3)/3 \times 10^8 \\ &= 0.004\text{ nm}\end{aligned}$$

3 If you stand beside a railway track and a train comes towards you then the note emitted by the hooter of the train will be doppler-shifted. Draw a graph to show how the frequency varies with the position of the train if you are standing a few metres from one side of the track.

4 The doppler effect has been used in a very sensitive type of burglar alarm. Suggest how this might work. (Remember that the doppler effect is only observed with objects in relative motion.)

5 A train sounds its horn while it is passing an observer who is standing beside the track. The observer notices a fractional change of frequency of 7/5. What is the speed of the train?

6 A whistle fixed to the end of a piece of string is whirled round in a horizontal circle of radius 1 m at a speed of 30 m s^{-1}. If the frequency of the note emitted by the whistle is 1024, calculate the maximum and minimum frequencies heard by a stationary observer standing some distance away. (Velocity of sound = 330 m s^{-1}.)

The radar speed trap

In the radar speed trap a beam is transmitted from a stationary source, reflected from a moving car and then detected by a stationary receiver.

The frequency used by the police is about 10.7 GHz (corresponding to a wavelength of about 2.8 cm) which is in the microwave region of the spectrum.

To determine the velocity of the car the reflected signal is made to beat with the outgoing signal, the beat frequency being easily found. It is left for the reader to show that the velocity v of a car moving towards a radar speed trap is given by the formula

$$v = \frac{c\Delta f}{2f}$$

where f is the frequency of the transmitter and Δf is the observed frequency change.

7 Calculate the beat frequency produced if a car travels towards a radar speed trap at 30 m s^{-1}, the operating frequency of the speed trap being 10.7 GHz. (Take the velocity of light to be 3 × 10^8 m s^{-1}.)

8 Calculate the change in frequency of the radar echo received from an aeroplane moving at 250 m s^{-1} if the operating wavelength of the radar set is 1 m.

9 Discuss the possible applications of the doppler effect in astronomy.
The wavelength of a line in the solar spectrum emitted at the pole of the Sun is 600 nm and this is changed by 4×10^{-3} nm at that part of the Sun's equator which is moving in the line of sight. Calculate the linear velocity of the Sun's equator.

10 If you are in a car driving up to a set of traffic lights that are red, how fast would you need to be going to make the lights appear green? (Take the velocity of light to be 3×10^8 m s^{-1}, the wavelength of red light to be 620 nm and the wavelength of green light to be 540 nm.)

The Mach effect

So far we have only considered cases where $v < c$. The problem of the case where $v > c$ is solved by Mach in 1936 (he received the Nobel prize for Physics in 1958).
Consider a source S moving with velocity v ($> c$). In one second the source will have moved from S to S′, a distance v, and in that time the waves will have moved from S to P, a distance c (Figure 27.12).

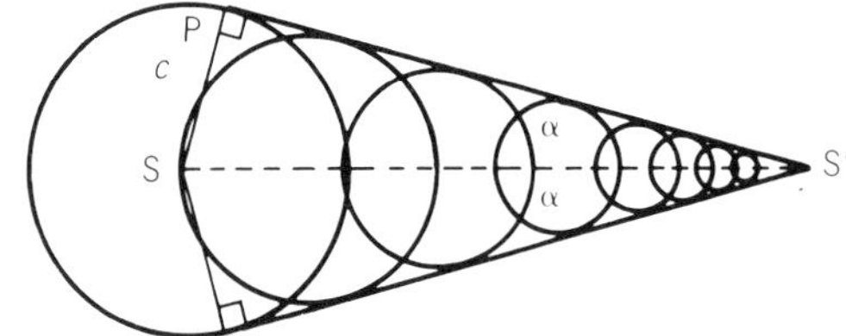

Figure 27.12

The envelope of the waves will be a cone of semiangle α, where $\sin\alpha = c/(v)$: the greater the value of v, the narrower the cone will be.

Examples of this are a sonic boom, the bow wave from a ship and shock waves from a bullet.

The same effect is also observed with light, as **Cerenkov radiation.** In some materials electrons from an accelerator can move faster than the velocity of light in that material and as the electrons travel through the solid or liquid a bluish radiation, a kind of shock wave, is observed, (for example, in water-moderated nuclear reactors).

11 A radar beam is reflected from a fast approaching aircraft and it is found that when the transmitted beam is made to beat with the reflected beam, the beat frequency is 950 Hz. If the wavelength of the radar waves is 10 cm, calculate the speed of approach of the aircraft.

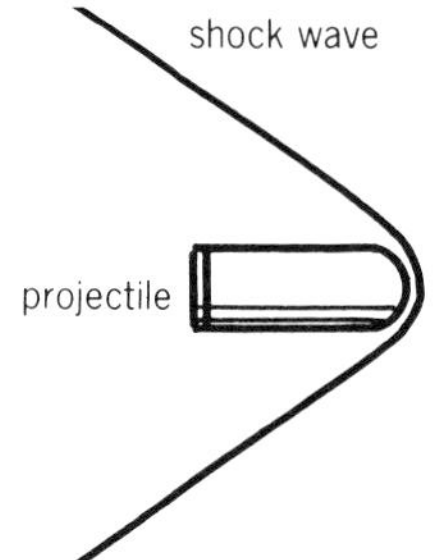

Figure 27.13

12 Figure 27.13 shows a projectile travelling through a material at supersonic speed. The shock wave produced by the projectile is clearly visible. If the velocity of sound in that material is 380 m s^{-1}, calculate the velocity of the projectile. (Refractive index = 1.5).

The doppler broadening of spectral lines

In a plasma (a gas at very high temperature) the atoms move at very high velocities. The light emitted by the atoms will be therefore doppler-shifted. Since some atoms will be moving towards an observer and others away, the result will be that each line in the spectrum will be broadened.

The width Δλ of a given line of wavelength λ can be shown to be:

$$\Delta\lambda = \frac{2v\lambda}{c}$$

where v is the r.m.s velocity of the atoms.
From the gas laws, however, we have that

$$v = \sqrt{\frac{3RT}{M}}$$

where M is the molar mass of the gas, R the gas constant and T the absolute temperature of the gas.

Combining these two equations thus gives us a means of finding the temperature of the gas from the doppler broadening of the spectral lines:

$$T = \frac{\Delta\lambda^2 c^2 M}{12\lambda^2 R}$$

Example

Calculate the broadening of a line of mean wavelength 656 nm in a hydrogen plasma at 10^6 K. (Take the molar mass of hydrogen in a plasma to be 0.001 kg.)

$$\Delta\lambda = \sqrt{\frac{12\lambda^2 RT}{c^2 M}}$$
$$= \sqrt{\frac{4.29 \times 10^{13}}{9 \times 10^{13}}}$$
$$= 0.69 \text{ nm}$$

28 · Sound waves

Sound waves are longitudinal waves propagated through a material by the transfer of kinetic energy from one molecule to another

(*a*) in solids and liquids by intermolecular forces and collisions,

(*b*) in gases by intermolecular collisions alone.

Hence the velocity of sound is greater in solids and liquids than in gases (the intermolecular forces in a gas are very small or zero).

The velocity of sound in a gas will thus be slightly less than the root mean square velocity of the gas molecules themselves (see page 251). It will increase with increasing temperature since this will give a larger molecular velocity.

The table below gives the velocity of sound in a number of materials.

Material	*Velocity of sound ($m\ s^{-1}$)*
Air (273 K)	330
Water (298 K)	1430
Steel	5060
Vulcanised rubber	54
Granite (293 K)	6000
Hydrogen (273 K)	1286
Lead	1230
Aluminium	5100
Copper	3650
Iron	5130
Glass	4000–5500
Pine	3313
Oak	3837
Elm	4108

The velocity of sound v in a solid in the form of a rod or wire may be found from the formula:

$$v = \sqrt{E/\rho}$$

where E is the Young modulus for the material and ρ is its density.

For an ideal gas the formula becomes:

$$v = \sqrt{\frac{\gamma P}{\rho}}$$

where P is the gas pressure and γ the ratio of the principal specific heat capacities of the gas (see page 241). Substituting for P from $PV = RT$ we have:

$$v = \sqrt{\frac{\gamma RT}{M}}$$

where M is the molar mass of the gas.

This last equation shows that the velocity of sound in an ideal gas is:

(*a*) independent of the gas pressure,

(*b*) directly proportional to the square root of the absolute temperature,

(*c*) directly proportional to the square root of γ, and

(*d*) inversely proportional to the square root of the molar mass of the gas.

It is for this reason that the velocity of sound at high altitude is low since the air there is cooler. The speed of an aircraft relative to the speed of sound (its Mach number) is therefore greater when it flies at high altitude even though its actual speed may be the same as that before it began to climb. The change in the velocity of sound with temperature also explains why an instrument such as a flute becomes sharp when taken into a warm concert hall, the frequency change being greater than any effects due to the expansion of the instrument.

1 A small explosion is set off on a railway line and an observer 1 km away with one ear to the rail hears two reports. Using only the following data find the time interval between them.

The Young modulus for steel = 2×10^{11} Pa, density of steel = 7800 kg m^{-3}; density of air = 1.3 kg m^{-3}; ratio of the principal specific heat capacities for air = 1.4; atmospheric pressure = 10^5 Pa. [L]

2 It is possible to make a toy telephone from two tins with a taut stretched string between them. How does this work? Why is the transmitted sound louder than the sound travelling through air for the same distance?

3 When sound waves travel from air into water which of the following change: frequency, wavelength, velocity?

All musical instruments rely on the vibration of air to produce a note. The air is usually set in vibration either by a moving string or by the oscillation of air enclosed in a pipe.

Stringed instruments are set in vibration either by a bow (as with a violin or cello), by a hammer (piano) or by plucking (guitar, harpsichord).

Wind instruments are all basically tubes in which the air is made to vibrate. Woodwind instruments are of two kinds:

(*a*) instruments with reeds such as the clarinet, saxophone and oboe (Figure 28.1), and

(*b*) instruments where the passage of air across a hole causes the air in the tube to vibrate such as the flute, recorder and organ.

In brass instruments the air is vibrated by a mouthpiece, the tension of the player's lips or the length of the tube altering the pitch of the note.

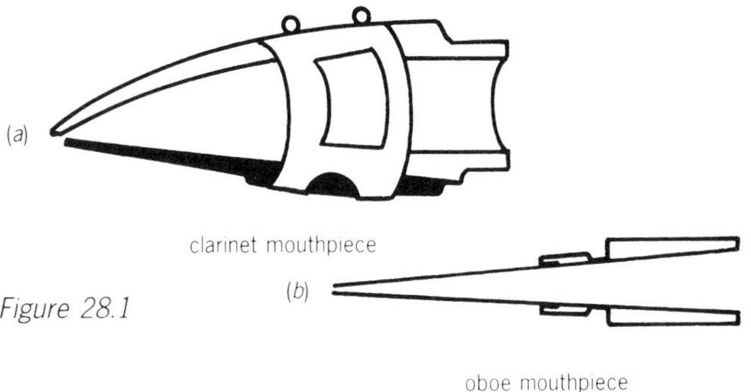

Figure 28.1

Vibrating strings

If a string stretched between two points is plucked it vibrates, and a wave travels along the string. Since the vibrations are from side to side the wave is transverse. The velocity of the wave along the string can be found as follows.

Velocity of waves along a stretched string

Assume that the velocity of the wave v depends upon

(*a*) the tension in the string (T),

(*b*) the mass of the string (M) and

(*c*) the length of the string (l) (Figure 28.2).

Therefore

$$v = kT^xM^yl^z$$

Solving this gives $x = \frac{1}{2}$, $z = \frac{1}{2}$, $y = -\frac{1}{2}$. The formula is

$$\text{velocity of waves on a stretched string} = \sqrt{\frac{T}{m}}$$

since the constant k can be shown to be equal to 1 in this case and the mass per unit length $m = M/l$.

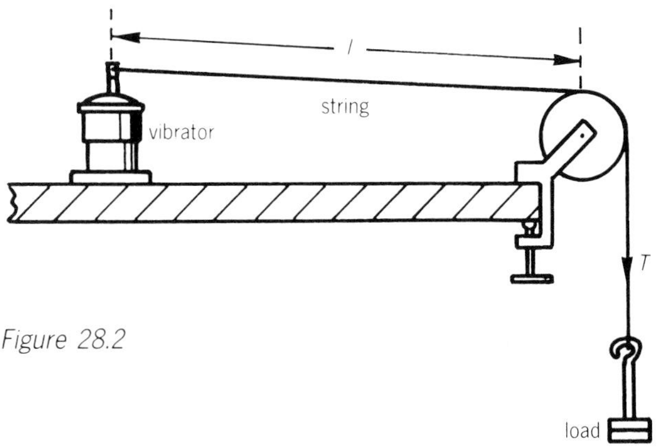

Figure 28.2

The Physics of vibrating strings

A string is fixed between two points and made to vibrate by displacing the centre of the string. This causes a transverse wave to travel along the string. The pulse then travels outwards along the string and when it reaches each end of the string it is reflected (Figure 28.3).

Figure 28.3 *Wave motion and sound*

The two travelling waves then interfere with each other (see the discussion of the principle of superposition on page 170) to produce a standing wave in the string. In the **fundamental** mode of vibration there are points of no vibration or **nodes** at each end of the string and a point of maximum vibration or **antinode** at the centre.

The first three harmonics for a vibrating string are shown in Figures 28.4 to 28.6.

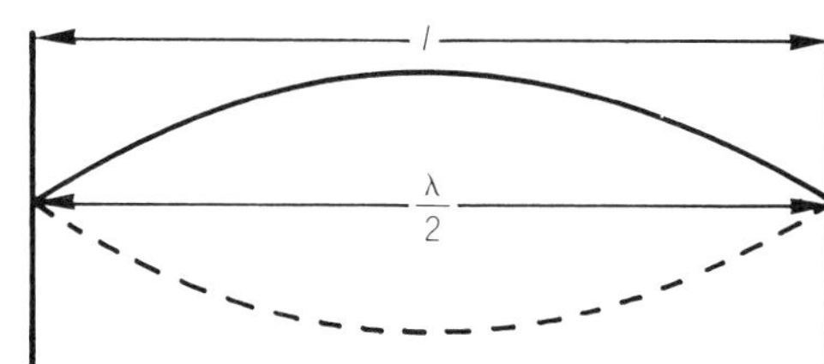

Figure 28.4

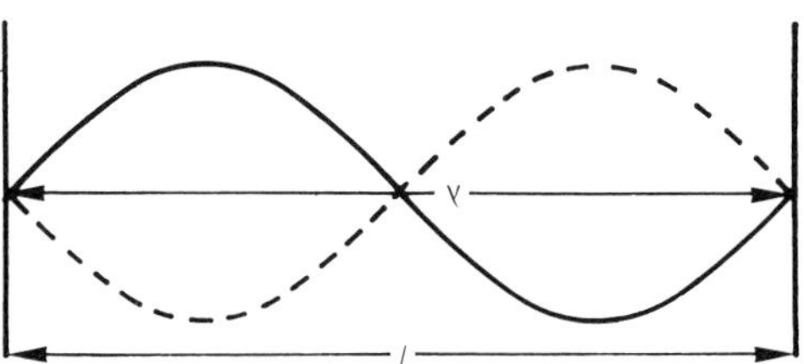

Figure 28.5

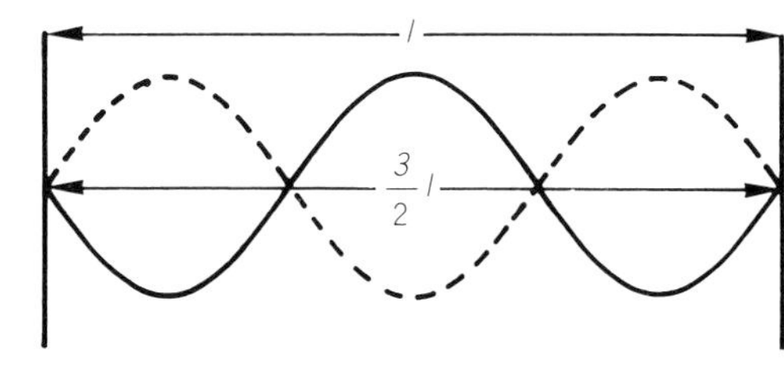

Figure 28.6

(*a*) As has already been shown, for a string of length l and mass per unit length m under a tension T the fundamental frequency is given by

$$f = \frac{1}{2l}\sqrt{\frac{T}{m}}$$

(*b*) First overtone or second harmonic:

$$f = \frac{1}{l}\sqrt{\frac{T}{m}}$$

(*c*) Second overtone or third harmonic:

$$f = \frac{3}{2l}\sqrt{\frac{T}{m}}$$

The sonometer

This instrument was devised to verify the laws of the vibrating string proposed by Mersenne in 1636. He stated that the frequency of a stretched string was:

(*a*) proportional to the square root of the tension,
(*b*) inversely proportional to the length of the string, and
(*c*) inversely proportional to the square root of the mass per unit length of the string.

The sonometer itself consists of a string stretched between two supports or bridges on a wooden sounding box. The tension of the string may be varied either by a screw or by hanging weights on one end of it (Figure 28.7).

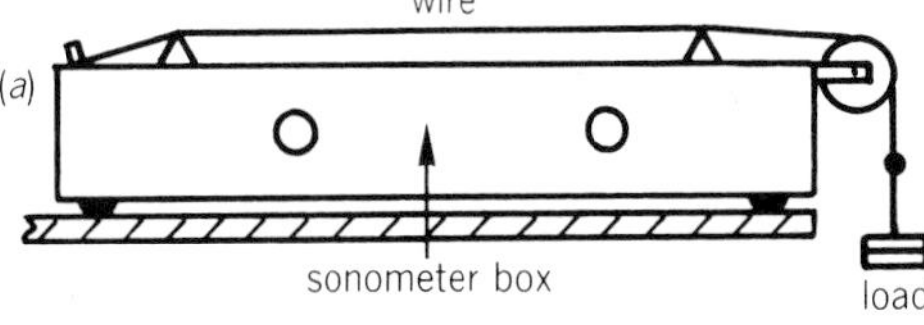

Figure 28.7

The purpose of the sounding box is to make a larger mass of air vibrate and so amplify the very small sounds produced by the vibrating string itself. The same principle is applied in stringed instruments such as the guitar or cello.

The frequency at which the string is vibrating can be found by using a tuning fork of known frequency, which is made to vibrate and held with its base on the sounding box. The string is then tuned to give the same note. A small piece of paper may be placed on the centre of the wire and when the frequency of the wire is tuned to that of the fork resonance occurs and the wire will vibrate, throwing the piece of paper off. The tension, length and mass per unit length of the string can then easily be measured.

Student investigation

If the wire on the sonometer is metal it can be used as a simple electric guitar. Set up the apparatus as shown in Figure 28.8, with the large magnet placed with its poles on either side of the sonometer wire. When the wire is plucked the movement of the wire in the magnetic field induces an e.m.f. in the wire (see page 316). If this alternating e.m.f. is fed to an amplifier and speaker a note will be heard.

Since the e.m.f. induced is proportional to the rate at which the magnetic flux is cut, how will the volume and pitch produced by the speaker be affected by the amplitude of the vibration of the wire?

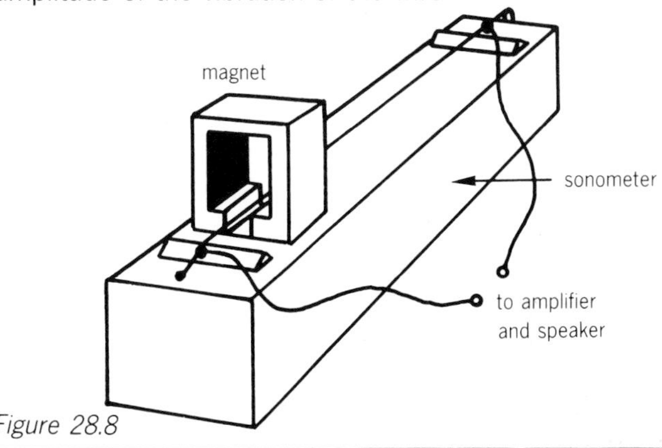

Figure 28.8

4 A horizontal metal wire is fixed in a state of tension between two vertical supports. When plucked it gives a fundamental frequency f_0. What change, if any, will be observed in this fundamental frequency if the wire is now immersed in water and plucked again? Explain your answer.

5 A steel wire is hung from one end and kept in a state of tension by a mass of iron fixed to the lower end. When the wire is plucked in air it emits a note of frequency 256 Hz. What will be the new frequency if the wire is suspended vertically in water?
(Density of iron = 7800 kg m^{-3}; density of water = 1000 kg m^{-3}.) [AEB]

6 Calculate the following:
(*a*) the frequency of BBC Radio 4, wavelength 1500 m;
(*b*) the wavelength of the sound of frequency 256 Hz (middle C) in air at 273 K;
(*c*) the fundamental frequency of a string of length 1 m and mass per unit length 2*g* when the tension in the string is 10 N;
(*d*) the velocity of the travelling waves in (*c*).

7 Find the ratio of the frequencies of transverse and longitudinal vibrations in a steel sonometer wire of diameter 1.5 mm and tension 100 N. (Young's modulus for steel = 2 × 10^{11} Pa)

Measurement of the frequency of the mains

If a current is passed through a wire in a magnetic field then the wire will move. If this current is alternating, as in the mains supply, the wire will vibrate, the fundamental resonant frequency of vibration being equal to the frequency of the mains supply.

An a.c. supply is passed from a *low-voltage* transformer to a stretched wire placed between the poles of a strong magnet (Figure 28.9) and the tension adjusted until resonance occurs. The frequency of vibration and hence the frequency of the supply (f_0) may then be found from the equation:

$$f_0 = \frac{1}{2l}\sqrt{\frac{T}{m}}$$

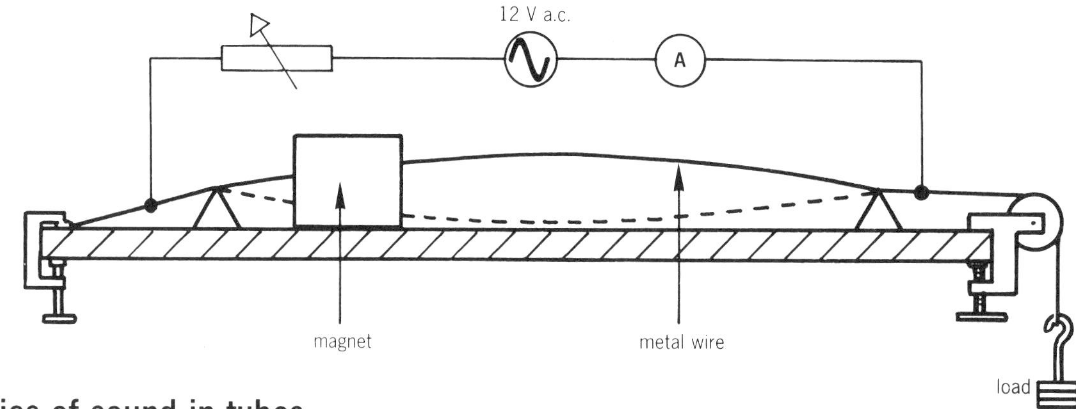

Figure 28.9

The Physics of sound in tubes

This part of the Physics of sound is the basis of all wind instruments, from the piccolo to the organ. Basically the ideas are very simple but they can become complex for a specific musical instrument. For that reason we will confine ourselves to a general treatment of the production of a note from a uniform tube.

The stationary waves set up by the vibrations of the air molecules within the tube are due to the sum of two travelling waves moving down the tube in opposite directions. One of these is the initial wave and the other its reflection from the end of the tube.

> All air-filled tubes have a resonant frequency and if the air inside them can be made to oscillate they will give out a note at this frequency. This is known as the **fundamental frequency** or **first harmonic.**

Higher harmonics or **overtones** may also be obtained and it is the presence of these harmonics that gives each instrument its individual quality. A note played on a flute will be quite unlike one of exactly the same pitch played on a bassoon!

> A **harmonic** is a note whose frequency is an integral multiple of the particular tube's or string's fundamental frequency.

Tubes in musical instruments are of two types:

(*a*) open at both ends, or

(*b*) open at one end and closed at the other.

The vibration of the air columns of these types of tube in their fundamental mode are shown in Figure 28.10.

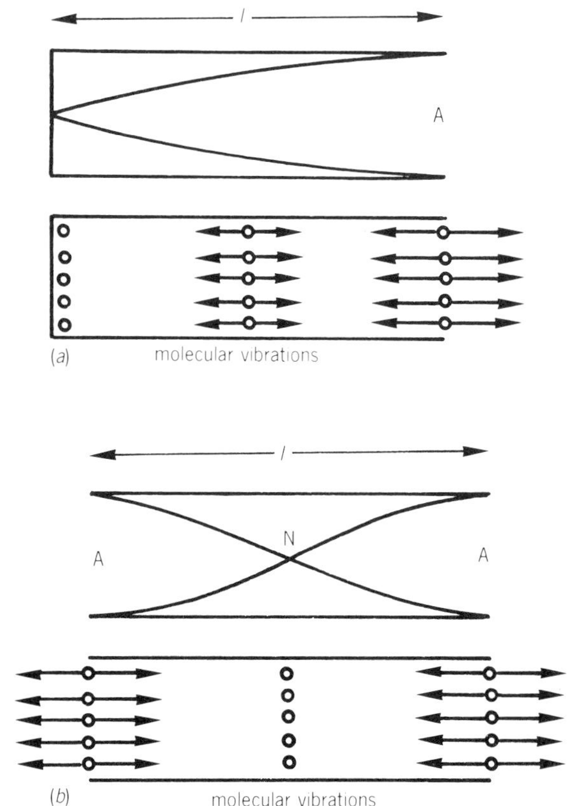

Figure 28.10

Notice that the tubes have areas of no vibration or **nodes** at their closed ends and areas of maximum vibration or **antinodes** at their open ends. An antinode also occurs at the centre of a tube closed at both ends in this mode.

Nodes are areas of *zero displacement* but of *maximum pressure variation*, while the reverse is true for antinodes.

Some of the higher harmonics for the different tubes are shown in Figure 28.11. Notice that a closed tube gives odd-numbered harmonics only, while the open tube will give both odd- and even-numbered.

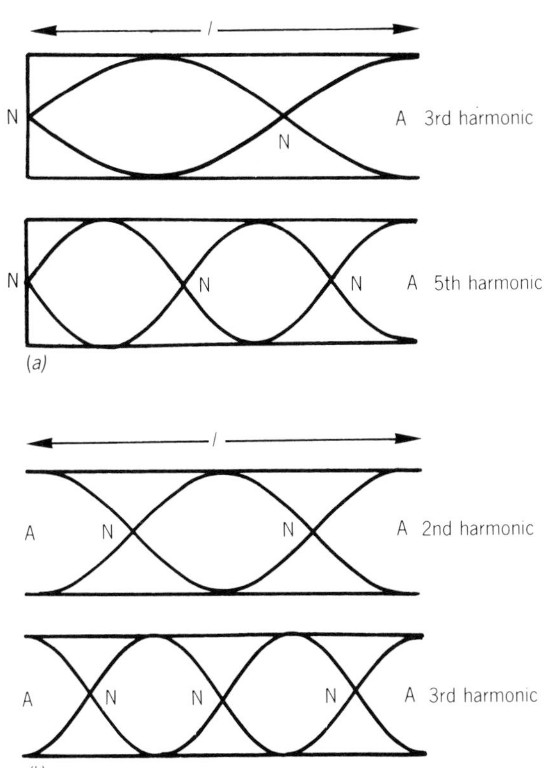

Figure 28.11

If the velocity of sound is denoted by v and the length of a tube by l, then for a tube closed at one end the fundamental frequency f is given by

$$f = \frac{v}{4l}$$

For a tube open at both ends the fundamental frequency is given by

$$f = \frac{v}{2l}$$

End corrections

The vibrations within the tube will be transmitted to the air just outside the tube, and the air will then also vibrate. In accurate work we must also allow for this effect, by making an **end correction** (Figure 28.12).

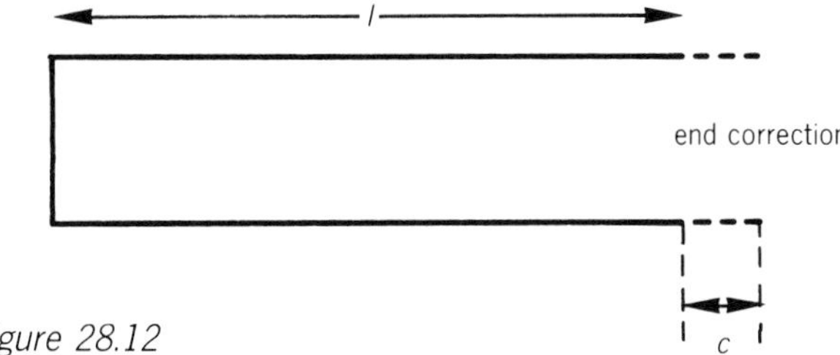

Figure 28.12

This means that we consider that the tube is effectively longer than its measured length by an amount c, that is, that the true length $= l + c$. The equation for a closed tube then becomes

$$f = \frac{v}{4(l + c)}$$

Measurement of the velocity of sound

The velocity of sound in air may be found quite simply by using the resonance of a column of air in a tube. A glass cylinder contains water into which is placed an open-ended tube, as shown in Figure 28.13, so that the water closes the bottom end of the tube. If a tuning fork of known frequency is sounded over the upper end the air in the tube vibrates and a note is heard.

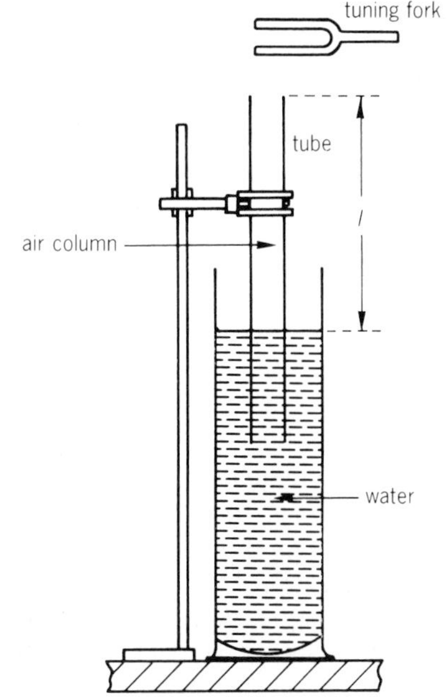

Figure 28.13

The length of the air column is adjusted by raising the tube out of the water until a point is found where resonance occurs and a loud note is produced. At this point the frequency of the tuning fork is equal to the fundamental frequency of the air column in the tube.

In its fundamental mode the wavelength λ is four times the length of the air column (l), that is:

$$\lambda = 4l$$

Since velocity = frequency × wavelength the velocity of sound may be found (since the frequency of the tuning fork is known). For accurate determinations the following precautions should be taken:

(*a*) the temperature of the air should be taken, since the velocity of sound is temperature-dependent, and

(*b*) the end correction should be allowed for. This may be done by finding the resonance for the second harmonic with the same tuning fork.

Student investigation

The velocity of compression waves in a metal rod may be studied using the apparatus shown in Figure 28.14. The metal rod under test is suspended from another rod by rubber bands so that it is free to vibrate.

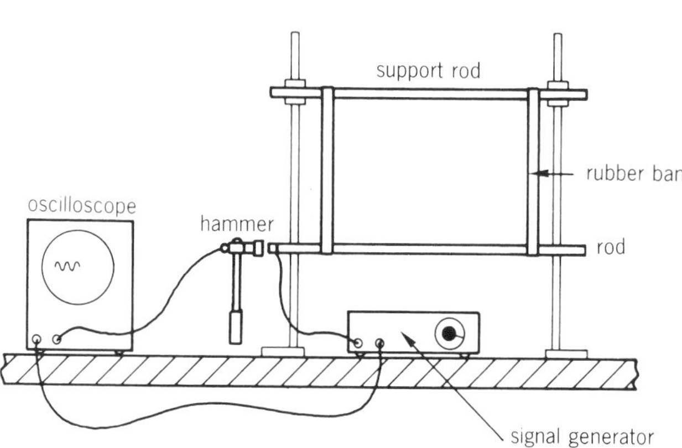

Figure 28.14

The signal generator should be adjusted to give an output of about 6 V at 25 kHz and the oscilloscope should be set for a time base of 100 μs and a sensitivity of 5 V cm^{-1}. The end of the rod is now given a sharp tap with the hammer. A pulse of compression waves will pass along the rod and be reflected at the far end. When they reach the hammer the contact with the hammer will be broken. (Why is this?) The time of contact can be found from the length of the trace on the oscilloscope screen. (The oscilloscope should have its stability control adjusted as far anticlockwise as possible so that a trace is only formed when contact is made between the hammer and the rod.)

The experiment should be repeated with a series of rods of different metals and the validity of the equation $v = \sqrt{E/\rho}$ should be checked.

The Physics of musical sounds

What makes a pleasant musical sound is something that varies from person to person – some prefer pop and some jazz, while others only listen to Bach! All types of music are built up from basically the same set of notes, however. So an even more fundamental thing than the type of music we prefer are the actual frequencies of the notes that make up what we call a scale.

The situation is complicated by the fact that there are actually *two* different scales:

(*a*) the **scientific scale** based on middle C having a frequency of 256 Hz, also known as the **diatonic scale,** and

(*b*) the **musicians' scale** based on A having a frequency of exactly 440 Hz, also known as the **equally tempered scale.** On this scale middle C has a frequency of 261.6 Hz.

The frequency ratio for two notes one octave apart is 2:1 while for a fifth it is 1.5:1. On the equally tempered scale the frequency ratio for each semitone is 1.0595:1. The ratio for the tone interval is the sixth root of 2 and that for the semitone the twelfth root of 2.

The two scales are shown below:

Note	*Frequency* *Scientific scale*	*Musicians' scale*	Note	*Frequency* *Scientific scale*	*Musicians' scale*
C	32	32.6	C	256	261.6
D	36	36.6	D	288	293.7
E	40	41.2	E	320	329.6
F	47.6	43.7	F	341	349.2
G	48	48.9	G	384	392
A	53.3	55	A	427	440
B	60	61.7	B	480	493.9
C	64	65.4	C	512	523.3
D	72	73.3	D	576	587.4
E	80	82.4	E	640	659.4
F	85.2	87.3	F	682	698.7
G	96	98.0	G	768	784.3
A	106.7	110	A	864	880
B	120	123.5	B	960	987.8
C	128	130.8	C	1024	1046.6
D	144	146.7	D	1152	1174.6
E	160	164.8	E	1296	1318.8
F	170.5	174.6	F	1365	1396.7
G	192	196	G	1536	1567.9
A	213.5	220	A	1728	1760
B	240	247	B	1944	1975.7
C	256	261.6	C	2048	2093.2

Some other notes, with their frequencies (corresponding to those of the musicians' scale) are as follows:

C sharp 277
D sharp 311
F sharp 370
G sharp 415
A sharp 466

Student investigation

Make a set of wooden blocks from a piece of knot-free hardwood. All the pieces should be of cross-section 3 cm × 0.5 cm with the lengths being 22.0 cm, 22.8 cm, 24.2 cm, 25.8 cm, 27.2 cm, 28.3 cm, 29.5 cm and 30.5 cm. (It is important to cut the blocks exactly to size.)

Now drop them one after the other in order on to a hard floor so that they fall with one end hitting the floor slightly before the other. Record and explain what you hear.

You might like to try some other lengths, but keep to the same cross-section.

Quality of notes

The **quality** or **timbre** of the note is also important. For example, middle C sounds quite different when it is sung and when it is played on a cello or oboe.

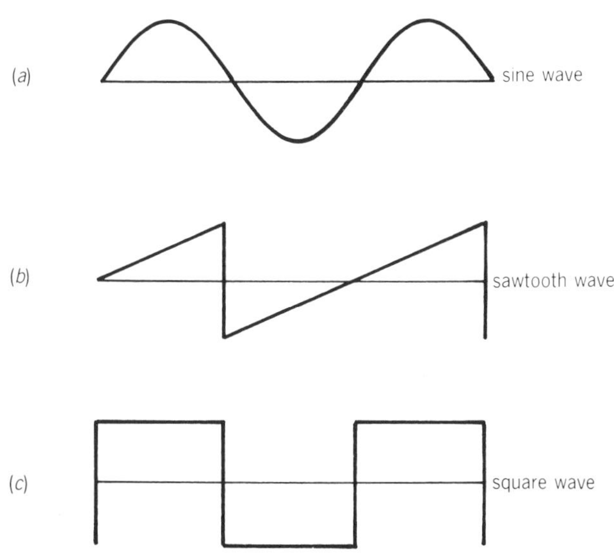

Figure 28.15

Figure 28.15 shows the effect of the quality of various notes. They all have the same frequency but note (*a*) will have a much smoother sound than either (*b*) or (*c*). The more jagged the waveform the sharper (in texture, not in pitch) will be the sound produced by it. Note that (*a*) is a pure sine wave while the others may be formed from one basic wave plus many harmonics.

8 In a resonance tube experiment using a tuning fork with a frequency of 512 Hz the first two resonant positions occur with tube lengths of 13.6 cm and 43.5 cm respectively. Calculate
(*a*) the velocity of sound, and
(*b*) the end correction for the tube.

9 Two organ pipes 80 cm and 81 cm long are found to give a beat frequency of 2.6 Hz when each is sounding its fundamental note. Neglecting end corrections calculate from these results
(*a*) the velocity of sound in air, and
(*b*) the frequencies of the two notes.

Applications of acoustics

The importance of sound is not limited to hearing. What we call sound is really only a small section of a broad spectrum of longitudinal elastic waves which may be propagated through many different types of material. We will consider some of the other applications of these oscillations below.

Ultrasonics

One very important use of sound in recent years has been that of ultrasonics. The human ear is sensitive to sounds with a frequency of up to about 18 kHz although this upper limit of hearing does decrease with age. Ultrasonics, however, is concerned with sounds with frequencies of at least 20 kHz and often into the megahertz range.

Ultrasound has many uses in medicine, including the detection of tissue (the absorption of ultrasound varies considerably for muscle, fat and bone), for scanning unborn children without the risks of X-rays, for selectively destroying tumours and in physiotherapy as a treatment for arthritis and related problems.

The doppler effect (see page 172) can be used with ultrasonics to measure the speed of the blood in different parts of the body.

Ultrasound is also useful as a cleaning agent. Sonar, in which an ultrasonic beam is transmitted and the reception of the reflected beam is monitored, is used to detect underwater objects such as fish, wrecks and submarines.

Geological uses

The analysis of elastic waves within the Earth can often give a guide to the geological nature of the upper part of the Earth's crust. This is vital in the search for minerals and oil.

Sound levels and damage to the ears

It is possible that listening to very loud music over long periods can damage the ears. Playing in a rock group may cause problems of this type.

The level of sound intensity is defined by the **decibel.** The ratio of the intensities (I_1 and I_0) of two sounds is given in decibels (dB) by the formula:

$$\text{decibel level} = 10 \log (I_1/I_0)$$

The human ear has a threshold of hearing which at 1000 Hz is taken as 10^{-12} W m^{-2}. The table below gives the decibel values and power densities for a number of different sounds.

	Sound intensity/dB	*Power density/W m^{-2}*
Threshold of pain	120	1
Riveter	95	3.2×10^{-3}
Elevated tram	90	10^{-3}
Busy street traffic	70	10^{-5}
Ordinary conversation	65	3.2×10^{-6}
Quiet car	50	10^{-7}
Quiet radio in a house	40	10^{-8}
Whisper	20	10^{-10}
Rustle of leaves	10	10^{-11}
Threshold of hearing	0	10^{-12}

Although the noise level produced by the high-power amplifiers of a rock group may be 90 dB or more, a personal stereo may give levels at your ears that can rise to as much as 100 dB, and are therefore even more dangerous.

Physics and music

Physics has had many impacts on music over the years, we shall just consider a few interesting effects.

The increase in volume and brilliance of the sound of a violin over the centuries has been due partly to the skill of the violin maker and partly to the much greater understanding of the Physics of the instrument.

Those of you who play a brass instrument will know that a much clearer sound can be produced on an instrument without valves. Holes in the tube tend to reduce the clarity of the sound produced.

When you next see a clarinet being played, think about where the sound is coming from. Most comes from the side holes with only a few high frequencies coming from the bell bottom. In fact the instrument acts as a simple diffraction grating with a set of sources. The sound that you hear, if any, depends on where you sit!

The use of instruments such as the sampling piano means that many new and interesting sounds may be created. For example, you may blow across a bottle top or twang a ruler and the sampling piano will record the sound. The 'shape'or quality of this sound is stored digitally and it may then be replayed at the same frequency, or the frequency may be changed, by pressing the keys of the piano, to produce a tune.

The development of computers has led to the production of computerised sound, some computers have even been made to sing. One of my favourite pieces of computer music is a recording of the Queen of the Night aria from Mozart's opera *The Magic Flute* which is sung superbly by a computer in Paris.

Sound and music, of whatever kind and however produced, depend critically on the physics of their sources. Even a full-sized symphony orchestra could be regarded as an experiment in practical physics with some superb results.

Light

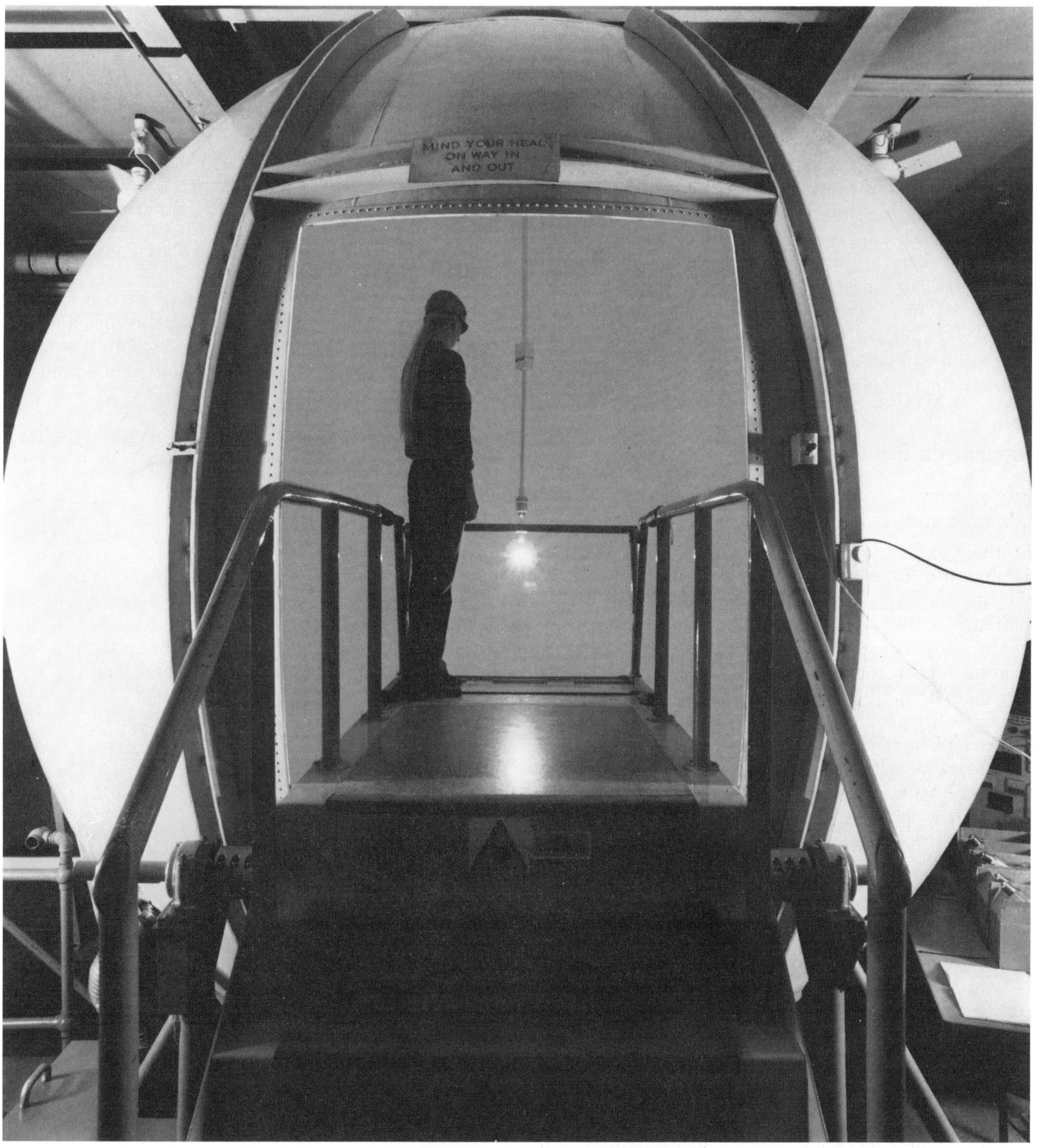

A 5 m diameter sphere used for the measurement of the luminous flux from very large or powerful light sources (National Physical Laboratory, England)

29 · The velocity of light

The problem of the nature of light puzzled scientists for many centuries, and it was not until the sixteenth century that some definite ideas were proposed.

Descartes (1596–1650) believed that light was propagated in a similar way to pressure, that is, instantaneously. In 1679, however, Römer proposed that light did have a finite velocity and by measuring the time intervals between successive eclipses of the moons of Jupiter was able to measure this velocity. He found that the times measured were not the same as those predicted on the basis of an infinite velocity of light. From his observations he predicted that the velocity of light was about 190 000 miles per second, or some 3.11×10^8 m s^{-1}.

In 1905 Einstein showed that the velocity of light was a fundamental constant, in fact the 'ultimate' velocity for any object.

Measuring the velocity of light

Communication with radio or light waves is limited by the velocity with which the waves can travel. For instance, signals sent to the deep space probe Pioneer 10 take five hours at present to go from the Earth to the spacecraft, so that course corrections have to be sent at least five hours before they are required!

The knowledge of the value of the velocity of light is important in the measurement of the light year in astronomy.

The main problem with the measurement of the velocity of light is its very large value. We therefore have to use very large distances or very accurate timing methods. Most of the methods to be described here rely on chopping up the light into short pulses; the method of doing this varies from one experiment to another.

Fizeau's rotating wheel

This was the first terrestrial method for measuring the velocity of light and was performed in 1849.

Light from a source S is focused by a lens L_1 on to the edge of a toothed wheel W which has N teeth. It passes through the gaps between the teeth and on to a second lens L_2, which produces a beam of parallel light. This travels across a known distance d to a third lens L_3 and on to a concave mirror M. It is then reflected back and when it meets plate P it is reflected into the eyepiece E (Figure 29.1).

The wheel is now rotated until a speed is reached at which the pulse of light leaving through one gap returns to the wheel when the next tooth has taken the place of the gap (Figure 29.2). No light will therefore be observed reaching the eyepiece. If the wheel is rotating at n revolutions per second then

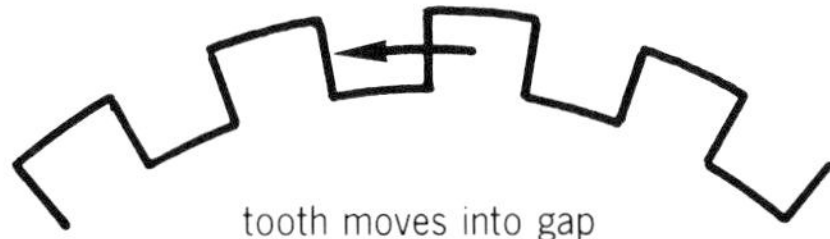

Figure 29.2

Distance travelled by light $= 2d$

Transit time $= \dfrac{1}{2nN}$

velocity of light (c) = $4nNd$

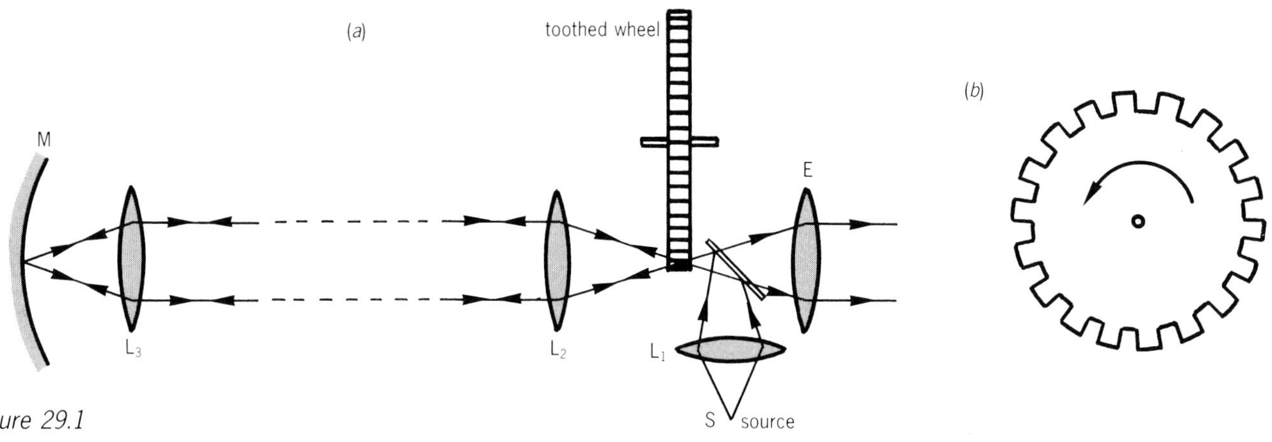

Figure 29.1

Fizeau's values were:

$2d = 17.26$ km, $N = 720$, $n = 12.6$ revs per second, giving a value of 3.13×10^8 m s^{-1} for the velocity of light.

The light must be monochromatic to give a parallel beam and the teeth on the wheel should be blackened to stop unwanted reflections.

1 A wheel with 720 teeth is rotated at a uniform speed and light passing through one slot is reflected back along its own path from a mirror 20 km away. If the light is to return through the next slot, determine the speed of rotation of the mirror. (Velocity of light = 3.0×10^8 m s^{-1}) [c]

2 In Fizeau's rotating wheel experiment the first eclipse occurs when the angular velocity of the wheel is ω. Calculate the speed at which
(*a*) the light will be visible again,
(*b*) the second eclipse will occur, and
(*c*) the third eclipse will occur.

Foucault's rotating mirror

First performed in 1862, this experiment can be carried out in the laboratory and is the basis of commercially available apparatus for schools. Light from the source S is converged by a lens L towards a plane mirror M. After reflection the light travels to a concave mirror N and then reflects back along its original path to M and thence into the eyepiece forming an image at I. The plane mirror is now rotated at angular velocity ω. During the time the light was travelling from M to N and back again the plane mirror will have rotated through a small angle θ and so the light reflected from M will be turned through 2θ and therefore the image seen in the eyepiece will have moved from I to I′ (Figure 29.3).

Let the distance from M to N be d and let the number of revolutions per second of M be n.

$$\theta = \omega t = \omega \times 2d/c = 2\pi n \times 2d/c = 4\pi n d/c$$

But $TT' = 2\theta d$ and $\frac{TT'}{d+b} = \frac{II'}{a}$

Therefore

$$\theta = \frac{II'(d+b)}{2ad}$$

Therefore the velocity of light c is given by the equation:

$$c = \frac{8\pi n d^2 a}{II'(d+b)}$$

Foucault used a mirror with a radius of curvature of 20 m and with a rate of rotation of 800 revolutions per second. II′ was 0.7 mm.

M and N could be placed in water so that Foucault was able to measure the velocity of light in a liquid. He showed that light travelled slower in water than it did in air, in fact:

velocity of light in air = refractive index of water × velocity of light in water

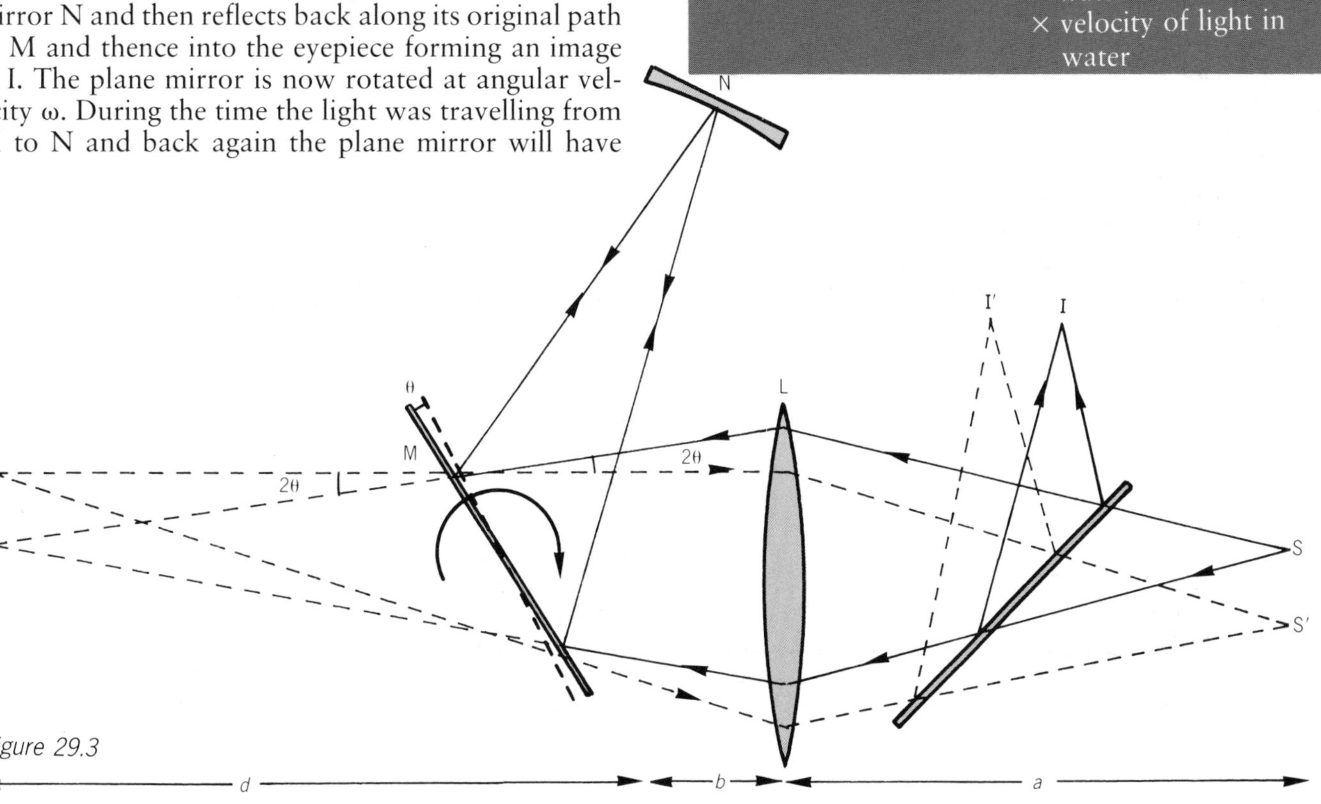

Figure 29.3

3 A rotating mirror method similar to that described above was used to measure the velocity of light in a liquid. Calculate the refractive index of the liquid using the following data:

Velocity of light in air	$= 3.0 \times 10^8$ m s^{-1}
Number of revolutions per second	= 600
Deflection of image	= 2.0 mm
Source to lens	= 1.50 m
Lens to concave mirror	= 20 m
Lens to plane mirror	= 10 cm

4 In a simple version of Foucault's apparatus for measuring the velocity of light, the distance between the rotating mirror and the concave reflector was 1 km, the distance from the eyepiece and the rotating mirror was 5 m, the measured value of the velocity of light was 2.98×10^8 m s^{-1}. What was the speed of rotation of the mirror when the image was displaced through a distance of 20 mm?

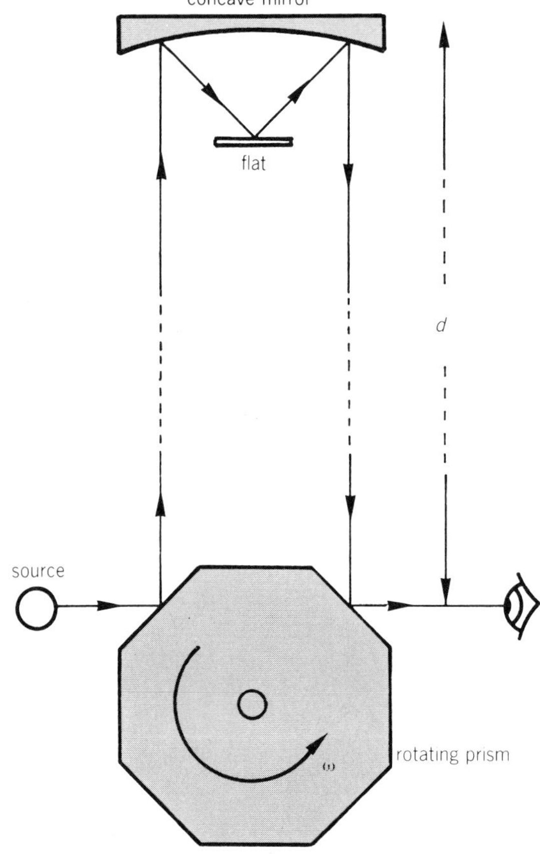

Figure 29.4

Michelson's rotating prism

Michelson used a rapidly rotating prism to chop up the light beam in an experiment first carried out in 1879.

He mounted the prism on Mount Wilson in the USA and placed a reflector on Mount San Antonio, 35 km away. Light from the source S was reflected from one face of the prism and on to the distant reflector. When the light returned the prism had rotated, and if light was to be observed at the eyepiece it must have rotated by one-eighth of a turn (Figure 29.4).

One facet of the prism must have replaced its predecessor in the time it takes the light to travel to the distant reflector and back. If d is the distance to the distant reflector and n the number of revolutions per second then:

velocity of light (c) $= 16nd$

Michelson rotated the prism with an air jet at 528 revs s^{-1} and measured the frequency with an electrically driven tuning fork that was compared stroboscopically with the rotating prism. He obtained a value for the velocity of light of $2.999\ 10 \times 10^8 \pm 50$ m s^{-1}.

This value was based on a measurement of the distance between the two mountains which was accurate to within one inch (2.5 cm). Between this measurement and Michelson's experiment, however, there was an earthquake which may have altered it by over a metre! It still represented a measurement of very high accuracy.

Michelson also measured the velocity of light in an evacuated pipe 7.5 cm in diameter and 1.6 km long in order to eliminate the correction due to the refractive index of air.

5 In an experiment to measure the velocity of light using Michelson's rotating eight-sided prism, the distance between the prism and the distant reflector was 35 km.

If the velocity of light is 3.0×10^8 m s^{-1}, calculate the least possible speed of rotation of the prism to give a steady reflected signal at the eyepiece.

What is the next speed of rotation that would give the same effect?

6 If the velocity of light in a vacuum is 3.0×10^8 m s^{-1}, calculate its velocity in

(*a*) water (refractive index 1.33),
(*b*) glass (refractive index 1.45), and
(*c*) diamond (refractive index 2.42).

Kerr cell

This experiment uses the electro-optic shutter developed by Kerr in 1875 and used in 1950 by Bergstrand to measure the velocity of light. Light is pulsed by allowing it to fall on a tank of nitrobenzene which becomes optically active when an electric field is placed across it. Crossed Polaroids are put at the two ends of the tank and so normally light cannot pass through it (Figure 29.5). By adjusting the frequency of the field results similar to those obtained with Fizeau's rotating wheel can be obtained, although in this case the frequency can be very large. This reduces the time interval and hence the distance over which the light must travel. For this reason the apparatus can be used in the laboratory.

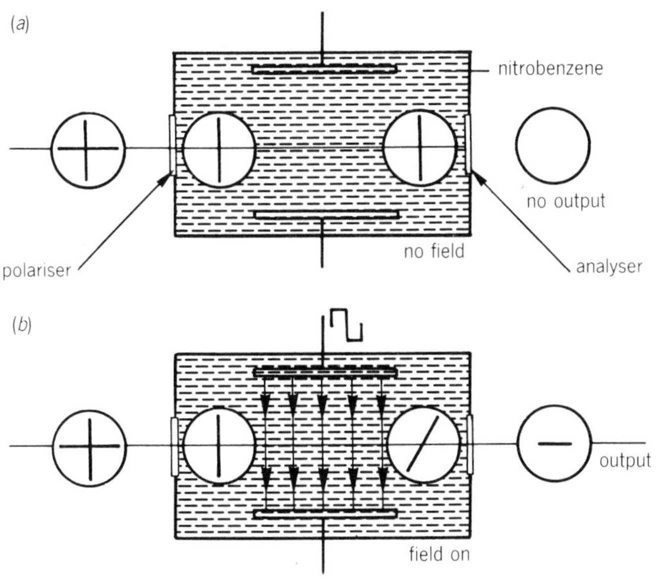

Figure 29.5

An electronic measurement of the velocity of light

A recent method for the determination of the velocity of light is described below and is shown in a simplified form in Figure 29.6.

A modulated light beam is produced by applying a sinusoidal voltage to a light-emitting diode (LED). This beam is allowed to fall on to a photodiode where the modulated light signal is converted back into a sinusoidal voltage. The velocity of this modulation is the group velocity of the light beam, which in air is very nearly equal to the wave velocity.

The phase difference at two points along the direction of travel (the LED and the photodiode) is found by applying one of the signals to the Y plates of an oscilloscope and the other to the X plates. If the modulation frequency is f, the phase difference between the two signals is ϕ, and d is the distance over which this phase difference is measured, then it can be shown that:

$$\text{velocity of light } (c) = \frac{360\,d}{\phi}f$$

where ϕ is measured in degrees. In practice the LED and the photodiode are mounted at the same ends of an optical bench, the outgoing signal being returned to the photodiode by a right-angle prism (see Figure 29.6).

The modulating frequency is very large (58 MHz) and the phase difference is usually adjusted to be 0° or 180°. The actual experiment is rather more complex and interested readers are referred to the Department of Physics and Astronomy at University College, London, for further details.

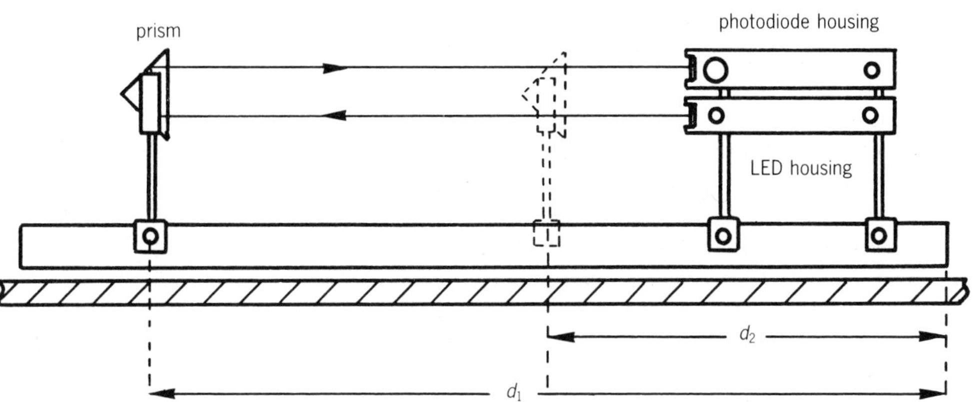

Figure 29.6

30 · Theories of light

In the seventeenth century two rival theories of the nature of light were proposed, the wave theory and the corpuscular theory.

The Dutch astronomer Huygens (1629–1695) proposed a **wave theory** of light. He believed that light was a longitudinal wave, and that this wave was propagated through a material called the 'aether'. Since light can pass through a vacuum and travels very fast Huygens had to propose some rather strange properties for the aether: for example, it must fill all space and be weightless and invisible. For this reason scientists were sceptical of his theory.

In 1690 Newton proposed the **corpuscular theory** of light. He believed that light was shot out from a source in small particles, and this view was accepted for over a hundred years. (See page 190 for a full treatment.)

The **quantum theory** put forward by Max Planck in 1900 combined the wave theory and the particle theory, and showed that light can sometimes behave like a particle and sometimes like a wave. We will consider this further in the section on quantum theory.

Wave theory of Huygens

As we have seen, Huygens considered that light was propagated in longitudinal waves through a material called the aether. We will now look at his ideas more closely.

Huygens published his theory in 1690, having compared the behaviour of light not with that of water waves but with that of sound. Sound cannot travel through a vacuum but light does, and so Huygens proposed that the aether must fill all space, be transparent and of zero inertia. Clearly a very strange material! Even at the beginning of the twentieth century, however, scientists were convinced of the existence of the aether. One book states 'whatever we consider the aether to be there can be no doubt of its existence'.

We now consider how Huygens thought the waves moved from place to place.

Consider a wavefront initially at position W, and assume that every point on that wavefront acts as a source of secondary wavelets. The new wavefront W_1 is formed by the envelope of these secondary wavelets since they will all have moved forward the same distance in a time t (Figure 30.1).

There are however at least two problems with this

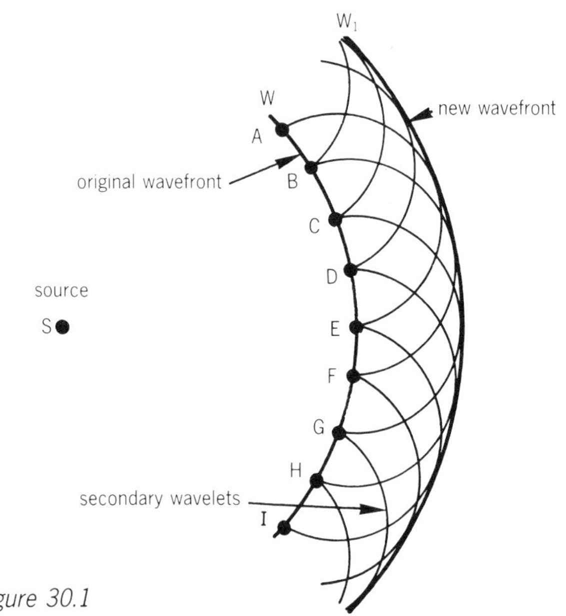

Figure 30.1

idea and these led Newton and others to reject it:

(*a*) the secondary waves are propagated in the forward direction only, and

(*b*) they are assumed to destroy each other except where they form the new wavefront.

Newton wrote: 'If light consists of undulations in an elastic medium it should diverge in every direction from each new centre of disturbance, and so, like sound, bend round all obstacles and obliterate all shadow.' Newton did not know that in fact light does do this, but the effects are exceedingly small due to the very short wavelength of light.

Huygens' theory also failed to explain the rectilinear propagation of light.

The reflection of a plane wavefront by a plane mirror is shown in Figure 30.2. Notice the initial position of the wavefront (AB), the secondary wavelets and the final position of the wavefront (CD).

The shape of the wavefront is not affected by reflection at a plane surface.

The lines below the mirror show the position that the wavefront would have reached if the mirror had not been there.

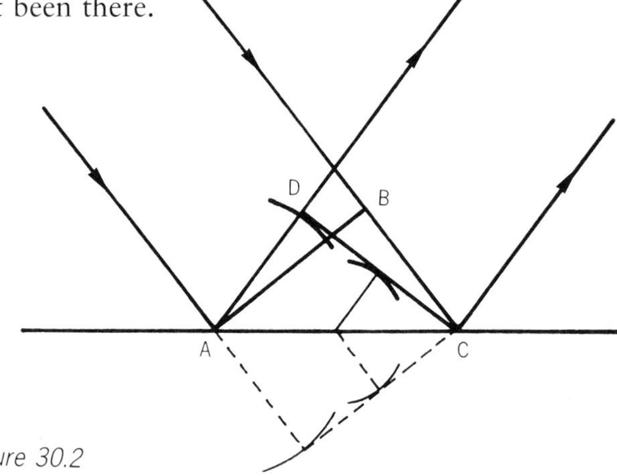

Figure 30.2

We will now show how Huygens' wave theory can be used to explain reflection and refraction.

(*a*) Reflection

Consider a parallel beam of monochromatic light incident on a plane surface, as shown in Figure 30.3. The wavefronts will be plane both before and after reflection, since a plane surface does not alter the shape of waves falling on it.

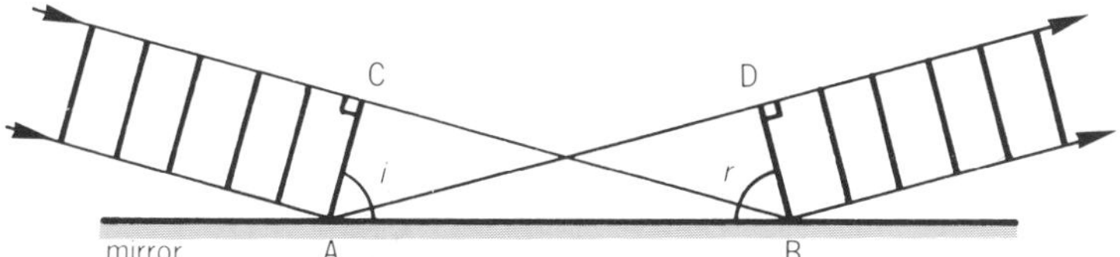

Figure 30.3

Consider a point where the wavefront AC has just touched the mirror at edge A. While the light travels from A to D, that from C travels to B. The new envelope for the wavefront AC will be BD after reflection. Therefore

AD = CB
$A\hat{C}B = A\hat{D}B = 90°$
AB is common

Therefore $\Delta ACB \equiv \Delta BDA$ therefore $C\hat{A}B = B\hat{A}D$. Therefore $\hat{\imath} = \hat{r}$, and the law of reflection is proved.

(*b*) Refraction

Consider a plane monochromatic wave hitting the surface of a transparent material of refractive index n. The velocity of light in the material is c_m and that in air c_a. Now in Figure 30.4,

$CB = AB \sin i$
$AD = AB \sin r$

The same argument applies about the new envelope as in the case of reflection:

time to travel CB = $CB/c_a = AB \sin i/c_a$
time to travel AD = $AD/c_m = AB \sin r/c_m$

But these are equal and therefore:

$$\frac{c_a}{c_m} = \frac{\sin i}{\sin r} = {}_a n_m$$

This is Snell's law, and it was verified later by Foucault and others.

Notice that since the refractive index of a transparent material is greater than 1, Huygens' theory requires that the velocity of light in air should be greater than that in the material.

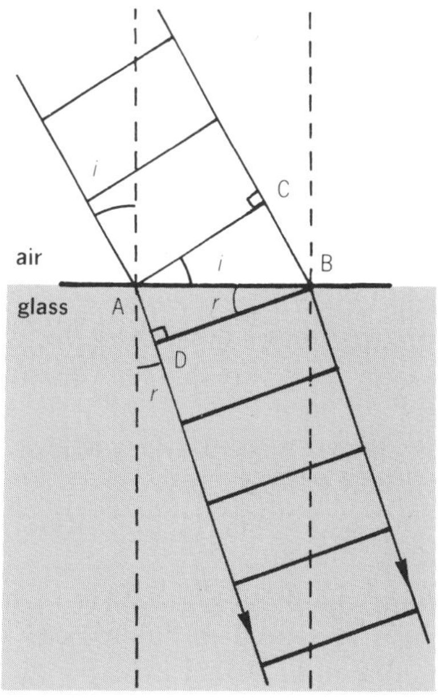

Figure 30.4

1 Using Huygens' wave theory, show by means of a scale diagram how a plane wave may be totally internally reflected at a glass–air boundary. The angle of incidence of the wave is 50° and the refractive index of the glass is 1.5.

2 Use Huygens' wave theory to show that a series of light waves diverging from a point source will appear to be diverging from a second point after reflection at a plane mirror. Find the position of this point.

3 A plane wave of wavelength 1.0 cm is incident at an angle of 30° on a boundary between two media. If the refractive index of the second medium relative to the first is 2.4, use Huygens' wave theory to construct a scale diagram to calculate the angle of refraction of the wave in the second medium and the wavelength in that medium.

4 Light travelling through water in a parallel beam is incident on the horizontal water–air boundary. If the velocity of light in water is 2.2×10^8 m s^{-1} and that in air 3.0×10^8 m s^{-1}, calculate the maximum angle that the light can make with the vertical if light is to escape into the air.

How will this be affected if a thick layer of oil of refractive index 1.45 is floated on the surface of the water?

Corpuscular theory of Newton

Newton proposed that light is shot out from a source as a stream of particles. He argued that light could not be a wave because although we can hear sound from behind an obstacle we cannot see light – that is, light shows no diffraction. He stated that particles of different colours should be of different sizes, the red particles being larger than the blue.

Since these particles are shot out all the time, according to Newton's theory, the mass of the source of light must get less!

We can use Newton's theory to deduce the laws of reflection and refraction.

(*a*) Reflection

Consider a particle of light in collision with a mirror. The collision is supposed to be perfectly elastic, and so the component of velocity perpendicular to the mirror is reversed while that parallel to the mirror remains unaltered. From Figure 30.5,

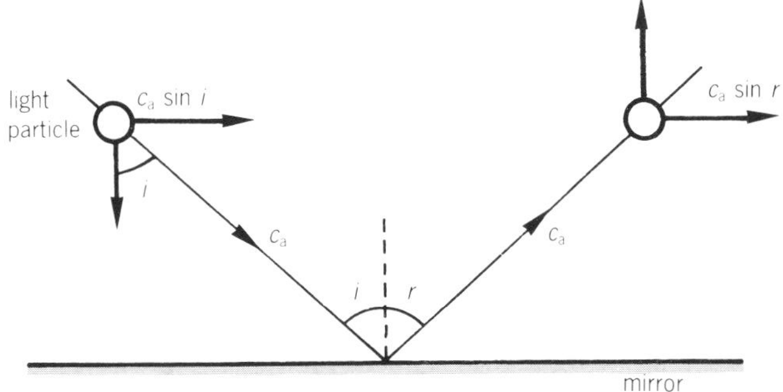

Figure 30.5

component of velocity before collision parallel to the mirror $= c_a \sin i$

component of velocity after collision parallel to the mirror $= c_a \sin r$

Therefore:

$$c_a \sin i = c_a \sin r$$
$$\hat{\imath} = \hat{r}$$

and so the law of reflection is proved.

(*b*) Refraction

Newton assumed that there is an attraction between the molecules of a solid and the particles of light, and that this attraction acts only perpendicularly to the surface and only at very short distances from the surface. (He explained total internal reflection by saying that the perpendicular component of velocity was too small to overcome the molecular attraction.) This has the effect of increasing the velocity of the light in the material.

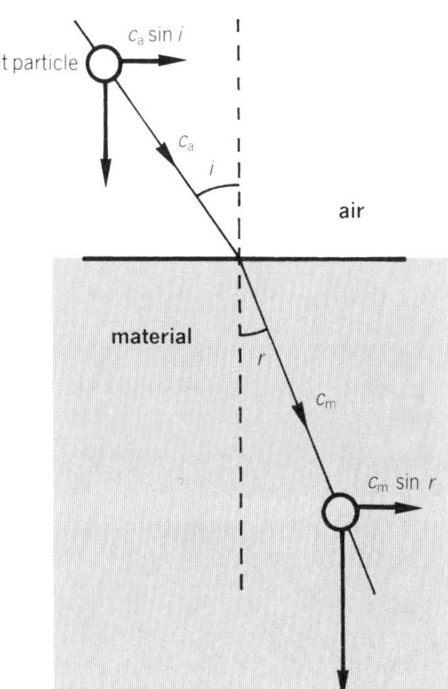

Figure 30.6

Let the velocity of light in air be c_a and the velocity of light in the material in Figure 30.6 be c_m. The velocity parallel to the material is unaltered and therefore:

$$c_a \sin i = c_m \sin r$$

Therefore:

$$\frac{c_m}{c_a} = \frac{\sin i}{\sin r} = {}_a n_m$$

This ratio is the refractive index, but because $n > 1$ the velocity of light in the material must be greater than that in air. Newton accepted this result and other scientists preferred it to that of Huygens, mainly because of Newton's eminence.

A problem of the corpuscular theory was that temperature has no effect on the velocity of light, although on the basis of this theory we would expect the particles to be shot out at greater velocities as the temperature rises.

Classical and modern theories of light

It is interesting to compare the two classical theories of light and see which phenomena can be explained by each theory. The following table does this.

Wave theory	*Corpuscular theory*
reflection	reflection
refraction	photoelectric theory
diffraction	
interference	

Notice that neither theory can account for polarisation, since for polarisation to occur the waves must be transverse in nature.

Modern theories

Twentieth-century ideas have led us to believe that light is

(*a*) a transverse electromagnetic wave with a small wavelength, and

(*b*) emitted in quanta or packets of radiation of about 10^{-8} s duration with abrupt phase changes between successive pulses.

5 Give an account of the fundamental differences between Huygens' wave theory and the accepted modern theory of the nature of light.

Christiaan Huygens 1629 – 1695 (Ann Ronan Picture Library)

Isaac Newton 1642 – 1727

31 · Diffraction

When a wave hits an obstacle it does not simply go straight past: it bends round the obstacle. The same type of effect occurs at a hole – the waves spread out the other side of the hole. This phenomenon is known as **diffraction** and examples of the diffraction of plane waves are shown in Figure 31.1.

The effects of diffraction are much more noticeable if the size of the obstacle is small, while a given size of obstacle will diffract a wave of long wavelength more than a shorter one.

Diffraction can be easily demonstrated with sound waves or microwaves. It is quite easy to hear a sound even if there is an obstacle in the direct line between the source and your ears. By using the 2.8 cm microwave apparatus owned by many schools very good diffraction effects may be observed with obstacles a few centimetres across.

One of the most powerful pieces of evidence for light being some form of wave motion is that it also shows diffraction. The problem with light, and that which led Newton to reject the wave theory, is that the wavelength is very small and therefore diffraction effects are hard to observe. You can observe the diffraction of light, however, if you know just where to look.

The coloured rings round a street light in frosty weather, the coloured bands viewed by reflection from a record and the spreading of light round your eyelashes are all diffraction effects. Looking through the material of a stretched pair of tights at a small torch bulb will also show very good diffraction. A laser will also show good diffraction effects over large distances because of the coherence of laser light (see page 218). Diffraction is essentially the effect of removing some of the information from a wave front; the new wavefront will be altered by the obstacle or aperture. Huygens' theory explained this satisfactorily.

Grimaldi first recorded the diffraction of light in 1665 but the real credit for its scientific study must go to Fresnel, Poisson and Arago, working in the late eighteenth and early nineteenth centuries.

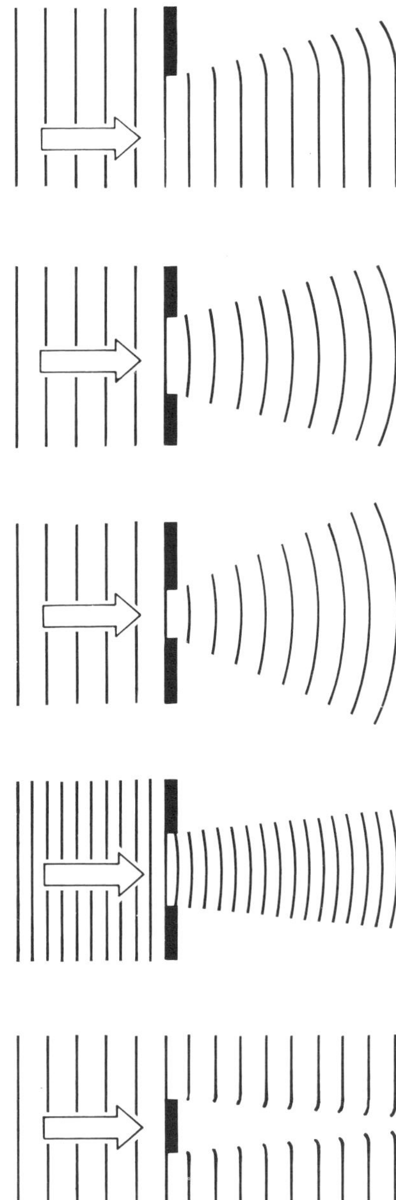

Figure 31.1

We can define two distinct types of diffraction:

(*a*) **Fresnel diffraction** is produced when light from a point source meets an obstacle, the waves are spherical and the pattern observed is a fringed image of the object.

(*b*) **Fraunhofer diffraction** occurs with plane wavefronts with the object effectively at infinity. The pattern is in a particular direction and is a fringed image of the source.

Fresnel diffraction

Fresnel diffraction can be observed with the minimum of apparatus but the mathematics are complex. We will therefore only treat it experimentally here.

If a razor blade is placed between the observer and a point source of monochromatic light, dark and bright diffraction fringes can be seen in the edges of the shadow. The same effects can be produced with a pinhead, when a spot of light will be seen in the centre of the shadow. Fresnel was unhappy about Newton's explanation of diffraction in terms of the attraction of the light particles by the particles of the solid, because diffraction was found to be independent of the density of the obstacle: a spider's web, for example, gave the same diffraction pattern as a platinum wire of the same thickness. The prediction and subsequent discovery of a bright spot within the centre of the shadow of a small steel ball was final proof that light was indeed a wave motion.

If the intensity of light is plotted against distance for points close to the shadow edge results like those shown in Figure 31.2 will be obtained.

Fresnel diffraction with a double slit will produce two single slit patterns superimposed on one another. This is exactly what happens in the Young's slit experiment (see page 202): the diffraction effects are observed as well as those due to the interference of the two sets of waves.

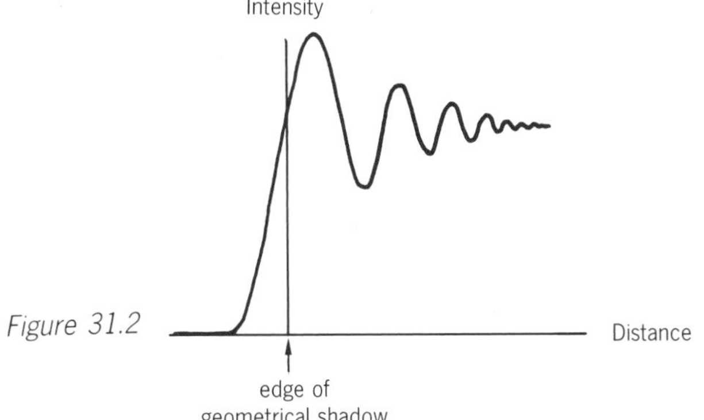

Figure 31.2

1 Explain what is seen when a small torch bulb is viewed through
(*a*) a handkerchief,
(*b*) the material of a pair of tights.
In each case state what can be deduced about the weave of the two materials. What would be the effect of substituting a handkerchief of much finer weave?

2 Explain why coloured halos may be seen around white street lights on foggy nights.

Student investigation

This investigation takes the form of two experiments with microwaves.

Use the 2.8 cm wavelength microwaves to investigate the diffraction from a single slit when the width of the slit is reduced to close to, and below, the wavelength of the microwaves. Plot graphs of both the position of the first maximum and the magnitude of the first maximum against slit width.

It has been stated that the flatness required for a reflector depends on the wavelength of the radiation that it is required to reflect. Using the metal polarisation grille supplied with the microwaves kit, investigate this claim. Make a set of grids from wire mesh of different grades and record how the reflected intensity varies with mesh size.

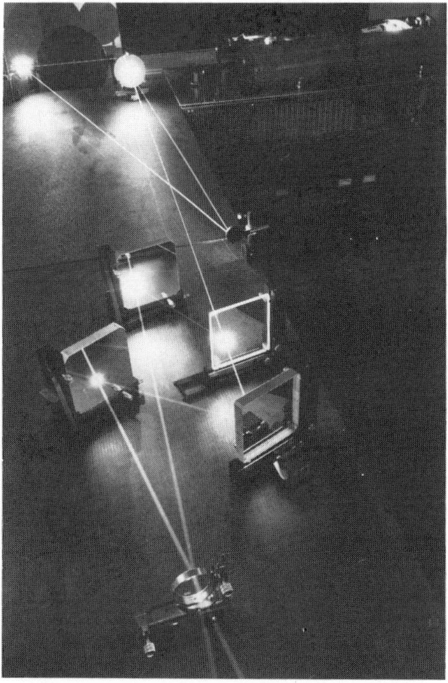

The production of interference gratings using a laser – the interference pattern produced by the laser is recorded on a photographic plate and this is then used as the grating (National Physical Laboratory, England)

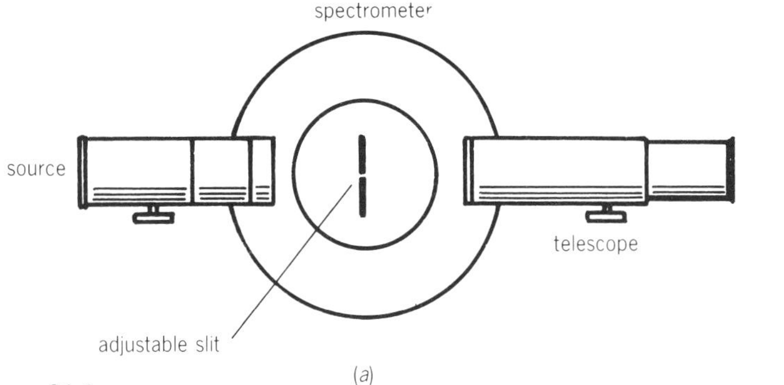

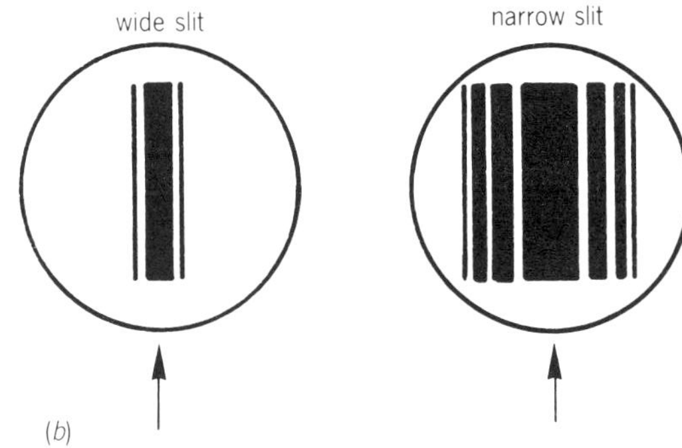

Figure 31.3

Fraunhofer diffraction

(*a*) A single slit

The Fraunhofer diffraction due to a single slit is very easy to observe. An adjustable slit is placed on the table of a spectroscope and a monochromatic light source is viewed through it using the spectroscope telescope (see Figure 31.3(*a*)). An image of the slit is seen as shown in Figure 31.3(*b*). As the slit is narrowed a broad diffraction pattern spreads out either side of the slit, only disappearing when the width of the slit is equal to or less than one wavelength of the light used.

The diffraction at a single slit of width a is shown in Figure 31.4(*a*). Plane waves arrive at P due to diffraction at the slit AB. Waves coming from the two sides of the slit have a path difference BN and therefore interference (see page 200) results.

But $BN = a \sin\theta$, and if this is equal to the wavelength of the light (λ) a minimum is observed at P. This is because if the path difference between the two extremes of the slit is exactly one wavelength then there will be points in the upper and lower halves of the slit that will be half a wavelength out of phase and so will cancel out.

Therefore the general condition for a *minimum* for a single slit is

$$m\lambda = a \sin\theta$$

where $m = 1, 2, 3, 4$ and so on.

If the intensity distribution for a single slit is plotted against distance from the slit, a graph similar to that shown in Figure 31.4(*b*) will be obtained.

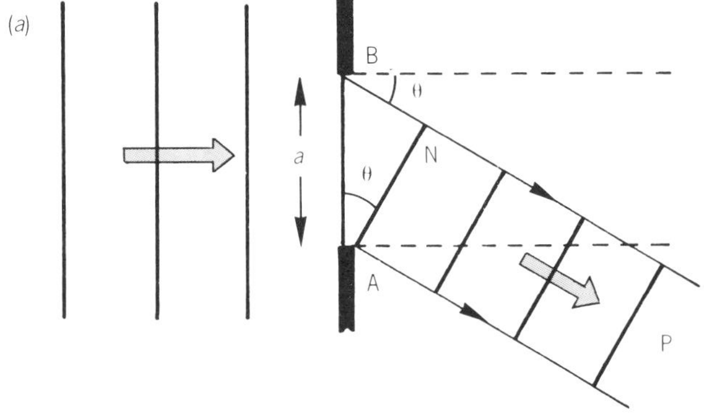

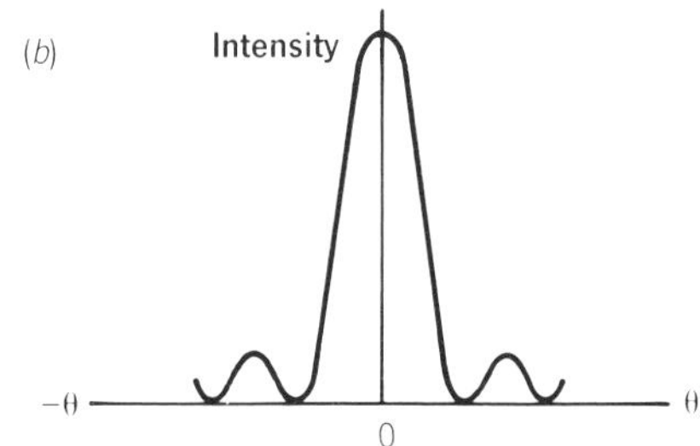

Figure 31.4

3 An adjustable slit is set up on the table of a spectrometer and the instrument is used to view a monochromatic light source. Explain carefully what is observed when the width of the slit is slowly reduced from about 2 mm to zero.

4 A parallel beam of light of wavelength 589 nm falls on a single slit 1.2 mm wide. The resulting diffraction pattern is observed on a screen 2 m from the slit. What is the distance between the two minima on either side of the central bright fringe?

(*b*) A double slit

For the double slit we simply have light from two adjacent slits meeting at the eyepiece. In this case the formula for a maximum is:

$$m\lambda = d \sin \theta$$

where d is the distance between the centres of the two slits (Figure 31.5). The intensity of the interference pattern produced by two sources is simply varied by the diffraction effects.

We will have $\cos^2 \theta$ fringes modulated by the diffraction pattern for a single slit.

The intensity distribution is shown in Figure 31.6.

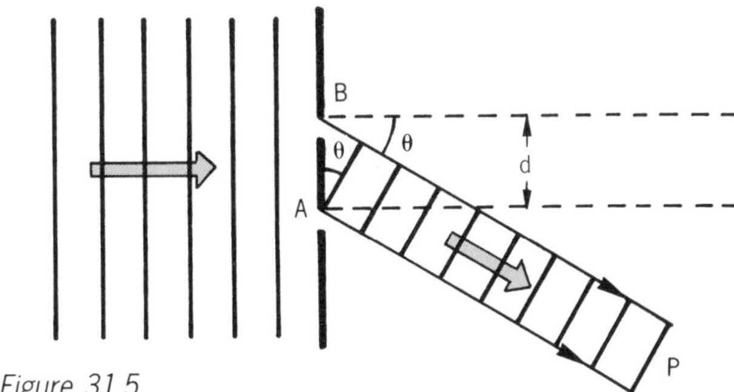

Figure 31.5

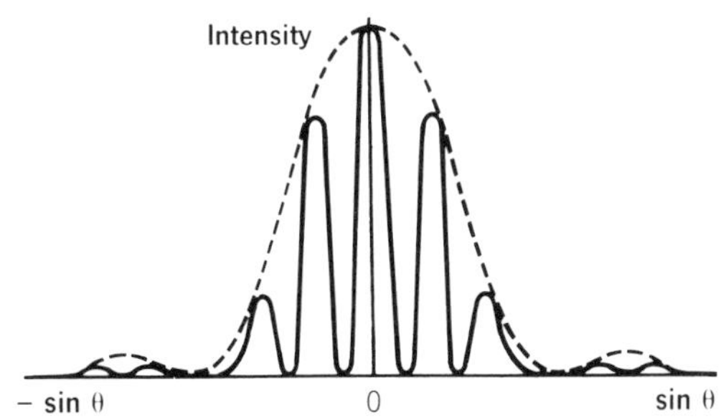

Figure 31.6

> **5** Laser light of wavelength 650 nm falls normally on a pair of slits 0.1 mm wide and 0.5 mm apart. The resulting diffraction pattern is focused on a screen 1 m from the slits.
>
> Calculate the distances of the first and second diffraction maxima from the centre of the fringe pattern.

The phasor treatment of diffraction

The phasor treatment of diffraction is a useful visual way of explaining the diffraction pattern at a point.

If we consider the single slit to be broken up into a large number of very small parts then all points on a given strip have the same path length to a point P on the screen where the diffraction pattern is formed. At the centre of the pattern light from each point is in phase and so the phase shift between adjacent strips is zero – the resulting intensity is then given simply by the algebraic sum of the intensities due to each strip (Figure 31.7(*a*)). As we move away from the centre of the pattern there is a definite phase difference between adjacent strips and the final intensity (E_θ) is shown by (Figure 31.7(*b*)).

A further movement across the pattern will give the first minimum (Figure 31.7(*c*)) where the resultant intensity is zero and the second maximum (Figure 31.7(*d*)).

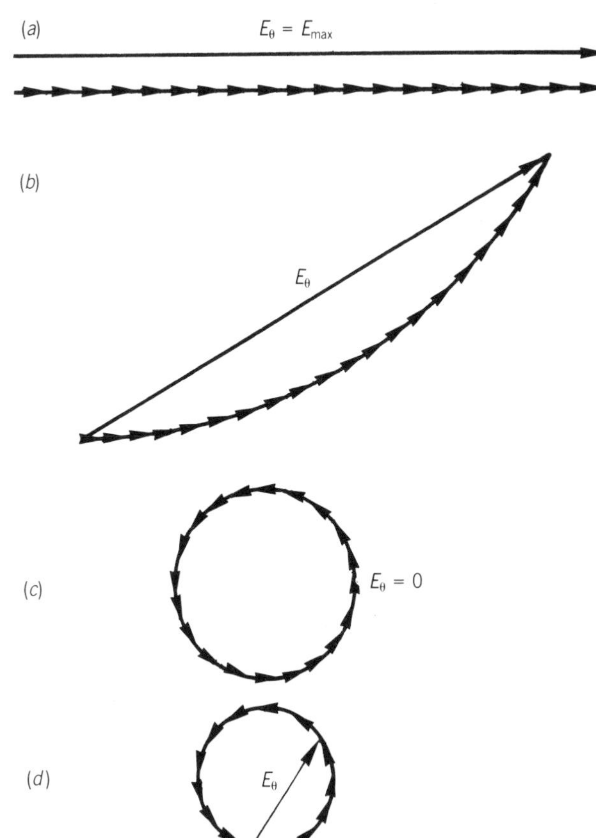

Figure 31.7

(*c*) Diffraction gratings

If the number of slits is now increased we will see that the sharpness of the pattern is improved, the maxima getting narrower. Obstacles with a large number of slits (more than, say, 20 to the millimetre) are called diffraction gratings. These were first developed by Fraunhofer in the late eighteenth century and they consisted of fine silver wire wound on two parallel screws giving about 30 obstacles to the millimetre.

Since then many improvements have been made, in 1882 Rowland used a diamond to rule fine lines on glass, the ridges acting as the slits and the rulings as the obstacles (Figure 31.8). Using this method it is possible to obtain diffraction gratings with as many as 3000 lines per millimetre although 'coarse' gratings with about 500 lines per millimetre are better for general use. In many schools two types are in common use, one with 300 lines per mm and the other with 80 lines per mm. Reflection gratings are also used, where the diffracted image is viewed after reflection from a ruled surface.

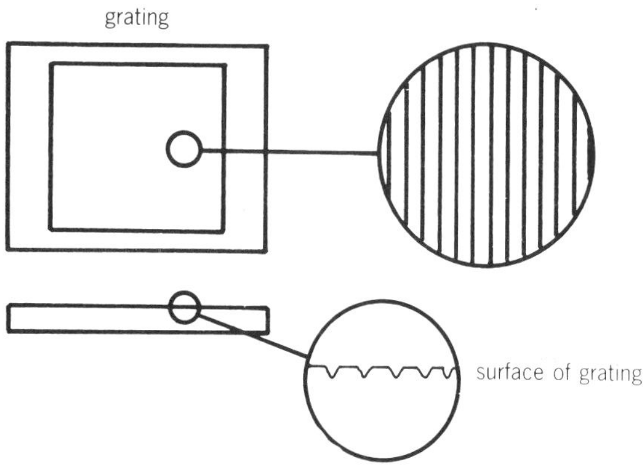

Figure 31.8

Student investigation

The diffraction of cadmium and mercury light is used to determine the separation of two lines on an integrated circuit. The following results were obtained for the second-order diffracted images for different wavelengths. Use them to plot an appropriate linear graph and thence determine the mean spacing of the lines on the circuit.

Wavelength/nm	Angle of diffraction/°
468	28.0
480	28.7
509	31.0
546	33.0
577	35.5
644	40.0

Figure 31.9 shows the Huygens construction for a grating. You can see how the circular diffracted waves from each slit reinforce each other to give a plane diffracted wave which is the envelope of all the secondary waves.

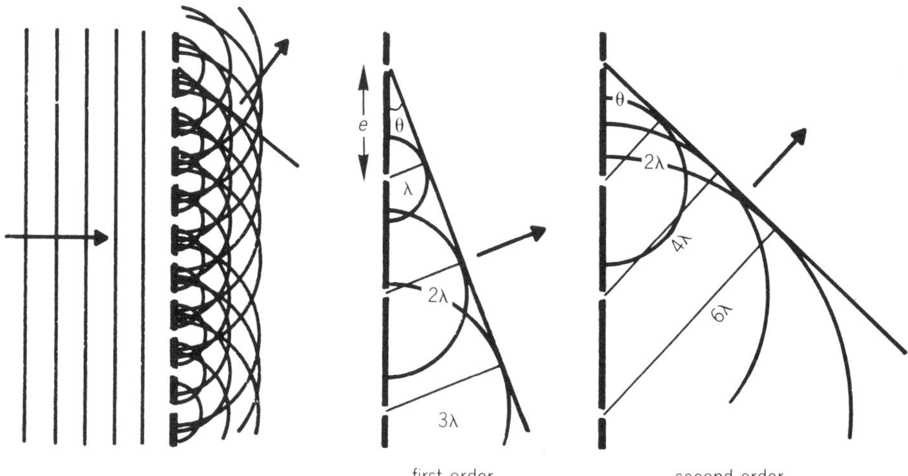

Figure 31.9

Consider a parallel beam of light incident normally on a diffraction grating with a grating spacing e (the grating spacing is the inverse of the number of lines per unit length). Consider light diffracted at an angle θ to the normal and light coming from corresponding points on adjacent slits (Figure 31.10). Then, for a maximum,

path difference = AC = $m\lambda$

But AC = $e \sin \theta$. Therefore for a maximum:

$$m\lambda = e \sin \theta \text{ where } m = 0, 1, 2, 3\ldots$$

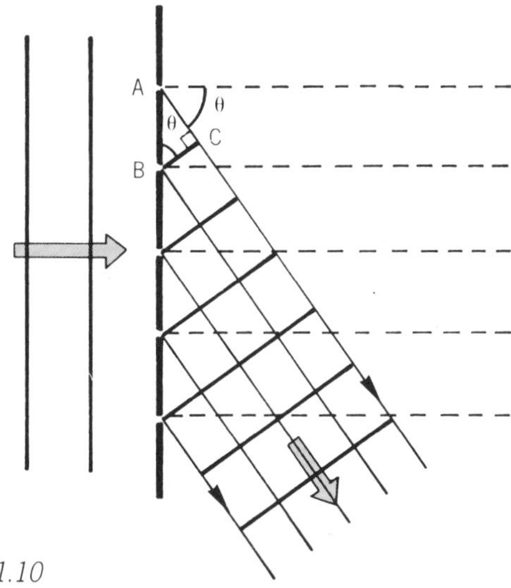

Figure 31.10

The number m is known as the **order** of the spectrum, that is, a first-order spectrum is formed for $m = 1$, and so on.

If light of a single wavelength, such as that from a laser, is used, then a series of sharp lines occur, one line to each order of the spectrum. With a white light source a series of spectra is formed with the light of the shortest wavelength having the smallest angle of diffraction.

6 Light of wavelength 589 nm is incident normally on a diffraction grating which has 6000 lines per centimetre.

(*a*) At what angle will the second-order image be seen?

(*b*) Determine whether it is possible to obtain a third-order image.

(*a*)

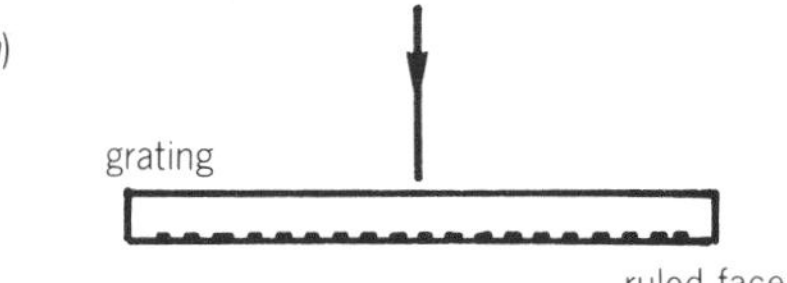

(*b*)

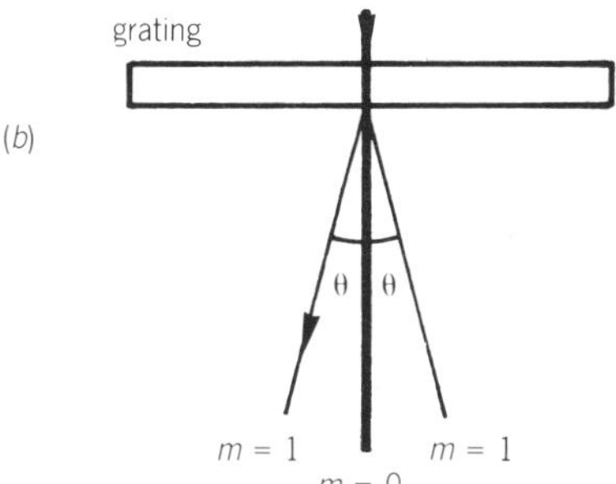

Figure 31.11

The number of orders of spectra visible with a given grating depends on the grating spacing, more spectra being visible with coarser gratings. The ruled face of the grating should always point away from the incident light to prevent errors due to refraction in the glass.

In deriving the formula above, we assumed that the incident beam is at right angles to the face of the grating. Allowance must be made if this is not the case. The simplest way is to measure the position of the first-order spectrum on *either side* of the centre, record the angle between these positions and then halve it, as shown in Figure 31.11.

The intensity distribution for a large number of slits is shown in Figure 31.12. Notice that the maxima become much sharper; the greater the number of slits per metre, the better defined are the maxima.

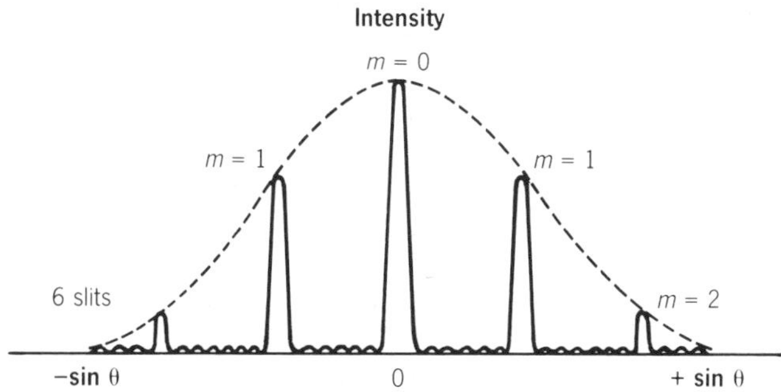

Figure 31.12

Example

Calculate the maximum number of orders visible with a diffraction grating of 500 lines per millimetre, using light of wavelength 600 nm.

Maximum angle of diffraction = 90°

Therefore $m = \frac{e \sin\theta}{\lambda} = \frac{2 \times 10^{-6}}{600 \times 10^{-9}} = 3.33.$

Therefore maximum number of orders = 3.

7 A diffraction grating having 6300 lines per centimetre is set up on the table of a spectrometer and is illuminated normally with monochromatic light. Bright images are formed on the cross-wires of the telescope for the following scale settings: 80° 54′, 107° 28′, 130° 0′, 152° 12′, 179° 6′. Explain this, and calculate the wavelength of the light. [O]

8 Explain carefully the effect on the spectrum observed by a plane transmission diffraction grating if the ruled face is presented to the incident light rather than the unruled face.

9 A diffraction grating with 5.0×10^4 lines per metre is set up on a spectrometer table. If the telescope lens of the spectrometer has a focal length of 0.3 m, what will be the separation of the third-order sodium D line images on the cross-wires? (The wavelengths of the sodium D lines are 589.0 nm and 589.6 nm.) [L]

10 A parallel beam of monochromatic light of wavelength 580 nm is incident normally on a diffraction grating having a large number of regular slits each of width 7.0×10^{-7} m. After passing through the grating the light will have, as the result of interference, intensity maxima in certain directions. Calculations predict that for the first-, second- and third-order interference maxima the values of the angle θ, between the direction of the incident light and the directions of these maxima, should be approximately 16°, 34° and 56° respectively.

(*a*) At what value of θ would light diffracted by a *single* slit of width 7.0×10^{-7} m have its first intensity *minimum*? Show the steps in your calculation.

(*b*) Draw a sketch graph to show how the intensity of the light varies with the angle θ, and mark the points 16°, 34° and 56° on the axis.

Resolving power of optical instruments

All optical instruments give images that are affected by the diffraction at the objective lens, so if we have two points on the object that are close together it is possible that their images may possess diffraction patterns that will overlap. If they are too close the images will be indistinguishable from one another.

For two images of equal intensity to be resolved the central maximum of one diffraction pattern must fall no closer than the first minimum to the centre of the second diffraction pattern (Figure 31.13). Using the formula for a rectangular aperture we have:

$$\lambda = a \sin \phi$$

where a is the aperture of the objective and λ the wavelength of radiation used.

For a circular aperture and a small angle:

$$\phi = \frac{1.22\lambda}{a}$$

You can see that higher resolution is possible with large apertures or with short-wavelength radiation such as ultraviolet light, X-rays or even electrons.

The eye can resolve fine detail rather better if the lighting is not too strong, so that the pupil will have a large aperture.

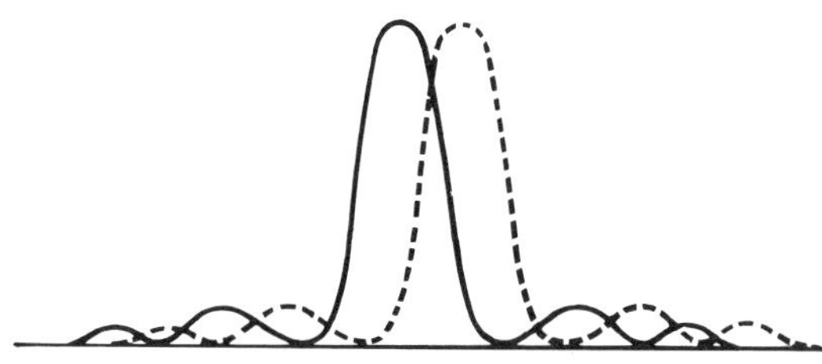

Figure 31.13

The problem with very large optical telescope mirrors has been overcome to some extent by the use of **multiple mirror** telescopes. These instruments use a number of smaller mirrors mounted to give the same light-gathering power and resolving power as a very large single mirror.

11 Using as a source a plunger vibrating with supersonic frequency 10^8 Hz, stationary waves are established in a liquid contained in a transparent vessel and the regular pattern of the resulting variations in the density of the fluid behaves in the same way as does a diffraction grating towards a beam of light directed on to it at right angles. The first-order diffraction maximum occurs at an angle of 6.2° for light of wavelength 540 nm. Find the velocity of the supersonic waves in the liquid. [O]

12 Two cyclists cycle towards you side by side at night with their front lamps on. If the two lamps are 0.90 m apart, how close do they have to be to you such that they are just resolved by your eye? (Take the mean wavelength of the light from the lamps to be 600 nm and the diameter of your pupil to be 0.45 cm.)

13 Find the separation of two points on the Moon's surface that can just be resolved under ideal conditions by the following instruments:

(*a*) the eye (pupil diameter 5 mm)
(*b*) a pair of 10 × 50 binoculars
(*c*) a 7.6 cm (3 inch) refracting telescope
(*d*) a 15.2 cm (6 inch) reflecting telescope
(*e*) the Mount Palomar 5 m (200 inch) reflecting telescope

Take the mean wavelength of light reflected from the Moon to be 600 nm and the mean distance of the moon from the Earth to be 3.8×10^8 m.

14 The Jodrell Bank radio telescope has a diameter of 80 m and operates at a wavelength of 0.21 m.

(*a*) Calculate the resolving power of the instrument.

(*b*) What would be the diameter of a stop in front of the eye that would give the same resolving power? (Take the mean wavelength of visible light to be 550 nm.)

15 In a practical exam a student is given a sodium discharge lamp, a wooden metre rule graduated in millimetres and a 30 cm steel rule graduated in 0.5 mm, and asked to measure the wavelength of sodium light. She decides to use the steel rule as a reflection diffraction grating. With light falling at a grazing angle of incidence of 1° the first maximum is at 2.5° to the rule.

What is the wavelength of the sodium light suggested by these results?

Student investigation

The resolving power of a system may be studied by the following simple experiment. Set up a multiple light source (Figure 31.14) and view it through a single adjustable slit in front of which is a green filter. Observe the change in the appearance of the source as the width of the slit is changed.

Replace the green filter with first a red one and then a blue one to study how the resolution depends on the wavelength of light.

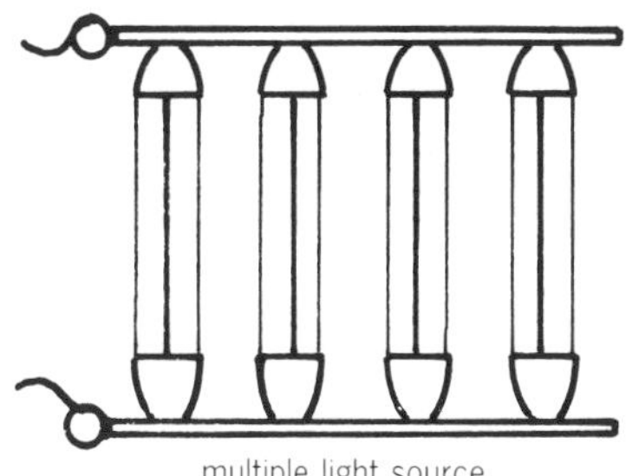

Figure 31.14

32 · Interference

When two wave trains meet and overlap they **interfere** with each other, the resultant amplitude at a point being the sum of the amplitudes of the two waves at that point. If the waves are always in phase then the resulting intensity will be large and this is known as **constructive interference**; while if they are out of phase by π and of equal amplitude then the resulting intensity will be zero, and this is known as **destructive interference**. This phase difference may be produced by allowing the two sets of waves to travel different distances – this difference in distance of travel is called the **path difference** between the two waves.

There may be many intermediate conditions between these two extremes that will give a small variation in intensity but we will confine ourselves to total constructive or total destructive interference for the moment.

The diagrams below show two waves of equal amplitudes with different phase and path differences between them. The first pair have a phase difference of π or 180° and a path difference of an odd number of half-wavelengths. The second pair have a phase difference of zero and a path difference of a whole number of wavelengths, including zero.

Figure 32.1(*a*) shows destructive interference and Figure 32.1(*b*) constructive interference.

To obtain a static interference pattern at a point (that is, one that is constant with time) we must have

(*a*) two sources of the same wavelength, and

(*b*) two sources which have a constant phase difference between them.

Sources with synchronised phase changes between them are called **coherent** sources and those with random phase changes are called **incoherent** sources.

Two separate light sources cannot be used as sources for a static interference pattern because although they may be monochromatic the light from them is emitted in a random series of pulses of around 10^{-8} s duration and the phase difference that may exist between one pair of pulses emitted from the source may well be quite different from that between the next pair of pulses. Although the interference pattern still occurs, it changes so rapidly that you get the impression of uniform illumination. We must therefore use one light source and split the waves from it into two in some way.

There are two ways of doing this:

(*a*) *division of amplitude*, where the amplitude at all points along the wavefront is divided between the two secondary waves, and

(*b*) *division of wavefront*, where the original wavefront is divided in two, half of it forming each of the secondary waves.

However, the length of each pulse limits the path difference that we may obtain between even these two waves from the same source. Since the pulses are only about 10^{-8} s long the maximum path difference is 3 m, although in practice good results are only obtained with shorter path differences than this.

Stokes' theorem

It is possible to introduce a phase difference between two wave trains without an actual path difference, using reflection. If a wave reflects from a more dense medium than the one in which it was travelling then a phase change of π is produced, corresponding to an effective path difference of half a wavelength.

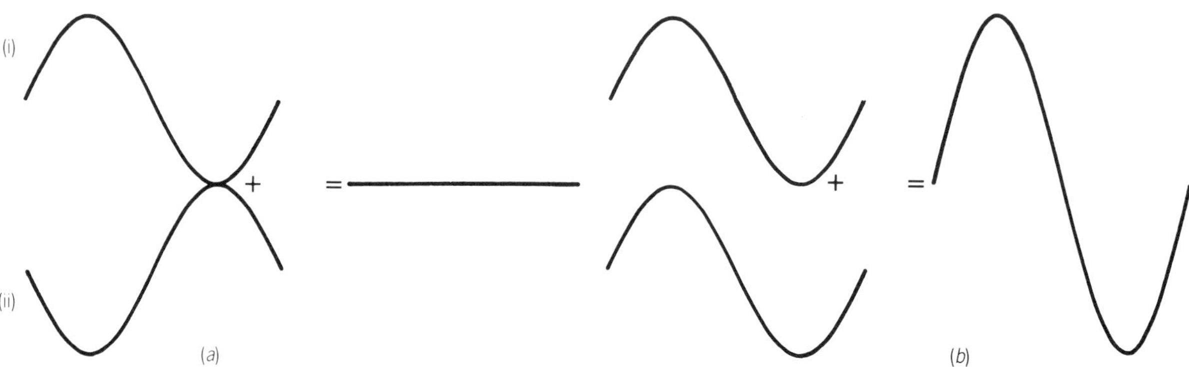

Figure 32.1

Student investigation

It has been suggested that a way to reduce the noise in a room would be to record the sound in it and then to replay it, delaying it by half a wave.

Investigate this theory using a signal generator emitting a pure tone through one speaker and a circuit for delaying the note emitted by the other speaker.

Consider the problems due to reflections at the walls of the room.

Interference between two waves

The diagrams in Figure 32.2 show two sources S_1 and S_2 emitting waves – they could be light, sound or microwaves. You can see at the different points on the screen the waves from S_1 have travelled a different distance from those from S_2. In Figure 32.2(*a*) the path difference is zero, in (*b*) half a wavelength, in (*c*) one wavelength and in (*d*) one and a half wavelengths.

The plan view of the waves in diagram (*e*) shows the lines along which the path differences will give maxima or minima. It should be realised that between these extremes the path differences will change gradually from one extreme to the other.

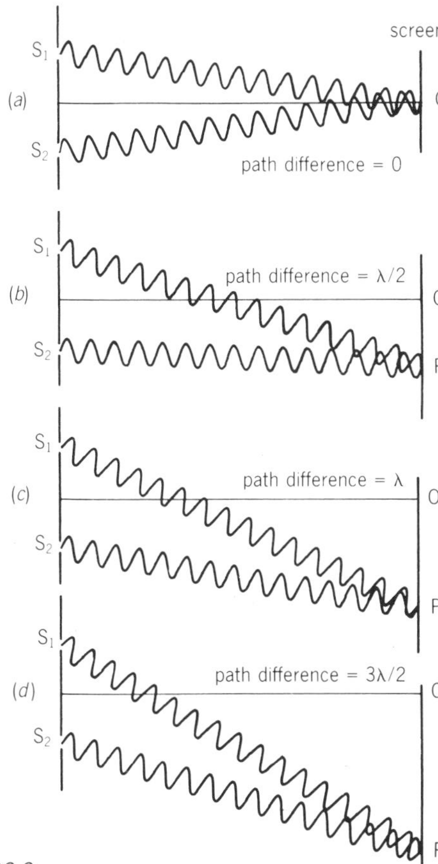

Figure 32.2

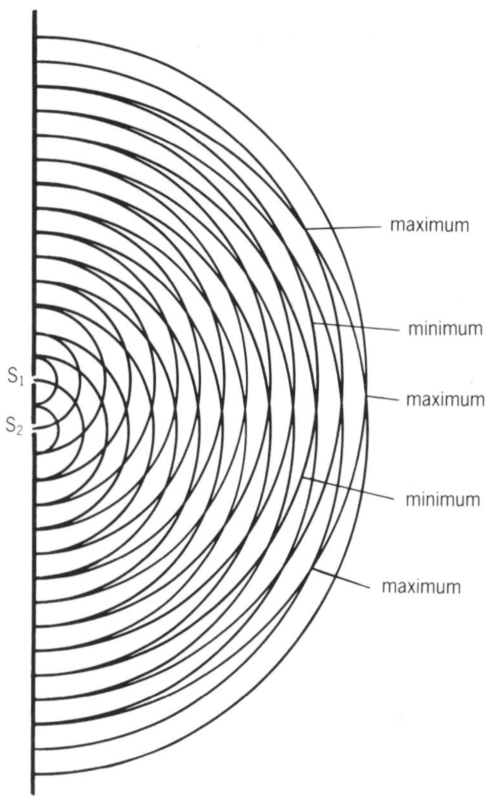

Figure 32.2(e)

Path length in a material

When light passes through a material of refractive index n it is slowed down, its velocity in the material being $1/n$ times that in a vacuum. For example, the velocity of light in glass is about 2.0×10^8 m s^{-1} compared with about 3.00×10^8 m s^{-1} in a vacuum.

The time light takes to pass through a given length of the material is therefore n times that which it takes to pass through the same length of air.

The path length in a material of length l and refractive index n is therefore nl (Figure 32.3). If one part of a light beam travels a distance l in air and the other a distance l in the material then a path difference will exist between them of $l(n - 1)$ and if the two beams are made to overlap an interference pattern will result.

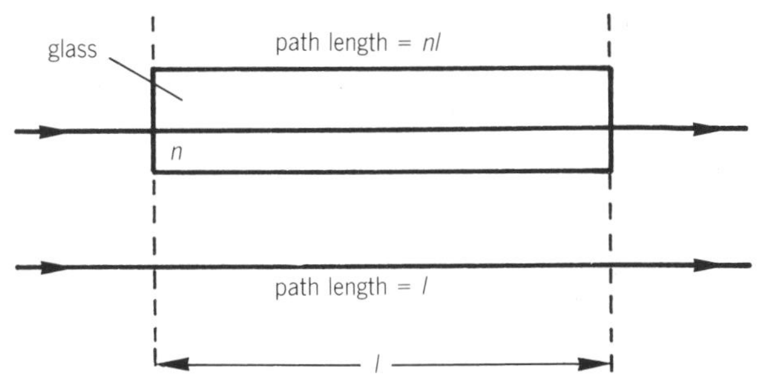

Figure 32.3

Interference by division of wavefront

Young's slits

This experiment to use the effects of interference to measure the wavelength of light was devised by Thomas Young in 1801, although the original idea was due to Grimaldi. The method produces non-localised interference fringes by division of wavefront, and a sketch of the experimental arrangement is shown in Figure 32.4.

Light from a monochromatic line source passes through a lens and is focused on to a single slit S. It then falls on a double slit (S_1 and S_2) and this produces two wave trains that interfere with each other in the region on the right of the diagram. The interference pattern at any distance from the double slit may be observed with a micrometer eyepiece or by placing a screen in the path of the waves. The separation across the double slit should be less than 1 mm, the width of each slit about 0.3 mm, and the distance between the double slit and the screen between 50 cm and 1 m. The single slit, the source and the double slit must be parallel to produce the optimum interference pattern.

The formula relating the dimensions of the apparatus and the wavelength of light may be proved as follows.

Consider the effects at a point P a distance x_m from the axis of the apparatus (Figure 32.5). The path difference at P is $S_2P - S_1P$.

For a bright fringe (constructive interference) the path difference must be a whole number of wavelengths and for a dark fringe it must be an odd number of half-wavelengths (Figure 32.6).

Consider the triangles S_1PR and S_2PT.

$$S_1P^2 = (x_m - d/2)^2 + D^2$$
$$S_2P^2 = (x_m + d/2)^2 + D^2$$

Therefore:

$$S_2P^2 - S_1P^2 = 2x_m d$$

$$(S_2P - S_1P)(S_2P + S_1P) = 2x_m d$$

But $S_2P + S_1P = 2D$.

Therefore

$$S_2P - S_1P \approx x_m d/D$$

For a bright fringe:

$$m\lambda = x_m d/D$$

For a dark fringe:

$$(2m + 1)\lambda/2 = x_m d/D$$

Figure 32.6

The distance between adjacent bright fringes is called the **fringe width** (x) and this can be used in the equation as

$$\lambda = xd/D$$

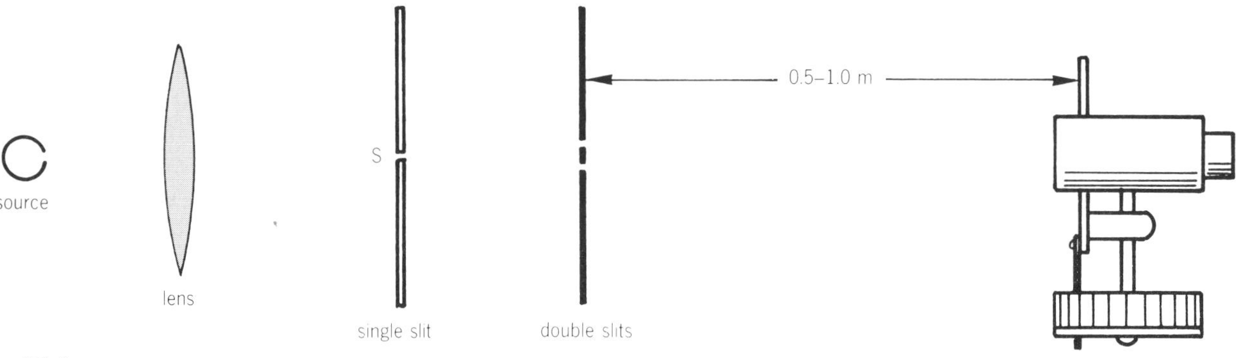

Figure 32.4

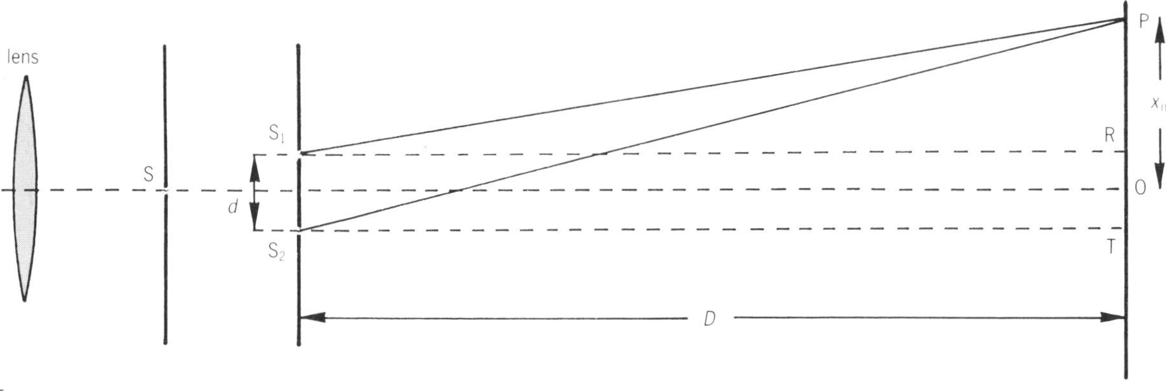

Figure 32.5

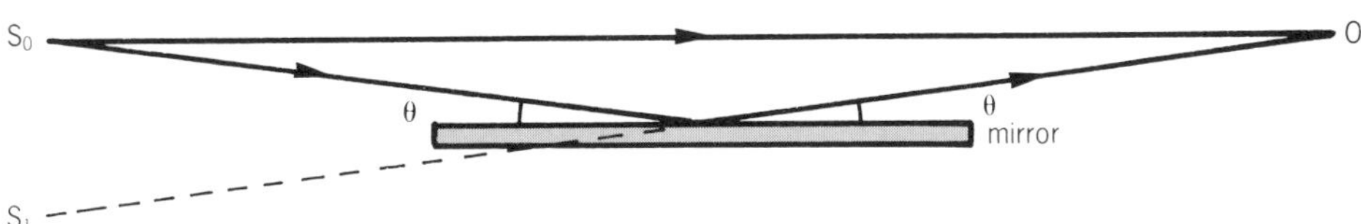

Figure 32.7

Note that the fringe width is directly proportional to the wavelength, and so light with a longer wavelength will give wider fringes.

If white light is used a white centre fringe is observed, but all the other fringes have coloured edges, the blue edge being nearer the centre. Eventually the fringes overlap and a uniform white light is produced.

Example

Calculate the fringe width for light of wavelength 550 nm in a Young's slit experiment where the double slits are separated by 0.75 mm and the screen is placed 0.80 m from them.

Fringe width (x) $= \lambda D/d$

$= 550 \times 10^{-9} \times 0.80/0.75 \times 10^{-3}$

$= 3.3 \times 10^{-4}$ m

$= 0.33$ mm

1 A set of fringes is formed in a Young's double slit experiment using monochromatic yellow light. State the effect on the fringes of:

(*a*) using light of a longer wavelength,

(*b*) twisting the single source slit about a vertical axis,

(*c*) making the single source slit wider,

(*d*) moving the source slit sideways,

(*e*) using white light,

(*f*) moving the source slit towards the double slit,

(*g*) moving the screen away from the double slit,

(*h*) putting a piece of Polaroid over one of the double slits,

(*i*) putting a thin piece of glass in front of one of the double slits.

2 If a Young's double slit interference experiment was carried out under water what effect, if any, would there be on the fringe width? Explain your answer.

3 Would you expect to observe beats between the light from (*a*) two small monochromatic torch bulbs, (*b*) between two lasers? Explain your answers.

Lloyd's mirror

This is another method for finding the wavelength of light by the division of wavefront. Light from a slit S_0 falls on a silvered surface at a very small grazing angle of incidence as shown in Figure 32.7. A virtual image of S_0 is formed at S_1.

Interference occurs between the direct beam from S_0 to the observer (O) and the reflected beam. The zeroth fringe will be black because of the phase change due to reflection at the surface.

4 In a Lloyd's mirror experiment the source slit S_0 and its virtual image S_1 lie in a plane 0.20 m behind the left edge of the mirror. The mirror is 0.3 m long and a screen is placed at the right edge. Calculate the distance from this edge to the first maximum if the perpendicular distance from S_0 to the mirror is 2 mm and the light used has a wavelength of 600 nm.

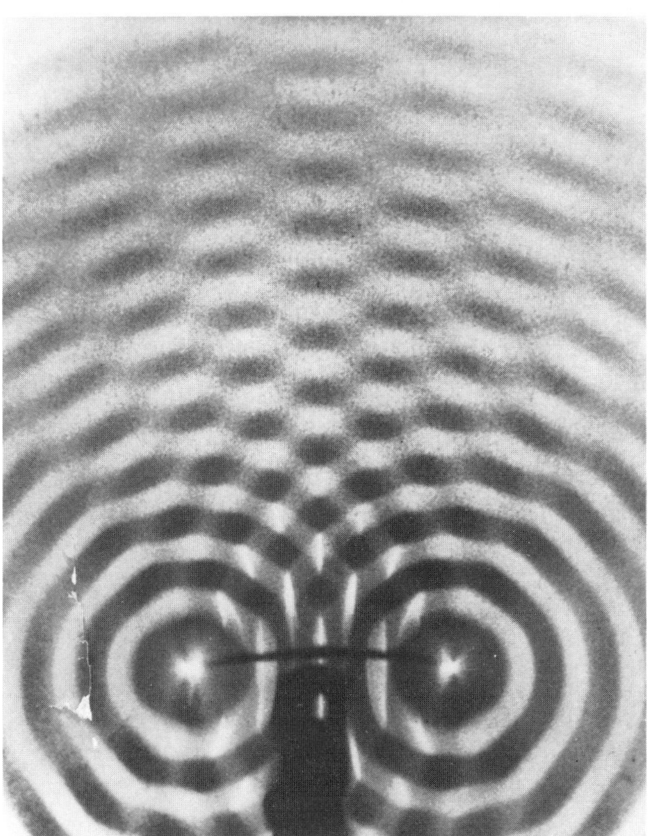

Interference demonstrated in a ripple tank

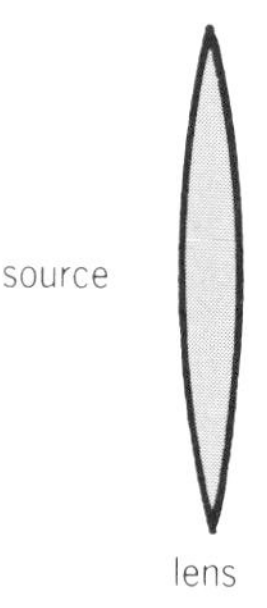

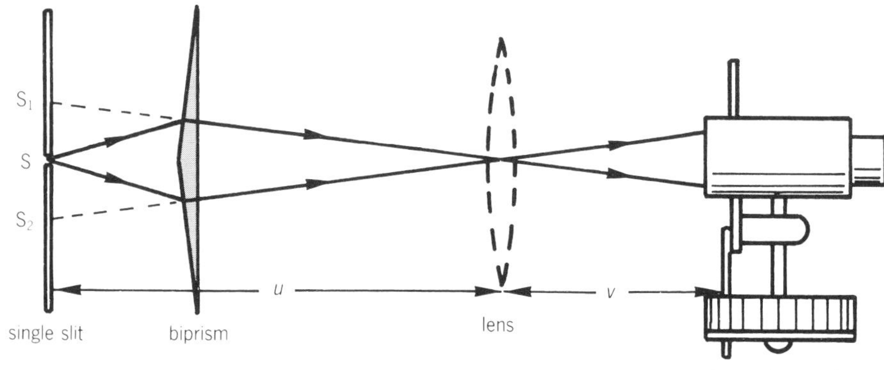

Figure 32.8

Fresnel's biprism

An alternative method is that due to Fresnel. The apparatus is shown in Figure 32.8.

Monochromatic light from a narrow slit S falls on the biprism, the axis of which must be in line with the slit. The refracting angles of the biprism are very small, usually about 0.25°. This prism forms two virtual images of the slit S_1 and S_2 in the plane of S, and these two virtual images act as the sources for two sets of waves which overlap and produce an interference pattern on the screen.

The fringes are much brighter than those produced by Young's slits, because of the very much greater amount of light that can pass through the prism compared with that passing through the double slit arrangement.

The formula used is the same as for Young's slits, the only problem being the measurement of the separation of the two virtual sources S_1 and S_2.

This can be done by placing a convex lens between the biprism and the screen or eyepiece and measuring the separation (s) of the images of S_1 and S_2 produced by the lens. If the object and image distances (u and v) are found, the value of d can be calculated from

$$\frac{d}{s} = \frac{u}{v}$$

Using a two position method removes the need to measure u and v. If s_1 and s_2 are the separations of the two image slits in the two positions then:

$$d = \sqrt{s_1 s_2}$$

Example

In a Fresnel's biprism experiment the refracting angles of the prism were 1.5° and the refractive index of the glass was 1.5. With the single slit 5 cm from the biprism and using light of wavelength 580 nm, fringes were formed on a screen 1 m from the single slit. Calculate the fringe width.

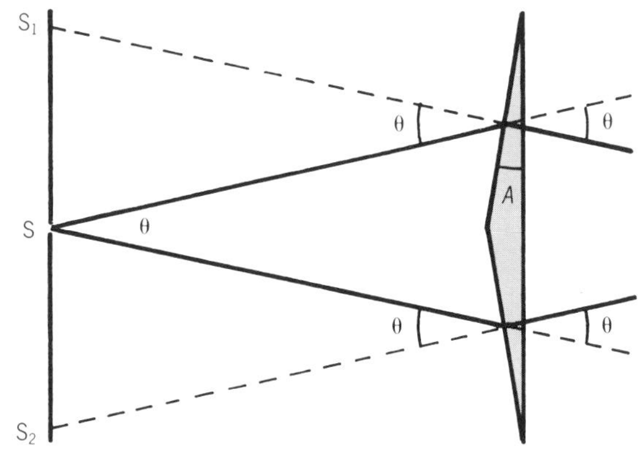

Figure 32.9

For a thin prism (Figure 32.9),

$$\text{deviation } \theta = (n-1)A = \frac{(1.5-1)1.5\pi}{180}$$

$$\text{Therefore } S_1S = \frac{5 \times 0.75\pi}{180} \text{ cm}\cdot$$

However, $S_1S_2 = 2S_1S = \dfrac{75\pi}{180} = 0.131$ cm; therefore the fringe width is given by:

$$x = \frac{\lambda D}{d} = \frac{580 \times 10^{-7} \times 100}{0.131} = 0.044 \text{ cm}$$

5 In an experiment with Fresnel's biprism the fringe width as measured with a micrometer eyepiece is 0.02 cm and the distance between the source slit and the cross-wires of the eyepiece is 75 cm.

When a converging lens is placed between the biprism and the eyepiece two positions of the lens can be found which give two clear images of the slit. The distance between these images is 3.73 mm and 1.24 mm respectively.

Calculate the wavelength of the light used in the experiment. [c]

Student investigation

The Young's double slit experiment is much easier to perform if a laser is used as the source. The brightness of the beam makes the interference pattern visible some metres from the double slit and therefore the width of a number of fringes is easily measurable with a ruler.

Set up the apparatus as shown in Figure 32.10 and measure the wavelength of the laser light. You should be able to see the single slit diffraction pattern crossing the $\cos^2$ fringes produced by interference.

Warning: laser light can be dangerous. Consult your teacher before proceeding.

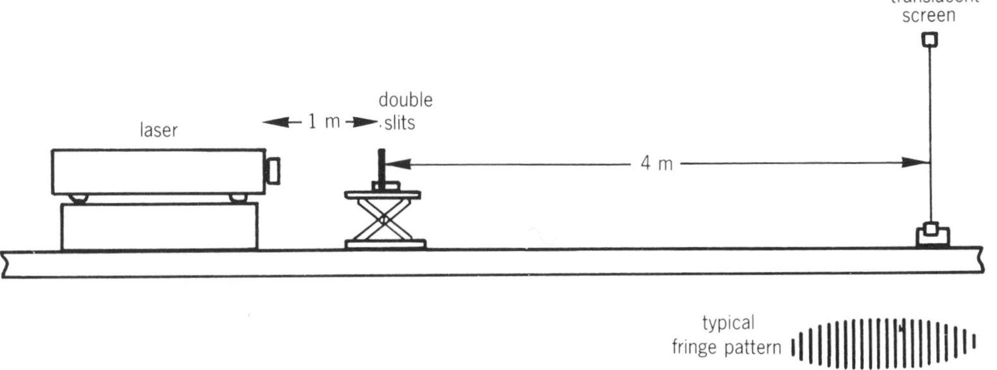

Figure 32.10

6 Find the value of m for which the $(m + 1)$th blue fringe coincides with the mth red fringe in a Young's slits experiment if the separation of the slits is 0.5 mm and they are 1.2 m from the screen. Take the wavelength of red light as 780 nm and that of blue light as 520 nm.

Student investigation

The following investigations demonstrate the principle of the stellar interferometer – a device for measuring the diameter of stars or the separation of double stars.

(*a*) Look at a distant light bulb first through a card with a pinhole in it and then through one with two pinholes. Compare the definition of the image seen in the two cases.

(*b*) Set up the microwaves arrangement shown in Figure 32.11. The apparatus on the left should be capable of rotating about a vertical axis through the receiver. Adjust the angle of the plates for maximum signal. Compare the sharpness of the fringe pattern recorded as the instruments on the left are rotated slightly first with only one plate A and then with both plates A and B.

Find out how a real stellar interferometer works, at both optical and radio wavelengths.

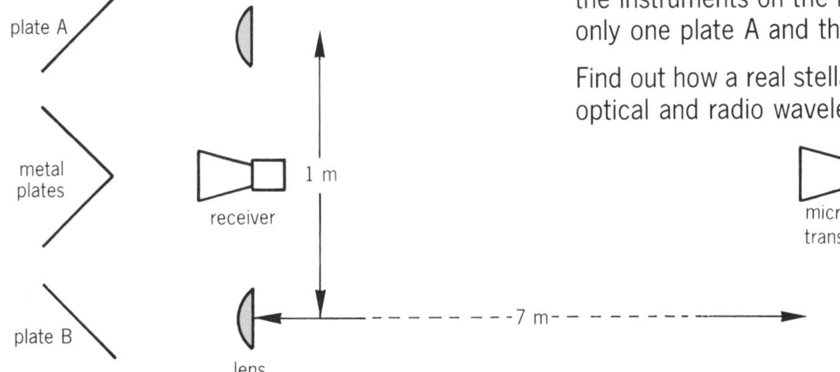

Figure 32.11

Newton's rings

This method for determining the wavelength of light was proposed by Sir Isaac Newton in his book *Opticks*, published in 1717. The experimental arrangement is shown in Figure 32.12.

A plano-convex lens of large radius of curvature R is placed on a plane glass plate with its curved surface downwards and is illuminated from above with a parallel beam of monochromatic light. Some of the light is reflected from the upper surface of the glass plate and some from the lower surface of the lens; interference thus occurs by **division of amplitude**, the fringes being localised in the air gap between the lens and plate.

At any point a distance r from the axis of the lens the path difference will be $2h$, where h is the distance between the lens and the plate at that point. The interference fringes are circular because the system is symmetrical about the centre of the lens. The radius of any ring is given by:

$$(2R - h)h = r^2$$

But h^2 is small compared with $2Rh$ and so we can write

$$2Rh = r^2$$

The path difference ($2h$) is therefore r^2/R.

A phase change of π occurs when the light reflects from the top surface of the plate but not at the lower surface of the lens, and therefore

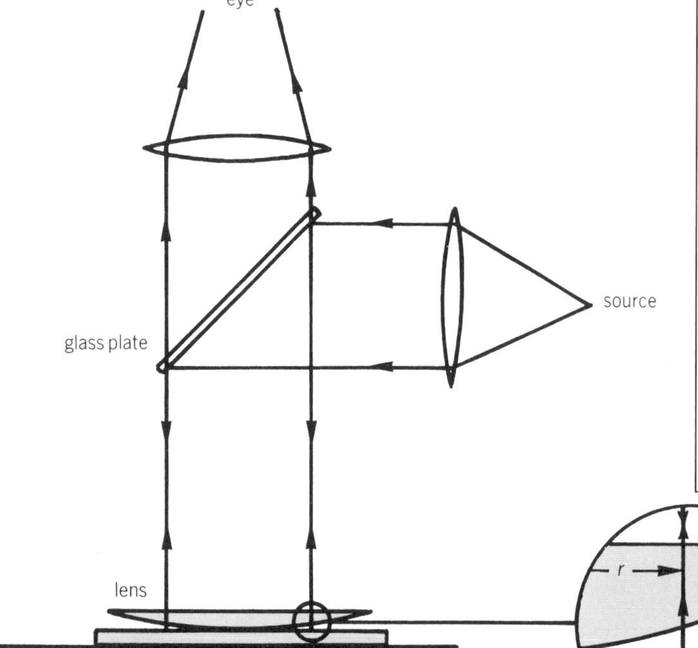

Figure 32.12

For a *bright* ring viewed by reflection:

$$(2m + 1)\lambda/2 = r_m^2/R$$

For a *dark* ring viewed by reflection:

$$m\lambda = r_m^2/R$$

If a graph is plotted of r^2 against m for the dark rings a straight line should be produced with a gradient given by:

$$(r_m^2 - r_1^2)/(m - 1) = \lambda R$$

where r_1 and r_m are the radii of the first and mth rings respectively (Figure 32.13).

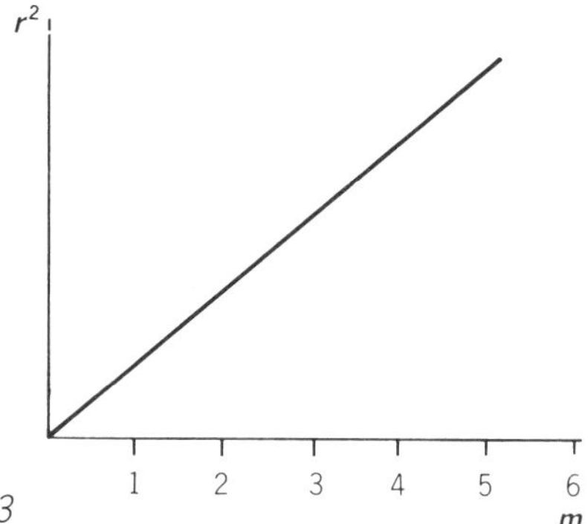

Figure 32.13

Example

A series of rings formed in Newton's rings experiment with sodium light was viewed by reflection. The diameter of the nth dark ring was found to be 0.28 cm and that of the $(n + 10)$th 0.68 cm. If the wavelength of sodium light is 589 nm, calculate the radius of curvature of the lens surface.

For the nth ring: $$\frac{(0.14 \times 10^{-2})^2}{R} = n \times 589 \times 10^{-9}$$

and for the $(n + 10)$th ring:

$$\frac{(0.34 \times 10^{-2})^2}{R} = (n + 10) \times 589 \times 10^{-9}$$

where R is the radius of curvature of the lens surface. Therefore:

$$\frac{0.34^2}{0.14^2} = \frac{(n + 10)}{n}$$ giving $n = 2$.

Therefore, substituting for n, $R = 1.66$ m.

When doing the experiment it is much easier (and more accurate) to measure the diameter of the rings and then calculate their radius. A dark central spot should be obtained when viewed by reflection.

The rings can be viewed by transmission by putting the microscope below the plate, and if this is done the equations for bright and dark rings should be interchanged as two phase changes will occur, producing an effective path difference of 2π. A bright central spot should be obtained.

If white light is used a few coloured rings will be seen due to the different wavelengths of the different colours of light.

Newton's rings and the refractive index of a liquid

Putting a liquid of refractive index n between the lens and the plate (Figure 32.14) will change the path difference to $2nh$ and give a formula for the mth dark ring of

$$m\lambda = \frac{nr_m^2}{R}$$

The radius of any given ring will be less with the liquid in place than without it.

This effect may be used to measure the refractive index of the liquid; the method is a good one since it is accurate and easy to perform, and only a small amount of the liquid is needed.

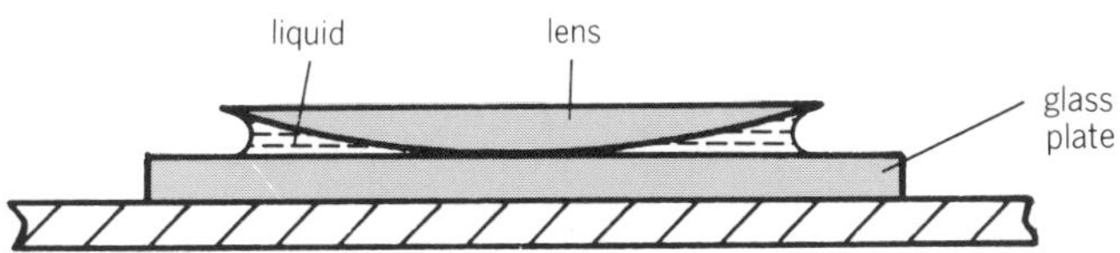

Figure 32.14

Example

Calculate the ratio of the diameters of the fifth interference rings with and without water (refractive index 1.33) between the lens and the plate in Figure 32.15 if the radius of curvature of lens is 0.50 m.

Without water: $r_m^2 = Rm\lambda = 0.5 \times 5 \times \lambda$

With water: $r_m^2 = \frac{Rm\lambda}{n} = \frac{0.5 \times 5 \times \lambda}{1.33}$

Therefore ratio of radii $= \frac{1}{\sqrt{1.33}} = 0.87.$

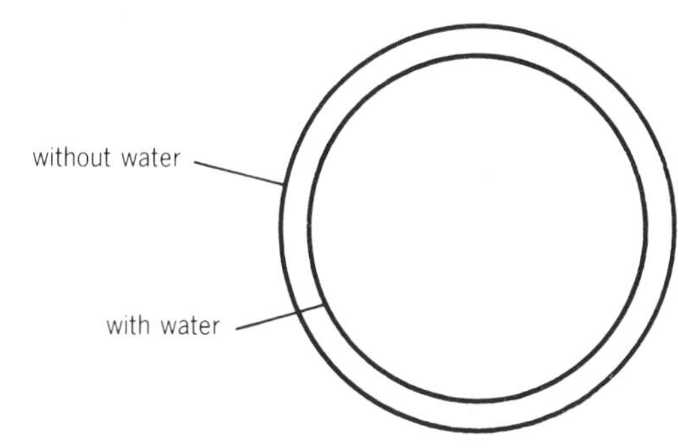

Figure 32.15

7 A plano-convex lens rests on a metal cylinder 6.0 mm long which stands on a flat glass plate. The lens is illuminated from above with light of wavelength 590 nm and Newton's rings are formed in the space between the lens and plate. The temperature of the metal cylinder is now raised by 150 K and the rings move so that the twenty-fifth ring now occupies the position where the fifth ring originally was.

Explain this effect, and use the data to calculate the linear expansivity of the metal of the cylinder.

8 A drop of oil of refractive index 1.58 is placed between a plano-convex lens and a glass plate on which the lens rests. The lens and plate are of the same refractive index, 1.50. Calculate the diameter of the fifth bright ring if the radius of curvature of the lens surface is 2.00 m and light of wavelength 589 nm is reflected normally from the system.

What effect will be observed when the plate is replaced by another of refractive index 1.65? Explain your answer.

9 In a Newton's rings experiment the diameter of the fifteenth dark ring viewed by reflection is 0.60 cm. The radius of curvature of the lens surface in contact with the plate is 100 cm.

What value does that give for the wavelength of the sodium light used?

Interference in thin films

The beautiful colours in soap films and in oil floating on water are due to interference by reflection. We will first consider the interference due to a parallel-sided film as shown in Figure 32.16. Interference at O occurs by division of amplitude, some light being reflected from each side of the film.

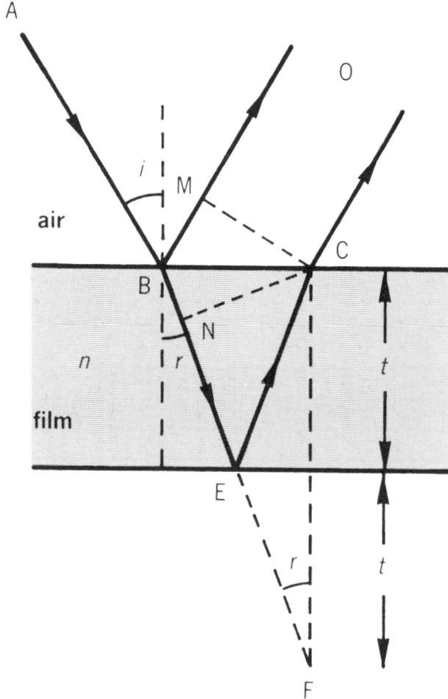

Figure 32.16

$$\begin{aligned}\text{The path difference} &= 2n\text{BE} - \text{BM}\\ &= 2n\text{BE} - n\text{BN}\\ &= n(\text{BE} + \text{EF} - \text{BN})\\ &= n\text{NF}\\ &= 2nt\cos r = (m + \tfrac{1}{2})\,\lambda\end{aligned}$$

where n is the refractive index of the film of thickness t, and $m = 0, 1, 2$, etc.

For a soap film in air a phase change will occur at the first face, while for an oil film on water the phase changes will depend on the refractive index of the oil.

If we now consider the soap film and normal incidence, it is easy to see why thick films reflect light but do not show coloured effects and appear transparent and why very thin films appear 'black' i.e. do not reflect light. Consider a soap film of refractive index 1.33 illuminated by white light.

For $t = 10^{-7}$ m and $m = 0$, $\lambda = 5.32 \times 10^{-7}$ m (green)
$m = 1$, $\lambda = 1.77 \times 10^{-7}$ m (ultraviolet)

Therefore only one colour is visible at this thickness at normal incidence.

For $t = 10^{-6}$ m and $m = 0$, $\lambda = 5.32 \times 10^{-6}$ m (infrared)
$m = 4$, $\lambda = 5.91 \times 10^{-7}$ m (yellow)
$m = 5$, $\lambda = 4.75 \times 10^{-7}$ m (blue)

All higher values of m give wavelengths in the ultraviolet region, so only two colours are visible.

For $t = 10^{-5}$ m and $m = 0$, $\lambda = 5.32 \times 10^{-5}$ m (infrared)
$m = 36$, $\lambda = 7.28 \times 10^{-7}$ m (red)
$m = 59$, $\lambda = 4.52 \times 10^{-7}$ m (violet)

All higher values of m give wavelengths in the ultraviolet region, so 24 wavelengths give maxima and so the appearance is very nearly white.

For thicker films still many more wavelengths can 'fit in', and so all thicker films appear to reflect white light.

For very thin films the distance travelled inside the film is insignificant and so the two reflected waves are almost exactly out of phase with each other (due to the phase change at one surface); they interfere destructively and the film appears 'black'.

Example

A film of oil 0.0005 mm thick and of refractive index 1.42 lies on a pool of water. Which colour will be missing from the spectrum when a point on the film is viewed at 40° to the vertical?

Destructive interference occurs:

$$m\lambda = 2nt\cos r$$
$$m\lambda = 2 \times 1.42 \times 5 \times 10^{-7} \times \cos r$$

But from Snell's law $r = 27°$; therefore $\cos r = 0.89$. Therefore

$$m\lambda = 2 \times 1.42 \times 5 \times 10^{-7} \times 0.89$$

If $m = 1$ then $\lambda = 1.26 \times 10^{-6}$ m (infrared).
If $m = 2$ then $\lambda = 6.33 \times 10^{-7}$ m (orange).
If $m = 3$ then $\lambda = 4.22 \times 10^{-7}$ m (ultraviolet).

Thus the only colour missing from the visible part of the spectrum will be an orange line of wavelength 6.33×10^{-7} m.

10 In an experiment in which Newton's rings were observed by reflected light the surface of the lens had a radius of curvature of 50.0 cm, and the diameters of the first, third, fifth, seventh, ninth and eleventh dark rings measured by a travelling microscope were found to be 0.74, 1.65, 2.22, 2.66, 3.05 and 3.39 mm respectively.

Plot a graph to show the relation between the squares of the radii of the rings and the ring numbers. Comment on the form of the graph and deduce a value of the wavelength of the light used in the experiment. [O and C]

11 (*a*) Find the least thickness of a film of refractive index 1.20 deposited on glass which will cut out reflection of light of wavelength 600 nm.

(*b*) Explain why brilliant colours are seen when a film of oil spreads over water.

(*c*) Explain why a static interference pattern cannot be observed using two separate torch bulbs even if monochromatic filters are placed in front of them.

The colours in a soap film can be observed clearly by projecting them on to a screen. A wire ring with a soap film formed across it should be mounted vertically in the beam of a high-intensity light source in such a way that the light is focused just behind the film. A further lens may then be used to project the colours formed on to a screen. As the water runs from the film it gets progressively narrower at the top and turns black when it is about to break. Beautiful effects may be obtained by blowing gently on the film.

12 A thin film 4×10^{-5} cm thick is illuminated with white light normal to its surface. If the refractive index of the film is 1.5, what wavelengths will be intensified in the visible spectrum?

Student investigation

It has been suggested that the gun turrets on a ship (Figure 32.17) may be made more stable by using interference damping. This means feeding an oscillation into the mounting of the same type and amplitude as that causing the vibration, but out of phase with it by half a period.

Test this in the laboratory using two vibrators and a signal generator and a method for delaying the output of one vibrator.

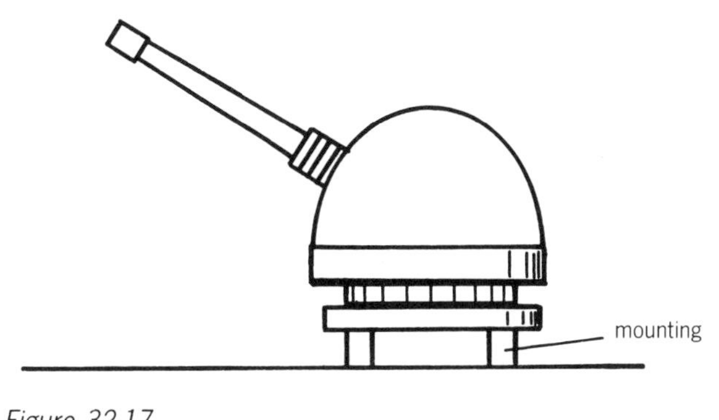

Figure 32.17

Wedge fringes

If two glass plates are placed face to face with one end separated by a piece of paper an air wedge will be formed between them. If monochromatic light is shone on the plates a series of straight line fringes will be seen parallel to the line along which they touch (Figure 32.18). This is due to interference by division of amplitude, as with Newton's rings. Some light is reflected from the bottom surface of the top plate and some from the top surface of the bottom plate.

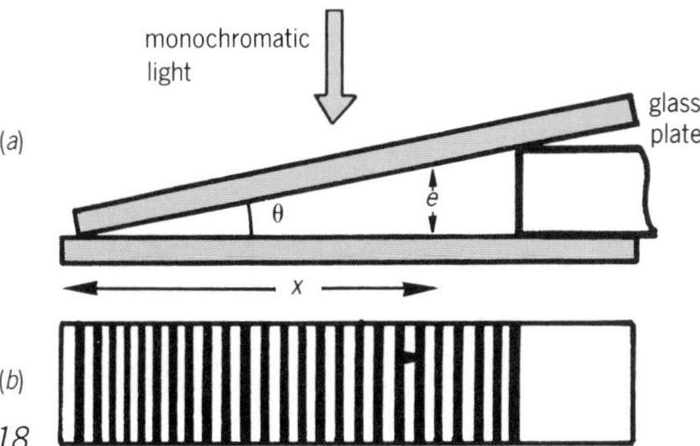

Figure 32.18

To see the fringes clearly the angle must be small, something like 4 minutes of arc. You should also look for fringes close to the join of the plates where the air gap is smallest, since the fringes are not well defined for path differences of more than some hundred wavelengths (0.058 mm for sodium light – compare this with the thickness of a sheet of paper).

Consider a point a distance x from the join.

Path difference $= 2e = 2x\theta$

where θ is the angle between the plates in radians (this angle is small, so $\tan \theta = \theta$ in radians). For an air wedge there is a phase change on reflection at the top surface of the lower plate and so:

$2e = 2x\theta = m\lambda$ for a *dark* fringe,
$2e = 2x\theta = (2m + 1)\lambda/2$ for a *bright* fringe.

The travelling microscope or the eye must be focused close to the upper surface of the air wedge since this is where the fringes are localised.

Pressing down gently with your finger on the plates will move the interference pattern, since only a very small movement is needed to alter the path difference significantly.

A good example of wedge fringes may be seen in a vertical soap film: this takes the form of a wedge of very small angle as the soap drains to the bottom. When the top part goes black the film is about to break.

The flatness of a glass surface may be tested by placing it on a test surface which is known to be flat and illuminating them with monochromatic light; any imperfections will show up as loop-shaped interference fringes around bumps or depressions on the surfaces.

13 A series of experiments to demonstrate that all waves will show interference is set up using a double slit arrangement. Calculate how far apart the two slits must be so that adjacent maxima subtend an angle of 4.0×10^{-2} rad at the double slits for the following waves:

(*a*) sound waves of wavelength 0.8 m,
(*b*) ultrasonic waves of wavelength 0.1 m,
(*c*) microwaves of wavelength 2.8 cm,
(*d*) infrared radiation of wavelength 10 μm,
(*e*) light of wavelength 600 nm.

Student investigation

Use the interference patterns formed between two glass sheets to investigate the elastic properties of glass. If possible your investigation should include a determination of the Young modulus for glass.

Example

An air wedge is formed by placing a sheet of foil between the edges of two glass plates 75 mm from their point of contact. When the wedge is illuminated with light of wavelength 5.8×10^{-7} m the fringes are 1.30 mm apart. Calculate the thickness of the foil.

Number of bright bands in air wedge $= 75/1.30 = 57.7 = m\lambda$.

Change in vertical height from one fringe to the next $= \lambda/2$.

Therefore vertical height for 57.7 fringes

$$= \frac{5.8 \times 10^{-7} \times 57.7}{2} = \frac{3.34 \times 10^{-5}\ \text{m}}{2}$$

and the foil thickness is therefore 1.67×10^{-5} m.

14 Two similar rectangular glass plates are placed in contact along one edge and separated by a strip of paper along the opposite edge, so forming an air wedge of very small angle between them. When the wedge is illuminated normally with sodium light of wavelength 589 nm the wedge is crossed by bright bands with a spacing of 1.20 mm.

Calculate the angle of the wedge in minutes of arc. How would this spacing alter if green light had been used instead of the yellow sodium light? [L]

Non-reflecting coatings

You may have noticed that many good camera and projector lenses appear bluish or purplish; this is due to a coating designed to prevent unwanted reflections from the lens surface. The surface of the glass is coated with a material which is transparent and has a refractive index between those of air and glass: magnesium fluoride, MgF_2, with a refractive index of 1.38, is often used. The thickness t of the film is chosen to give destructive interference between the beam reflected from the surface of the coating and that reflected from the surface of the lens (Figure 32.19). This is given by $2nt \cos r = \lambda/2$, or $2nt = \lambda/2$ for normal incidence; a value of t of around 10^{-5}cm is typical.

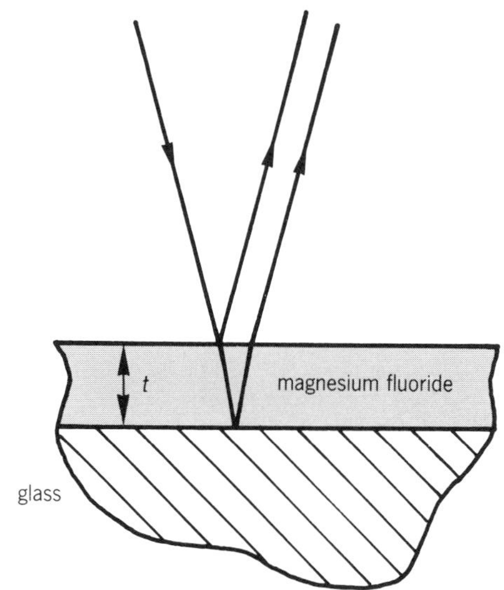

Figure 32.19

The value of the wavelength chosen is around 530 nm, because this is the wavelength to which the eye is most sensitive. Removing light of this region from the spectrum leaves a predominance of blue and red, thus giving the characteristic purplish colour.

It can be shown that the two reflected waves from the coating and the glass have the same intensity if the refractive index of the coating is equal to the square root of the refractive index of the glass.

If the refractive index of the coating is greater than that of the glass then the reflection is *increased*!

The following uses of interference are not considered in detail here, but the interested student can follow them up in reference books:

testing flat and curved surfaces;
expansion of materials;
measurement of refractive indices of gases;
Michelson–Morley experiment;
interferometers to measure stellar diameters;
distance measurement by laser interference.

15 (*a*) Two glass plates 4 cm long touch at one edge and are separated by a piece of paper 0.02 mm thick at the other, so making an air wedge between them. If the wedge is illuminated with light of wavelength 589 nm, calculate the separation of the bright interference bands produced, and how many of them will be seen.

(*b*) What will be the separation between the interference bands if glycerol, refractive index 1.47, is placed between the plates in part (*a*)?

(*c*) Why do the lenses of some cameras appear purple in colour?

(*d*) If I wet my glasses to clean them I find that they become markedly less reflecting as the water evaporates from them. Why is this?

16 A non-reflecting layer has a refractive index of 1.334. Find the necessary thickness for zero reflection at the following wavelengths: (*a*) 450 nm, (*b*) 600 nm, (*c*) 700 nm.

17 Anodising is the electroplating process which forms a thin film of aluminium oxide on a polished aluminium surface.

(*a*) Aluminium oxide is a colourless transparent material and yet if the thickness is correctly chosen the surface can look coloured. Explain why this is so.

(*b*) If the oxide layer is 250 nm thick and has a refractive index of 1.77, what colour will it look when viewed in white light at normal incidence? (Assume no phase change at the aluminium metal surface.)

(Note that anodised aluminium commercially produced usually contains dyes which add to the colour effects.)

33 · Polarisation

As you know, waves can be either transverse or longitudinal in nature. If the vibrations of a *transverse* wave are in one plane only then that wave is said to be **plane-polarised.** (Longitudinal waves cannot be plane-polarised.)

The phenomenon of the polarisation of light was known to Newton and was inexplicable in terms of longitudinal waves. Later theory showed that light is a transverse wave motion and in fact polarisation is very good evidence for this type of wave motion. Polarisation was first recorded by Bartholinus in 1669 when he noticed the double refraction in Iceland spar, a crystalline form of calcium carbonate (double refraction is discussed later in this chapter).

In 1808 Malus found that if he looked through two tourmaline crystals and then rotated one through 90° the light was cut out. He also looked through a tourmaline crystal at the windows of the palace in Luxembourg which were reflecting the setting Sun and found that this reflected light could be cut off by rotating the crystal. This showed that the reflected light was polarised.

Light is a transverse electromagnetic wave with the vibrations occurring in any plane at right angles to the direction of travel of the light (see Figure 33.1(*a*)). When light is plane-polarised the vibrations are made to occur in one plane only (see Figures 33.1(*b*) and (*c*)). The human eye cannot distinguish between polarised and non-polarised light; what we actually register is the intensity of light. Some materials can be used to detect polarisation, however, by allowing light to pass through them only if the vibrations are in a particular plane, called the **plane of polarisation** of the material.

One such material is herapathite, a sulphate of iodoquinine discovered in 1852. The plastic known as Polaroid, developed by Land in 1932, is a sheet of nitrocellulose with millions of herapathite crystals embedded in it, and is often used in the laboratory to polarise light.

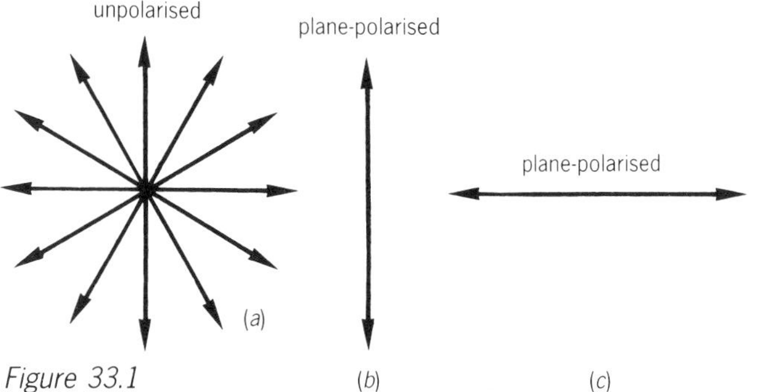

Figure 33.1 (*b*) (*c*)

Student investigation

This experiment studies the polarisation of GHz waves.

Many schools have a set of apparatus that will produce and detect oscillations with a frequency of about 1 GHz (10^9 Hz). The wavelength of these is therefore 0.3 m.

Set up the apparatus as shown in Figure 33.2 and record the strength of the signal received by the receiver when it is rotated about a horizontal axis. Plot a graph of intensity against angle. It is important to avoid all unwanted reflections that might interfere with the result.

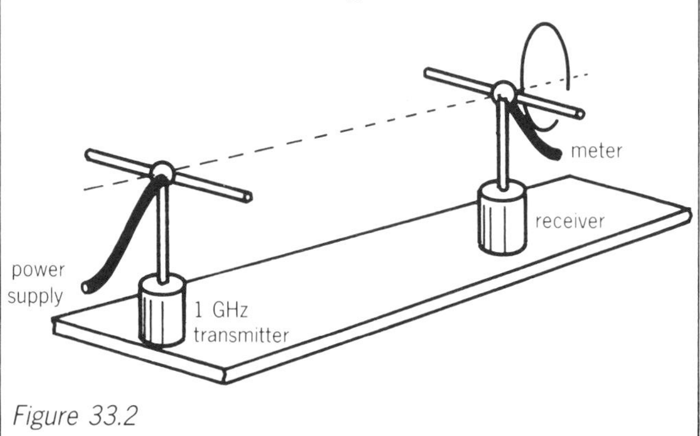

Figure 33.2

Student investigation

How good is a pair of Polaroid sunglasses? Using two pairs of similar Polaroid glasses, study the light that is transmitted when they are placed one over the other and rotated. Also see if they remove the reflection from a shiny surface such as a wet board or the surface of a swimming pool.

Malus' law

Light from an unpolarised source is allowed to fall on a piece of Polaroid P. This plane-polarises the light (it is therefore known as the **polariser**), which then falls on a second piece of Polaroid A. (Figure 33.3(*a*)). This second piece is called the **analyser** because it is used to analyse the polarisation of the beam from P.

As A is rotated the intensity of the light emerging from it slowly changes (Figure 33.3(*b*)), being a maximum at one point and a minimum after a further 90° rotation. Rotating A by another 90° will bring back a maximum once more. The theory of this was proposed by Malus in 1810.

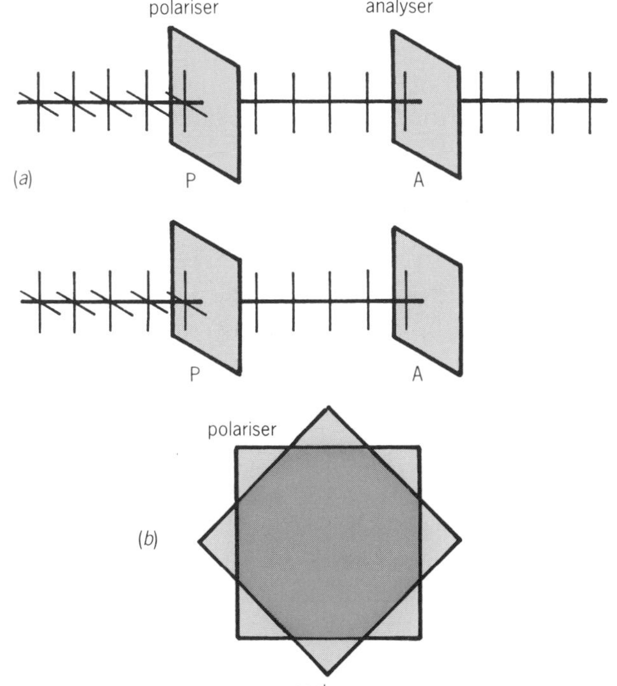

Figure 33.3

Assume that light of amplitude E_0 is incident on a piece of Polaroid which has its plane of polarisation at an angle to the direction of polarisation of the light (see Figure 33.4).

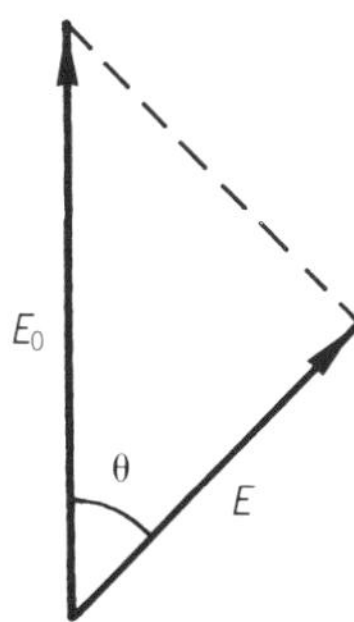

Figure 33.4

Let the transmitted amplitude be E. Now $E = E_0 \cos \theta$, and since the intensity I is proportional to the square of the amplitude we have:

$$I = I_0 \cos^2 \theta$$

This is known as **Malus' law**. Plotting a graph of $\cos^2 \theta$ against I should give a straight line.

Polarisation by reflection

Polaroid sunglasses will cut out the reflected glare from roads because the reflected beam is partly or totally polarised. This polarisation occurs when light is reflected from any non-conductor of electricity. Whether the polarisation is total depends on the surface and the angle of incidence.

For a particular angle p, the beam is completely plane-polarised, the reflected light being polarised as shown in Figure 33.5; p is known as the **polarising angle** for that material.

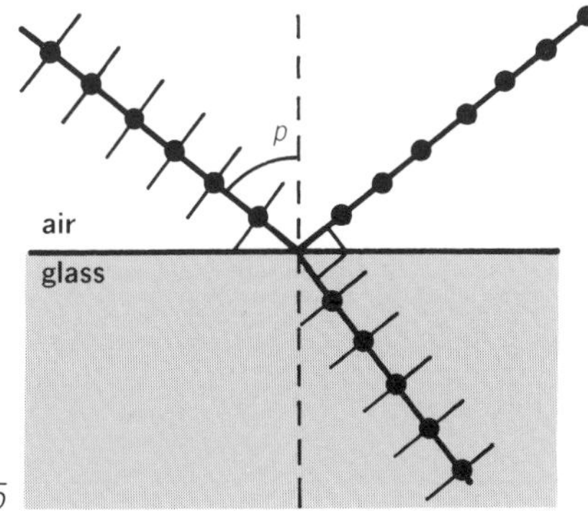

Figure 33.5

Brewster found that

$$\tan p = n$$

where n is the refractive index of the material. It is simple to show that when light meets a surface at the polarising angle the reflected and refracted beams are at right angles to each other. Notice also that the reflected and refracted light has vibrations along the surface at the point of incidence.

For glass with $n = 1.54$ the polarising angle is 57°. Since n varies with the colour of the light, white light can never be perfectly polarised by reflection.

Figure 33.6 shows how we can use two mirrors as a polariser and analyser arrangement.

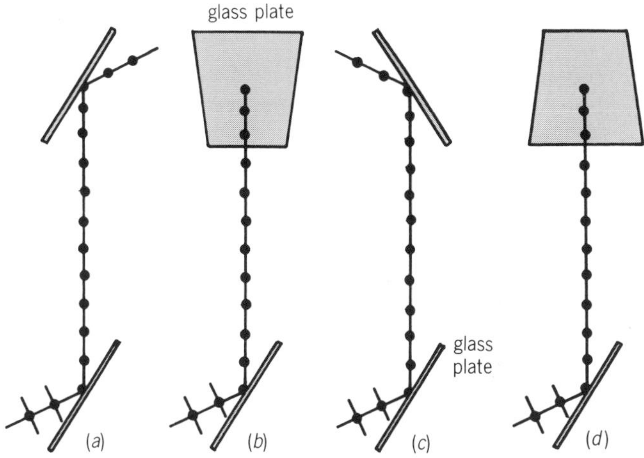

Figure 33.6

1 A beam of light is shone through two pieces of Polaroid arranged with their axes at right angles to each other. Describe what will be observed if a third piece of Polaroid is placed above the two fixed pieces and rotated through 360°.

The third piece is now placed *between* the other two and rotated through 360°. What is observed now? [o]

2 In a Young's slit experiment a piece of Polaroid is placed over one of the two slits and rotated. What difference, if any, will this make to the interference pattern? Explain your answer.

3 Calculate the polarising angle for the following materials:
(*a*) glass – refractive index 1.53;
(*b*) water – refractive index 1.33;
(*c*) diamond – refractive index 2.42.

4 Two Polaroids are inclined to each other at an angle of 35° and a light beam is shone on one. What is the ratio of the transmitted intensity to the incident intensity?

Double refraction

Double refraction was observed by Bartholinus in 1669. He placed a crystal of Iceland spar (calcite) above some words written on a piece of paper and found that he obtained *two* sets of images.
When unpolarised light hits a crystal of calcite *two* refracted rays are formed, as shown in Figure 33.7. One is called the **ordinary ray** (O), because it obeys the normal laws of refraction, and the other the **extraordinary ray** (E).

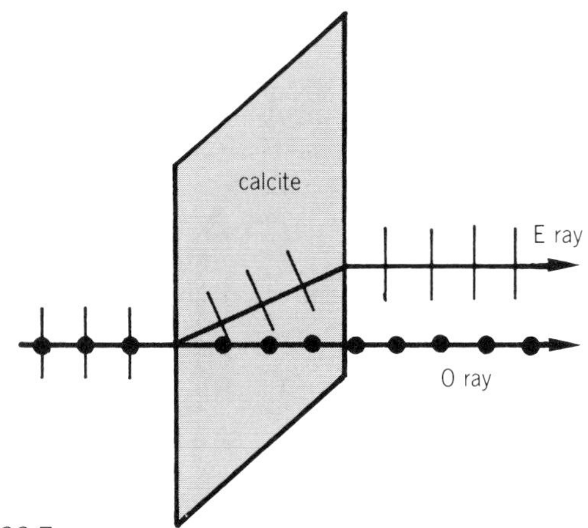

Figure 33.7

It was soon discovered that these two rays were totally plane-polarised at right angles to each other. If we could separate the rays then we would have a very good method of producing polarised light. A method was found by the Scottish physicist William Nicol, who in 1828 devised the **Nicol prism**. This is simply a crystal of calcite cut through the centre and then stuck together again with a glue called Canada balsam.

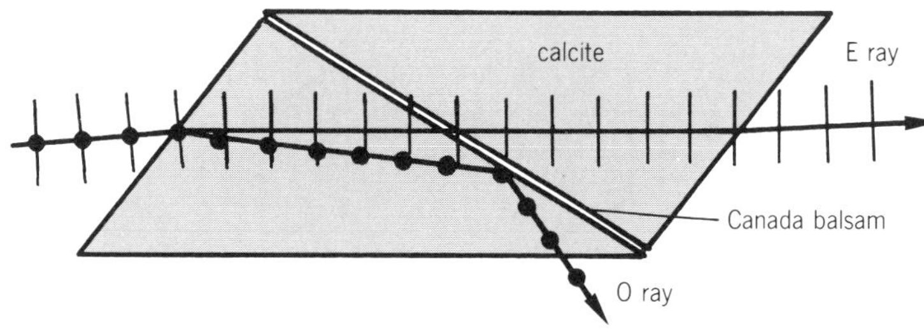

Figure 33.8

The paths of the ordinary and extraordinary rays through such an arrangement are shown in Figure 33.8. The importance of the glue is that its refractive index is less than that of the calcite for the ordinary ray and greater than that of the calcite for the extraordinary ray. This means that total internal reflection can, and does, occur for the ordinary ray but not for the extraordinary ray.

The polarised nature of the two rays is easy to show using a piece of calcite and a sheet of Polaroid. Place the calcite over a line drawn on a piece of paper and view the double image produced through the Polaroid sheet. Rotate the Polaroid; you will see that each image disappears at certain points in each rotation.

Photoelasticity

Some materials, including glass, celluloid, Bakelite and some other plastics, become doubly refracting when subjected to stress. If a piece of such material is placed between two crossed Polaroids the stress patterns can be observed. Different colours of light are affected differently and some very beautiful effects can be obtained. Models of components such as gears, turbine blades or hooks can be made and the stress patterns in them observed to check their design.

These patterns can be seen in car windscreens. The patterns stored in them are due to the stresses produced during their manufacture.

The Kerr effect

In 1875 Kerr discovered that glass becomes doubly refracting when subjected to an intense electric field. It was later found that many liquids (nitrobenzene is one example) also showed this effect, the ordinary ray being in the direction of the field and the extraordinary ray perpendicular to the field. The effect follows the variation of the field very closely in nitrobenzene, disappearing within one nanosecond of the field being removed.

Polarisation by scattering

Light is scattered when it meets a particle of similar size to its own wavelength. This can be seen in the scattering of sunlight by dust in the atmosphere. In 1847 Brucke showed that the scattering is proportional to the fourth power of the frequency of the light, that is blue light is scattered more than red, and this acounts for the blue of the sky (Figure 33.9). It also explains why most babies have blue or blue-grey eyes at birth. The scattering is more marked from smaller particles such as the shorter molecules in the irises of babies; in many children these join up as they grow and the eye colour alters from blue or blue-grey to brown.

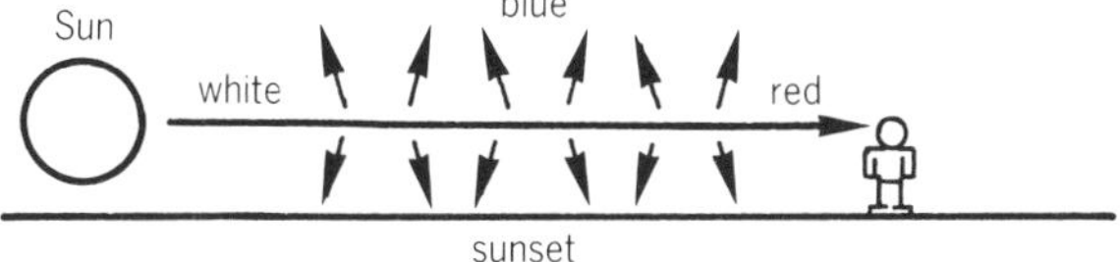

Figure 33.9

You can produce polarisation by scattering in the laboratory by passing a strong beam of light through a tank of water to which a few drops of milk have been added, producing a suspension of tiny globules of fat which scatter the light. Light scattered in this way is plane-polarised in two directions at right angles to each other (Figure 33.10).

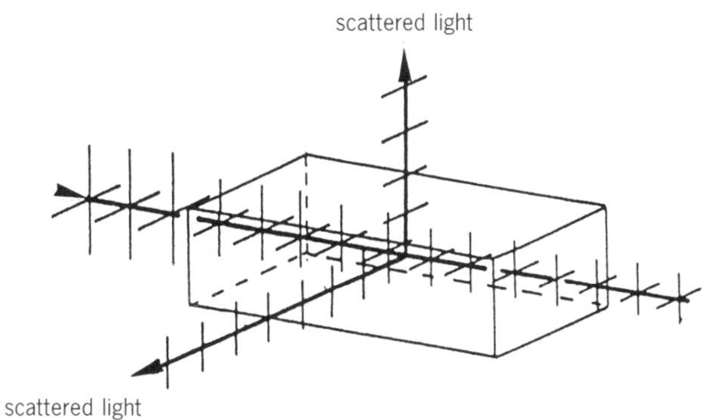

Figure 33.10

Optical activity

Some materials can rotate the plane of polarisation of light as it passes through them. Those that rotate it in a left-handed direction are called **laevorotatory** and those that rotate it in a right-handed direction **dextrorotatory**. They are said to be **optically active.** The rotation produced is roughly proportional to the inverse square of the wavelength. A plate of quartz 1 mm thick produces a rotation of 16° for red light and about 47° for violet at 20 °C.

Some liquids, such as sugar or turpentine and solutions of tartaric acid are optically active. The amount of rotation (δ) is found to be proportional to:

(*a*) the length of the liquid column l, and

(*b*) the concentration of the solution c.

We define a quantity known as the **specific rotation** of a solution (s) by the formula:

$$\delta = slc$$

The polarimeter

The specific rotation of a given liquid may be found using a polarimeter as shown in Figure 33.11. The two Polaroids are adjusted to give a minimum light intensity, and the scale reading noted. A measured length of solution of known concentration is then placed in the inner tube and the Polaroids readjusted to regain a minimum and the scale is read again. The rotation of the solution may then be found from the difference in the two scale readings.

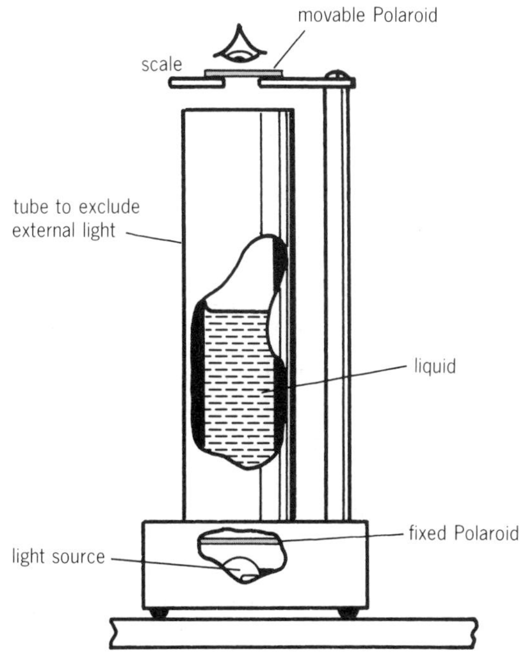

Figure 33.11

5 Write an account of the uses of polarised light.

6 Describe carefully two methods of producing polarised light other than by using a piece of Polaroid.

7 Why can't sound waves be polarised?

8 Why are the stress patterns in car windscreens sometimes visible? Why do they become much more clearly visible if you use Polaroid sunglasses?

Student investigation

Photoelastic stress patterns may be observed very easily as follows.

Place a piece of Polaroid on the top of an overhead projector and blank off the rest of the transmitted light. Put the object under test, such as a protractor or clear plastic ruler, on top of the Polaroid and place a second piece of Polaroid on top of the specimen. The projection on the screen will show the photoelastic patterns clearly.

Alternatively a slide projector may be used, one piece of Polaroid being placed in the slide holder and the second piece taped on the front of the projector lens. The test object can then be hung between the two. Using this method differing loads may be applied to the bottom of the specimen and the resulting change in the stress pattern observed.

Summary of the development of the theory of light

1637	Descartes' *Dioptrique*
1657	Fermat's Principle
1664	Hooke's *Micrographia*
1665	Grimaldi discovers diffraction
1670	Bartholinus discovers the double refraction of Iceland spar
1676	Romer measures the velocity of light
1690	Huygens' *Traité de la Lumière*
1704	Newton's *Opticks*
1770	Euler's *Dioptrica*
1801–3	Young's papers on interference
1850	Foucault shows experimentally that the velocity of light in water is less than that in air
1865	Maxwell's electromagnetic theory of light
1887	Michelson–Morley experiment
1901	Planck's quantum theory
1905	Einstein's special theory of relativity and the explanation of the photoelectric effect
1922	De Broglie's theory of electron waves
1925	Development of quantum mechanics

34 · Lasers

The laser has become part of our lives and will be used much more in the years to come so we will start this section with a look at a few of the purposes for which lasers are used at the time of writing:

repairing damaged retinas
a modification of the Michelson–Morley experiment to check the existence of the aether
distance measurement
production of very high temperatures in fusion reactors
holography – three-dimensional images (see page 219)
surveying – checking ground levels
making holes in the teats of babies' bottles
cutting microelectronic circuits
cutting metal and cloth
laser video and audio discs ('compact discs') (see page 219)
neurosurgery – cutting and sealing nerves
sterilisation
physiotherapy – using laser energy to raise the temperature of localised areas of tissue
removing tongue tumours
laser lances for unblocking heart valves
removal of tattoos or birth marks
laser guidance systems for weapons
laser defence systems ('Star Wars')
communication via modulated laser light in optical fibres (see page 142)

Theory and development of the laser

We will now look at the development and some simple theory behind the operation of the laser.

A radio transmitter can emit a beam of electromagnetic radiation that is far purer than that emitted by a light source – in other words, much more energy is generated with a small spread of frequency.

It would be good to be able to generate electromagnetic waves in the visible region so precisely and this did in fact become possible in the 1960s with the invention of the optical maser or **laser**, the name deriving from **l**ight **a**mplification by the **s**timulated **e**mission of **r**adiation.

Atoms in hot gases are continuously being raised to higher energy states and their electrons then fall back at random, so giving a disorderly outpouring of quanta. This is also true of the electrons in a hot tungsten filament lamp. Conventional light sources are therefore incoherent sources, since we have no control over when an atom is going to lose energy in the form of radiation. The light that comes from a laser, however, is **coherent, parallel, monochromatic** and **in unbroken wave chains.**

We can make a normal light source more coherent by making it smaller, so reducing the number of atoms that may emit quanta, but if we do this the intensity is reduced. The total energy radiated by the Sun is about 7 kW per square centimetre of surface, and although this may sound a large amount it must be remembered that this energy is spread out over a very large range of frequency across the solar spectrum. If we try and filter out a narrow band of light 1 MHz wide in the region of the Sun's greatest intensity (at about 480 nm) then we find that 1 cm^2 of surface will give an output of only 0.000 01 W! So to get 1W we would need to concentrate the light from 10 square metres of solar surface and of course using this large area would completely destroy the coherence of the source.

The width of a standard television channel is about 4 MHz but the visible region of the solar spectrum alone has a width of some 320 million MHz, and could therefore contain about 80 million television channels! Modern transmitters will emit up to 250 kW in the television region, however, in a band less than 1 MHz wide. The search therefore began for powerful coherent light sources.

A high-powered laser in use for hard surfacing a Rolls-Royce engine turbine blade (Rolls-Royce)

The production of laser light

The first attempt was made by generating electromagnetic waves by electronic means, but even with a microwave resonator the shortest wavelength possible was about 1 mm (1 000 000 nm).

Researchers then had the idea of using atoms and molecules at the resonant structures, but unfortunately the power available from just one electron transition is very small and it only occurs intermittently. They therefore had to try and persuade *all* the atoms in a specimen to react *simultaneously* since this would produce a powerful coherent wave. This was made possible using the **maser** principle discovered by Charles Townes at Columbia University in 1954.

The basis of the maser is that of **stimulated emission** and is shown in Figure 34.1. Figure 34.1(*a*) shows an electron in its ground state (E_0); in Figure 34.1(*b*) a photon with just the right energy raises the electron to an excited state E_1, and in Figure 34.1(*c*) another photon reacts with the atom causing the electron to fall back to level E_0. The photon produced adds its energy to that of the stimulating photon.

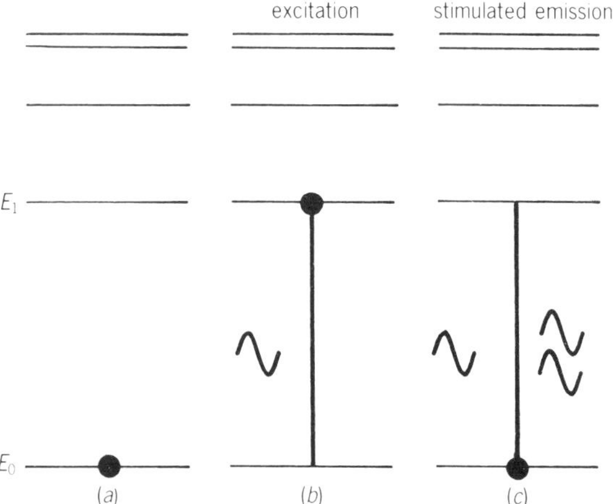

Figure 34.1

If this process goes on through the body of a specimen a beam of radiation will be produced which is perfectly coherent and parallel.

The first successful optical maser (or laser) was constructed by Maiman in 1960 using a small ruby rod; ruby is a form of aluminium oxide in which a few of the aluminium atoms have been replaced by chromium.

Light is absorbed from a flash tube wrapped round the rod and this raises the electrons up to an excited level E_3. They fall back rapidly to the metastable level E_2, after which further light will stimulate laser action back to level E_0 (Figure 34.2(*a*)). The light emitted is red with a wavelength of 693.2 nm.

One end of the rod is silvered and the other end half silvered so that the beam reflects backwards and forwards along the rod, and a pulse of light is emitted from one end.

The original laser used a ruby rod 4 cm long and 0.5 cm in diameter, producing an intense red beam for 0.0005 s. Figure 34.2(*b*) is a diagram of the structure of the laser and Figure 34.2(*c*) illustrates the idea of stimulated emission: one photon moving parallel with the axis of the tube stimulates a second atom to emit a photon, these stimulate further atoms to emit and so on. The result is an intense beam of laser light moving parallel to the axis of the rod.

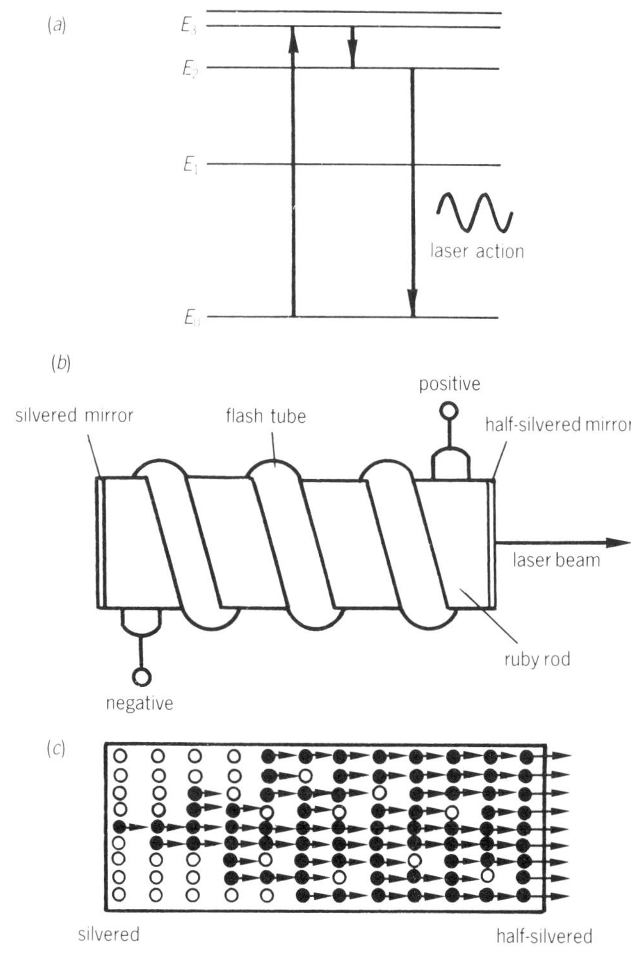

Figure 34.2

The ruby laser gives up to 10 kW in a beam less than 1 cm^2 in cross-sectional area, and with other lasers even greater powers have been produced. The carbon dioxide laser, for instance, will give 1 kJ of energy in 1 ns, producing a power of 10^{12} W, or one million megawatts.

The laser disc

One of the important uses of laser technology is in the development of the laser disc system. The BBC have used this system for a video disc to hold their new version of the Domesday Book, since the amount of information that may be carried on a laser disc is enormous: one video disc can carry as much information as a whole set of the *Encyclopaedia Britannica*.

The laser disc is superficially similar to a record, in that it is a 30 cm diameter disc with a spiral track running round it; there the similarity ends, however.

On the laser disc the track is only about 1 μm wide and is made of a series of tiny pits, each pit some 0.16 μm deep and of varying length (Figure 34.3). These pits are scanned by a fine laser beam only 0.9 μm in diameter. The reflected light from the flat part of the disc is detected by a photodiode and this modulated beam is converted into a television picture. The disc is given a thin metallised coating and the whole thing is protected by a plastic cover through which the laser light can pass.

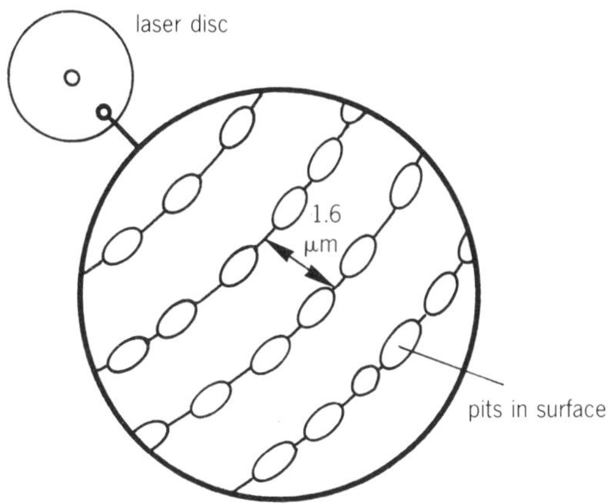

Figure 34.3

With a constant angular velocity (CAV) disc about 54 000 television frames may be carried, with some 28×10^9 bits of information per side!

The hologram

The idea of the hologram was first proposed in 1948 by Dr D Gabor who named it from the Greek word *holos*, meaning whole. A hologram contains the whole of the information of the wave from the object, phase as well as amplitude.

Unlike a normal two-dimensional image formed on a piece of paper by a lens, a hologram provides a true three-dimensional record of the object. The hologram itself is two-dimensional but using a laser a three-dimensional image may be constructed.

The hologram is formed by allowing a reference beam to interfere with the light scattered from the object, using a mirror and photographic plate (Figure 34.4(*a*)).

The image of the object may be reconstructed from the hologram by allowing laser light to fall on it. (Figure 34.4(*b*)). If you move your head and view the image from different positions you will see that it is truly three-dimensional.

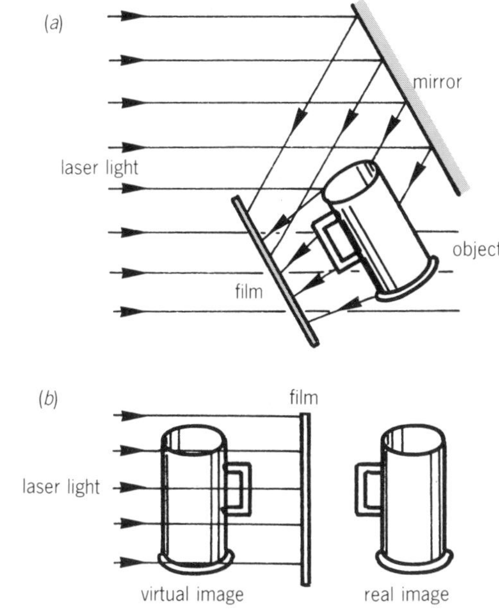

Figure 34.4

If you break a hologram the full image can still be reconstructed from each of the broken pieces, since diffracted beams from any point on the object will reach all parts of the photographic plate.

1 In what ways does laser light differ from the light from a filament lamp?

2 Explain carefully why a laser can be used to give a static interference pattern with a path difference of many metres while this is impossible with a 'normal' light source.

35 · Electromagnetic radiation

Electromagnetic radiation is the name given to a whole range of transverse radiation having differing wavelengths but six common properties, namely:

(*a*) it is propagated by varying electric and magnetic fields oscillating at right angles to each other;
(*b*) it travels with a constant velocity of 299 792 458 m s^{-1} in a vacuum;
(*c*) it is unaffected by electric and magnetic fields;
(*d*) it travels in straight lines in a vacuum;
(*e*) it may be polarised;
(*f*) it can show interference and diffraction.

The oscillating fields are represented by Figure 35.1. For a light beam with an intensity of 100 W m^{-2} the amplitude of the electric vector can be shown to be 200 V m^{-1} and that of the magnetic vector 10^{-6} T.

In optics the electric vector is the more important, partly because of the ability of electric fields to affect *static* charges.

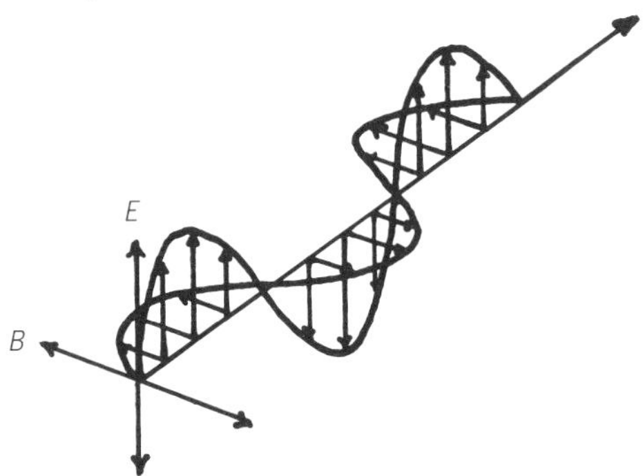

Figure 35.1

Regions of the electromagnetic spectrum

For convenience the electromagnetic spectrum is divided into the following regions:

gamma-rays;
X-rays;
ultraviolet radiation;
visible light;
infrared radiation;
microwaves;
radio waves.

Figure 35.2 shows that many of these regions overlap, the distinction between one region and another lying in the way in which the radiations are produced. The range of wavelength, frequency and energy per quantum are also shown: the scales for both frequency and wavelength are logarithmic. There follows a summary of the production, properties and detection of the different regions of the electromagnetic spectrum.

Gamma-radiation (see also page 437)

This radiation is normally produced by transitions within the excited nucleus of an atom and usually occurs as the result of some previous radioactive emission.

Gamma-radiation can result from fission or fusion reactions or the destruction of a particle–antiparticle pair, such as an electron and a positron (see page 451). It is used in some medical treatment and also for checking flaws in metal castings, and it may be detected by photographic plates or radiation detectors such as the Geiger tube or scintillation counter.

X-radiation (see also page 432)

This occurs due to electron transitions between the upper and lower energy levels of heavy elements, usually excited by electron bombardment or by the rapid deceleration of electrons (known as *bremsstrahlung* or braking radiation). X-rays are primarily used in medicine and dentistry, and may be detected using photographic film.

Ultraviolet radiation

This is produced by fairly large energy changes in the electrons of an atom. It may occur with either heavy or light elements. The Sun produces a large amount of ultraviolet radiation, most of which is absorbed by the ozone layer in the upper atmosphere.

Ultraviolet radiation will cause fluorescence and ionisation, promote chemical reactions, affect photographic film and produce photoelectric emission. It will also give you a sun tan although since radiation of the required wavelength will not pass through glass you will not go brown unless you are exposed to sunlight directly! Like the preceding radiations it can be dangerous in large doses, particularly to the eyes. Its main uses are in spectroscopy and mineral analysis (some minerals exhibit strong fluorescence under ultraviolet radiation).

Visible light

This is due to electron transitions in atoms. It affects a photographic film, stimulates the retina in the eye and causes photosynthesis in plants.

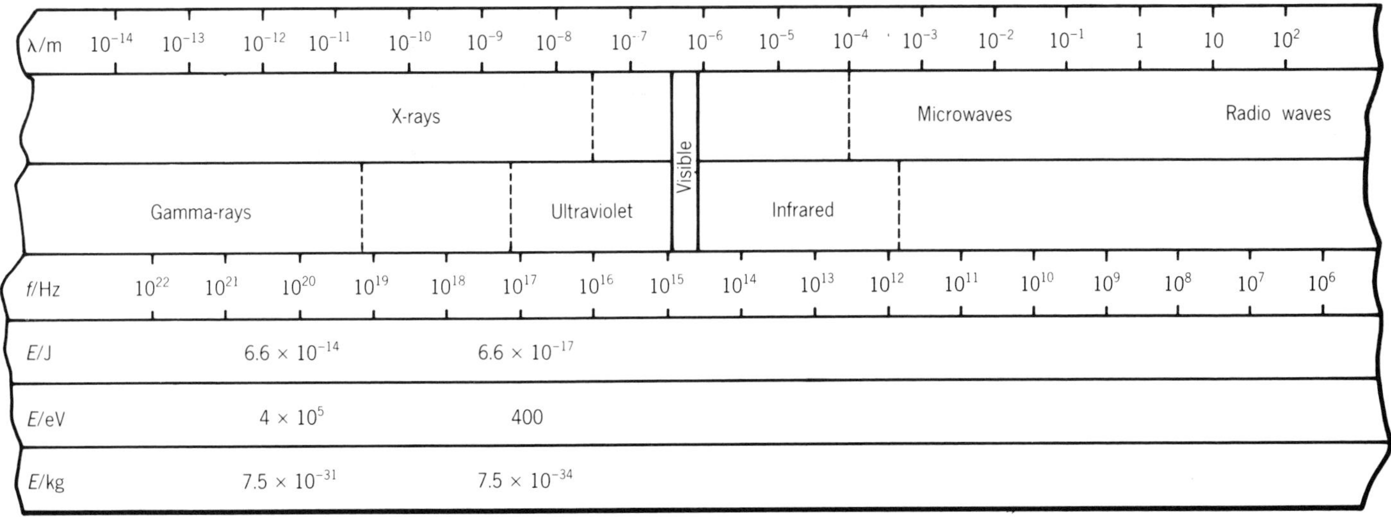

Figure 35.2

Infrared radiation (see also page 268)

This is due to small energy changes of an electron in an atom or to molecular vibrations. It may be detected by a thermopile or special photographic film. Since it is less scattered by fine particles than visible light (because of its longer wavelength) infrared radiation is useful for haze photography. It is also used by earth resource satellites to detect healthy crops; most of us are familiar with its use for heating, both in the home and in hospitals. It may be refracted by rock salt.

> **Student investigation**
>
> It was stated on page 220 that glass is opaque to ultraviolet radiation. How true is this statement? Design and carry out an experiment to test it.
>
> Test the amount of radiation transmitted by various numbers of glass plates by recording the blackening of a photographic negative placed under them. The blackening may be tested after development by measuring the transmitted light from a standard source with a phototransistor or other suitable detector. Plot a graph of glass thickness against the transmitted intensity.
>
> The wavelength of the u.v. lamp that you use will be specified by the manufacturer. If possible you should investigate two different wavelengths if a second lamp is available.
>
> **Ultraviolet light is dangerous. Protect your eyes during this experiment.**

Microwaves

These are produced by valves such as a magnetron or with a maser (see page 217). They are used in radar, telemetry and electron spin resonance studies and in microwave ovens. In a microwave oven the food is heated because it contains water which is a strong absorber of microwaves. The microwaves excite the water molecules, the velocity of the molecules rises and therefore the temperature of the food rises. This explains why the food is heated but the temperature of the containers does not rise very much. Microwave ovens are useful because they reduce cooking time considerably since they cook the food from within.

Microwaves may be detected with crystal detectors or solid-state diodes. The radiation from interstellar hydrogen has a wavelength of 21 cm (0.21 m) and so lies at the edge of the microwave region: the detection and analysis of this radiation has added greatly to our knowledge of the structure of the universe.

Radio waves

These waves have the longest wavelengths of any region of the electromagnetic spectrum and therefore the smallest frequency and hence the lowest energy per quantum. They are produced by electrical oscillations and may be detected by resonant circuits in radio receivers. Their use is of course in radio and television communications.

Information may be transmitted on an electromagnetic wave. Initially we have a wave, say a radio wave, known as the **carrier wave**. The carrier wave is then modulated, either in frequency or amplitude, by the signal (Figure 35.3).

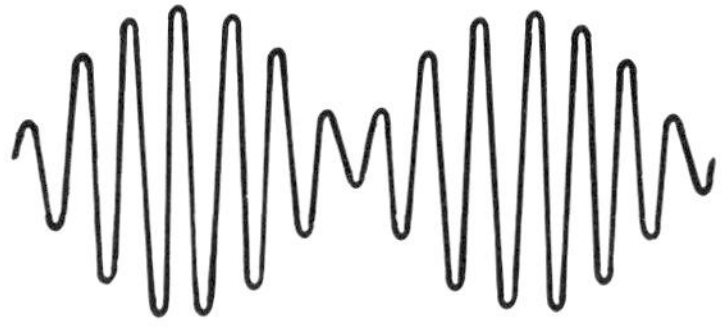

Figure 35.3 (*a*) amplitude modulation

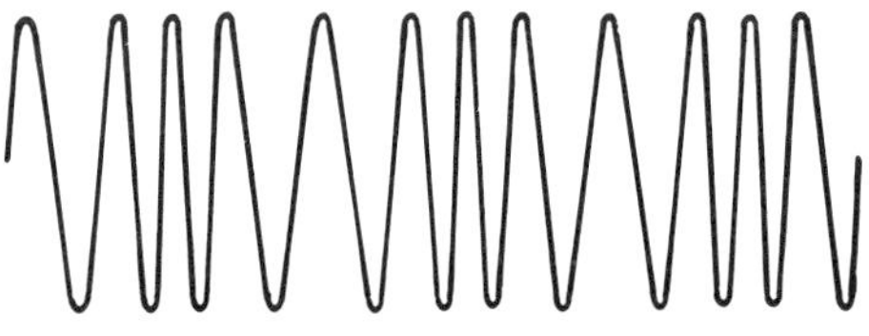

(*b*) frequency modulation

In amplitude modulation amplitude is varied with time while with frequency modulation it is the frequency that is changed.

The velocity of electromagnetic waves in free space (ie a vacuum with no boundaries) is given by the following equation:

$$c = \frac{1}{\sqrt{\epsilon_0 \mu_0}}$$

where ϵ_0 is the permittivity of free space and μ_0 is the permeability of free space. This equation is used to find ϵ_0.

Thermal properties

A 1.2 cm thick steel plate being cut by a 40 kW plasma torch (ECRC)

36 · Heat energy and thermometers

Over the past few centuries scientists have put forward some very strange theories concerning the nature of heat. One of these was that heat was some sort of fluid that you added to a body to make it hot and removed from a body to cool it down! Whatever heat was, the result of its addition or removal was clear – the temperature of the body rose or fell. We must therefore consider the change in temperature of a body to be related to the change in the heat content of that body.

During the last century two men, Rumford and Joule, proposed that heat was related to energy, indeed that heat was itself a form of energy. Davy showed that even cold objects like blocks of ice could be melted if they were rubbed together. In 1843 Joule performed his classic paddle wheel experiment, in which water was heated by friction from a rotating paddle wheel driven by the loss of potential energy from a falling mass. We can summarise their results as:

To heat up a body requires energy. This energy increases the internal energy of the body by increasing the kinetic energy of its molecules and so the temperature of the body rises.

Temperature scales

The **temperature** of a body is a property of the body that determines how hot or cold the body is. It depends on the amount of heat energy absorbed by the body and also the nature of the body and its mass. Temperature is measured with a thermometer but before we can take any readings we have to set up a temperature scale.

The **thermodynamic scale** is the one that is used for scientific measurement. It is measured in units called **kelvins** (K), the temperature itself being given the letter *T*. It is defined using one fixed point – the **triple point** of water (see page 259). This is the temperature where saturated water vapour, pure water and ice are all in equilibrium at a temperature of 273.16 K.

The **Celsius scale** is now defined by $\theta = T - 273.15$. The two fixed points on this scale are the ice point (0 °C) and the steam point (100 °C). The ice point and the triple point differ by 0.01 K.

A temperature scale depends on the particular property on which it is based. In setting up a scale of temperature we must:

(*a*) choose a property that varies with temperature,

(*b*) assume that it varies uniformly with temperature.

If we denote the property by *F*, then on the Celsius scale:

$$\frac{\theta}{100} = \frac{F_\theta - F_0}{F_{100} - F_0}$$

where θ is the temperature to be measured, and F_0 its value at 0 °C, F_θ its value at θ °C and F_{100} its value at 100 °C.

Standard temperature and pressure (STP). This set of conditions which is usually applied to gases is defined as a temperature of 273 K and a pressure of 760 mm of mercury (1.013×10^5 Pa). At STP 1 mole of any gas has a volume of 22.4×10^{-3} m^3.

Types of thermometer

The following properties or instruments have all been used to measure temperatures and are thus the basis of thermometers.

liquid in glass	vapour pressure	optical pyrometer
gas	strain	transistor
platinum resistance	bimetallic strip	thermistor
thermocouple	liquid pressure	

1 Suggest appropriate ways of measuring the following temperatures. Give examples of the difficulties that might be experienced in each measurement.

(*a*) The temperature of the human body.

(*b*) The temperature of the surface of the Sun.

(*c*) The temperature of liquid helium.

(*d*) The temperature of the exhaust gases in a jet engine.

(*e*) The temperature of the plasma in a fusion reactor.

(*f*) The melting point of gold.

(*g*) The change in temperature as water is slowly added to anhydrous copper sulphate.

Liquid-in-glass thermometer

This type of thermometer is probably the most widely used and consists of a liquid in a thin-walled glass bulb to which is fixed a thin capillary tube (Figure 36.1). The property that varies with temperature is the volume of the liquid, which is measured by reading the length of the liquid thread, assuming the bore of the capillary tube to be uniform.

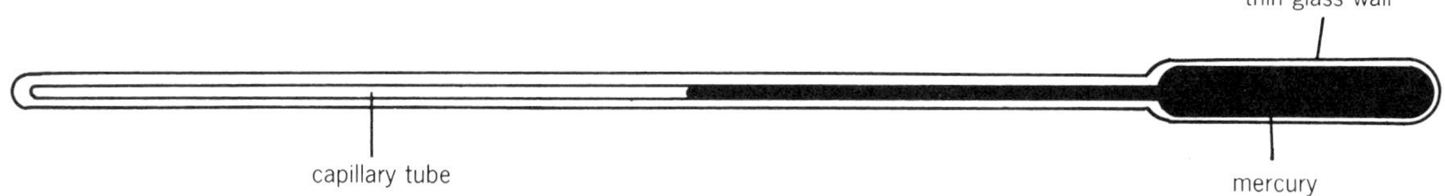

Figure 36.1

The ranges of the most common liquid-in-glass thermometers are as follows:

Mercury-in-glass	−39 °C to +357 °C
Pressurised mercury-in-glass	−39 °C to +500 °C
Pressurised mercury-in-quartz	−39 °C to +800 °C
Alcohol-in-glass	−120 °C to +60 °C
Pentane-in-glass	−200 °C to +30 °C

(Mercury boils at 365.58 °C and freezes at −39 °C (normal pressure).)

The mercury-in-glass thermometer has the advantages that it is direct-reading and that mercury is opaque, does not wet glass, is easily purified and does not distil at low temperatures. The relative expansion of mercury, though uniform, is fairly small, however, and the movement of the liquid thread is sometimes jerky. This thermometer is subject to various errors, of which the largest is due to the expansion of the glass bulb with rising temperature, which may be up to 10 per cent of the mercury expansion, while with falling temperatures the glass contracts relatively slowly. There is also a small long-period expansion of the glass, known as the secular change (around 0.01 °C per year). Further errors may arise if the bore of the capillary tube is not uniform, in marking the fixed points and from internal and external pressure on the bulb. Finally, a correction for the exposed mercury column may be required: this is equal to $0.000\,16n\,(t - t_m)$, where n is the number of exposed Celsius degrees, t is the indicated temperature and t_m is the mean temperature of the stem. The error may be as much as 10 °C at 400 °C.

The thermocouple

If two dissimilar metals are joined together and the junctions between them maintained at different temperatures, then an e.m.f. will be generated across the junctions. This e.m.f. is proportional to the temperature difference as long as this is not too large. A measurement of this e.m.f., normally with a potentiometer, will therefore give us a measure of the temperature difference (see page 291).

Joining an intermediate metal into the circuit will not affect this e.m.f., providing that the points where it is joined are at the same temperature.

These thermometers have the advantage of a very low thermal capacity, they are small and they can be made direct-reading. They can therefore be used to measure varying temperatures and they will detect changes in temperature of about 0.001 °C.

The ranges of various pairs of wires and the e.m.f. generated for a temperature difference of 100 °C are given below.

Copper/constantan	0 °to + 300 °C	4.00 mV
Platinum/platinum + rhodium	0 ° to + 1600 °C	0.65 mV
Iron/constantan	0 ° to + 1090 °C	5.30 mV

Gas thermometers

There are two main types of gas thermometer, one operating at constant volume and the other at constant pressure. The constant-volume gas thermometer is by far the more widely used and so we will deal with it alone.

The ideal gas equation states that for n moles of a gas:

$$PV = nRT$$

and therefore for a gas at constant volume V the absolute temperature T is directly proportional to the pressure of the gas P.

A simple form of constant-volume gas thermometer is shown in Figure 36.2. The gas is enclosed in the bulb B and the pressure recorded by the difference in levels (h) of the mercury columns. The mercury level at R is always adjusted so that it coincides with the mark. The pressure of the gas within the bulb is then given by $P = A + h$, where A is the atmospheric pressure.

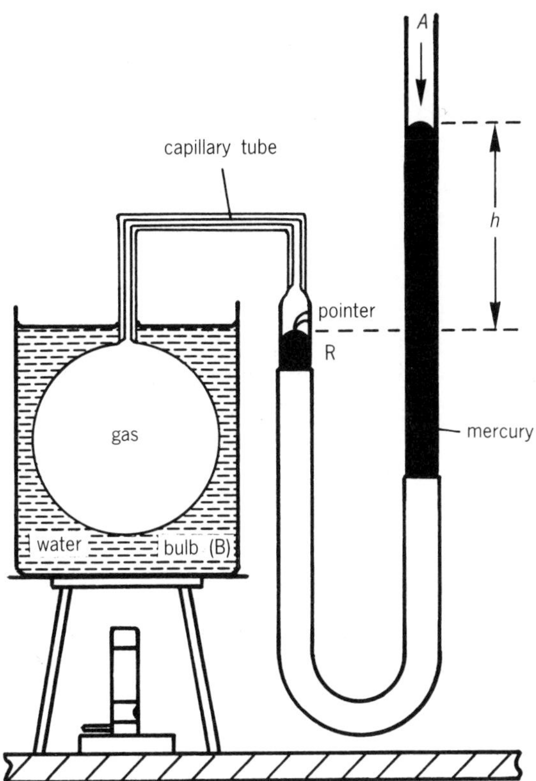

Figure 36.2

If the atmospheric pressure varies during the experiment allowance must be made for this, since it is the *total* gas pressure that is measured.

The gas in the bulb can be air, hydrogen, helium or nitrogen, although it is the constant-volume hydrogen gas thermometer that is taken as standard.

The simple form of constant-volume gas thermometer is subject to errors due to changes in volume of the glass and of the mercury (due to temperature variations), to pressure on the bulb and to the exposed column 'dead space', that is, the volume of gas that is outside the region of which the temperature is being measured. It has the further disadvantages that it is not direct-reading, and that it cannot be used to measure varying temperatures, because gases are such poor conductors of heat.

A more accurate form of constant-volume thermometer has been designed where some of these errors are reduced, the dead space is made as small as possible and the bulb containing the gas is large (1.6 litres).

By using different gas thermometers a wide range of temperatures can be measured:

Hydrogen	−200 °C to +500°C
Nitrogen	+500 °C to +1500 °C
Helium	−270 °C to +1500 °C

These thermometers can be very accurate, to within 0.005 °C from 0 °C to 100 °C, 0.1 °C around 500 °C and to within 2 °C at 1500 °C.

The platinum resistance thermometer

This type of thermometer, devised by Callendar in 1877, uses the change in the resistance of a platinum wire with temperature to measure the change in temperature (see page 288). The equation for such a change is:

$$R_\theta = R_0(1 + \alpha\theta + \beta\theta^2)$$

where θ is the temperature change and α and β are constants, β being much smaller than α. We therefore ignore the term $\beta\theta^2$ and assume that the resistance of the wire varies uniformly with temperature: α is the temperature coefficient of resistance of the material, being 3.8×10^{-4} °C^{-1} for platinum.

A simple form of the platinum resistance thermometer is shown in Figure 36.3. It consists of a platinum wire wound non-inductively on a mica former and held in a glass tube by silica spacers. The resistance of the wire is measured with a Wheatstone bridge network and to allow for the change in resistance of the leads a set of dummy leads are included in the opposite arm of the bridge (see Figure 36.4).

This type of thermometer has a large range, from −200 °C to +1100 °C and this can be extended by the use of different wires. Bronze has a range starting at −260 °C and using carbon temperatures as low as −270 °C can be measured.

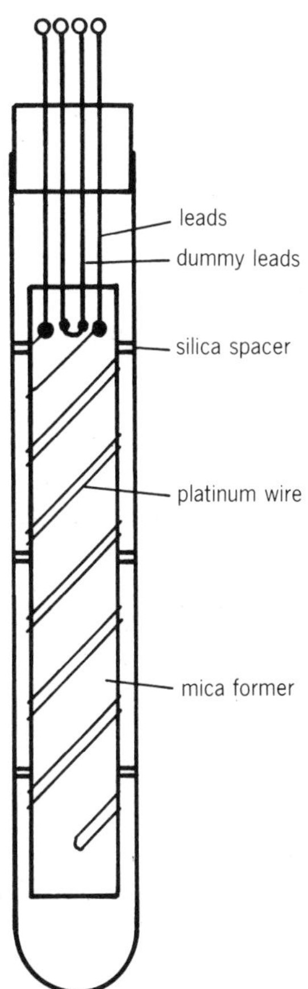

Figure 36.3

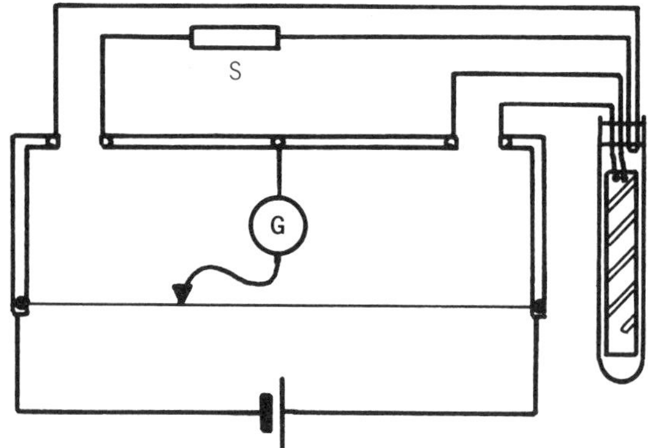

Figure 36.4

The advantages of the resistance thermometer are its convenient size, wide range and high sensitivity (0.000 05 °C). It can only be used for steady readings, however, and is not direct-reading.

The accuracy obviously depends on how accurately the bridge can be balanced.

Secondary fixed points

The following temperatures are used as practical fixed points in different temperature ranges:

Equilibrium between gaseous and liquid oxygen	−182.97 °C
Equilibrium between liquid sulphur and its vapour	444.60 °C
Freezing point of silver	960.5 °C
Freezing point of gold	1063 °C

Student investigation

Devise experiments to measure the following temperatures:

(*a*) the temperature at which paper burns,

(*b*) the temperature of the base of a domestic electric iron for various settings.

The quest for absolute zero

One method used to reach very low temperatures – within 0.01 °C of absolute zero – is that of adiabatic demagnetisation. A paramagnetic crystal of potassium chromium alum is held by an insulating support in a flask of helium gas surrounded by liquid helium at a temperature of about 1 K, the whole being in a vacuum flask (Figure 36.5). A large magnetic field is placed across the specimen and the heat generated by the magnetisation is conducted away through the gas. The flask is then evacuated. Finally the field is removed, the specimen becomes demagnetised and therefore cools, the energy to give the random alignment of the molecular magnets coming from the internal kinetic energy of the specimen.

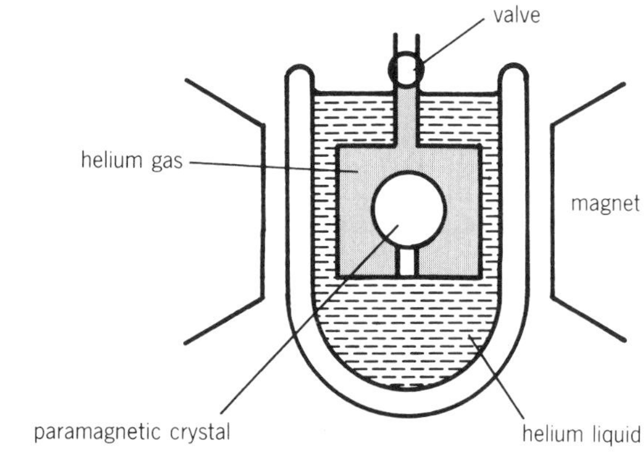

Figure 36.5

At very low temperatures such as these strange things happen. The viscosity of these liquids drops to virtually zero (**superfluidity**). This enables some of these liquids to flow uphill! The resistance of a metal wire also falls to zero (**superconductivity**) and in these conditions currents may flow in conductors forever with no energy input! (See also page 289.)

The internal structure of He^3 –He^4 dilution refrigerator, the lower vessel can reach temperatures as low as 10 mK (University of Birmingham Physics Department)

37 · The expansion of solids and liquids

When a substance is heated the molecules within it gain energy. The potential energy of two adjacent molecules is shown on page 98, and you will notice that as energy is gained the separation of the molecules increases. The material therefore expands on heating.

This expansion must be allowed for in the construction of buildings and bridges where large steel girders are used and where very great stresses develop.

It has been found experimentally that the change in dimension depends on:

the original dimension of the specimen,
the change in temperature, and
the material of which the specimen is made.

For a change in length this can be expressed as:

change in length = α × original length × temperature change

where α is the **linear expansivity** of the material, defined as the fractional change in length for a unit rise in temperature, or

$$\alpha = \frac{l - l_0}{l_0\theta}$$

where l_0 is the original length, l the final length and θ the change in temperature. The units for α are K^{-1} or $°C^{-1}$.

The linear expansivities for a number of solid materials are given in the following table:

Material	*Linear expansivity* ($\times 10^{-6}/K^{-1}$)
Aluminium	23
Brick	9
Copper	17
Diamond	very nearly zero
Invar	0.9
Iron	12
Quartz	0.4
Rubber	220
Zinc	31

Example

Calculate the increase in length of a 20 m steel girder in a building when the temperature changes from 0 °C to 30 °C.

$$\text{Change in length} = l_0 \alpha (\theta_2 - \theta_1) = 20 \times 1.2 \times 10^{-5} \times 30 = 7.2 \text{ mm}$$

Student investigation

Suspend a metre length of resistance wire between two supports and hang a weight from the centre as shown in Figure 37.1. Record the position of the weight and then pass a current through the wire so that the wire heats up and expands. Record the new position of the weight and hence find the extension of the wire. Measure the current and the p.d. between the ends of the wire. Using the known value of the expansivity of the material of the wire, estimate the mean temperature of the wire.

Repeat for various power inputs and plot a graph of temperature against power.

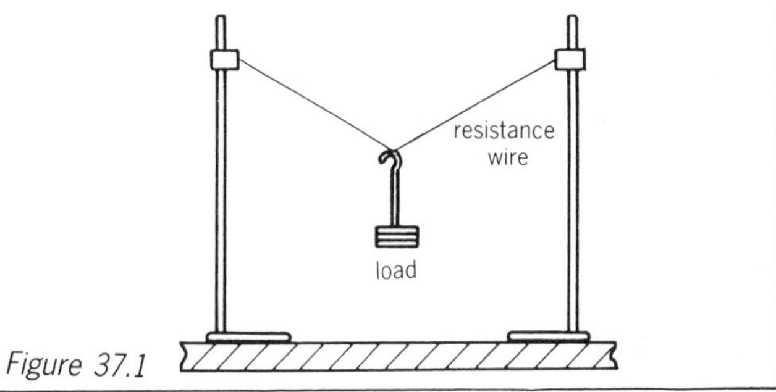

Figure 37.1

Other expansivities

It can be shown that the **superficial** (or **area**) **expansivity** is about twice that of the linear expansivity and that the **cubical** (or **volume**) **expansivity** is roughly three times the linear expansivity.

Applications and effects of solid expansion

The effects of solid expansion are used in the bimetallic thermostat and the hot-wire ammeter, and must be allowed for in the design of a parallel-plate condenser, the compensated pendulum and telephone wires. Special low-expansion glass is used in precision optical devices such as telescope mirrors.

Expansion of liquids

When considering the increase in the volume of a liquid with temperature we must use its cubical expansivity. Allowance should also be made for the expansion of the container, although this may be ignored except in accurate work, since the expansivities of liquids are usually greater than those of solids – for example, the expansivity of ethanol is some 100 times that of iron!

The strange behaviour of water around 4 °C is covered in most GCSE textbooks.

38 · Heat capacity and specific heat capacity

The amount of heat needed to change the temperature of a body depends on

(*a*) the material of the body,
(*b*) the mass of the body, and
(*c*) the change in temperature (positive or negative).

For a given body we can define a quantity known as the **thermal capacity** as the heat energy needed to raise its temperature by 1 K. A rather more useful quantity is the **specific heat capacity** of a material defined as follows:

The specific heat capacity of a material is the heat energy needed to raise the temperature of 1 kg of the material by 1 K.

The units of thermal capacity are joules per kelvin (J K^{-1}) and those of specific heat capacity joules per kilogram kelvin (J kg^{-1} K^{-1}). Therefore:

heat energy = mass × specific heat capacity × temperature change

The values of some specific heat capacities are given in the following table.

Substance	*Specific heat capacity* /J kg^{-1} K^{-1}	*Substance*	*Specific heat capacity* /J kg^{-1} K^{-1}
Water	4200	Copper	385
Ethanol	2500	Lead	126
Paraffin oil	2130	Aluminium	913
Turpentine	1760	Sodium	1240
Hydrogen	14 300	Iron	106
Air	993	Steel	420
Helium	5240	Concrete	3350
Oxygen	913	Polypropylene	2100
Granite	820	Marble	900
Beryllium	1970		

It is interesting to note the large specific heat capacity of water compared with other liquids, which makes it useful as a coolant. Sodium too has a high specific heat capacity and is used in liquid form as a coolant in some nuclear reactors (see page 456).

The specific heat capacity of air is also deceptive; it actually requires quite a large amount of energy to raise the temperature of a kilogram of air. Remember, however, that at normal atmospheric pressure this mass of air has a volume of about 1 m^3.

Example

A block of metal of mass 0.5 kg initially at a temperature of 100 °C is gently lowered into an insulated copper container of mass 0.05 kg containing 0.9 kg of water at 20 °C. If the final temperature of the mixture is 25 °C, calculate the specific heat capacity *c* of the metal of the block. (Assume no loss of heat and that no water is vaporised.)

Heat lost by block = 0.5 × c × (100 − 25) = 37.5c.
Heat gained by water and container = (0.9 × 4200 × 5) + (0.05 × 385 × 5) = 18 996 J.
Therefore 37.5c = 18 996

$$c = \frac{18\,996}{37.5} = 506.6 \text{ J kg}^{-1}\text{ K}^{-1}$$

1 When a block of metal of mass 0.11 kg and specific heat capacity 400 J kg^{-1} K^{-1} is heated to 100 °C and quickly transferred to a calorimeter containing 0.20 kg of a liquid at 10 °C the resulting temperature is 18 °C. On repeating the experiment with 0.40 kg of liquid in the same container and at the same initial temperature of 10 °C the resulting temperature is 14.5 °C. Calculate
(*a*) the specific heat capacity of the liquid
(*b*) the thermal capacity of the container.

2 (*a*) When a hot body warms a cool one, are their temperature changes equal in magnitude? Explain your answer, with examples.
(*b*) Explain why the sea tends to moderate the temperature changes of nearby land masses.
(*c*) Can heat be added to a substance without causing its temperature to rise? Explain your answer.

3 Estimate the rise in temperature of the brake discs in a car of mass 1200 kg travelling at 30 m s^{-1} which is brought to rest by the application of the brakes alone. The brake discs have a total mass of 5 kg. Assume that there is no heat loss and that the material of the four brake discs has a specific heat capacity of 800 J kg^{-1} K^{-1}.

All specific heat capacities have been found to vary with temperature: the variation for three solids is shown in Figure 38.1. The exact reasons for this variation are complex and outside the scope of this book.

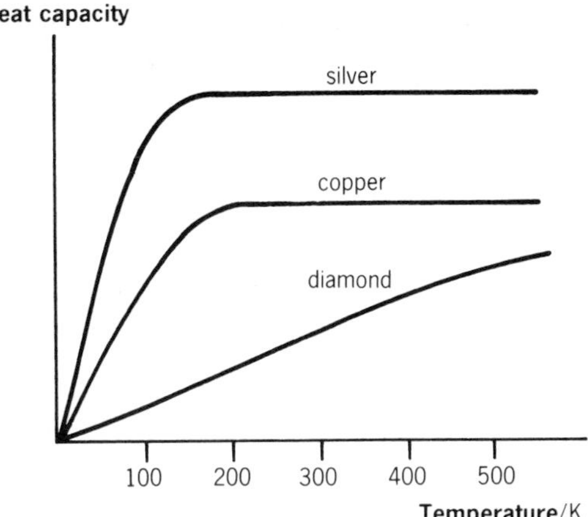

Figure 38.1

Molar heat capacities

If the molar heat capacities (the heat required to raise the temperature of one mole of a substance by 1 K) of metals are considered, then it is found that they are all approximately the same and equal to about 25 J mol^{-1} K^{-1}, a fact first noticed by Dulong and Petit in 1819.

It follows that the heat required to raise the temperature of a sample of metal depends on *how many* particles the sample contains, and not on the mass of an individual molecule. The specific heat capacity is therefore directly related to the molecular structure of the material.

Student investigation

At some time you will have sat down to what you hoped would be a hot meal only to find that parts of it have gone cold. You will also have met with the scalding pudding that you have to sit and look at while it cools off before you can attempt to eat any of it, and the jam sponge where the jam is so much hotter than the sponge.

Using a thermocouple or small probe digital thermometer, investigate the cooling of different foods. Also find out just how hot food has to be before it becomes difficult to eat, and how cold it must be before it is unpleasant.

Be careful not to burn yourself.

How does the surface area and texture of the food affect the cooling?

If possible, investigate the rate of rise of temperature during the thawing of some frozen food such as a loaf of bread taken from a freezer.

If the food is to be eaten at any point in the experiment make sure that all the apparatus with which it may come into contact is cleaned carefully before starting the experiment.

The cooling of a body

Before considering methods by which the specific heat capacity of a material may be found we must think about what happens in any experiment where heat is added to a body. The body will gain energy but it will also lose energy to the surroundings. The law governing the rate of loss of heat from a body to its surroundings was first proposed by Newton in 1701 and is therefore known as **Newton's law of cooling.** He proposed that:

> The rate of loss of heat of a body by cooling in a steady stream of air is proportional to the excess temperature $(\theta - \theta_s)$ of the body above its surroundings.

This can be expressed mathematically as:

$$\frac{-\mathrm{d}H}{\mathrm{d}t} = k(\theta - \theta_s)$$

and if C is the thermal capacity of the body

$$\frac{-C\,\mathrm{d}\theta}{\mathrm{d}t} = k(\theta - \theta_s)$$

This has been found to hold very well for forced convection, where the air velocity is >4 m s^{-1}, but not too well in still air, that is, for natural convection.

For natural convection the law has been shown experimentally to be a 5/4 power law. That is:

$$\frac{-\mathrm{d}H}{\mathrm{d}t} = k(\theta - \theta_s)^{5/4}$$

The following set of results may be used to investigate the law of natural convection.

Excess temperature/°C	20	30	40	50	60	70
Rate of loss of heat	0.212	0.350	0.501	0.660	0.830	1.01

If a graph is plotted of log(excess temperature) against log(rate of heat loss) the validity of the law can be checked.

Heat losses can be useful, in fact essential in some cases. Engines are cooled with water or air, integrated circuits that work at relatively high power are set in a piece of blackened aluminium and the Earth itself must be able to lose heat to space, otherwise the so-called 'greenhouse effect' would occur.

The cooling correction

If we add heat to a perfectly insulated body at a steady rate then a graph of the temperature of the body against time will be a straight line (Figure 38.2(*a*)). However, if we now take into account the loss of heat a graph similar to Figure 38.2(*b*) will be obtained.

Clearly the final temperature in Figure 38.2(*b*) needs to be corrected for this loss of heat.

The simplest way to do this is to cool the object to a few degrees below room temperature before heating begins. The object therefore *gains* heat from the surroundings in the first part of the heating process and loses it in the second (see Figure 38.2(*c*)).

Figure 38.2(*b*) also shows the cooling of the body after the supply of energy has been switched off at t_0. To enable us to correct the rise of temperature for heat loss we will assume forced convection and that Newton's law of cooling holds. It can be shown that

$$\Delta\theta = \frac{\phi S_1}{S_2}$$

where $\Delta\theta$ is the cooling correction, and hence the true final temperature due to heating can be calculated.

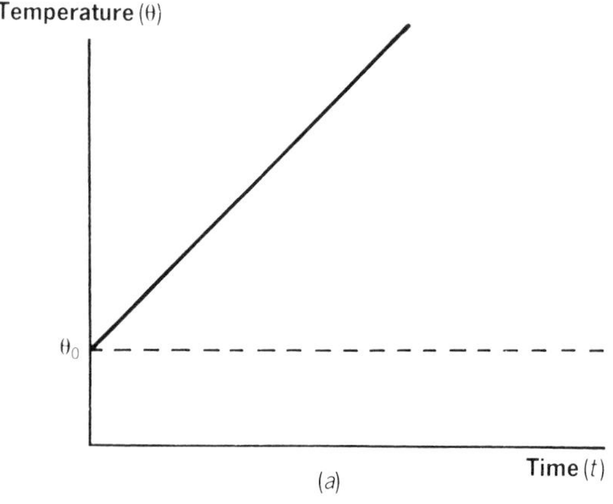

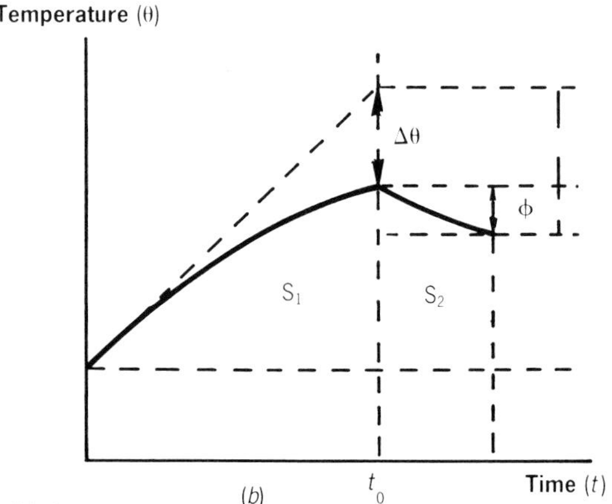

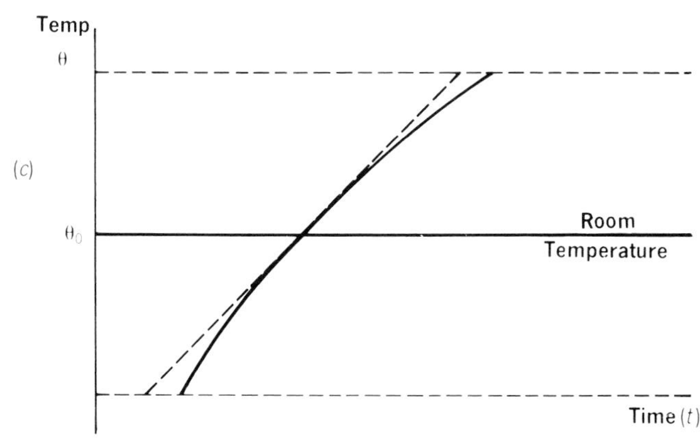

Figure 38.2

4 It is decided to replace the 1 kW fire that is used to heat a room during the day by a cubical block of concrete that is heated overnight and then allowed to release its heat energy during the day.

Calculate the length of the sides of the concrete block if the heat it gives out in cooling from 70 °C to 30 °C is the same as that given out by the electric fire in 8 hours. (Density of concrete = 2700 kg m^{-3}; specific heat capacity of concrete = 850 J kg^{-1} K^{-1}.)

5 If there was no friction in the bearings a motor would raise a certain lift of mass 1500 kg at 8.5 m s^{-1}, but this is reduced to 7.0 m s^{-1} by friction. How much oil, initially at 20 °C, is needed to keep the temperature of the bearings down to 70 °C? (Specific heat capacity of oil = 2100 J kg^{-1} K^{-1}; g = 10 m s^{-2})

6 An artificial satellite made entirely of aluminium orbits the Earth at a constant velocity of 9000 m s^{-1}.

(*a*) Calculate the ratio of its kinetic energy to the energy required to raise its temperature by 600 °C.

(*b*) Discuss the bearing of your answer on the problem of re-entry of such a satellite into the Earth's atmosphere.

(Specific heat capacity of aluminium = 913 J kg^{-1} K^{-1};
melting point of aluminium = 660 °C.) [z]

7 You have run a bath but the water is much too hot to get into. You also have a bucket full of cold water. If you want to be able to get into the bath as soon as possible, should you add the cold water straight away or wait for the hot water to cool down a little before adding the cold water? Explain your answer.

Measurement of specific heat capacities

There are several simple methods for measuring the specific heat capacities of both solids and liquids, such as the method of mixtures, but we will consider here only electrical methods. (You will find a consideration of the method of mixtures in the example earlier in this chapter, (on page 230.) Since the specific heat capacity varies with temperature, we have seen it is important to record the mean temperature at which the measurement is made.

Electrical calorimeters

Figure 38.3(*a*) and (*b*) show possible arrangements for electrical calorimeters for a solid and a liquid specimen.

The material under investigation is heated by an electrical heater and the input energy (E) and the rise in temperature that this produces are measured. If the mass of the specimen (solid or liquid) is m and its specific heat capacity c, then:

$$E = mc(\theta_1 - \theta_0) + h$$

where θ_0 and θ_1 are the initial and final temperatures of the specimen and h is the heat loss. Using the cooling correction, the value of h may be found. This simple method can be used for liquids or solids, although in the case of a liquid allowance has to be made for the thermal capacity of the container, and the liquid should also be stirred to allow even distribution of the heat energy throughout its volume. This is necessary since liquids are such poor conductors (see page 262).

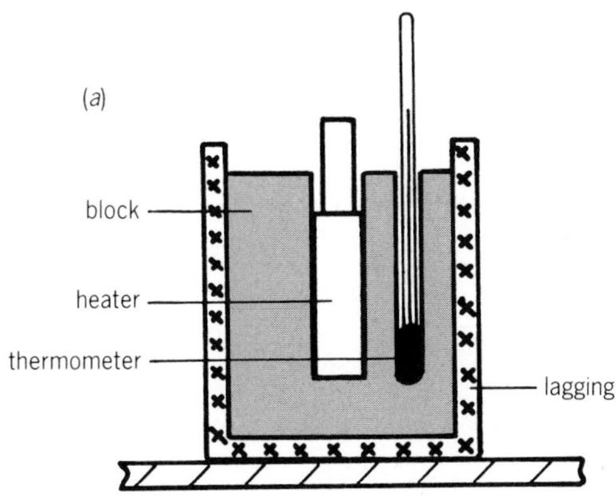

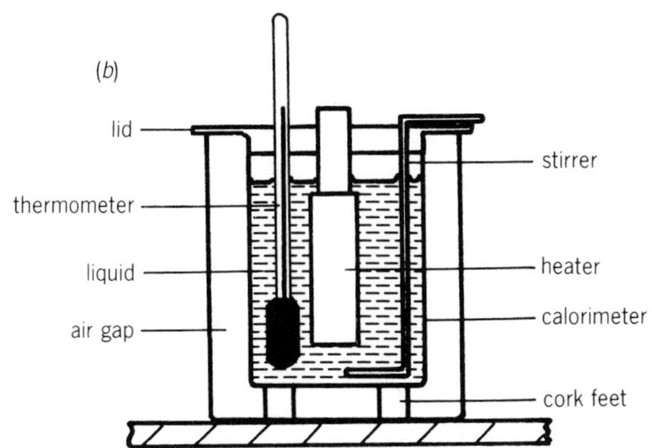

Figure 38.3

The Nernst calorimeter

This apparatus was first used by Nernst and Lindemann in 1913; Figure 38.4 shows a simplified version. The solid C in the form of a cylinder has a plug P of the same material inserted in it with the heating coil wrapped round it. The plug and the cylinder are insulated from each other by paraffin waxed paper but good *thermal* contact between the plug and cylinder is ensured by making the plug thicker at the top. The whole arrangement is suspended in a vacuum jacket. Energy is now applied to the heater and the temperature rise is recorded using the heater coil as a resistance thermometer. The vacuum jacket is surrounded by a constant-temperature bath, kept at the temperature at which the measurement of the specific heat capacity is required. The vacuum jacket and the constant-temperature bath virtually eliminate heat losses.

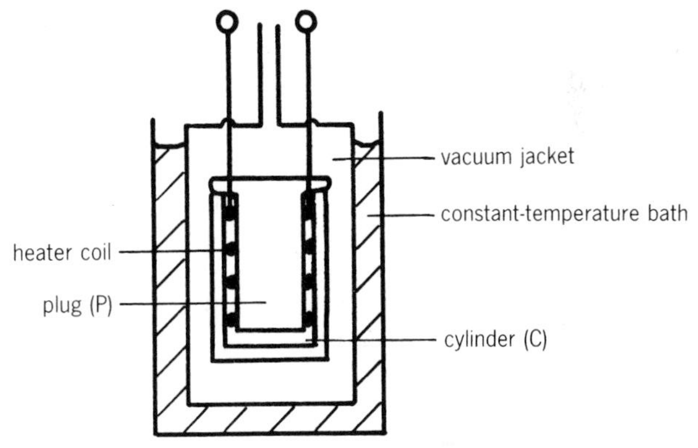

Figure 38.4

The continuous-flow calorimeter

This was first developed by Callender and Barnes in 1902 for the measurement of the specific heat capacity of a liquid, and is shown in Figure 38.5. Its main advantage is that the thermal capacity of the apparatus itself need not be known.

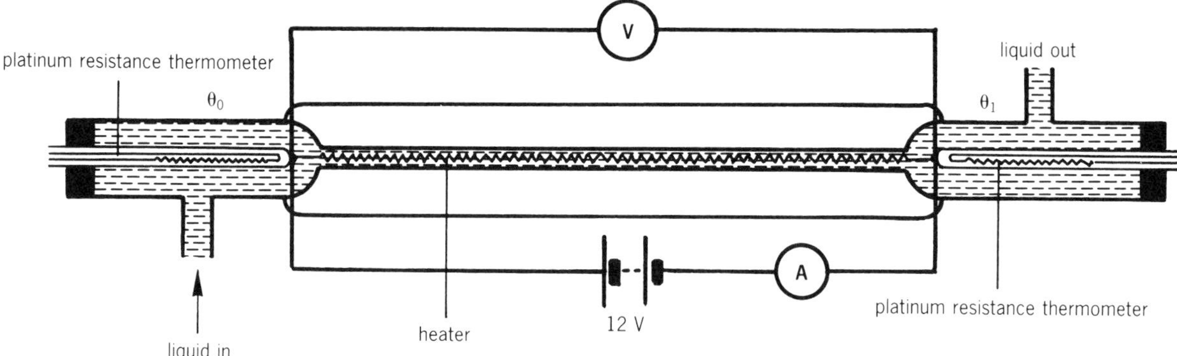

Figure 38.5

Liquid flows in from a constant-head apparatus at a constant rate past a thermometer (θ_0). It then flows around the heater coil and out past a second thermometer where the outlet temperature (θ_1) may be measured. When steady-state conditions have been reached (a temperature difference between inlet and outlet points of 5 °C is reasonable) the temperatures and the flow rate of the liquid are measured. A vacuum jacket round the heater coil reduces heat losses.

The electrical energy supplied to the heater coil ($E = VIt$) may be found directly with a joulemeter or with an ammeter and voltmeter.

For a first experiment we have:

$$E_1 = V_1I_1t_1 = m_1c(\theta_1 - \theta_0) + H$$

where c is the specific heat capacity of the liquid and H is the heat loss to the surroundings and to the apparatus.

The flow rate and rate of energy input are now altered to give a second set of results. However, if the inlet and outlet temperatures are the same as in the first experiment the heat loss will also be the same. Therefore:

$$E_2 = V_2I_2t_2 = m_2c(\theta_1 - \theta_0) + H$$

Eliminating H gives

$$c = \frac{E_2 - E_1}{(m_2 - m_1)(\theta_1 - \theta_0)}$$

A modified form of this apparatus (the Cleapse calorimeter) eliminates heat losses, and a similar type is used to measure the specific heat capacities of gases (see page 242).

8 Compare and contrast the following three methods for determining the specific heat capacity of water, suggesting advantages and disadvantages of each:
   (*a*) the electrical calorimeter;
   (*b*) the method of mixtures;
   (*c*) the continuous-flow calorimeter.

9 A student uses the continuous-flow calorimeter to determine the specific heat capacity of water. The first experiment was performed with a flow rate of 40 g per minute and a power unit of 30 W. The steady-state readings on the two thermometers were 18.5 °C for the input water temperature and 26.5 °C for the outlet water temperature.

The flow rate was adjusted to 20 g per minute and a power input of 18.25 W was found to give the same temperature difference as before.

Use the results to calculate the specific heat capacity of water.

10 In a determination of the specific heat capacity of water using the continuous flow method the following readings were taken:

First experiment
E.m.f. = 3.05 V. Current = 6.55 A. 0.431 kg of water pass through the apparatus in 20 minutes giving a rise of temperature of 11.5 °C.
Second experiment
E.m.f. = 3.15 V. Current = 7.54 A. 0.524 kg of water pass through in 20 minutes and give the same temperature rise as before.

Use these values to calculate the specific heat capacity of water.

Change of state and latent heat

When a substance changes from one state to another energy is either absorbed or liberated. This heat energy is called the **latent heat**, and part of it is the energy used to overcome the forces of attraction between the molecules (see page 98).

It is clearly useful to know the energy required to change the state of unit mass of the substance. This is known as the specific latent heat and is defined as follows:

> The **specific latent heat** is the energy required to change the state of 1 kg of the substance

Any material has two specific latent heats:

> The **specific latent heat of fusion** is the heat energy needed to change 1 kg of the material in its solid state at its melting point to 1 kg of the material in its liquid state, and that released when 1 kg of the liquid changes to 1 kg of solid

> The **specific latent heat of vaporisation** of a liquid is the heat energy needed to change 1 kg of the material in its liquid state at its boiling point to 1 kg of the material in its gaseous state, and that released when 1 kg of vapour changes to 1 kg of liquid

It is important to realise that no temperature change occurs *during* the change of state. The temperature will only rise or fall when *all* the specimen has changed from one state to the other. Figure 38.6 shows how the temperature of a specimen might alter with time due to a steady heat input – heat losses to the exterior have been ignored here. Figure 38.7 shows the molecular arrangements suggested by the graph.

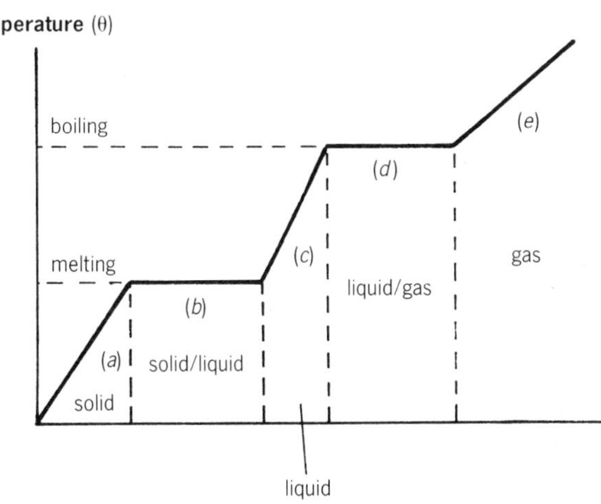

Figure 38.6

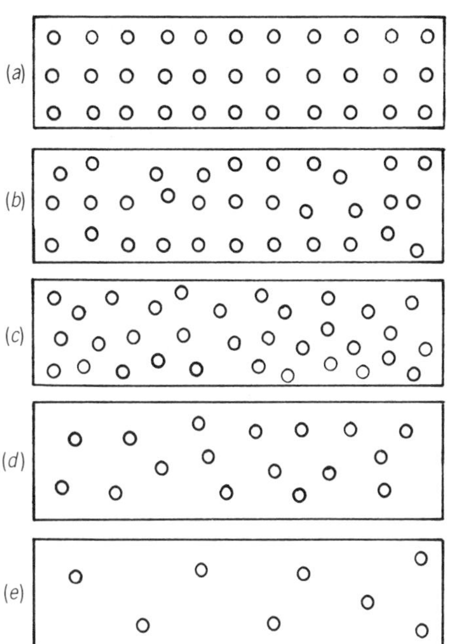

Figure 38.7

If a volatile liquid is allowed to evaporate from the surface of an object then its latent heat of vaporisation may be used to cool the object: the heat energy needed to evaporate the liquid is drawn from the object itself and so its temperature falls.

Some examples of specific latent heats are given in the following tables:

	Specific latent heats of fusion/J kg^{-1}
Aluminium	390 000
Water	330 000
Iron	270 000
Copper	210 000
Naphthalene	150 000
Solder	70 000
Lead	2 600
Mercury	1 300

	Specific latent heats of vaporisation/J kg^{-1}
Turpentine	270 000
Ether	350 000
Benzene	400 000
Ethanol	850 000
Water	2 260 000

Generally the specific latent heats of vaporisation are greater than the specific latent heats of fusion. The change of state from a liquid to a gas results in a large increase of volume and therefore a large amount of work has to be done against the surrounding atmosphere.

Thus in general energy is needed to

(*a*) change the state of the material at a constant temperature (and pressure), and

(*b*) to do external work if there is a change of volume during the change of state.

This external work is usually positive, although there are exceptions. Ice contracts when it melts, the volume of a sample of water being a minimum at 4 °C, and therefore the external work done on melting is negative.

Example

A double-walled flask containing water is heated with a 16 W heater and it is found that it takes 30 minutes for the temperature to rise from 20 °C to 100 °C.

(*a*) Estimate an upper limit for the value of the specific heat capacity of the inner flask and its contents.

(*b*) Calculate the mass of water that would be vaporised after 30 minutes of steady heating when the power is supplied at a rate of 60 W. Take the specific latent heat of vaporisation of water to be 2.26×10^6 J kg^{-1}.

Initial energy input = 16 × 30 × 60 = 28 800 J.
Therefore (assuming no heat losses) the upper limit for the specific heat capacity of the inner flask and contents would be 28 800/80 = 360 J kg^{-1} K^{-1}.
New energy input = 60 × 30 × 60 = 108 000 J.
Of this, 28 000 J is required to heat the flask and contents, and therefore a further 79 200 J is available to vaporise the water.

$$\text{Mass of water vaporised} = \frac{79\,200}{2.26 \times 10^6}$$
$$= 3.5 \times 10^{-2}\ \text{kg} = 3.5\ \text{g}$$

This result assumes that there are no heat losses from the flask during the boiling phase and therefore no energy is needed to keep the flask at 100 °C.

The enormous pressure at the base of a glacier will cause melting of the ice (ZEFA)

Student investigation

A shiny electric kettle (Figure 38.8) is used in a simple determination of the specific latent heat of vaporisation of water. The kettle and its contents are weighed and the kettle is then boiled for a given time and the loss of weight is found.

Assuming the value given above for the specific latent heat capacity of water, make measurements to find the heat lost by the kettle during this time and thence estimate the accuracy of a measurement made by this method.

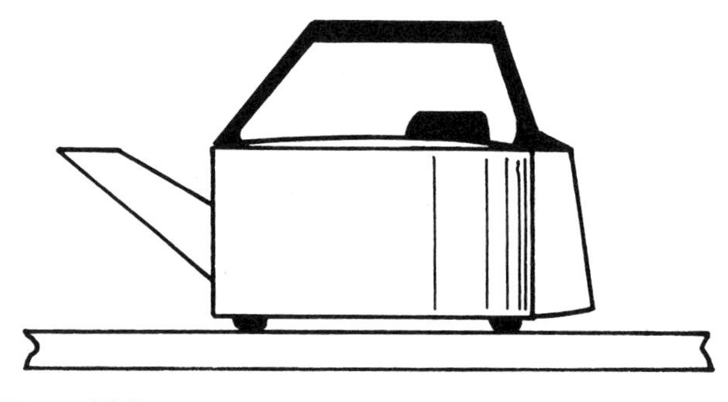

Figure 38.8

11 A shiny electric kettle with a 2.0 kW heating element has a thermal capacity of 400 J K^{-1}. 1.00 kg of water at 20 °C is placed in the kettle. The kettle is then switched on and 0.5 kg of water remain after 13 minutes. Ignoring heat losses, calculate the value for the specific latent heat of vaporisation of water. (Specific heat capacity of water = 4200 J kg^{-1} K^{-1})

If heat losses had been taken into account, how would your answer be modified?

12 An ice cube whose mass is 50 g is taken from a fridge at −10 °C and dropped into a glass of water at 0 °C. If no heat is gained or lost from the outside, how much ice will freeze on to the cube? (Specific latent heat of fusion of water = 330 000 J kg^{-1})

13 2 g of iron wire at 15 °C are dropped into liquid oxygen maintained at its boiling point in a vacuum flask. The volume of oxygen driven off, measured at 20 °C and 1.2×10^5 Pa, is 4.32×10^{-4} m^3. Find the specific latent heat of vaporisation of oxygen. (Specific heat capacity of iron = 106 J kg^{-1} K^{-1}; boiling point of oxygen = −184° C; density of oxygen at s.t.p. = 1.43 kg m^{-3}) [O and C]

Measurement of the specific latent heat of vaporisation

The specific latent heat of a liquid may be measured by a modification of the method of Ramsey and Marshall (1896). The apparatus is shown in Figure 38.9.

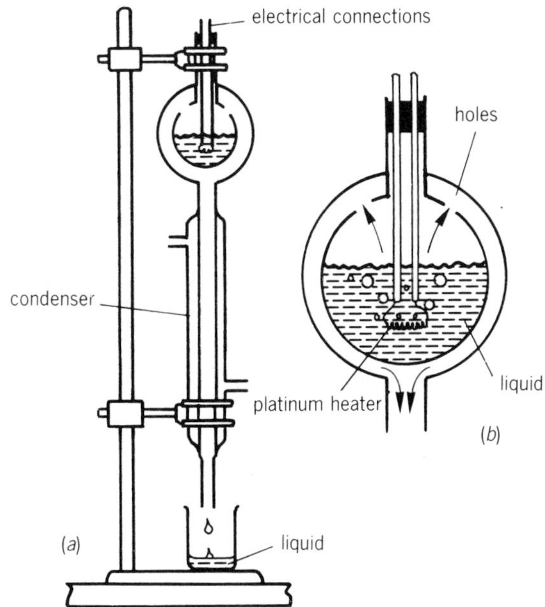

Figure 38.9

The double-walled glass vessel is fitted to a condenser and mounted vertically. The inner section contains the liquid in which is a heater made of platinum wire. When the liquid boils the vapour passes through small holes into the outer vessel and then down into the condenser. Here it condenses, runs down and is collected in the beaker. It is essential that evaporation is rapid, for then the vapour in the outer vessel acts as a heat shield and eliminates heat losses from the inner vessel.

When a steady state has been reached – that is, when liquid drips into the beaker at a constant rate – a clean beaker is placed under the condenser and the mass of liquid m condensing, and hence being evaporated, in a measured time t can be found.
The specific latent heat of vaporisation L of the liquid can then be found from the equation

$$mL = VIt$$

where VI is the power supplied to the coil. If a joulemeter is available the energy input E may be measured directly; then

$$E = mL$$

The large specific latent heat of water explains why it is much more painful to be scalded by steam at 100 °C than by an equal mass of liquid water at 100 °C. The steam first condenses before it cools to your body temperature and in doing so releases roughly ten times as much heat energy as it does in the cooling phase.

Measurement of the specific latent heat of fusion of ice

The simplest method for measuring this quantity is the method of mixtures. Ice is dropped into water a few degrees above room temperature, and the resulting fall in temperature is recorded after all the ice has melted. Since the water falls from a few degrees above the temperature of the surroundings to a few degrees below the heat losses may be ignored – the mixture is assumed to gain as much heat as it losses and a cooling correction need not be applied.

The effect of pressure and impurities on freezing

If pressure is applied to ice its freezing point falls. The effect is known as **regelation.** This explains why snowballs can be made. When the snow is compressed the pressure between the snow crystals causes melting and refreezing takes place when the pressure is removed. Gentle pressure with the hands may result in a local pressure of 100 atmospheres where the crystals touch and this will lower the freezing point by about 0.75 °C. This is not enough to melt the snow if the external temperature is −1.0 °C, however, which is why snowballs cannot be made on a very cold day.

You will probably have seen the famous experiment with a wire cutting through a block of ice in your GCSE course. This can be explained by regelation. Why will the experiment not work if string is used rather than a copper wire?

When salt is added to an ice–water mixture at 0 °C the freezing point of the mixture is lowered. Students should investigate the temperature that can be reached with different concentrations of salt.

14 A student measures the specific latent heat of ethanol using an electrical method as described above. He makes two measurements, the results of which are given below.

Experiment 1: heater voltage 8.90 V, heater current 2.10 A, mass of ethanol evaporated 174 g in 15 minutes.

Experiment 2: heater voltage 7.30 V, heater current 1.74 A, mass of ethanol evaporated 111 g in 15 minutes.

Calculate the specific latent heat of ethanol from these results.

39 · Ideal gases

We will define an **ideal gas** as one which obeys the following gas laws exactly under all conditions and one whose molecules do not exert any appreciable attraction on each other.

Pressure–volume changes

Consider first a change of pressure and volume at a constant temperature – Boyle's law:

> pressure × volume = constant
>
> for a given mass of gas at a constant temperature

The graphs in Figure 39.1 show the variation of pressure P with volume V and the variation of the product PV with pressure or volume. The lines showing the variation of P with V at a constant temperature are known as **isothermals**, that is, lines joining points of equal temperature.

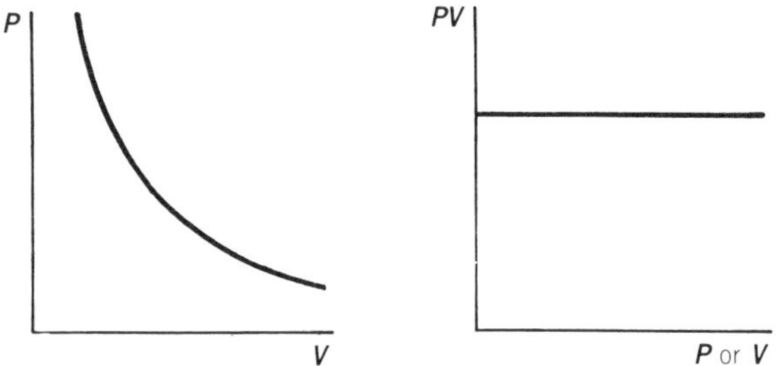

Figure 39.1

Temperature changes

If the temperature changes then Boyle's law does not apply, and the behaviour of the gas can be described by two separate equations:

(*a*) The pressure law

> pressure = constant × temperature

(*b*) Charles's law

> volume = constant × temperature

The variations of pressure with temperature and of volume with temperature are shown in Figure 39.2.

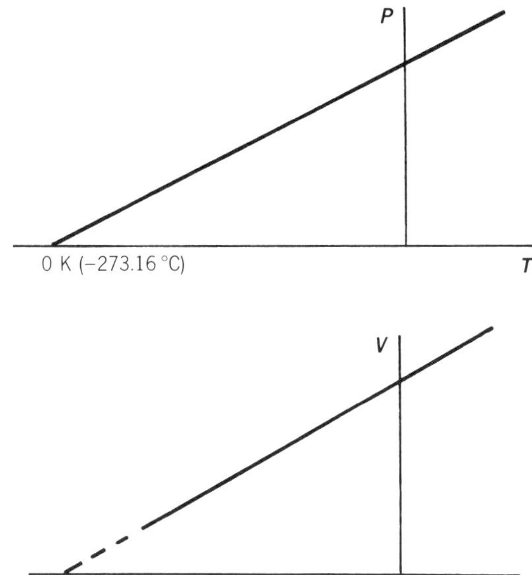

Figure 39.2

It is clear that as the temperature is reduced the volume and pressure both reduce, and a point is reached where theoretically the volume and pressure both become zero. Clearly the volume of a gas, even an ideal one, can never be zero but the pressure can. At this point all molecular motion ceases and therefore the gas does not exert any pressure on the walls of the container.

This temperature is called **absolute zero** (−273.16 °C) and temperatures measured with this point as the zero of the scale are known as **absolute** or **thermodynamic** temperatures, and are measured in **kelvins** (K).

This is the lowest temperature that it is possible to obtain. Scientists have reached within a few thousands of a degree of absolute zero by sophisticated methods such as adiabatic demagnetisation. A brief account of such a method is given on page 228.

The rate at which the volume of a gas changes with temperature can be expressed by defining a quantity known as the **expansivity** or volume coefficient (α):

$$\alpha = \frac{\text{volume at } \theta\ ^\circ\text{C} - \text{volume at } 0\ ^\circ\text{C}}{\text{volume at } 0\ ^\circ\text{C} \times \theta}$$

The value of α is about 1/273 or 0.00366. In other words, the volume of an ideal gas increases by 1/273 of its volume at 0 °C for every degree (°C or K) rise in temperature.

This is **Charles's** or **Gay-Lussac's law.**

The ideal gas equation

These laws may be combined to give the ideal gas equation:

pressure × volume = constant × temperature

For *one mole* of gas we have

$$PV = RT$$

where R is the **molar gas constant.** It has a value of $8.31\ \mathrm{J\ mol^{-1}\ K^{-1}}$ (see page 241) and generally for n moles we have:

$$PV = nRT$$

The equation of state for 1 kg of the gas is:

$$PV = \frac{RT}{M} = rT$$

where M is the molar mass in kg (2×10^{-3} for hydrogen and 32×10^{-3} for oxygen, for example). Therefore for m kg of the gas we have:

$$PV = \frac{mRT}{M} = mrT$$

For a fixed mass of gas whose conditions are changed from P_1, V_1 and T_1 to P_2, V_2 and T_2 the equation of state can be written:

$$P_1V_1T_2 = P_2V_2T_1$$

Note that the temperature must always be measured in kelvins.

Avogadro's law

Avogadro's law can be stated as:

Equal volumes of all gases at the same temperature and pressure contain equal numbers of molecules.

This can be verified using the ideal gas equation. Consider two gases 1 and 2. The gas equation for each gas is:

Gas 1: $P_1V_1 = n_1RT_1$ Gas 2: $P_2V_2 = n_2RT_2$

Now if $P_1 = P_2$, $V_1 = V_2$ and $T_1 = T_2$ we have that $n_1 = n_2$ and so Avogadro's law is proved.

1 A barometer tube 90 cm long contains a small amount of air above the mercury. The barometer reading is 75.0 when the true pressure is 76 cm and the temperature is 15 °C. What is the true pressure when the reading is 75.5 and the temperature 6 °C?

2 A gas has a volume of 64 $\mathrm{cm^3}$ at 0 °C and 88 $\mathrm{cm^3}$ at 100 °C. What value does this give for absolute zero?

3 When it is fully inflated with hydrogen gas a balloon has a radius of 12 m at a temperature of 20 °C. It was filled from gas in cylinders which had a volume of 25 $\mathrm{m^3}$ at 10 °C. If the final pressure in the balloon was 10^5 Pa, what was the pressure of the gas in the cylinders?

Dalton's law of partial pressures

If two or more gases are mixed in a container then the final pressure can be found from Dalton's law, which states that:

The pressure in a container is the sum of the partial pressures of the gases that occupy the container.

The **partial pressure** of a gas is that pressure that the gas would exert if it alone occupied the container. For example, consider a container with a volume V and a temperature T. Let the container be occupied by two different gases, there being n_1 moles of gas 1 and n_2 moles of gas 2 (Figure 39.3). Let the partial pressures of the gases be P_1 and P_2.

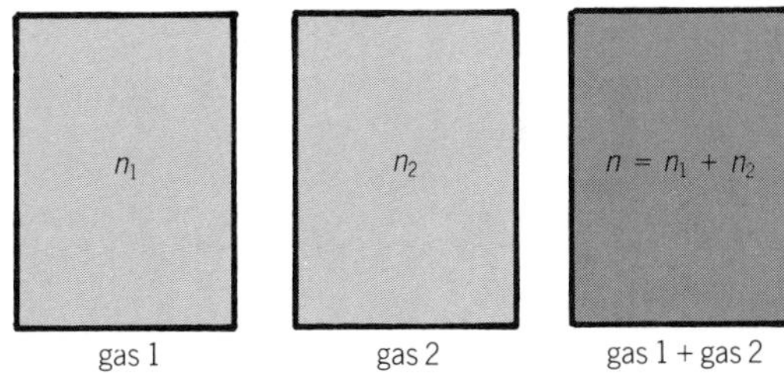

Figure 39.3

Now $P_1V = n_1RT$ and $P_2V = n_2RT$. But the total pressure in the container is P, where $PV = nRT$ for $n = n_1 + n_2$, the total number of moles of whatever type occupying the container. Therefore

$$P_1 = \frac{n_1RT}{V} \quad P_2 = \frac{n_2RT}{V} \quad \text{and} \quad P = \frac{nRT}{V}$$

and since $n = n_1 + n_2$ we have

$$\frac{P_1V}{RT} + \frac{P_2V}{RT} = \frac{PV}{RT} \qquad \text{or} \qquad P = P_1 + P_2$$

which is Dalton's law.

A useful application of this law is in cases where volumes of the same gas occupy separate but connected containers at differing temperatures.

Example

A volume of gas V at a temperature T_1 and a pressure p is enclosed in a sphere (Figure 39.4). It is connected to another sphere of volume $V/2$ by a tube and stopcock. The second sphere is initially evacuated and the stopcock is closed.

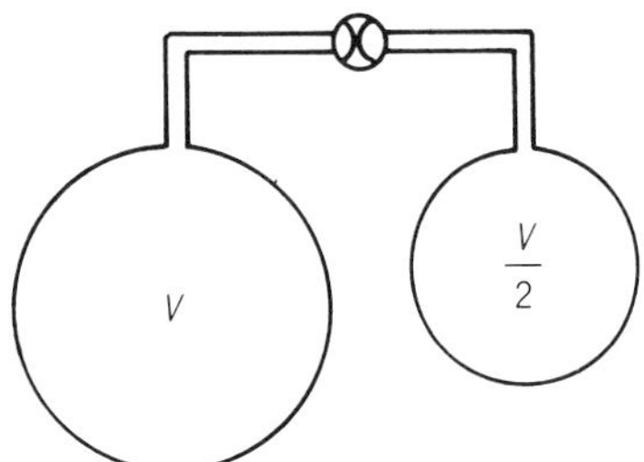

Figure 39.4

If the stopcock is opened the temperature of the gas in the second sphere becomes T_2. The first sphere is maintained at a temperature T_1. Show that the final pressure p' within the apparatus is

$$p' = \frac{2pT_2}{2T_2 + T_1}$$

Let there be n molecules of gas, and let there be n_1 molecules in the larger sphere and n_2 molecules in the smaller sphere after the stopcock is opened.

Now $n = n_1 + n_2$, but $pV = nRT$. So

$$\frac{pV}{RT_1} = \frac{p'V}{RT_1} + \frac{p'V}{2T_2R}$$

Therefore

$$\frac{p}{T_1} = p'\left(\frac{1}{T_1} + \frac{1}{2T_2}\right)$$

$$p' = \frac{2pT_2}{2T_2 + T_1}$$

The first law of thermodynamics

When heat energy is supplied to a gas two things may happen:

(*a*) the internal energy of the gas will alter, and
(*b*) the gas will do external work by expanding.

Let the amount of heat energy be dQ, the change in internal energy be dU and the external work done be dW. (Note that dU represents changes in both kinetic energy dE and potential energy dI, but because we are considering an ideal gas for the present $dI = 0$, since there is no intermolecular attraction.)

The first law of thermodynamics states that the heat energy input = change in internal energy of the gas + amount of external work done **by** the gas, or

$$dQ = dU + dW$$

Work done by an ideal gas during expansion

Consider an ideal gas enclosed in a cylinder by a frictionless piston of area A. Let the pressure of the gas be P (Figure 39.5).

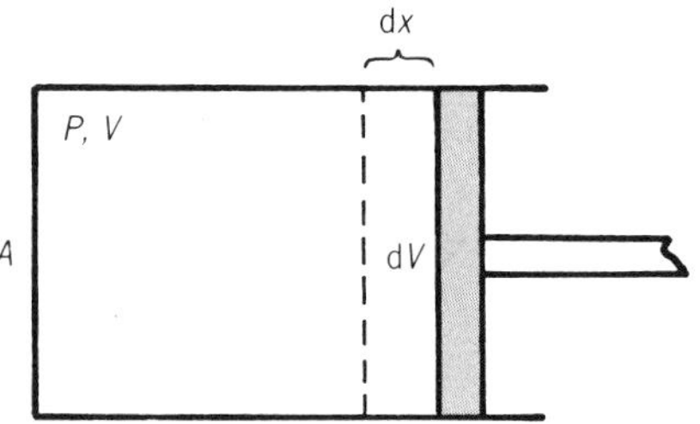

Figure 39.5

The gas now expands, pushing the piston back a distance dx, the volume of the gas increasing by dV. Let the work done by the gas during this expansion be dW.

Force on the piston = PA. Then

Work done during expansion $= PA\,dx$
$= P\,dV$

Therefore $dW = P\,dV$

Using this formula the first law of thermodynamics can be written as:

$$dQ = dU + dW = dU + P\,dV$$

4 An ideal gas undergoes isothermal expansion at 0 °C from 0.010 m^3 to 0.200 m^3. For 5 moles of gas, calculate
(*a*) the work done,
(*b*) the heat added, and
(*c*) the change in internal energy.

5 A gas cylinder contains 6.4 kg of oxygen at a pressure of 5 atmospheres. An exactly similar cylinder contains 4.2 kg of nitrogen at the same temperature. What is the pressure of the nitrogen? (Relative molecular masses: oxygen = 32, nitrogen = 28. Assume that each behaves as a perfect gas.)

6 A hot air balloon when inflated contains 1 500 m^3 of hot air at atmospheric pressure (10^5 Pa). The temperature outside the envelope is 300 K and the mass of the balloon (excluding the hot air) and its passengers is 250 kg. Assuming that the air may be treated as an ideal gas of molar mass 29×10^{-3} kg mol^{-1}, find the mean temperature to which the air in the balloon must be heated if the balloon is just to rise. (Take the molar gas constant R to be 8.3 J mol^{-1} K^{-1}.)

The universal gas constant (R)

At STP (273 K and 1.013×10^5 Pa) 1 mole of any gas has a volume of 22.4×10^{-3} m^3. Substituting these values in the ideal gas equation gives:

$$PV = RT; \quad \text{therefore} \quad R = PV/T$$

$$R = \frac{1.013 \times 10^5 \times 22.4 \times 10^{-3}}{273}$$

$$= 8.31 \text{ J mol}^{-1} \text{ K}^{-1}$$

The specific heat capacities of gases

For solids and liquids we define the specific heat capacity as the quantity of energy that will raise the temperature of unit mass of the body by 1 K. For gases, however, it is necessary to specify the conditions under which the change of temperature takes place, since a change of temperature will also produce large changes in pressure and volume.

For solids and liquids we can neglect this pressure change and the specific heat capacity that we measure for them is essentially one where the pressure on the body is unaltered. We call this the specific heat capacity at constant pressure (C_p).

The principal specific heat capacities of a gas

The specific heat capacity of a gas will depend on the conditions under which it is measured and since these could vary considerably we will restrict ourselves to the following, called the **principal specific heat capacities of a gas:**

(*a*) The **specific heat capacity at constant volume** (c_v) is defined as the quantity of heat required to raise the temperature of 1 kg of the gas by 1 K if the volume of the gas remains constant.

(*b*) The **specific heat capacity at constant pressure** (c_p) is defined as the quantity of heat required to raise the temperature of 1 kg of the gas by 1 K if the pressure of the gas remains constant.

The molar heat capacity at constant volume (C_v) is the quantity of heat required to raise the temperature of 1 mole of the gas by 1 K if the volume of the gas remains constant. The molar heat capacity at constant pressure (C_p) is the quantity of heat required to raise the temperature of 1 mole of the gas by 1 K if the pressure of the gas remains constant.

c_p is always greater than c_v, since if the volume of the gas increases work must be done by the gas to push back the surroundings.

The table below gives the principal specific heat capacities for some well-known gases.

Gas	*Specific heat capacity at constant volume*	*Specific heat capacity at constant pressure*
Air	714	993
Argon	314	524
Carbon dioxide	640	834
Carbon monoxide	748	1050
Helium	3157	5240
Hydrogen	10 142	14 300
Nitrogen	741	1040
Oxygen	652	913
Water vapour		2020

All specific heat capacities are in J kg^{-1} K^{-1}. The value for water vapour is at 373 K.

Connection between C_p and C_v

Imagine a mole of gas enclosed in a cylinder of initial volume V by a frictionless and weightless piston.

The gas is now heated, the volume being kept constant (Figure 39.6). If the rise in temperature is dT then the heat input is $C_v\, dT$, and all this energy goes to raising the internal energy and hence the temperature of the gas; no work is done in expanding the gas.

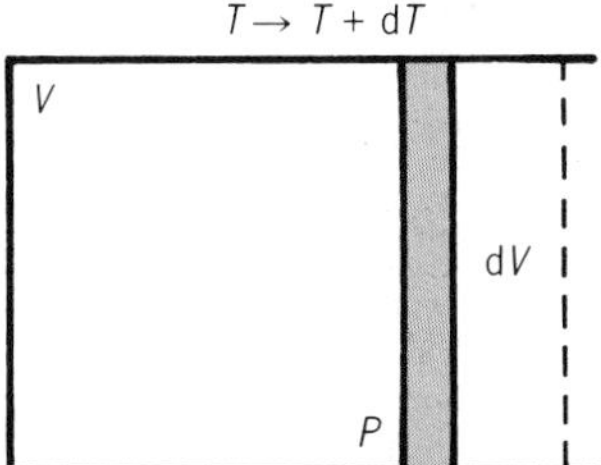

Figure 39.6

If we now return to the initial conditions and heat the gas again but this time allow it to expand, keeping the pressure constant, the energy input for a temperature rise of dT is $C_p\, dT$.

This not only has to raise the temperature of the gas but also must do external work in expanding it by dV. Therefore

$$C_p\, dT = C_v\, dT + dW$$
$$C_p\, dT = C_v d\,T + P\, dV$$

We assume that the gas obeys the ideal gas equation $PV = RT$, and therefore $P\, dV = R\, dT$. Substituting for dV we have:

$$C_p - C_v = R$$

This formula was first derived in 1842 by Robert Mayer.

The ratio of the two principal specific heats of a gas is denoted by the Greek letter γ. Therefore:

$$\frac{C_p}{C_v} = \gamma$$

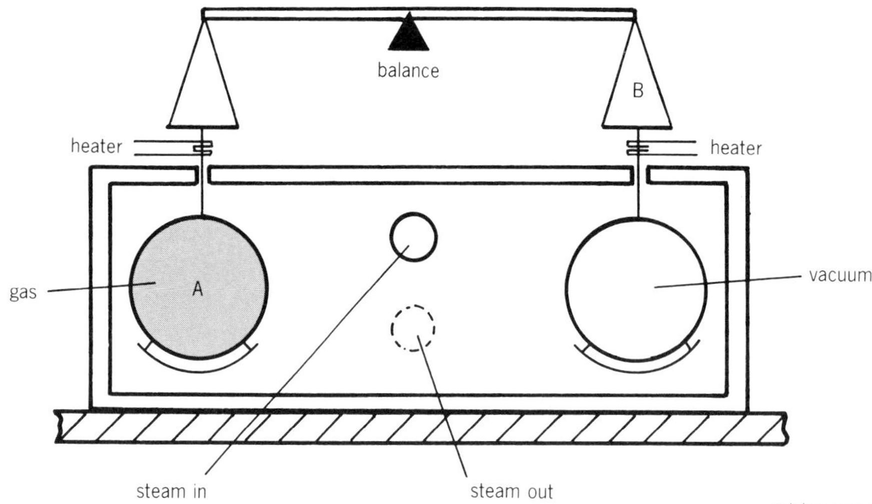

Figure 39.7

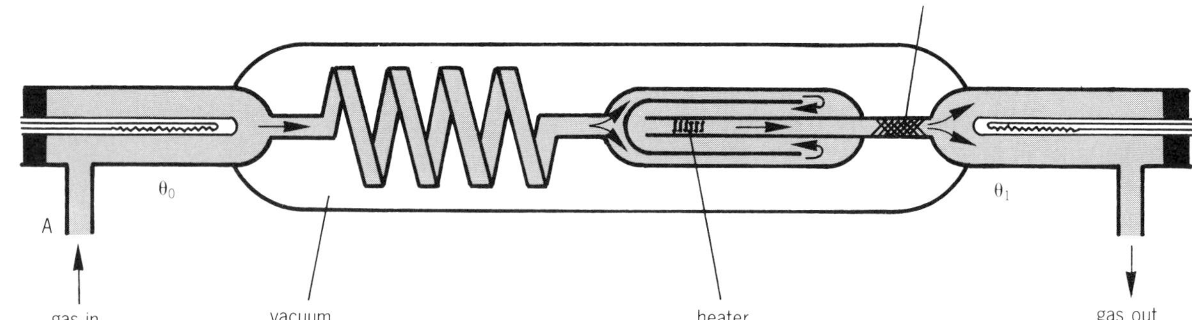

Figure 39.8

Measurement of the principal specific heat capacities of a gas

(*a*) Specific heat capacity at constant volume

C_v can be measured using the differential steam calorimeter invented by Joly in 1886 (Figure 39.7).

Two hollow copper spheres identical in size and mass are suspended by wire from the two pans of a beam balance. One of the spheres contains a mass of gas M at high pressure (Joly used 22 atmospheres) and the other is evacuated. The spheres are surrounded by a box through which steam is passed.

Steam will condense on the cool spheres, more steam condensing on the one with the greater thermal capacity, that is, the one filled with gas. After some time a mass m has to be placed on pan B to counterbalance the extra mass of steam that has condensed on sphere A.

If C_v is the specific heat capacity of the gas at constant volume and θ_0 and θ_1 the initial and final temperatures of the sphere, then

$$C_v = \frac{mL}{M(\theta_1 - \theta_0)}$$

where L is the specific heat of vaporisation of water. The two wires are heated to vaporise any liquid condensing on them, and baffles are provided to prevent water dripping off the roof of the box on to the spheres. A control experiment is performed to check the amount of steam condensing on the spheres when both are empty.

(*b*) Specific heat capacity at constant pressure

C_p can be measured using the continuous-flow calorimeter devised in 1862 by Regnault. The modern method is a modification of the constant-flow method first used by Swann in 1909.

The apparatus is shown in Figure 39.8. Gas is passed round a series of tubes in a water bath to ensure that it has reached a constant temperature and is then fed into the apparatus at A. Here its temperature is measured using a platinum resistance thermometer (θ_0). It passes over a heater where its temperature is raised, then through a mixing gauze and finally out at B where its temperature is measured again (θ_1). When steady state has been reached the temperatures are recorded, and hence C_p can be calculated from

$$VIt = MC_p(\theta_1 - \theta_0) + H$$

where VIt is the energy supplied to the heater in a time t, M is the mass of gas passing through in that time and H is the heat lost. As usual with continuous-flow experiments, by doing two measurements with the same temperature difference but with a different rate of flow H can be eliminated.

The measurement of the ratio of the principal specific heat capacities of a gas

The measurement of the velocity of sound in a gas (see pages 179 and 180) is the most convenient way of finding γ, but a direct method is described below.

This method was devised by Clement and Desormes in 1819. It is based upon the adiabatic expansion of a gas in a large flask. A laboratory version of their apparatus is shown in Figure 39.9.

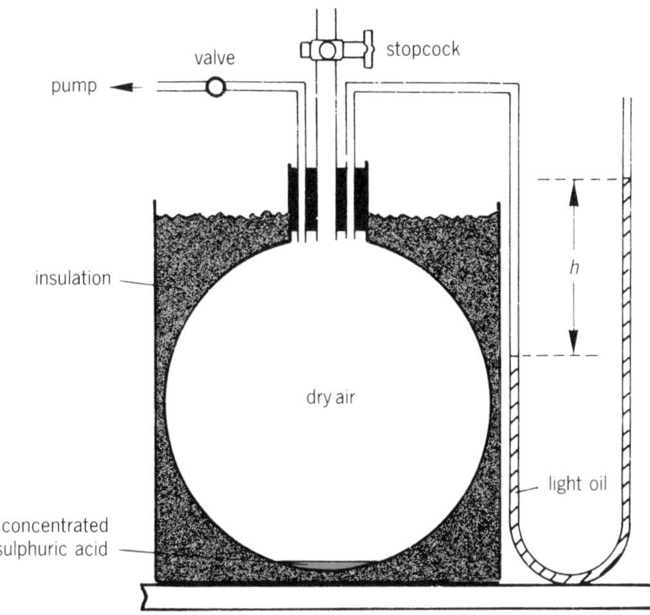

Figure 39.9

A large glass flask of at least 10 litres (0.01 m^3) capacity contains air at atmospheric pressure. The flask is fitted with a large bung containing a bicycle tyre valve, a large stopcock and a tube connecting the flask to a manometer filled with a light oil. The flask is usually surrounded by insulation although this is really unnecessary since the air is a bad conductor of heat and the resulting expansion is rapid. A little concentrated sulphuric acid may be placed in the flask to dry the air.

The pressure in the flask is raised using the bicycle pump until the manometer reads a pressure 10–15 cm of oil above that of the surroundings. The valve is then closed and the flask allowed to stand until the manometer levels are steady and the air in the flask has regained its original temperature. The manometer head h_1 is recorded. The stopcock is then opened for a second or two and then closed rapidly. The air in the flask expands adiabatically, the temperature drops and the pressure drops to atmospheric causing the manometer level to fall. The flask is then allowed to stand until the levels become steady. The new pressure head h_2 is then recorded. A $P-V$ diagram of the experiment is shown in Figure 39.10.

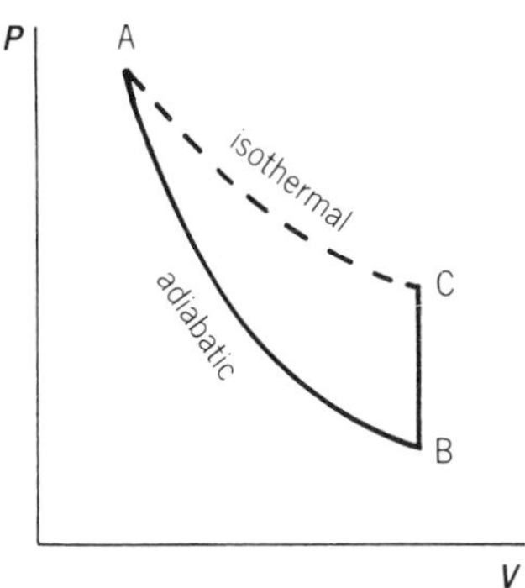

Figure 39.10

It can be shown that if the pressure heads are small compared with atmospheric pressure then the value of the ratio of the principal specific heat capacities of the gas γ is given by the equation:

$$\gamma = \frac{h_1}{h_1 - h_2}$$

within the limits of the experiment.

One serious disadvantage of the method is that if the stopcock is large enough to allow a rapid expansion the air inside the flask oscillates, and it is impossible to tell when to close the stopcock since this must be done after one expansion phase only.

7 Two grams of helium gas at 27 °C are contained in a chamber by a frictionless piston at atmospheric pressure 1.0×10^5 Pa. Calculate

(*a*) the number of molecules per unit volume in the chamber,

(*b*) their mean kinetic energy, and

(*c*) the internal energy of the gas.

Ten grams of neon gas are pumped into the chamber, which is maintained at constant volume. Calculate the final pressure in the chamber when both gases are present and their temperature is 27 °C. How are the values of the quantities in (*a*) to (*c*) changed?

The chamber, which has negligible heat capacity, is then thermally insulated and the gas is allowed to return to atmospheric pressure slowly and adiabatically. Treating the gas as ideal, explain qualitatively whether the internal energy and temperature of the gas will rise, fall or stay the same.

Why is such a cumbersome device as the constant volume gas thermometer used as the standard thermometer over a range of temperatures? Why are several different pressures of gas used in the thermometer to ensure a correct temperature measurement?

($R = 8.3$ J mol^{-1} K^{-1}; $L = 6.0 \times 10^{23}$ mol^{-1};
$M_{He} = 0.004$ kg mol^{-1}; $M_{Ne} = 0.020$ kg mol^{-1})
[(O and C)(part)]

8 Air under a pressure of 10^6 Pa in a closed vessel is suddenly released by opening and closing a tap. If the external pressure is 1 atmosphere, what fraction of the original air remains in the vessel?

If the initial temperature is 300 K, find

(*a*) the temperature just after the tap is closed,

(*b*) the pressure some time after the tap is closed.

9 An ideal gas is trapped in a cylinder by a movable piston. Initially it occupies a volume of 8×10^{-3}m ^{3} and exerts a pressure of 108 kPa.

(*a*) It first undergoes an isothermal expansion until its volume is 27×10^{-3}m ^{3}. Calculate the new pressure.

(*b*) It is then compressed adiabatically back to a volume of 8×10^{-3}m ^{3}. Calculate the final pressure.

(*c*) State what single process will bring the gas back to its initial condition.

(*d*) Sketch and label the three stages on a *P–V* diagram. (Ratio of the principal molar heat capacities of the gas = 5/3)

[AEB 1985]

Adiabatic and isothermal changes

When a gas is compressed or expanded there are many possible connections between the changes of pressure, volume and temperature. We will restrict ourselves to looking at just two basic variations.

(i) Isothermal expansion or compression
The *temperature* of the gas is kept constant during the change in pressure and volume by adding or removing heat energy from the system. For this reason isothermal changes should take place in thin-walled, conducting containers.

For this type of change $T=$ constant and therefore $PV =$ constant; the gas obeys Boyle's law (Figure 39.11).

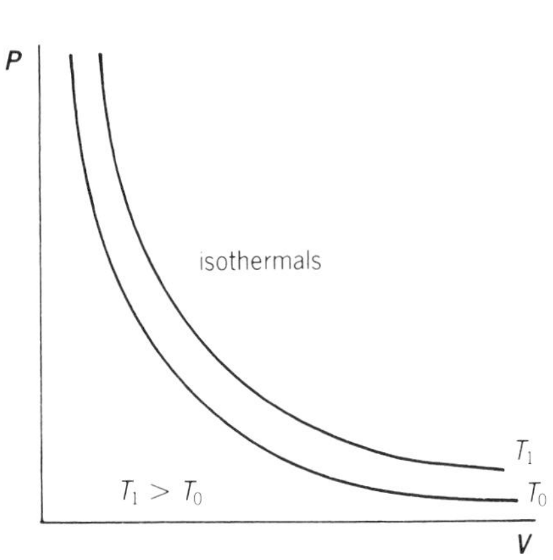

Figure 39.11

(ii) Adiabatic expansion or compression
The *total heat content* of the system is kept constant and therefore the temperature of the gas will alter; no heat must enter or leave the system. This type of change should occur in an insulated container.

Since the temperature of the gas changes the adiabatic curves for PV will be steeper than those for an isothermal change (Figure 39.12). True adiabatic changes are difficult to produce in reality, but the expansion of air from a burst tyre or the expansion and compression of air through which a sound wave is passing are very close to adiabatic changes.

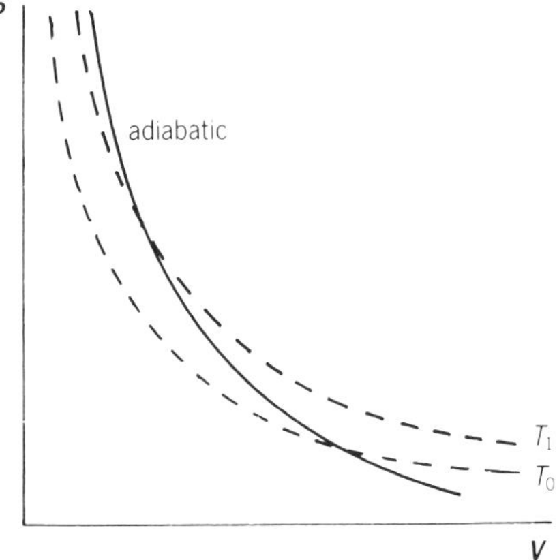

Figure 39.12

Temperature variation in a reversible adiabatic change

When a gas in an insulated container is compressed or expanded it suffers a change in temperature, the molecules of gas gaining energy from, or losing energy to, the moving walls of the container.

Consider a volume of gas enclosed in an insulating container by a frictionless piston. Let the initial velocity of a molecule moving in the x-direction be u.

(*a*) If it collides with a stationary wall of the container its velocity after collision will be $-u$ (see Figure 39.13(*a*)).

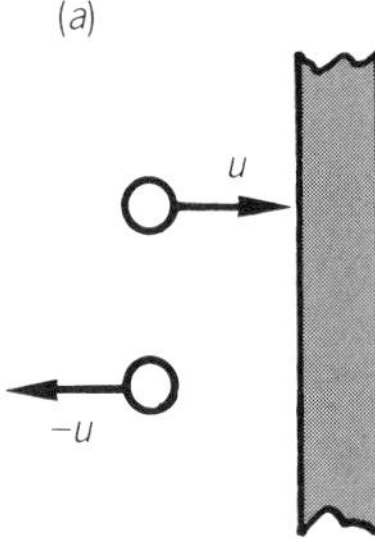

Figure 39.13(a)

Now consider the case when the wall is moving at velocity v, first an expansion and then a compression (Figures 39.13(*b*) and (*c*)).

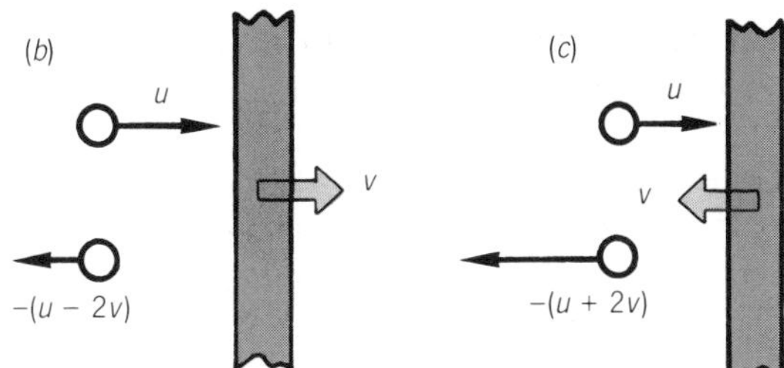

Figure 39.13(b and c)

(*b*) The velocity of the molecule relative to the wall = $u - v$. After collision,

velocity relative to the wall = $-(u - v)$
velocity relative to the Earth = $-(u - 2v)$

The final velocity is less than the initial velocity by $2v$, and so the gas has cooled. Notice that this cooling only takes place *while* the wall of the container is moving.

(*c*) Similarly for the compression we can say that, after collision,

velocity relative to the Earth = $-(u + 2v)$

This shows an increase in velocity, and therefore the temperature of the gas will be raised.

Equation for an adiabatic change

We can now consider the equation for an adiabatic expansion or compression. The proof of the equation will be outside the scope of some courses, so the result will be quoted first. The proof is then given for interested students (page 247).

The pressure P and volume V of a gas undergoing an adiabatic change are related by the formula:

$$PV^\gamma = \text{constant}$$

where γ is a constant for the gas. We will see later that γ is the ratio of the two principal specific heats of the gas and has a value between 1.3 and 1.67.

Now when a gas expands or contracts reversibly and adiabatically it still obeys the ideal gas equation ($PV = nRT$) and therefore we have some alternative ways of expressing an adiabatic change, namely:

$$PV^\gamma = \text{constant}$$
$$TV^{\gamma-1} = \text{constant}$$
$$P^{(1-\gamma)}T^\gamma = \text{constant}$$

The equations may also be written in the form:

$$P_1V_1^\gamma = P_2V_2^\gamma \text{ etc.,}$$

where P_1V_1 and P_2V_2 are the initial and final conditions of the gas respectively.

Example

An ideal gas at 27 °C and a pressure of 760 mm of mercury is compressed isothermally until its volume is halved. It is then expanded reversibly and adiabatically to twice its original volume. If the value of γ for the gas is 1.4, calculate the final pressure and temperature of the gas.

For the isothermal change:

$PV = P_1V_1$ $\quad 760 \times V = P \times V/2 \quad P = 1520$ mm of mercury

For the adiabatic change:

$$PV^\gamma = P_2V_2^\gamma$$
$$1520 \times (V/2)^{1.4} = P_2 \times (2V)^{1.4}$$
$$P_2 = 1520/6.97 = 218 \text{ mm of mercury}$$

Therefore, from $\dfrac{PV}{T_1} = \dfrac{P_2V_2}{T_2}$, we have $\dfrac{1520 \times V}{300 \times 2}$

$= \dfrac{218 \times 2V}{T_2} \qquad T_2 = 172 \text{ K} = -101\ °\text{C}.$

10 Air at 20 °C is allowed to expand under adiabatic conditions until its pressure has fallen to one-third of its original value. What is the final temperature of the air? (Ratio of the principal specific heats of air = 1.4)

11 A certain volume of helium at 15 °C is expanded adiabatically until its volume is trebled. Calculate the temperature of the gas immediately after the expansion has taken place. (Ratio of the principal specific heat capacities of helium = 1.67)

12 Some nitrogen at 20 °C is expanded isothermally to twice its original volume. It is then cooled at constant volume to −10 °C and finally compressed adiabatically to its original pressure and volume.
(*a*) Draw a *pV* diagram to show this change.
(*b*) Calculate the pressure after the isothermal expansion.
(*c*) Calculate the pressure after the cooling at constant volume.

13 The density of neon at 27 °C and a pressure of 1.00×10^5 Pa is 0.90 kg m^{-3}. Calculate the mass of neon in a neon discharge tube of volume 250 cm^3 if the pressure inside it is 1.00×10^5 Pa at a temperature of 150 °C.

14 Two identical glass bulbs are joined with a thin glass tube and filled with air which is initially at 20 °C. What will the pressure in the apparatus become if one bulb is immersed in steam and the other in melting ice?

The pressure–volume cycle for an ideal gas

We have shown that the work done by an ideal gas which undergoes a change of volume $\mathrm{d}V$ at a pressure P is $P\,\mathrm{d}V$ (see page 240).

This may be integrated to give the total work done for a large volume change. For an isothermal change $PV = nRT$, and so for a volume change from V_0 to V_1:

$$\text{work done} = \int_{V_0}^{V_1} P\,\mathrm{d}V = \int_{V_0}^{V_1} \frac{RT\,\mathrm{d}V}{V} = RT\log\frac{V_1}{V_0}$$

If the gas changes its volume at a constant pressure, the work done on it is given simply by:

$$\text{work done at constant pressure} = P(V_1 - V_0)$$

Example

An ideal gas with a volume of $0.1\ \mathrm{m}^3$ expands at a constant pressure of 1.5×10^5 Pa to treble its volume. Calculate the work done by the gas.

Work done = $1.5 \times 10^5 \times (0.3 - 0.1) = 3 \times 10^4$ J.

We may represent the work done by a pressure–volume or PV diagram as shown in Figure 39.14.

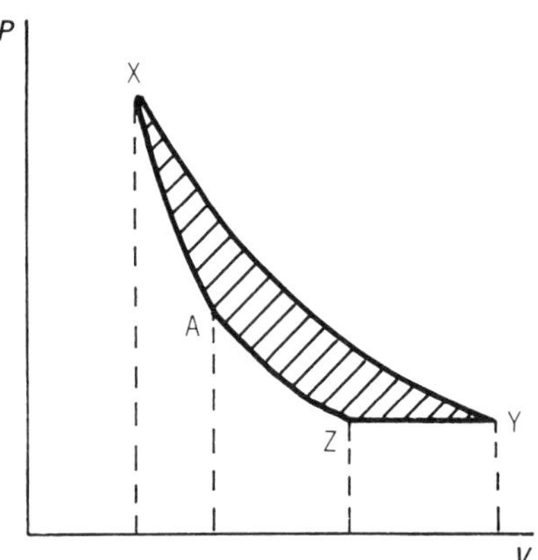

Figure 39.14

Consider a gas at X (volume V and pressure P). Let the gas expand isothermally to Y and then let it be cooled to Z with no change of pressure. It is then compressed isothermally to A and finally compressed adiabatically to X.

The area XYZA enclosed by these PV changes represents the work done by the gas.

The first law of thermodynamics and isothermal and adiabatic changes

On page 240 the first law of thermodynamics was stated as:

$$\mathrm{d}Q = \mathrm{d}U + P\,\mathrm{d}V$$

where $\mathrm{d}Q$ is the heat input, $\mathrm{d}U$ the increase in internal energy and $P\,\mathrm{d}V$ the work done by the gas. Particular cases of this law will now be considered.

(*a*) An isothermal change

In such a change the temperature of the gas remains constant and therefore for an ideal gas there is no change in internal energy of the gas ($\mathrm{d}U = 0$). The first law for such a change becomes:

$$\mathrm{d}Q = P\,\mathrm{d}V$$

(*b*) A reversible adiabatic change

In this case the change in the heat content of the gas is zero ($\mathrm{d}Q = 0$) and the first law becomes:

$$0 = \mathrm{d}U + P\,\mathrm{d}V \quad \text{or} \quad \mathrm{d}U = -P\,\mathrm{d}V$$

This shows that for an ideal gas an increase in volume results in a drop in temperature of the gas.

(*c*) A change at constant volume

In this case $\mathrm{d}V = 0$ and the first law becomes:

$$\mathrm{d}Q = \mathrm{d}U$$

This means that for an ideal gas an input of energy goes purely to raise the temperature of the gas as long as the volume of the gas remains constant.

15 When a gas expands adiabatically it does work on its surroundings although there is no heat input to the gas. Where does this energy come from?

16 A mass of 1 g of hydrogen at 20 °C and 10^5 Pa has its volume halved by an adiabatic change. Calculate the change in the internal energy of the gas. (Ideal gas constant = 8.31 J mol^{-1}; ratio of the principal specific heats for hydrogen = 1.40)

Proof of the formula for a reversible adiabatic change

We will assume that we are dealing with an ideal gas and therefore the first law of thermodynamics becomes:

$$dQ = dE + dW$$

This gives

$$dQ = C_v\, dT + P\, dV$$

For an adiabatic change $dQ = 0$.
Let the gas expand from V to $V + dV$ at constant pressure and let the temperature fall from T to $T - dT$. Then

$$C_p\, dT + P\, dV = 0$$

But $PV = nRT$. Therefore for one mole:

$$C_v \frac{dT}{T} + \frac{R\, dV}{V} = 0$$

But since $C_p - C_v = R$ for an ideal gas,

$$C_v \frac{dT}{T} + (C_p - C_v)\frac{dV}{V} = 0$$

Writing $C_p/C_v = \gamma$ we have

$$\frac{dT}{T} + (\gamma - 1)\frac{dV}{V} = 0$$

which when integrated becomes $TV^{(\gamma-1)} =$ constant.

From this the other versions of the adiabatic equation may be obtained.

17 A mass of air with an initial volume of 5 litres at a temperature of 0 °C and a pressure of 10^5 Pa is compressed isothermally to 2.5 litres, and then allowed to expand adiabatically to 12.5 litres.
Show the process on a *PV* diagram and calculate the final pressure and temperature of the air. At what volume was the pressure momentarily atmospheric? (Assume γ for air = 1.40.)

18 State the first law of thermodynamics. How is the equation modified for:
(*a*) an adiabatic change,
(*b*) an input of heat at constant volume.
Explain how the composition of the term for internal energy for a real gas differs from that for an ideal one.

Enthalpy

From the first law of thermodynamics we can write Q as the heat input, U as the change in internal energy and PV as the work done. We can then define a new quantity known as the **enthalpy**. This quantity is useful when considering the flow of gas through a hole from one cylinder to another – the so called **throttling process** (see below).

enthalpy $(H) = U + PV$

and so

$$C_p = \frac{\Delta H}{\Delta T}$$

where ΔH is the change of molar enthalpy measured at constant pressure.

The throttling process

Consider a perfectly insulated cylinder with two pistons as shown in Figure 39.15. The net work done is $P_1V_1 - P_2V_2$, and so the change in internal energy $U_1 - U_2 = P_1V_1 - P_2V_2$. Therefore:

$$U_1 + P_1V_1 = U_2 + P_2V_2$$

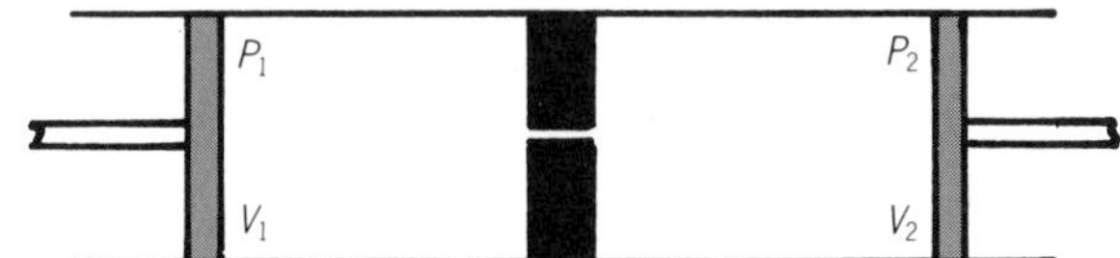

Figure 39.15

In other words, the enthalpy of the system is constant. This is known as the **law of conservation of enthalpy.** The gas must pass slowly through the hole so that there is no change in its kinetic energy.

Robert Mayer 1814 – 1887 (Ann Ronan Picture Library)

The Carnot cycle and the ideal heat engine

Any device for converting heat energy into mechanical energy is called a **heat engine**. Internal combustion engines and steam engines are both examples of heat engines.

A heat engine takes in heat energy at a high temperature and emits some of it at a lower temperature.

The *net* amount of heat flowing into an engine is equal to the *net* amount of work done by the engine. This can be represented by Figure 39.16. An amount of heat Q_1 is taken in at the higher temperature T_1 and an amount of heat Q_2 is emitted at the lower temperature T_2.

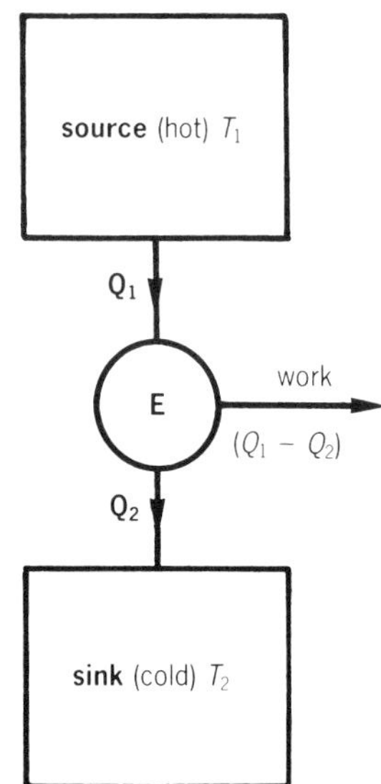

Figure 39.16

The efficiency of such a cycle is given by the equation:

$$\text{efficiency } (\eta) = \frac{Q_1 - Q_2}{Q_1}$$

The approximate efficiencies of some practical heat engines are given below:

internal combustion	56 per cent
steam	40 per cent
diesel	68 per cent

The concept of the ideal heat engine was first developed by the French scientist Sadi Carnot in 1824. He imagined an engine that was free from friction and where the working substance, usually a gas, was taken through a completely reversible cycle consisting of two isothermal and two adiabatic changes.

The Carnot cycle is shown in the *PV* diagram in Figure 39.17. The changes represented are:

(*a*) an isothermal expansion (AB) in which the working substance takes in an amount of heat Q_1 from a source at high temperature T_1;

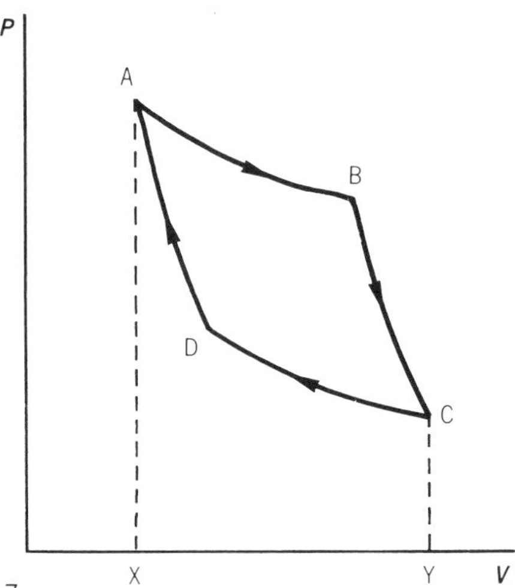

Figure 39.17

(*b*) an adiabatic expansion (BC) where the temperature falls to T_2;

(*c*) an isothermal compression (CD) where an amount of heat Q_2 is emitted to the sink at T_2; and

(*d*) an adiabatic compression (DA) where the temperature rises to T_1.

The work done *by* the gas is given by the area ABCYXA and the work done *on* the gas is given by the area CDAXYC. The *net* work done *by* the gas is therefore represented by the area ABCD.

The efficiency of a heat engine is defined as:

$$\text{efficiency} = \frac{Q_1 - Q_2}{Q_1} \text{ and this is equal to } \frac{T_1 - T_2}{T_1}$$
for a Carnot cycle

This shows that the efficiency of an ideal heat engine depends only on the temperatures of the source and sink, and also that a heat engine can never be 100 per cent efficient. For example, for Dungeness power station steam at 400 °C (673 K) is used to drive a turbine and is emitted to the sea at 300 K. This gives a maximum efficiency of 55 per cent.

19 Suppose that you wanted to increase the efficiency of a Carnot engine. Would it be better to increase the temperature T_1 or to decrease the temperature T_2 by an equal amount? Explain your answer.

20 A Carnot engine operates between two reservoirs at 300 K and 400 K. What is the efficiency of the cycle?

21 A Carnot engine whose low-temperature reservoir is at 280 K has an efficiency of 40 per cent. By how much must the temperature of the high-temperature reservoir be raised if the efficiency is to be increased to 50 per cent, the temperature of the low-temperature reservoir being unchanged?

22 A substance is taken slowly from a state A (P_0, V_0) to a state B ($2P_0$, $3V_0$) along the path ACB shown in the diagram. In this process the substance absorbs 80 J of heat (30 J along AC and 50 J along CB), and does 30 J of work.

(*a*) What are the internal energy differences $U_B - U_A$ and $U_C - U_A$?

(*b*) How much heat flows during the return path BDA indicated in the diagram, and is the heat absorbed or given out by the substance?

(*c*) Explain whether the cycle as indicated would describe the operation of an engine or a refrigerator.

(*d*) At which of the states A, B, C or D would you expect the substance to have the highest temperature, and why?

(O and C, part)

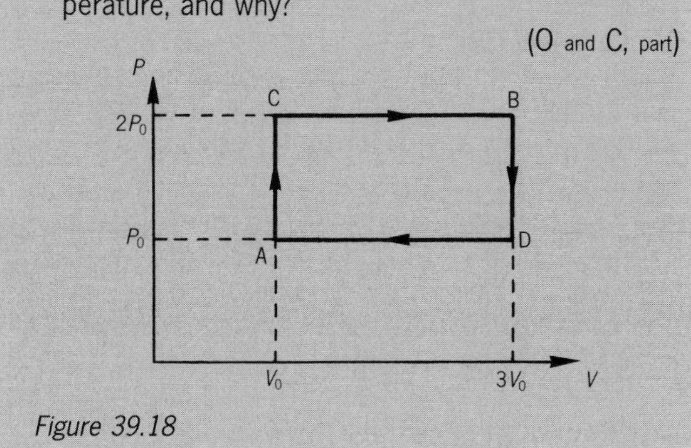

Figure 39.18

Entropy and the second law of thermodynamics

The first law of thermodynamics relates the input of heat energy to the mechanical work that may be obtained from it. It says nothing about the way that this conversion may take place, however, nor does it put any restrictions on it.

The second law of thermodynamics states the way in which these changes of energy may take place. It is considered by many eminent scientists to be one of the most fundamental laws of Physics and yet in one of its forms it may be stated in the following very simple manner:

> It is impossible for there to be a net transfer of heat from a cold body to a hot body in an isolated system

To study the second law further we have to define a new quantity known as the **entropy** of a body. The entropy is best considered as a measure of the *disorder* of the body and you will see later that the total entropy of the universe can never decrease, only remain constant (for a reversible process) or increase (for an irreversible change).

The entropy change (ΔS) of a system is defined as follows:

$$\Delta S = \int_1^2 \frac{dQ}{T}$$

where dQ is the heat taken in reversibly by the system at temperature T and the integral is taken from state 1 to state 2.

If the change occurs at a fixed temperature – that is, an isothermal change – then

$$\Delta S = \frac{Q}{T}$$

For example, the entropy change of 1 kg of ice when it turns to water at 273 K is the latent heat of fusion Q divided by the temperature and is 1223 J K^{-1}.

It is easy to show that the change of entropy is consistent with the second law of thermodynamics. Let a hot body give out heat Q at temperature T_1 and let this heat be absorbed by a cold body at T_2 (where T_1 is obviously greater than T_2).

Now the entropy change of the universe is given by:

$$dS = \frac{dQ}{T_2} - \frac{dQ}{T_1}$$

and since $T_1 > T_2$ there is a net increase in entropy of the universe. This entropy increase is consistent with heat being able to pass from a hot body to a cold one (an irreversible process).

The first law of thermodynamics is thus a law of *energy* while the second law of thermodynamics is a law of *entropy*.

In all heat engines energy is taken in as 'high-grade energy' and only some of it is converted into useful work, the remainder being emitted as 'low-grade energy' at a lower temperature.

The fundamental idea of an increase of the entropy of a system can give us a way of checking the passage of time. If you watch a film of a pile of bricks falling over it is easy to tell if the film is being run backwards since in only one case is the entropy or disorder increasing. Mixing hot and cold water to give a bucket of lukewarm water shows an entropy increase – you would not expect the lukewarm water to unmix itself!

We can put this idea on a cosmic scale. If we look into the universe we see discrete sources of energy – the stars. Their energy is being spread out throughout space, however, and if we could return many aeons in the future we would find this energy smeared out through the universe. The entropy and hence the disorder of the universe would have increased.

40 · The kinetic theory of matter

The ancients such as the philosophers Democritus and Lucretius held that matter was composed of minute particles. They also maintained that these particles were in a state of continuous random motion within solids, liquids and gases. The theory was therefore called the **kinetic theory of matter**, after the Greek work *kinema* – motion. Strong evidence for the existence of molecules is provided by the following observations:

(*a*) the diffusion of gases and liquids – diffusion in solids has actually also been observed: a slab of lead was clamped to a slab of gold for some years, and diffusion of each metal a few millimetres into the other was demonstrated by chemical analysis.

(*b*) the mixing of two liquids to give a final volume which is less than the sum of their original volumes;

(*c*) dissolving a solid in a liquid.

It was not until 1827, however, that actual experimental evidence for these particles existed. This was provided by the Scottish physicist Robert Brown. He observed a weak solution of milk and later pollen grains in suspension with a high-powered microscope, and saw that the particles of milk and the pollen grains showed a violent and random motion. Brown wrongly attributed what he saw to living organisms, and the true explanation was not given until some thirty years later when the Frenchman Carbonelle proposed that the motion was due to the impacts of the liquid molecules on the milk particles or pollen grains. The motion is now known as **Brownian movement**.

A simple modern version of Brown's experiment is the smoke cell. A small cell of air is placed under a microscope and illuminated strongly from the side. Some smoke is then blown into it. Through the microscope the particles of smoke can be seen to be in violent random motion just like Brown's pollen grains. This motion is due to the collisions of the air molecules with the much larger particles of smoke. Heating the cell makes the smoke particles' motion even more violent due to the increased velocity of the air molecules.

Various phenomena dealt with elsewhere in detail may be explained in terms of the kinetic theory:

(*a*) evaporation – molecules in the surface of a liquid gain sufficient energy to escape from it (page 258);

(*b*) saturated vapour pressure – there is a dynamic equilibrium between molecules entering and leaving a liquid surface in an enclosed space (page 258);

(*c*) surface tension – the intermolecular forces at a liquid surface explain capillary rise, liquid drop shapes, the wetting of surfaces and so on (page 102);

(*d*) latent heat – energy is required to overcome the intermolecular attraction to change the state of a substance (page 235);

(*e*) viscosity – the movement of molecules between adjacent layers of a moving fluid and their attraction gives the effect of viscous drag (page 120);

(*f*) the behaviour of gases, both ideal and real, may be explained in terms of molecules.

1 If hot air rises why is it cooler at the top of a mountain than at sea level?

2 In the kinetic theory of gases we have assumed that the force exerted by the gas molecules on the container walls is constant. How is this justified?

3 A bottle of strongly smelling perfume is dropped on to a hard floor in a long, straight draught-free corridor and smashes. Say how the kinetic theory of gases explains

(*a*) the time taken for the sound to reach the other end of the corridor,

(*b*) the time taken for the smell to reach the other end of the corridor.

Account for the large difference between these times.

Derivation of the kinetic theory formula

Remember that what follows applies to ideal gases only; the assumptions that we make certainly do not all apply to solids and liquids.

This proof was originally proposed by Maxwell in 1860. He considered a gas to be a collection of molecules and made the following assumptions about these molecules:

molecules behave as if they were hard, smooth, elastic spheres;
molecules are in continuous random motion;
the average kinetic energy of the molecules is proportional to the absolute temperature of the gas;
the molecules do not exert any appreciable attraction on each other;
the volume of the molecules is infinitesimal when compared with the volume of the gas;
the time spent *in* collisions is small compared with the time *between* collisions.

Consider a volume of gas V enclosed by a cubical box of sides l. Let the box contain N molecules of gas each of mass m, and let the density of the gas be ρ. Let the velocities of the molecules be $u_1, u_2, u_3 \dots u_n$.

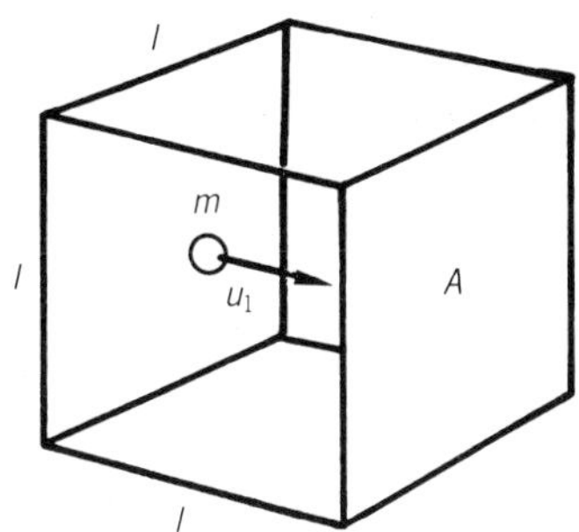

Figure 40.1

Consider a molecule moving in the x-direction towards face A with velocity u_1 (Figure 40.1). On collision with face A the molecule will experience a change of momentum equal to $2mu_1$.

It will then travel back across the box, collide with the opposite face and hit face A again after a time t, where $t = 2l/u_1$.

The number of impacts per second on face A will therefore be $1/t = u_1/2l$.

Therefore rate of change of momentum $= \dfrac{mu_1{}^2}{l}$

= force on face A due to one molecule.

But the area of face A $= l^2$, so

$$\text{pressure on face A} = \frac{mu_1{}^2}{l^3}$$

But there are N molecules in the box and if they were all travelling along the x-direction then

$$\text{total pressure on face A} = \frac{m}{l^3}(u_1{}^2 + u_2{}^2 + \ldots + u_n{}^2)$$

But on average only one-third of the molecules will be travelling along the x-direction. Therefore

$$\text{pressure} = \frac{1m}{3l^3}(u_1{}^2 + u_2{}^2 + \ldots + u_n{}^2)$$

If we rewrite $N\overline{c^2} = u_1{}^2 + u_2{}^2 + \ldots u_N{}^2$ where $\overline{c^2}$ is the **mean square velocity** of the molecules, then

$$\text{pressure} = \tfrac{1}{3}\frac{mN\overline{c^2}}{l^3}$$

But l^3 is the volume of the gas and therefore

$$PV = \tfrac{1}{3}mN\overline{c^2}$$

and this is the kinetic theory equation.

Now the total mass of the gas $M = mN$, and since $\rho = M/V$ we can write

$$P = \tfrac{1}{3}\rho\overline{c^2}$$

The **root mean square velocity** or r.m.s. velocity is written as $c_{\text{r.m.s.}}$ and is given by the equation:

$$\text{r.m.s. velocity} = \sqrt{\overline{c^2}} = \sqrt{\frac{u_1^2 + u_2^2 + u_3^2 \ldots + u_N^2}{N}}$$

We can use this equation to calculate the root mean square velocity of gas molecules at any given temperature and pressure.

Example

The density of nitrogen at s.t.p. = 1.251 kg m^{-3}. Calculate the r.m.s. velocity of nitrogen molecules.

$$\overline{c^2} = \frac{3P}{\rho} = \frac{3 \times 9.81 \times 13\,600 \times 0.76}{1.251}$$

$$= 2.432 \times 10^5$$

Therefore $c_{\text{r.m.s.}} = 493$ m s^{-1}

The table below gives some further values of the root mean square velocity at s.t.p. for other gases.

Gas	*R.m.s. velocity m s^{-1}*
Hydrogen	18.39×10^2
Helium	13.10×10^2
Oxygen	4.61×10^2
Carbon dioxide	3.92×10^2
Bromine	2.06×10^2

Use of the formula to prove the gas laws

(i) Boyle's law

We have $PV = \frac{1}{3}mN\overline{c^2}$, but $\overline{c^2}$ is proportional to the absolute temperature T.

Therefore for a given mass of gas at constant temperature $\frac{1}{3}mN\overline{c^2}$ is constant.

Therefore PV is constant and this is Boyle's law.

For one mole of gas we have $PV = RT$, where R is the gas constant, and therefore:

$$PV = \tfrac{1}{3}mL\overline{c^2} = RT$$

where L is the Avogadro constant. Therefore

$$\tfrac{1}{3}m\overline{c^2} = \frac{RT}{L}$$

and the quantity R/L is known as **Boltzmann's constant** k (see also page 253). The equation for one molecule may therefore be rewritten as:

$$\tfrac{1}{3}mc^2 = kT$$

4 'When two gases are mixed, if they are to be in thermal equilibrium they must have the same molecular speed.' Comment on this statement.

5 Two similar rubber balloons are filled to the same pressure, one with hydrogen and one with oxygen. Which balloon will go down first and why?

(ii) Charles's law
The total mass of gas is $mN = M$, therefore:

$$PV = \frac{1}{3}M\overline{c^2}$$

But if the temperature of the gas is changed from T_1 to T_2 with a resulting change in volume from V_1 to V_2, the pressure being kept constant:

$$PV_1 = \frac{1}{3}M\overline{c_1^2} \quad \text{and} \quad PV_2 = \frac{1}{3}M\overline{c_2^2}$$

Therefore

$$\frac{PV_1}{PV_2} = \frac{\frac{1}{3}M\overline{c_1^2}}{\frac{1}{3}M\overline{c_2^2}}$$

Therefore

$$\frac{V_1}{V_2} = \frac{\frac{2}{3}(\text{k.e.})_1}{\frac{2}{3}(\text{k.e.})_2} = \frac{T_1}{T_2}$$

So the volume is directly proportional to the absolute temperature, and this is Charles's law.

(iii) Avogadro's law
Maxwell showed that the average kinetic energies of molecules are equal at the same temperature, that is:

$$\frac{1}{2}m_1\overline{c_1^2} = \frac{1}{2}m_2\overline{c_2^2} \quad \text{but} \quad P_1V_1 = \frac{1}{3}m_1N_1\overline{c_1^2}$$

$$\text{and} \quad P_2V_2 = \frac{1}{3}m_2N_2\overline{c_2^2}$$

Now if $P_1 = P_2$ and $V_1 = V_2$, $m_1N_1\overline{c_1^2} = m_2N_2\overline{c_2^2}$; therefore

$$N_1 = N_2$$

and this is Avogadro's law (equal volumes of all gases at the same temperature and pressure contain equal numbers of molecules).

(iv) Dalton's law of partial pressures
For a mixture of gases:

$$PV = \frac{1}{3}(m_1N_1\overline{c_1^2} + m_2N_2\overline{c_2^2} + \ldots)$$

$$P = \frac{1}{3}\left(\frac{m_1N_1\overline{c_1^2}}{V} + \frac{m_2N_2\overline{c_2^2}}{V} + \ldots\right) \text{velocity}$$

$$P = P_1 + P_2 + \ldots$$

where $P_1, P_2 \ldots$ are the partial pressures of the gases, and this is Dalton's law (the sum of the partial pressures of all the gases occupying a given volume is equal to the total pressure).

(v) Graham's law of diffusion
The rate of diffusion of a gas is directly proportional to the mean velocity of the gas molecules, and this is also proportional to $\sqrt{\overline{c^2}}$.

$$\frac{\text{Rate of diffusion of gas A}}{\text{Rate of diffusion of gas B}} = \frac{u_A}{u_B} = \sqrt{\frac{\overline{c_A^2}}{\overline{c_B^2}}} = \sqrt{\frac{\rho_B}{\rho_A}}$$

This is Graham's law (the rate of diffusion of a gas varies inversely as the square root of the density of the gas).

The difference in mass and hence in the diffusion rates of the two isotopes of uranium (^{238}U and ^{235}U) is used in the nuclear industry to separate them, although the differences are small, and so a series of diffusion processes have to be used to obtain sufficient purity.

Student investigation

The following investigation is designed to study the absorption of sound in different gases.

Set up a horizontal tube 5 cm in diameter and 3 m long (a piece of water pipe is suitable) with a loudspeaker directed into one end.

(*a*) Using a signal generator, investigate the propagation of sound of frequency 8000 Hz in the tube when it is filled first with air and then with carbon dioxide.

(*b*) Reduce the frequency to 2000 Hz and repeat the experiment.

Suggest possible reasons for what you observe.

6 The surface of the Sun has a temperature of about 6000 °C and consists largely of hydrogen. Find the r.m.s. velocity and kinetic energy of a hydrogen molecule there.

7 Smoke particles in air have a mass of about 10^{-16} kg. The Brownian motion of these particles results from collisions with air molecules.
Calculate the r.m.s. velocity of the Brownian motion for such a particle in air at 300 K.

8 What is the average translational energy of an oxygen molecule at 300 K?

9 At a height of 300 km above the Earth's surface the air pressure is 10^{-6} mm of mercury. Calculate the molecular temperature that will just allow nitrogen molecules to escape from the atmosphere at this height. (Further data for this question may be found in the Appendix.)

Degrees of freedom

So far we have only been considering monatomic gases. We must now extend the ideas to cover gases of higher atomicity, that is, molecules with more than one atom per molecule.

If we go back to the kinetic theory formula, $PV = \frac{1}{3}mNc^2 = RT$, you can see that

$$RT = \tfrac{2}{3}(\text{average kinetic energy of the molecules})$$

since k.e. $= \frac{1}{2}mNc^2$. Therefore

$$\text{kinetic energy} = \tfrac{3}{2}RT$$

We have considered the motion of these molecules to be in three directions; we say that the molecule has three **degrees of freedom**. It is therefore sensible to suppose that one-third of the total energy is associated with each degree of freedom, and this is known as **Boltzmann's law of equipartition of energy**. Thus each degree of freedom has an amount of energy $\frac{1}{2}RT$ associated with it.

If a gas has its temperature raised at constant volume the energy input is the increase in k.e. of the gas molecules. So for a unit mass and for a rise in temperature dT we have:

$$C_v\, dT = \text{k.e.} = \tfrac{3}{2}R\, dT$$

But $C_p - C_v = R$, so for a monatomic gas:

$$C_v = \tfrac{3}{2}R \quad \text{and} \quad C_p = \tfrac{5}{2}R$$

Now consider a diatomic molecule. In addition to three translational degrees of freedom it can also rotate about three axes X, Y and Z (Figure 40.2).

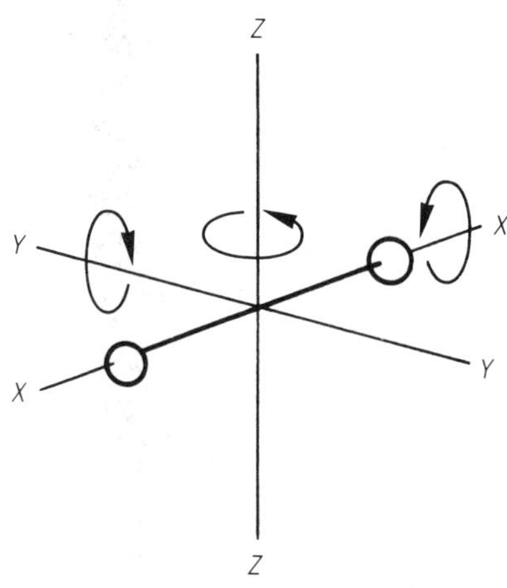

Figure 40.2

The energy associated with axis X is very small, however, and so we say that the molecule has five degrees of freedom. If we assume that the energy associated with each rotational degree of freedom is the same as that for each translational degree of freedom then the total energy of the molecule will be $5 \times \frac{1}{2}RT = \frac{5}{2}RT$. (The vibrational energy of the molecule is insignificant except at very high temperatures.)

Using the same argument as for the monatomic gas, we have for the two principal molar specific heats of a diatomic gas:

$$C_v = \tfrac{5}{2}R \quad \text{and} \quad C_p = \tfrac{7}{2}R$$

at temperatures around room temperature.

We therefore have for the ratio C_p/C_v (γ):

For a monatomic gas, $\gamma = 5/3 = 1.66$
For a diatomic gas, $\gamma = 7/5 = 1.40$

For more complex molecules we have that

$$\gamma = 1 + \frac{2}{n}$$

where n is the total number of degrees of freedom.

The table below gives the value of γ for a number of common gases.

Gas	*Value of* γ
Air	1.410
Ammonia	1.31
Argon	1.66
Carbon dioxide	1.30
Carbon monoxide	1.40
Helium	1.66
Hydrogen	1.41
Oxygen	1.40

These results show very good agreement with theory. The preceding section has dealt with one mole of a gas. If we now consider a sample of gas containing n moles we have:

$$\tfrac{2}{3}N(\tfrac{1}{2}m\overline{c^2}) = nRT$$

and this gives

$$\tfrac{1}{2}m\overline{c^2} = \tfrac{3}{2}\frac{R}{L}T$$

where L is the Avogadro constant. The quantity $\frac{R}{L}$ is known as the Boltzmann constant (k) and its value can be shown to be:

$$1.38 \times 10^{-23}\ \text{J K}^{-1}$$

The average translational energy of a single molecule is therefore:

$$\tfrac{3}{2}kT$$

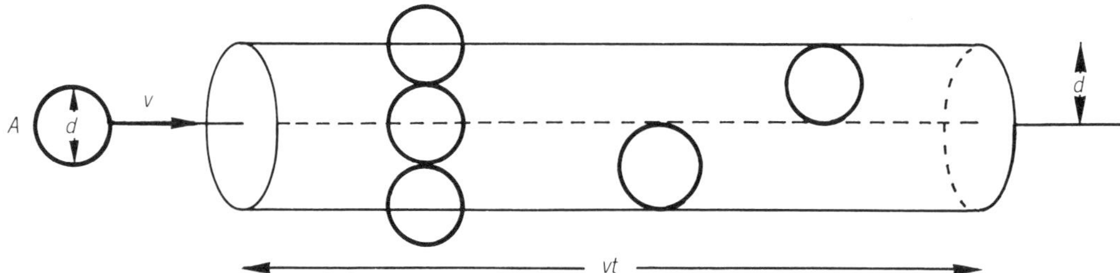

Figure 40.3

Mean free path of molecules in a gas

The molecules in a gas are assumed to be in continuous random motion making collisions with each other and with the walls of the container. The mean distance that the molecules travel between one collision and the next is called the **mean free path** of the molecules.

Consider a molecule A with an effective diameter d travelling with a velocity v. In a time t the molecule will travel a distance vt and collide with πd^2vtn molecules, where n is the number of molecules per unit volume (Figure 40.3). The molecule collides with all molecules whose centres are within a cylinder of length vt and cross-sectional area πd^2.

The mean free path is the total distance covered (vt) divided by the number of collisions. Therefore the mean free path l is given by

$$l = \frac{vt}{\pi d^2 nvt} = \frac{1}{\pi nd^2}$$

This proof assumes that all the other molecules remain at rest. If we consider the case of moving molecules the formula must be modified and becomes:

$$l = \frac{1}{\sqrt{2}\pi nd^2}$$

For air at 0°C and at a pressure of 1 atmosphere $d = 2 \times 10^{-10}$ m and $n = 3 \times 10^{25}$ m^{-3}. This gives a mean free path for air molecules in these conditions of 2×10^{-7} m or 200 nm, about a thousand molecular diameters and each molecule makes about five thousand million collisions per second!

At an altitude of 100 km the mean free path is 1 metre and at 300 km it is nearly 10 km.

At a depth of 5 000 m in a mine the density of air has risen to 2.32 kg m^{-3} and the mean free path is then reduced to about 75 nm.

10 State the assumptions usually made in deriving the kinetic theory formula for an ideal gas, and discuss the accuracy that you consider each assumption to have.

A further practical study of the mean free path in a gas may be made with the bromine diffusion experiment. In this experiment bromine vapour is allowed to diffuse through air at atmospheric pressure in a closed tube. The average distance d that the bromine diffuses in a certain time t is found by measuring the progress of the 'middle brown' colour of the bromine gas.

Now it can be shown statistically that d is related to the mean free path of the gas l by the formula:

$$d = l\sqrt{N}$$

where N is the number of collisions made while the bromine is diffusing through the distance d.

However, the total distance travelled by an individual molecule of bromine is D, where $D = Nl$, and therefore

$$l = \frac{d^2}{D}$$

Using the kinetic theory formula the velocity of the gas molecules may be found and hence the total distance D travelled in a certain time T. The mean free path can then be found.

Example

Using the data in the text calculate the number of air molecules per cubic metre n at the following places in the atmosphere.

(*a*) a height of 100 km
(*b*) a height of 300 km
(*c*) a depth of 5000 m in a mine.

$$n = \frac{1}{\sqrt{2}\pi ld^2}$$

(*a*) $n = 5.627 \times 10^{18}/1 = 5.6 \times 10^{18}$
(*b*) $n = 5.627 \times 10^{18}/1 = 5.6 \times 10^{14}$
(*c*) $n = 5.627 \times 10^{18}/1 = 7.5 \times 10^{25}$

Maxwell's distribution of molecular speeds

Maxwell showed on the basis of statistical mechanics that the actual distribution of molecular speeds within a gas was as shown in Figure 40.4.

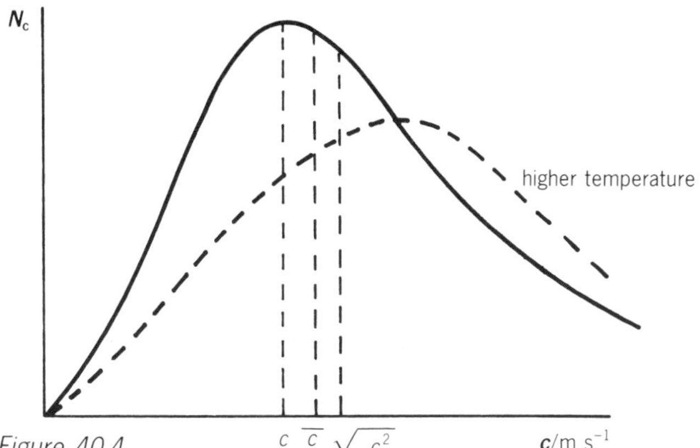

Figure 40.4

The number of molecules N_c having velocities between c and $(c + \Delta c)$ is plotted against the velocity (c). It can be shown that

$$c{:}\bar{c}{:}\sqrt{\overline{c^2}} = 1{:}1.13{:}1.23$$

where c is the most probable speed, $\bar{c}$ is the mean speed and $\sqrt{\overline{c^2}}$ is the root mean square speed.

The distribution can be investigated experimentally by passing a stream of gaseous molecules through three rotating discs with a slot in each. The discs are rotated on a common shaft separated by a known distance, the slots being at an angle θ to each other. Only those molecules with the correct velocity will be able to pass through all the slits.

A simplified diagram of the apparatus is shown Figure 40.5.

Consider a molecule that passes through S_1. If it is to pass through S_2 then the second disc must have rotated through an angle θ during the time that the molecule was travelling between the two discs, where θ is given by

$$\theta = 360nt = \frac{360l}{v}$$

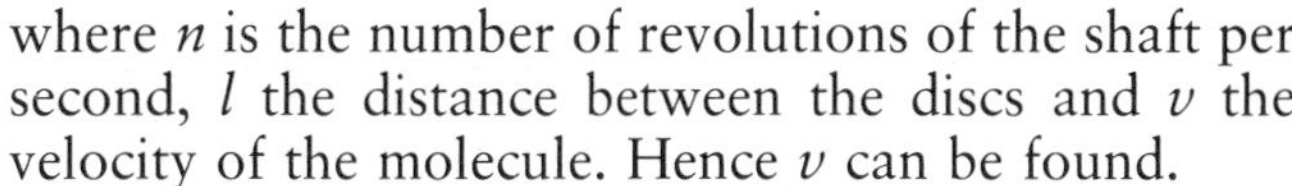

where n is the number of revolutions of the shaft per second, l the distance between the discs and v the velocity of the molecule. Hence v can be found.

11 Calculate the specific heat capacities of helium at constant volume and constant pressure if the density of helium at s.t.p. is 0.18 kg m^{-3}.

12 (*a*) What is meant by 'degrees of freedom' of a gas molecule?
(*b*) How is a knowledge of the degrees of freedom useful in determining the number of atoms per molecule for a given gas?

13 If there are 2.71×10^{25} molecules in 1 m^3 of a gas at a temperature of 20 °C and at a pressure of 10^5 Pa calculate the number per cubic metre at
(*a*) 0 °C and 10^{-4} mm of mercury pressure,
(*b*) 50 °C and 10^{-4} mm of mercury pressure.

14 For an ideal gas distinguish between:
(*a*) the mean velocity,
(*b*) the mean square velocity,
(*c*) the most common velocity, and
(*d*) the root mean square velocity.

15 Find the root mean square velocity of the molecules of nitrogen at 27 °C. (The relative molecular mass of nitrogen is 28 and the ideal gas constant is 8.31 J mol^{-1} K^{-1}.)

16 A closed vessel contains hydrogen which exerts a pressure of 20.0 mm of mercury at a temperature of 50 K.
(*a*) At what temperature will it exert a pressure of 180 mm of mercury?
(*b*) If the r.m.s. velocity of the molecules at 50 K was 800 m s^{-1}, what will be their velocity at this new temperature?
Assume that there is no change in the volume of the vessel.

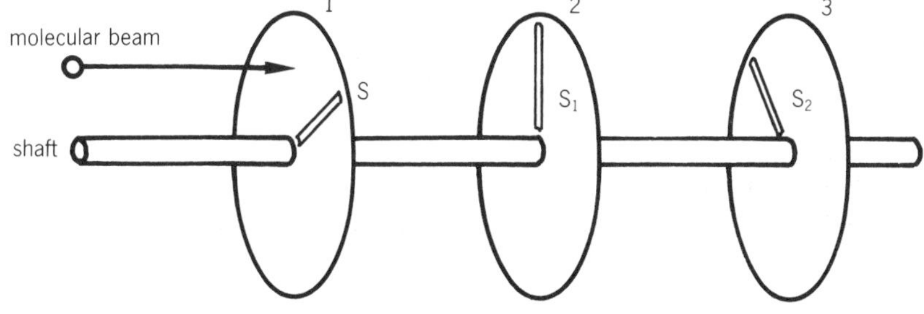

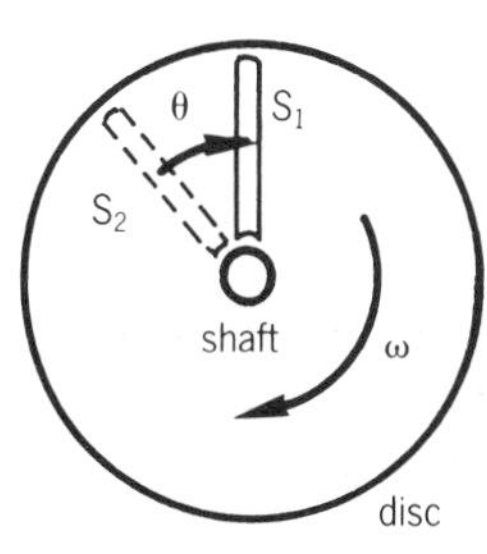

Figure 40.5 (*a*) (*b*)

41 · The behaviour of real gases

In our consideration of gases so far we have assumed that the intermolecular forces are zero and therefore that they follow the kinetic theory of gases exactly. This is not the case with actual gases, however.

A gas which follows the gas laws precisely is known as an **ideal gas** and one which does not is called a **real gas**.

In 1847 Regnault constructed *PV* curves up to 400 atmospheres and found that Boyle's law was not obeyed at these high pressures. Amagat went a stage further in 1892, working with nitrogen to pressures of some 3000 atmospheres (3×10^8 Pa) down a coal mine.

The idea that actual gases did not always obey the ideal gas equation was first tested by Cagniard de la Tour in 1822, using the apparatus shown in Figure 41.1.

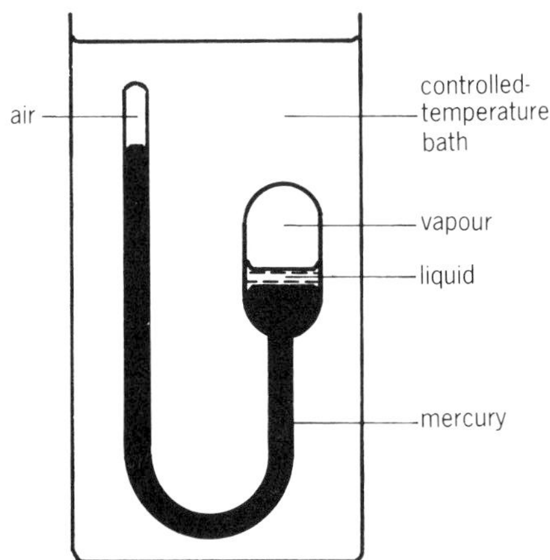

Figure 41.1

A liquid such as water or ether was trapped in a tube and the end of the tube placed in a bath whose temperature could be controlled. The temperature was then varied and the behaviour of the liquid observed. The space above the liquid is obviously filled with vapour and it was noticed that at a particular temperature no difference could be seen between the liquid and vapour states – this was called the **critical temperature**. This phenomenon was not predicted by Boyle's law, which says nothing about the liquefaction of gases.

The classic experiment on the behaviour of gases was devised by Andrews in 1863 and used carbon dioxide as the test gas. Using the apparatus shown in Figure 41.2, he plotted a series of isothermals (*PV* curves) to test the validity of Boyle's law over a wide range of pressures. The gases were compressed by tightening

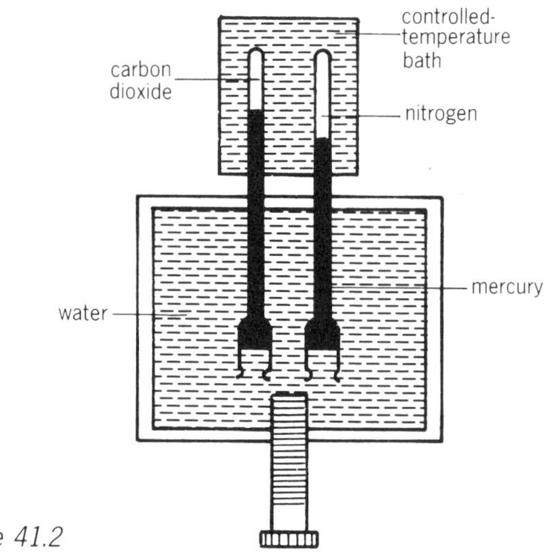

Figure 41.2

the screw and the pressure was estimated using the nitrogen assuming that under the conditions of the experiment it still obeyed Boyle's law. The capillary tubes were very strong and Andrews obtained results up to pressures of 10^7 Pa.

The results are shown in the two graphs in Figure 41.3. Above about 50 °C Boyle's law was fairly closely obeyed. But as you can see, the behaviour of the 'gas' is different above and below about 30 °C – in fact Andrews found that the **critical temperature** for carbon dioxide was 30.9 °C.

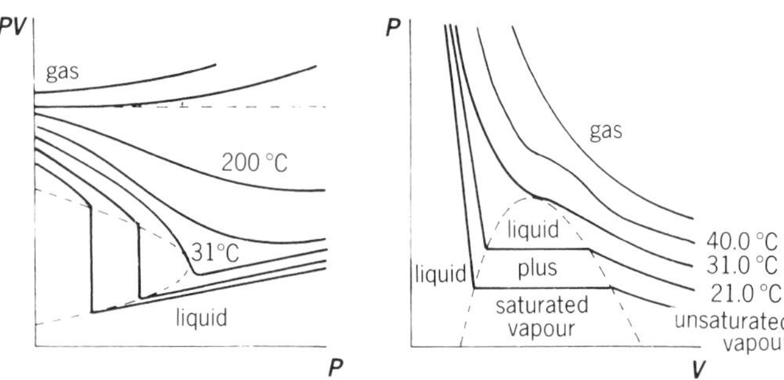

Figure 41.3

Above this temperature carbon dioxide could not be liquefied by pressure alone while below this temperature an increase in pressure would finally result in liquid carbon dioxide. At the critical point the gas and liquid are in equilibrium.

These ideas form the basis for a useful definition of a vapour:

A vapour is a gas below its critical temperature.

Some critical temperatures are shown in the following table.

Substance	*Critical temperature/°C*	*Boiling point/°C*
Helium	−268	−269
Hydrogen	−240	−253
Nitrogen	−147	−196
Air	−140	−190
Oxygen	−118	−183
Carbon dioxide	30.9	−78.2
Chlorine	146	−34
Water	374	100

To liquefy a gas by pressure alone it must first be cooled below its critical temperature.

The equation of state for a real gas

The most common form and the most accurate simple equation for the behaviour of a real gas is that proposed by van der Waals in 1872. He modified the ideal gas equations to allow for the fact that two of the assumptions made in their derivation may not be correct, that is:

(*a*) the volume of the molecules may not be negligible when compared with the volume of the gas, and

(*b*) the forces between the molecules may not be negligible.

Clearly both these effects become much more noticeable at high pressures and small volumes when the molecules are packed tightly together.

Consider first the volume of the molecules. The actual volume given in the equation must be reduced because the number of collisions will be greater. The equation becomes:

$$P(V - b) = RT$$

where b is the effective volume of the molecules. (It has been found to be about 4.2 × volume of the molecules.)

Considering now the attractive forces between the gas molecules, you can see that the pressure in the body of the gas is higher than that at the edges since molecules are pulled back into the centre by other molecules. We assume the attraction to be proportional to the number of molecules per unit volume (that is, to N/V).

The number of impacts per second is also affected and both these numbers are proportional to the density. So

$$\text{pressure reduction} = a/V^2$$

where a is a constant. Taking both these corrections into consideration, van der Waals' equation for one mole of a gas thus becomes:

$$(P + a/V^2)(V - b) = RT$$

where the observed pressure and volume are P and V.

Van der Waals' equation fits the isothermals of actual gases above the critical temperature, but below this the equation must be modified considerably.

The Joule–Kelvin effect: expansion of a real gas

This famous experiment performed in 1852 was a follow-up to those of Gay-Lussac (1807) and Joule (1845) and demonstrated that there were indeed attractive forces acting between gas molecules. In theory, if attractive forces do exist then when a gas expands its temperature should drop. The potential energy of the gas molecules has been increased and therefore in an isolated system its kinetic energy, and thus its temperature, should fall.

The apparatus used is shown in Figure 41.4. The experiment is often known as the porous plug experiment because gas at high pressure was allowed to expand through a cotton wool plug. The plug prevented eddies forming and the gas did not gain any kinetic energy in bulk. The initial temperature of the gas was maintained by the constant-temperature bath.

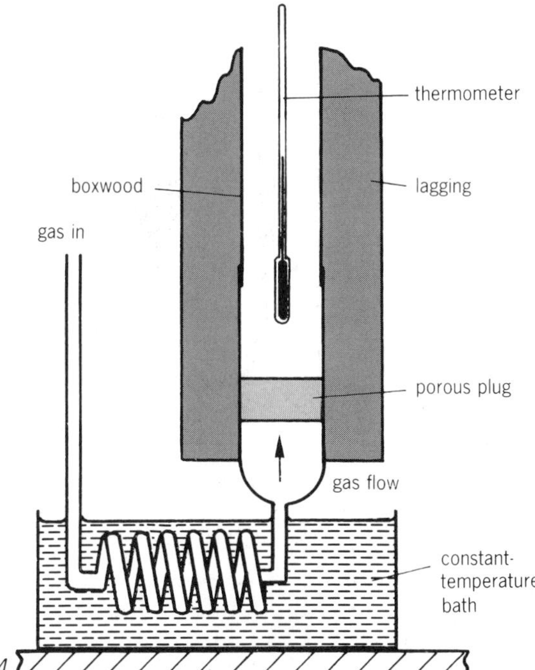

Figure 41.4

All gases showed a temperature change when passing through the plug but for some it was a cooling and for others a heating. The change in temperature was proportional to the pressure difference between the two sides of the plug: this can be understood if it is realised that work is done *on* the gas in forcing it through the plug and *by* the gas when it expands on emerging. For every gas there is an **inversion temperature**; if the initial temperature of the gas is above this then heating occurs and if it is below this cooling.

For helium this inversion temperature is 30 K, for hydrogen 190 K and for most other gases it is well above room temperature.

The table below gives the temperature changes per atmosphere observed in the experiment.

Gas	*Temperature change*/°C atm^{-1}
Nitrogen	−0.249
Oxygen	−0.253
Air	−0.208
Carbon dioxide	−1.005
Hydrogen	+0.039

Vapours and saturated vapour pressure

The molecules in a liquid are in a state of continuous motion and some of those at the liquid surface will gain sufficient energy to escape from the surface altogether. The molecules that have left the surface are said to be in the **vapour** state. The difference between a vapour and a gas is purely one of temperature, a vapour being a gas below its critical temperature (see page 256).

This phenomenon is known as **evaporation**. The number of molecules leaving the surface, and hence the rate of evaporation, will increase with temperature as the liquid contains more energy at a higher temperature. The effect of the evaporation of a liquid can be shown clearly by the following experiment.

Some ether is run into the flask, as shown in Figure 41.5. It will evaporate in the enclosed space and the pressure that it exerts on the water will force a jet of water out of the tube. Warming the liquid will increase this evaporation and give a more powerful jet.

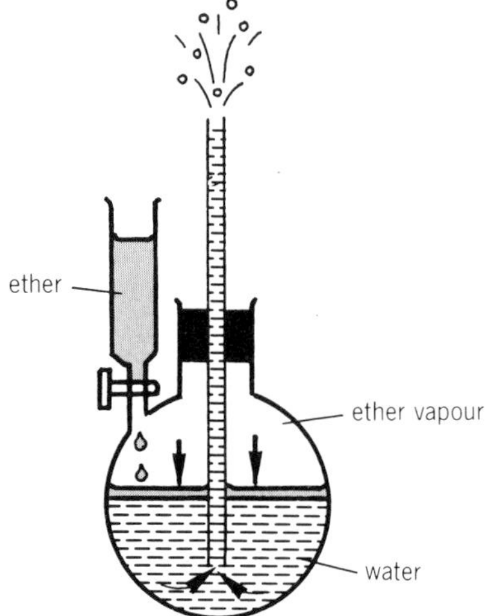

Figure 41.5

You can show that the rate of evaporation may be increased by

(*a*) warming the flask gently,
(*b*) increasing the area of the liquid surface,
(*c*) blowing a stream of air across the surface, and
(*d*) reducing the pressure above the liquid surface.

Saturated vapours

When a liquid is in a closed container the space above the liquid is full of vapour, and the vapour is then described as a **saturated vapour** – this means that the density of the liquid molecules in the air is a maximum. This is due to molecules continually escaping and re-entering the liquid. At any moment the number of molecules leaving the surface will be equal to the number returning to it and so a dynamic equilibrium is set up.

The properties of saturated vapours were first investigated by Dalton around 1800. This is shown in Figure 41.6(*a*), which shows a state before saturation has been reached (when there will be more molecules leaving the surface than returning to it) and Figure 41.6(*b*), which shows the saturated state. This vapour will exert a pressure and if there is sufficient liquid the air above the liquid surface will be saturated with vapour; the pressure that this saturated vapour exerts is known as the **saturated vapour pressure** (s.v.p.) of the liquid at that temperature. Notice that since the velocity of the molecules increases with temperature the saturated vapour pressure also increases with temperature, and therefore the temperature of the vapour must be specified when quoting its s.v.p.

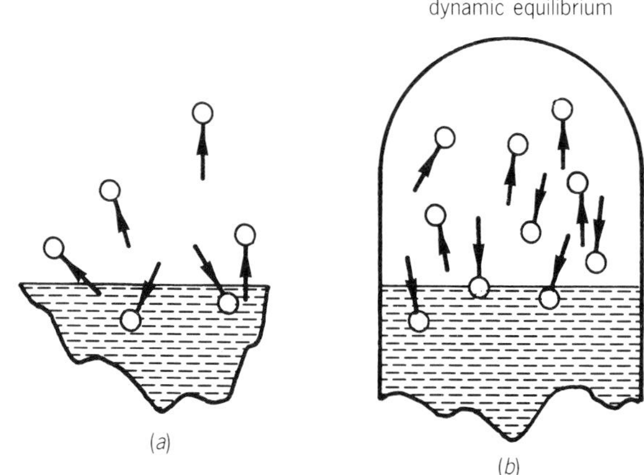

Figure 41.6

> The **saturated vapour pressure** of a liquid at a given temperature is defined as the pressure of the vapour in equilibrium with excess liquid at that temperature.

The saturated vapour pressure at 293 K is 2337 Pa for water and 0.16 Pa for mercury. These values rise to 101 325 Pa and 36.4 Pa at 373 K.

The following table gives the variation of the saturated vapour pressure of water with temperature.

Temperature/°C	*S.v.p.*/MPa	*Temperature*/°C	*S.v.p.*/MPa
10	0.001 227	50	0.012 34
15	0.001 704	60	0.019 92
20	0.002 337	70	0.031 16
25	0.003 166	80	0.047 36
30	0.004 242	90	0.070 11
40	0.007 375	100	0.101 325

Measurement of the s.v.p. of water

The saturated vapour pressure of a liquid – ether, for instance – may be measured using the apparatus shown in Figure 41.7. Ether is introduced into the space above the mercury in a barometer tube, using a special pipette, and the resulting depression of the mercury column is measured. The drop in level is the saturated vapour pressure of ether at that temperature. For an accurate determination we should allow for the effects of the weight of excess ether and for its surface tension, although these are small and are usually neglected. The barometer tube should also be kept in a water bath at a constant temperature.

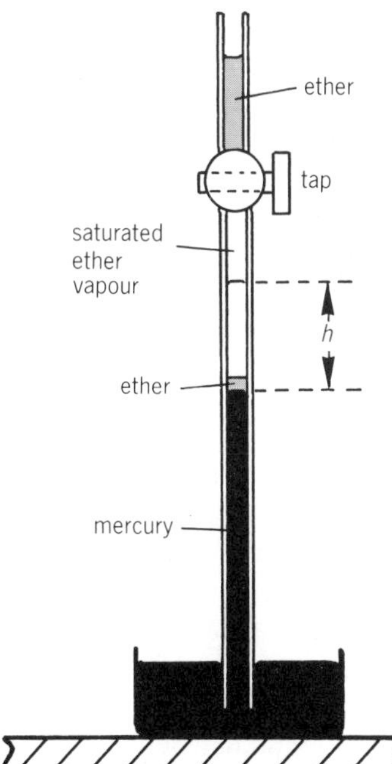

Figure 41.7

The s.v.p. of ether at 20 °C is 44 cm of mercury and this falls to 36 cm of mercury at 18 °C. The corresponding values for water at these temperatures are 1.8 cm and 1.5 cm, while for mercury the s.v.p. at 20 °C is only 1.2×10^{-3} mm.

The triple point of water

This is a most important point in the definition of the thermodynamic scale of temperature (see page 225). The graph of pressure plotted against temperature in Figure 41.8 explains how it is defined. Three lines are shown:

(*a*) the boiling curve (AB) is the locus of points where water and its vapour can exist in equilibrium;

(*b*) the sublimation curve (AC) is the locus of points where ice and its vapour can exist together in equilibrium;

(*c*) the solidification curve (AD) is the locus of points where water and ice can exist together.

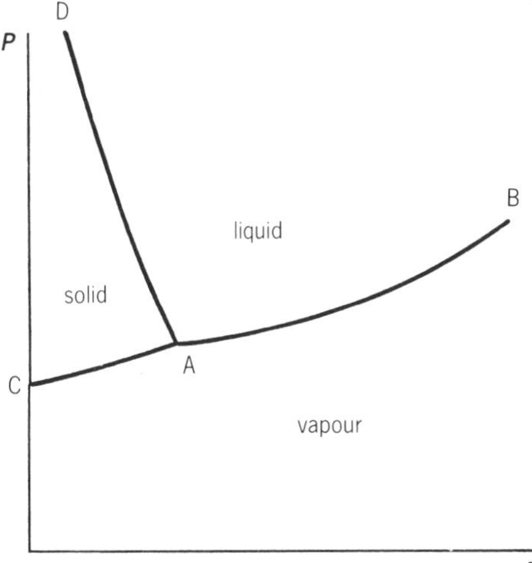

Figure 41.8

The **triple point** is at A where these three lines intersect and where water, water vapour and ice can exist in equilibrium. The temperature at which this occurs is defined as 273.16 K on the thermodynamic temperature scale. (The triple point is not exactly at 0 °C because under the pressure of its own vapour ice melts at about 0.0075 °C.)

1 A sealed flask contains a mixture of air and water vapour in contact with excess water vapour at 27 °C and a pressure of 77.7 cm of mercury. The temperature is now raised to 60 °C and the pressure in the flask becomes 98.1 cm of mercury. If the saturated vapour pressure of water at 27 °C is 2.7 cm of mercury, what will it be at 60 °C?

2 A uniform capillary tube, sealed at one end, contains a small plug of water so that the trapped air is saturated with water vapour. If the length of the air column at 40 °C is 25 cm and that at 60 °C 30.5 cm, calculate the atmospheric pressure. (S.v.p. of water at 40 °C = 7373 Pa and at 60 °C 19 920 Pa)

Supersaturated vapours

It can be shown by consideration of surface tension effects that droplets of liquid always tend to evaporate, due to the excess pressure at their surfaces, and that small drops evaporate faster than large ones. If this is the case, how do droplets condense at all? In fact they find it very difficult unless there is a nucleus, such as a dust particle or a charged ion, on which the drop can begin to grow. This means that the pressure of a vapour can exceed its saturated vapour pressure at a given temperature before condensation takes place. Such a vapour is said to be in a **supersaturated state**. Condensation will begin rapidly if a suitable nucleus is introduced into the vapour; this is of great importance in the cloud chamber (see page 441).

The capillary tube method for finding the s.v.p. of water

This is a simple method, for which the apparatus is shown in Figure 41.9: a capillary tube closed at one end containing a short column of air with a water plug stands in a glass of water. The air trapped in the tube is of course saturated since there is excess water present.

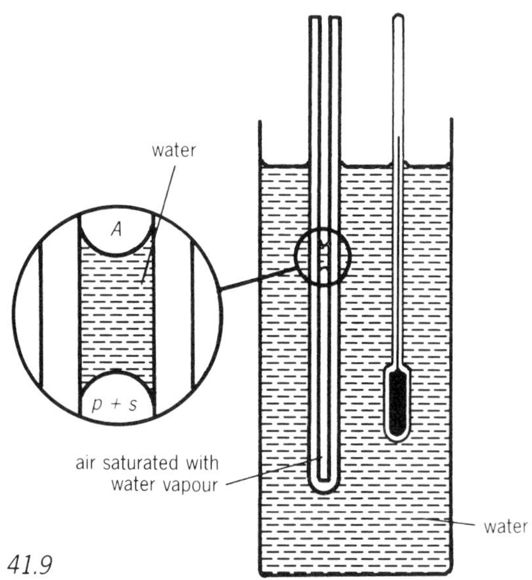

Figure 41.9

Let the atmospheric pressure be A, let the air pressure in the tube be p and the s.v.p. of water at that temperature be s. Neglecting the weight of the small amount of water in the plug, we have

$$A = p + s$$

Therefore:

$$p = A - s$$

Now saturated vapours do not obey Boyle's law, since their pressure is constant at a given temperature and is independent of the volume of air. Therefore for the *air* in the tube we have:

$$\frac{(A - s)\,V}{T} = \text{constant}$$

where V is the volume of air in the tube and T is its temperature.

We can therefore measure the s.v.p. of water if its value at one temperature is known.

The results obtained for water are shown in Figure 41.10. Notice that the s.v.p. rises with temperature as predicted, and that its value at 100 °C is the value of standard atmospheric pressure. This fact can be explained as follows. Consider a bubble below the surface of the liquid: the pressure within the bubble is the saturated vapour pressure of that liquid, neglecting the hydrostatic pressure which is comparatively

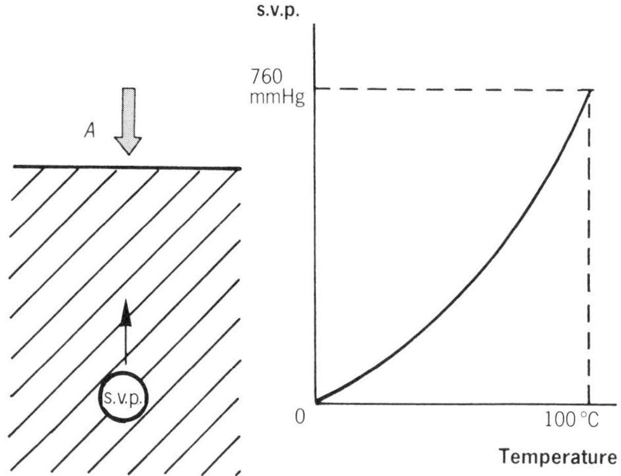

Figure 41.10

small. Now when the liquid boils bubbles rise to the surface of the liquid and escape so the pressure within them must be equal to the external pressure. We can say, therefore, that

A liquid boils when its saturated vapour pressure is equal to the external pressure.

Example

A column of air was sealed into a horizontal uniform-bore capillary tube by a water plug. When the atmospheric pressure was 762.5 mm of mercury and the temperature was 20 °C the air column was 15.6 cm long. When the tube was immersed in a water bath at 50 °C the length of the air column became 19.1 cm, the atmospheric pressure remaining the same. If the s.v.p. of water at 20 °C is 17.5 mm of mercury, deduce its value at 50 °C.

Remembering that a saturated vapour does *not* obey the gas laws, we have:

initial air pressure = 762.5 − 17.5 = 745 mm.

Therefore final air pressure p can be found from:

$$\frac{745 \times 15.6}{293} = \frac{p \times 19.1}{323}$$

Therefore p = 670.8 mm, giving a value for the s.v.p. at 50 °C of (762.5 − 670.8) = 91.7 mm of mercury.

3 (*a*) Explain what is meant by a saturated vapour.

(*b*) Draw graphs to show the relationship between pressure and temperature (i) for an ideal gas, (ii) for saturated water vapour and (iii) for a mixture of the ideal gas and the saturated water vapour. The curves should be drawn on axes extending from 0–100 °C (*x* axis) and 0–1.2 × 10^5 Pa (*y* axis) and should be reasonably accurate. The initial pressure of the ideal gas at 0 °C is to be taken as 0.2 × 10^5 Pa. (Normal atmospheric pressure is *approximately* 10^5 Pa.)

(*c*) Describe how you would measure the saturated vapour pressure of water at various temperatures between 10 °C and 80 °C.

(*d*) A mass of saturated water vapour at 50 °C occupies a volume of 1.00 × 10^{-2} m^3. When converted to steam at 100 °C and pressure 1.01 × 10^5 Pa it occupies 1.60 × 10^{-3} m^3. Assuming that, up to saturation point, the vapour behaves like an ideal gas, calculate the saturated vapour pressure of water at 50 °C. [AEB 1983]

Dynamic method for the determination of the s.v.p. of water

A method of measuring the s.v.p. of water based on the above idea was developed by Ramsay and Young in 1886. A simplified diagram of their apparatus is shown in Figure 41.11.

The liquid in the flask is heated until it boils and the pressure within the apparatus measured with a manometer. The large flask is included in the apparatus to minimise the effects of rapid changes of pressure during the experiment. The source of heat is then removed and the flask allowed to cool slowly. Boiling can be achieved at any temperature by reducing the pressure within the apparatus using the vacuum pump. The water can be made to boil at 30 °C with a simple tap-mounted pump, the s.v.p. of water being about 3 cm of mercury at this temperature.

Water vapour in the atmosphere

The amount of water vapour in the atmosphere is known as its **humidity**. The ease with which our bodies lose water vapour depends on the humidity of the air, that is, how much water vapour is already present in it. Water vapour will condense from the air when it is saturated, and since saturation varies with temperature cooling down a sample of air will often result in condensation occurring. The formation of clouds and rain is governed by these effects. The formation of a cloud in the cloud chamber is caused by cooling the air containing meths vapour (by expansion or by the use of 'dry ice') to a point where it becomes saturated and liquid is forced to condense (see below).

The humidity of the atmosphere is measured by an instrument known as a **hygrometer**, the most common types of this being the wet and dry bulb hygrometer and the hair hygrometer. Further study of this topic is outside the scope of this book.

4 An amateur astronomer brings her 15 cm mirror into the kitchen after an hour or so of observing outside on a winter evening. Explain why a layer of water condenses on it.

Student investigation

Write an essay on the cycle of water vapour in the atmosphere, with particular reference to the measurement of the relative humidity. Explain also how evaporation from a surface will cool that surface.

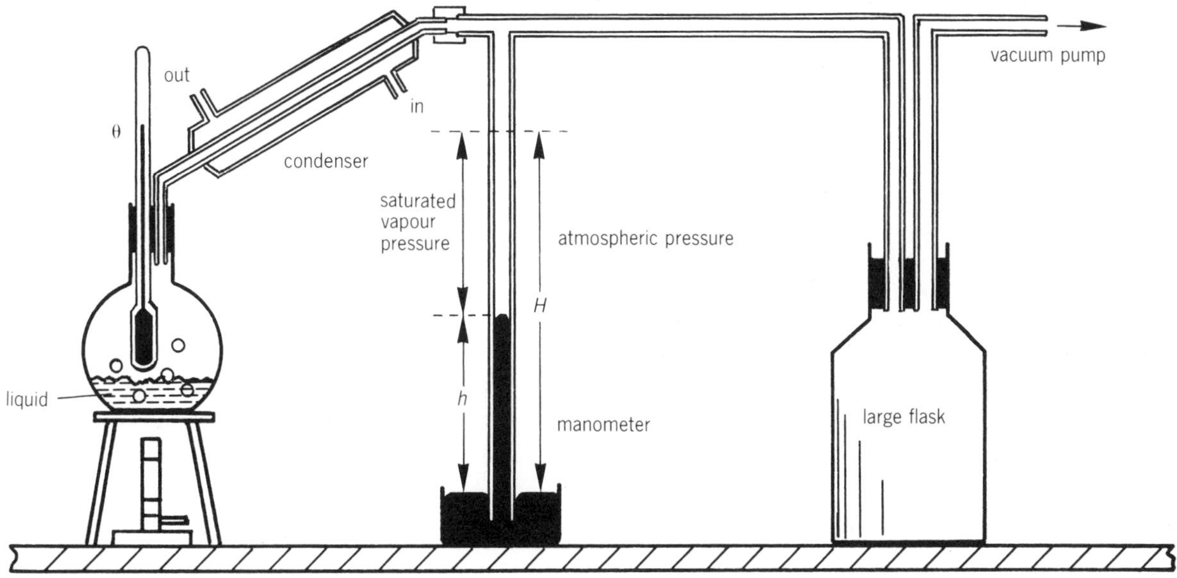

Figure 41.11

42 · Transfer of heat

Conduction

The transfer of heat energy from one place to another through a substance without the movement of the substance as a whole is known as **conduction.**

Conduction of heat is most important in the insulation of houses because much of the heat produced in the house is lost by conduction through the walls, roof, windows and floor and knowledge of materials that can be used to reduce this loss is of great importance (see page 265).

If we consider a specimen of length dx and cross-sectional area A, with a temperature difference dθ between the opposite faces (Figure 42.1), then the rate of flow of heat energy through it will depend on

(*a*) the cross-sectional area of the face,

(*b*) the temperature difference between the faces, and

(*c*) the inverse of the distance between the faces.

Therefore:

$$\text{rate of flow of heat } \frac{dH}{dt} = -kA\frac{d\theta}{dx}$$

where k is a constant known as the **thermal conductivity** of the material, which is measured in W m^{-1} K^{-1}.

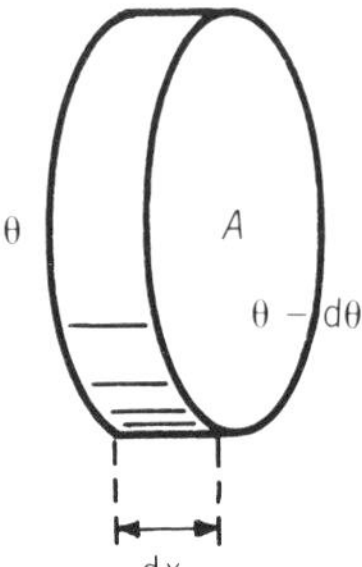

Figure 42.1

> The **thermal conductivity** is defined as the rate of flow of heat between two surfaces of unit area separated by unit distance when the temperature difference between them is 1 K

(Notice the negative sign: this implies that the temperature will decrease as the distance down the bar increases.)

The value of k for various materials is given in the table below.

Material	k/W m^{-1} K^{-1}	*Material*	k/W m^{-1} K^{-1}
Silver	419	Copper	385
Aluminium	200	Iron	80
Glass	0.8	Brick	0.6
Water	0.59	Methylated spirits	0.20
Wood	0.15	Cork	0.05
Air	0.024	Chlorine	0.007

1 Calculate the rate of flow of heat down the following specimens if the temperature difference between the two ends of the specimens is maintained at 100 °C:

(*a*) a copper rod 10 cm long with a diameter of 0.4 cm;

(*b*) an iron rod of the same dimensions;

(*c*) a 'slab' of air 5 cm thick and with an area of 0.5 m^2;

(*d*) a brick 20 cm long with ends 10 cm by 7 cm.

Assume in each case that no heat energy is lost from the sides of the specimen.

Student investigation

You may have performed a simple experiment in your GCSE course to investigate the conductivities of various metal rods by holding one end of them in a bunsen flame and seeing which one you have to put down first when it becomes too hot to hold. How much of this effect is due to the thermal conductivity of the specimen and how much to the rate at which the specimen can be warmed up, that is, to its specific heat capacity?

Using a thermocouple and either a potentiometer or an instrument such as a Vela, investigate the rate of rise of temperature at different points along a metal rod when one end is placed in a bunsen flame. Plot a graph of temperature against time and attempt to deduce the form of the equation relating these two quantities. Try different metals, and also specimens with different cross-sectional areas.

How would lagging the rods affect your results?

A comparison between the flow of heat down a bar and the flow of matter and electricity is given on page 123.

We will now consider the flow of heat down a bar, assuming that it is perfectly lagged so that no heat escapes from the sides. All the heat energy entering one end of the bar eventually leaves the other end; this is known as parallel heat flow. The drop in temperature is linear.

With an unlagged bar, however, heat is lost and so the rate of fall of temperature varies down the bar.

The temperature variation and the heat flow are shown for both bars in Figure 42.2(*a*) and (*b*).

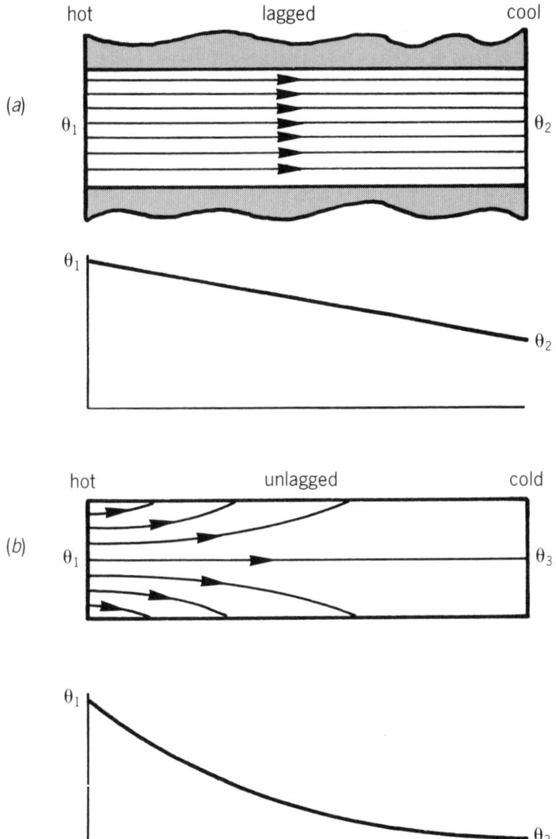

Figure 42.2

Note that this is the flow of heat down a bar when steady state has been reached. Initially the temperature distribution will depend on the rate at which a pulse of heat energy can travel down the bar, and this depends on the specific heat capacity of the material and not the thermal conductivity.

> **Example**
>
> Calculate the rate of loss of heat through a window of thickness 6 mm and area 2 m^2 if the temperature difference between the two sides is 20 ° C.
>
> $$\frac{dH}{dt} = -kA\frac{d\theta}{dx} = \frac{0.8 \times 2 \times 20}{6 \times 10^{-3}} = 5.3 \text{ kW.}$$

Clearly this is a very large value: the heat loss from a normal house in winter would seem to be enormous. However, when heat is conducted through the glass it warms the layer of air just outside the window, thus raising the temperature of the outer glass surface (Figure 42.3). This reduces the temperature gradient and hence the loss of heat is also reduced.

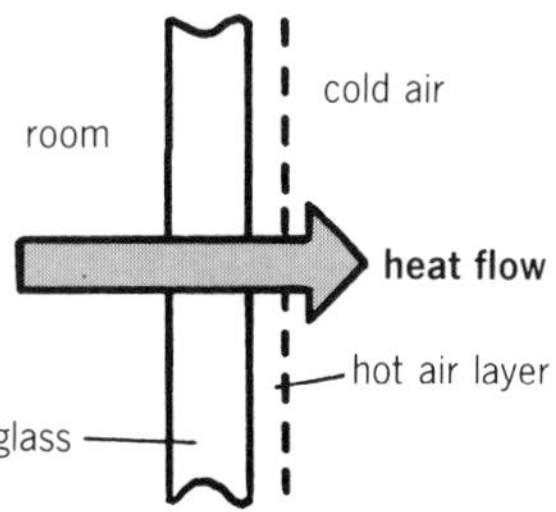

Figure 42.3

The mechanism of conduction

(i) Metals

If one end of a metal rod is heated the atoms gain energy and their vibrations increase. This energy is then passed on to the other atoms and to the numerous free electrons in the metal. Since the electrons are very small they can travel rapidly around within the specimen, transferring their energy by collision to other electrons and other atoms. In metals, therefore, heat is carried mainly by the motion of these free electrons, although some energy is of course transferred by interatomic vibration.

The conductivity of metals does vary with temperature and at very low temperatures the lattice vibrations carry the heat energy more easily than the free electrons do.

(ii) Non-metals

In non-metallic solids there are virtually no free electrons, and therefore the only way that heat can travel through the specimen is by the direct transfer of energy from one atom to another. Debye suggested that the energy was transferred by some sort of elastic wave propagated through the specimen. These waves are sometimes called **phonons**, and travel with the speed of sound through the solid.

Wiedmann and Franz showed that the ratio of thermal conductivity to electrical conductivity is the same for all metals, and this supports the view that a good conductor of electricity is also a good conductor of heat.

The composite bar

Consider a bar made of two materials, both of the same cross-sectional area A, one a good conductor and the other a poor conductor, and assume that the bar is perfectly lagged, so that no heat leaves its sides (Figure 42.4(a)).

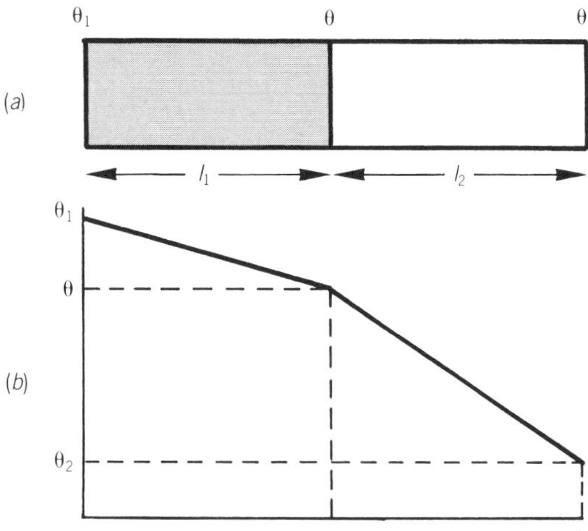

Figure 42.4

The heat flowing into one end of the bar is equal to that flowing out the other end, and so the rate of flow of heat in one material is equal to that in the other material.

Therefore if the temperature of one end of the bar is θ_1 and that of the other end θ_2, and if the temperature of the join is θ, then:

For the good conductor: $$\frac{dH}{dt} = \frac{-k_1A(\theta_1 - \theta)}{l_1}$$

For the poor conductor: $$\frac{dH}{dt} = \frac{-k_2A(\theta - \theta_2)}{l_2}$$

where k_1 and k_2 are the thermal conductivities of the two materials and l_1 and l_2 are the lengths of the two sections of the bar. Since the rates of heat flow are equal, we have

$$\frac{k_1A(\theta_1 - \theta)}{l_1} = \frac{k_2A(\theta - \theta_2)}{l_2}$$

So if the lengths are equal, the temperature drop through the good conductor will be much less than that through the poor conductor (Figure 42.4(b)).

2 In a domestic heating system, a room is warmed by a 'radiator' through which water passes at a rate of 0.12 kg s^{-1}. The steady-state difference between the inlet and outlet temperatures of the water is 6.0 K. The radiator is made of iron of thermal conductivity 80 W m^{-1} K^{-1} and has an effective surface area of 1.5 m^2 with walls 2.0 mm thick. At what rate is heat supplied to the room? What is the mean temperature difference between the inner and outer surfaces of the radiator walls?
[Specific heat capacity of water
= 4.2×10^3 J kg^{-1} K^{-1}] [c]

3 The Earth has a crust (thin compared with the radius of the Earth) of thermal conductivity approximately 2 W m^{-1} K^{-1}. On average the temperature of the crust increases by about 20 °C for each kilometre below the surface. Estimate the total rate at which heat leaves the Earth's surface by conduction through the crust. (Take the radius of the Earth to be 6×10^6 m.) [c]

Thermal conductivity and kinetic theory

Consider three horizontal planes in the gas each of area A (Figure 42.5). The heat conducted downwards through A per second is then $-kA\frac{d\theta}{dz}$.

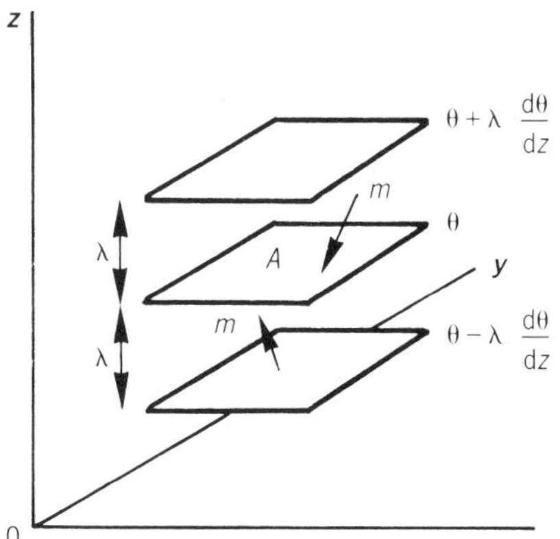

Figure 42.5

However, each second a mass of gas m at a temperature θ_1 crosses A moving downwards and a mass of gas m at a temperature θ_2 crosses A moving upwards. Now

$$m = \frac{\rho c A}{6} \quad \theta_1 = \theta + \lambda\frac{d\theta}{dz} \quad \text{and} \quad \theta_2 = \theta - \lambda\frac{d\theta}{dz}$$

Therefore, since heat = $mc\theta$, the net transfer of heat downwards is $\frac{-\rho c A}{6}\lambda\frac{2d\theta}{dz}C_v$. But this must equal $-kA\frac{d\theta}{dz}$, and therefore:

$$k = \tfrac{1}{3}\rho c\lambda C_v \qquad \text{and since } \eta = \tfrac{1}{3}\rho c\lambda \qquad k = \eta C_v$$

Radial heat flow through the sides of a tube

In most of our homes hot water flows through pipes to taps or in hot water systems. If these pipes are not lagged a great deal of heat will be lost. It is no use turning on the hot tap to find that so much heat has been lost that the water is cold before it reaches you from the hot water tank!

Consider a tube of inner radius r and outer radius R. Let the temperature on the outer surface be θ_1 and that inside the tube θ_2. The rate of flow of heat through the walls is then given approximately by

$$\frac{dH}{dt} = -kA\frac{d\theta}{dx}$$

$$= -kA\frac{(\theta_2 - \theta_1)}{(R - r)}$$

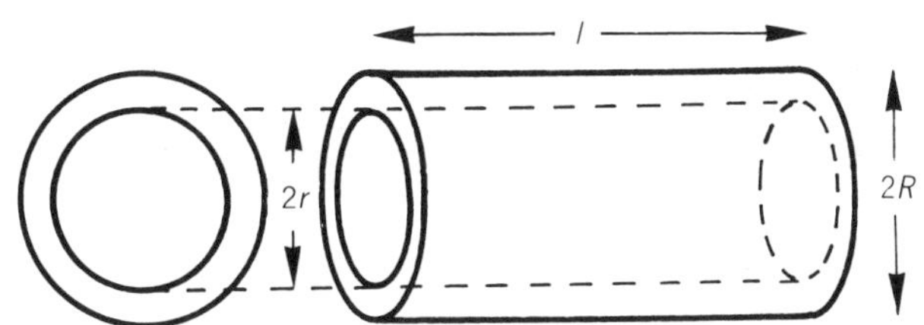

Figure 42.6

where A is the mean surface area of the inner and outer walls of the tube. However, if the walls of the tube are not too thick we can take A as $\frac{2\pi(R + r)l}{2}$ $= \pi l(R + r)$, for a length of tube l. Therefore

$$\frac{dH}{dt} = -k\pi l\frac{(R + r)}{(R - r)}(\theta_2 - \theta_1)$$

The loss of heat from unlagged central heating pipes can be found by this method. We start by assuming that the temperature outside the pipe is the air temperature but in reality this will not be so.

Student investigation

Keeping warm in bed can be very important, especially for old people. In this investigation you will study the insulation properties of blankets and continental quilts of various types.

Fill a metal can with water at 100 °C and fix the probe of a digital thermometer to the outside of the can. (If such a thermometer is not available a thermocouple will do instead.)

Place the quilt or blanket over it and record the temperature at regular time intervals.

Repeat the procedure for several types of bed covering. Which type would you recommend?

Example

Consider a copper hot water pipe that delivers a flow of water at 0.2 kg s^{-1} (m). If the pipe has a length of 20 m and the inlet temperature is 60 °C, calculate the outlet temperature if the exterior of the pipe is at a temperature of 50 °C. (Thermal conductivity of copper (k) = 385 W m^{-1} K^{-1} and specific heat capacity of water (c) = 4200 J kg^{-1} K^{-1})

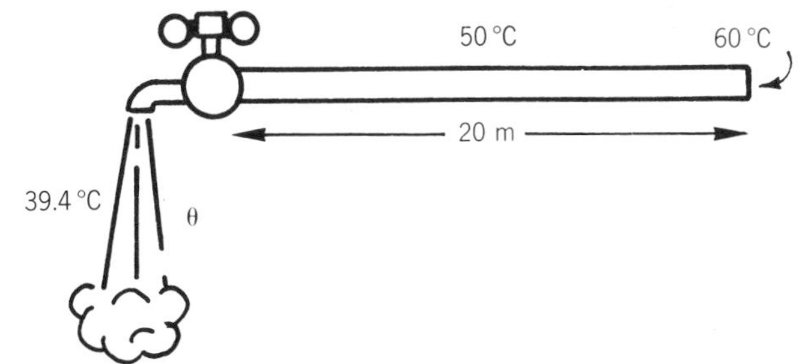

Figure 42.7

Let the pipe have an internal diameter of 2.0 cm and an exterior diameter of 3.5 cm.
Let the outlet temperature be θ. Therefore

$$mc(60 - \theta) = kA\frac{d\theta}{dx} = \frac{kA}{\Delta r}(50 - \tfrac{1}{2}(\theta + 60))$$

This gives θ = 39.4 °C (Figure 42.7).

Insulation of houses

Much detailed work has been done on this topic and a few results are quoted below.

Part of house	*Rate of loss of heat*/(W m^{-2})
Glass window	112
Double-glazed window	60
Single brick wall	66
Cavity wall	19
Foam-filled cavity wall	10
Uninsulated roof	30
Roof with 50 mm glass wool	10.4
Roof with 75 mm glass wool	7.8
Solid floor	9

All these figures are for a temperature difference across the surfaces of 20 °C. Of course, even perfect insulation is no use at all unless you cut out all the draughts!

4 An insulated wire whose resistivity is $5 \times 10^{-7}\,\Omega$ m and diameter 1 mm carries a current of 5 A. The insulation material is 1 mm thick and has a coefficient of thermal conductivity of 0.2 W m^{-1} K^{-1}.

Find the temperature difference between the inner and outer surfaces of the insulating material when steady state has been reached.

The measurement of the thermal conductivity of a good conductor

The method uses an apparatus called Searle's bar, shown in Figure 42.8. A specimen of the material in the form of a bar, polished on the outside to reduce radiation losses, is heavily lagged and placed in a wooden box. The length of the bar is large compared with its diameter so that a measurable temperature gradient can be produced.

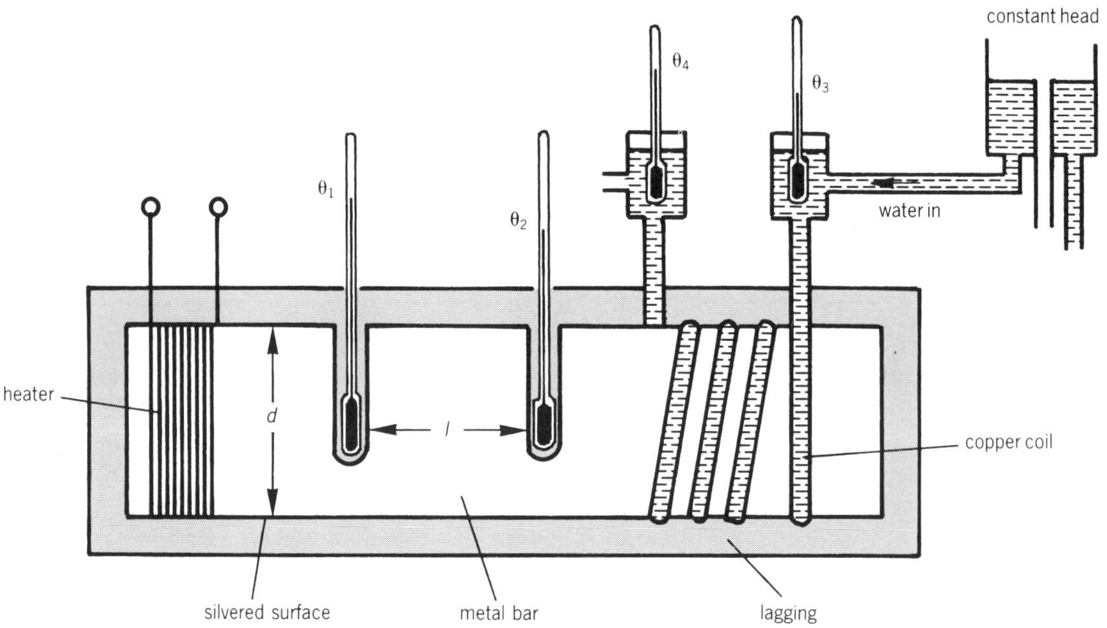

Figure 42.8

A heating coil wrapped round one end provides a heat input at a constant rate and the heat is removed at the other end by water flowing slowly through a copper tube which is soldered round the bar at the other end. The temperature gradient is measured by two thermometers placed in holes in the bar; these holes may be filled with mercury to increase thermal contact. When steady state has been reached the incoming temperature (θ_3) and outgoing temperature (θ_4) of the water is recorded as is its rate of flow (m) in kg s^{-1}. The cooling water must flow from a constant-head apparatus so that the rate of flow does not vary.

The diameter of the bar is measured at a number of different points using a pair of vernier calipers and a mean value found. From this the cross-sectional area (A) can be found. The value of k is found from the following equation:

$$\frac{dH}{dt} = \frac{-kA(\theta_1 - \theta_2)}{l} = mc_w(\theta_4 - \theta_3)$$

where θ_1 and θ_2 are the temperatures of the thermometers in the bar, l is their separation and c_w is the specific heat capacity of the water.

5 Explain how the temperature varies along a uniform metal bar which is
(*a*) unlagged,
(*b*) lagged all along its length.
Assume that heat is supplied at a constant rate to one end and that a steady state has been reached.
In case (*b*) suppose heat flows along the bar, which is of 20 cm^2 cross-section, at the rate of 600 J s^{-1}. If the temperature at a certain distance from the heated end is 60 °C, where will the temperature be 40 °C? (The coefficient of thermal conductivity of the bar is 400 W m^{-1} K^{-1}.)

6 Bars of copper and iron of equal length are welded together end to end and lagged. Determine the temperature of the interface when the free end of the copper is at 100 °C and the free end of the iron is at 0 °C and conditions are steady.
Sketch the variation down the two bars of (*a*) the rate of flow of heat through the bars, and (*b*) the temperature of the bars. (The thermal conductivity of copper is 385 W m^{-1} K^{-1} and that of iron is 80 W m^{-1} K^{-1}.) [c]

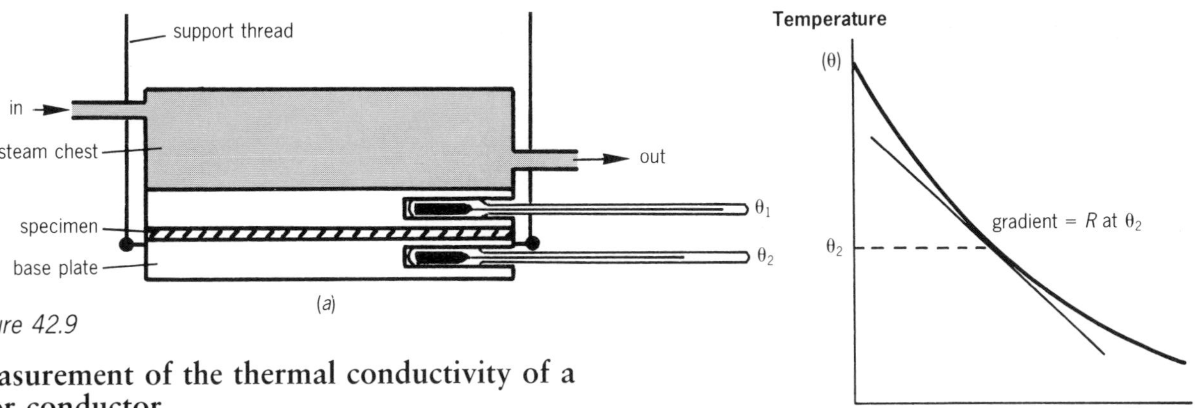

Figure 42.9

Measurement of the thermal conductivity of a poor conductor

With a poor conductor the rate of flow of heat will be small and so a thin specimen with a large cross-sectional area has to be used. The apparatus is known as Lee's disc, and is shown in Figure 42.9(*a*).

The specimen rests on a brass baseplate and a steam chest is placed on top. Steam is passed through the chest and the temperature of the baseplate and the base of the steam chest is measured. The thermometers are set in good thermal conductors and therefore the temperatures that they measure are effectively those of the faces of the specimen. Vaseline may be placed in the holes to ensure even better contact.

When a steady state has been reached the temperatures θ_1 and θ_2 are recorded. The rate of loss of heat from the baseplate being by radiation and convection, the baseplate is polished so that radiation losses are small and Newton's law of cooling can be applied. We can assume that the heat lost from the sides of the specimen itself is negligible.

The rate of loss of heat from the baseplate can be found as follows. The specimen is removed and the baseplate heated directly by the steam chest to nearly 100 °C. The steam chest is then removed, the specimen replaced and a cooling curve plotted for the baseplate and specimen (Figure 42.9(*b*)). The rate of cooling R at the temperature θ_2 can be found by taking the gradient of the curve at that point, and if the mass m and specific heat capacity c of the material of the baseplate are known, its rate of loss of heat can be found.

The thickness l and cross-sectional area A of the specimen can be found using vernier calipers, and then

$$\frac{kA(\theta_1 - \theta_2)}{l} = mcR$$

Hence k can be calculated.

The growth of ice on a pond

An interesting application of thermal conductivity is the calculation of the rate of growth of ice on top of a pond.

Let the air temperature be θ °C and the water temperature just below the ice be 0 °C. At a certain time let the thickness of the ice be x, and let it increase by a further thickness dx in a time dt (Figure 42.10). The

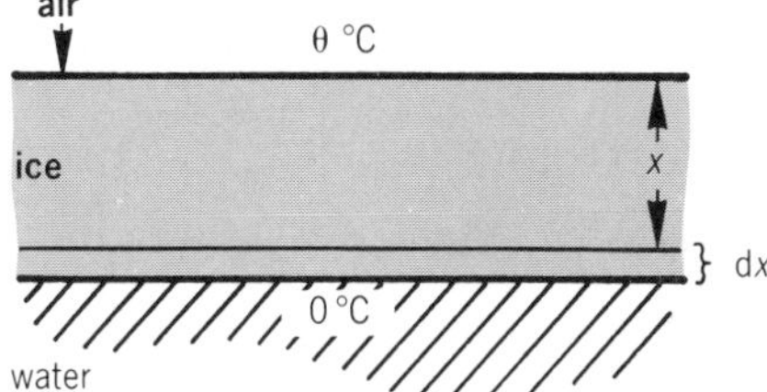

Figure 42.10

latent heat released on melting has to be conducted away through the ice layer as the water freezes and therefore we have:

$$\text{quantity of heat lost due to increase } dx = \rho L A dx$$

where ρ is the density of ice, L the specific latent heat of fusion of water and A the area of the ice surface. Then, if x is the thickness of the ice after a time t,

$$\text{rate of loss of heat} = LA\rho\frac{dx}{dt} = \frac{k\theta A}{x}$$

$$\therefore \quad \frac{dx}{dt} = \frac{k\theta}{L\rho x}$$

Integrating gives

$$x^2 = \frac{2k\theta t}{L\rho}$$

7 (*a*) A sheet of glass has an area of 2.0 m^2 and a thickness of 8.0 × 10^{-3} m. The glass has a thermal conductivity of 0.80 W m^{-1} K^{-1}. Calculate the rate of heat transfer through the glass when there is a temperature difference of 20 K between its faces.

(*b*) A room in a house is heated to a temperature 20 K above that outside. The room has 2 m^2 of windows of glass similar to the type used in (*a*). Suggest why the rate of heat transfer through the glass is much less than the value calculated above.

(*c*) Explain why two sheets of similar glass insulate much more effectively when separated by a thin layer of air than when they are in contact. [AEB 1986]

Infrared radiation

All bodies emit radiation, the intensity and wavelength distribution depending on the nature of the body itself and its temperature. **Infrared** radiation is invisible to the human eye. The detection of infrared radiation is much used, however, in Earth resource satellites, by the military in night glasses, for spotting areas of high heat loss from buildings and by the electricity boards in detecting hot spots in power cables.

Infrared radiation was first detected by Herschel in 1800, when he showed that there was radiant energy beyond the red end of the visible spectrum. (Ultraviolet radiation was detected beyond the violet end, and this is dealt with fully on page 220.)

We will begin by looking at the methods by which infrared radiation may be detected.

Infrared detectors

You can easily detect infrared radiation with your hand but there are much more sensitive methods.

As was shown by Leslie with his cube in 1804, blackened surfaces are better detectors of heat than shiny ones are, and this fact is used in several of the detectors described below.

(i) A liquid-in-glass thermometer with a blackened bulb

Heat is absorbed by the bulb and the liquid level rises.

(ii) The ether thermoscope

This consists of a tube with a glass bulb at either end; one is clear and the other is blackened (Figure 42.11). The tube is partly filled with ether and therefore both bulbs contain a mixture of air and ether vapour. When infrared radiation falls on the apparatus more is absorbed by the blackened bulb than by the shiny one, and the pressure inside this bulb rises and pushes the ether along the tube.

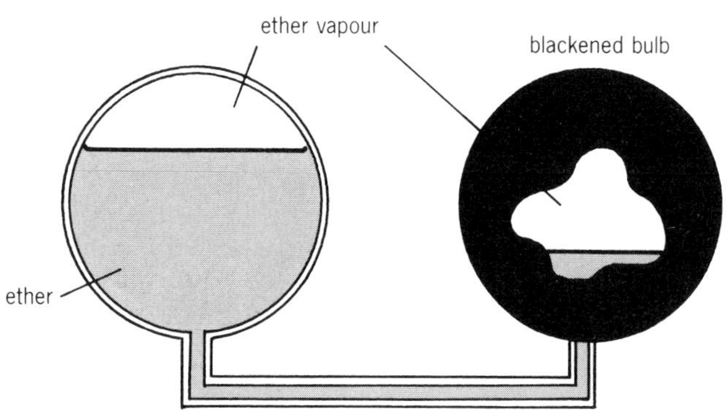

Figure 42.11

(iii) Crookes' radiometer

A vane mounted on a vertical pivot is enclosed in a glass bulb filled with air at low pressure. One side of each part of the vane is blackened and the other is silvered (Figure 42.12). When infrared radiation falls on the radiometer the black surfaces absorb more energy than the shiny ones and so become hotter. The air molecules hitting one of these blackened surfaces will gain energy and rebound with an increased velocity so pushing the vane round. The black surfaces are the trailing surfaces in this case.

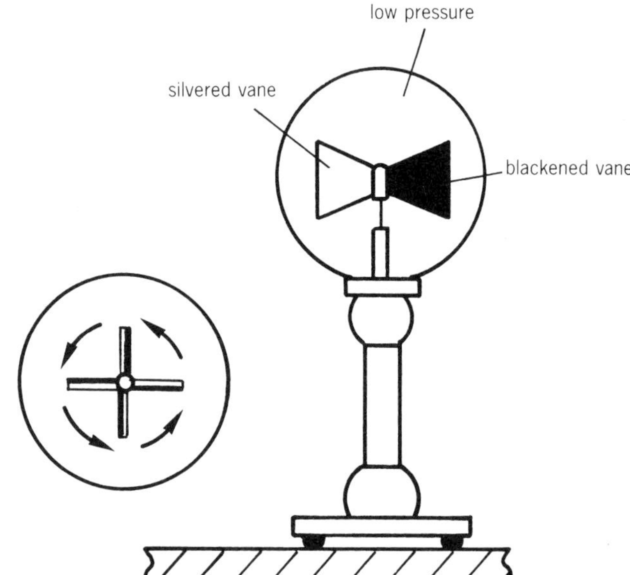

Figure 42.12

If the pressure of air in the bulb is reduced nearly to that of a vacuum the vane will begin to rotate in the opposite direction. This is because of the actual pressure of radiation on the shiny surfaces; the quanta of radiation rebound strongly from these surfaces so pushing the vane round. The shiny surfaces are now the trailing surfaces.

(iv) The bolometer

This instrument was invented by Langley in 1881. It is simply a blackened strip of platinum (Figure 42.13) and the radiation falling on it is measured by the resulting change in the resistance of the strip. This is measured by connecting the strip into one arm of a Wheatstone bridge.

Figure 42.13

(v) The thermopile
The principle of the thermocouple was used by Nobili and Melloni in 1830 to measure the intensity of radiation. A series of thermocouple junctions were connected in series, so that the final e.m.f. generated was much larger than that due to one junction (Figure 42.14). They called this arrangement a thermopile.

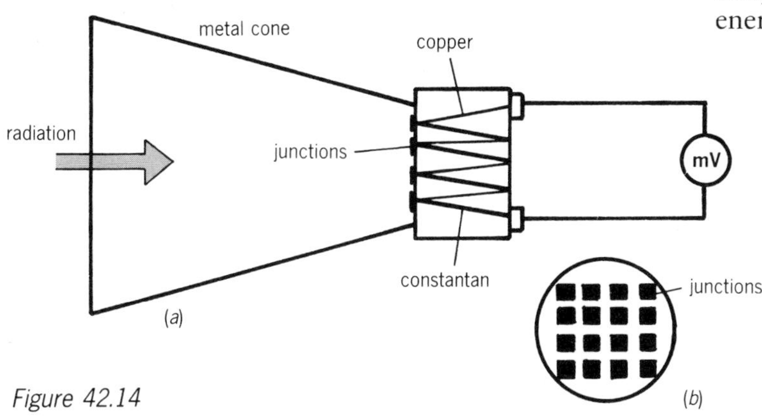

Figure 42.14

The junctions on to which radiation is to fall are blackened. The thermocouple has been used to measure the radiation from the planets and hence their temperatures may be found.

(vi) The transistor
A phototransistor can be used to measure the intensity of radiation, because the leakage current through it increases with temperature. Such a device is very simple to use.

(vii) The disappearing filament pyrometer
This consists of a telescope which has a lamp filament in the focal plane of the eyepiece. Radiation from the source is focused on to the filament. The lamp filament and the source are viewed through a red filter and the temperature of the filament is adjusted by altering the current through it until the filament disappears. The instrument is calibrated by comparison with a source of known temperature.

(viii) The thermistor
One type of this semiconductor device has a negative temperature coefficient of resistance – its resistance decreases with increasing temperature.

Prévost's theory of exchanges

It had been thought that only 'hot' bodies emitted radiation, but of course what may be 'hot' when compared with one set of surroundings may be 'cold' when compared with another. For example, a candle flame (700 °C) seems hot compared with your hand (37 °C) but cold when compared with the surface of the Sun (6000 °C).

In 1792 Prévost suggested that *all* bodies radiate energy, but that those with a higher temperature radiate more energy than those at lower temperatures.

If we consider two isolated bodies A and B initially at different temperatures (T_1 and T_2) with A being hotter than B (Figure 42.15), then each body will radiate heat to the other. The result will be equal temperatures (T), a kind of 'smearing out' of heat energy over the whole system.

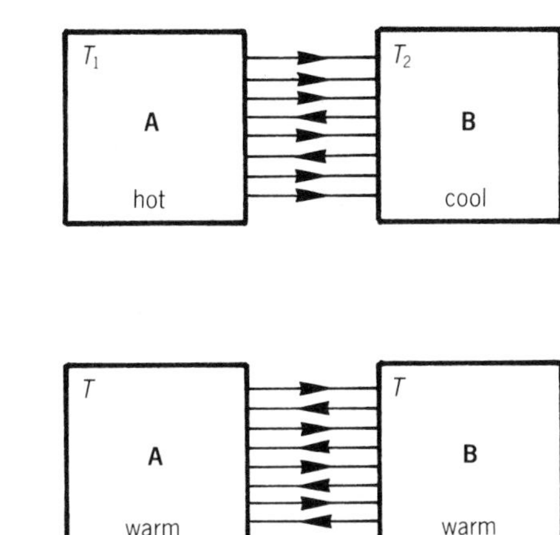

Figure 42.15

Notice that it is finally a case of dynamic equilibrium, both bodies radiating an equal amount of energy to each other.

Kirchhoff's law

When radiation falls on a surface three things may happen to it:

(*a*) a certain amount R will be reflected,
(*b*) a certain amount A will be absorbed, and
(*c*) a certain amount T will be transmitted.

The total amount of incident energy (I) is divided between these three possibilities. We can therefore write

$$I = R + A + T$$

For a shiny surface such as silver R will be large and both A and T small.

For a black surface such as coal R will be small, A large and T small.

For glass R will be average, A small and T large.

The energy absorbed by a body can be emitted later, and clearly if a surface cannot absorb radiation strongly it will be unable to emit strongly. Kirchhoff summarised this by saying that **a good emitter is also a good absorber**.

The nature of infrared radiation

Infrared radiation can be shown to be electromagnetic in nature and to have a wavelength rather longer than that of visible light. In fact the infrared region of the spectrum extends from about 750 nm to some 400 000 nm.

We can demonstrate the reflection of infrared radiation quite easily because the surfaces do not need to be very flat to give good reflection. Refraction is a little more difficult because many materials are opaque to infrared radiation. Glass is one of these, only short-wavelength infrared radiation passing through. Glass will transmit up to 3000 nm, fluorite up to 9000 nm and rock salt up to 15 000 nm so clearly prisms for refracting infrared radiation should be of rock salt.

An infrared filter of a solution of iodine in carbon disulphide can be made that will transmit infrared but is completely opaque to visible light.

The velocity of infrared radiation can be inferred from a solar eclipse; infrared radiation and light are cut off at the same instant. This simple observation suggests that in free space the velocity of infrared radiation is the same as that of light.

Black body radiation

The amount of heat radiation emitted by a body depends on three things:

(*a*) the surface area of the body,
(*b*) the type of surface, and
(*c*) the temperature of the body.

Consider first the type of surface. As we have seen, simple experiments with apparatus such as Leslie's cube show us that black surfaces are the best emitters and absorbers of radiation at a given temperature, and that a matt black surface is better than a shiny one.

Student investigation

The above information is that normally accepted, but how accurate is it?

Devise and carry out your own experiment using a thermopile to measure the radiation emitted by the different surfaces of a Leslie's cube.

Also compare the amounts of heat emitted by different coloured articles of clothing.

What conclusions do you draw from your results?

8 Discuss Newton's and Stefan's laws of cooling, pointing out the processes to which they refer and the conditions under which each is valid.

How would these laws apply to the cooling of a hot jacket potato, and how could its rate of cooling be increased?

An ideal absorber of heat would be one that absorbed *all* the radiation that fell on it and from Kirchhoff's law also emitted the maximum amount of radiation possible for that area at that temperature. Such a body is known as a **black body** and the radiation emitted by it as **black body radiation.**

We can get very close to the ideal body in the laboratory by using a sphere with a very small hole in it and with a blackened interior surface (Figure 42.16). Virtually all the radiation that falls on this hole will be absorbed. If the sphere is heated then radiation will be emitted from this hole, and this will

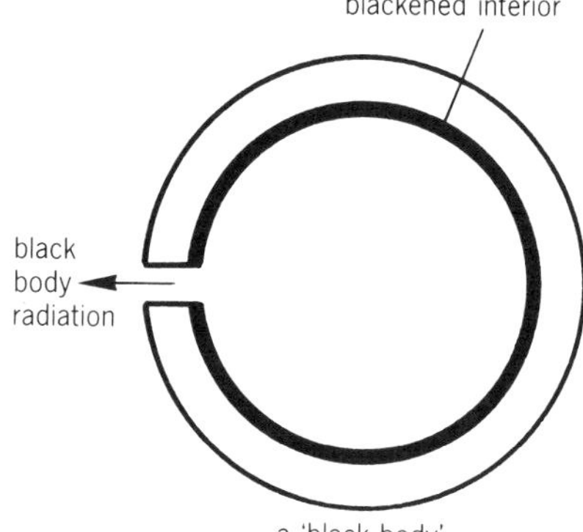

Figure 42.16 a 'black body'

also be black body radiation. Since it comes from a hole it is sometimes called **cavity radiation.** Since the hole is a perfect absorber it will emit black body radiation and will emit more energy per second than any other surface of the same area at that temperature.

The standard laboratory black body was designed by Lummer and Pringsheim in 1899 to define a scale for black body radiation.

9 Explain or discuss the following.

(*a*) The temperature of the inside of a greenhouse is higher than that outside on a sunny day, although glass is opaque to infrared radiation.

(*b*) Cavity walls are filled with foam although foam is a better conductor of heat than air.

(*c*) The wavelength at which most energy is radiated by a body may be used to determine its temperature.

(*d*) The colour of an incandescent body changes as its temperature rises.

(*e*) What factors affect the rate at which steady state is achieved when one end of a cold metal rod is heated?

(*f*) The emission of radiation from a body forms the basis of the quantum theory.

(*g*) A block of wood and a block of metal are kept at the same temperature. When the blocks feel cold the metal feels colder than the wood and when the blocks feel hot the metal feels hotter than the wood. Explain this. At what temperature will the blocks feel equally hot?

Laws of black body radiation

Using Lummer and Pringsheim's apparatus the energy emitted by a black body may be measured over a range of different temperatures and in many different regions of the spectrum. The results obtained can be summarised as follows.

(*a*) The total energy (E) emitted by a black body per unit area of surface per second is proportional to the fourth power of the body's absolute temperature T (Figure 42.17(*a*)). This is known as **Stefan's law** and can be written as:

$$E = \sigma T^4$$

σ is known as **Stefan's constant** and can be shown to have a value of 5.7×10^{-8} W m^2 K^{-4}.

(*b*) If the body is surrounded by an enclosure at temperature T_0 there will be an exchange of heat energy between the enclosure and the body, since both will radiate heat (Figure 42.17(*b*)). The *net* loss of energy by the body per unit area will be:

$$E = \sigma(T^4 - T_0^4)$$

(*c*) For a body of surface area A the total energy emitted per second will be:

$$E = \sigma A T^4$$

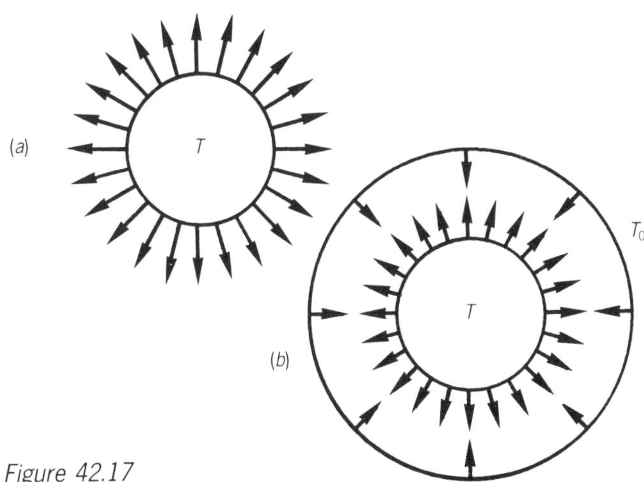

Figure 42.17

(*d*) If the body is not a black body, then the energy it emits at any temperature will be less than that emitted by a black body of similar surface area at the same temperature. The emission equation is modified as follows:

$$E = e\sigma A T^4$$

where e is the **emissivity** of the body, always less than unity.

This equation agrees with the ideas of Prévost. It is important to realise the difference between the basis of this equation and the basis of Newton's law of cooling. Stefan's law applies to loss of energy by *radiation*, whilst Newton's law of cooling applies to loss of energy by *convection* and *conduction*. Both laws are found to hold for temperature differences of hundreds of degrees.

Example

Calculate the net rate of loss of heat energy from a spacecraft of surface area 25 m^2 and at a temperature of 300 K if the radiation that it receives from the Sun is equivalent to a temperature in space of 50 K. Assume that the spacecraft behaves as a perfect black body.

Net rate of loss of energy $= \sigma A(T^4 - T_0^4)$
$= 5.7 \times 10^{-8} \times 25 \times (300^4 - 50^4)$
$= 1.15 \times 10^4$ W
$= 11.5$ kW

10 The normal operating conditions of a variable-intensity car headlamp are 2.5 A and 12 V. The temperature of the filament is 1750 °C. The intensity is now altered so that the lamp runs at 2.2 A and 12.5 V. Calculate the new operating temperature assuming that the filament behaves as a black body.

11 The average distance of Pluto from the Sun is about 40 times that of the Earth's. If the Sun behaves as a black body at 6000 K, and if it has a radius of 7.0×10^8 m and is 1.5×10^{11} m from the Earth, calculate the surface temperature of Pluto.

12 A certain integrated circuit operates at 70 °C and generates heat at a rate of 2.5 W. It is fixed to an aluminium rod 20 mm long and of cross-sectional area 50 mm^2. The other end of the rod is fixed to a finned heat sink that can transfer heat to its surroundings at 90 W m^{-2} of its surface per kelvin of excess temperature above its surroundings.

(*a*) If the surroundings are at 20 °C, what area of heat sink is needed and what is its equilibrium temperature?

(*b*) Discuss whether the equilibrium temperature will be different if the integrated circuit does not make good contact with the rod. [O]

(Thermal conductivity of aluminium = 200 W m^{-1} K^{-1})

13 The surface area of a domestic hot water radiator made of iron 2 mm thick is 4 m^2. If the water in the pipes is maintained at 60 °C and the temperature of the room is 20 °C, calculate the quantity of heat supplied to the room per hour. (Assume the emissivity of the radiator surface is 0.4.)

The solar constant

The energy that the Earth receives from the Sun is about 1400 J m^{-2} s^{-1}, and this quantity is known as the **solar constant.** Assuming that the Sun is a black body, we can use this information to determine the temperature of the surface of the Sun.

Energy emitted by the Sun $= \sigma T^4 4\pi r^2$.
Area of sphere with a radius equal to that of the Earth's orbit $= 4\pi R^2$. Therefore

$$\sigma T^4 4\pi r = 4\pi R \times r^2 \, 1400$$

$$T = 5800 \text{ K}$$

This radiation also exerts a very small pressure on the Earth of about 0.45×10^{-5} Pa; compare this with the atmospheric pressure at sea level of 10^5 Pa.

14 A black body radiates heat at 2 W m^{-2} when at 0 °C. Find the rate of fall in temperature of a copper sphere of radius 3 cm when at 1000 °C in air at 0 °C. (Assume that the density of copper is 8930 kg m^{-3} and its specific heat capacity is 385 J kg^{-1} K^{-1}.)

15 Given that the energy received from the Sun at the surface of the Earth is 1400 J m^{-2} s^{-1} determine the effective solar temperature, assuming that the Sun behaves as a perfect black body.

16 Find the net rate of energy lost by radiation from the following black bodies:
(*a*) a sphere of radius 10 cm at a temperature of 500 °C in an enclosure whose temperature is 20 °C;
(*b*) a person of surface area 1.2 m^2 at a temperature of 37 °C in an enclosure whose temperature is 0 °C. Comment on your answer.

17 A certain 100 W tungsten filament lamp operates at a temperature of 1500 °C. Assuming that it behaves as a perfect black body, estimate the surface area of the filament.

18 A black body at 1000 K emits radiation, with maximum energy emitted at a wavelength of 2500 nm. Calculate the wavelengths at which maximum energy is emitted by the following, assuming that they all behave as black bodies:
(*a*) a piece of iron heated in a bunsen flame to 800 °C,
(*b*) a star with a surface temperature of 7000 °C,
(*c*) the plasma in a fusion reaction at 10^6 °C.

19 Using the information given at the start of question 18, calculate the temperatures of black bodies which emit maximum energy at the following wavelengths: (*a*) 5 nm, (*b*) 50 nm, (*c*) 500 nm, (*d*) 5000 nm, (*e*) 50 000 nm.

Distribution of energy within the spectrum

Stefan's law gives the total energy radiated by a body, but tells us nothing about how this energy is distributed across the spectrum. If measurements are made of the energy emitted at different wavelengths by a black body at different temperatures results like those in Figure 42.18 will be obtained. Here the vertical axis shows the energy density (that is, energy emitted per square metre per second in a small wavelength range from λ to $\lambda + d\lambda$) and the horizontal axis shows the wavelength.

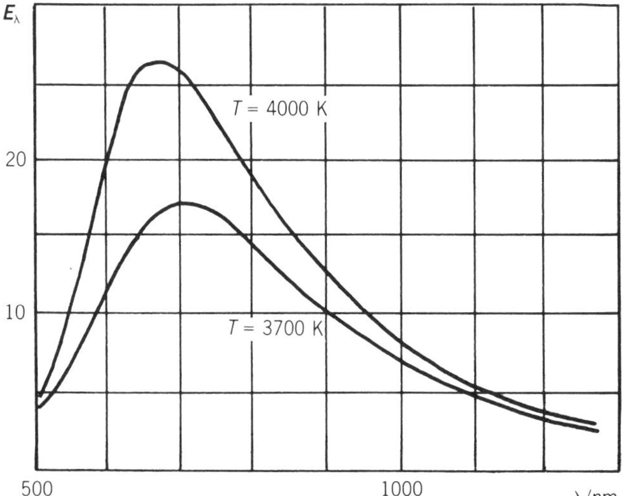

Figure 42.18

Some important facts can de deduced from these curves.

(*a*) The area between any curve and the wavelength axis gives the total energy emitted by the body at that temperature (σT^4).

(*b*) The maxima of the curves tend towards short wavelengths at higher temperatures.

(*c*) The curves at lower temperatures lie completely inside those of higher temperature.

It was found that:

(*a*) $\lambda_m T$ = constant, where λ_m is the wavelength at which most energy is emitted, that is, the peak of the curve. The value of the constant is 2.5×10^{-3} m K.

(*b*) The energy emitted at this wavelength is proportional to T^5.

These two results are shown as **Wien's laws.**

20 A metal sphere of 1 cm diameter, whose surface acts as a black body, is placed at the focus of a concave mirror with an aperture of 60 cm directed towards the Sun. If the solar constant is 1400 W m^{-2} and the mean temperature of the surroundings is 27 °C, calculate the maximum theoretical temperature that the sphere could attain, stating any assumptions that you make.

The values of λ_m for a range of temperatures are shown in the table below (it must be remembered that they apply to black bodies only).

Temperature/K	*Wavelength* (λ_m)/nm
500	5000
750	3300
1000	2500
1100	2300
1750	1400
2000	1250
3000	833
4000	625
5000	500
6000	420

You can see that if λ_m for a body lies in the red region of the spectrum then the object will appear red-hot, and as it gets hotter the peak moves nearer to the violet end of the visible spectrum. A white-hot body will give high emission across the full visible range. If we know the value of λ_m for one black body at a known temperature we can use Wien's law to calculate the temperature of another black body provided the wavelength at which maximum energy is emitted for this second body is known. This has been used extensively in astronomy for determining the temperature of stars.

Example

A black body at 2000 K emits radiation with λ_m = 1250 mm. Use this result to calculate the surface temperature of the star Sirius if λ_m for Sirius is 71 nm. (Assume that Sirius behaves like a black body.)

$$\lambda_{m1}T_1 = \lambda_{m2}T_2$$

$$1250 \times 10^{-9} \times 2000 = 71 \times 10^{-9} \times T_2$$

Therefore $T_2 = 35\ 200$ K

Quantum theory and an equation for the black body curves

When scientists were attempting to deduce equations that would fit the black body curves they encountered considerable difficulty – none of the equations that they produced using classicial Physics would fit the experimental results.

In 1900, however, Max Planck solved the problem by proposing a radical new law to govern the emission and absorption of radiation. He suggested that the energy was not radiated in a continuous wave but in discrete packets which he called **quanta**, and that the energy of each quantum E was given by the equation:

$$E = hf$$

where h is the Planck constant and f the frequency of the emitted radiation. (A fuller consideration of this equation is given on page 427.)

Furthermore each quantum could only have certain energy values, but no values in between these. This fact would not be obvious to us in our large-scale world, but is something that becomes vitally important at an atomic level.

It was thus here in the study of heat radiation and not in the realms of nuclear Physics that the quantum theory was born!

Planck deduced an equation for the energy distribution of black body radiation based on his quantum theory which fitted the experimental results exactly. His equation is outside the scope of this book but it is quoted for interest:

$$E_\lambda = \frac{8\pi hc\lambda^{-5}}{(e^{a/\lambda T} - 1)}$$

where E_λ the energy density
λ the wavelength
T the absolute temperature of the body
h Planck constant
c the velocity of light
a a constant equal to ch/k where k is Boltzmann's constant ($a = 1.44 \times 10^{-2}$ m K).

Non-equilibrium conditions

If a black cloth and a white cloth are placed out in sunlight the black cloth will warm up much more quickly than the white one. This may seem a little strange because if good absorbers are also good emitters you would expect the black cloth to *absorb* more radiation but also *emit* it at a greater rate than the white one.

The two cloths are not in equilibrium with their surroundings, however. Since they are both very much colder than the Sun they emit radiation at a much slower rate than they receive it and therefore the temperature of the one with the greater absorptive power – the black cloth – will rise much more rapidly than that of the other. This can be summarised as follows:

When a black body is receiving energy from hotter surroundings it will heat up quicker than any other body of the same surface area.

When a black body is emitting energy to cooler surroundings it will cool down quicker than any other body of the same surface area.

The greenhouse effect and global warming

When solar radiation falls on the Earth the energy is distributed in a number of ways. Some is absorbed by the atmosphere, some is reflected by the land and the remainder is absorbed by the Earth's surface. This absorbed energy warms the land which then re-radiates this energy as infrared.

Of this radiated energy, some escapes into space and the rest is absorbed by the atmosphere. This is known as the **greenhouse effect**. The shorter wavelength solar radiation can penetrate the atmosphere, while the longer wavelength infrared radiated from the Earth cannot.

This warming of the atmospheric blanket is important. Without it the Earth would be some 30 °C colder. However, too much warming may become a serious problem for the human race.

Not all gases absorb the infrared. The most important absorbers are water vapour, carbon dioxide and other gases such as methane, nitrous oxide and chlorofluorocarbons (CFCs).

It is estimated that at the present time 110 000 million tons of carbon dioxide enter the atmosphere from biological processes every year, but people add a further 5000 million tons. The destruction of the rain forest removes a vital carbon dioxide absorber – trees.

However CFCs are about 20 000 times more important than carbon dioxide as greenhouse gases. Their long lifetime of around a hundred years and the fact that they absorb radiation strongly in a region of the infrared where little other natural absorption occurs means that they are a real cause for concern. In 1989 their emission was increasing at a rate of 4% per year. The emission of 540 million tons of methane into the atmosphere every year, with an annual increase of 1%, further adds to the problem.

It is very difficult to predict exactly what the result of this global warming may be, but a rise in temperature of the Earth and some melting of the polar ice caps are possibilities. Estimates suggest a rise in temperature of between 0.5 °C and 1.5 °C in the next 40 years leading to perhaps a 0.4 m rise in sea level.

We can conserve energy to reduce the burning of fossil fuels and we can recycle some materials to save resources. The human race will have to adapt to a changing world whether we like it or not!

Electrical and magnetic properties

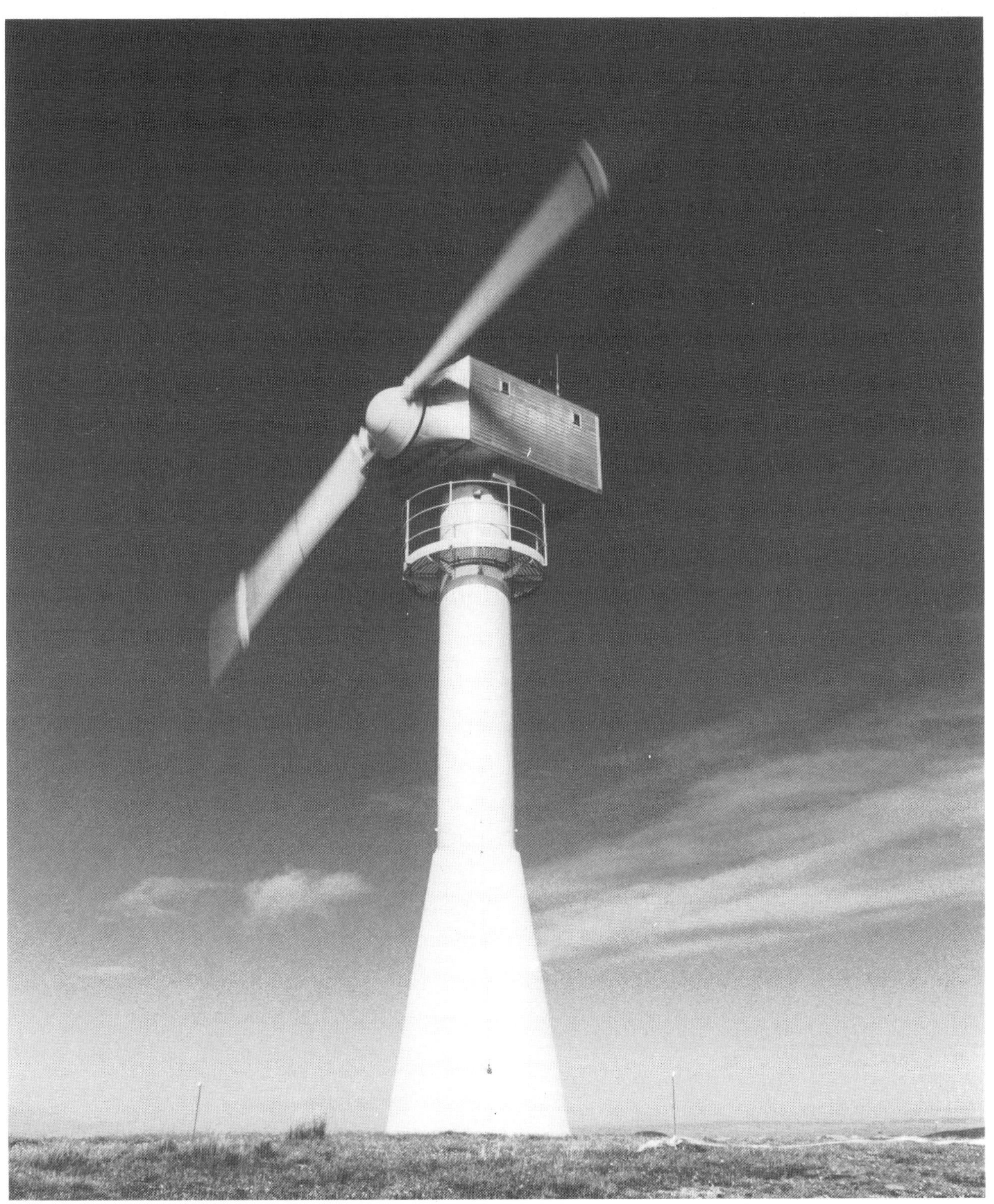

Production of electricity using a 250 kW wind turbine at Burger Hill in the Orkneys, Scotland (Martin Bond)

43 · Current electricity

Electrical energy

The flow of electricity down a wire will cause an energy change, converting the electrical energy into heat energy, chemical energy or magnetic energy (or into one or more of these). We will first consider the nature of this electric current.

As you know, matter consists of atoms. Inside the atoms there are electrons, which are usually bound to the nucleus. In many solids, however, and especially in metals, a large number of electrons are free to wander between one atom and another.

Electric current in a metal is the flow of **free electrons** through a material. The number of free electrons and the ease with which they flow depends on the energy band structure of the material. In metals the large number of free electrons (about 10^{28} m^{-3} for copper) are free to move within the conduction band with the addition of a very small amount of energy (see page 360 for further details).

The electrons are always present in the metal and are in constant random motion rather like the molecules in a gas. If a source of e.m.f. such as a battery is joined to the two ends of a wire it attracts the electrons so that they move generally in one direction (it does *not* put electrons into the wire).

An electron has a very small charge and so we use a larger unit when measuring quantities of electrical charge. This is the **coulomb.** It can be shown that the charge carried by one electron is 1.6×10^{-19} C (see the description of Millikan's experiment on page 410). The electrical charge passing any point in the wire per second is called the **electric current.** It is measured in **amperes** (amps or A), defined by the following:

a current of one ampere is flowing in a circuit when a charge of one coulomb passes any point in the circuit in one second.

charge = current × time

$Q = It$

For example, when a current of 1 A flows 6.2×10^{18} electrons pass any point in the circuit every second!

We will see later that the ampere can also be defined from basic units as follows:

a current of one ampere is flowing in two parallel conductors placed one metre apart in a vacuum when there is a force between them of 2×10^{-7} N m^{-1}.

Sources of electrical energy

These are covered in detail in other parts of the book (see the Index); they are simply listed here:

- primary cells – simple, Leclanché, Daniell, fuel, mercury, cadmium
- secondary cells – lead acid, Nife
- electromagnetic induction – dynamo
- photoelectric cell
- thermocouple
- microphone
- piezoelectric effect

All these effects are reversible changes although the efficiency of the conversion to or from electrical energy is never 100 per cent.

All the above are sources of electrical energy. Raising an electric charge to a higher electrical energy (voltage or potential) is exactly analogous to lifting up an object against the pull of gravity. When the object falls down again this energy is released, and this is just what happens when charge flows round the circuit. The energy given to it by the supply is released in the form of heat, light, motion, sound or magnetic energy.

Large solar energy complex situated in a desert area in California, USA – the complex consists of large number of flat orienting mirrors (seen here from the underside) forming a near circular pattern on the desert floor (Science Photo Library)

Primary and secondary cells

We will give here a brief survey of primary and secondary cells. Further details will be found in GCSE Science books.

Primary cells

The zinc–carbon cell
This contains a zinc negative electrode, a manganese(IV) oxide positive electrode and an electrolyte of ammonium chloride which in the dry cell is in the form of a paste. Down the cell runs a carbon rod which acts as a current collector (Figure 43.1).

No hydrogen is produced in the cell and most of the polarisation is prevented.

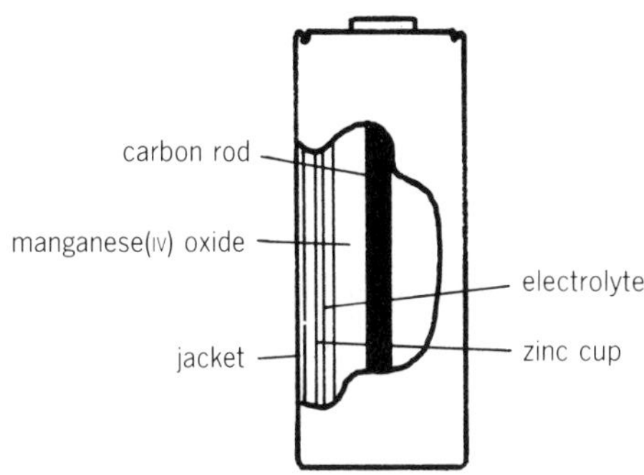

Figure 43.1

The zinc–air cell
In this cell the negative electrode is zinc powder, the electrolyte is alkaline and the positive electrode is the air. A catalyst within the cell helps the oxygen to react and a layer of PTFE allows air in but prevents the electrolyte leaking out (Figure 43.2). This type of cell is made in a button shape and is used in hearing aids.

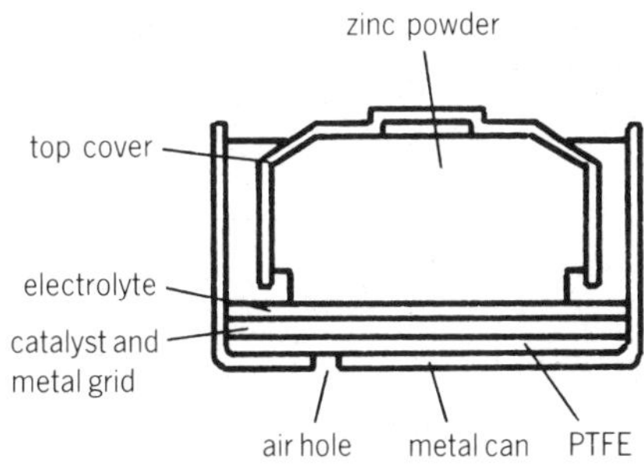

Figure 43.2

The alkaline magnesium cell
This uses the same electrodes as the zinc–carbon cell, the difference being that the electrolyte is a solution of potassium hydroxide. These cells will last longer and give higher continuous currents than the zinc–carbon cell can.

The fuel cell
This type of cell is extensively used in spacecraft and will continue to operate as long as the necessary chemicals are provided. The most common fuel cell uses hydrogen and oxygen which react to form water, producing an e.m.f between two porous electrodes made of a metal such as nickel. In spacecraft the water produced has the advantage that it can be used for drinking.

Secondary cells

The nickel–cadmium cell
This was developed as the first dry secondary cell. It contains a positive electrode of a complex nickel compound, a cadmium negative electrode and an electrolyte of potassium hydroxide. This is held in the sponge-like separator (Figure 43.3). The cell has two disadvantages. Firstly, they may be ten times as expensive as other dry cells. Secondly, great care has to be taken when recharging because if they are charged in the wrong direction hydrogen may be produced and the cell may explode!

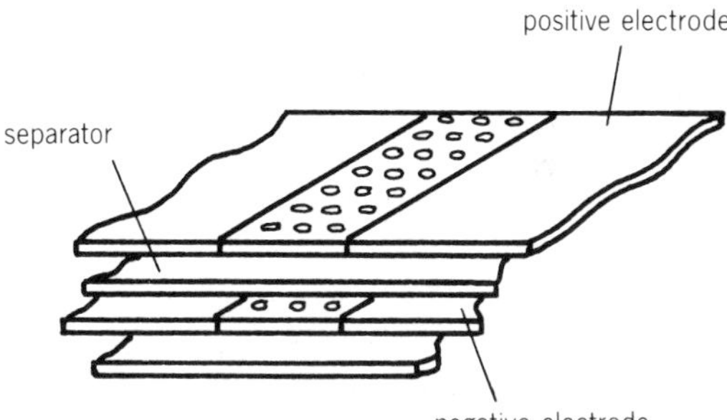

Figure 43.3

Student investigation

The following set of data was obtained for tests on an electric car. Comment on the advantages and disadvantages of the different types of battery used.

Battery details	*Battery weight* /kg	*Total weight* /kg	*kWh*	*watt h per kg*	*Discharge rate* /min^{-1}	*Average range at 48 km h^{-1}*/km
8 12 V, 40 A h lead–acid	110	455	1.9	18	40	30
12 12 V 40 A h lead–acid	173	510	3	18.3	60	48
80 cells (96 V) 46 A h nickel–cadmium	355	700	4.4	12.2	70	55

Electrolysis

When an electric current passes through certain liquids a chemical reaction occurs at both electrodes. This is known as **electrolysis** and the liquid in which this takes place is known as an **electrolyte**. At the negative electrode (**cathode**) the product liberated is always either a metal or hydrogen while at the positive electrode (**anode**) it is oxygen or a non-metal, or the anode may dissolve into the solution.

Not all liquids will conduct electricity, only those that contain ions. Pure anhydrous sulphuric acid is an insulator, as is pure water, but if a few drops of sulphuric acid are added to water the resulting solution becomes conducting.

By experiment it can be shown that the amount of a substance liberated at either electrode depends on:

(*a*) the substance being liberated,

(*b*) the current passed through the electrolyte, and

(*c*) the time for which this current is passed.

Faraday's laws of electrolysis

The reactions may be summarised by Faraday's laws of electrolysis.

Faraday's first law

The mass m of a given element liberated in electrolysis is directly proportional to the quantity of electricity Q that has passed, that is:

$$m = ZQ = ZIt$$

where Z is a constant for each element known as its **electrochemical equivalent**, and is the mass of that element liberated by the passage of one coulomb.

Faraday's second law

The number of moles of different elements liberated in electrolysis by the passage of the same charge are simply related to each other.

The quantity of electric charge required to liberate or dissolve one mole of any singly charged ion in electrolysis is known as the **Faraday constant** (F). Its value is found to be 9.65×10^4 C mol^{-1}.

Now the charge on one monovalent ion is e, the electron charge, and there are L ions in one mole where L is the Avogadro constant. The total charge on one mole is Le and so:

$$F = Le$$

This equation can be used to determine a value for the charge on the electron which is more accurate than that obtained by Millikan's experiment (see page 410).

1 An athletics cup with a surface area of 500 cm^2 is to be silver-plated. If the layer of silver is to be of a uniform thickness of 25 μm, how long must a current of 0.5 A flow in the electroplating tank to achieve this? (Density of silver = 10 500 kg m^{-3}; silver is monovalent with a relative atomic mass of 108. Take the Faraday constant to be 96 500 C mol^{-1}.)

Velocity of electrons in a wire

The electrons in a wire have three distinct velocities associated with them:

(*a*) the random velocity – some 10^5 m s^{-1};

(*b*) the velocity of electrical energy transfer through the wire – around 10^8 m s^{-1};

(*c*) the drift velocity of the electrons as a whole when a current flows in the wire.

Student investigation

It is not possible to measure the electron drift velocity directly but you can get an idea of its magnitude by measuring the drift velocity for the ions in a liquid. We assume that they will have a velocity similar to that of the electron. A crystal of potassium manganate(VII) is placed on a filter paper clipped to a microscope slide. The filter paper is soaked with ammonium hydroxide and a high voltage placed across it, as shown in Figure 43.5. The coloured manganate(VII) ions can be seen to move and their velocity can be measured.

Record the ionic drift velocity for a series of voltages in the range 50–250 V.

Take care not to touch the h.t. outlets during the experiment.

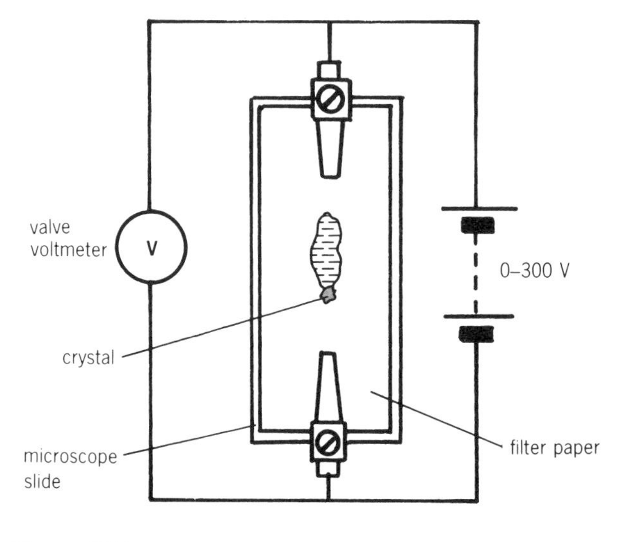

Figure 43.5

Student investigation

The velocity of energy transfer may be found as follows. The two ends of a length of coaxial cable are connected to the Y terminals of a double beam oscilloscope and a pulse of electricity fed into one end. A suitable circuit is shown in Figure 43.4. This gives a pulse on one trace.

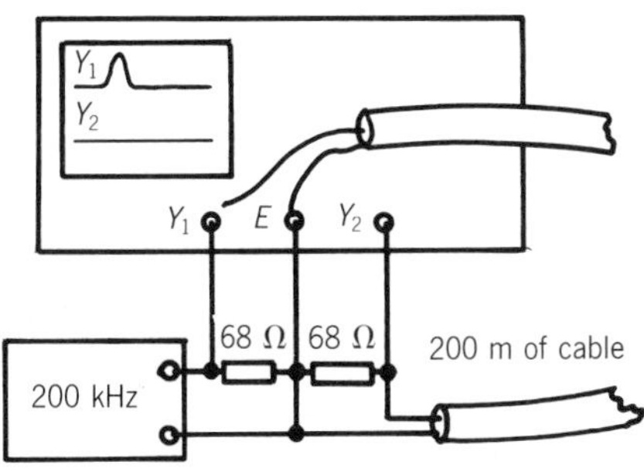

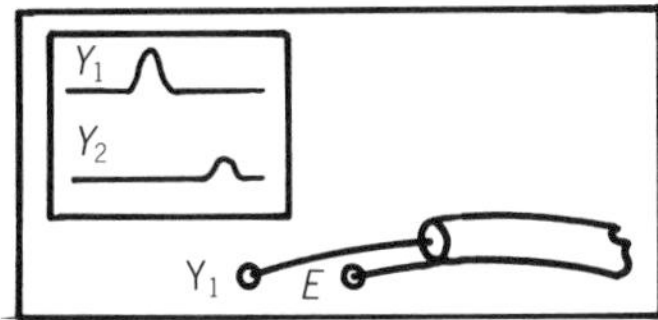

Figure 43.4

This pulse travels down the wire and when it reaches the other end a pulse is obtained on the other trace. The time between these pulses can be found from the time base speed, and hence the velocity of the electro magnetic wave in the cable can be found if the length of cable is known. Because of the large value of this velocity some 200–300 m of cable are needed. The resistors are included to prevent unwanted reflections from the ends of the cable.

Carry out this experiment and if possible compare the velocity of the electrical energy pulse in different cables.

2 Using the data in Question 1 and the current cost of silver and electricity calculate the cost of electroplating the cup.

Electron drift velocity

We will now consider the proof of an equation for electron drift velocity.

Consider a wire of cross-sectional area A carrying a current I. Let the velocity of the electrons be v and let there be n electrons per cubic metre (Figure 43.6).

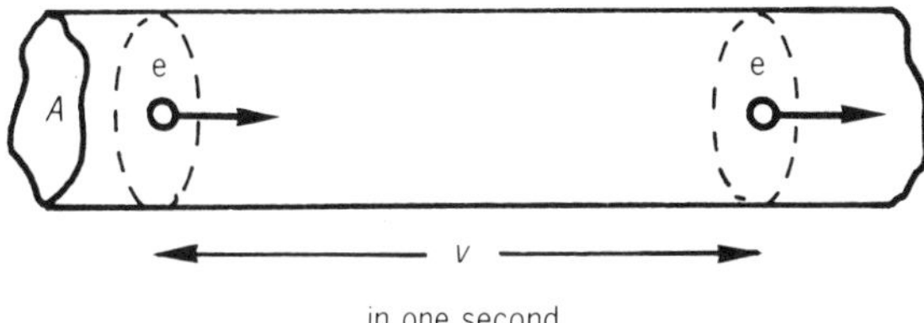

Figure 43.6

In one second an electron will have moved a distance v down the wire. But since there are n electrons per cubic metre the total number moving this distance will be nAv. Therefore the current I (which is the rate of flow of charge past a point in the wire) is:

$$I = nAve$$

Now copper contains some 10^{29} free electrons per cubic metre, and if we take a copper wire of cross-sectional area 2×10^{-7} m^2 (0.5 mm diameter) carrying a current of 1 A then

$$v = \frac{I}{nAe} = 3.1 \times 10^{-4} \text{ m s}^{-1}$$

This is a very small value; it has been calculated that a given electron would take some 300 years to cross the Atlantic in a cable, and that it might only make one circuit of a torch before the battery ran out!

You can see from the formula that the electron drift velocity is greater for thin wires than for thick ones carrying the same current.

Some values for the number of free electrons per cubic metre (n) are shown in the following table.

Metal	*Free electron concentration*/m^{-3}
Lithium	3.7×10^{28}
Sodium	2.5×10^{28}
Potassium	1.5×10^{28}
Caesium	0.8×10^{28}
Copper	11×10^{28}
Silver	7.4×10^{28}
Gold	8.7×10^{28}

3 A metal wire containing 1.5×10^{29} free electrons m^{-3} and a diameter of 0.3 mm carries a current of 0.5 A. If the electron charge is 1.6×10^{-19} C, calculate the mean drift velocity of the electrons down the wire.

4 The current flowing through a copper wire is increased. State what happens to the following:
(*a*) the number of free electrons,
(*b*) the concentration of free electrons,
(*c*) the mean electron drift velocity, and
(*d*) the velocity with which energy is propagated down the wire.

Electrical potential

The energy of a unit charge at a point in the circuit is called the **potential** at that point and the difference in energy between one point and another is the **potential difference** between the two points (often called the **voltage**). (For further details and definitions see page 332.)

Figure 43.7 shows how the potential varies round four simple circuits.

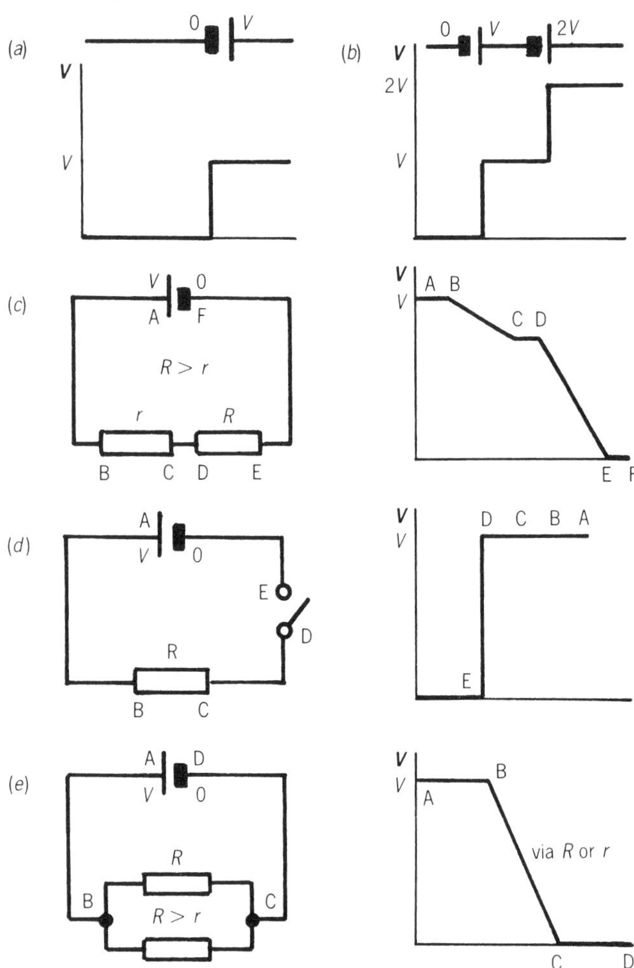

Figure 43.7

You can see how there is a large drop in potential where there is a large energy loss. We assume a steady, but very small, loss of energy in the connecting wires and usually we ignore this energy loss completely.

Potential difference

The potential difference between two points is defined as **the work done per unit charge in moving from one place to the other**, that is:

volts = joules/coulomb
joules = volts × coulombs

Power is the rate of doing work or the rate of energy conversion, and so:

$$\text{power} = \text{volts} \times \frac{\text{coulombs}}{\text{time}}$$

power = volts × amps

5 Calculate how much electrical energy a 6 V battery supplies when
(*a*) a charge of 1 C passes through it,
(*b*) a charge of 25 C passes through it,
(*c*) a current of 3 A flows through it for 2 minutes.

6 You have five 1.5 V cells. Explain how they would be connected
(*a*) to give the highest output potential,
(*b*) to deliver a current of 0.5 A for the longest possible time

Student investigation

Mount three pieces of fuse wire of the same material and the same length but of different diameters in parallel between two copper bars, and apply a variable potential between the bars. Observe and explain what happens when the applied voltage is slowly increased.

Variation of current with voltage

There are several ways in which the current through a conductor can be altered. Elastic strain, temperature and illumination can all vary the current. Figure 43.8 shows how current varies with voltage for various different conditions.

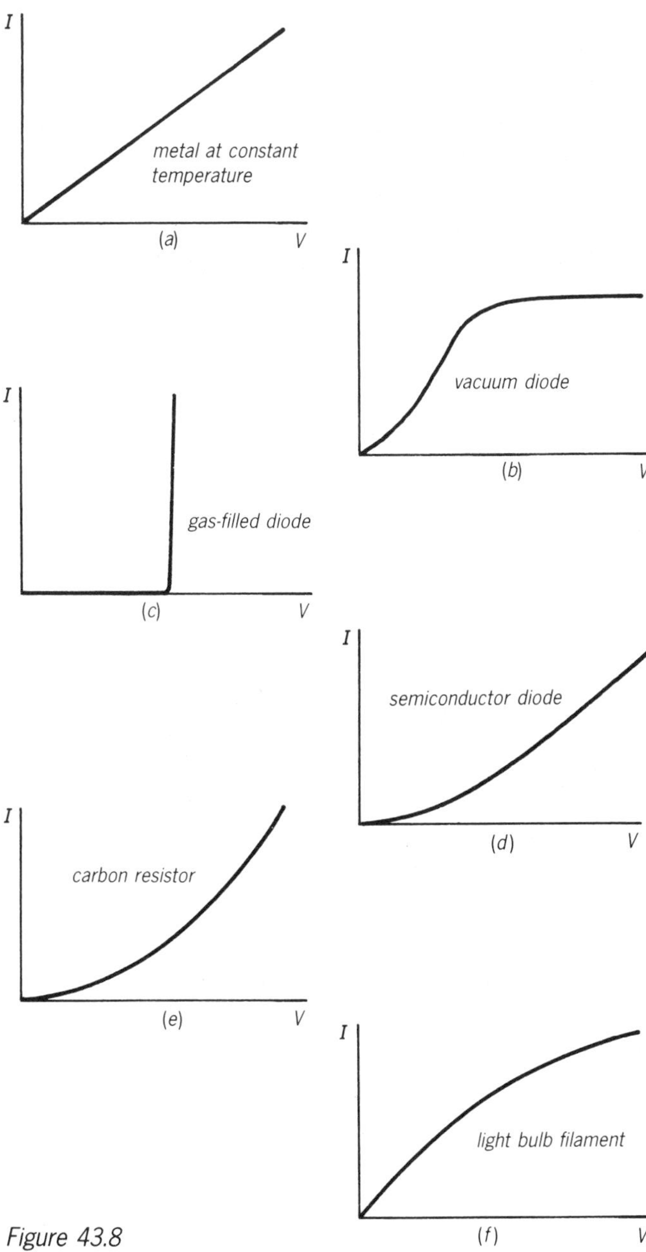

Figure 43.8

7 Discuss the way in which the current varies with the potential difference applied across the following:
(*a*) the filament of an electric lamp;
(*b*) two platinum electrodes immersed in slightly acidulated water;
(*c*) the electrodes of a vacuum diode;
(*d*) a semiconductor diode;
(*e*) a gas-filled diode.

Ohm's law

As free electrons move through a metal due to an applied potential difference they collide with each other and with the atoms of the metal crystal lattice (Figure 43.9).

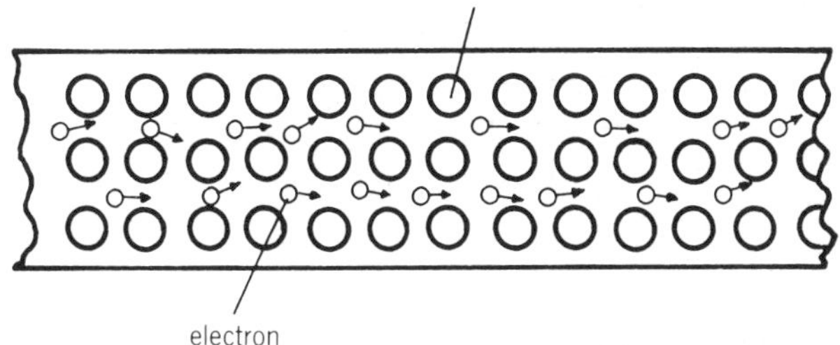

Figure 43.9

The property of the material that restricts this movement is known as the **resistance** of the conductor (a fuller consideration of the electron theory of resistance is given on page 286).

For a metallic conductor at a constant temperature the current varies linearly with the voltage (Figure 43.10) – this is known as Ohm's law. **That is, the ratio of the potential difference V to the current I is a constant for any conductor, and is known as its resistance R.**

Ohm's law can be expressed as:

$$V = IR$$

Resistance are measured in **ohms** (Ω); larger values are given in kilohms (kΩ) or megohms (MΩ).

It is important to realise that Ohm's law only holds if the temperature is kept constant. For example, if the current and voltage in a wire are measured while its temperature is held steady at, say, 10 °C the variation of current with voltage will be linear and the resistance at 15 °C may be found.

If the temperature of the wire is now raised to, say, 75 °C and a second set of readings taken the variation will still be linear but the gradient of the line, and hence the resistance of the wire, will be different.

Two such lines are shown in Figure 43.11.

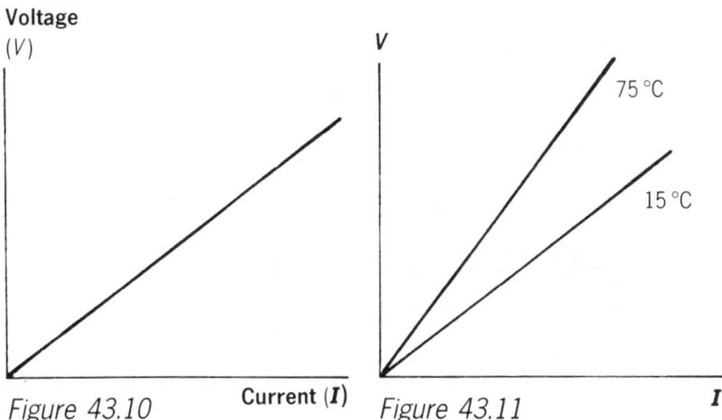

Figure 43.10 Figure 43.11

Resistivity

The resistance of a piece of material depends not only on the material itself but also on its dimensions. For a given volume, the greater the length and the smaller the cross-sectional area the greater the resistance will be.

It is therefore useful to discuss the property of a material in general rather than that of a particular specimen. For this reason a property known as the **resistivity** of a material is used, defined as **the resistance of a specimen with unit length and unit crosssecional area**:

$$\text{resistivity } (\rho) = \frac{\text{resistance } (R) \times \text{area } (A)}{\text{length } (l)}$$

Resitivity is measured in ohm metres (Ω m): the higher the resistivity of a material the greater will be the resistance of a sample of a given size.

The reciprocal of resistivity is known as the **conductivity** of the material (σ).

$$\text{conductivity} = \frac{1}{\rho} = \frac{l}{RA}$$

Conductivity is measured in **siemens per metre** ($\mathrm{Sm^{-1}}$).

Silver has one of the highest conductivities, followed by copper. In spite of this, aluminium is used for overhead power cables because although it has a lower conductivity it is lighter and cheaper than copper or silver.

Impurities in a metal do not affect the number of conduction electrons very much but they do affect their freedom of movement and therefore increase the resistivity.

The following table gives the resistivities of some well known materials.

Material	*Resistivity* /ohm metre	*Material*	*Resistivity* /ohm metre
Copper	1.69×10^{-8}	Non-metals	10^4
Nichrome	130×10^{-8}	Insulators	10^{13}–10^{16}
Aluminium	3.21×10^{-8}	Germanium	0.65
Eureka	49×10^{-8}	Silicon	2.3×10^3
Lead	20.8×10^{-8}	Carbon	33–185×10^{-8}
Manganin	44×10^{-8}	Silver	1.6×10^{-8}

The resistivities of solutions cannot be quoted generally because they depend on the concentrations and are therefore variable quantities. As an example, however, the resistivity of pure water is about 2.5×10^5 Ω m and that of a saturated solution of sodium chloride about 0.04 Ω m at 20 °C.

8 The following table gives the current/voltage readings for two filament lamps A and B that are connected in series:

Current in A/A	0	0.05	0.10	0.15	0.20
p.d. across A, V_A/V	0	0.40	1.1	2.8	6.5
p.d. across B, V_B/V	0	1.25	2.6	5.0	9.1

(*a*) On the same graph, using *I* as the y-axis, draw a graph of *I* against *V* for each lamp.

(*b*) The two lamps are connected in parallel. Find the tabulate corresponding values of the current *I* and the voltage *V* across the lamps up to 6 V. Draw the *I*–*V* graph on the same axes you used in (*a*). [O]

9 If the resistivity of copper is 1.7×10^{-8} Ω m, calculate the resistance of 1 cm^3 of copper

(*a*) when in the form of a wire of diameter 0.02 cm,

(*b*) when in the form of a thin sheet 2.5 mm thick, the current passing through the sheet perpendicularly to its faces.

10 Two wires, A and B, have lengths which are in the ratio 4:5 and diameters which are in the ratio 2:1, and are made of materials of resistivity in the ratio 3:2. If the wires are arranged in parallel and a current of 1 A enters the arrangement, find the current in each branch. [T]

11 Assuming that the rate of heat loss from the surface of a wire carrying a current is proportional to the temperature difference between the wire and its surroundings for small temperature differences, show that the final temperature reached by the wire is

(*a*) proportional to the square of the current,

(*b*) inversely proportional to the cube of the diameter of the wire, and

(*c*) proportional to the resistivity of the wire.

Series and parallel resistors

Resistors are rarely found singly in circuits so we must consider the case of two or more resistors joined in series or parallel.

For the circuits in Figure 43.12, the formula for the resistors in series is:

$$R = R_1 + R_2$$

and that for resistors in parallel:

$$\frac{1}{R} = \frac{1}{R_1} + \frac{1}{R_2}$$

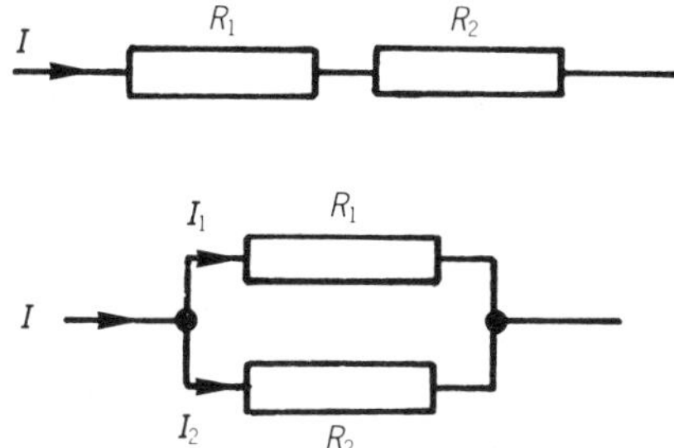

Figure 43.12

For the proof of these formulae the reader should consult any standard GCSE science textbook.

The formulae for two parallel resistors may be rewritten as:

$$R = \frac{R_1 R_2}{R_1 + R_2}$$

It should be noted that the formulae for three resistors is *not* a simple extension of this version, the actual equation being:

$$R = \frac{R_1 R_2 R_3}{R_1 R_2 + R_1 R_3 + R_2 R_3}$$

Note that for resistors in series the addition of a further resistor *reduces* the total current in the circuit, while for resistors in parallel the addition of a further resistor *increases* the total current.

A series of puzzle boxes containing two or more resistors may be investigated to practise the use of the preceding equations.

A widely used example of series and parallel resistors is in the calculation of the shunt or series resistors used to convert a galvanometer into an ammeter or a voltmeter (see also page 305).

The potential divider

If two resistors R_1 and R_2 are joined in series and a p.d of V is placed across them and an output taken from the point P, at the join of the two resistors, and the opposite end of R_2, the arrangement is known as a **potential divider**. The p.d across R_2 is V_2 where

$$V_2 = \frac{R_2}{R_1 + R_2}$$

Example

Consider a moving coil galvanometer with a resistance of 1000 Ω and a full scale deflection of 100 μA.

(i) Conversion to an ammeter reading 5 A

A low resistance *R* is connected in parallel with the meter to allow 100 μA to flow through the meter and the remaining 4.9999 A through *R*.

The voltage drop across the meter and *R* must be the same and is 100 μA × 1000 Ω = 100 mV.

Therefore *R* = 100/4.9999 = 0.02 Ω (Figure 43.13).

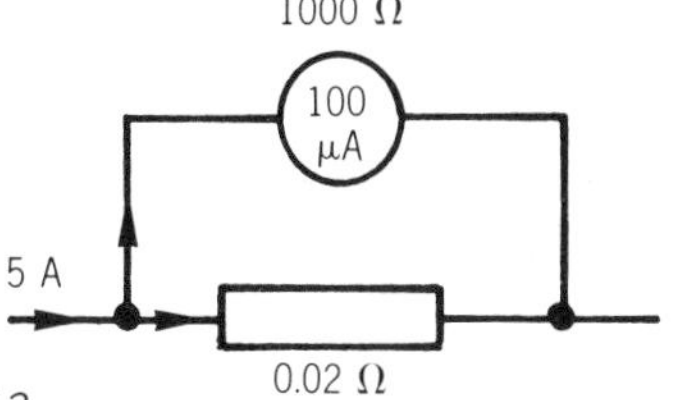

Figure 43.13

(ii) Conversion to a voltmeter reading 5 V

A high resistance *R* is connected in series with the meter to allow a potential drop of 100 mV across the meter and the remaining 4.9 V across the resistor.

The current through both the meter and the resistor is 100 μA.

Therefore *R* = 4.9/100 = 49 000 Ω = 49 kΩ (Figure 43.14).

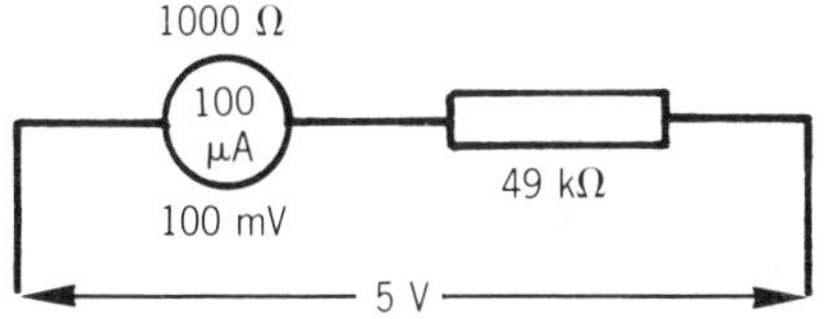

Figure 43.14

12 A cube is composed of twelve resistors each of 2 Ω resistance. If a current of 2 A enters at one corner of the top face and leaves by the opposite corner of the top face, what is the potential drop across the arrangement?

13 A infinitely long chain of resistors is constructed as shown in Figure 43.15. If each component has a resistance *r*, calculate the effective resistance of the chain between A and B.

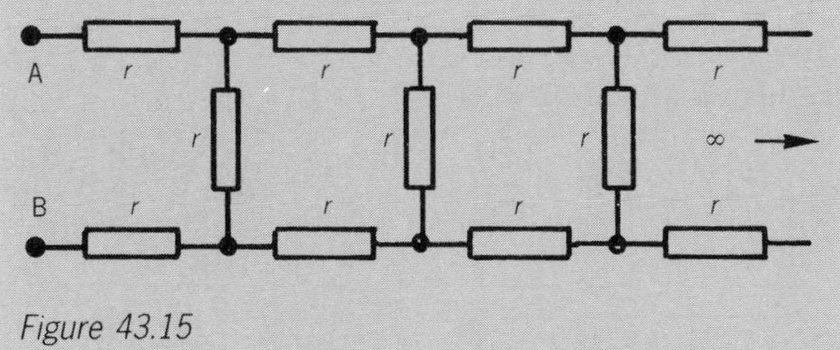

Figure 43.15

Practical forms of resistor

1. Carbon composite resistors – the stability of this type is poor: heating causes permanent damage and Ohm's law is then not obeyed.
2. Carbon film resistors – these are ceramic rods heated in methane so that a film of carbon is deposited on the surface. The resistance depends on the thickness of the film, and grooves can be cut in the surface to change the resistance.
3. Wire wound resistors – these are made with nichrome wire and are used as standard resistors. These must be non-inductively wound to eliminate self-inductance (see page 321) and such coils are used in resistance boxes.

Resistors used in radios are colour coded as shown in Figure 43.16. The first band gives the first digit of the code number, the second band the second digit and the third band the number of zeros. Some resistors also have a fourth band that shows the precision of the rating: red signifies that the resistance is within 2 per cent of the stated value, gold 5 per cent and silver 10 per cent, while the absence of a coloured band means within 20 per cent of the stated value.

Colour	*Digit*	*Colour*	*Digit*
Black	0	Green	5
Brown	1	Blue	6
Red	2	Violet	7
Orange	3	Grey	8
Yellow	4	White	9

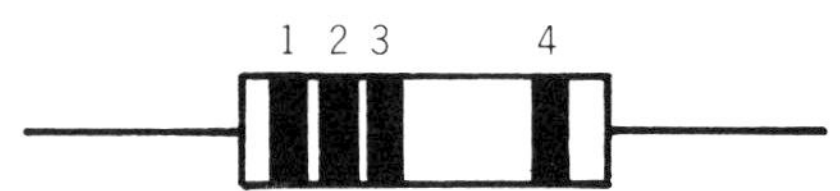

Figure 43.16

A new way of writing down resistance values (for use in practical electronics only) has been adopted recently:

1.5Ω would be written as 1R5
1.5kΩ would be written 1K5
150kΩ would be written 150K or M15
1.5MΩ would be written 1M5.

Student investigation

Design and carry out an experiment to measure the conduction of electricity by pencil lines on a sheet of paper.

The table below gives the resistances per metre of some common materials in the form of wire of stated gauges, with the equivalent diameters.

Gauge	*Diameter* /mm	*Resistance per metre* Ω/*Copper*[1]	*Eureka*[2]	*Nichrome*[3]	*Manganin*[4]
16	1.63	0.008	0.228	0.200	0.204
20	0.91	0.026	0.722	0.888	0.645
24	0.56	0.071	1.93	2.37	1.73
26	0.46	0.105	2.89	3.55	2.58
28	0.38	0.155	4.27	5.25	3.82
30	0.32	0.222	6.08	7.48	5.45

[1] Copper is used for connecting leads because of its low resistance since we require the energy loss in the leads to be as small as possible.
[2] Eureka is an alloy containing 60 per cent of copper and 40 per cent of nickel.
[3] Nichrome is an alloy of nickel, copper and chromium, used in electric fires since it does not oxidise at 1000 °C.
[4] Manganin contains 84 per cent copper, 12 per cent manganese and 4 per cent nickel, and is used in resistance boxes.

14 Calculate the effective resistance of the following combinations of resistors:
(*a*) two resistors in series, each of 25 Ω;
(*b*) two resistors in parallel, each of 25 Ω;
(*c*) one resistor of 25 Ω connected in series with two others, each of 25 Ω, in parallel;
(*d*) four resistors in parallel, each of 25 Ω;
(*e*) two resistors of 25 Ω in parallel connected in series to three of 25 Ω in parallel.

Electrical power

We can use Ohm's law to derive an alternative formula for electrical power.

Since $V = IR$, and power $= VI$, we have

$$\text{power} = I^2R = \frac{V^2}{R}$$

15 A copper water tank of mass 20 kg and containing 0.125 m^3 of water is heated using a 3 kW immersion heater. If 15 per cent of the energy is lost, find out how long it takes to raise the temperature of the water from 20 ° to 60°C.

Electromotive force and internal resistance

When current flows round a circuit energy is used to drive it, not only through the external resistors but also through the source of energy itself. If we think of a simple cell then the liquid of the cell has resistance; we call this the **internal resistance** of the cell. The voltage produced by the cell is known as the **electromotive force** or e.m.f. and this produces a voltage drop across the cell and across the external resistor.

The e.m.f. of a cell can be defined as **the maximum potential difference that the cell can produce across its terminals**, or **open circuit potential difference**, since in that condition no energy will be lost within it.

Consider the circuit shown in Figure 43.17. Let the e.m.f. of the cell be E and the internal resistance r. If the cell is connected to an external resistance R, then

$$E = IR + Ir$$

The quantity IR is the useful energy per coulomb available outside the cell, and Ir is the energy lost per coulomb within the cell itself.

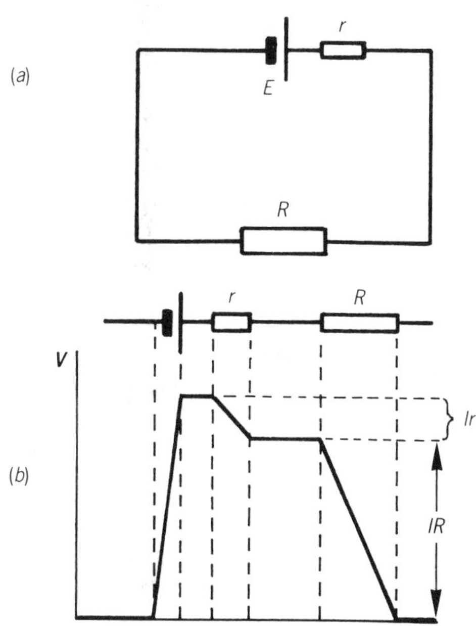

Figure 43.17

We usually require the internal resistance to be as small as possible to reduce the energy loss; however, it is sometimes helpful to have a rather larger internal resistance to prevent large currents from damaging the cell.

Example

A cell of e.m.f. 12 V and internal resistance 0.1 Ω is used in two circuits. Calculate the voltage at the terminals of the cell (i) when it is connected to a 10 Ω resistance, (ii) when it is connected to a 0.2 Ω resistance.

(i) Total resistance = 10 + 0.1 = 10.1 Ω.
Therefore current = 12/10.1 = 1.19 A.
Loss of energy per coulomb in the cell = 1.19 × 0.1 = 0.119 V.
Therefore voltage at the terminals of the cell = 12 – 0.119 = 11.88 V.

(ii) Total resistance = 0.1 + 0.2 = 0.3 Ω.
Therefore current = 12/0.3 = 40 A.
Loss of energy per coulomb in the cell = 40 × 0.1 = 4 V.

Therefore voltage at the terminals of the cell = 12 – 4 = 8 V.

16 Three cells of e.m.f.s 2.0, 1.5 and 1.1 V with internal resistances of 0.2, 2 and 5 Ω respectively are connected in parallel with their like poles together.
Calculate the potential drop across the terminals of this arrangement when an external resistance of 10 Ω is joined in the circuit.

17 Two batteries A and B have their positive terminals connected by a wire of resistance 8 Ω and their negative terminals connected by a wire of resistance 12 Ω. A 5 Ω wire connects the midpoint of these two wires.
What is the p.d. across the 5 Ω wire if the battery A has an e.m.f. of 4.2 V and internal resistance 0.1 Ω and battery B has an e.m.f. of 4.5 V and an internal resistance of 4.0 Ω? [o]

18 A given cell is connected in series with a variable resistance while at the same time a high-resistance voltmeter is connected across the terminals of the cell. The voltmeter reads 1.30 V when the variable resistance is fixed at 13 Ω, and 1.20 V when this resistance is 8 Ω. Calculate
(*a*) the e.m.f. of the cell,
(*b*) the internal resistance of the cell.

Maximum power transfer theorem

The external resistance will affect the current drawn from a source of e.m.f., and therefore the energy lost within it. It is possible to find the value of this external resistance R that will give the greatest power output.

In the circuit in Figure 43.18, consider the variation of output power with R.

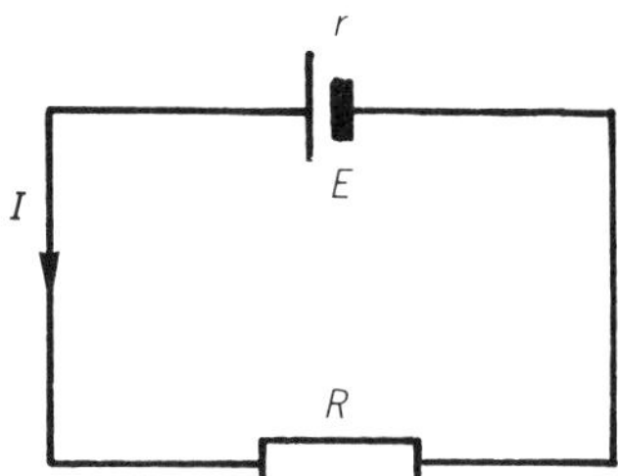

Figure 43.18

$$E = IR + Ir$$
$$EI = I^2R + I^2r$$

Therefore

$$\frac{d(I^2R)}{dR} = E\frac{dI}{dR} - 2Ir\frac{dI}{dR} = 0 \text{ for a maximum.}$$

$$\text{Therefore } E\frac{dI}{dR} = 2Ir\frac{dI}{dR} \quad \text{and so} \quad E = 2Ir$$

This therefore gives $r = R$ for maximum power output. This is the case for an amplifier and loudspeaker; the output impedance of the amplifier should be matched to that of the speaker. This condition does not give the most efficient operation of the system, however.

19 A voltmeter of resistance 100 Ω reads 1.30 V when connected across a cell of e.m.f. 1.40 V. If a 10 Ω resistor is joined in series with the cell and the voltmeter, what will the latter now read?

20 (*a*) When a torch battery delivers a current of 0.5 A, the potential difference between its terminals is 1.2 V. When the current is 1.0 A, the terminal potential difference is 0.8 V. Calculate the e.m.f. and internal resistance of the battery, assuming that both remain constant.

(*b*) Two resistors each having a resistance equal to the internal resistance of the battery, are connected across the battery (i) in series, (ii) in parallel. Show that the power dissipated *in each resistor* is the same in the two cases. [JMB]

Electron theory of resistance

We can consider the electrons in a solid to have a random motion similar to a cloud of gas molecules.

An electric field of intensity E is placed across a length l of the conductor. Let the conductor be of resistivity ρ and resistance R, and have n conduction electrons per unit volume.

$$E = \frac{V}{l} \quad \text{and therefore} \quad Ee = \frac{Ve}{l} = F$$

where F is the force on the electron. The acceleration of an electron due to this field is then given by

$$\text{acceleration} = \frac{Ve}{ml}$$

where m is the electron mass. If the time between electron collisions is t, then (Figure 43.19) the velocity v' just before a collision is

$$v' = \frac{Vet}{lm}$$

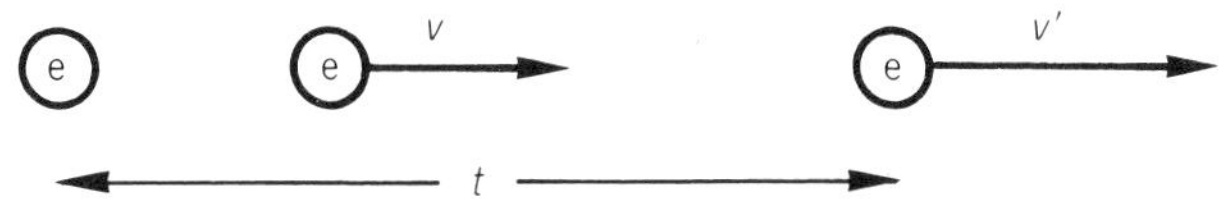

Figure 43.19

The average velocity between collisions is therefore $\frac{Vet}{2lm} = v$, but since $I = nAve$ (see page 279) we have

$$I = \frac{e^2tnAV}{2lm}$$

and this gives for the resistance:

$$R = \frac{2lm}{e^2tnA}$$

If we consider the thermal velocity of the electrons to be around 10^6 m s^{-1}, then the time between collisions in copper is 5×10^{-14} s and the distance travelled is some 5×10^{-8} m, much greater than the interatomic spacing which is about 2×10^{-10} m.

Kirchhoff's laws

It is often necessary to solve the current, resistance and p.d. values for a more complex circuit and Kirchhoff's laws help us to do this. These laws describe the flow of current round a circuit, and state

(*a*) the algebraic sum of the currents at a junction is zero;

(*b*) the algebraic sum of the (current × resistance) round a circuit is equal to the algebraic sum of the e.m.f.s round that circuit.

Consider the two simple circuits shown in Figure 43.20.

In circuit (*a*) the e.m.f. is E and the sum of the products of (current × resistance) IR is $IR_1 + IR_2$. Kirchhoff's second law simply states that

$$E = IR_1 + IR_2$$

In circuit (*b*), applying Kirchhoff's first law to the junction at A we have

$$I + (I_1 + I_2) = 0$$

Applying the second law to loop ABCDFA gives

$$I_1R_1 - I_2R_2 = 0$$

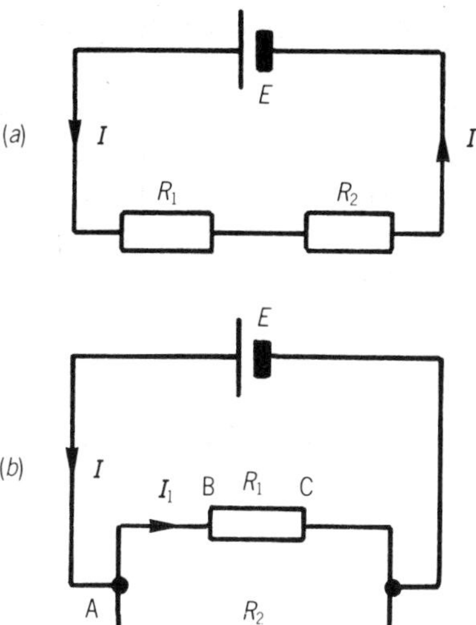

Figure 43.20

Kirchhoff's laws may be used to calculate the resistance of a complex network of resistors. One such version is shown below.

Example

In the circuit shown in Figure 43.21, using Kirchhoff's first law, we have

Round ABDA: $2i_1 + i_3 - i_2 = 0$
Round BCDB: $3(i_1 - i_3) - 2(i_2 + i_3) - i_3 = 0$
Round FABCF: $2i_1 + 3(i_1 - i_3) = 3$

Solving these equations gives:

$$i_1 = \frac{24}{43}\,\text{A} \qquad i_2 = \frac{45}{43}\,\text{A} \qquad i_3 = \frac{-3}{43}\,\text{A}$$

Notice that the sign of i_3 implies that it is flowing in the opposite direction from that shown in the diagram.

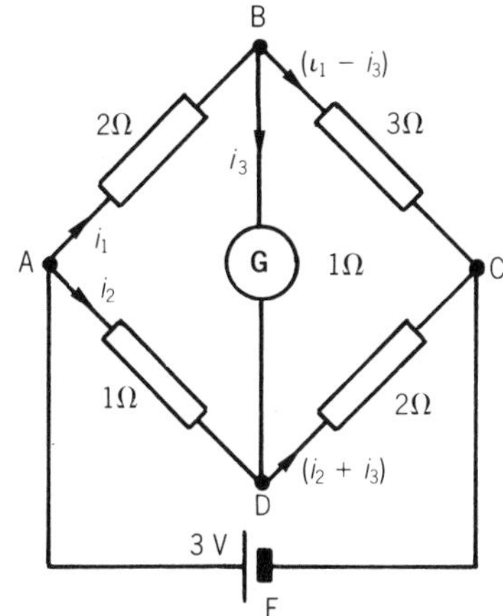

Figure 43.21

Example

Consider a cube made by twelve equal resistors r (Figure 43.22). Calculate the effective resistance R between points A and B.

The voltage drop along any path between A and B must be equal no matter which path we take. Therefore consider the path ACDB.

At A (by symmetry) a current of $i/3$ flows in each branch, and for the same reason the current along sides ED, EG ... is $i/6$. Therefore along ACDB:

$$iR = \frac{ir}{3} + \frac{ir}{6} + \frac{ir}{3}$$

$$= \tfrac{5}{6}ir$$

$$R = \tfrac{5}{6}r$$

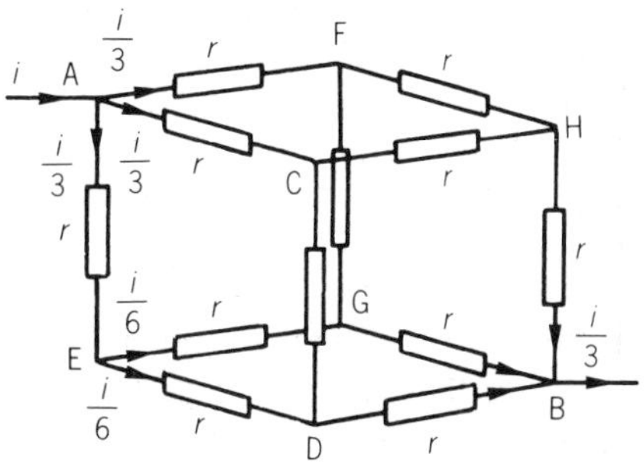

Figure 43.22

21 A galvanometer in series with a resistor of R ohm and one of 1000 Ω gives a scale deflection of 23.7 divisions when connected to a cell of negligible internal resistance. On successively cutting out the 1000 Ω and R the deflections are 61.4 and 81.0 divisions respectively. If the current is proportional to the deflection of the galvanometer, calculate R and the resistance of the galvanometer. [D]

The temperature coefficient of resistance

When a material is heated its resistance will change due to the increased thermal motion of the atoms in the specimen. The equation for this variation is:

$$R_\theta = R_0(1 + \alpha\theta + b\theta^2 + \ldots)$$

where R_θ is the resistance at some temperature θ °C and R_0 the resistance at 0 °C. But since $b << \alpha$ we can express this change by the following simplified linear equation, as long as the rise in temperature is not too great:

$$R_\theta = R_0(1 + \alpha\theta)$$

Here α is the **temperature coefficient of resistance,** defined as **the increase in resistance per degree rise divided by the resistance at 0 °C:**

$$\alpha = \frac{R_\theta - R_0}{R_0\theta}$$

It is important to realise that you must use R_0 as the resistance at 0 °C and not take θ as simply the rise in temperature.

For a metal the temperature coefficient of resistance is positive – in other words, as the temperature increases so does the resistance. This can be explained by considering the motion of the atoms and free electrons within the solid. At low temperatures the thermal vibration of the atoms is small, but as the temperature is increased this motion increases. This means that the electrons are much more likely to collide with an atom and so their motion through the metal is restricted, and the resistance therefore increases with temperature. (This is not the case with semiconductors – see page 361.)

Example

If the resistance of a copper wire is 4 Ω at 20 °C, calculate its resistance at 50 °C. (α for copper = 43×10^{-4} K^{-1}.)

Calculate first the value of R_0.

$$R_{20} = R_0(1 + \alpha \times 20)$$

$$R_0 = \frac{4}{1 + 43 \times 10^{-4} \times 20}$$

$$= \frac{4}{1.086} = 3.68\ \Omega$$

Therefore resistance at 50 °C is

$$R_{50} = 3.68(1 + 43 \times 10^{-4} \times 50) = 4.47\ \Omega$$

In a light bulb the filament is at about 2700 °C when the bulb is working, and its resistance when hot is about ten times that when cold. (For one light bulb tested the resistance at room temperature was 32 Ω, rising to 324 Ω at its working temperature.)

We can also define the change in resistivity with temperature by the equation:

$$\rho_\theta = \rho_0(1 + \beta\theta)$$

where β is the **temperature coefficient of resistivity.** We require that the variation of resistance in circuits should be small, so β should be as small as possible for thermal stability.

22 (*a*) What length of copper wire of diameter 0.1 mm is required to make a coil with resistance 0.5 Ω?

(*b*) If on passing a current of 2 A the temperature of the coil rises by 10 °C, what error would arise in taking the potential drop across the coil as 1 V? (Temperature coefficient of resistance of copper = 0.0043 K^{-1}; resistivity = 1.69×10^{-8} Ω m.) [T]

The following table gives the temperature coefficients of resistivity for various materials.

Material	*β × 10⁻⁴ K⁻¹*	*Material*	*β × 10⁻⁴ K⁻¹*
Copper	43	Aluminium	38
Lead	43	Nichrome	1.7
Eureka	0.2	Manganin	0.2
Iron	62	Platinum	38
Carbon	−0.5	Tungsten	60

A further point on circuits

When considering circuit problems you should always look at the circuit first to see if a simple method may be used to solve it. One such circuit is shown in Figure 43.23. The p.d. between the points A and B may be found by using the ratio of the voltage drop down the resistors in each branch of the circuit. We therefore have, taking the potential at C as zero,

potential at A = 6 V
potential at B = 4 V

Therefore

p.d. between A and B = 2 V

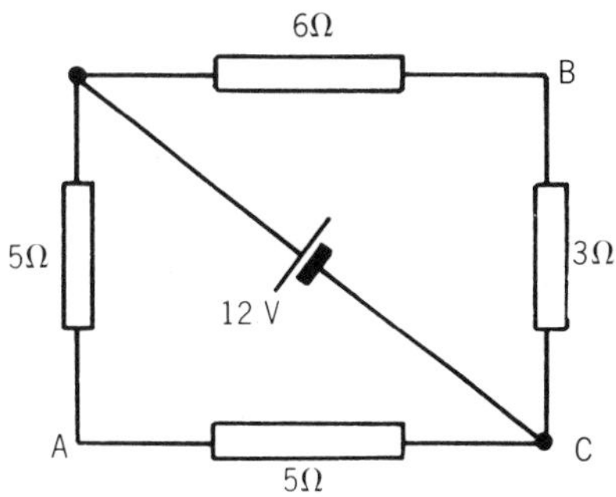

Figure 43.23

Student investigation

The currents at which wires fuse may be found using the circuit in Figure 43.24. Test wires of different materials and different gauges. For each different material record the diameter of the wire and the current at which if fuses. Plot a graph of current I against the log of the diameter d, and use it to determine the value of the constants a and n in the equation:

$$I = ad^n$$

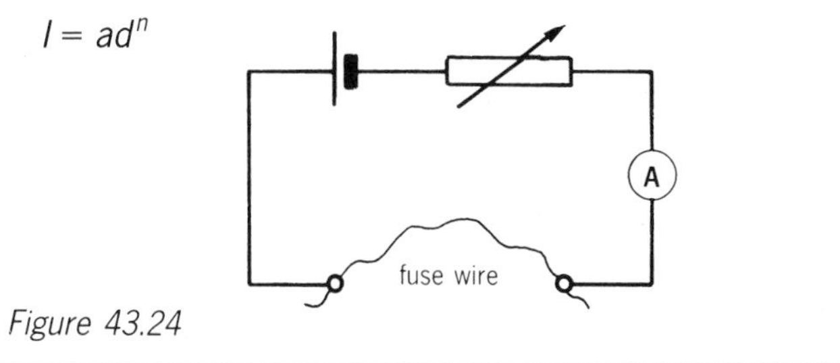

Figure 43.24

23 The temperature at which the tungsten filament of a 12 V 36 W lamp operates is 1750 °C. If the temperature coefficient of resistance of tungsten is 6×10^{-3} K^{-1}, find the resistance of the lamp at a room temperature of 20 °C.

Superconductivity

At very low temperatures some materials become **superconducting**, that is, their resistance drops to a vanishingly small value. For niobium this occurs at 9.46 K and for copper at 1.19 K. In these conditions a current will flow for a long period of time without the need of an external e.m.f. In 1911 Kammerlingh Onnes showed that under superconducting conditions a current could continue flowing in a coil for several hours *after* the source of electrical energy had been disconnected.

A simple version of his apparatus is shown in Figure 43.25. Switch S_1 was closed and a current passed through the coil, which was cooled to superconducting conditions. S_2 was now closed and S_1 opened, and the compass needle still showed a deflection proving that a current was still flowing in the coil.

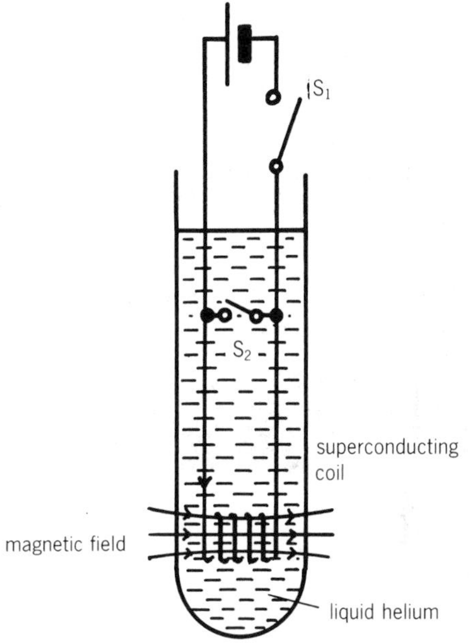

Figure 43.25

A magnet can be made to float over a dish made of superconducting lead, held there by the repulsion due to the induced currents formed as the magnet was lowered down!

Much research is in progress on the development of superconducting motors and the use of superconducting material in computer circuits. Unfortunately there is a **critical field** above which superconductivity breaks down. This means that the actual strength of a superconducting magnet is limited.

In 1987 great advances were made in this field. The temperature at which some ceramic materials could be made superconducting was raised to 230 K and it is predicted that the discovery of materials that are superconductors at room temperature is not far off.

The potentiometer

The potentiometer, devised by Poggendorf in 1850, is a very useful instrument for a number of measurements in electricity. In its simplest form it is simply a piece of resistance wire, usually a metre long, fixed between two points A and B with a cell of output voltage V connected between the two ends (Figure 43.26). The potential drop along AB is assumed to be uniform and that in the connecting leads zero.

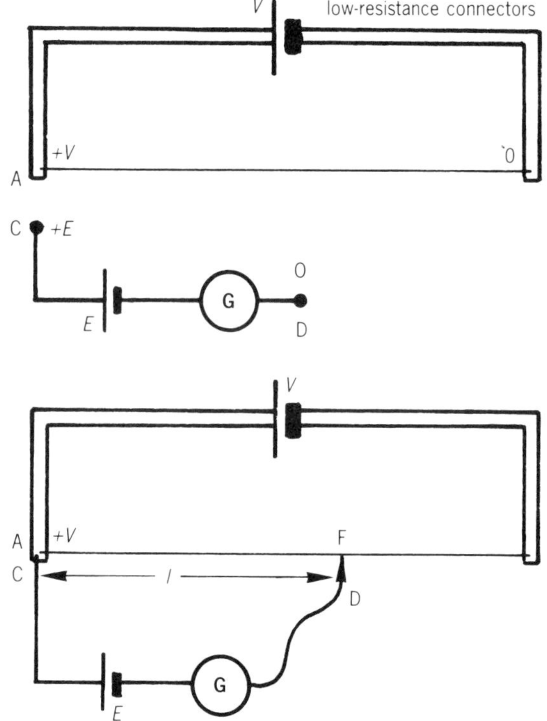

Figure 43.26

Consider a source of e.m.f. E. The potential at C will be $+E$ and that at D will be zero; there will be a p.d. across the source and galvanometer of E volts.

If C is now connected to A the potential at junction AC becomes $+V$ and that at D becomes $(V - E)$.

If D is now connected to the wire at a point F then if no current is to flow through the galvanometer the potential drop down the wire must be equal to that across the source and meter, that is

p.d. across AF must equal p.d. across CD

Since we know the p.d. across AB then, assuming that it reduces uniformly down the wire, E can be found.

Let length AB = 1 m
Let length AF = l m

Then:

$$E = \frac{V}{l} \text{ volts}$$

Notice that E must be less than V.

In practice the source is connected to the potentiometer wire by a sliding contact (or *jockey*) and the position of the jockey varied until zero deflection is observed on the galvanometer.

The potentiometer is a very good instrument for the measurement of e.m.f., since when it is balanced no current is being drawn from the source. This is known as a **null** method. The circuit is shown in Figure 43.27. A key is used to cut out the supply e.m.f. to prevent overheating of the potentiometer wire. A protective resistor is included in series with the galvanometer to prevent damage when far from the balance point. Once the balance point is found this resistor may be shorted out.

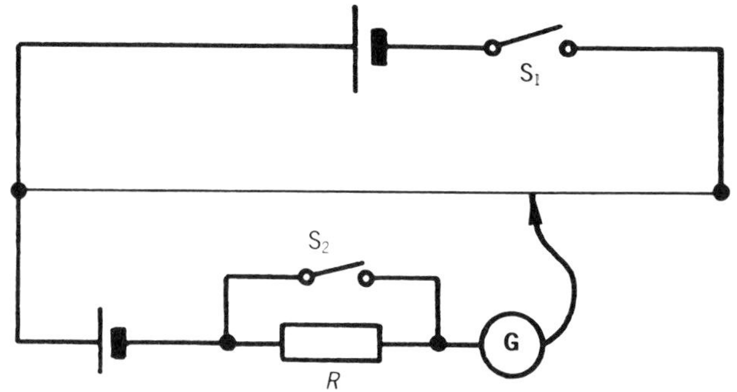

Figure 43.27

Note that although no current flows in the galvanometer when the balance condition is reached the driver cell supplies current throughout.

Example

A potentiometer is set up as shown in Figure 43.28 and the balance point for the unknown e.m.f. V found at 74.5 cm from the left-hand end of the metre wire.

If the driver cell has an e.m.f of 1.5 V and negligible internal resistance find that of the unknown e.m.f.

$V = 1.5 \times 74.5/100 = 1.12$ V.

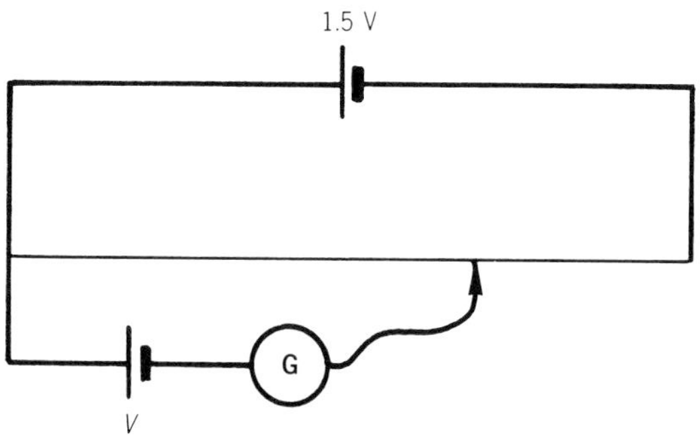

Figure 43.28

Uses of the potentiometer

Some of the purposes for which the potentiometer may be used are discussed in this section.

(i) Comparison of e.m.f.s

The circuit used is shown in Figure 43.29. E_1 is the unknown e.m.f. and E_0 is a standard cell of known e.m.f.

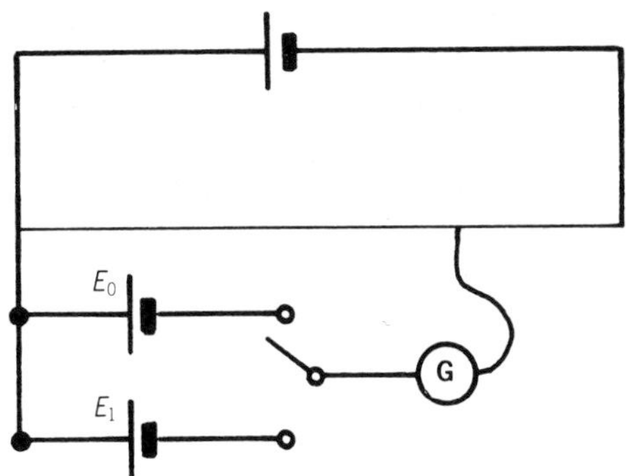

Figure 43.29

The balance point is first found with the standard cell (l_0 and then with the unknown e.m.f. (l_1). The ratio of the e.m.f.s is then found from:

$$\frac{E_0}{E_1} = \frac{l_0}{l_1}$$

A commonly used standard cell is the Weston cadmium cell, having an e.m.f. of 1.0186 V (see page 306).

(ii) Measurement of internal resistance

The cell of e.m.f. E and internal resistance r is connected in parallel with a resistance R and switch S (Figure 43.30).

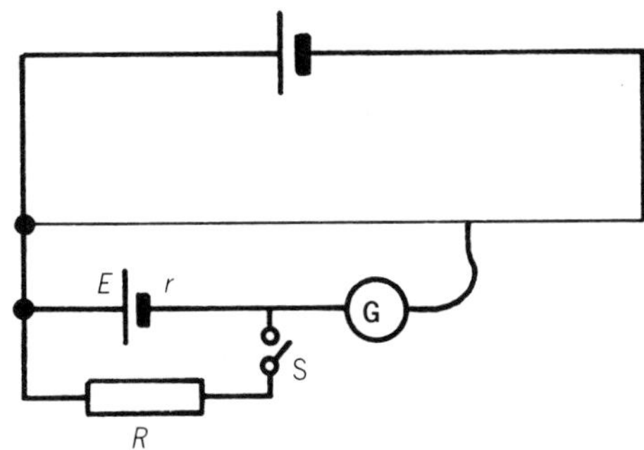

Figure 43.30

The balance point (l_0) is found with the switch open; this measures E, since no current is flowing from the cell ($l_0 \propto E$).

The switch is now closed and a second balance point (l_1) is found. This measures the output voltage of the cell (V) ($l_1 \propto V$).

Since $E/V = l_0/l_1$ and $E = V + Ir$,

$$\frac{E}{R + r} = \frac{V}{R} = \mathrm{I}$$

Therefore

$$r = \left(\frac{l_0}{l_1} - 1\right)R$$

(iii) Measurement of small e.m.f.s – the thermocouple

The balance length l is proportional to the e.m.f. and therefore with very small e.m.f.s (a few mV) like those produced by a thermocouple the balance point would be very close to one end of the wire and therefore very difficult to measure.

A resistance R (usually a few hundred ohms) is placed in series with the potentiometer wire (Figure 43.31). Therefore there is a large p.d. across R and only a small p.d. across the wire. The effect on the balance position can be shown by a simple example.

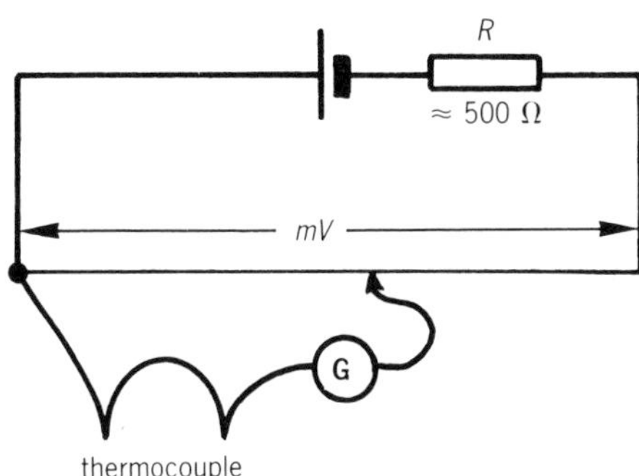

Figure 43.31

Let the driver cell have an output voltage of 1.5 V and the potentiometer wire have a resistance of 5 Ω. If R = 500 Ω, then the voltage drop down the potentiometer wire is

$$\frac{5 \times 1.5}{505} = 14.85 \text{ mV}$$

Therefore balance points may be found that lie well down the wire for small e.m.f.s.

> **Example**
>
> Using the resistance values given above, calculate the balance point for a thermocouple giving an e.m.f. of 6 mV.
>
> Drop down 100 cm = 15 mV.
> Therefore for a drop of 6 mV, length $= \dfrac{6 \times 100}{15} = 40$ cm.

(iv) Measurement of current

Set up the circuit shown in Figure 43.32. The potential drop across R can be found by finding the balance point, and hence if R is known the value of the current can be found. This principle can be used to calibrate an ammeter or voltmeter.

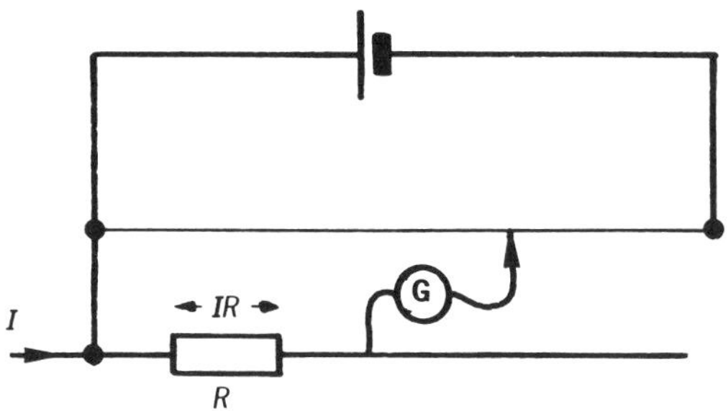

Figure 43.32

(v) Comparison of resistances

The circuit is set up as shown in Figure 43.33, and the balance point found first for one resistance (l_1) and then the other (l_2). Then

$$\frac{l_1}{l_2} = \frac{IR_1}{IR_2} = \frac{R_1}{R_2}$$

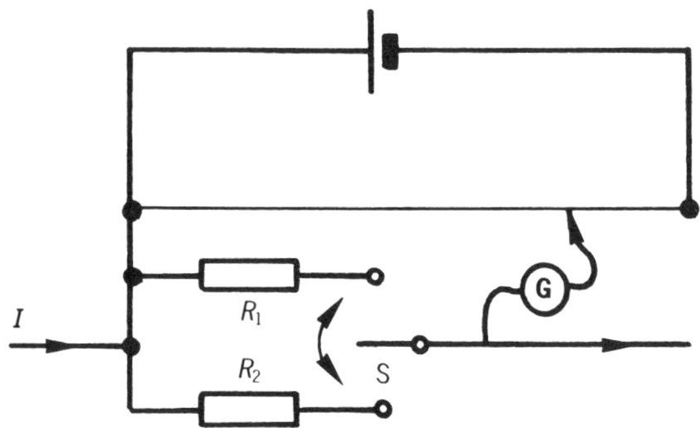

Figure 43.33

The advantages of the potentiometer are:

(*a*) the scale can be made as long as we choose, within reason, for maximum accuracy;

(*b*) the adjustment and measurement is by a 'null' method;

(*c*) no current is drawn from the circuit under test;

(*d*) the connecting wires may be thin since no current passes through them;

(*e*) direct calibration with a standard cell is possible,

(*f*) it has a wide range limited only by the value of the e.m.f. of the driver cell and the resistance of the series resistor R.

It has certain disadvantages, however:

(*a*) it is relatively cumbersome and slow to use;

(*b*) faults may arise due to breaks in the circuit or incorrect connection;

(*c*) the temperature of the wire must remain constant;

(*d*) the wire is assumed to be of uniform thickness.

It is important that the e.m.f. to be measured is always connected correctly, that is, with the positive to the positive of the potentiometer wire.

For accurate work allowance must be made for the resistance of the contacts at either end of the wire – the so-called **end effects**. These can be eliminated by reversing the driver cell and then connecting the e.m.f. to the opposite end of the wire.

24 A potentiometer is set up with a thermocouple to measure changes of temperature. Suppose that in such a determination the thermocouple is balanced against a length of potentiometer wire with a resistance of 4 Ω, the galvanometer having a resistance of 10 Ω. The thermocouple has a resistance of 1 Ω and gives an e.m.f. 0.03 mV per °C temperature difference between its junctions. Find the smallest change in temperature of the hot junction that will be detectable by the galvanometer if it is unaffected by currents of less than 1 μA. [D]

25 A certain cell is connected to a potentiometer and a balance point (no galvanometer deflection) is obtained at 84.0 cm along the wire. When its terminals are connected by a 5 Ω resistor the balance point changes to 70 cm.

Calculate the internal resistance of the cell, and the balance point when the 5 Ω resistor is changed to one of 4 Ω.

26 A cell of 1.5 V and internal resistance 0.2 Ω is used as the driver cell in a potentiometer with a metre wire of resistance 10 Ω. If the potentiometer is to be used with a thermocouple to measure a temperature of 60 °C, calculate the value of the resistor that must be placed in series with the cell to give a balance point 80 cm from the end connected to the thermocouple. The thermocouple gives an output of 1.5 mV per degree.

27 A steady current is passed through two resistances P and Q connected in series. If two leads are taken from the end of P a balance is obtained against 22.1 cm of a given potentiometer wire. When the leads are transferred to the ends of Q a balance is found at 56.0 cm, whereas if the leads are taken across P and Q together a balance is found at 78.6 cm.

How do you account for these observations, and what is the resistance of Q if P has a resistance of 10 Ω? [T]

Wheatstone bridge

The Wheatstone bridge, devised in 1843, provides an accurate method of determining the resistance of an unknown resistor. The circuit is shown in Figure 43.34. Four resistors are joined as shown, one of them being an unknown resistor whose resistance is to be measured and one a standard resistor. We will assume that R_4 is the unknown. R_3 can be varied and it is adjusted until no current flows in the galvanometer. In this condition

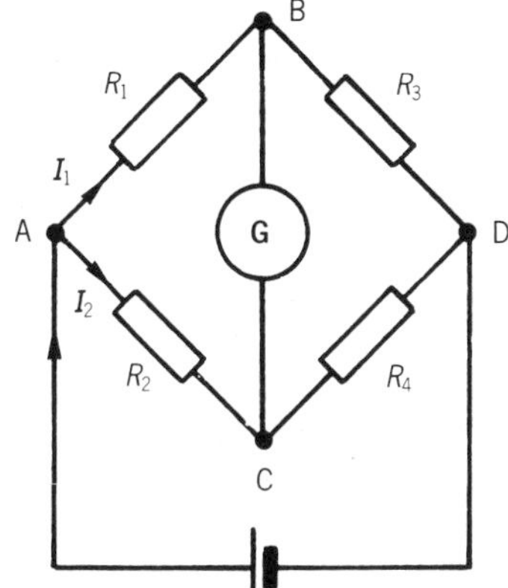

Figure 43.34

p.d. across AB = p.d. across AC

also

p.d. across BD = p.d. across CD

Therefore $I_1R_1 = I_2R_2$ and $I_1R_3 = I_2R_4$

$$\frac{R_1}{R_3} = \frac{R_2}{R_4}$$

The arms AB and BD are known as the **ratio arms** of the bridge.

It can be shown that for the highest sensitivity the galvanometer must be connected from the junction of the highest resistances to the junction of the lowest.

Accuracy should be of the order of 0.2 per cent. A switch is usually incorporated in the circuit in series with the cell, to prevent current flowing through the bridge at points other than the balance point and thus heating the components and changing their resistance.

Practical arrangements of the Wheatstone bridge

(i) Metre bridge

The ratio arms are the two sections of a metre wire as shown in Figure 43.35.

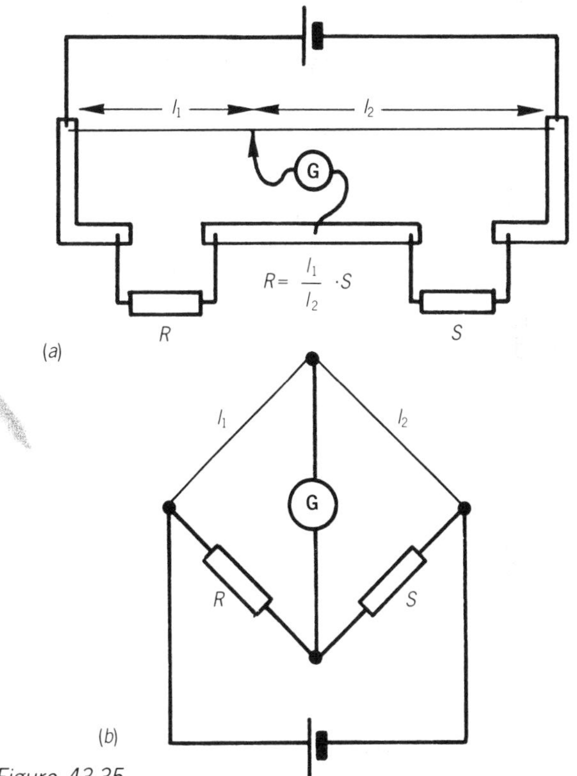

Figure 43.35

(ii) Metre bridge for a.c.

A.c. bridges are used for the measurement of the resistance of liquids to eliminate the effects of polarisation at the electrodes. Changing the values of the two ratio arms will affect the sensitivity of the instrument.

(iii) Post office box

A Wheatstone bridge arrangement is in use by British Telecom for testing cables. If a short occurs, its distance from the test point can be found if the resistance per metre of the cables is known.

Example

A short occurs in a telephone cable having a resistance of 0.45 Ω per metre. The circuit is tested with a Wheatstone bridge. The two resistors in the ratio arms of the Wheatstone bridge network have values of 100 Ω and 1110 Ω respectively. A balance condition is found when the variable resistor has a value of 400 Ω.

Calculate the distance down the cable where the short has occurred.

Let the total resistance of the two parts of the cable be R.

$$\frac{100}{1110} = \frac{R}{400}$$

Therefore $R = 36.04\ \Omega$. Therefore distance down the cable $= \dfrac{36.04}{2 \times 0.45} = 40$ m.

28 In a Wheatstone bridge the four resistors in the arms of the bridge are 2 Ω (AB), 4 Ω (BC), 1 Ω (AD) and 3 Ω (DC). The terminals of a cell of e.m.f. 2 V and negligible internal resistance are connected to A and C. If a galvanometer of resistance 10 Ω is connected between B and D, find the current in the galvanometer. [O and C]

29 If a potentiometer circuit fails to balance, how would you attempt to find the cause of the trouble?

30 Why is it necessary to aim to get a balance point well down the wire in a potentiometer but close to the centre in a metre wire bridge?

31 A telephone line BCD 30 km long has a fault due to earthing at an unknown point C. The end B is joined to the end D through resistances *P, Q, R* in series and in that order. A battery is connected from the end B to the junction of the resistances *Q* and *R* and a galvanometer is connected from the junction of P and Q to earth. The resistance of *R* is equal to that of 7.8 km of the telephone line. When *P* = 1500 Ω and *Q* = 1425 Ω the galvanometer is not deflected.

Where is the fault in the line?

32 A 120 cm length of wire of diameter 0.5 mm is placed in one gap of a metre bridge, a standard one ohm coil being placed in the other gap. A balance point is obtained 57.7 cm from the end of the bridge wire corresponding to the one ohm coil. Calculate the resistivity of the 120 cm of wire.

33 Consider the circuit shown in Figure 43.36. Calculate
(*a*) the effective resistance of the circuit,
(*b*) the current in each of the resistors.
The cell may be considered to have zero internal resistance.

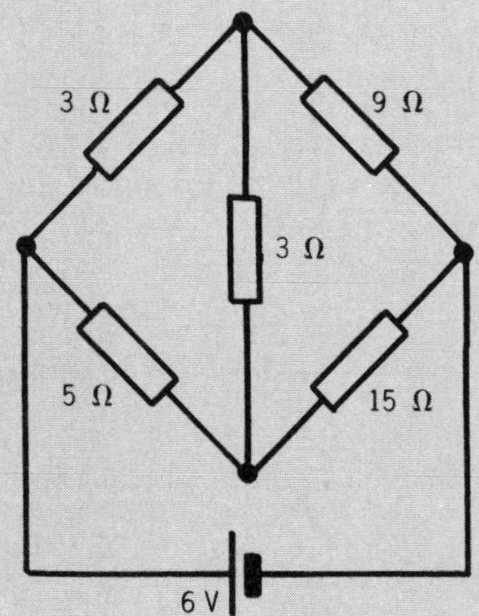

Figure 43.36

Student investigation

Set up the circuit shown in Figure 43.37. Heat the water slowly and calculate the resistance of the iron coil by balancing the bridge about every 10 °C.

Plot a graph of resistance against temperature, and hence determine the temperature coefficient of resistance of the iron wire.

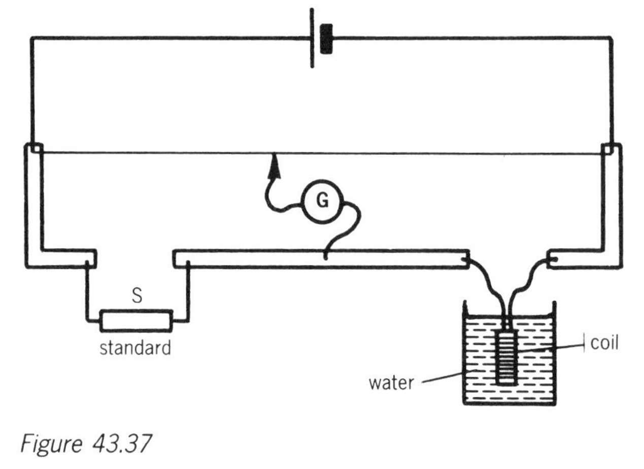

Figure 43.37

Accuracy of a potentiometer and a metre wire bridge

The accuracy of a potentiometer and a metre wire bridge (see page 293) may be found as follows:

(i) Measurement of e.m.f. with a potentiometer
Let the balance length with the standard cell of e.m.f E_0 be l_0 and that with the unknown cell (of e.m.f. E) be l. The fractional error in E is given by the equation:

$$\frac{\Delta E}{E} = \frac{\Delta E_0}{E_0} + \frac{\Delta l_0}{l_0} + \frac{\Delta l}{l}$$

Therefore if the balance point may be found with a given accuracy (that is, if Δl is fixed) then the larger the value of l, the greater will be the accuracy. The balance point must be well down the wire.

(ii) Measurement of resistance with a metre wire bridge
Let the unknown resistor be R, the standard resistor be S and the two lengths of wire at the balance point be l_1 and l_2 (Figure 43.35(a)).

Therefore the fractional error in R is given by:

$$\frac{\Delta R}{R} = \frac{\Delta S}{S} + \frac{\Delta l_1}{l_1} + \frac{\Delta l_2}{l_2}$$

Therefore the greatest accuracy is obtained when $l_1 = l_2$ for a given value of Δl. The balance point must be in the centre of the wire.

44 · Magnetic effect of an electric current

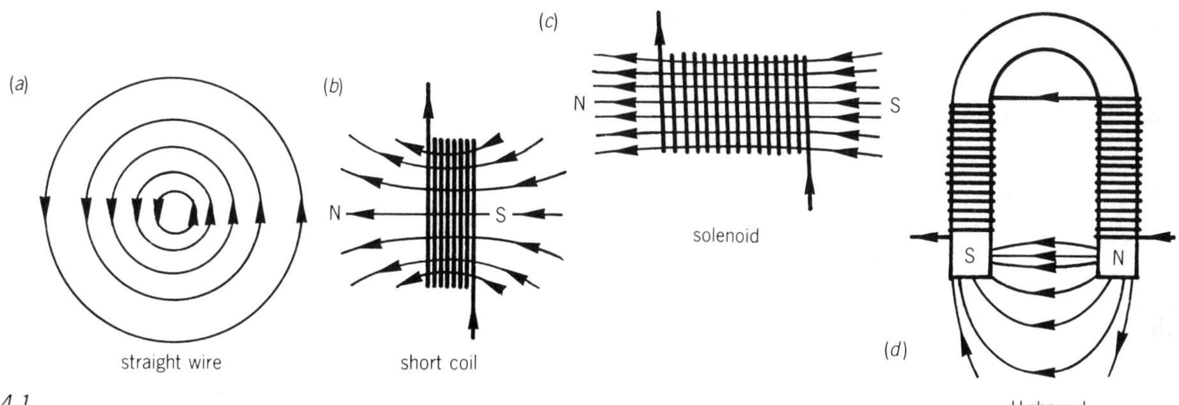

Figure 44.1

An electric current will produce a magnetic field, a fact discovered by Oersted in 1820. The intensity and shape of this field depends on the strength of the current and the arrangement of the wires carrying it. In 1820 Sturgeon also showed that the strength of the field in a coil could be increased considerably by placing an iron core in the coil.

Magnetic fields have a large number of uses in the modern world in, for instance, particle accelerators, plasma bottles, lifting magnets, linear induction motors, tape recording heads and many other applications. Knowledge of those fields has also helped in the studies of the Physics of the van Allen radiation belts, quasars and aurorae.

You will have seen some magnetic field arrangements in your GCSE course and we will be considering these and other field arrangements in detail.

The shapes of the magnetic fields for some simple arrangements are shown in Figure 44.1. You can see that these fields are not uniform and it is found that the strength of the field depends on the closeness of the lines of magnetic flux (see page 296).

The direction of the magnetic force can be found by **Maxwell's corkscrew rule.** If we imagine ourselves driving a corkscrew in the direction of the current, then the direction of rotation of the corkscrew is the direction of the lines of force.

The polarity of a coil of wire can be found by **Fleming's right-hand grip rule,** where the fingers of the right hand indicate the current direction and the thumb the north pole of the solenoid.

A single wire connected to a cell and doubled back on itself has no net magnetic field – the field produced by the current in one direction cancels that produced by the current in the other. This is known as non-inductive winding; it is used in resistance boxes and in the platinum resistance thermometer.

Student investigation

Figure 44.2 is a simplified version of the bubble chamber photograph of the discovery of a new fundamental particle, the Ω^-.

A magnetic field was placed across the bubble chamber when the photograph was taken. A proton track is marked *p* and the dotted lines represent the path of a particle with no charge.

(*a*) In which general direction was this field?

(*b*) What can you say about the particles that produced tracks *a*, *b*, *c* and *d*?

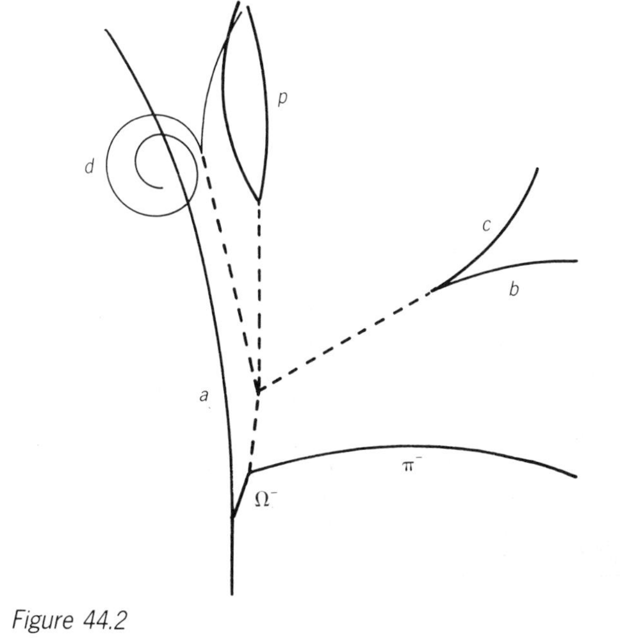

Figure 44.2

Force on a current in a magnetic field

The strength of a magnetic field is usually measured in terms of a quantity called the **magnetic flux density** of the field, B. A definition of B requires a consideration of the forces produced by electromagnetic fields.

You will know that when a wire carrying a current is placed in a magnetic field the wire experiences a force due to the interaction between the field and the moving charges in the wire. A very good demonstration is the so-called catapult field experiment in which a wire carrying a d.c. current can be made to move in the field of two flat magnets.

The fields of the wire, the magnets and the combined fields are shown in Figure 44.3. Notice that the wire moves away from the area of highest field intensity (where the magnetic field lines are closest) to a region of lower intensity.

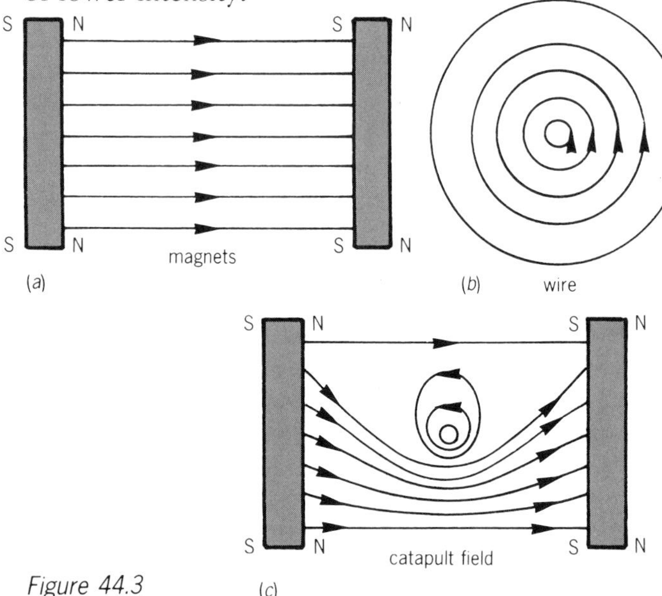

Figure 44.3

The force F on the wire in Figure 44.4(a) can be shown to be proportional to

(a) the current on the wire I,

(b) the length of the conductor in the field l,

(c) the sine of the angle that the conductor makes with the field θ, and

(d) the strength of the field – this is measured by a quantity known as the **magnetic flux density** B of the field. The force is given by the equation:

$$F = BIl \sin \theta$$

The units for B are **tesla** (T).

The greatest force occurs when $\theta = 90°$, that is, when the conductor is at right angles to the field (Figure 44.4(b)).

The flux density of a field of one tesla is therefore defined as the **force per unit length on a wire carrying a current of one ampere at right angles to the field.**

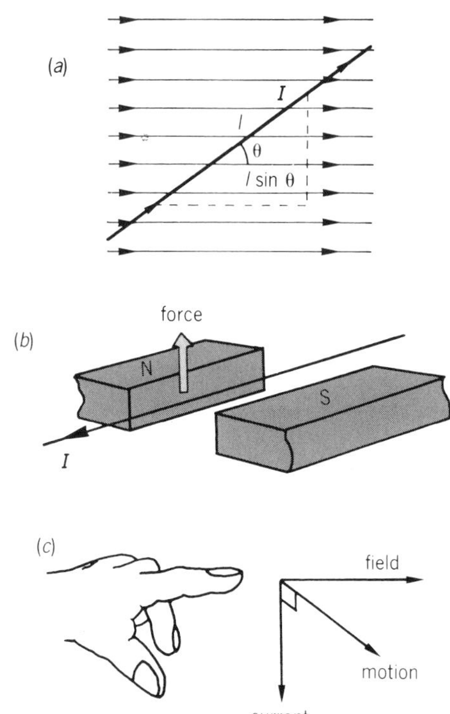

Figure 44.4

Fleming's left-hand rule gives the direction of motion for the case when field and current are at right angles. The *F*irst finger represents the *F*ield direction (N to S), the Se*C*ond finger the *C*urrent direction (+ to −) and the thu*M*b the direction of *M*otion (Figure 44.4(c)).

For a large permanent magnet of the type used in schools the flux density between the poles is about 1 T, magnadur magnets have a flux density of some 0.08 T close to their poles and the horizontal component of the Earth's magnetic field (see page 310) is about 10^{-5} T.

Having defined B we can express the **magnetic flux** passing through a surface as BA where A is the area of the surface at right angles to the field. Magnetic flux (Φ) is measured in **webers** (Wb).

Example

Calculate the force on a power cable of length 200 m carrying a current of 200 A in a direction N 30°E at a place where the horizontal component of the Earth's magnetic field is 10^{-5} T.

The wire will experience an upward force given by

$F = BIl \sin \theta$

$= 10^{-5} \times 200 \times 200 \times 0.866 = 0.35$ N

Equations for electromagnetic fields

Consider a wire carrying a current I (Figure 44.5). The flux density B at a point P due to a length of wire dl is given by:

$$dB \propto \frac{I\,dl \sin\theta}{x^2}$$

This is known as the **Biot–Savart rule**, after two French physicists. The constant of proportionality in this formula is known as the **permeability** of the medium and is denoted by μ. The unit of permeability is the **henry per metre** (H m^{-1}).

The **permeability of free space** (a vacuum) is written as μ_0 and is $4\pi \times 10^{-7}\ \text{H m}^{-1}$. This can be deduced as shown on page 299.

In a vacuum the field for a short current element is given by

$$dB = \frac{\mu_0}{4\pi}\frac{I\,dl \sin\theta}{x^2}$$

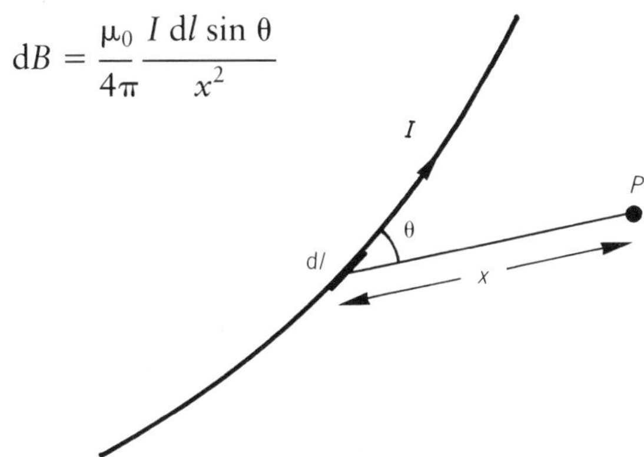

Figure 44.5

Using this formula the fields due to various arrangements of currents in a vacuum can be found. For the present we will quote them without deriving them.

(*a*) At distance r from a long straight wire carrying a current I (Figure 44.6).

$$B = \frac{\mu_0 I}{2\pi r}$$

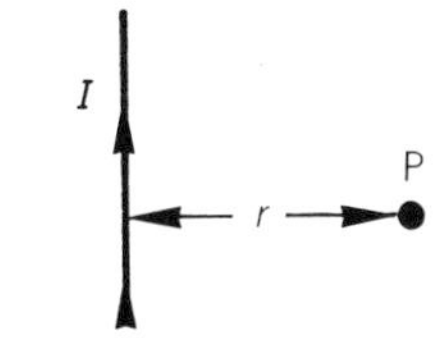

Figure 44.6

(*b*) At the centre of a plane circular coil, radius r, of N turns and carrying a current I (Figure 44.7):

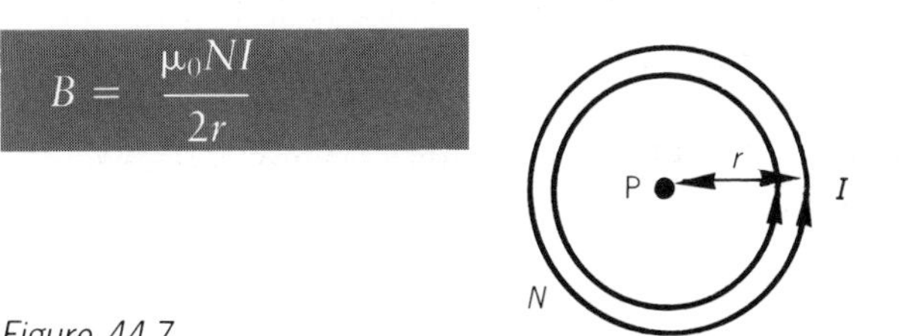

$$B = \frac{\mu_0 NI}{2r}$$

Figure 44.7

(*c*) At the centre of a long solenoid of n turns per metre carrying a current I:

$$B = \frac{\mu_0 NI}{l} = \mu_0 nI$$

where N is the total number of turns on the solenoid of length l (Figure 44.8).

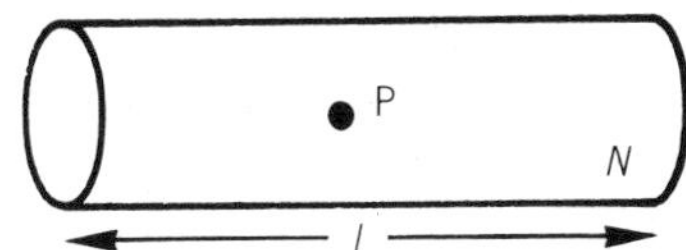

Figure 44.8

(*d*) At the end of a long solenoid (Figure 44.9):

$$B = \frac{\mu_0 nI}{2} = \frac{\mu_0 NI}{2l}$$

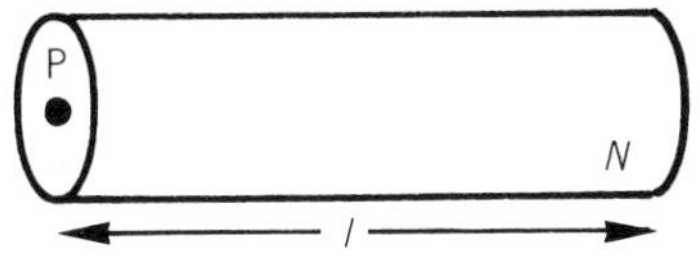

Figure 44.9

(*e*) Helmholtz coils – two coils of radius r, each of N turns, carrying a current I and placed as shown in Figure 44.10:

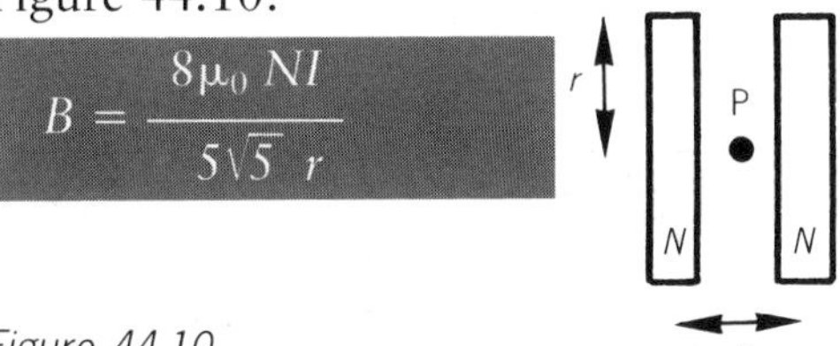

$$B = \frac{8\mu_0 NI}{5\sqrt{5}\,r}$$

Figure 44.10

This arrangement gives a fairly uniform field in the space between the two coils.

Force on a moving charge in a magnetic field

Consider a wire carrying a current I in a field of flux density B (Figure 44.11). We have

$I = nAve$ and $F = BIl \sin\theta$

Therefore the force on a charge e is:

$$F = Bev \sin\theta$$

and this becomes $F = Bev$ for a particle moving at right angles to the field.

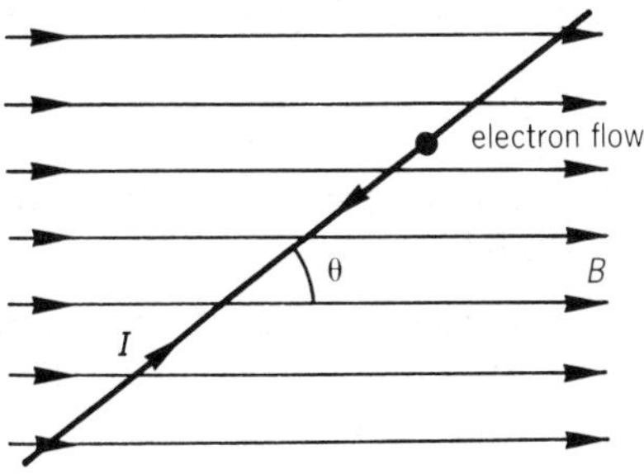

Figure 44.11

The forces between currents

As we have seen, when a current flows in a wire a magnetic field is produced around the wire. If two conductors are placed close together then the field of one wire affects the other and a force exists between the two wires.

This may be demonstrated simply by using the apparatus shown in Figure 44.12, where a direct current of some 5 A is allowed to flow along two pieces of cooking foil. When the currents in the two pieces of foil are in the same direction the strips of foil attract each other and when they are in opposite directions they repel each other.

The force between the conductors is directly proportional to the current flowing in them and this therefore forms the basis for a definition of the ampere.

The ampere is defined as **the constant current which, when flowing in two infinitely long, straight and parallel conductors of negligible cross section placed 1 m apart in a vacuum causes a force between them of 2×10^{-7} N per metre of their length.**

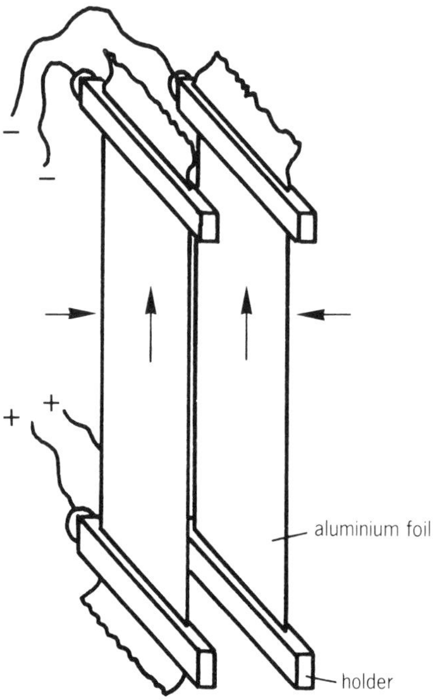

Figure 44.12

The magnetic fields for the two wires are shown in Figure 44.13, (*a*) for currents in the same direction and (*b*) for currents in opposite directions. Points where there is a zero resultant field are known as **neutral points.**

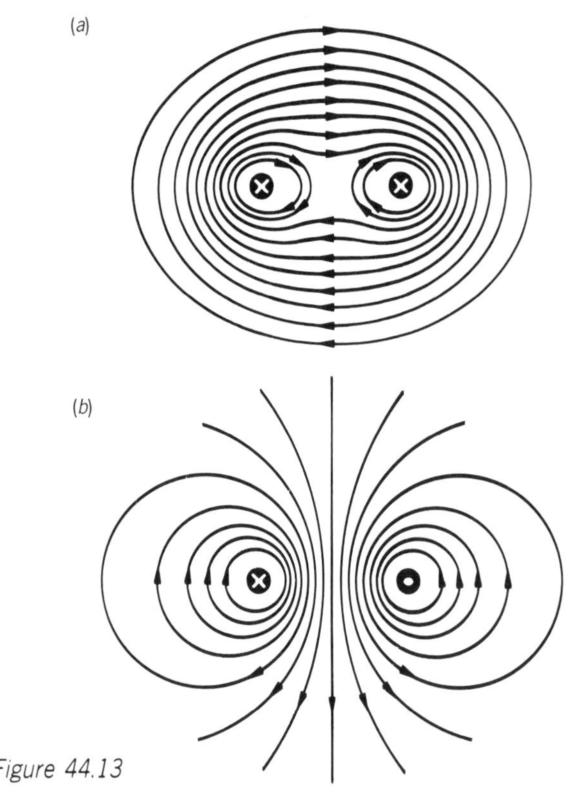

Figure 44.13

1 Calculate the magnetic flux density at the following places:
(*a*) 2 m from a long straight wire carrying a current of 3 A;
(*b*) at the centre of a solenoid of 2000 turns 75 cm long and carrying a current of 1.5 A;
(*c*) at the end of the solenoid given in part (*b*);
(*d*) at the centre of a short coil of 200 turns and 15 cm diameter carrying a current of 20 mA;
(*e*) 20 cm to the west of a long vertical wire carrying a current of 100 mA flowing up the wire, if the horizontal component of the Earth's field at that point is 1.8×10^{-5} T.
(The flux density of the Earth's magnetic field may be ignored unless specifically stated.)

2 Calculate the force per unit length between two long straight wires placed 3 cm apart in a vacuum and each carrying a current of 5 A in the same direction. State whether the force is an attraction or a repulsion.

3 A horizontal wire carrying a current of 10 A lies in a vertical magnetic field of flux density 0.5 T. Calculate the force on the wire per metre.

4 A horizontal wire 6 cm long and with a mass of 1.5 g is placed at right angles to a uniform horizontal magnetic field of flux density 0.5 T. If the resistance of the wire is 4.5 Ω, calculate the current that must be passed through the wire so that it is just self-supporting.

The value of μ_0

Consider the force of attraction between two infinitely long wires, each carrying a current I (Figure 44.14).

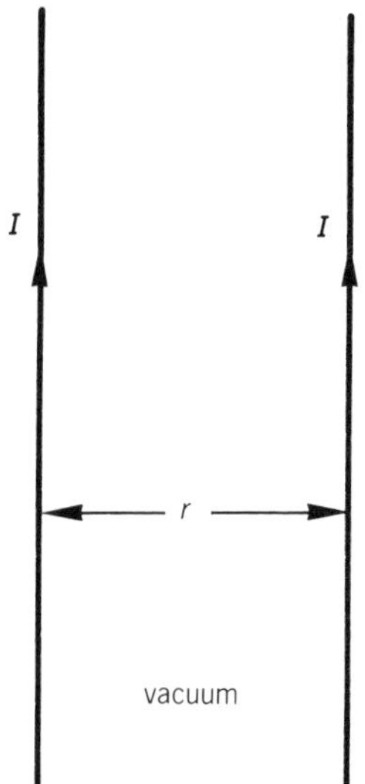

Figure 44.14

The field B at one wire due to the other wire is

$$B = \frac{\mu_0 I}{2\pi r}$$

where r is the distance between the two wires. The force F on a length l of this wire is therefore

$$F = BIl = \frac{\mu_0 I^2 l}{2\pi r}$$

If the wires are carrying a current of 1 A and are 1 m apart in a vacuum and we consider unit length, then by the definition of the ampere we have

$$r = 1\text{ m} \qquad I = 1\text{ A} \qquad F = 2 \times 10^{-7}\text{ N}$$

Therefore:

$$\mu_0 = 4\pi \times 10^{-7}\text{ H m}^{-1}$$

Ampere's law

This law is an alternative to the Biot–Savart law for deriving the expressions for the magnetic flux density of a field. It states that **the line integral of the flux density around a closed path is equal to the product of the current enclosed by the path and the permeability of the material**, that is:

$$\int B \cos\theta \, dl = \mu_0 I$$

where θ is the angle between a short length of path dl and the direction of the field at that point.

For example, the line integral for a straight wire in a path around the wire is $2\pi r$, and so the equation becomes

$$B2\pi r = \mu_0 I \qquad \text{therefore} \qquad B = \frac{\mu_0 I}{2\pi r}$$

Example 1

Calculate the magnetic flux density at the centre of a solenoid of 2000 turns and 50 cm long if a current of 0.5 A flows in the coil.

$$B = \frac{\mu_0 NI}{l} = \frac{4\pi \times 10^{-7} \times 2000 \times 0.5}{0.5}$$

$$= 2.5 \times 10^{-3}\text{ T}$$

Example 2

What current must flow in an infinitely long straight wire to give a flux density the same as the above at 0.3 m from the wire?

$$B = \frac{\mu_0 I}{2\pi r} \quad \text{Therefore } I = \frac{2.5 \times 10^{-3} \times 2 \times \pi \times 0.3}{\mu_0}$$

$$= 3570\text{ A!}$$

If the magnetic field exists in a material other than a vacuum, the permeability in the equation is that of the material and not a vacuum. The permeability of a material is written as μ but it is usual to speak of the **relative permeability** of the material. This is the ratio of the permeability of the material to that of a vacuum, and is written as μ_r (note that μ_r is a pure number with no units or dimensions). Therefore $\mu = \mu_r \mu_o$

Some values for relative permeabilities are given below. The value for iron is many thousands of times that of air; this is why the introduction of an iron core into a solenoid produces a very large increase in the field within it.

Material	*Relative permeability*
Mild steel	2000
Silicon–iron (4.25 % Si)	9000
Supermalloy (Fe 16%, Ni 79%, Mo 5%)	1 000 000

5 A solenoid of length 25 cm, with an iron core, is wound with 100 turns of wire and a current of 2 A is passed through it. If the magnetic flux density produced at the centre of the core is 2.5 T, calculate the relative permeability of the core.

The measurement of magnetic fields

The flux density of magnetic fields may be measured by various methods, three of which are described below. The first and third methods are only suitable for constant magnetic fields while the second may be used for either steady or varying fields.

(*a*) *The Hall probe* (see also page 362)

This is simply a slice of semiconducting material with a small current passing through it. When it is placed in the magnetic field a p.d. that is directly proportional to the magnetic flux density is produced across the slice at right angles to the current direction.

The instrument must first be calibrated by placing it in a magnetic field of known flux density, such as the centre of a long solenoid. The sensitivity of the probe in millivolts per tesla can then be found. The probe is then placed in the unknown field and its flux density found.

(*b*) *The search coil*

This method can be used to measure both constant and varying fields and we will consider first its use for varying fields.

(i) Measuring varying magnetic fields

The search coil is a small flat coil of fine insulated wire with a large number of turns. Those in use in schools usually have between 500 and 2000 turns with an average diameter of 0.5 cm. It is mounted on an insulated handle as shown in Figure 44.15.

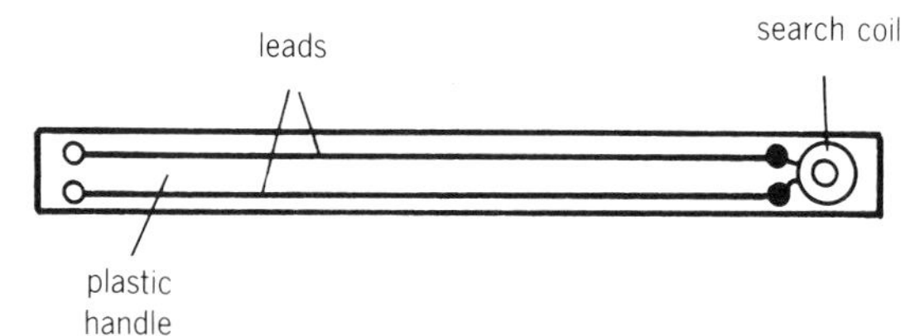

Figure 44.15

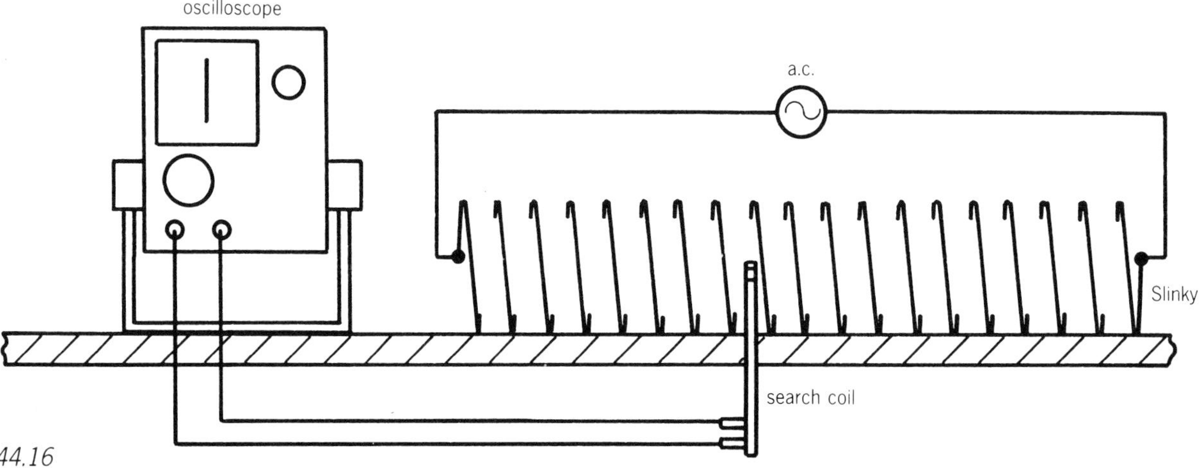

Figure 44.16

When the coil is placed in a varying magnetic field an e.m.f. is induced in it which is directly proportional to the flux density of the field. If this e.m.f. is measured the strength of the field may be found.

The search coil is connected to an oscilloscope and calibrated in a known field. The induced e.m.f. is displayed most conveniently as a vertical line, the time base of the oscilloscope being switched off (Figure 44.16). The coil is then placed in the unknown field and the value of this field found.

6 (*a*) Pairs of conductors carrying current in and out of equipment are sometimes twisted together to reduce magnetic field effects. Why does this help?

(*b*) A direct current was passed through a spiral spring and the spring appeared to contract as if it had been compressed. Why?

What would have happened if alternating current had been used?

Student investigation

Use a Hall probe to investigate the variation of magnetic field of a magnadur magnet with the distance from the magnet. Repeat the experiment using the other side of the magnet.

(ii) Measuring steady magnetic fields

In the measurement of steady magnetic fields the search coil is connected to a ballistic galvanometer (see page 306).

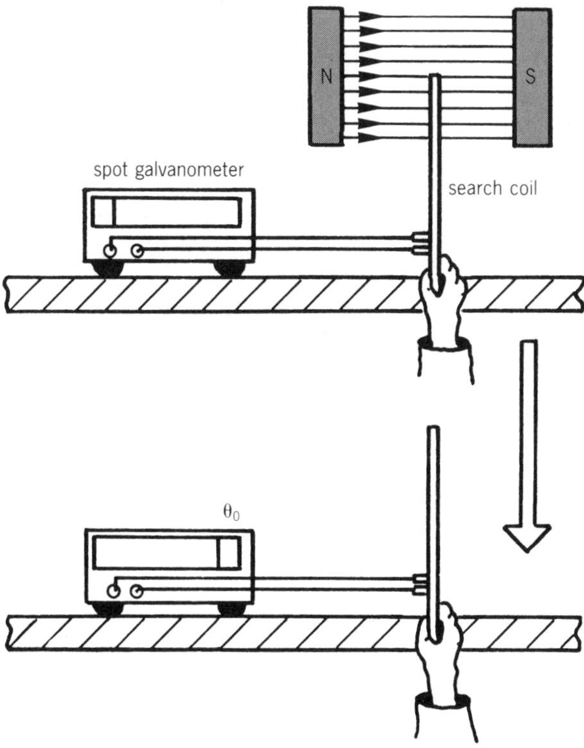

Figure 44.17

Consider a coil of area A and n turns at right angles to a field of flux density B (Figure 44.17). Suppose the the coil is now removed to a large distance from the field and therefore the change in flux in the coil is NAB. Suppose that a charge Q flows in the coil due to this change of flux. It can be shown that:

$$Q = \frac{NAB}{R}$$

where R is the total resistance of the complete circuit, including the ballistic galvanometer. Notice that the charge does not depend on the time taken to remove the search coil from the field. Since the charge should pass through the galvanometer before the coil of the instrument can make an appreciable deflection, however, the search coil should be removed as quickly as possible.

If the maximum deflection of the ballistic galvanometer is θ_0, then:

$$B = \frac{\theta_0 R}{sNA}$$

where s is the charge sensitivity of the ballistic galvanometer. If the charge sensitivity is known the value of B may be found.

(c) The Earth inductor

This instrument, as its name suggests, is used primarily for the measurement of the flux density of the magnetic field of the Earth. The principle is the same as that described for the search coil, but since the flux density of the Earth's field is low a coil of many turns and large area is needed.

The coil is placed in the position shown in Figure 44.18(*a*) and rotated suddenly through 180°; the resulting kick on the galvanometer is proportional to the charge passed which is proportional to the flux cut. Therefore if the experiment is repeated starting with the coil in position shown in Figure 44.18(*b*) the ratio of the two deflections gives the ratio of the vertical and horizontal components of the Earth's field, that is, the tangent of the angle of dip (see page 310).

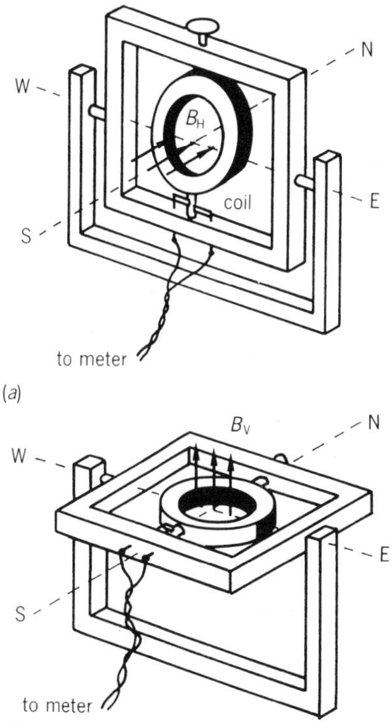

Figure 44.18

> **7** Mercury is contained in a vertical U-tube of uniform square cross-section. Electrodes are sealed inside the upper and lower walls of the horizontal arm of the U-tube. What will happen when a current is passed in a vertical direction between the electrodes if a horizontal magnetic field is applied across the bottom of the tube and perpendicular to its plane?
>
> If the side of the tube has an area of 16 mm^2, the current is 10 A and the field has a flux density of 0.3 T, calculate the difference in the mercury levels in the two arms of the U-tube. (Density of mercury = 13 600 kg m^{-3})

Torque on a coil in a magnetic field

If a coil carrying a current is placed in a magnetic field it will experience a force on two of its sides in such a way as to make the coil rotate (Figure 44.19(*a*)). This effect is the basis of all moving coil meters and electric motors.

You can see why the coil will rotate from the 'double catapult' field diagram in Figure 44.19(*b*). Since the current moves along the two opposite sides of the coil in opposite directions the two sides receive a force in opposite directions also, thus turning the coil.

Consider a rectangular coil with sides of length *a* and *b* placed in a magnetic field of flux density *B* and free to rotate about an axis perpendicular to the paper, as shown in Figure 44.19(*c*).

The field exerts a force on the sides *b* given by

$$F = BNIb$$

where *n* is the number of turns on the coil.

If the perpendicular to the coil is at an angle θ to the field direction, then the torque exerted on the coil is *Fd* where $d = a \sin\theta$. Therefore the torque *C* is given by

$$C = Fa \sin\theta$$

$$= BnIba \sin\theta, \text{ or}$$

$$C = BANI \sin\theta$$

where *A* (= *ab*) is the area of the coil.

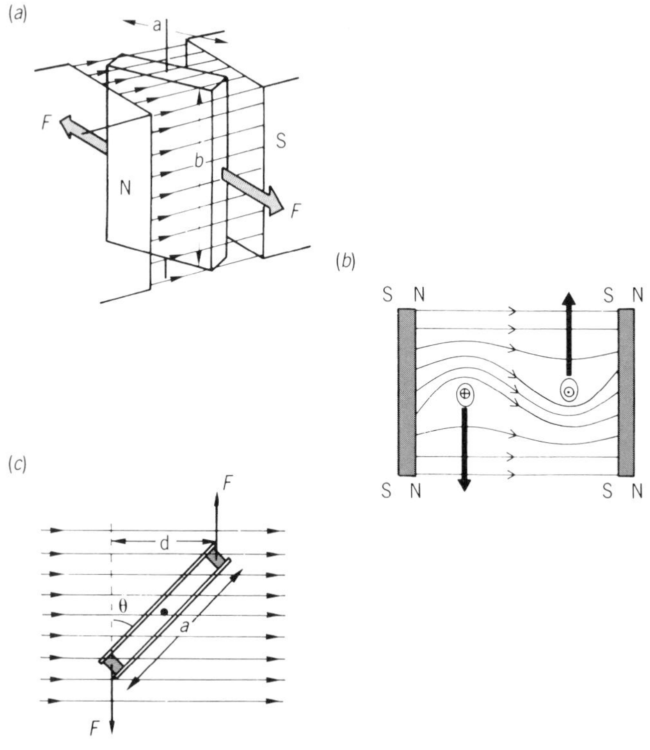

Figure 44.19

The maximum torque occurs when the plane of the coil is lying along the field lines ($\theta = 90°$ and $\sin\theta = 1$). At this point, shown in Figure 44.20,

$$C_0 = BANI$$

The minimum value of the torque is zero, when $\theta = 0°$.

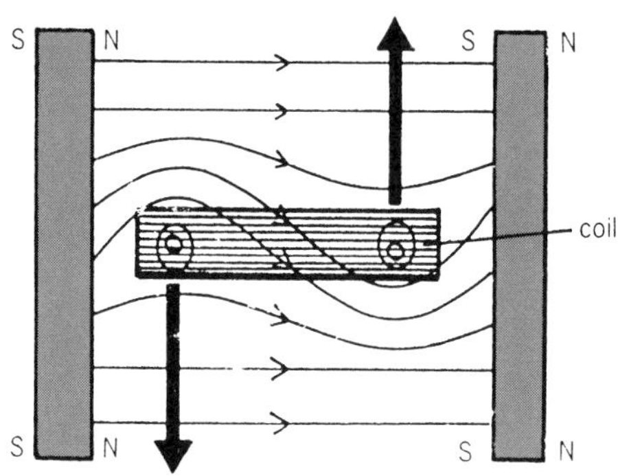

Figure 44.20

Magnetic moment of a coil

The quantity *NIA* is called the **magnetic moment** of the coil, and is usually defined as the torque exerted on it when placed with its plane parallel to a field of unit magnitude.

> **Example**
>
> Calculate the torque needed to hold a coil of area 8 cm^2 at an angle of 60° to a field of flux density 0.1 T if the coil carries a current of 0.5 A.
>
> $$\text{Torque} = BANI \sin\theta$$
> $$= 0.1 \times 8 \times 10^{-4} \times 0.5\ A \sin 60$$
> $$= 3.46 \times 10^{-5} \text{ N m}$$

8 A flat circular coil of 50 turns of mean diameter 40 cm is in a fixed vertical plane and has a current of 5 A flowing through it. A small coil, 1 cm square and having 120 turns, is suspended at the centre of the circular coil in a vertical plane at an angle of 30° to that of the larger coil. Calculate the torque that will act on the small coil when it carries a current of 2 mA. [L]

9 A fixed vertical coil has a diameter of 15 cm and 120 turns. At the centre of this coil is a small coil of radius 2 cm and 100 turns, pivoted through its centre so that it can rotate about a horizontal axis which lies along the diameter of the larger coil.

A rider of mass 0.05 g must be moved 13.0 cm from the axis of the small coil along an arm fixed to the small coil to keep the plane of the latter horizontal when a current is passed through both coils.

What is the current? [D]

Student investigation

This investigation will enable you to determine the value of μ_0, the permeability of free space. The apparatus used is known as an ampere balance and one can easily be constructed as part of the experiment, two views being shown in Figure 44.21. The small coil (area A) is pivoted on a horizontal axis which passes through the centre of the large coil (radius R).

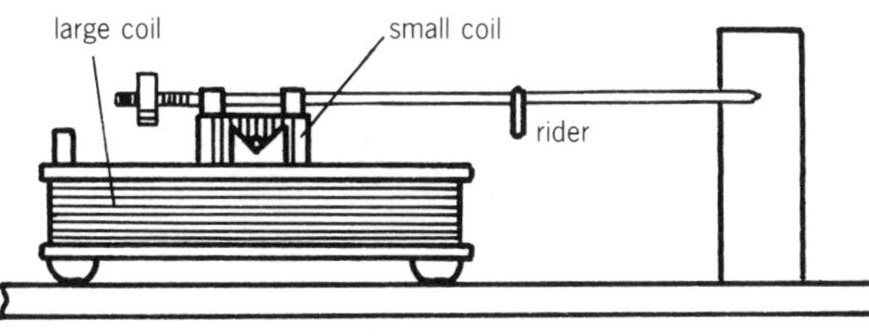

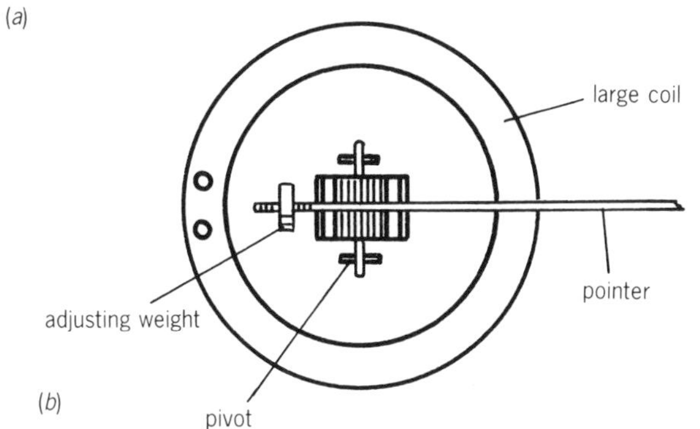

Figure 44.21

The apparatus should be set up with the two coils connected in series. The balance screws and the rider on the small coil should be adjusted until the pointer fixed to it is perfectly horizontal as shown by the vertical scale. A known current I should then be passed through the coils and the position of the rider adjusted to bring the pointer back to the horizontal once more.

The field at the centre of the large coil is given by

$$B = \frac{\mu_0 N I}{2R}$$

and due to this the small coil will experience a torque $BAnI$, which may be balanced by an opposing torque mgd, where d is the distance that the rider has to be moved to rebalance the pointer.

Therefore $mgd = \dfrac{\mu_0 NI}{2R} AnI$

and hence μ_0 may be found. Comment on the accuracy of your value for μ_0.

10 A coil of radius 7.5 cm and of 500 turns is suspended vertically with the plane of the coil in the east–west direction. If the horizontal component at the centre of the coil is 1.8×10^{-5} T, what current must be passed through the coil to just neutralize this field?
Explain why there are two answers.

11 It is found that at a distance of 5.0 cm from a long vertical wire in which a current is flowing the resultant magnetic field is zero, that is, the magnetic field produced by the wire cancels that due to the Earth's horizontal component. Calculate the current flowing in the wire, assuming that the horizontal component of the Earth's field at that point is 1.8×10^{-5} T.

12 A circular coil of 100 turns and mean radius 10 cm is set up with its plane vertical and at right angles to the magnetic meridian. A short magnetic needle suspended at its centre makes 8 oscillations per minute when slightly deflected. How many oscillations per minute will the needle make when a current of 0.5 A flows in the coil, if the horizontal component of the Earth's field is 2.0×10^{-5} T? Explain clearly why there are two possible answers.

The electromagnetic pump

This is a very useful application of the force on a current in a magnetic field. A steady magnetic field is placed across a tube carrying a conducting liquid, as shown in Figure 44.22. A current is passed through the liquid at right angles to the magnetic field, and therefore a force is exerted on the liquid which pushes it down the pipe.

This type of pump is particularly useful since there are no moving parts. It has found application in two widely different fields: for pumping liquid sodium coolant round a nuclear reactor, and for pumping blood round the body if the heart is damaged.

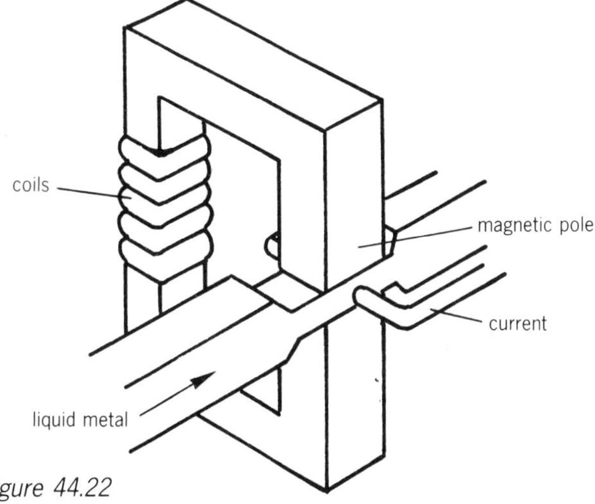

Figure 44.22

The moving coil galvanometer

A very common use of the forces on a coil in a magnetic field is that of the moving coil galvanometer, shown diagrammatically in Figure 44.23.

The coil is suspended between the poles of a magnet on jewelled bearings and is held in place by two finely coiled springs (S_1 and S_2) through which the current to be measured passes in and out of the coil.

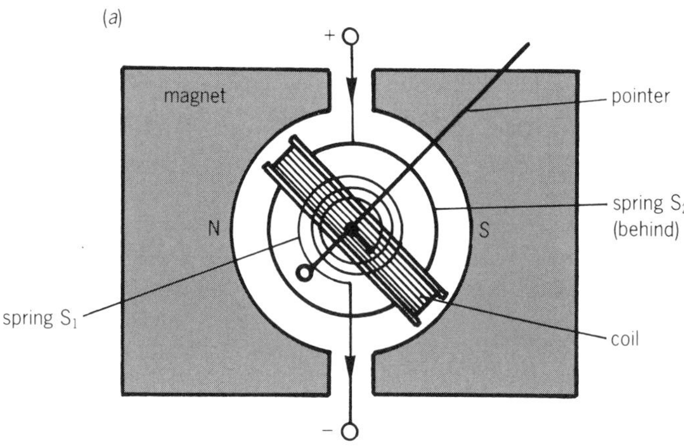

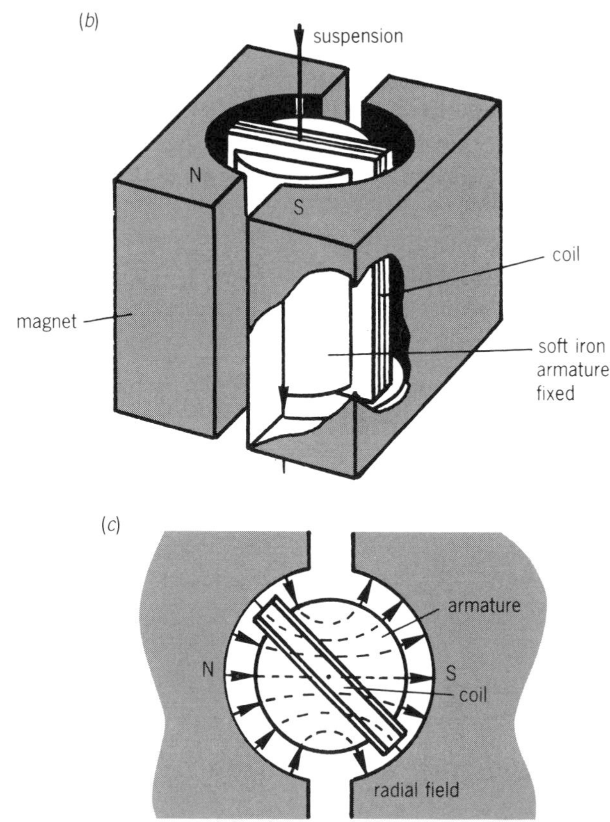

Figure 44.23

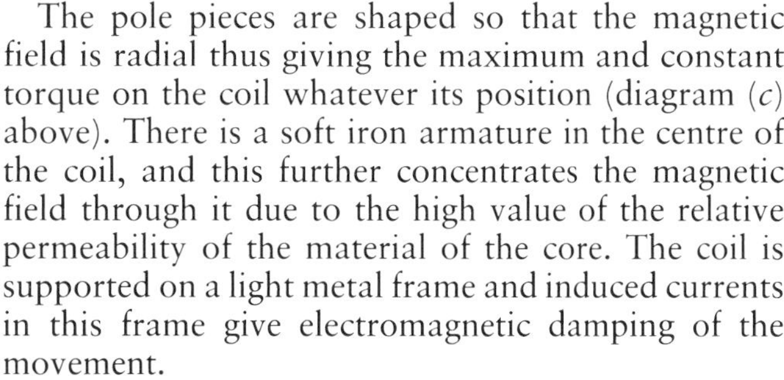

The pole pieces are shaped so that the magnetic field is radial thus giving the maximum and constant torque on the coil whatever its position (diagram (*c*) above). There is a soft iron armature in the centre of the coil, and this further concentrates the magnetic field through it due to the high value of the relative permeability of the material of the core. The coil is supported on a light metal frame and induced currents in this frame give electromagnetic damping of the movement.

When it is in equilibrium with a current passing through it, the torque on the coil produced by the magnetic field is balanced by an opposing torque due to the rigidity of the springs. Clearly, the more delicate the springs the bigger the deflection for a given current.

Some meters are of the suspended coil type; the coil is mounted on a fine phosphor bronze wire and the deflection measured with a lamp and scale. A small mirror mounted above the coil reflects a beam of light on to a scale, the angle of twist of the light beam being double the angle of rotation of the coil. Such instruments have a framework of brass or aluminium.

Galvanometers are often made with a protective series resistor since too large a current will burn out the springs or the coil. When the correct range for the meter has been found this protective resistor may be shorted out.

13 The coil in a certain galvanometer is rectangular, with sides of 3 cm and 2 cm and with 100 turns. Calculate the initial deflecting couple due to a current of 5 mA in the coil, if the magnetic field has a flux density of 0.05 T.

14 A moving coil galvanometer has the following characteristics:

number of turns on coil = 80
area of coil = 50 mm^2
flux density of the radial field = 0.2 T
torsional constant of the suspension wire = 5×10^{-9} N m rad^{-1}
resistance of coil = 20 Ω

Calculate the angular deflection produced by
(*a*) a current of 0.01 mA,
(*b*) a potential difference of 0.01 mV.

15 A galvanometer has a rectangular coil 3 cm × 2 cm and of 30 turns. It is suspended with the long side vertical in a radial magnetic field of 0.6 T by means of a phosphor bronze fibre, which produces a restoring couple of 0.35 N m per radian of twist. What is the deflection produced when a current of 15 A passes through it? [T]

Sensitivity of a galvanometer

(i) *Current sensitivity*
Consider a coil of N turns and cross-sectional area A, carrying a current I in a field of flux density B as shown in Figure 44.24. The torque C due to the magnetic field is given by

$$C = BANI$$

for a radial field, and the opposing torque due to the twist of the suspension is $k\theta$ where k is the torsion constant for the wire and θ is the angle of twist.

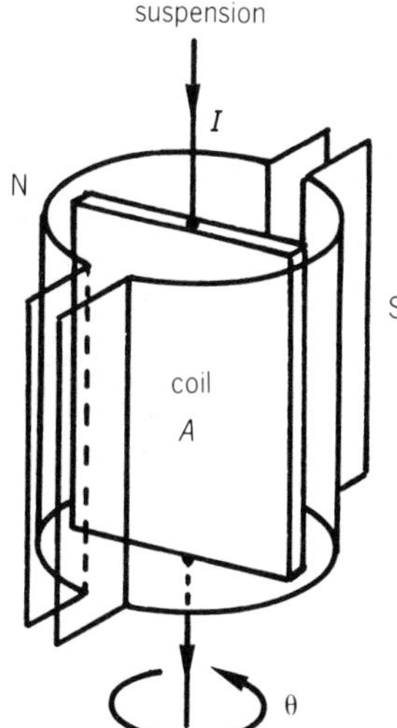

Figure 44.24

The radial field is important since it gives $B \sin\theta$ as constant and therefore the angle of twist θ is directly proportional to the current I for all positions of the coil. In equilibrium:

$$k\theta = BANI$$

The angular twist per unit current (θ/I) is called the **current sensitivity** of the meter and is given by:

$$\text{current sensitivity } (\theta/I) = \frac{BAN}{k}$$

To increase this (that is, to make the meter more sensitive) we require:

(*a*) large magnetic flux density (B), that is, the gap between the poles as small as possible,
(*b*) a coil with a large area (A),
(*c*) a large number of turns (N), and
(*d*) a small value of k – that is, a very thin wire or one with a very low rigidity.

Unfortunately (*b*) and (*c*) tend to make the coil both bigger and heavier and so cause problems with (*a*) and (*d*). A compromise has to be reached.

(ii) *Voltage sensitivity*
Given that the resistance of the meter is R, its **voltage sensitivity** is given by:

$$\text{voltage sensitivity } (\theta/V) = \frac{BAN}{kR}$$

when the voltage across it is V volts.

Example

The coil of a lamp and scale galvanometer has an area of 4 cm^2 and 200 turns. A torque of 2×10^{-7} N m causes it to twist through 180° against the torsion of the suspension. If the field acting on the coil is 0.2 T, find the current that will cause the spot of light on a scale 1 m away to be deflected through 1 mm.

Original torque = $2 \times 10^{-7} = k\theta_0$.

Therefore $k = 2 \times 10^{-7}/\theta_0$.

New angle (θ) is given by:

$$\frac{\theta}{I} = \frac{0.2 \times 4 \times 10^{-4} \times 200 \times \pi}{2 \times 10^{-7}}$$

Angle of deflection = $10^{-3}/1 = 10^{-3}$ radians

$$\text{Therefore current } I = \frac{2 \times 10^{-7} \times 10^{-3}}{0.2 \times 4 \times 10^{-4} \times 200 \times \theta}$$

$$= \frac{2 \times 10^{-10}}{5.02 \times 10^{-2}}$$

$$= 4 \times 10^{-9} \text{ A}$$

$$= 4 \times 10^{-3}\ \mu\text{A}$$

Conversion to ammeter or voltmeter

A typical moving coil meter such as those used in schools may have a full scale deflection (f.s.d.) of 100 μA and a resistance of 1000 ΩA. This means that the pointer will deflect right across the scale when a current of 100 μA is passed through the meter. When this occurs the p.d. between the terminals of the meter will be 100 μA × 1000 Ω = 100 mV. Clearly this is quite inadequate when measurements of currents of say 5 A or voltages of 12 V are required. External resistors may be used to extend the range of the meter and these are known as shunts and series resistors (see page 283).

So that as little current as possible is drawn from a circuit under test a good voltmeter should have a resistance of at least 1000 Ω per volt – for example, a meter designed to read voltages up to 10 V should have a resistance of 10 kΩ. This also requires a galvanometer with a high current sensitivity.

The moving coil galvanometer can also be used as an ohmmeter and a wattmeter.

There has been a considerable increase in the use of direct-reading digital meters in the last few years. These rely on a totally different principle, that of the integrated circuit, for their operation and have no moving parts. The digital voltmeter has a very high resistance (of the order of 10 MΩ on d.c.) but it does need a small internal battery to power the instrument. The input voltage to be measured is compared with a steadily rising voltage produced by a ramp generator (see page 384). The time taken for the rising voltage to reach that of the input voltage is measured and this time is directly proportional to the voltage. The output reading is scaled to give a direct reading in volts.

Measurement of alternating current

It should be clear that none of the preceding moving coil instruments are suitable for the measurement of an alternating current or voltage. The coil would tend to oscillate between a positive and a negative reading. In Britain, however, the frequency of the mains is 50 Hz and the inertia of a coil will prevent it from moving far before the current reverses, so it simply vibrates slightly.

The following types of meter can be used to measure alternating currents:

moving iron instruments – using the repulsion between two metal rods in the field
hot wire instruments – using the expansion of a wire
rectifier instruments
dynamometer instruments
electrostatic voltmeter
diode valve voltmeter
cathode ray oscilloscope

Electrical standards

(*a*) Weston cell

This cell is used as a voltage standard, since its e.m.f. can be found very accurately. The positive electrode is mercury and the negative electrode an amalgam of cadmium in mercury, the electrolyte being cadmium sulphate solution. At temperatures between 0 °C and 40 °C the e.m.f. is 1.0186 V.

If currents of more than 10 μA are drawn from the cell it will depolarise, and so these cells must always be operated with a protective series resistor and *never* used as a source of current.

(*b*) Current balance

This instrument balances the gravitational attraction on a small rider against the electromagnetic force provided by a known length of wire carrying a current in a magnetic field. Sensitive current balances are accurate to five parts in a million; simpler current balances can be made, however, to check the calibration of ammeters.

The ballistic galvanometer

When a pulse of current passes through a moving coil instrument the coil is given an impulse which sets is swinging. If the duration of the pulse is short compared with the natural period of oscillation of the coil (T), then the amplitude of the oscillation does not depend on the way in which the current varies during the pulse. Such an instrument therefore uses a heavy coil wound on an insulating former giving little or no damping. The mass of the coil gives it a large moment of inertia and therefore makes it swing slowly.

If the duration of current is small compared with T, then it can be shown that the first deflection θ_1 is directly proportional to the charge passed, that is, $Q = k\theta_1$. In fact,

$$\theta_1 = \frac{2\pi S}{T} Q$$

where S is the sensitivity of the instrument, BAN/k.

After the pulse has passed through it the motion of the coil depends on

(*a*) the restoring couple due to the suspension,
(*b*) the damping due to air currents and any eddy currents in the circuit.

The coil therefore oscillates with an exponential decrease of amplitude, as shown in Figure 44.25.

For the Pye spot galvanometer $T = 2$ s, the instrument is critically damped for an external resistance of 100 Ω. A 1 mm deflection is obtained for about 10^{-8} C.

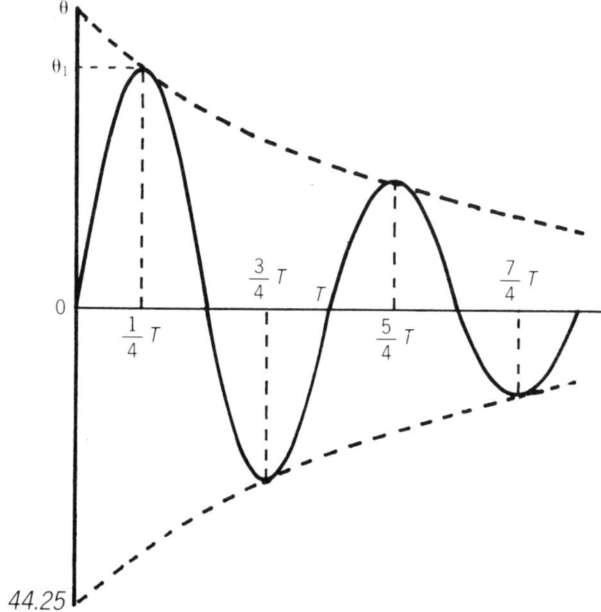

Figure 44.25

The ballistic galvanometer may be calibrated using:
(*a*) a standard capacitor,
(*b*) a standard mutual inductor.

The ballistic galvanometer may be used to compare or to determine the value of either capacitors or magnetic fields.

Proof of the formula for the flux density inside a long solenoid

Although most of the formulae for magnetic fields have been quoted without proof, it is interesting to read through one example. This one uses Ampere's law.

Consider a closed path PQRS around a long thin solenoid (Figure 44.26). The field outside is negligible compared with that inside, and if the solenoid is thin we can also ignore sections QR and SP. This leaves only the length inside the solenoid RS.

Figure 44.26

The field due to each element of the solenoid is parallel to RS and so:

$$\text{line integral} = \int B \cos\theta \, dl = B \times RS$$

But RS = l, the length of the solenoid, and if the solenoid has N turns and carries a current I we have:

$$Bl = \mu_0 NI \qquad \text{and so} \qquad B = \mu_0 \frac{NI}{l}$$

The electric motor

The electric motor is a device that converts electrical energy into rotational kinetic energy by the action of the force on a coil pivoted in a magnetic field. It differs from the moving coil galvanometer in that in practical motors there is usually more than one coil and these coils are free to rotate. A cylindrical laminated iron core provides inertia and a radial field.

The d.c. motor

Figure 44.27 shows the essential features of a d.c. motor.

The d.c. motor consists of:

(*a*) a number of coils of fine wire wound on
(*b*) a laminated soft iron armature;
(*c*) a set of brushes to allow current to enter and leave the windings;
(*d*) a commutator to reverse the current in the coils;
(*e*) a set of external field coils.

To understand the operation of the motor, consider Figure 44.28(*a*) which shows a simple arrangement with only one coil.

A current flows round the coil and one side is forced up by the magnetic field and the other is forced down Figure 44.28(*b*). The motion is made continuous by reversing the current direction through the coil by means of a split ring commutator and two brushes (Figure 44.28(*c*) and (*d*). The coil is kept rotating during the short time interval when there is no force acting on it by its own inertia.

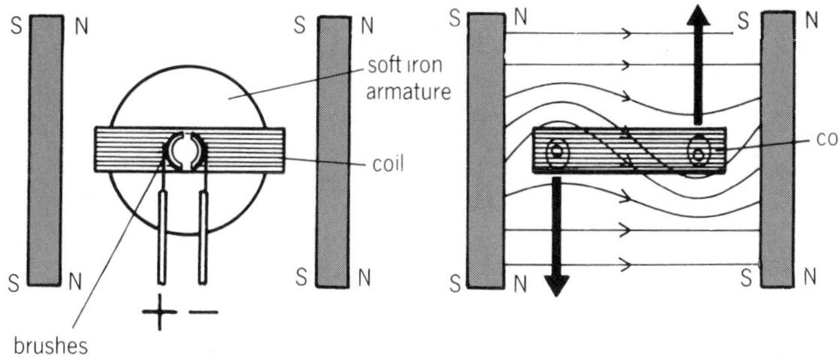

Figure 44.27

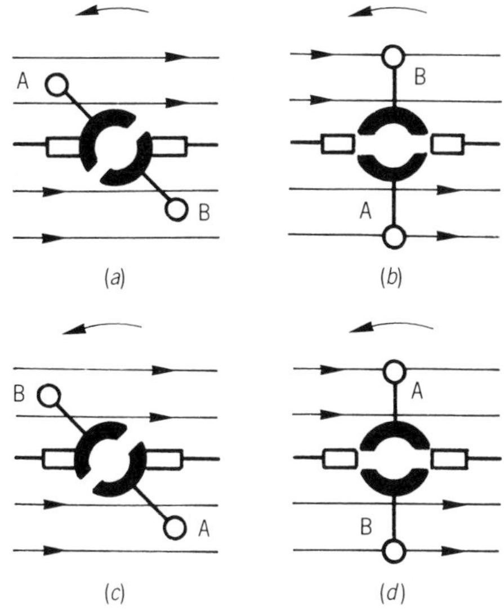

Figure 44.28

Practical d.c. motors

By having a set of coils instead of the single armature coil, the time when the armature 'freewheels' is reduced and the number of 'kicks' per rotation greatly increased. This makes the torque applied by the motor very nearly constant. The distance between the field coils and the armature is made as small as possible by using magnets with curved pole pieces to increase the flux density, and the armature core is laminated to reduce eddy current losses (Figure 44.29).

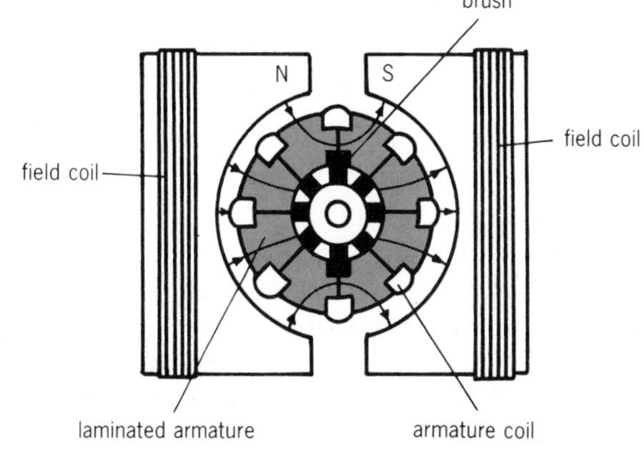

Figure 44.29

The back e.m.f. in the d.c. motor

As soon as the coil starts rotating, a back e.m.f. will be induced in it due to the flux that it cuts, and this will tend to reduce the current through it.

Let the supply e.m.f. be E, the back e.m.f. be ϵ, the resistance of the coil R and the current through the coil I. Then

$$I = \frac{E - \epsilon}{R}$$

For practical motors with $E = 100$ V, the back e.m.f. may be as great as 95 V!

The resistance of the coil R is usually small (less than 1 Ω) and therefore when it is at rest a large current may flow through it. When the coil speeds up this is reduced, since the back e.m.f. is proportional to the rate of rotation of the coil. The starting current can be as large as 1000 A, and a protective resistor must be incorporated in series with the coil during starting. This can be removed when the motor is running.

This is why a d.c. motor that is running should never be stopped with the supply connected. If this is done the back e.m.f. will fall to zero, the current will become very large and the coil may burn out.

Figure 44.30 shows an electric car run by a 60 V battery going over a hill. It should help to explain what happens when the motor runs at different speeds.

As the car climbs the hill AB on the left the motor is running slowly, the back e.m.f. is therefore low (say 5 V) and this means that a large current flows through the motor, giving a large torque. Chemical energy from the battery is converted to potential energy of the car.

The car now goes up section BC. The slope is much shallower, the motor speeds up and so the back e.m.f. rises to say 59 V. The current through the motor is therefore low.

The car now descends the section CD. The speed increases so that the back e.m.f. rises to 60 V, and energy is supplied to just overcome friction. Further down the hill, however, the back e.m.f. is greater than 60 V and so the motor acts as a dynamo, storing up energy in the battery. The current flowing produces a torque which tends to oppose the motion and so acts as a brake.

As long as electromagnets are used for the field, a d.c. motor will run on a.c., although very inefficiently owing to the large self-inductance of its coils.

16 A small electric motor with permanent magnets to produce the field is connected to a 12 V supply of negligible internal resistance. With no load the motor rotates with a frequency of 10 Hz and the armature current is 2 A. If the armature resistance is 1.5 Ω, calculate the rate of rotation when a load is applied that causes the current to rise to 5 A.

Series-wound and shunt-wound motors

Although the field coils of the motor may be separately excited they are usually connected to the armature in one of two ways:

(*a*) series wound (Figure 44.31(*a*)) or
(*b*) shunt wound (Figure 44.31(*b*)).

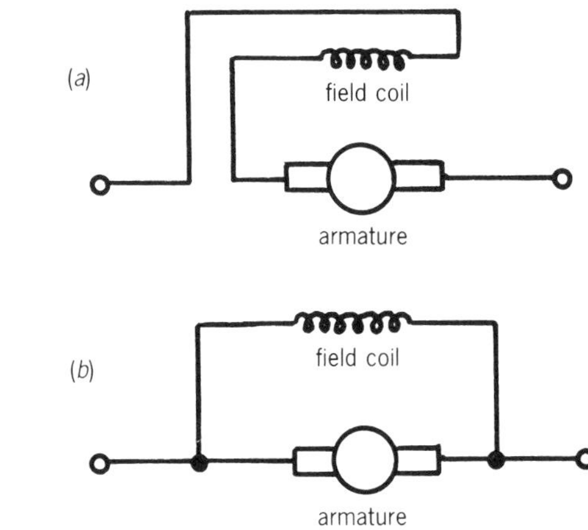

Figure 44.31

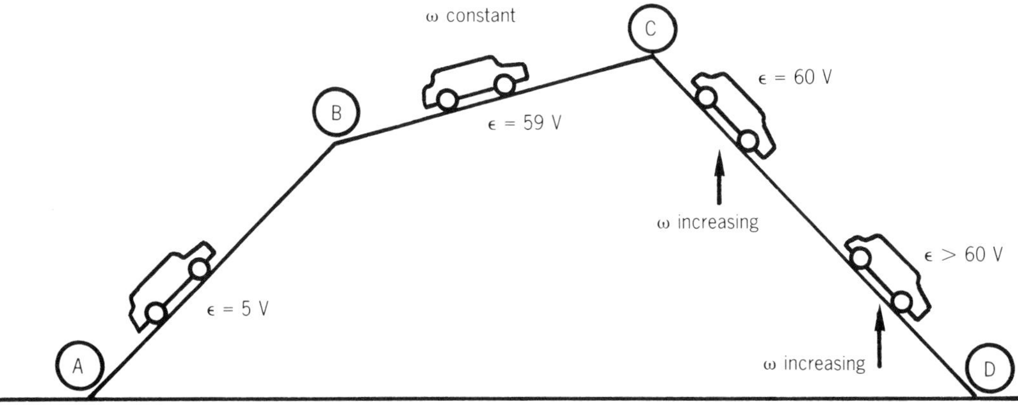

Figure 44.30

In **series-wound motors**, the current varies considerably with the load and speed control is difficult, but the starting torque is large. This type of motor is therefore used for cranes and winches and for high-speed motors such as those used in fans and grinding wheels where speed control is not important.

In **shunt-wound motors**, the speed varies little with the load and it can be easily controlled; however, the starting torque is not as great as that of a series-wound motor. Shunt-wound motors are used in machines where the speed is important, such as record players and machine tools.

Student investigation

The following experiment is designed to study the effect of various loads on the speed of an electric motor and hence on the back e.m.f. produced.

Set up the motor as shown in Figure 44.32, with a variable-tension friction brake around a wheel on the motor axle.

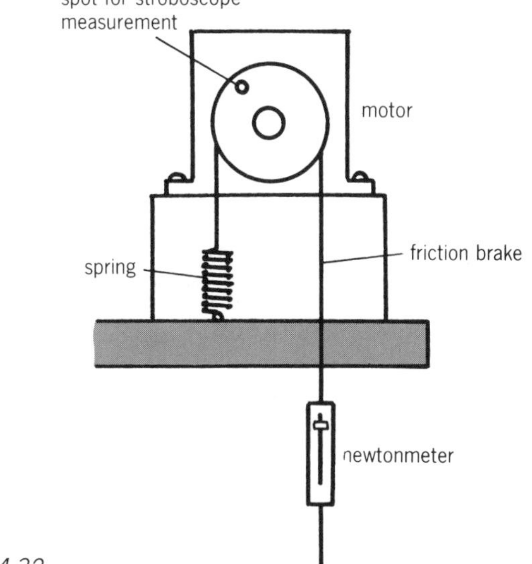

Figure 44.32

Using a very small armature voltage (say 0.5 V, not enough to rotate the motor) measure the resistance of the armature coils.

Set the output of the power supply to a known value (E) near the maximum required for the motor, and then connect the motor to it. Measure the tension in the friction brake, the voltage across the motor and the current through it.

Hence calculate the back e.m.f. Measure the speed of rotation of the motor with a stroboscope.

Vary the tension in the friction brake and record a set of values for the above variables. Plot graphs of both the current in the motor and the back e.m.f. against the angular velocity and tension.

17 A shunt-wound motor is connected to a 240 V supply. With no load it rotates at 15 Hz and the armature current is 2.5 A. When the motor is loaded its rate of rotation falls to 5 Hz and the armature current rises to 25 A. What is the resistance of the armature?

18 You mow your lawn using an electric lawn-mower with an armature resistance of 0.5 Ω. When running freely and connected to the 240 V supply the motor takes 3 A, but when the mower is on full load when cutting through long grass the current rises to 50 A. Calculate
(*a*) the back e.m.f. in each case,
(*b*) the electrical efficiency in the second case.

The a.c. motor

Several types of a.c. motor are in use.

(i) The series-wound commutator motor

As we saw above, such a motor will work with a.c., although rather inefficiently. The motor will be a high-speed motor whose speed is rather variable if the load is changed.

The shunt-wound motor cannot be used in this way, since self-inductive effects in the field coils would result in the peaks of the field in the armature and field coils getting out of phase, and so very little torque would be obtained.

(ii) The three-phase synchronous motor

Such a motor has a single armature coil but three sets of field coils, as shown in Figure 44.33.

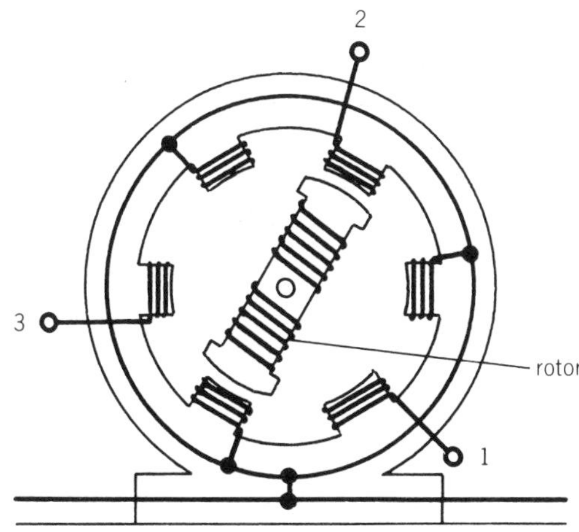

Figure 44.33

The peaks of the current in each field coil occur at different times and so the torque on the armature is fairly constant. If the rotor can be made to rotate at the same rate as the field, it will be locked on to it and rotate at a constant speed with the field.

(iii) The three-phase induction motor
This type of motor uses a set of three field coils, as in the synchronous motor, but the rotor is of entirely different construction. It is made of a set of copper bars fixed to two copper rings as shown in Figure 44.34, an arrangement known as a squirrel cage. The rotating magnetic field in the field coils induces currents within these bars and the interaction between these eddy currents and the field in the coils makes the rotor rotate.

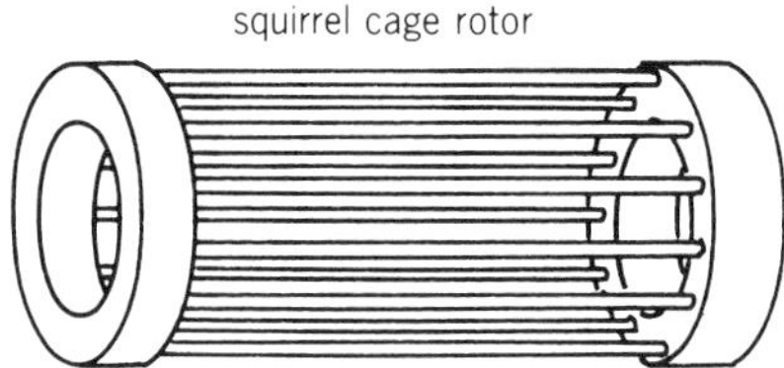

Figure 44.34

(iv) The single-phase induction motor
This employs a similar rotor to the previous type but uses single-phase a.c. To get the motor to the speed of the field an auxiliary coil and capacitor are used, to give a signal 90° out of phase with that in the main coils.

The linear induction motor

The linear motor had its first major development in the early 1960s. This type of motor is essentially a cylindrical induction motor that has been cut along its length and unrolled, as shown in Figure 44.35. The field moves down the windings of what used to be the stator at a velocity v given by $v = 2pf$, where p is the distance between the pole pieces and f is the frequency of the field. In the example shown a field is induced in the 'rotor' and this is then propelled along between the fixed field windings.

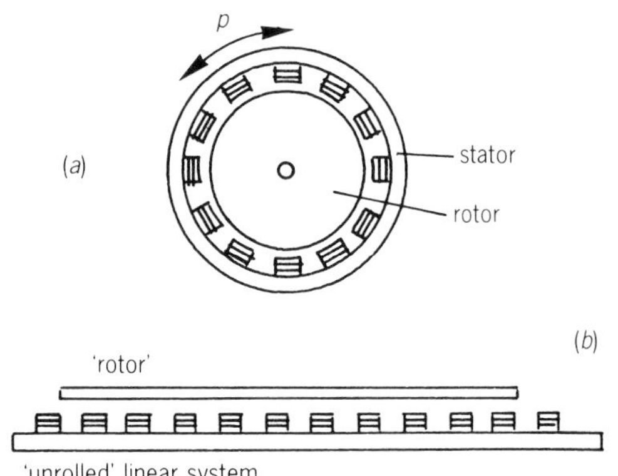

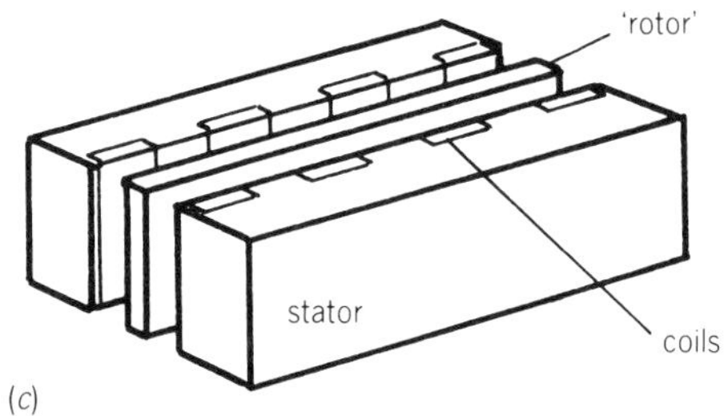

Figure 44.35

Very high speeds may be achieved and these motors have been used to propel shuttles on textile looms, as aircraft launchers, to move conveyor belts and at low speed even to open and close curtains!

The magnetic field of the Earth

The Earth's magnetic field closely resembles that of a uniformly magnetised sphere, or at least one with a magnetic dipole at its centre. The field is not constant with time; it changes over periods as short as a few hundred years. It is thought that it is due to the motion of molten material within the Earth's core – a sort of self exciting dynamo. The field has also undergone periods of reversal, the direction changing by 180 °. The reasons for this are not too well understood but a study of the magnetisation of rocks, a science known as paleomagnetism, has been of considerable help in developing our knowledge of the movement of the Earth's crust: continental drift.

At any point on the Earth the resultant magnetic field may be considered in two components: (*a*) the vertical component and (*b*) the horizontal component. The direction of the resultant field makes an angle ϕ with the horizontal, and this angle is known as the **angle of dip**.

This is related to the two components by the formula:

$$\tan\phi = \frac{\text{vertical component}}{\text{horizontal component}}$$

45 · Magnetism

Magnetic properties of materials

The science of magnetism has come a long way since 600 B.C. when the Greeks discovered that the iron ore lodestone (first found in Magnesia in Asia Minor and now known as magnetite) had some interesting properties. A piece of lodestone suspended by a thread, would always point in the same direction. The word *lodestone* comes from the Saxon *loedan* (to lead).

Permanent magnetic materials are now used in many applications from magnetic ink on cheques to magnetic door catches. Magnetic materials possess a property known as **susceptibility** (χ) defined as follows:

$$B = \mu_0(H + M)$$
$$= \mu_0 H(1 + M/H)$$

where the quantity M/H is the susceptibility.

Magnetic materials are of three types: (*a*) diamagnetic, (*b*) paramagnetic and (*c*) ferromagnetic.

(*a*) Diamagnetics

If a sample of diamagnetic material is placed in a magnetising coil and a current passed through the coil, then a field is produced in the specimen that *opposes* the direction of the original magnetising field. The susceptibility is therefore negative (-1.7×10^{-8} for bismuth, for example).

The electron magnetic moments will cancel out in a diamagnetic material, because of their orbital motion and spin.

The value of the relative permeability for diamagnetics is slightly less than 1, usually about 0.9999.

(*b*) Paramagnetics

An application of an external field produces a field within the specimen in the *same direction* as the initial magnetising field. The susceptibility is therefore positive ($+0.82 \times 10^{-8}$ for aluminium).

In the paramagnetic material the electron magnetic moments tend to add up; thermal motion disturbs them but if an external field is applied they realign. Paramagnetism is temperature-dependent, since at low temperatures there is little thermal motion and so the susceptibility is higher.

The value of the relative permeability of paramagnetic materials is slightly greater than 1, usually about 1.001.

(*c*) Ferromagnetics

In ferromagnetic materials there is a strong linkage between neighbouring atoms to form what are known as **magnetic domains**. The relative permeability of ferromagnetics is large, of the order of 10^4, but does depend on the past history of the specimen. The only ferromagnetic *elements* are iron, nickel, cobalt, gadolinium and dysprosium, but there are many ferromagnetic alloys. Modern quantum physics actually predicts that ferromagnetism will only occur for the elements listed above.

When a ferromagnetic material is heated the domain boundaries are destroyed, and above a certain temperature known as the **Curie point** (about 770 °C for iron) ferromagnetics become paramagnetics.

The Barkhausen effect

The existence of domains in a ferromagnetic material may be shown by the Barkhausen effect, using the apparatus shown in Figure 45.1. If the north pole of the magnet is moved slowly across the top of the bundle of iron wires a rushing sound is heard from

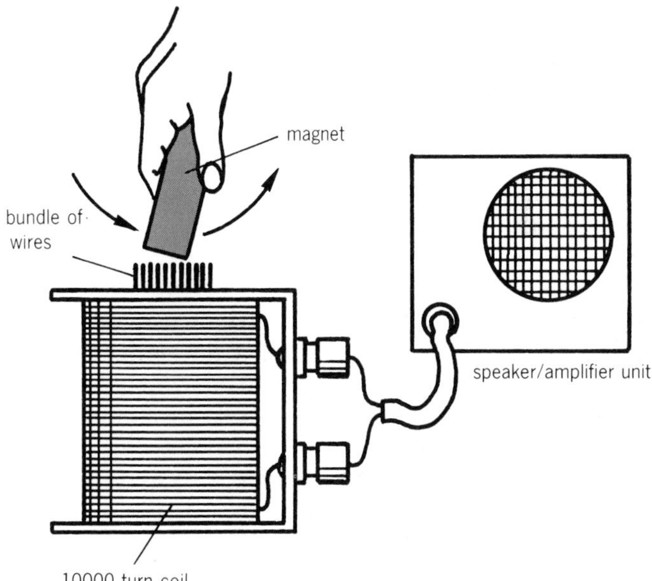

Figure 45.1

the loudspeaker. This is due to currents induced in the coil as the molecular domains align themselves during magnetisation. No subsequent noise is produced if the north pole is moved across again, the effect returning only if a south pole is used.

Hysteresis

Hysteresis (the name comes from the Greek word meaning 'delay') describes the relation between the magnetising field and the magnetisation produced within a specimen.

Figure 45.2 shows the relation between the magnetising force and the resultant magnetisation of the specimen. You will see that there is a maximum flux that can be produced within a given specimen, shown as B_m on the graph. This is known as **saturation.**

If a specimen is fully magnetised and then demagnetised, it will not return to a condition where both the magnetising field and the magnetisation produced in the specimen are both zero.

When the magnetising field is reduced to zero there will still be a small amount of magnetisation left in the specimen. This is known as the **remanent flux** and the effect as **remanence** (B_r). This is shown by the length OA in Figure 45.2.

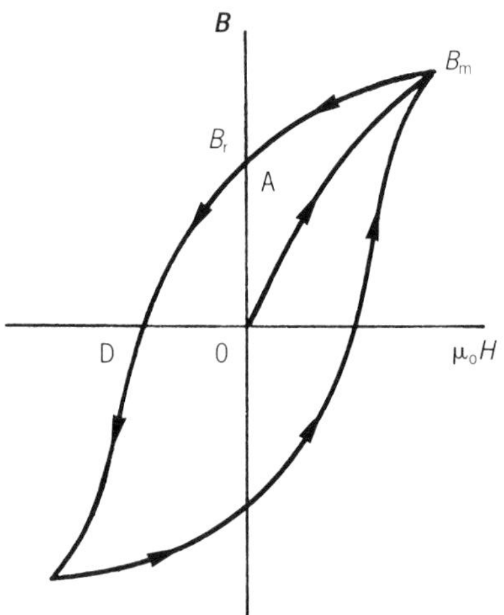

Figure 45.2

The reverse field needed to reduce the magnetisation in the specimen to zero is known as the **coercivity** (H) of the specimen and is shown as OD in Figure 45.2.

The loop produced when the magnetising field is taken through a full cycle is called a **hysteresis loop.** One very important factor is the area within the loop, since this represents the loss of energy within the specimen when it is magnetised and demagnetised. This energy is lost as heat within the specimen, and the larger the area within the loop the more energy is lost in magnetising and demagnetising the specimen.

A soft magnetic material (soft iron) will have a small energy loss and therefore a narrow hysteresis loop while that for a hard magnetic material (steel) will be wider. Figure 45.3 shows the effect of hysteresis in two different types of specimen.

The table below gives the remanence and coercivity for a number of magnetic materials.

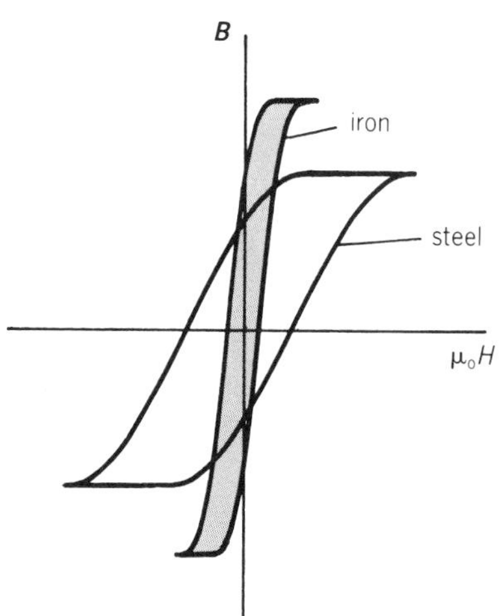

Figure 45.3

Material	*Composition/%*	*B/T*	*H/A* m^{-1}
Carbon steel	98 Fe, 0.86 C, 0.9 Mn	0.95	3.6×10^3
Cobalt steel	52 Fe, 36 Co, 7 W, 3.5 Cr 0.5 Mn, 0.7 C	0.95	18×10^3
Alnico	55 Fe, 10 Al, 17 Ni, 12 Co, 6 Cu	0.76	42×10^3
Magnadur	Ba, Fe	0.36	110×10^3
Mumetal	76 Ni, 17 Fe, 5 Cu, 2 Cr	0.5	0.002×10^3

Permanent magnets are made with hard magnetic materials with a high remanence, so that the magnet will retain its magnetism after magnetisation, and a high coercivity so that stray fields will not affect it.

Soft magnetic materials are used in transformer cores so that the energy losses are small. For example, at a frequency of 50 Hz the power loss per kilogram of mumetal is 0.2 W for a saturation field of 0.1 T. This rises to 175 W for a frequency of 2.4 kHz!

46 · Electromagnetic induction

The discovery of electromagnetic induction by Faraday

The following is an extract from Michael Faraday's own notebook.

August 29th 1831

1. *Experiments on the production of Electricity and Magnetism etc.*

2. *Have an iron ring made (soft iron), iron round and $\frac{7}{8}$ inches thick and ring 6 inches in external diameter. Wound many coils of copper wire round one half, the coils being separated by twine and calico – there were three lengths of wire each about 24 feet long and they could be connected as one length or used as separate lengths. By trial with a trough each was insulated from the other. Will call this side of the ring A. On the other side but separated by an interval was wound wire in two pieces together amounting to about 60 feet in length the direction being as with the former coils. This side call B.*

3. *Charged a battery of 10 pairs plates 4 inches square. Made the coil on B side one coil and connected its extremities by a copper wire passing to a distance and just over a magnetic needle (3 feet from iron ring). Then connected the ends of one of the pieces on A side with battery. Immediately a sensible effect on needle. It oscillated and settled at last in original position. On breaking connection on side A with battery again a disturbance of the needle.*

4. *Made all the wires on side A one coil and sent current from battery through the whole. Effect on needle much stronger than before.*

5. *The effect on the needle then but a very small part of which the wire communicating directly with the battery could produce.*

6. *Changed the simple wire from B side for one carrying a flat helix and put the helix in plane of the magnetic meridian to the west of the south pole of the needle so as to show best its influence when a current passed through it – the helix and needle were about 3 feet from the iron ring and the ring about a foot from the battery.*

7. *When all was ready the moment the battery was communicated with both ends of wire at A side, the helix strongly attracted the needle. After a few vibrations it came to a state of rest in its original and natural position and then on breaking the battery connection the needle was strongly repelled and after a few oscillations came to rest in the same place as before.*

8. *Hence effect evident but transient but its recurrence on breaking the connection shews an equilibrium somewhere that must be capable of being rendered more distinct.*

9. *The direction of the pole towards the helix was when the contact was first made as if the helix round B was part of that at A, i.e. the electric currents in both were in the same direction, but when contact with the battery was broken the motion of the needle was as if a current in the opposite direction existed for a moment.*

10. *Had a short cylinder of iron $\frac{7}{8}$ inches thick, 4 inches long and coiled round with 4 pieces of wire each about 14 feet long; made these coils into one and substituted this in place of the flat helix. The needle was affected as before but not all as if the iron had helped to develop magnetic power – not more than helices round it would probably have done without the iron. It was the same transient and inverted states as before.*

August 30

14. *Repeated 6. Continued the contact of A side with battery but broke and closed alternately contact of B side with flat helix. No effect at such times on the needle. Depends upon the change at battery side. Hence is no permanent or peculiar state of the wire from B but effect due to a wave of electricity caused at moments of breaking and completing at A side.*

15. *Tried to perceive a spark with charcoal at flat helix junction B side but could find none. Wave apparently very short and sudden. No use trying platina wire. Not sure large battery would not produce spark.*

Then disjoined the three portions of wire on A side – made two into one helix and sent battery current through that – and connected the third portion with the flat spiral and needle etc. so as to represent B side. Effects on needle stronger than before but same in character, occurring inversely etc. on breaking battery connections etc.

16. *A larger bar magnet brought in contact with the ring caused no change at the flat helix.*

17. *May not these transient effects be connected with causes of difference between power of metals in rest and in motion in Arago's expts?*

18. *Took the iron cylinder (10) and connecting two of the wires into one helix and the other two into another connected one of these helices with the flat spiral and needle and the other with the battery – immediately a sharp short pull upon the needle the effects being exactly as before but not as strong. Hence a ring magnet is not wanted.*

19. *Brought the poles of stong magnets in contact with ends of the iron cylinder but found no difference upon the needle at the flat spiral. All these effects seem due to the electrical current only.*

1 Put the account into your own words.

2 Explain the effects that Faraday observed.

3 You are asked to give a Christmas lecture to young people at the Royal Institution. How would you demonstrate the effects mentioned in the extract?

Electromagnetic induction

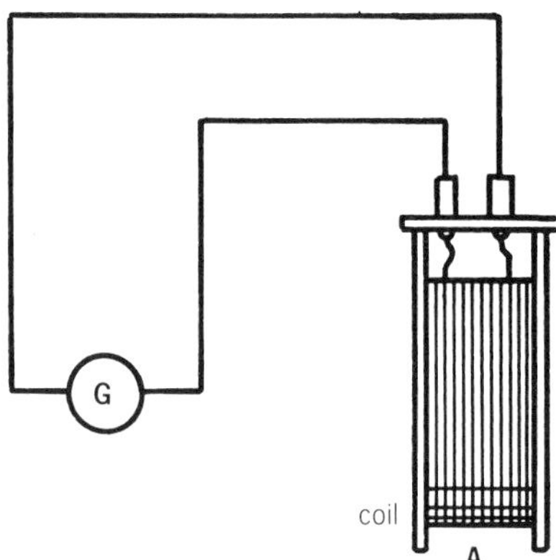

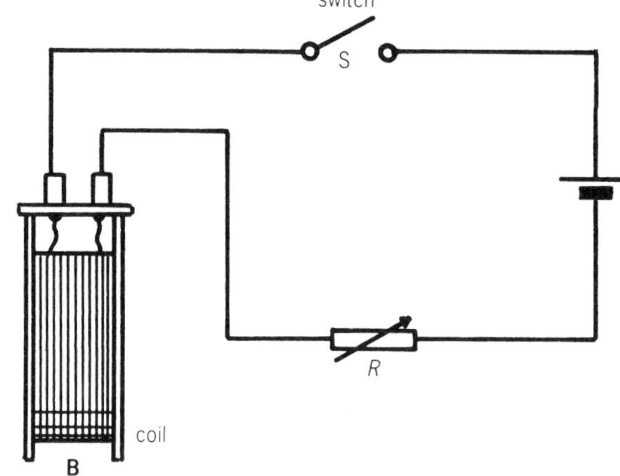

Figure 46.1

Induced e.m.f.s

If the magnetic flux through a coil is altered then an e.m.f. will be generated in the coil. This effect was first observed and explained by Ampere and Faraday (see page 313) between 1825 and 1831. Faraday discovered that an e.m.f. could be generated by

(*a*) either moving the coil or source of flux relative to each other

(*b*) or changing the magnitude of the source of flux in some way.

Note that the e.m.f. is only produced *while* the flux is changing.

For example, consider two coils as shown in Figure 46.1.

Coil A is connected to a galvanometer and coil B is connected to a battery and has direct current flowing through it. Coil A is within the magnetic field produced by B and an e.m.f. can be produced in A by moving the coils relative to each other or by changing the size of the current in B. This can be done by

(*a*) using the rheostat R,

(*b*) switching the current on or off, or

(*c*) using an a.c. supply for B.

(An e.m.f. could also be produced in A by replacing B with a permanent magnet and moving this relative to A.)

Faraday's laws

Faraday summarised the results of his experiments as follows:

(*a*) An e.m.f. is induced in a coil if the magnetic flux through the coil changes

(*b*) The magnitude of the induced e.m.f. depends on

(i) the rate of change of flux,

(ii) the number of turns on the coil, and

(iii) the cross-sectional area of the coil.

Points (ii) and (iii) simply refer to the amount of change of flux. The faster the flux is changed the greater is the e.m.f. produced.

Lenz's law

The direction of the induced e.m.f. was explained by Lenz who proposed the following law in 1835:

The direction of the induced e.m.f. is such that it tends to oppose the change that produced it.

We can explain this law by considering the energy changes that occur when a magnet is moved towards a coil, as shown in Figure 46.2. Assume that the magnet is moved towards the coil with its north pole facing towards the coil. Now by Lenz's law this should induce a current in the coil such that the right-hand end of the coil (B) nearest the magnet is also a north pole. If this is true then it should repel the magnet and work must be done on the magnet to move it in against this repulsion.

The energy used goes to produce the induced e.m.f. in the coil. This would agree with Lenz's law.

However, if we assume that the e.m.f. produced is in the opposite sense and gives a *south* pole at B then as the magnet is moved in it will experience an attraction due to the e.m.f. in the coil. This will accelerate it, the e.m.f. produced will increase in size, the acceleration will increase and so on. Clearly energy is being produced from nothing and this is impossible.

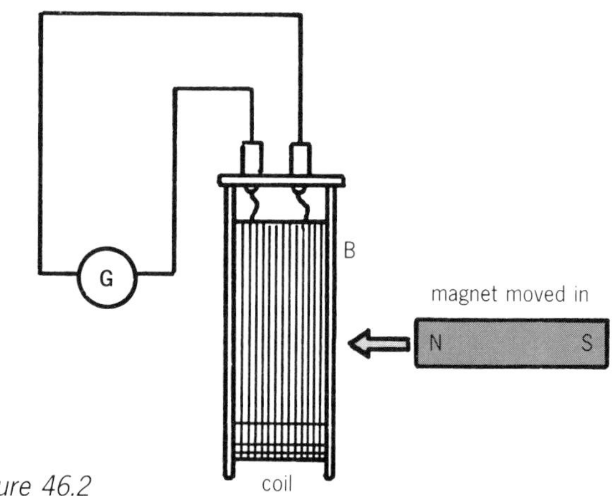

Figure 46.2

Faraday's right-hand rule

Faraday proposed a simple rule for giving the direction of the induced current as follows:

If the thumb and first two fingers of the right hand are held at right angles and the first finger is pointed in the direction of the magnetic field and the thumb in the direction of motion then the second finger gives the direction of the induced current (Figure 46.3).

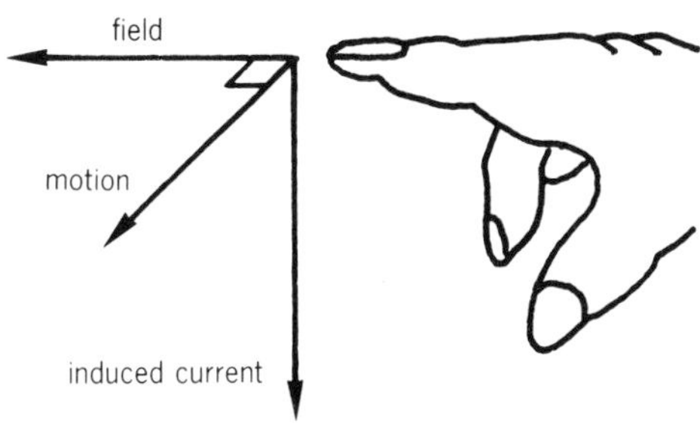

Figure 46.3

Faraday's and Lenz's laws may be tested by the following simple experiments:

(*a*) rotating a metal disc at a constant rate in a magnetic field and measuring the e.m.f. generated between the rim and the axle;

(*b*) moving a bar magnet within a solenoid connected to a meter;

(*c*) rotating a magnet near a coil connected to a cathode ray oscilloscope.

Eddy currents

Before we consider the mathematical treatment of Faraday's laws we will look at the phenomenon of eddy currents. These are induced currents in metal objects larger than pieces of wire; the e.m.f.s induced may not be very great but because the resistance of a lump of metal is low the induced currents can be large.

Since the induced currents always act so as to oppose the motion (Lenz's law) eddy currents can be used as a very effective electromagnetic brake. A simple example of this is shown in Figure 46.4.

A piece of metal is swung between the poles of magnet and currents are induced in the metal which quickly damp the oscillation. But if slots are cut in the metal its resistance is increased, the induced currents are reduced and the damping is very much less.

Eddy currents become a problem in the cores of transformers where they could cause large energy losses. For this reason the cores are made of thin laminations, thus increasing the resistance and limiting the eddy current flow. The energy loss is proportional to the square of the lamination thickness and the square of the frequency of the current.

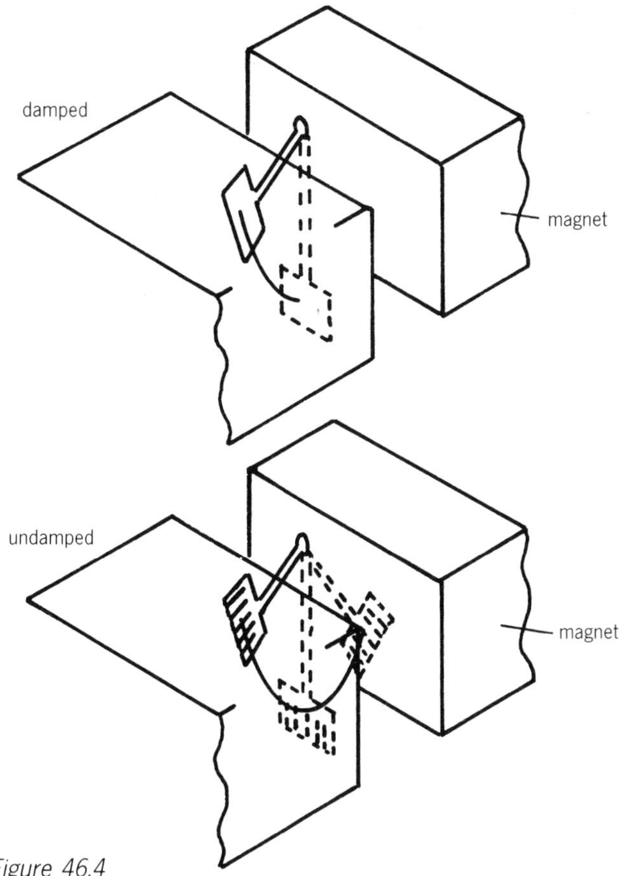

Figure 46.4

Eddy currents can be used as electromagnetic damping, to melt metals in a vacuum, so giving metals of a high purity free from atmospheric contamination, and to heat metal parts of valves.

Student investigation

Suspend a copper cylinder from a thread between the poles of an Eclipse major magnet and twist the thread so that the cylinder performs torsional oscillations. Time how long the cylinder takes to come to rest. Repeat the experiment but this time use a pile of 1 p pieces.

Explain what you observe.

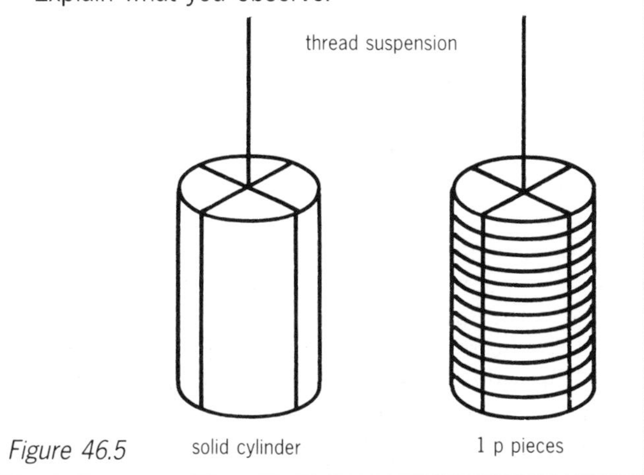

Figure 46.5

The laws of electromagnetic induction

When the magnetic flux through a coil changes, the e.m.f. E generated in the coil can be expressed as

$$E = \frac{-\mathrm{d}(N\phi)}{\mathrm{d}t}$$

where N is the number of turns in the coil and ϕ the flux. The quantity $N\phi$ is known as the **flux linkage** and is measured in webers, and therefore $\mathrm{d}(N\phi)/\mathrm{d}t$ is the rate of change of flux linkage in webers per second.

Example

Calculate the e.m.f. induced in a coil of 200 turns placed in a field where the rate of change of flux is 0.01 Wb s^{-1}.

E.m.f. = −200 × 0.01 = −2 V.

If we think of a conductor moving through a magnetic field (Figure 46.6) then the equation becomes:

$$E = \frac{-N\,\mathrm{d}\phi}{\mathrm{d}t}$$

where N is the number of conductors cutting the flux.

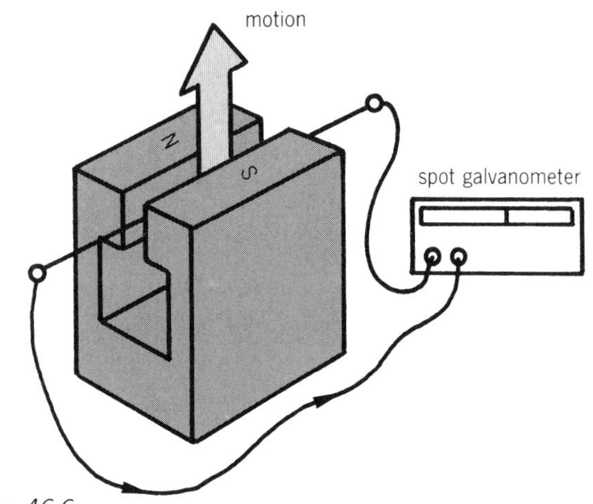

Figure 46.6

Back e.m.f.

Since the e.m.f. generated opposes the changes that produces it, it is known as a **back e.m.f.** This effect is particularly important in electric motors (see page 308).

E.m.f. induced in a straight conductor

When a straight conductor is moved through a magnetic field an e.m.f. is induced between its ends. This movement must be in such a direction that the conductor cuts through the lines of magnetic flux, and will

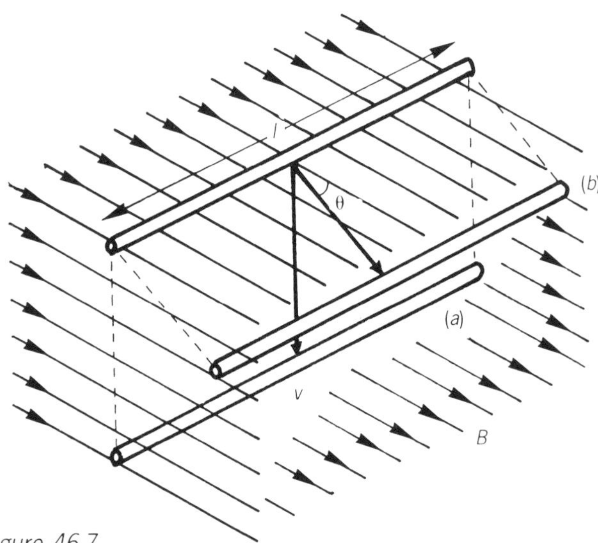

Figure 46.7

be a maximum when it moves at right angles to the field ((*a*) in Figure 46.7).

Let the length of the conductor be l and the flux density of the field be B.

If the conductor moves with velocity v at right angles to the field then the flux cut per second will be Bvl (since the conductor will sweep out an area vl every second).

But the rate of cutting flux is equal to the e.m.f. induced in the conductor. Therefore

$$E = Blv$$

If the conductor cuts through the flux at an angle θ ((*b*) in Figure 46.7) the equation becomes

$$E = Blv \sin\theta$$

Example 1

Calculate the e.m.f. generated between the wing tips of an aircraft that is flying horizontally at 200 m s^{-1} in a region where the vertical component of the Earth's magnetic field is 4.0×10^{-5} T, if the aircraft has a wingspan of 25 m.

$E = 4 \times 10^{-5} \times 25 \times 200$

$= 0.2$ V

Example 2

Calculate the e.m.f. generated between the fixed and the free ends of a helicopter blade 9.45 m long that is rotating at 3.5 revs per second. The vertical component of the Earth's field has a flux density of 4.0×10^{-5} T.

E.m.f. = $BAn = 4.0 \times 10^{-5} \times \pi \times 89.3 \times 3.5 = 39.3$ mV.

1 A Boeing 747 with a wingspan of 60 m flies due south at a constant altitude in the northern hemisphere at 260 m s^{-1}. If the vertical component of the Earth's magnetic field in that area was 4×10^{-5} T, calculate the e.m.f. between the wing tips and state which wing tip is positive.

The aircraft now dives at 10° to the horizontal. Calculate the change in induced e.m.f. Horizontal component of the Earth's magnetic field at this point $= 2 \times 10^{-5}$ T.

2 A copper wire 0.5 m long, of resistance 0.001 Ω and with a mass of 0.01 kg, falls through a horizontal magnetic field of flux density 0.2 T with its ends sliding smoothly down two thick vertical rails, the top ends of which are connected by a wire of negligible resistance. Explain why the wire reaches a terminal velocity and calculate its value. [O, modified]

3 A magnetised compass needle is allowed to oscillate first above a sheet of glass and then above a sheet of copper. Describe and explain what happens in each case. [C]

Calculation of the e.m.f. produced due to forces on charged particles

Consider a conductor of length l moving with velocity v at right angles to magnetic field of flux density B that is perpendicular to the paper (Figure 46.9).

At equilibrium the magnetic force on an electron in the conductor must be balanced by an electrostatic force between its ends.

Magnetic force: $F = Bev$

Electrostatic force: $F = \dfrac{eV}{l}$

At equilibrium: $Bev = \dfrac{eV}{l}$

Therefore e.m.f. between the ends of the conductor is:

$$V = Blv$$

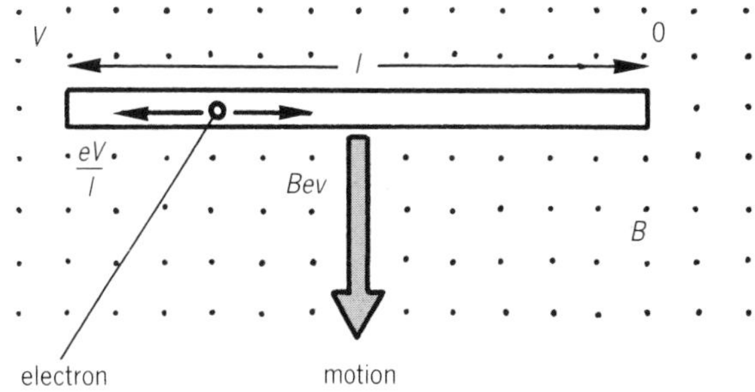

Figure 46.9

Student investigation

The electromagnetic metal separator, used in car scrap yards, may become a very important industrial application of electromagnetic induction. A car sent for scrapping contains a large amount of metal that may be recycled. Until recently only the steel could be separated by simply passing the crushed scrap along a belt over a d.c. electromagnet (see Figure 46.8(*a*)). The ferrous metal was attracted and passed round under the magnetic roller while the rest of the scrap fell into a hopper. The remainder of the scrap contained plastic, rubber and a large amount of aluminium and it was this aluminium that it was desirable to separate.

This further separation can now be achieved as follows. The remaining scrap is passed along a belt over an a.c. electromagnet (see Figure 46.8(*b*)). This induces eddy currents in the aluminium metal scrap, which is then repelled by the field and flies off sideways while the remaining non-metal scrap continues along the belt. A very high purity for the aluminium separated by this method has been claimed. It has also proved extremely effective for separating bottle tops from crushed glass bottle waste.

Construct a small-scale aluminium metal separator in the laboratory and test its effectiveness. A mixture of old milk-bottle tops and small stones is suitable.

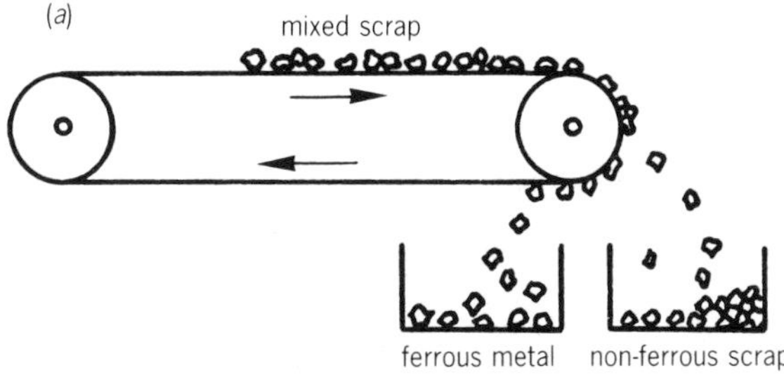

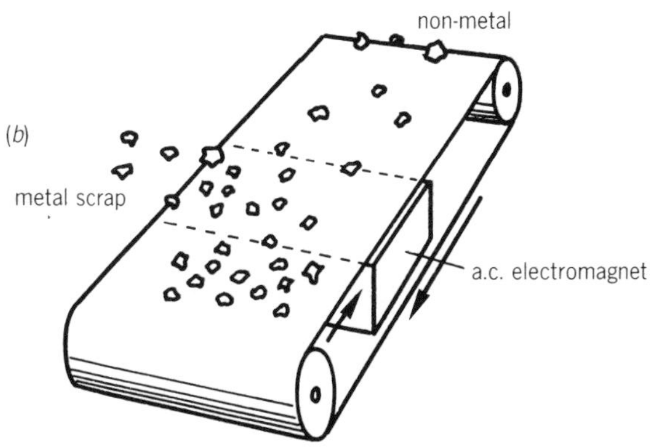

Figure 46.8

E.m.f. generated in a rotating coil

Consider a coil of N turns and area A being rotated at a constant angular velocity ω in a magnetic field of flux density B, its axis being perpendicular to the field (Figure 46.10). When the normal to the coil is at an angle θ to the field the flux through the coil is $BAN \cos \theta = BAN \cos (\omega t)$, since $\theta = \omega t$.

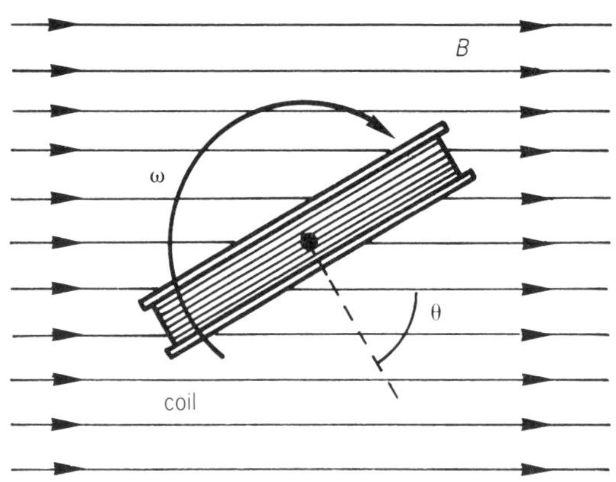

Figure 46.10

Therefore the e.m.f. E generated between the ends of the coil is:

$$E = -\frac{d(\phi)}{dt}$$

$$= -\frac{d(BAN\cos\theta)}{dt}$$

Therefore

$$E = BAN\omega \sin(\omega t)$$

The maximum value of the e.m.f. ($\mathbf{E}_0$) is when θ ($= \omega t$) $= 90^\circ$ (that is, the coil is in the plane of the field, Figure 46.11) and is given by

$$E_0 = BAN\omega$$

The r.m.s. value of the e.m.f. is

$$E = \frac{BAN\omega}{\sqrt{2}}$$

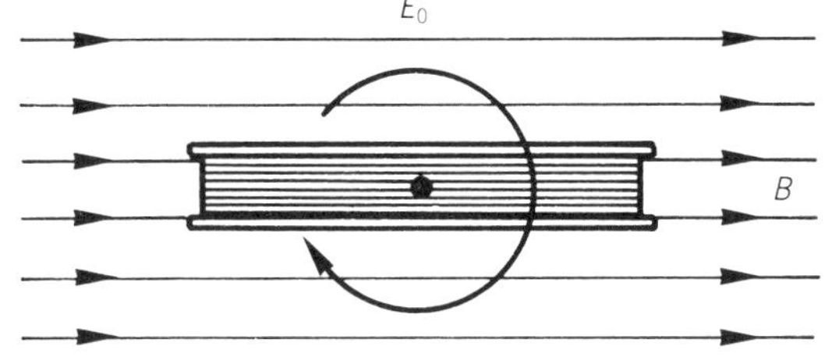

Figure 46.11

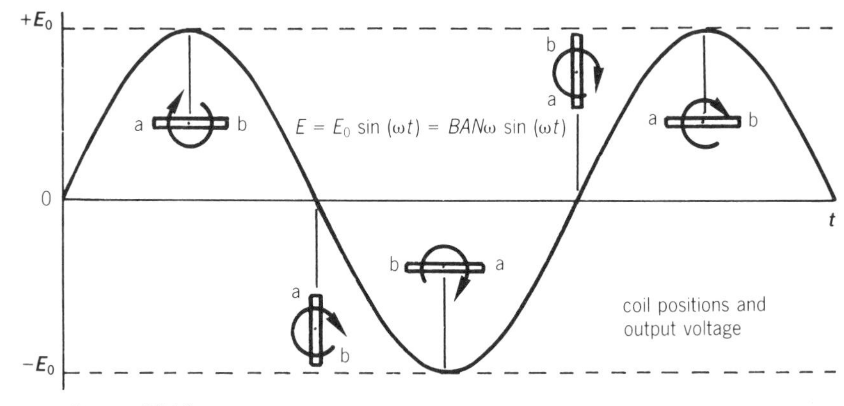

Figure 46.12

Example

Calculate the maximum value of the e.m.f. generated in a coil with 200 turns and of area 10 cm^2 rotating at 60 radians per second in a field of flux density 0.1 T.

$$E = BAN\omega = 0.1 \times 10^{-3} \times 200 \times 60$$

$$= 1.2 \text{ V}$$

4 A circular coil of 100 turns, each of radius 10 cm, is rotated at 10 revs per second about an axis at right angles to a field of flux density 0.1 T. Find the position of the coil when the e.m.f. across its ends is a maximum and calculate this e.m.f.

5 The metal frame of a window in the west wall of a house forms a circuit of total resistance 5×10^{-3} Ω. The area of the glass is 1.5 m^2. How much charge will flow round the frame if the window is opened until it is at right angles to the wall? The horizontal component of the Earth's field at that point is 2×10^{-5} T.

6 A moving coil galvanometer using electromagnetic damping has a coil resistance 0.002 Ω and 10 mm by 20 mm suspended in a radial field of flux density 0.3 T. What is the damping torque on the coil when it turns at 10 rad s^{-1}? (N = 100 turns)

Generators

As we have seen, if a coil is rotated in a magnetic field then an e.m.f. is induced in the coil. This is the basis of all generators.

The a.c. generator or alternator

A simple form of the a.c. generator is shown in Figure 46.13(*a*).

A coil (the **rotor**) is rotated between the poles of a d.c. electromagnet (energised by the **field coils**), except in the case of a bicycle dynamo where a permanent magnet is used, and the e.m.f. generated is taken from the ends of the coil. These are connected to sliding contacts known as **slip rings** on the axle, and contact is made with these by two pieces of carbon (the **brushes**) which press against the slip rings. As the coil rotates it cuts through the lines of magnetic flux producing an induced e.m.f., the variation of which with time is shown by Figure 46.12 on page 318. A much smoother output is obtained by having a number of coils wound on an iron core which is laminated to reduce eddy currents. The output of such a generator is shown in Figure 46.13(*b*).

In generators where the output current may be very large, as in a power station, it is the magnet that rotates while the coil remains at rest. A simplified version of this is shown in Figure 46.13(*c*). The advantage of this is that the slip rings and brushes have to carry only the small current needed to magnetise the rotating electromagnet while the current produced the static field coils may be many hundreds of amps. In fact in modern alternators installed in a power station the e.m.f. generated will be some 25 kV and the current produced over 1000 A!

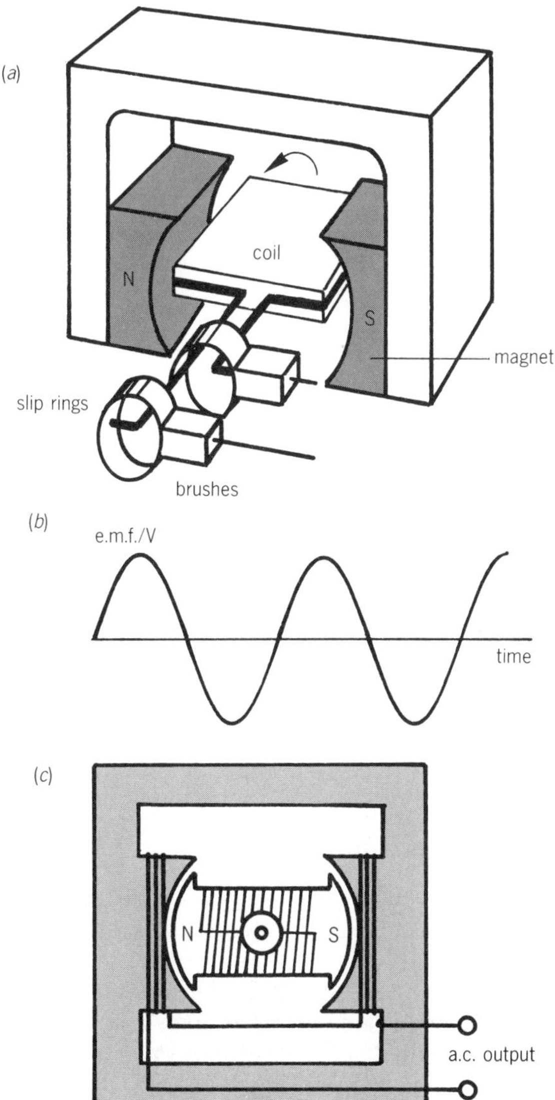

Figure 46.13

7 A coil of 300 turns and with an area of 0.05 m^2 is rotated 20 times per second in a field of flux density 0.2 T. Calculate

(*a*) the maximum e.m.f. produced across the ends of the coil,

(*b*) the torque required to maintain this rate of rotation if the current in the coil is 0.8 A when the e.m.f. generated is a maximum.

Student investigation

The induction motor (see page 310) relies on the phenomenon of electromagnetic induction for its operation and a simple investigation will demonstrate this. (Remember that to obtain an induced e.m.f. *either* the conductor *or* the magnetic field may move.)

Set up the apparatus as shown in Figure 46.14 and switch on the electric drill. As the copper disc speeds up, observe and explain the effect on the magnet.

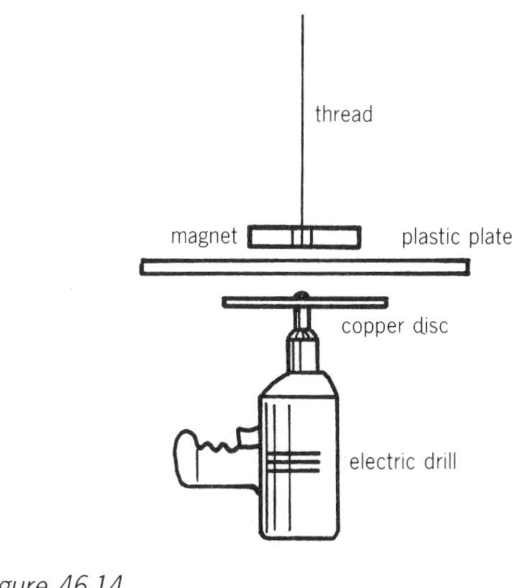

Figure 46.14

The d.c. generator

In the d.c. generator the output from the rotor assembly is fed to a **commutator** where the brushes press against a split ring of copper. This means that a varying but unidirectional e.m.f. will be produced. A d.c. generator and its output is shown in simplified form in Figure 46.15.

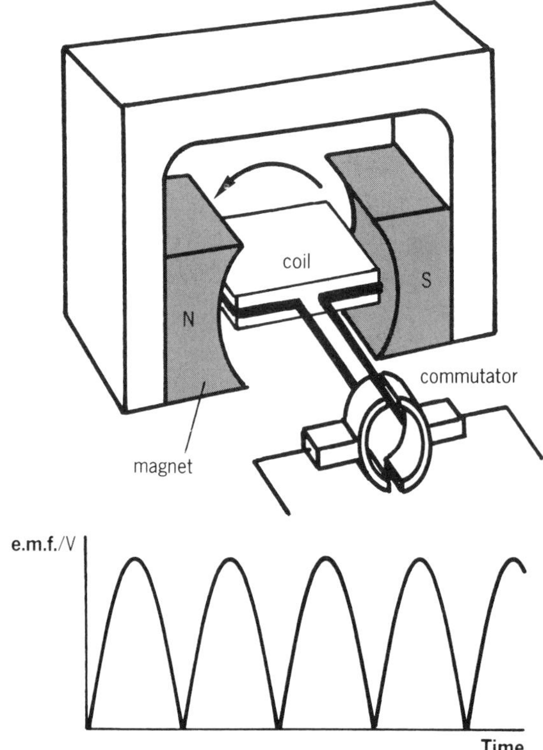

Figure 46.15

As with the a.c. generator, the d.c. machine usually uses rotating field coils, a series of them being wound in slots in the core; the rotating coils and the core are known as the **armature**. The output is then much steadier, a ripple effect being obtained. The d.c. generator may be made 'self-exciting' by putting the field coils and armature in series or parallel, the current required for the field coils being produced by the generator itself. There is nearly always some residual magnetism in the core of the armature to aid the starting of such a generator.

Characteristics of the series- and shunt-wound d.c. generators

The two graphs in Figure 46.16 show how the voltage generated varies with the load current drawn from it for both a series-wound and a shunt-wound machine.

For the series-wound generator the voltage between the terminals rises with the current whereas for the shunt-wound machine the current variation is much smaller, a slow decrease being observed.

Can you explain these effects?

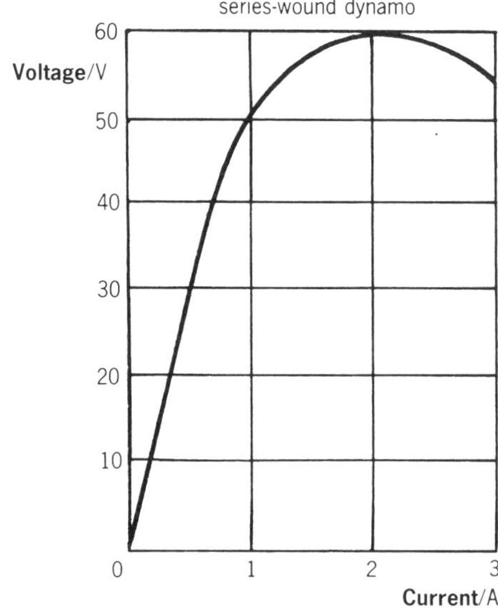

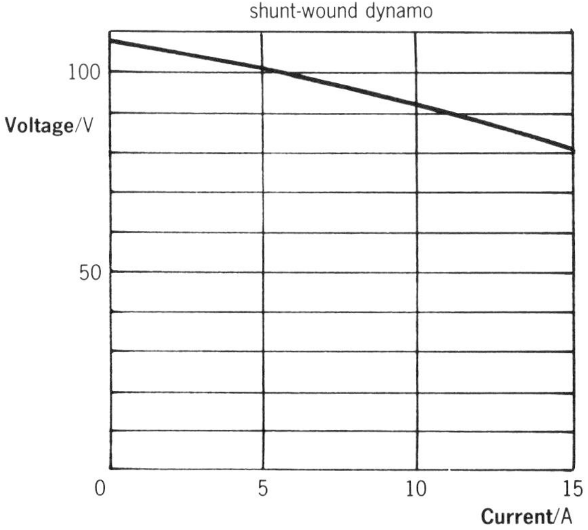

Figure 46.16

Student investigation

The following experiment is designed to investigate the variation of output voltage with rotation speed for a d.c. generator.

Set up a d.c. generator which may be rotated from rest by a motor. Use a voltmeter or an instrument such as a Vela to record the instantaneous values of the e.m.f. generated as the speed of rotation is slowly increased from zero. Explain your results.

Self-inductance

If the current through a coil is altered then the flux through that coil also changes, and this will induce an e.m.f. in the coil. This effect is known **self-induction** and the property of the coil is the **self-inductance** (L) of the coil, usually abbreviated as the inductance.

The e.m.f. generated is given by the equation

$$E = -L\frac{dI}{dt}$$

The unit of inductance is the **henry** and it is defined as **the inductance of a coil (or circuit) in which an e.m.f. of one volt is induced when the current changes at the rate of one ampere per second.** The unit can be expressed as $1\ \mathrm{H} = 1\ \mathrm{V\,s\,A^{-1}}$.

A very simple demonstration uses the apparatus shown in Figure 46.17.

An air-cored inductor is connected in series with a d.c. supply and a 12 V bulb. The resistance of the solenoid will be low so that it barely affects the light emitted by the bulb, and placing an iron core inside the inductor will make no difference to the bulb's brightness.

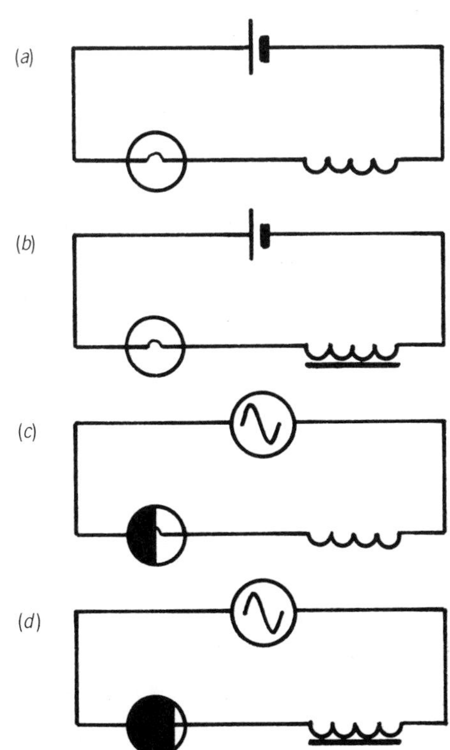

Figure 46.17

If the experiment is repeated using a.c. with an air core, the inductance will probably prevent the lamp from reaching its full brightness. If an iron core is placed inside the solenoid, however, its inductance is increased considerably and the lamp goes out due to the increased self-inductance and resulting back e.m.f. in the coil.

The coil and iron rod are called a **choke.**

Inductance of a solenoid

Consider an air-cored solenoid of length l, cross-sectional area A and N turns carrying a current I (Figure 46.18) The field B in the solenoid is

$$B = \mu_0\frac{NI}{l}$$

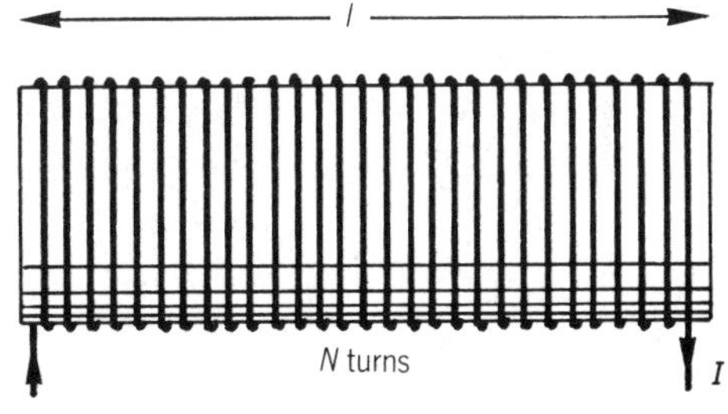

Figure 46.18

The flux ϕ through each turn is BA, and the flux linkage for the solenoid is $N\phi = BAN$. Therefore

$$N\phi = \mu_0\frac{AN^2I}{l}$$

Let the current now change by an amount dI in a time dt, giving a change of flux linkage $d(N\phi)$. But from Faraday's law

$$E = \frac{-d(N\phi)}{dt} = \mu_0\frac{AN^2}{l}\frac{dI}{dt}$$

Therefore, since $E = -L\frac{dI}{dt}$, we have

$$-L\frac{dI}{dt} = -\frac{\mu_0 AN^2}{l}\frac{dI}{dt}$$

and so for a solenoid

$$L = \mu_0\frac{AN^2}{l}$$

Example

Calculate the inductance of a solenoid 0.5 m long, of cross-sectional area 20 cm^2 and with 500 turns.

$$L = \frac{4\pi \times 10^{-7} \times 20 \times 10^{-4} \times 500^2}{0.5}$$

$$= 1.25 \times 10^{-3}\ \mathrm{H}$$

$$= 1.25\ \mathrm{mH}$$

Energy stored in an inductor

Since a changing current in an inductor causes an e.m.f. if the source supplying the current is to maintain a p.d. between its terminals the inductor must gain energy.

Let the inductor carry an instantaneous current i which is changing at the rate of $\mathrm{d}i/\mathrm{d}t$. The induced e.m.f. is $L\,\mathrm{d}i/\mathrm{d}t$ and the power P supplied to the inductor is

$$P = Ei = Li\,\frac{\mathrm{d}i}{\mathrm{d}t}$$

The energy $\mathrm{d}W$ supplied in time $\mathrm{d}t$ is $P\,\mathrm{d}t$, or $\mathrm{d}W = Li\,\mathrm{d}i$. Therefore:

$$\text{energy stored in inductor} = \tfrac{1}{2}Li^2$$

This energy is used to produce the magnetic field in and around the coil. If the current is suddenly interrupted a spark may occur as the energy is dissipated.

Self-inductance can be a problem in circuits, where the breaking of the circuit can induce a large e.m.f., and so the switches may be immersed in oil to quench the arc. Alternatively a capacitor may be connected across the terminals to slow down the decay of current and so reduce the induced e.m.f.

The solenoid plays a rather similar role with relation to magnetic fields as the capacitor does to electric fields – the ability to store energy.

8 Calculate the self-inductance of a solenoid 50 cm long, 4 cm in diameter and of 5000 turns, neglecting end effects.

9 Explain why iron-cored solenoids are used for high inductances. Why does the inductance tend to decrease in size as the current in the solenoid increases?

10 If a wire carrying a high-frequency alternating current is wrapped round a pencil, the current in it is reduced. Explain why this is so.

11 The current in a coil rises from zero to 4.0 A in 1.5 s. If the inductance of the coil is 0.20 H, calculate the magnitude of the e.m.f. induced in the coil.

12 A current of 5 A flowing in a flat circular coil of 30 turns is found to produce a magnetic flux through the coil of 4×10^{-5} Wb. Calculate the inductance of the coil in millihenries.

Student investigation

When drilling a wall to put up a shelf, it is most important not to drill through a mains power cable carrying power to a light or to a power socket. Devise and test a simple detector based on electromagnetic induction that could be used to trace the path of a cable carrying a.c. mains.

Student investigation

Study the transmission of sound from one coil to another using the output from a cassette recorder fed into the primary coil. The primary should be of about five turns of insulated copper wire wrapped round the edges of a laboratory table and the secondary coil should be placed within it.

Would you consider this to be a suitable method for the transmission of messages to workers in a noisy room? What problems would there be?

Growth and decay of current in an inductor

When a battery of emf E is connected across a resistor and an inductor in series the current does not rise to its final value instantaneously. There is a rise time that is due to the back emf in the inductor.

The equation is:

$$E - L.\frac{\mathrm{dI}}{\mathrm{dt}} = IR$$

and this can be shown to have the solution

$$I = E/R(1 - \mathrm{e}^{-t(R/L)})$$

and this shows that the growth of current is exponential towards a final value E/R.

A similar argument can be applied to the decay of current when the cell is disconnected, the equation in this case being:

$$I = \frac{E}{R}\mathrm{e}^{-t(R/L)}$$

Mutual inductance

When the current in a coil is changing an e.m.f. will be induced in a nearby circuit due to some of the magnetic flux produced by the first circuit linking the second. The phenomenon is known as **mutual induction.** It is important to realise that the induced e.m.f. lasts only as long as the current in the first circuit is changing.

The mutual inductance M is defined by the equation

$$M = -\frac{E}{\mathrm{d}I/\mathrm{d}t}$$

where E is the e.m.f. induced in the secondary coil and $\mathrm{d}I/\mathrm{d}t$ the rate of change of current in the primary.

Two coils are said to have a mutual inductance of 1 H if an e.m.f. of 1 V is induced in the secondary when the current in the primary changes at the rate of 1 A s^{-1}.

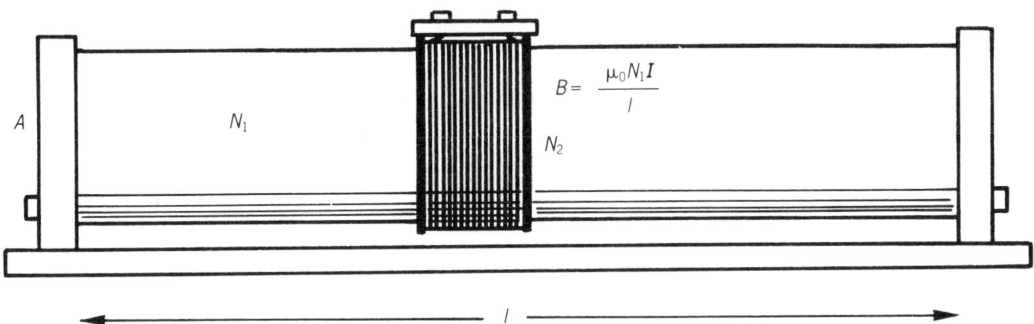

Figure 46.19

Induction coils such as this are used in car ignition circuits, and used to be a source of high voltage for research.

Consider the mutual inductance of a long solenoid and a coil (Figure 46.19).

Suppose that a short coil of N_2 turns is wound round a solenoid of N_1 turns, with a cross-sectional area A, length l and carrying a current I. The flux at the centre of the solenoid is:

$$B = \frac{\mu_0 N_1}{l} I$$

The flux linking the short coil is $\phi = BA$ and therefore the flux linkage of the short coil is

$$N_2\phi = BAN_2 = \mu_0 \frac{N_1}{l} IAN_2$$

If the current in the primary changes by $\mathrm{d}I$ in time $\mathrm{d}t$, giving a change in flux linkage of $\mathrm{d}(N\phi)$ in the secondary, then the e.m.f. induced in the secondary will be

$$E = -\frac{\mathrm{d}(N\phi)}{\mathrm{d}t} = -\mu_0 \frac{AN_1}{l} N_2 \frac{\mathrm{d}I}{\mathrm{d}t}$$

Writing M as the mutual inductance, we have that

$$E = -M\frac{\mathrm{d}I}{\mathrm{d}t}$$

and therefore

$$M = \mu_0 \frac{AN_1N_2}{l}$$

Example

Calculate the mutual inductance of a pair of coils if the primary has 1000 turns of radius 2 cm and is 1 m long, while the secondary has 1200 turns and is wound round the centre of the primary.

$$M = \frac{4\pi \times 10^{-7} \times \pi \times 4 \times 10^{-4} \times 1000 \times 1200}{1}$$

$$= 1.90 \times 10^{-3}\ \mathrm{H} = 1.90\ \mathrm{mH}$$

13 A long solenoid of 2000 turns, cross-sectional area 10 cm^2 and length 0.5 m is wound on a plastic tube. A short coil of 500 turns is then wound tightly round the centre of the solenoid. Calculate

(*a*) the flux density in the solenoid when it carries a steady current of 4 A,

(*b*) the flux linked in the solenoid in these conditions,

(*c*) the self-inductance of the solenoid,

(*d*) the mutual inductance between the solenoid and the short coil,

(*e*) a lower limit to the self-inductance of the short coil,

(*f*) the size of the e.m.f. induced in the short coil when the current in the solenoid is changing at 8 A s^{-1}. [O]

14 The mutual inductance of the two coils of an induction coil is 30 H. If a current in the primary of 1.5 A falls to zero in 0.003 s, calculate the e.m.f. induced in the secondary coil.

15 Discuss the following statement. 'If a permanent bar magnet is dropped down a vertical copper pipe it will reach a terminal velocity, even if the air resistance is neglected.'

16 A farmer claims that large voltages can be induced in a wire fence due to a high-voltage transmission line that runs above and parallel to it. Is this likely?

The absolute measurement of resistance – Lorentz rotating disc

This apparatus enables a measurement of resistance to be made that uses only fundamental units.

A copper disc is mounted on an axle inside a long solenoid (Figure 46.20).

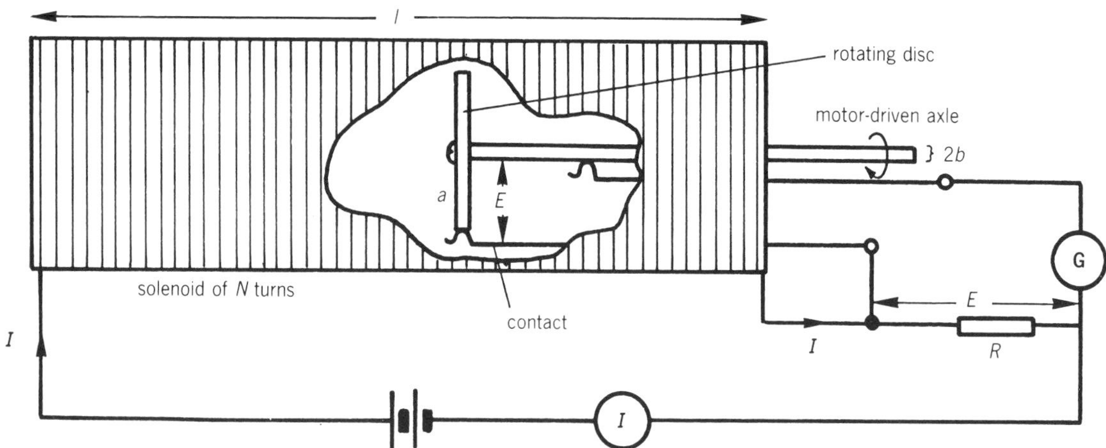

Figure 46.20

The solenoid carries a current and there is therefore a uniform magnetic field of flux density B along its axis. The disc is rotated by a motor and the e.m.f. generated between its rim and its axle is balanced by that produced between the ends of the resistance R to be measured. The current through the solenoid also runs through R, as shown.

The speed of rotation of the disc is varied until the galvanometer shows no deflection. The number of revolutions of the disc per second (r) is measured with a stroboscope.

Let the axle diameter be $2b$ and the disc diameter be $2a$ (Figure 46.21). Then

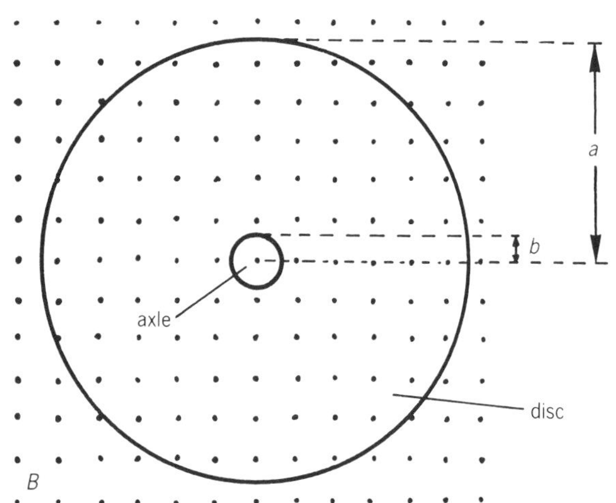

Figure 46.21

area swept out by the disc per second

$$= \pi(a^2 - b^2)r = \frac{dA}{dt}$$

However, $B = \dfrac{\mu_0 NI}{l}$ and $E = -\dfrac{d(BA)}{dt}$

Therefore

$$E = IR = \mu_0 \frac{N\pi(a^2 - b^2)}{l} rI$$

and so:

$$R = \mu_0 \frac{N\pi(a^2 - b^2)}{l} r$$

The experiment is difficult to perform, as the e.m.f.s generated are usually very small. Also friction between the contacts and the disc causes thermoelectric e.m.f.s which may not be negligible compared with those produced by induction. Allowance should also be made for the magnetic field of the Earth and for the fact that the field of the solenoid is not quite uniform over the area of the disc.

Example

Calculate the e.m.f. produced by a disc rotating at 20 revs per second inside a solenoid of 1000 turns and length 1 m carrying a current of 1 A.
The radii of the disc and axle are 2 cm and 0.25 cm respectively.

E.m.f. generated
$= 4\pi \times 10^{-7} \times 1000 \times \pi \times 3.34 \times 10^{-4}$
$= 1.36 \times 10^{-6}$ V
$= 1.36$ μV

17 A Westland Lynx helicopter has a rotor with four blades each 6.4 m long and hovers in an area where the vertical component of the Earth's field is 4×10^{-5} T. If, as the rotor rotates, the tips of the rotor blade move with a speed of 200 m s^{-1}, calculate the induced e.m.f.
(*a*) between the tip of one blade and the axle,
(*b*) between the tips of two diametrically opposite blades, and
(*c*) between the tips of two adjacent blades.

18 A magnetised needle is rotated at a constant rate above an aluminium disc which is itself free to rotate about a similar axis. Describe and explain what happens to the disc.

19 A short bar magnet is dropped through an aluminium ring placed with its plane horizontal. Describe and explain what happens to any currents in the ring.

The induction coil

This device, which is the basis of many ignition systems for cars, uses the mutual inductance between two coils to produce a high voltage. A simplified diagram of an induction coil is shown in Figure 46.22.

A primary coil consisting of a small number of turns of thick copper wire is wound round a bundle of soft iron rods which are insulated from each other. The secondary coil, which may consist of many hundreds of metres of fine wire, is wound over the primary.

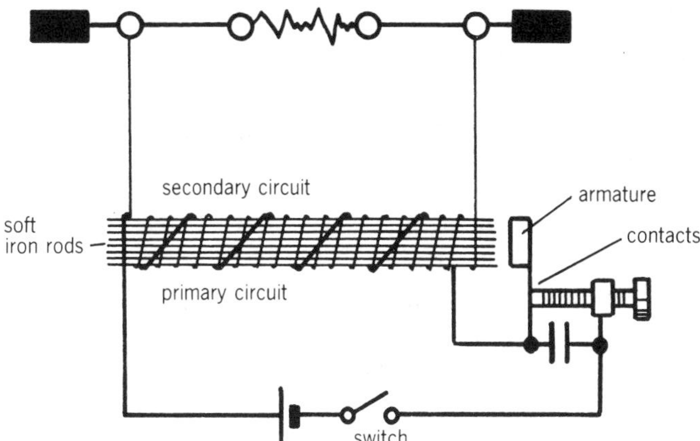

Figure 46.22

On closing the switch a current flows in the primary and magnetises the core, which attracts the armature and breaks the circuit. The magnetic field dies away; the armature is pulled back by the spring and the current flows again. The process then repeats itself.

The rapidly changing magnetic field produces a high voltage in the primary coil; the greater the rate at which this field changes, the greater is the induced voltage. A capacitor is connected across the make and break contacts; this reduces sparking and also causes the field to die away much more rapidly than if the capacitor had not been present. As a result the induced voltage in the secondary is much greater when the circuit is broken than when it is made. The secondary current therefore pulsates, but it is always in the same direction. Sparks of several centimetres in length may be obtained through air at atmospheric pressure with quite small induction coils, and larger coils were originally used to power X-ray tubes.

Figure 46.23 shows how the primary and secondary voltages produced by the induction coil vary with time. Note the rapid decrease of primary voltage at the break and the corresponding high value of the e.m.f. induced in the secondary.

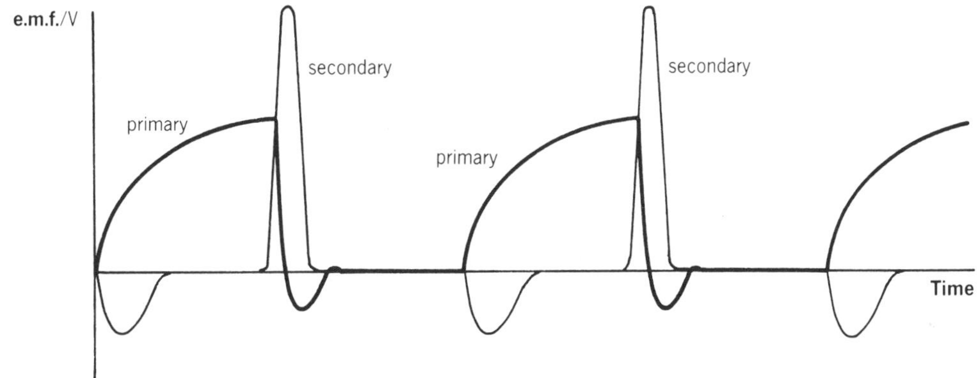

Figure 46.23

The transformer

The transformer uses the property of mutual inductance to change the voltage of an alternating supply. It may be used in the home to give a low-voltage output from the mains for a cassette recorder or train set, or in a power station to produce very high voltages for the National Grid.

In its simplest form it consists of two coils known as the primary and secondary, wound on a laminated iron former that links both coils (Figure 46.24). The **former**, or **core** as it may be called, must be laminated otherwise large eddy currents would flow in it (see page 315). The laminations are usually E-shaped, and the primary and secondary are wound one on top of the other to improve magnetic linkage.

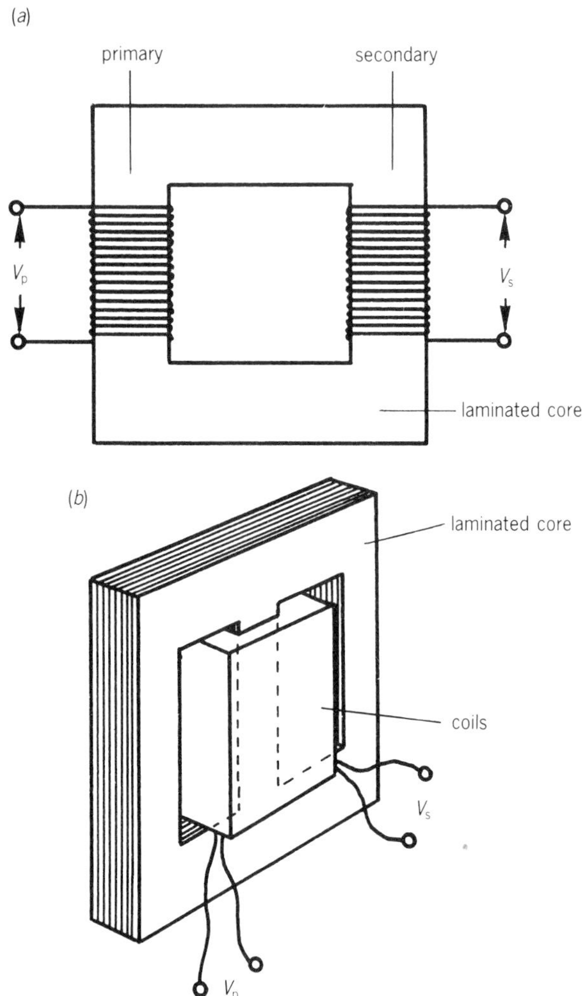

Figure 46.24

An a.c. voltage is applied to the primary and this produces a changing magnetic field within it. This changing magnetic field links the secondary coil and therefore induces an e.m.f. in it. The magnitude of this induced e.m.f. (V_s) is related to the e.m.f. applied to the primary (V_p) by the equation:

$$\frac{V_s}{V_p} = -\frac{n_s}{n_p}$$

where n_p and n_s are the number of turns on the primary and secondary coils respectively. The negative sign means that the voltage induced in the secondary is 180 ° (or π) out of phase with that in the primary. If the output voltage is greater than the input voltage the transformer is known as a **step up** transformer and if the reverse is true it is called a **step down** transformer.

The current in the secondary produces its own magnetic flux, which is opposite to that of the primary. When the current in the secondary is increased by increasing the load the flux in the core is reduced. The back e.m.f. in the primary therefore falls and the current in the primary increases. Eventually the situation will stabilise.

The output voltage may be measured with a meter but a better method is to use an oscilloscope since it draws no current from the transformer.

We have assumed here that there is no leakage of flux, that is, that all the flux produced by the primary links the secondary and that there are no energy losses. In practice, however, energy is lost from a transformer in the following ways:

(*a*) heating in the coils – this can be reduced by keeping their resistance low;

(*b*) eddy current losses in the core – reduced by the laminated core already mentioned;

(*c*) hysteresis loss – every time the direction of the magnetising field is changed some energy is lost due to heating as the magnetic domains in the core realign. This is reduced by using a 'soft' magnetic material for the core such as permalloy or silicon–iron. For soft magnetic materials the loss might be about 0.02 J per cycle.

Despite these energy losses transformers are remarkably efficient (up to 98 per cent efficiency is common) and they are in fact among the most efficient devices ever developed.

If we now assume the transfer of energy from primary to secondary to be 100 per cent efficient, then

power in primary = power in secondary

and therefore:

$$\frac{I_s}{I_p} = \frac{n_p}{n_s}$$

and so a step up transformer for voltage will be a step down transformer for current, and vice versa.

This stepping up of the current can be demonstrated by two exciting demonstrations, the primary coil being connected to the mains in both cases.

In the first experiment the secondary coil is of only six turns and is shorted by a nail. When the power is switched on the current in the nail is so great that it melts. An arc can then be struck between the two broken ends, so welding them together again.

In the second experiment the secondary is simply an aluminium trough which contains water. When the power is switched on the current in the aluminium is so great that the water boils!

The transmission of electricity

The transformer is a vital part of the National Grid which distributes electrical energy around the country.

Electrical energy is generated in power stations by generators at a potential of 25 kV. It is first stepped up to 400 kV by a transformer and then transmitted across the country in aluminium cables roughly 2 cm in diameter.

High voltages are used because the power loss per kilometre (I^2R) for a given power output will be much less at high voltage and low current than at low voltage and high current. Despite this, even after the current has been reduced many transmission lines carry up to 2500 A! (What must the current output from the generators be in these cases?)

In Britain the grid system can meet a simultaneous demand of 56 000 MW supplied through some 8000 km of high-voltage transmission line. Alternating current is used in the National Grid, although this has not always been the case, because it may be transformed to high voltage. However, the underground cross-Channel link between Britain and France uses d.c. because of the large losses in the dielectric with a.c.

A simplified diagram of part of the grid system is in Figure 46.25.

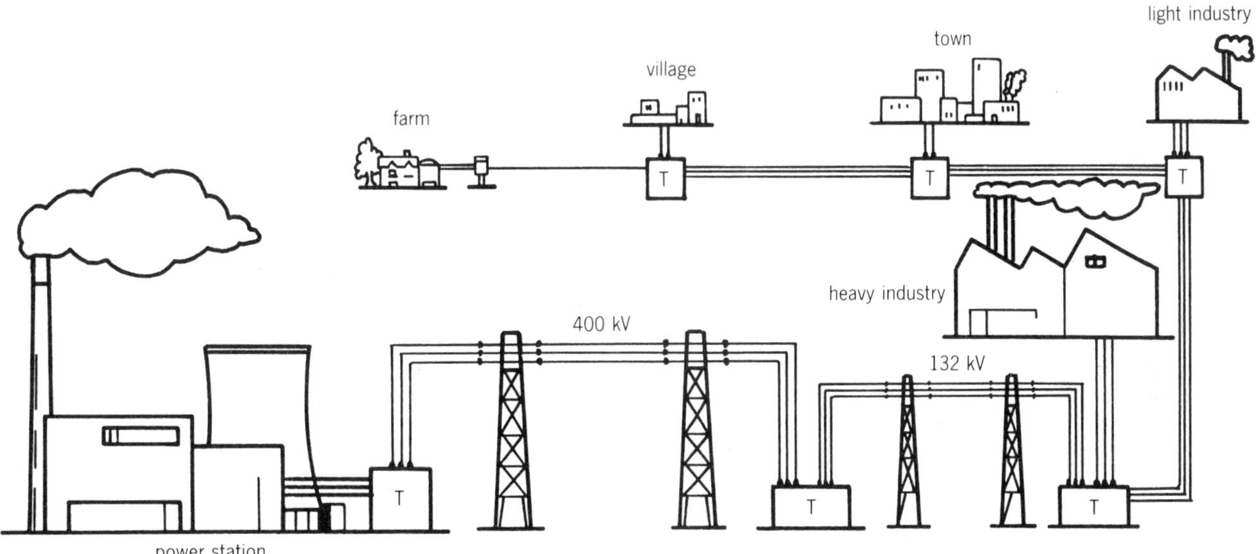

Figure 46.25

> **Student investigation**
>
> Construct a model power line using a 12 V power supply as the 'power station' and two 1 m lengths of constantan wire as the power lines. Investigate the power losses with 12 V d.c. and then with 12 V a.c., and finally with two 20:1 transformers. A lamp should be placed at the power station end and another at the house end.

20 Estimate the power loss per kilometre in an aluminium alloy cable 2 cm in diameter carrying a current of 2500 A, if the resistivity of the aluminium alloy is 5×10^{-8} Ω m.

47 · Electrostatics

Static electricity may be defined as **electric charge at rest.**

There are many effects due to static electricity that can easily be observed. It is well known that if you wear a woollen jumper over a nylon blouse then small sparks can be made when you take it off and a piece of polythene rubbed with a duster will attract small pieces of paper. A plastic comb rubbed with a cloth will make someone's hair stand on end if it is placed near it. If you rub a balloon on a jumper the balloon will often stick to the wall. Next time you look at a television screen notice the way that dust collects on it.

The uses of static electricity include electrostatic paint sprays (a charge is placed on the metal to be sprayed and an opposite charge on the paint spray), garden sprays (charging the droplets makes them stick to the leaves) and electrostatic dust collectors in chimneys.

The discovery of static electricity is usually attributed to Thales in around 600 B.C., and to detect it we normally either investigate the electric field that it produces or else discharge the charged body and observe the small current produced.

One early recorded use of static was the spinning of silk on an amber spindle by the Greeks. The friction between the silk and the amber caused the amber to become charged and this helped the silk to stick to it. The word for electricity itself comes from the Greek word for amber – *elektron*.

Gilbert (1540–1603) found that he could not charge metal objects but in 1734 du Fay succeeded in doing this but used an insulating handle. In 1729 Gray found that static electricity could be discharged from an object through the human body thus giving the idea of conductors and insulators.

In 1745, du Fay discovered that there were two types of static charge, positive and negative, and no more. This was later confirmed by Benjamin Franklin (1706–1790).

Glass rubbed with silk becomes positively charged. Ebonite rubbed with fur becomes negatively charged. Polythene rubbed with a duster becomes negatively charged.

It is easy to show that two like charges repel each other while two unlike charges attract by using the apparatus shown in Figure 47.1(*a*). The two graphite-coated polystyrene balls will either swing together or apart depending on the nature of their charge.

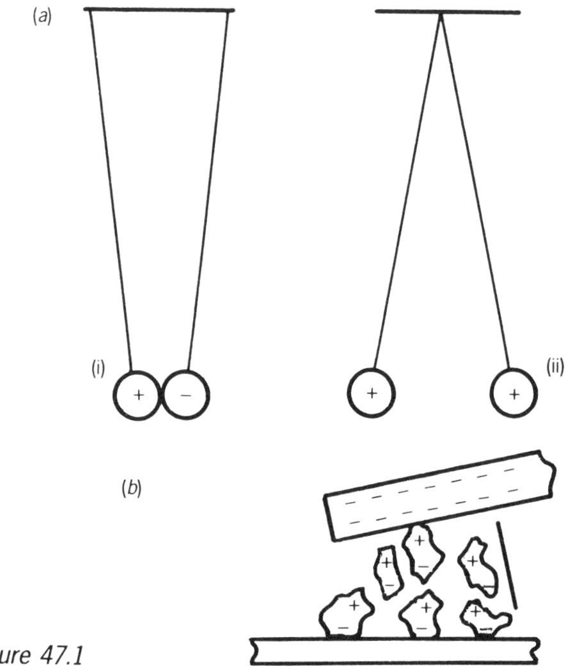

Figure 47.1

Uncharged pieces of paper will be attracted to a charged rod because of movement of charge within the paper (see Figure 47.1(*b*)).

The actual magnitude of this attractive or repulsive force is given by Coulomb's law – (see page 330).

Charged conductors

In any conductor there are charge carriers that are free to move. If two regions of the conductor at different potentials then charge will move until the potential becomes the same at all points within it.

Since the potential is the same at all points there is no change of potential with distance, that is $\mathrm{d}V/\mathrm{d}x = 0$. Now the electric field intensity (E) is given by the formula $E = -\mathrm{d}V/\mathrm{d}x$ (see page 332) and so E is also zero, that is,

There is no electric field within a charged conductor.

Using Gauss's theorem (see page 330) it can be shown that this requires the following:

(*a*) there is no excess charge within a charge conductor, that is, any excess charge is on the surface of the conductor;

(*b*) the excess charge is entirely on the *outer* surface of a hollow charged conductor.

The field at the surface of a charged conductor must be perpendicular to the surface at all points. If this were not true there would be a component of electric field intensity in the surface, so causing a further movement of charge.

The electric field

An electric field may be described in terms of lines of force in much the same way as can a magnetic field. These lines of force represent the directions of motion of a small positive charge placed at that point in the field, assuming that the charge is so small that the field is not changed significantly by the presence of the charge.

We will deal with the mathematical aspects of electric fields later (see page 332), but some of their properties will be considered here.

Figure 47.2 shows an alternative way of considering an electric field – by considering the potential at any point in the field. If we then imagine all points in the field at equal potential to be joined, we form what are known as **equipotential surfaces.**

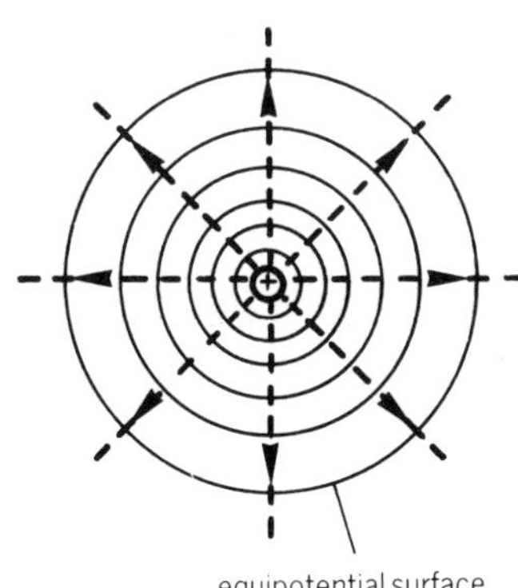

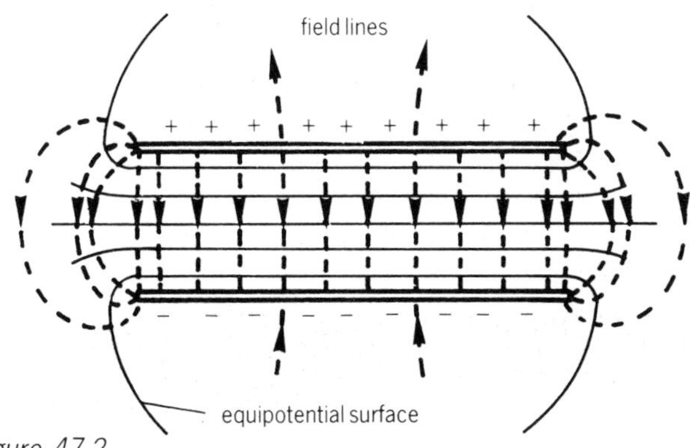

Figure 47.2

The direction of a line of force is always at right angles to an equipotential surface.

The distribution of charge over a surface depends on the curvature of the surface, the charge density being greater on sharply curved surfaces. The distribution

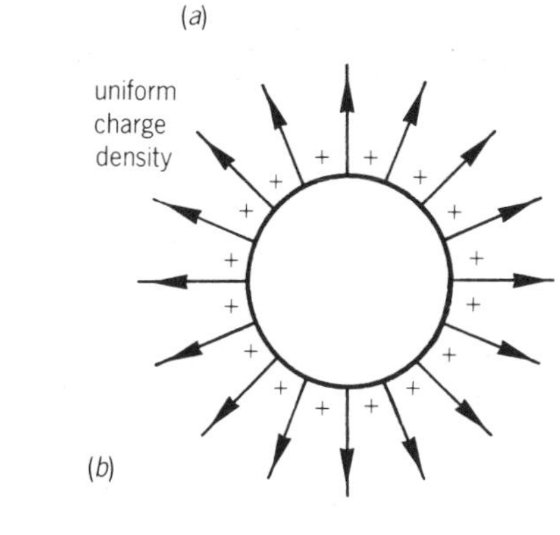

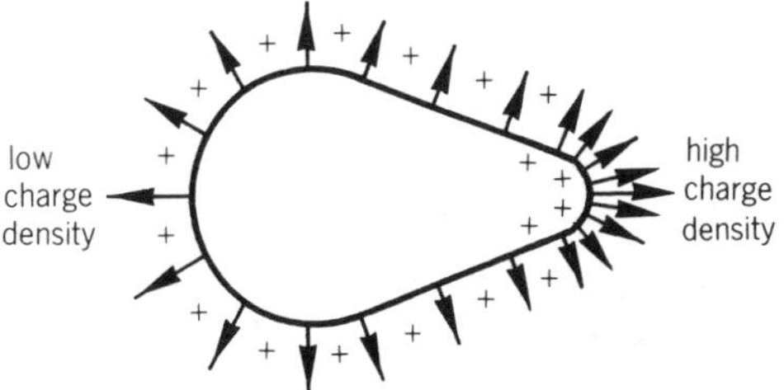

Figure 47.3

of charge and lines of force for two differently shaped objects are shown in Figure 47.3.

Electric field flux

Suppose that the electric field of intensity E makes an angle θ with a small surface of area ΔA (figure 47.4) then the electric field flux ψ is defined as:

$$\psi = E \cos \theta \, \Delta A$$

For any closed surface the flux is taken as positive if the lines of flux point outwards ($\theta < 90°$) and negative if they point inwards ($\theta > 90°$).

For a closed surface the flux emerging from it is written as:

$$\psi = \int E \cos \theta \, \mathrm{d}A$$

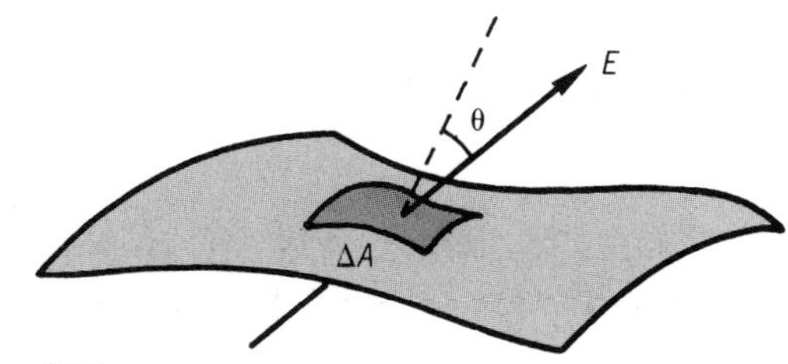

Figure 47.4

For example, for a unit charge the flux emerging through an imaginary sphere of radius r drawn round the charge:

$$\psi = \int E \cos \theta \, \mathrm{d}A = 4\pi r^2 E$$

Coulomb's law

If we consider two isolated point electric charges Q_1 and Q_2 separated by a distance d, then the force between them is given by Coulomb's law, proposed in 1785:

$$F = \frac{1}{4\pi\epsilon}\frac{Q_1 Q_2}{d^2}$$

where ϵ is a constant known as the **permittivity** of the medium in which the charges are situated. You can see from the formula that ϵ will have units $C^2\ N^{-1}\ m^{-2}$ but it is usually expressed in farads per metre ($F\ m^{-1}$). The reason for this will be seen later. If the charges are in a vacuum then the formula becomes

$$F = \frac{1}{4\pi\epsilon_0}\frac{Q_1 Q_2}{d^2}$$

where ϵ_0 is the **permittivity of free space**, the value of ϵ_0 being $8.85 \times 10^{-12}\ F\ m^{-1}$.

We can compare the permittivity (ϵ) of a material with that of free space (ϵ_o) and define a quantity known as the **relative permittivity** (ϵ_r) as permittivity/permittivity of free space. Then

$$\epsilon = \epsilon_r \epsilon_0$$

The table below gives the relative permittivities (ϵ_r) of a number of common substances at 293 K.

Solid		*Liquid*		*Gas*	
Amber	2.8	Propanone	21.3	Air	1.000 0536
Ebonite	2.8	Castor oil	4.5	Carbon dioxide	1.000 986
Glass	5–10	Ethoxyethane	4.3	Helium	1.000 07
Mica	5.7–6.7	Glycerol	43	Hydrogen	1.000 27
Wax	2–2.3	Paraffin	2.2	Nitrogen	1.000 580
Polystyrene	2.55	Nitrobenzene	35.7	Oxygen	1.000 53
PVC	4.5	Turpentine	2.23	Water vapour (393 K)	1.000 60
Teflon	2.1	Water	80.4		

Values for gases are at STP.

Gauss's theorem

Gauss's theorem states that for any closed surface:

$$\epsilon_0 \psi \doteq \Sigma Q$$

where ΣQ is the algebraic sum of the charges enclosed within that surface. This means that if a surface encloses a pair of equal but opposite charges the net charge is zero.

1 Calculate the electrostatic force between two electrons separated by a distance of 10^{-10} m (roughly the diameter of an atom). (Charge on the electron = 1.6×10^{-19} C)

2 The dimensions of atomic nuclei are of the order of 10^{-14} m. If two alpha-particles are separated by that distance, calculate

(*a*) the electrostatic force that one alpha-particle exerts on the other,

(*b*) the resulting acceleration of the alpha-particle.

Each alpha-particle has a positive charge of $+3.2 \times 10^{-19}$ C and a mass of 6.68×10^{-27} kg.

3 Two small conducting spheres each of mass 10 mg suspended from the same point by non-conducting threads 10 cm long. They are then each given the same charge and the threads each become inclined at 30° to the vertical. Calculate the charge on each sphere.

4 Two oil droplets 0.1 mm in diameter acquire a charge of 10^{-10} C by being sprayed through a nozzle. Calculate

(*a*) the force between them when they are separated by 1 mm in air,

(*b*) the resulting acceleration.

(Density of oil = 850 kg m^{-3})

Testing a cardiac pacemaker in a high intensity electric field (Reproduced with the kind permission of the National Grid Company)

Electrostatic and gravitational attraction

It is interesting to compare the electrostatic and gravitational forces for, say, the electron circling a hydrogen atom.

The gravitational attraction to the nucleus is:

$$F = \frac{GmM}{r^2} = 4 \times 10^{-47}\ \text{N}$$

and the electrostatic attraction:

$$F = \frac{1}{4\pi\epsilon_0}\frac{e^2}{r^2} = 8 \times 10^{-8}\ \text{N}$$

This shows that the electrostatic force is some 10^{39} times stronger than the gravitational force and it is therefore the electrostatic force that is responsible for binding

(*a*) electrons to nuclei to form atoms,
(*b*) atoms to atoms to form molecules, and
(*c*) molecules to molecules to form solids and liquids.

For large bodies carrying a small charge the gravitational force predominates.

5 (*a*) Bits of paper are attracted to a charged comb even though they have no charge. Why?
(*b*) Petrol tankers sometimes have chains dangling down on to the road behind them. Why?
(*c*) It was once thought that car sickness was due to the electric field inside the car. Comment on this.
(*d*) Clingfilm can be made to stick simply by stretching it across a container and pressing it against the sides. Why?
(*e*) 'The gold leaf electroscope is an instrument for measuring total potential rather than charge.' Comment on this statement.

The repulsion of like charges may be demonstrated very simply by placing some small pieces of paper on the dome of a Van de Graaff generator. When the machine is switched on the paper gains the same charge as the dome and is repelled from it violently, the paper pieces moving rapidly outwards.

Student investigation

This experiment is a modern version of one proposed by Faraday using an ice bucket and is therefore often called Faraday's ice pail experiment.

Set up the apparatus as shown in Figure 47.5. Charge the small metal disc and then lower it into the sphere being careful not to touch the inner surface. Observe the following:

(*a*) the deflection of the meter with the disc well inside the sphere,
(*b*) the deflection of the meter when the disc touches the inside of the sphere and is then taken out of it.

The results should show that

(*i*) if a charged body is placed inside a hollow conductor then it induces an equal and opposite charge on the inside of the conductor and an equal and similar charge on the outside, and
(*ii*) the *net* charge inside a hollow charged conductor is zero and therefore the field is also zero.

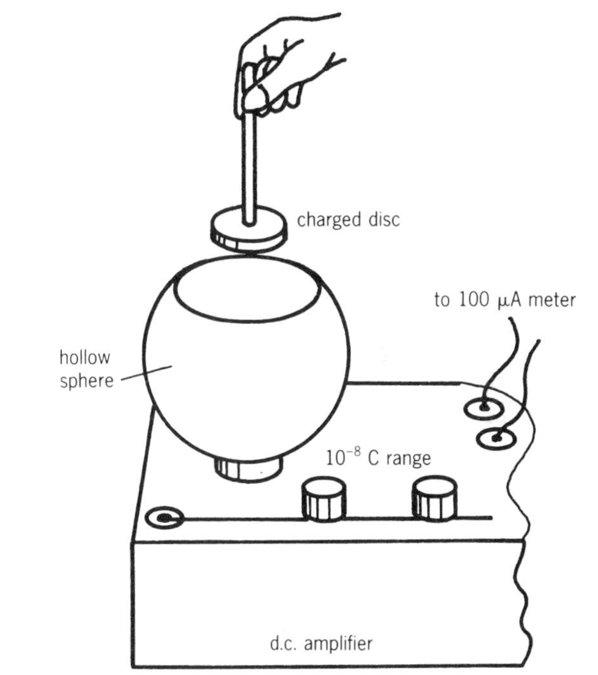

Figure 47.5

Potential and field strength

The **potential** at a point is defined as **the energy transformed in bringing a unit positive charge from infinity to that point against the action of the field.** The units are volts (V) or joules per coulomb ($J\ C^{-1}$).

The **potential difference** between two points is therefore the energy transformed when unit charge is moved from one point to the other. We take the practical zero of potential as the Earth and the theoretical zero of potential as infinity, but since we are nearly always dealing with potential difference this apparent contradiction is a not a problem.

Potential due to a point charge

Consider the potential due to a charge Q as shown in Figure 47.6.

Figure 47.6

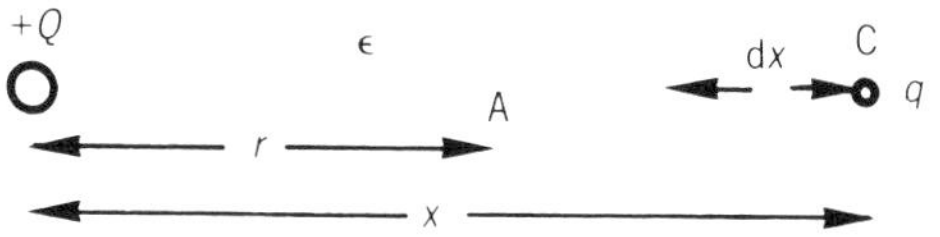

The force on a small charge q at C is assumed to remain constant as q is moved a small distance dx towards Q against the repulsion of the field. Therefore the work done by an external force acting on q and the energy transformed is:

$$dW = F\,dx \qquad \text{but} \qquad F = \frac{1}{4\pi\epsilon}\,\frac{Qq}{x^2}$$

$$\text{therefore} \qquad dW = \frac{Qq}{4\pi\epsilon}\,\frac{-dx}{x^2} \qquad \text{and so}$$

$$W = \frac{-Qq}{4\pi\epsilon}\int_{\infty}^{r}\frac{dx}{x^2} = \frac{Qq}{4\pi\epsilon}\,\frac{1}{r}$$

Therefore if we consider unit charge then this becomes the potential at that point.

$$V = \frac{W}{q} = \frac{1}{4\pi\epsilon}\,\frac{Q}{r}$$

For a sphere of radius r carrying a charge Q the potential at its surface is given by:

$$V = \frac{1}{4\pi\epsilon}\,\frac{Q}{r}$$

The electric field strength

An electric field is present at a point if a force of electrostatic origin acts on a charge placed at that point. The electric field E at the point is defined as **the force per unit charge at that point**:

$$E = \frac{F}{Q}$$

The units for E are newtons per coulomb ($N\ C^{-1}$) or volts per metre ($V\ m^{-1}$).

Consider a charge Q in an electric field of intensity E. Now the work (δE) done in moving this charge from A to B (Figure 47.7) is given by:

$$\delta W = \text{force} \times \text{distance} = F\,\delta x = EQ\,\delta x$$

If the potential difference between A and B is δV, then

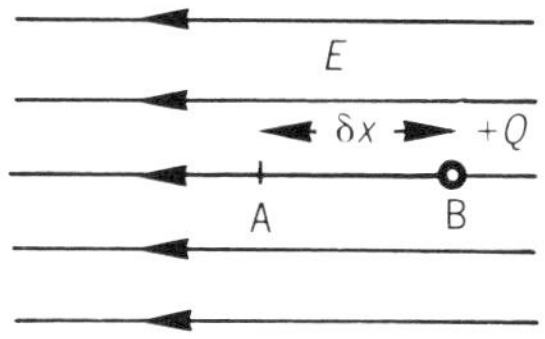

Figure 47.7

$$\delta V = \text{work done per unit charge} = -\frac{\delta W}{Q} = -E\,\delta x$$

Therefore:

$$\delta V = -E\delta x \qquad \text{or} \qquad E = -\frac{\delta V}{\delta x}$$

In the limit this becomes:

$$E = -\frac{dV}{dx}$$

The electric field intensity E is the negative potential gradient at a point in the field.

Graphs of the variation of field and potential for a sphere

The graphs in Figure 47.8 show how the electric field intensity and potential vary around a sphere. You can

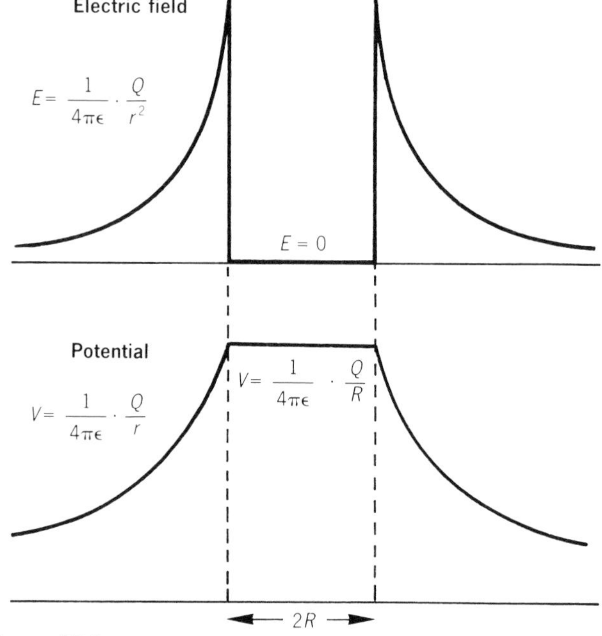

Figure 47.8

see that the electric field intensity is zero inside a hollow charged sphere and this in fact applies to any hollow charged conductor, whatever its shape.

Example

Calculate the charge carried by a sphere of radius 10 cm in air if the potential at its surface is 100 kV. (These figures are approximately those for a school Van de Graaff generator.)

$$Q = 10^5 \times 4\pi \times 1.000\,053 \times 0.1$$
$$= 1.25 \times 10^5 \text{ C}$$

But since the charge carried by one electron is 1.6×10^{-19} C, this charge is equivalent to 7.8×10^{23} electrons!

The field due to a point charge

Consider the field at a point P a distance d from a point charge Q (Figure 47.9). The force on a small charge q placed at P is:

$$F = -\frac{1}{4\pi\epsilon_0}\frac{Qq}{d^2}$$

Therefore the electric field at P is:

$$E = \frac{F}{q} = \frac{1}{4\pi\epsilon_0}\frac{Q}{d^2}$$

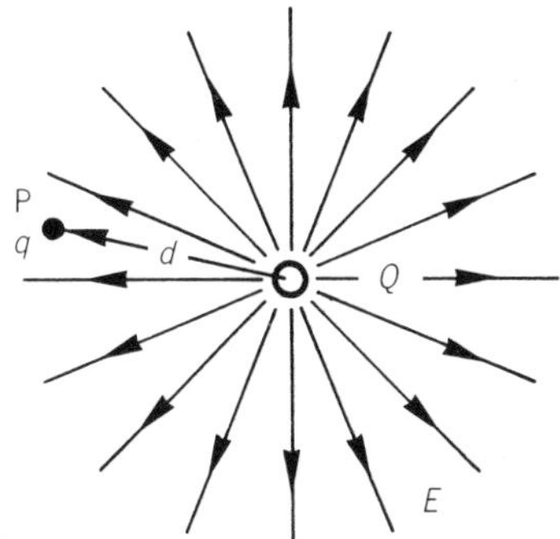

Figure 47.9

6 The high-voltage terminal of a Van de Graaff generator consists of a sphere of radius 0.20 m. Calculate
(*a*) the maximum potential to which it can be raised in air, for which the breakdown potential is 3.0×10^6 V m^{-1},
(*b*) the charge stored on the sphere in this condition,
(*c*) the energy stored on the sphere, and
(*d*) the time taken to achieve this potential if the current conveyed to the sphere by the belt is 0.1 μA.

The electric dipole

This consists of two unlike charges $+q$ and $-q$ separated by a distance d, as shown in Figure 47.10. The **dipole moment** is defined as:

$$p = qd$$

In a uniform electric field a dipole experiences a torque but no resultant force. Since $F = Eq$, we have

$$\text{torque} = Fd\sin\theta = Eq\,d\sin\theta$$
$$= pE\sin\theta$$

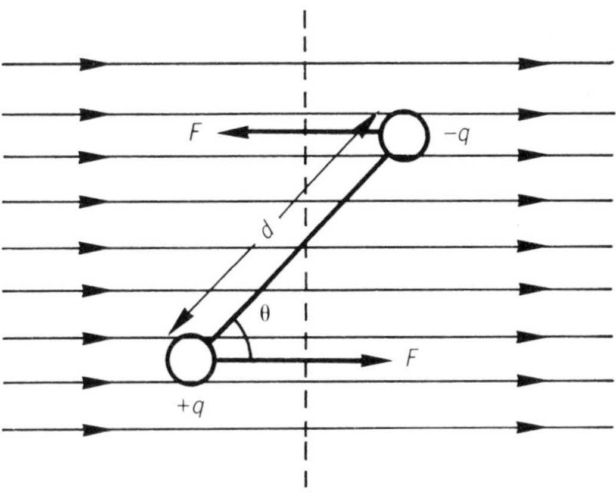

Figure 47.10

If the field is non-uniform the dipole will not only rotate, it will also move along the field direction.

7 Explain whether it is possible for:
(*a*) the potential at a point to be zero when the electric field intensity at that point is not zero,
(*b*) the electric field intensity at a point to be zero while the potential at that point is not zero,
(*c*) charge to be distributed in such a way that both the potential and the electric field are zero.

8 Calculate
(*a*) the work done in charging a sphere of radius 5 cm to a potential of 1000 V,
(*b*) the electric field intensity at distances of 1, 2, 5 and 10 cm from a charge of 10 μC,
(*c*) the potential energy of an electron in a hydrogen atom if it is separated from the proton by a distance of 5×10^{-11} m, the charge on the electron and proton being equal and opposite and of magnitude 1.6×10^{-19} C.

Charge density

The charge density σ on a surface of area A is defined as:

$$\sigma = Q/A$$

and since for an isolated charge Q a spherical surface round the charge at a distance r has an area of $4\pi r^2$ we have:

$$E = \frac{1}{4\pi\epsilon_0}\frac{Q}{r^2} \quad \text{and} \quad \sigma = Q/A$$

Therefore

$$E = \frac{\sigma}{\epsilon_0}$$

and this is true for a surface of any shape as r tends to infinity.

The gold leaf electroscope

The charge may be detected using a gold leaf electroscope. Strictly speaking the gold leaf electroscope measures the repulsion between a plate and a small piece of gold leaf that is fixed to it.

Figure 47.11 shows the basic form of the electroscope. Any charge placed on the plate will distribute itself over the leaf and rod as well, and so the leaf will be repelled. The greater the charge the greater the repulsion.

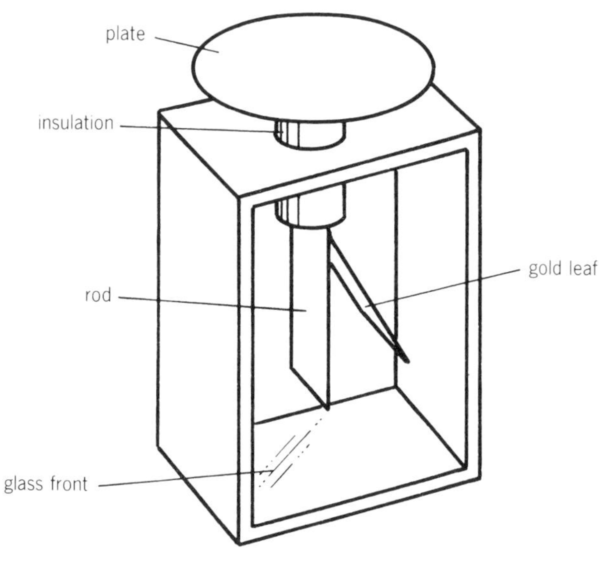

Figure 47.11

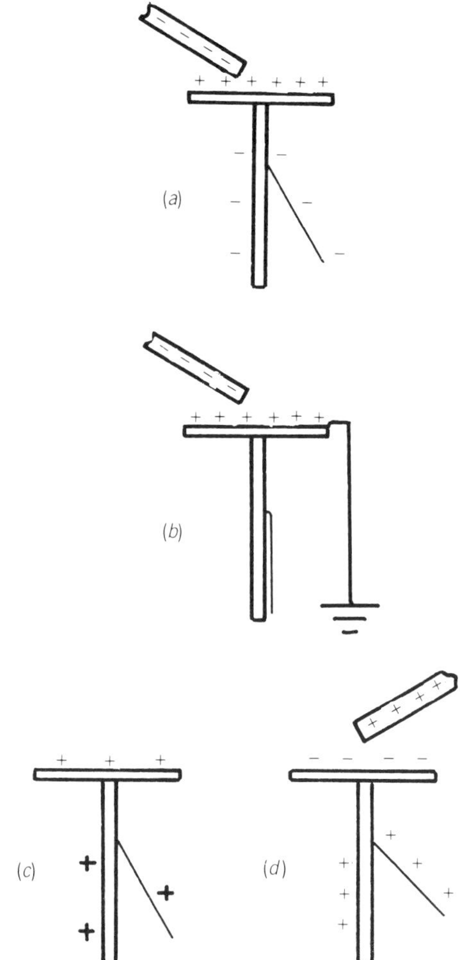

Figure 47.12

The electroscope may be charged by induction as shown in Figure 47.12. The negatively charged rod induces a positive charge on the plate and the leaf therefore becomes negative. If the plate is now earthed while the rod is still there the negative charges flow to earth and the electroscope is left positively charged. It should be noticed that in Figure 47.12(*b*) the electroscope carries a charge but the leaf does not diverge. It is at zero potential and so the divergence of the leaf indicates potential rather than charge.

If a positively charged body is brought close to the leaf (Figure 47.12(*d*)) the leaf diverges further. The electroscope can therefore be regarded as an electrostatic voltmeter.

9 The electric field near the surface of the Earth is 100 V m^{-1}. Calculate the surface charge density on the Earth's surface.

Induction

It is possible to charge a body without actually touching it – this process is known as **induction** and can be demonstrated by the following simple experiment. In this case no charge is lost by the charging body.

Student investigation

Two insulated conducting spheres A and B are placed in contact and a negatively charged rod is brought up close to, but not touching sphere A (Figure 47.13(*a*)). The spheres are then separated (Figure 47.13(*b*)) and after this the rod is removed.
To investigate the charge on the two spheres they may be touched in turn on to the brass rod on the electrometer (set to 10^{-8} C range).

Both spheres are now seen to be charged and in opposite senses, although neither was touched by the charged rod and the charged rod did not lose any charge.This can be explained as follows: electrons within A are repelled from the rod and flow to B thus leaving A with a positive charge. The reverse would happen if a positively charged rod were used.

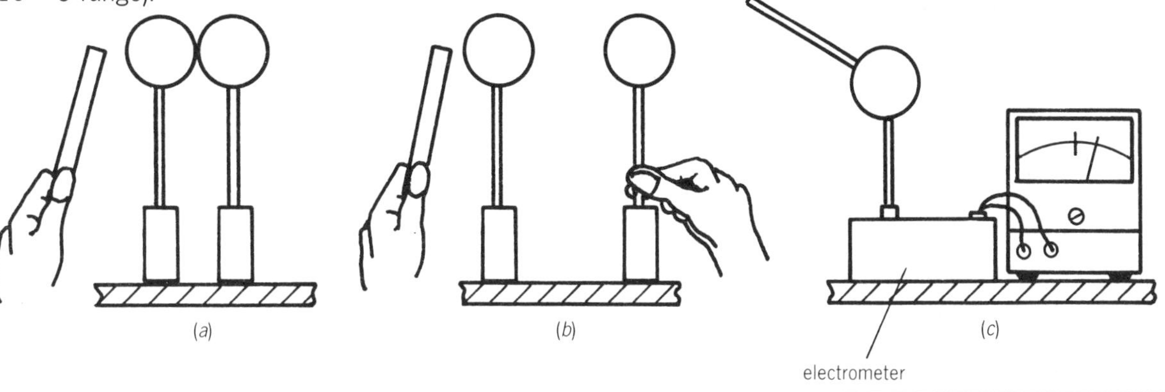

Figure 47.13

The electrophorus

The principle of electrostatic induction is demonstrated very well by the electrophorus, which is a device for supplying large quantities of charge and which may therefore be used to raise an insulated conductor to a high potential. The diagrams in Figure 47.14 demonstrate its operation.

A polythene slab in a metal dish is rubbed so that it acquires a negative charge on its upper surface. A metal plate fixed to an insulating handle is now placed on the polythene and so it acquires an induced charge, positive below and negative above. The plate is now earthed and then removed from the polythene, thus carrying away a positive charge. This may be transferred to another insulated conductor. The process may be repeated until the charge on the polythene leaks away, thus raising the potential of the second insulated conductor to a high value.

It is important to realise that the energy required to produce the charge comes from the mechanical energy used to separate the metal plate from the polythene (Figure 47.14(*e*)).

10 An electrophorus may be used to produce a high potential without loss of charge from the source.
(*a*) Does this violate the law of conservation of energy? Explain.
(*b*) If not, where does the energy come from to produce this potential?

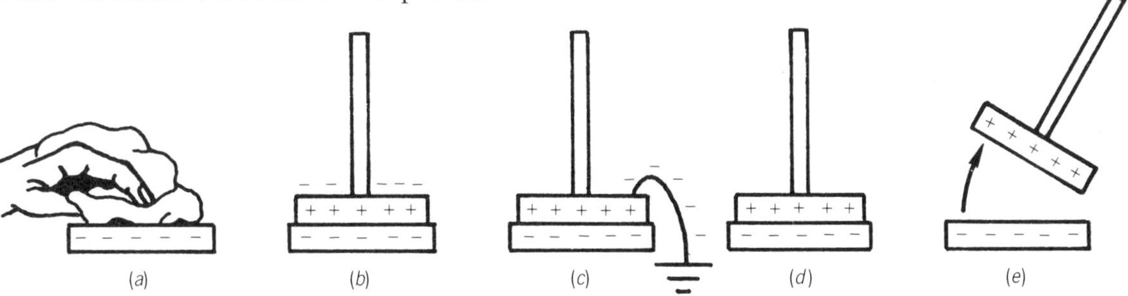

Figure 47.14

48 · Capacitors

Any two conductors separated by an insulator are known as a **capacitor**. The two conductors usually carry an equal and opposite charge such that the net charge on the capacitor as a whole is zero. In what follows when we speak of a capacitor as having a charge Q we mean that the conductor at the higher potential has a charge $+Q$ and that at the lower potential a charge $-Q$.

A capacitor may be thought of as an electrical device that will store electric charge. It can be compared with a bucket that will store water.

> The ability to store charge is called the **capacitance** of the capacitor.

Capacitance corresponds to the volume of our bucket.

Capacitors have many applications in electrical circuits, including the following:

tuning in radio circuits
smoothing rectified current from power supplies
elimination of sparking in switches
in timing circuits
storing large quantities of charge for use in research such as nuclear fusion

General formula and the farad

If the potential across the capacitor changes by V when a charge Q is placed on it then the capacitance is given by the formula:

$$\text{capacitance } (C) = \frac{\text{charge } (Q)}{\text{potential difference } (V)}$$

The capacitance of a capacitor is measured in **farads** (F), one farad being defined by

> A capacitor has a capacitance of 1 farad if the potential across it rises by 1 volt when a charge of 1 coulomb is placed on it.

The farad is a large capacitance. Using the formula on page 337 for the parallel-plate capacitor you can show that if the plates of a 1 F capacitor were separated by a distance of 1 mm in a vacuum, the plates would have an area of $1.13 \times 10^8\ \text{m}^2$. This corresponds to a square with sides about 6.5 miles long!

For this reason capacitances are usually expressed in microfarads (μF) or picofarads (pF). One micro farad = 10^{-6} F and one picofarad = 10^{-12} F.

Student investigation

This experiment illustrated in Figure 48.1 will help you to investigate the properties of a parallel-plate capacitor.

To charge the capacitor, simply touch its top surface with the flying lead from the h.t. supply. To measure the charge on it, touch it with the lead from the input socket of the electrometer.

You should try variations in both the spacing of the plates and their area of overlap.

Plot suitable graphs to show the relation between these quantities.
(The electrometer should be used on its 10^{-8} C range.)

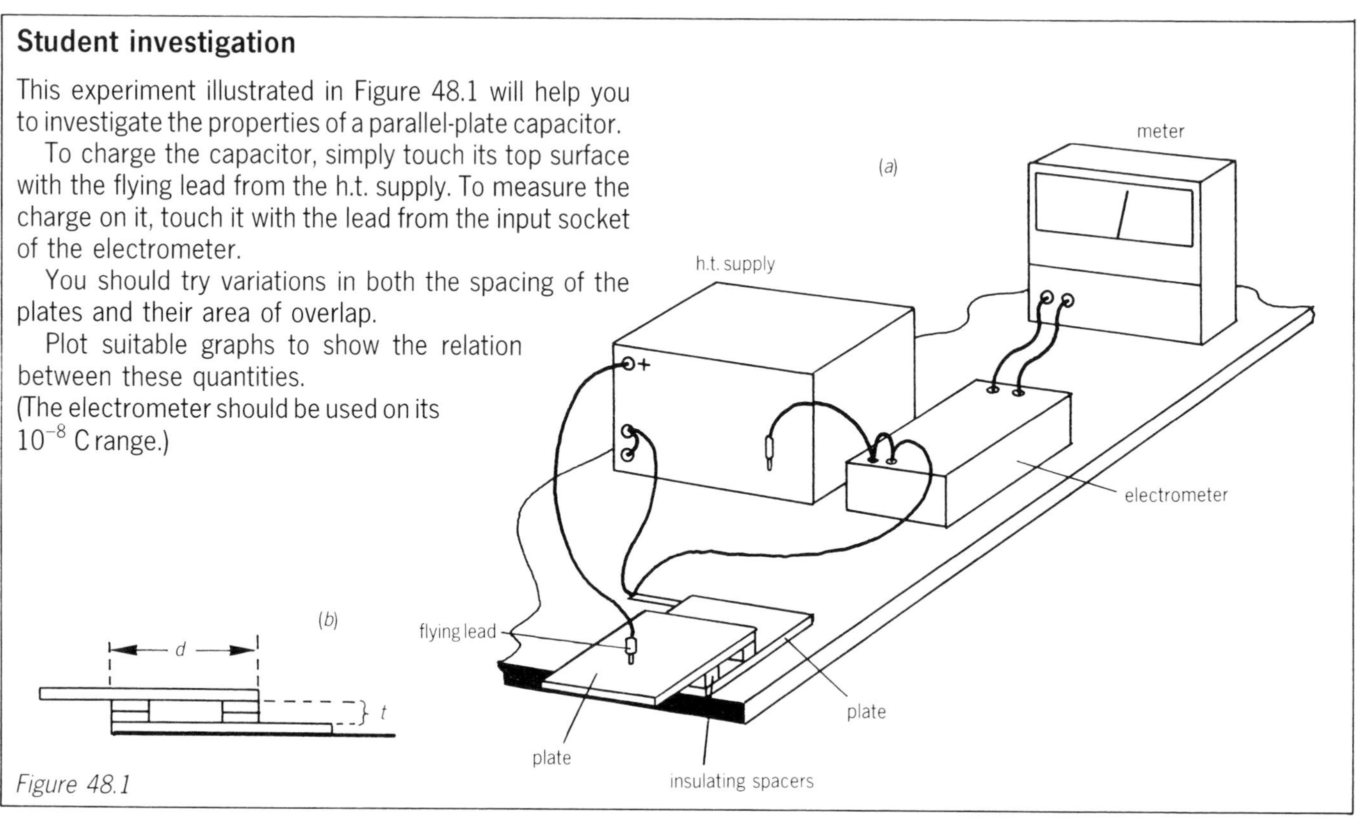

Figure 48.1

The parallel-plate capacitor

It is useful to consider a simple form of capacitor, that in the form of two metal plates with a material of permittivity ϵ filling the space between them as shown in Figure 48.2.

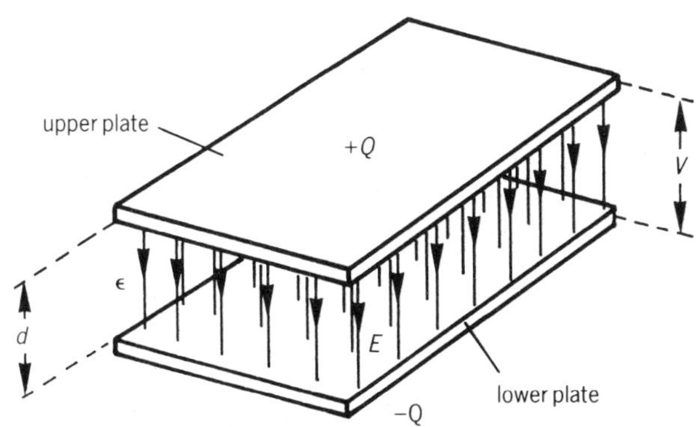

Figure 48.2

Let the area of the plates be A and their separation d; let one plate have a charge $+Q$ and the other $-Q$, and let the capacitance be C. Assume the field between the plates to be uniform and that the charge density is also uniform.

The charge density on the plates (σ) is Q/A and therefore the electric field intensity E between the plates is given by

$$E = \frac{\sigma}{\epsilon} = \frac{Q}{\epsilon A}$$

But if V is the potential difference between the plates we have:

$$E = \frac{V}{d} = \frac{Q}{\epsilon A}$$

and therefore, since $C = Q/V$

$$C = \frac{\epsilon A}{d}$$

Therefore the capacitance increases if the area of the plates is increased or their separation decreased.

You can see that the insertion of a material with a high permittivity will increase the capacitance of a capacitor. An explanation of this is given on the following page.

Example

Calculate the capacitance of a pair of parallel plates of area 25 cm^2 if they are separated by a piece of Perspex 0.1 mm thick. Take the relative permittivity of Perspex to be 3.5.

$$\text{Capacitance} = \frac{8.85 \times 10^{-12} \times 3.5 \times 25 \times 10^{-4}}{10^{-4}}$$

$$= 7.43 \times 10^{-10} = 0.74 \text{ nF.}$$

If we consider the formula for the parallel-plate capacitor we can see what happens as we change the plate separation. There are two different cases to consider:

(*a*) where the capacitor remains connected to the source of electrical potential, and

(*b*) where the capacitor is disconnected after the initial charge Q has been placed on the plates.

(*a*) The potential V remains constant and therefore the charge on the plates varies since $V = Q/C$ and $C = \epsilon A/d$. As the separation of the plates is increased the charge on them decreases to maintain a constant value of V. The electric field intensity between the plates therefore falls.

(*b*) If the supply is disconnected, however, then it is the charge on the plates that remains constant and the potential difference between them increases as the plates are separated. The electric field intensity remains constant in this case. This can be explained by the fact that work has to be done on the plates to separate them.

Student investigation

Using a parallel-plate air capacitor similar to that shown above, investigate the effect of placing a slab of polythene between the plates.

Position the two metal plates vertically side by side, the gap between them being slightly greater than the thickness of the polythene. Charge the capacitor plates and then disconnect them from the power supply. Carefully lower the piece of polythene into the gap between the plates and observe the variation in potential across the plates.

Record the p.d. variation and plot a graph of p.d. against the area of polythene within the plates.

The action of a dielectric

When a dielectric material is placed between the plates of a parallel-plate (or other) capacitor the capacitance increases. The reason for this is shown in Figure 48.3.

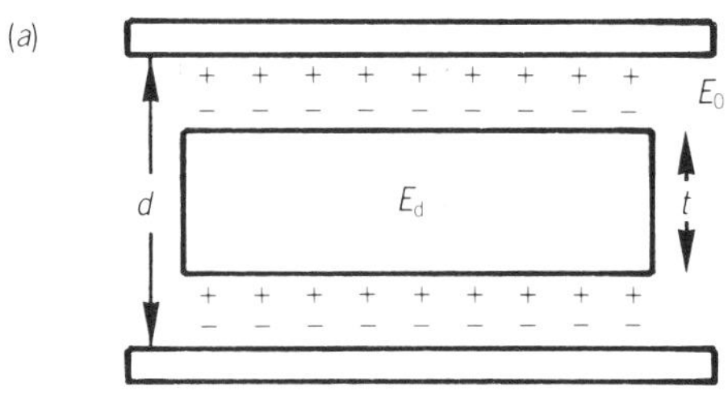

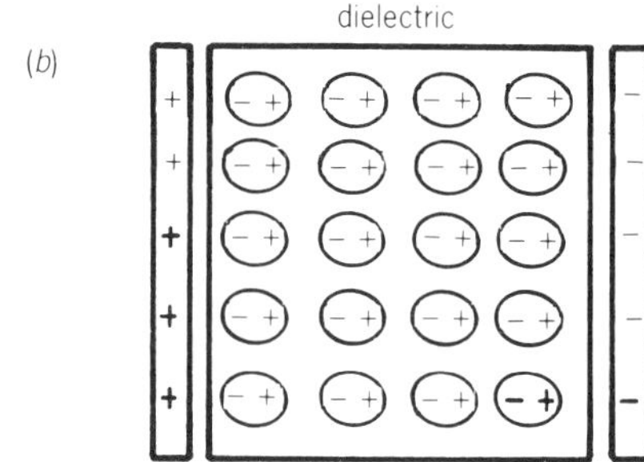

Figure 48.3

The charges on the plates of the capacitor induce opposite charges on the two surfaces of the dielectric. This has the effect of reducing the p.d. across the capacitor.

This can be explained as follows. Under the action of the electric field within the dielectric the molecules become polarised and are aligned as shown in Figure 48.3(b).

Since the capacitance of a capacitor is given by the formula $C = Q/V$, if the p.d. (V) across the capacitor is reduced the capacitance must be increased.

The capacitance of a parallel-plate capacitor with a material of relative permittivity ϵ_r filling the space between the plates is

$$C = \frac{\epsilon_0 \epsilon_r A}{d}$$

where ϵ_r is the ratio of the capacitance of the capacitor to the capacitance it would possess if the dielectric were removed.

The capacitance of a capacitor when only a thickness t of the air space is filled is

$$C = \frac{\epsilon_0 \epsilon_r A}{\epsilon_r (d - t) + t}$$

The following example should illustrate how to deal with some of the problems of dielectrics and capacitors.

Example

A parallel-plate capacitor has an area of 100 cm^2, a plate separation of 1.0 cm and is charged initially to a potential of 100 V (call this V_0).

The supply is disconnected and a slab of dielectric, 0.5 cm thick and of relative permittivity 7, is then placed between the plates as shown in Figure 48.4.

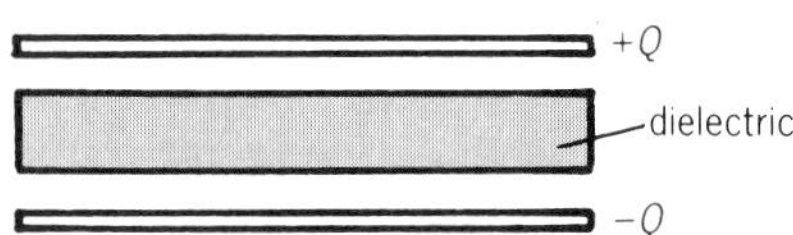

Figure 48.4

Calculate

(a) the capacitance C_0 before the slab is inserted,

(b) the charge on the plates Q,

(c) the electric field strength in the gap between the plates and the dielectric,

(d) the electric field strength within the dielectric,

(e) the potential difference between the plates after the dielectric is inserted, and

(f) the capacitance when the dielectric has been inserted.

(a) $C_0 = \dfrac{\epsilon_0 A}{d} = \dfrac{8.9 \times 10^{-12} \times 10^{-2}}{10^{-2}} = 8.9 \times 10^{-12}$ F.

(b) $Q = C_0 V_0 = 8.9 \times 10^{-12} \times 100 = 8.9 \times 10^{-10}$C.

(c) $E_0 = \dfrac{Q}{\epsilon_0 A} = \dfrac{8.9 \times 10^{-10}}{8.9 \times 10^{-12} \times 10^{-2}} = 10^4$ V m^{-1}.

(d) $E_1 = \dfrac{Q}{\epsilon a} = \dfrac{E_0}{\epsilon_r} = \dfrac{10^4}{7} = 0.14 \times 10^4$ V m^{-1}.

(e) p.d. $= \dfrac{0.5 \times 10^4 + 0.5 \times 0.14 \times 10^4}{100} = 57$ V.

(f) $C = \dfrac{\epsilon A}{\epsilon_r (d - t) + t} = \dfrac{7 \epsilon_0 A}{0.04} = 15.2 \times 10^{-12}$ F.

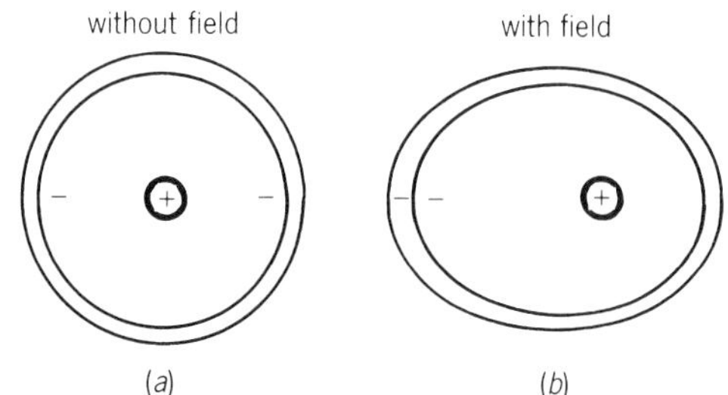

Figure 48.5

Measurement of capacitance

(*a*) Capacitance comparison using a ballistic galvanometer

If we charge up a capacitor (C) to a known potential V and then discharge it through a ballistic galvanometer the charge passed through the galvanometer is proportional to the first deflection of the instrument (θ_1). That is,

$$Q_1 \propto \theta_1$$

If the experiment is repeated with a second capacitor using the same potential we have

$$Q_2 \propto \theta_2$$

Since $Q = CV$ we can write $Q_1 = C_1V_1$ and $Q_2 = C_2V_2$; therefore $C_1 \propto \theta_1$ and $C_2 \propto \theta_2$. This gives

$$\frac{C_1}{C_2} = \frac{\theta_1}{\theta_2}$$

and so if the value of one of the capacitors is known the capacitance of the other may be found. (Notice that this method can only compare one capacitor with another.)

(*b*) Capacitance comparison by the vibrating reed method

This method is based on a rapid charge and discharge process to give a very nearly constant current from the capacitor. The circuit used is shown in Figure 48.6.

The reed switch itself contains a springy steel strip which becomes magnetised when placed inside the coil as shown. If an a.c. signal is applied to the coil the switch vibrates backwards and forwards between the two contacts 1 and 2.

It can be seen from the diagram that when the strip is in position 1 the capacitor is being charged, and when the strip is in position 2 the capacitor is discharging through the resistor R and the microammeter. The frequency of the supply is high, usually some 400 Hz, and the use of the rectifier means that the number of discharges per second is equal to the frequency of the a.c. signal f.

As long as the frequency is high enough the meter will show a steady deflection recording the average current I passing though it.

Therefore $I = Qf$ where Q is the charge given to the capacitor each time the switch is in position 1. Hence $Q = I/f$, and since $C = Q/V$ the capacitance of the capacitor is given by

$$C = \frac{I}{fV}$$

A further method using the discharge of the capacitor and a measurement of its time constant is given on page 345.

1 A certain capacitor consists of two parallel square metal plates with sides 20 cm long and initially separated by 5 mm of air. Calculate
(*a*) the capacitance of the capacitor;
(*b*) the charge stored on each plate if the p.d. between them is (i) 12 V, (ii) 100 V, (iii) 1000 V;
(*c*) the capacitance when a piece of waxed paper of relative permittivity 2.7 and 0.1 mm thick is placed between the plates.

2 Two insulated conducting plates are placed parallel to each other and about 2 cm apart. Each is connected to the cap of a gold leaf electroscope. State and explain what the electroscope shows when
(*a*) A is given a positive charge,
(*b*) B is earthed, and
(*c*) a slab of paraffin wax is placed between A and B while B is still earthed.

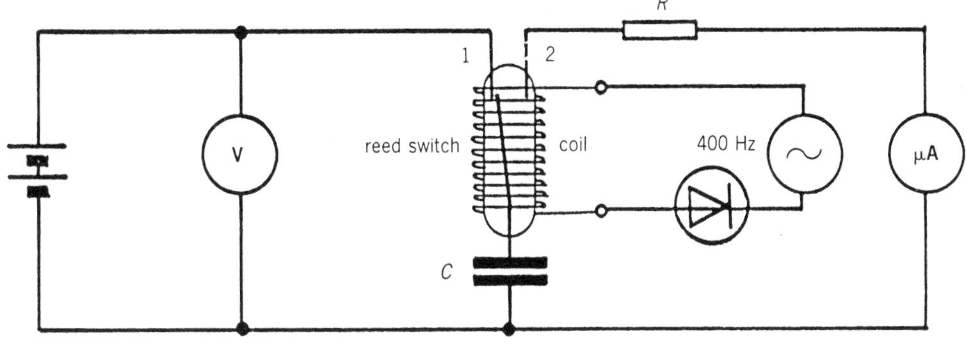

Figure 48.6

Energy of a charged capacitor

Since capacitors have the ability to store charge they are also a source of electrical energy. Care must be taken when touching capacitors because although they may be disconnected from a supply they may still retain a charge, and this stored energy can give you a serious shock!

Consider a parallel-plate capacitor as shown in Figure 48.7. Imagine that one plate carries a charge $+Q$ and that the other plate is earthed. If we take a small charge dq from one plate to the other, the work done will be $v\,dq$ where v is the potential across the plates. If the initial charge on the positive plate is Q then the total energy lost in completely discharging the capacitor is

$$\text{Energy} = \int -v\,dq = \int_0^Q \frac{q\,dq}{C} = \tfrac{1}{2}\frac{Q^2}{C} = \tfrac{1}{2}CV^2 = \tfrac{1}{2}QV$$

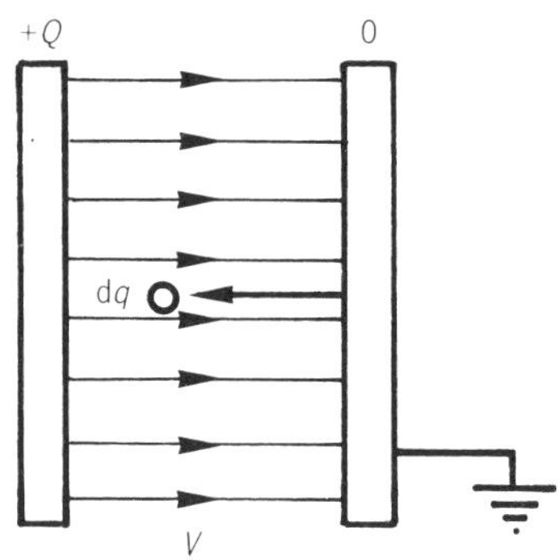

Figure 48.7

> **3** Find the energy stored in a 6 μF capacitor charged to a p.d. of 2000 V.

Example

A parallel-plate air capacitor of area 25 cm^2 and with plates 1 mm apart is charged to a potential of 100 V.

(*a*) Calculate the energy stored in it.

(*b*) The plates of the capacitor are now moved a further 1 mm apart with the power supply connected. Calculate the energy change.

(*c*) If the power supply had been disconnected before the plates had been moved apart, what would have been the energy change in this case?

(*a*) $\text{Energy} = \tfrac{1}{2}CV^2 = \tfrac{1}{2}\frac{\epsilon_0 AV^2}{d}$

$$= \frac{8.85\times10^{-12}\times25\times10^{-4}\times10^{-4}}{2\times0.001}$$

$$= 1.1\times10^{-7}\text{ J}$$

(*b*) New plate separation = 0.002 m; potential across plates is still 100 V.
New energy = 0.5 × original energy = 0.55×10^{-7} J
The difference in energy is explained by the movement of charge in the wires as the capacitor partly discharges to maintain the potential.

(*c*) New plate separation = 0.002 m; the charge on plates is unchanged but the potential increases.

$$\text{New energy} = \tfrac{1}{2}\frac{Q^2}{C} = \tfrac{1}{2}\frac{Q^2t}{\epsilon_0 A}$$

and since t is doubled the energy will be doubled to 2.2×10^{-7} J.

This increase in energy is explained by the addition of energy in the movement of the plates apart against their mutual attraction.

Capacitance formulae

The formulae for capacitors of some other common shapes are given below, although the proofs of these formulae are outside the scope of this book.

Sphere (radius a)	$4\pi\epsilon a$
Concentric spheres (radii a and b)	$\frac{4\pi\epsilon ab}{b-a}$
Concentric cylinders (radii a, b, length l)	$\frac{2\pi\epsilon l}{\ln(b/a)}$
Two long, parallel wires (separation d, radius a, length l, $d \gg a$)	$\frac{\epsilon l}{\ln(d/a)}$
Parallel-plate capacitor of area A containing a thickness x of dielectric and thickness b of air	$\frac{\epsilon A}{(\epsilon_r b + x)}$

A 750 kV capacitor bank fixed to the fuselage of a Hawker Hunter aircraft to simulate the effect of lightning strikes on the electrical components of the aircraft (AEA Technology, Culham Laboratory)

Student investigation

The energy stored by a large capacitor may be studied using the following three experiments using a capacitor of large capacitance – 10 000 μF is suitable. In the first experiment the energy is converted to potential energy as a small motor lifts a small load while in the second heat energy is used to light one or more light bulbs. In the final experiment heat energy is produced in a heating coil.

Experiment 1

Set up the apparatus shown in Figure 48.8. First charge the capacitor to 10 V and then by throwing the switch allow it to discharge through the motor. Measure the height through which the weight is raised and hence calculate the mechanical energy gained.

The initial electrostatic energy stored in the capacitor was $1/2(CV) = 0.5$ J

Compare this with the mechanical energy gained. Where else has the initial energy gone?

Experiment 2

Set up the circuit shown in Figure 48.9. Charge the capacitor to 3 V and then discharge it through one lamp. Then charge it to 6 V and discharge it first through two lamps in series and then two lamps in parallel. Compare and contrast the brightness and the time for which the lamps light in each case.

Experiment 3

Set up the apparatus shown in Figure 48.10.

Charge the capacitor to 30 V and then discharge it through the heating coil. This coil should consist of 2 m of 32 s.w.g. constantan wire. The temperature rise produced in the coil should be measured with a copper–constantan thermocouple. The effect on the temperature of a number of charges and discharges should be investigated.

Do these experiments confirm the preceding equations for the energy stored in a charged capacitor?

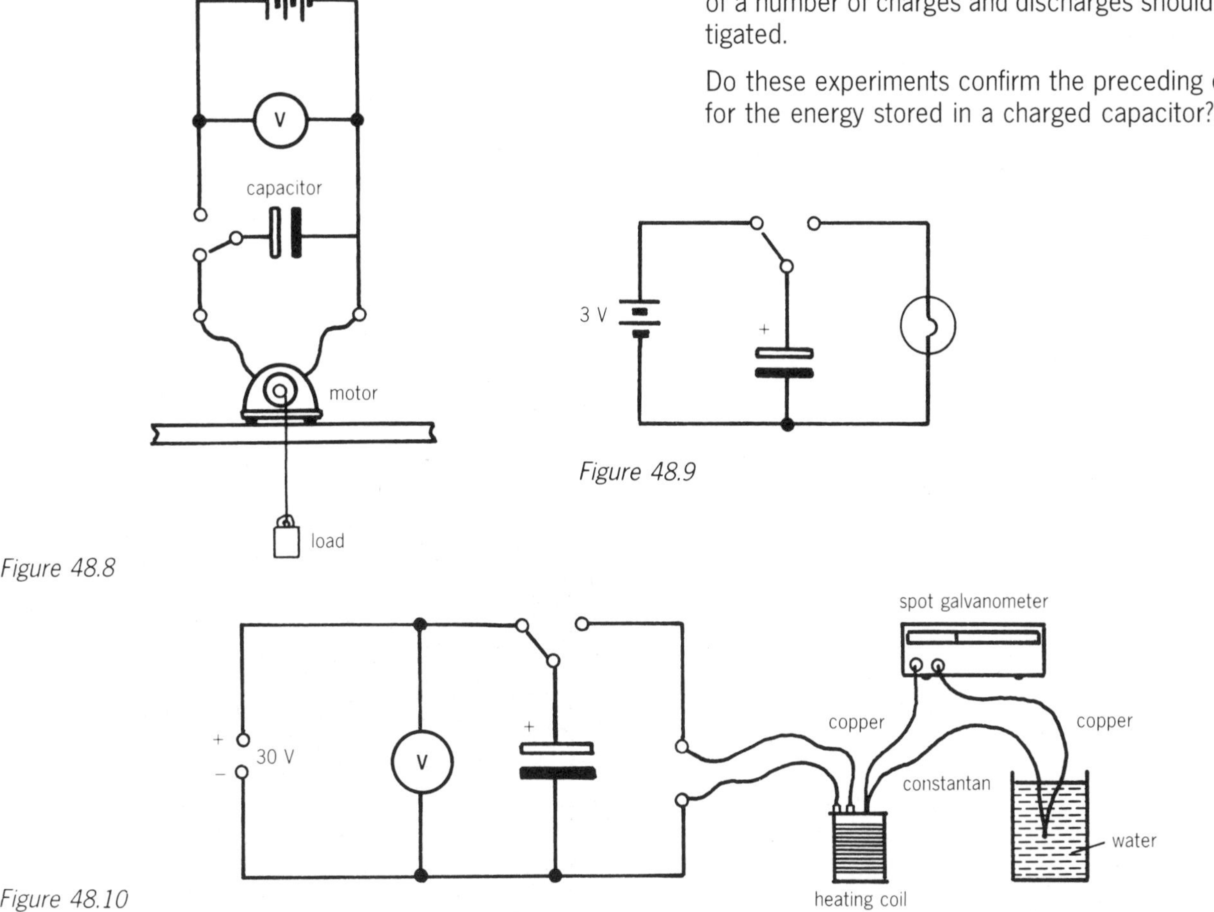

Figure 48.8

Figure 48.9

Figure 48.10

4 A parallel-plate air capacitor is made from two plates with an area of 100 cm^2 and with plates 2 mm apart. If it is charged to potential of 100 V, calculate
   (*a*) the charge on the plates, and
   (*b*) the energy stored in the capacitor.

The plates are now separated to 5 mm with the power source still connected. Calculate
   (*c*) the new capacitance, and
   (*d*) the new stored energy.
   (*e*) Where has this energy come from?

Capacitor networks

We will consider the cases of capacitors in parallel and in series.

(*a*) Capacitors in parallel

Consider two capacitors connected in parallel as shown in Figure 48.11.

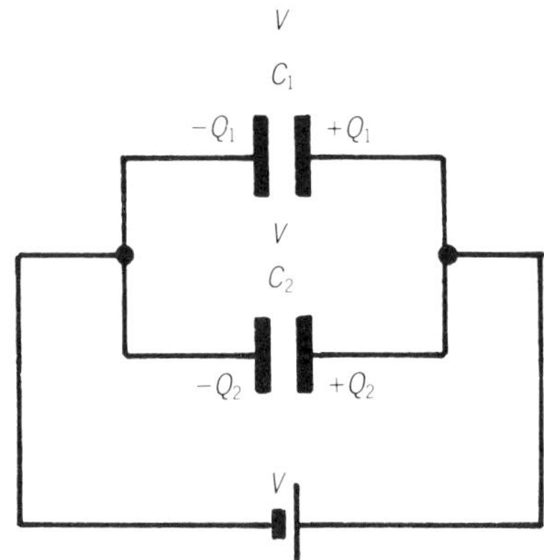

Figure 48.11

The potential across both capacitors is the same (V) and let the charges on the capacitors be Q_1 and Q_2 respectively. Now $Q = CV$, and so $Q_1 = C_1V$ and $Q_2 = C_2V$. But the total charge stored $Q = Q_1 + Q_2$, therefore

$$Q = Q_1 + Q_2 = V(C_1 + C_2)$$

giving

$$C = C_1 + C_2$$

where C is the capacitance of the combination.

(*b*) Capacitors in series

In this case the capacitors are connected as shown in Figure 48.12.

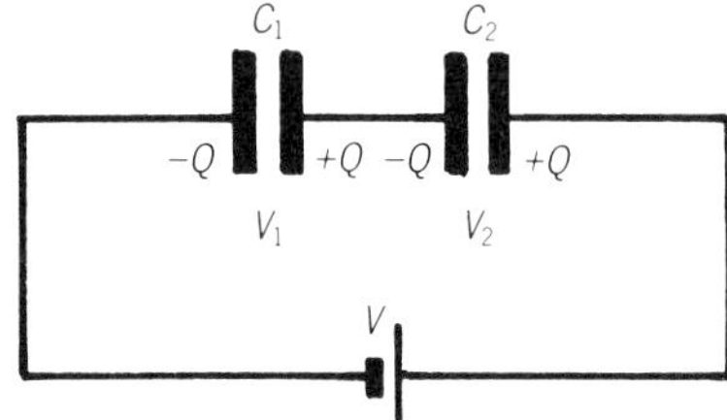

Figure 48.12

The charge stored by each capacitor is the same. If V_1 and V_2 are the potentials across C_1 and C_2 respectively then $V_1 = Q/C_1$ and $V_2 = Q/C_2$. Therefore

$$V = V_1 + V_2 = Q(1/C_1 + 1/C_2)$$

Hence:

$$\frac{1}{C} = \frac{1}{C_1} + \frac{1}{C_2}$$

Example

Two capacitors of 0.10 and 0.20 μF respectively are connected in series to a supply of 100 V. Calculate the charge on each capacitor.

Combined capacitance (C) is given by

$$\frac{1}{C} = \frac{1}{0.1} + \frac{1}{0.2} = \frac{1}{0.067}$$

Therefore $C = 0.067$ μF.

So charge $Q = CV = 0.067 \times 100 = 6.7$ microcoulombs.

5 A capacitor of capacitance 5000 μF is charged to a potential difference of 24 V and is discharged through a small electric motor. The motor is arranged to lift a load of mass 150 g.

(*a*) Calculate the energy stored in the charged capacitor.

(*b*) Assuming that the system is 20% efficient, calculate the height through which the load is raised. (Assume that $g = 10$ m s^{-2}.)

Give two reasons why the efficiency of such an arrangement is not 100%. [AEB 1983]

6 A thundercloud and the Earth can be regarded as a parallel-plate capacitor. Taking the area of the thundercloud to be 50 km^2, its height above the Earth as 1 km and its potential as 100 kV, calculate the energy stored in it.

7 A parallel-plate air capacitor with a plate separation of 3.0 mm and area 8 cm^2 is charged to a p.d. of 150 V and then isolated. The separation of the plates is now increased to 4.5 mm. Calculate

(*a*) the new p.d. between the plates,

(*b*) the charge stored on each plate, and

(*c*) the change in the energy stored by the capacitor.

(*d*) How do you account for this energy change?

8 Repeat all parts of question 7, but this time considering the capacitor to remain connected to the 150 V supply.

Joining two charged capacitors

If two capacitors are joined together as shown in Figure 48.13 then:

(*a*) there is no change in the total charge stored by the system;

(*b*) the potential across the two capacitors becomes equal, and

(*c*) the combined capacitance of the two capacitors in parallel becomes

$$C = C_1 + C_2$$

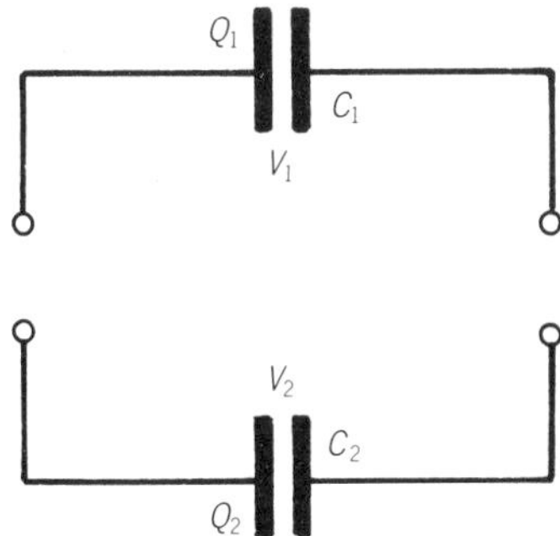

Figure 48.13

There is usually a loss in energy when the two capacitors are joined; this is because unless the potential differences across them are equal, charge will flow to equalise this difference. The flow of charge results in heating in the connecting wires and a consequent loss of energy.

Example

A capacitor of 10 μF with a p.d. of 100 V across it is joined to one of 50 μF with a p.d. of 50 V across it. Calculate the change in energy of the system.

Initial energies:

Capacitor 1 : $E_1 = \frac{1}{2} \times 10^{-5} \times 10^4$

Capacitor 2 : $E_2 = \frac{1}{2} \times 5 \times 10^{-5} \times 2500$

Therefore $E_1 = 5 \times 10^{-2}$ J and $E_2 = 6.25 \times 10^{-2}$ J

Initial total energy = 11.25×10^{-2} J
Final capacitance = 60 μF
Initial and final charge
= $10 \times 10^{-6} \times 100 + 50 \times 10^{-6} \times 50 = 3.5 \times 10^{-3}$ C
Therefore final energy =

$$\frac{1}{2}\frac{Q^2}{C} = \frac{(3.5 \times 10^{-3})^2}{2 \times 60 \times 10^{-6}} = 0.10 \text{ J}$$

Loss of energy = 1.25×10^{-2} J.

9 Three 1.0 μF capacitors are (*a*) connected in series to a 2.0 V battery, (*b*) connected in parallel with each other and a 2.0 V battery. Calculate the charge on each of the capacitors in (*a*) and (*b*).

Account without calculation for the difference in energy stored in each capacitor in both cases.

10 If you have several 2.0 μF capacitors each capable of withstanding 200 V without breakdown, how would you assemble a combination having an equivalent capacitance of (*a*) 0.40 μF, (*b*) 1.2 μF, each capable of withstanding 1000 V?

11 A parallel-plate air capacitor has plates of area 5.0×10^{-2} m^2 which are 2.5 mm apart. It is charged to a p.d. of 100 V and then disconnected from the supply. The charged capacitor is now connected in parallel to a second capacitor having plates of half the area but twice the distance apart. Calculate

(*a*) the final charge on each capacitor,

(*b*) the p.d. across each capacitor, and

(*c*) the energy stored by each part of the system before and after joining the two capacitors together.

12 A capacitor is made from a pile of 100 sheets of tinfoil, each 100 cm^2 in area, successive sheets being separated by waxed paper 0.5 mm thick with relative permittivity 2.0. Alternate sheets of foil are connected to form the two terminals of the capacitor. Calculate the capacitance of the device. [W]

13 A parallel-plate capacitor consists of two plates 3.5 cm apart with a piece of glass 2 cm thick filling part of the space between them. When the glass is removed the plates' separation has to be reduced to 2 cm to restore the capacitance to its original value.

Explain why this happens and calculate the relative permittivity of the glass

The charge and discharge of a capacitor

When a voltage is placed across the terminals of a capacitor the potential cannot rise to its final value instantaneously. As the charge builds up it tends to repel the addition of further charge.

The rate at which a capacitor can be charged or discharged depends on:

(*a*) the capacitance of the capacitor, and

(*b*) the resistance of the circuit through which it is being charged or is discharging.

This fact makes the capacitor a very useful if not vital component in timing circuits from clocks to computers.

Discharge of a capacitor through a resistor

In Figure 48.14, let the charge on a capacitor of capacitance *C* be *q*, and let *V* be the potential difference across it at any instant. The current in the discharge is therefore

$$I = -\frac{dq}{dt}$$

But $V = IR$ and $q = CV$.

Therefore we have

$$V = -CR\frac{dV}{dt}$$

Rearranging and integrating gives

$$V = V_0 e^{-(t/RC)}$$

where V_0 is the initial voltage applied to the capacitor. The equation for the charge on the capacitor is therefore

$$Q = Q_0 e^{-(t/RC)}$$

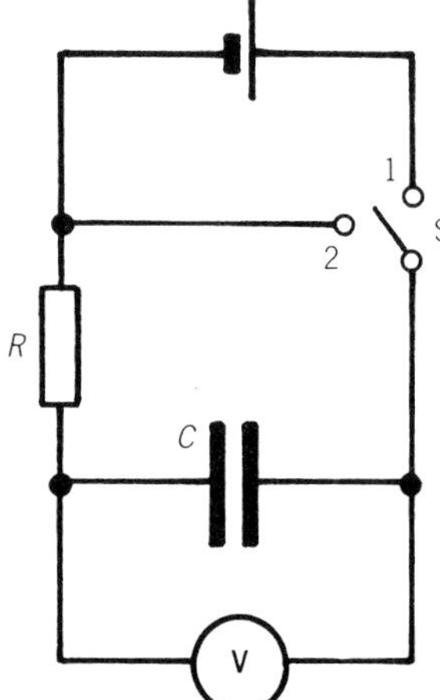

Figure 48.14

A graph of this exponential discharge is shown in Figure 48.15.

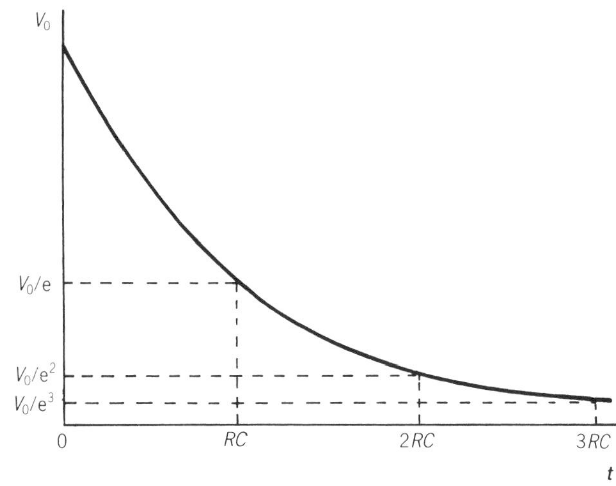

Figure 48.15

You should realise that the term *RC* governs the rate at which the charge on the capacitor decays. When $t = RC$, $V = V_0/e = 0.37\ V_0$ and the product *RC* is known as the **time constant** for the circuit.

The value of *C* can be found from this discharge curve if *CR* can be found from the decay curve and *R* is known.

Student investigation

The capacitance of a capacitor may be found from the following investigation.

Set up the circuit as shown in Figure 48.16 such that the capacitor may be discharged through the resistance *R*. (This should be a few thousand ohms for capacitances thought to be of the order of thousands of microfarads.) Connect the Vela across *R* and select the slow transient program.

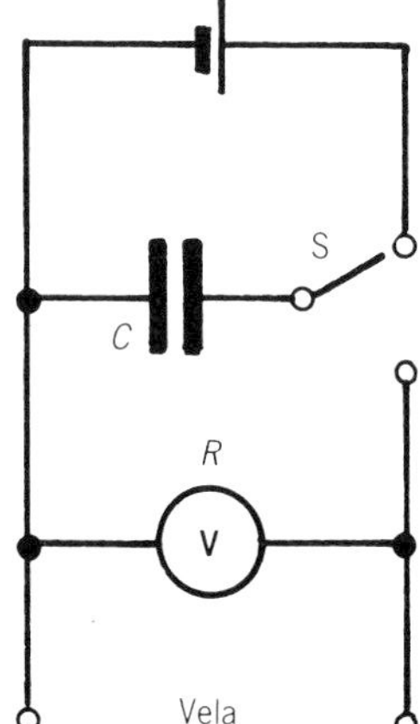

Figure 48.16

Set the interval between readings at a few seconds and discharge the capacitor, starting the program. The Vela will record the voltage at set intervals of time and the complete discharge may be displayed on an oscilloscope or recorded from the Vela on a graph. (If a chart recorder is available it may be printed out directly.)

Example 1

A capacitor is discharged through a 10 MΩ resistor and it is found that the time constant is 200 s. Calculate the value of the capacitor.
$RC = 200$. Therefore $C = 200/10 \times 10^6 = 20\ \mu F$.

Example 2

Calculate the time for the potential across a 100 μF capacitor to fall to 80 per cent of its original value if it is discharged through a 20 kΩ resistor.

$V = 0.8\ V_0$. Therefore $0.8 = e^{-t/20 \times 10^3 \times 100 \times 10^{-6}}$
Therefore

$$\ln(1/0.8) = \frac{t}{20 \times 10^3 \times 100 \times 10^{-6}}$$

This gives $t = 2 \times \ln(1/0.8) = 0.45$ s.

14 A 1000 μF capacitor is charged to 5000 V, disconnected from the power supply and then allowed to discharge through a 100 kΩ resistor. Calculate the time taken for the voltage across the capacitor to fall to (*a*) 200 V, (*b*) 100 V, (*c*) 1 V.

15 It is required that the output from a 1000 V power supply should fall to 10 V within a maximum of 5 s of the supply being switched off. If a 2000 μF capacitor is connected across the terminals inside the power supply, what resistor must be connected across the capacitor in series to satisfy this condition?

16 A 2500 μF capacitor is charged through a 1 kΩ resistor by a 12 V d.c. source. Calculate
(*a*) the voltage across the capacitor after 5 s,
(*b*) the charging current after 0.5 s, and
(*c*) the charge stored by the capacitor after 1 s.

Charging a capacitor

When a capacitor is being charged through a resistance to a final potential V_0 the equation relating the voltage across the capacitor at any time t is

$$V = V_0(1 - e^{-t/RC})$$

and the variation of potential with time is shown in Figure 48.17.

As the capacitor charges the charging current decreases, since the potential across the resistance decreases as the potential across the capacitor increases.

Figures 48.17 and 48.18 show how both the potential difference across the capacitor and the charging current vary with time during charging.

The area below the current–time curve in both charging and discharging represents the total charge held by the capacitor.

Warning
Some badly made power supplies have a capacitor connected across their outputs and so remain live even after the power supply has been switched off. Always be careful when handling apparatus containing capacitors.

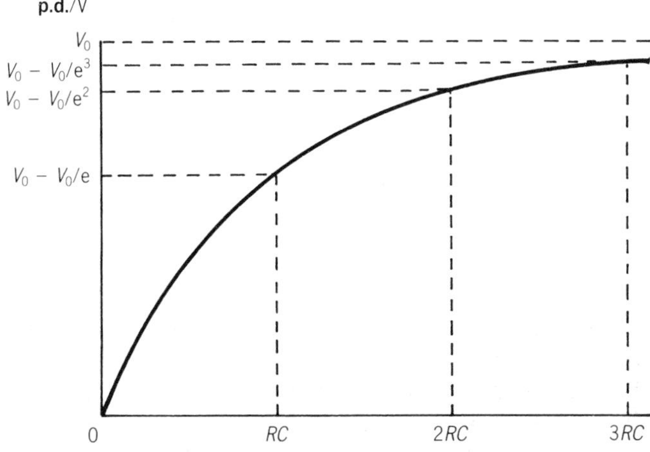

Figure 48.17

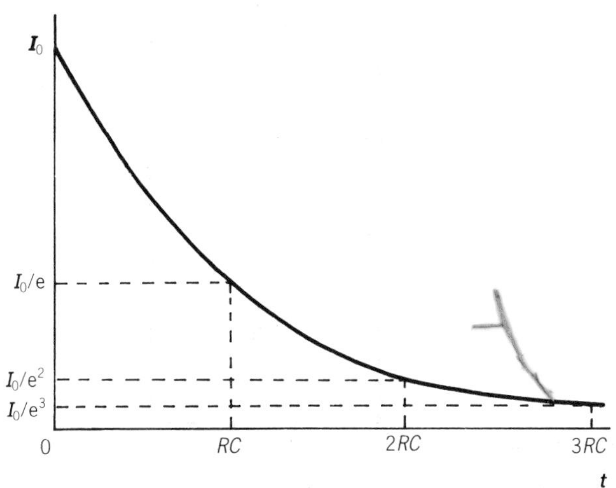

Figure 48.18

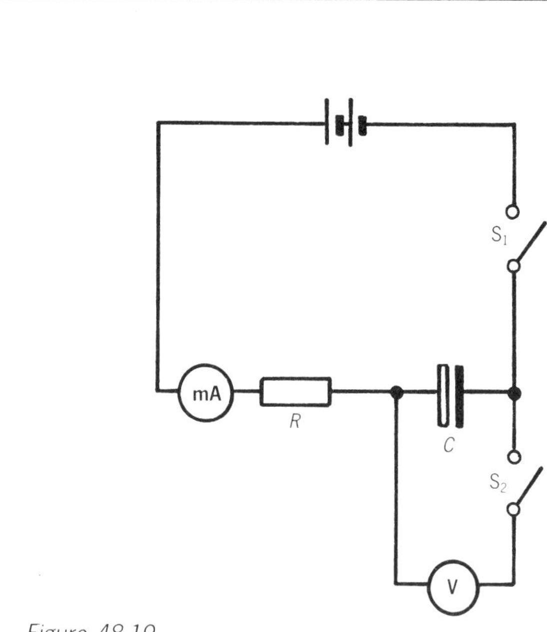

Figure 48.19

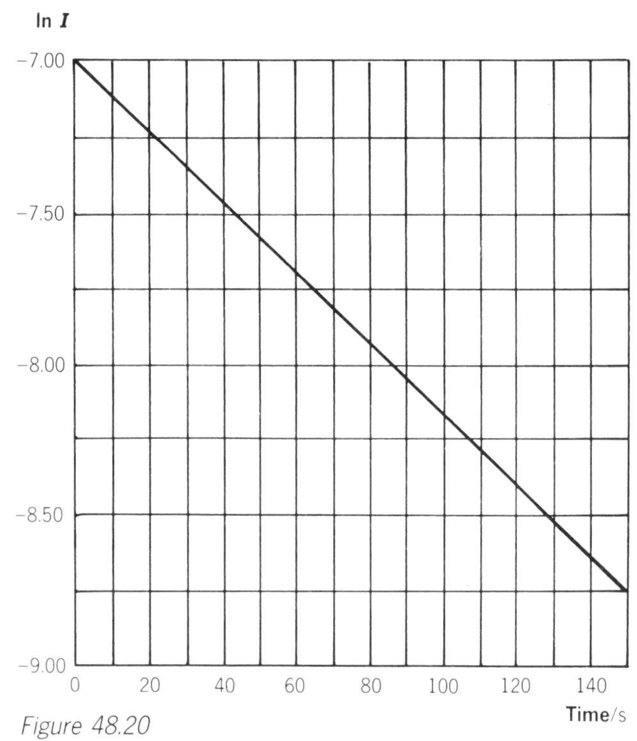

Figure 48.20

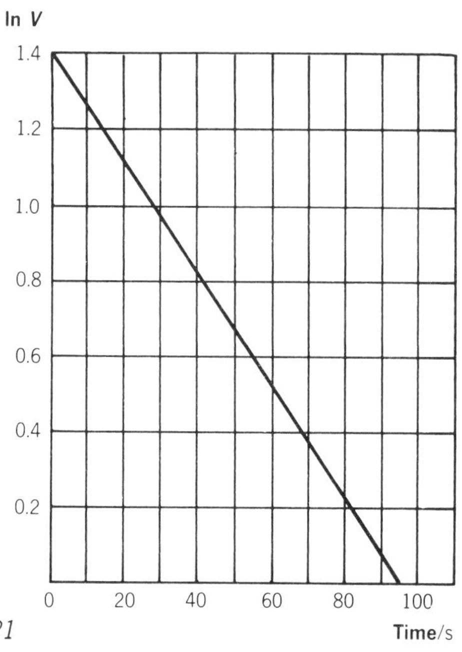

Figure 48.21

Student investigation

An experiment was set up to measure the capacitance of a large capacitor and also to determine the resistance of the milliammeter and its series resistance, using the circuit in Figure 48.19.

Figure 48.20 shows the charging current I to the capacitor and the time, the graph being of ln I against t.

Figure 48.21 shows the voltage across the capacitor during discharge and the time, the graph being of ln V against t.

Use the graphs to determine the capacitance of C, and the combined resistance of the milliammeter and its series resistance.

The force between two charged plates

The two plates of a parallel-plate capacitor attract each other, since they are oppositely charged.

When the plates are allowed to move together so that they touch, the work done by the force of attraction is equal to the original energy of the capacitor. If the plates were originally a distance d apart, the work done is Fd where F is the force between them.

Therefore:

$$Fd = \tfrac{1}{2}QV \quad \therefore F = \tfrac{1}{2}\frac{QV}{d} = \tfrac{1}{2}QE$$

The charge on the insulated plate contributes half the field and that induced on the earthed plate the other half; the force on the charge on one plate is due to the field set up by the charge on the other. This explains the factor of $\frac{1}{2}$ in the above formulae.

Practical forms of capacitor

Most capacitors are of the parallel-plate type, either as two flat plates or as a 'swiss roll' arrangement, with the plates and dielectric rolled into a cylinder (Figure 48.22).

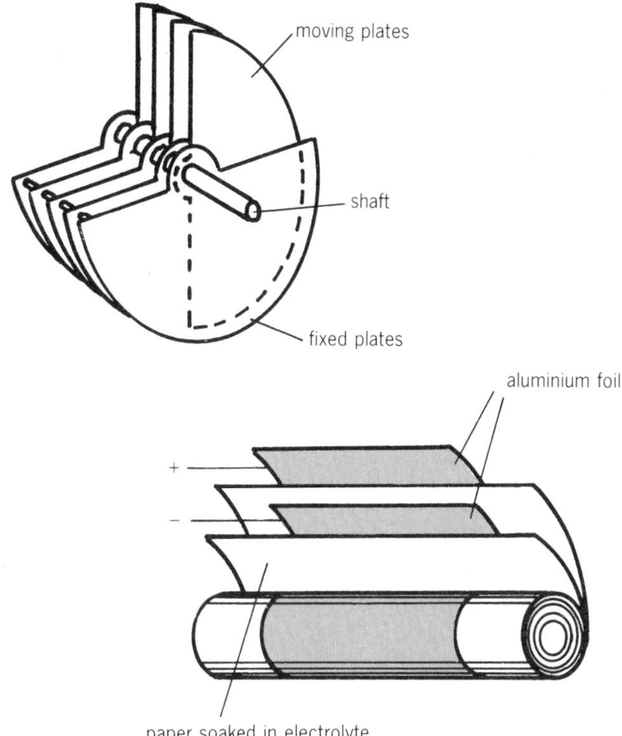

Figure 48.22

Air capacitors

The air capacitor has the advantage of being simple to make and having a precisely known capacitance with almost perfect properties at all frequencies. It has a low insulation strength, however, only about one-twentieth of that of impregnated paper.

The tuner in a radio is a variable air capacitor, consisting of two sets of plates in air overlapping each other. The overlap of the plates and hence the capacitance may be varied by moving one set of plates into the other.

Paper capacitors

The two plates are thin metal sheets, with the paper dielectric of relative permittivity about 5 between them. They are then rolled into a cylinder. The whole arrangement is packed in a cylinder of metal or plastic. Clearly there will be a breakdown potential and this can be increased by waxing the paper.

Such capacitors are not very stable but they are cheap to make. They have capacitances between 10^{-3} μF and 10 μF and are suitable for applied p.d.s in the frequency range 100 Hz to 100 MHz.

Electrolytic capacitors

When an electric current is passed through a solution of aluminium borate using aluminium electrodes, a very thin layer of oxide forms on the anode. The thickness of this layer depends on the applied p.d. and on the time for which the current is passed. This oxide film is used as the dielectric in electrolytic capacitors. It may be very thin, less than 10^{-7}m, but it has a very high insulation strength of some 10^9 V m^{-1}.

17 A metal sphere 4 m in diameter is charged to a potential of 3 million volts by a Van de Graaff generator. Calculate the heat generated when the sphere is earthed through a long resistance wire. [O and C]

18 A charged capacitor of capacitance 100 μF is connected across the terminals of a voltmeter of resistance 100 kΩ. When time $t = 0$, the reading on the voltmeter is 10.0 V. Calculate

(*a*) the charge on the capacitor at $t = 0$,

(*b*) the reading on the voltmeter at $t = 20.0$ s,

(*c*) the time which must elapse, from $t = 0$, before 75% of the energy stored in the capacitor at $t = 0$ has dissipated. [JMB]

19 Calculate the capacitance of the Earth, taking its radius to be 6.4×10^6 m.

20 A capacitor consists of two plates each of area 100 cm^2 and 1.0 cm apart, with a slab of glass (relative permittivity 10) 0.8 cm thick filling most of the space between them. One of the plates is earthed and the other given a charge of 0.030 μC.

Calculate the potential of the insulated plate and also its electrical energy.

The slab of glass is now removed. What are the new values of potential and energy of the insulated plate? Where did this extra energy come from?

21 (*a*) Discuss the differences and similarities when (i) a dielectric slab and (ii) a conducting slab are inserted between the plates of a parallel-plate capacitor. (Assume the slab thicknesses to be one-third of the plate separation.)

(*b*) An isolated conducting sphere is given a positive charge. Does its mass increase, decrease or remain the same?

(*c*) Explain whether it is possible for the potential at a point to be zero while the electric intensity at that point is not zero.

(*d*) Can a 1 μF capacitor be made in a microcircuit with a dielectric of relative permittivity 22 and thickness 400 nm?

49 · Alternating currents

We define an alternating current or voltage as one which varies with time about a mean value. Some examples of this variation are shown in Figure 49.1, which illustrates variations that are (*a*) sinusoidal, (*b*) square, (*c*) sawtooth and (*d*) irregular.

There are three reasons why we shall restrict ourselves mainly to considering sinusoidal variations:

(i) they may be produced by a rotating coil;

(ii) the mains supply in the United Kingdom varies in this way;

(iii) all other variations can be considered as com binations of sine waves of different amplitudes, wavelengths and phases.

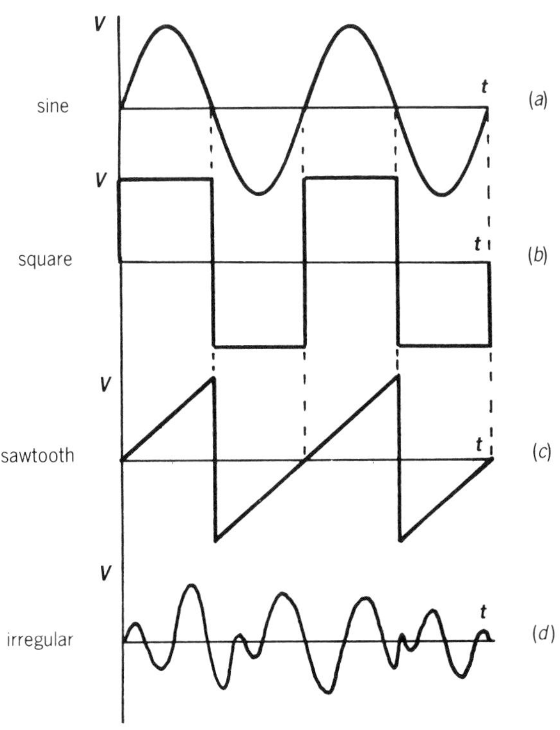

Figure 49.1

Important definitions in a.c. theory

Consider the sine wave shown in Figure 49.3.

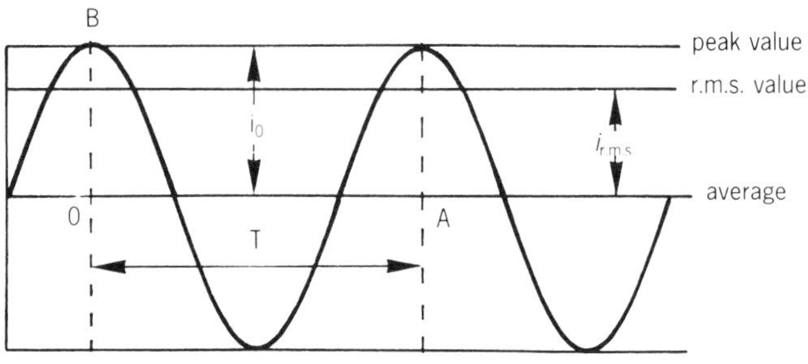

Figure 49.3

Imagine that this represents the variation of current with time. The current is not constant but alternates sinusoidally between two extremes.

The **period** (T) of the variation is the time for one complete oscillation (OA in Figure 49.3).

The **frequency** (f) of the variation is $1/T$.

There are several ways in which we can express the size of the current since it is not constant with time:

(*a*) The **average** value of the current is zero – as much of the curve lies below the central line as lies above it.

(*b*) The **mean** value or **half-cycle average**; this is the average value taken over half a cycle.

(*c*) The **peak** value of the current (i_0) is the distance from the *average* value to the crest or trough of the wave. This is clearly also the **amplitude** of the wave. (OB in Figure 49.3).

(*d*) The **root mean square** (r.m.s.) value. This is defined as the square root of the mean value of the *square* of the current, taken over a whole cycle.

Student investigation

Investigate the smoothing effects of the circuit in Figure 49.2 in which a square wave is applied to a capacitor and resistor in series. Record both the input waveform and the waveform across the capacitor for various capacitances.

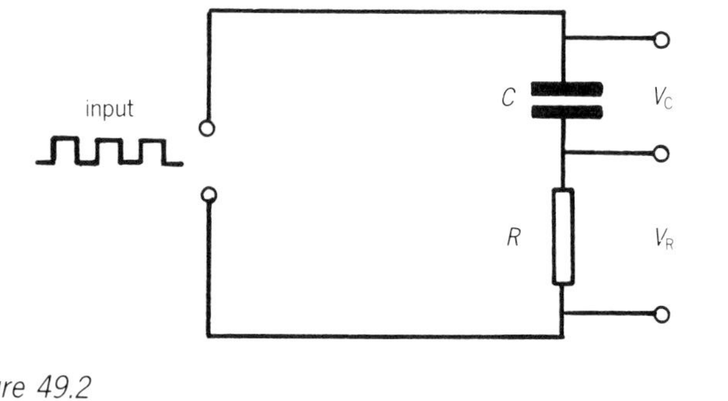

Figure 49.2

The reason for using what seems a rather complicated definition is as follows. The power P used in a resistor R is proportional to the square of the current:

$$P = i^2R$$

But with alternating current the value of i and therefore of P changes, and so:

$$\text{mean value of } P = (\text{mean value of } i^2) \times R = I^2R$$

where $I = \sqrt{(\text{mean value of } i^2)}$ = r.m.s. current.

We can therefore define the r.m.s. value as that current that would dissipate power at the same rate as a d.c. current of the same value.

The relation between the peak and r.m.s. values for a sinusoidal wave can be seen in Figure 49.3. It can be shown that the r.m.s. value of current I is related to the peak value i_0 by the equation:

$$I = \frac{i_0}{\sqrt{2}} = 0.707\, i_0$$

Similarly, for the voltage we have:

$$V = \frac{v_0}{\sqrt{2}} = 0.707\, v_0$$

In Britain the voltage supply is 240 V; this is the r.m.s. value, and so the peak value is 240/0.707 or about 340 V.

Proof of the value of the r.m.s. current

Let the current vary with time in the following way:

$$i = i_0 \sin(\omega t)$$

where ω is a constant related to the frequency f by the equation $\omega = 2\pi f$. By definition the r.m.s. current I is

$$I = \sqrt{(\text{mean value of } i^2)}$$
$$= i_0 \sqrt{(\text{mean value of } \sin^2(\omega t))}$$

But $\sin^2(\omega t) = \frac{1}{2} - \frac{1}{2}\cos(2\omega t)$, and the mean value of $\cos(2\omega t)$ is 0. Therefore the mean value of $\sin^2(\omega t) = \frac{1}{2}$, and therefore

$$I = i_0\sqrt{\tfrac{1}{2}} = \frac{i_0}{\sqrt{2}}$$

It is important to realise that the general definition of r.m.s. value applies to *any* type of varying signal and not simply to one that varies sinusoidally. For example, it is quite possible for a square wave to have an r.m.s. value.

The variation of both $\sin(\omega t)$ and $\sin^2(\omega t)$ are shown in Figure 49.4.

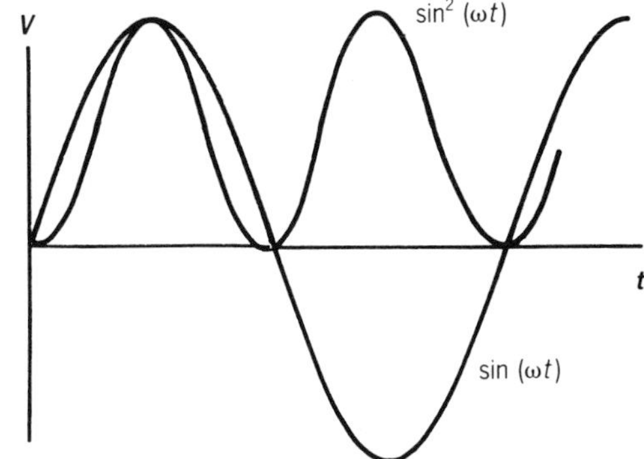

Figure 49.4

Vector diagrams

It is very useful to represent the variation of current or voltage by a rotating vector model, as shown in Figure 49.5(*a*).

If the vector OP is rotated at a steady angular velocity ω, then its projections on OA and OB respectively are:

$$\text{ON} = \text{OP} \sin(\omega t) \qquad \text{and} \qquad \text{OM} = \text{OP} \cos(\omega t)$$

If OP is the maximum value of the current through a component, then ON represents the magnitude of the current at a time t.

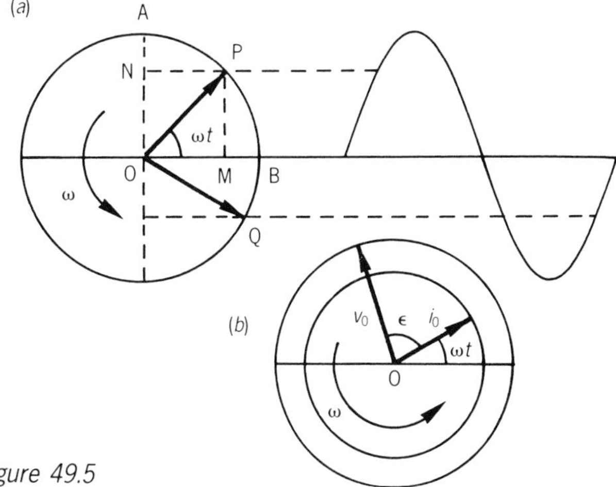

Figure 49.5

If the current and voltage are of the same frequency but not in phase then we have the situation shown in Figure 49.5(*b*). There is a **phase difference** ϵ between them. The equations for current and voltage are:

$$i = i_0 \sin(\omega t) \qquad \text{and} \qquad v = v_0 \sin(\omega t + \epsilon)$$

The magnitude and direction of the current through a piece of apparatus can be represented by such a vector diagram and we will use this treatment when considering the flow of a.c. through resistive, capacitative and inductive circuits.

Resistive circuits

In a circuit containing only resistance the current and voltage are in phase, and the equations for their variation with time are:

$$i = i_0 \sin(\omega t) \quad \text{and} \quad v = v_0 \sin(\omega t)$$

Capacitative circuits

When a capacitor is connected to a voltage supply the result is quite different for an a.c. supply from that for d.c.

In the circuit in Figure 49.6(*a*) no current flows and the lamp does not light. But if the supply is a.c., as in Figure 49.6(*b*), the lamp lights showing that some current must be flowing through it. This can be explained as follows.

When a capacitor is connected to an a.c. supply the plates of the capacitor are continually charging and discharging, and so an a.c. current flows in the connecting wires. Current does not actually flow *through* the capacitor itself.

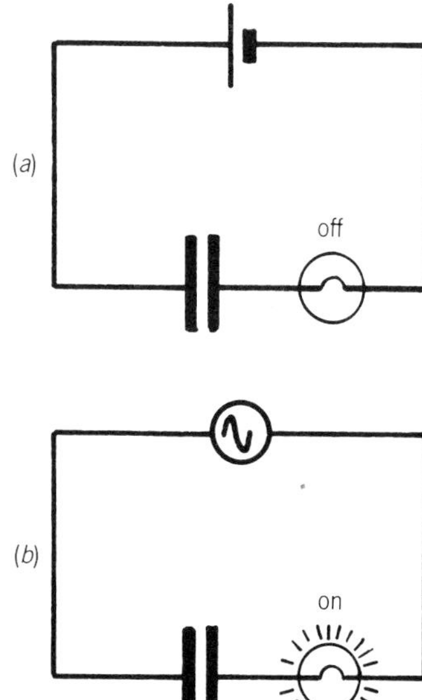

Figure 49.6

The current and voltage shown in Figure 49.7 are not in phase; in fact, the current is 90° ahead of the voltage, as shown by the vector diagram.

In a capacitative circuit the current leads the voltage by 90°.

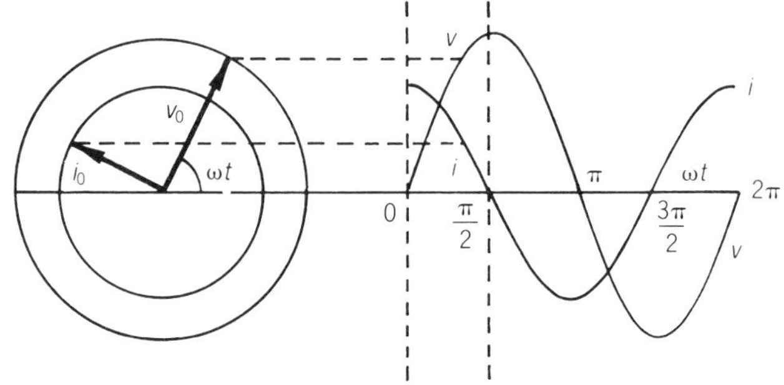

Figure 49.7

This can be shown mathematically as follows. Let the voltage applied to the capacitance C be

$$v = v_0 \sin(\omega t)$$

The charge q on the capacitor plates is given by

$$q = Cv = Cv_0 \sin(\omega t)$$

But the current

$$i = \frac{dq}{dt} = \omega C v_0 \cos(\omega t) = \omega C v_0 \sin(\omega t + \pi/2)$$

This shows that the current leads the voltage by 90°, i.e. by $\pi/2$.

1 Calculate (i) the average voltage, (ii) the root mean square voltage for:
(*a*) a sine wave of peak value 200 V and frequency 50 Hz;
(*b*) a square wave of peak value 200 V and frequency 50 Hz;
(*c*) a half-wave-rectified sine wave of peak value 200 V and frequency 50 Hz;
(*d*) a half-wave-rectified square wave of peak value 200 V and frequency 50 Hz.

2 A capacitor of 1000 μF is connected to a 16 V peak value a.c. supply of 50 Hz. Calculate
(*a*) the maximum charge on the capacitor plates;
(*b*) the charge on the plates 10^{-3} s after the applied voltage is zero;
(*c*) the a.c. current through the capacitor at these times.
(*d*) Repeat the above calculations using a 1 F capacitor.

3 When a sinusoidal a.c. is passed through a 100 Ω resistor whose ends are connected to the Y-plates of an oscilloscope, there is a trace 30 mm high on the screen. A steady potential applied between the plates gives a deflection of 0.5 mm per volt. Calculate the r.m.s. value of the alternating p.d.

Inductive circuits

Like a capacitative circuit, a pure inductive circuit behaves quite differently from one containing resistance alone. Consider the circuit in Figure 49.8(*a*).

When the switch is closed the lamp (L_1) in series with the inductance lights more slowly than lamp L_2 suggesting that the inductance resists a changing current.

A coil with an iron core has a much greater inductance than one with an air core, and using the circuit in Figure 49.8(*b*) you can show that the lamp will dim markedly or even go out when the iron core is placed in the coil. If d.c. were used, however, the lamp would remain alight whether there was an iron core or not.

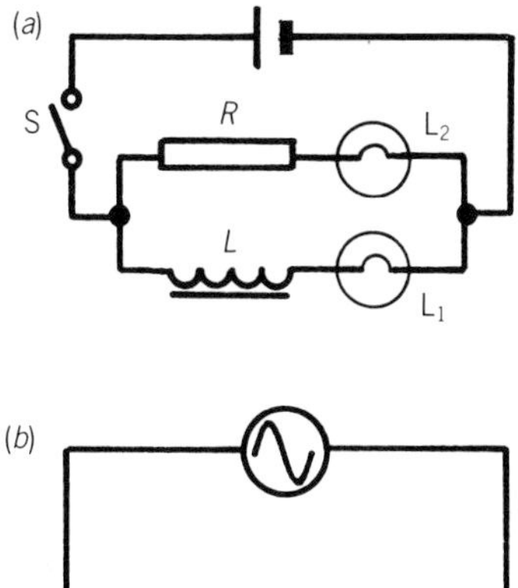

Figure 49.8

In the inductive circuit the current and voltage are not in phase; in fact, the current lags behind the voltage by 90° as shown by the vector diagram in Figure 49.9.

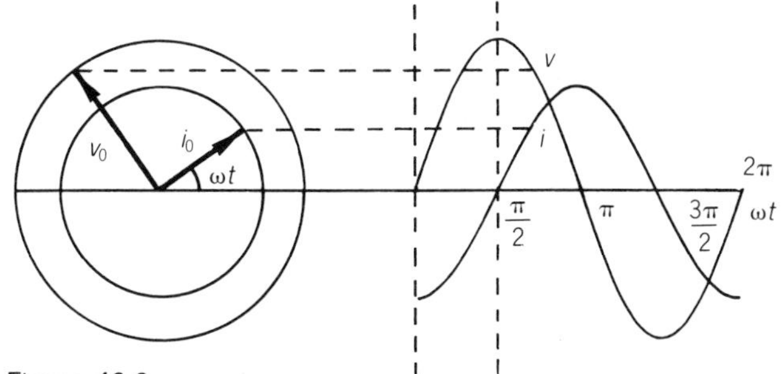

Figure 49.9

In inductive circuits the voltage leads the current by 90 °.

This can be shown mathematically as follows. Let the current flowing through an inductance L be

$$i = i_0 \sin(\omega t)$$

Now the back e.m.f. produced is

$$E = -\frac{L\,di}{dt} = -\omega L i_0 \cos(\omega t)$$

The applied p.d. is therefore

$$-E = v = \omega L i_0 \cos(\omega t) = \omega L i_0 \sin(\omega t + \pi/2)$$

This shows that the voltage leads the current by 90° or π/2.

4 A long solenoid connected to a 12 V d.c. source passes a steady current of 2 A. When the solenoid is connected to a source of 12 V r.m.s. at 50 Hz the current flowing is 1 A r.m.s.. Calculate the inductance of the solenoid.

5 A solenoid of inductance 10 mH is connected to a 16 V peak a.c. supply with a frequency of 50 Hz. Calculate
(*a*) the peak current in the circuit;
(*b*) the current 10^{-3} s after a zero of the supply voltage;
(*c*) the voltages across the inductance at these times.
(*d*) Repeat these calculations for a solenoid of inductance 1 H.

Reactance

The term **reactance** is given to the effective resistance of a component to a.c. It is given the symbol X and is defined as:

$$X = \frac{\text{amplitude of the voltage across a component}}{\text{amplitude of the current flowing through it}} = \frac{v}{i}$$

(*a*) For a capacitor, $i = \omega C v$ giving

$$X_C = \frac{v}{\omega C v} = \frac{1}{\omega C}$$

The reactance of a capacitor is therefore inversely proportional to the frequency of the applied p.d. (since $\omega = 2\pi f$).

(*b*) For an inductor, $v = \omega L i$ giving

$$X_L = \frac{v\omega L}{v} = \omega L$$

The reactance of an inductor is therefore directly proportional to the frequency of the applied p.d.

Example

Calculate the reactance of the following components at frequencies of 50 Hz and 200 kHz (long wave radio):

(*a*) a resistor of 1000 ohms,

(*b*) a capacitor of 1000 microfarads, and

(*c*) a solenoid of length 10 cm, diameter 1 cm, with 5000 turns (relative permeability of core 2000).

(*a*) The resistance of the resistor for a.c. or d.c. is constant and equal to 1000 Ω.

(*b*) For the capacitor,

(i) at 50 Hz, reactance

$$= \frac{1}{2\pi fC} = \frac{1}{2\pi \times 50 \times 1000 \times 10^{-6}} = 3.18\ \Omega$$

(ii) at 200 kHz, reactance

$$= 8 \times 10^{-4} = 0.0008\ \Omega$$

(*c*) For the inductor, inductance

$$= \mu_0 AN/l = \frac{4\pi \times 10^{-7} \times 2000 \times 7.85 \times 10^{-5} \times 5000}{0.1}$$

$$= 9.86 \times 10^{-3}\ \text{H}$$

(i) at 50 Hz, reactance

$$= 2\pi fL = 2\pi \times 50 \times 9.86 \times 10^{-3} = 3.1\ \Omega.$$

(ii) at 200 kHz, reactance

$$= 12\,390\Omega = 12.39\ \text{k}\Omega.$$

The *C–R* (capacitance–resistance) circuit

The circuit shown in Figure 49.10 contains both resist ance and capacitance, and therefore both the components and the frequency of the supply voltage affect the final current in the circuit.

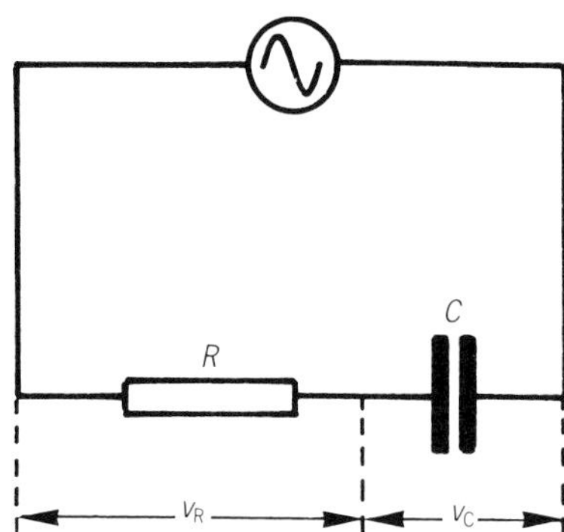

Figure 49.10

The a.c. resistance of such a circuit is known as the **impedance** of the circuit and is denoted by the symbol Z. Impedance is measured in ohms.

We will now deduce the impedance of the circuit using the vector treatment.

Consider the voltages round the circuit. The supply voltage will be denoted by v_0 and the voltages across the resistor and capacitor by $v_{R,0}$ and $v_{C,0}$ respectively.

We know that for a resistor the current and voltage are in phase, while for a capacitor the current leads the voltage by 90°; $v_{R,0}$ therefore leads $v_{C,0}$ by 90°, as shown in the vector diagram in Figure 49.11. The resultant voltage v_0 is given by

$$v_0^2 = v_{R,0}^2 + v_{C,0}^2 = i_0^2 R^2 + i_0^2 X_C^2$$

Therefore the current in the circuit is given by:

$$i_0 = \frac{v_0}{\sqrt{X_c^2 + R^2}}$$

and the impedance Z by:

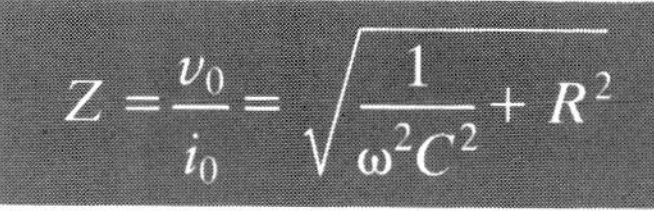

$$Z = \frac{v_0}{i_0} = \sqrt{\frac{1}{\omega^2 C^2} + R^2}$$

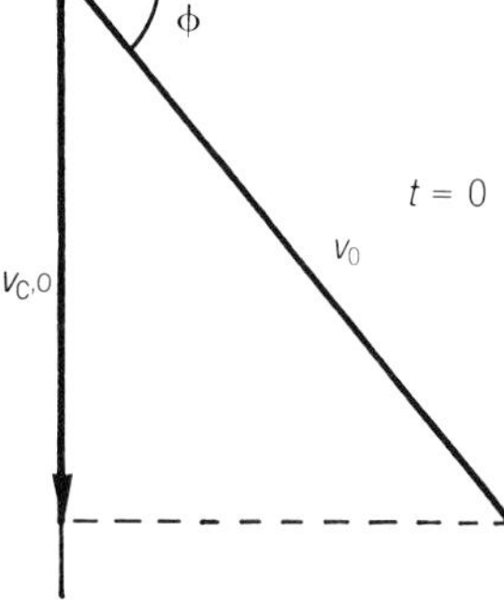

Figure 49.11

The angle φ that the resultant vector makes with v is known as the **phase angle** of the voltage. You can see from Figure 49.12 that

$$\tan\phi = \frac{v_{C,0}}{v_{R,0}} = -\frac{1}{\omega CR}$$

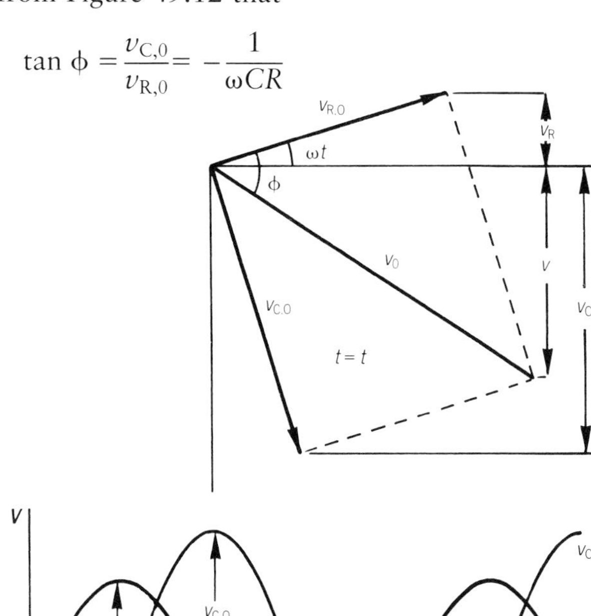

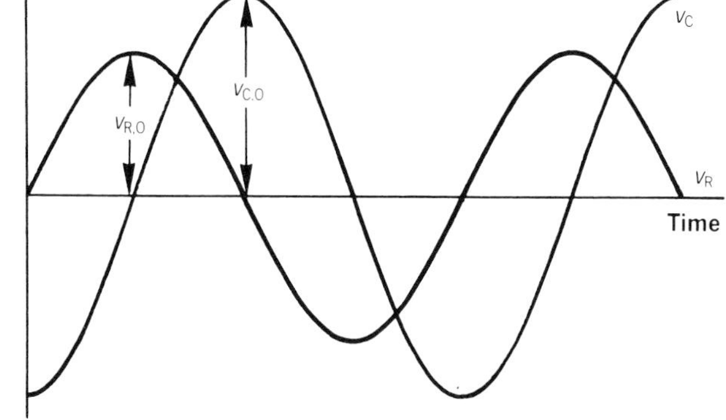

Figure 49.12

The *L–R* (inductance–resistance) circuit

The circuit in Figure 49.13 contains both inductance and resistance. As with the capacitance–resistance circuit, the current through it depends on the value of both the components and the frequency of the supply voltage.

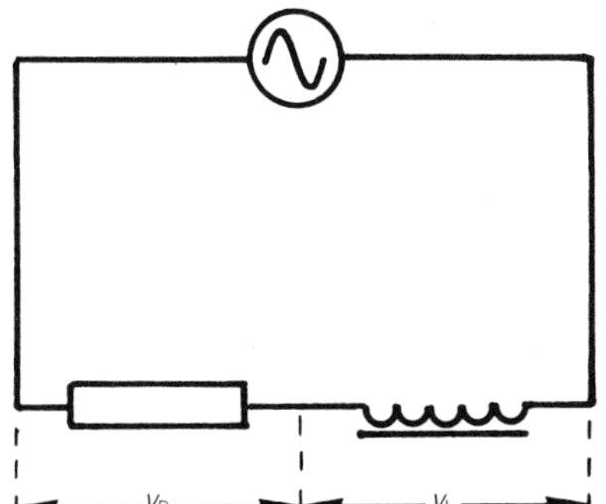

Figure 49.13

Let the supply voltage be v_0 and the voltages across the inductor and the resistor be $v_{L,0}$ and $v_{R,0}$ respectively. Now we know that for a resistor the current and voltage are in phase, while for an inductor the voltage leads the current by 90°; $v_{L,0}$ therefore leads $v_{R,0}$ by 90°, as can be seen from Figure 49.14. The resultant voltage is given by

$$v_0^2 = v_{R,0}^2 + v_{L,0}^2 = i_0^2R^2 + i_0^2X_L^2$$

The current in the circuit is therefore

$$i_0 = \frac{v_0}{\sqrt{X_L^2 + R^2}}$$

and the impedance is

$$Z = \sqrt{X_L^2 + R^2} = \sqrt{\omega^2L^2 + R^2}$$

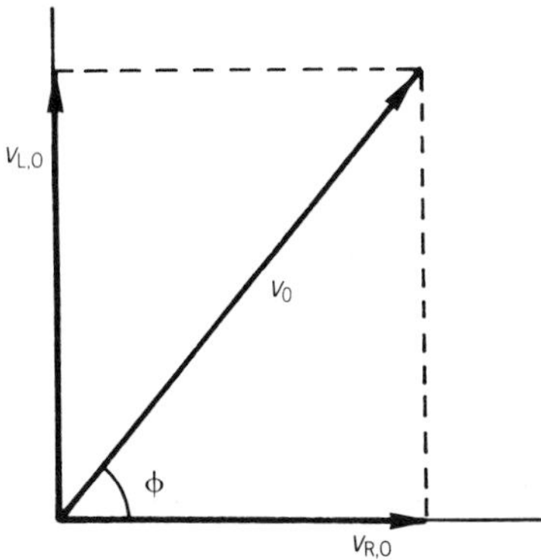

Figure 49.14

6 Calculate the impedance of a 100 mH inductor of negligible resistance at (*a*) 10 Hz, (*b*) 50 Hz, (*c*) 1 MHz.

7 Distinguish between the reactance and the resistance of a coil, and show how they are related.

and the phase angle for this circuit ϕ (see Figure 49.15) is given by

$$\tan\phi = \frac{v_{L,0}}{v_{R,0}} = \frac{\omega L}{R}$$

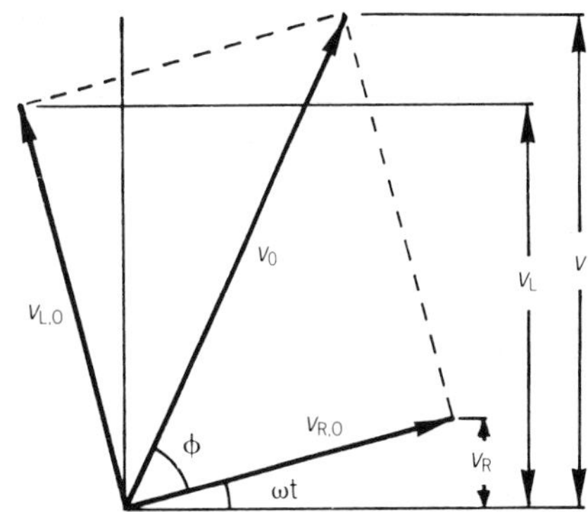

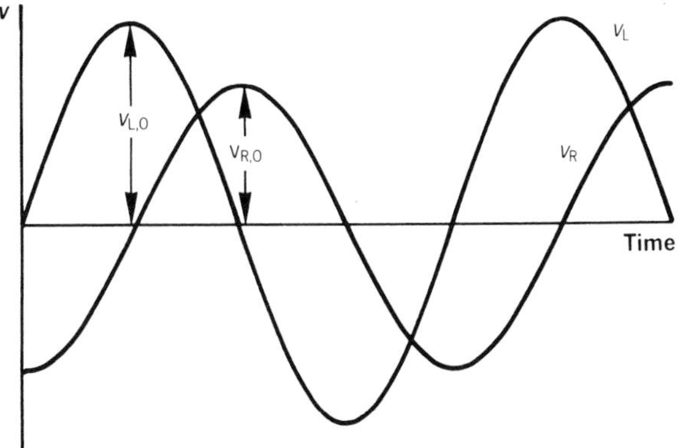

Figure 49.15

8 An 8 μF capacitor is placed across a 200 V, 50 Hz supply. Calculate the r.m.s. current that flows in the circuit. What is the peak value of the voltage across the capacitor?

9 Find the magnitude and phase of the current when the following are connected to a 200 V, 50 Hz supply:
(*a*) a coil of inductance 0.2 H and negligible resistance;
(*b*) a capacitor of 60 μF;
(*c*) a coil of inductance 0.2 H and a resistance of 20 Ω;
(*d*) a coil of inductance 0.2 H and resistance 20 Ω in series with a capacitor of 60 μF.

10 A 150 mH inductor is connected in series with a variable capacitor which can be varied between 500 pF and 20 pF. What are the maximum and minimum frequencies to which the circuit can be tuned?

The *L–C–R* series circuit

The circuit shown in Figure 49.16 contains all three components in series. In the vector diagram in Figure 49.17, notice the directions of the voltage vectors showing the phase differences between them and the resultant voltage.

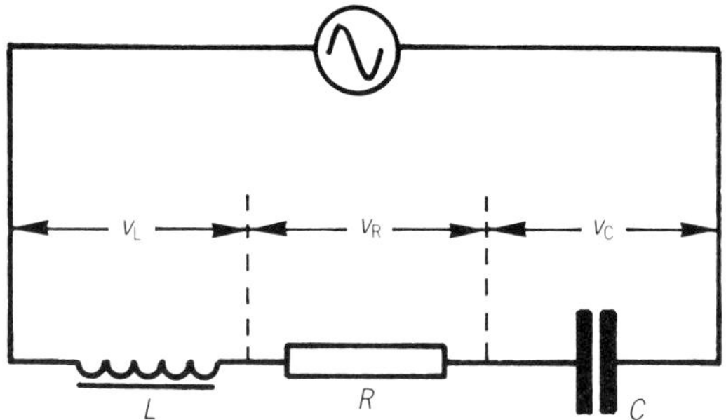

Figure 49.16

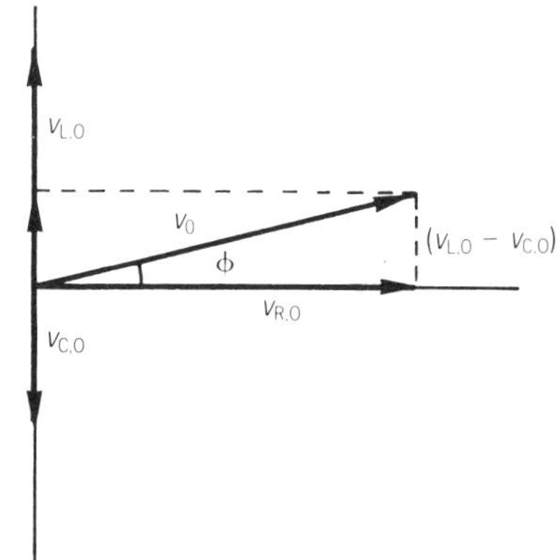

Figure 49.17

The voltages across the inductor and the capacitor (v_{L0} and v_{c0}) are 180° out of phase, and the result of the addition of these two must be added vectorially to v_{R0} to give the resultant voltage, which is therefore given by:

$$v_0^2 = (v_{L0} - v_{C0})^2 + v_{R0}^2 = (i_0X_L - i_0X_C)^2 + i_0^2R^2$$

This means that the impedance of the circuit is:

$$Z = \sqrt{(X_L - X_C)^2 + R^2}$$

It should be realised that since the voltages across the capacitor and the inductor are 180° out of phase they may be individually greater than the supply voltage – see the example.

Example

Consider an *L–C–R* series circuit where $R = 300\ \Omega$, $L = 0.9$ H, $C = 2.0\ \mu$F and the supply frequency has a frequency of 50 Hz and an r.m.s. voltage of 240 V. Therefore $\omega = 314$ radians per second.

$$X_L = \omega L = 314 \times 0.9 = 283\ \Omega$$

$$X_C = \frac{1}{314 \times 2 \times 10^{-6}} = 1592\ \Omega$$

The reactance X of the capacitor–inductor components is $283 - 1592 = -1309\ \Omega$.

The reactance Z is given by:

$$Z = \sqrt{X^2 + R^2} = 1342\ \Omega$$

The phase angle will be 77 ° and the current in the circuit 0.18 A.

Summarising:

For the resistor: $v_R = iR = 0.18 \times 300 = 54$ V
For the inductor: $v_L = iX_L = 0.18 \times 283 = 51$ V
For the capacitor: $v_c = iX_c = 0.18 \times 1592 = 287$ V

11 A capacitor, an inductor and a resistor are connected in series and an a.c. supply of 130 V, 50 Hz placed across them. An a.c. voltmeter connected in turn across the terminals of the capacitor, the inductor and the resistor reads 30 V, 80 V and 120 V respectively.

(*a*) Explain with the help of a diagram the phase relation between these voltages and show how they can be reconciled with the applied voltage.

(*b*) Calculate the values of *C*, *L* and *R* if a current of 1.5 A flows in the circuit. [o]

12 A 600Ω resistor, a 5 μF capacitor and a 0.8 H inductor are connected in series with a 240 V, 50 Hz mains supply.

(*a*) Determine the current flowing and the potential difference across each component.

(*b*) Explain why the sum of the potential differences is not 240 V. [w]

Resonance

One very important consequence of this result is that the impedance of a circuit has a *minimum* value when $X_L = X_C$. When this condition holds the current through the circuit is a *maximum*.

This is known as the **resonant condition** for the circuit. You can see that since X_L and X_C are frequency-dependent, the resonant condition depends on the frequency of the applied a.c.

Every series a.c. circuit has a frequency for which resonance occurs, known as its **resonant frequency** (f_0). This is given by the equation

$$\frac{1}{2\pi f_0 C} = 2\pi f_0 L \quad \text{or} \quad f_0 = \frac{1}{2\pi\sqrt{LC}}$$

For the circuit given in the above example the resonant frequency is 119 Hz. (see also the example below).

Figure 49.18 shows how X_L, X_C, R and Z vary with frequency for a series circuit. The value of f_0 is clearly seen.

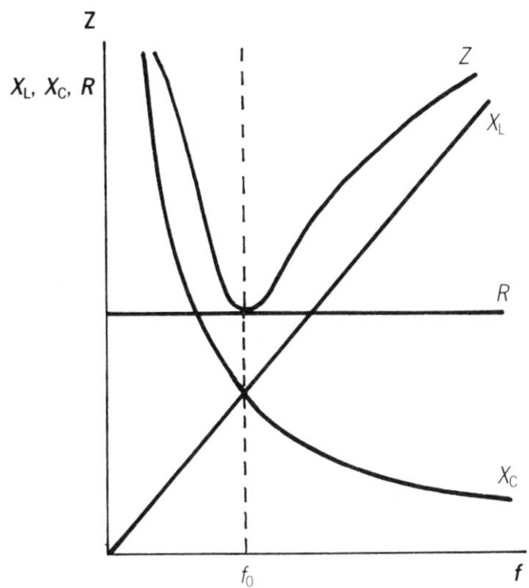

Figure 49.18

Example

A capacitor of 20 pF and an inductor are joined in series. Calculate the value of the inductor that will give the circuit a resonant frequency of 200 kHz (Radio 4).

Resonant frequency (f_0) = $2 \times 10^5 = 1/2\pi\sqrt{LC}$. Therefore

$$L = \frac{1}{4 \times 10^{10} \times 20 \times 10^{-9} \times 4\pi^2} = 0.03 \text{ mH}$$

13 A coil of inductance 0.2 mH and negligible resistance is connected in series with a capacitor of capacitance 0.005μF. Calculate the resonant frequency of the circuit.

14 A coil of inductance 0.1 mH is connected in series with a variable capacitor. If this simple arrangement is to be used as a tuner for Radio 3 (wavelength 247 m), what is the value of the capacitor required?

15 Write a short account of the phenomenon of resonance, taking examples from mechanics, light and electricity.

Power in a.c. circuits

The power consumed in any circuit is given by the equation

$P = vi$

Now for a capacitor
$v = v_0 \sin(\omega t)$ and $i = i_0 \cos(\omega t)$.

The power dissipated is therefore

$$P = i_0 v_0 \sin(\omega t).\cos(\omega t) = \tfrac{1}{2} i_0 v_0 \sin(2\omega t)$$

But the average value of $\sin(2\omega t)$ is zero, and therefore the power dissipated in a purely capacitative circuit is also zero.

The same argument shows that the power dissipated in a purely inductive circuit is also zero. For this reason capacitors and inductors are often used in a.c. circuits to limit the current, since they do not waste any energy.

16 A 110 V, 60 W lamp is run from a 240 V a.c. mains supply using a capacitor in series with the lamp instead of a resistor. Calculate

(*a*) the value of the capacitor required and the r.m.s. voltage across it when in use;

(*b*) if a resistor had been used instead of the capacitor, the value of resistor that would have been needed;

(*c*) the power that would be dissipated in the resistor;

(*d*) the advantage of using a capacitor instead of a resistor.

(*e*) Repeat parts (*a*) and (*d*), using an inductor instead of a capacitor.

Electrical oscillations

The oscillations of the current within an electrical circuit are of fundamental importance in the generation of waveforms of a variety of shapes for radio, oscilloscopes, signal generators and so forth. One of the simplest circuits for producing these oscillations is a capacitor and an inductor connected as shown in Figure 49.19. In understanding these oscillations it is helpful to compare them with the mechanical oscillations in a spring.

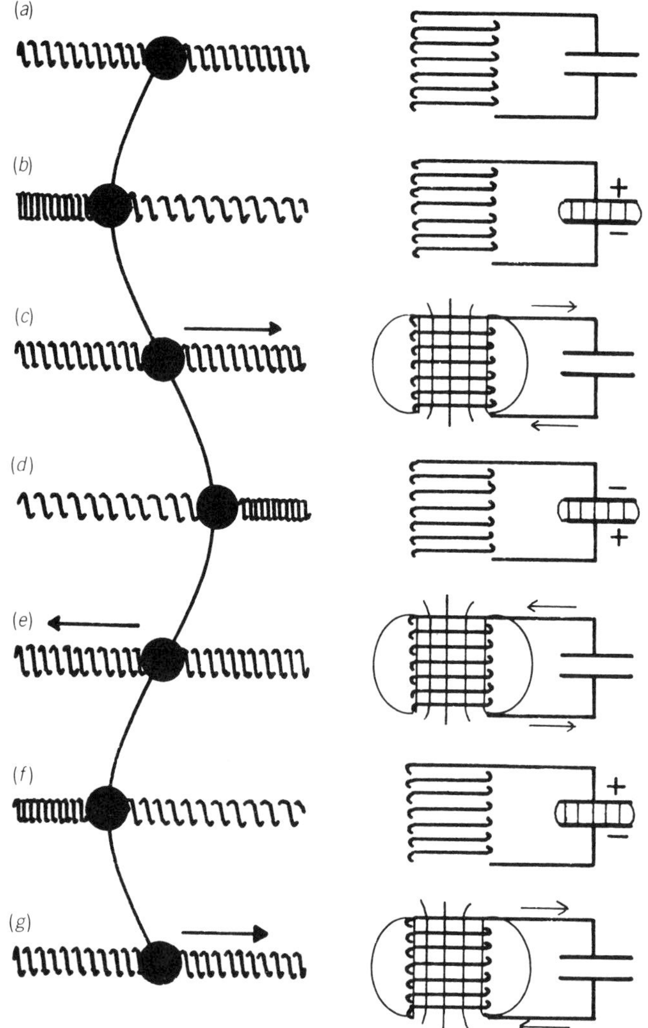

Figure 49.19

Consider the diagram. The mass on the spring oscillates, transferring stored potential energy in the spring to kinetic energy of the mass and back again. The charge in the electrical circuit also oscillates, transferring stored energy in the electric field of the capacitor to energy in the magnetic field in the inductor.

(*a*) This diagram represents the initial zero energy situation for both systems. The mass is at rest and the springs are in equilibrium and no energy exists as stored charge in the capacitor or current in the inductor.

(*b*) The mass is displaced from its rest position, and therefore potential energy is stored in the spring. The capacitor is charged, thus possessing potential energy.

(*c*) As soon as the mass is released it moves to the right, gaining kinetic energy. The capacitor begins to discharge through the inductor, producing a magnetic field in it.

(*d*) The mass is now at rest; all the energy is stored as potential energy in the spring. The charge has now stopped moving and all energy is stored in the capacitor, which is charged in the opposite sense from its original state.

(*e*) This process now repeats itself, the mass oscillating backwards and forwards and the charge continually charging and discharging the capacitor.
A continuous exchange of energy occurs from potential to kinetic energy in the springs

$$\tfrac{1}{2}Fe \text{ going to } \tfrac{1}{2}mv^2$$

and from electric to magnetic energy in the electrical circuit

$$\tfrac{1}{2}QV \text{ going to } \tfrac{1}{2}Li^2$$

The amplitudes of the oscillations decrease with time, since energy is lost as other forms: (*a*) in the spring as heating in the coils and air resistance, (*b*) in the inductor and connecting wires as heat due to the flow of current within them.

Filters and tuned circuits

The resonance effects in an *L–C* circuit may be used to filter out selected regions of the frequency spectrum.

Figure 49.20(*a*) shows an **acceptor** filter where frequencies of $1/2\pi\sqrt{(LC)}$ will be passed by the filter. Figure 49.20(*b*) shows a **rejector** filter where all frequencies *except* those of frequency $1/2\pi\sqrt{(LC)}$ will be passed by the filter.

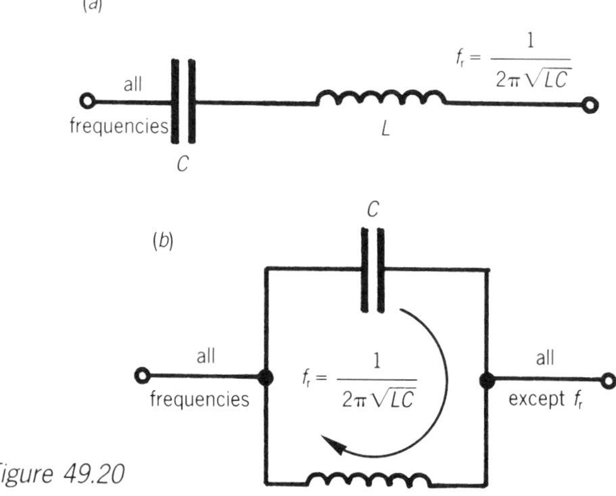

Figure 49.20

If the capacitor (or inductor) is variable, then the circuit may be tuned to resonate at a particular frequency. This is used in the tuning of a radio set. The aerial receives a broad band of frequencies and the capacitor is varied so that the circuit resonates at the frequency of the required station. A simple circuit for the tuner section of a radio receiver is shown in Figure 49.21(*a*). The response of the circuit with frequency is shown in Figure 49.21(*b*), in which R is the total series resistance of the tuned circuit.

A simple radio receiver

In a radio transmitter the audio signal is combined with a wave of high frequency, called the carrier wave. This is known as **modulation**. Either the amplitude or the frequency may be varied. The effects of both amplitude and frequency modulation are shown in Figure 49.22.

In the receiver the frequency to which the aerial must be tuned is that of the carrier wave. The carrier wave must be demodulated so that the audio signal may be detected.

The full circuit for a simple receiver is shown in Figure 49.23, the functions of the various sections being indicated.

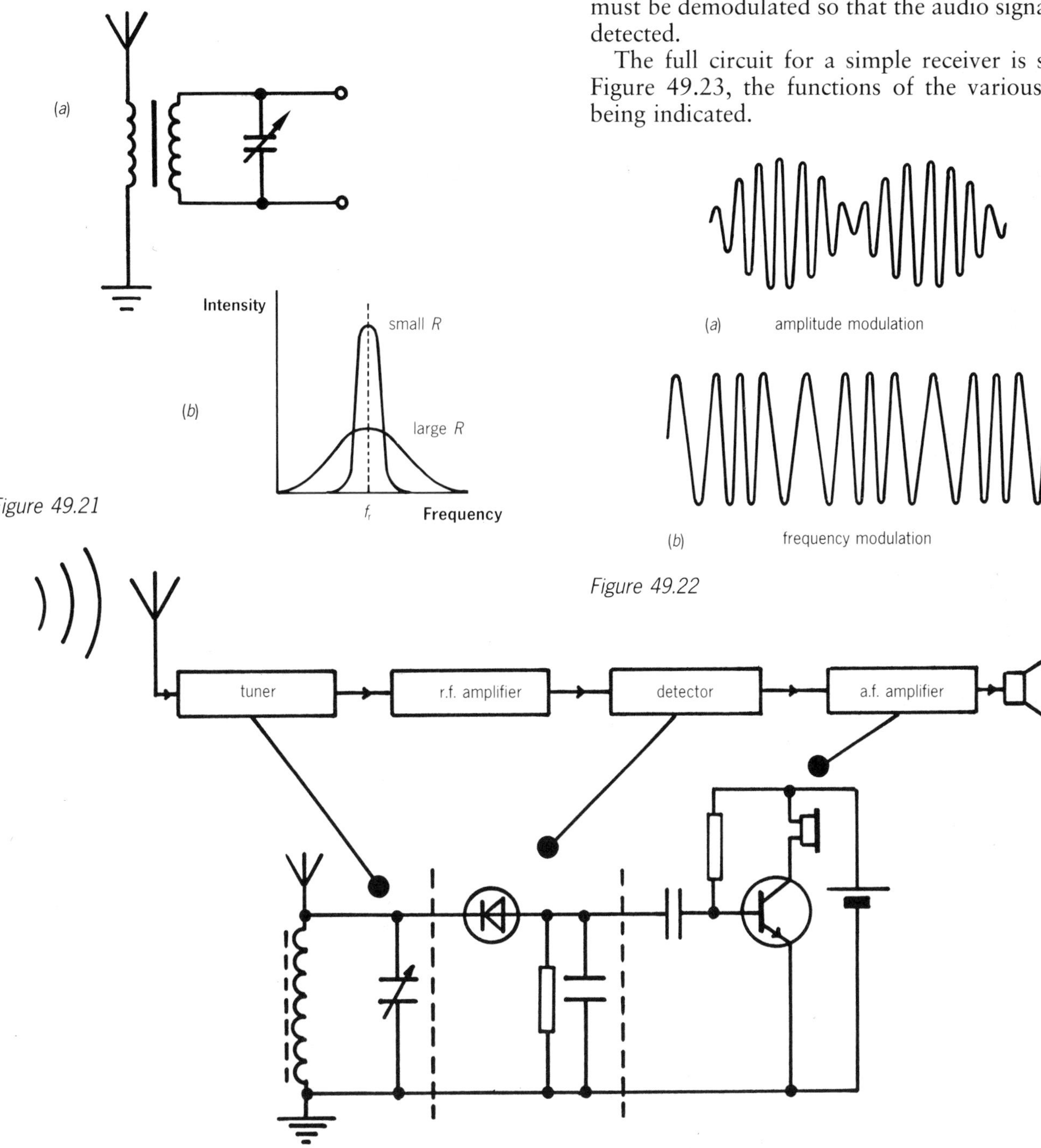

Figure 49.21

Figure 49.22

Figure 49.23

Semiconductor devices

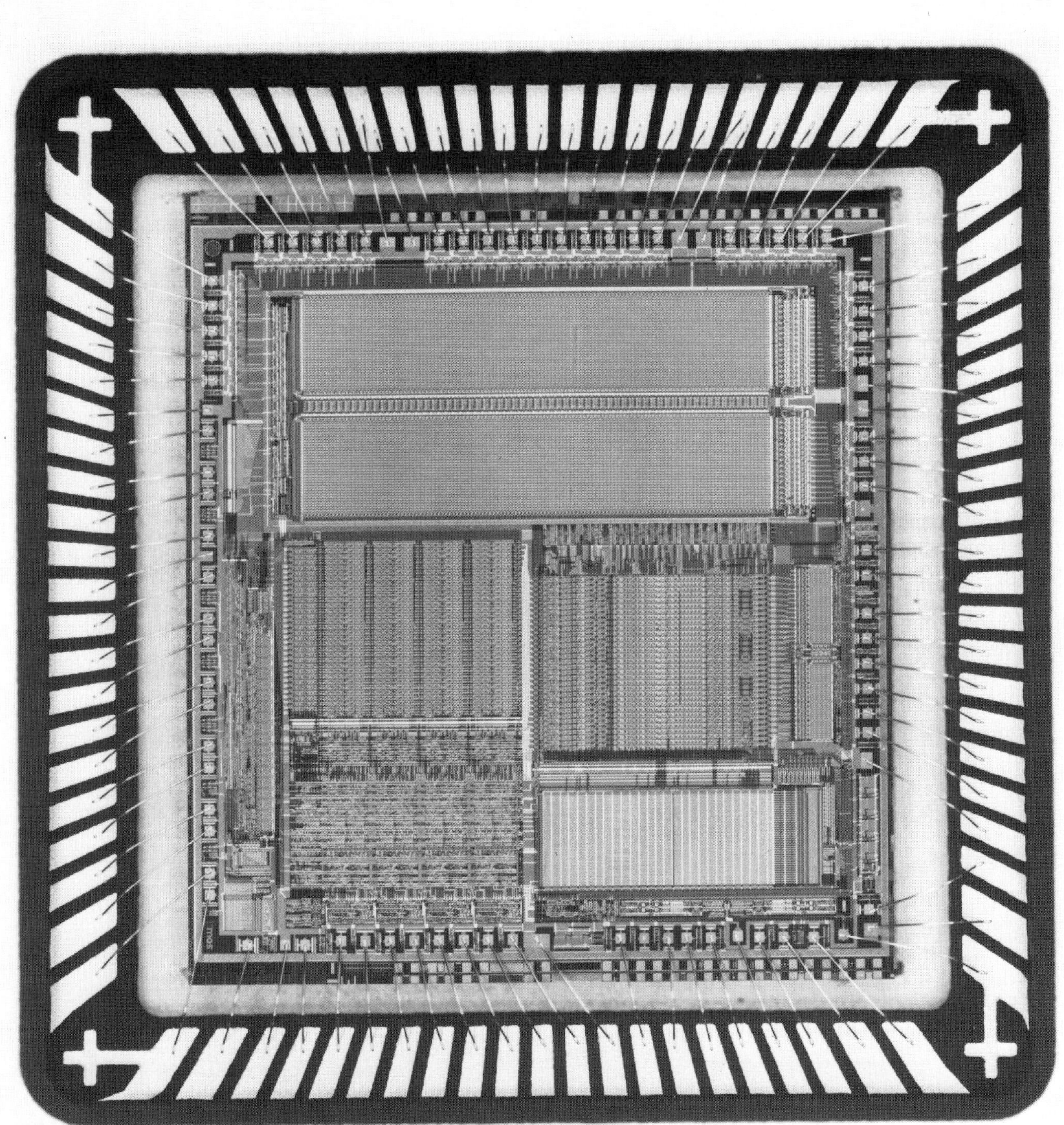

The INMOS 32 bit transputer (Institute of Physics)

50 · What are semiconductors?

The advent of the semiconductor has revolutionised our lives, since it is the basis of all integrated circuits and microprocessors.

To distinguish between the electrical properties of materials we can group them into three sections:

(*a*) conductors,
(*b*) semiconductors and
(*c*) insulators.

You are probably aware of many conductors and insulators such as copper and rubber; semiconductors include materials such as silicon, germanium, carbon, selenium, gallium arsenide, lead sulphide and so on. The important difference between conductors, semiconductors and insulators lies in the number of free electrons present in the material. Perhaps the best way to consider the differences between them is to use the **band theory of solids**.

As you may know, electrons in an individual atom are restricted to well-defined energy levels and energy changes within the atom only take place between one level and another (see page 415).

In a solid the atoms are linked together and the electrons can occupy a whole series of energy levels grouped into **bands** (see Figure 50.1). The difference in energy between levels within the band is very small compared with the energy gap between the bands. The electrical differences between one type of solid and another lie in the different arrangements of the bands.

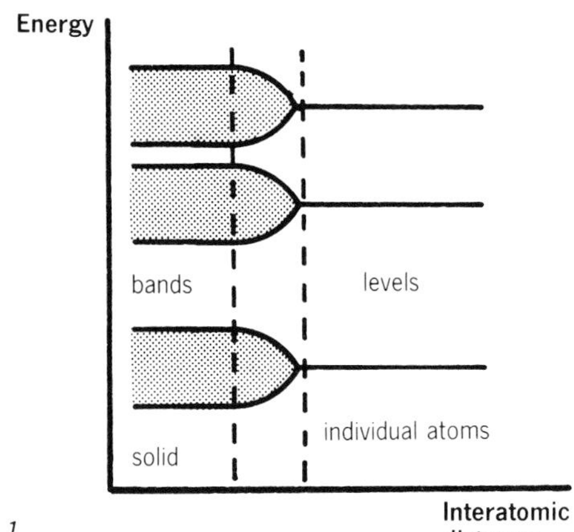

Figure 50.1

The band structures of a conductor, semiconductor and insulator are shown in Figure 50.2.

Conductors

In a conductor the valence band is full of electrons, while the conduction band is only partly filled. The addition of a very small amount of energy will allow electrons to move within the conduction band, some rising to a higher level and others returning to lower levels. This movement of electrons constitutes electrical conduction.

In some conductors the valence band and the conduction band actually overlap. This effectively gives a partly filled top band.

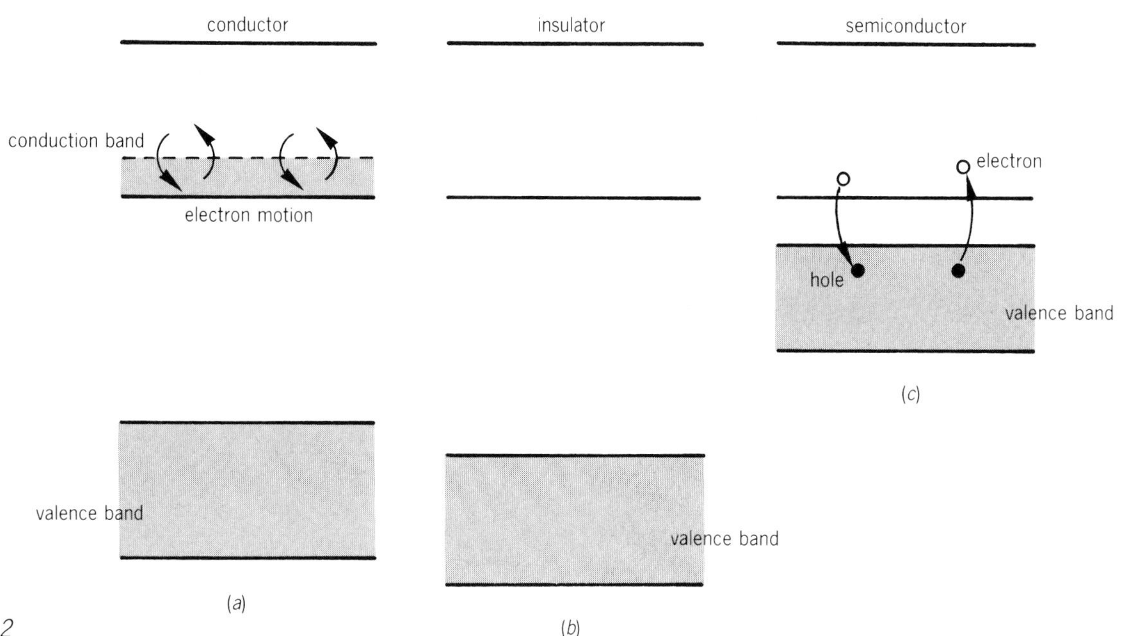

Figure 50.2

Intrinsic semiconductors

We will deal first with the **intrinsic semiconductor.** This is a material that is a semiconductor 'in its own right' – nothing has been added to it.

In the intrinsic semiconductor the valence band is full once more, but the conduction band is empty at very low temperatures. However, the energy gap between the two bands is so very small that electrons can jump across it by the addition of thermal energy alone; in other words, heating the specimen is sufficient to cause electrical conduction. The conductivity increases with temperature as more and more electrons are liberated. Semiconductors therefore have negative temperature coefficients of resistance.

For germanium the energy gap is 0.66 eV and for silicon it is 1.11 eV at 27 °C. When an electron jumps to the conduction band it leaves behind it a space or **hole** in the valence band. This hole is effectively positive and since an electron can jump into it from another part of the valence band it is as if the hole itself was moving! Conduction can take place either by negative electrons moving within the conduction band or by positive holes moving within the valence band. A semiconductor may be thought of as similar to an almost full multistorey car park, the cars representing the electrons and the spaces the holes (no cars are allowed to enter or leave the car park, however, only to drive round within it!).

If this idea of holes seems odd to you, think of a pile of earth and the hole in the road from which it came. Both the pile (electron) and the hole (hole) have a physical effect on you if you run into them on a bike! Conduction by positive holes is rather like workmen digging up a road; in a way, they are only moving a hole from one place to another.

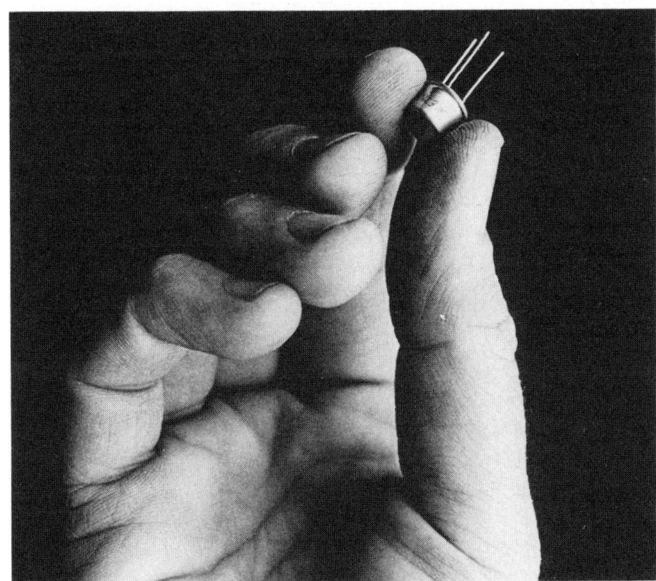

A transistor

Student investigation

The thermistor is a semiconductor device whose resistance changes markedly with temperature. Using a negative temperature coefficient thermistor, set up the circuit shown in Figure 50.3 and record values of the current and voltage for a range of temperatures. Hence plot a graph of resistance against temperature.

Finally plot a second graph, choosing suitable axes to give a linear graph.

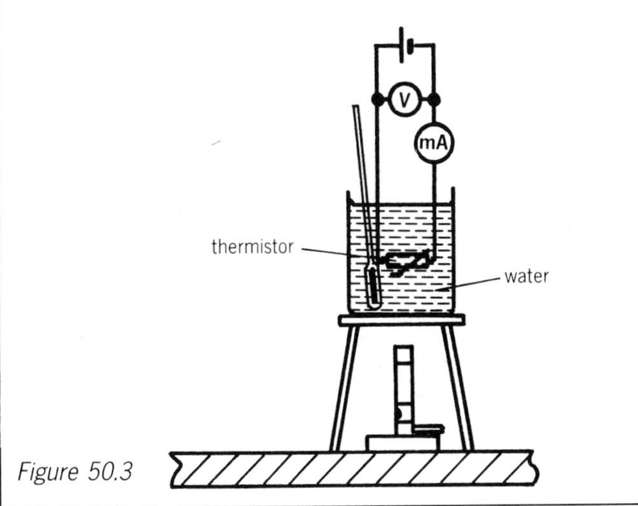

Figure 50.3

Insulators

In the insulator the valence band is full once again, but in these substances the energy gap between this and the empty conduction band is very large. It would take a great deal of energy to make an electron jump the gap and to cause the insulator to break down. At very high temperatures or under very large electric fields breakdown will occur, and like semiconductors the greater the temperature the greater the conduction. Insulators, like semiconductors, have negative temperature coefficients of resistance.

Student investigation

Investigate how the conductivity of glass varies with temperature. A short glass rod should be connected to the mains supply by winding copper wire round each end. An a.c. ammeter and voltmeter should be included in the circuit. The glass rod should then be heated strongly with a bunsen burner until conduction takes place. The current may produce sufficient heat to allow the bunsen to be switched off. Record the conductivity under different conditions during the experiment.

WARNING: This experiment should only be performed in a laboratory under strict staff supervision.

The Hall effect

This effect was discovered by Edwin Hall in 1879 using a strip of gold foil. He showed that a p.d. could be built up *across* a conductor in a magnetic field when an electric current is passed through it.

The sign of the charge carriers in a given material can be found using the Hall effect. A specimen of the material has a small current passed through it while it is placed in a magnetic field so that the field acts at right angles to the face of the specimen (see Figure 50.4). The magnetic field will exert a force on the charge carriers so that they move to one side of the specimen or the other. This will build up a potential difference across the material which will just balance the magnetic force at equilibrium. The sign of the potential will determine whether the charge carriers are positive or negative.

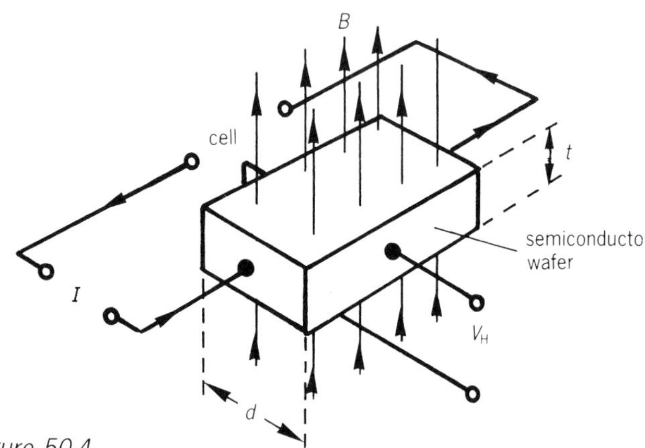

Figure 50.4

If E is the electric field intensity, e the charge on an electron, v the velocity of charge carriers and B the flux density of the field then:

$$Ee = Bev \qquad \text{and so} \qquad \frac{V_H e}{d} = Bev$$

Therefore, since $I = nAve$ where n is the number of charge carriers per cubic metre and A the cross-sectional area of the specimen, d its width and t its thickness,

$$V_H = \frac{BI}{net}$$

The value of the Hall voltage V_H depends on the current, flux density, electron charge and thickness of the specimen. It also depends on n. The more free charge carriers there are in the material, the smaller the Hall voltage will be. For a metal such as copper $n = 10^{29}$ and the Hall voltage will be only 0.06 microvolts for $B = 1$ T, $I = 1$ A and $t = 1$ mm. For semiconducting materials $n = 10^{25}$ and so a voltage of 0.6 millivolts is produced.

A Hall probe may be used to find the number or sign of the charge carriers or to measure the flux density of a steady magnetic field (see page 300).

1 (*a*) What properties of a material may be determined using the Hall effect?

(*b*) What other quantity is often measured using the Hall effect?

(*c*) A small slice of gold 0.05 mm thick and with a free electron concentration of 8.7×10^{28} m^{-3} lies with its plane perpendicular to a steady magnetic field of flux density 1.5 T. If it has a current of 400 mA passed through it, calculate the Hall voltage developed across the slice. (Electron charge $= 1.6 \times 10^{-19}$ C)

2 A germanium slice 1 mm thick is placed with its plane perpendicular to a steady magnetic field of flux density 0.8 T. If a current of 50 mA flows through the slice and the Hall voltage developed is 25 mV, calculate the density of free electrons in germanium. (Electron charge $= 1.6 \times 10^{-9}$ C)

3 (*a*) A piece of semiconductor with Hall coefficient 6.3×10^{-4} m^3 C^{-1} is used to make a Hall probe. A current of 2.0 mA is passed along the 10.0 mm length of the probe. The width of the face to be placed perpendicular to the magnetic flux density to be measured is 5.0 mm and the thickness is 1.0 mm. Estimate the Hall potential difference which would be obtained when B is 0.3 T.

(*b*) A plane circular coil C_1 has 200 turns of diameter 0.6 m. It is mounted with its plane vertical and is connected in series with a much smaller coil C_2 of diameter 0.07 m containing 100 turns of wire. C_2 is placed with its plane horizontal at the centre of C_1. Show that, when a current i is passed through the two coils. C_1 exerts a couple on C_2 proportional to i^2 tending to rotate it out of the horizontal plane.

Estimate the value of this couple when $i = 4$ A, indicating any assumption made.

Suggest a means of measuring the couple.

[O and C part]

The quantity $1/ne$ is known as the Hall coefficient for a material.

Extrinsic semiconductors

An **extrinsic semiconductor** is basically a semiconductor to which a very small amount of impurity has been added. About one atom per million is replaced by an impurity atom; this process is called **doping**.

Doping with an impurity can have quite marked effects on the electrical properties of the material. The addition of one impurity atom in one hundred million will increase the conductivity of germanium by twelve times at 300 K. Very precise doping may be achieved by neutron irradiation.

We will consider the effects of doping a piece of silicon. Silicon is made up of tetravalent atoms joined in a lattice, as shown in Figure 50.5. Two types of semiconductor can be made by doping with different impurities:

(*a*) **n-type**, by doping with pentavalent material such as phosphorus;

(*b*) **p-type**, by doping with trivalent material such as aluminium.

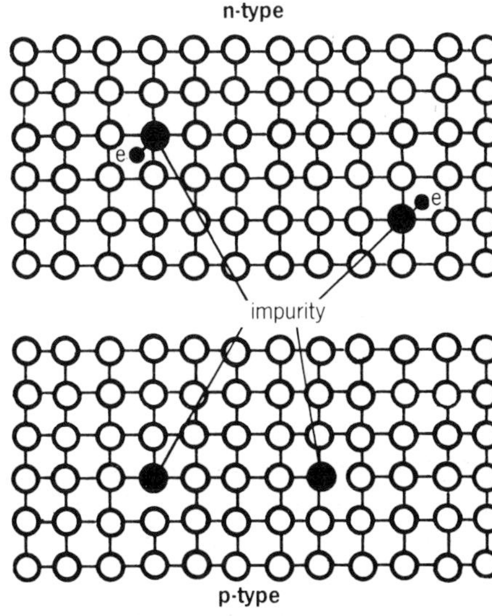

Figure 50.5

The effect of both types of doping is shown in the diagram. With the p-type each impurity atom has one fewer electron than the silicon atom, while with the n-type they have one extra electron.

Figures 50.6 and 50.7 show how the impurity atoms fit into the energy level diagram of the solid as a whole. In the p-type material the aluminium levels fall just above the full valence band of the silicon. These levels are very close to this band and so electrons can easily jump into them from the valence band. For this reason they are called **acceptor** levels. When an electron jumps up to these levels it leaves behind a hole in the valence band; it is the movement of holes within the valence band that causes the greatest conduction in p-type material. In the n-type material the phosphorus energy levels fall just below the empty conduction band of the silicon, and very close to it. For this reason electrons can very easily jump from them into the conduction band, and they are therefore called **donor** levels. In n-type material conduction takes place mainly due to the movement of these electrons.

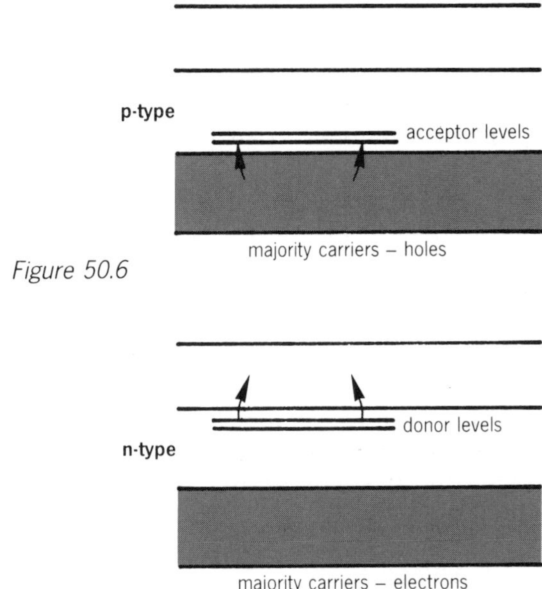

Figure 50.6

Figure 50.7

4 Explain how the conductivity of a semiconductor varies with (*a*) temperature, (*b*) the addition of impurities.

5 Describe the structure of
(*a*) an extrinsic semiconductor,
(*b*) an n-type extrinsic semiconductor, and
(*c*) a p-type extrinsic semiconductor.

6 Explain why the addition of an impurity atom of valency different from that of the main crystal atoms does not produce a change of charge of the specimen.

Conduction occurs in both types of extrinsic semiconductor by the movement of both holes and electrons. The particles that contribute most to conduction are called **majority carriers** and the other **minority carriers**.

In a p-type material the majority carriers are holes, and in an n-type semiconductor the majority carriers are electrons.

51 · Diodes and transistors

The p–n junction

If a region of p-type material and a region of n-type material are formed side by side in a piece of silicon, a p–n junction is formed. It is important that this is made in one piece of the material so that the crystal lattice extends across the boundary. It is not sufficient just to have two pieces in contact.

Both the p-type and the n-type material are electrically neutral, but they both contain an imbalance of conduction electrons or holes. At the boundary, holes drift from the p-type towards the n-type material and electrons drift from the n-type to the p-type to reduce this imbalance. This diffusion of holes and electrons across the boundary sets up a potential barrier which prevents further change, the p-type region becoming slightly negative and the n-type becoming slightly positive. The barrier has a p.d. across it of about 0.1 V, although the exact size of the potential barrier depends on the material. These effects only occur over a very small region (about 10^{-3} mm on either side of the boundary) known as the **depletion layer**. They are summarised in Figure 51.1.

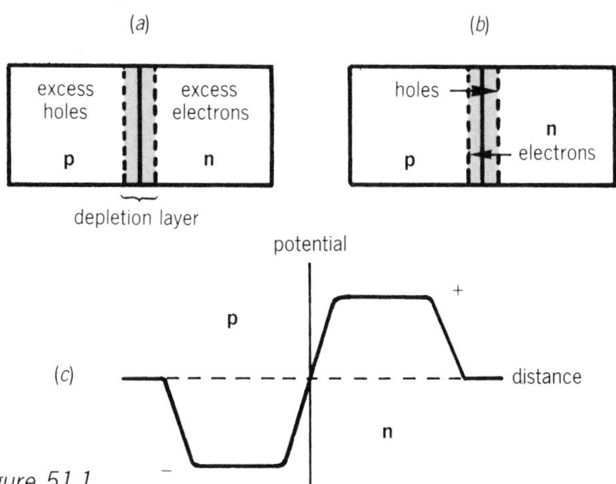

Figure 51.1

The p–n junction forms a semiconductor diode. If current is to flow through the diode, then the latter must be connected in a circuit in such a way as to reduce the height of the potential barrier, that is, the p-type material must be made positive to attract more electrons and the n-type must be made negative.

Connecting it in such a way is called **forward bias**, and round the other way is known as **reverse bias**. A reverse bias tends to increase the width of the depletion layer while a forward bias will reduce the width of this layer (see Figure 51.2).

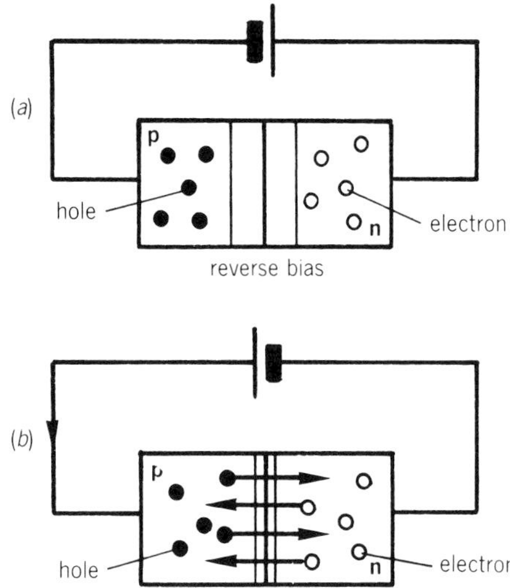

Figure 51.2

> **Student investigation**
>
> Use an insulated semiconductor diode to see how the current through it is affected by the temperature of the diode for a fixed input voltage. The diode should be immersed in a beaker of water which is then heated gently.

Characteristics of a p–n junction diode

The characteristics of a germanium junction diode are shown in Figure 51.3. When in the forward biased direction, as the p.d. across it is increased the current increases almost linearly, a p.d. of a volt giving a current of a few milliamps. In the reverse direction

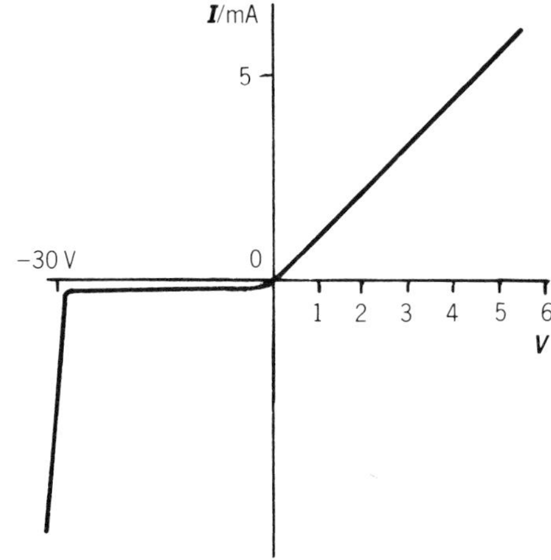

Figure 51.3

the current is only a few microamps until the diode breaks down, this occuring at a reverse p.d. of some 30 V.

Diodes must be protected from excess temperature, otherwise their structure will be destroyed. The limit for germanium is about 100 °C, and that for silicon about 200 °C.

Semiconductor diodes have several advantages over thermionic diode valves. They are smaller, require less voltage to operate, do not waste so much energy as heat and are quick and cheap to manufacture. At the time of writing a small thermionic diode valve costs about £3, while the same money would buy about thirty semiconductor diodes!

Rectification using a diode

The diode can be used as a simple rectifier because of the difference in its forward and reverse bias properties. The effect of a single diode on an a.c. voltage is shown in Figure 51.4(*a*) and (*b*); this is known as **half-wave rectification.** The addition of a capacitor will produce a smoothing effect on the output, as shown in Figure 51.4(*c*).

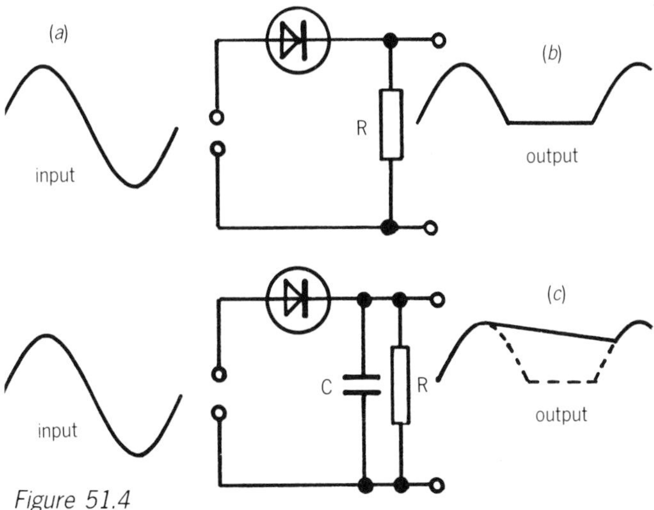

Figure 51.4

> **Student investigation**
>
> Using a bridge rectifier similar to that in Figure 51.5 with a sinusoidal signal applied to points A and B, investigate the output voltage between the following points: (*a*) A and C, (*b*) A and D, (*c*) C and D, (*d*) C and B.

Full-wave rectification may be obtained using the bridge rectifier circuit. This is basically four diodes connected in a square (Figure 51.5) and once again the smoothing effect of a capacitor is shown.

The action of the bridge rectifier can be explained as follows. If point A is positive diode 2 conducts, making D positive. If B is positive diode 4 conducts, still keeping D positive.

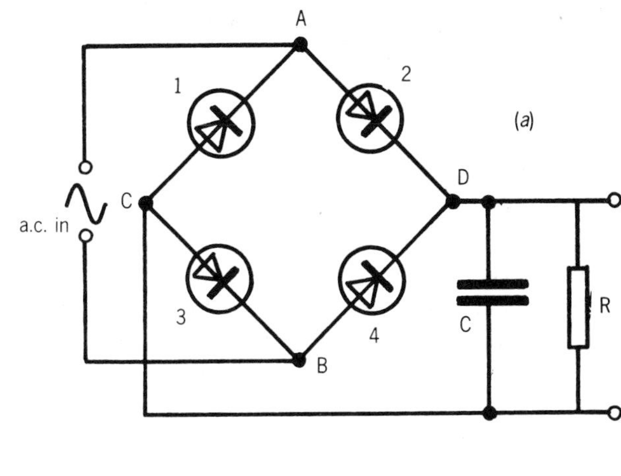

Figure 51.5

1 Explain the action of the circuit in Figure 51.6. For a sinusoidal input sketch the output and input voltages on the same axes. If the peak voltage induced between A and B is 12 V, what is the peak across (*a*) *R*, (*b*) D_1?

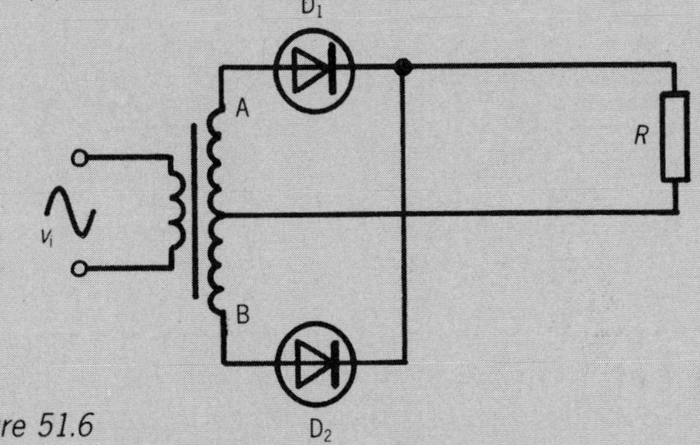

Figure 51.6

2 Why does the resistance of *pure* silicon fall as the temperature rises?

3 The following questions concern the semiconductor diode.
(*a*) What is meant by (i) reverse bias, (ii) forward bias?
(*b*) What is meant by the *depletion layer*?
(*c*) Explain the way in which the width of the depletion layer varies for the two conditions described in part (*a*).

4 In a bridge rectifier circuit containing four semiconductor diodes, one diode breaks so that an open circuit occurs at that point.
Describe and explain the shape of the resulting output waveform for a sinusoidal a.c. input.

5 Explain why a reverse biased semiconductor diode may be used to detect alpha-particles.

The transistor

In 1948 some work was carried out at the Bell Telephone Laboratories in America that has changed our lives. This was the invention of the **transistor** by Shockley, Brattain and Bardeen.

The transistor, basically a semiconductor triode, consists of a thin central layer of one type of semiconductor between two relatively thick pieces of the other type. The junction transistor can be of two types, as shown in Figure 51.7: pnp or npn. The pnp transistor consists of a very thin piece of n-type material sandwiched between two pieces of p-type, while the npn transistor has a central piece of p-type. The pieces at either side are called the **emitter** and the **collector** while the central part is known as the **base.** The base is lightly doped compared with the emitter and the collector, and is only about 3–5 μm thick.

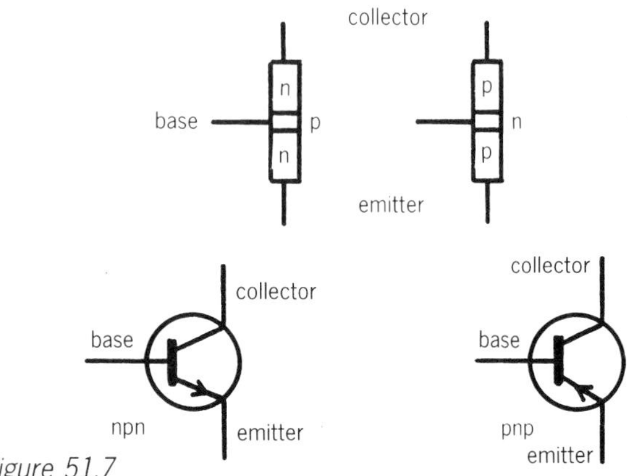

Figure 51.7

From now on we will consider only the npn transistor as it is now in more common use in schools. The npn silicon transistor is connected into the circuit as shown by Figure 51.8. The emitter–base junction is forward biased and the base–collector junction is reverse biased.

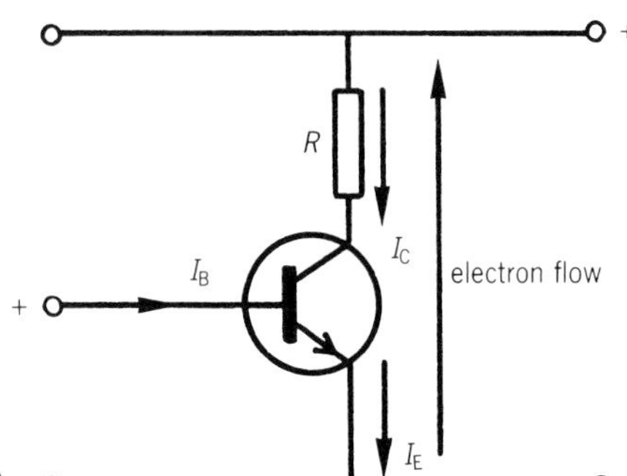

Figure 51.8

When the base–emitter voltage is 0.6 V current will flow through the transistor, electrons flowing through the base from the emitter to the collector. No current will flow without this base–emitter voltage, since it is needed to overcome the potential barrier formed at the junction. Electrons flow into the collector, although the base–collector junction is reverse biased because the base is very thin. You should see that the emitter current (I_E) is the sum of the base current (I_B) and the collector current (I_C):

$$I_E = I_B + I_C$$

I_C is usually over 99 per cent of I_E and I_B less than 1 per cent.

The name 'transistor' comes from the words 'transfer of resistance': the emitter–base junction is forward biased and therefore has a low resistance, while the base–collector is reverse biased and has a high resistance.

The properties of the transistor described above lead us to consider it as a current amplifier.

Student investigation

A very small current, known as a **leakage current**, will flow through the transistor even if there is no supply to the base. This experiment is designed to investigate how the leakage current varies with temperature.

Set up the circuit as shown in Figure 51.9, taking care not to let the transistor leads get in the water. Slowly heat the water and record a set of values of leakage current against temperature. Be sure to connect the transistor with the correct polarity.

Suggest why the current varies in the way you have observed.

Plot a graph of your results and then use the transistor to measure the temperature of your hand.

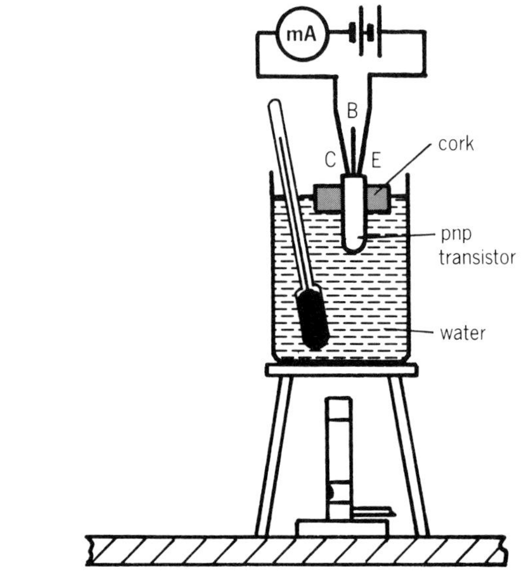

Figure 51.9

Example circuits with the npn transistor

For its basic operation, the circuit is set up as shown in Figure 51.10, and the value of *R* is chosen so that the transistor is switched on, that is, the potential at the base is at least 0.6 V.

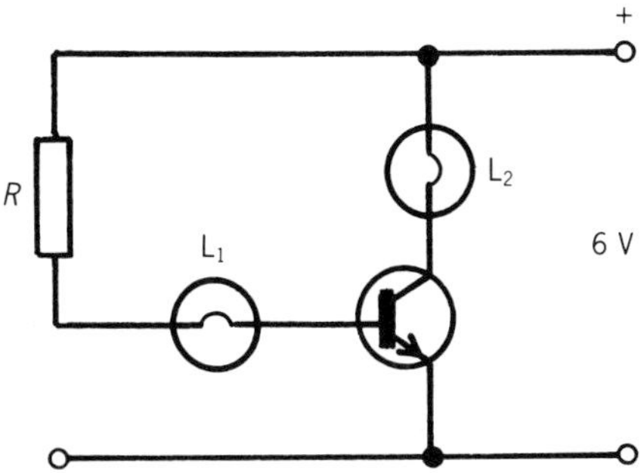

Figure 51.10

Lamp L_2 lights but L_1 does not, showing that the collector current must be much larger than the base current. If L_1 is removed, however, L_2 goes out because no potential is being applied to the base.

The transistor as a switch

As you have seen the transistor will not conduct (that is, no current will flow through from the collector to the emitter) unless there is a p.d. between the emitter and the base of at least 0.6 V. This property enables the transistor to be used as a switch: it is 'on' when the base–emitter p.d. is bigger than 0.6 V and 'off' when it isn't.

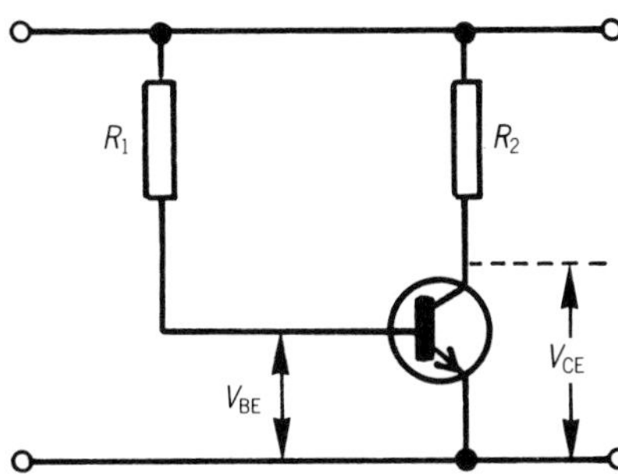

Figure 51.11

If you consider the circuit in Figure 51.11, then when the transistor is off, that is, there is no current flowing through it, the p.d. across the emitter–collector (V_{CE}) is high. As soon as the transistor starts to conduct this p.d. falls to very close to zero (Figure 51.12). So the output p.d. (V_{CE}) is small when the input p.d. (V_{BE}) is large, and large when the input p.d. is small (< 0.6 V). This is the basic NOT logic gate circuit (see page 387 for a further treatment).

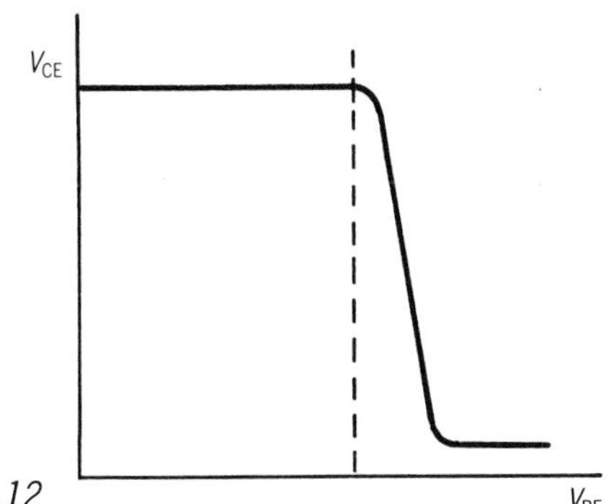

Figure 51.12

Student investigation

The switching characteristics of a transistor may be investigated using the circuit in Figure 51.13. Consult the Vela manual, and then record the V_{CE}/V_{BE} characteristic on the oscilloscope.

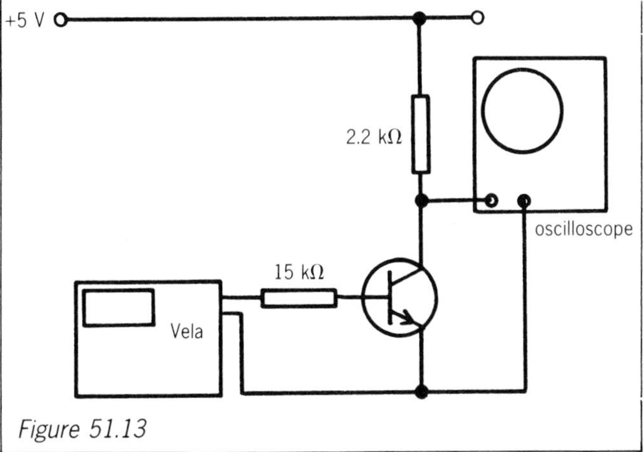

Figure 51.13

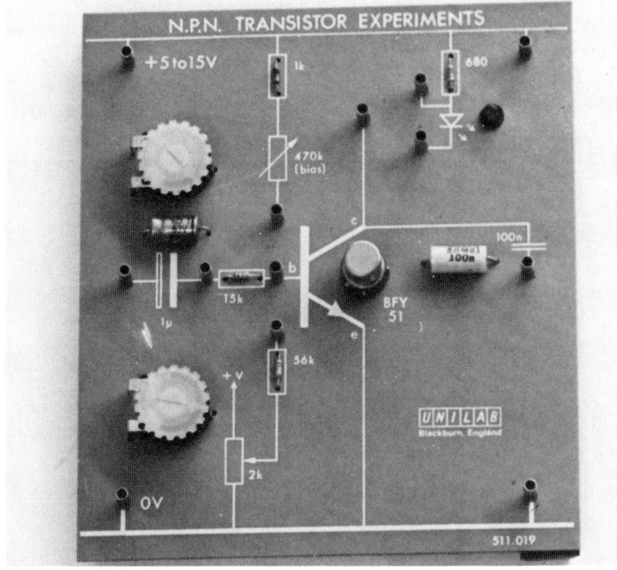

A transistor board for the investigation of the properties of a transistor (UNILAB Ltd.)

We will now consider two circuits in which the switching action of a transistor is important.

(i) Making a light come on in the dark
The circuit includes a light-dependent resistor (LDR), the resistance of which changes with illumination. A table showing the variation for a light-dependent resistor in common use is shown below.

Conditions	*Resistance*
Darkness	> 10 MΩ
60 W bulb at 1 m	2.4 kΩ
1 W bulb at 0.1 m	1.1 kΩ
Fluorescent lighting	275 Ω
Bright sunlight	10 Ω

The circuit used is shown in Figure 51.14. Since the resistance of the light-dependent resistor varies so will the voltage drop across it, and therefore the potential at the base will change. The less light that shines on the LDR the higher its resistance, and therefore the larger V_{BE} will be. If this is above 0.6 V the transistor switches on, and so when the LDR is in darkness the transistor conducts and the lamp L comes on.

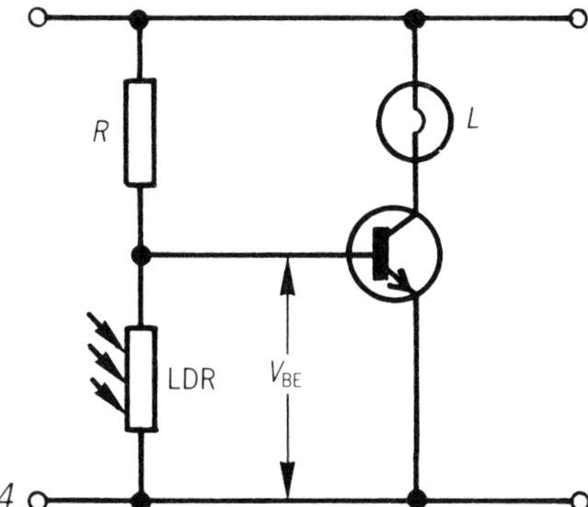

Figure 51.14

(ii) Moisture detector
The circuit is shown in Figure 51.15. If the base circuit is broken at XY then the transistor is off, but if the probes XY are placed in a conducting liquid the transistor switches on. This could be used as a liquid level indicator for a blind person, the lamp L being replaced by a buzzer.

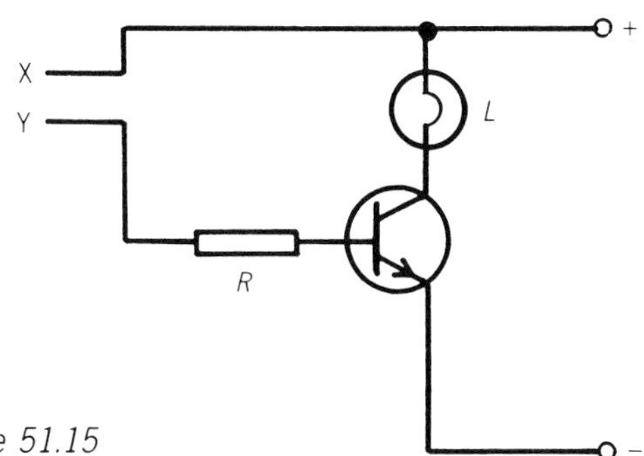

Figure 51.15

> **Student investigation**
>
> Design and build a simple fire alarm based on the switching action of a transistor and using a thermistor as a heat sensor. Explain how you would be able to vary the temperature at which the alarm is triggered.

> **Student investigation**
>
> Design and build a circuit based on the switching action of a transistor that will close the contacts of a relay after a certain time. (Note that a diode should be connected in parallel with the relay to protect the transistor from the large e.m.f. induced in the relay coil when the current falls to zero when the circuit is switched off.)

Saturation

We have seen that when V_{BE} >0.6 V the transistor switches on, and Figure 51.16 shows that as V_{BE} is increased above this value V_{CE} falls and reaches a steady value (close to zero) when V_{BE} is about 1.4 V. Any further increase in V_{BE} does not change V_{CE}.

In this condition the transistor is said to have bottomed or be **saturated**.

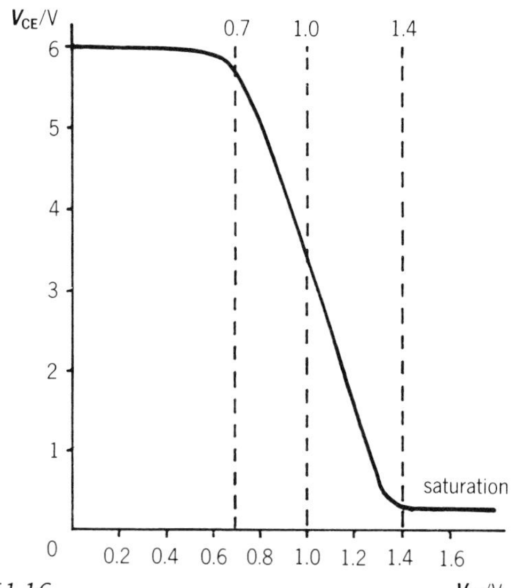

Figure 51.16

Transistor characteristics

The characteristics of the npn transistor can be found using the circuit shown in Figure 51.17.

Three characteristics are usually measured and these are shown in Figure 51.18:

(*a*) the variation of base current (I_B) with base–emitter voltage (V_{BE}),

(*b*) the variation of collector current (I_C) with base current, and

(*c*) the variation of collector current with collector–emitter voltage (V_{CE}).

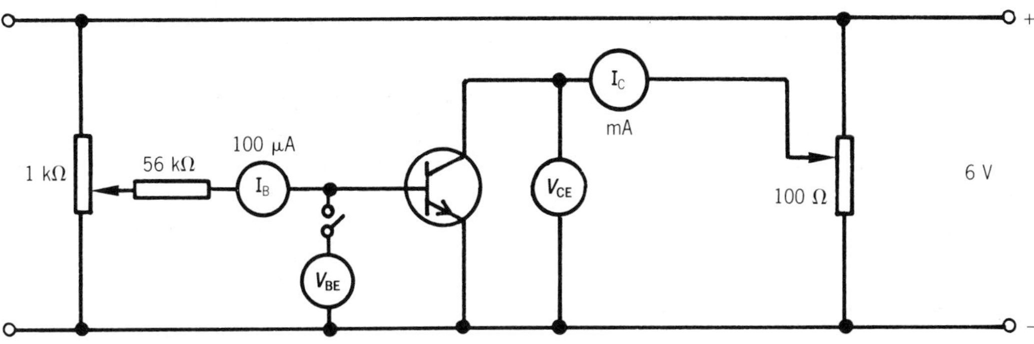

Figure 51.17

Figure 51.18(*a*) shows the 'switching on' of the transistor. There is no significant base current until the base–emitter voltage reaches about 0.6 V.

Figure 51.18(*b*) shows how the collector current varies when there is a change in the base current. You can see that a change in base current (ΔI_B) of a few *microamps* will produce a collector current change (ΔI_C) of a few *milliamps*. This shows the **amplifying action** of the transistor and also that this amplification is current-controlled rather than voltage-controlled. The ratio of the change in collector current to the change in base current is called the **current gain** of the transistor, and is written as h_{FE}. Thus

$$h_{FE} = \frac{\Delta I_C}{\Delta I_B}$$

This usually has a value of between 100 and 200 for an npn silicon transistor.

Figure 51.18(*c*) shows the variation of collector current with collector–emitter voltage. There are several curves, each representing a different base current.

6 The following table of values of collector current (I_C) and collector–emitter voltage at various base currents were obtained for an npn junction transistor. Plot a graph of I_C against V_{CE} and use it to determine
(*a*) the current gain at 9 V, and
(*b*) the output resistance for a base current of 40 μA.

V_{CE}	I_B = 20 μA	40 μA	60μA	80 μA
4	0.91	1.60	2.30	3.00
6	0.93	1.70	2.50	3.35
8	0.97	1.85	2.70	3.55
10	1.00	2.05	3.00	4.05

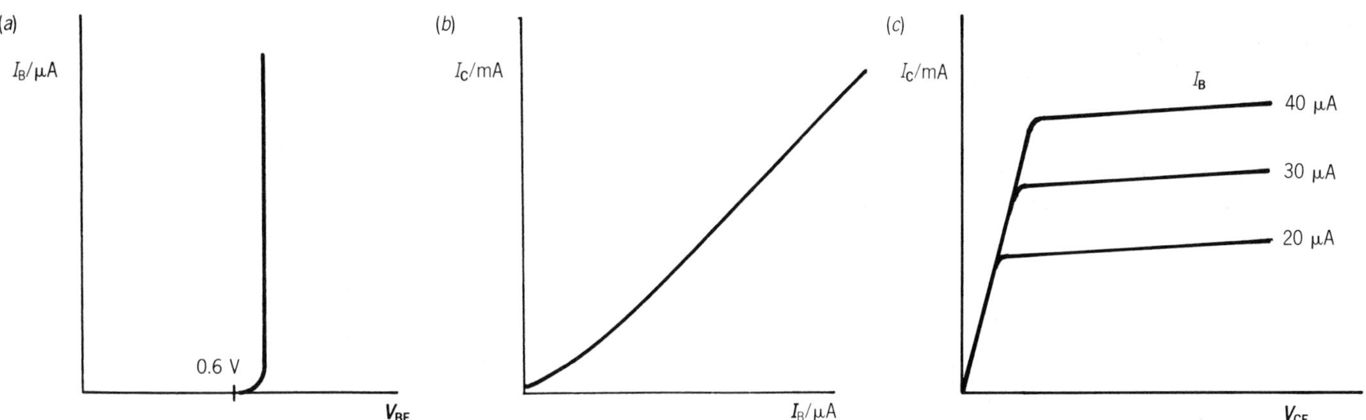

Figure 51.18

Consider the circuit shown in Figure 51.19. Let the supply voltage be 6 V, and let h_{FE} for the transistor be 100. We will assume that the transistor is switched on and so $V_{BE} = 0.6$ V. Therefore voltage drop across $R_B = 6 - 0.6 = 5.4$ V.

Taking 50 μA as a possible base current, we have

$$R_B = \frac{5.4\ \text{V}}{50\ \mu\text{A}} = 108\ \text{k}\Omega$$

The collector current is given by

$$I_C = h_{FE} I_B = 100 \times 50\ \mu\text{A} = 5\ \text{mA}$$

If we choose that the collector is at 3.5 V, then the drop across R_L is $6 - 3.5 = 2.5$ V. Therefore

$$R_L = \frac{2.5\ \text{V}}{5\ \text{mA}} = 500\ \Omega$$

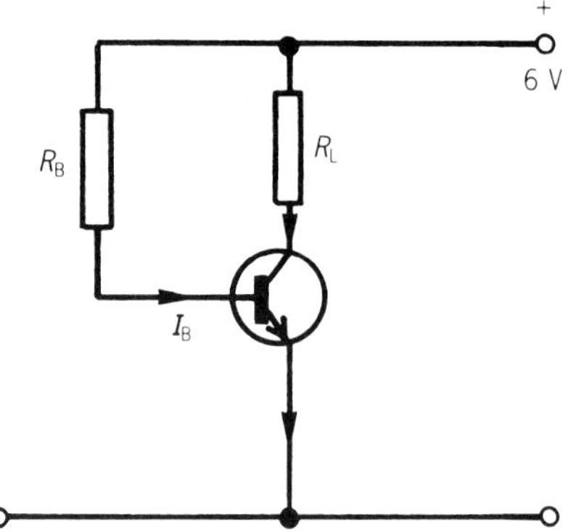

Figure 51.19

7 (*a*) Explain why the resistance of a photoconductive cell of cadmium sulphide decreases when light falls on it.

(*b*) Such a cell is used in the circuit shown in Figure 51.20. The relay closes when a current of 25 mA flows through it. Calculate the resistance of the cell when this occurs. (Current gain for the transistor = 120.)

8 The transistor shown in Figure 51.21 has a value of h_{FE} of 120. What is the minimum value that R can have so that the transistor will saturate? What is the collector current in this condition? (Assume $V_{BE} = 0.7$ V and $V_{CE} = 3$ V.)

9 In the circuit shown in Figure 51.22, assume that $V_{BE} = 0.7$ V and that $h_{FE} = 75$. Calculate

(*a*) the base current,

(*b*) the collector current, and

(*c*) the collector current and base currents when the transistor saturates.

10 The current amplification of the circuit shown in Figure 51.23 is 75. What is the approximate p.d. between A and B?

11 The transistor circuit in Figure 51.24 is used as a sensitive switch.

(*a*) For a silicon transistor, what is the value of V_{BE}, required to switch the transistor on?

(*b*) What will the p.d. then be across R_1?

(*c*) What is the current in R_1?

(*d*) If the transistor is saturated, what will be the p.d. across R_2?

(*e*) What will be the current in R_2?

(*f*) Calculate the value of h_{FE} for the transistor. State any assumptions that you have made.

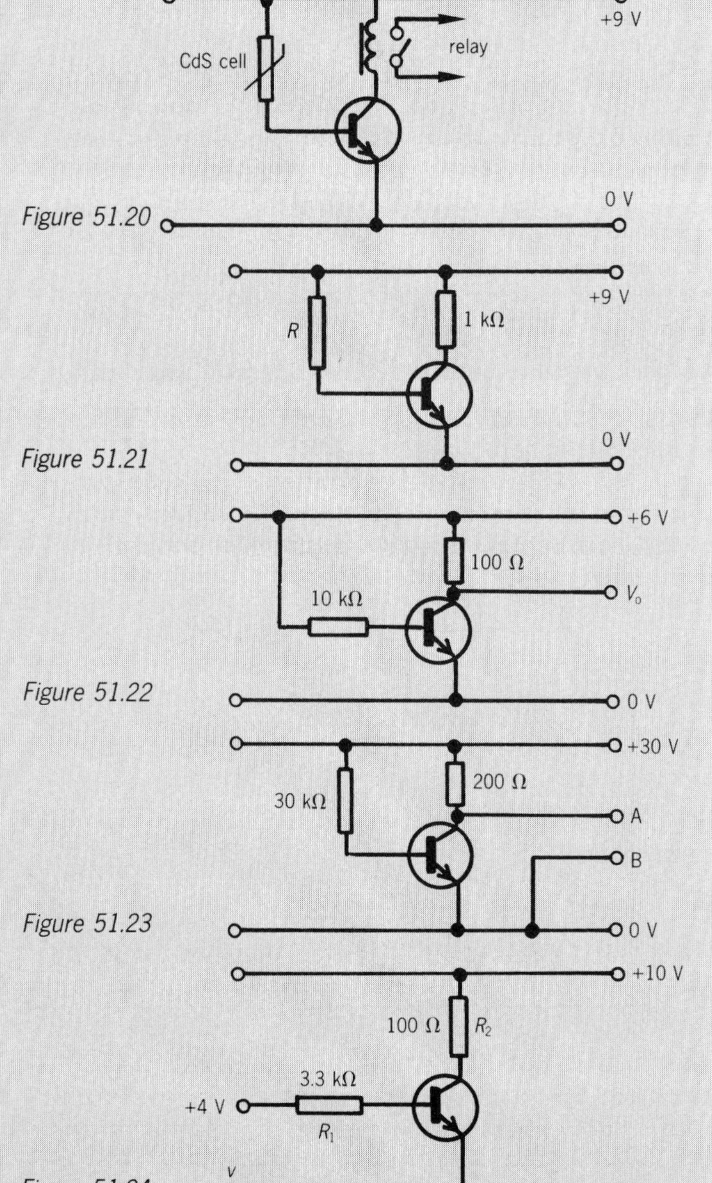

Figure 51.20

Figure 51.21

Figure 51.22

Figure 51.23

Figure 51.24

Consider now the circuit shown in Figure 51.25.

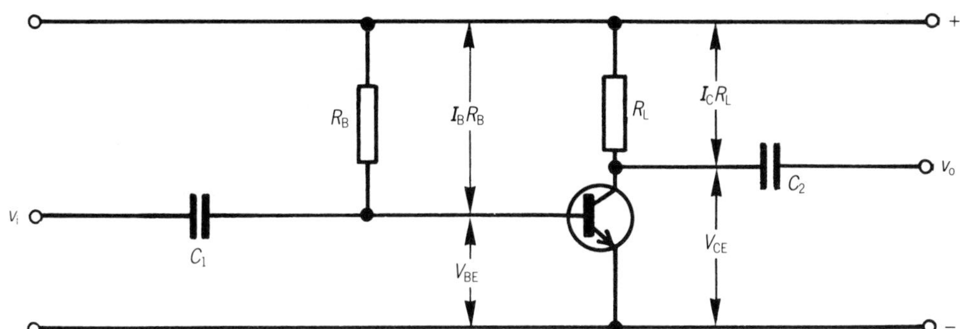

Figure 51.25

The drop in voltage across the load resistor, I_CR_L, plus that across the transistor (V_{CE}) is equal to the supply voltage (V_{CC}).

The supply voltage is also equal to the voltage drop across R_B plus that across the base–emitter junction. Therefore:

$$V_{CC} = I_CR_L + V_{CE} \text{ and } V_{CC} = I_BR_B + V_{BE}$$

If we take $I_C = 5$ mA, $V_{CC} = 6$ V, $V_{CE} = 4.0$ V and $h_{FE} = 75$, then

$$R_L = \frac{V_{CC} - V_{CE}}{I_C} = \frac{(6 - 4.0)\text{V}}{5 \text{ mA}} = \frac{2.0\text{V}}{5 \text{ mA}}$$

$$= 500\ \Omega$$

and

$$I_B = \frac{5 \text{ mA}}{75} = 66.7\ \mu\text{A}$$

Therefore

$$R_B = \frac{V_{CC} - V_{BE}}{I_B} = \frac{5.4 \text{ V}}{66.7\ \mu\text{A}} = 81\ \text{k}\Omega$$

If we now increase the current in the base by applying a small voltage v_i to the input, then the collector current will also increase. This rise in collector current increases the voltage drop across R_L. Since V_{CC} is constant and $V_{CC} = I_CR_L + V_{CE}$, this will reduce the voltage drop across the transistor (V_{CE}) and so the output voltage will drop. Therefore:

> An increase in the input voltage (v_i) will result in a decrease in the output voltage (v_0).

This means that the output voltage is 180° out of phase with the input voltage – a rise in one produces a fall in the other.

If an a.c. signal is applied to the base as shown in Figure 51.26(a), the output voltage will vary as shown in Figure 51.26(b).

(a)

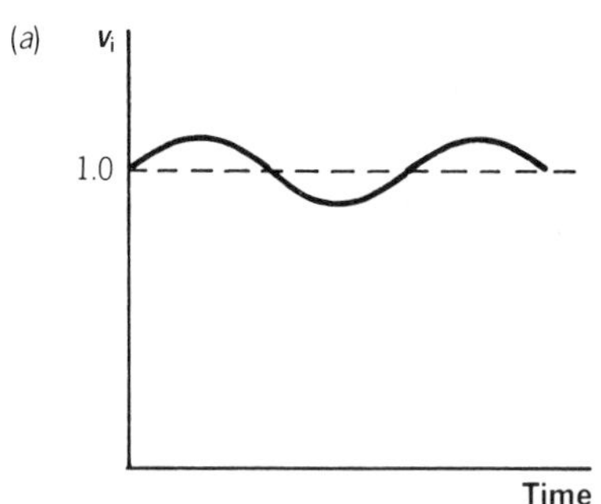

(b)

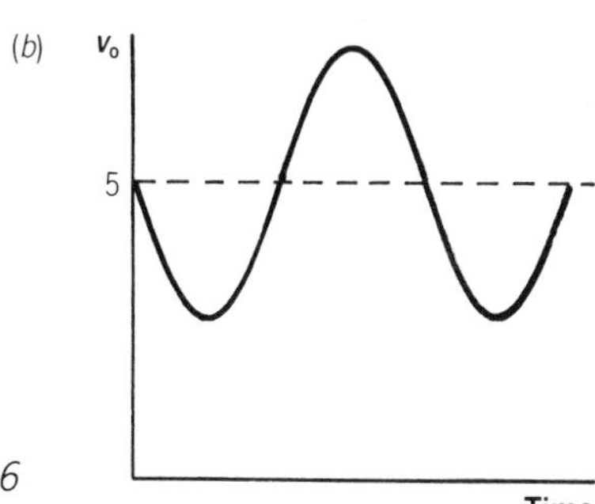

Figure 51.26

Consider the base–emitter voltage to be 1.0 V. The base voltage is made to vary a little above and below this value by the application of a signal to the base, keeping V_{BE} greater than 0.6 V, and so the transistor always remains switched on.

There is also a variation in the amplification of the transistor with frequency. The current gain (h_{FE}) is constant but the voltage gain is variable (this is discussed below). Because the transistor is a solid-state device electrons and holes cannot move very quickly through it, and so the amplification drops off at very high frequencies – over 4 MHz for a junction transistor.

You will notice the presence of the two capacitors C_1 and C_2 in the circuit. Their purpose is to prevent the flow of d.c. current past the transistor. They allow the passage of the alternating signals only.

12 A switch S is used to select one of five resistors, as shown in Figure 51.27. They are used in conjunction with two transistors to control the brightness of the lamp. If the current amplification (h_{FE}) for each transistor is 50, which resistor must be used to give a current through the lamp of 150 mA? Justify your answer.

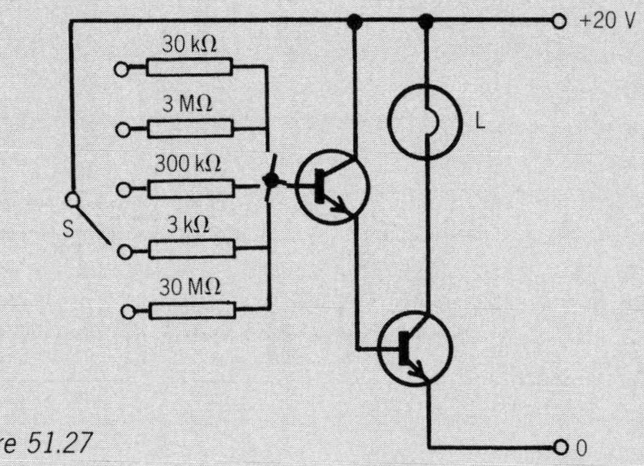

Figure 51.27

13 The circuit in Figure 51.28 includes an npn transistor whose current amplification (h_{FE}) is 75.

Assume that the transistor is in a saturated condition, and calculate the following when the input voltage is 1.5 V:

(*a*) the base current,
(*b*) the emitter current, and
(*c*) the output voltage.

(*b*) +6 V
V_o
6 kΩ
V_i

Figure 51.28

0 V

14 A transistor amplifier is connected in the common-emitter mode as shown in Figure 51.29(*a*) and the characteristics for that transistor in Figure 51.29(*b*).

Given that the supply voltage is 6 V and that the collector–emitter voltage is 3.5 V, calculate the following:

(*a*) the value of the resistor R_L,
(*b*) the value of the resistor R_B, and
(*c*) the value of h_{FE} for the transistor,

if I_C = 2mA.

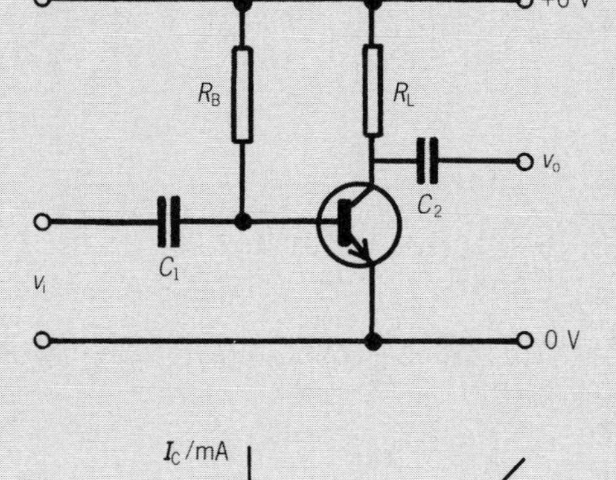

(*b*)

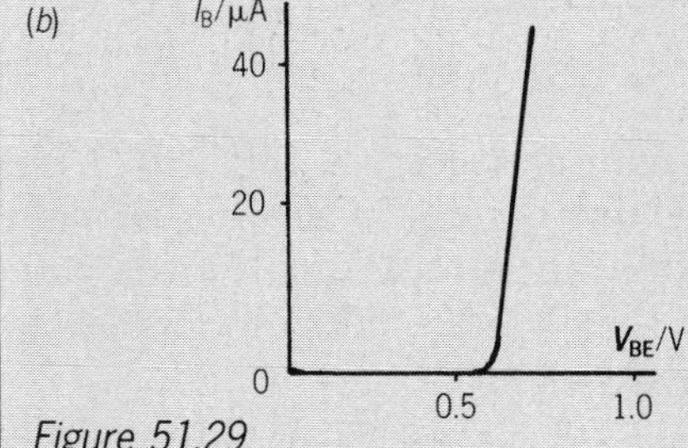

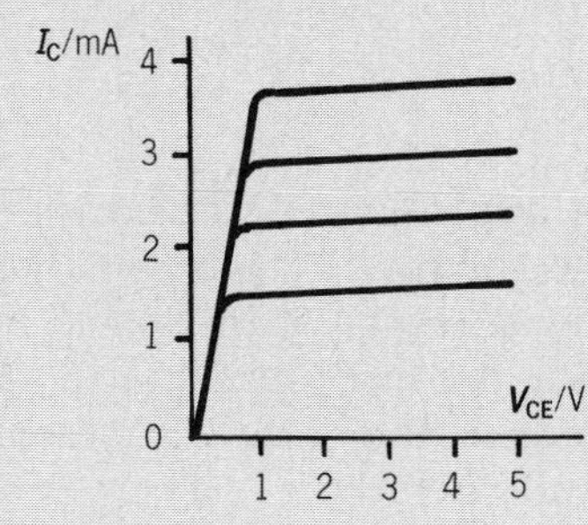

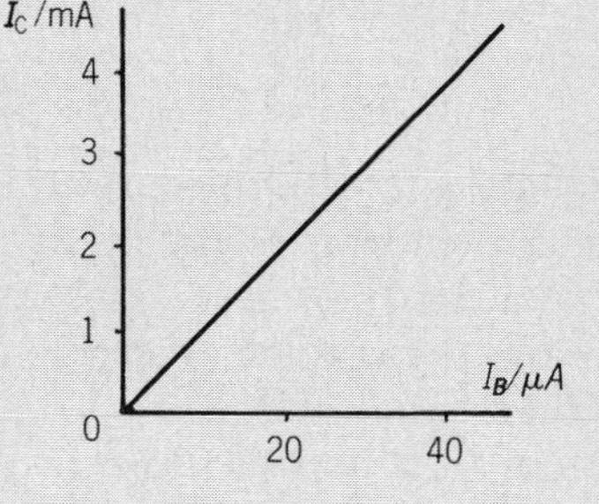

Figure 51.29

Student investigation

Devise and construct a simple circuit including one npn transistor that could be used as an intercom system.

Modify your circuit so that the variation of amplification with input signal frequency may be studied.

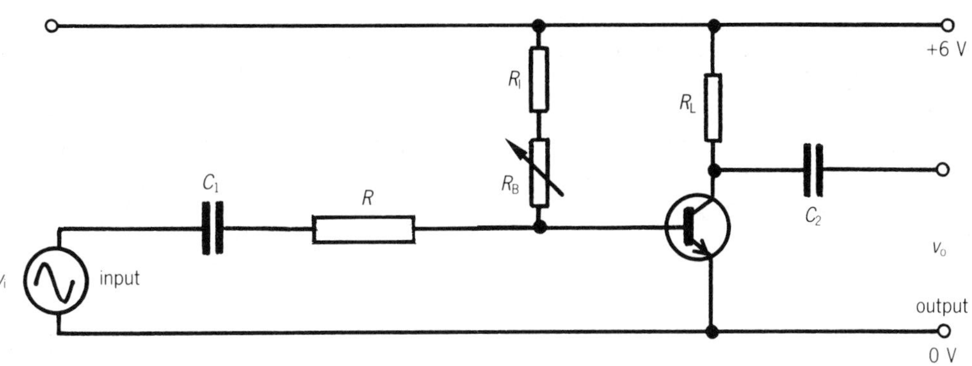

Figure 51.30

The voltage gain of a transistor amplifier

The transistor and load together give voltage amplification, since a change in collector current will also change the collector potential and hence the collector–emitter voltage. The circuit is shown in Figure 51.30. We can define the voltage gain of a transistor amplifier as A, where

$$A = \frac{v_0}{v_i}$$

v_0 and v_i being the changes in the quiescent (static) voltages V_{CE} and V_{BE}. The change in base current ΔI_B produced by a change in base voltage V_{BE} is given by

$$\Delta I_B = \frac{v_i}{R + r}$$

where $r \left(= \frac{V_{BE}}{I_B} \right)$ is the input resistance of the transistor. This change produces a collector current change of ΔI_C, and therefore a collector voltage change v_0 (ΔV_C) where v_0 is given by

$$v_0 = \Delta I_C \times R_L$$

However $\Delta I_C = h_{FE} \times \Delta I_B$, and so we have for v_0:

$$v_0 = h_{FE} \times \frac{R_L}{R + r} \times v_i$$

This means that the voltage amplification A is

$$A = \frac{v_0}{v_i} = h_{FE} \times \frac{R_L}{R + r}$$

15 Determine the voltage amplification of a transistor with current amplification of 100 if the input resistance is 1 kΩ, the load resistance 2.2 kΩ and the value of the resistor in the base circuit is 20 kΩ.

16 The circuit in Figure 51.31 shows a transistor amplifier.
(*a*) If the collector voltage is 3 V and the collector current 6 mA, what is the p.d. across the earphone?
(*b*) What is the resistance of the earphone?
(*c*) If h_{FE} is 60, what is the base current?
(*d*) If the base current changes by 10 μA, what is the resulting p.d. change across the earphone?

17 The circuit in Figure 51.32 shows a simple transistor amplifier. The collector current is 1.2 mA, the collector–emitter voltage 4.5 V, and the current amplification (h_{FE}) 50. Calculate (*a*) the base current, (*b*) the values of R_1 and R_2.
The base current is now changed by 5 μA due to a base emitter voltage change of 10 mV. Calculate (*c*) the change in collector–emitter voltage, (*d*) the voltage amplification of the transistor.

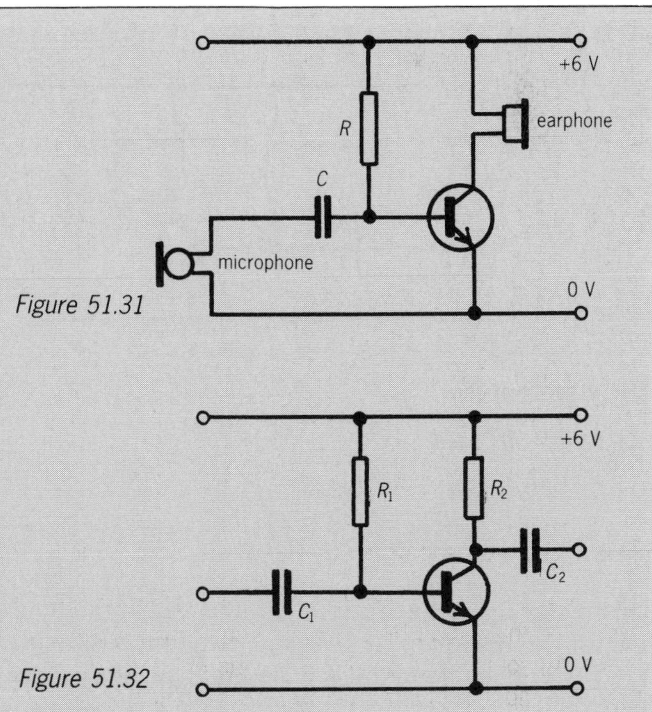

Figure 51.31

Figure 51.32

18 The circuit shown in Figure 51.33 represents a transistor voltage amplifier. The collector current I_C is 2 mA and the collector–emitter voltage is 4.5 V. If the current gain for the transistor is 75, calculate

(*a*) the base current,
(*b*) the value of R_1,
(*c*) the value of R_2.

19 What is meant by the d.c. *Current gain* (h_{FE}) for a transistor? Over what region of operation is the definition that you give valid?

20 Figure 51.34 shows the variation of collector current (I_C) with collector–emitter voltage (V_{CE}).

Draw a circuit to show how such a graph may have been obtained.

Copy the diagram and use it to calculate the change in V_{CE} for base current change of 10 μA.

Suggest the range of V_{CE} over which the transistor should operate to give linear amplification.

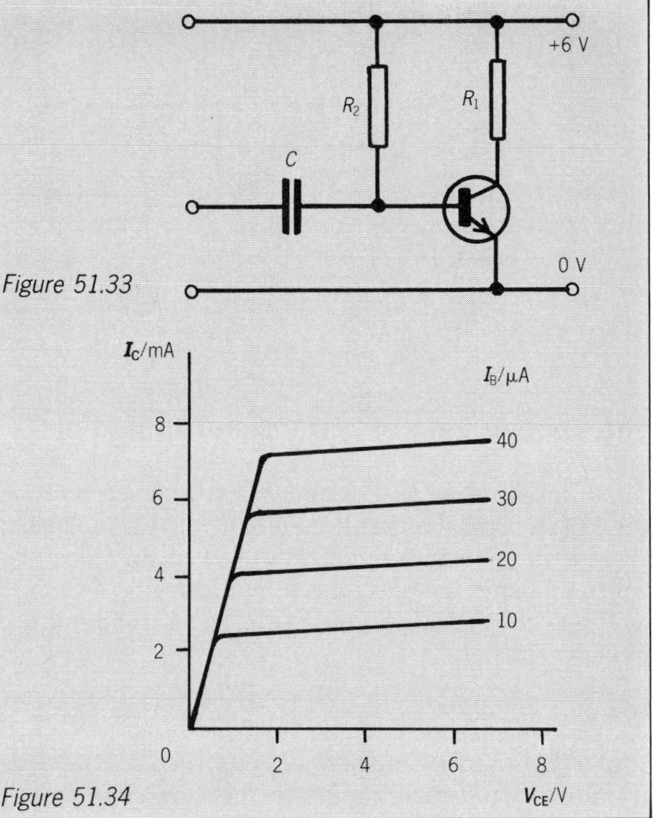

Figure 51.33

Figure 51.34

The load line

It is important to know the best operating conditions for a transistor amplifier and this can be found using the load line. Consider the circuit shown in Figure 51.35.

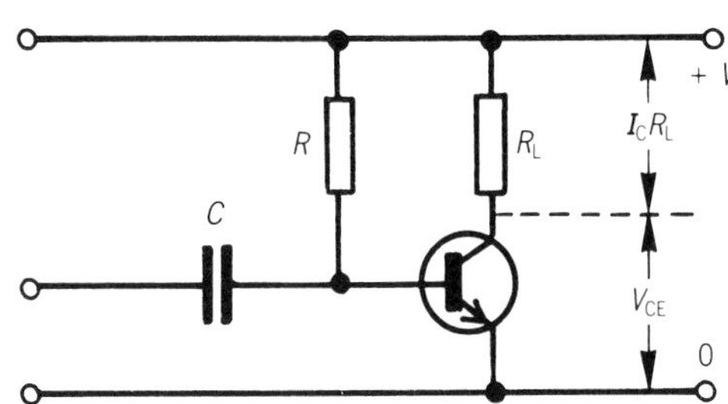

Figure 51.35

The equation for V is:

$$V = I_C R_L + V_{CE}$$

$$V_{CE} = V - I_C R_L$$

$$I_C = \frac{V}{R_L} - \frac{1}{R_L} V_{CE}$$

This is the equation of a straight line, called the **load line** for the transistor. It gives the variation of I_C with V_{CE} for a given value of R_L, the gradient of the line being $-1/R_L$.

If we draw the load line on the graph of I_C against V_{CE} we see that it cuts through the curves. Now the best operating conditions will be somewhere in the middle of the load line, where the I_C/V_{CE} curves are linear.

The graph in Figure 51.36 shows two different load lines for two different values of R_L. Consider a transistor with $V_{CE} = 3$ V and $I_b = 30$ μA. If I_B now varies by ±10 μA due to a change in base input voltage of, say, ±20 mV (see I_B/V_{BE} curves) then V_{CE} varies by 1.5 V. The voltage gain of the transistor is therefore:

$$\frac{V_o}{V_i} = \frac{3}{0.04} = 75$$

You can see that the variation occurs on the straight part of the I_C/V_{CE} curves, thus giving an undistorted output.

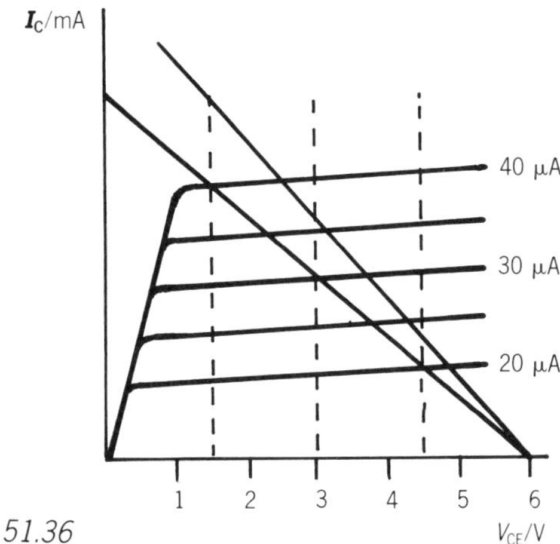

Figure 51.36

The astable multivibrator

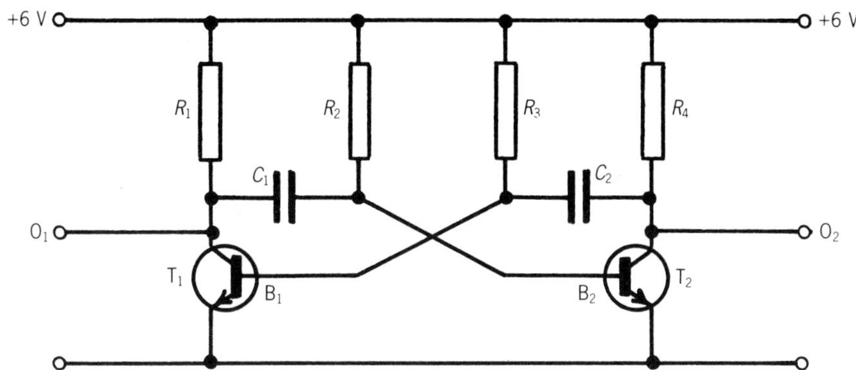

Figure 51.37

This uses two transistors, one or the other being on at any time; when one switches on the other switches off. For this reason it is sometimes called a 'flip-flop' circuit. The ability to control the rate at which the circuit flip-flops makes it the basis for many timers.

The circuit is shown in Figure 51.37.

We will assume that transistor T_1 is on initially and T_2 is off.

When T_1 is on, O_1 is at 0.2 V because the transistor is conducting and therefore there will be only a small voltage drop across it. Since it is on, the potential at the base of T_1, B_1, will be 0.6 V.

Transistor T_2 is off; O_2 is therefore at 6 V, because since the transistor is not conducting no current flows through resistor R_4 and so there is no voltage drop across it. B_2 is at −5.4 V; we will see the reason for this shortly.

C_1 therefore charges up through R_2, since there is a p.d. of some 11.4 V across it. As soon as the potential of B_2 reaches +0.6 V transistor T_2 switches on, and the potential at O_2 drops to nearly zero, say 0.2 V. This means that B_1 must also fall by about 6 V, since the p.d. across the capacitor C_2 cannot change instantly and must therefore remain at about 6 V. The potential at B_1 therefore becomes −5.4 V and T_1 switches off, since its base is well below 0.6 V. The cycle now repeats itself for the other transistor.

The graphs in Figure 51.38 show the variation of the potentials at different points in the cycle.

Changing the value of any of the resistors or capacitors will alter the rate of switching. If this frequency is in the correct range an audible signal can be produced by connecting a speaker in series with R_1 or R_4. This can be the basis of a simple electronic organ.

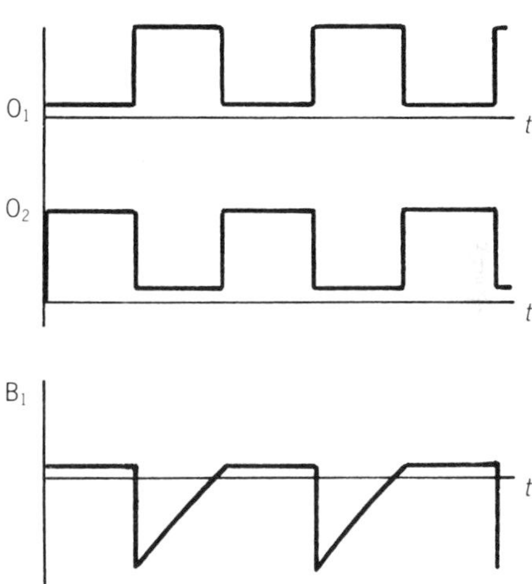

Figure 51.38

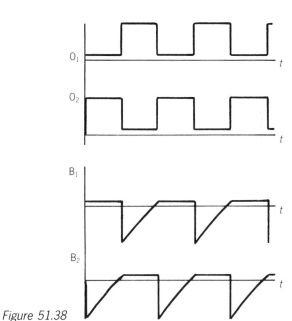

Student investigation

Use the astable multivibrator circuit as the basis for the design and construction of the following;

(*a*) a morse buzzer,
(*b*) a light-operated burglar alarm,
(*c*) an electronic organ.

21 Draw a graph plotting the two collector–emitter voltage outputs against time for an astable multivibrator.

How will the results change if *one* of the capacitors is increased in value?

22 (*a*) Using the graph in question 20, plot a load line for a load resistor of 1 kΩ.

(*b*) What would happen if load resistors of (i) 500 Ω or (ii) 2 kΩ had been used instead?

(*c*) Explain why the voltage amplification of a junction transistor varies with frequency.

Further semiconductor devices

The zener diode

If the reverse bias applied to the diode is great enough the diode will break down and give a large increase in the reverse current. The critical voltage is known as the **breakdown voltage** or **zener voltage**.

The zener diode is a diode that uses this breakdown voltage when the diode is operated in the reverse direction. The symbol for a zener diode and its characteristics are shown in Figure 51.39.

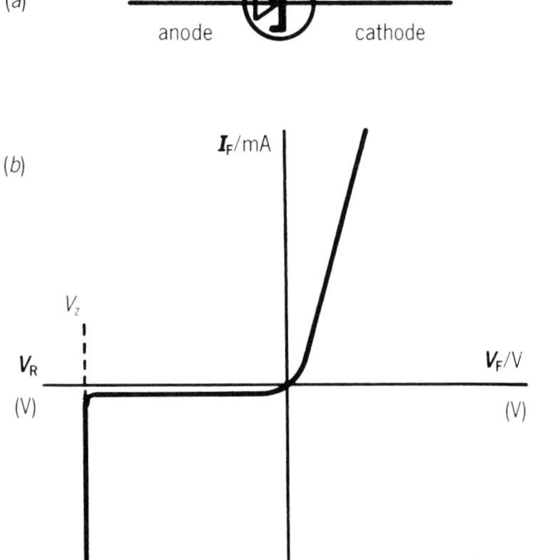

Figure 51.39

It can be seen from the characteristics that the voltage across the diode remains constant over a wide range of reverse current. This reverse current must be limited by a resistor, otherwise overheating will occur and the diode will be ruined. The power rating depends on the diode used, but is usually of the order of hundreds of milliwatts.

The reverse breakdown potential may be designed to be anything between 3 V and 150 V by controlling the doping; this makes it a very useful component, particularly in voltage stabiliser circuits such as the one shown in Figure 51.40. Here the output voltage across the load R_L remains constant over a reverse current range of tens of milliamps even if the input changes, although it must remain a little greater than V_Z.

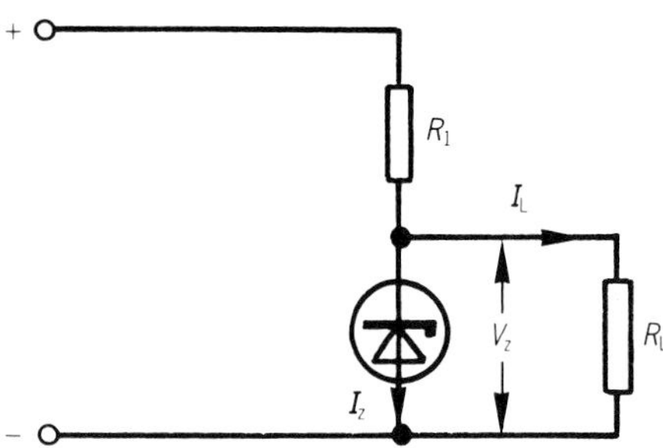

Figure 51.40

Zener diodes are also used to protect voltmeters from overload, and also to 'clip' the tops of waveforms to restrict them to a certain maximum. When used in this way the diode is known as a **voltage limiter**.

Liquid crystal displays

These are now becoming more and more widely used because of their low power requirements and low cost.

They are formed in a seven-segment arrangement (like the LED, page 377) but operate on a completely different principle. A small amount of liquid-crystalline material is sandwiched between two thin glass plates and an electric field is placed across the plates. The field causes disturbances in the liquid which cause light falling on the cell to be reflected. These cells do *not* emit light themselves and are therefore not good in low external light levels.

The thermistor

This is a semiconductor device whose resistance changes with temperature. Thermistors are made from metal oxides such as those of manganese and nickel. There are two types of thermistor:

(*a*) thermistors having a negative temperature coefficient (NTC), the resistance of which decreases approximately exponentially with temperature and

(*b*) thermistors having a positive temperature coefficient (PTC), whose resistance rises abruptly to a value of several thousands of ohms at a definite temperature, usually around 100–150 °C.

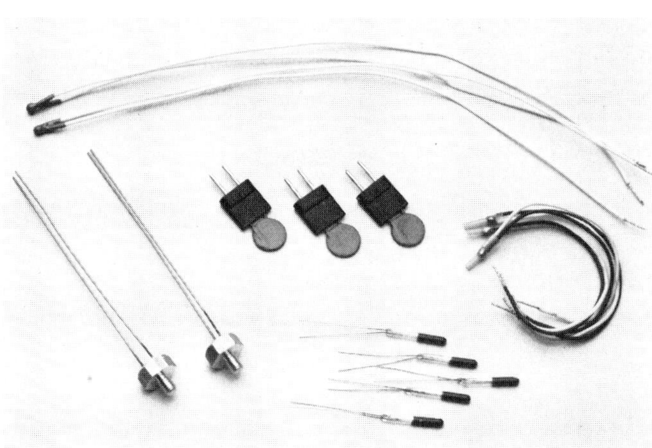

Thermistors (STC)

These devices have many applications, for example:

(*a*) water temperature sensor in cars (NTC) or as an ice sensor on aircraft wing surfaces;

(*b*) baby alarms, where the air flow from an air bed cools a thermistor (NTC) while the baby is moving and breathing – if the baby stops breathing the air flow ceases, the thermistor heats up and an alarm sounds;

(*c*) overload protection in a razor socket (PTC) – if the circuit heats up the resistance of the thermistor rises rapidly to cut off the current.

The light-emitting diode (LED)

The light-emitting diode is made of either gallium arsenide or gallium phosphide, and when forward biased it emits red, yellow or green light (the colour depends on the exact composition of the material). This light is due to the recombination of electrons and holes at the p–n junction. The symbol for the LED is shown in Figure 51.41.

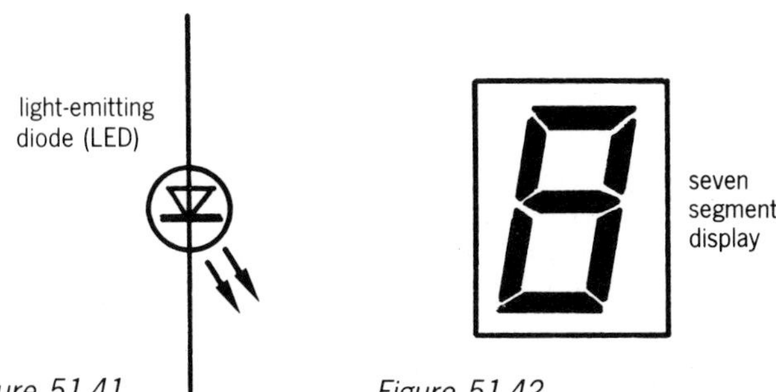

Figure 51.41 *Figure 51.42*

The energy produced is given off as light which escapes from the diode because the junction is formed very close to the surface of the material. LEDs are used as indicator lamps and also in the seven-segment displays (Figure 51.42) in clocks, calculators and so on. They have two great advantages over normal filament lamps: they last longer, and they use very little energy.

The thyristor

The thyristor (Figure 51.43) is yet another form of diode. This type will not allow current to flow through it in *either* direction unless a signal is applied to another electrode known as the **gate**.

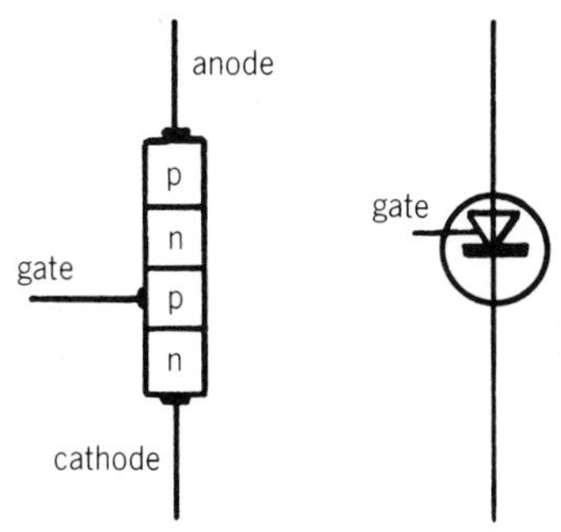

Figure 51.43

One type of thyristor is the silicon-controlled rectifier, or SCR. This will not conduct in the reverse direction and will only conduct in the forward direction when a signal is applied to the gate. It will then behave like a normal diode until it is switched off again. This happens when the forward current falls below a certain value known as the holding current. A control signal of a few tens of milliwatts enables an SCR to turn on a signal a million times as great!

The field effect transistor (FET)

The main parts of the field effect transistor are as follows:

(*a*) the **source** (S), the electrode where the majority carriers enter the bar;

(*b*) the **drain** (D), the electrode where the majority carriers leave the bar;

(*c*) the **gate** (G), the heavily doped p-region;

(*d*) the **channel**, the region in the bar between the two gate electrodes, through which the majority carriers move from source to drain.

The symbol and structure of an n-channel and a p-channel FET are shown in Figure 51.44.

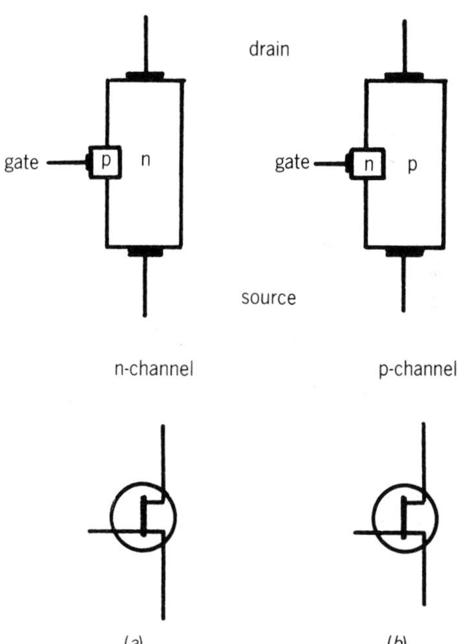

Figure 51.44

A field effect transistor has a higher input impedance, is less noisy and is thermally more stable than a bipolar junction transistor, but it cannot operate at such high frequencies.

52 · Integrated circuits and the op amp

The integrated circuit

In the early days of solid-state electronics (as distinct from vacuum tube electronics) computing circuits were made from individual components such as diodes, transistors and capacitors. It was realised in the 1950s, however, that it would be possible to form all the components required for such circuits in a single wafer of semiconductor material, and this became known as the **integrated circuit.**

There are two main types of integrated circuit:

(*a*) **linear** or **analogue**, containing amplifying circuits, and

(*b*) **digital**, containing switching circuits. The two types of digital integrated circuit are:

(i) **TTL** (transistor–transistor logic) give faster switching but require a stabilised power supply and larger quiescent currents;

(ii) **CMOS** (complementary metal-oxide semiconductor logic) give slower switching but can work from any power supply in the range 3 to 15 V. A larger density of components may be achieved with CMOS circuits, and this makes large-scale integration (LSI) easier.

As the years have passed it has become possible to put more and more components on to one chip, and the 'one chip' microprocessor is now being developed.

Four basic steps are needed to create very small regions that form MOS transistors on the silicon slice (they are illustrated in Figure 52.1):

(*a*) **oxidation** – a layer of silicon oxide is grown on the top of the silicon;

(*b*) **photomasking** – parts of the oxide layer are selectively removed;

(*c*) **Diffusion** – unprotected layers of silicon are changed to p- or n-type by diffusion of other materials;

(*d*) **Metallization** – a thin metal layer is placed over the slice to connect the transistors and diodes electrically.

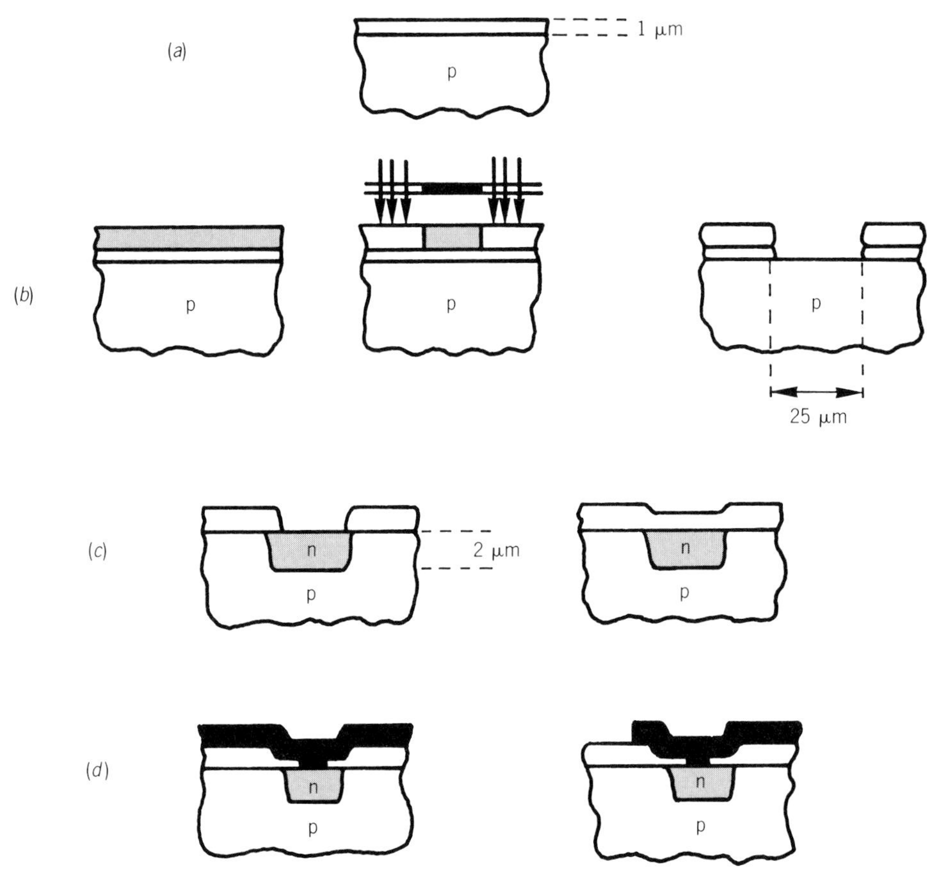

Figure 52.1

We will look at these in a little more detail.

(*a*) The first process is to oxidise the surface of a p-type silicon slice to form a protective layer of silicon oxide (glass) over it by heating it in a furnace with oxygen and steam.

(*b*) A light-sensitive plastic film is then formed on the surface of the slice – this film will harden wherever ultraviolet light hits it. A mask containing the circuit design is placed over the wafer and ultraviolet light shone through it, so hardening parts of the film. The soft parts of the plastic film are now washed away and the unprotected areas of the oxide film are dissolved. The remainder of the plastic coating is then chemically removed.

(*c*) Next, n-type atoms in a phosphorus gas are passed over the slice in a furnace at 1200 °C to change the exposed areas of silicon from p-type to n-type, by the diffusion of n-type atoms.

(*d*) Further oxide is then grown on as before and by a further masking process contact regions are formed and aluminium strips connected to these.

Digital and analogue signals

There are two main branches of electronics. **Digital electronics** is concerned with circuits that can exist in one of two states, these states usually being represented by a voltage output. This output may either be high (say +6 V) or low (near 0 V). Such electronics are found in digital computers and the control systems of machinery. An example of the variation of a digital signal with time is given in Figure 52.2.

In **analogue electronics** the signals are electrical representations of the physical quantities that produce them. For example, the electrical signal produced by a microphone and then displayed on a CRO screen is an *analogue* of the sound wave that produced it; the signal changes in phase with the sound wave. The variation of an analogue signal with time is shown in Figure 52.3.

Student investigation

The development of the integrated circuit and its applications has often been termed the Electronic Revolution. Discuss the possible social effects of the integrated circuit, with particular mention of the development of new industries and unemployment.

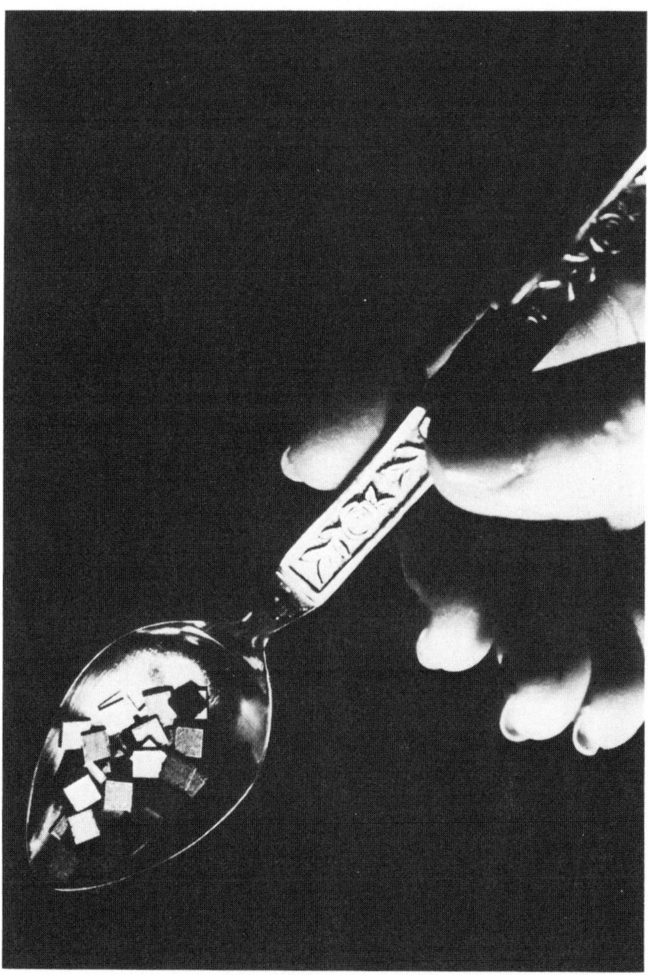

A spoonful of computers (IBM)

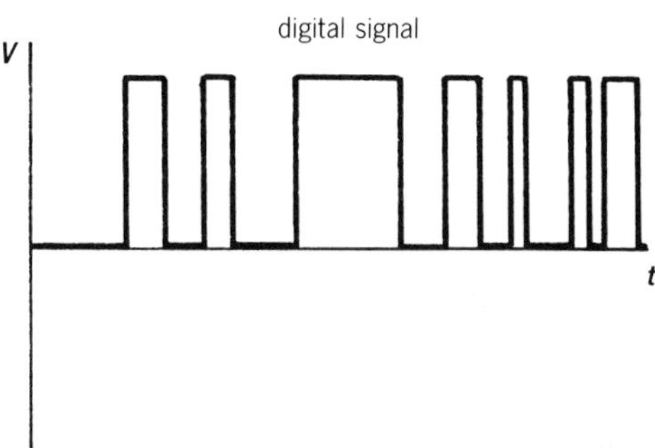

Figure 52.2

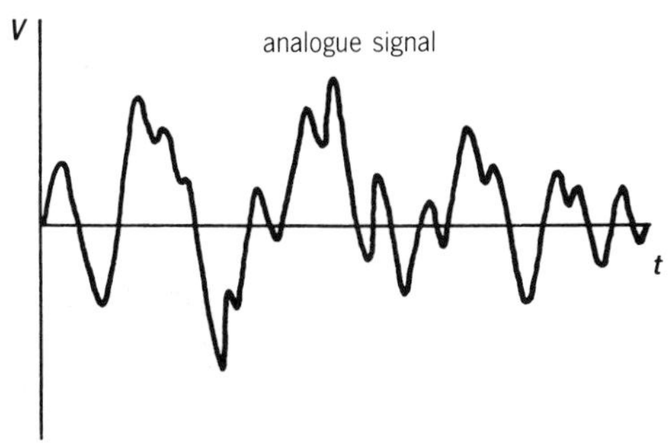

Figure 52.3

The operational amplifier

This particular integrated circuit has come to have wide applications because of its very high gain, its ability to carry out simple mathematical functions such as addition and subtraction, multiplication, differentiation and integration, and its use as a voltage comparator circuit or oscillator. It owes its usefulness to the following properties:

(*a*) a very high open loop voltage gain (A_o) – up to 10^5 for d.c. – although this does decrease with frequency (see later);

(*b*) a very high input resistance so that it draws virtually no current from the input signal;

(*c*) a very low output resistance;

(*d*) it is a **differential** amplifier, giving an amplified output signal proportional to the **difference** between the two input signals providing that this difference is not too large (see later).

A common form of op amp used in schools is the type 741. This is made in what is called an 'eight-pin dual in line form' and is shown diagrammatically in Figure 52.4 together with the symbol for an op amp.

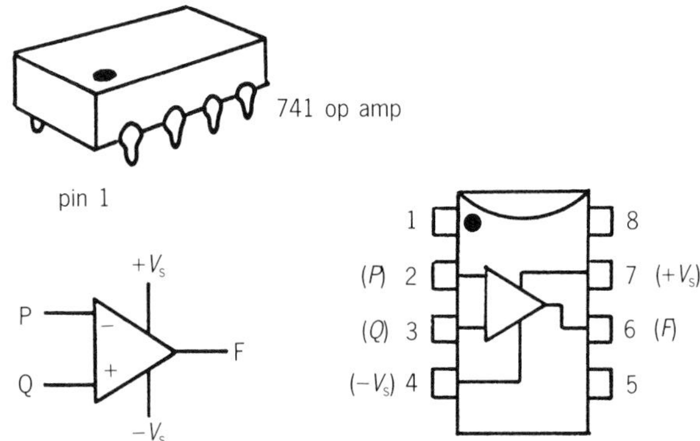

Figure 52.4

Of the eight pins on the op amp we are interested in only five:

(*a*) the inverting input (P) – inputs here will be changed in sign (pin 2)

(*b*) the non-inverting input (Q) – inputs here will not be changed in sign (pin 3)

(*c*) the output (F) (pin 6)

(*d*) the positive supply ($\pm V_s$) (pin 7)

(*e*) the negative supply ($-V_s$) (pin 4)

We shall call the voltage at the inverting input V_1 and that at the non-inverting input V_2.

The positive and negative supply connections are shown on the above diagram but they will be assumed and omitted from the following circuits.

The internal circuitry of an op amp is complex and outside the scope of this book (the 741 containing twenty transistors, eleven resistors and one capacitor). We shall treat it as a 'black box' that will perform certain functions if connected into a circuit correctly.

The circuit symbol represents an **'open loop'** amplifier with an **'open loop gain'** A_o. The output potential (V_o) is proportional to the DIFFERENCE in the potential between P and Q (ie to ($V_2 - V_1$)).

In fact it is given by the equation:

$$V_o = A_o (V_2 - V_1)$$

This is true providing the output potential is less than that of the supply voltage V_s. When V_o reaches V_s the op amp is said to SATURATED. This can be seen from Figure 52.5 which is known as the **transfer characteristic** for the op amp.

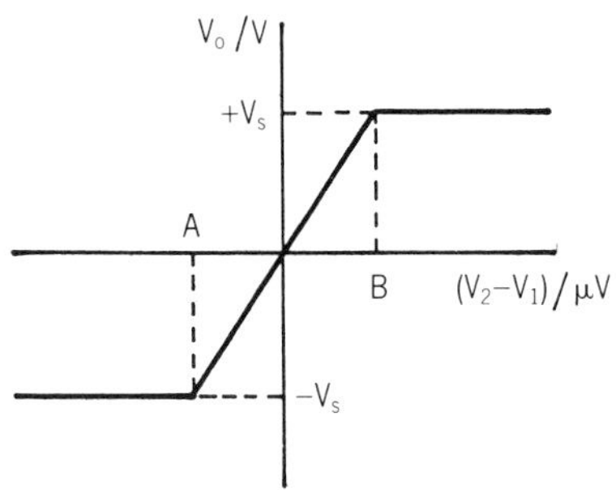

Figure 52.5

It can be seen that the output voltage lies between $+V_s$ and $-V_s$. The supply voltage used in most examples in this book is 15 V and so V_o must be between +15 V and −15 V.

You can see that there is a small region between A and B where the graph rises linearly and it is in this region that the op amp is operated as an amplifier.

Since A_o is about 100 000 the op amp will saturate for a difference of potential between P and Q of more than 150 μV.

If the difference is more than 150 μV the output will be +15 V if $V_1 < V_2$ and −15 V if $V_1 > V_2$.

As was said earlier that the open loop gain varies with frequency and this is shown in Figure 52.6. As the frequency of the input signal increases so the open loop gain falls. This can be explained by the decreased mobility of the charge carriers through the semiconductor material.

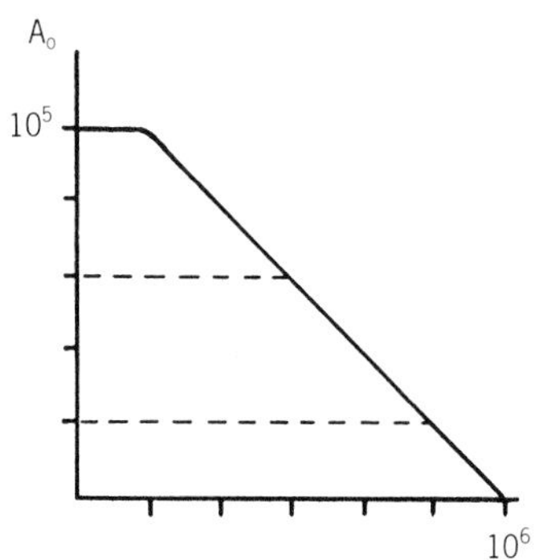

Figure 52.6

Feedback

An important property in various areas of Physics, particularly in electronics is that of **feedback**.

Feedback is the term used to describe the situation where a certain fraction of the output of a device is fed back to the input.

There are two types of feedback:

(*a*) negative feedback – this tends to reduce the output. A simple example of this is the flow of silty water through a hole. The slower the flow the more silt settles and the quicker the hole fills up and the slower the rate becomes and so on;

(*b*) positive feedback – this tends to increase the output. This is shown by a snowball rolling down a hill, the bigger it is the more snow it picks up and the bigger it becomes, and so on.

The op amp as an amplifier

For the op amp to work as a amplifier the **difference** between V_2 and V_1 must be less than 150 μV. (More generally it must be less than V_s/A_o.) This is achieved in different ways by the two types of amplifier described here. Remember that the output voltage can never exceed the supply voltage.

The non-inverting voltage amplifier

In this circuit, shown in Figure 52.7, the input voltage is applied to the non-inverting input (*Q*). This gives an output voltage that is in phase with the input voltage.

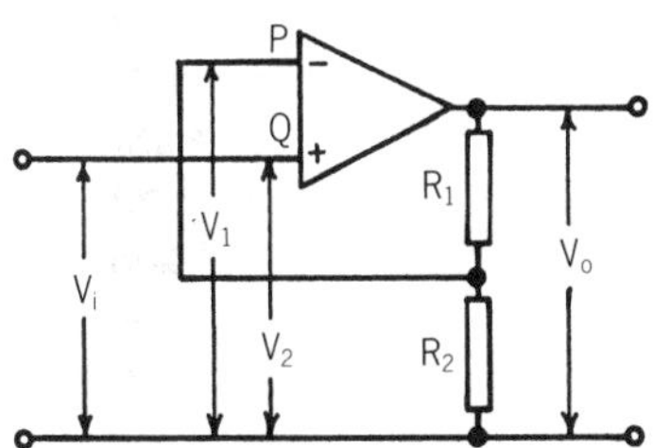

Figure 52.7

A certain fraction (β) of this output is fed back to the inverting input. This gives negative feedback and the feedback fraction is given by the equation:

$$\beta = \frac{R_2}{R_1 + R_2}$$

However for negative feedback we have $V_o = A_0(V_i - \beta V_o)$ but since the closed loop gain (A) is V_o/V_i and we have that $A = A_o/(1 + \beta A_o)$. However since usually $\beta A_o \gg 1$ this gives $A = 1/\beta$ approximately.

Therefore for the non-inverting amplifier:

Closed loop gain $(A = V_0/V_i = 1/\beta = 1 + R_1/R_2$

As with the inverting voltage amplifier this is dependent only on the external resistors R_1 and R_2.

> **Example**
>
> Calculate the closed loop voltage gain of a non-inverting voltage amplifier with $R = 3$ kΩ and $R = 1$ kΩ.
>
> Closed loop gain $(A) = 1 + 3/1 = 4$.

The inverting voltage amplifier

In this use the input is applied to the inverting input and the non inverting input is earthed (Figure 52.8). So that the value of $(V_2 - V_1)$ is less than 150 μV a resistor R_1 is placed in the input circuit. Hence V_2 is 0 and V_1 is less than 150 μV. A resistor R_2 forms a feedback loop and since the inverting input is used the feedback is out of phase with the input and is therefore negative feedback.

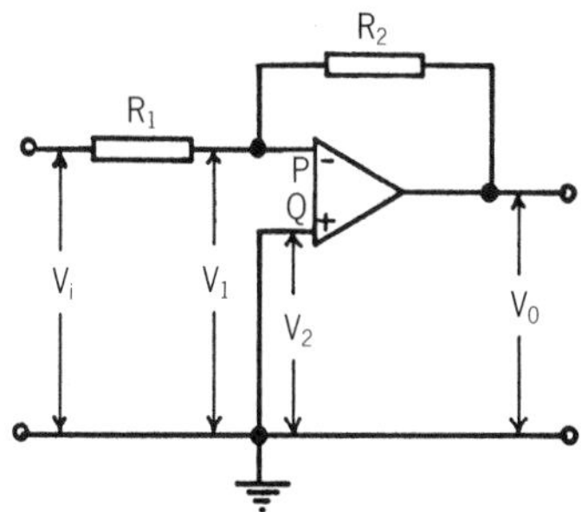

Figure 52.8

The maximum value of V_1 at P will be 150 μV when the output is V_s and so we can consider V_1 to be virtually zero. P is said to be a **virtual earth**. The p.d. across R_1 is therefore virtually V_i and the p.d. across R_2 is virtually V_o (but reversed in sign). Since almost no current flows through the op amp, the current (*I*) in R_2 is equal to that in R_1 and so we can write:

$$I = \frac{V_i}{R_1} = \frac{-V_o}{R_2}$$

the voltage gain of the amplifier (A) is known as the **closed loop gain** and is given by the formula:

$$\text{Closed loop gain } (A) = \frac{V_o}{V_i} = \frac{-R_2}{R_1}$$

Notice that this depends only on the values of the two external resistors.

> **Example**
>
> Calculate the closed loop gain of an inverting voltage amplifier with $R = 3\ k\Omega$ and $R = 1\ k\Omega$.
>
> Closed loop gain (A) = −3/1 = −3.

Voltage comparator

A voltage comparator circuit, as its name suggests, is used to compare one voltage with another. The op amp can do this.

If both inputs of the op amp are used at the same time the output voltage V_o is given by

$$V_o = A_o(V_2 - V_1)$$

where V_1 is the inverting input and V_2 is the non-inverting input (Figure 52.9). The voltage *difference* between the two inputs is therefore amplified and appears at the output.

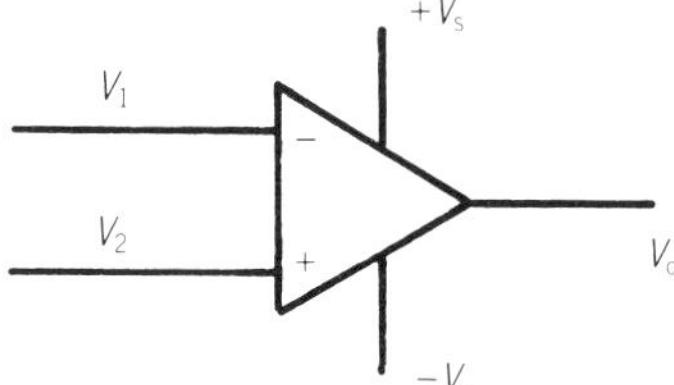

Figure 52.9

Alternatively, we can regard the circuit as one in which voltage 1 is amplified, voltage 2 is inverted and then amplified, and the difference between these final voltages is found.

Two practical uses of the voltage comparator are as a flame sensor and as a heat sensor.

(i) Flame sensor

The circuit in Figure 52.10 might be used in a gas boiler to monitor the pilot light. The alarm is required to sound when the flame of the pilot light goes out.

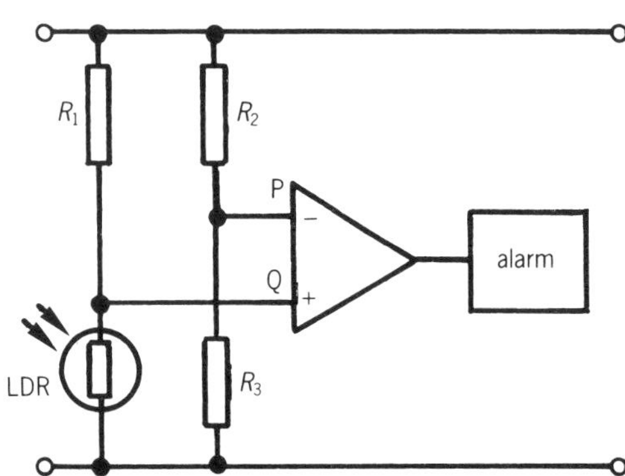

Figure 52.10

A light-dependent resistor (LDR) is the sensor: its resistance is low in light and high in the dark. When the flame is on the resistance of the LDR is low, the voltage at Q (V_2) is low, ($V_2 - V_1$) is negative and the alarm is off. If the flame goes out, however, V_2 rises such that ($V_2 - V_1$) becomes positive, the op amp switches to positive saturation and the alarm is switched on.

(ii) Heat sensor

This sensor (Figure 52.11) is designed to operate one of two LEDs to show whether the heat sensor, the thermistor, is hot or cold.

When the thermistor is cold its resistance is large, the voltage at Q (V_2) is large, and the op amp is in a positively saturated condition, that is, the output voltage (V_o) is positive. LED 1 therefore conducts.

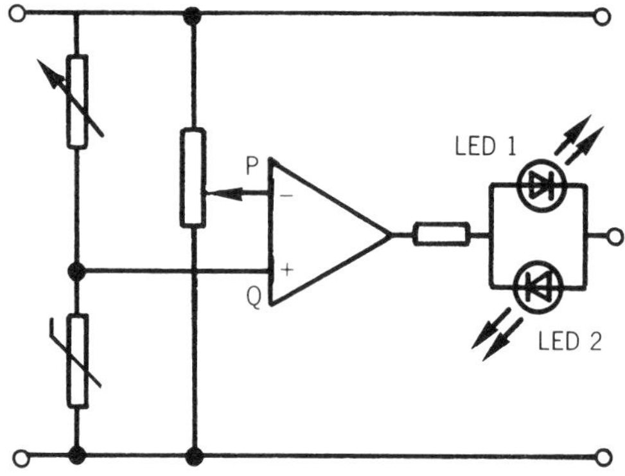

Figure 52.11

When the thermistor warms up a point will be reached when the voltage at Q falls below that at P; ($V_2 - V_1$) is therefore negative, the output voltage is negative and LED 2 conducts.

> **1** The resistors R_1 and R_2 in Figure 52.12 have values of 10 kΩ and 150 kΩ respectively. Calculate the output voltage when the input is (*a*) 0.2 V, (*b*) 1.0 V.
>
> 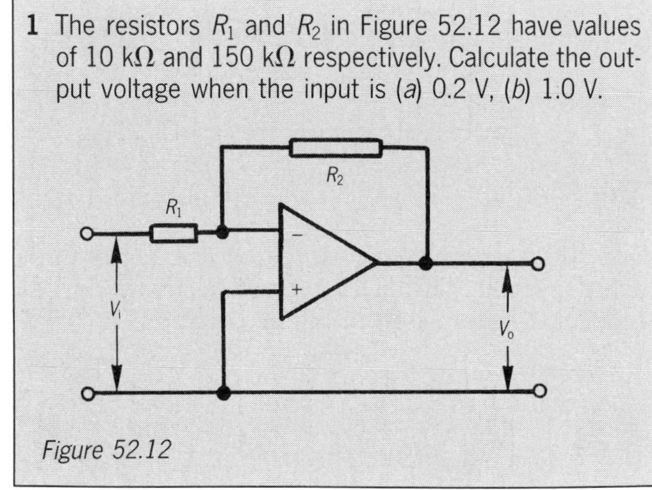
>
>
> *Figure 52.12*

2 If the open loop gain of an op amp is 10^5 and the supply voltage is ± 15 V calculate the output voltages for the following inputs:

(*a*) $V_1 = 10\ \mu V$ $\quad V_2 = 120\ \mu V$
(*b*) $V_1 = 10$ mV $\quad V_2 = 8$ mV
(*c*) $V_1 = 2$ V $\quad V_2 = 1.5$ V
(*d*) $V_1 = 10.2$ mV $\quad V_2 = 10.3$ mV

3 The non-inverting input of an op amp is connected to the junction of two resistors, one of 5 kΩ and the other of 15 kΩ. The other ends of the resistors are connected to the +15 V supply and 0 V respectively. A sinusoidal ac signal with a peak value 12 V is now applied to the inverting input.

(*a*) sketch the circuit
(*b*) what is the voltage at the join of the two resistors
(*c*) sketch the output voltage

4 Calculate the gain of the op amp circuit shown in Figure 52.13.

A second input is added as shown in Figure 52.14, and the waveforms applied to the two inputs are shown in the graphs in Figure 52.15. Sketch the variation of the output voltage. [AEB]

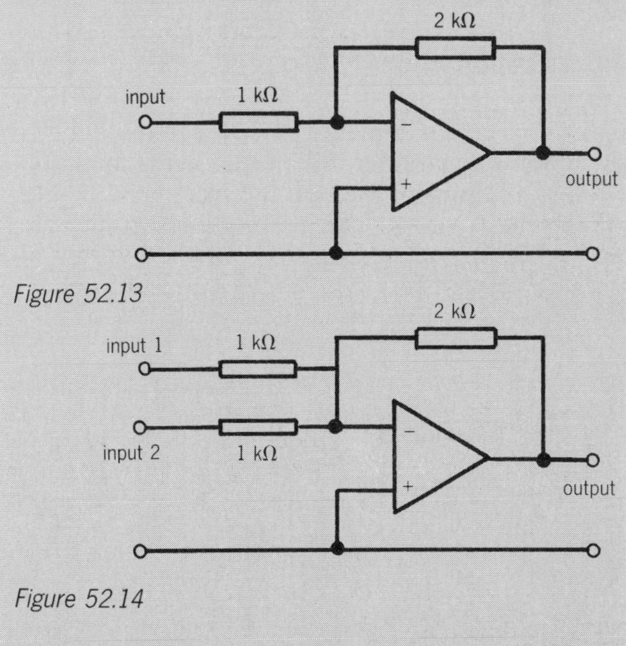

Figure 52.13

Figure 52.14

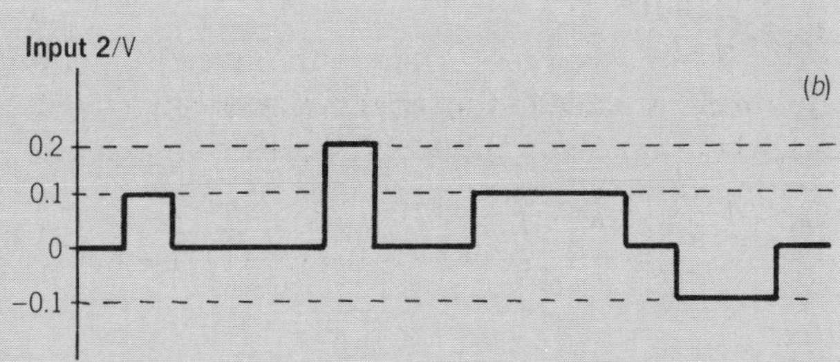

Figure 52.15

5 Large potted plants are kept as a decoration in many modern offices, but they need to be kept moist even when the offices are closed. It is proposed to achieve this by means of an electronic system which will monitor the state of the soil around the roots every twenty minutes and allow a small amount of water to be added if the soil is too dry.

A warning light is to be illuminated if the soil is too dry and a buzzer should sound if no water flows when the supply is turned on, indicating that the reservoir tank is empty.

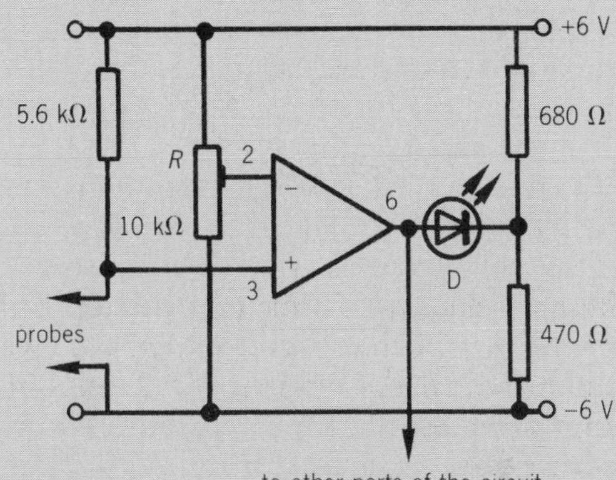

Figure 52.16

The circuit in Figure 52.16 has been suggested for the detector unit which monitors the amount of moisture in the soil. The moisture level will determine the resistance between the probes. The power supply connections to the op amp are not shown.

(*a*) With the variable resistor *R* set at its midpoint position, D is lit when the probes are pushed into dry soil and not lit when pushed into wet soil. In dry soil the probe to probe resistance is at least 50 kΩ and when in wet soil it is no greater than 1 kΩ. Briefly explain how the circuit operates.

(*b*) Calculate for wet soil conditions and with *R* set at its midpoint position:

(i) the voltage at pin 2 of the op amp;
(ii) the voltage at the junction of the 470 Ω and 680 Ω resistors;
(iii) the voltage at pin 6 of the op amp.

(*c*) What is the purpose of making *R* variable?

(*d*) Design a circuit to make the buzzer sound when the tank is empty. [AEB]

Ramp generator

If the feedback resistor of the inverting voltage amplifier is replaced by a capacitor, as shown in Figure 52.17, a ramp generator or integrator is formed.

If the input voltage V_i is constant and $RC = 1$ s, then the output voltage V_o after a time t is given by

$$V_o = V_i t$$

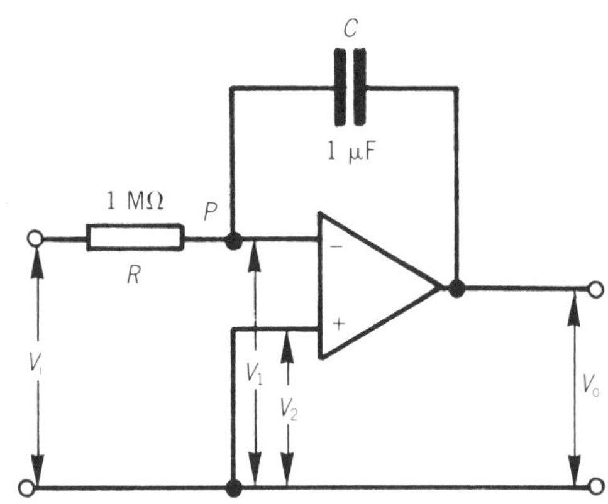

Figure 52.17

This means that the output voltage rises steadily with time (hence the name of ramp generator). This increase continues until the op amp saturates at a voltage just less than the supply voltage.

The variation of the voltage output against time is shown in Figure 52.18. Since P is almost zero (a virtual earth) the voltage across the input resistor R will be the input voltage V_i and the voltage across the capacitor C will be the output voltage V_o. If we assume that no current flows into the inverting input of the op amp, then all the input current I flows to the capacitor C and so charges it up.

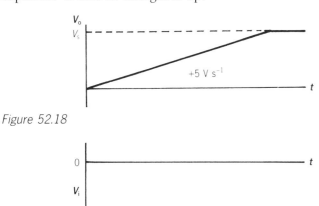

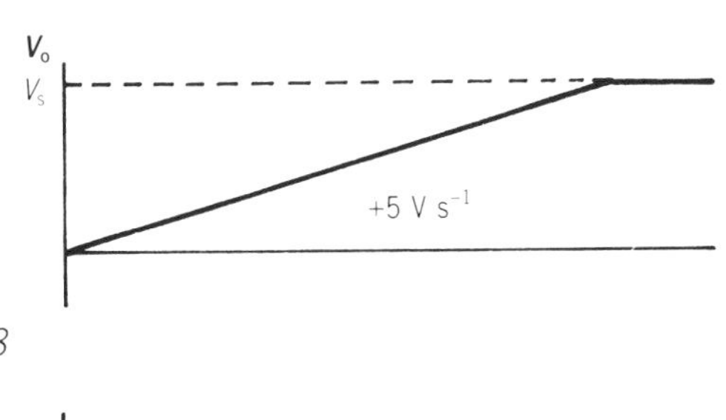

Figure 52.18

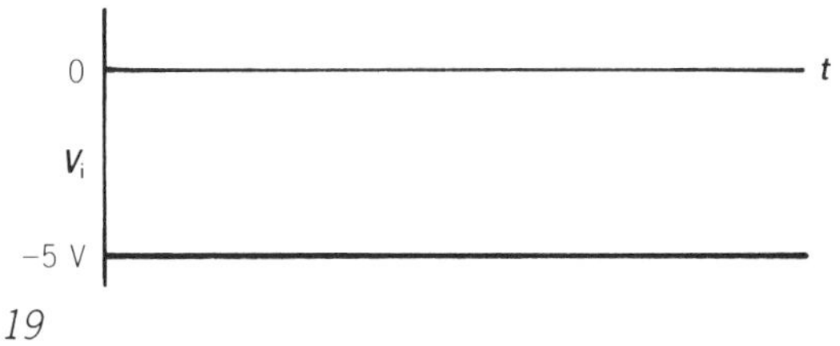

Figure 52.19

If V_i is constant then I will be constant (see Figure 52.19), and its value will be given by

$$I = \frac{V_i}{R}$$

C therefore charges at a constant rate.

If Q is the charge on C at a time t and if p.d. across it changes from 0 to V_o in that time, then (since I is constant)

$$Q = V_o C = It$$

Therefore combining this with the equation above gives

$$-V_o C = \frac{V_i t}{R} \qquad \text{or} \qquad -V_o = \frac{1}{RC} V_i t$$

If C and R are chosen such that $CR = 1$ then

$$V_o = V_i t$$

A more general case is where V_i varies and then

$$V_o = -\frac{1}{RC}\int V_i \, dt$$

This last equation is the reason why this circuit is known as an **integrator**, since the value of V_i is integrated over a certain time interval.

This type of circuit will be found in most oscilloscopes as a means of producing the steadily rising voltage needed for the time base. The ramp generator is also used in the digital voltmeter, the a–d converter and in digital recording.

The summing amplifier

If there are two inputs to the inverting input of the op amp, as shown in Figure 52.20, then it will behave as a **summing amplifier**, the output being an amplification of the *sum* of the two inputs.

Using the symbols shown it can be proved that

$$V_o = -R_3(V_1/R_1 + V_2/R_2)$$

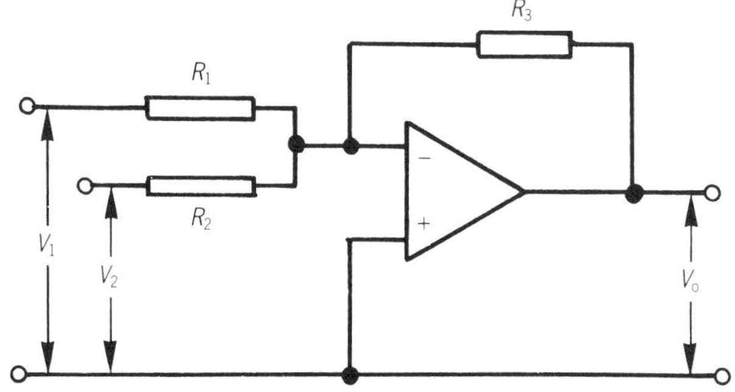

Figure 52.20

Oscillator

The op amp voltage comparator may be used as an oscillator if positive feedback is used. The circuit and waveforms are shown in Figures 52.21 and 52.22.

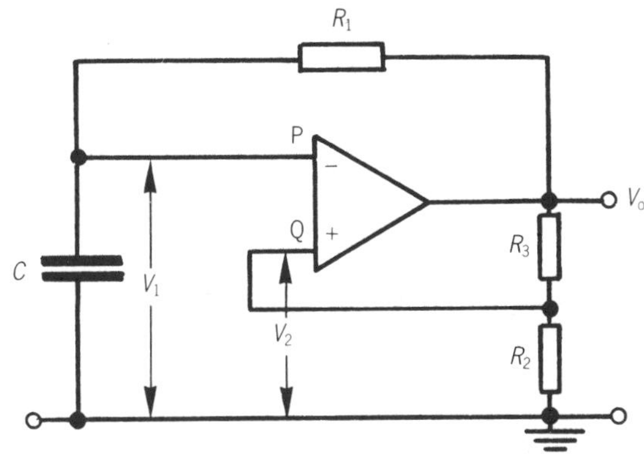

Figure 52.21

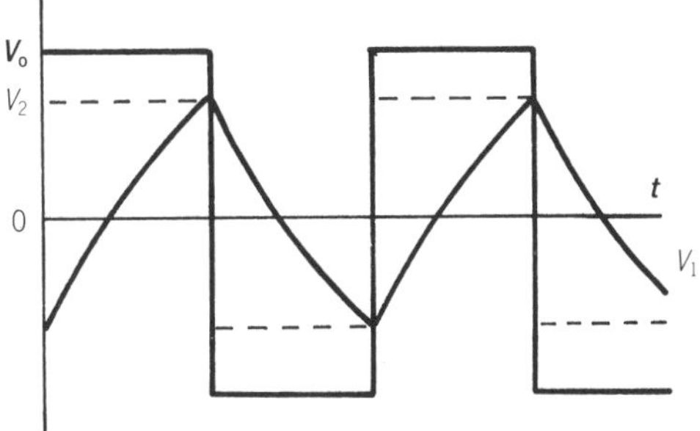

Figure 52.22

Suppose that the output voltage is positive at a particular instant. A certain fraction β of the output voltage V_o is fed back to the non-inverting input, and V_o is fed back to the inverting input via R_1.

The feedback fraction β is given by the equation:

$$\beta = \frac{R_2}{R_2 + R_3}$$

V_1 therefore rises exponentially as C is charged.

After a certain time that depends upon the time constant CR_1, the voltage at P exceeds that at Q, that is, $V_1 > V_2$. The op amp therefore switches to negative saturation ($V_o = -V_s$), and as a result of the positive feedback Q becomes negative.

C now charges in the opposite direction, and the voltage at P falls until $V_1 < V_2$, at which point the op amp switches to positive saturation and the cycle repeats itself. The output voltage is therefore a square wave, as can be seen from the graphs in Figure 52.22.

The equation for the frequency f of such a system is

$$f = \frac{1}{2R_1C \ln(2R_2/R_3 + 1)}$$

Inverting amplifier with a varying input voltage

If the input to the inverting input is a sine wave, then the op amp will saturate every time the difference between the voltages at the inverting input and the non-inverting input exceeds about 150 μV.

The saturation will swing from positive to negative as this voltage difference becomes positive or negative.

This will result in a square wave output, as shown in Figure 52.23.

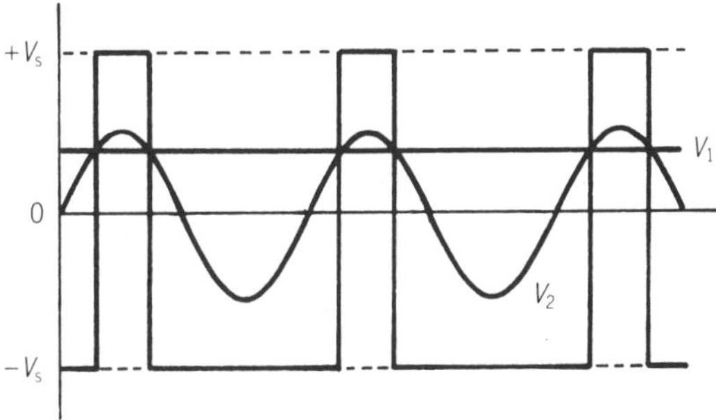

Figure 52.23

6 Explain what is meant by *voltage gain* and *negative feedback* in relation to electronic circuits.

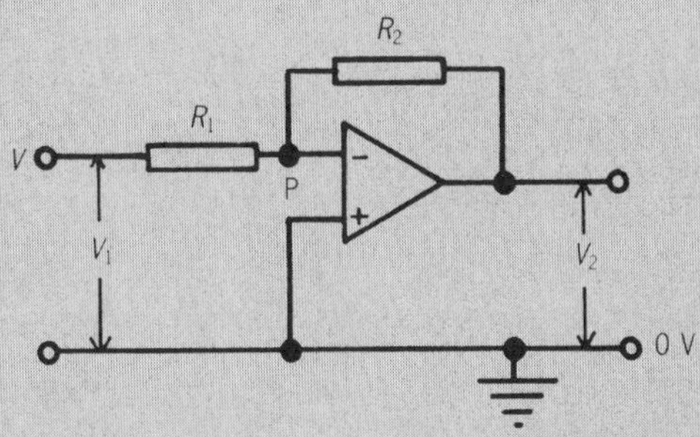

Figure 52.24

Figure 52.24 shows a circuit containing an ideal operational amplifier where the point P is usually referred to as a *virtual earth*. Explain what you understand by *virtual earth* in this context and hence derive an expression for V_2 in terms of V_1 and the values of the circuit components.

The current, I, through a certain device varies with applied potential difference, V, according to the relation

$$I = I_0 e^{kV}$$

where I_0 and k are constants. If R_2 is replaced by this device, write down an expression for the feedback current in terms of V_2. Hence show that V_2 is given by the expression

$$V_2 = 1/k \ln(V_1/R_1 I_0)$$

What is the possible advantage of this type of amplifier over a linear amplifier when a wide range of input signal amplitudes must be displayed? [c]

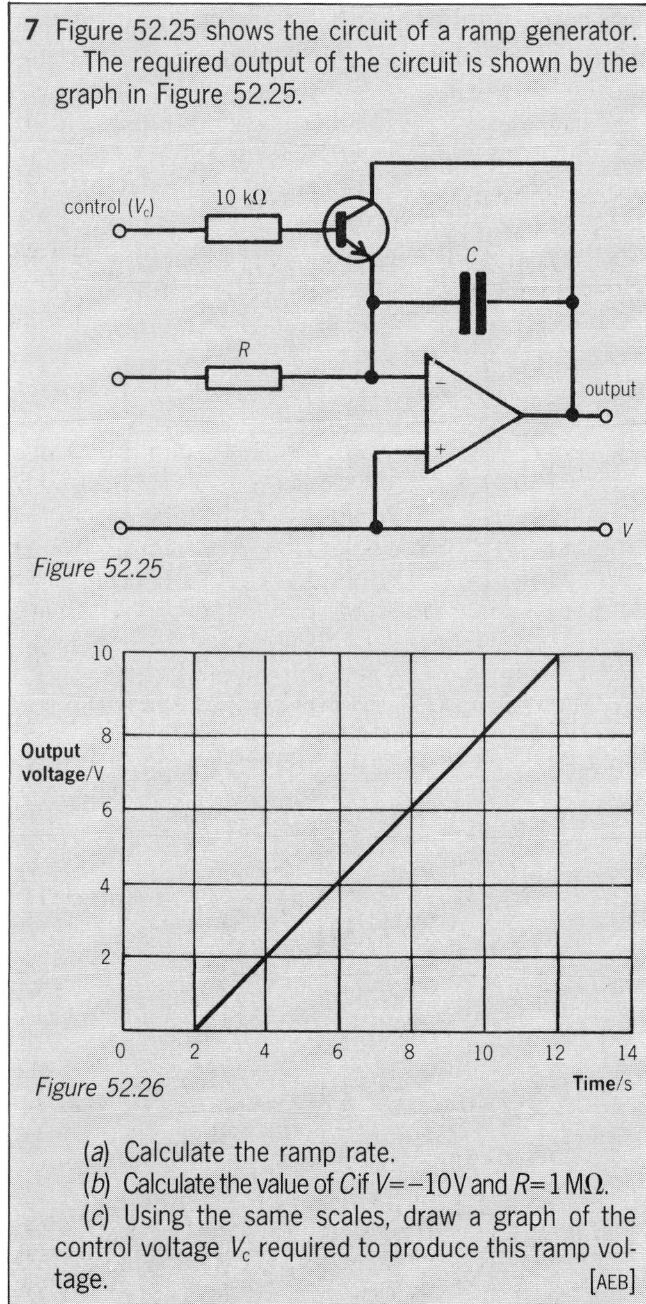

7 Figure 52.25 shows the circuit of a ramp generator.

The required output of the circuit is shown by the graph in Figure 52.25.

Figure 52.25

Figure 52.26

(*a*) Calculate the ramp rate.

(*b*) Calculate the value of *C* if $V = -10$ V and $R = 1$ MΩ.

(*c*) Using the same scales, draw a graph of the control voltage V_c required to produce this ramp voltage. [AEB]

8 An alternating p.d. of r.m.s. value 1 V and frequency 50 Hz is connected across a resistor of resistance 1 kΩ and a capacitor of capacitance 10 μF in turn. For each case, calculate the r.m.s. current delivered by the supply and draw sketch graphs, with appropriate scales, of the p.d. across the component and the current in the circuit, as functions of time.

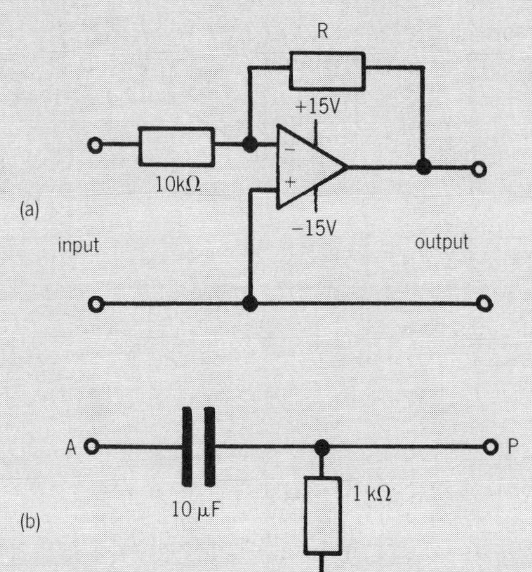

Figure 52.27

Circuit (*a*) shows an operational amplifier with feedback to give an overall voltage gain of 10. Calculate the value of the resistor R.

A 0.5 V r.m.s. 50 Hz sinusoidal alternating p.d. is applied to the input of the amplifier. Sketch graphs, with appropriate p.d. scales and the same time axes, of the input and output waveforms.

The input p.d. is increased in amplitude to 5 V r.m.s.; describe and sketch the resulting output waveform.

Describe, including sketch graphs, the waveform at PQ in circuit (*b*) when (i) a sine wave, and (ii) a square wave, both of frequency 50 Hz, is applied to the input terminals AB of circuit (*b*). [O and C]

A delayed switch-off system

The op amp can be used in a circuit that will switch off an indicator after a set time, as is shown in Figure 52.28. Initially the op amp output is high and the LED is on. The capacitor then begins to charge up through R; when the voltage at P exceeds that at Q the output becomes negative and the LED goes off. The time delay can be adjusted by the variable resistor.

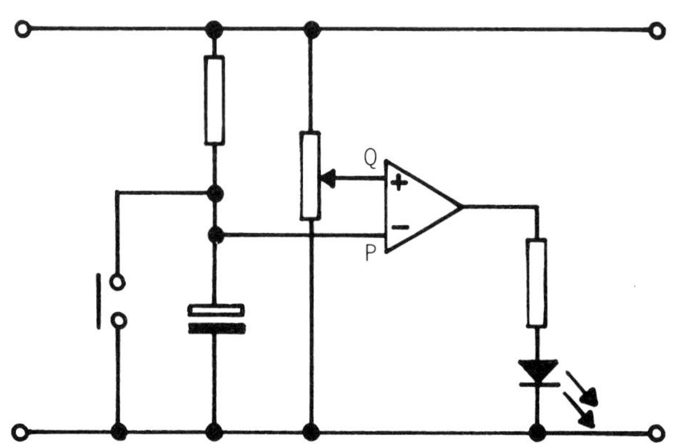

Figure 52.28

53 · Logic gates

The switching action of the transistor makes it especially suitable for use in digital logic circuits where the output is either 1 or 0 depending on the input. Applications for such circuits include (among many others):

(*a*) making a light come on in the dark,
(*b*) a burglar alarm that will sound when someone breaks a light beam or treads on a pressure pad,
(*c*) counting circuits,
(*d*) a fire alarm.

If you refer back to the switching circuit for the transistor (see page 367) you will see that the output voltage is **high** (consider this as 1) when the input voltage is **low** (consider this as 0). This is the basic NOT gate – there is an output when there is *not* an input.

Combinations of these switching circuits can be made into **logic gates** that will perform simple decisions within a microprocessor. These logic gates are the basis of all decisions within computers and from now on we will consider their effects rather then their internal structure. We will consider the following types of logic gate:

(*a*) NOT gate – this gives an output 1 for an input of 0
(*b*) NOR gate – this gives an output 1 for *neither* of two inputs 1
(*c*) OR gate – this gives an output 1 for *either* of two inputs 1 and both inputs 1
(*d*) AND gate – this gives an output 1 for *both* two inputs 1
(*e*) NAND gate – this gives an output 1 for *either but not both* of two inputs 1 or both inputs 0
(*f*) EXCLUSIVE-OR – this gives an output 1 for *either but not both* of two inputs 1
(*g*) EXCLUSIVE-NOR – this gives an output 1 when *both* inputs are 0 or 1

Because of its wide use in modern digital electronics the NAND gate will be considered as a basic building block for a variety of logic circuits. In fact a number of other logic gates can be constructed from NAND gates as is shown on page 389. The circuit in Figure 53.1 shows how a NAND gate might be constructed from discrete components, although it would normally be in the form of an integrated circuit.

There will be a large output voltage across the transistor as long as at least one of the inputs is made low.

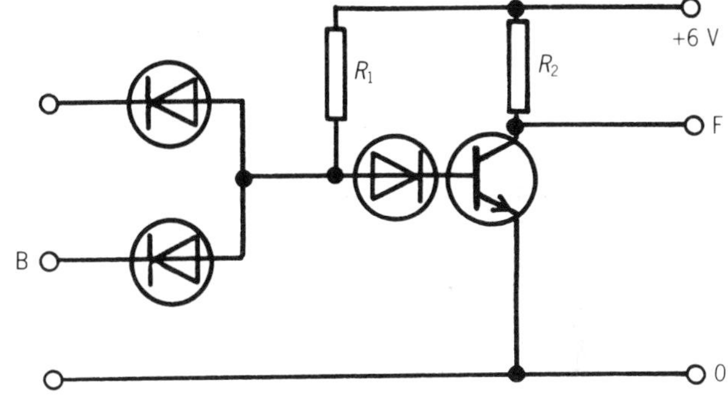

Figure 53.1

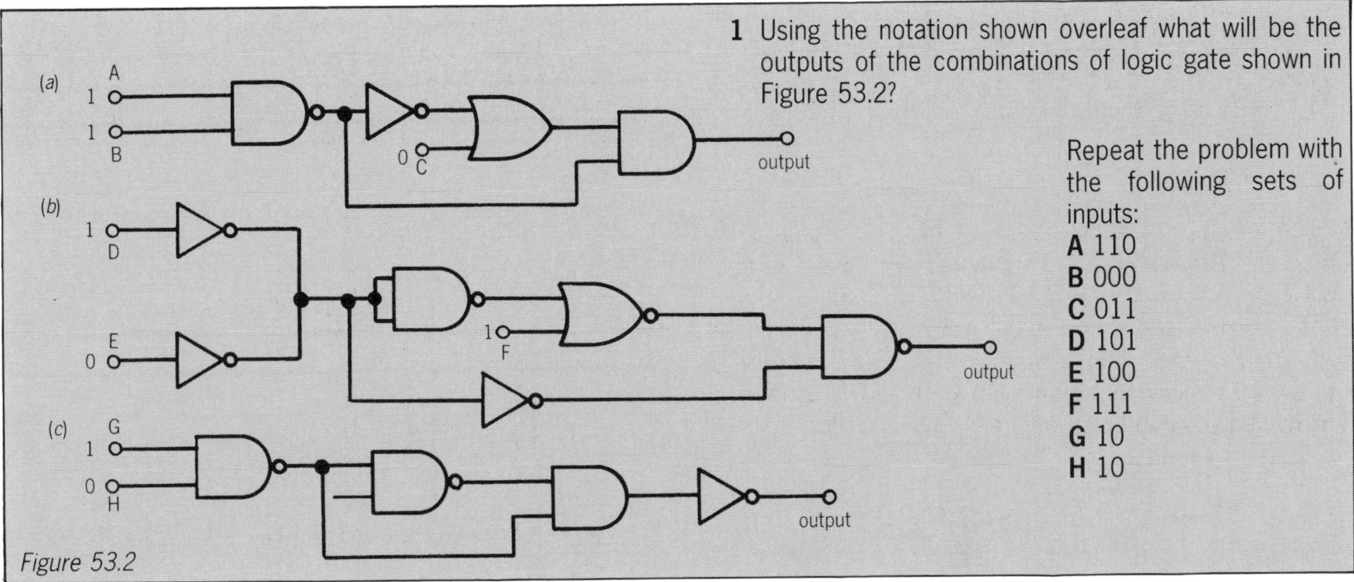

Figure 53.2

1 Using the notation shown overleaf what will be the outputs of the combinations of logic gate shown in Figure 53.2?

Repeat the problem with the following sets of inputs:
A 110
B 000
C 011
D 101
E 100
F 111
G 10
H 10

The symbols and truth tables of the logic gates

The symbols and properties (TRUTH TABLES) of the logic gates are shown in Figures 53.3 to 53.9. Both the British and American symbols are shown but only the American symbols, shown here on the right are used in the following circuit diagrams.

Figure 53.3

Input	*Output*
I	F
0	1
1	0

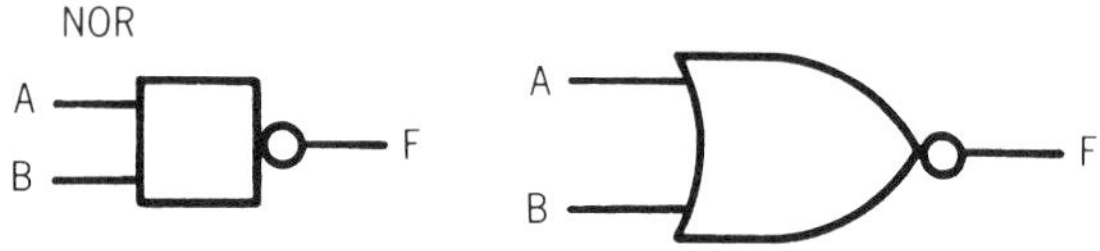

Figure 53.4

Input		*Output*
A	*B*	*F*
0	0	1
0	1	0
1	0	0
1	1	0

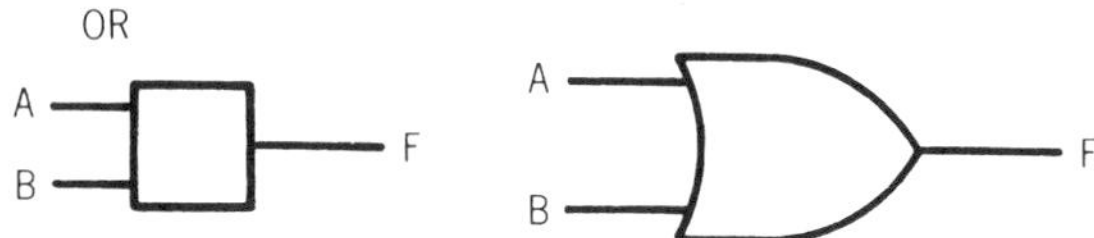

Figure 53.5

Input		*Output*
A	*B*	*F*
0	0	0
1	0	1
0	1	1
1	1	1

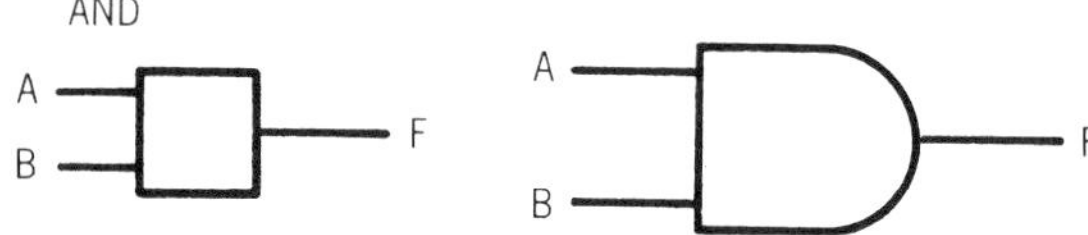

Figure 53.6

Input		*Output*
A	*B*	*F*
0	0	0
1	0	0
0	1	0
1	1	1

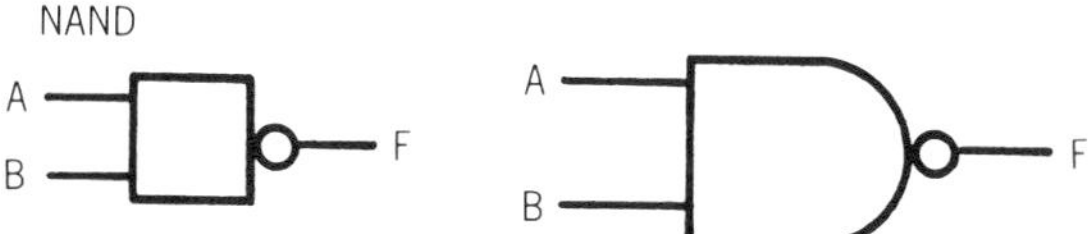

Figure 53.7

Input		*Output*
A	*B*	*F*
0	0	1
1	0	1
0	1	1
1	1	0

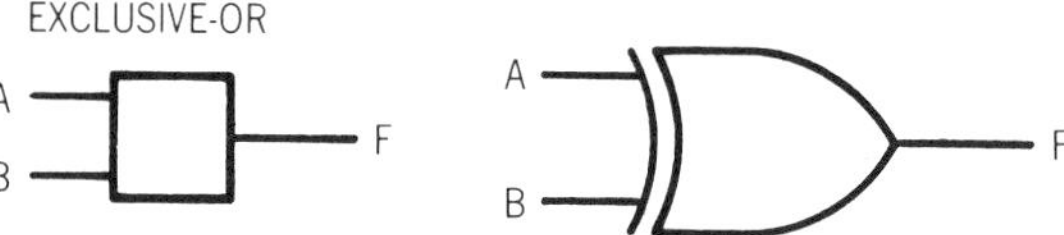

Figure 53.8

Input		*Output*
A	*B*	*F*
0	0	0
0	1	1
1	0	1
1	1	0

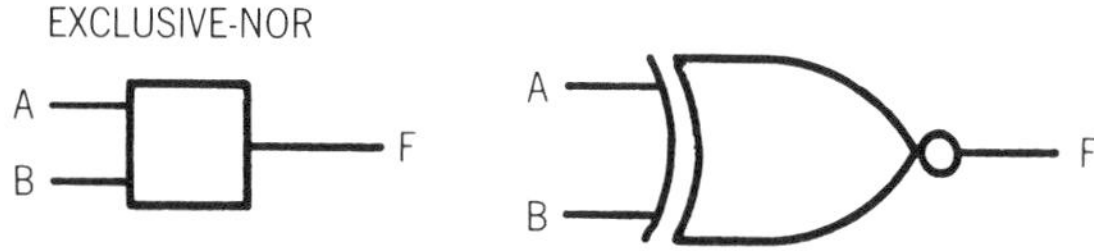

Figure 53.9

Input		*Output*
A	*B*	*F*
0	0	1
0	1	0
1	0	0
1	1	1

Other circuits from the NAND gate

The NAND gate is a very useful circuit and all other logic gates may be constructed from a combination of NAND gates.

Figure 53.10 shows how this may be done. In subsequent work in this section NAND gate versions of all circuits will be given.

Remember that if an input to a NAND gate is not connected (that is, it is a flying lead) the input to that lead is effectively high, logic value 1. You can see this by considering the transistor version of the NAND gate on page 387.

(a)

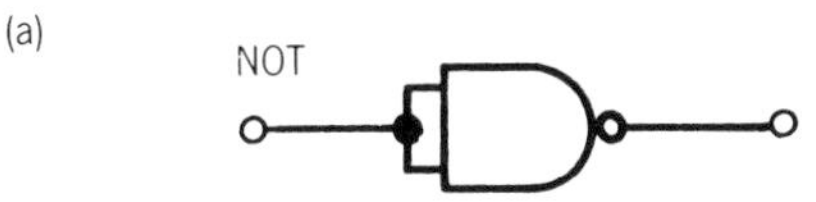

(b)

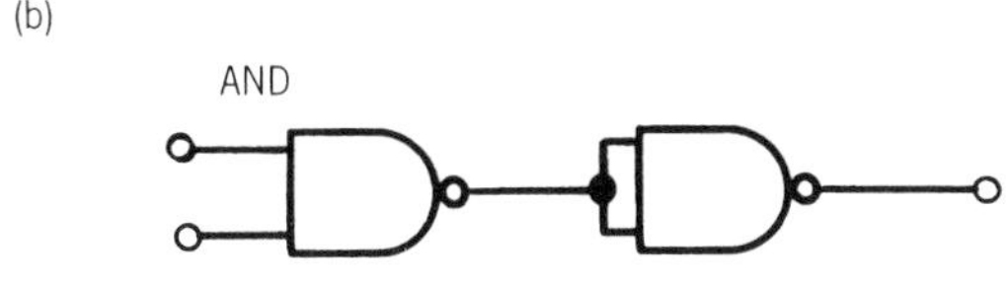

(c)

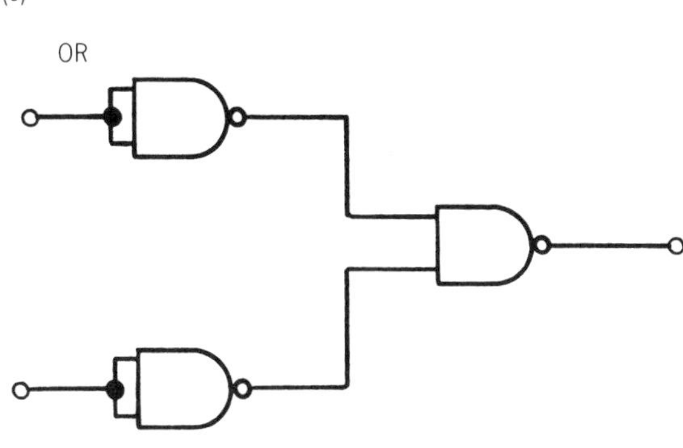

(d)

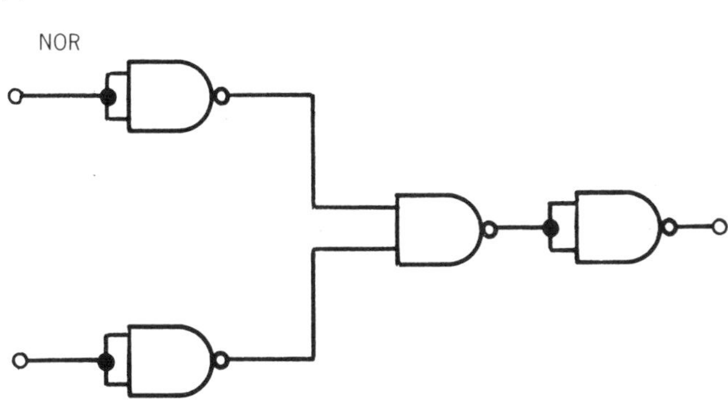

Figure 53.10

Applications of NAND gates

There are many applications of logic gates but we will only consider two here for the moment.

Figure 53.11 shows a length detector. If the length of the object is greater than *d* (the separation of the two LDRs) then their resistance will increase, thus the input to the first gate goes high, the output from the second gate is then high and the buzzer sounds.

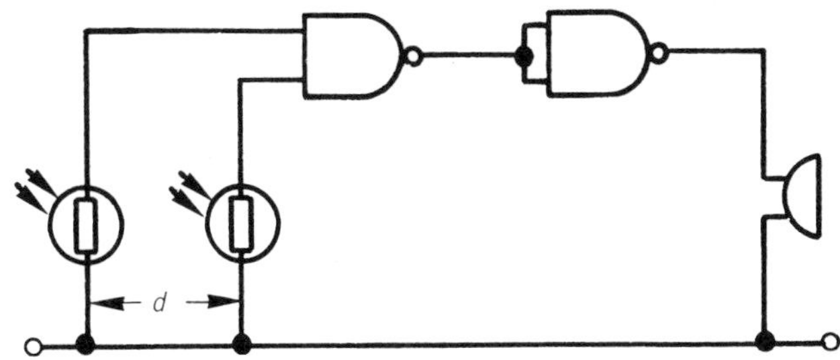

Figure 53.11

Figure 53.12 is a temperature sensor. If the temperature of the thermistor increases its resistance falls, the input falls and the output of the NAND gate is high and the buzzer sounds.

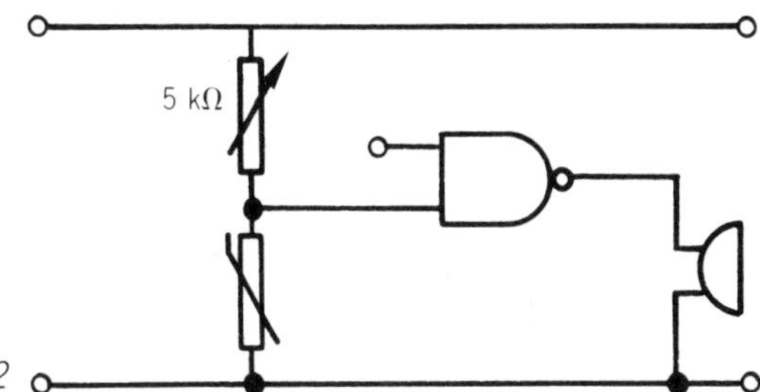

Figure 53.12

2 Devise circuits using logic gates to perform the following functions (you should try to give the simplest version possible and then the version using only NAND gates).

(*a*) Switch a light on in the dark.

(*b*) Open the curtains of a room when it gets light but is not too cold.

(*c*) Sound alarm when the water level in a tank is above a certain level and the temperature falls below a certain value.

(*d*) Allow water to be run into a bath when a switch is pressed only if its temperature is between two preset values.

(*e*) Allow the door of a dark room to be opened only if the safe light and the enlarger light are both off and the main light in the dark room is on.

(*f*) Switch on three coloured LEDs in the same order as the British traffic lights when four binary codes are applied to the two inputs in ascending order (that is, from 00 to 11).

If possible, construct and test the circuits that you suggest.

Problem circuits using logic gates

The following four circuits demonstrate some further practical applications of logic gates, the function of each circuit being explained. Some of the actual logic gates have been omitted, however, the position of each being denoted by a circle. What is the simplest logic gate that will replace each of the circles?

A push-button lock (Figure 53.14)

To open the lock the solenoid must be activated and this can be done by pressing both switches A and B. If B is pressed before A, however, the buzzer will sound.

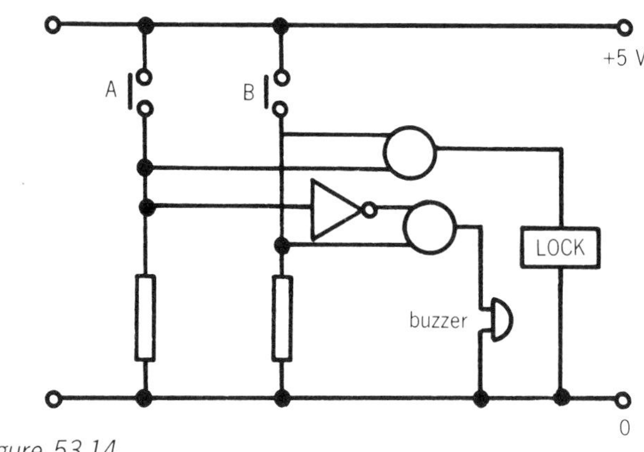

Figure 53.14

A light-activated burglar alarm (Figure 53.15)

When the switch is in position A the buzzer stays off whatever the illumination of the light-dependent resistor. If the switch is closed in position B the buzzer will come on, however, and stay on when a brief flash of light (perhaps from the torch of a burglar) falls on the light-dependent resistor. The buzzer may only be turned off by returning the switch to position A.

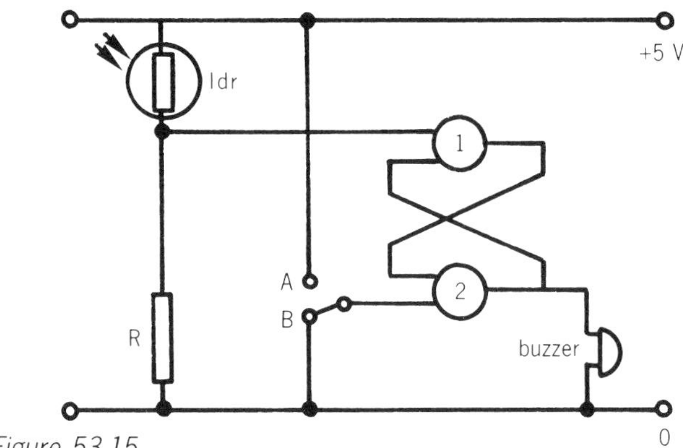

Figure 53.15

A safety thermostat (Figure 53.16)

The two contacts X and Y are near the top of the hot water tank and are normally covered with water so that there is a contact between them. The thermistor is also in the water. If the water is too cold and if the contacts are also covered the heater comes on. The temperature at which this occurs may be set by the variable resistor R.

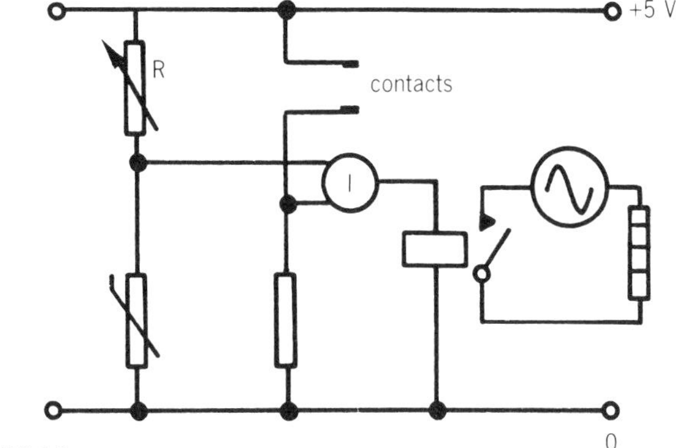

Figure 53.16

An automatic watering system (Figure 53.17)

This is designed to water plants only if the contacts, which may be buried in the soil, are too dry and it is night-time. The relay closes and starts the pump only if *both* these conditions are fulfilled. (Presumably somebody waters the plants in the daytime because if the switch is pressed the water pump works regardless.)

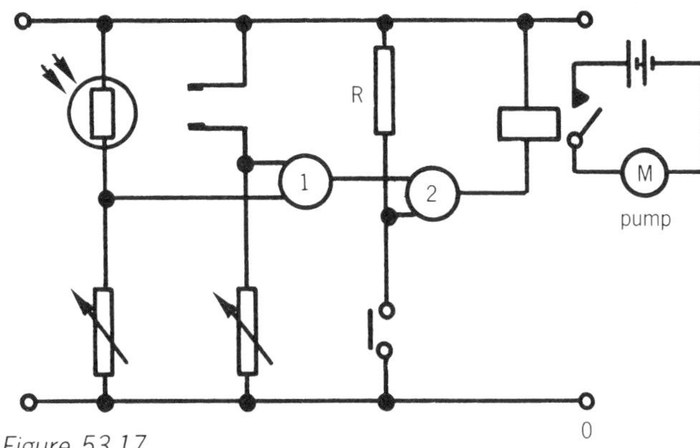

Figure 53.17

Boolean algebra

In 1847 George Boole devised a simple method of analysing logic circuits, over a century before the first integrated circuit had been produced. Boolean algebra, as this branch of mathematics is called, operates with the following rules.

If A is the input to a circuit and the notation $\overline{A}$ means NOT A then:

1 $A + 0 = A$	4 $A.1 = A$	7 $A.\overline{A} = 0$
2 $A + 1 = 1$	5 $\overline{\overline{A}} = A$	8 $A + \overline{A} = 1$
3 $A.0 = 0$	6 $A.A = A$	9 $A + A = A$

Using this notation we can write down the outputs from the logic gates that we have considered.

OR output $= A + B$
AND output $= A.B$
NOT output $= \overline{A}$
NAND output $= \overline{A.B}$
NOR output $= \overline{A + B}$

Now we can *handle* expressions in Boolean algebra in exactly the same way as normal algebra; however, the results will not mean the same as in normal algebra. For example:

$$A.(B + C) = A.B + A.C$$

but if we now give A, B and C values with $A = 1$, $B = 1$, $C = 0$ then the final result using the rules above is:

$$1 + 0 = 1$$

Draw the logic gates that will fulfil those conditions.

We can apply these rules to the slightly more complex circuit in Figure 53.18.

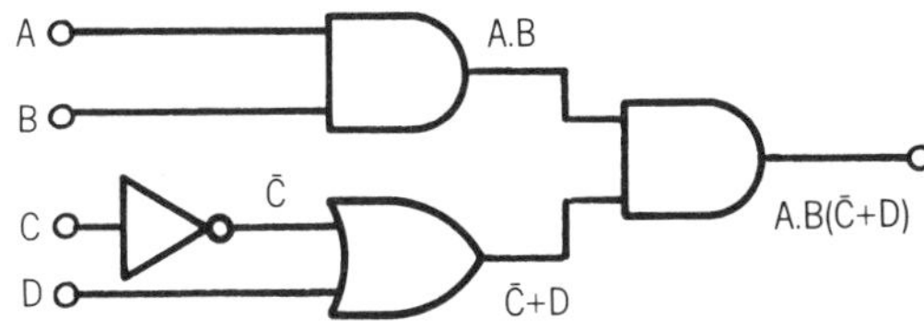

Figure 53.18

The final output is $A.B(\overline{C} + D)$ and this can be multiplied out to give $A.B.\overline{C}. + A.B.D$
Using the values $A = 1, B = 1, C = 0, D = 1$ gives:

$$A.B.\overline{C} + A.B.D = 1 + 1 = 1$$

3 Apply the rules of Boolean algebra to the EXCLUSIVE-OR gate on page 388 and hence obtain an equation for the final output.

4 Apply the rules of Boolean algebra to solve the following circuit for these input values.
1 $A = B = 1$, $C = D = 0$
2 $A = 0$, $B = C = 1$, $D = 0$

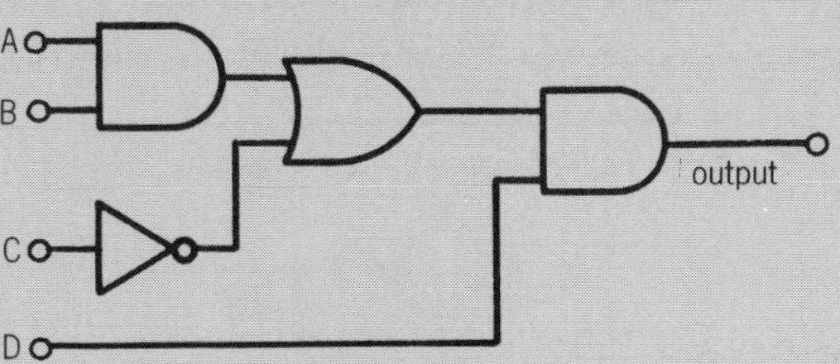

Figure 53.19

5 The following circuit may be used in a coconut shy. There are three coconuts on pressure-sensitive stands and the light should come on when all three have been knocked off. Write down the Boolean algebra expression for the circuit.

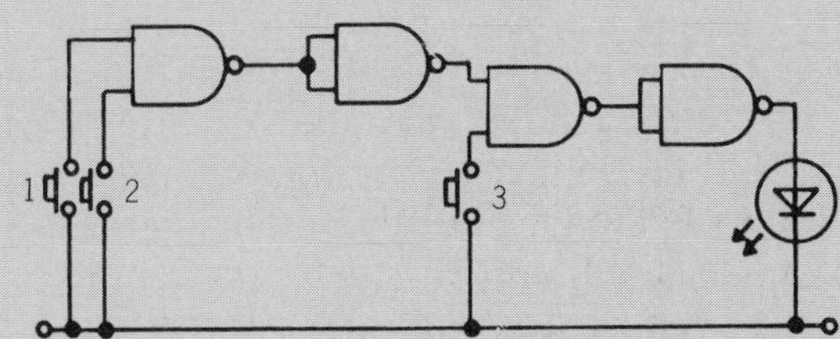

Figure 53.20

6 Write down the Boolean algebra expressions for the length detector and temperature sensor on page 389.

7 Write down the Boolean algebra expression for the EXCLUSIVE-NOR gate. Expand the simple version and draw a circuit for this gate based on your results.

8 Devise circuits that will give the following Boolean algebra expressions.
What would be the output of each circuit when $A = 1$, $B = 0$ and $C = 1$?
(*a*) $A.\overline{B}. + A.B$
(*b*) $A.B. + \overline{A.B}$
(*c*) $A.\overline{B}.C. + A.B.\overline{C}$
(*d*) $\overline{A}.B.\overline{C} + A.B.C$

The NAND gate bistable multivibrator

A very useful electronic circuit is one which is set into one of two stable states by one input switch and will not change its state until the other input switch is pressed. An example of a use of such a circuit is a burglar alarm fitted to a car, the alarm comes on when the burglar opens the door and does not go off until the owner presses a reset switch within the car.

Such a circuit may be made with two NAND gates connected as shown by the following diagram.

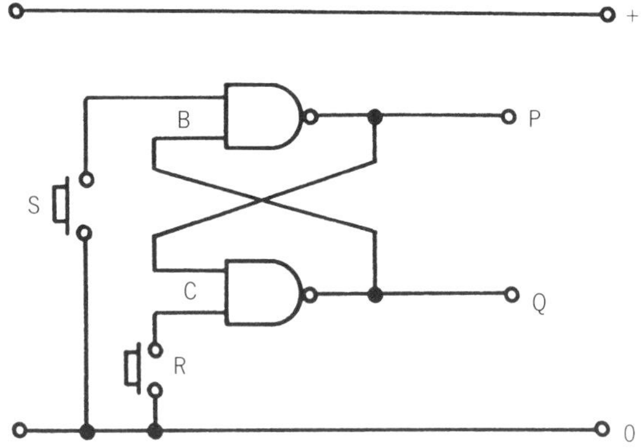

Figure 53.21

The two inputs are two simple push switches, they will be LOW when the switch is pressed but spring open to become HIGH when the switch is released. We will call the inputs S (set) and R (reset) and the two outputs P and Q. The other inputs to the NAND gates are labelled B and C.

Initially suppose that P is LOW (0) and Q is HIGH (1). Now if S is pressed the output P becomes HIGH (1) and the output Q becomes LOW (0) since C becomes 1. The input B therefore becomes LOW (0). Releasing S and then pressing it again will not alter the output states. This can only be done by pressing R.

The truth table for the bistable circuit is shown below.

S	R	B	C	P	Q
1	1	1	0	0	1
0	1	0	1	1	0
1	1	0	1	1	0
1	0	1	0	0	1

Student investigations

Design and build logic circuits using NAND gate bistables that will:

(*a*) act as a burglar alarm sensitive to a light beam,
(*b*) control stop-go traffic lights,
(*c*) act as a control circuit for a quiz game,
(*d*) move a truck backwards and forwards between two light beams.

The fire alarm

A circuit using a NAND gate bistable that will act as a fire alarm is shown below.

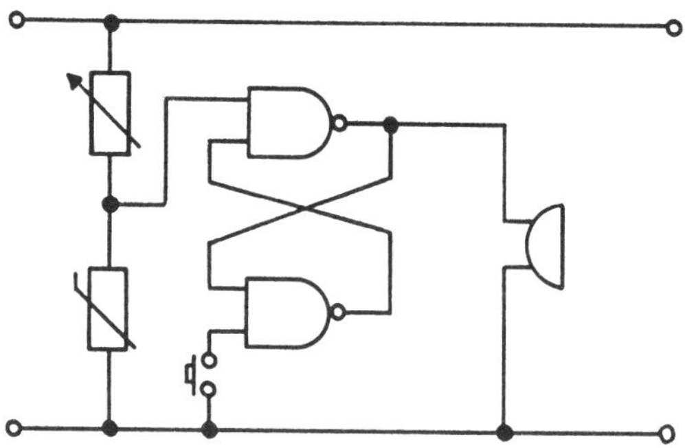

Figure 53.22

To start with the buzzer is off and so the output from gate A must be 0. This means that the output from gate B must be 1. The thermistor is cold, its resistance is high and so the two inputs to gate A are both 1. When the thermistor is warmed its resistance falls and the lower input to gate A becomes 0. Gate A now switches and its output becomes high (1) and the buzzer sounds.

It is left for the student to show that cooling the thermistor will not switch the alarm off. To do this the reset switch R must be pressed.

The NAND gate astable multivibrator

On page 375 we considered the transistor astable multivibrator. Figure 53.24 shows the NAND gate version of this useful circuit.

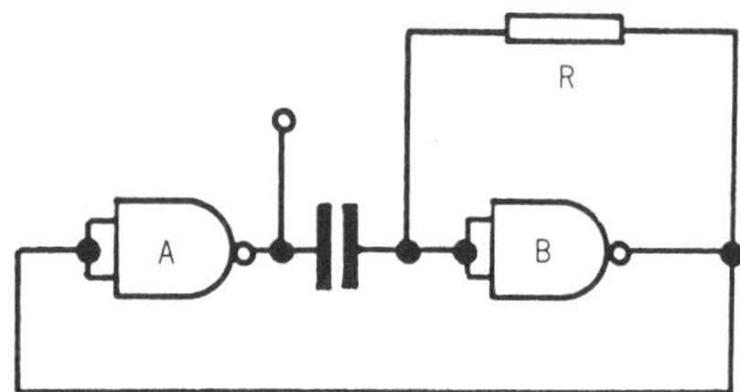

Figure 53.23

We will call the output voltage from the circuit *V*. Imagine that initially the input to A is high, this means that the output from A is low and the output from B is high. If the output from B is high the input to B must be low.

The capacitor C therefore charges up through R and the potential at the input to B rises. When this potential is high enough B switches making the output to B low. This means that the input to A is low and therefore the output from A is high. C now discharges through R until B switches to a high output; the process then repeats itself. The switching rate and therefore the output frequency depends on the values of R and C.

The EXCLUSIVE-OR gate

On page 388 the truth table for the exclusive OR gate was shown. This is a gate where the output is high only if one or other inputs is high but not both.

The Boolean algebra equation for such a circuit is:

$$\text{Output} = \bar{A}.B + A.\bar{B}$$

You should see that this is therefore simply two sets of NOT and AND gates followed by an OR gate, as shown in Figure 53.24.

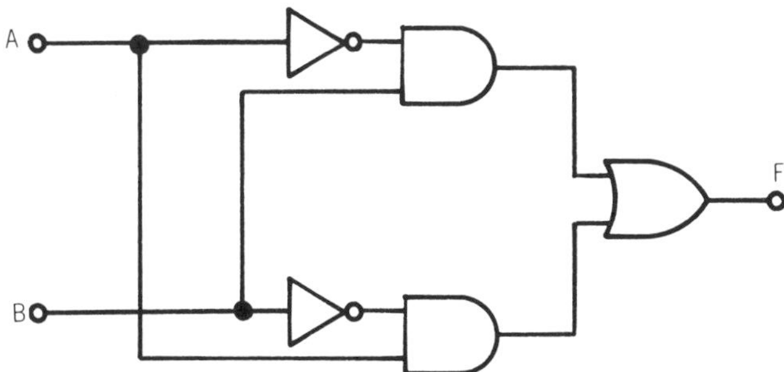

Figure 53.24

The NAND gate version of this circuit is shown in Figure 53.25.

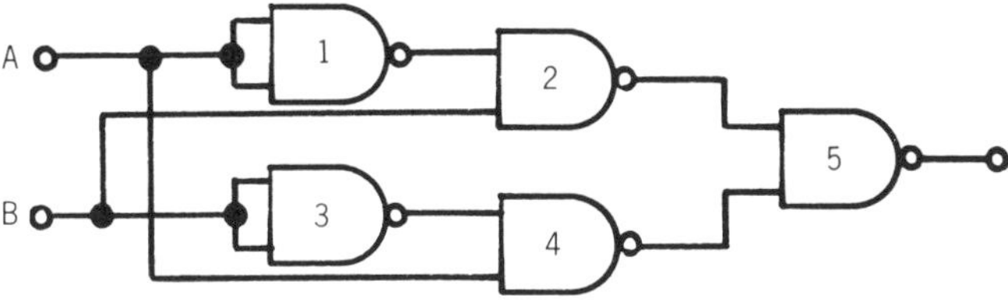

Figure 53.25

The EXCLUSIVE-NOR gate

This gate gives a high output when its two inputs are equal, that is, both 0 or both 1. It is therefore known as the parity or equivalence gate.

This circuit may be realised with two NOT gates, two AND gates and an OR gate, as shown in Figure 53.26.

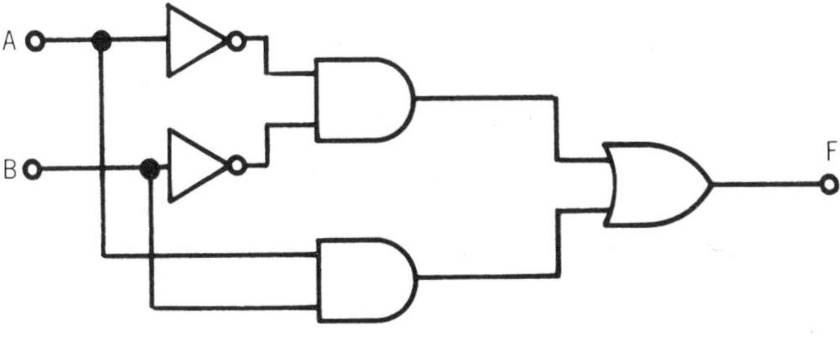

Figure 53.26

The half adder

By a small extension of the EXCLUSIVE-OR gate we can obtain a circuit that will not only add two simple binary digits but also give a carry bit.

We need a circuit where the sum bit is 0 if the two inputs are either both 0 or both 1 and where the carry bit is 1 only if both inputs are 1.

Using Boolean algebra notation and taking the inputs as A and B we can obtain the following equations for the sum bit (S) and the carry bit (C):

The sum bit (S) is given by $S = \bar{A}.B + A.\bar{B}$
The carry bit (C) is given by $C = A.B$

You should see that the sum bit will be given by an EXCLUSIVE-OR gate and the carry bit by an AND gate. A circuit for the full half adder is shown below.

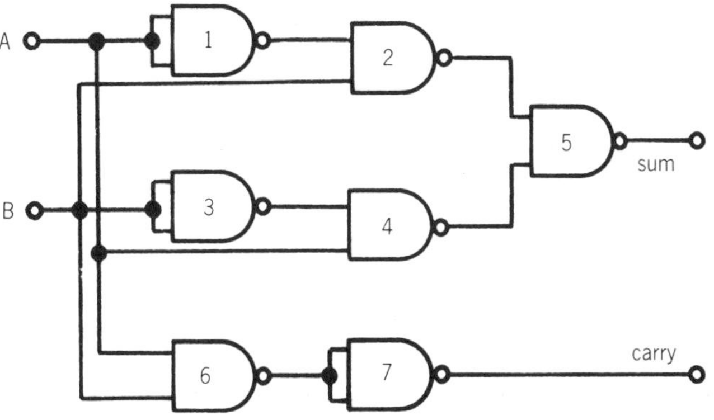

Figure 53.27

You should follow through the circuit checking the condition at each NAND gate to see that it produces the required output.

Student investigation

Construct and operate a full half adder circuit using two quad NAND gates. Check the output for all input combinations.

Using two half adders and an OR gate a full adder circuit may be produced that will add three bits A, B and C.

The Boolean notation for such a circuit is:

SUM bit $= \bar{A}.\bar{B}.C + \bar{A}.B.\bar{C} + A.\bar{B}.\bar{C} + A.B.C$
CARRY bit $= \bar{A}.B.C + A.B.\bar{C} + A.\bar{B}.C + A.B.C$

9 Attempt to devise the NAND gate version of the full adder circuit.

10 Devise the NAND gate circuit for the EXCLUSIVE-NOR gate. Suggest a practical use for such a circuit.

54 · The microprocessor

An integrated circuit that is designed to carry out a series of commands is known as a **microprocessor.** The microprocessor has had an enormous impact on people's lives over the past few years; these are just some of its uses:

calculator	control of machinery
word processor	data storage
computer-aided design	games
stock control	spacecraft guidance

The logic circuits that make up the microprocessor have basically two conditions: *on* (1) and *off* (0). The microprocessor will recognise a series of such conditions and interpret that as an instruction.

For this reason, **binary numbers** form the basis for computer instructions. The decimal numbers with their binary equivalents are shown below for numbers up to decimal 12.

1	01	5	101	9	1001
2	10	6	110	10	1010
3	11	7	111	11	1011
4	100	8	1000	12	1100

Binary numbers are unwieldy, however: decimal 64 is 1000000, while decimal 256 is 100000000. So to keep the numbers manageable many microprocessors use the **hexadecimal** notation – numbers to the base 16. The numbers from 0 to 9 are used and then the letters A to F. Some examples of hexadecimal numbers are given below.

1	1	15	F	30	1E
5	5	16	10	32	20
10	A	17	11	40	28
11	B	25	19	256	100

This notation becomes very useful for large numbers. For example, the binary number 1010 0111 can be written simply as A7 in hex (167 in decimal), while in the 16-bit microprocessor the address (see below) 1111 1101 0010 1110 is replaced by the corresponding hex value FD2E.

It would be very tedious to write programs for a microprocessor using binary or hex notation and so a program is built into the microprocessor that will convert the instructions that we type in into something that the machine will 'understand'.

We type in a so-called high-level language such as BASIC and the microprocessor decodes this, turning it into **machine code.** Writing a program in BASIC is much quicker and easier for the operator, but the program is much slower and more difficult for the machine to deal with. The word 'slower' is probably misleading here, since a modern calculator will add two numbers together in 0.7 μs and it will add together all the numbers from 1 to 100 in less than one-hundredth of a second!

The microcomputer

The block diagram in Figure 54.1 shows the essential parts of a microcomputer.

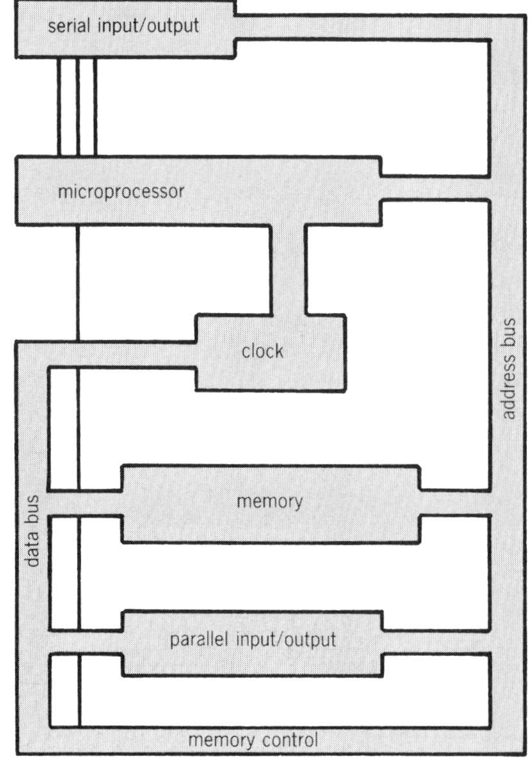

Figure 54.1

At the heart of the micro is the **microprocessor**, which tells the other parts of the circuit what to do and when to do it.

The **memory** remembers and stores information that may be needed later by the system. Memory may be in **software** form, as magnetic signals recorded on disc or tape, or **hardware** as a memory chip in the computer.

This latter form of memory can be of two types. The first is **read only memory** (ROM) – each memory cell contains a fixed piece of data (ROM cannot be altered by the user). The second type is **random access memory** (RAM): data can be added to or removed from any cell in RAM.

The microcomputer also contains an electronic **clock**. This produces a pulse every 2 microseconds, and this sets a time scale for the operation of a program. Only one computer operation can take place during one clock pulse.

The microcomputer also has input and output connections or **interfaces** through which it communicates with the outside world. These may be a screen, a printer or a piece of machinery.

In the next chapter we will consider some of the programs that can be written for the BBC model B microcomputer, since many schools have this machine.

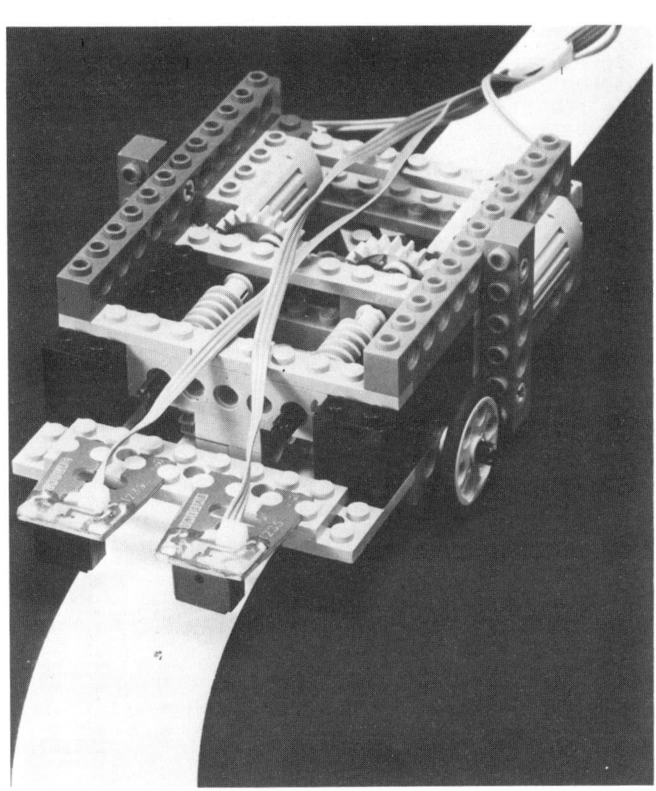

A computer controlled buggy (UNILAB Ltd)

It is important to realise that the computer is not just an expensive calculator or a means of playing arcade games, although it can fulfil both these functions. In the author's school the uses made of the BBC computers have included

(*a*) teaching programs for the classroom,
(*b*) pupil records,
(*c*) cricket scoreboard,
(*d*) graphic designer,
(*e*) word processor for letters/booklets,
(*f*) with apparatus in the science laboratories,
(*g*) computer controlled lathe,
(*h*) information technology,

and many others.

Some excellent books have been written about the use of the BBC computer. Here we shall simply outline some straightforward programs, to enable those who know little of computing to make the machine do something interesting for them, together with one longer program on the photoelectric effect.

If you have a BBC microcomputer load these programs in turn, and find out what they do; some explanation is given in the REM statements within the first few programs. (These can be omitted when the programs are typed in since they do not affect the running on the program.)

55 · Program listings

Greet

```
1. GREETING
   10 CLS
   20 PRINT TAB(15,10);CHR$(141)"GREETING"
   30 PRINT TAB(15,11);CHR$(141)"GREETING"
   35 REM LINE 40 IS A TIME DELAY
   40 FOR H= 1 TO 2000:NEXT H
   50 PRINT TAB(2,14);"HELLO, I'M A BBC COMPUTER"
   55 FOR B=1 TO 1000:NEXT B
   60 PRINT TAB(2,17);"WHAT IS YOUR NAME?"
   65 REM COMPUTER WAITS FOR A NAME
   70 INPUT NAME$
   72 FOR J= 1 TO 1000:NEXT J
   75 CLS
   77 FOR J= 1 TO 1000:NEXT J
   80 PRINT TAB(15,10);CHR$(141);"HELLO ";NAME$
   90 PRINT TAB(15,11);CHR$(141);"HELLO ";NAME$
```

Tables

```
2. TABLES
    5 MODE 7
   10 CLS
   20 PRINT TAB(11,10);CHR$(141)"TIMED TABLES"
   30 PRINT TAB(11,11);CHR$(141)"TIMED TABLES"
   40 FOR D=1 TO 2000:NEXT D
   50 CLS
   60 PRINT:PRINT:PRINT
   70 PRINT"THIS PROGRAM WILL TEST YOUR TABLES
      BUT YOU ONLY HAVE A CERTAIN TIME TO TYPE
      IN THE ANSWER"
   80 PRINT
   90 INPUT"WHAT LEVEL OF DIFFICULTY(1-10)",L
  100 CLS
  110 PRINT:PRINT
  120 LET D=INT(10/L)
  130 T=0
  140 REPEAT
  150 FOR X=0 TO 18
  160 FOR G= 1 TO 2000:NEXT G
  170 PRINT TAB(20,6);"CORRECT ANSWERS  ";T
  180 A=RND(12):B=RND(12):PRINT TAB(2,X+2);A;"x"B;"="
  190 B$=""
  200 REPEAT
  210 A$=INKEY$(200*D)
  220 PRINT A$;
  230 IF A$=CHR$(127)B$=LEFT$(B$,LEN(B$-1))
      ELSE B$=B$+A$
  240 UNTIL A$="" OR A$=CHR$(13)
  250 IF A$="" PRINT TAB(2,X+4)"TOO SLOW":GOTO 300
  260 ELSE REQUIRED$=B$
  270 NUMBER = VAL(B$)
  280 IF NUMBER =A*B THEN PRINT TAB(2,X+4);"CORRECT"
      ELSE PRINT TAB(2,X+4);"WRONG"
  290 IFNUMBER =A*B THEN T=T+1
  300 X=X+3
  310 NEXT X
  320 PRINT
  330 INPUT"ANOTHER GO",Z$
  340 IF Z$="Y" THEN  90
  350 IF NOT(Z$="Y") THEN  360
  360 END
```

Histogram

```
3. HISTOGRAM

   10 CLS
   20 MODE 7
   30 PRINT TAB(12,10);CHR$(141)"HISTOGRAM"
   40 PRINT TAB(12,11);CHR$(141)"HISTOGRAM"
   50 FOR D= 1 TO 1000:NEXT D
   60 PRINT:PRINT
   70 PRINT TAB(4)"PRESS SPACE BAR TO CONTINUE"
   80 REPEAT UNTIL GET = 32
   90 GOTO 100
  100 MODE 4
  110 VDU 28,5,20,34,10
  120 PRINT "THIS PROGRAM WILL DRAW A HISTOGRAM.
      YOU WILL BE ASKED TO TYPE IN THE NUMBER FOR
      EACH OF TWELVE VALUES"
  130 PRINT:PRINT
  140 PRINT"PRESS SPACE BAR TO CONTINUE"
  150 REPEAT UNTIL GET =32
  160 GOTO 170
  170 CLS
  180 VDU 28,0,31,39,0
  190 MOVE 95,125
  200 FOR X =95 TO 1280 STEP 5
  210 DRAW X,125
  220 NEXT X
  230 FOR Z= 0 TO 25 STEP 5
  240 IF Z<10 GOTO 280
  250 IF Z>=10 GOTO 260
  260 PRINT TAB(0,28-Z);Z
  270 GOTO 290
  280 PRINT TAB(1,28-Z);Z
  290 NEXT Z
  300 FOR P=1 TO 12
  310 PRINT TAB(3*P+1,30);P
  320 NEXT P
  330 MOVE 95,125
  340 FOR Y = 125 TO 1000 STEP 5
  350 DRAW 95,Y
  360 NEXT Y
  370 VDU 23,240,255,255,255,255,255,255,255,255
  380 FOR X = 3 TO 36 STEP 3
  390 PRINT TAB(20,2);"ENTER NUMBER"
  400 PRINT TAB(19,4);"    "
  410 PRINT TAB(20,4);
  420 INPUT N
  430 IF N=0 GOTO 540
  440 IF N>27 N=27
  450 VDU 19,128,0,0,0,0
  460 VDU 19,1,3,0,0,0
  470 FOR H = 1 TO N
  480 PRINT TAB(X,28-H);CHR$(240)
  490 PRINT TAB(X+1,28-H);CHR$(240)
  500 PRINT TAB(X+2,28-H);CHR$(240)
  510 NEXT H
  520 IF X=36 GOTO 570
  530 NEXT X
  540 PRINT TAB(X,27-N);CHR$(255)
  550 IF X = 36 GOTO 570
  560 NEXT X
  570 PRINT TAB(1,5);"PRESS SPACE BAR FOR ANOTHER
      HISTOGRAM"
  580 REPEAT UNTIL GET = 32
  590 GOTO 100
```

Circle

```
4. CIRCLE
   5 REM THIS PROGRAM DRAWS A CIRCLE
  10 CLS
  20 PRINT TAB(15,10);"CIRCLES"
  30 FOR T= 1 TO 3000:NEXT T
  40 CLS
  50 MODE 4
  60 PRINT "PLEASE TYPE IN THE RADIUS (<=5)"
  70 INPUT R
  80 MOVE 600,500+R*100
  90 FOR X=0 TO 320 STEP 4
 100 DRAW 600+100*R*SIN(X/50),500+100*R*COS(X/50)
 110 NEXT X
```

Motion

```
5.MOTION
  10 MODE1
  20 A%=500:B%=500
  30 PROCBOX
  35 REM THESE LINES MOVE THE BOX
  40 IF INKEY-122PROCBOX:A%=A%+10:PROCBOX
  50 IF INKEY-26PROCBOX:A%=A%-10:PROCBOX
  60 IF INKEY-58PROCBOX:B%=B%+10:PROCBOX
  65 REM THESE LINES GROW THE BOX
  70 IF INKEY-42PROCBOX:B%=B%-10:PROCBOX
  80 IF INKEY-85PROCBOX:H%=H%+10:PROCBOX
  90 IF INKEY-38PROCBOX:H%=H%-10:PROCBOXCI
 100 IF INKEY-34PROCBOX:W%=W%+10:PROCBOX
 110 IF INKEY-67PROCBOX:W%=W%-10:PROCBOX
 120 GOTO40
 130 DEFPROCBOX
 140 GCOL3,7
 150 MOVEA%,B%
 160 DRAWA%+W%,B%
 170 DRAWA%+W%,B%+H%
 180 DRAWA%,B%+H%
 190 DRAWA%,B%
 200 ENDPROC
```

Wordsort

```
6. WORDSORT
  10 CLS
  20 PRINT TAB(12,10);CHR$(141)"WORD SORT"
  30 PRINT TAB(12,11);CHR$(141)"WORD SORT"
  40 PRINT TAB(0,13);"THIS  PROGRAM  WILL SORT
     TWENTY
     WORDS INTO ALPHABETICAL ORDER"
  50 PRINT TAB(6,20);"PRESS ANY KEY TO CONTINUE"
  60 LET A$=INKEY$(0)
  70 IF A$<>"" GOTO 90
  80 GOTO 60
  90 CLS
 100 DIM NAME$(20)
 110 PRINT TAB(3,1);"UNSORTED"
 115 PRINT TAB(20,1);"SORTED"
 120 FOR I=1 TO 20
 130 READ NAME$(I)
 140 PRINT TAB(4,I+3);NAME$(I)
 150 NEXT I
 160 FOR K=1 TO 19
 170 FOR L = K+1 TO 20
 180 IF NAME$(L) >=NAME$(K) THEN 220
 190 LET T$= NAME$(L)
 200 LET NAME$(L) = NAME$(K)
 210 LET NAME$(K)=T$
 220 NEXT L:NEXT K
 240 FOR T=1 TO 1000:NEXT T
 250 PRINT TAB(20,1);"SORTED"
 260 FOR I = 1 TO 20
 270 PRINT TAB(20,I+3)NAME$(I)
 280 NEXT I
 290 DATABOX,TABLE,CHAIR,CARPET,BOOK,
     SHELF,STOOL,FLOOR,ROOF,GARDEN,
     DESK,PENCIL,PAPER,KETTLE,CUP,TREE,
     FLOWER,CAR,CARAVAN,MIST
```

Tune

```
7. THE NATIONAL ANTHEM
   5 THIS PROGRAM PLAYS THE NATIONAL ANTHEM
  10 CLS
  15 MODE7
  20 PRINT TAB(15,10);CHR$(141)"MUSIC"
  30 PRINT TAB(15,11);CHR$(141)"MUSIC"
  40 FOR T=1 TO 2000:NEXT T
  50 PRINT TAB(12,15);CHR$(141)"PLEASE STAND"
  60 PRINT TAB(12,16);CHR$(141)"PLEASE STAND"
  70 FOR P=1 TO 2000:NEXT P
  80 VDU23;8202;0;0;0
  90 SOUND 1,-15,81,16
 100 SOUND 1,0,81,1
 110 SOUND 1,-15,81,16
 120 SOUND 1,-15,89,16
 130 SOUND 1,-15,77,24
 140 SOUND 1,-15,81,8
 150 SOUND 1,-15,89,16
 160 SOUND 1,-15,97,16
 170 SOUND 1,0,97,1
 180 SOUND 1,-15,97,16
 190 SOUND 1,-15,101,16
 200 SOUND 1,-15,97,24
 210 SOUND 1,-15,89,8
 220 SOUND 1,-15,81,16
 230 SOUND 1,-15,89,16
 240 SOUND 1,-15,81,16
 250 SOUND 1,-15,77,16
 260 SOUND 1,-15,81,16
 270 SOUND 1,0,81,1
 280 SOUND 1,-15,81,8
 290 SOUND 1,-15,89,8
 300 SOUND 1,-15,97,8
 310 SOUND 1,-15,101,8
 320 SOUND 1,-15,109,16
 330 SOUND 1,0,109,1
 340 SOUND 1,-15,109,16
 350 SOUND 1,0,109,1
 360 SOUND 1,-15,109,16
 370 SOUND 1,0,109,1
 380 SOUND 1,-15,109,24
 390 SOUND 1,-15,101,8
 400 SOUND 1,-15,97,16
 410 SOUND 1,-15,101,16
 420 SOUND 1,0,109,1
 430 SOUND 1,-15,101,16
 440 SOUND 1,0,109,1
 450 SOUND 1,-15,101,16
 460 SOUND 1,0,109,1
 470 SOUND 1,-15,101,24
 480 SOUND 1,-15,97,8
 490 SOUND 1,-15,89,16
 500 SOUND 1,-15,97,16
 510 SOUND 1,-15,101,8
 520 SOUND 1,-15,97,8
 530 SOUND 1,-15,89,8
 540 SOUND 1,-15,81,8
 550 SOUND 1,-15,97,24
 560 SOUND 1,-15,101,8
 570 SOUND 1,-15,109,16
 580 SOUND 1,-15,117,8
 590 SOUND 1,-15,101,8
 600 SOUND 1,-15,97,16
 610 SOUND 1,-15,89,16
 620 SOUND 1,-15,81,48
 640 FOR H=1 TO 7500:NEXT H
 650 PRINT TAB(12,10);CHR$(141);"YOU MAY SIT NOW"
 660 PRINT TAB(12,11);CHR$(141);"YOU MAY SIT NOW"
 670 END
```

```
8. PHOTOELECTRIC EFFECT
  10 MODE7
  15 VDU23;8202;0;0;0;
  20 CLS
  30 PRINT TAB(7,9);CHR$(132);CHR$(141);"PHOTOELECTRIC EFFECT"
  40 PRINT TAB(7,10);CHR$(132);CHR$(141);"PHOTOELECTRIC EFFECT"
  50 PRINTTAB(3,23);CHR$(129);"PRESS THE SPACE BAR TO CONTINUE"
  60 REPEAT UNTIL GET = 32
  70 CLS
  80 PRINT "When light falls on a metal surface electrons are
     sometimes emitted."
  90 PRINT "This is known as the"
 100 PRINTTAB(7,4);CHR$(131);"PHOTOELECTRIC EFFECT"
 110 PRINT
 120 PRINT"It has been found that"
 130 PRINT"1. the NUMBERof electrons emitted per second
     depends on the INTENSITY of the incident radiation"
 140 PRINT"2. the ENERGY of the emitted electrons  depends
     on the FREQUENCY of the incident radiation"
 150 PRINT
 160 PRINT "This can be explained by thinking of the light
     as being composed of packets of energy called QUANTA"
 170 PRINTTAB(3,23);CHR$(132);"PRESS THE SPACE BAR TO CONTINUE"
 180 REPEAT UNTIL GET = 32
 190 CLS
 200 PRINT
 210 PRINTTAB(10,4);CHR$(132);"POTENTIAL WELL"
 220 PRINT
 230 PRINT"You can think of the electrons as being bound into the
     metal in a kind of well."
 240 PRINT"In just the same way that a stone in a  hole in the ground
     requires energy to get out so an electron needs energy to escape
     from the potential well"
 250 PRINT "This energy can be provided in the form of a quantum of
     radiation"
 260 PRINT
 270 PRINT"The following simulation enables you to see the
     effect of irradiating a surface with quanta of different
     frequency and  therefore different energy"
 280 PRINTTAB(3,23)CHR$(130);"PRESS THE SPACE BAR TO CONTINUE"
 290 REPEAT UNTIL GET = 32
 300 MODE1
 305 VDU23;8202;0;0;0;
 310 VDU 19,2,2,0,0,0
 320 VDU 19,3,5,0,0,0
 330 VDU 24,10;100;500;550;
 340 GCOL 0,134
 350 CLG
 360 VDU 24,700;100;1200;550;
 370 GCOL 0,134
 380 CLG
 390 VDU 24,500;100;700;200;
 400 GCOL 0,134
 410 CLG
 420 VDU 24,500;200;700;900;
 430 VDU 23,240,28,28,8,127,8,20,34,65
 440 VDU 5
 450 MOVE 500,235
 460 PRINTCHR$(240)
 470 VDU4
 480 PRINT
 490 PRINT"TYPE IN THE COLOUR OF LIGHT"
 500 PRINT"RED,GREEN OR VIOLET"
 510 INPUT I$
 520 IF LEFT$(I$,1) = "R" THEN W=1
 530 IF LEFT$(I$,1) = "V" THEN W=3
 540 IF LEFT$(I$,1) = "G" THEN W=2
 550 MOVE 600,1000
 560 FORA%=0TO810STEP15
 570 GCOL0,W
 580 DRAW600+80*SIN(RAD(W*A%)),1000-A%
 590 NEXTA%
 600 GCOL0,128
 610 CLG
 620 VDU 5
 630 GCOL0,W
 640 VDU 23,240,28,28,8,127,8,20,34,65
 650 FOR H = 0 TO 200+(W-1)*(W-1)*200 STEP 10
 660 MOVE 500,200+H
 670 PRINT CHR$(240)
 690 VDU 9,127
 700 NEXT H
 710 VDU 4
 720 IF W = 1 GOTO 750
 730 IF W = 2 GOTO 930
 740 IF W = 3 GOTO 1000
 750 VDU 5
 760 GCOL0,W
 770 FOR H = 200*W TO 0 STEP -10
 780 MOVE 500,200+H
 790 PRINT CHR$(240)
 800 VDU 11,9,127
 810 NEXT H
 820 GCOL 0,W
 830 PRINT CHR$(240)
 840 VDU 4
 850 FOR T = 1 TO 3000:NEXT T
 860 MODE7
 865 VDU23;8202;0;0;0;
 870 PRINT
```

```
880 PRINT"The energy in a quantum of red light is not sufficient
    to eject the electron from the surface"
890 PRINTTAB(3,23);CHR$(129);"PRESS THE SPACE BAR TO CONTINUE"
900 REPEAT UNTIL GET = 32
910 MODE7
920 GOTO 1080
930 FOR T = 1 TO 3000:NEXT T
940 MODE7
950 PRINT
955 VDU23;8202;0;0;0;
960 PRINT"The energy of a quantum of green light is just
    sufficient to raise the electron to the surface with no
    remaining kinetic energy"
970 PRINTTAB(3,23);CHR$(130);"PRESS THE SPACE BAR TO CONTINUE"
980 REPEAT UNTIL GET = 32
990 GOTO 1080
1000 FOR T = 1 TO 3000:NEXT T
1010 MODE7
1015 VDU23;8202;0;0;0;
1020 PRINT
1030 PRINTTAB(0,8)"The energy in a quantum of violet light is
     sufficient to eject the electron from the surface with a certain
     amount of kinetic energy"
1040 PRINTTAB(3,23);CHR$(132);"PRESS THE SPACE BAR TO CONTINUE"
1050 REPEAT UNTIL GET = 32
1060 GOTO 1080
1070 PRINT"2. the ENERGY of the electrons emitted depends on the
     FREQUENCY of the incident radiation"
1080 CLS
1090 PRINT
1100 PRINTTAB(0,8);CHR$(131);"DO YOU WISH TO RUN THE POTENTIAL WELL "
1110 PRINTCHR$(131);"SIMULATION AGAIN"
1120 PRINT
1130 INPUT R$
1140 IF R$ = "Y" GOTO 300 ELSE GOTO 1150
1150 CLS
1170 PRINTTAB(0,10);"THE ENERGY NEEDED TO ALLOW AN ELECTRON TO ESCAPE
     FROM THE SURFACE WITH NO REMAINING KINETIC ENERGY IS CALLED THE"
1180 PRINTTAB(10,15);" WORK FUNCTION"
1190 PRINTTAB(10,18);" OF THE METAL"
1200 PRINT TAB(3,23);"PRESS THE SPACE BAR TO CONTINUE"
1210 REPEAT UNTIL GET = 32
1220 CLS
1230 PRINTTAB(2,5);"METAL"
1240 PRINTTAB(15,4);"WORK FUNCTION "
1250 PRINTTAB(15,5);"J"
1260 PRINT TAB(29,5);"eV"
1270 PRINT
1280 PRINT"SODIUM       2.8x10(-19)       1.75"
1290 PRINT"CAESIUM      3.7x10(-19)       1.88"
1300 PRINT"SILVER       7.6x10(-19)       4.75"
1310 PRINT"PLATINUM    10.0x10(-19)       6.75"
1320 PRINT:PRINT
1330 PRINT"The table above gives the work functions for some
     common metals"
1340 PRINT"Choose a metal to investigate in a simulation of the
     photoelectric effect experiment"
1350 PRINT
1360 PRINT" 1. SODIUM"
1370 PRINT" 2. CAESIUM"
1380 PRINT" 3. SILVER"
1390 PRINT" 4. PLATINUM"
1400 INPUT M
1410 CLS
1420 MODE1
1425 VDU23;8202;0;0;0;
1430 GCOL 0,2
1440 IF M = 1 W = 1.75: GOTO 1480
1450 IF M = 2 W = 1.88: GOTO 1490
1460 IF M = 3 W = 4.75: GOTO 1500
1470 IF M = 4 W = 6.75: GOTO 1510
1480 PRINTTAB(10,1);"SODIUM":GOTO1520
1490 PRINTTAB(10,1);"CAESIUM":GOTO1520
1500 PRINTTAB(10,1);"SILVER":GOTO1520
1510 PRINTTAB(10,1);"PLATINUM":GOTO1520
1520 FOR T = 1 TO 10:NEXT T
1530 MOVE 100,100:DRAW 100,1000:MOVE100,100:DRAW1200,100
1570 VDU 5
1580 MOVE 800,80
1590 PRINT"FREQUENCY "
1600 MOVE 750,40
1610 PRINT"(x10(14)Hz)"
1620 MOVE 200,80
1630 PRINT"4"
1640 MOVE 600,80
1650 PRINT"10"
1660 MOVE 20,900
1670 PRINT "VOLTS"
1680 MOVE 30,850
1690 PRINT"(V)"
1700 MOVE 40,320
1710 PRINT"1"
1720 MOVE 40,510
1730 PRINT"2"
1740 MOVE 40,700
1750 PRINT"3"
1760 VDU4
1770 h = 6.64E-34
1780 e = 1.6E-19
1790 VDU 28,16,8,39,3
1800 N = 1
1810 PRINT"INPUT WAVELENGTH (nm)"
1820 INPUT L
1830 F = 3E8/(L*1E-9)
1840 V =  (h/e)*F - W
1850 V$=STR$(V)
1860 PRINT LEFT$(V$,4);"V"
1870 MOVE80+50*(F*1E-14),100+(200*V):
     DRAW120+50*(F*1E-14),100+(200*V):
     MOVE100+50*(F*1E-14),120+(200*V):
     DRAW100+50*(F*1E-14),80+(200*V)
1880 N = N+1
1890 IF N = 10 GOTO 1910
1900 GOTO 1810
1910 CLS
1920 PRINT"WORK FUNCTION = ";W;"V"
1930 T = (W*e)/h
1940 T$ =STR$(T)
1950 PRINT"THRESHOLD FREQUENCY "
1960 IF M = 3 OR 4 GOTO 1990
1970 PRINT"          =";LEFT$(T$,3);"x10(14)Hz"
1980 GOTO 2000
1990 PRINT"          =";LEFT$(T$,3);"x10(15)Hz"
2000 PRINT"ANOTHER METAL ?"
2010 INPUT R$
2020 MODE7
2030 IF R$ = "Y" GOTO 1360
2040 IF R$ = "N" GOTO 2050
2050 END
```

56 · Applications of the microcomputer in sixth form Physics

We will concern ourselves here specifically with the BBC computer, although what is said may apply to many other microcomputers.

The microcomputer can be used in sixth form Physics in several different ways.

(*a*) Testing

Here you will follow through a pre-programmed test on the computer where at each stage a correct answer is required before you may proceed further. It may also be used to teach students about a subject, but unlike a textbook it is interactive – you can react to the program by entering material as the program runs. This is known as **computer assisted learning** (CAL).

(*b*) Simulation

You will carry out a simulation of an 'experiment' on the computer without any recourse to apparatus. Suitable experimental simulations that have been used at the author's school include:

capacitor discharge where the parameters of the circuit may be varied

simple harmonic motion, both free and damped

the photoelectric effect – see page 399 for a full listing of this program

Lissajous figures – the amplitude, frequency and phase difference may be varied

beats between two waves; see page 171 for a full listing

gravitational or nuclear collisions, where the paths of colliding bodies may be plotted

radioactive decay – the half-life may be varied

the cathode ray oscilloscope – various inputs and timebase speeds may be tested.

Other examples which require machine code programming (which is outside the scope of the present book) include wave reflection and molecular motion.

It is important that the use of the computer in this way should never replace the actual experiment but only act as a further aid to understanding.

1 Write programs that simulate the following:
(*a*) radioactive decay,
(*b*) damped simple harmonic motion,
(*c*) the motion of electrons across an evacuated tube under the action of electric and magnetic fields,
(*d*) the motion of a projectile (the effects of air resistance could be included).
All the techniques required for these will be found in the example listings in the preceding pages.

(*c*) Interfacing

You will use the computer with a suitable interface as part of an actual experiment. These devices enable the computer to display and store data during an experiment, and if a disc is used the information may be recalled at a later date. It is not the intention to give full experimental details here, only to suggest the types of experiments to which the computer may be applied. The interested student will be able to think of many more. Examples of its use in this way include the following:

a high speed timer – this has many applications such as a fast timer in collision experiments or in measuring the length of a square wave pulse

a digital multimeter – this is an obvious application; the measured voltage may be displayed in large digits on the screen

a current–voltage plotter – these two parameters may be measured simultaneously and their variation plotted on the screen

a chart recorder – this measures four voltages at the analogue port and displays them on the screen; a machine code program may then be used to scroll the screen sideways as a chart recorder

control of a simple robot – the movement of a buggy or a robot arm may be controlled from the computer. A very good example of this is the material developed for the Microelectronics Education Program.

You will find it useful to see some kind of demonstration of computer control during your Physics course, as an illustration of its application in industry.

Atomic and nuclear physics

Part of the 52 m diameter 800 MeV synchrotron of the ISIS facility at Rutherford Appleton Laboratory in Oxfordshire, England; one of the large bending magnets can be seen at the top left of the photograph (RAL)

57· Atomic structure and electron Physics

The development of the atomic theory has considerable importance in Physics and we will begin this section with a short summary of the development of the ideas of atomic structure over the centuries.

The following people put forward the key concepts of the atomic theory:

500 B.C.	Anaxagoras – germ of an atomic theory
450 B.C.	Empedocles – the elements (earth, air, fire and water)
420 B.C.	Democritus – open spaces between atoms
384–322 B.C.	Aristotle – rejected the above idea
1743–1794	Lavoisier – law of conservation of mass
1766–1844	Dalton – founder of the modern atomic theory, and framer of the law of multiple proportions
1800	Dalton published the atomic theory, suggesting the existence of tiny indivisible atoms, and that atoms of the same element are identical in weight
1896	Thomson – the 'plum pudding' idea of the atom (that is, a positive 'pudding' with negative 'plums' in it)
1909	Rutherford – alpha-particle experiments (carried out by Geiger and Marsden) showed the existence of a heavy central nucleus
1906	Planck – quantum theory
1910	Rutherford – predicted the decay of the electron orbit in 10^{-10} s
1913	Franck–Hertz – critical potentials tube, and the idea of a central heavy nucleus with electrons moving round it in stable orbits
1913	Bohr – overcame the theoretical spiralling inwards of the electron by application of the quantum theory, showing that the electron has only certain allowed orbits
1914	Planck – electrons can change from one energy level to another with the emission or absorption of radiation
1919	Proton discovered
1925	Pauli – exclusion principle (no two electrons in an atom may exist in the same quantum state)
1932	Positron – the first particle of antimatter – discovered by Anderson

The structure of the atom

The idea that atoms were very small particles was first suggested by the Greeks some two thousand years ago but it was not until the nineteenth century that any ideas about the *inside* of an atom were proposed.

The English scientist J.J. Thomson suggested that an atom was a neutral particle made of positive charge with lumps of negative charge within it. This model was called the **plum pudding model** of the atom, the positive charge being the 'pudding' and the negative particles the 'plums'.

In 1906 Rutherford proposed a classic experiment to investigate the structure of the atom, which Geiger and Marsden carried out a few years later. A very thin sheet of gold (about 1 μm thick) was bombarded with alpha-particles and the resulting paths of the alpha-particles recorded. As was expected, many of the alpha-particles passed straight through the foil, meaning that they had not suffered any collisions with gold atoms. Some of the alpha-particles made very large changes of direction, however, about 1 in 8000 being deflected by more than 90°. This can only be explained by assuming that the atom has a small but heavy central nucleus with a positive charge surrounded by a cloud of negative charge – the electrons.

The positively charged alpha-particles make elastic collisions with the nucleus and their deflection depends on their initial direction (Figure 57.1). It can be shown that the path of the alpha-particle is hyperbolic whilst it is in the region of repulsion of the nucleus.

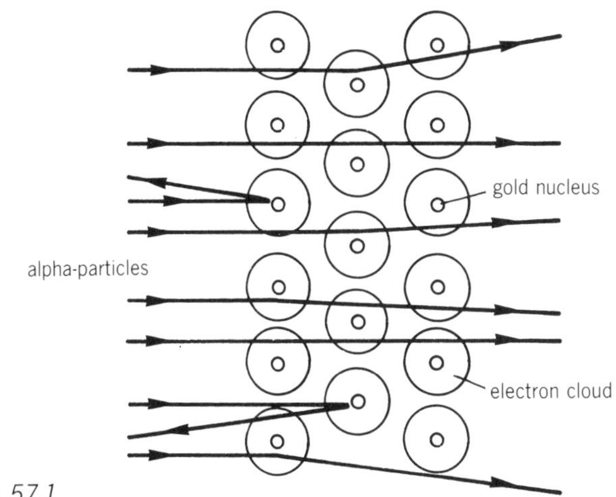

Figure 57.1

Figure 57.2 shows the path of an alpha-particle which passes close to the nucleus. The deflection ϕ depends on the distance between the centre of the nucleus and the line of the alpha-particle's motion when it is far from the nucleus.

These experiments suggested that the nucleus has a diameter of about 10^{-15} m.

1 Find the distance of closest approach of alpha-particles with an initial kinetic energy of 5.0 MeV which make a head-on collision with a gold nucleus, which has an atomic (proton) number of 79. (Charge on the electron = 1.6×10^{-19} C; permittivity of free space = 8.84×10^{-12} F m^{-1})

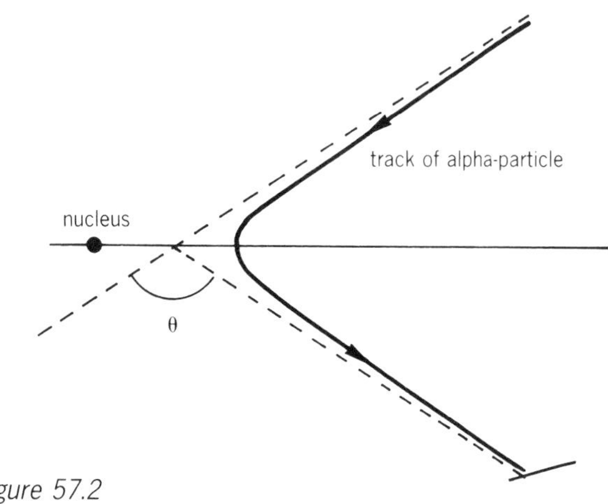

Figure 57.2

The Thomson and Rutherford models of the atom

It is possible to calculate the electric field strengths at the surface of both a Thomson atom and a Rutherford nucleus. Consider a gold atom, for example: Thomson would have said that 'the atom has a radius of some 1.0×10^{-10} m' while Rutherford would have said that 'the positive charge is concentrated on a nucleus of radius 6.9×10^{-15} m'. Using the formula for the electric field given on page 333 we have:

field strength at surface of Thomson atom
$= 1.4 \times 10^{11}$ V m^{-1}
field strength at surface of Rutherford nucleus
$= 3.0 \times 10^{19}$ V m^{-1}

a difference of some 10^8 times greater in the case of the Rutherford model. This shows why the deflecting forces of the nucleus are so great.

The structure of the nucleus

The atomic nucleus itself was found to consist of two types of particle:

(*a*) the **proton** – a positively charged stable particle;
(*b*) the **neutron** – a neutral particle which is stable while it is in the nucleus.

All nuclei (except that of hydrogen, which consists of a single proton) contain both types of particle, there being usually more neutrons than protons. They are held together in the nucleus by the **strong nuclear force** that acts only over the very small distances in the nucleus. At these small distances the nuclear force is great enough to overcome the electrostatic repulsion between the protons, which would otherwise force the nucleus apart.

The number of *protons* in the nucleus is known as the **proton number** (Z) (previously called the 'atomic number').

The number of *protons plus neutrons* in the nucleus is known as the **nucleon number** (A) (previously called the 'mass number').

Lists of the nucleon and proton numbers of the elements are given in a table in the Appendix (see page 485). You can see from this table that for heavy nuclei the number of neutrons exceeds the number of protons, the excess increasing with nucleon number (see also Figure 59.6 on page 423).

The electron

The discovery of the electron and its properties were crucial stages in our understanding of the structure of the atom. The following series of dates show the way in which our knowledge of the electron developed.

1869 Hittorf – Maltese cross tube

1876 Goldstein – first used the term 'cathode rays' for the radiation that appeared to come from the cathode.

1879 Crookes – deflected the rays with a magnetic field, thus establishing the sign and direction of flow of the current carriers

1897 Thomson – showed that the value of e/m was always the same, demonstrated the Maltese cross tube and assumed that the charge carried was the same as that in electrolysis and hence calculated the mass of the electron. From the Maltese cross tube we can see that the electrons are not electromagnetic radiation like light, since

	light is not deflected by electromagnetic fields
1909	Millikan – measurement of the electron charge

Electric and magnetic fields

(*a*) Electric fields
Consider an electron that is accelerated through a potential difference V by an electric field of intensity E:
Energy gained $= eV$ Force on electron $= eE$
(*b*) Magnetic fields
Consider an electron moving with velocity v at right angles to a magnetic field of flux density B:
Force on electron $= Bev$

The electron volt

When an electron is accelerated through a p.d of one volt, the energy gained is known as an **electron volt** (eV) ($= 1.6 \times 10^{-19}$ J
$1\ \text{MeV} = 10^6\text{eV}$ and $1\ \text{GeV} = 10^9\ \text{eV}$

Thermionic emission

In 1880 Edison noticed that a current could flow in an evacuated bulb from a glowing filament to another filament *if* the hot filament was negatively charged; this did not happen if the filament was positively charged. This emission of electrons was called **thermionic emission.**

Thermionic emission is the emission of free electrons from a hot metal surface. The energy required to cause this emission varies with the metal concerned.

Many of the basic properties of the electron may be studied using thermionic emission. The emitting surface was usually a metal plate in an evacuated valve indirectly heated with a hot wire. The cloud of electrons produced near the plate could be accelerated away by placing a second plate in the valve and applying a potential difference between the two plates, forming a simple thermionic diode (Figure 57.3(*a*)). A current was found to flow across the valve if the anode was positive with respect to the cathode and the cathode was hot. The hotter the cathode the greater the current, since more electrons are emitted per second; this is shown in Figure 57.3(*b*), the lower curve representing a lower heater temperature.

(*a*)

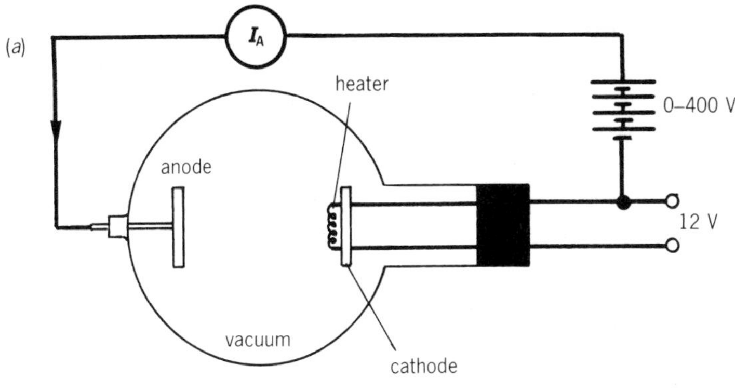

(*b*)

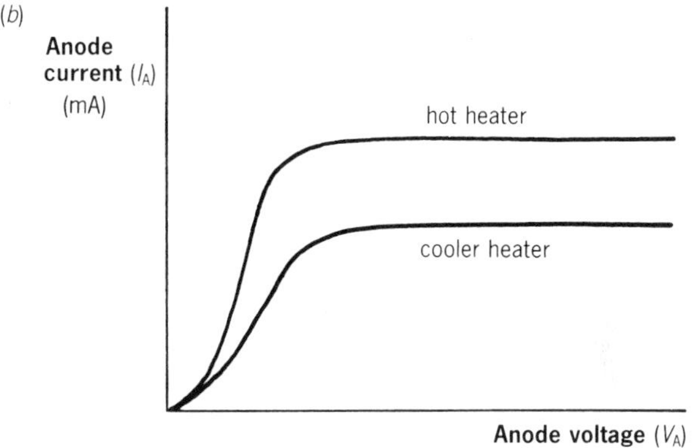

Figure 57.3

The greater the potential difference across the tube (that is, the greater the anode potential) the greater the electron velocity will be.

Thermionic emission occurs because the *free* electrons within the metal are given sufficient energy to escape from the surface. This energy is provided by the heater of the filament.

The fact that the streams of electrons were emitted from the cathode led to them being called **cathode rays.** It was shown that the cathode rays had the following properties:

(*a*) rectilinear propagation;
(*b*) they cause fluorescence;
(*c*) they possess kinetic energy which is changed to heat when they are brought to rest;
(*d*) they are deflected by electric and magnetic fields, travelling in circles in magnetic fields at right angles to their motion and in parabolas in electric fields at right angles to their motion – the nature of the deflection shows that they have a negative charge;
(*e*) they can produce X-rays if they are of sufficiently high energy.

The electron gun

When electrons are emitted from a hot metal surface they may be accelerated towards a positvely charged anode. If a hole is made in the anode then most of the electrons pass through. The device is known as an electron gun (Figure 57.4).

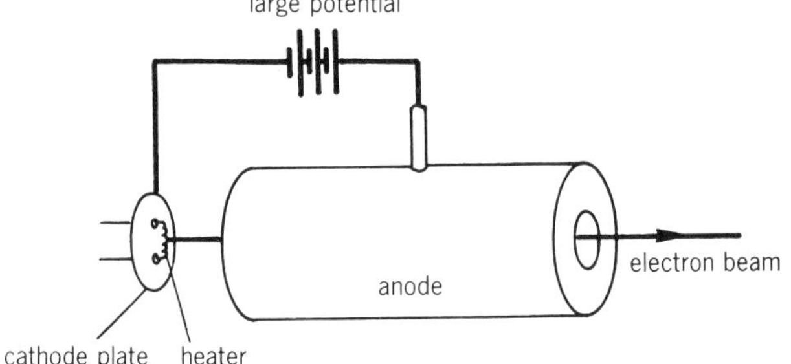

Figure 57.4

The gain in kinetic energy of the electrons comes from their loss of electrical energy:

gain in k.e. $= \frac{1}{2}mv^2$
loss of electrical energy $= eV$

where V is the voltage applied to the anode and e the electron charge. Therefore

$$\text{electron velocity} = \sqrt{\frac{2eV}{m}}$$

The Maltese cross tube

This is basically an evacuated tube containing an elec tron gun, with a metal cross held in the path of the electron beam (Figure 57.5). The side of the tube opposite the electron gun is coated with a material that

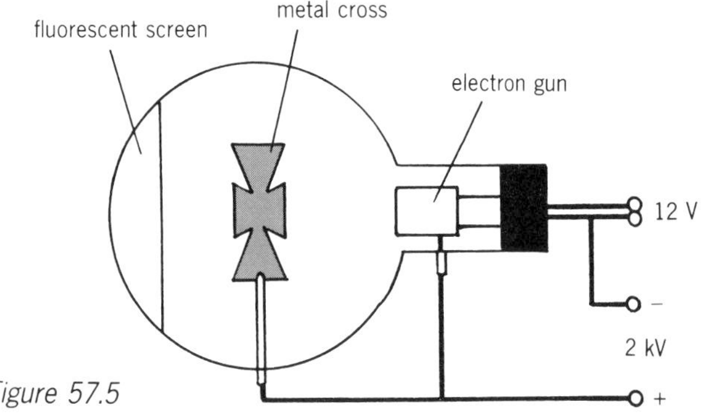

Figure 57.5

will fluoresce when electrons collide with it. The accelerating voltage is a few kV, and when this or the heater voltage is increased the screen glows more brightly due to greater electron energy or more electron collisions per second. A sharp silhouette of the cross is formed on the screen, showing that the electrons travel in straight lines. Placing a magnet near the tube will show the effect of a magnetic field on the electron beam.

Example

Calculate the electron velocity for an accelerating potential of (*a*) 5000 V and (*b*) 10 000 V.

The equation can be written as
$v = \sqrt{2e/m} \times \sqrt{V}$

and since we know the value of e/m for the electron is 1.76×10^{11} C kg^{-1} (see page 407), this becomes

$v = 5.93 \times 10^5\sqrt{V}$

This gives:
(*a*) $v = 4.19 \times 10^7$ m s^{-1}
(*b*) $v = 5.93 \times 10^7$ m s^{-1}
if relativistic effects are ignored.

Specific charge

The charge to mass ratio of a charged particle (q/M) is known as its **specific charge**. For the electron this quantity is denoted by e/m.

In questions 2 to 5, the following data may be used if needed:
Charge on the electron = -1.6×10^{-19} C
Mass of the electron = 9×10^{-31} kg

2 An electron is initially at rest between two parallel plates 4.0 cm apart. An alternating p.d. of peak value 35 V and frequency 50 MHz is applied between the plates and the electron oscillates up and down with simple harmonic motion. Find the amplitude of the electron's motion, and its maximum k.e. [H]

3 An electron with a velocity of 2.0×10^6 m s^{-1} enters a magnetic field of uniform magnetic flux density 0.2 T. The path of the electron is initially at an angle of 60° to the field direction. The subsequent path of the electron will be a helix. Calculate the distance between successive turns of the helix.

4 In a bubble chamber the track of a subatomic particle are shown by a track of bubbles in the superheated liquid. A magnetic field is applied at right angles to the plane of the chamber to deflect the particles into circular paths. One such path is found to have a radius of 0.35 m when the magnetic flux density is 1.5 T. From other measurements the velocity of the particle is found to be 2.5×10^6 m s^{-1}. Calculate the specific charge (q/M) for the particle.

5 An electron beam, after being accelerated from rest through a potential of 5000 V, is allowed to fall normally on a fixed surface. If the incident current is 50 μA, calculate the force exerted by the electrons on the surface assuming that it brings them to rest.

Measurement of *e/m* for cathode rays (electrons)

In 1897 J.J. Thomson measured the value of *e/m* for an electron, using crossed electric and magnetic fields (see Figure 57.6, which shows the apparatus seen (*a*) from the side and (*b*) end-on).

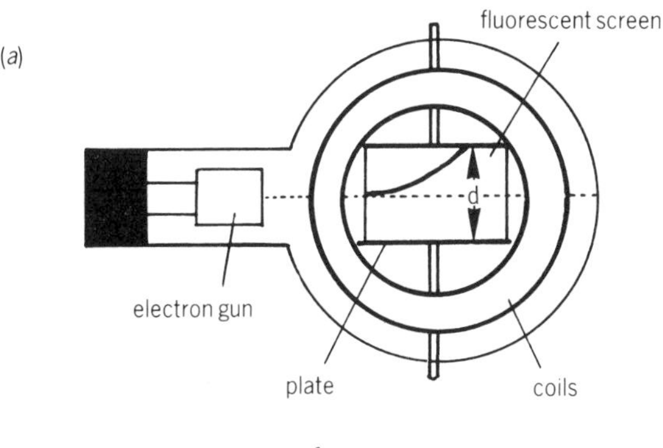

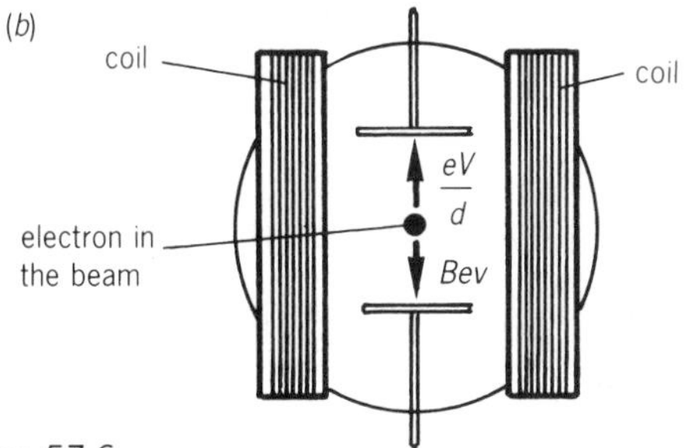

Figure 57.6

The electrons are accelerated by a potential V and when they pass into the centre of the tube they are acted upon by two forces, one due to the magnetic field B produced by the Helmholtz coils and the other due to the electrostatic field E produced by the voltage V applied between two plates of separation d.

The electrostatic force = Ee, and the magnetic force = Bev. Then

kinetic energy of the electron $= \frac{1}{2}mv^2 = eV$.

Therefore, if the forces due to the two fields act in opposite directions and are adjusted so that the beam is undeflected, then

$$Bev = Ee$$
$$e/m = E^2/(2B^2V)$$

Therefore $e/m = V/(2B^2d^2)$

The field produced by the coils is given by the equation:

$$B = \mu_0 8NI/(5\sqrt{5}r)$$

where N is the number of turns on the coil, I is the current in the coils and r the radius of the coils.

We have assumed that the fields are uniform within the space between the plates. Remember that when the electrons leave the space between the plates they are only acted on by the magnetic field produced by the coils.

Thomson used a slightly different method. Having balanced the fields and calculated v, he then removed the magnetic field and measured the deflection due to the electric field alone (Figure 57.7). The distance D on the screen is measured and hence s can be found. Using the equation:

$$s = \frac{Ee}{2m}\left(\frac{l}{v}\right)^2$$

the value of *e/m* can be found. (It is left as an exercise for the student to deduce the above equation.)

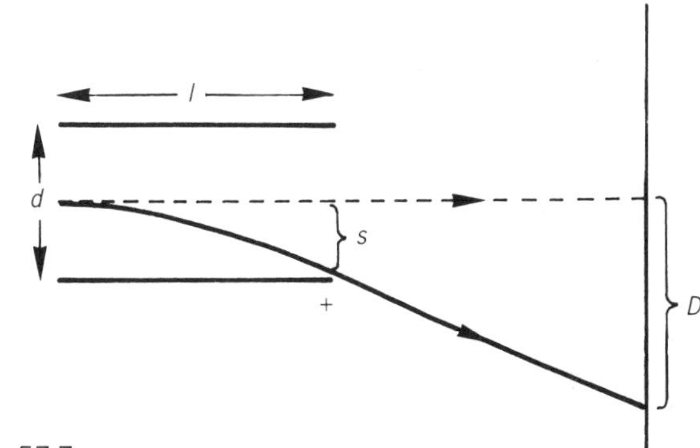

Figure 57.7

Example

Electrons, accelerated from rest through a potential difference of 3000 V, enter a region of uniform magnetic field, the direction of the field being at right angles to the motion of the electrons. If the flux density is 0.010 T, calculate the radius of the electron's orbit.

Magnetic force = $Bev = mv^2/r$, where r is the radius of the orbit.

But also $\frac{1}{2}mv^2 = eV$; therefore

$$r = \sqrt{\frac{2Vm}{B^2e}}$$

giving $r = 1.85$ mm.

As an example, Helmholtz coils of 320 turns and of radius 6.5 cm carrying a current of 0.25 A give a field of 1.11×10^{-3} T, and an anode voltage of 3000 V gives an electron velocity of 3.3×10^7 m s^{-1}, if relativistic effects are ignored.

It should be remembered that the electrostatic force acts along the line of the field and affects both stationary and moving particles. The electromagnetic force acts at right angles to the lines of magnetic flux, however, and affects only charges in motion.

For the electron $e/m = 1.76 \times 10^{11}$ C kg^{-1}

Magnetron valve

This valve is basically a diode with a cylindrical anode surrounding a linear cathode. A solenoid is placed over the valve with its axis coincident with that of the cathode (Figure 57.8(*a*)).

With no current in the coil electrons travel straight across from the anode to the cathode, but as the magnetic field strength is increased they follow paths that become more and more curved (see Figure 57.8(*b*)). A point will be reached for a critical field B_C where the electrons just fail to reach the anode (Figure 57.8(*c*)).

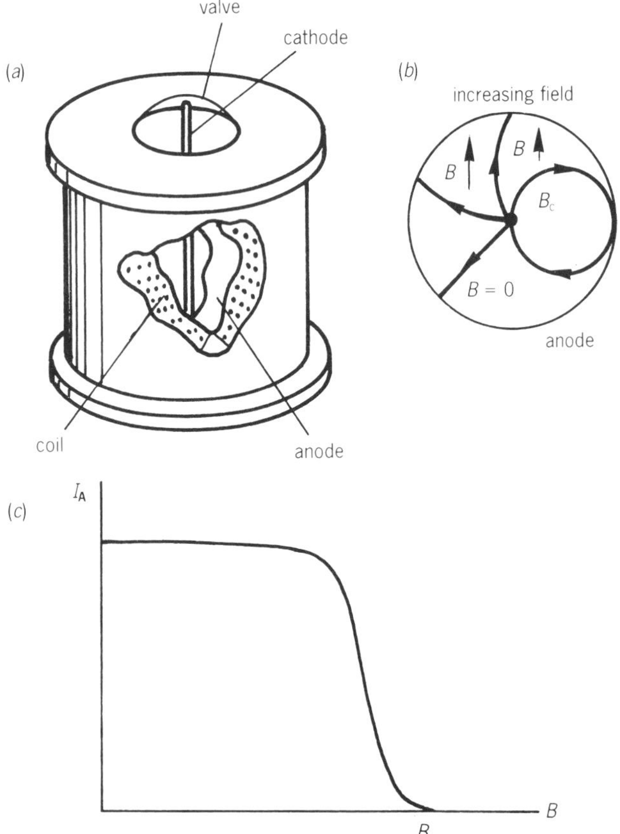

Figure 57.8

With a field of flux density B we have:

$$Bev = mv^2/r \quad \text{and} \quad \tfrac{1}{2}mv^2 = eV$$

Therefore

$$e/m = 2V/(B^2r^2)$$

If R is the radius of the anode ($R = 2r$),

$$e/m = 8V/(B_c^2R^2)$$

The value for the critical field can be found when the anode current drops to zero. At this point the electrons just fail to reach the anode and so are travelling in paths of diameter R.

In the magnetron valve we must assume that the cathode is very narrow, so that the field at its surface is high. If we do this the electron experiences most of its acceleration close to the cathode, and its velocity across the rest of the valve is virtually uniform.

Example

A magnetron has a potential of 200 V between the anode and cathode and an anode diameter of 24 mm. If the specific charge on the electron (e/m) is 1.76×10^{11} C kg^{-1}, calculate the flux density of the field for which the valve just ceases to conduct.

The radius of the electron orbit in this condition is 6 mm = 6×10^{-3} m. Therefore

$$\text{critical field } (B_c) = \sqrt{\frac{8V}{(e/m)R^2}} = 7.95 \times 10^{-3}\ \text{T}$$

6 An electron moving at 5.0×10^6 m s^{-1} is shot parallel to an electric field of strength 1×10^3 N C^{-1} arranged so as to retard its motion.

(*a*) How far will the electron travel in the field before coming momentarily to rest?

(*b*) If the field ends suddenly after 0.75 cm, what fraction of its initial energy will the electron lose in passing through it?

7 A vacuum diode consists of a cylindrical cathode of radius 0.05 cm mounted coaxially inside a cylindrical anode of radius 0.45 cm. If the anode–cathode voltage is 400 V and the electron leaves the anode with zero speed, calculate its speed when it strikes the anode.

What is the flux density of the magnetic field that must be applied along the axis in order to just prevent the electrons from striking the anode?

8 Calculate

(*a*) the force on an electron which is stationary in (i) a magnetic field of flux density 2.5 T, (ii) an electric field of intensity 1000 V m^{-1};

(*b*) the force on an electron moving with a velocity of 1.5×10^6 m s^{-1} at right angles to (i) a magnetic field of flux density 1.5 T, (ii) an electric field of intensity 2000 V m^{-1}.

The double-beam tube

This tube is different from those previously described in that it contains low-pressure helium gas. The gas is excited by the passage of the electron beam and emits a bluish glow that enables the path of the beam to be seen. The tube is also unusual in that it contains *two* electron guns: one firing a beam radially across the tube, and one firing a beam tangentially (see Figure 57.9).

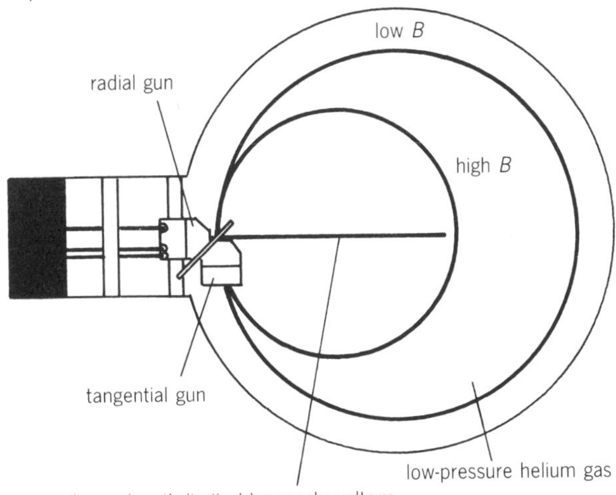

Figure 57.9

Using the radial gun, the range of the electron beam can be shown to be proportional to the accelerating voltage on the anode and hence to the energy of the electrons.

If a pair of Helmholtz coils is placed around the tube and a current passed through them, a magnetic field is formed across the tube. This field acts on the electrons, and if the tangential beam is used it can be bent into a circle as shown in the diagram. Clearly, for a given anode voltage the radius of the circle decreases with increasing field flux density.

If the accelerating voltage on the anode is V and the flux density of the field is B, then for an orbit of radius R we have:

$$eV = \tfrac{1}{2}mv^2 \qquad Bev = \frac{mv^2}{R}$$

where v is the electron velocity. This gives

$$\frac{e}{m} = \frac{2V}{B^2R^2}$$

9 If the specific charge of an electron is 1.76×10^{11} C kg^{-1}, calculate the orbit radii for electrons accelerated through a p.d. of 2 kV in fields of flux density (*a*) 1 T, (*b*) 1.8×10^{-5} T.

10 Calculate the maximum field required to hold a proton in orbit in the 7 GeV proton synchrotron at the Rutherford Laboratory in Oxfordshire. The orbit has a radius of 50 m and the specific charge on a proton 9.58×10^7 C kg^{-1}.

11 What is the velocity of an electron after it has been accelerated through a potential difference of 1 kV?

12 An electron enters a magnetic field with a flux density of 1.2 T at right angles to the path of the particle. What is the intensity of the electric field that must be applied to neutralise the effect of the magnetic field, and in which direction should it be applied, if the electron velocity is 2×10^5 m s^{-1}?

13 An electron moves with a velocity of 2×10^7 m s^{-1} along the axis of a tube between two horizontal plates. If the electric field between the plates is 2×10^4 m s^{-1}, the plate length is 40 mm and the separation of the plates is 20 mm, at what angle to the axis will the electron leave the field?

14 Estimate the velocity of electrons in a copper wire of cross-sectional area 2×10^{-3} mm when carrying a current of 150 mA.

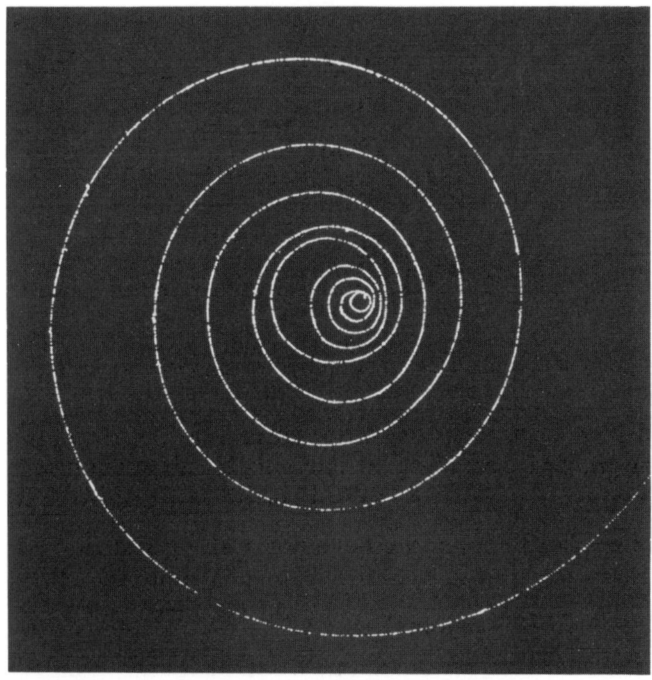

The path of an electron in a magnetic field in a bubble chamber, the path is a spiral because of the loss of energy as the electron collides with the molecules of the liquid (Science Photo Library)

The charge on the electron – Millikan's experiment

This experiment was devised in 1909 to measure the charge on the electron. Small oil droplets were sprayed through a hole into the space between two plates where they were illuminated by a strong light source and viewed with a microscope. The droplets became charged by friction at the spray nozzle and Millikan also used an X-ray beam to ensure that they all became charged.

In a simplified form of the experiment, the oil droplets are held between the plates by the application of an electrostatic field, the upper plate being positive relative to the lower one. When a droplet is held at rest, the upward electrostatic force just balances the downward gravitational attraction. If V is the potential difference between the plates and m is the mass of a droplet carrying a charge Q, then

$$\frac{QV}{d} = mg$$

where d is the separation between the plates.

Millikan himself used a more elaborate version of the method, in which the droplets were first allowed to fall at their terminal velocity between the plates (Figure 57.10(*a*)).

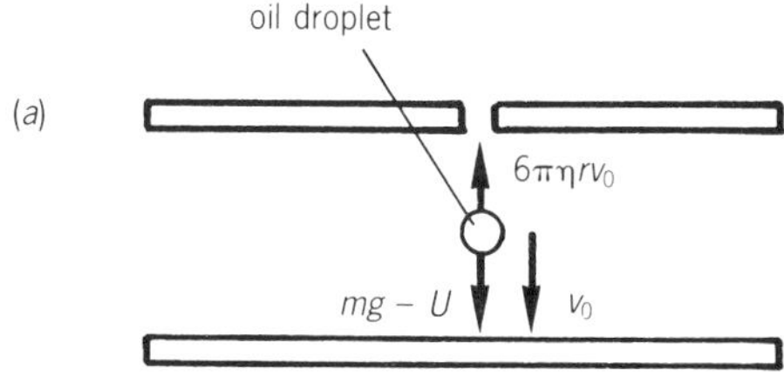

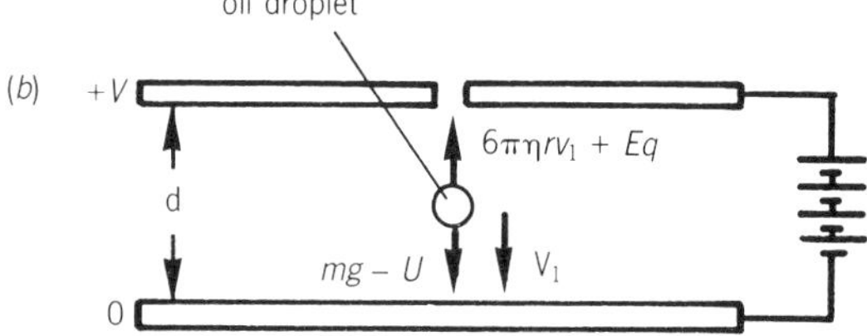

Figure 57.10

(*a*) Consider a drop of oil of density ρ and radius r falling at velocity v_0 through air of density σ. The frictional force F is balanced by the effective weight of the drop:

$$6\pi\eta r v_0 = \tfrac{4}{3}\pi r^3 g(\rho - \sigma)$$

where η is the viscosity of the air.

(*b*) A potential V is then applied across the plates, the upper plate being positive, and the experiment is repeated. This time the total upward force is the sum of the electrostatic attraction and the frictional drag.

$$6\pi\eta r v_1 + q\frac{V}{d} = \frac{4}{3}\pi r^3 g(\rho - \sigma)$$

where q is the charge on the droplet and d the separation of the plates. Note the new terminal velocity v_1.

Example

In a version of Millikan's experiment it is found that a charged droplet of mass 1.8×10^{-15} kg just remains stationary when the p.d. between the plates, which are 12 mm apart, is 150 V. If the droplet suddenly gains an extra electron,

(*a*) calculate the initial acceleration of the droplet, and

(*b*) find the voltage needed to bring the droplet to rest again.

(*a*) $mg = Vq/d$, so $1.8 \times 10^{-15} \times 10 = 150q/0.012$.
Therefore $q = 1.44 \times 10^{-18}$ C or nine electrons.
Therefore final charge is ten electrons.
Net force $= eE = 2 \times 10^{-15}$ N
$= ma = 1.8 \times 10^{-15}\ a$.
Therefore $= a = 1.11$ m s^{-2}.

(*b*) New voltage $= \dfrac{1.8 \times 10^{-15} \times 10 \times 0.012}{10 \times 1.6 \times 10^{-19}} = 135$ V.

From the first experiment the radius of the drop r can be found and by using this value in the second equation a value of q, the charge on the drop, can be found. The experiment was repeated many times and a series of values q_1, q_2, q_3 .... were found for the charges on different droplets. All these charges were found to be multiples of one basic charge and this was therefore considered to be the charge on one electron. No experiments to date have shown a smaller unit of charge (see, however, the brief discussion of the quark on page 465).

The value of the charge on one electron (e) is accepted as being -1.6×10^{-19} C.

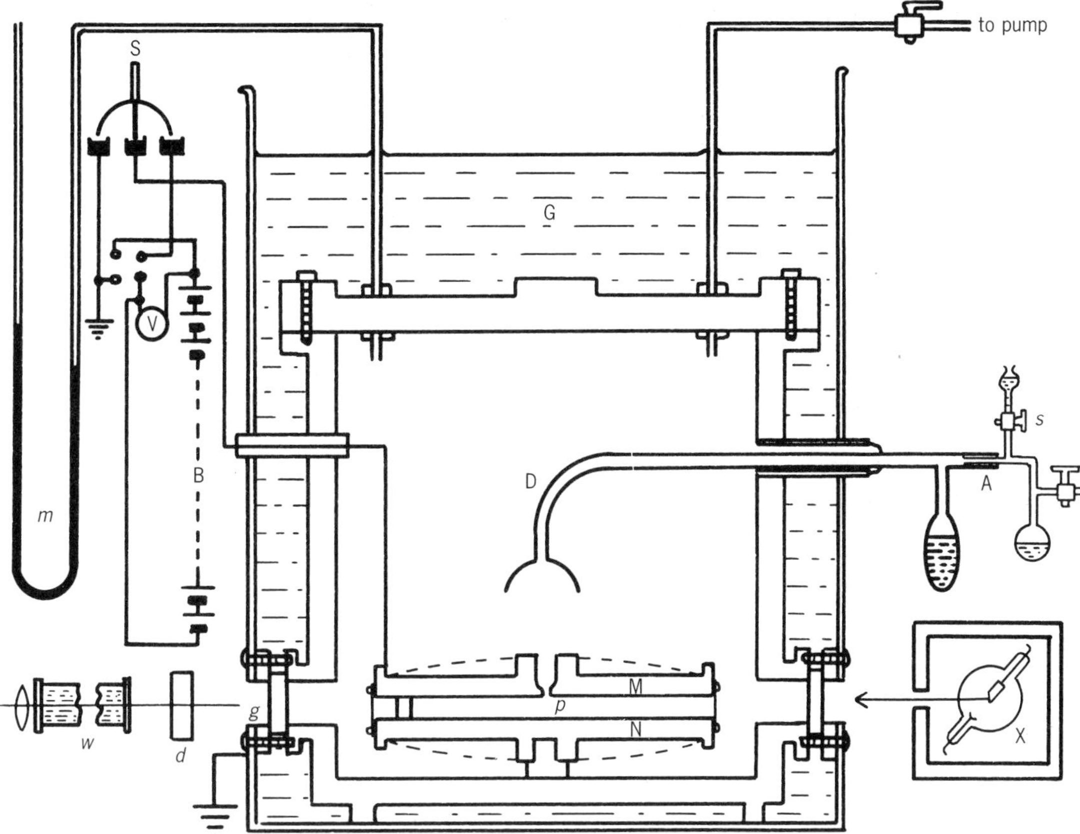

Figure 57.11

Figure 57.11, taken from Millikan's own book *The Electron*, shows the apparatus for the classic experiments which enabled him to measure the charge on the individual electron. *A* indicates the atomiser through which the oil spray is blown into the cylindrical vessel *D*, which is surrounded by a constant-temperature bath *G*. *M* and *N* are brass plates between which an electrical field is produced when the battery *B* is switched on. Light from an arc lamp passes through *w* and *d* (to remove heat radiation) and enters the chamber through the glass window *g*; it illuminates the oil droplet *p* between the brass plates through the pinhole in *M*. Additional ions are produced about *p* by X-rays from the X-ray tube *X*.

15 (*a*) Describe Millikan's experiment, or a school laboratory version, to determine the charge on the electron.

(*b*) A charged oil drop of mass 2.0×10^{-15} kg is stationary between two horizontal metal plates supported parallel to each other in air. The plates are 5.0 mm apart and the top plate is at a potential of +208 V relative to the lower plate. Calculate the magnitude of the charge on the drop and state the sign of the charge.

(*c*) Both the plates described in (*b*) are tilted so as to be at 30 ° to the horizontal, parallel to each other and with the same separation. Calculate (i) the direction and magnitude of the initial acceleration of the drop, and (ii) the potential difference which would have to be applied across the plates so that the drop acquired no vertical component of velocity. [JMB]

16 In a version of the Millikan experiment a charged drop of oil is found to fall with a velocity of 0.04 mm s^{-1} when no voltage is applied to the plates. The same drop can be held stationary between the plates when a voltage of 23.7 V is applied between them. If the drop has a diameter of 1 mm and the plates are 10 mm apart, calculate

(*a*) the charge on the drop, and

(*b*) the new velocity of the drop when a potential difference of 50 V is applied between the plates.

17 An electron is at rest between two parallel plates. If a high potential is now placed between the plates, the left plate being positive, describe the subsequent motion of the electron. Your answer should include a mention of any changes in position, velocity, force and acceleration. (The field between the plates may be considered to be uniform and the effects of gravity may be ignored.)

How will your answer differ if the field is not uniform, but increasing towards the left?

The cathode ray oscilloscope

This versatile instrument was developed by Brown in 1897 from the cathode ray tube. It has many uses, including voltage measurement, observation of wave forms, frequency comparison and time measurement. Figure 57.12 is a simplified diagram of a cathode ray oscilloscope.

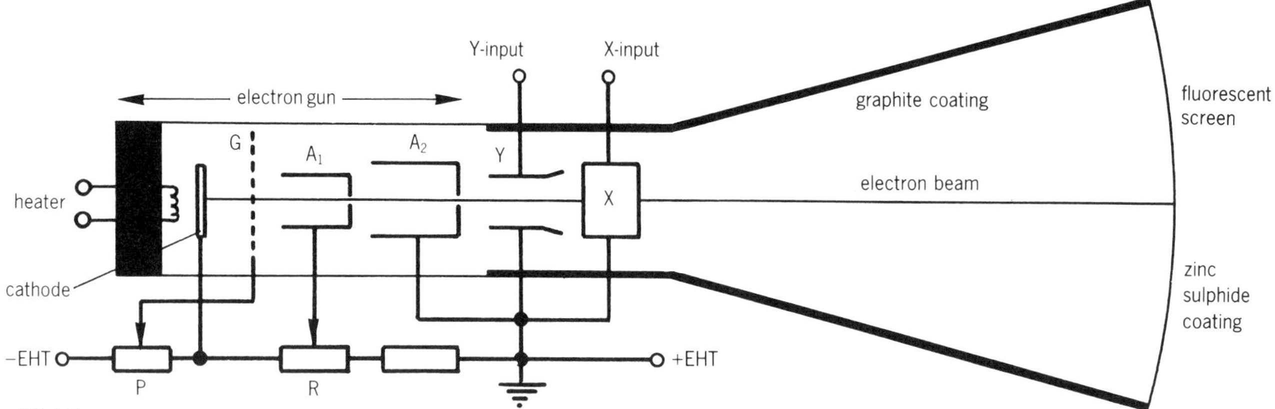

Figure 57.12

At the centre of the instrument is a highly evacuated cathode ray tube with the following features:

(*a*) a heated cathode C to produce a beam of electrons – a typical beam current is of the order of 0.1 mA;

(*b*) a grid G to control the brightness of the beam;

(*c*) an accelerating anode A_2 – a typical potential difference between A_2 and the cathode would be about +1000 V;

(*d*) a pair of plates Y_1 and Y_2 to deflect the beam in the vertical direction;

(*e*) a pair of plates X_1 and X_2 to deflect the beam in the horizontal direction;

(*f*) a fluorescent screen F on which the beam of electrons falls – in many modern oscilloscopes this is coated with zinc sulphide, which emits a blue glow when electrons collide with it, while there are other coatings that glow for some seconds after the beam has passed so enabling transient events to be seen more clearly;

(*g*) a graphite coating to shield the beam from external electric fields and to provide a return path for the electrons (see below);

(*h*) a mumetal screen which surrounds the tube and shields it from stray magnetic fields.

The focusing and accelerating systems are connected at different points along a resistor chain. Focusing is achieved by varying the voltage applied between the two anodes A_1 and A_2.

Since secondary electrons are emitted from the screen when the electron beam hits it, the phosphor coating of the screen and the inner graphite layer of the tube are both earthed to prevent a large build-up of static charge on the tube.

In the double beam oscilloscope there are two Y plates with an earthed plate between them to split the beam into two. Two traces are then observed on the screen. This can be most useful when comparing phase differences or making lapsed time measurements.

> **18** (*a*) Why is the cathode ray oscilloscope such an excellent instrument for measuring e.m.f.?
> (*b*) Is the magnetic field of Earth going to affect the path of an electron in a school oscilloscope significantly? Justify your answer.

The deflection system

The beam may be moved 'manually' in the X- and Y-directions by applying a d.c. or a.c. voltage to the X- and Y-plates. Alternatively it can be moved using the **time base** system.

The time base circuit applies a sawtooth waveform to the X-plates, as shown in Figure 57.13. The beam is moved from the left-hand side of the screen to the right during the time that the voltage rises to a maximum, and then is returned rapidly to the left as the voltage returns to zero. This **fly-back time** should be as short as possible.

The rise time is usually between 1 μs and 1 s for most oscilloscopes used in schools, but time base speeds of many seconds or of fractions of a microsecond can be obtained on more elaborate instruments.

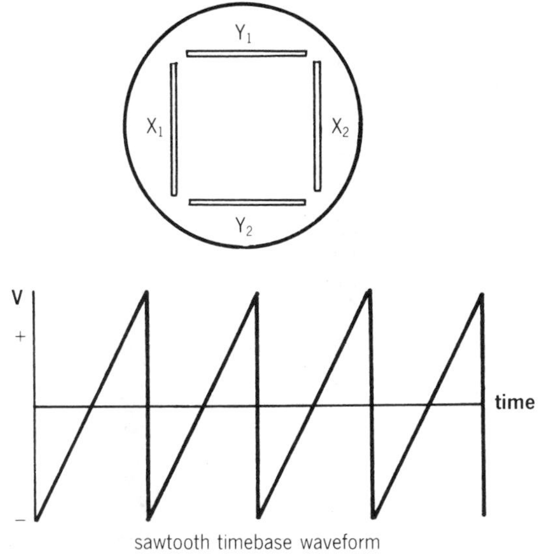

Figure 57.13

If a voltage is now applied to the Y-inputs, the variation of this voltage with time may be displayed on the screen. Some such variations are shown in Figure 57.14, together with the effect of various alterations of time base speed or input frequency.

Cathode ray oscilloscope traces

Figure 57.14 shows the appearance of the oscilloscope screen when a variety of different signals are applied to the Y-plates. Diagrams (*a*) to (*d*) show traces made with the time base off, and the remainder were made with the time base on.

(*a*) No input
(*b*) Top plate positive
(*c*) Bottom plate positive
(*d*) A.c. input
(*e*) No input
(*f*) D.c. input top plate positive
(*g*) D.c. input, bottom plate positive
(*h*) A.c. input
(*i*) A.c. input, greater Y gain
(*j*) A.c. input, slower time base
(*k*) A.c. input with diode
(*l*) D.c. input, top plate positive

Diagram (*i*) may also represent a larger input voltage, while diagram (*j*) may also represent a higher input frequency.

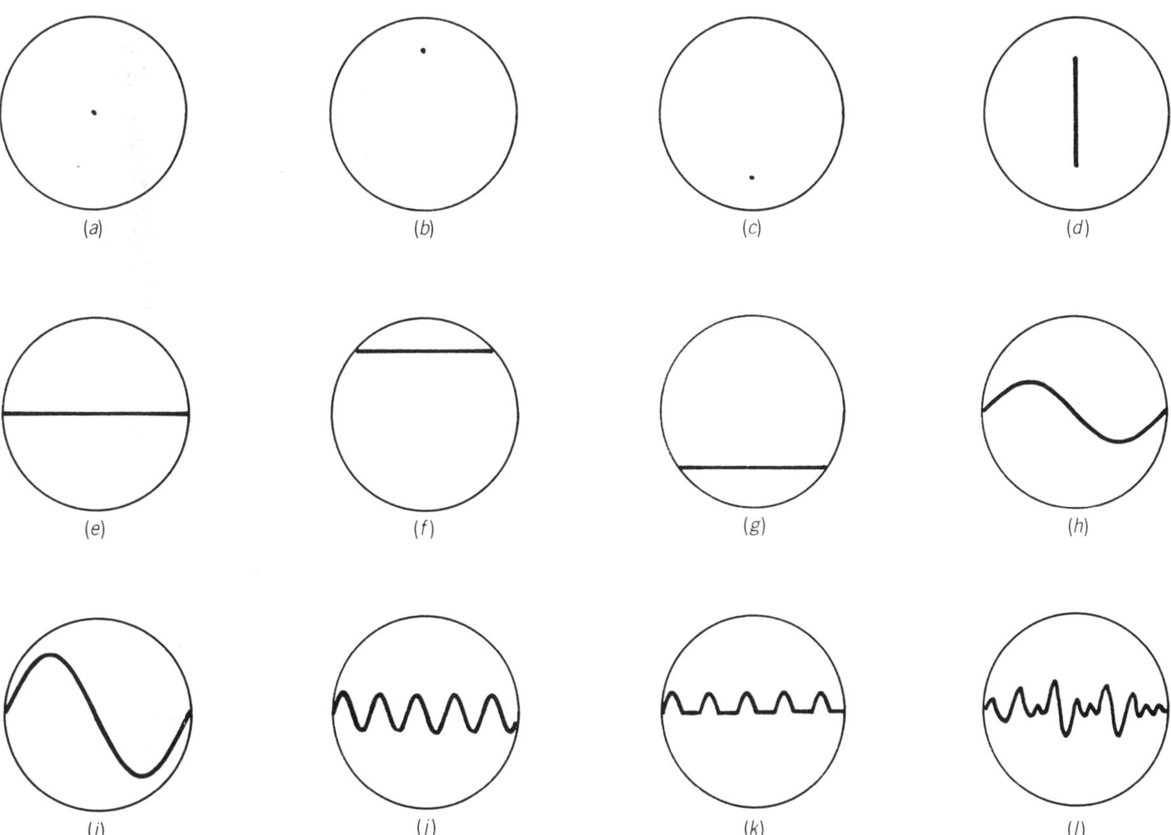

Figure 57.14

Measurements with the cathode ray oscilloscope

The primary uses of the cathode ray oscilloscope (CRO) are to measure voltage, to measure frequency and to measure phase.

(i) Measuring voltage

Because of its effectively infinite resistance, the CRO makes an excellent voltmeter. It has a relatively low sensitivity, but this can be improved by the use of an internal voltage amplifier.

The oscilloscope must first be calibrated by connecting a d.c. source of known e.m.f. to the Y-plates and measuring the deflection of the spot on the screen. This should be repeated for a range of values, so that the linearity of the deflection may be checked. The unknown e.m.f. is then connected and its value found from the deflection produced.

Most oscilloscopes have a previously calibrated screen giving the deflection sensitivity in volts per cm or volts per scale division. In this case a calibration by a d.c. source may be considered unnecessary.

(ii) Measuring frequency

Using the calibrated time base the input signal of unknown frequency may be 'frozen', and its frequency found directly by comparison with the scale divisions.

Alternatively the internal time base may be switched off and a signal of known frequency applied to the X-input. If the signal of unknown frequency is applied to the Y-input, Lissajous figures are formed on the screen (see page 81). Analysis of the peaks on the two axes enables the unknown frequency to be found.

(iii) Measuring phase

The internal time base is switched off as above and the two signals are applied as before. The frequency of the known signal is adjusted until it is the same as that of the unknown signal. An ellipse will then be formed on the screen and the angle of the ellipse will denote the phase difference between the two signals (Figure 57.15).

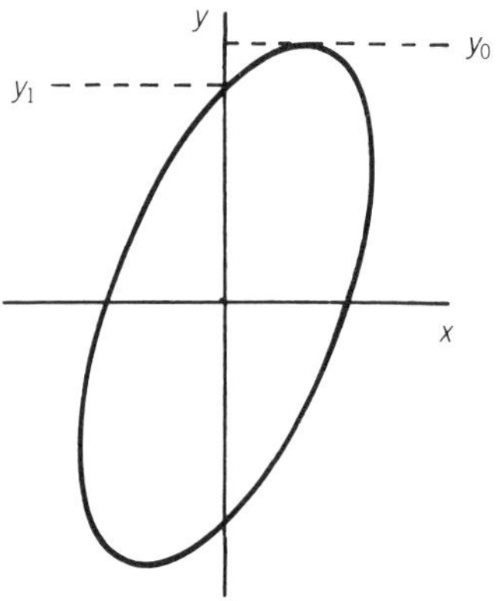

Figure 57.15 phase measurement

Consider the diagram. If ϕ is the phase difference then:

$$x = x_0 \sin(\omega t) \qquad \text{and} \qquad y = y_0 \sin(\omega t + \phi)$$

But when $x = 0$, $\sin(\omega t) = 0$, giving $\omega t = 0$.

At this point $y = y_1 = y_0 \sin\phi$, and hence ϕ may be found.

19 In a television tube of length 0.35 m there are on average 3.5×10^8 electrons per metre in the beam beween the cathode and the fluorescent screen.

(*a*) If the average velocity of the electrons is 5.0×10^7 m s^{-1}, what is the energy carried per electron to the screen? (Relativistic effects may be ignored.)

(*b*) What is the total energy that reaches the screen per second?

(*c*) What is the potential difference between the anode and cathode in the tube?

20 (*a*) Draw a labelled diagram to show the essential parts of a cathode ray oscilloscope that uses electrostatic deflection.

(*b*) Give an account of the energy transformations that occur within such an oscilloscope.

(*c*) An electron is projected along the axis of a cathode ray tube at a velocity of 1.5×10^7 m s^{-1}. There is a unifom electric field of 30 000 V m^{-1} between the plates, the upper plate being positive. If the plates have a separation of 2.5 cm and are 3.5 cm long, calculate how far above the axis the electron will be when it leaves the space between the plates.

If the fluorescent screen is 15 cm from the end of the plates, how far above the axis will the electron beam strike the screen?

58 · Emission of radiation from atoms

At the beginning of this century scientists believed that the atom was composed of a heavy central nucleus, positively charged and with a swarm of negatively charged electrons orbiting round it. Now in 1910 Rutherford showed that such a system would be unstable, and would decay in about 10^{-10} s as the attractive force between the nucleus and the electrons caused the latter to spiral inwards, producing a burst of radiation. In 1913, however, Niels Bohr overcame this difficulty by applying the quantum theory to the problem. This theory was developed in 1900 by Max Planck to explain the black body radiation curves.

Planck stated that the electron's energy was quantised, that is, that the electron could only have certain distinct values of energy – these could be represented as allowed orbits around the nucleus. In each orbit the electron is at a different energy level. In other words, the spiralling in is simply not allowed – the electron could only lose its energy in well-defined steps. This means that the angular momentum of the electron within an atom is quantised (for further details see page 463).

A change of energy level is always accompanied by the emission or absorption of radiation depending on the size of the energy change.

The Franck and Hertz experiment

This experiment, which was a direct verification of Bohr's energy level model of the atom, was first performed in 1914. Franck and Hertz used a three-electrode tube containing mercury vapour at a pressure of about 1 mm of mercury (about 10^2 Pa). This is shown in Figure 58.1.

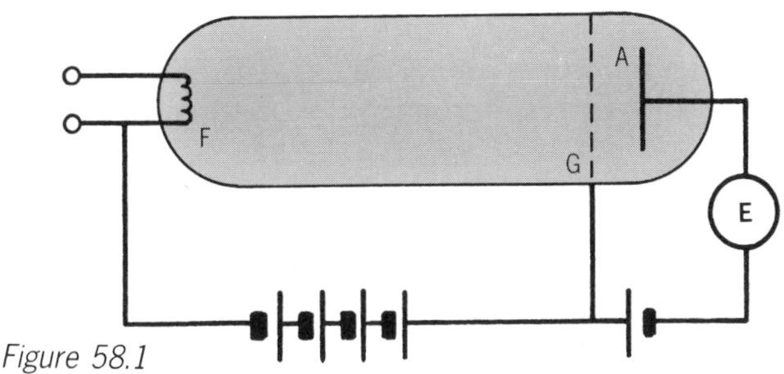

Figure 58.1

The distance between the filament F and the grid G was considerably greater than the mean free path of the electrons in the gas at this pressure, so that many collisions were made in this region. The distance from the grid to the anode was made relatively small, however. The anode A was slightly negative compared with the grid G, so that electrons were retarded between G and A. The accelerating potential between the filament and the grid was slowly increased from zero and the current in the electrometer E rose. When a potential V_C was reached, however, the current fell a little before rising again, and this also happened for other values of the potential ($2V_C$, $3V_C$) and so on – see Figure 58.2).

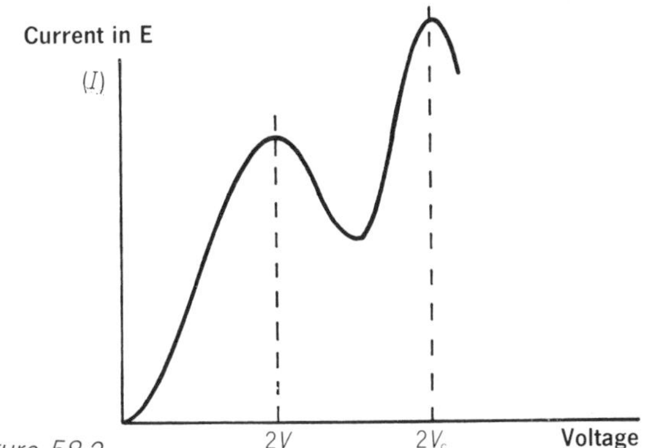

Figure 58.2

This can be explained as follows. As the voltage across the tube is increased the current increases, as the electrons collide *elastically* with the atoms of the gas, but when it reaches V_C *inelastic* collisions occur, and the electrons are brought practically to rest. The electric field in most of the tube is small since most of the potential drop occurs near the very thin wire of the filament. Therefore when the electrons reach the grid they have insufficient kinetic energy to overcome the retarding field between the grid and anode, and cannot reach the anode, so the anode current falls.

This shows that no increase in the energy of the atom can occur if the energy of the electrons is less than eV_C. The existence of a definite series of energies with no intermediate values suggests that the atom must have a set of well-defined **energy levels.** A further drop at $2eV_C$ shows electrons losing energy to two atoms in successive collisions.

The transition of electrons from one energy level to another gives the characteristic spectrum of the material. No two elements have identical energy level structures and therefore the spectrum of an element is unique. Notice that energy must be *put in* to raise the electrons within the atom to higher energy states.

The hydrogen spectrum

For simplicity we will now consider only the hydrogen atom with its single electron. We take an electron that is at rest outside the atom to have zero energy, and so the levels within the atom have negative energy values. Each level is given a number – the **quantum number** for that level – with the higher numbers representing the states of greater energy.

When an electron in an atom falls from one of the upper energy levels to one lower down, energy is emitted in the form of radiation: the bigger the energy difference, the greater will be the energy of the emitted quantum. The frequency f of the emitted radiation is given by Planck's formula:

$$E = hf$$

Where E is the energy difference and h is Planck's constant (6.67×10^{-34} J s).

Each energy change gives rise to a quantum of radiation of frequency f and therefore to a line in the hydrogen spectrum.

A diagram of the energy levels in the hydrogen spectrum is shown in Figure 58.3. The values of the energy levels can be calculated from Bohr's formula (see page 420). These are shown in the table.

n	Energy/eV	Energy/J
1	−13.60	-2.18×10^{-18}
2	−3.39	-5.42×10^{-19}
3	−1.51	-2.42×10^{-19}
4	−0.85	-1.36×10^{-19}
5	−0.54	-8.71×10^{-20}

The lowest level, with $n = 1$, is called the **ground state.** The electron will always occupy this lowest level unless it absorbs energy. This is also the lowest energy state for the *atom*.

The other levels are called **excited states** and the top level, with $n = \infty$, is the **ionisation state.** An electron raised to this level will be removed from the atom.

An electron will only be raised to an excited state if the input quantum of energy exactly matches the difference between the ground state and an excited level, or between two excited states if an electron already exists in an excited state. For other energies an incoming electron will suffer elastic scattering.

When an electron in a high energy state falls back to a lower level, energy is emitted in the form of radiation. This type of emission of radiation is called **spontaneous emission.** The loss of energy of an atom is a random process and we therefore cannot tell when a particular electron within an atom may fall to a lower energy level.

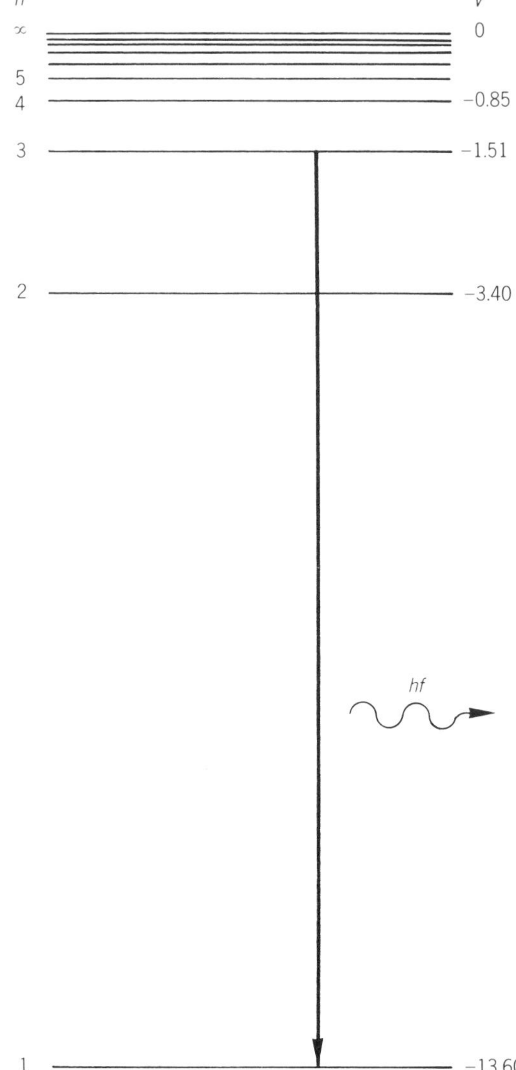

Figure 58.3

Turning the energy level diagram in Figure 58.3 on its side will give a diagram that represents the line spectrum of hydrogen (Figure 58.4). You can see how the lines get closer together towards the blue end of the spectrum, corresponding to the closer energy levels near $n = \infty$.

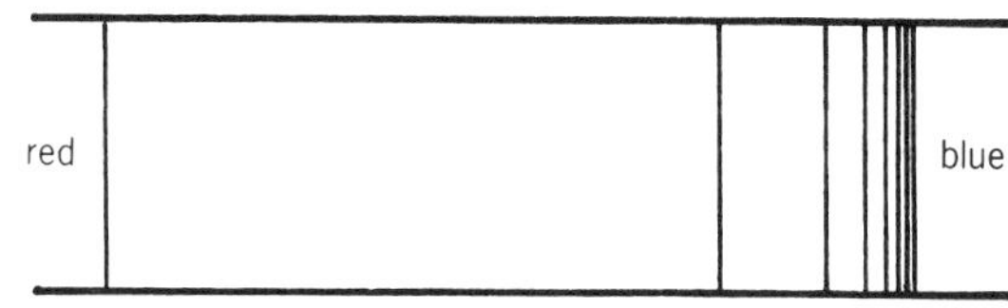

Figure 58.4

Calculation of wavelengths from the energy level diagram

Knowing the values of the energy levels gives us a way of calculating the frequency and wavelength of a given transition.

It is important that the energy values used in calculations is always in **joules.** (See example).

Example

Calculate the energy released and the wavelength of the emitted radiation when an electron falls from level $n = 3$ (−1.51 eV) to $n = 2$ (−3.4 eV).

Energy difference (E) = −1.51 − (−3.4)
= 1.89 eV
= 3.0×10^{-19} J

Therefore wavelength emitted = hc/E

$$= \frac{6.6 \times 10^{-34} \times 3 \times 10^{8}}{3.0 \times 10^{-19}}$$

= 6.6×10^{-7} m
= 660 nm

1 Figure 58.5 shows the energy level diagram for the hydrogen atom. Calculate the wavelength and frequency of the emitted radiation due to transitions between the following levels:
   (*a*) ∞ to 1,
   (*b*) 5 to 1,
   (*c*) 5 to 4,
   (*d*) 3 to 2, and
   (*e*) 2 to 1.
   State also the region of the spectrum in which each emission occurs.

2 The sodium spectrum contains two bright yellow lines of wavelengths 589.6 nm and 589.0 nm. Calculate the energy of the electron transition producing each line.

3 Explain how the velocity of recession (radial velocity) of a galaxy can be determined by analysis of its spectrum.

4 Calculate the speed of an electron that would just ionise a hydrogen atom that was initially in its ground state. (Mass of electron = 9×10^{-31} kg.)

5 State what happens when electrons of the following energies are incident on some hydrogen atoms initially in the ground state: (*a*) 2 eV, (*b*) 10.20 eV, (*c*) 12.09 eV, (*d*) 12.5 eV.

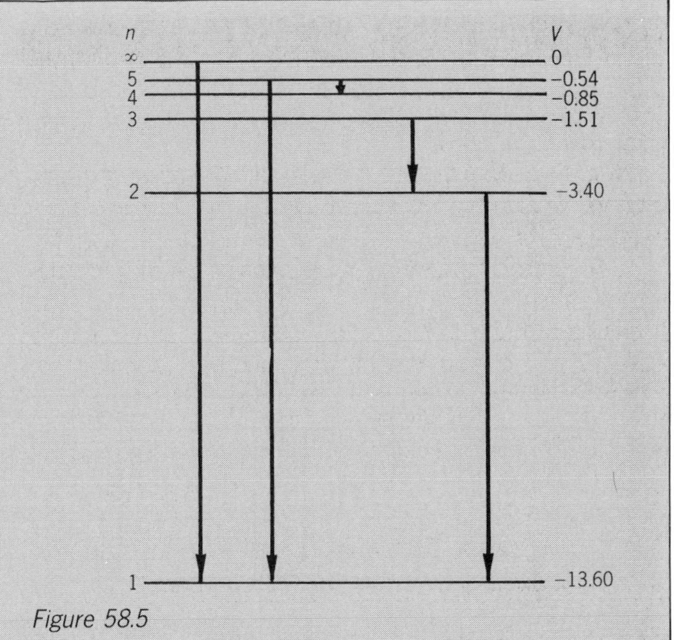

Figure 58.5

Spectral series

The spectrum of hydrogen contains distinct groups of lines known as **spectral series.** These are shown in Figure 58.6 and represent groups of electron transitions that end on levels $n = 1, 2, 3, 4$ and so on.

The series ending on $n = 1$ shows the largest energy transitions and gives lines in the ultraviolet region of the spectrum. This is known as the **Lyman series.** The series ending on $n = 2$ lies mostly in the visible region of the spectrum and is called the **Balmer series.** Other series ending on $n = 3$ and above lie in the infrared region. Notice how the lines in a given spectral series get closer together as the wavelength decreases, reaching a so-called **series limit** at the short-wavelength end.

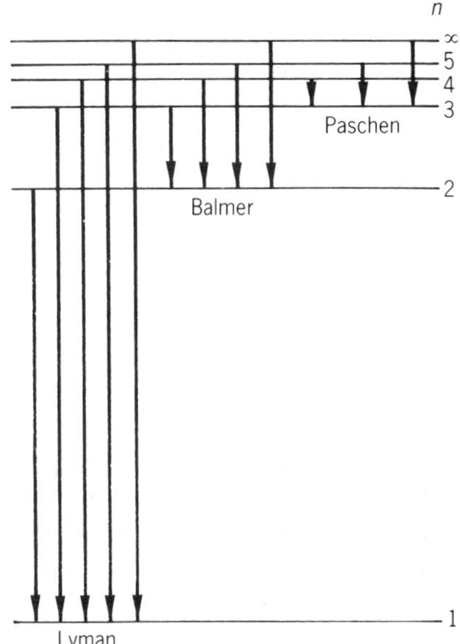

Figure 58.6

Types of spectrum

There are two main types of spectrum

(*a*) **emission spectra**, where light is given out by a source, and

(*b*) **absorption spectra,** where light from a source is absorbed when it passes through another material, usually a gas or a liquid.

(*a*) Emission spectra

These show different characteristics that depend on the nature of the source.

(i) **A continuous spectrum** contains all the wavelengths in a certain region of the spectrum. A continuous spectrum in the visible region may be emitted by a hot solid at a temperature above some 800 K. The Sun emits a more or less continuous spectrum, as does a piece of iron heated in a flame. This is because the atoms in the crystal of the solid are linked and any energy changes in one atom will affect the others.

(ii) **A line spectrum**, where – as its name suggests – only certain lines are visible, is emitted by a monatomic gas (Figure 58.7). This is because the atoms in a gas are not linked and you are simply getting a brighter version of the spectrum of one atom.

The lines may be broadened due to the motion of the atoms, giving a doppler shift to the radiation.

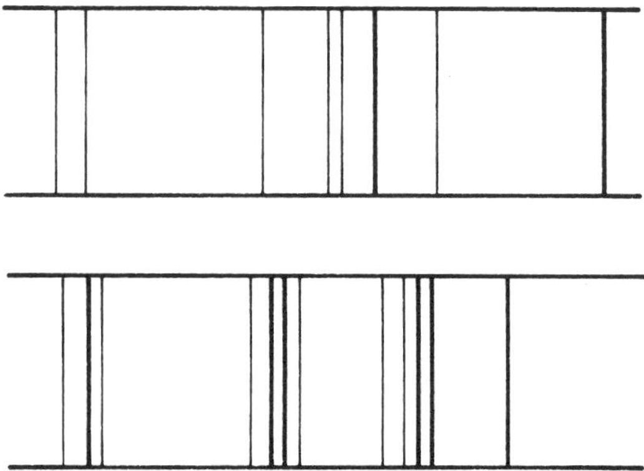

Figure 58.7

(iii) A **band spectrum** consisting of a series of bands is emitted by gases or liquids such as oxygen, carbon monoxide, blood or potassium manganate(VII) solution, consisting of molecules. Here the linkages between two or more atoms give groups of lines (Figure 58.8).

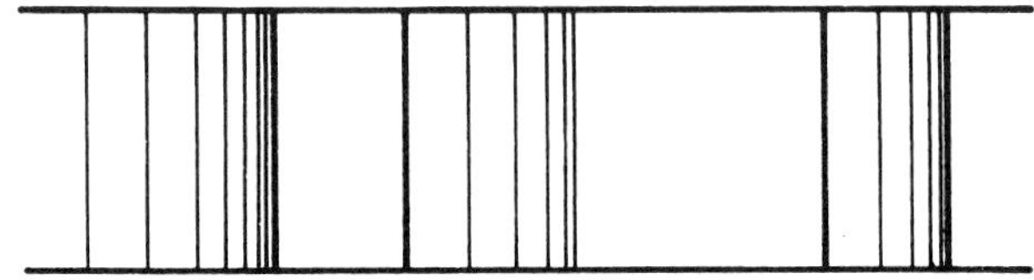

Figure 58.8

(*b*) Absorption spectra

If light from a white light source is passed through a gas then the continuous spectrum is crossed by a series of dark lines that correspond exactly to the lines observed in the emission spectrum which involve transitions to the ground state. This is because in a gas almost all the atoms are in their ground state.

Absorption occurs by the electrons in the atom absorbing the energy from the incoming radiation and then reradiating it in *all* directions. Thus the energy that was originally travelling in one direction is spread out, and compared with the rest of the spectrum these wavelengths appear dark (Figure 58.9).

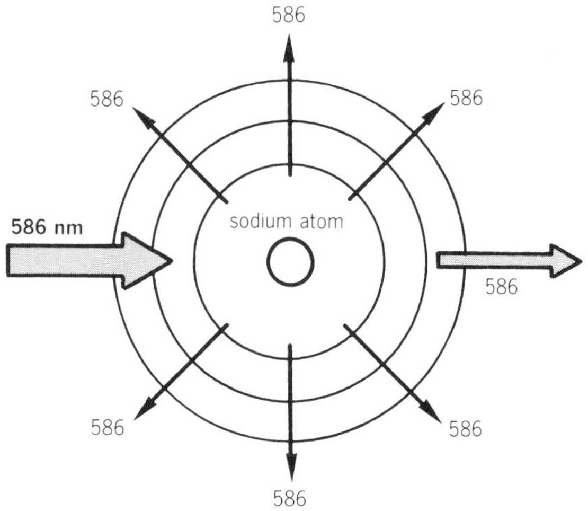

Figure 58.9

Absorption spectra can be shown clearly by heating a stick of sodium chloride in a bunsen flame. If light from a sodium vapour lamp is now shone on to the flame a shadow of the flame can be formed on a screen. Experiments show that shadows are *not* produced when materials that do not contain sodium are heated in the flame in the path of sodium light.

In 1814 Fraunhofer discovered that the spectrum of the suns radiation is crossed by many dark absorption lines, sometimes called **Fraunhofer lines**. These are due to absorption by the outer gaseous layers of the Sun and a study of such lines gives the astronomer a method for determining the composition of the Sun or, indeed, of any other star.

Student investigation

As we have seen the composition of a transparent material may be determined by a study of the absorption spectrum that it gives when white light is passed through it.

The following results are from an experiment which was performed by the author while a sixth former.

The spectroscope was set up with a grating of 575 lines per mm and a white light source was viewed through it. A rectangular beaker of cerium(III) chloride was placed in the beam and the absorption spectrum shown in Figure 58.10 was obtained.

The zero order was at a telescope setting of 334° 10′.

The following table of results gives the telescope settings for the other 16 points measured in the spectrum.

1	316° 05′	5	314° 31′	9	313° 14′	13	312° 44′
2	315° 30′	6	314° 23′	10	313° 06′	14	312° 26′
3	315° 22′	7	314° 12′	11	313° 01′	15	311° 08′
4	314° 37′	8	314° 08′	12	312° 50′	16	310° 46′

Use these results to calculate the wavelengths at the different parts of the spectrum, and draw a scale diagram of the spectrum.

If possible repeat the experiment, and also study the absorption spectrum of a solution containing manganate (VII) ions.

A further interesting study is the absorption spectrum of blood. Your teacher will give you a sample of blood which should be examined both before and after carbon dioxide or oxygen has been passed through it.

Figure 58.10

6 In the X-ray spectrum of copper there is a line of wavelength 0.02 nm. Calculate the energy associated with this transition in electronvolts.

7 In a sodium atom we will assume that radiation of wavelength 590 nm is emitted when an electron makes a transition from the first excited level to the ground state.

(*a*) What is the energy of the photon emitted in this transition?

(*b*) What is the temperature of the gas whose molecules have an average kinetic energy equal to that photon energy?

(*c*) If the average temperature of a gas flame is 2000 K, why does excitation occur at all?

8 What is the minimum velocity of two hydrogen atoms that, in a collision, might lead to ionisation in one of them?

9 Some of the energy levels in the mercury spectrum are shown in Figure 58.11. In the unexcited state all levels above −10.4 eV are unoccupied.

Calculate the wavelengths of the electron transitions between the energy level (*a*) 0 to −5.5 eV, and (*b*) 0 to −10.4 eV.

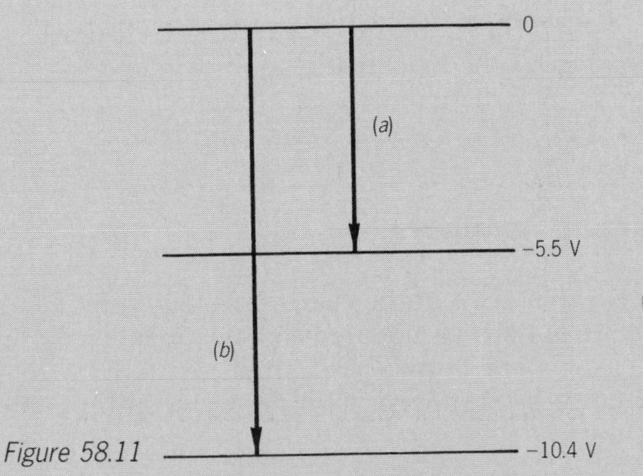

Figure 58.11

10 Construct the energy level diagram for sodium from the following transition wavelengths, showing the values of the energy levels in eV:

Transition	Wavelength/nm
B–A	589
C–A	330
D–A	285
E–B	514

(These values have been simplified.)

Bohr's equation for the hydrogen atom

Bohr derived an equation to give the values of the energy levels in the hydrogen atom.

The proof of this equation is outside the scope of this book, but we will quote the result here. Bohr showed that the energy levels were proportional to $1/n^2$, where n is an integer.

When an electron falls from one energy level E_2 to another level E_1 radiation of frequency f will be emitted. Bohr showed that the energy difference ($E_2 - E_1 = hf$) was given by the equation:

$$E_2 - E_1 = hf = \frac{me^4}{8\epsilon_0{}^2h^2}\left\{\frac{1}{n_1{}^2} - \frac{1}{n_2{}^2}\right\}$$

where n_1 and n_2 are integers (1, 2, 3. . .) and the other constants have their usual meanings.

The equation can be expressed in the form of **wave number** ($1/\lambda$) as:

$$\frac{1}{\lambda} = \frac{me^4}{8\epsilon_0{}^2ch^3}\left\{\frac{1}{n_1{}^2} - \frac{1}{n_2{}^2}\right\}$$

The term $\dfrac{me^4}{8\epsilon_0{}^2ch^3}$ is known as **Rydberg's constant** (R):

$R = 1.097 \times 10^7\ \text{m}^{-1}$.

Putting $n_1 = 1, 2$ or 3 will give us three series of energy changes and therefore three series of wavelengths:

$n_1 = 1$ gives the Lyman series (ultraviolet);
$n_1 = 2$ gives the Balmer series (visible);
$n_1 = 3$ gives the Paschen series (infrared).

Quantum numbers

The full treatment of the electron energy in terms of quantum numbers is not predicted by the simple Bohr model. It is not normally required for study at this level but a brief summary will be included for completeness.

Every electron within an atom is considered to have four quantum numbers:

(*a*) the **principal quantum number** (n), representing the energy level;

(*b*) the **orbital quantum number** (l), which may have any integral value from 0 to $n - 1$;

(*c*) the **magnetic quantum number** (m), which may have any integral value from $-l$ to $+l$;

(*d*) the **spin quantum number** (s), which may have values of $+\frac{1}{2}$ or $-\frac{1}{2}$.

Related to these quantum numbers is the **Pauli exclusion principle** which states that no two electrons in an atom may exist in the same quantum state. This important statement may be used to predict the numbers of electrons in the shells of an atom. Consider the K-shell and L-shell.

(*a*) In the K-shell, $n = 1$. The only possible values for l and m are 0, s can be $+\frac{1}{2}$ or $-\frac{1}{2}$, and so only two electrons can exist in this shell.

(*b*) In the L-shell, n = 2. In this shell eight electrons are possible, as shown by the following table:

n	l	m	s	n	l	m	s
2	0	0	$+\frac{1}{2}$	2	0	0	$-\frac{1}{2}$
2	1	-1	$+\frac{1}{2}$	2	1	-1	$-\frac{1}{2}$
2	1	0	$+\frac{1}{2}$	2	1	0	$-\frac{1}{2}$
2	1	$+1$	$+\frac{1}{2}$	2	1	$+1$	$-\frac{1}{2}$

59 · Ionic physics

The conduction of electricity through gases

We are all familiar with the electric spark formed when a high-voltage discharge occurs across a region of air, and also with the bright yellow light emitted by a sodium vapour lamp. Both these are examples of the conduction of electricity through gases – the differing results being due not only to the different gases but also the different pressures under which conduction takes place. (The pressure in a neon lamp is about 10 mm of mercury.)

The effects of different gases are considered elsewhere (page 422), and we will consider here only the effect of pressure changes on the discharge in air.

In dry air at atmospheric pressure a voltage of 30 kV is required to produce a spark between two spherical electrodes 1 cm apart. In a thunderstorm, even allowing for the moisture in the air, you can appreciate the truly enormous voltages that are required for one lightning flash. (For pointed electrodes the p.d. is reduced to 12 kV due to the higher field at a point.) For small potential differences, a gas is an almost perfect insulator.

At lower pressures the potential difference to give sparking is reduced. This is because the mean free path of the electrons is longer and they can therefore be accelerated to higher speeds before collision with an atom; they therefore have more chance of causing ionisation.

The following table shows the mean free path (in metres) of an electron in various gases at different pressures.

Gas	*Pressure*			
	760 mm	10 mm	1 mm	0.001 mm
Hydrogen	1.83×10^{-7}	1.4×10^{-5}	1.4×10^{-4}	0.14
Oxygen	9.95×10^{-8}	7.56×10^{-6}	7.56×10^{-5}	0.076
Nitrogen	9.44×10^{-7}	7.17×10^{-6}	7.17×10^{-5}	0.017

The discharge through gases at low pressure may be investigated using a **Geissler tube**. This is simply a glass tube containing air, the pressure of which may be varied, with electrodes at either end. It is unsafe to use a Geissler tube at p.d.s above about 5–6 kV, because above this X-rays may be generated by electron impact with the anode and walls of the tube.

Figures 59.1 to 59.4 show the appearance of the discharge in air for various pressures.

At 20 mm pressure, violet streamers pass between cathode and anode (Figure 59.1).

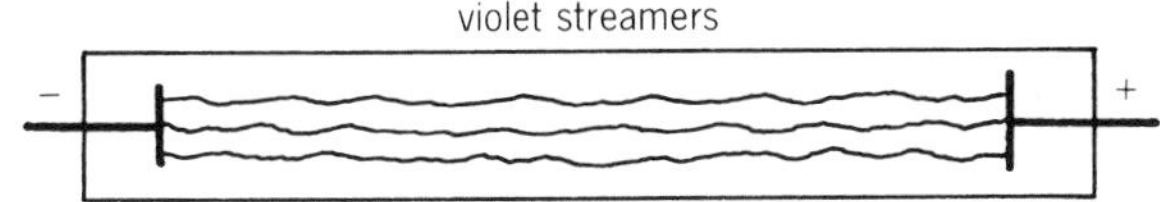

Figure 59.1

At 5 mm pressure, a pink positive column and a negative glow appear near the cathode. These two regions are separated by **Faraday's dark space** (Figure 59.2).

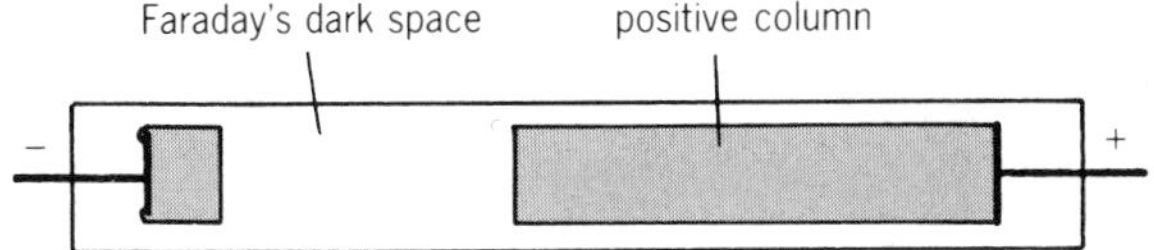

Figure 59.2

At 0.1 mm pressure the positive column becomes striated, the negative glow moves away from the cathode, **Crookes' dark space** appears and the cathode glow appears round the cathode (Figure 59.3). Most of the p.d. in the tube exists across the Crookes' dark space.

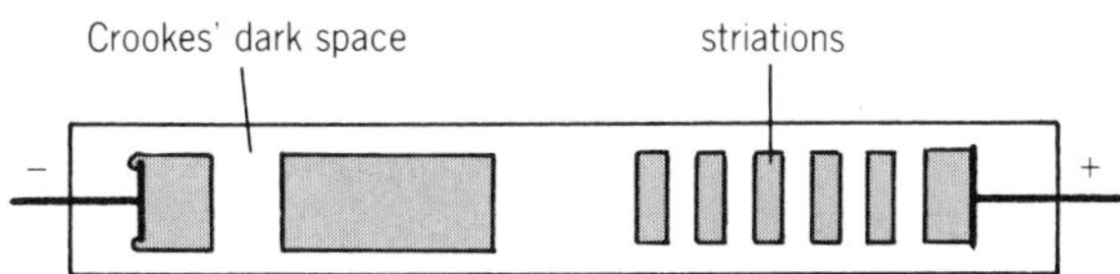

Figure 59.3

At 0.01 mm pressure or less, Crookes' dark space fills the whole tube and the glass fluoresces due to electron impact (Figure 59.4). In 1858 Plucher demonstrated that the fluorescence could be moved about by a magnet, showing that it was due to charged particle motion.

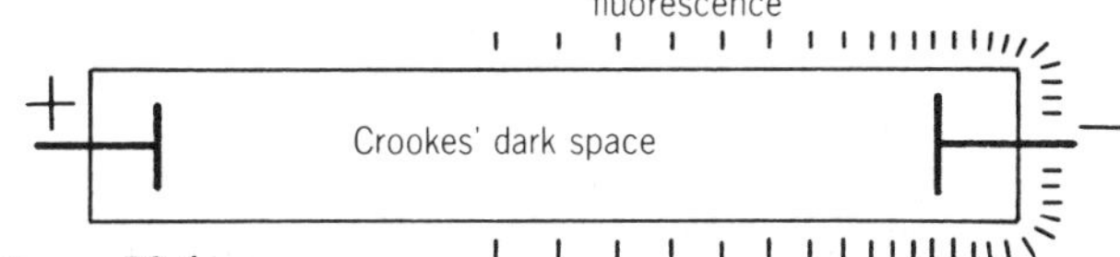

Figure 59.4

As the pressure is reduced still further the potential difference needed to maintain the discharge rises again, and below pressures of about 10^{-3} mm of mercury the tube usually becomes a good insulator again.

Positive rays

In 1896 Goldstein noticed that when a discharge occurred in a tube of low-pressure gas rays appeared to be produced originating from the anode. These he called **positive rays**, sometimes known as **canal rays**.

The rays originated within the gas itself, none being produced if the tube were totally evacuated.

It was realised that these positive rays were composed of particles, and that these particles were positive ions of the gas in the tube. The properties of the positive rays were investigated by Thomson in 1906, using the apparatus shown in Figure 59.5(*a*).

(*a*)

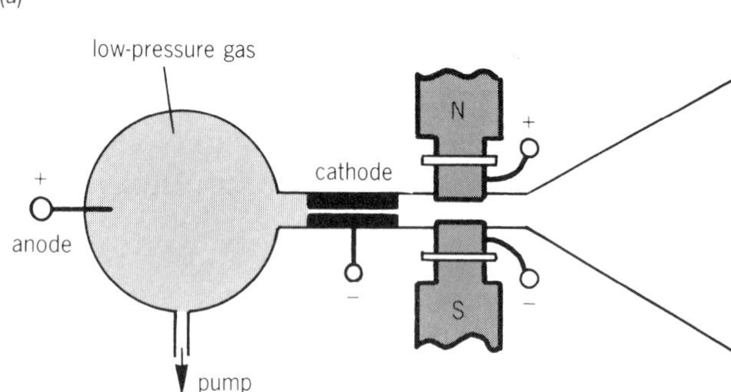

(*b*)

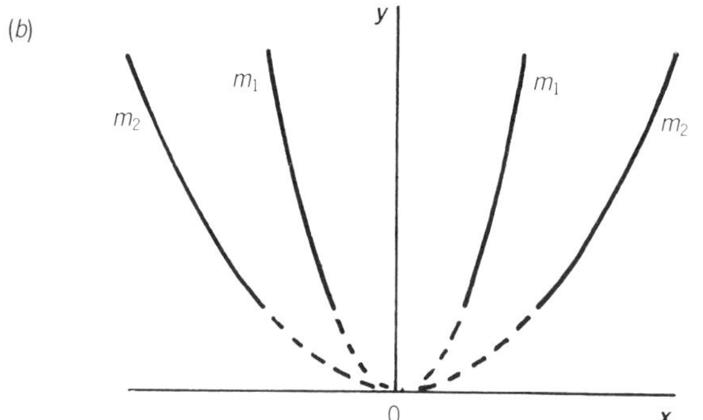

Figure 59.5

A discharge occurs in the low-pressure gas in the bulb at the left-hand end of the apparatus, producing positive rays that pass through the anode and into the right-hand end of the tube. Here they go through electric and magnetic fields that act in the Y-direction; the electric and magnetic forces on the particles are therefore at right angles to each other.

When the particles strike the fluorescent screen a parabola (Figure 59.5(*b*)) is produced by particles having different velocities, those with the highest velocities having originated closest to the anode (since an ion with zero velocity near the anode will have a longer distance over which to accelerate before it reaches the cathode if it makes no collisions on the way). The positive rays showed the following properties:

(*a*) they could be deflected by electric and magnetic fields;
(*b*) they showed a spectrum of velocities;
(*c*) they were dependent on the gas in the tube;
(*d*) they could cause ionisation;
(*e*) they caused fluorescence and affected photographic plates.

It was assumed that the particles were gaseous ions of mass m and charge q.

Thomson found that the value of q/m for the particles in the positive rays with hydrogen in the tube was of the order of 10^8 C kg^{-1}. This must mean that the particle that makes up positive rays has either a smaller charge than that of the electron or a much greater mass, and it is the latter that has been accepted.

Isotopes

With some gases in the tube more than one parabola was produced, and this was eventually thought to mean that the gas was composed of particles of different masses. There was only one gas in the tube, and the difference in mass was much greater than could be attributed to a difference in the number of electrons.

These different parabolas were due to different **isotopes** of the same gas.

Isotopes are particles which have the same position in the Periodic Table, that is, they are atoms of the same chemical element but their nucleon numbers are different. Isotopes of an element have nuclei with the same number of protons but different numbers of neutrons. Neon, for instance, has three isotopes with nucleon numbers of 20, 21 and 22, corresponding respectively to 10, 11 and 12 neutrons in the nucleus. The most common isotopes of uranium are uranium-235 and uranium-238 (143 and 146 neutrons respectively.)

It is important to realise that since the number of electrons is identical for all isotopes of the same element, the *chemical* properties of isotopes of the same element are identical. Since the structure of the nuclei are different, however, their nuclear properties will be different and, since their relative atomic masses are different, some of their physical properties are different as well. For example, the boiling point of 'heavy water' (water containing the isotope of hydrogen with a neutron in the nucleus) is 104 °C.

In 1906 isotopes were discovered in radioactive elements (although their nature was not understood) and in 1912 Thomson discovered the three isotopes of neon with the nucleon numbers shown above.

The following table shows some of the more common isotopes of a few elements.

Element	*Nucleon numbers of isotopes*
Hydrogen	1, 2, 3
Helium	3, 4
Carbon	12, 14
Oxygen	16, 17, 18,
Neon	20, 21, 22
Calcium	40, 42, 44
Iron	56, 57
Mercury	198, 199, 200, 201, 202
Lead	206, 207, 208
Uranium	235, 238

(For a more complete list of isotopes see page 485.)

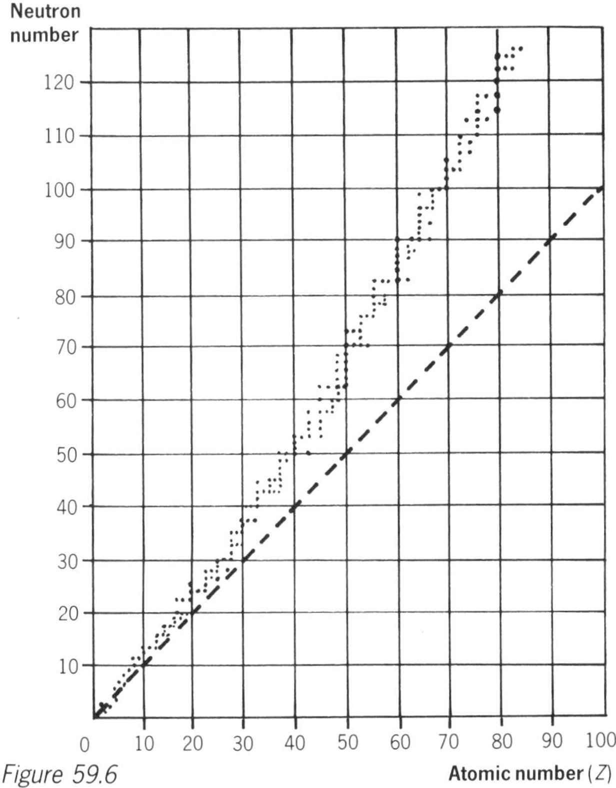

Figure 59.6

Figure 59.6 shows the increase in neutron number with the number of protons in the nucleus (proton or atomic number). You can see that there are many more neutrons than protons in the nuclei of atoms that have large proton numbers.

Separation of isotopes

There are several methods for separating isotopes.

(*a*) Centrifuge

Due to the difference in the masses of the two isotopes of uranium, a centrifuge method can be used to separate them. The mass difference is three neutron masses and this is sufficient to make this method effective.

(*b*) Gaseous diffusion

This method is used when the difference in mass is small, for example one neutron mass as in the case of hydrogen (1p) and deuterium (1p, 1n). It is also used to enrich uranium.

(*c*) Electromagnetic/electrostatic deflection

Where a very high purity is required the sample may be built up particle by particle, by deflection and collection in a mass spectrometer.

An ion current of 0.1 mA gives 6.21×10^{14} particles per second, assuming that the ions are singly charged. To produce 10^{-4} mole of the sample by this method would take 1.33 days!

A uranium mine – the Ranger in Australia (United Kingdom Atomic Energy Authority)

The mass spectrograph

In 1919 Aston developed the first really good mass spectrograph, an instrument for measuring the masses of isotopes. His apparatus gave accuracies of 1 part in 1000.

A simpler form of the mass spectrograph than Aston's is that due to Bainbridge (1933) and a plan view of this is shown in Figure 59.7(*a*).

Ions are formed at D and pass through the cathode C and then through a slit S_1. They then travel between two plates A and B, between which is applied a potential. A magnetic field is applied at right angles to the

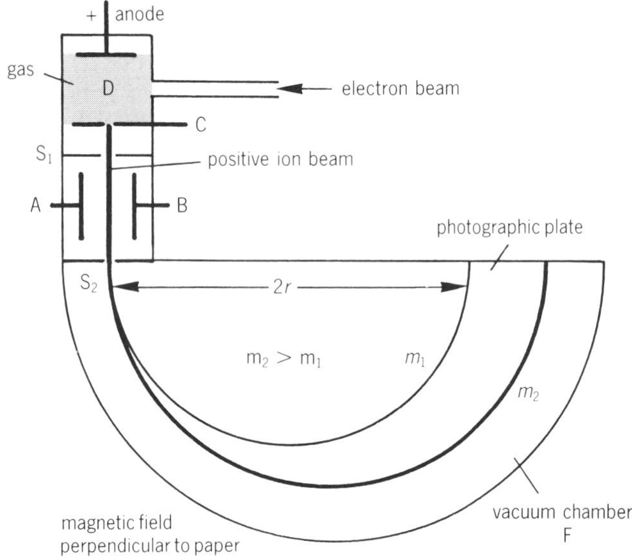

Figure 59.7 (*a*)

electrostatic field and so the electrostatic and electromagnetic forces act in opposite directions to each other. Only if the resultant force is zero will the particle pass though the next slit S_2. If the forces are equal, then

$$Bqv = qE$$

Therefore, for the particle to pass through S_2,

$$v = E/B$$

But this is a constant, and so only particles with a certain velocity enter the deflection chamber F. For this reason the combination of slits and deflecting plates is called a velocity selector.

In the deflection chamber the ions are affected by the magnetic fields alone and therefore move in circular paths, the lighter ions having the larger path radius. If the mass of an ion is M, its charge q and its velocity v then:

$$Bqv = Mv^2/r$$

where r is the radius of the path. Therefore

$$r = Mv/(Bq) \qquad \text{and} \qquad M = rB^2q/E$$

so the radius is directly proportional to the mass of the ion.

Figure 59.7 (*b*)

The detection is by either a photographic plate or a collector that produces a small current when the ions fall on it. The magnetic field may be varied, so changing the radii of the particles' paths so that ions of different masses fall on a fixed collector.

This method of analysis is very accurate and can detect differences in the masses of two ions as small as one part in 10^9.

Figure 59.7(*b*) shows the appearance of the photographic plate when a gas containing two isotopes is used. Note the wider line for the mass m_2, showing its relatively greater abundance.

Student investigation

Figure 59.8 represents the photographic plate taken from a Bainbridge mass spectrometer. It is drawn one-quarter full size and shows the collection of two different isotopes. Assuming that the isotopes are singly charged find

(*a*) the mass number of each of the isotopes,
(*b*) the gas used in the experiment.

Figure 59.8

The magnetic field across the apparatus is 0.01 T and the electric field in the velocity selector 100 V m^{-1}.

1 A Bainbridge mass spectrograph is used to examine the mass spectrum of germanium. The isotopes present had mass numbers of 70, 72, 73, 74 and 76. If the magnetic field across the deflection chamber was 0.05 T and the electric field in the velocity selector was 50 V m^{-1}, find the radius of each orbit assuming that the ions are singly charged. (Electron charge = 1.6×10^{-19} C; 1 a.m.u. = 1.66×10^{-27} kg)

2 In the Bainbridge mass spectrograph described above it is required that the radius of path of the ion with a mass number of 72 be exactly 1 m. If the field in the velocity selector remained the same, what must be the magnetic field across the deflection chamber?

Isotopes and relative atomic masses

The following in an extract from an article by Dr F.W.Aston first published in *Nature* in 1920.

In the atomic theory put forward by John Dalton in 1801 the second postulate was 'Atoms of the same element are similar to one another and equal in weight'. For more than a century this was regarded by chemists and physicists alike as an article of scientific faith. The only item among the immense quantities of knowledge acquired during that productive period which offered the faintest suggestion against its validity was the inexplicable mixture of order and disorder among the elementary atomic weights [relative atomic masses]. The general state of opinion at the end of the last century may be gathered from the two following quotations from Sir William Ramsay's address to the British Association at Toronto in 1897:

'There have been almost innumerable attempts to reduce the differences between atomic weights to regularity by contriving some formula which will express the numbers which represent the atomic weights with all their irregularities. Needless to say such attempts have in no case been successful. … The idea has been advanced that what we call the atomic weight is a mean; that when we say the atomic weight of oxygen is 16 we merely state that the average atomic weight of oxygen is 16; and it is not inconceivable that a certain number of oxygen molecules have a weight somewhat higher than 32 and a certain number have a lower weight.'

This idea was placed on an altogether different footing some ten years later by the work of Lord Rutherford and his colleagues on radioactive transformations. The results of these led inevitably to the conclusion that there must exist elements which have chemical properties identical for all practical purposes, but the atoms have different weights. This conclusion has been recently confirmed in a most convincing manner by the production in quantity of specimens of lead from radioactive and other sources, which, although perfectly pure and chemically indistinguishable, give atomic weights differing by amounts quite outside the possible experimental error. Elements differing in mass but chemically identical have been called *isotopes* by Professor Soddy.

The work of Sir J.J.Thomson before the war led to the belief that neon also existed as a mixture of two isotopes with atomic weights of 20 and 22, the accepted atomic weight being 20.2. The methods available were not accurate enough to distinguish between 20 and 20.2 with certainty but in 1913 a diffusion experiment gave positive results, an apparent change in density of 0.7 per cent between the lightest and heaviest fractions being obtained after many thousands of operations.

By the time work was started again after the war the isotope theory had been generally accepted so far as the radioactive elements were concerned and a good deal of theoretical speculation had been made as to its applicability to the elements generally. As separation by diffusion is at best extremely slow and laborious attention was again turned to positive rays in the hope of increasing the accuracy of measurements to the required degree.

[A description of the Aston mass spectrograph then follows. I will continue the extract at the point where the results are considered.]

By far the most important result obtained from this work is the generalisation that, with the exception of hydrogen, all atomic weights so far measured are exactly whole numbers on the scale O = 16. Hydrogen is found to be 1.008, which agrees with the value accepted by the chemists. This exception from the whole number rule is not unexpected, as on the Rutherford 'nucleus' theory the hydrogen atom is the only one not containing any negative electricity in its nucleus.

The results which have been so far obtained with eighteen elements make it possible that the higher the atomic weight of an element, the more complex it is likely to be, and that there are more complex elements than simple. It must be noticed that, though the whole number rule asserts that a pure element must have a whole number atomic weight, there is no reason to suppose that all elements having atomic weights approximating to integers are therefore pure.

1 Why was the existence of isotopes initially thought to be unlikely?

2 Write an account of Rutherford's work on radioactive decay.

3 Assuming that neon occurs as two isotopes of atomic weights 20 and 22, what proportion of naturally occurring neon is neon-20 if the atomic weight of neon is 20.2? (Ignore other isotopes.)

4 What is the modern unit for 'atomic weights', and why was it chosen?

5 Why did hydrogen appear to be an exception to the whole number rule?

60 · The photoelectric effect

In 1888 Hallwachs discovered that electrons could be emitted from a metal surface when electromagnetic radiation fell on the surface. For some surfaces, such as sodium, this radiation had to have a short wavelength (X-rays or ultraviolet) to cause electron emission while for others such as caesium electrons were emitted when irradiated by the much longer-wavelength infrared radiation. The effect is known as **photoelectric emission.**

A simple experiment to investigate these effects can be performed with a gold leaf electroscope.

A freshly cleaned zinc plate is connected to the top of a positively charged electroscope (Figure 60.1).

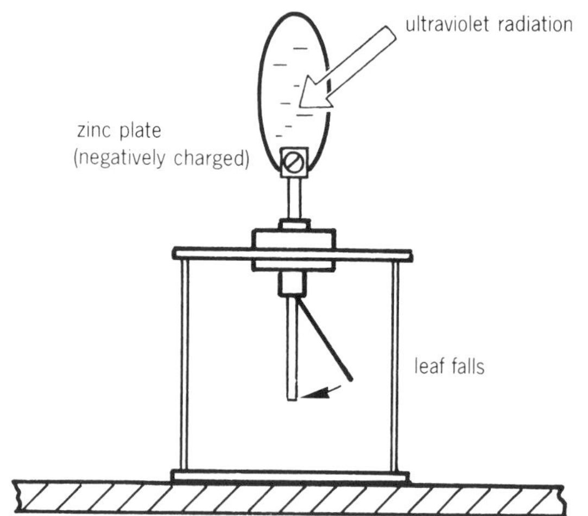

Figure 60.1

If the plate is then illuminated with ultraviolet radiation nothing happens, but if the electroscope is initially charged negatively the leaf moves down immediately when the ultraviolet radiation falls on the plate. No effect can be produced with radiation of a longer wavelength, no matter how intense the radiation may be or how long the surface is exposed to it.

The particles emitted from the plate were shown to be electrons by Lennard, who measured their specific charge.

These effects can be summarised as follows:

(*a*) No electrons are emitted from the positive plate because of the mutual attractive force between the electrons and the plate.

(*b*) The *number* of photoelectrons emitted per second is directly proportional to the *intensity* of the incident radiation.

(*c*) The *energy* of the emitted electrons depends upon the *frequency* of the incident radiation.

(*d*) There exists a **threshold frequency** (f_0) for all surfaces, and below this frequency no electrons are emitted no matter how intense the radiation or for how long it falls on the surface.

If we try to explain these effects using the wave theory we find that (*a*) and (*b*) can be explained but not (*c*) or (*d*).

Student investigation

A more accurate investigation of the photoelectric effect may be performed using the d.c. electrometer with a strip of magnesium ribbon. Clean the magnesium ribbon thoroughly and set up the apparatus shown in Figure 60.2. With the strip of magnesium ribbon connected to the negative terminal, investigate the following by observing the output meter deflection.

(*a*) Shine the light from a quartz–iodine lamp on the magnesium.

(*b*) Shine ultraviolet light on the magnesium.

(*c*) Try varying the intensity of the ultraviolet radiation.

(*d*) Observe the effect of placing sheets of glass or polythene between the lamp and the magnesium.

(*e*) Reverse the power supply and repeat the experiments with the magnesium strip positively charged.

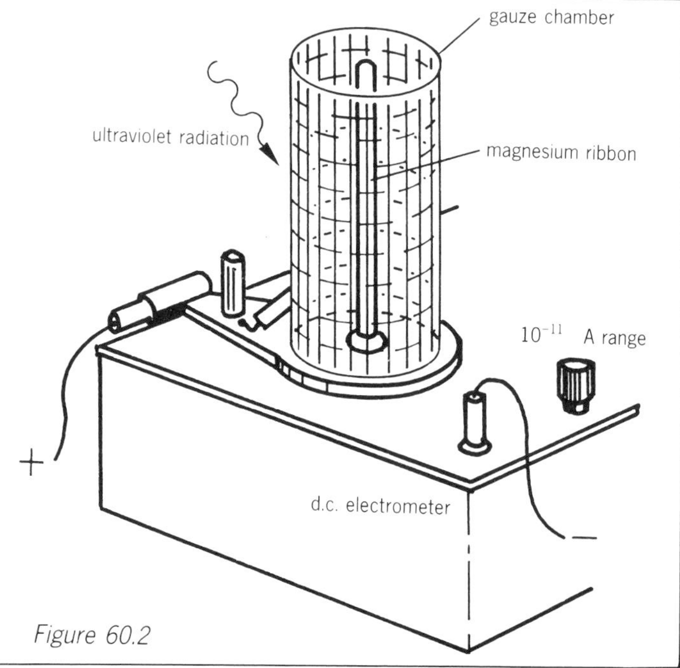

Figure 60.2

As long as we use radiation with a frequency above the threshold value, then emission of electrons is instantaneous; the electrons do not seem to have to 'build up' energy received from the radiation over a period of time.

The photoelectric effect and the quantum theory

To explain the photoelectric effect we therefore have to resort to the quantum theory, already used in 1900 by Max Planck to account for the energy distribution curves of black bodies. This states that radiation is emitted in **quanta** or packets of energy. The energy E of a quantum of radiation is given by

$$E = hf$$

where h is the Planck constant and f is the frequency of the radiation.

1 Given that the mass of the electron is 9×10^{-31} kg and that the velocity of light is 3×10^{8} m s^{-1}, calculate the following:
(*a*) the kinetic energy of a gas molecule of mass 5×10^{-26} kg moving with a velocity of 400 m s^{-1};
(*b*) the kinetic energy of an electron moving with a velocity of 2×10^{6} m s^{-1};
(*c*) the energy of a quantum of green light of wavelength 550 nm;
(*d*) the energy of a quantum of ultraviolet radiation of wavelength 100 nm.

The work function

As has been found from experiments, only quanta of sufficient energy and therefore of sufficiently high frequency would produce photoelectric emission from a metal surface. The minimum energy needed to remove an electron from the surface can be written as

$$E_0 = hf_0$$

and is known as the **work function** (W) of the metal. Some values for the work functions of metals are given in the table below.

Metal	*Work function*/J	*Work function*/eV	*Minimum f*/Hz	*Maximum* λ/nm
Sodium	3.8×10^{-19}	2.40	5.8×10^{14}	520
Caesium	3.0×10^{-19}	1.88	4.5×10^{14}	666
Lithium	3.7×10^{-19}	2.31	5.6×10^{14}	560
Calcium	4.3×10^{-19}	2.69	6.5×10^{14}	462
Magnesium	5.9×10^{-19}	3.69	8.9×10^{14}	337
Silver	7.6×10^{-19}	4.75	11.4×10^{14}	263
Platinum	10.0×10^{-19}	6.75	15.1×10^{14}	199

It is useful if we imagine the electrons in a **potential well**, rather like a hole in the ground. In just the same way that a stone in the bottom of the hole requires energy to get out, so the electrons must be given energy to escape from the potential well. This is provided in the form of a quantum of radiation.

If a quantum of energy greater than E_0 falls on the surface then the electrons will be emitted with a certain amount of kinetic energy. You should see now why the emission is instantaneous – one quantum of radiation will carry with it all the energy needed to liberate one electron if its frequency is sufficiently high.

The quantum theory also explains why the number of electrons emitted is greater when the intensity of the incident radiation and hence the number of quanta arriving per second is greater.

2 (*a*) What is meant by a photon?
(*b*) A quantum of energy 4.5 eV is incident on a calcium surface. What is the energy of the emitted electron?
(*c*) Express 2.5 eV in joules.
(*d*) What is the velocity of an electron of energy 2.5 eV?

An application of the photoelectric effect – solar cells on the space probe Giotto which was used to investigate Halley's comet (British Aerospace)

Einstein's photoelectric equation

In 1905 Einstein proposed his photoelectric equation, known as **Einstein's equation**. This relates the energy of the incident quantum to the work function and the kinetic energy of the emitted electron. If the work function of the metal is W and the incident frequency is f, Einstein's photoelectric equation can be written as

$$E = hf = W + \tfrac{1}{2}mv^2$$

Writing W as hf_0, we have

$$\tfrac{1}{2}mv^2 = h(f - f_0)$$

(see Figure 60.3). If we place the emitting surface in a vacuum and put a collecting electrode in front of it, we can collect the photoelectrons and record them as a small current. Changing the frequency of the radiation will not have any effect on this current as long as it is above f_0 but the current will be directly proportional to the intensity of the radiation.

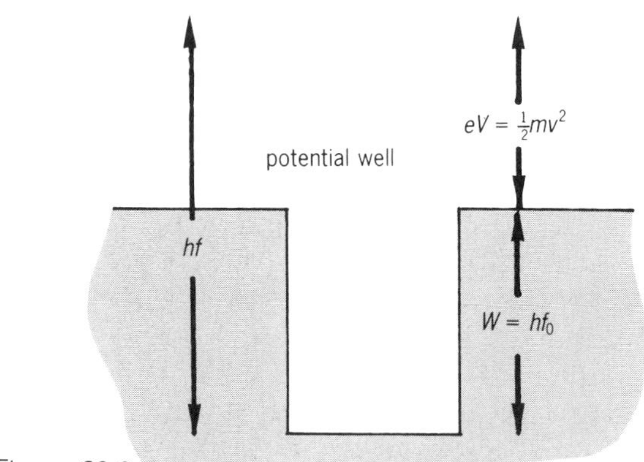

Figure 60.3

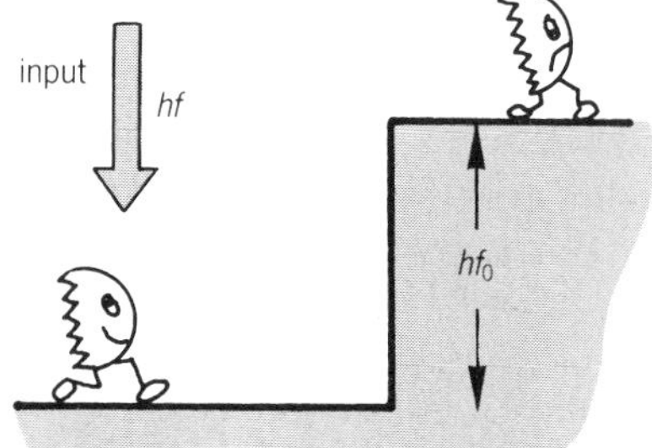

Figure 60.4

If a potential is now applied between the collecting electrode and the emitting surface, so that the collecting electrode is negative, no electrons will be detected unless their energy is greater than the energy of the potential barrier.

The idea of a potential hill that the electrons have to climb is shown in Figure 60.5. Electrons are detected if

$$\tfrac{1}{2}mv^2 > eV$$

where V is the potential applied. So the potential barrier that must be applied to just stop the current is given by

$$\tfrac{1}{2}mv^2 = eV$$

and Einstein's equation can be re-written as

$$eV = h(f - f_0)$$

Figure 60.5

3 The maximum wavelength of radiation that will eject electrons from a calcium surface is 462 nm.
If such a surface is illuminated with radiation of wavelength 300 nm, what is the maximum velocity with which photoelectrons may be emitted from it?

4 If a sodium surface in a vacuum is illuminated with a beam of monochromatic ultraviolet light with a wavelength of 200 nm, what is the maximum velocity with which electrons can be emitted? (Take the work function of sodium as 2.4 eV.) [AEB]

5 Explain Einstein's application of the quantum theory of radiation to the understanding of photoelectric emission.

6 Radiation of wavelength 180 nm ejects electrons from a potassium plate whose work function is 2.0 eV.
(*a*) What is the maximum energy of the emitted electrons?
(*b*) What is the maximum wavelength that will cause electron emission?

7 A calcium surface is illuminated with radiation of different wavelengths and the kinetic energies of the photoelectrons emitted at the wavelengths recorded in the following table:

Wavelength/nm	415	387	368	345	325	315
Energy/J $\times 10^{-19}$	0.5	0.8	1.1	1.5	1.75	2.00

Use these results to plot a graph of frequency against electron energy and use it to determine
(*a*) the work function of calcium,
(*b*) the value of the Planck constant.

Determination of the Planck constant

The photoelectric effect can be used as the basis of an experiment to determine the value of the Planck constant, h. White light is shone on to a photocell through a series of different coloured filters and the voltage applied to the electrode to reduce the current to zero is recorded for each colour. The potential is known as the **stopping potential**, V. A graph is plotted of the frequency f against V (Figure 60.6) and the slope V/f is determined. Hence h can be found if e is known using Einstein's equation in the form

$$eV = h(f - f_0)$$

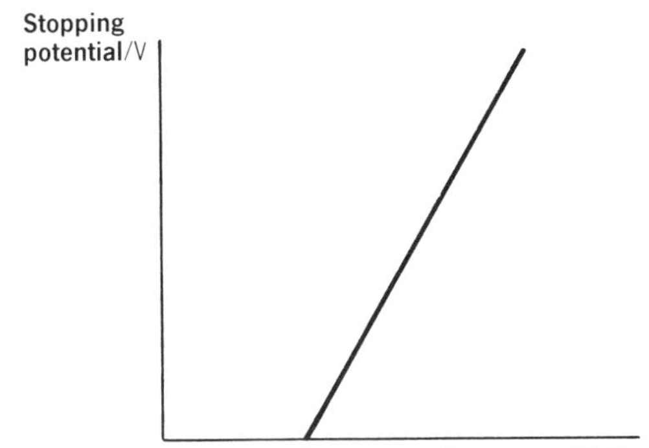

Figure 60.6

The original test of Einstein's equation and the measurement of the Planck constant was carried out by Millikan in 1916 using the apparatus shown in Figure 60.7.

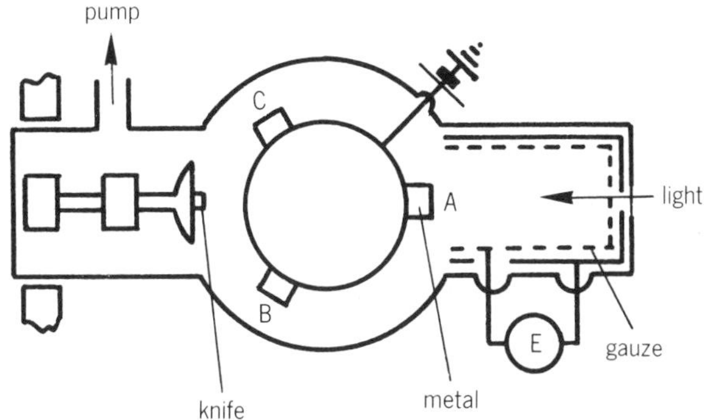

Figure 60.7

Targets of different metals (A, B and C) were fixed to a rotatable table inside an evacuated glass tube about 30 cm long. Monochromatic light was allowed to fall on the target and, if the frequency was high enough, photoelectrons were emitted. These electrons were collected by the gauze and the electrometer registered a small current. The potential of the target was then raised to a value at which the current in the electrometer fell to zero; this potential was the stopping potential for the target metal. By varying the incident frequency a graph can be plotted as shown in Figure 60.6. The Planck constant can be found from the graph by using either the gradient or the intercept. Since V is the stopping potential for a frequency f, then

$$eV = hf - hf_0 = \tfrac{1}{2}mv^2$$

If $V = 0$ then $f = f_0$, and the gradient $= h/e$.

Since the metal surface must be perfectly clean to obtain good results Millikan used a knife in the tube which could scrape the metal surfaces to remove any impurities such as an oxide film.

From such experiments the value of the Planck constant h was found to be 6.63×10^{-34} J s.

8 Explain the phenomenon of photoelectric emission using the potential well model.

9 The work function of potassium is 2.0 eV. What potential would have to be applied between a potassium surface and the collecting electrode to just prevent the emission of photoelectrons when the surface is illuminated with light of wavelength 350 nm?

What would be the speed and kinetic energy of the most energetic electrons emitted in this case? [L]

10 The work function for caesium is 1.88 eV.

(*a*) What is the longest wavelength that can cause photoelectric emission from a caesium surface?

(*b*) What is the maximum velocity with which electrons will be emitted from a caesium surface if light of wavelength 400 nm falls on it?

(*c*) What potential difference will just prevent a current from passing through a caesium photocell illuminated with light of wavelength 400 nm? [O]

11 When ultraviolet light of wavelength 150 nm falls on a certain well-insulated metal surface in a vacuum, the metal attains a potential of +6.6 V relative to its surroundings. For wavelengths of 300 nm and 450 nm the corresponding potentials are +2.4 V and 1.0 V respectively.

(*a*) Calculate Planck's constant, the threshold wavelength and the work function of the metal. (Velocity of light = 3×10^8 m s^{-1}; charge on the electron = 1.6×10^{-19} C)

(*b*) Show how the quantum theory explains

(i) the effect of increasing the intensity of the light falling on the surface, and

(ii) the effect of illuminating the surface simultaneously with light of all three wavelengths, the surface being initially at earth potential in each case.

Example

Calculate the stopping voltage for a photocell containing a caesium emitting surface if light of wavelength 500 nm is shone on to it. The work function for caesium is 3.0×10^{-19} J.

Threshold frequency is given by:

$$W = hf_0 = 3.0 \times 10^{-19}$$

$$\text{Therefore } f_0 = \frac{3.0 \times 10^{-19}}{6.63 \times 10^{-34}} = 4.52 \times 10^{14} \text{ Hz}$$

Frequency of incident light $f = c/\lambda$
$= 3 \times 10^8/500 \times 10^{-9}$
$= 6 \times 10^{14}$ Hz

Therefore the stopping voltage can be found from Einstein's equation in the form

$$eV = h(f - f_0)$$

$$eV = 6.63 \times 10^{-34} \times (6 \times 10^{14} - 4.52 \times 10^{14})$$

$$V = \frac{6.63 \times 10^{-34} \times 1.48 \times 10^{14}}{1.6 \times 10^{-19}}$$

$$= 0.61 \text{ V}$$

That is, the stopping voltage = 0.61 V.

We can also use this result to calculate the velocity of the photoelectrons as they leave the emitting surface, since $eV = \frac{1}{2}mv^2$. If the mass of the electron is 9.1×10^{-31} kg, then:

$$1.6 \times 10^{-19} \times 0.61 = \frac{9.1 \times 10^{-31}}{2} \times v^2$$

Therefore $v^2 = 2.14 \times 10^{11}$.
giving $v = 4.63 \times 10^5$ m s^{-1}.

12 A point source of monochromatic light of wavelength 247.5 nm radiates equally in all directions a total power of 0.4 W. The light falls normally on a metal surface of area 10^{-2} m^2 at a distance of 1 m. An electrode at a positive potential with respect to the surface collects all the emitted electrons and a current of 1 μA is measured. With the collector at a negative potential with respect to the surface, the current is zero if the potential difference is greater than 2 V. With a similar source emitting monochromatic light of wavelength 309.4 nm, the maximum collector current is 2 μA and the current is reduced to zero by a reverse potential difference of 1 V.

Interpret these results, including in your discussion a calculation of the number of photons reaching the photoelectric surface per electron emitted, for each wavelength. Comment on these results. ($h = 6.6 \times 10^{-34}$ J s; $e = 1.6 \times 10^{-19}$ C) [C]

Photoelectric cells

Photocells are devices whose electrical properties are affected by light. They may be used in cameras as light meters, in television cameras, in the audio part of a cine film, in solar batteries, in electronic ignition circuits and so on.

These are various devices that can be used to measure the intensity of incident light.

(*a*) **Photoemissive cells**: light falls on a sensitive surface and electrons are emitted, the number of photoelectrons produced being proportional to the intensity of the incident light;

(*b*) **Photovoltaic cells**: light is incident on a p–n junction – essentially a **photodiode** – and electron–hole pairs are produced, giving a small p.d. across the junction. In full sunlight such a silicon cell will give about 0.6 V on open circuit. Many spacecraft use large panels of up to 5000 such cells giving 100 W at 30 V. The phototransistor is simply a junction transistor in which light is able to fall on the base region producing electron–hole pairs. This small current is then amplified by the transistor (see page 369).

(*c*) **Photoconductive cells**, in which the resistance of the cell changes due to light.

One very common type of photoconductive cell is the light-dependent resistor (LDR). The characteristics of one such LDR (the ORP12) are shown in Figure 60.8. The surface of the cell is made of cadmium sulphide, the resistance of which decreases with increasing illumination. This is due to the energy of the light quanta releasing more conduction electrons. A cell made of lead sulphide sensitive to infrared radiation is used in electronic ignition circuits.

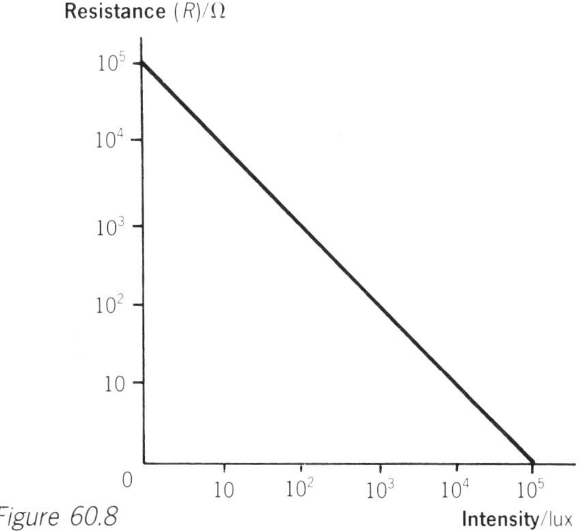

Figure 60.8

The space telescope solar cell array

Power for the space telescope (see page 163) is provided by two roll-out panels of solar cells with a total area of 33 m^2. The 48 760 cells with a mass of less than 64 kg will give a total power output of 5 kW at 34 V at the start of their five-year life in orbit.

It has been estimated that the surface of the Earth receives at most 75 per cent of the radiation that falls on the upper level of the atmosphere, and so the output of the space telescope array would be correspondingly less at sea level.

13 Using the data given above, calculate the following:
(*a*) the power output of each cell,
(*b*) the current produced by the array, and
(*c*) the current produced by each cell.

14 Assuming that the value of the solar constant at the Earth's surface is 1400 W m^{-2}, use the above data to calculate
(*a*) the energy falling on each square metre of the array per second,
(*b*) the efficiency of the array,
(*c*) the power output of the array at sea level, and
(*d*) the area of similar cells required to give an output of 1000 MW (that of a large power station).

Student investigation

Investigate the properties of the ORP12, using it to measure the energy output from a 12 V lamp. Devise and carry out experiments to investigate

(*a*) how the current through the cell varies with the power applied to the lamp,

(*b*) how the current through the cell varies with the wavelengths of the incident radiation.

Final inspection of the huge double-roll-out arrays for the Hubble space telescope, the arrays contain over 48 000 solar cells in a total area of 34 m^2 (British Aerospace)

61 · X-rays

In 1895 Roentgen was working with discharge tubes when he discovered that photographic plates placed near the tubes had become fogged although they had not been exposed to light. He decided that this effect must be due to the emission of some form of radiation from the discharge tube, and he named the radiation **X-rays**.

He deduced that these rays were electromagnetic in nature (it was later shown that their wavelength was much shorter than that of visible light). He realised that X-rays were produced when a beam of high-energy electrons hit a metal target: the greater the electron energy, the higher the frequency of the X-rays.

X-ray tubes

A diagram of a modern X-ray tube is shown below.

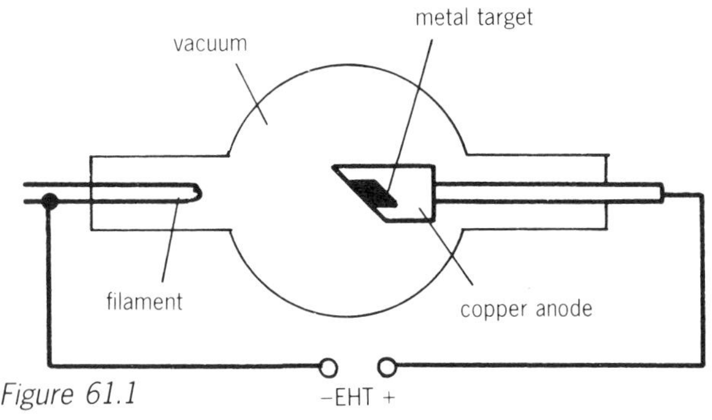

Figure 61.1

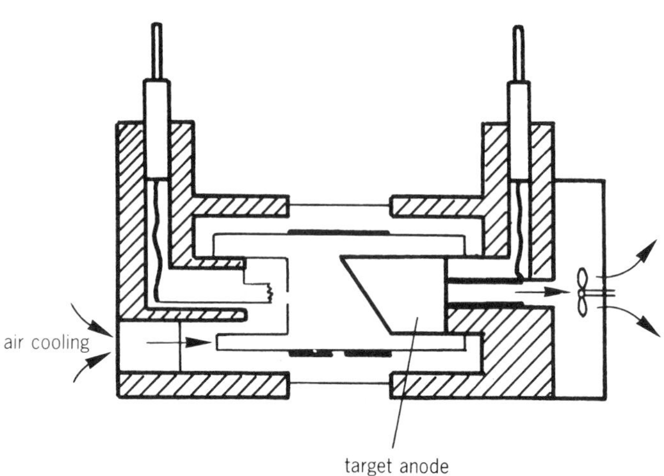

Figure 61.2

This type of tube was devised by Coolidge in 1913; it can operate with either a hot or a cold cathode. In the hot-cathode tube electrons are emitted by thermionic emission and then accelerated by voltages usually of the order of 20 kV, giving relatively long-wavelength X-rays called 'soft' X-rays. With a cold cathode, however, the voltages required to cause electron emission are much greater – around 100 kV – and these tubes produce 'hard' X-rays of much shorter wavelength, between 10^{-9} and 10^{-13} m, depending on the voltages used. For some applications potential differences of up to 1 000 000 V are used.

The intensity of the X-ray beam depends on the number of electrons striking the target per second and in the hot-cathode tubes this is controlled by the heater current. The wavelength depends on the voltage across the tube. The *penetrating power* of the X-rays is thus dependent on the accelerating voltage and the *intensity* of the beam on the heater voltage.

When the electrons collide with the target anode they lose their kinetic energy; some of this energy is converted into X-radiation, but much of it produces heat. In fact, less than 0.05 per cent of the kinetic energy of the electrons becomes X-ray energy.

To prevent damage to the anode it has to be cooled, either by air cooling, using fins, or by pumping cooling liquid through it. It may even be rotated during use to spread the wear over a larger area.

Uses of X-rays

X-rays were put to practical use less than three months after Roentgen discovered them. A few of their present-day applications are as follows:

art: detecting covered paintings;
engineering: checking metal castings for defects;
crystal analysis.
medical uses of X-rays: there are two main areas

(*a*) *diagnostic*. In a simple form, this would be the detection of a broken bone or a tooth cavity. With the addition of an absorber such as barium or iodine, X-rays may be used to check respiratory or digestive disorders.

(*b*) *therapeutic*. This use is almost completely restricted to the treatment of malignant cancers.

It is great importance in the use of X-rays for medical purposes that the dose given to both the patient and the operator is carefully controlled. X-rays can damage living tissue – hence their use for the destruction of tumours.

Calculation of X-ray wavelengths

If electrons are accelerated to a velocity v by a potential difference V and then allowed to collide with a metal target, the maximum frequency f of the X-rays emitted is given by the equation:

$$\tfrac{1}{2}mv^2 = eV = hf$$

Therefore

$$f = eV/h$$

This shows that the maximum frequency is directly proportional to the accelerating voltage.

Example

Calculate the minimum wavelength of X-rays emitted when electrons accelerated through 30 kV strike a target.

$$f = \frac{1.6 \times 10^{-19} \times 3 \times 10^4}{6.63 \times 10^{-34}}$$

Therefore the wavelength λ (= c/f) is 0.41×10^{-10} m = 0.041 nm (compared with some 600 nm for yellow light).

1 Calculate the frequency and wavelength of the highest-energy X-rays emitted by an X-ray tube operating at the following voltages: (*a*) 10 kV, (*b*) 25 kV, (*c*) 150 kV, (*d*) 200 KV.

2 The voltage of a certain X-ray tube is 45 kV. Only 0.5 per cent of the energy of the electron beam is converted to X-rays, and the rate of heat production in the anode is 500 W. Calculate
 (*a*) the current passing through the tube, and
 (*b*) the velocity of the electrons.
Comment on your answer to part (*b*).

Properties of X-rays

X-rays were shown to have the following properties:

(*a*) they pass through many materials more or less unchanged (but see the discussion of their absorption, below);

(*b*) they cause fluorescence in materials such as rock salt, calcium compounds or uranium glass;

(*c*) they affect photographic plates, causing fogging;

(*d*) they cannot be refracted;

(*e*) they are unaffected by electric and magnetic fields;

(*f*) they discharge electrified bodies by ionising the surrounding air;

(*g*) they can cause photoelectric emission;

(*h*) they are produced when a beam of high-energy electrons strike a metal target (the higher the nucleon number of the target the greater the intensity of the X-rays produced).

Absorption of X-rays

When X-rays pass through matter such as a human body they will lose energy in one or more of the following ways:

(*a*) The photoelectric effect – an X-ray photon transfers all its energy to an electron which then escapes from the atom.

(*b*) Compton scattering – an X-ray photon collides with a loosely-bound outer electron. At the collision the electron gains some energy and a scattered X-ray photon is produced travelling in a different direction from the incident photon and with a lower energy.

(*c*) Pair production – an X-ray photon with an energy greater than 1.02 MeV enters the intense electric field at the nucleus. It may be converted into two particles, a positron and an electron.

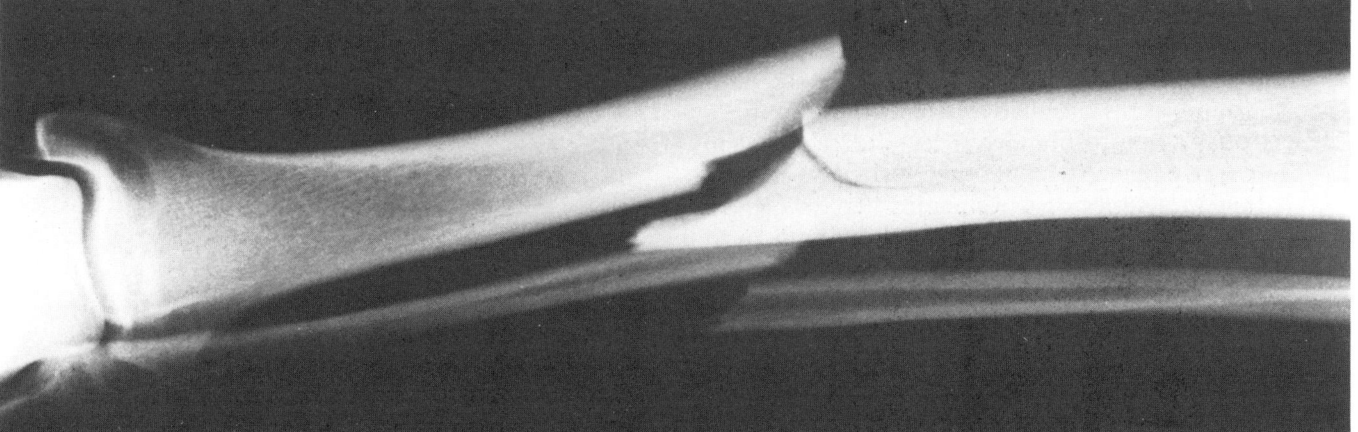

X-ray showing severe fracture of tibia and fibula (Addenbrookes Hospital)

3 What is the minimum potential difference between the cathode and anode of an X-ray tube if the tube is to produce X-rays of wavelength 0.05 nm?

4 An X-ray tube is operating at a potential of 125 000 V and 10 mA.

(*a*) If only 1 per cent of the electrical power is converted to X-rays, at what rate is the target being heated per second?

(*b*) If the target has a mass of 0.3 kg and is made of a material with a specific heat capacity of 150 J kg^{-1} K^{-1}, at what average rate would the temperature rise if there were not thermal losses?

5 In an X-ray tube the current through the tube is 1.0 mA and the accelerating potential is 15 kV. Calculate

(*a*) the number of electrons striking the anode per second,

(*b*) the speed of the electrons on striking the anode assuming that they leave the cathode with zero speed,

(*c*) the rate at which cooling fluid, entering at 10 °C, must circulate through the anode if the anode temperature is to be maintained at 35 °C. Neglect any of the kinetic energy of the electrons which is converted to X-radiation.

(Electronic charge = 1.6×10^{-19} C; mass of electron = 9.1×10^{-31} kg; specific heat capacity of liquid = 2.0×10^3 J kg^{-1} K^{-1}) [AEB 1984]

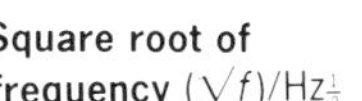

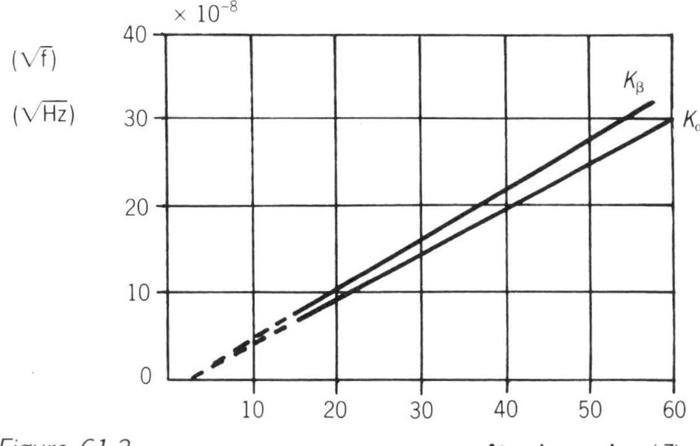

Figure 61.3

Moseley's law

In 1914 Moseley proposed a law showing how the X-ray frequency can be related to the proton (atomic) number Z of the target material. If f is the X-ray frequency, then

$$f = k(Z - b)^2$$

where k and b are constants, k having a value of 2.48×10^{15}.

Plotting a graph of Z against $\sqrt{f}$ will give a straight line (Figure 61.3), and in fact Moseley predicted the existence of elements 43, 61, 72 and 75 by the gaps that he found in his original version of the graph.

Electrons falling to the lowest level (or K-shell) in the atom (see page 420) from other excited levels give out X-rays in a series of wavelengths like an optical spectrum. This is known as the K-series, and individual lines are denoted by K_α, K_β and so on. Electron transitions ending on the second level are known as the L-series.

The following table shows the wavelengths of the K_α lines for some elements.

Element	*Proton number*	*Wavelength*/nm
Aluminium	13	0.823
Calcium	20	0.335
Manganese	25	0.210
Iron	26	0.194
Cobalt	27	0.179
Nickel	28	0.166
Copper	29	0.139
Bromine	35	0.104
Silver	47	0.056
Tungsten	74	0.021
Uranium	92	0.017

6 Do you think that it would be possible to produce X-rays from a tube with a target anode of hydrogen? Explain the reasons for your answer.

X-ray spectra

Using X-ray diffraction the spectrum produced by an X-ray tube can be investigated. Such a spectrum is shown in Figure 61.4, in which the two curves represent two different accelerating voltages.

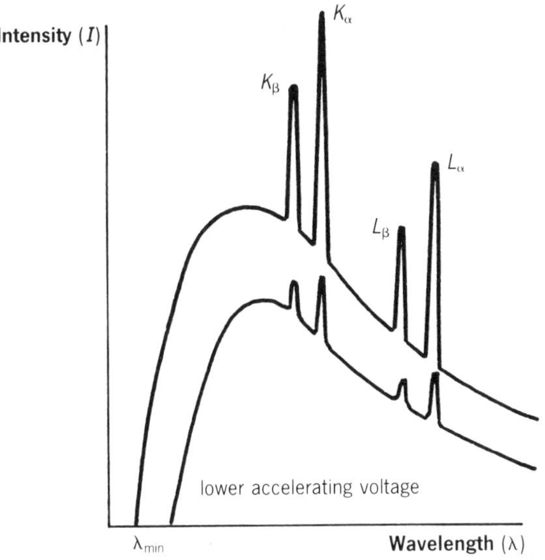

Figure 61.4

The X-ray spectrum can be considered in two parts:

(a) a continuous background, and

(b) a series of sharp peaks.

The background is due to radiation emitted as the electrons are slowed down by electromagnetic attraction of the nuclei of the material. The minimum wavelength – and therefore the maximum energy and frequency – of an X-ray in this spectrum is produced when an electron is stopped by just one nucleus. The rest of the curve is produced by electrons losing only part of their energy during collisions with many nuclei. The minimum wavelength λ_m is given by the equation:

$$\lambda_m = \frac{hc}{eV}$$

where V is the accelerating voltage and c the velocity of light: the smaller the value of V, the greater the minimum wavelength will be and the smaller the maximum frequency.

The peaks on the spectrum are characteristic of the particular target material. Electrons from the inner shells are removed completely by the bombarding electrons. An electron from an outer energy level falls back to fill the vacancy emitting a photon of a definite wavelength, thus giving a sharp peak on the spectrum.

7 Using the graphs in Figure 61.5 answer the following questions:

(a) explain why graph (a) shows four curves although the same single metal target was used for each;

(b) calculate the energies associated with the K_α and K_β lines shown in graph (b);

(c) calculate the accelerating voltages for each line on both graphs.

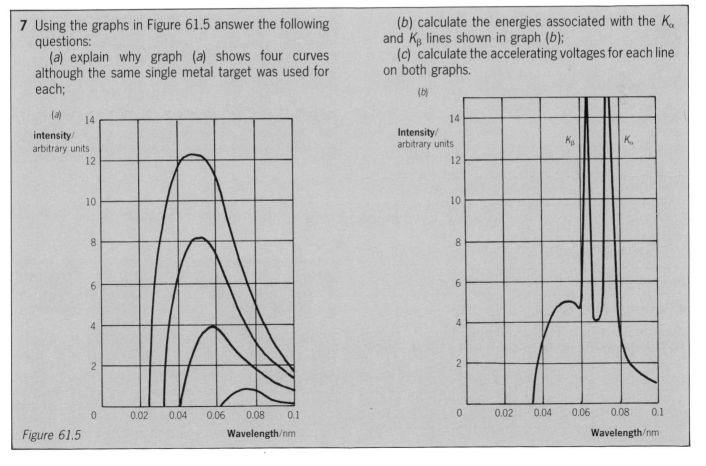

(a)

intensity/ arbitrary units

Wavelength/nm

(b)

Intensity/ arbitrary units

K_β K_α

Wavelength/nm

Figure 61.5

X-ray diffraction

The measurement of X-ray wavelengths proved to be very difficult because they are so short. In 1912, however, von Laue used a crystal in an attempt to diffract the X-rays after failing to do this with ordinary optical-style diffraction gratings, and was successful.

His work was followed up by Friedrich and Knipping, and good X-ray diffraction patterns were produced. To give diffraction the obstacles must be only a few wavelengths apart and so the atoms in a crystal lattice were ideal for X-ray diffraction since their separation is about 10^{-10} m (0.1 nm). Sir William and his son Sir Lawrence Bragg used a crystal as a reflection diffraction grating.

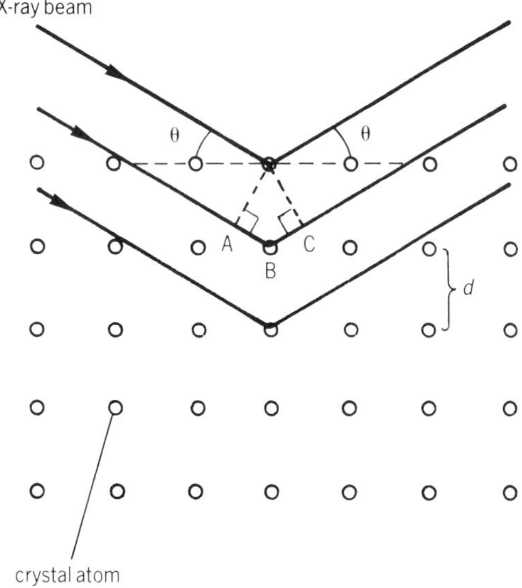

Figure 61.6

In Figure 61.6 a beam of X-rays of wavelength is incident at a **glancing angle** θ on a crystal where the atomic planes are separated by a distance *d*. The path difference between the waves reflected at the top plane and those reflected at the second plane is ABC $= 2d \sin\theta$.

Constructive interference occurs when this path difference is equal to a whole number of wavelengths. Therefore

$$2d \sin\theta = m\lambda$$

where *m* is a whole number. (**Bragg's Law**)

This equation is useful in determining the structure of a crystal, because if the X-ray wavelength is known the atomic spacing in the crystal can be found.

If the interatomic spacing can be found from X-ray diffraction, then the Avogadro constant can be calculated. The electron charge can then be found, from $F = Le$.

Alternatively X-ray diffraction can provide a means of calculating X-ray wavelengths if the interatomic spacing is known.

Example

A beam of X-rays of wavelength 0.3 nm is incident on a crystal, and gives a first-order maximum when the glancing angle is 9.0 degrees. Find the atomic spacing.

$$d = \frac{\lambda}{2\sin\theta} = \frac{0.3}{2 \times 0.156}$$
$$= 0.96 \text{ nm}$$

8 A beam of X-rays of wavelength 0.15 nm is incident on the face of a crystal of calcite. The smallest angle at which there is a strongly reflected beam is 15° to the cleavage face. Calculate the distance between successive layers of the crystal lattice.

9 Sketch the spectrum showing X-ray intensity and wavelength for a given metal target. Explain any important features of your curve.
Also sketch on the same axes a curve that represents a smaller accelerating voltage for the same target.

10 The potential difference between the target and cathode of an X-ray tube is 50 kV and the current in the tube is 20 mA. Only 1% of the total energy supplied is emitted as X-radiation.
(*a*) What is the maximum frequency of the emitted radiation?
(*b*) At what rate must heat be removed from the target in order to keep it at a steady temperature?
(The Planck constant, $h = 6.6 \times 10^{-34}$ J s; electron charge, $e = 1.6 \times 10^{-19}$ C)

The use of a 2.7 cm microwaves to model the investigation of crystal structure by X-ray diffraction (UNILAB Ltd.)

62 · Radioactivity

In 1896 Henri Becquerel, who was Professor of Physics at the University of Paris, discovered that uranium salts could fog a photographic plate even if the plate was covered. He deduced that the salts were emitting some form of radiation that could pass through the wrapping. He also found that this radiation could ionise a gas, causing a charged electroscope to discharge.

In the same year Marie Curie and Schmidt discovered that thorium also produced this radiation.

In 1898 Marie Curie extracted a much more active material from the ore pitchblende, which is 80 per cent uranium oxide. She called the radiation **radioactivity** and the active material radium. Radium is so active that its compounds stay a few degrees above the temperature of their surroundings.

In 1900 the radioactive gases thoron and radon were discovered by Rutherford and Dorn.

Research showed that there were three different types of radioactivity and these were denoted by the Greek letters alpha (α), beta (β) and gamma (γ). The table below sets out the main properties of these radiations.

	Alpha-radiation	*Beta-radiation*	*Gamma-radiation*
Penetration	small	large	very large
Range in air	few cm	tens of cm	many metres
Charge	positive	+ or −	no charge
Deflection by electric or magnetic fields	some	large	none
Ionisation	10 000	1000	1
Velocity	$0.05c$	$0.9c$	c
Mass	heavy	light	none
Nature	helium nuclei	electrons	e.m. radiation

The energy of a radioactive particle is usually expressed in million electron volts (MeV); 1 MeV is the energy acquired by an electron when accelerated through a potential of one million volts.

$$1 \text{ MeV} = 1.6 \times 10^{-13} \text{ J}$$

Alpha-particles

The magnetic deflection of alpha-particles is difficult to produce; a field of 1 tesla gives a path of radius 39 cm for an alpha particle of energy 1.8 MeV, while a similar field acting on beta-particles of the same energy would give a radius of 0.75 cm. This suggests either that alpha-particles are heavier than electrons or that they move more slowly. It was found that both are true! They were also found to be very heavily ionising particles (this accounts for their short range in air) and to have a positive charge of $+2e$.

Rutherford and Royds made a direct identification of the alpha-particle in 1909. The apparatus they used is shown in Figure 62.1. Radon gas, an alpha-emitter, was enclosed in a glass tube A that had walls only 0.01 mm thick. The tube B was originally evacuated.

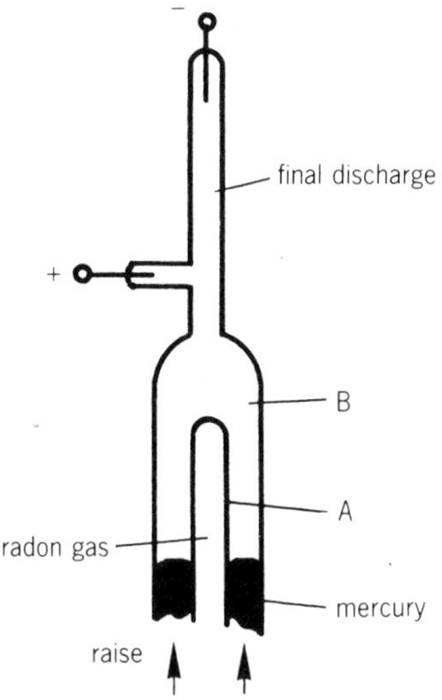

Figure 62.1

After a week the mercury level in B was raised and a discharge struck, forming a spectrum. On examination it was found to be the spectrum of helium. When the experiment was repeated with A initially filled with helium no spectrum was seen when a discharge was struck in B.

Rutherford reasoned that the alpha-particles produced by the radon collected electrons from the glass as they passed through the walls of tube A, thus becoming helium atoms.

The alpha-particles emitted by a source have a well-defined energy. Sometimes a source will emit alpha-particles of two different energies, but these two values are distinct and separate.

The distinct nature of these energies is very good evidence for the fact that the alpha-particle is emitted on its own, not in conjunction with another particle. Only two particles are involved, the alpha-particle and the nucleus that has emitted it.

Beta-particles

From measurements of their charge-to-mass ratio Becquerel showed that beta-particles were in fact electrons, but relativistic effects have to be taken into account in the measurement, as some beta-particles are emitted with 90 per cent of the velocity of light. It can be shown from the special theory of relativity that at this velocity their mass is some 2.4 times their rest mass (see page 469). How electrons come to be emitted from the *nucleus* of an atom will be considered below.

If we record an energy spectrum of the beta-particles emitted from a radioactive source, it is found that they have a range of energies between about zero and a maximum (Figure 62.2). The reason is that the beta-particles come from the decay of a neutron into a proton and an electron and also a very light particle called a neutrino ν:

$$\mathrm{n} \rightarrow \mathrm{p} + \mathrm{e} + \nu$$

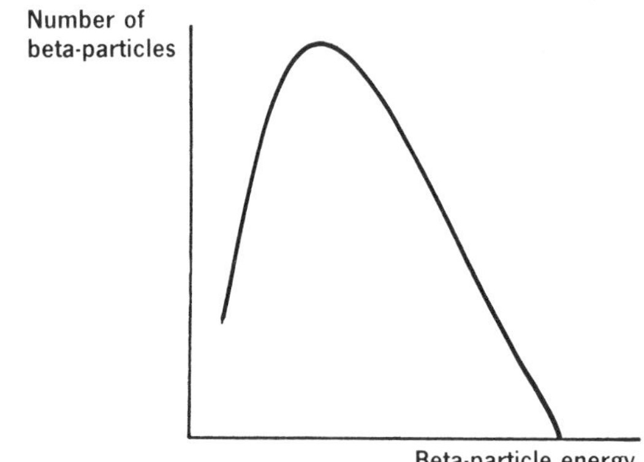

Figure 62.2

The variation in beta-particle energy arises from the way in which the energy is shared out between these three products: sometimes more energy goes to the electron and sometimes more to the neutrino.

Gamma-rays

In 1914 Rutherford and Andrade managed to diffract gamma-rays by a crystal, showing them to be electromagnetic in nature with a wavelength of about 10^{-13} m. Gamma-rays are the result of an initial emission of a alpha-particle, a beta-particle or a neutron from a nucleus, leaving the nucleus in an excited state. The nucleus then loses energy, just as an excited atom does, but the nucleus does not radiate visible light but gamma-radiation. Sources of gamma-radiation show a line spectrum similar to that obtained for X-rays; for example, cobalt-60 gives two gamma-rays of energies 1.17 and 1.33 MeV.

The absorption of radiation

In a vacuum the range of either alpha-, beta- or gamma-radiation is infinite, since no ions are produced. The intensity of gamma-radiation decreases with distance, following the inverse square law since it is electromagnetic radiation.

Alpha-particles have a very short range in materials and their range is difficult to measure. The absorption of gamma-radiation can be studied quite easily, however, and it is found that the intensity of the radiation I varies with distance through the material t, according to the equation

$$\log I = a - \mu t$$

where μ is a constant for the material.

Student investigation

The absorption of gamma-radiation is of crucial importance in the nuclear power industry and this investigation is designed to measure this.

(*a*) **Absorption in air**
Set up the Geiger tube and scaler as shown in Figure 62.3, and compare the count rates at different distances from the source. Plot a linear graph of the results.

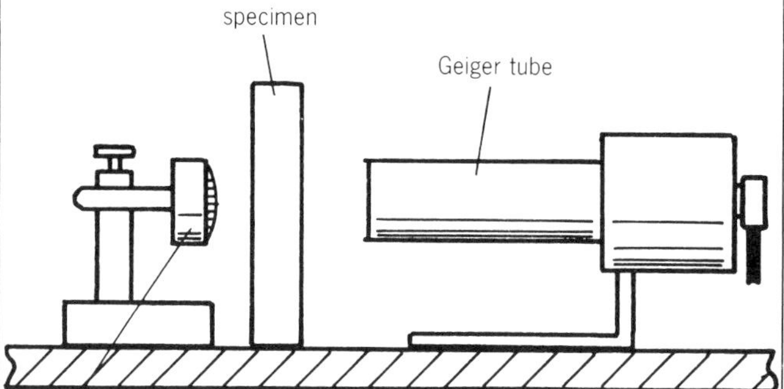

Figure 62.3

(*b*) **Absorption in building materials and soil**
Prepare a suitable series of absorbers of concrete, brick and soil. Using the Geiger tube and scaler as before, measure the intensity of the gamma-beam with different thicknesses in place. Plot linear graphs relating count rate to absorber thickness, and deduce the thickness of each absorber required to reduce the gamma-ray flux to one-tenth of the original value.

Observe the normal radioactivity safety procedures when carrying out these investigations.

Detectors of radioactivity

The following instruments are used for detecting radioactivity.

(*a*) **Photographic plates.** Though these are not good for gamma-radiation, as there is insufficient ionisation, alpha- and beta-particles produce visible tracks in the plate where they pass.

(*b*) **Electroscope.** The leaf falls, due to ionisation of the surrounding air. This is rather a crude method and is not good for gamma-radiation.

(*c*) **Ionisation chamber.** This is a can with a coaxial wire electrode. A 5 μC source will give a current of about 10^{-9} μA in a small chamber.

(*d*) **Scintillation counter.** Particles or gamma-rays produce a flash of light in a crystal (zinc sulphide and silver for alpha- and beta-radiation, sodium iodide and tellurium for gamma-rays). This is detected by a photomultiplier tube and the electrical pulse recorded.

(*e*) **Bubble chamber.** Radiation creates tracks of bubbles in a superheated liquid such as hydrogen or propane. The bubble chamber is a much more effective detector of radiation than the cloud chamber, because of the much greater number of atoms per unit volume of the liquid in it. This means that there is a much greater chance of a collision occurring between an incoming particle and a nucleus.

(*f*) **Solid-state detector.** This is a reverse biased p–n junction of semiconductor material, and when ionising radiation falls on it ion pairs are formed at the junction, thus producing a current through it.

Other important detectors are the spark counter, the Geiger counter and the cloud chamber. We shall consider these now in detail.

Student investigation

The ionising ability that forms the basis of many detectors of radioactivity may be investigated by the following experiment.

Use a d.c. amplifier as shown in Figure 62.4, with a wire gauze connected around a central brass electrode. Set the meter to the 10^{-11} A range and connect the output to a 1 mA range meter.

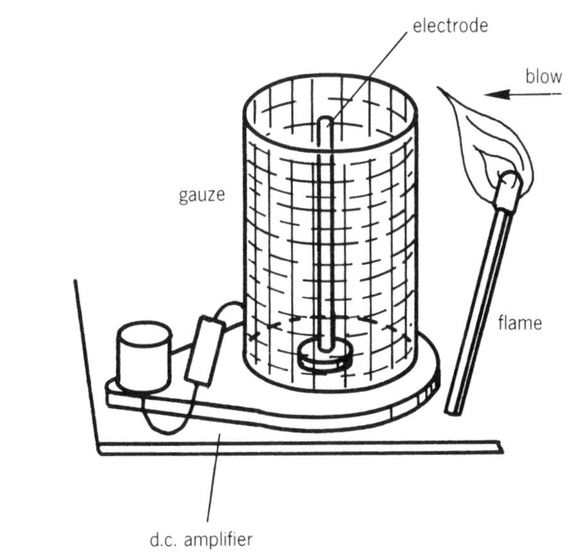

Figure 62.4

(*a*) Hold a lighted splint just outside the gauze and blow the flame gently towards the electrode.

(*b*) Hold a 5 μC radium source, just above the rod using a pair of tweezers.

In each case observe the meter current.

The spark counter

This consists of a fine metal gauze mounted about a millimetre away from a thin wire (Figure 62.5). A voltage is applied between the two so that sparking takes place between them – this usually requires some 4000–5000 V. The voltage is then reduced until sparking just stops.

If an alpha-source is brought up close to the gauze it will ionise the air, and sparks will occur between the gauze and wire. With beta- and gamma-sources, however, insufficient ions are usually produced for sparking to take place. The spark counter can be used to measure the range of alpha-particles, and in nuclear research a stack of spark counters is used to show the track of a particle as a line of sparks.

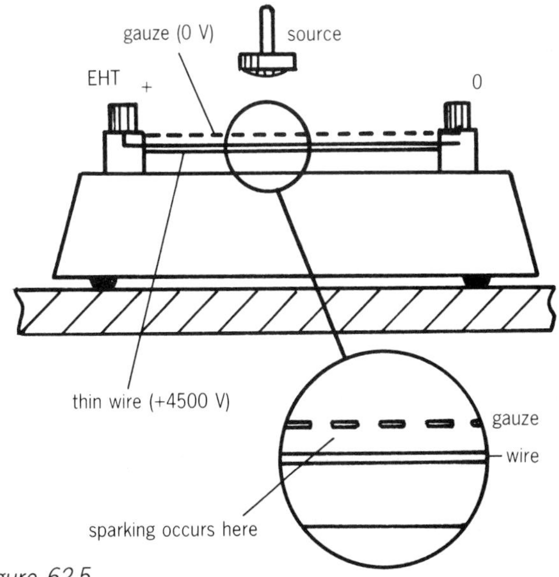

Figure 62.5

The Geiger–Mueller tube

A diagram of a Geiger–Mueller tube is shown in Figure 62.6.

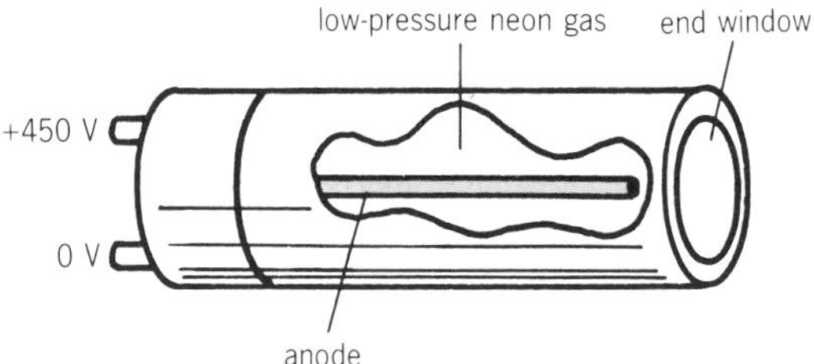

Figure 62.6

This device is basically a gas-filled cold-cathode diode, in which the anode is a metal rod fixed along the axis of a cylindrical cathode. The anode should be thin, so that an intense electric field is produced near it when a potential is connected between the anode and cathode. The end of a tube is closed by a 'window', the thickness of which varies from tube to tube depending on the type of radiation it is designed to detect.

The thickness of the end window is quoted in mg cm^{-2}; for alpha-particles it is about 2, for beta-particles about 25 and for gamma-rays many hundred. The tube contains neon at about 10 cm of mercury pressure, and a potential of about 450 V is applied between anode and cathode.

When a particle enters through the end window ions are produced in the gas; the positive ions travel towards the cathode while the electrons move towards the anode (Figure 62.7). As they move they produce further ions by collisions, a process known as **secondary ionisation**, and an avalanche of ions reaches the detecting electrodes. For an electron about 10^8 ions are produced in a few microseconds. This pulse is amplified in an external circuit and detected as either a meter reading or a sound. To prevent continuous secondary ionisation a little bromine gas is added to the tube, acting as a 'quenching agent' and absorbing the kinetic energy of the positive ions.

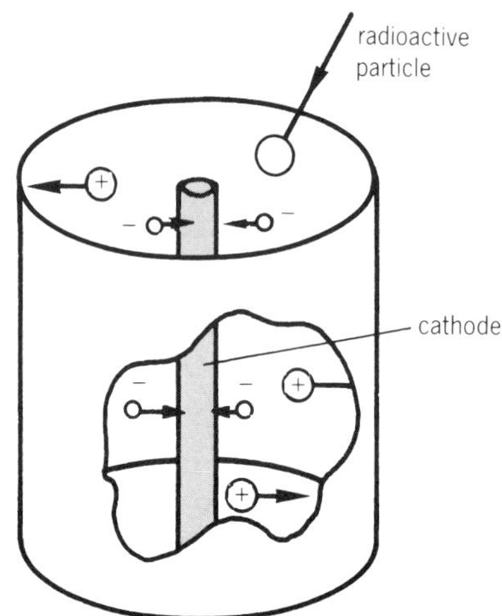

Figure 62.7

A typical Geiger tube can detect separate particles as long as they arrive more than 200 microseconds apart and therefore it has a maximum count rate of 5000 counts per second.

If the characteristics of the Geiger tube (the anode voltage related to the count rate) are recorded as shown in Figure 62.8, it can be seen that the tube should be operated in the so-called **plateau** region. In this area a small change of anode potential will have little effect on the count rate.

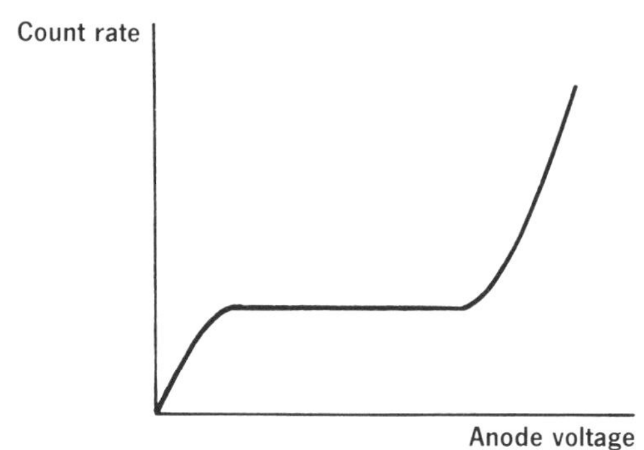

Figure 62.8

The Geiger tube may be fitted to a variety of detectors for investigating the activity of a radioactive source:

(*a*) a scaler – this device simply records the total number of pulses;

(*b*) a speaker and an amplifier – this will give an audible signal that becomes a continuous crackle when the activity is high;

(*c*) a ratemeter – this actually records the count rate (dN/dt – see page 444) and the output may be fed to a meter or to a storage facility such as a Vela.

If a Geiger tube with a thin end window is used in a darkened room, flashes of light may be observed in the tube when it is used to detect particles from an alpha source.

1 The energy of an alpha-particle emitted by polonium-210 is 3.9 MeV, and its range in air at s.t.p. is 35 mm. As it passes through the air the alpha-particle produces ion pairs, the energy required to produce each ion pair being about 30 eV.

(*a*) Estimate the number of ion pairs formed per mm.

(*b*) The ionisation per mm increases towards the end of the path. Suggest a reason for this.

If the pressure was reduced to one-hundredth of the original value, how would this affect the number of ions per mm? Explain your answer.

The cloud chamber

The first cloud chamber was made in 1911 by C.T.R.Wilson. Its main use is to show the tracks of radioactive particles rather than to measure the intensity of the radiation.

There are two types of cloud chamber: the expansion type and the diffusion cloud chamber. Their final results are similar but they use different methods to achieve it.

When a radioactive particle passes through air which is supersaturated with the vapour of a liquid the ions it produces act as centres on which the liquid can condense, and so a line of liquid droplets is formed along the track of the particle. The liquid condenses more readily on the ions because they are larger than the uncharged gas molecules. The length of the track is proportional to the energy of the particle.

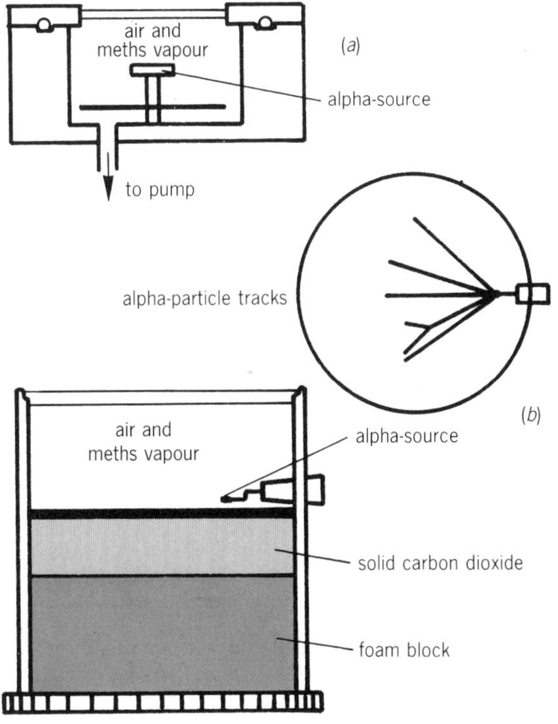

Figure 62.9

In the expansion cloud chamber shown in Figure 62.9(*a*), the supersaturated state is produced by rapidly lowering the pressure in the chamber, while in the diffusion cloud chamber (Figure 62.9(*b*)) solid carbon dioxide cools the chamber so that at one level the air is supersaturated. In both cloud chambers the liquid used is methylated spirits. As was mentioned earlier the cloud chamber, and more recently the bubble chamber, have been of considerable use in studying the tracks of particles and hence obtaining knowledge of their relative masses.

It can be shown that, for an incoming particle of mass m striking a stationary nucleus of mass M,

(*a*) if $m < M$ then $\theta < 90°$ and $\alpha > 90°$
(*b*) if $m = M$ then $\theta = 90°$ and $\alpha = 90°$
(*c*) if $m > M$ then $\theta > 90°$ and $\alpha < 90°$

where α is the angle between the final tracks of the two particles (Figure 62.10) and $\theta = 180° - \alpha$. The collisions are assumed to be perfectly elastic. Examples of such collisions would be:

(*a*) an alpha-particle striking a nitrogen nucleus,
(*b*) an alpha-particle striking a helium nucleus,
(*c*) an alpha-particle striking a hydrogen nucleus.

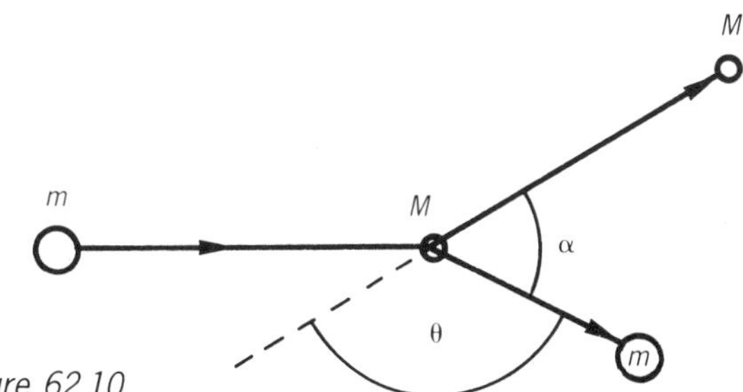

Figure 62.10

Neutral *K*-particle

Figure 62.11 is drawn from a photograph of an event that occurred in the bubble chamber at the Brookhaven National Laboratory in the USA. The neutral *K*-particle or kaon, formed in a collision of a negative pion with a proton, decays into a pair of oppositely charged pions. The positive pion decays further to a muon and a neutrino, which leaves no bubble track.

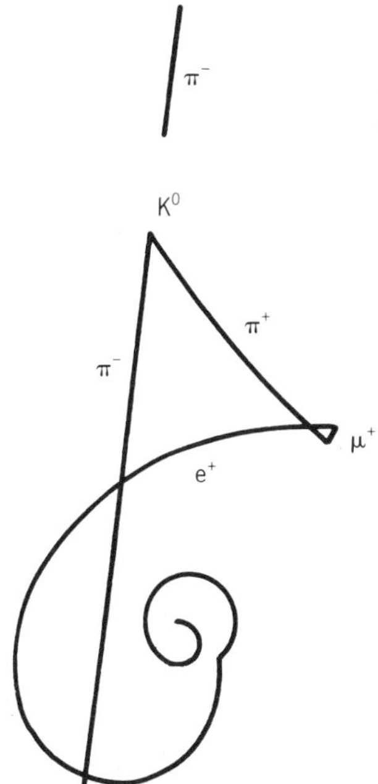

Figure 62.11

Finally the muon decays to a positron and two invisible neutrinos. A neutral lambda-particle was presumably made together with the *K*-particle, but it left the chamber without decaying and so left no track.

Safety precautions and the biological effects of radiation

Unfortunately the early workers with radioactivity did not know of its dangers; Marie Curie, for instance, died of leukaemia, a disease of the blood produced by prolonged exposure to radiation. With all types of radioactivity shielding is important, the thickness and type of shielding depending on the type of radiation.

Alpha-particles are not penetrating and aluminium sheet will stop them. Their only biological effects are to the surface of the skin, with the production of radiation 'burns'. The term burns is perhaps misleading – although the temperature rise produced is only a few thousandths of a degree, the burns do not heal since the molecular structure of the cells has been destroyed.

The penetration of beta-particles is rather greater and thicker aluminium is needed to stop these. Gamma-radiation is intensely penetrating, and many centimetres of lead are required to reduce the intensity from a large source to safe levels. Since gamma-radiation obeys the inverse square law in air, the best thing is to get as far away from a gamma-source as possible. Gamma-radiation also affects the internal organs of the body due to its high penetrating power.

Neutron radiation presents special problems. Because neutrons are uncharged they produce few ions and so have a relatively long range in body tissue, but because of their large mass they cause considerable damage when they collide with living cells. A neutron has about the same mass as a hydrogen nucleus, and since the body contains large numbers of hydrogen nuclei in its cells the neutrons lose a lot of energy and thus the cells are severely damaged. For the same reason neutrons are best stopped by materials containing a large number of hydrogen atoms – paraffin wax is effective.

Safety precautions

The following safety precautions should be observed when using radioactive sources.

1. If you are under 16 do not use the sources.
2. Never handle a source directly. Always use tongs or tweezers.
3. Never point a source towards anyone, including yourself.
4. Always return the source to its lead container after use.
5. Keep the sources locked away in a secure cupboard when not in use.
6. Keep as far away from a source as possible.
7. Never open a sealed radioactive source.
8. Report any accidents **immediately**.

Radiation can cause immediate damage such as radiation burns but possibly its long-term effects are even more serious. Besides leukaemia, it causes cancer and genetic damage since it affects the rapidly dividing cells in the body, such as those in the liver and the reproductive organs. Radiation can also damage the eye, causing cataracts which destroy clarity of vision. For these reasons radioactive sources must always be handled carefully and sensibly.

Units for radiation measurement

The unit of activity of a radioactive source used to be the curie (3.7×10^{10} disintegrations per second) but this has now been superseded by the **becquerel** (Bq). A source has an activity of 1 Bq if it emits 1 particle per second; thus a source labelled 1 curie has an activity of 3.7×10^{10} Bq.

The energy liberated by radiation within a material is known as the **radiation dose** and is measured in units known as **grays**. A gray is an energy liberation of 1 J per kilogram of the material.

Different radiations affect the body more than others, each having what is known as a **relative biological effectiveness** (RBE). Then

$$\text{effective dose} = \text{radiation dose} \times \text{RBE}$$

The relative biological effectiveness of some radiations are given below.

Radiation	*RBE*
beta, gamma, X	1
n (slow)	3
n (fast)	10
alpha	10–20
fission fragments	20

Wherever radioactive materials are in use the symbol shown in Figure 62.12 should always be displayed to warn other people, since radioactivity is invisible.

Figure 62.12

Radioactive decay

A radioactive isotope will emit radiation and therefore its activity will decrease as time passes.

The radiation emitted can be either alpha-, beta- or gamma-radiation, and a given source may emit radiation of more than one type in its decay process to a stable isotope. It is important to realise that this decay is a completely random process.

During radioactive decay the *mass* of the sample will decrease, due to the emission of alpha- or beta-particles, but the *total number of atoms* will remain constant. Gamma-emission takes place from an excited nucleus with no change of nucleon or proton number. Alpha-emission reduces the nucleon number by four and the proton number by two. Beta-emission leaves the nucleon number unchanged but increases or decreases the proton number by one. Examples of these three decay processes are given below, and illustrated in Figure 62.13:

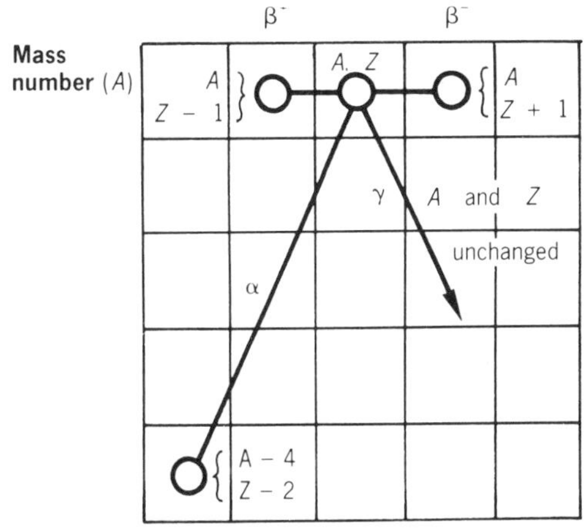

Figure 62.13

Alpha-emission: $^{231}_{91}\text{Pa} \rightarrow {}^{4}_{2}\text{He} + {}^{227}_{89}\text{Ac}$

Beta-emission: $^{11}_{4}\text{Be} \rightarrow {}^{0}_{-1}\text{e} + {}^{11}_{5}\text{B}$

Gamma-emission: $^{60}_{27}\text{Co} \rightarrow {}^{0}_{0}\gamma + {}^{60}_{27}\text{Co}$

The emission of beta-particles from the nucleus is explained by the decay of a neutron into a proton, an electron and a **neutrino**. The neutrino is a particle with no charge and a very small mass compared with that of the electron. The existence of the neutrino is a necessary part of nuclear Physics but we will not consider it further at this stage.

The radioactive decay of a sample will proceed at the same rate regardless of any changes in the physical or chemical conditions in its surroundings and it therefore gives a very precise and reproducible method of measuring time.

2 (*a*) How many alpha-particles are emitted altogether by an atom of uranium-238 when it decays to lead-206?

(*b*) As a result of a series of successive decay processes, the nucleon number of a radioactive atom decreases by 4 while its proton number is unchanged. What is the smallest number of particles that might be emitted, and what are they?

Student investigation

It is said that the emission of particles from a radioactive source is a purely random process, that is, if the activity of the source has an average value of 100 Bq then the count rate will not always be 100 but will vary on either side of this value. Theory suggests that if the number of occasions that a given count rate is observed is plotted against the count rate, a Gaussian distribution will be produced. The following experiment is to investigate this.

Set up the apparatus as shown in Figure 62.14, and select the appropriate program from the Vela handbook. Sample the count rate every second. The output may be stored in the Vela or displayed on a oscilloscope.

Draw a graph of your results.

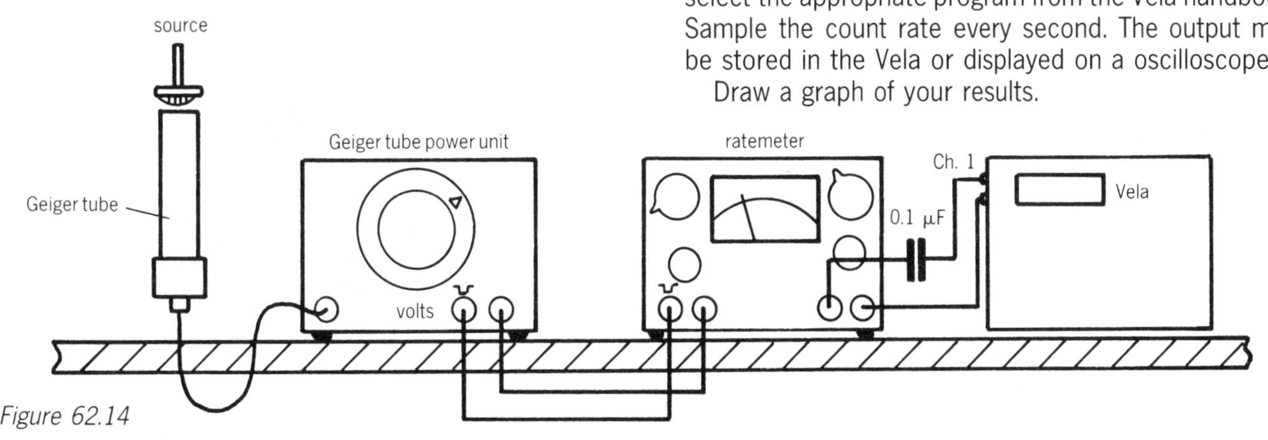

Figure 62.14

The radioactive decay law

We will now derive the law relating to the decay of a radioactive sample. Assume that the number of radioactive nuclei (dN) decaying in a time dt is proportional to the number (N) present at that instant. We can write this as:

$$\frac{dN}{dt} = -\lambda N \quad \text{or} \quad dN = -\lambda N\,dt$$

where λ is a constant known as the **radioactive decay constant** or **disintegration constant**. The negative sign shows that the number of radioactive nuclei decreases with time.

The quantity dN/dt is called the **activity** of the sample, and is measured in becquerels (see page 442).

If there are N_0 undecayed nuclei at time $t = 0$, then

$$\frac{dN}{N} = -\lambda\,dt$$

which when integrated becomes

$$N = N_0 e^{-\lambda t}$$

You can see from the equation that radioactive decay is a random process following an exponential decay curve.

The constant λ may be written as

$$\lambda = \frac{-dN}{N\,dt}$$

which is the fractional number of nuclei present in the specimen that decay in unit time, as long as that time interval is small.

Figures 62.15 and 62.16 show how these results may be presented (both ignore the background radiation – see page 447).

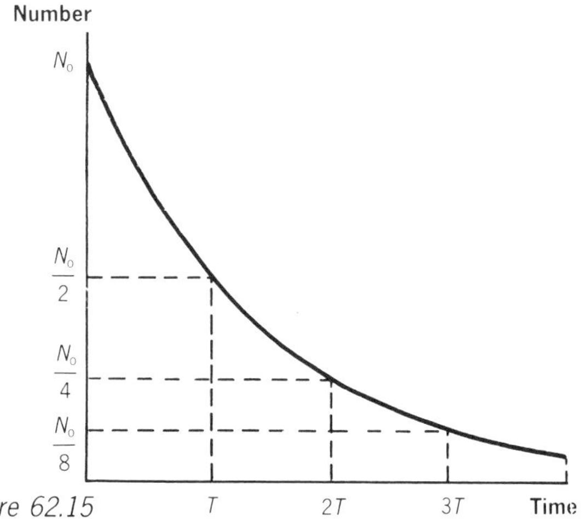

Figure 62.15

The graph of $\ln N$ against t, shown in Figure 62.16, is useful because it gives a straight line graph from which λ may be found, since the gradient of the line is $-\lambda$.

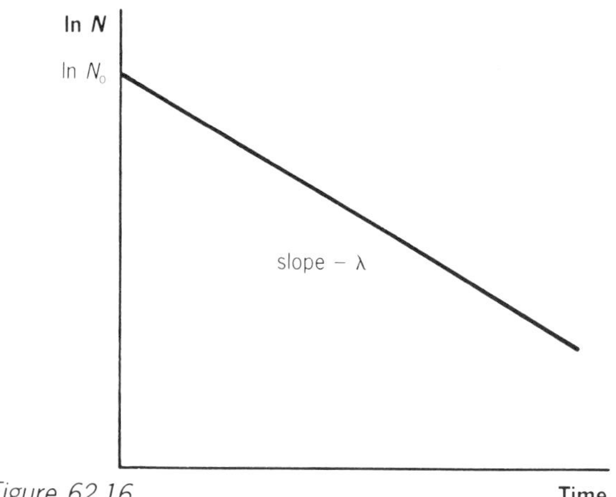

Figure 62.16

The half-life of a source

A very useful concept is the **half-life** T of a radioactive sample, which is defined as the time it takes for the activity of the sample to fall to half its original value. This is also the time it takes for the number of radioactive nuclei in the sample to reduce to half. The half-life is shown clearly in Figure 62.15.

Since this would be represented by $N/N_0 = \frac{1}{2}$, we can write

$$\ln(N/N_0) = -\lambda T$$
$$\ln 2 = \lambda T$$
$$T = \frac{0.693}{\lambda}$$

Some values of the half-lives and decay constants of some well-known isotopes are given in the following table.

Isotope	*Half-life*	*Decay constant/s*$^{-1}$
Uranium-238	4.5×10^{9} years	5.0×10^{-18}
Plutonium-239	2.4×10^{4} years	9.2×10^{-13}
Carbon-14	5570 years	3.9×10^{-12}
Radium-226	1622 years	1.35×10^{-11}
Radon-222	31.1 minutes	3.7×10^{-4}
Free neutron	10.8 minutes	1.1×10^{-3}
Bismuth-214	1.6×10^{-4} s	4.33×10^{3}
Helium-5	6×10^{-20} s	1.2×10^{19}

Isotopes with short half-lives will have large decay constants, and vice versa.

Example

A sample of material is found to contain 2 g of the isotope gold-199. How much of this isotope will remain 10 days later? (The half-life of gold-199 is 3.15 days.)

$$N = N_0 e^{-\lambda t}$$
$$= 2 \times e^{-2.55 \times 10^{-6} \times 8.64 \times 10^5}$$
$$= 0.22 \text{ g}$$

We could work with the time in years, days or seconds as long as the units for λ are consistent.

Student investigation

Determine the half-lives of the two radioactive samples represented by the two graphs in Figure 62.17.

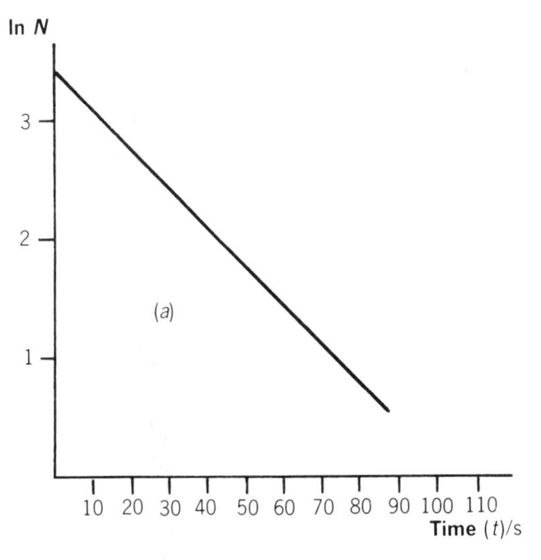

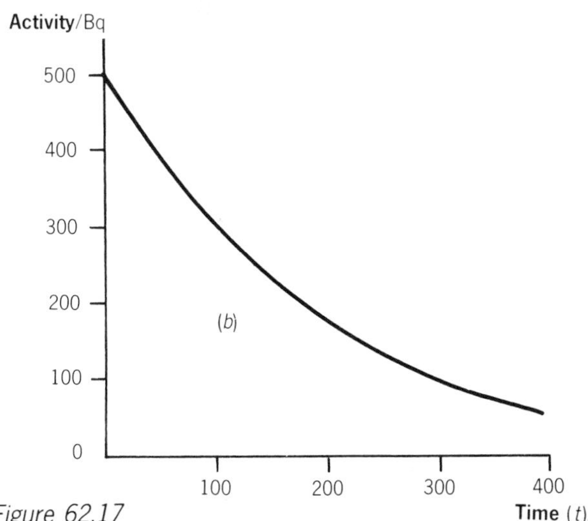

Figure 62.17

3 Two radioactive sources A and B initially contain equal numbers of radioactive atoms. Source A has a half-life of one hour and source B a half-life of two hours. Calculate the ratio of the rate of disintegration of source A to that of source B
(*a*) initially,
(*b*) after 2 hours,
(*c*) after 10 hours. [O & C]

4 The following measurements (after correction for the background count) were obtained from a piece of silver that contains a small quantity of the radioactive isotope silver-112.

Time/hours	0	0.5	1.0	1.5	2.0	
Counts/minute^{-1}	409	258	326	270	254	
Time/hours	2.5	3.0	3.5	4.0	4.5	5.0
Counts/minute^{-1}	226	206	180	163	149	129

Plot the results to give a linear graph and hence determine the half-life of silver-112.

5 What mass, in grams, of an original 4 g of radium would remain after a lapse of 200 years, given that the half-life of radium is 1600 years?

6 A school science department bought a strontium beta-source in 1965. If the activity of the source was such that it emitted 10^4 beta-particles per second initially, calculate the activity in 1986 given that the half-life of strontium-90 is 28 years.

Power from radioactive decay

The energy from radioactive decay can be used to power devices such as cardiac pacemakers, atomic lights (materials that give out visible light due to the energy released as radiation passes through them) and spacecraft. The heat produced by the decay may be found as in the example shown below.

Example

Consider the decay of radium-226. The molar mass is 226 and therefore each gram contains 2.66×10^{21} atoms. Radium emits alpha-particles with an energy of 4.7 MeV and has a half-life of 1622 years or 5.12×10^{10} s. The initial power output of the source is therefore 0.03 W.

Of course, sources with shorter half-lives and emitting alpha-particles of similar energies will produce greater powers.

Measurement of half-life

(i) Short half-lives

If an isotope's half-life is less than a few days or so it can be measured directly. This is simply done by plotting the activity A against time t and reading off the half-life T from the graph.

Alternatively a second graph can be plotted of ln A against time t, and this should give a straight line with slope $-\lambda$. Since $T = 0.693/\lambda$, we can then calculate T.

The radioactive gas thoron (radon-220) is often used in school experiments, since it has a half-life of about 53 s, and readings taken over a few minutes will give a satisfactory decay curve. The equation for the decay is:

$$^{220}_{86}\text{Rn} \rightarrow {}^{216}_{84}\text{Po} + {}^{4}_{2}\text{He}$$

Student investigation

When carrying out this experiment remember that you are using **radioactive gas**, and observe all the normal safety procedures carefully.

The apparatus is shown in Figure 62.18. The output of the electrometer can be to a meter or to an instrument such as a Vela.

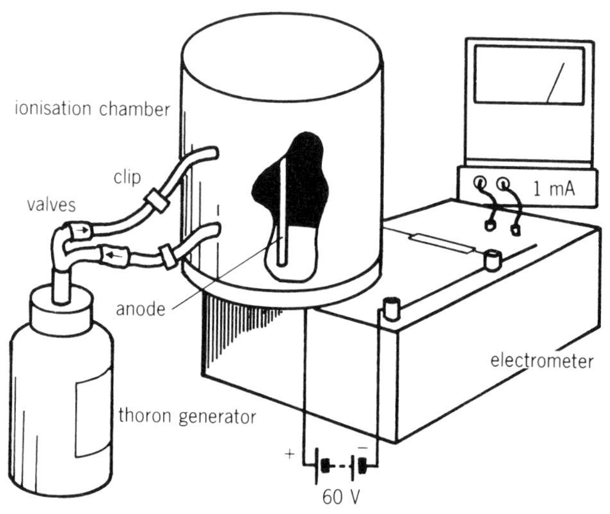

Figure 62.18

Check that the meter is correctly zeroed with the tube clamps closed, then open the clamps and puff radioactive gas into the ionisation chamber until the reading on the meter nears full scale deflection.

Close the clamps and start the stopclock, recording the meter reading every five seconds. Two minutes of readings should be sufficient.

Plot the results as suggested above, and thence determine the half-life of thoron.

7 A pupil uses the ionisation chamber method to measure the half-life of thoron and obtains a result of 55 s.

The lab assistant refuses to pack the apparatus away until the count rate due to the decay of thoron is 10 per cent of that found at the end of the experiment. How long must she wait before clearing the apparatus away?

(ii) Long half-lives

Clearly method (i) is quite impractical for isotopes with long half-lives. The decay over a few days for an isotope with a half-life of say 10^6 years would be negligible. The following method can be adopted for these isotopes.

The radioactive decay equation is:

$$N = N_0 e^{-\lambda t}$$

Therefore $$\frac{dN}{dt} = -\lambda N$$

But the number of particles of the long-lived isotope in the specimen (N) will be more or less constant over a short time and so we can write

$$N = \frac{mL}{A}$$

where L is the Avogadro constant (6.02×10^{23}), m is the mass of the specimen in grams and A is the relative atomic mass of the material.

Therefore if the count rate (dN/dt) is measured we can calculate the half-life T from the equation:

$$\frac{dN}{dt} = \frac{-\lambda mL}{A} = \frac{-0.693mL}{TA}$$

(iii) Very short half-lives

When the half-life is very small (a second or less, say) both these methods are unsuitable. Such half-lives may be found either from the tracks in cloud or bubble chambers or from the equilibrium condition for a decay series. (For full details of this method see page 448.)

Example

A sample of ore is found to contain 0.1 g of bismuth-214 and 0.015 µg of polonium-214. If the half-life of bismuth-214 is 1200 s, find the half-life of polonium-214.

Using the relationship from page 448, we have

$$\text{half-life of polonium-215} = \frac{214 \times 1200 \times 0.015 \times 10^{-6}}{214 \times 0.1} = 1.8 \times 10^{-4}\ \text{s}$$

Background radiation

Any experiments with radioactivity should allow for the radiation from natural sources. This is known as **background radiation**, and may come from several origins:

(*a*) cosmic radiation;

(*b*) radioactive rocks – background radiation is greater over rocks such as granite;

(*c*) radioactive contamination of the apparatus;

(*d*) fallout and other artificial effects – we may hope that this is negligible;

(*e*) radioactive potassium and carbon in the body;

(*f*) X-rays from television screens.

The sum total of all these sources is likely to be small – some 20 to 50 counts per minute at most. Their relative proportions are shown in the table below.

Source	*% activity*
Radiation from rocks	43
Cosmic rays	28
Potassium-40 in body	20
Radon in body	2
Radon in air	1
Carbon-14 in body	1
Other	5

An alternative version of the content of background radiation is shown below (by permission of the UKAEA).

Source	*% activity*
Radon gas	33
Medical	20.7
Rocks and soil	16
Internal	16
Cosmic radiation	13
Fallout	0.4
Occupational	0.4
Miscellaneous	0.4
Nuclear waste	0.1

The background radiation received by a person in a year is roughly equal to the dose that would be received in 5 minutes due to a 1 curie source of cobalt-60 placed one metre away. Since the body receives the background radiation over a long period the cells are able to regenerate.

For example, a piece of granite from the edge of Dartmoor near Ivybridge gave a count rate of 34 counts per minute when measured in Taunton, while the normal background count rate in Taunton is some 19 to 20 counts per minute (although this did rise after the Chernobyl accident). (See page 457)

Even eighteen months after the destruction of the reactor at Chernobyl (see page 457) there were restrictions on the sale of lambs from North Wales and the Finnish government has put a safety limit of 1200 Bq per kg on reindeer meat.

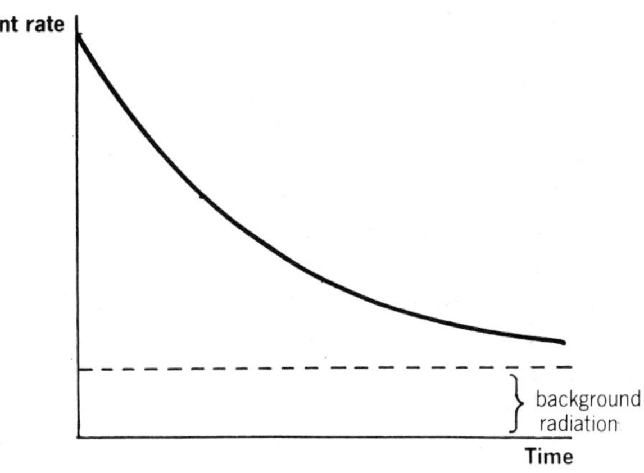

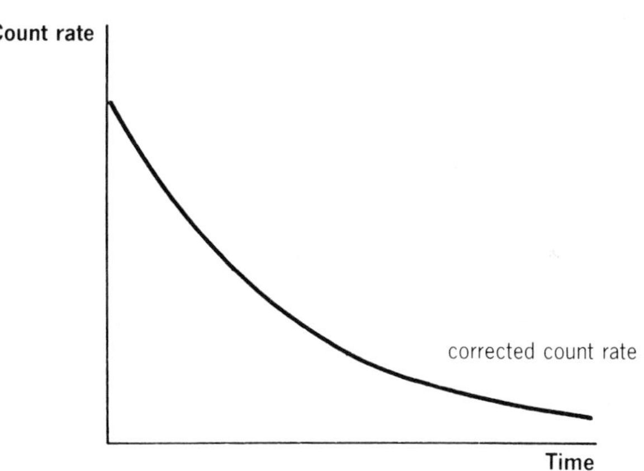

Figure 62.19

Allowance for background radiation

In accurate experiments where measurements of radiation are taken, an allowance should be made for the background radiation.

The two graphs in Figure 62.19 show the effect of allowance for this background count.

Example

Calculate the count rate produced by 0.1 μg of Caesium 137. (The half life of Cs 137 = 28 years = 8.83×10^8 s)

$$\text{Number of atoms} = mL/A = \frac{0.1 \times 10^{-6} \times 6.02 \times 10^{23}}{137} = 4.39 \times 10^{14}$$

$$\text{Count rate} = \frac{dN}{dt} = -\lambda N = -7.8 \times 10^{-10} \times 4.39 \times 10^{14} = 3.45 \times 10^5 \text{ Bq}$$

8 Define the decay constant λ of a radioactive isotope. Deduce the time dependence of the decay of emission from a radioactive source.

A target of gold ^{197}Au is irradiated with thermal neutrons. The isotope ^{198}Au (half-life 2.7 d) is produced at a constant rate of 1 atom of ^{198}Au per 10^{12} atoms of ^{197}Au per second. At time t during the irradiation the number of ^{198}Au atoms in the target is $N(t)$. By considering both production and decay of ^{198}Au atoms in the target at time t, write down an equation for the rate of change of $N(t)$ with time. Show that the equation is satisfied by

$$N(t) = N_\infty(1 - e^{-\lambda t}),$$

where N_∞ is the number of ^{198}Au atoms in the target after a long irradiation. Why does the number of ^{198}Au atoms reach a maximum value which is independent of the length of a long irradiation?

The irradiation lasts 24 h and the target finally contains 10^4 Bq of ^{198}Au (1 Bq equals one decay per second). Find the mass m of the target, neglecting the number of ^{197}Au atoms changed to ^{198}Au. Why is it unnecessary to take the number of atoms changed into account? [O and C]

Uses of radioactive isotopes

These materials have a variety of uses and a selection of these are listed below.

(*a*) dating geological specimens, using uranium;
(*b*) dating archaeological specimens, using carbon-14;
(*c*) thickness measurement by back-scattered beta-radiation;
(*d*) treatment of tumours;
(*e*) sterilisation of foodstuffs;
(*f*) nuclear pacemakers for the heart;
(*g*) liquid flow measurement;
(*h*) tracing sewage or silt in the sea or rivers;
(*i*) checking blood circulation and blood volume;
(*j*) atomic lights using krypton-85;
(*k*) checking the silver content of coins;
(*l*) radiographs of castings and teeth;
(*m*) testing for leaks in pipes;
(*n*) tracing phosphate fertilisers using phosphorus-32;
(*o*) sterilisation of insects for pest control.

Some isotopes used in medical physics

(*a*) Iodine-131 with a half-life of 8.0 days and activity of 8μC may be taken as liquid or in a capsule.

(*b*) Technetium-99 with a half-life of 6 hours gives gamma-rays of 140 keV energy.

(*c*) Iodine-123 is suitable for medical studies since it gives no beta-radiation.

(*d*) Cobalt-60 sources of up to 10 000 curies have been used; such a source gives 200 R per minute at 1 m. Treatment is typically 3 grays (<2 m) a day for 20 days. (1 gray = 100 rads.)

Radioactive decay series

If the isotope that results from a radioactive decay is itself radioactive then it will also decay and so on. The sequence of decays is known as a **radioactive decay series,** and each isotope in the series a **daughter product** of the isotope above it in the series.

When uranium-238 decays to thorium-234 it is the start of a series of decay products that ends with the stable isotope lead-206. The decay of uranium is one example of a radioactive decay series and it is shown below.

Isotope	*Emissions*	*Half-life*
Uranium-238	α,γ	4.5×10^9 y
Thorium-234	β,γ	24 d
Protoactinium-234	β,γ	1.2 min
Uranium-234	α,γ	2.5×10^5 y
Thorium-230	α,γ	8.0×10^4 y
Radium-226	α,γ	1620 y
Radon-222	α	3.8 d
Polonium-218	α	3.1 min
Lead-214	β,γ	27 min
Bismuth-214	β,γ	20 min
Polonium-214	α	1.6×10^{-4} s
Lead-210	β, γ	19 y
Bismuth-210	β	5.0 d
Polonium-210	∝	138 d
Lead-206	stable	stable

The half-life of uranium-238 is so long that its disintegration rate is very nearly constant, and this is equal to the disintegration rate of each member of the series in equilibrium with it. It can be shown that for a radiaoctive series in equilibrium:

$$\lambda_1 N_1 = \lambda_2 N_2 = \lambda_3 N_3 = ...$$

and so on

$$N \propto \frac{1}{\lambda}$$

But the half-life of an isotope is given by $T = 0.693/\lambda$, and therefore

$$N \propto T$$

for a series. The mass of m of any isotope present is proportional to its relative atomic mass A and the number of atoms N, therefore

$$m \propto AT$$

There are also radioactive decay series beginning with thorium-232 and uranium-235.

Radioactive dating

(*a*) Carbon dating

It is worth considering this use more closely. The half-life of carbon-14 (5570 years) is just the right sort of length for use in dating archaeological specimens with ages up to a few thousand years.

Carbon-14 is continually being formed in the upper atmosphere. Cosmic rays can produce neutrons, and the following reaction may then occur:

$$^{14}_{7}\mathrm{N} + {}^{1}_{0}\mathrm{n} \rightarrow {}^{14}_{6}\mathrm{C} + {}^{1}_{1}\mathrm{H}$$

The carbon-14 is then absorbed by plants; these in turn are eaten by animals which may then be eaten by other animals. As soon as the animal dies the intake of radioactive carbon-14 stops and the proportion in the body starts to decrease (Figure 62.20). Therefore if the proportion of carbon-14 to carbon-12 is known at the start, the age of the specimen can be found once the amount of carbon-14 remaining in it has been measured. It has been found that the activity of carbon-14 in living materials is about 19 counts per minute per gram of specimen.

This method of dating can be used with success to determine not only the ages of animal remains but also those of wood, paper, cloth and other organic material.

One difficulty with this method is that it has to be assumed that the cosmic ray intensity has remained constant, and in fact this has been found not to be the case. By comparison with the tree rings in the extremely old bristlecone pines, however, a corrected carbon date can be found for objects over about 1500 years old. The trees are themselves dated by the carbon-14 method using dead parts in the bark. A comparison between the carbon date and that due to the tree rings is shown on the graph in Figure 62.21.

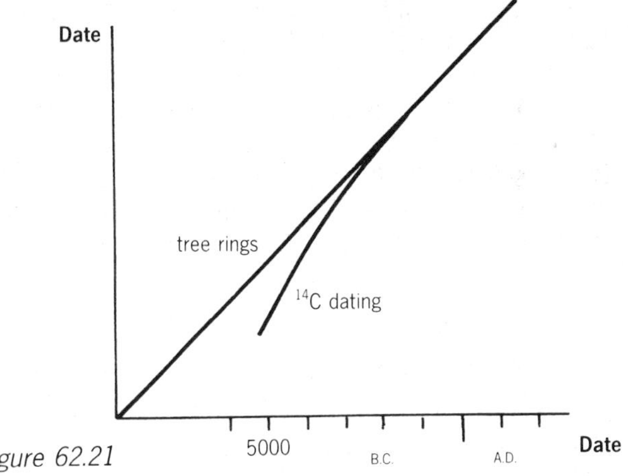

Figure 62.21

Example

A piece of bone from an archaeological site is found to give a count rate of 15 counts per minute. A similar sample of fresh bone gives a count rate of 19 counts per minute. Calculate the age of the specimen.

The activity A of a sample is proportional to the number of radioactive atoms within it. Therefore

$$A = A_0 e^{-\lambda t} \qquad \text{giving} \qquad 15 = 19e^{-\lambda t}$$

Therefore

$$0.236 = \lambda t$$

$$t = \frac{0.236}{\lambda} = \frac{0.236 \times 5570}{0.693} = 1897 \text{ years.}$$

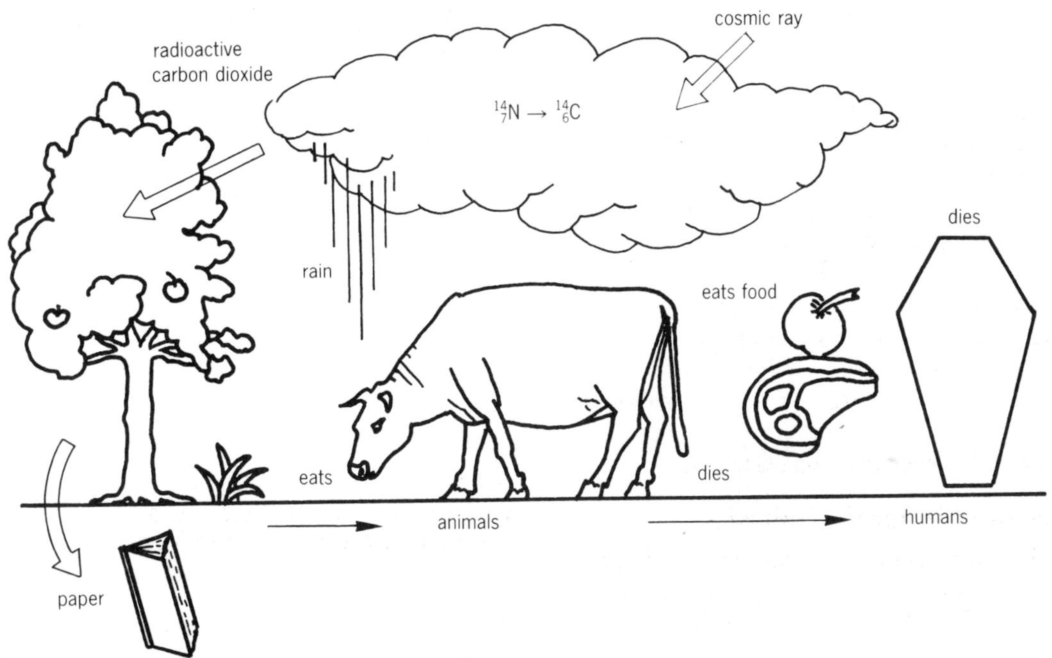

Figure 62.20

(*b*) Uranium dating

The very long half-life of uranium-238 (4.5×10^9 years) makes it particularly suitable for finding the age of rocks.

You can see from the uranium series on page 448 that the final stable isotope is lead-206, and if we assume that there was no lead in the rock when it was formed the ratio of the number of atoms of lead-206 (N_{Pb}) to the number of atoms of uranium-238 (N_U) will give us the age of the sample.

Example

Consider a rock sample in which the ratio of lead-206 to uranium-238 is 0.7.

Now the number of atoms initially (N_0) is the sum of the numbers of lead N_{Pb} and uranium N_U atoms present when the sample was analysed. Therefore

$$N_u = (N_U + N_{Pb})e^{-\lambda t}$$

where λ is the decay constant for uranium-238 and t is the time that has elapsed since the rock was formed. Therefore we can show that

$$1.7 = e^{\lambda t}$$

and so

$$\lambda t = 0.53$$

But $\lambda = 5 \times 10^{-18}\ s^{-1}$, and therefore

$$t = \frac{0.53}{5 \times 10^{18}}$$

$$= 1.06 \times 10^{17}\ s$$

$$= 3.36 \times 10^9\ \text{years}$$

The body of the 'bog man' discovered in Lindow Moss, Cheshire in 1984. Radio carbon dating was used to tell the age of the body – results varied from 500 BC to AD 500. (Topham Picture Library)

9 The ratio of the mass of lead-206 to the mass of uranium-238 in a certain rock is measured to be 0.42. If the rock originally contained no lead-206, estimate its age. (Half-life of uranium-238 $= 4.5 \times 10^9$ years)

10 A Geiger counter was used to measure the age of a piece of wood taken from the tomb of the Egyptian king Tutankhamun.

A solution containing 1.00 g of carbon from the wood was placed in the detecting tube and the count rate recorded was 1000 counts per hour. The background count at the time was 300 per hour and when living material containing 1.00 g of carbon was placed in the tube the count rate was 1600 counts per hour. If the half-life of carbon-14 is 5570 years, calculate the age of the wood.

11 The isotope $^{40}_{19}K$ with a half-life of 1.37×10^9 years decays to $^{40}_{18}Ar$ which is stable. Moon rocks from the Sea of Tranquillity show that the ratio of these potassium atoms to argon atoms is 1:7. Estimate the age of the rocks.

12 A patient was given an injection containing a small amount of the isotope sodium-24, which is a beta-emitter with a half-life of 15 hours. The initial activity of the sample was 60 Bq. After a period of 8 hours the activity of 10 ml sample of blood was found to be 0.08 Bq.

(*a*) Estimate the volume of the patient's blood from these measurement.

(*b*) What assumptions have you made in your determination?

13 The activity of carbon found in living specimens is 19 counts per minute, due to the carbon-14 present. The charcoal from the fire pit of an Indian camp site has an activity of 13 counts per minute. How long was it since the fire pit was last used?

63 · Nuclear properties

The Einstein mass–energy relation

In 1905 Albert Einstein published his special theory of relativity. One of the conclusions from this is that mass and energy are equivalent, and are related by the equation

$$E = mc^2$$

where E is the quantity of energy produced if a mass m is destroyed, and c is the velocity of light.

If a mass of 1 kg of *any* matter whatever could be destroyed, a huge amount of energy would be produced. By Einstein's equation,

$$\begin{aligned} E &= 1 \times (3 \times 10^8)^2 \\ &= 9 \times 10^{16}\ \text{J} \end{aligned}$$

If we think of this vast amount of energy in terms of electrical energy used in the home it is 2.5×10^{10} kW h. This would heat each of the 10 000 houses in a town with a 1 kW fire for nearly 300 years! Think of how much useful energy we could produce simply from the destruction of everyday rubbish.

Unfortunately no means has yet been devised for doing this on a large scale, but the conversion of mass to energy, and of energy to mass, can be observed at a nuclear level. When an electron and a positron collide and annihilate each other, two gamma-rays are produced showing matter being converted to energy!

The reverse of this is also observed. A 1 MeV gamma-ray can be converted into mass, giving 1.78×10^{-30} kg or roughly twice the mass of an electron – this explains the production of electron–positron pairs.

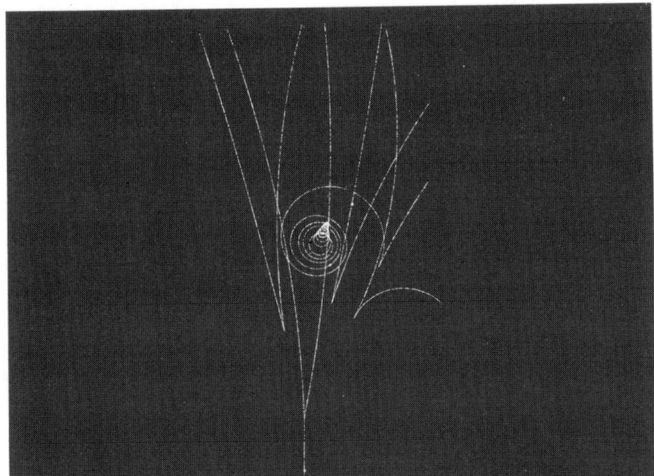

Matter and antimatter – the production of electron positron pairs and their tracks in a bubble chamber (Science Photo Library)

The masses of atomic particles are so small that it is convenient to define a new unit to measure them. This is known as the **atomic mass unit** (u). One atomic mass unit is defined as one-twelfth of the mass of one atom of the carbon-12 isotope. Using the conversion given above this gives:

$$\begin{aligned} 1\ \text{u} = \tfrac{1}{12}(19.92 \times 10^{-27})\ \text{kg} &= 1.66 \times 10^{-27}\ \text{kg} \\ &= 931\ \text{MeV} \\ &= 1.54 \times 10^{-10}\ \text{J} \end{aligned}$$

The following tables lists the masses of some of the most common particles on this scale.

Electron	0.000 548 u
Proton	1.007 275 u
Hydrogen atom	1.007 825 u
Neutron	1.008 665 u
Alpha-particle	4.001 508 u
Helium atom	4.002 604 u

1 Convert
(*a*) 1 MeV into J, kg, u,
(*b*) 1 J into kg, u, MeV.

2 What mass of coal must be burnt to release the same amount of energy as the destruction of 1 kg of matter? (Calorific value of coal = 3.528 MJ kg^{-1})

3 When an electron and a positron annihilate each other two gamma-rays of equal energy are produced. If the masses of the electron and the positron are both 0.000 548 u, calculate the energy of the gamma-rays.
Explain why the gamma-rays are at 180 ° to each other.

The positron and LEP

In 1932, Carl Anderson discovered the first known particle of antimatter – the positron. Its properties were later explained by the Cambridge physicist Paul Dirac. It has exactly opposite properties to the electron and so it has a positive charge.

In the huge accelerator of the Large Electron-Positron Collider (LEP), which has a circumference of 27 km and is situated in underground laboratories near Geneva, bursts of positrons and electrons collide at speeds close to that of light. They create new particles when they collide.

In calculations about the decay of radioactive atoms it is often convenient to use the atomic masses of the particles rather than their nuclear masses (the electrons being conserved on either side of the equation).

In calculations about the decay of radioactive atoms it is often convenient to use the atomic masses of the particles rather than their nuclear masses (the electrons being conserved on either side of the equation).

Example

Consider the decay of a radium-226 atom into an alpha-particle and radon-222. We can build up a mass–energy sum as follows:

mass of radium-226 atom = 226.0254 u
mass of radon-222 atom = 222.0175 u
mass of helium atom = 4.0026 u

The sum of the masses of the products of the reaction is 226.0201 u, which is 0.0053 u, less than the mass of the original nucleus. This difference is known as the **mass defect** of the reaction and appears as kinetic energy of the alpha-particle and recoil energy of the residual radon atom. The kinetic energy is equivalent to 8.16×10^{-13} J.

4 The radioactive isotope $^{210}_{84}$Po emits alpha-particles of single energy, the product nuclei being $^{206}_{82}$Pb.

(*a*) Using the data below calculate the energy in MeV released in each disintegration.

(*b*) Explain why not all this energy appears as kinetic energy of the alpha-particle

(*c*) Calculate the kinetic energy of the alpha-particle, taking integer values of the nuclear masses.

Nucleus	*Mass*/u
$^{210}_{84}$Po	209.936 730
$^{206}_{82}$Pb	205.929 421
Alpha-particle	4.001 504

Binding energy

The neutrons and protons in a stable nucleus are held together by nuclear forces and energy is needed to pull them apart. This energy is called the **binding energy** of the nucleus; the greater the binding energy, the more stable is the nucleus.

This energy shows itself as a difference between the mass of the nucleus and the sum of the masses of the nucleons within it. For example, consider the alpha-particle, or helium-4 nucleus, which contains two protons and two neutrons:

mass of proton = 1.007 276 u
mass of neutron = 1.008 665 u
Therefore mass of two protons plus two neutrons = 4.031 882 u

But the mass of a helium nucleus = 4.001 508 u.
Therefore the binding energy (the difference between the mass of the nucleons and the nucleus) = 4.031 882 − 4.001 508 = 0.030 374 u = 28.3 MeV.

Another useful concept is the **binding energy per nucleon**: this is the energy that has to be given to the nucleus to remove one nucleon from it. In the case of the isotope helium-4 this is 28.3/4 = 7.1 MeV, that is, 7.1 MeV of energy is required to remove one nucleon from the helium-4 nucleus. The helium nucleus is actually a very stable particle.

The variation in the binding energy per nucleon (E/A) is shown in Figure 63.2.

By considering the binding energy we can say whether a nucleus is stable or unstable. If the binding energy is positive then the nucleus is stable, but if it is negative the nucleus will decay spontaneously.

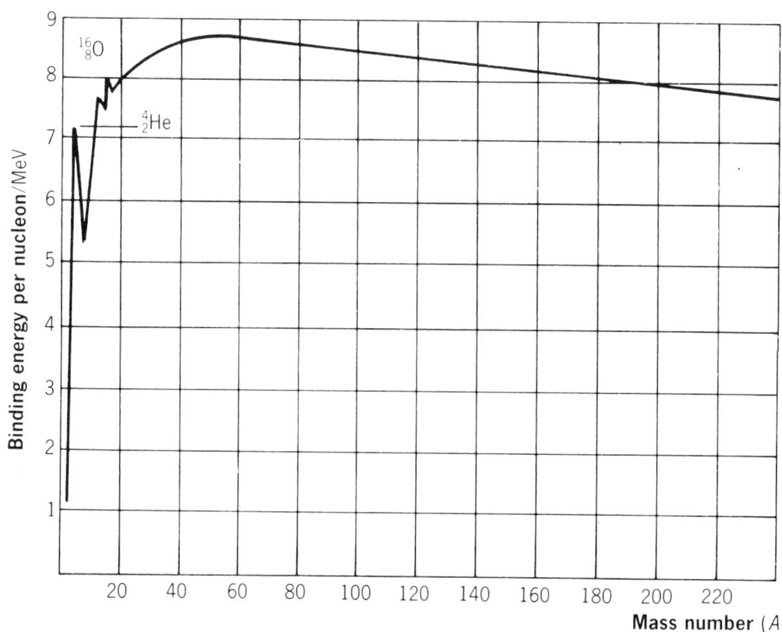

Figure 63.2

Example

Calculate the energy involved in the following reactions:

(*a*) $^{14}_{7}N + ^{1}_{0}n \rightarrow ^{14}_{6}C + ^{1}_{1}H$

(*b*) $^{14}_{7}N + ^{1}_{0}n \rightarrow ^{12}_{6}C + ^{3}_{1}H$

Use the data for the hydrogen atom and neutron masses given on page 451 and the following:

mass of nitrogen-14 atom	= 14.003 07 u
mass of carbon-14 atom	= 14.003 24 u
mass of carbon-12 atom	= 12.000 00 u
mass of hydrogen-3 atom	= 3.016 05 u

(*a*)

Mass of nitrogen-14 + neutron	= 15.011 74 u
Mass of carbon-14 + hydrogen	= 15.011 06 u
Therefore energy available	= 0.000 68 u
	= 0.63 MeV

This appears as kinetic energy of the products of the reaction.

(*b*)

Mass of nitrogen-14 + neutron	= 15.011 74 u
Mass of carbon-12 + hydrogen-3	= 15.016 05 u
Therefore energy difference	= −0.004 31 u
	= −4.01 MeV

Energy must be given to the original nuclei to produce this reaction.

The nuclear force saturates between pairs of particles or pairs of pairs; it does not act between one nucleon and all others within that nucleus. This means that nuclei containing nucleons in groups of four are likely to be very stable particles – for example, the nuclei of helium-4, carbon-12 and oxygen-16.

5 The mass of the nucleus of the isotope, $^{7}_{3}Li$ is 7.014351 u. Find its binding energy given the masses of the proton and neutron on p.451.

The discovery of the neutron

In 1932 Bothe and Becker bombarded a piece of beryllium with alpha-particles using the apparatus shown diagrammatically in Figure 63.3. They observed a penetrating radiation which they took to be gamma-rays. When a piece of paraffin wax was placed in the path of the beam, however, the reading on the detector actually increased!

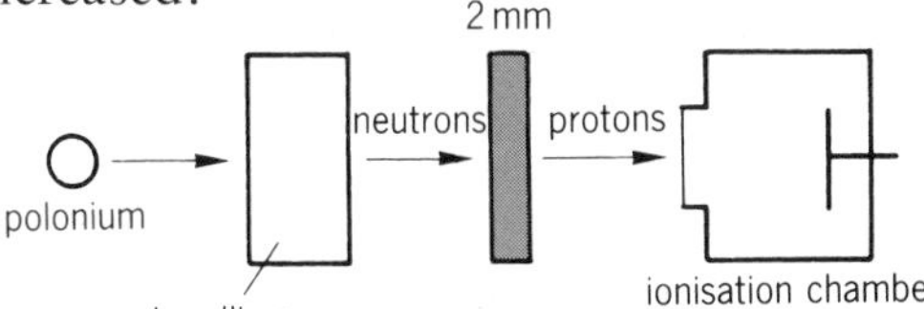

Figure 63.3

It was realised that the increase in reading was due to the emission of protons from the wax. If this proton emission had been due to bombardment by gamma-radiation, then the gamma-rays would have to have an energy of some 16 MeV and this is very large for such a reaction.

Chadwick realised that the radiation produced by the alpha-particles was not gamma-radiation at all but particles with very nearly the same mass as the proton. The high penetration was explained by assuming that the particle was uncharged and could therefore pass through material without any electrostatic scattering.

The particle was named the **neutron**, a name suggested years before by Rutherford as a combination of the proton and electron. The reaction of the beryllium nucleus that produces neutrons is

$$^{9}_{4}Be + ^{4}_{2}He \rightarrow ^{12}_{6}C + ^{1}_{0}n$$

The neutrons collide elastically with the atoms of a hydrogenous material such as wax and lose much more energy to a light atom than to a heavy one. For this reason the neutron is particularly dangerous to human tissue which contains large numbers of hydrogen atoms, the mass of which is similar to that of the neutron.

The neutron is now known to have a mass slightly greater than that of the proton, the neutron's mass being 1.008 665 u compared with the proton's 1.007 276 u. Free neutrons are unstable, decaying into a proton and an electron with a half-life of 650 s (10.8 minutes).

The most common large-scale source of neutrons is the nuclear reactor (see page 456). Materials are often placed in reactors to see how they stand up to neutron bombardment. The effect of other radiations may also be studied in this way. For example, when hypodermic syringes are sterilised by gamma-radiation the plastic of the syringes will deteriorate if the period of irradiation is too long. Tests were therefore made in reactors to determine the best irradiation time for a given sample.

6 A typical fission reaction is

$$^{235}_{92}U + ^{1}_{0}n \rightarrow ^{95}_{42}Mo + ^{139}_{57}La + 2^{1}_{0}n + 7\,^{0}_{-1}e$$

Calculate the total energy released by 1 g of uranium-235 undergoing fission by this reaction, neglecting the masses of the electrons.

Mass of neutron	= 1.009 u
Mass of molybdenum-95 atom	= 94.906 u
Mass of lanthanum-139 atom	= 138.906 u
Mass of uranium-235 atom	= 235.044 u
Number of atoms in one mole	= 6.02×10^{23}
Velocity of light	= 3×10^{8} m s^{-1}

7 Using the data given in question 4 and that the mass of the deuterium (^2_1H) atom is 2.014 102 u, calculate the binding energies of ^3_2He and ^3_1H from the following reactions:

$$^2_1H + ^2_1H \rightarrow ^3_2He + ^1_0n + 3.34 \text{ MeV}$$

$$^2_1H + ^2_1H \rightarrow ^3_1H + ^1_1H + 4.0 \text{ MeV}$$

$$^2_1H + ^3_1H \rightarrow ^4_2He + ^1_0n + 17.6 \text{ MeV}$$

8 Calculate the mass defect, the binding energy and the binding energy per nucleon of the common isotope of oxygen ^{16}O. You may use the data on page 485.

9 A radioactive isotope of thallium, $^{207}_{81}Tl$, emits beta-particles (β^-) with an average energy of 1.5 MeV. The half-life of the isotope is 135 days, and it is thought to emit gamma-radiation.

(*a*) (i) Describe simple tests which could be used to confirm that beta-particles are emitted, and to check for the presence of gamma-radiation.

(ii) What will be the atomic number and the atomic mass of the new isotope formed by the emission of a beta-particle? What will happen to the nucleus of the new isotope if a gamma-ray photon is emitted?

(*b*) (i) What is meant by an 'energy of 1.5 MeV', and what form does the energy take in this case?

(ii) What is meant by a half-life of 135 days?

(iii) Calculate the decay constant.

(*c*) Assuming that 207 g of thallium-207 contains 6×10^{23} atoms, calculate

(i) the total energy, in joules, available from the beta-particles emitted from 1 g of the isotope; (electronic charge = -1.6×10^{-19} C)

(ii) the initial rate at which beta-particles are emitted from 1 g of the freshly prepared isotope;

(iii) the initial power, in watts, available from the beta-particles emitted at the rate calculated in (ii).

(*d*) It has been suggested that thallium-207 could be used to power the amplifiers built into underwater telephone cables. Use the data and your answers to (*c*) to discuss whether the suggestion is worth pursuing. [AEB 1984]

10 When lithium-6 is bombarded with deuterons (deuterium nuclei) alpha-particles are produced, two for every lithium nucleus that reacts with a deuteron. Write down an equation for the reaction and calculate the energy of each alpha-particle, assuming that the energy of the deuterons is negligible. (Lithium-6 atom = 6.015 13 u, deuterium atom = 2.014 10 u and helium-4 atom = 4.002 60 u)

Artificial transmutations

Through the ages the alchemists claimed that they could change one metal into another, particularly base metals into gold. One possibility was to change lead into gold but any gold found after the reaction was probably from the spectacle frames of the experimenters!

In 1919, however, an experiment was performed that did change one material to another – although not into gold – when alpha-particles colliding with nitrogen nuclei were found to give off protons. Two reactions were possible, either

$$^{14}_7N + ^4_2He \rightarrow ^{13}_6C + ^1_1H + ^4_2He$$

or

$$^{14}_7N + ^4_2He \rightarrow ^{17}_8O + ^1_1H$$

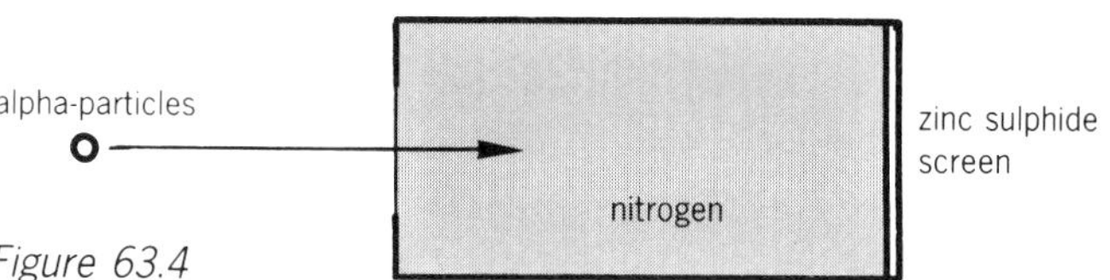

Figure 63.4

By studying the tracks of the product in a cloud chamber it was shown that it was the second reaction that had occurred: the alpha-particle had actually been *absorbed* by the nucleus and had not simply 'chipped' off a proton. The reaction had changed nitrogen into oxygen!

A simple diagram of the apparatus is shown in Figure 63.4.

The alpha-source produced a reaction in the gas and the protons produced were detected by the zinc sulphide screen. (With heavy elements Rutherford scatttering occurs instead.)

Now 1 mg of radium emits about 37 000 000 alpha-particles per second, but even this enormous number does not cause many interactions because of the large spaces between atoms. It required the development of particle accelerators before sufficiently high particle densities could be obtained (see page 466).

In 1932, using a 400 000 V accelerator, Cockcroft, Walton and Rutherford were able to transmute lithium:

$$^7_3Li + ^1_1H \rightarrow 2\ ^4_2He$$

Nuclear fission

In 1934 Fermi used neutrons to bombard thorium and uranium nuclei. The result was a highly radioactive material. He concluded that he had produced a transuranic element, that is, one with a proton number greater than 92 (transuranic elements).

Then in 1939 Hahn and Strassman analysed the products of these reactions and found that they had a proton number of around 56! Obviously they were *not* transuranic elements.

In the same year Meitner and Frisch suggested that when uranium is bombarded with neutrons two roughly equal fragments are produced, with the release of a large amount of energy. The original uranium nucleus had split in half and the process was called **nuclear fission.**

We can explain this idea by the liquid drop model of the nucleus. In just the same way that a drop of water might become unstable if another small drop hits it, so the uranium nucleus becomes unstable and breaks up when hit by a neutron.

One possible equation for the fission of uranium-235 is

$$^{235}_{92}\text{U} + \ ^{1}_{0}\text{n} \rightarrow \ ^{236}_{92}\text{U} \rightarrow \ ^{144}_{56}\text{Ba} + \ ^{90}_{36}\text{Kr} + 2\,^{1}_{0}\text{n} + 200\,\text{MeV}$$

A further reaction could be

$$^{235}_{92}\text{U} + \ ^{1}_{0}\text{n} \rightarrow \ ^{236}_{92}\text{U} \rightarrow \ ^{148}_{57}\text{La} + \ ^{85}_{35}\text{Br} + 3\,^{1}_{0}\text{n} + \text{energy}$$

The mass equation for the second reaction is

$$235.124 + 1.009 \rightarrow 147.961 + 84.938 + 3.027$$

This gives a difference in mass of 0.207 u, or $0.207 \times 931 = 193$ MeV. So the energy from the fission of one uranium atom $= 3.20 \times 10^{-11}$ J.

But in 1 kg of uranium-235 there are $1000 \times 6.02 \times 10^{23}/235.124 = 2.56 \times 10^{24}$ atoms. So the energy available from the fission of *all* the nuclei in 1 kg of uranium is 8.19×10^{13} J, or 2.28×10^{7} kW h!

Chain reactions and the nuclear reactor

If one of the neutrons produced by the first fission reaction hits a second uranium nucleus the latter will also split: the process will continue, causing an avalanche of fission reactions (Figure 63.5). This is called a **chain reaction.**

To sustain a chain reaction there must be sufficient uranium, known as the **critical mass** or too many neutrons will be lost from the sides before they can cause further fission. The uranium fuel must also be stacked in a pile (hence the name 'atomic pile').

The neutrons produced in fission are travelling too fast to cause further fission of uranium-235, so they have to be slowed down. This is done by a **moderator,** which is usually carbon or heavy water (^2H_2O).

The first small atomic pile was made by Heisenberg in 1941 using heavy water from Rjukan as moderator, but it was Fermi who produced the first workable reactor in 1942. He built this in a squash court in Chicago using six tonnes of uranium and forty tonnes of uranium oxide as fuel. His moderator was carbon in the form of graphite.

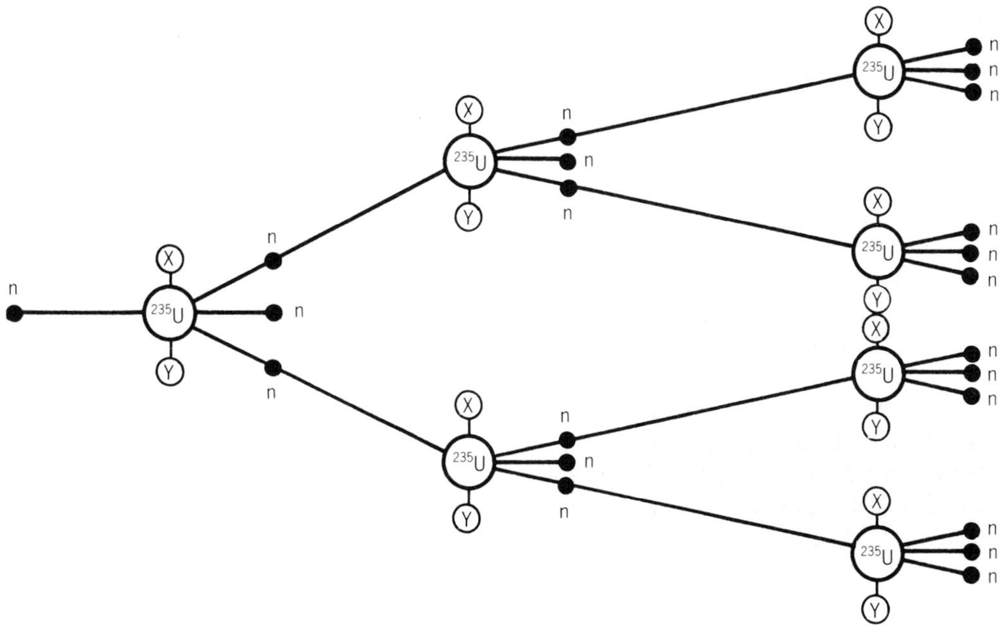

Figure 63.5

The nuclear fission reactor

The nuclear reactor represents the development of the peaceful uses of nuclear energy to generate electricity.

The fission reaction takes place in the core of the reactor. The fuel in the early British nuclear reactors was enriched uranium-238 (99.3 per cent ^{238}U and 0.7 per cent ^{235}U) held in magnesium alloy cans (hence the name 'Magnox' for the early British reactors) with cooling fins on the outside. Although there is so little uranium-235 in the fuel, the probability of fission of uranium-235 by slow neutrons is so much greater than that of uranium-238 by fast neutrons that it is worth deliberately slowing down the neutrons to use the fission of uranium-235. The uranium fuel rods are grouped together in the core of the reactor, which in a typical reactor (600 MW) is about 14 m in diameter and 8 m high. In the Hinkley Point 'A' reactors the cores contain 4500 fuel element channels with a total fuel mass of 3.55×10^5 kg. The design of the core must ensure that sufficient neutrons remain in the core to sustain the fission reaction.

In the fission of uranium-235 high-velocity neutrons are produced, and these must be slowed down before fission can take place. This is achieved by the moderator which in the case of the early British reactors is carbon in the form of graphite blocks. The neutrons collide with the carbon nuclei and lose energy; these slower neutrons are known as **thermal neutrons** and it is these that cause fission of further uranium-235 nuclei. The graphite also reflects neutrons back into the core of reactor.

To control the rate of the fission reaction control rods are used. Hollow stainless steel rods filled with boron are placed in channels between the uranium fuel elements. The boron absorbs neutrons and the fission can be controlled by adjusting the height of the rods within the core.

The core of a reactor of the Hinkley Point 'A' type, shown diagrammatically in Figure 63.6, is surrounded by a steel pressure vessel 7.62 cm thick and with an internal diameter of 20.4 m. The pressure vessel is surrounded by a 5 m thick concrete biological shield to protect the operators from neutron and gamma-radiation. The coolant is carbon dioxide pumped through the pressure vessel at a pressure of 12.75 atmospheres, and the heat from the reactor core raises its temperature from 180 °C to 360 °C. The carbon dioxide then passes into a heat exchanger where it heats water. The water is superheated to 350 °C at a pressure of 45 atmospheres. Its energy is then transferred to turn more water into steam in a second heat exchanger, and it is this steam that is passed through the turbines which in turn drive the generators. The steam that drives the turbines is thus not radioactive (or at least only very slightly so) because of the use of the secondary heat exchanger.

From then on the generation of electricity is just the same as a conventional coal-fired power station.

Student investigation

Consider the following points:

(*a*) Is uranium mining any more dangerous than coal mining?

(*b*) What are the economic considerations in the building of a nuclear power station?

(*c*) How will a nuclear power station affect the local biosystem?

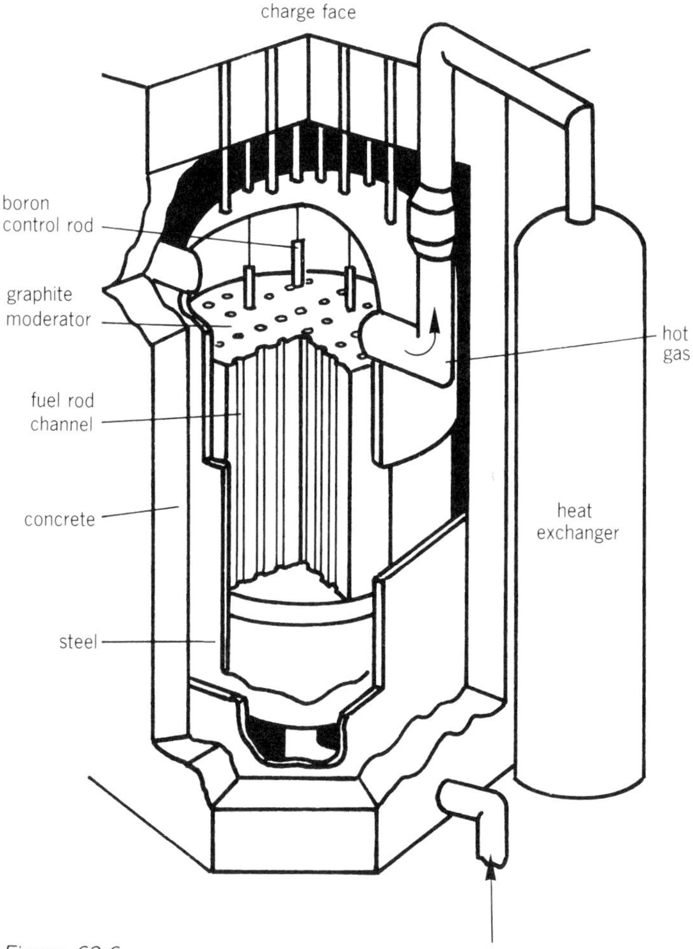

Figure 63.6

Advanced reactors

A development of the early Magnox reactors is the **Advanced Gas-cooled Reactor** (AGR). This type of reactor uses fuel with a greater percentage of uranium-235 (2.3 per cent), it has stainless steel fuel element containers and a smaller core than that of a Magnox reactor, and it operates at a higher temperature. The reactor is more efficient, giving a greater power output than Magnox reactors of similar size.

Another type of reactor is the **Candu** (Canadian deuterium–uranium). The short fuel bundles lie in hundreds of horizontal channels and the coolant (heavy water) flows past in double-walled tubes. The moderator is also heavy water.

Much publicity has been given to the **Pressurised Water Reactor** (PWR) developed mainly in the USA and the Soviet Union as a compact propulsion system for ships. This type of reactor uses water as both moderator and coolant and uranium fuel enriched with 3.2 per cent of uranium-235. The core of a reactor of this type designed to give an output of 700MW is only 3.0 m in diameter and 3.7 m high.

In the **Fast Reactor** the fuel is enriched with 20 per cent of plutonium, and no moderator is needed as the fission occurs with fast neutrons. The coolant is liquid sodium pumped round by an electromagnetic pump.

Liquid metal fast breeder reactors are, as their name suggests, reactors that use sodium as a coolant and breed plutonium-239 in their cores from the uranium fuel. Plutonium-239 is also a fissile material and is used in a core surrounded by a blanket of uranium-238.

In 1986 a serious failure in the reactor at the Chernobyl power station in the USSR caused the release of large amounts of radioactive material, which contaminated parts of northern Europe. The Chernobyl reactor was a graphite-moderated but water-cooled type, the moderator being blanketed with a mixture of nitrogen and helium. It operated at much higher temperatures (some 700 °C) than those in graphite-moderated British reactors and it is thought that the failure was due to a loss of coolant which allowed the graphite to reach unacceptably high temperatures and therefore to catch fire.

It is clear from the Chernobyl accident that the highest safety standards, both in design and construction, must always be applied to nuclear power stations.

11 The accident at Chernobyl affected the reindeer of Northern Lapland. Produce a scenario for such an effect, considering and giving estimates of
(*a*) fallout particle size;
(*b*) altitude reached by fallout;
(*c*) distance from the reactor to the site of contamination;
(*d*) time lapse until the safety level is reached;
(*e*) effect of wind and rain;
(*f*) half-life of the contamination.

The disposal of nuclear waste

One important problem that has to be considered when dealing with nuclear power reactors is the disposal of the waste products formed by the fission process. The wastes are classified into two types: those of low activity and those of high activity.

Most of the waste products of the reactor are dealt with during reprocessing of the fuel for re-use and a small amount of low-activity material is discharged. This discharge is subject to stringent government regulations and is carefully monitored. The reprocessing is based on solvent extraction. After extraction of unused uranium or plutonium a small amount, some 3 per cent, of highly radioactive waste products remains.

The high-level waste from all of Britain's nuclear power stations to date has a volume equal to that of two ordinary family houses.

The most likely method of treatment for the highly radioactive waste is vitrification – enclosing the material in glass. It can then be buried deep underground where it will cool and decay. A plant to convert high-level liquid waste into glass is planned to be in operation at Sellafield in Britain by the 1990s.

Student investigation

Discuss the following questions.

(*a*) How should radioactive waste be transported around the country?

(*b*) Should this waste be transported through areas of population?

(*c*) How great is the world need for energy?

(*d*) Should high-level waste be buried underground or at sea?

(*e*) Should we fire nuclear waste into the Sun?

(*f*) Is there a danger of plutonium being stolen from a reprocessing plant by terrorists?

Fusion

If two light nuclei are joined together energy can be released, this process is called **nuclear fusion**. To see how this is possible consider the following reaction, in which two deuterons (heavy hydrogen nuclei) are fused to produce helium-3 and a neutron:

$$^{2}_{1}\mathrm{H} + ^{2}_{1}\mathrm{H} \rightarrow \ ^{3}_{2}\mathrm{He} + ^{1}_{0}\mathrm{n} + \text{energy}$$

If we calculate the masses before and after the reaction we find that there is a difference of 0.004 u or 3.27 MeV, that is,

$$\text{energy released per deuteron} = 3.04 \times 10^{-13}\ \mathrm{J}$$

This is much less than the energy released for the fission of one atom of uranium (compare page 455) but because there are many more atoms in a kilogram of hydrogen than in a kilogram of uranium the energy released per kilogram for the fusion reaction is larger. Since there are 3×10^{26} deuterons in one kilogram,

$$\text{energy released per kilogram} = 9.12 \times 10^{13}\ \mathrm{J} = 2.5 \times 10^{7}\ \mathrm{kW\,h}$$

The biggest problem with the fusion reaction is making the nuclei fuse, because the electrostatic repulsion between them at very small distances becomes enormous. For this reason the hydrogen gas has to be raised to very high temperatures in excess of 10^{6} °C, even under quite high pressure, thus giving the nuclei sufficient thermal kinetic energy to overcome the electrostatic repulsion. Under such conditions the hot gas or plasma has to be held in a magnetic field as it would vaporise a normal container. A likely reaction for an all-hydrogen system is

$$5\,^{2}_{1}\mathrm{H} \rightarrow \,^{3}_{2}\mathrm{He} + \,^{4}_{2}\mathrm{He} + \,^{1}_{1}\mathrm{H} + 2\,^{1}_{0}\mathrm{n} + 24.88\ \mathrm{MeV}$$

that is, the energy available from five deuterons is 24.88 MeV. Now one mole of deuterium gas has a mass of 2 g and contains 6.02×10^{23} atoms. Therefore the energy available from 1 kg of deuterium is 2.996×10^{27} MeV or 4.79×10^{14} J!

The high temperatures required can be obtained by passing a very large current through the plasma; at present this method enables temperatures of 40 MK to be reached. A further increase of temperature may be obtained by other methods such as radiofrequency heating. In the USA a bank of high-powered lasers are used to vaporise a pellet of material.

Natural hydrogen contains about 1 part in 5000 of deuterium, and so sea water gives us a cheap and easily available source; using the deuterium from sea water would give enough energy to supply the world at its present rate of consumption for some 10 thousand million years. There would be a neutron flux which would cause some radioactivity in the structure but the lifetime of this could be reduced by a suitable choice of the materials used. The material would not be volatile and should not present any storage problems.

The largest single project in European fusion research is at Culham in Oxfordshire, and is known as the JET (Joint European Torus) project. This is a European Community venture involving fourteen European nations. The plasma is held in a toroidal magnetic field and raised to a very high temperature by passing a large current through it.

The torus is 6 m in diameter with an elliptical bore of 2.5 m by 4.2 m and has a mass of 100 000 kg. At present it operates with ordinary hydrogen or deuterium plasmas. The final phase of the project, which is to use deuterium and tritium together, is planned for 1992, though it could be delayed until 1995/6. The structure will then become radioactive.

At present temperatures of up to 70 MK have been reached for a few seconds, with heating currents up to 7 MA supplemented with 35 MW of additional heating. One major difficulty is the control of impurities, arising from plasma interaction with the vessel walls, which reduce the fusion reaction rate.

The fusion reactor at the Joint European Torus Project (JET – Joint undertaking)

Stellar energy

It was soon realised that the energy of the stars was produced by nuclear fusion, the temperatures required in the stars being lower than those needed in the laboratory because of the enormous pressures in the stellar interiors.

Heavier and heavier nuclei can be produced by successive fusion reactions. The types of reaction taking place in the Sun are shown below:

$$^{12}_{6}C + {}^{1}_{1}H \rightarrow {}^{13}_{7}N + \text{energy}$$

$$^{13}_{7}N \rightarrow {}^{13}_{6}C + e^{+}$$

$$^{13}_{6}C + {}^{1}_{1}H \rightarrow {}^{14}_{7}N + \text{energy}$$

$$^{14}_{7}N + {}^{1}_{1}H \rightarrow {}^{15}_{8}O + \text{energy}$$

$$^{15}_{8}O \rightarrow {}^{15}_{7}N + e^{+}$$

$$^{15}_{7}N + {}^{1}_{1}H \rightarrow {}^{12}_{6}C + {}^{4}_{2}He$$

The net result of this series of reactions is:

$$4\,{}^{1}_{1}H \rightarrow {}^{4}_{2}He + 2e^{+} + \text{energy}$$

In other words, 564 million tonnes of hydrogen are being converted into 560 million tonnes of helium every second, producing a staggering output of 3.90×10^{20} MW – equivalent to some million million million large power stations!

Although the Sun is converting four million tonnes of mass into energy every second it is thought that it will continue to last for a further 10^9 years.

The life and death of a star

Even though the lifetime of the Sun, or in fact of any star, is enormous there will be changes as time goes by and one day the Sun will cease to exist in the form that we know it today. There are various possibilities.

(*a*) The radiation pressure from within the star may decrease to a point where the star simply 'goes out'.

(*b*) The radiation pressure will increase to such a point that it will overcome the gravitational attraction and the size of the star will increase – this may happen explosively, as in a nova or supernova.

(*c*) The gravitational attraction will increase to the point where the star may collapse in on itself, to form one of the strangest objects in the Universe – a 'black hole'. The surface of a black hole is not material – it is simply a boundary. Once entered the boundary may never be recrossed, since the escape velocity within it is greater than the velocity of light. The matter which has fallen inside a black hole will attain unimaginable densities, possibly to be crushed out of existence in a 'space–time' singularity where the normal laws of Physics as we know them may cease to exist.

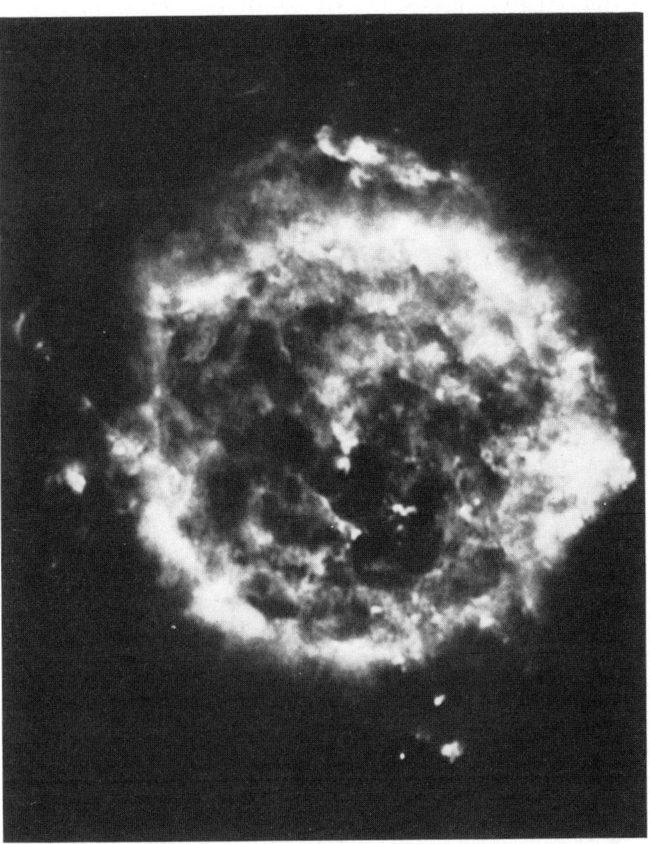

Radio emission from the Cassiopeia A supernova remnant mapped at the Mullard Radio Astronomy Observatory, University of Cambridge. A star about ten times the size of the sun exploded 300 years ago – the shell of ejected matter is now a strong source of radio waves.

The life and death of the universe

It is now generally believed that the Universe as we know it began as an enormous fireball some 10 000 million years ago. We call this the Big Bang. In just the same way that echoes of an explosion can be heard a short while after it happened, so the Big Bang has left an echo. Even after 10 000 million years astronomers have detected background radiation in deep spaces corresponding to a temperature of 3 K – this is the echo of the Big Bang.

What about the end of the Universe, if it is ever to have an end? Space appears to be expanding and cooling but it is not certain whether this process will go on for ever. Some astrophysicists believe that the universe will continue to undergo a period of expansion but will then contract to give an oscillating universe that can expand and contract forever.

The atomic and thermonuclear bombs

It is appropriate to include a mention of atomic and thermonuclear weapons in this book, since although not part of most school courses they exemplify the most terrible misuse of science in history.

The first atomic bomb was developed at Los Alamos in the United States by an international team of scientists and exploded in the Alamogordo desert in New Mexico on 16 July 1945. A leading statesman at the time quoted from the book of Hosea in the Bible: 'They have sowed the wind, they shall reap the whirlwind'.

Fortunately for our world, only two atomic bombs have ever been dropped in war but now the superpowers have sufficient stockpiled nuclear warheads to destroy every man, woman and child on the planet.

Statistics often mean little and sources do not always agree, but it seems that about 100 000 people died in Hiroshima on 6 August 1945 when the first atomic bomb was dropped, and thousands more died later as a result of the burns and radiation they had received. Three days later, on 9 August 1945, a second bomb was dropped on Nagasaki – 70 000 people died.

The bomb dropped on Hiroshima was 0.71 m in diameter and 3 m long; it had a mass of 4000 kg and a destructive power equivalent to 20 000 tonnes of high explosive. It was exploded 300 m above ground to achieve the 'maximum effect'.

To get some idea of the power of such weapons, consider the speed at which the fireball travelled. Such a fireball produced in a nuclear explosion would reach a diameter of 150 m in 0.006 s, 300 m in 0.016 s and 1 km only 1 s after the explosion. The temperature in the Hiroshima fireball reached 7000 °C – hotter than the surface of the Sun – and wooden buildings two miles from the explosion were obliterated. It is true that terrible destruction occurred in Coventry, in Munich and in Dresden but that was due to continuous bombing. The cities of Hiroshima and Nagasaki were each destroyed by *only one bomb*. But the present nuclear stockpile is equivalent to some 50 000 warheads, equivalent to 1.5 *million* Hiroshima bombs.

Atomic and thermonuclear bombs also produce a high degree of fallout, that is, material that has been irradiated and sucked up by the great uprush of hot air and subsequently deposited over a wide area of the Earth.

One possible result of a full-scale nuclear war, and one that is especially sobering to contemplate, has been suggested by scientists only in the last few years: the effect of the huge clouds of dust that would be carried up into the atmosphere, so reducing the amount of sunlight reaching the Earth's surface. The resulting change in climate has become known as the 'nuclear winter'. It has been estimated that the mid-summer temperature would drop to below freezing in the latitude of London and that even the deserts would eventually freeze. These conditions, which could be brought about by the detonation of 10 per cent of the present stockpile of warheads, could last from six months to three years. During that time the sunlight would be reduced to some 1 per cent of its present amount, the sea would start to freeze, forests would die and much of the Earth's oxygen-producing plants would therefore be destroyed.

Amazingly, it has been estimated that out of a present population of the Earth of some 4800 million about 1000 million might survive to try to start all over again. There is absolutely no doubt that civilisation as we know it would have disappeared for ever.

There were many military reasons why it was considered necessary to drop the atomic bombs on Japan in 1945 and there is a view that they brought the Second World War to a close more quickly. However, I believe that it is up to all of us to try to see that such weapons are never used again to save our planet and our civilisation from annihilation.

We began this book with some lines from a poem:

This is the morning I would not forget
For then we stood in awe
And saw the world created in a day.

Let us be sure that we do not see it destroyed – it is likely that there would be no second chance.

64 · The wave nature of matter

The growth of the wave–particle duality theory

Although this theory is not usually studied fully at A level, such an important part of Physics should not be omitted totally from the course. An elementary introduction to wave–particle duality follows.

This theory suggests that there is no basic distinction between a particle and a wave. The differences that we observe arise simply from the particular experiment that we are doing at the time.

Some important steps in the development of the wave–particle theory were as follows:

1923 discovery of the Compton effect
1923 de Broglie's matter–wave theory
1927 the diffraction of electrons
the uncertainty principle of Heisenberg

An interesting idea concerning waves and particles was put forward by G.I. Taylor in 1924. He reasoned that if light only behaved like a particle, then in an interference experiment such as Young's slits it would be possible to reduce the intensity to a point where only one photon was passing through the apparatus at a particular time and you would therefore expect there to be no interference – the photon could not interfere with itself. This does *not* happen, however, – the interference pattern is always visible although very faint, suggesting some kind of wave property of the photon.

Diffraction appears to be some kind of statistical behaviour of each individual photon, and not a reaction between photons. If we attempt to determine which slit a given photon has passed through we destroy the diffraction pattern, because we have altered the nature of the experiment.

The Heisenberg uncertainty principle

If it were possible to measure the exact position and velocity of every particle in the universe at a certain time, then by applying the basic laws of Physics we should be able to predict their state at any future time – for example, we could say how much rain would fall on Taunton on the third of January in the year 2000!

The uncertainty principle of Heisenberg states that it is actually impossible to make such a measurement.

In fact, if ΔE, Δx and Δp represent the smallest uncertainty with which the energy, position and momentum of a particle and Δt the smallest uncertainty in the time of measurement, then

$$\Delta x . \Delta p = \hbar$$
$$\Delta E . \Delta t = \hbar$$

where $\hbar$ is the Planck constant divided by 2π.

The concept of the detached observer of classical Physics is a myth, since a completely isolated universe cannot be observed. An observer must always form part of an experiment – otherwise there *is* no experiment.

The 'true' nature of a particle, or at least the modern view of it, is that it has both wave and particle properties described by the wave mechanical model of Schroedinger. This model is complex but simply states that we cannot fix the position of a particle (as in classical Physics) but can only predict the *probability* of it being at a given point at a certain time. It could therefore be anywhere, but is in fact more likely to be at one place than another. The square of the amplitude of the wave associated with a particle at a given point in space and time is proportional to the probability of the particle being at that point.

Further consideration of this subject is beyond the scope of this book, but it is hoped that this very brief introduction has been sufficient to demonstrate the uncertainty of Physics on a nuclear level. Remember that all the world around us is composed of matter waves, even ourselves. As you read this, there is only a probability that you are there at all!

Student investigation

The Planck constant is actually a very small number but imagine that we lived in a world where the Planck constant was 1J s.

Write an essay discussing how different this world might be.

De Broglie's equation

After the discovery of the photoelectric effect it was realised that waves can possess particle-like properties, and a search was made to see if particles could indeed behave like waves.

In 1923 Louis de Broglie proposed that a particle of mass m travelling with a velocity v would have a wavelength λ given by the equation:

$$\lambda = \frac{h}{mv}$$

where h is the Planck constant. The intensity of the wave represented the probability of the particle being found at that point.

The formula allows us to calculate the wavelength associated with a moving cricket ball.

Example

Find the wavelength of a cricket ball of mass 0.15 kg moving at 30 m s^{-1}.

$$\lambda = \frac{6.7 \times 10^{-34}}{0.15 \times 30} = 1.49 \times 10^{-34} \text{ m}$$ – a *very* small number!

For electrons accelerated through a p.d. of v volts, $\frac{1}{2}mv^2 = eV$. Therefore, substituting values for the charge and mass for the electron,

$$\lambda = \frac{12.27 \times 10^{-10}}{\sqrt{V}}$$

Example

Calculate the wavelength of an electron accelerated through a p.d. of (*a*) 10 kV, (*b*) 100 V.

(*a*) $\lambda = 1.23 \times 10^{-11}$ m.
(*b*) $\lambda = 1.23 \times 10^{-10}$ m.

This is the true beginning of wave–particle duality, since sometimes the particle would behave like a wave and sometimes like a particle. Even more strangely, the way in which it behaved seemed to be influenced by the nature of the experiment used.

We can also use the formula to calculate the 'mass' of a quantum of light, or **photon**. For yellow light of wavelength 600 nm the calculated mass is 3.7×10^{-36} kg, as compared with a mass of 9×10^{-31} kg for the electron. Using these ideas it is possible to calculate the recoil velocity of an atom which emits a quantum of light.

(For the following problems, use where necessary the values of the electron mass, the Planck constant and the electron charge given in the Appendix.)

1 Calculate the wavelength of an electron accelerated through a p.d. of:
(*a*) 15 000 V in a colour television tube,
(*b*) 200 000 V in an electron microscope, and
(*c*) 10 MV in a linear accelerator.

2 What would be the velocity of an electron with a wavelength of 0.1 nm?

3 A sodium atom with a mass of 23 u emits a photon with a wavelength of 589.6 nm. What is the recoil velocity of the sodium atom?

Electron diffraction

If the electron has wave properties, then it ought to be possible to observe these: electrons should show the characteristics of waves such as interference and diffraction. This is clearly a difficult concept if we are used to thinking of the electron as a particle. We must, however, abandon the out-of-date idea that the electron, or in fact *any* particle, always behaves like a solid object!

The very small wavelength of electrons means that the obstacles used to diffract them must also be very small, and as with X-rays it was the atomic lattice that was eventually found to be suitable.

The diffraction of electrons was first shown by Davisson and Germer in 1927 and it can now be observed easily in schools with the correct apparatus. A very good example is manufactured by Teltron Ltd, in which a beam of electrons is accelerated in an electron gun to a potential of between 3500 and 5000 V and then allowed to fall on a very thin sheet of graphite (Figure 64.1(*a*)). The electrons diffract from the carbon atoms and the resulting circular pattern on the screeen (Figure 64.1(*b*)) is very good evidence for the wave nature of the electrons.

The diffraction pattern observed on the screen is a series of concentric rings. This is due to the regular spacing of the carbon atoms in different layers in the graphite. It is an example of Bragg scattering (see p.436).

If the voltage on the anode is increased the energy of the electrons is increased, and the diameter of a given ring gets less. This is exactly similar to the observation that blue light is diffracted less strongly than red light, which arises because the wavelength of blue light is smaller than that of red and hence its energy is larger.

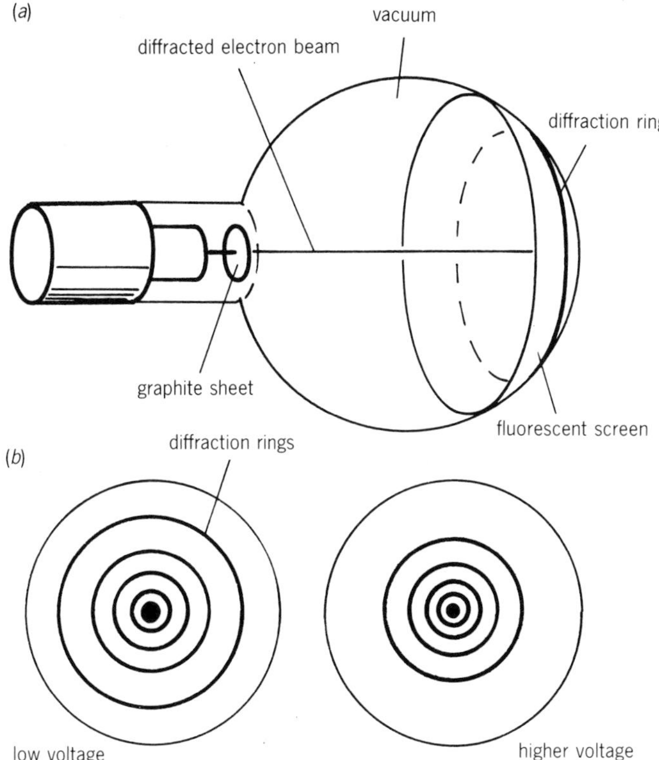

Figure 64.1

Quantised orbits

The simple Rutherford model of the atom had one serious disadvantage concerning the stability of the orbits. Bohr showed that in such a model the electrons would spiral into the nucleus in about 10^{-10} s, due to electrostatic attraction. He therefore proposed that the angular momentum of the electron should be quantised, in line with Planck's quantum theory of radiation.

He stated that the allowed values of the angular momentum would be integral multiples of $h/2\pi$, that is,

$$\text{angular momentum} = \frac{nh}{2\pi}$$

This implied a series of discrete orbits for the electron (see page 415). From the Schroedinger wave equation we can imagine the electron as existing as a wave that fits round a given orbit an integral number of times. In other words, if r is the orbit radius and λ the wavelength,

$$2\pi r = n\lambda$$

A very simple analogy of this is seen if we fit a circle of copper wire to a vibrator and then oscillate it as shown in Figure 64.2. A series of resonance positions can be found where an integral number of waves fit round the orbit.

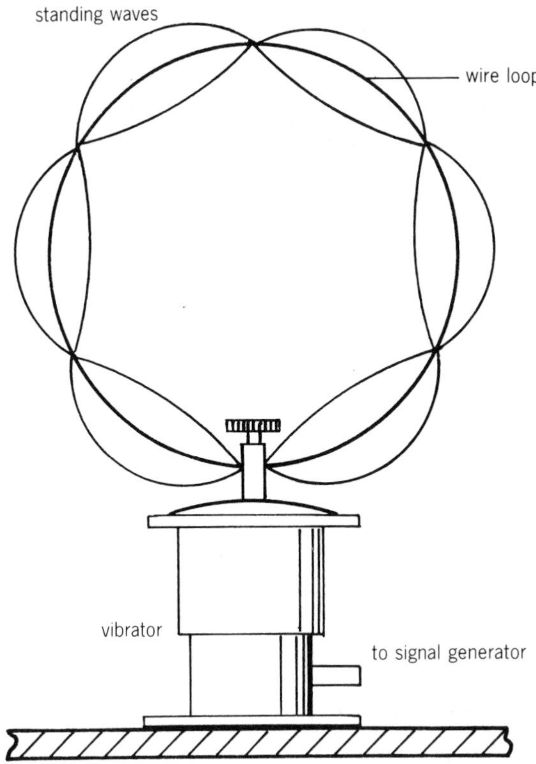

Figure 64.2

Verification of Bohr's principle

The idea of the electron's discrete or quantised orbits within an atom can now be verified. We have two proposals:

(*a*) that of Schroedinger, suggesting that n electron waves can be fitted around an orbit, that is

$$2\pi r = n\lambda$$

(*b*) that of de Broglie, who proposed that electrons have a wavelength:

$$\lambda = \frac{h}{mv}$$

Therefore

$$2\pi r = \frac{nh}{mv} \qquad \text{and so} \qquad mvr = \frac{nh}{2\pi}$$

But the quantity mvr is the angular momentum of the electron, and therefore Bohr's original proposal had been confirmed, since n is an integer. (As we have seen, the quantity $h/2\pi$ is usually written as $\hbar$.)

Within a few years of 1923 the wave hypothesis was developed into the theory known as wave mechanics, by Schroedinger and others.

Each electron also possesses an internal angular momentum called **spin**, which must be conserved in nuclear and atomic processes. Spin gives rise to a magnetic moment of the electron within the atom.

The electron microscope

The electron microscope is based on the discovery by Thomson, Davisson and Germer that electrons have wave properties. If an electron is accelerated through a p.d. of 500 000 V, then the wavelength associated with it is 1.73×10^{-3} nm. This means that if it can be used in a microscope the resolving power (which depends on wavelength – see page 198) would be very large.

Electrons are also affected by magnetic fields, and magnetic focusing had been used for some time in the cathode ray tube. Then in 1926 it was realised that a suitable magnetic field arrangement could be used to act as a magnetic lens, bringing electrons of a given velocity to a focus and so giving an image of an object (see Figure 64.3(*a*)).

By combining several such magnetic lenses a succession of magnifications may be obtained, and Figure 64.3(*b*) shows the similarity between an electron microscope and its optical counterpart. The condenser lens produces a parallel beam of electrons, which strike the object. Some electrons are absorbed by the object, some are transmitted and some are scattered sideways. These scattered electrons cannot pass through the small slit placed in front of the object, and in order to reduce the number of scattered electrons the object must be very thin.

The transmitted electrons pass through one or two magnifying lenses and the final image is formed on a screen or on a photographic plate.

The whole interior of the apparatus must be maintained at a very high vacuum, otherwise scattering of the electron beam from gas particles would ruin the image.

The magnification may be varied by altering the current in the magnetic lenses.

Accelerating voltages of 1 MV have been achieved, and for such an instrument the field in the lenses reaches a maximum of some 2.5 T using currents of 5 A in 3000 turns, giving a focal length of about 5 mm. Such lenses must be cooled and work has been carried out on superconducting magnets for use in magnetic lenses. Theoretically the resolution of such an instrument would be very high, but aberration in the lenses limits it to about 0.1 nm. Magnifications of over 100 000 times are quite feasible, however.

Other problems exist at these very high magnifications: the objects that we are trying to view are little larger, by a factor of 1000 or so, than the electrons in the beam and so the electron beam distorts the object. Also the very high-energy electrons leak across the viewing screen, so blurring the image further.

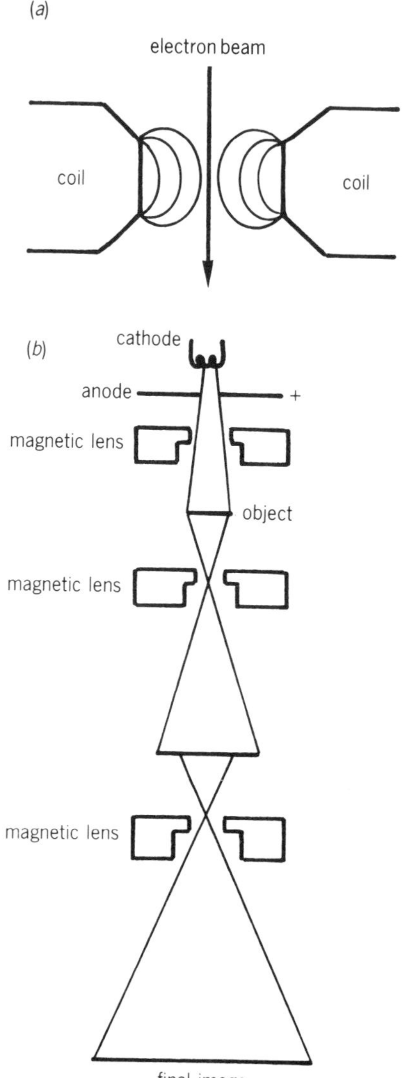

Figure 64.3

65 · Particles and accelerators

The particles of Physics

The following table gives the main properties of the fundamental particles of Physics. It is a very much simplified version.

The masses are given in terms of the mass of the proton.

Particle	*Symbol*	*Mass*	*Charge*	*Lifetime*
Electron	e	0.000 548	negative	infinite
Neutrino	ν	very small	zero	infinite
Muon	μ	0.11	negative	2.2×10^{-6} s
Pion	π	0.14	0 or +1	
Kaon	K	0.5		
Proton	p	1	1	infinite
Neutron	n	1	0	650 s (free)
Lambda	λ	1.1	0	10^{-10} s
Sigma	Σ	1.2		10^{-10} s
Xi	Ξ	1.3		
Quark			$+\frac{2}{3}$ or $-\frac{1}{3}$	
Omega minus	Ω^-	1.8	negative	10^{-10} s

Antimatter

The idea of antimatter originates from an equation produced by Paul Dirac in 1928, describing the motion of an electron in the presence of electromagnetic radiation. He found that to make his results consistent with relativity theory he would have to have two solutions for particles and not just one. One solution gave the properties of the well-known electron, but the other suggested a particle of the same mass as the electron but of opposite electrical charge. He named this the **positron** and this became the first so-called **antiparticle** to be proposed. In fact, the positron was first detected by Anderson in 1932.

When a particle of matter such as an electron meets a particle of antimatter such as the positron they annihilate each other, and a burst of radiation is produced consistent with Einstein's mass–energy equation.

The idea of the quark

For many years physicists have been fascinated by the possibility that nuclear particles such as protons and neutrons might consist of even more fundamental particles, and these have come to be known as **quarks**. (I prefer the name to rhyme with parks rather than corks, but others think differently!)

The modern idea of the quark was proposed independently in 1964 by Murray Gell-Mann and George Zweig. They suggested three different types of quark:

(*a*) the *up* quark, charge $+\frac{2}{3}$;
(*b*) the *down* quark, charge $-\frac{1}{3}$;
(*c*) the *strange* quark, charge $-\frac{1}{3}$.

The proton is thought to be the combination of two *up* quarks (each with a charge $+\frac{2}{3}$) and one *down* quark (charge $-\frac{1}{3}$) giving a total charge of $\frac{2}{3} + \frac{2}{3} - \frac{1}{3} = +1$.

The neutron, however, is thought to consist of two *down* quarks and one *up* quark, giving a total charge of zero.

At the time of writing it is unlikely that any free quarks have been observed – if this is indeed possible.

Accelerators

To investigate the structure of the nucleus, and even that of subnuclear particles, one particle is usually fired at another at high energy – a method that has been compared to trying to find out what a watch contains by throwing two watches together and seeing what bits fly out.

If a composite particle requires a certain amount of energy to separate its constituents, one way of providing this energy is by a high-energy projectile such as another particle. The acceleration of particles to high energies is therefore of great importance in nuclear research, and we will consider here some of the ways in which this may be done.

All the accelerators are for charged particles, the kinetic energy of the particle being increased by an electrostatic field.

A Cockcroft and Walton accelerator being operated by Walton himself (University of Cambridge, Cavendish Laboratory)

(*a*) Simple electrostatic accelerator

This is simply a tube containing a number of electrodes, with a p.d between successive pairs of 50–100 kV. The apparatus is evacuated to a pressure of about 10^{-5} mm of mercury and the maximum p.d. obtained is about 5 MV.

(*b*) Van de Graaff generator (1931)

This instrument can produce a high potential difference by a steady accumulation of static charge. It has been particularly useful as an accelerator for the production of beams of high-energy charged particles for use in nuclear physics research (see page 465). A simplified version of the Van de Graaff generator is shown in Figure 65.1.

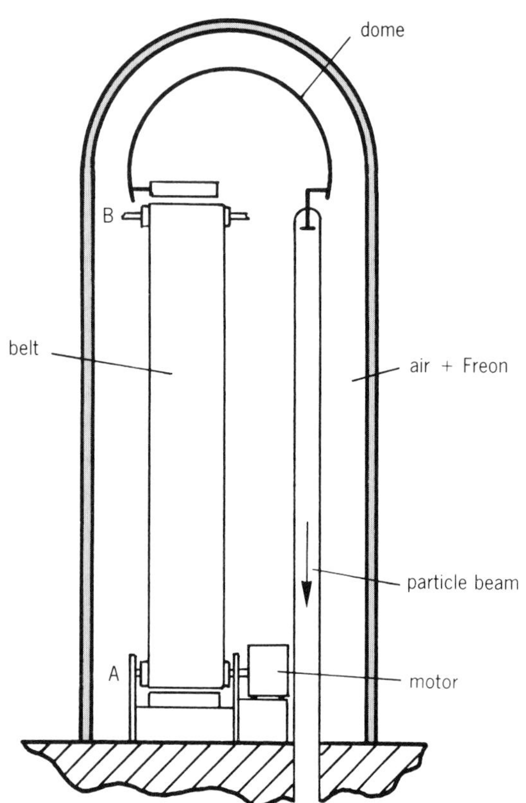

Figure 65.1

A belt made of insulating material runs past two sets of points A and B. Charge is sprayed on to the belt at A, either by a power pack or by friction between the belt and roller. This charge is carried up to B and induces a negative charge at B, which then streams on to the belt. The effect of this is to produce a positive charge at B, and so positive charge effectively is transferred by the belt from A to B. The point B is connected to a conducting sphere and therefore the charge on the sphere steadily builds up. This process continues until the potential of the sphere is so great that a spark jumps from it to any nearby earthed object – such as a finger! Very high voltages of more than 100 000 V can be reached even with school machines, and it is therefore *never* safe to allow a spark to jump to your head or even to subject yourself to prolonged sparking to other parts of the body.

In larger machines the belt is enclosed in an evacuated tube or one containing air (mixed with Freon to reduce sparking), enabling potentials of over 12 MV to be achieved.

(*c*) The linear accelerator

This type of accelerator was invented by Wideroe, and is the first of the important modern accelerators. It accelerates particles down a straight tube without the use of very high voltages. Some of these machines are very large, the one at Stanford, USA, being over 2 miles long.

The particles move down a vacuum tube under the influence of a travelling wave, which appears regularly with correct phase at the electrode gaps (see Figure 65.2).

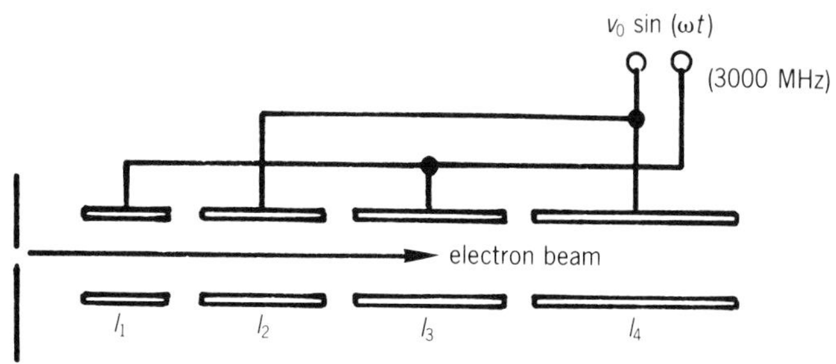

Figure 65.2

Alternate pairs of electrodes are connected together and an a.c. signal applied to them. Notice that the electrodes have to get longer as the particle gets further down the tube, since the particles will travel further during each cycle of the field. At very high velocities relativistic effects have to be allowed for.

With electron linear accelerators the particles are injected at about 4 MeV from a small electrostatic accelerator, and in the Stanford machine they are accelerated to energies in excess of 10 GeV (1000 MeV). The average beam current is about 15 μA.

(*d*) The cyclotron

The idea of dividing the accelerating voltage into small steps works better still if the particles are travelling in a circular path, and it was this fact that led to the development of the first circular accelerator or cyclotron by Lawrence in 1932.

The path of a charged particle in a magnetic field is circular for a given velocity and so a large path length may be achieved for a small amount of space. As the particle passes across the gap between the D-shaped electrodes it receives a pulse of energy, and thus the resulting path is a spiral of ever-increasing radius as the particle's energy increases (Figure 65.3).

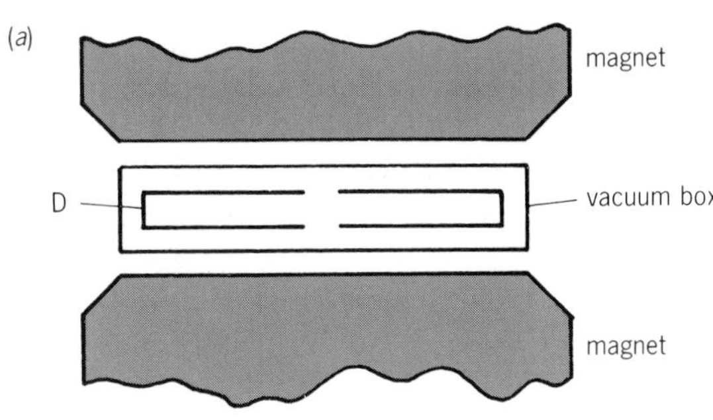

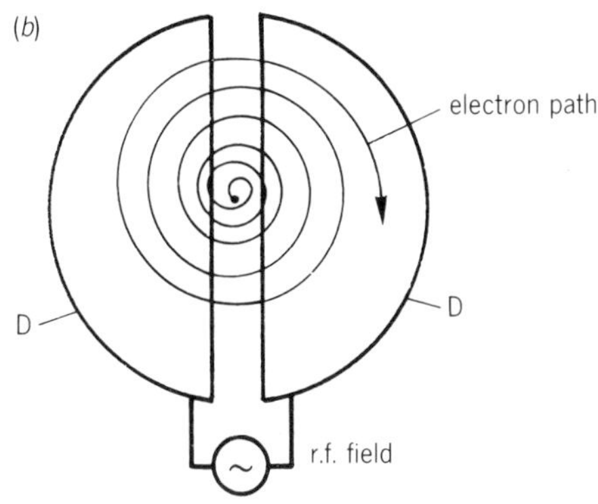

Figure 65.3

(*e*) The proton synchrotron

In the proton synchrotron the particles are made to accelerate in an orbit of constant radius in a toroidal vacuum tube. They are kept in this orbit by a magnetic field produced by a series of electromagnets placed around the tube, as shown in Figure 65.4(*a*). Figure 65.4(*b*) shows the approximate shape of the required field across the vacuum tube. To achieve this constant orbit radius the magnetic field is increased as the particles reach higher and higher energies. As in the cyclotron, they are accelerated by an electric field each time they pass through a pair of electrodes in the tube.

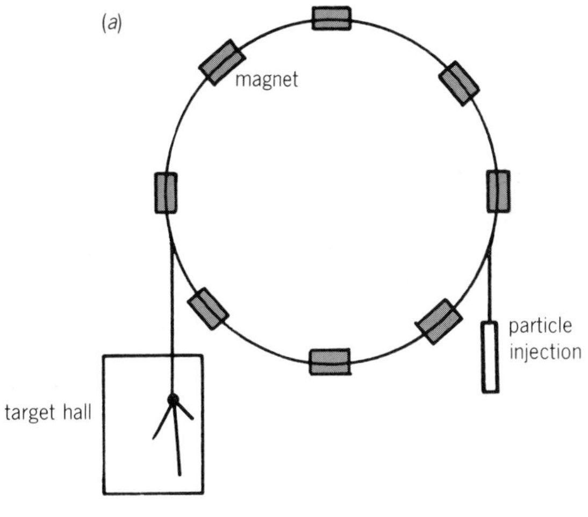

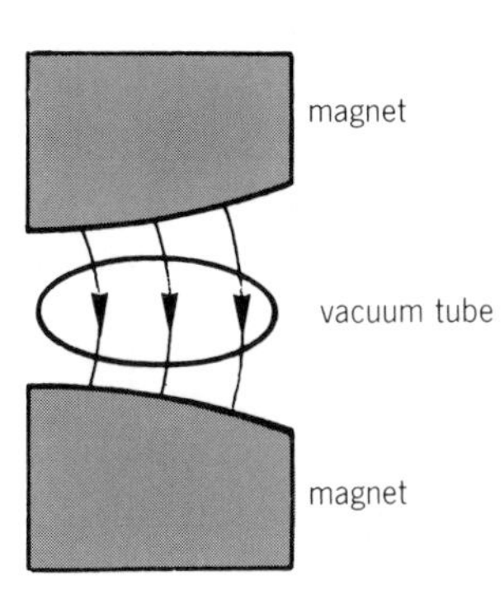

Figure 65.4

The CERN proton synchrotron at Geneva produces protons with energies up to 28 GeV. The maximum field is 1.4 T and the orbit diameter about 172 m, each proton pulse contains some 10^{11} protons and during acceleration the protons travel roughly 8×10^4 km or 50 000 miles. The super proton synchrotron (1978) at Geneva can accelerate protons to energies of 500 GeV.

The Large Electron Project (LEP) at CERN uses a synchrotron with a circumference of some 27 km!

(*f*) Intersecting particle storage rings

Very large energies can be made available if two particles, both moving at high speed but in opposite directions, are made to collide head on. Such collisions are produced in SPEAR at Stanford in the USA. Try and imagine the different effects of two charging elephants meeting head on and of one charging elephant hitting a stationary mouse. The former represents the situation in SPEAR, in which the energy available for annihilation is some 30 GeV; the latter represents the collision of a particle with a stationary target – the available energy is much less.

66 · Theory of relativity

The theory of relativity proposed by Albert Einstein in 1905 deals, as its name suggests, with measurements made in systems that are in motion relative to each other. Such a system is known as a **frame of reference.** For example, consider a train moving along a railway track. Measurements made in the train are relative to the train and the train is therefore one frame of reference, while measurements made at the side of the track are relative to the ground, the other frame of reference.

While you read this you are probably sitting still – but 'still' relative to what? Even if you are in a building, the building is fixed to the Earth which is itself rotating and also travelling round the Sun. The Sun is moving within our galaxy and the galaxy is moving relative to others in the universe.

There are basically two types of relativity:

(*a*) **special relativity**, that deals with frames of reference in uniform relative motion, and

(*b*) **general relativity**, that deals with frames of reference in non-uniform relative motion, for example, one frame accelerating relative to the other.

The laws of Newtonian Physics, such as $F = ma$, hold very well for our everyday lives but at speeds close to that of light considerable divergencies occur. Relativity is not considered in detail here, but some of its important facts and consequences are briefly surveyed. Certain basic facts must be assumed:

(*a*) physical laws are obeyed in all frames of reference,

(*b*) the velocity of light in free space is constant in all inertial frames of reference.

If we assume these, then we must abandon some of our other more traditional ideas, namely the constancy of mass, length and time. This means that if one object is moving relative to a frame of reference, then the mass and length of the body measured from the frame of reference will be different from those measured with instruments travelling with the body. Even more unusual, time measured by a clock travelling with the body will differ from that measured by a clock at rest in the frame of reference! Length appears to get smaller, mass increases and time appears to pass more slowly in a moving frame of reference when viewed from a stationary frame. Any such differences are very small, however, unless the relative velocities are very large, that is, approaching that of light.

The consequences of special relativity

Imagine for a moment that we live in a world where the velocity of light is small, say 32 m s^{-1} (about 70 m.p.h.). Then the predictions of the theory of special relativity would become much more obvious.

If we stood at a street corner in this strange world and watched traffic passing by, then all the cars would appear shortened and even people would appear a little thinner than they were when standing still.

If you tried to pull a trolley along with a rope, not only would it seem to get thinner but you would also find that as you went faster and faster the trolley would seem heavier and heavier and so become more difficult to accelerate.

Imagine that you had gone to the station in the morning to say goodbye to your friends who were going by train to the nearest town (at no more than 70 m.p.h.) and agreed to meet them there in the evening. They would seem to have aged little, but to them you would have looked a lot older – time for a moving frame of reference runs more slowly than for one at rest!

Effects similar to these have been observed in the real world, but because of the very large velocity of light they are much more difficult to see.

The slowing down of time has been noticed in atomic clocks that have been carried in satellites and some high-energy fundamental particles have been observed at sea level even though knowledge of their half-life indicates that they should have decayed long before they reached the ground.

The increase of mass becomes a problem in high-energy accelerators where as the particles approach the speed of light they become more and more difficult to accelerate further. Even the electrons in our colour television tubes are moving so fast that their actual masses are some 21 per cent heavier than those of electrons at rest.

A further consequence, and indeed a requirement of special relativity, is the fact that the velocity of light in free space is constant. This means that the relative velocity of two photons approaching each other in free space, when measured from one or the other, is c and not $2c$.

The equations of special relativity

Consider an object of rest mass m_0 and length l_0, moving with velocity v relative to a stationary frame of reference.

The following equations give the mass m, length l and time t as measured from the frame of reference.

$$m = \frac{m_0}{(1 - v^2/c^2)^{\frac{1}{2}}}$$

$$l = l_0(1 - v^2/c^2)^{\frac{1}{2}}$$

$$t = \frac{t_0}{(1 - v^2/c^2)^{\frac{1}{2}}}$$

Example

An interstellar starship travels through space at high speed. Find the mass of an object with a rest mass of 1 kg, the length of a bar of rest length 1 m and the new value of the second when all these quantities are measured relative to a frame of reference at rest outside the starship. Consider three cases:

(*a*) the starship has a velocity of 10^4 m s^{-1};
(*b*) the starship has a velocity of 2×10^8 m s^{-1};
(*c*) the starship has a velocity of 2.95×10^8 m s^{-1}.

Using the above equations we have:

(*a*) $m = 1.00$ kg, $l = 1.00$ m, $t = 1.00$ s;
(*b*) $m = 1.34$ kg, $l = 0.75$ m, $t = 1.34$ s;
(*c*) $m = 5.5$ kg, $l = 0.18$ m, $t = 5.5$ s.

The equivalence of mass and energy

Elsewhere in this book we have used Einstein's famous equation relating matter to energy, $E = mc^2$. We will now show how it can be deduced starting with the first equation of special relativity:

$$m = \frac{m_0}{(1 - v^2/c^2)^{\frac{1}{2}}}$$

therefore

$$m^2c^2 - m^2v^2 - m_0{}^2c^2 = 0$$

and so

$$c^2 2m \frac{dm}{dt} - 2mv \frac{d(mv)}{dt} = 0$$

therefore

$$c^2 2m \frac{dm}{dt} = 2mv \frac{d(mv)}{dt}$$

However,

$$\frac{dE}{dt} = Fv \quad \text{and so} \quad \frac{dE}{dt} = Fv = v\frac{d(mv)}{dt} = c^2 \frac{dm}{dt}$$

and therefore

$$E = mc^2$$

General relativity

The theory of general relativity does not restrict itself to frames of reference that are moving relative to each other at a constant velocity. In the general theory accelerated frames are considered, as are gravitational fields – in fact, it can be shown that the effects of acceleration and gravitational field are equivalent. General relativity theory predicts the following:

(*a*) that light bends in a gravitational field – light just grazing the surface of the Sun has been observed to be deviated by some 1.75 seconds of arc;

(*b*) that the perihelion of Mercury, (its nearest point to the Sun), shows precession;

(*c*) that physical processes such as the vibrations within an atom are slowed down in a high gravitational field, and therefore the light coming from the stars is reddened slightly.

According to the general theory, if a very large triangle were to be surveyed near the Sun or other large astronomical body the angles would not add up to 180°, suggesting that space is curved in a gravitational field!

This last idea extends the problem to the whole universe, and so I will end this book with some questions – maybe one day one of you who read this will find the answers.

If space is actually curved, which way does it curve?

Has space a positive curvature like the surface of the Earth and therefore a finite size? Or has it a negative curvature like the saddle between two mountain peaks?

Is the universe expanding without limit? Or is it pulsating, so that one day it will collapse back on itself and then expand once more and so on for ever?

If it does this, will another human race like ourselves develop to populate the planet we call Earth – if another Earth ever exists?

Appendices

Useful data

The following table of data should be useful as a back up for your course. It is *not* expected that these numbers be learnt off by heart but some idea of their approximate value is useful.

Quantity	Symbol	Value
Acceleration due to gravity	g	$9.81\ \mathrm{m\ s^{-2}}$
Universal constant of gravitation	G	$6.67 \times 10^{-11}\ \mathrm{N\ m^2\ kg^{-2}}$
Stefan constant	σ	$5.7 \times 10^{-8}\ \mathrm{W\ m^{-2}\ K^{-4}}$
Permittivity of free space	ϵ_0	$8.84 \times 10^{-12}\ \mathrm{F\ m^{-1}}$
Permeability of free space	μ_0	$4\pi \times 10^{-7}\ \mathrm{H\ m^{-1}}$
Velocity of sound in air at s.t.p.	v	$340\ \mathrm{m\ s^{-1}}$
Molar gas constant	R	$8.3\ \mathrm{J\ mol^{-1}\ K^{-1}}$
Faraday constant	F	$9.65 \times 10^4\ \mathrm{C\ mol^{-1}}$
Molar volume at s.t.p.	V_m	$22.4 \times 10^{-3}\ \mathrm{m^3\ mol^{-1}}$
Atomic mass unit	u	931 MeV or 1.66×10^{-27} kg
Mass of proton	m	1.67×10^{-27} kg or 1.0076 u
Mass of electron	m	9.1×10^{-31} kg
Mass of neutron		1.0090 u
Mass of alpha-particle		4.0026 u
Electron charge	e	1.6×10^{-19} C
Specific charge of electron	e/m	$1.76 \times 10^{11}\ \mathrm{C\ kg^{-1}}$
Velocity of light	c	$3.0 \times 10^8\ \mathrm{m\ s^{-1}}$
Planck constant	h	6.63×10^{-34} J s
Boltzmann constant	k	$1.38 \times 10^{-23}\ \mathrm{J\ K^{-1}}$
Avogadro constant	L	$6.02 \times 10^{23}\ \mathrm{mol^{-1}}$
Half-life of free neutron	T	650 s
Half-life of carbon-14	T	5570 y
Curie	Ci	3.7×10^{10} Bq
1 million electron volts	MeV	1.6×10^{-13} J
Light year		9.5×10^{15} m
Critical temperature of air		−190 °C (183 K)
Helium point		2.186 K
Absolute zero		−273.16 °C
Boiling point of sulphur		444.6 °C
E.m.f. of Leclanché cell		1.46 V
E.m.f. of Daniell cell		1.08 V
E.m.f. of Nife cell		1.4 V
E.m.f. of Weston cell		1.0186 V
Refractive index of glass	n_g	1.5 (typical)
Refractive index of water	n_w	1.33
Refractive index of paraffin	n_p	1.42
Metre	m	Distance travelled by electromagnetic waves in free space in 1/299 792 458 second.
Second	s	9 192 631 770 cycles of a transition in caesium-137
Specific latent heat of fusion of water	L	$3.34 \times 10^5\ \mathrm{J\ kg^{-1}}$
Specific latent heat of vaporisation of water	L	$2.26 \times 10^6\ \mathrm{J\ kg^{-1}}$
Specific heat capacity of water	c_w	$4200\ \mathrm{J\ kg^{-1}\ K^{-1}}$
Specific heat capacity (copper)	c_c	$385\ \mathrm{J\ kg^{-1}\ K^{-1}}$
R.m.s. velocity of helium atom at s.t.p.		$900\ \mathrm{m\ s^{-1}}$
Thermal conductivity of copper	k	$385\ \mathrm{W\ m^{-1}\ K^{-1}}$
Thermal conductivity of glass	k	$1.0\ \mathrm{W\ m^{-1}\ K^{-1}}$
Linear expansivity of steel	α	$1.2 \times 10^{-5}\ \mathrm{K^{-1}}$
Linear expansivity of copper	α	$1.7 \times 10^{-5}\ \mathrm{K^{-1}}$
Horizontal component of Earth's magnetic field	B_0	1.8×10^{-5} T
Young modulus for steel	E	$2.1 \times 10^{11}\ \mathrm{N\ m^{-2}}$ (Pa)
Young modulus for copper	E	$1.3 \times 10^{11}\ \mathrm{N\ m^{-2}}$ (Pa)
Viscosity of water (20 °C)	η_w	$1.002 \times 10^{-3}\ \mathrm{N\ s\ m^{-2}}$
Viscosity of air (20 °C)	η_0	$1.8 \times 10^{-5}\ \mathrm{N\ s\ m^{-2}}$
Earth's average radius	R	6.37×10^6 m
Earth's mass	M	5.972×10^{24} kg
Earth's average density		$5.517 \times 10^3\ \mathrm{kg\ m^{-3}}$
Moon's mean distance		3.844×10^8 m
Moon's density		$3.33 \times 10^3\ \mathrm{kg\ m^{-3}}$
Moon's mass		7.33×10^{22} kg
Moon's radius		1.738×10^6 m
Moon's gravitational acceleration		$1.619\ \mathrm{m\ s^{-2}}$
Sun's mean distance		1.495×10^{11} m
Sun's mean radius		6.960×10^8 m
Sun's mass		1.99×10^{30} kg
Sun's energy production		3.90×10^{26} W
Solar constant		$1400\ \mathrm{W\ m^{-2}}$
Wavelength of sodium D-lines		589.0 and 589.6 m
Diameter of 24-gauge wire		0.5588 mm
Resistance of 28-gauge copper wire		$0.155\ \Omega\ \mathrm{m^{-1}}$
Resistance of 28-gauge eureka wire		$4.41\ \Omega\ \mathrm{m^{-1}}$
Free electrons in copper		$10^{29}\ \mathrm{m^{-3}}$

Useful Mathematics for A level Physics

As you will realise a knowledge of Mathematics will be very useful to you in parts of the A level Physics course.

The following suggests the basic requirements in mathematics for most A level Physics syllabuses together with some extensions for more advanced Physics papers. It *does not* attempt to teach or explain the topics but simply lists them. You should consult your Mathematics or Physics teachers for further help. (Some of these topics may not be required for all syllabuses, however.)

Many of the topics include references to pages in the book where their use is demonstrated.

Students should be able to do the following:

Carry out calculations involving numbers in decimal form.

Make sensible evaluations of numerical expressions using reasonable approximations such as $\pi = 3$.

Express small fractional changes as percentages and vice versa.

Use scientific notation and work out problems in this form.

Change the subject of an algebraic equation.

Solve algebraic equations of the form $ax^2 + bx + c = 0$ using the formula

$$\text{roots} = \frac{-b \pm \sqrt{b^2 - 4ac}}{2a}$$

Recognise the shape of various graphs (pages 12–13).

Recognise the equivalent forms of the logarithms of ab, a/b, n^n and e^{kx}.

$$\log (ab) = \log a + \log b$$
$$\log (a/b) = \log a - \log b$$
$$\log (x^n) = n \log x \qquad \ln (e^{kx}) = kx$$

Use the binomial theorem to express quantities such as $(1 + x)^n$; for small x,

$$(1 + x)^n = 1 + nx$$

Calculate areas of triangles, circumferences and areas of circles, and volumes of rectangular blocks, cylinders and spheres.

Use and apply simple theorems such as Pythagoras'.

Translate from degrees to radians and vice versa, where θ radians $= 2\pi\theta°/360$.

Use sine, cosines and tangents, and recall and use the expansions of $\sin (A + B)$ and $\cos (A + B)$ as follows:

$$\sin (A + B) = \sin A \cos B + \cos A \sin B$$
$$\cos (A + B) = \cos A \cos B + \sin A \sin B$$

Recall the following identities;

$$\sin^2 A + \cos^2 A = 1$$
$$\sin 2A = 2 \sin A \cos A$$
$$\cos 2A = 1 - 2 \sin^2 A$$

Recall the sketch graphs of $\sin A$, $\sin (A + e)$ (where e is a constant) and $\cos A$ (see pages 74 and 167).

Recall that, when θ tends to zero,

$$\sin \theta \to \theta^c, \ \cos \theta \to 1 \text{ and } \tan \theta \to \theta^c$$

Find the resultant of two vectors and the components of a vector in two perpendicular directions (page 22).

Use graphical methods to display variables or find values for quantities, choosing suitable values for the axes and suitable scales (see pages 12–13).

Understand the use of the area below a curve when this has a physical significance.

Understand the use of the slope of a tangent to a curve to express rate of change (page 26).

Understand the meaning of the sum Σx.

Be able to perform simple differentiation and integration:

$$\frac{d(x^n)}{dx} = nx^{n-1} \qquad \frac{d(\sin rx)}{dx} = r \cos rx$$

$$\frac{d(\cos rx)}{dx} = -r \sin rx \qquad \frac{d(e^{kx})}{dx} = ke^{kx}$$

$$\int x^n \, dx = \frac{x^{n+1}}{n+1} + C \qquad \int \frac{dx}{x} = \ln x + C$$

$$\int \sin x = -\cos x + C \qquad \int \cos x = \sin x + C$$

Understand the relation between the derivative and the slope of the curve (page 26) and also that between the integral and the area below a curve.

Be able to find the maxima and minima of a curve by differentiation.

Useful numbers: e = 2.7183; 1 radian = 57.3 °.

Electrical symbols

The following table shows the recognised symbols that should be used in all diagrams of electrical circuits.

Description	*Symbol*
Direct current or steady voltage	—
Alternating	~
Positive polarity	+
Negative polarity	−
Rectifier	
Variability	
Primary or secondary cell	
Battery of primary or secondary cells	
Alternative symbol	
Earth	
Aerial (antenna)	
Signal lamp	
Filament lamp	
Electric bell	
Crossing of conductor symbols on diagram (no electrical connection)	
Junction of conductors	
Double junction of conductors	
Plug (male)	
Socket (female)	
Fuse	
Fixed resistor	
Variable resistor	
Resistor with moving contact	
Voltage divider with moving contact	

Description	*Symbol*
Heater	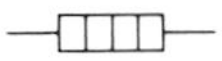
Thermistor	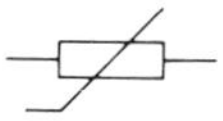
Capacitor: general symbol	
Polarised capacitor	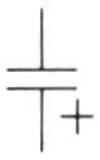 +
Polarised electrolytic capacitor	 +
Capacitor with preset adjustment	
Winding	
Inductor + core	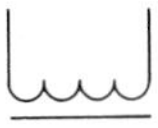
Transformer	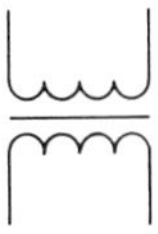
Ammeter	 A
Voltmeter	 V
Wattmeter	 W
Galvanometer	
Oscilloscope	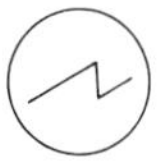
Motor	 M
Generator	 G
Microphone	
Earphone (receiver)	
Loudspeaker	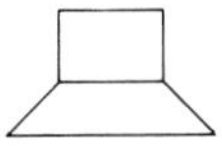

Description	*Symbol*
Clock (and slave clock)	
Make contact (normally open)	
Break contact (normally closed)	
Relay make contact-unit	
break contact-unit	
Neon lamp	
pn diode	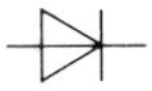
Alternative symbol	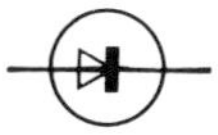
Light-sensitive pn diode	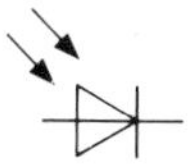
Light-emitting diode (LED)	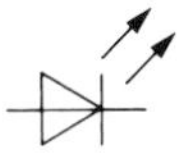
Zener diode	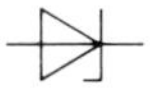
pnp transistor	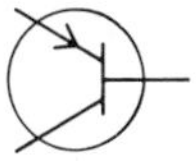
npn transistor	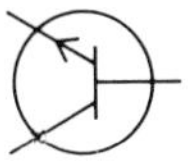
Amplifier	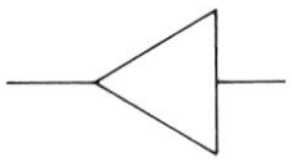

Essay topics

Whatever sixth form Physics course you are studying, it is important that you read around the subject. This should give added interest to your study even if some of the topics may not actually be examined at the end. The following suggested essay titles are designed to encourage this broadening of your knowledge of Physics, its history and its applications. Do attempt a few of them; you will find it a rewarding experience.

The Physics of the atmosphere
Lightning
The Coriolis effect
The quest for absolute zero
Physics in the 18th century
Physics in the 19th century
Physics in the 20th century
Physics in the 21st century
Uncertainty
Radioactivity and time
Supersonic transports
The evolution of the galaxies
Antimatter
Black holes
Superconductivity
Continental drift
Particle accelerators
The discovery of the Ω^-
The hunting of the quark
Space re-entry
Steam engines
The Stirling engine
Fundamental particles
Earth resource facilities
The Crab nebula
The Physics of Halley's comet
The future of nuclear fusion
The nuclear fission reactor
Energy resources
The red shift
Radio galaxies
Atomic clocks
Masers
The uses of the laser

The transistor
The Physics of glass
Carbon fibre structures
The dual nature of light
Radioisotopes in industry
Parity – left- and right-handedness
Diesel engines
Aircraft wing shapes
Wernher von Braun: the space race
Robert Oppenheimer: the bomb
Thomas Young: interference
Isaac Newton: the laws of motion
Galileo Galilei: the Solar System
Henry Cavendish: the measurement of G
Michael Faraday: electromagnetism
James Rutherford: the nuclear atom
The Physics of Music
Sound recording
Nobel prizewinners in Physics
The Physics of the tides
The unit of length
The unit of time
Biophysics
The autogyro
Audio amplifiers
The history of photograph
The charm particle
Gravity waves
Physics and religion
The microcomputer
Space physics
Electronic music
The linear motor
Physics of the mind

The quantum
Colour television
Video discs
Communication systems
Tidal and wave power
Geothermal energy
Solar energy
Windmills
Energy conservation
The Rutherford Laboratory
The National Physical Laboratory
The Science Museum
Harwell
The Cavendish Laboratory
The integrated circuit
Artificial intelligence
Logic circuits
The teaching of Physics
Propulsion in space
Vibration in machinery
The fourth dimension
The design of bridges
Modern building techniques
Industrial archaeology
Man-powered flight
Fibre optics
The Physics of sport
Photoelasticity
Liquid crystals
White holes in space
Electric vehicles
High-speed boats
Chaos Theory

Units in Physics

Quantity	*Unit*	*Symbol*
length	metre	m
mass	kilogram	kg
atomic mass	atomic mass unit	u
time	second	s
electric current	ampere	A
thermodynamic temperature	kelvin	K
luminous intensity	candela	cd
amount of substance	mole	mol
frequency	hertz	Hz
force	newton	N
pressure and stress	pascal	Pa
work, energy, heat	joule	J
power	watt	W
electric charge	coulomb	C
electric potential difference	volt	V
electromotive force	volt	V
electric resistance	ohm	Ω
electric conductance	siemens	S
electric capacitance	farad	F
magnetic flux	weber	W
magnetic flux density (magnetic induction)	tesla	T
inductance	henry	H
luminous flux	lumen	lm
illuminance	lux	lx
activity (of radioactive source)	becquerel	Bq
gravitational field strength	$N\ kg^{-1}$	g
gravitational potential	$J\ kg^{-1}$	V
specific heat capacity	$J\ kg^{-1}\ K^{-1}$	c
specific latent heat	$J\ kg^{-1}$	L
momentum	N s	P
moment of a force	N m	M
torque	N m	T
electrical resistivity	Ω m	ρ
electrical conductivity	$S\ m^{-1}$	σ
current density	$A\ m^{-2}$	j
permittivity	$F\ m^{-1}$	ϵ
electric field strength	$N\ C^{-1}$ or $V\ m^{-1}$	E
capacitance	F	C
permeability	$H\ m^{-1}$	μ
moment of inertia	$kg\ m^2$	I
angular momentum	J s	L
Young modulus	Pa	E
surface tension	$N\ m^{-1}$	σ
viscosity	$N\ s\ m^{-2}$	η
gravitational constant	$N\ m^2\ kg^{-2}$	G
thermal conductivity	$W\ m^{-1}\ K^{-1}$	k

Advances in Physics since 1750

The following are a series of important discoveries in the realms of Physics since 1750. They will not be needed for examination purposes but they are included because they show the development of scientific thought and progress.

1750 Nature of lightning – Franklin
1758 Achromatic lens – Dolland
1781 Uranus – Herschel
1785 Law of force between charges
1787 Charles's law
Gold leaf electroscope
1798 Cavendish experiment – measurement of G
1800 Dalton's atomic theory
1801 Young's slits
1808 Polarisation by reflection – Malus
1814 Photography
1820 Fraunhofer lines
1816 Photoelectric effect
1820 Electromagnetism – Oersted
1821 Diffraction grating
1824 Electromagnetic induction
1827 Brownian motion
1831 Dynamo – Faraday
1833 Wheatstone bridge
1834 Electric motor – Jacobi
Lenz's law
1841 Potentiometer – Poggendorf
1842 Doppler effect
1845 Electromagnetic theory of light
1846 Planet Neptune discovered
1847 Kirchhoff's laws of electricity
1849 Fizeau's method for measuring c
1850 Second law of thermodynamics
1852 Joule–Kelvin effect
1854 Airy's measurement of G
Thermodynamic temperature scale
1857 Kinetic theory – Clausius
Lissajous figures
1858 Plucher – magnetic effect on cathode rays
1860 Kirchhoff's laws of heat
Distribution of velocities – Maxwell
1861 Andrew's experiment with carbon dioxide
1862 Continuous-flow calorimeter – Regnault
1864 Electromagnetic wave theory – Maxwell
1865 Entropy – Clasius
Leclanché cell
1866 Velocity of sound in dust tube
1868 Doppler effect in stellar spectra
1870 Fibre optics – Tyndall
1872 Van der Waals' equation
1873 Selenium photocell
1874 Electron named
1875 Kerr effect
1876 Telephone
1876 Cathode rays – Goldstein
1877 Gramophone
Oxygen liquefied
Resistance thermometer – Callendar
1878 Electric light
Wimshurst machine
1879 Velocity of light – Michelson
Stefan's law
Cathode ray tube – Crookes
1880 Piezoelectric effect
1881 Bolometer – Langley
1882 Diffraction grating – Rowland
1885 Balmer series
Transformer – Stanley
1886 Dynamic method for saturated vapour pressure
Canal rays – Goldstein
1887 Motor car
Photoelectric effect
Wireless waves – Hertz
Michelson–Morley experiment
1892 Blooming of lenses
Dewar flask
1893 Fitzgerald contraction
1895 X-rays – Roentgen
Boys' method for G
1896 Radioactivity – Becquerel
Curve for black body – Wien
Zeeman effect
1897 Infrared radiation – Lummer and Pringsheim
Cathode ray oscilloscope – Brown
Measurement of e/m for the electron – Thomson
1898 Hydrogen liquefied
Radium discovered – Curies
Lee's disc
Polonium discovered
1899 Hydrogen solidified
Alpha-, beta- and gamma-rays
1900 Searle's apparatus for elasticity studies
Quantum theory – Planck

1901 Black body curve – Planck
1903 Thermionic emission theory
1905 Relativity – Einstein
1906 *e/m* for alpha-particle
Lyman series
1908 Helium liquefied
1909 Alpha-particle scattering
1911 Superconductivity
Measurement of *e* – Millikan
1912 Cloud chamber – Wilson
X-ray diffraction – Laue
1913 X-ray spectrometer – Bragg
X-rays – Moseley's law
Bohr's theory of the atom
X-ray tube – Coolidge
Geiger counter
1915 General theory of relativity
1918 Barton's pendulums
1919 Deflection of light in solar eclipse
Proton discovered
1923 Compton effect
1924 de Broglie equation
1925 Exclusion principle – Pauli
1926 Wave mechanics – Schroedinger
1927 Electron diffraction
Uncertainty principle – Heisenberg
1928 Velocity of light – Kerr cell
1929 Television tube – Zworykin
Electrostatic accelerator – Cockcroft and Walton
1930 Quantum mechanics – Dirac
1931 Neutrino – Pauli
Van de Graaff accelerator
1932 Positron – Anderson
1932 Cyclotron – Lawrence
1932 Neutron – Chadwick
1933 Magnetron
1934 Tritium discovered
Cerenkov radiation
1936 Neutron diffraction
Radar
1937 Electron microscope
1938 Superfluidity – Kapitza
Fission – Hahn and Strassman
1942 Plutonium discovered
Nuclear chain reaction – Fermi
1945 Synchrocyclotron
First nuclear explosion
1946 Linear accelerator built
Electron synchrotron
1947 Photomultiplier tube
British atomic pile
1948 *K*-particle
Transistor
1949 Holography – Gabor
Colour television
1950 Vacuum tube computer
1952 Bubble chamber – Glaser
CERN established
1953 Conservation of strangeness
1954 Maser
1955 Unified field theory – Einstein
1956 Antineutrino
Calder Hall
Antiproton
Neutrino detection
1957 Sputnik 1 launched
1958 ZETA
1959 Mössbauer effect
Integrated circuit
1960 Laser – Schawlow
1963 Quasars
1964 Ω^- particle
1969 Quark proposed
Man lands on Moon
Eight fold way
1971 One chip calculator
1974 Charmed quark
1976 Viking spacecraft land on Mars
1977 One chip 16 bit microprocessor
1979 Voyager 1 and 2 reach Jupiter
1980 Holographic bubble chamber
Voyager 1 and 2 reach Saturn
1982 Quarks in the proton
1983 Charge-coupled device (CCD)
40 million MeV proton accelerator proposed
Decay of proton (?)
1985 1000 GeV accelerator – Fermilab
1986 *Giotto* spacecraft encounters Halley's comet
Chernobyl disaster
Voyager 2 reaches Uranus
1987 4.2 m William Herschel telescope

Experiment list

The following list of experiments is not intended to be exhaustive. Many schools cover most of them, many will do more open-ended investigations, while others do not have the apparatus to perform some. It is included merely to provide some suggestions for practical work at this level suitable for use in most schools in the country.

g using Venner stopclock
g using vibrating spring
g using simple pendulum
g by turntable method
g using a.c. vibrator
g using linear air track
Measuring instruments
Newton's second law
Statics board
Water path in gravity
Coefficient of restitution
Torsion balance
Capillary rise
Jaeger's method
Drop weight
Ferguson's method
Soap film
Vibrating cantilever
Compound pendulum
Radius of gyration
Moment of inertia (flywheel)
Torsional oscillations
Young modulus (wire)
Fishing line extension
Stokes' law
Fluid flow in tubes
Centripetal force (turntable)
Bifilar suspension
Bending of a beam
Damped s.h.m.
Melde's experiment
Interrupted pendulum
Floating test-tube
Coefficient of friction
Mechanical resonance
Sonometer
Velocity of sound using CRO
Resonance tube
Lissajous figures
Doppler effect (3 cm waves)
Photoelectric effect
Newton's rings
Fresnel biprism
Absorption spectrum
Energy distribution in spectrum
Polarimeter
Malus' law
Neon spectrum
Young's slits
Single slit diffraction
Thermocouple
Constant-volume thermometer
Platinum resistance thermometer
Specific heat – rotating drum
Specific latent heat of vaporisation
Specific heat of liquids (electric method)
Specific heat by cooling
Specific heat (steam–water)
Boyles' law
Charles's law
Lee's disc
Searle's bar
Constant-flow calorimeter
Conductivity of sand
Linear expansivity (projector)
Linear expansivity of metal
Cubical expansivity (liquids)
Dynamic method for s.v.p.
Regnault hygrometer
Conductivity of rubber tubing
Thermopile
Sound in rods
Frequency of the mains
Microwaves
Magnification of lenses
Defects of lenses
Grease spot photometer
Wheatstone bridge
Electrical puzzle boxes
Flow of electrical charge
Ohm's law and lamps
Ohm's law (tangent galvo)
Post Office box
Capacitance (reed switch)
Internal resistance of cells
Ampere balance
Conductivity of electrolytes
Electrochemical equivalent
Current balance
Tangent galvanometer (B)
Magnetic fields (search coil)
Hysteresis
Resistivity of wires
Earth inductor
Sound transmission (coils)
Demountable transformer
Hall effect
Field near straight wire
Capacitance comparison
Time constant (capacitors)
Temperature coefficient of resistance
npn transistor (Unilab)
Demountable CRO
e/m by double beam tube
e/m by deflection tube
e/m by magnetron
e/m by electrolysis of water
Vacuum diode (EA 50)
Vacuum diode (Teltron)
Semiconductor diode
Locktronics circuits
Op amp
Radioactive decay (water)
Radioactive decay (thoron)
Radioactive decay (protoactinium)
Geiger tube characteristics
Gamma-ray absorption
Beta-ray absorption
Photography
Capacitance in a.c. circuits
Electric fields
Photoelasticity
Programming the BBC microcomputer
Resonant circuits
Hysteresis (Hall probe)
Ionisation levels
Magnetic fields (Hall probe)
Ballistic galvanometer
Fusing currents in wires
Clement and Desormes experiment
GHz oscillations
Analogue computer
Control with the BBC microcomputer
Vela
BBC buggy
Logic circuits
MEP boards
Newton's law of cooling (transistor)
Transistor thermometer

Thermistor
Boltzmann's constant
n by minimum deviation
n by concave mirror
n by air cell
n by real/apparent depth
f by minimum deviation
f by two-position method
f of convex/concave lens
Image location (concave mirror)

The following is a short list of some possible investigations; you will probably be able to think of many more that will interest you.

At what temperature does paper burn?
Which way does a ball spin?
Frequency response of a transistor
Force in a long jump take-off
Sound output from a stereo
How dark is a dark room?
Magnetic field of a cassette tape
How much will glass bend?
How good an insulator is polystyrene?
Impact properties of polystyrene
Sound transmission in a room
Flame-retardant properties of paint
Strength of polythene bags
Temperature variation in a room
Detector for wires in walls
Temperature effects on an integrated circuit
Electronic dice
Absorption spectra
Surge of current in a light bulb
Absorption properties of soil
What makes a discord?
Stress in gear wheels
Improving the efficiency of a bicycle
Marbles in a circular track
Directional emission of light from a lamp
The strength of bone
The Physics of the lariat
The Physics of the yo-yo
A model of Flettner's rotors

Formulae list

Most of these formulae should be memorised during your A level course. It is most important that you are sure of the meaning of all the symbols.

Equations of motion $s = vt$
$v = u + at$
$v^2 = u^2 + 2as$
$s = ut + \frac{1}{2}at^2$

Momentum $M = mv$
Impulse $I = Ft$
Newton's second law $F = \frac{d(mv)}{dt} = ma$
Impulse and momentum $Ft = mv - mu$
Kinetic energy k.e. $= \frac{1}{2}mv^2$
Potential energy p.e. $= mgh$
Work work $= Fs\cos\theta$
Power power = work/time
power $= Fv$
Weight $F = mg$
Pressure pressure = force/area
Pressure in a liquid pressure $= h\rho g$
Density $\rho = m/V$
Couple torque of a couple $= Fd$
Upthrust $U = V\rho g$
Projectiles
Range range $= u^2 \sin 2\theta/g$
Maximum height $h = u^2 \sin^2\theta/2g$
Time of flight $t = 2u \sin\theta/g$
Motion in a circle
Angular velocity $\omega = \theta/t$
Linear and angular velocity $v = r\omega$
Time of rotation period $T = 2\pi/\omega$
Centripetal force $F = mv^2/r = m\omega^2 r$
Rotational dynamics
Moment of inertia $I = \Sigma mr^2$
Angular momentum $M = I\omega$
Rotational k.e. k.e. $= \frac{1}{2}I\omega^2$
Couple $C = I\alpha$
Work done $W = C\theta$
Simple harmonic motion
Acceleration $a = -\omega^2 x$
Displacement $x = r\sin(\omega t)$
Velocity $v = \pm\omega(r^2 - x^2)^{\frac{1}{2}}$
Acceleration $a = -\omega^2 r \sin(\omega t)$
Velocity $v = \omega r \cos(\omega t)$
Kinetic energy k.e. $= \frac{1}{2}m\omega^2(r^2 - x^2)$
Potential energy p.e. $= \frac{1}{2}m\omega^2 x^2$
Total energy $E = \frac{1}{2}m\omega^2 r^2$

Simple harmonic motion examples:
Pendulum $T = 2\pi(l/g)^{\frac{1}{2}}$
Helical spring $T = 2\pi(e/g)^{\frac{1}{2}}$
$= 2\pi(m/k)^{\frac{1}{2}}$
Gravitation
Kepler's third law T^2/r^3 = constant
Newton's law $F = GMm/d^2$
Potential energy p.e. $= -GMm/r$
Kinetic energy k.e. $= +GMm/2r$
Total energy $E = -GMm/2r$
Potential $V = -GM/r$
g_0 and G $g_0 = GM/R^2$
g and g_0 $(r > R)$ $g = g_0R^2/r^2$
g and g_0 $(r < R)$ $g = g_0 r/R$
Escape velocity $v = (2Rg_0)^{\frac{1}{2}}$
Elasticity
Stress stress $= F/A$
Strain strain $= e/l$
Young modulus $E = Fl/eA$
Bulk modulus $K = -\Delta p/(\Delta v/v)$
Rigidity or shear modulus (G)
$G = (F/A)/\theta$
p.e. stored p.e. $= \frac{1}{2}Fe$
$= \frac{1}{2}\frac{EAe^2}{l}$
Energy per unit volume
energy $= \frac{1}{2}$stress $\times$ strain
Thermal expansion $F = EA\alpha\theta$
Coefficient of friction (μ) $F = \mu R$
Viscosity
Coefficient of viscosity (η)
$F = \eta A \times$ velocity gradient
Stokes' law $F = 6\pi\eta rv$
Poiseuille's formula volume $s^{-1} = \pi h\rho g r^4/8\eta l$
Surface tension
Capillary rise (h) $T\cos\theta = hr\rho g/2$
Excess pressure in air bubble $p = 2T/r$
Excess pressure in soap bubble
$p = 4T/r$
Refractive index $n = (\sin i)\,(\sin r)$
$n = \frac{\text{real depth}}{\text{apparent depth}}$
Related to wave velocities $n = c_v/c_m$
Serial relation for n $n_1 \sin\theta_1 = n_2 \sin\theta_2$

Thin prism	$d = (n-1)A$
Minimum deviation	$n = \dfrac{\sin((D+A)/2)}{\sin(A/2)}$
Critical angle	$n = 1/\sin c$
Lens formulae	$1/f = 1/u + 1/v$
	$1/F = 1/f_1 + 1/f_2$
	$1/f = (n-1)(1/R_1 + 1/R_2)$
	$f^2 = xy$
	$m = v/u$
Telescope magnification	$m = f_o/f_e$
Angular magnification	$M = -(D/f + 1)$
Resolving power	$\phi = 1.22\lambda/a$
Constructive interference	path difference $= m\lambda$
Destructive interference	path difference $= (2m+1)\lambda/2$
Young's slits	$m\lambda = x_m d/D$
Newton's rings (dark ring viewed by reflection)	$m\lambda = r_m^2/R$
Thin film interference	$m\lambda = 2nt\cos r$
Diffraction grating (max)	$m\lambda = e\sin\theta$
Brewster's law (polarisation)	$\tan p = n$
Malus' law	$I = I_0\cos^2\theta$
Doppler effect	
Moving source	$\lambda' = \lambda(1 - v/c)$
Moving observer	$f' = f(1 - v/c)$
Travelling wave	$y = a\sin(\omega t - kx)$
	$= a\sin 2\pi(t/T - x/\lambda)$
Standing wave	$y = 2a\cos(2\pi x/\lambda)\sin(2\pi t/T)$
Velocity of sound	$v = (\gamma p/\rho)^{\frac{1}{2}}$
Frequency of stretched string	$f = (1/2l)(T/m)^{\frac{1}{2}}$
Fundamental frequency (closed tube)	$f = v/4l$
Intensity of wave	$I \propto a^2$
Beat frequency	$f = f_1 - f_2$
Organ pipes	
Open pipe	$f = (m+1)f_0$
Closed at one end	$f = (2m+1)f_0$
Scale of temperature	$\dfrac{t}{100} = \dfrac{(F_t - F_0)}{(F_{100} - F_0)}$
Linear expansivity (α)	$l_\theta = l_0(1 + \alpha\theta)$
Area expansivity	$\beta = 2\alpha$
Volume expansivity	$\gamma = 3\alpha$
Specific heat capacity (c)	$H = mc\theta$
Specific latent heat (L)	$H = mL$
Electrical heating	$H = VIt$

Density change	$\rho_\theta = \rho_0(1 + \gamma\theta)$
Ideal gas equation	$PV = nRT$
Isothermal change	$PV =$ constant
Adiabatic change	$PV^\gamma =$ constant
Charles's law	$V/T =$ constant
Van der Waals' equation (one mole)	$(P + a/V^2)(V - b) = RT$
Conduction of heat	$dH/dt = -kA\,d\theta/dx$
Stefan's law	$E = \sigma A(T^4 - T_0^4)$
Wien's law	$\lambda_{max}T =$ constant
Principal specific heats of a gas	$C_p - C_v = R$
	$C_p/C_v = \gamma$
First law of thermodynamics	$dQ = dU + dW$
	$= dU + P\,dV$
Work done in isothermal change	$W = nRT\ln(V_2/V_1)$
Kinetic theory equation	$PV = \frac{1}{3}mn\overline{c^2}$
Mean square velocity	$\overline{c^2} = u_1^2 + u_2^2 + + \dots u_n^2/n$
Energy/degree of freedom	$E = \frac{1}{2}kT$
Graham's Law	$\sqrt{\overline{c^2}} = (3p/\rho)^{\frac{1}{2}}$
Mean free path	$\lambda = 1/(r_0^2 n)$
Thermal conductivity	$k = \frac{1}{3}c\rho C_v\lambda$
Viscosity	$\eta = \frac{1}{3}\rho c\lambda$
Charge	$Q = It$
Current	$I = nAve$
Electrical energy	energy $= QV$
Force on charge	$F = QE = QV/d$
Ohm's law	$V = IR$
Internal resistance	e.m.f. $= I(R + r)$
Resistivity	$\rho = RA/l$
Temperature variation of resistance	$R_\theta = R_0(1 + \alpha\theta)$
Series resistance	$R = R_1 + R_2$
Parallel resistance	$1/R = 1/R_1 + 1/R_2$
Power	$W = VI = I^2R = V^2/R$
Wheatstone bridge	$R_1/R_2 = R_3/R_4$
Faraday constant	$F = Le$
Mass liberated in electrolysis	$m = zIt$
Electric field strength	$E = -dV/dx$
Force between point charges	$F = \dfrac{1}{4\pi\epsilon}\dfrac{Q_1Q_2}{d^2}$
Field due to point charge Q	$E = Q/(4\pi\epsilon d^2)$
Potential	$V = W/Q_0$
Potential due to charge Q	$V = Q/(4\pi\epsilon d)$
Capacitance	$C = Q/V$
Capacitance of a sphere	$C = 4\pi\epsilon r$
Parallel-plate capacitor	$C = \epsilon A/t$

Concentric spheres	$C = 4\pi\epsilon ab/(a-b)$
Parallel capacitors	$C = C_1 + C_2$
Series capacitors	$1/C = 1/C_1 + 1/C_2$
Energy stored	$E = \frac{1}{2}QV = \frac{1}{2}CV^2$
Capacitance comparison	$C_1/C_2 = \theta_1/\theta_2$
Capacitor discharge	$V = V_0 e^{-t/RC}$
Capacitor charge	$V = V_0(1 - e^{-t/RC})$
Force on current	$F = BIl \sin\theta$
Couple of coil	$C = BANI \sin\theta$
Field at centre of coil	$B = \mu_0 NI/2r$
Field in solenoid	$B = \mu_0 nI$ (n turns m^{-1})
Field at end of long solenoid	$B = \mu_0 nI/2$
Helmholtz coils	$B = 8\mu_0 NI/(125)^{\frac{1}{2}} r$
Field near straight wire	$B = \mu_0 I/2\pi r$
Velocity of e.m. waves	$c = 1/(\epsilon_0\mu_0)^{\frac{1}{2}}$
Current sensitivity	$\theta = BANI/c$
Voltage sensitivity	$\theta/V = BAN/cr$
Self-inductance	$L = N\phi/I$
Mutual inductance	$M = N_s\phi_s/I_p$
Induced e.m.f. (ϵ)	$\epsilon = -L\, dI/dt$
Induced e.m.f. (ϵ_s)	$\epsilon_s = -M\, dI_p/dt$
Induced e.m.f. in a rotating coil	$\epsilon = BAN\omega \sin\theta$
Induced e.m.f. (Neumann's law)	$\epsilon = -N\, d\phi/dt$
Ballistic galvanometer	$Q \propto \theta$
Transformer	$n_p/n_s = V_p/V_s$ $I_p/I_s = n_s/n_p$
Root mean square current (I)	$I = i_0/\sqrt{2}$
Alternating current	$i = i_0 \sin(\omega t)$
Capacitative reactance	$X_c = 1/(\omega C)$
Inductive reactance	$X_L = \omega L$
Impedance (series RCL)	$Z = (R^2 + (X_L - X_C)^2)^{\frac{1}{2}}$
Resonance condition for I	$X_L = X_c$
Electrostatic force on electron	$F = eE$
Electromagnetic force on electron	$F = Bev$
Crossed fields	$eE = Bev$
Energy gain	$E = eV$
Kinetic energy	$eV = \frac{1}{2}mv^2$
Circular orbit	$Bev = mv^2/r$
Mass spectrometer	$q/M = v/Br$
X-ray diffraction	$m\lambda = 2d \sin\theta$
Quantum energy	$E = hf$
Relativistic mass–energy relation	$E = mc^2$
de Broglie equation	$\lambda = h/mv$
Moseley's law	$f = k(Z - b)^2$
Work function	$W = hf_0$
Einstein's p.e. equation	$hf = hf_0 + \frac{1}{2}mv^2$
Photoelectric effect	$hf = eV$
Radioactive decay	$N = N_0 e^{-\lambda t}$
Half-life	$T = 0.693/\lambda$
Serial relation	$\lambda_1 N_1 = \lambda_2 N_2$
Hall voltage	$V = BI/net$
Current gain of transistor	$h_{FE} = I_c/I_B$
Op amp	
Closed loop gain	$\frac{V_0}{V_i} = -\frac{R_2}{R_1}$
Voltage comparator	$V_0 = A_0(V_2 - V_1)$
Ramp generator	$V_0 = V_i t$

Table of the elements

The following table gives the most abundant or most stable isotope for each element, together with a few others.

Proton number	*Nucleon number*	*Symbol*	*Name*	*Atomic mass(u)*	*Half-life*	*Decay mode*
		e	Electron	0.000 548		
1	1	p	Proton	1.007 276		
1	1	n	Neutron	1.008 665	10.8 minutes	β
1	1	H	Hydrogen	1.007 825		
1	2	D	Deuterium	2.014 102		
1	3	T	Tritium	3.016 049	12.3 years	β
2	3	He	Helium	3.016 030		
2	4	He	Helium	4.002 604		
3	7	Li	Lithium	7.016 005		
4	9	Be	Beryllium	9.012 186		
5	11	B	Boron	11.009 305		
6	12	C	Carbon	12.000 000		
6	14	C	Carbon	14.003 242	5570 years	β
7	14	N	Nitrogen	14.003 074		
8	16	O	Oxygen	15.994 915		
8	18	O	Oxygen	17.999 160		
9	19	F	Fluorine	18.998 40		
10	20	Ne	Neon	19.992 440		
11	23	Na	Sodium	22.989 773		
12	24	Mg	Magnesium	23.985 045		
13	27	Al	Aluminium	26.981 635		
14	28	Si	Silicon	27.976 93		
15	31	P	Phosphorus	30.973 763		
15	32	P	Phosphorus	31.973 908	14.5 days	β
16	32	S	Sulphur	31.927 074		
17	35	Cl	Chlorine	34.968 85		
18	40	Ar	Argon	39.962 384		
19	39	K	Potassium	38.963 71		
19	41	K	Potassium	40.961 83		
19	42	K	Potassium	41.962 4	12.5 hours	β
20	40	Ca	Calcium	39.962 59		
21	45	Sc	Scandium	44.955 92		
22	48	Ti	Titanium	47.947 95		
23	51	V	Vanadium	50.943 98		
24	52	Cr	Chromium	51.940 51		
25	55	Mn	Manganese	54.938 88		
26	54	Fe	Iron	53.939 62		
26	56	Fe	Iron	55.934 93		
26	57	Fe	Iron	56.935 39		
27	59	Co	Cobalt	58.933 19		
27	60	Co	Cobalt	59.933 81	5.29 years	γ
28	58	Ni	Nickel	57.935 34		
29	63	Cu	Copper	62.929 59		
30	64	Zn	Zinc	63.929 15		

Proton number	*Nucleon number*	*Symbol*	*Name*	*Atomic mass(u)*	*Half-life*	*Decay mode*
31	69	Ga	Gallium	68.925 7		
32	74	Ge	Germanium	73.921 2		
33	75	As	Arsenic	74.921		
34	80	Se	Selenium	79.916 51		
35	79	Br	Bromine	78.918 4		
35	85	Br	Bromine	84.938		
36	84	Kr	Krypton	83.911 50		
37	85	Rb	Rubidium	84.911 7		
38	88	Sr	Strontium	87.905 6		
38	89	Sr	Strontium	88.907	51 days	β
38	90	Sr	Strontium	89.9073	28 years	β
39	89	Y	Yttrium	88.905		
40	90	Zr	Zirconium	89.904 3		
41	93	Nb	Niobium	92.906 0		
42	98	Mo	Molybdenum	97.906		
43	101	Tc	Technetium	100.905 9		
44	102	Ru	Ruthenium	101.903 7		
45	103	Rh	Rhodium	102.904 8		
46	106	Pd	Palladium	105.903 6		
47	107	Ag	Silver	106.905		
47	111	Ag	Silver	110.905 2	7.5 days	β
48	114	Cd	Cadmium	113.903 6		
49	113	In	Indium	112.904 3		
49	115	In	Indium	114.904 1	6×10^{14} years	β
50	120	Sn	Tin	119.902		
51	121	Sb	Antimony	120.903		
52	122	Te	Tellurium	121.903		
53	127	I	Iodine	126.904 35		
53	128	I	Iodine	127.905 83	25 minutes	β
53	131	I	Iodine	130.906 13	8.1 days	β
54	129	Xe	Xenon	129.904 78		
54	132	Xe	Xenon	131.904 16		
55	133	Cs	Caesium	132.905 1		
55	137	Cs	Caesium	136.906 8	28 years	β
56	138	Ba	Barium	137.905 0		
56	139	Ba	Barium	138.908 6	85 minutes	β
56	140	Ba	Barium	139.910 5	12.8 days	β
57	139	La	Lanthanum	138.906 1		
57	148	La	Lanthanum	147.961		
58	140	Ce	Cerium	139.905 3		
59	141	Pr	Praseodymium	140.907 4		
60	142	Nd	Neodymium	141.907 5		
61	147	Pm	Promethium	146.914 9	2.6 years	β
62	152	Sm	Samarium	151.919 5		
63	151	Eu	Europium	150.919 6		

Proton number	*Nucleon number*	*Symbol*	*Name*	*Atomic mass(u)*	*Half-life*	*Decay mode*
64	158	Gd	Gadolinium	157.924 1		
65	159	Tb	Terbium	158.925 0		
66	164	Dy	Dysprosium	163.938 4		
67	165	Ho	Holmium	164.930 3		
68	166	Er	Erbium	165.930 4		
69	169	Tm	Thulium	168.934		
70	174	Yb	Ytterbium	173.939 0		
71	175	Lu	Lutetium	174.940 9		
72	180	Hf	Hafnium	179.946 8		
73	181	Ta	Tantalum	180.948 0		
74	184	W	Tungsten	183.951 0		
75	185	Re	Rhenium	184.953		
76	190	Os	Osmium	189.958 3		
77	193	Ir	Iridium	192.963 3		
78	195	Pt	Platinum	194.964 82		
79	197	Au	Gold	196.966 55		
80	202	Hg	Mercury	201.970 62		
81	205	Tl	Thallium	204.974 46		
82	206	Pb	Lead	205.974 46		
82	208	Pb	Lead	207.976 64		
82	209	Pb	Lead	209.981 0	3.3 hours	β
83	209	Bi	Bismuth	208.980 42		
84	209	Po	Polonium	208.982 46	200 years	α
85	210	At	Astatine	209.987	8.3 hours	α
86	220	Rn	Radon	220.011 4	52 seconds	α
86	222	Rn	Radon	222.017	3.83 days	α
87	223	Fr	Francium	223.019 8	22 minutes	β
88	226	Ra	Radium	226.025 36	1600 years	α
89	227	Ac	Actinium	227.027 81	22 years	β
90	232	Th	Thorium	232.038 21	1.41×10^{10} years	α
91	231	Pa	Protoactinium	231.035 94	3.4×10^4 years	α
92	235	U	Uranium	235.043 9	7.1×10^8 years	α
92	238	U	Uranium	238.050 7	4.5×10^9 years	α
93	237	Np	Neptunium	237.048 03	2.2×10^6 years	α
94	242	Pu	Plutonium	242.058 7	3.8×10^5 years	α
95	243	Am	Americium	243.061 38	8×10^3 years	α
96	245	Cm	Curium	245.065 34	10^4 years	α
96	248	Cm	Curium	Fission	5×10^5 years	
97	247	Bk	Berkelium	247.070 18	10^4 years	α
98	249	Cf	Californium	249.075 70	360 years	α
99	253	Es	Einsteinium	253.084 68	20 days	α
100	250	Fm	Fermium	250.079 48	30 minutes	
101	255	Md	Mendelevium	255.090 6	30 minutes	α
102	253	No	Nobelium		10 minutes	α
103	254	Lw	Lawrencium			

Physics examinations

The aim of this section is to help you to plan for an examination at A level in Physics and to give you a guide as to how to revise and how to approach the paper once you are in the examination room.

Before the examination

1 Have a look at the syllabus. Are there any optional sections or must it all be studied?

2 As far as possible, find out the structure of the exam. You will need to know
  (*a*) how many papers there are,
  (*b*) how long each paper is,
  (*c*) whether data or formulae sheets are provided,
  (*d*) what type of questions there are:
    multiple choice questions
    short answer questions
    long answer structured questions
    comprehension section with questions
    practical examinations;
  (*e*) which parts of the syllabus are examined on which paper,
  (*f*) whether there is a restriction as to how many questions may be answered on a given section,
  (*g*) whether electronic calculators are allowed.

3 Go over as many past papers as possible. Answer some by looking up things that you cannot do but try others under exam conditions, looking nothing up and trying to allocate the correct time to each section.

4 Revision is *not* simply sitting in a comfortable chair in the sun and reading through your notes or the text book. You need to write something down or talk about it. The best way to revise is to answer questions of the type that you will get in the examination. In addition you should learn the formulae if required (see pages 482–484).

Go through this book and make special note of the information highlighted. Make your own revision notes, but be sure that they are not too long. Get one of the family or a friend to test you on the work. Try not to get the feeling that you are working in isolation; many thousands of students will be taking the exam as well as yourself.

Select questions at random from each chapter, particularly those on sections that you find a little more difficult. There is little point in revising things that you know well; it may make you feel good but it gets you nowhere.

Don't revise with the television on; music in the background does help some people, however.

Plan your revision carefully many weeks before the examination so that you know which sections you are going to revise during a given week.

It's not the time spent revising that is important, it's what you actually do in that time.

Do ask for help from anyone that you can – your friends, your family and most of all your teachers. They will be only too willing to help.

The examination itself

Practical examinations were considered on page 15; here are some suggestions to help with the theory exams.

1 Don't panic! The only person to suffer will be yourself.

2 Arrive at the exam in good time.

3 Bring with you anything you may need; for an A level Physics examination this might include pen (with spare ink or cartridges), HB pencil (plus spare), pencil sharpener or penknife, rubber, ruler (30 cm clear plastic), calculator (do check the batteries in advance), pair of compasses.

4 Read the paper carefully, and if there are optional sections choose which questions you are going to attempt. If there is a choice be sure to attempt the correct number of questions, and choose them from the right sections.

5 Plan the time, so that you know roughly how long you can spend on each part. Look at the marks allotted by the examiners to parts of the structured long answer questions. There is little point in spending fifteen minutes out of a three hour exam on a question that is only worth 2 per cent of the marks for the paper.

6 Answer the questions that have been asked, *not* those that you hoped had been asked.

7 In general, show all your working; marks may be given for the working even if the final answer is wrong. Remember that multiple choice papers are not designed to be answered in your head. Use rough work if necessary to work out an answer, but don't hand it in.

8 Do write clearly, for your own sake as well as the examiner's. If you cannot read your own figures there is little hope for anyone else! Make any alterations clearly so that it is obvious what you intend the answer to be.

9 If there are questions that you can't do, don't worry – leave them out and return to them later.

10 Don't forget the units after every numerical answer.

11 Write clearly and precisely – it's not how much you write that is important but its content.

12 After the examination – forget it! Don't go over the paper with friends, it will only make you feel bad. There is nothing that you can do about it then anyway, except wait for the results. Try not to be one of those who says 'If only I had worked harder earlier in the course'.

Finally, good luck to you. I hope that it has all been worth it and that you will have gained something from your study of Physics at this level and will maintain an interest in it in the future.

Answers

Chapter 3

3a (i) 2.15×10^3 mm^3, 2.15 cm^3, 2.15×10^{-6} m^3 (ii) 1.5, 2.9 (iii) 14.9 g cm^{-3} (iv) 0.32 (v) 0.35 (vi) 690 mm^3 (vii) 5.2×10^3 kg m^{-3}
b $2.2 \times 10^3 \pm 0.7 \times 10^3$ mm^3
c $15.0 \times 10^3 \pm 5.0 \times 10^3$ kg m^{-3}
7 a 13%
b 9.2%
8 a 3.25% 0.1 m s^{-1}
b 7.9% 0.16 g cm^{-3}

Chapter 4

7 0.11, 0.008

Chapter 7

3 215 s
4 1005 m
5a 1.55 s **b** 34.5 m
7 74.4 years
8 58.2 m
9a 167 m
b 5.57 m s^{-1}
c 7.2 m s^{-1}
d 0.18 m s^{-2}
e 0
f −0.27 m s^{-2}
10 10^{15} m s^{-2}
11 $s/(u^2 - v^2)^{\frac{1}{2}}$
12a 11.2 m s^{-1} 296°
b 11.2 m s^{-1} 117°
c 5.7 km
15 27.2 m s^{-1}
16a 2.14 m
b 6.01 m
c 1.31 s
d 1.80 m
e 8 m s^{-1}

Chapter 9

2 1.41 N
3a 45 000 N
b 3 m s^{-2}
c 24 000 N
4 a 700 N
b 1.76 m s^{-2}

Chapter 10

1a 744 N
c (i) 25 kJ
(ii) 47 kJ
2a 111 m s^{-2}
b 7200 N
3 3.2×10^{-9} J
4a 0.174 N
b 4.5 m s^{-2}
c 0.09 N
5 11600 N 17900 W
6 8 m s^{-1}
8a 2.26×10^8 m^2
b 8.78 kg
11a 11.2 m s^{-1}
b 2500 m s^{-2}

Chapter 11

2 32.7 m s^{-1}
5 a 4.45 N
b 0.05 J
c 0.82
6a 4.0 kg
b 24 kN
c 96 J 72 J
7 2.65×10^6 m s^{-1} 45°
9 58
10 1.84×10^4 N
11 71 N
12 5.9×10^{-2} Pa
13a 37.5 N
b 56.3 W
c 28.1 W

Chapter 12

6 44 cm–73 cm
7a 130 N
b 50 N 150 N
8a 342 N
b 940
9a 324 N
b 1291 N
14.5° with the vertical
11a 546 N 146 N
b 346 N
13 5036 N
14a 750 kg
b 270 kg
16 59.5 kg

Chapter 13

1 0.6
2a 3.5 Hz
b 3.8 Hz
c 5.0 Hz $T = 1.44 \times 10^5$ N
3a 1.35 rad s^{-1}
b −0.015 rad s^{-1}
c 79
4a 5 N
b 15 N
5 17°
8a 450 m
b 4800 N
9 4.8×10^6 m s^{-1}
10 0.45 rad s^{-1}
11a 25.2 N
b 24.7
13b 12 m s^{-1}

Chapter 14

1 0.003 J
2a 13.5 kg m^2
b 192 J
c 256 N
3 4.5×10^5 J
4a 0.31 J
b 11.1 J
5 1.73 m
7 a 1.97×10^7 J
b 1052 s
c 9.87 km
8a 2304 J
b 38.4 kg m^2 rad s^{-1}
c 0.42 N
d 91.4 s
9 0.72 rad s^{-1}
12 4.98 N 0.996 J
13 81 m
14b negligible
15a 50 rad s^{-1}
b 0.055 Nm
16 0.2 kg

Chapter 15

1a 39.5 m s^{-1}
b 34.2 m s^{-1}
c 31 m s^{-2}
2a 3.5
b 4
c 1.57
d 2.95
e 14
3 2.05 pm
4 1.6 Hz
5a 100 Hz
b 149
c 0.5π
d 2×10^{-16} J
6a 3.38×10^{-3} J
b 3.45 N 2.55 N
7 0.2 s
8a 10.8 m
b 2697 N
c 14.6 kJ
10a 9.99 m s^{-2}
b 4.47 m
11 9.63×10^{11} Hz
12 4.70 cm 5.45×10^{-4} J
13a 0.89 s
b 0.63 s
15a 0.6 m
b 4 s
c 0
d 0 0.94 m s^{-1}
e 1.33 J
f π

g $3\pi/2$
h 0.3π

Chapter 16

2 Mercury 0.24 years
Venus 0.63 years
Mars 1.9 years
Jupiter 11.86 years
Saturn 28.5 years
Uranus 85 years
Neptune 164 years
Pluto 247 years
4 2.7×10^{-7} N
5 1.4×10^{-5} rad s^{-1}
6 6.14×10^{24} kg
7 3.5×10^{4} m
8 4.5×10^{12} m
9 3.3×10^{5}
11a 9.21 N kg^{-1}
b 7.8 km s^{-1}
c 5250 s
12 3.6×10^{7} m
13a 9.975 m s^{-2}
b 9.988 m s^{-2}
14a 6.33×10^{6} m
b 4×10^{14} N kg^{-1}
15a 5.45×10^{11} J
b 12 m^{3}
16 1229 m
17 3.93×10^{3} kg m^{-3}
18a (i) 274 N kg^{-1} (ii) 24.8 N kg^{-1}
(iii) 7.1×10^{-3} N kg^{-1}
b (i) 6.2×10^{5} m s^{-1}
(ii) 6.0×10^{4} m s^{-1}
(iii) 13.4 m s^{-1}
19 11.2 km s^{-1}
20 2.6×10^{5} m
21 3.75×10^{8} m
22 2513 s

Chapter 18

2a 11.1
b 6.6×10^{24}

Chapter 19

2 4.42×10^{-2} N m^{-1}
3a 0.7 mm
b 6 cm
4a 2.8 Pa
b 2.2×10^{-3} J
6 0.25 mm
7 2.8 cm
8 4.1 N

Chapter 20

1 8.33×10^{-3} J
2 9.9×10^{5} Pa
3a 1.41×10^{4} kg
b depends on density of load
4 1.1 mm
5 112 g
6 9.95×10^{-10} m
7 0.25 mm
8a 126 °C
b 1.65×10^{4} N
9 1.25×10^{4} N
10a 6.25 J
b 50 m s^{-1}
c 125 m
12 9.8 cm
15a 134 N
b 25 N
16 4.2×10^{8} kW

Chapter 21

1a 1.73
b 1.75
2 1.21×10^{6} Pa
3 AB = 0.6 cm BC = 2.4 cm of water
4 1.06×10^{-3} Pa s
5a 45 m s^{-1}
b 0.5 mm s^{-1}
6 1.62×10^{5} s 1620 km
7 3.6×10^{-8} N
9 9.6×10^{-6} m
10 3.8 times faster
11 0.13 m s^{-1}

Chapter 22

1a 5.4 m s^{-1}
b 0.38 m from the top
2 16 cm^{2}
3 9352 kg
4 4.47 m s^{-1} 112 kg

Chapter 23

1 0.42 m
2a 180°
b 180°
3 0.9 m
5 20 cm
6a 0.81 m
b 1.3 cm s^{-1}
7 0.36 m
8 7 cm
9 1.2 cm
10 u=10 cm f=20 cm
mirror is concave
12 −3.3 cm

Chapter 24

2 35°
3 0.82 m
7 1.88
9 24°
10 from within turps
11 37.18°

Chapter 25

1a v=−16.7 cm 1.67 cm high
b 2.81 cm
c u=3.3 cm 1.67 cm high
2 f=21 cm 1 cm from end
3a 0.29 m
b 1.4 and 0.7
c 0.7 m and 0.5 m from screen
4 −14 D
5a converging
b (i) 15 cm (ii) 19 cm
c 37.5 cm, 1.5 cm high, real
d 15 cm from lens
6a 0.8 m
b 1.48
c 7.07 cm
8 u=6.38 cm 0.64 cm high
9 10 cm, 60 cm
10a 7.5 cm in front of B
b in B
c 15 cm behind B
d 10 cm in front of B
11 0.074 mm
12 1°

Chapter 26

1 0.25 mm
2 3.3 times
3 2.52 km, 30.5 m
4a 5
b 1 cm
c 120 cm
5 15.7 cm, 0.15″
6a 1.15 mm
b 153 times
c 200 times
8 f_o=2.47 cm f_e=11.5 cm
9 74

Chapter 27

1b (i) 33.4 m s^{-1}
(ii) 6.6×10^{-5} m s^{-1}
c 4.7×10^{-8} m
d 2.2×10^{-8} m
2 310 Hz
5 94 m s^{-1}
6 1117 Hz 930 Hz
7 2.14 kHz
8 500 Hz
9 2000 m s^{-1}
10 4.4×10^{7} m s^{-1}
11 47.5 m s^{-1}
12 393 m s^{-1}

Chapter 28

1 2.85 s
5 239 Hz
6a 2×10^{5} Hz
b 1.29 m

c 35.3 Hz
d 70.7m s^{-1}
7 0.17
8a 306 m s^{-1}
b 1.35 cm
9a 337 m s^{-1}
b 105.3 Hz 102.7 Hz

Chapter 29

1 10.4 revs per sec
2a 2ω
b 3ω
c 5ω
3 1.33
4 47.4 revs per sec
5 536 revs s^{-1} 1072 revs s^{-1}
6a 2.26×10^8 m s^{-1}
b 2.07×10^8 m s^{-1}
c 1.24×10^8 m s^{-1}

Chapter 30

4 47.1°

Chapter 31

4 1.96 mm
5 1.08 mm
6a 45°
b no
7 608 nm
9 0.027 mm
10 56°
11 500 m s^{-1}
12 5530 m
13a 55.6 km
b 5.56 km
c 3.66 km
d 1.83 km
e 55.6 m
14a 0.18°
b 0.21 mm
15 600 nm

Chapter 32

4 0.075 mm
5 5.74×10^{-7} m
6 2
7 1.31×10^{-5} K^{-1}
8 4.05 mm
9 6.0×10^{-7} m
11 125 nm
12 480 nm
13a 20 m
b 2.5 m
c 0.7 m
d 0.25 mm
e 0.015 mm
14 0.42′
15a 0.59 mm 68
b 0.40 mm

16a 1.69×10^{-7} m
b 2.25×10^{-7} m
c 2.62×10^{-7} m
17 590 nm 442 nm

Chapter 33

3a 56.8°
b 53.1°
c 67.5°
4 0.67

Chapter 38

1a 1925 J kg^{-1} K^{-1}
b 66 J K^{-1}
3 135 K
4 0.68 m
5 214 g s^{-1}
6a 74
9 4406 J kg^{-1} K^{-1}
10 4234 J kg^{-1} K^{-1}
11 2.38×10^6 J kg^{-1} K^{-1}
12 6.36 g
13 6.19×10^4 J kg^{-1}
14 8.55×10^4 J kg^{-1}

Chapter 39

1 76.5 cm
2 −267 °C
3 2.8×10^7 Pa
4a 14.7 kJ
b −14.7 kJ
c 0
5 3.75 atmospheres
6 350 K
7a 3×10^{23}
b 6.2×10^{-21}
c 1.87 kJ 200 kPa
8 0.19
a 155 K
b 1.93×10^5 Pa
9a 32 kPa
b 243 kPa
10 194 K
11 138 K
12b 0.5 P_0
c 0.45 P_0
13 0.16 g
14 1.08 P_0
16 608 J
17 2.10×10^4 Pa 143 K
20 25 %
21 93.4 K
22a AB 30 J BC 20 J
b 35 J
d C

Chapter 40

6 9×10^3 m s^{-1} 1.3×10^{-19} J
7 1.1 cm s^{-1}
8 6.21×10^{-21} J
9 1.96×10^5 K
11 C_p=29.05 J mol^{-1} K^{-1}
C_v = 20.75 J mol^{-1} K^{-1}
13a 3.96×10^{18}
b 3.34×10^{18}
15 516 m s^{-1}
16a 450 K
b 2400 m s^{-1}

Chapter 41

1 14.9 cm of mercury
2 1.05×10^5 Pa
3d 1.4×10^4 Pa

Chapter 42

1a 4.8 W
b 1.0 W
c 24 W
d 2.1 W
2 3.024 kW 5.04×10^{-2} K
3 1.8×10^7 MW
4 12.7 K
5 2.67 cm further down the bar
6 82.8° C
7a 4 kW
10 1706 K
11 0.35 K
12a 6.2 cm^2 65 °C
13 2.3×10^{10} J
14 4.34 K s^{-1}
15 5800 K
16a 2505 W
b 251 W
17 3.46 cm^2
18a 3125 nm
b 357 nm
c 2.5×10^{-3} nm
19a 5×10^5 K
b 5×10^4 K
c 5×10^3 K
d 500 K
e 50 K
20 2170 K

Chapter 43

1 2.35×10^4 s
3 2.9×10^{-4} m s^{-1}
5a 6 J
b 150 J
c 2160 J
6a series
b parallel
9a 17.2 Ω
b 1.06×10^{-7} Ω
10 I_A=0.77 A I_B=0.23 A
12 3 V
13 2.73r
14a 50 Ω
b 12.5 Ω

c 37.5 Ω
d 6.25 Ω
e 20.8 Ω
15 8.4×10^3 s
16 1.96 V
17 1.99 V
18a 1.5 V
b 2 Ω
19 1.19 V
20a 1.6 V
b 0.8 Ω
21 R=152 Ω r=476.5 Ω
22 23.2 cm
p.d 4.1% less than true value
23 0.39 Ω
24 0.5 °C
25 1 Ω 67.2 cm
26 123 Ω
27 25.34 Ω
28 0.014 A
31 19.4 km
32 1.2×10^{-7} Ωm
33a 7.5 Ω
b 0.3 A 0.5 A 0 A

Chapter 44

1a 3×10^{-7} T
b 5.0×10^{-3} T
c 2.5×10^{-3} T
d 3.35×10^{-5} T
e 1.79×10^{-5} T
2 1.67×10^{-4} N
3 5 N
4 0.5 A
5 2500
7 5.5 mm
8 9.4×10^{-9} Nm
9 0.72 A
10 4.29 mA
11 4.5 A
12 7.88 and 8.27 vibrations per minute
13 1.5×10^{-5} Nm
14a 1.6 radians
b 0.08 radians
15 0.46 radians
16 5 Hz
17 6.62 Ω
18a 238.5 V 215 V
b 6%

Chapter 46

1 0.62 V 9.5 mV
2 1 cm s^{-1}
4 19.7 V
5 9.4×10^{-3} C
6 0.18 Nm
7a 376 V
b 2.4 Nm
8 0.8 mH
11 0.53 V
12 0.24 mH
13a 2.0×10^{-2} T
b 4.02×10^{-2} Wb
c 10 mH
d 2.5 mH
e 0.7 mH
f 20 mV
14 15 kV
17a 25.6 mV
b 0
c 0
20 995 kW

Chapter 47

1 2.3×10^{-8} N
2a 9.21 N
b 1.38×10^{27} m s^{-2}
3 8.01×10^{-9} C
4 8.99×10^{-5} N 2.02×10^5 m s^{-2}
6a 6×10^5 V
b 1.33×10^{-5} C
c 8 J
d 133 s
8a 5.56×10^{-6} J
b 8.99×10^8 V m^{-1}
2.25×10^8 V m^{-1} 3.6×10^7 V m^{-1}
8.99×10^6 V m^{-1}
c 4.6×10^{-18} J
9 8.85×10^{-10} C m^{-2}

Chapter 48

1a 7.08×10^{-11} F
b (i) 8.5×10^{-10} C
(ii) 7.1×10^{-9} C
(iii) 7.1×10^{-8} C
c 7.2×10^{-11} F
3 12 J
4a 4.4×10^{-9} C
b 2.2×10^{-7} J
c 1.77×10^{-11} F
d 8.85×10^{-8} J
5a 1.44 J
b 19.2 cm
6 2215 J
7a 225 V
b 3.54×10^{-10} C
c 1.33×10^{-8} J
8a 150 V
b 2.36×10^{-10} C
c 3.54×10^{-8} J
9a 6.7×10^{-7} C
b 2×10^{-6} C
10a 5 in series
b 3 sets of five in series, all in parallel
11a 1.42×10^{-8} C 3.54×10^{-9} C
b 80 V
c 8.9×10^{-7} J 5.68×10^{-7} J
1.42×10^{-7} J
12 1.77×10^{-8} F
13 4
14a 322 s
b 391 s
c 852 s
15 542 Ω
16a 10.4 V
b 9.82 mA
c 2.59×10^{-2} C
17 1000 J
18a 10^{-3} C
b 1.35 V
c 6.93 s
19 711 μF
20 949 V 1.42×10^{-5} J 3390 V
5.08×10^{-5} J

Chapter 49

1a 0 141.4 V
b 0 200
c 50 V
d 50 V 141.2 V
2a 1.6×10^{-2} C
b 4.9×10^{-3} C
c (i) 0 (ii) 4.78 A
d (i) 16 C (ii) 4780 A
3 21.2 V
4 33 mH
5a 5.09 A
b 4.84 A
c 16 V 15.2 V
d 0.05 A 48.4 mA 16 V 15.2 V
6a 6.28 Ω
b 31.4 Ω
c 6.28×10^5 Ω
8 0.5 A 200 V
9a 4.5 A
b 5.3 A
c 0.7 A
d 0.71 A
10 9.2×10^4 Hz 1.84×10^4 Hz
11b 159 μF 170 mH 80 Ω
12a 0.18 A V_c = 116 V
V_L = 45.7 V V_R = 109 V
13 1.6×10^5 Hz
14 0.17 pF
16a 8.1 μF
b 391 Ω
c 116 W

Chapter 50

1 0.86 μV
2 10^{22}
3a 0.38 mV
b 2.6×10^{-3} Nm

Chapter 51

1a 6 V
b 6 V
7 39.8 kΩ
8 101 kΩ
9a 0.53 mA

b 39.8 mA
c 0.46 mA 34.5 mA
10 15 V
11a 0.7 V
b 3.3 V
c 1 mA
d 10 V
e 100 mA
f 127 (V_{CE} = 0 at saturation)
12 300 kΩ
13a 16.7 μA
b 1.27 mA
c 0
14a 1.25 kΩ
b 251 kΩ
c 100
15 10.5
16a 3 V
b 500 Ω
c 100 μA
d 0.3 V
17a 24 μA
b 221 kΩ 1.25 kΩ
c 0.31 V
d 31
18a 26.7 μA
b 750 Ω
c 198.5 kΩ

Chapter 52

1a 3 V
b 15 V
2a 11 V
b 15 V
c 15 V
d 10 V
3 3.75 V
5 a 0 V
b −1.1 V
c −5 V
7 a 1 V s^{-1}
b 10 μF
8 resistor 1 mA capacitor 3.14 mA
R = 100 kΩ

Chapter 53

1a 0
b 1
c 1
d 0 1 1
e 1 1 1
f 1 1
3 A + B
41 0
2 0
5 (1.2)3
6a $\overline{A.B}$
b $\underline{A.B}$
7 A + B
8a 1
b 1
c 1
d 0

Chapter 57

1 4.6×10^{-14} m
2 1.6 mm 1.13×10^{-19} J
3 0.175 mm
4 4.8×10^{6} C kg^{-1}
5 1.18×10^{-8} N
6a 7.0 cm
b 0.11
7 1.19×10^{7} m s^{-1} 1.67×10^{-2} T
8a (i) 0 (ii) 1.6×10^{-16} N
b (i) 3.6×10^{-13} N
(ii) 3.2×10^{-16} N
9a 0.1 mm
b 5.9 m
10 0.062 T
11 1.9×10^{7} m s^{-1}
12 2.4×10^{5} V m^{-1}
13 19.5°
14 4.26 mm s^{-1}
15b -4.8×10^{-19} C
c (i) 5.18 m s^{-2} 15° to horizontal
(ii) 416 V
16a 2.86×10^{-15} C
b 0.044 mm s^{-1} upwards
19a 1.13×10^{-15} J
b 19.7 J
c 7032 V
20a 1.07
b 11.7 cm

Chapter 58

1a 91 nm 3.3×10^{15} Hz
b 95 nm 3.25×10^{15} Hz
c 4000 nm 7.5×10^{13} Hz
d 667 nm 4.5×10^{14} Hz
e 121 nm 2.48×10^{15} Hz
2 3.37×10^{-19} J 3.38×10^{-19} J
4 2.2×10^{6} m s^{-1}
6 6.2×10^{4} eV
7a 3.37×10^{-19} J
b 16 268 K
8 3.6×10^{4} m s^{-1}
9a 2.26×10^{-7} m
b 1.20×10^{-7} m

Chapter 59

1 14.5 mm 14.9 mm 15.1 mm
15.4 mm 15.8 mm
2 0.006 T

Chapter 60

1a 4×10^{-21} J
b 1.8×10^{-18} J
c 3.6×10^{-19} J
d 2×10^{-18} J
2b 2.9×10^{-19} J
c 4.0×10^{-19} J
d 9.4×10^{5} m s^{-1}
3 7.13×10^{5} m s^{-1}
4 1.16×10^{6} m s^{-1}
6a 7.9×10^{-19} J
b 622 nm
9a 1.54 V
b 7.4×10^{5} m s^{-1} 2.5×10^{-19} J
10a 661 nm
b 2.6×10^{5} m s^{-1}
c 1.74 V
11 6.72×10^{-34} J s 700 nm 1.82 eV
12 156 250
13a 0.1 W
b 147 A
c 3 mA
14a 1.87 kJ
b 8 %
c 3.75 kW
d 8.8 km^{2}

Chapter 61

1a 2.4×10^{18} Hz 0.12 nm
b 6.03×10^{18} Hz 0.049 nm
c 3.62×10^{19} Hz 0.0083 nm
d 4.83×10^{19} Hz 0.0062 nm
2a 13.4 mA
b 1.26×10^{8} m s^{-1}
3 24.8 kV
4a 1238 W
b 27.5 K s^{-1}
5a 6.25×10^{15}
b 7.3×10^{7} m s^{-1}
c 0.3 g s^{-1}
8 0.28 nm
10a 1.21×10^{19} Hz
b 1000 J s^{-1}

Chapter 62

1a 3714
2a 8
b 3
3a 0.5
b 1
c 0.0625
5 3.67 g
6 5947 Bq
7 183 s
8 1.39×10^{-8} kg
9 2.3×10^{9} years
10 4974 years
11 4.11×10^{9} years
12 5.95×10^{-3} m^{3}
13 3050 years

Chapter 63

1a 1.65×10^{-13} J 1.78×10^{-30} kg
1.07×10^{-3} u
b 1.08×10^{-17} kg 6.49×10^{9} u
6.05×10^{12} MeV
2 2.551×10^{10} kg
3 0.51 MeV
4a 5.4 MeV

b 5.30 MeV
5 39.1 MeV
6 207.6 MeV 8.5×10^{10} J
7 0.0018 u 0.0091 u
8a 0.136 u
b 128 MeV
c 7.97 MeV

9a (ii) 82 207
b (i) 2.4×10^{-13} J
(iii) 8.6×10^{-8} s^{-1}
c (i) 6.96×10^{8} J
(ii) 1.72×10^{14} Bq
(iii) 41.3 W
10 11.18 MeV

Chapter 64

1a 1.0×10^{-11} m
b 2.7×10^{-12} m
c 3.9×10^{-13} m
2 7.3×10^{6} m s^{-1}
3 3 cm s^{-1}

Acknowledgements

I am grateful to the following for permission to reproduce material:

British Standards Institution [BSI]
Cambridge University Press
Harwell Laboratory,
United Kingdom Atomic Energy Authority [UKAEA]
Institute of Physics
National Aeronautics and
Space Administration [NASA]
University of Chicago Press
Davey, *Advanced and Scholarship Test Papers in Physics*, Methuen and Co [D]
Hackett and Wilson, *Inquiring into Physics*, E.J. Arnold [H]
Nature [N]
Sears, Zemansky and Young, *University Physics* (1976), Addison-Wesley [Z]
Problems in Physics for Advanced and Scholarship Candidates, Edward Arnold [T]
The Royal Institution for extracts from Faraday's diary

and to the following examining bodies:

Associated Examining Board [AEB]
Joint Matriculation Board [JMB]
Oxford and Cambridge Schools Examination Board [O and C]
University of Cambridge Local Examinations Syndicate [C]
University of London Schools Examination Board [L]
University of Oxford Delegacy of Local Examinations [O]
Welsh Joint Education Committee [W]

The publishers would like to thank the following for supplying photographs:–

Addenbrookes Hospital; Ann Ronan Picture Library; British Aerospace plc; British Nuclear Fuels plc; The Cavendish Laboratory, University of Cambridge; Electricity Council Research Centre; IBM United Kingdom Ltd.; Institute of Physics Publishing Ltd.; INMOS Ltd.; Japan Meteorological Agency; Topham Picture Library; Martin Bond; Mullard Radio Astronomy Laboratory, University of Cambridge; National Engineering Laboratory, Scotland (Crown Copyright); National Grid Company; National Physical Laboratory, England (Crown Copyright); Natural History Photographic Agency; Ove Arup and Partners; Powergen; Rolls Royce plc; Royal Greenwich Observatory; Rutherford Appleton Laboratory; Science Photo Library; Standard Telephones and Cables plc; UKAEA Culham Laboratory; Unilab Ltd. The Science Park, Hutton Street, Blackburn, England, BB13BT; University of Birmingham Physics Department and ZEFA Picture Library (UK) Ltd.

Cover illustration by Mick Armson.

Index